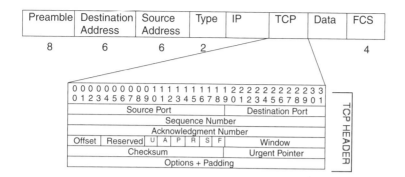

Preamble	Destination Address	Source Address	Type	IP	TCP	Data	FCS
8	6	6	2				4

```
0 0 0 0 0 0 0 0 0 0 1 1 1 1 1 1 1 1 1 1 2 2 2 2 2 2 2 2 2 2 3 3
0 1 2 3 4 5 6 7 8 9 0 1 2 3 4 5 6 7 8 9 0 1 2 3 4 5 6 7 8 9 0 1
```

Source Port						Destination Port
Sequence Number						
Acknowledgment Number						
Offset	Reserved	U A P R S F	Window			
Checksum					Urgent Pointer	
Options + Padding						

TCP HEADER

TCP Header

Field	Description
Source port (16 bits):	Number of the calling port.
Destination port (16 bits):	The number of the called port. Examples include:

Keyword	Description
bgp	Border Gateway Protocol (179)
chargen	Character generator (19)
cmd	Remote commands (rcmd, 514)
daytime	Daytime (13)
discard	Discard (9)
domain	Domain Name Service (53)
echo	Echo (7)
exec	Exec (rsh, 512)
finger	Finger (79)
ftp	File Transfer Protocol (21)
ftp-data	FTP data connections (used infrequently, 20)
gopher	Gopher (70)
hostname	NIC hostname server (101)
ident	Ident Protocol (113)
irc	Internet Relay Chat (194)
klogin	Kerberos login (543)
kshell	Kerberos shell (544)
login	Login (rlogin, 513)
lpd	Printer service (515)
nntp	Network News Transport Protocol (119)
pim-auto-rp	PIM Auto-RP (496)
pop2	Post Office Protocol v2 (109)
pop3	Post Office Protocol v3 (110)
smtp	Simple Mail Transport Protocol (25)
sunrpc	Sun Remote Procedure Call (111)
syslog	Syslog (514)
tacacs	TAC Access Control System (49)
talk	Talk (517)
telnet	Telnet (23)
time	Time (37)
uucp	Unix-to-Unix Copy Program (540)
whois	Nicname (43)
www	World Wide Web (HTTP, 80)

For a complete list of IP/TCP/UDP ports please see www.iana.org/assignments/port-numbers
NIC-Government Systems, Inc., DDN Network Information Center
14200 Park Meadow Drive, Suite 200
Chantilly, VA 22021

Field	Description
Sequence Number (32 bits):	A sequence number assuring the correct arrival and sequence of the data. This number indicates the byte sequence number of the first octet in the TCP data block and is incremented according to the number of octets transmitted in each TCP segment.
Acknowledgment Number (32 Bits):	A piggyback acknowledgment of the next expected TCP octet.
Data offset (4 bits):	The number 32 bit words in the TCP header.
Reserved (6 bits):	Set to Zero.
Flags (6 bits):	Control Functions such as the set up and termination of a session, expedited or urgent data flow, reset of a connection, or indication of the end of the data.

URG: Urgent pointer field significant
ACK: Acknowledgment field significant
PSH: Push function
RST: Reset connection
SYN: Synchronize sequence numbers
FIN: No more data from sender

Field	Description
Window (16 bits):	The receive wind size, indicating the number of octets-beginning with the one in the acknowledgment field-that the sender is willing to accept.
Checksum (16 bits):	Points to the first octet that follows the urgent data and allows the receiver to determine how much urgent data is coming.
Options (variable):	One option (maximum TCP segment size – MSS) is currently defined.
Padding (variable):	Ensures that the TCP header ends, and data begins, on a 32-bit boundary.

D1616010

CCIE Practical Studies
Volume II

Karl Solie, CCIE No. 4599
Leah Lynch, CCIE No. 7220

Cisco Press

Cisco Press
800 East 96th Street
Indianapolis, IN 46240 USA

CCIE Practical Studies
Volume II

Karl Solie, Leah Lynch, with contributions from Scott Morris

Copyright © 2004 Karl Solie and Leah Lynch

Published by:
Cisco Press
800 East 96th Street
Indianapolis, IN 46240 USA

Printed in the United States of America 2 3 4 5 6 7 8 9 0

Second Printing December 2003

Library of Congress Cataloging-in-Publication Number: 2001094973

ISBN: 1-58705-072-2

Warning and Disclaimer

This book is designed to provide information about selected topics for the CCIE exam for the Routing and Switching track. Every effort has been made to make this book as complete and as accurate as possible, but no warranty or fitness is implied.

The information is provided on an "as is" basis. The authors, Cisco Press, and Cisco Systems, Inc. shall have neither liability nor responsibility to any person or entity with respect to any loss or damages arising from the information contained in this book or from the use of the discs or programs that may accompany it.

The opinions expressed in this book belong to the author and are not necessarily those of Cisco Systems, Inc.

Trademark Acknowledgments

All terms mentioned in this book that are known to be trademarks or service marks have been appropriately capitalized. Cisco Press or Cisco Systems, Inc. cannot attest to the accuracy of this information. Use of a term in this book should not be regarded as affecting the validity of any trademark or service mark.

Feedback Information

At Cisco Press, our goal is to create in-depth technical books of the highest quality and value. Each book is crafted with care and precision, undergoing rigorous development that involves the unique expertise of members from the professional technical community.

Readers' feedback is a natural continuation of this process. If you have any comments regarding how we could improve the quality of this book, or otherwise alter it to better suit your needs, you can contact us through e-mail at feedback@ciscopress.com. Please make sure to include the book title and ISBN in your message.

We greatly appreciate your assistance.

Corporate and Government Sales

Cisco Press offers excellent discounts on this book when ordered in quantity for bulk purchases or special sales. For more information, please contact: **U.S. Corporate and Government Sales** 1-800-382-3419 corpsales@pearsontechgroup.com

For sales outside of the U.S. please contact: **International Sales** 1-317-581-3793 international@pearsontechgroup.com

Publisher	John Wait
Editor-in-Chief	John Kane
Cisco Representative	Anthony Wolfenden
Cisco Press Program Manager	Sonia Torres Chavez
Cisco Marketing Communications Manager	Scott Miller
Cisco Marketing Program Manager	Edie Quiroz
Executive Editor	Brett Bartow
Managing Editor	Patrick Kanouse
Development Editors	Greg Balas, Christopher Cleveland
Project Editor	San Dee Phillips
Copy Editor	Keith Cline
Technical Editors	Jennifer DeHaven Carroll, Greg Tillett, Kevin Turek
Team Coordinator	Tammi Ross
Book Designer	Gina Rexrode
Cover Designer	Louisa Adair
Production Team	Octal Publishing, Inc.
Indexer	Tim Wright

CISCO SYSTEMS

Corporate Headquarters
Cisco Systems, Inc.
170 West Tasman Drive
San Jose, CA 95134-1706
USA
www.cisco.com
Tel: 408 526-4000
    800 553-NETS (6387)
Fax: 408 526-4100

European Headquarters
Cisco Systems International BV
Haarlerbergpark
Haarlerbergweg 13-19
1101 CH Amsterdam
The Netherlands
www-europe.cisco.com
Tel: 31 0 20 357 1000
Fax: 31 0 20 357 1100

Americas Headquarters
Cisco Systems, Inc.
170 West Tasman Drive
San Jose, CA 95134-1706
USA
www.cisco.com
Tel: 408 526-7660
Fax: 408 527-0883

Asia Pacific Headquarters
Cisco Systems, Inc.
Capital Tower
168 Robinson Road
#22-01 to #29-01
Singapore 068912
www.cisco.com
Tel: +65 6317 7777
Fax: +65 6317 7799

Cisco Systems has more than 200 offices in the following countries and regions. Addresses, phone numbers, and fax numbers are listed on the **Cisco.com Web site at www.cisco.com/go/offices.**

Argentina • Australia • Austria • Belgium • Brazil • Bulgaria • Canada • Chile • China PRC • Colombia • Costa Rica • Croatia • Czech Republic Denmark • Dubai, UAE • Finland • France • Germany • Greece • Hong Kong SAR • Hungary • India • Indonesia • Ireland • Israel • Italy Japan • Korea • Luxembourg • Malaysia • Mexico • The Netherlands • New Zealand • Norway • Peru • Philippines • Poland • Portugal Puerto Rico • Romania • Russia • Saudi Arabia • Scotland • Singapore • Slovakia • Slovenia • South Africa • Spain • Sweden Switzerland • Taiwan • Thailand • Turkey • Ukraine • United Kingdom • United States • Venezuela • Vietnam • Zimbabwe

About the Authors

Leah Lynch, CCIE No. 7220 R/S, is a network engineer with a large financial institution. Leah has more than seven years of experience in the IT industry, with four years focused on heterogeneous internetwork environments, including banking, retail, medical, government, manufacturing, corporate, sales, network service provider, telecommunications, and 2.5/3G wireless networks. Leah also holds several other Cisco certifications and is currently working on her Communications and Services CCIE. She wrote Chapters 6 through 9 (the QoS and BGP chapters) and can be reached at leah.lynch@ieee.org.

Karl Solie, CCIE No. 4599, is a principal engineer for the consulting firm Solie Research, LLC. Karl has more than 14 years of experience in the field designing and implementing some of the largest IP- and SNA-based internetworks in the United States and abroad for companies such as McDonnell Douglas/Boeing, Unisys, and the Fulton and Los Angeles county governments. Karl is also active in Cisco professional development and, along with this volume, he has authored *CCIE Practical Studies,* Volume I, (Cisco Press, 2001). Karl can also be caught in the classroom, as a certified Cisco Systems instructor, training for the Ascolta Training Company in Minneapolis. Karl concentrated in applied mathematics at the University of Wisconsin-Stout and holds a bachelor of arts in law from the University of California, Irvine.

About the Contributing Author

Scott Morris, CCIE No. 4713, certified Cisco Systems instructor. Among several other certifications, Scott currently has four separate CCIE certifications (Routing and Switching, ISP/Dial, Security, and Service Provider) and is working on his fifth (Voice). He travels the world teaching and consulting on various projects. To not become bored or stagnant, he has also started branching out into the Juniper Networks world (JNCIS currently and growing) for added consulting and training interests. His primary areas of interest and expertise are in security, IP telephony, cable modem networks, and advanced routing. When not traveling, he resides in Lexington, Kentucky. At times, he has taught CCIE (Routing and Switching) boot camps for various companies, currently at IPExpert. He has contributed material to a few different books and has served as a technical editor on many others. He currently runs his own company Emanon.com, Inc. and markets as Uber-Geek.Net, too (http://smorris.uber-geek.net).

About the Technical Reviewers

Jennifer DeHaven Carroll, CCIE No. 1402, is a principal consultant with Lucent Technologies. She has planned, designed, and implemented many large networks over the past 15 years. She has also developed and taught theory and Cisco implementation classes on all IP routing protocols. Jenny is the coauthor of *Routing TCP/IP,* Volume II, (Cisco Press, 2001) with Jeff Doyle and can be reached at jennifer.carroll@ieee.org.

Greg Tillett, CCIE No. 5231, is currently working toward his second CCIE in the Security track. He has recertified twice since achieving his first CCIE. Greg is a consulting systems engineer with Cisco Systems focusing on security, virtual private networks, and campus technologies. In his current role, he supports Cisco Systems engineers and account managers with their customer base and presents these technologies to various audiences at Cisco seminars. Since joining Cisco in 1997, he has supported many customers, state and local governments, K-12 and higher educational customers, and several Fortune 100 customers with global networks. This experience gives him a unique perspective on designing and supporting extremely diverse types of multiservice networks.

Kevin Turek, CCIE No. 7284, is currently working as a network consulting engineer in the Cisco Federal Support Program in Research Triangle Park. He currently supports some of Cisco Department of Defense customers. Kevin is also a member of the Cisco internal QoS virtual team, which supports internal Cisco engineers and external Cisco customers with QoS deployment and promotes current industry best practices as they pertain to QoS. Kevin earned his bachelor of science degree in business administration at the State University of New York, Stony Brook.

Dedications

Leah Lynch: This book is dedicated to my husband, Chad Lynch, who always supports, listens to, and encourages me. I love you.

Karl Solie: This book is dedicated to my family—my mother and father, John and Linda Solie; and my two brothers, Mike and Jim. We have been blessed with a close family and have a king's wealth of a different kind. This book is also dedicated to my wife, Sandra, and my two daughters, Amanda and Paige, for all their sacrifices over the years and their enduring love. You three make every day warmer, brighter, and happier for me.

Acknowledgments

Leah Lynch: There are tons of people who worked together to get this book to this point. First, I would like to thank all the people from Cisco Press—Brett Bartow, Chris Cleveland, and Greg Balas, who helped take the raw material and create a real Cisco Press book; and the technical editors, Jenny Carroll, Greg Tillett, and Kevin Turek, who verified our work and found all the tiny errors you never see when you are the one writing. Thanks guys!

I also want to thank Karl Solie for spending so many nights on the phone discussing ideas and content. I cannot thank Karl without thanking his wife, Sandra, who tolerated all of our late-night discussions.

I also want to thank Jenny Carroll and Jeff Doyle for introducing me to the folks at Cisco Press and helping me take the beginning steps toward becoming an author.

I also want to thank Pan Chou, my very patient friend, for answering (or at least attempted to answer) my obscure BGP questions. And Scott Downing for letting me bounce ideas off him. I also want to thank Mike Flannagan for answering my odd QoS questions and Daniel Walton for his excellent BGP presentations and Q/A sessions at Networkers.

And, of course, I must thank my husband, Chad Lynch, who patiently waited for me to complete this project and provided on-the-spot editing. Thank you for tolerating the two years of constant work; now, we can go on vacation.

I also want to thank my friend Erin Heitz for helping me get into this field and motivating me to start a real IT career; thanks to my mentor, George Sereno, for all the good advice and honesty; and, finally, I want to thank my family, the Lynches and the Sifuentes, for their love and support.

Karl Solie: No project of this size would be possible without the dedication of many CCIEs, editors, technical people and friends. I first want to thank all the people Leah mentioned at Cisco Press, especially Editor-in-Chief John Kane for giving me the great opportunity to become a Cisco Press author.

I also want to thank my co-author, Leah Lynch, for all her hard work and long nights on this project. This text would not have been possible without her devotion to it.

Sincere thanks go to the other CCIEs involved with this work—Scott Morris, for contributing his expertise in multicast routing by writing Chapter 3, as well as the excellent work put in by our technical reviewers: Jennifer Carroll, Greg Tillett, and Kevin Turek.

I also want to say *thank you* to all the readers of *CCIE Practical Studies,* Volume I, especially for the kind letters that people have sent me about their quest to become CCIEs.

Finally, I once again want to thank the good Lord Jesus for His continued blessings and for always being there for me.

Contents at a Glance

Table of Contents

Icons Used in This Book

Router

Bridge

Hub

DSU/CSU

Catalyst
Switch

Multilayer
Switch

Modem

ATM
Switch

ISDN/Frame Relay
Switch

Communication
Server

Gateway

Access
Server

PC

PC with
Software

Sun
Workstation

Macintosh

Terminal

Cisco Works
Workstation

Web
Server

File
Server

Laptop

Printer

IBM
Mainframe

Front End
Processor

Cluster
Controller

Line: Ethernet

Line: Serial

Line: Switched Serial

Token Ring

FDDI

Network Cloud

Command Syntax Conventions

The conventions used to present command syntax in this book are the same conventions used in the Cisco IOS Command Reference. The Command Reference describes these conventions as follows:

- Vertical bars (|) separate alternative, mutually exclusive elements.

- Square brackets [ ] indicate optional elements.

- Braces { } indicate a required choice.

- Braces within brackets [{ }] indicate a required choice within an optional element.

- **Boldface** indicates commands and keywords that are entered literally as shown. In actual configuration examples and output (not general command syntax), boldface indicates commands that are manually input by the user (such as a **show** command).

- *Italics* indicate arguments for which you supply actual values.

Foreword

Preparing for the CCIE certification is a challenging and individual process, and there are as many paths to success as there are candidates. I've had the pleasure of meeting and talking to thousands of CCIE candidates, and there is no doubt in my mind that the single greatest factor in achieving certification is the amount of "hands-on" practice a candidate logs during their preparation. *CCIE Practical Studies*, Volume II, by Karl Solie and Leah Lynch provides a clear framework to make the all-important hands-on preparation more effective. The hallmark of any CCIE certification is the breadth of the content covered by the exam, and many candidates have difficulty choosing where and how to begin their preparation. This book and its companion, *CCIE Practical Studies*, Volume I, can help the candidate focus on key content likely to appear on the exam. In addition to the knowledge gained by reading and working through the sample lab scenarios, the book can act as a starting point for a more self-directed approach to study, in which candidates explore "what-if" type scenarios requiring true expert-level skills.

The CCIE certification is now ten years old and still stands in the top rank of certification programs in our industry. One measure of that vitality is the growth in quality preparation materials for the exam, and this volume is a worthy addition to the list of resources now available to CCIE candidates. Like its companion volume, I'm sure it will be an excellent addition to any preparation library.

Mike Reid
Manager, CCIE Programs
Cisco Systems, Inc.

Introduction

The CCIE is one of the most challenging certifications available. Most CCIE candidates spend several months studying and even take a few attempts at the lab exam before passing. If you are considering pursuing the CCIE, you are most likely aware of the amount of self-study, training, and experience required to undertake the laboratory exam. Despite the difficulties, pursuing the CCIE certification program is a very rewarding experience requiring candidates to refresh their skills in technologies that they are already familiar with, expand their skills in areas where they have less knowledge, and generally prepare for situations that require a great amount of technical expertise. The skills and hands-on experience working with a number of different technologies under pressure and time limitations add to one's ability to troubleshoot and add value to employers.

The CCIE lab exam is an extended one-day exam that tests the candidate's abilities to work with multiple protocols within a limited amount of time under a considerable amount of pressure. Candidates must use their knowledge of Cisco IOS Software to configure, test, and troubleshoot a network that they are not familiar with, proving their ability to work independently and under pressure. Because the CCIE program is constantly changing to keep up with industry needs, candidates frequently encounter technologies with which they do not have extensive experience working. This makes the CCIE program more versatile to candidates and employers because the candidates are not only tested in areas that apply to their current career situation, but also to situations in a number of different markets. The protocols and technologies covered by the Routing and Switching exam track apply to a number of different network types: corporate enterprise, retail, service providers, and others. This broad range of skills benefits the candidates, their employers, and their coworkers.

Cisco recommends that CCIE candidates have at least two years of experience with Cisco products, formal training with the technologies, and a considerable amount of time dedicated to self-study before undertaking the lab exam. This book is the second volume in a series intended to help CCIE candidates with the self-study part of their preparation. Over the course of this series, the books explore a number of technologies. You can to use the examples in the book to test your knowledge of the technologies through various hands-on lab scenarios. It is strongly recommended that you use each book in the series to prepare for the exam, reading through the theory, practicing the lab scenarios, and reviewing familiar technologies. After passing the CCIE exam, most people find a great feeling of accomplishment and are no longer intimidated by time limitations and pressure.

We will be honest with you; your journey on the path to becoming a CCIE will be long and formidable. It will challenge you mentally like nothing else. When it comes to the CCIE lab test, the testing standards are rigid and the proctors are stringent. You will not be able to argue or talk your way into becoming a CCIE. Prepare wisely; there are no shortcuts on the road to becoming a CCIE, so do not waste time looking for them. As long as your journey may be, when all is said and done and you are finally assigned your own CCIE number, the feeling is like nothing else. You will feel that all the hard work, the sacrifices, and the long lonely hours in the lab have paid off. You will have entered the ranks of the most elite group of network engineers on the planet—by becoming a CCIE.

CCIE Practical Studies, Volume I, stressed that there is no shortcut to becoming a CCIE, no "all-in-one" book on becoming a CCIE (including *CCIE Practical Studies,* Volume I and Volume II). There are no quick "buy this book and we guarantee you will pass" solutions that will replace a strong level of experience and dedication. It is assumed that most CCIE candidates already have at least some experience with most of the technologies covered in this series. The CCIE lab is ever changing, and the possible test content is deep and vast. For these reasons, it is difficult to create a "single source" for CCIE knowledge and study. This does not mean that boot camps and such are not valuable tools; they are, and should be treated as one of the many study techniques you can use.

Like Volume I, the text in Volume II does not, in general, go into great detail on specific protocols; instead, it is designed to provide practical configuration guidelines that you can use to help improve network skills and to introduce you to technologies that you might not yet have worked with in the field. Volume II, along with its companion, Volume I, presents a tremendous amount of information on many foundation or core network technologies and includes many new concepts that, if applied with a working network model, can help to produce even stronger network skills, furthering your preparation to take, and pass, the CCIE lab exam.

CCIE Practical Studies, Volume II, picks up where *CCIE Practical Studies,* Volume I, left off. *CCIE Practical Studies,* Volume I, focuses on modeling complex internetwork scenarios from ISO Layer 1 on up. It covers physical access, modeling LAN and WAN data-link protocols such as Frame Relay, HDLC, PPP, ATM, Ethernet, and Token Ring. *CCIE Practical Studies,* Volume I, details Cisco Catalyst platforms, including the Token Ring Catalyst 3924 and the Catalyst 35xx/5500/6500 family. Volume II continues with the Catalyst family of switches, focusing on the powerful new Catalyst 3550 intelligent Ethernet switch. The studies include Layer 3 switching and the new 802.1w and 802.1s Spanning Tree Protocols.

CCIE Practical Studies, Volume I, also covers Interior Gateway Protocols (IGPs), such as RIP, IGRP/EIGRP, and OSPF. *CCIE Practical Studies,* Volume II, takes the next step and concentrates on the primary Exterior Gateway Protocol (EGP) and Border Gateway Protocol (BGP)—more than 300 pages are devoted to BGP.

In addition to modeling routing protocols and Ethernet switching, this text takes a detailed look at quality of service (QoS). As with BGP, a significant portion of the text, more than 200 pages, is devoted to advance QoS techniques, including topics such as Resource Reservation Protocol (RSVP), Differentiated Services Code Point (DSCP) field, and Weighted Random Early Detection (WRED). QoS is also discussed as it relates to ATM and voice technologies.

How This Book Is Organized

The text is arranged into six sections, which provide technical details on specific technologies. It demonstrates how you can implement these technologies and guides you through more advanced technical implementations using practical examples. At the end of each configuration-based chapter, you can test your knowledge of the subject by completing a lab scenario that applies the technology that was just covered. After completing the lab, you can use the lab walkthrough to see how your configuration compares to the configurations created in our labs. The subjects discussed in this book are organized in the following manner:

- Part I: Ethernet Switching

- Part II: Controlling Network Propagation and Network Access

- Part III: Multicast Routing

- Part IV: Performance Management and Quality of Service

- Part V: BGP Theory and Configuration

- Part VI: CCIE Practice Labs

CCIE Practical Studies, Volume II, was designed to be a customizable study resource. The sections are divided into technology-specific areas that enable you to use your study time efficiently. Each chapter begins with basic theory and works up to configuration examples, which you can model in your own lab. Most chapters also include practical examples that apply more complex configuration topics and, with the lab walkthroughs, enable you virtually to work with the author configurations deployed during the writing process. If you have a problem with a certain technology or configuration step, go back to the theory and configuration section for a quick review and then try the example or lab again until you understand how it works. Do not be afraid to go beyond the limits of any of the labs to further investigate technologies or take time to explore one item in detail. The experience you gain working through these network models will add to any other training or experience you already have, preparing you for complex network implementations. When you feel comfortable with a section, move on to the next; and if you think you do not need the information in a section, skip to the end and try the lab scenario to verify that you have mastered the subject. Each chapter in this book also provides you with a "Further Reading" section that directs you to references that can provide additional detail on the subjects contained within for additional study. This book builds on the information covered in Volume I, assuming that you have the solid foundation skills required to configure core technologies such as IGP routing protocols, basic LAN switching concepts, and WAN protocol configuration experience, and that you know how to configure IP services such as Network Address Translation (NAT). For more information on these technologies, refer to the corresponding chapters in Volume I.

Part I takes an in-depth look at the new Cisco 3550 intelligent switching platform—exploring the capabilities of this new platform, reviewing the old-school switching technologies, and looking at new and improved applications of these switching technologies. You then use the full capabilities of this platform in routing and switching practical examples and practical lab scenarios.

Part II analyzes and demonstrates the use of the simple, but powerful, route maps and also covers frequently overlooked route maps. You will learn many of the ways to use route maps to change or influence routing behavior, control traffic based on protocol characteristics, or policy route traffic. Route maps are an integral part of many advanced routing schemes, and good route map configuration skills are a must for BGP routing. This part provides a fundamental look at route maps and their application and prepares you for some of the technologies covered later in this book.

Part III takes an in-depth look at multicast routing and switching on router and switch platforms, applying practical theory to network models—thereby, demonstrating the application of multicast routing for real-world scenarios.

Part IV comprehensively examines router performance management and QoS by first analyzing router performance with a brief section on performance-related router **show** commands. Using the information derived from these commands, you can provide the best level of service by applying some of the Cisco IOS Software extensive QoS technologies. ATM QoS is then covered—first, a review of ATM theory, comparing ATM to Frame Relay, and then a brief review of ATM PVC configuration using newer Cisco IOS Software ATM configuration commands. The focus then turns to ATM QoS mechanisms, and you apply these technologies to traffic based on network service level requirements. This information can also help enterprise network professionals understand some of the terminology that is frequently used by their service providers. This part also covers Layer 3 switching methods, demonstrating how to determine the right switching method for particular network characteristics and router hardware and interface types.

Chapter 5 removes the cloud of mystery surrounding the QoS integrated and differentiated services. This chapter reviews RSVP theory and configuration on Cisco routers, taking an in-depth look at RSVP **show** and **debug** commands. You apply RSVP configurations to one of the most popular RSVP network applications, Voice over IP. The chapter then examines the predominant differentiated services currently available for traffic marking and classification using the information stored in the IP Type of Service (ToS) field. This section explores IP precedence, the newly emerging IP Differentiated Services Code Point (DSCP) field, and WRED (the congestion-avoidance algorithm). After you explore the ways that traffic can be classified, you can apply these technologies in several network models using Voice over IP as a network application.

Chapter 6, a little book in itself, dives right in and provides a broad view of the current queuing, shaping, classification, and policing technologies available in Cisco IOS Software. This chapter begins by exploring the primary four basic queuing methods and then delves deeper into queuing theory by exposing newer, more advanced queuing methods such as Class-Based Weighted Fair Queuing and Low Latency Queuing—technologies that integrate many of the subjects covered up to this point in this book. The chapter then revisits traffic shaping and explores the newer, class-based shaping method. Because no QoS chapter would be complete without addressing traffic policing, this chapter demonstrates new policing methods that you can apply in the field as protective measures to prevent or contain the spread of certain viruses and undesirable protocols while maintaining certain levels of network performance.

Part V explores one of the most exciting and confusing protocols ever written: BGP. In this part, unlike the other parts, an entire chapter is dedicated only to BGP theory, Chapter 7. This chapter provides one of the newest, most comprehensive BGP theory descriptions available today by exploring the states of the BGP finite-state machine, five BGP messages, BGP attributes, route reflectors, and confederations. This chapter is geared specifically to Cisco BGP implementation but is derived from all BGP source information available; providing a concise BGP theory review that prepares you for the following chapters by providing the theory up front without jumping from theory to configuration.

Chapter 8 begins applying the BGP theory from Chapter 7, from a service provider and enterprise perspective, exploring basic BGP configurations, providing a few quick BGP configuration tips, and exploring the impact that BGP routing has on a router. This chapter includes numerous real-world implementation tips that you can use in the field. After reviewing the fundamentals, this chapter examines the heart of a successful BGP implementation—displaying configuration data and diagnosing problems using BGP **show** and **debug** commands. This chapter delves into previously undocumented items displayed during BGP debugging sessions, explaining **debug** output line by line. This information prepares you to handle almost any BGP problem by introducing a BGP troubleshooting methodology and showing which commands help you diagnose problems quickly with the least network impact.

Chapter 9 examines I-BGP and E-BGP implementations, how BGP uses its tables, advertising BGP networks, and integrating BGP with IGPs. This chapter helps alleviate many confusing or difficult concepts such as multihoming to two service providers and the common I-BGP full-mesh problem. This chapter—designed not just as a study guide but as a real-world field guide that can save you hours of troubleshooting in the field—builds on the information provided in the previous two chapters by delving straight into the good stuff: route reflectors, confederations, redistribution, route filtering, and conditional route advertisement. This chapter then takes an unprecedented look at one of the most confusing and difficult BGP topics: applying regular expressions. This chapter demonstrates how regular expressions work by applying several examples and using little-known **show** commands to find the right regular expression for the task. After exploring regular expressions, you use them to filter or modify routes by applying the information contained in BGP attributes. This chapter also covers the use of multiple paths, private autonomous system numbers, backdoors, peer groups, and aggregation. And, finally, you apply this information to several real-world type scenarios building a strong BGP foundation that should leave you confident to deal with any problems the BGP protocol can throw at you.

Part VI, Chapter 10, takes all the information from both volumes of the *CCIE Practical Studies* books and combines skills from all these areas to create five challenging lab scenarios. Based on input provided from readers of Volume I, we have included the lab configurations with the book to ease reference.

Final Notes

With only just more than 10,000 CCIEs worldwide in 10 years, the CCIE certification is still the most challenging certification one can attain. It is the only exam that requires knowledge in desktop protocols, routing protocols, Ethernet switching, and LAN/WAN skills, plus a strong knowledge of IP services. We sincerely hope *CCIE Practical Studies, Volume I and Volume II*, will be an indispensable tool for your CCIE preparation and in the field. Good luck and Godspeed!

—Karl Solie and Leah Lynch

PART I

Ethernet Switching

Chapter 1   Configuring Advanced Switching on the Cisco Catalyst 3550 Ethernet Switch

Configuring Advanced Switching on the Cisco Catalyst 3550 Ethernet Switch

Ethernet is often referred to as an evolutionary protocol rather than a revolutionary protocol. Over the years, Ethernet has evolved by building on various standards at astonishing speeds. Evolutionary protocols build on the current standard and provide some form of migration path, whereas revolutionary protocols involve some form of scientific break-through or use new technology. Revolutionary protocols use few parts, if any, of the existing infrastructure.

The evolution of Ethernet continues to be a remarkable one. The people of the IEEE committee have also been very busy ratifying many new standards, including updating the Spanning Tree Protocol with IEEE 802.1w. Wireless Ethernet IEEE 802.11a and IEEE 802.11b are giving promise to 802.11g operating at 54 Mbps. 10/100-Mbps Ethernet has moved to the home and 10 Gigabit IEEE 802.3ae products have started shipping offering OC-192 speeds! Industry experts predict it will be only a matter of time before Gigabit Ethernet hits the desktop and 40-Gb standards are drafted. Apple computer, for instance, has been shipping Gigabit Ethernet in its PowerBooks and its G4/G5 desktop systems bringing this closer to reality. One might say the evolution might give way to revolution in WANs and MANs. Imagine a day, perhaps not that far off, with Internet service providers (ISPs) using wireless Ethernet to their customers, and points of presence (POPs) connected with 10 Gigabit links! Bandwidth such as this could give way to the next *killer application* on the Internet.

As the role of Ethernet continues to evolve, so does the Cisco product line, being the first to market with many new Ethernet-based products. One such product that will play an increasing role in the enterprise is the Cisco Catalyst 3550 Intelligent Ethernet Switch. As you will see by the end of this chapter, Cisco does a fantastic job of integrating the Catalyst OS (CAT OS) features with the traditional Cisco IOS Software features. Many portions of the Catalyst 3550 configuration might be familiar to you in one form or another.

This chapter focuses on the software configuration of the Cisco Catalyst 3550 Intelligent Ethernet Switch. The discussion includes the technical aspects of the Catalyst 3550 followed by a detailed overview of Ethernet switching and spanning tree. This chapter presents a complete method for configuring VLAN, VLAN Trunking Protocol (VTP), and trunks, and covers other Layer 2/Layer 3 functionality. This chapter also discusses advanced configuration of the 3550, including Rapid Spanning Tree and Multiple Spanning Tree.

For more information on general Ethernet switching concepts and configuring the Cisco Catalyst 3900 Token Ring switch and the Cisco Catalyst 2900/3500 and 5500/6500 series switches, refer to *CCIE Practical Studies*, Volume I.

Enter the Cisco Catalyst 3550 Intelligent Ethernet Switch

The Cisco Catalyst 3550 is an intelligent Ethernet switch that provides impressive bandwidth, Layer 3 switching, and advanced quality of service (QoS) in a small footprint. The switch is called an *intelligent switch* because of many of the advanced features it brings to the traditional enterprise access switch. The switch can make decisions based on Layer 3 and Layer 4 information, thus making it *intelligent*. The Cisco Enhanced Multilayer Software Image (EMI) allows the switch to serve as a core switch in smaller networks providing inter-VLAN routing and Hot Standby Routing Protocol (HSRP). Figure 1-1 shows a Cisco Catalyst 3550.

Figure 1-1   *Cisco Catalyst 3550 Intelligent Ethernet Switch*

Some of the key features of the Catalyst 3550 include the following:

- **Superior redundancy and fault backup**—Features such as Uplinkfast, Backbonefast, and 802.1w Rapid Spanning Tree reduce recovery time significantly between failures. The EMI software feature allows for advance failsafe routing with HSRP.

- **Integrated Cisco IOS features for bandwidth optimization**—Features such as Layer 2 and Layer 3 EtherChannel provide very large paths between switches up to 16 Gbps! Per VLAN Spanning Tree Plus (PVST+) and VTP pruning allow for advanced spanning tree control.

- **Advanced QoS and queuing**—The Cisco 3550 supports 802.1p QoS and the Differentiated Services Code Point (DSCP) field, Weighted Round-Robin (WRR), and Weighted Random Early Detection (WRED).

Other features include advanced security and management, granular rate-limiting, and high-performance routing via Cisco Express Forwarding (CEF) with the EMI. Multicast routing is also supported with the EMI.

NOTE   This list highlights some of the more predominate features of the Cisco Catalyst 3550. For more information on these and other features, see www.cisco.com.

The Cisco 3550 also backs the latest in regulatory certifications and standards from the IEEE and other bodies. The following standards are available on the Catalyst 3550 Ethernet switch:

- IEEE 802.1x port-based authentication
- IEEE 802.1w Rapid Spanning Tree

- IEEE 802.1s Multiple Spanning Tree
- IEEE 802.3 Full Duplex on 10BASE-T, 100BASE-T, and 1000BASE-T ports
- IEEE 802.1d Spanning Tree Protocol
- IEEE 802.1p class of service (CoS) prioritization
- IEEE 802.1Q VLAN trunks
- IEEE 802.3 10BASE-T
- IEEE 802.3u 100BASE-TX
- IEEE 802.3ab 1000BASE-T
- IEEE 802.3z 1000BASE-X
- 1000BASE-X (GBICs): 1000BASE-SX, 1000BASE-LX/LH, and 1000BASE-ZX, 1000BASE-T, 1000BASE-CWDM, and the GigaStack GBIC
- Remote Monitoring (RMON) type I and RMON type II
- Simple Network Management Protocol (SNMP) v1 and SNMP v2c

The Catalyst 3550 currently comes in four base models with multiple variations of each, and the number of models is constantly growing. The Catalyst 3550-24 and 3550-48 come with the Standard Multilayer Software Image (SMI) or the EMI. The Catalyst 3550-12T and 3550-12G are shipped only with the EMI software, whereas the Catalyst 3550-24 and 3550-48 might be field upgraded to the EMI image. The EMI provides a set of enterprise-class features, such as hardware-based IP unicast and multicast routing, inter-VLAN routing, HSRP, and many other features that you would find on a router. Performance and capacity also vary from model to model. Table 1-1 lists the various models and capacities of the Catalyst 3550 switch.

Table 1-1   *Performance Characteristics of the Various Catalyst 3550s*

Switch/ Characteristic	Switch Fabric	Max Forwarding Bandwidth Layer 2/3	Port Memory	64-byte Forwarding Rate	Mac Addresses	Gbps Ports GBICs	10/100 Ports
3550-24	8.8 Gbps	4.4 Gbps	2 MB	6.6 Mpps	8000	2	24
3550-48	13.6 Gbps	6.8 Gbps	4 MB	10.1 Mpps	8000	2	48
3550-12T	24 Gbps	12 Gbps	4 MB	17 Mpps	12,000	2	10 -10/100/1000 BASE-T ports
3550-12G	24 Gbps	12 Gbps	4 MB	17 Mpps	12,000	10	2 -10/100/1000 BASE-T ports

*   All 3550 switches have 64 MB of dynamic random-access memory (DRAM) and 16 MB of Flash memory. The maximum transmission unit (MTU) and the number of unicast and multicast routes also vary by switch type. For more detailed information, see www.cisco.com.

Ethernet Switching Review

Before discussing the detailed configuration of the Cisco 3550, it's necessary to review some important technologies. The following sections briefly review VLANs, VTP, VLAN trunking, spanning-tree 802.1d, and port autonegotiation. If you have previously read *CCIE Practical Studies, Volume I (CCIE PSV1)*, you might want to glance only at this section, because it is intended as a review. For a more comprehensive explanation of these and other Ethernet switching principals, refer to *CCIE PSV1*.

Virtual LANs (VLANs)

There are many definitions for the term *VLAN*. For this discussion, the definition is very simple. Virtual LANs (VLANs) are broadcast domains that can extend geographical distances. Within the VLAN, unicast, broadcast, and multicast, frames are forwarded to members of that VLAN; this is referred to as intra-VLAN traffic. Members of separate VLANs do not forward traffic to each other; this can provide some form of inherent security. For one VLAN to communicate with another, some form of routing must be used. To put VLANs in their simplest form, remember the following:

A VLAN = A broadcast domain = A Layer 3 network (IP subnet)

In a nutshell, VLANs offer the following:

- Network segmentation
- Flexibility and management
- Security

When Ethernet switching is configured, every port is assigned to a VLAN by default. The default VLAN is always VLAN 1. When switches ship from the factory, they are in some ways "plug and play." Every port is assigned to VLAN 1; therefore, every port of the switch will be in a single broadcast domain. This makes migrating from shared Ethernet hubs to a basic switched network very easy. VLANs should always be thought of as just broadcast domains. Most VLANs eventually become IP/IPX subnets or bridging domains. The basic design rules that apply to broadcast domains also apply to VLANs, such as the following:

- There should be a single subnet per VLAN. Each VLAN is like a separate bridging domain.
- Do not bridge different VLANs together.
- VLANs can span across multiple switches and geographic areas.
- Trunks carry traffic for multiple VLANs by using a special encapsulation.
- A router or Layer 3 switch will be needed to route between VLANs.
- Spanning Tree Protocol runs a per-VLAN level to prevent loops. This can be disabled but is not recommend.

Table 1-2 lists the various VLAN default values for Catalyst switches.

Table 1-2   *Default VLAN Settings*

Feature	Default Value
Native VLAN	VLAN 1.
Default VLAN	VLAN 1.
Port VLAN assignments	All ports assigned to VLAN1; Token Ring ports are assigned to VLAN 1003 (TrCRF-default).
VTP mode	Server.
VTP name	Null.
VLAN state	Active.
Reserved VLAN range*	VLAN 0, VLAN 1006–VLAN 1009, VLAN 4095.
Normal VLAN range	VLAN 2–VLAN 1001.
VLAN extended range*	VLAN 1006–VLAN 4094.
MTU size	1500 bytes for Ethernet. 4472 bytes for Token Ring.
SAID value	100,000 plus VLAN number. Example: VLAN 2 = SAID 100002
Prune eligibility	VLANS 2–1000 are prune eligible; VLANs 1025–4094 are not.
MAC address reduction	Disabled.
Spanning-tree mode	PVST+ (128 spanning tree instances).
Default FDDI VLAN	VLAN 1002.
Default Token Ring TrCRF VLAN	VLAN 1003.
Default FDDI Net VLAN	VLAN 1004.
Default Token Ring TrBRF VLAN	VLAN 1005 with bridge number 0F.
Spanning-tree version for TrBRF VLANs	IBM.
TrCRF bridge mode	SRB.

*   The VLAN reserved range is used on the Catalyst 6000 series to map nonreserved VLANs to reserved VLANs. The VLAN extended range is available on the Catalyst 6000 series and 3550 series switches. The extended and reserved VLAN range is not propagated by VTP at this time and requires the switch to be in VTP transparent mode. Token Ring and FDDI VLANs are listed on Ethernet-only switches because it is global VTP information.

Now consider some of the basic switched networks; this discussion focuses on the differences in each one.

Figure 1-2 shows a basic LAN configuration. The switch has VLANs 1 and 2 configured on it and various ports assigned to those VLANs. Each VLAN is configured with a separate IP subnet. If information needs to pass from VLAN 1 to VLAN 2, a router is required. Here the router has an interface in each VLAN. Traffic going from VLAN 1 to VLAN 2 needs to first hit the router. This type of configuration requires a single interface for every VLAN that needs to be routed; therefore, it is very expensive and not very scalable.

Figure 1-2   *Per-Interface VLAN routing*

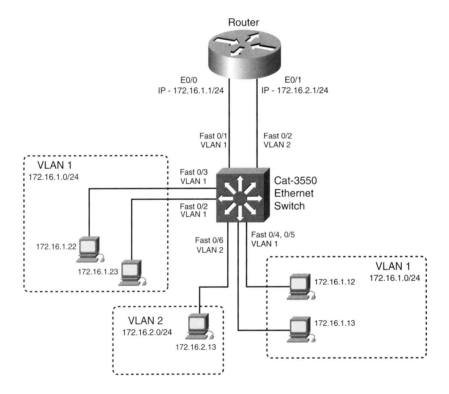

Figure 1-3 shows another basic VLAN configuration. The switch has VLANs 1 and 2 configured on it again. Here the router has a single 100-Mbps interface running a VTP, such as 802.1Q. Traffic going from one VLAN to the other must travel up the trunk to the router and then back down the same trunk. Using a single trunk to route between VLANs is one of the more economical ways to accomplish routing between VLANs. This type of configuration is often referred to as a "router on a stick."

The next evolution was to move the routing function from a standalone router to the switch itself. This move was only logical, because traffic is doubled up coming in and exiting the same interface. Switches such as the Catalyst 3550 with the EMI software support this type of configuration. Figure 1-4 illustrates Layer 3 Switching.

Figure 1-3   *Router on a Stick*

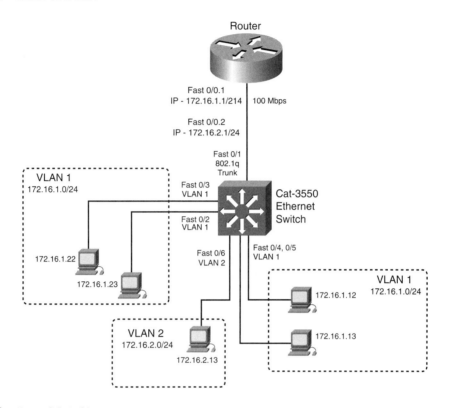

Figure 1-4   *Layer 3 Switching*

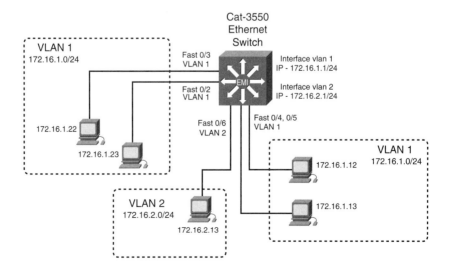

VTP and Trunking Protocols

A powerful function of VLANs is their capability to span geographic distance. The VLANs present on a switch are communicated from switch to switch by the means of a VLAN Trunking Protocol (VTP). VTP maintains global VLAN information between switches. This includes synchronizing the VLAN database and the management of additions, deletions, and VLAN name changes across the network. A VLAN management domain, or VTP domain, consists of one or more switches interconnected and sharing the same administrative responsibility. Anytime you desire the VLANs on one switch to have information about the VLANs on another switch, you must configure a VTP domain and a trunk. VTP also tracks all the VLANs in a VTP domain and propagates these in a client/server fashion from one switch to another. The intent of VTP is to ease management and provide a common VLAN database across the VTP domain. An advanced function of VTP includes VTP pruning, which helps control inter-VLAN broadcast traffic between switches.

VTP operates in one of three modes:

- **VTP server mode**—In VTP server mode, VLANs can be created, modified, and deleted. VLAN information is automatically sent to all adjacent VTP servers and clients in the same VTP domain. Always exercise caution when "clearing" a VLAN from the VTP server because that VLAN will be deleted on all VTP servers and clients in that VTP domain. If two devices are configured as servers, the switch/server with the highest VTP configuration revision serves as the primary server. VLAN information is stored in the switch's nonvolatile random-access memory (NVRAM).

- **VTP client mode**—In VTP client mode, VLANs cannot be created, modified, or deleted. Only the name and the VTP mode and pruning can be changed. The VTP client is at the mercy of the VTP server for all VLAN information. The client must still assign ports to a VLAN, but the VLAN will not be active on the switch unless the VTP server sends information to the client about that VLAN. On Catalyst 2900XL/3500XL/3550 series switches, VLAN information is stored in Flash memory in the VLAN.DAT file after it is received from the server. The Catalyst 4000/5500/6500 series of switches do not store the VLAN database on VTP client switches.

- **VTP transparent mode**—In VTP transparent mode, VLAN information that is local, or created, on the switch will not be advertised, and VTP will not synchronize VLAN databases between switches. VTP information received from other switches can be forwarded if *all* the switches are in the same VTP domain. For VTP updates to flow through a VTP transparent switch, the transparent switch and any other client or sever switches must be in the same VTP domain. VLANs can be created, modified, and deleted on transparent switches. Transparent switches also support extended-range VLANs. As a matter of fact, VLANs 1006 through 4094 can only be created on VTP transparent switches. VTP will also not propagate VLANs in this range. VLAN information is stored in Flash memory in the VLAN.DAT file on transparent switches on the Catalyst 2900XL/3500XL/3550 series switches. Table 1-3 highlights the various VTP modes and operation.

Table 1-3 *Various VTP Modes of Operation*

VTP Mode	Source VTP Messages	Propagate Local VLAN Database	Listen to VTP Messages	Create, Modify, and Delete VLANs	Sync VLAN Database to VTP Servers	VLAN Database Saved in NVRAM
Server	Yes	Yes	Yes	Yes	Yes	Yes
Client	Yes	N/A	Yes	No	Yes	Yes/No*
Transparent	No**	No	Yes**	Yes	No	Yes

* The Catalyst 4000/5500/6500 series of switches do not store the VLAN database on VTP client switches. The Catalyst 2900XL/3500G/3550 series of switches save VTP and VLAN information in the VLAN.DAT file in Flash memory. The switch will have the VLAN database upon initialization.

** In transparent mode, the switch will not participate in VTP; that is, it will not synchronize VLAN databases. However, VTP information received can be forwarded out other trunk ports. The trunks will not propagate local VLAN information.

Figure 1-5 illustrates how VTP information can be propagated across a LAN.

Figure 1-5 *VTP Modes and Propagation*

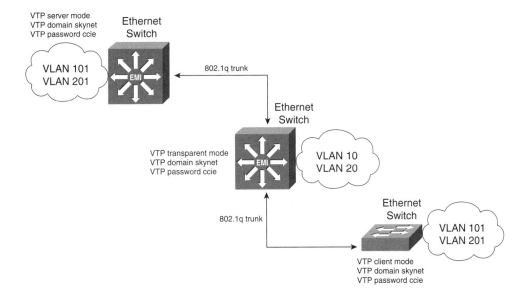

VTP advertisements are sent out on all trunk connections in Inter-Switch Link (ISL) frames, 802.1Q frames, IEEE 802.10, or ATM LAN Emulation (LANE) cells. VTP frames are sent to the destination MAC address of 0100.0ccc.cccc with a logical link control (LLC) code of SNAP (AAAA). IEEE 802.1Q frames have an Ethernet type code of 0x8100. VTP advertisements are also sent out every 5 minutes or when there is a change in a VLAN. For VTP messages to be successfully transmitted, the following must occur:

- **VTP domain name**—VTP server and client switches only accept messages with the same domain name. If authentication is configured for that VTP domain, the VTP passwords must also match. The VTP name and VTP password are case sensitive.

- **VTP version mode must match**—VTP only accepts messages with the same version: version I or version II. The VTP version is controlled by enabling/disabling V2 mode on both sides of the trunk. A switch might be VTP version II capable and have V2 mode disabled. This is the default setting. V2 mode is used only for Token Ring switches; therefore, you see it primarily on the Catalyst 3924s and the Catalyst 5500/6500 series switches with Token Ring switching modules installed.

- **VTP clients synchronize with VTP servers only if the client's VTP revision number is less than the VTP server's revision number**—If the VTP client's revision number is equal to or greater than the VTP revision number of the server, the VLAN databases will not synchronize, and the VTP client will not receive any VLAN information from the server.

When a trunk is established, VTP sends periodic advertisement out each trunk port, once every 5 minutes or when there is a change in a VLAN. The VTP advertisement contains the following:

- VLAN IDs (ISL and 802.1Q).
- Emulated LAN names for ATM LANE.
- 802.10 SAID values.
- VTP domain name and configuration revision number. The server with the highest revision number will become the primary server and send its VLAN database to the other switches. This process is referred to as *synchronization*. When VTP is synchronized, all VTP servers and clients will have the same VTP revision number. The VTP revision number is incremented every time a VLAN configuration change is made.
- VLAN configuration, VLAN ID, VLAN name, and MTU size for each VLAN.
- Ethernet frame format.

VTP has two versions: version I and version II. All the switches in the VTP domain must be on the same version. This rule does not apply to the transparent mode switches. VTP version II offers the following, the most important being support for Token Ring:

- **Token Ring support**—VTP version II supports Token Ring LAN switching and VLANs (Token Ring Bridge Relay Function [TrBRF]).

- **Unrecognized Type Length Value (TLV) support**—Unrecognized TLVs are saved in NVRAM when the switch is in VTP server mode.

- **Version-dependent transparent mode**—VTP forwards VTP messages that do not match the domain name and version to switches operating in VTP transparent mode version II switches. In transparent mode version I, VTP inspects the frame for a version number; if the numbers match, VTP forwards the frame. This inspection process does not happen in VTP version II.

- **Consistency checks**—Consistency checks are performed on VLAN names and values when information is changed from the command-line interface or Simple Network Management Protocol.

Table 1-4 lists the default VTP settings on the Catalyst 3550 switch.

Table 1-4   *Default VTP Settings on Catalyst 3550*

VTP Feature	Default Setting
VTP domain name	Null
VTP mode	Server
VTP version 2 updates	Disabled
VTP security/password	Disabled
VTP pruning	Disabled
VLAN trunking	DTP

VTP Pruning

VTP pruning basically controls broadcast, multicast, and unknown unicast traffic from crossing trunk lines where it is not needed. A common misconception is that VTP pruning controls Spanning Tree Protocol (STP) traffic, which it does not. With VTP pruning disabled, the default setting on the 3550, all broadcast, multicast, and unknown unicast traffic is forwarded down trunk lines on the switch to downstream switches, regardless of whether the switch needs or will discard the traffic. VTP pruning essentially only forwards broadcast, multicast, and unknown unicast traffic across a trunk if the downstream switch has an active port in the same VLAN as the VLAN that originated the traffic. If the destination switch is not adjacent, switches in between the source and destination switches receive and forward the traffic. In Figure 1-6, a workstation in VLAN 10 sends a broadcast, with VTP pruning disabled; all switches in the LAN will receive that broadcast.

In Figure 1-7, VTP pruning is enabled. With VTP pruning enabled, only switches with ports/interfaces in VLAN 10 will receive and forward VLAN 10's traffic, along with any intermediary switches.

VLAN Trunking Protocols

VTP requires trunks to transport VTP information. A trunk is considered a point-to-point link between Ethernet switch ports and another networking device, such as a router or another switch. Trunks have the capability to carry the traffic of multiple VLANs over a single link and extend VLANs across the internetwork. Without the use of VTP and trunks, an IP subnet could never be partitioned across switches. VTP trunks allow for an effective way to tie two broadcast domains together that are separated by geographical distance. Figure 1-8 illustrates how 802.1Q trunks tie VLANs 2 and 4 together.

Figure 1-6 *VTP Pruning*

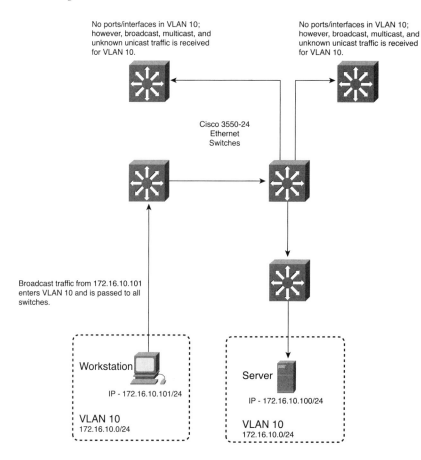

No ports/interfaces in VLAN 10; however, broadcast, multicast, and unknown unicast traffic is received for VLAN 10.

No ports/interfaces in VLAN 10; however, broadcast, multicast, and unknown unicast traffic is received for VLAN 10.

Cisco 3550-24 Ethernet Switches

Broadcast traffic from 172.16.10.101 enters VLAN 10 and is passed to all switches.

Workstation
IP - 172.16.10.101/24
VLAN 10
172.16.10.0/24

Server
IP - 172.16.10.100/24
VLAN 10
172.16.10.0/24

Figure 1-7   *VTP Pruning*

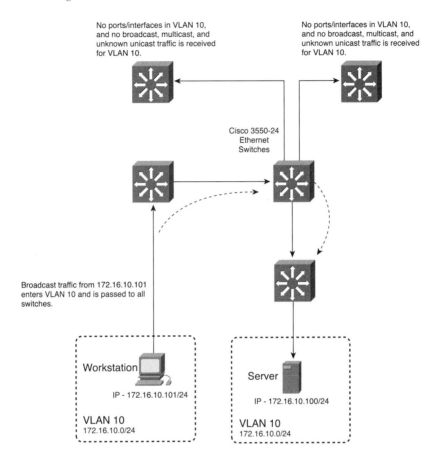

No ports/interfaces in VLAN 10,
and no broadcast, multicast, and
unknown unicast traffic is received
for VLAN 10.

No ports/interfaces in VLAN 10,
and no broadcast, multicast, and
unknown unicast traffic is received
for VLAN 10.

Cisco 3550-24
Ethernet
Switches

Broadcast traffic from 172.16.10.101
enters VLAN 10 and is passed to all
switches.

Workstation
IP - 172.16.10.101/24
VLAN 10
172.16.10.0/24

Server
IP - 172.16.10.100/24
VLAN 10
172.16.10.0/24

Three types of encapsulation are supported on the Cisco Catalyst family of switches: ISL, 802.1Q, and 802.10. The Catalyst 3550 Ethernet switch supports ISL and 802.1Q; therefore, this discussion focuses on these switches:

- **Inter-Switch Link (ISL)**—ISL is a Cisco proprietary trunking encapsulation. ISL is a frame-tagging protocol that allows for low-latency multiplexing of traffic from multiple VLANs to a single physical path. Ports configured as ISL trunks encapsulate each frame with a 26-byte ISL header followed by a 4-byte cyclic redundancy check (CRC) before forwarding it out the trunk. The encapsulation of each frame is a low-latency process. This operation is performed by application-specific integrated circuits (ASICs), so it is very fast. This is referred to as "wire speed." The frames on the link contain the standard Ethernet, or FDDI or Token Ring frame, and the VLAN information associated with that frame along with a bridge packet data unit (BPDU). ISL is supported on links that are 100 Mbps or greater in speed, and it can operate in full or half duplex. STP on ISL trunks is implemented on a per-VLAN basis, called PVST+. This means that every VLAN has a root bridge, and trunks go into a forward/blocking mode for each VLAN on each trunk. PVST+ is critical to control on large networks, as discussed later in this chapter.

- **IEEE 802.1Q**—802.1Q is the industry standard trunking protocol. An 802.1Q frame uses an Ethernet type code of 0x8100 and inserts VLAN information and recomputes the frame control sequence at the end of the frame. 802.1Q operates slightly different from ISL. For instance, it runs Mono Spanning Tree on the native VLAN for all VLANs in the VTP domain. The native VLAN 802.1Q uses by default is VLAN 1. In Mono Spanning Tree, one root bridge is elected for the entire VTP domain; this is called the Common Spanning Tree (CST) domain. All VLAN traffic follows one path in this type of configuration. Cisco, understanding the need to control spanning tree on large networks while controlling load, implements PVST+ on all 802.1Q VLANs in addition to Mono Spanning Tree. The following restrictions apply to 802.1Q trunks:

  — The native VLAN needs to be the same on both ends of the trunk. Mono Spanning Tree will run in this VLAN. It is critical that the native VLAN be the same on third-party switches interacting with Cisco switches.

  — As mentioned, 802.1Q uses Mono Spanning Tree. Cisco enhances this with PVST+. Because the BPDUs are handled differently between Cisco and third-party switches, care should be taken whenever integrating these domains, that spanning tree and the default VLANs are consistent in both switches. The entire non-Cisco domain will look like a single broadcast/spanning-tree domain to the Cisco PVST+ VTP domain. The Mono Spanning Tree of the non-Cisco domain will map to the CST of the Cisco domain, which is by default VLAN 1.

  — BPDUs on the native VLAN of the trunk are sent untagged to the reserved IEEE 802.1d spanning-tree multicast MAC address (0180.c200.0000). The BPDUs on all other VLANs on the trunk are sent and tagged on the reserved Cisco Shared Spanning Tree (SSTP) multicast MAC address (0100.0ccc.cccd).

Figure 1-8   *VLAN Trunking*

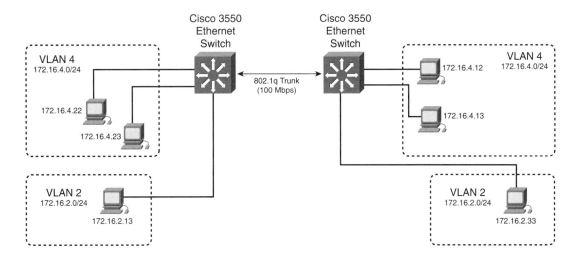

Dynamic ISL (DISL) and Dynamic Trunk Protocol (DTP)

Dynamic ISL was Cisco's first trunk negotiation protocol. DISL was slowly replaced with Dynamic Trunk Protocol (DTP) on newer versions of CAT OS and Cisco IOS Software. DTP is essentially DISL that attempts to automate ISL and 802.1Q trunk configuration. DTP uses the reserved destination multicast address of 0100.0ccc.cccc for LAN networks to negotiate trunks. In the default "auto" state, DTP messages are sent out every 30 seconds on all trunk lines. Depending on the "mode" of the port, the port might become an ISL or 802.1Q trunk. DTP operates in the following modes. (Note that these modes are not available on all switches and might differ slightly syntactically.)

- **On**—Puts the port in a permanent trunking state. It also tries to negotiate the link to be a trunk.

- **Off**—Turns the port into a nontrunk link, and thereby disables the trunk.

- **Desirable**—Makes the port attempt to convert to a trunk link. The port becomes a trunk if the neighboring port is set to on, desirable, or auto mode.

- **Auto**—The port converts to a trunk if the neighboring port is set to on or desirable mode.

- **Nonegotiate**—Puts the port into trunking mode but prevents the port from sending DTP frames.

In practicality, this is really too many options for a trunk. Network administrators either configure a port as trunk or they don't. It could even be argued that having dynamic trunks is a potential security risk. Table 1-5 charts the possible combinations of trunks and the modes on CAT OS. As you will see, the most reliable and simplest way to configure a trunk is to statically configure it on both sides of the link as a trunk and in the on mode.

Table 1-5   *Ethernet DTP Configuration Outcomes on CAT OS*

Neighbor Port	Trunk Mode and Trunk Encapsulation	Off	On	Desirable	Auto	On	Desirable	Auto	Desirable	Auto
Off	ISL or DOT1Q	Local: Nontrunk Neighbor: Nontrunk	Local: ISL trunk Neighbor: Nontrunk	Local: Nontrunk Neighbor: Nontrunk	Local: Nontrunk Neighbor: Nontrunk	Local: 1Q TRUNK Neighbor: Nontrunk	Local: Nontrunk Neighbor: Nontrunk	Local: Nontrunk Neighbor: Nontrunk	Local: Nontrunk Neighbor: Nontrunk	Local: Nontrunk Neighbor: Nontrunk
On	ISL	Local: Nontrunk Neighbor: ISL trunk	Local: ISL trunk Neighbor: ISL trunk	Local: ISL trunk Neighbor: ISL trunk	Local: ISL trunk Neighbor: ISL trunk	Local: 1Q trunk Neighbor: ISL trunk	Local Nontrunk Neighbor: ISL trunk	Local: Nontrunk Neighbor: ISL trunk	Local: ISL trunk Neighbor: ISL trunk	Local: ISL trunk Neighbor: ISL trunk
Desirable	ISL	Local: Nontrunk Neighbor: Nontrunk	Local: ISL trunk Neighbor: ISL trunk	Local: ISL trunk Neighbor: ISL trunk	Local: ISL trunk Neighbor: ISL trunk	Local: 1Q trunk Neighbor: ISL trunk	Local: Nontrunk Neighbor: ISL trunk	Local: Nontrunk Neighbor: ISL trunk	Local: ISL trunk Neighbor: ISL	Local: ISL trunk Neighbor: ISL
Auto	ISL	Local: Nontrunk Neighbor: Nontrunk	Local: ISL trunk Neighbor: ISL trunk	Local: ISL trunk Neighbor: ISL trunk	Local: Nontrunk Neighbor: Nontrunk	Local: 1Q trunk Neighbor: Nontrunk	Local: Nontrunk Neighbor: ISL trunk	Local: Nontrunk Neighbor: Nontrunk	Local: ISL trunk Neighbor: ISL	Local: Nontrunk Neighbor: Nontrunk
On	DOT1Q	Local: Nontrunk Neighbor: 1Q trunk	Local: ISL trunk Neighbor: 1Q trunk	Local: Non Neighbor: 1Q trunk	Local: Non Neighbor: 1Q trunk	Local: 1Q trunk Neighbor: 1Q trunk	Local: 1Q trunk Neighbor: 1Q trunk	Local: 1Q trunk Neighbor: 1Q trunk	Local: 1Q trunk Neighbor: 1Q trunk	Local: 1Q trunk Neighbor: 1Q trunk

Table 1-5   *Ethernet DTP Configuration Outcomes on CAT OS (Continued)*

Neighbor Port	Trunk Mode and Trunk Encapsulation	Off	On	Desirable	Auto	On	Desirable	Auto	Desirable	Auto
Desirable	DOT1Q	Local: Nontrunk Neighbor: Nontrunk	Local: ISL trunk Neighbor: Nontrunk	Local: Nontrunk Neighbor: Nontrunk	Local: Nontrunk Neighbor: Nontrunk	Local: 1Q trunk Neighbor: 1Q trunk	Local: 1Q trunk Neighbor: 1Q trunk	Local: 1Q trunk Neighbor: 1Q trunk	Local: 1Q trunk Neighbor: 1Q trunk	Local: 1Q trunk Neighbor: 1Q trunk
Auto	DOT1Q	Local: Nontrunk Neighbor: Nontrunk	Local: ISL trunk Neighbor: Nontrunk	Local: Nontrunk Neighbor: Nontrunk	Local: Nontrunk Neighbor: Nontrunk	Local: 1Q trunk Neighbor: 1Q trunk	Local: 1Q trunk Neighbor: 1Q trunk	Local: Nontrunk Neighbor: Nontrunk	Local: 1Q trunk Neighbor: 1Q trunk	Local: Nontrunk Neighbor: Nontrunk
Desirable	Negotiate	Local: Nontrunk Neighbor: Nontrunk	Local: ISL trunk Neighbor: ISL trunk	Local: ISL trunk Neighbor: ISL trunk	Local: ISL trunk Neighbor: ISL trunk	Local: 1Q trunk Neighbor: 1Q trunk	Local: 1Q trunk Neighbor: 1Q trunk	Local: ISL trunk Neighbor: ISL trunk	Local: ISL	Local: ISL Neighbor: ISL
Auto	Negotiate	Local: Nontrunk Neighbor: Nontrunk	Local: ISL Neighbor: ISL trunk	Local: ISL Neighbor: ISL trunk	Local: Nontrunk Neighbor: Nontrunk	Local: 1Q trunk Neighbor: 1Q trunk	Local: 1Q trunk Neighbor: 1Q trunk	Local: Nontrunk Neighbor: Nontrunk	Local: ISL Neighbor: ISL	Local: Nontrunk Neighbor: Nontrunk

Layer 2 and Layer 3 EtherChannel Trunks

EtherChannel combines multiple physical Fast Ethernet or Gigabit ports/interfaces into a single logical interface called a *channel group*. For instance, up to eight Fast Ethernet ports/ interfaces might be grouped together to provide a full-duplex 1600-Mbps logical link. Gigabit EtherChannel can group up to 8 ports together for an aggregate speed of 16 Gbps in full-duplex mode.

NOTE   GigaStack Gigabit Ethernet modules cannot be used as Gigabit EtherChannel trunks.

Figure 1-9   *Physical, Logical, and Channel Group Relationship*

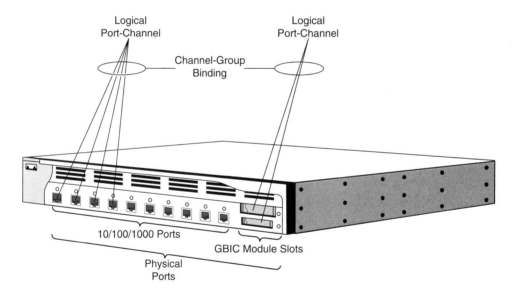

EtherChannel can serve as a great alternative when trunking Cisco switches together. One of the improvements it offers over normal multiple trunks is that STP will see normal multiple links as individual links to the same bridge; therefore, bandwidth will not be wasted by an interface in blocking mode. Traditionally, VLAN traffic can become tricky to load balance across, and bandwidth is limited because of STP blocking on redundant ports. In a link failure, STP will also have to wait a default of 50 seconds for convergence. EtherChannel load shares across all physical ports in the EtherChannel group. If a physical link goes down, the EtherChannel group only loses the bandwidth that the link provided. EtherChannel proves especially useful between core switches. Figure 1-10 illustrates two Cisco Catalyst 3550s serving as the core switches with the Gigabit Ethernet interfaces channeled into a single Gigabit EtherChannel port group.

Figure 1-10 *Gigabit EtherChannel on Catalyst 3550s*

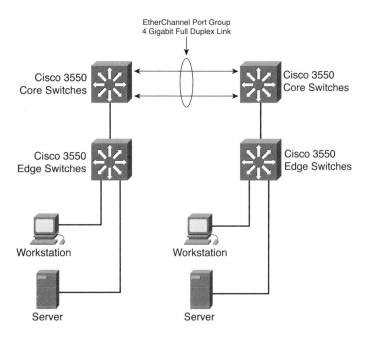

The number and type of interfaces that you can put into an EtherChannel port group varies from switch to switch. One standing rule is that you can only group Fast Ethernet together with Fast Ethernet ports, and Gigabit ports together with Gigabit ports. Because there exist very specific rules for which ports and how many you can group into a channel that are switch-type specific, check with Cisco at www.cisco.com as to the limitations that EtherChannel might have on the switch you are configuring.

Port Aggregation Protocol (PAgP) and Link Aggregation Protocol (LACP)

EtherChannel uses a protocol called *Port Aggregation Protocol* to dynamically build an EtherChannel port group between adjacent switches. Cisco defines PAgP and the way it operates as follows:

> Port Aggregation Protocol (PAgP) facilitates the automatic creation of EtherChannel port groups. By using PAgP, the switch learns the identity of adjacent switch capable of supporting PAgP and then learns the capabilities of each interface. It then dynamically groups similarly configured interfaces into a single logical link (channel or aggregate port); these interfaces are grouped based on hardware, administrative, and port parameter constraints. For example, PAgP groups the interfaces with the same speed, duplex, native VLAN, VLAN range, and the trunking status and type. After grouping the links into an EtherChannel, PAgP adds the group to the spanning tree as a single switch port.

For these reasons, it is extremely important to have the same physical VLAN and STP parameters configured on each interface in the channel group.

PAgP works along with LACP to negotiate the EtherChannel trunk. LACP is defined in IEEE 802.3AD and allows Cisco switches to manage Ethernet channels between switches that conform to the 802.3AD protocol.

Port Aggregation Protocol (PAgP) Modes

PAgP has four modes in the CAT OS and six in Cisco IOS Software:

- **Auto**—Auto mode places an interface into a passive negotiating state; the interface responds to PAgP frames it receives but does not initiate PAgP negotiation. This setting is the default and minimizes the transmission of PAgP.

- **Desirable**—Desirable mode places an interface into an active negotiating state, in which the interface initiates negotiations with other interfaces by sending PAgP packets.

- **On**—On forces the interface to channel without PAgP or LACP. With the on mode, a usable EtherChannel exists only when an interface group in the on mode is connected to another interface group in the on mode. An interface in the on mode that is added to a port channel is forced to have the same characteristics as the already existing on mode interfaces in the channel.

- **Off**—In this mode, the port will not form an Ethernet channel, and no PAgP frames will be exchanged.

- **Active (LACP)-IOS only**—Active sets the interface into an active negotiating state, in which the interface starts negotiations with other interfaces by sending LACP packets.

- **Passive (LACP)-IOS only**—Passive sets the interface into a passive negotiating state. In this mode, the interface responds to LACP packets that it receives but does not start LACP packet negotiation. This setting uses minimal LACP packets.

Switch interfaces exchange PAgP packets only with partner interfaces configured in the **auto** or **desirable** modes; interfaces configured in the **on** mode do not exchange PAgP frames. Interfaces can form an EtherChannel when they are in different PAgP modes as long as the modes are compatible. For example, an interface in **desirable** mode can form an EtherChannel with another interface that is in **desirable** or **auto** mode. However, an interface in **auto** mode cannot form an EtherChannel with another interface that is also in **auto** mode because neither interface initiates PAgP negotiation.

If your switch is connected to a partner that is PAgP capable, you can configure the switch interface for nonsilent operation. This is accomplished by using the **non-silent** keyword. If you do not specify the **non-silent** keyword with the **auto** or **desirable** mode, silent is assumed.

PAgP Physical Learners and Aggregate-Port Learners

Network devices are classified into two groups called *PAgP physical learners* and *aggregate-port learners*. A device is a physical learner if it learns addresses by physical ports and directs traffic based on that learning. A device is an aggregate-port learner if it learns addresses by aggregate (logical) ports.

When a device and its partner are both aggregate-port learners, they learn the address on the logical port channel. The device transmits frames to the source using any of the interfaces in the EtherChannel bundle.

PAgP cannot automatically detect when the partner device is a physical or aggregate port. You must manually set the learning method on the local device for source-based distribution by using the **pagp learn-method src-mac** interface configuration command. With source-based distribution, any given source MAC address is sent on the same physical port.

Some EtherChannel features and limitations are as follows:

- The number of interfaces you can put in a bundle is tightly related to the switch hardware. Be sure to check the Cisco website at www.cisco.com for the latest software and hardware limitations.

- Dynamic Trunking Protocol (DTP), VTP, and Cisco Discovery Protocol (CDP) can transmit and receive frames over the physical interfaces in the EtherChannel. Trunk ports transmit and receive PAgP protocol data units (PDUs) on the lowest-numbered VLAN.

- STP sends frames over the first interface in the EtherChannel group. STP views the channel group as a single physical link.

- The MAC address of a Layer 3 EtherChannel is the MAC address of the first interface in the port channel.

- PAgP transmits and receives PAgP PDUs only from interfaces that are up and have PAgP enabled for the **auto** or **desirable** mode. Statically configuring a trunk disables PAgP.

- EtherChannel will not form with ports that have different GARP VLAN Registration Protocol (GVRP), GARP Multicast Registration Protocol (GMRP), and QoS configurations.

- Port security cannot be used on EtherChannel ports.

- An EtherChannel will not form if one of the ports is a Switch Port Analyzer (SPAN) destination port. You can use the EtherChannel group as the source of SPAN to monitor the entire group.

- Speed, duplex, native VLAN, VLAN range, and trunk type (if you are trunking over the EtherChannel) must match on both ends of the EtherChannel link.

Layer 3 EtherChannel

Layer 3 EtherChannel is configuring EtherChannel on a routed interface on the switch. The EtherChannel group will have a single IP address assigned to it, and the port must have switching functions disabled with the interface command **no switchport**. For all practical purposes, Layer 3 EtherChannel operates in the same functional manner as Layer 2 EtherChannel. Layer 3 EtherChannel is only available with the EMI software installed on the switch.

Ethernet Physical Properties: Half- and Full-Duplex Ethernet

Half-duplex mode fundamentally operates Ethernet in the classic carrier sense multiple access collision detect (CSMA/CD) mode. Ethernet hubs are a good example of a device requiring half duplex. Half-duplex Ethernet has the follow characteristics:

- Unidirectional data flow.

- High potential for collisions.

- Operates on shared media devices such as a hub, or a workstation.

- Operational efficiency is rated at 50 percent to 60 percent of the total bandwidth of the link.

Full-duplex Ethernet allows for a station to simultaneously transmit and receive data. Ethernet frames are transmitted and received simultaneously on two pairs of unshielded twisted-pair (UTP) or a single pair of fiber. Full-duplex Ethernet is essentially Ethernet without CSMA/CD. Full-duplex mode basically doubles the bandwidth of Ethernet! To run full-duplex Ethernet, both Ethernet devices must be capable and configured for autonegotiation or full duplex. Figure 1-11 illustrates a common Ethernet network and the duplex setting of the links.

NOTE   A station not operating in the correct duplex mode will generate enormous amounts of collisions or frame check sequence (FCS) errors on the port to which it is connected. These collisions will most likely be registered as *late collisions*. Be sure the port on the switch and the end station are operating in the same duplex mode.

Ethernet Autonegotiation

To aid in simplifying the configuration of Ethernet devices, the IEEE committee defined normal link pulse (NLP) for 10BASE-T networks and fast link pulse (FLP) for 100BASE-T and 1000BASE-T networks. NLP and FLP are a series of pulses on the network that are able to deduce what the duplex and speed at which the link is operating. The station and the hub/switch agrees on the highest priority and configures the station in that manner. All autonegotiation occurs at the physical layer. Table 1-6 lists the priority FLP uses and the associated data transfer rate. For autonegotiation to work, both devices must support autonegotiation logic.

Figure 1-11   *Ethernet Network Duplex Settings*

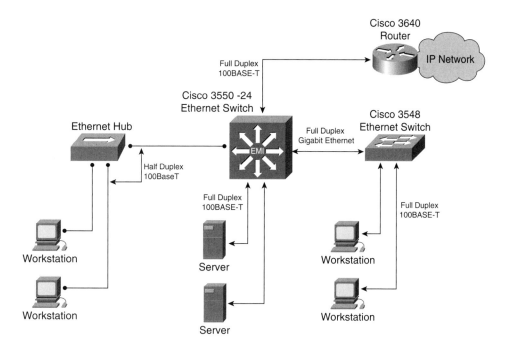

Table 1-6   *Ethernet Autonegotiation Prioritization*

Priority	Total Data Transfer Rate (Mbps)	Speed and Duplex Settings
1 (highest)	2000	1000BASE-T full duplex
2	1000	1000BASE-T half duplex
3	200	100BASE-T2 full duplex
4	200	100BASE-TX full duplex
5	100	100BASE-T2 half duplex
6	100	100BASE-T4 half duplex
7	100	100BASE-TX half duplex
8	20	10BASE-T full duplex
9 (lowest)	10	10BASE-T half duplex

Infrastructure devices, such as routers and servers, should always have speed and duplex settings fixed. Most 100-Mbps and greater network interface cards (NICs) support full duplex. Running at full duplex essentially doubles the capacity of Ethernet. Taking advantage of this is the cheapest network upgrade you will ever do!

NOTE   Duplex modes are a function of the hardware built in to the NIC. Software upgrades will not enable you to run full-duplex mode. For full-duplex mode to work, both stations must be capable of full-duplex operation.

IEEE 802.1d Spanning Tree Protocol (STP)

As Ethernet was evolving from a single shared cable to networks with multiple bridges and hubs, a loop detection and prevention protocol was needed. The 802.1d protocol, developed by Radia Perlman, provided this loop protection. As a matter of fact, it did such a good job at this that when most networks went from bridged networks to switched networks, the importance of spanning tree was almost forgotten. STP did an excellent job of preventing loops from occurring on redundant switched networks. For many network engineers, this protocol ran in the background on their networks without manual configuration. Because of this, spanning tree is probably the most used but least understood protocol in the modern switched LAN. Over the next few years, you might see LANs start to migrate from IEEE 802.1d STP to IEEE 802.1w Rapid STP. IEEE 802.1w networks allow for very quick convergence, using concepts originally developed by Cisco Systems, such as PortFast, UplinkFast, and BackboneFast. This section focuses on IEEE 802.1d STP; IEEE 802.1w and IEEE 802.1s are discussed in upcoming sections.

Spanning-Tree Operation

Spanning tree's sole purpose in life is to elect a *root bridge* and build loop-free paths leading toward that root bridge for all bridges in the network. When spanning tree is converged, every bridge in the network will have its bridged interfaces in one of two states: *forwarding* or *blocking*. STP accomplishes this by transmitting special messages called bridge protocol data units (BPDUs). 802.1d uses two types of BPDUs:

* A configuration BPDU, used for initial STP configuration
* A topology change notification (TCN) BPDU used for topology changes

BPDUs are transmitted using a reserved multicast address assigned to "all bridges." The BPDU is sent out on all bridged LAN ports and is received by all bridges residing on the LAN. The BPDU will not be forwarded off the LAN by a router.

The BPDU contains the following relevant information:

- **Root ID**—This is the ID of the bridge assumed to be root. Upon initialization, the bridge assumes itself to be root.

- **Transmitting bridge ID (BID) and port ID**—This is the bridge ID (BID) of the bridge transmitting the BPDU, and what port the BPDU originated from.

- **Cost to root**—This is the least-cost path to the root bridge from the bridge transmitting the BPDU. Upon initialization, because the bridge assumes itself to be root, it transmits a 0 for the cost to root.

- **Other STP information and timers**—The complete 802.1d frame is illustrated later in Figure 1-26. Here you will see the three STP timers listed along with other STP information.

Bridge ID

The BID is an 8-byte field composed from a 6-byte MAC address and a 2-byte bridge priority. The MAC address used for the BID is generated from a number of sources depending on the hardware in use for the bridge. Routers use a physical address, whereas switches use an address from the backplane or supervisor module. Figure 1-12 illustrates the BID. The priority value ranges from 0 to 65,535; the default value is 32,768.

Figure 1-12 *The Bridge ID (BID)*

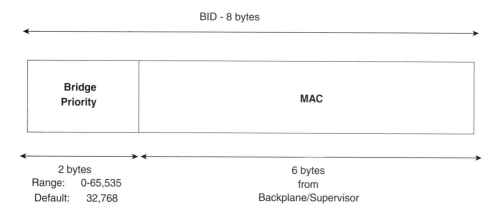

Extended System ID and IEEE 802.1T

IEEE 802.1T spanning-tree extensions address the fact that the priority value is really too large. 802.1T remedies these situations by using an extended system ID. The extended system ID was created in part to start to conserve MAC addresses. The IEEE 802.1d standard requires that each bridge/switch have a unique BID. In PVST+, each VLAN requires a unique BID; therefore, the same switch must have as many unique BIDs as VLANs configured on it. This can cause a limit on the number of STP instances a switch can run. STP uses the extended system ID, the switch priority, and the allocated STP MAC address to make a unique BID for each VLAN.

In Release 12.1(8)EA1 and later, Catalyst 3550 switches support the 802.1T spanning-tree extensions, and some of the bits previously used for the priority are now used as the extended system ID, which is set equal to the VLAN identifier. The result is that fewer MAC addresses are reserved for the switch, and a larger range of VLAN IDs can be supported, all while maintaining the uniqueness of the BID. Table 1-7 illustrates the switch priority value and the extended system ID.

Table 1-7 *Switch Priority Value and Extended System ID*

Switch Priority Value				Extended System ID (Set Equal to the VLAN ID)											
				Bit											
16	15	14	13	12	11	10	9	8	7	6	5	4	3	2	1
32,768	16,384	8192	4096	2048	1024	512	256	128	64	32	16	8	4	2	1

From Table 1-7, the 2 bytes previously used for the switch priority (Figure 1-12) are re-allocated into a 4-bit priority value and a 12-bit extended system ID value equal to the VLAN ID. To configure the switch to use the extended system ID, use the following global configuration command:

```
3550_switch(config)#spanning-tree extend system-id
```

The extended system ID is enabled by default on the Catalyst 3550 series switches.

If your switch is using the extended system ID, it will be noted with the **show spanning-tree summary** command and it will appear in the configuration listing.

STP Path Cost

Bridges to determine the best possible path to root use STP path cost. Path costs have recently been updated by the IEEE to include gigabit speeds and greater. The lower the path cost, the more preferable the path. Table 1-8 lists the STP cost values for LAN links.

Table 1-8 *STP Cost Values for LAN Links*

Bandwidth	*Revised STP Cost
4 Mbps	250
10 Mbps	100
16 Mbps	62

Table 1-8   *STP Cost Values for LAN Links (Continued)*

Bandwidth	*Revised STP Cost
45 Mbps	39
100 Mbps	19
155 Mbps	14
622 Mbps	6
1 Gbps*	4
10 Gbps	2

*   Before the IEEE standard was updated, the lowest cost STP could attain was 1. An STP cost of 1 was used for all links greater than, or equal to, 1 gigabit; a cost of 10 was used for 100-Mbps links, and a cost of 100 was used for 10-Mbps links.

STP has six primary states, and four states it transitions through during its operation, and Cisco switches have two additional proprietary states that can be assigned during operation. When STP converges, it will be in one of two states: forwarding or blocking. Table 1-9 lists the states of STP.

Table 1-9   *Various STP States*

STP State	STP Activity	User Data Being Passed
Disabled	Port is not active; it is not participating in any STP activity.	No
Broken	The 802.1Q trunk is misconfigured on one end, or the default/native VLANs do not match on each end. STP root guard is in effect.	No
Listening	Port is sending and receiving BPDUs.	No
Learning	Building loop-free bridging table.	No
Forwarding	Sending and receiving user data.	Yes
Blocking	Not permitting user traffic out the port.	No
PortFast*		Yes
UplinkFast*		Yes

*   PortFast and UplinkFast are Cisco proprietary states that allow user data traffic to be forwarding during the STP convergence process.

STP also assigns a port status to each port participating in the spanning tree. The STP port states are as follows:

- **Designated ports**—Designated ports are ports that lead *away* from the root bridge. On the root bridge, all ports are designated ports. Only one designated port is elected per segment. Designated ports are placed into the forwarding state.

- **Root ports**—The root port is the port that leads *toward* the root bridge. The root port is the lowest-cost path from the nonroot bridge to the root bridge. There is only one root port elected per nonroot bridge. Root ports are placed into the forwarding state.

- **Nondesignated ports**—Any port that is not elected as a root port or as a designated port becomes a nondesignated port. Nondesignated ports are placed into the blocking state.

NOTE   In some switch documentation, you might see STP bridges represented with the traditional bridge symbol. In practicality, there really exists no physical bridge, and the bridge icon is synonymous with the switch icon. This text uses the switch icon to represent switches and the STP bridge that resides on them.

The STP port and role relationship is represented in Figure 1-13.

A port transitions from one STP state to another, as depicted in Figure 1-14. The following sections examine each one of these states in more detail.

Disabled or Broken

The broken state occurs when a bridge is having problems processing BPDUs or a trunk is improperly configured. The broken state occurs when an 802.1Q trunk is misconfigured on one end, or the native VLANs do not match on each end of the trunk. The broken state also occurs on a trunk with STP root guard in effect. Disabled state occurs when the port is administratively down from an STP point of view.

Listening

When a bridge port initializes, or during the absence of BPDUs for longer than the max age timer (usually 20 seconds), STP transitions to the listening state. When STP is in this state, the port is actually blocking, and no user data is sent on the link. The port stays in this state for 15 seconds, called the *forward delay timer.*

Figure 1-13 *STP Ports and Roles*

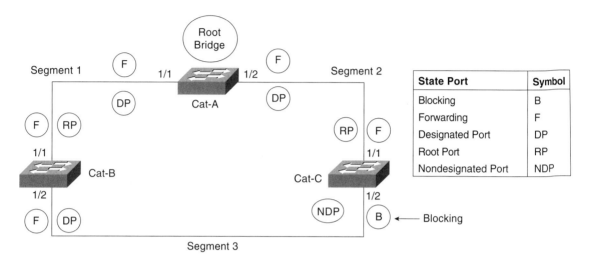

Figure 1-14 *The STP Transition*

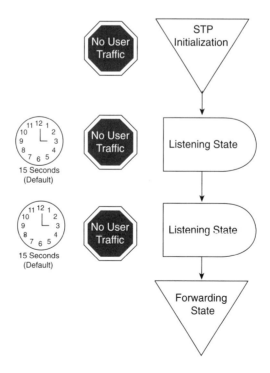

STP follows a three-step process for convergence:

1 **Elect one root bridge.** Upon initialization, the bridge begins sending BPDUs on all interfaces. A root bridge is chosen based on the bridge with the lowest BID. Recall that the BID is a combination of a priority and MAC address. Because the priority comes first in the BID, the bridge with the lowest priority is elected root bridge. In the event of a tie on bridge priority, the bridge with the lowest MAC address is chosen as root. All ports of the root bridge become designated ports and are put in the forwarding state.

2 **Elect one root port for every nonroot bridge.** After a single root bridge has been elected, STP elects a *single* root port on each nonroot bridge. The root port is the bridge's best path to the root bridge. When a root port is elected, it is put into the forwarding state. To determine what port should be a root port, STP follows this decision process:

    a. Lowest root BID; the BID from the root bridge

    b. Lowest path cost to root bridge; the cumulative cost of all the paths to Root

    c. Lowest sender BID; lowest port ID

    The primary variable that influences the root port election is the *cost to root bridge*. This is because most bridges are not adjacent to the root bridge.

    When a bridge receives a BPDU, it stores it in a bridge table for that port. As new BPDUs are received on that port, they are compared to existing BPDUs. BPDUs that are more attractive or have lower costs are kept, and the other ones are discarded; this might also cause the switch/bridge to change the port's state to forwarding or blocking.

3 **Elect one designated port on every segment.** For every segment, STP elects only one port that leads away from the root bridge, called the *designated port*. The designated port is put into the STP forwarding state.

All remaining ports become nondesignated ports and are put in the blocking state.

Learning

Ports that remain designated or root ports for a period of 15 seconds, the default forward delay, enter the learning state. The learning state is another 15 seconds that the bridge waits while it builds its bridge table; this is done to ensure that the bridge topology is stable.

Forwarding and Blocking

When the bridge reaches this phase, ports that do not serve a special purpose, such as a root port or designated port, are called *nondesignated ports*. All *nondesignated ports* are put into the STP blocking state. In the blocking state, a bridge does not send configuration BPDUs but still listens to BPDUs. A blocking port also does not forward user data.

STP Timers

STP has three basic timers that regulate and age BPDUs: hello, forward delay, and max age. The timers accomplish the following for STP:

- **Hello timer**—The default hello timer is 2 seconds; this is the length of time between configuration BPDUs sent by the root bridge.

- **Forward delay timer**—This timer is the default 15 seconds that the router waits while building its bridging table. The listening and learning stages each use this single 15-second timer.

- **Max age timer**—The default max age timer is 20 seconds. The max age timer is how long a BPDU is stored before it is flushed. If this timer expires before the interface receives a new BPDU, the interface transitions to the listening state. An expired max age parameter is usually caused by a link failure.

STP uses the hello timer to space BPDUs and has a keepalive mechanism. The hello timer should always prevent the max age value from being hit. When the max age timer expires, it usually indicates a link failure. When this happens, the bridge re-enters the listening state. For STP to recover from a link failure, it takes approximately 50 seconds: 20 seconds for the BPDU to age out, the max age, 15 seconds for the listening state, and 15 seconds for the learning state.

NOTE   There are two other forms of STP besides IEEE 802.1d. DEC and IBM are two other forms of spanning tree in use. The operation of all forms of STP is very similar. Cisco routers support all forms, whereas Cisco Ethernet switches currently support IEEE STP, and Token Ring switches support IBM STP.

Catalyst 3550 Configuration Modes and Terminology

Configuring a Catalyst 3550 is much like configuring the Cisco IOS Software found in predecessor switches, such as the Cisco Catalyst 3500XL series, or like configuring the combined routing and QoS features found on traditional Cisco IOS on router platforms. The upcoming sections focus on configuring the Catalyst 3550 family of switches with the EMI software installed.

The Catalyst 3550 CLI has different configuration modes and different interfaces types. For instance, *routed ports* are configured different from *switched virtual interfaces*, which are different from *access ports*. Each one of these interfaces is configured from different configuration modes. Therefore, it is important to have a common terminology when discussing the configuration of the Catalyst 3550.

These configuration modes might all be common to you in one form or another. The Catalyst 3550, however, is probably the first platform in which you will see them all together. Table 1-10 lists the configuration modes available and a brief description of them.

Table 1-10 *Configuration Command Modes on the Catalyst 3550*

Mode Name	Prompt	Starting Prompt*	Description
User exec	Switch>	Switch>	The default mode, used for basic **show** commands.
Privileged exec	Switch#	Switch>	Privileged mode is required for VLAN configuration modes and global configuration modes.
Global configuration	Switch(config)#	Switch#	Used to configure parameters that apply to the whole switch. Routing protocols are configured here.
VLAN interface	Switch(config-vlan)#	Switch(config)#	Used to create switched virtual interfaces (SVIs)** on the management VLAN. Extended VLANs are also created from this mode.
VLAN configuration	Switch(vlan)#	Switch#vlan database	Used to configure VLANs and VTP parameters for VLANs 1 to 1005, such as VTP and VLAN name on 1–1001.
Multiple spanning-tree configuration	Switch(config-mst)	Switch(config)#	Used to configure MST features, such as name, revision, and instances.
Interface configuration	Switch(config-if)#	Switch(config)#	Used to configure the parameters for the Ethernet interface, such as VLAN membership or duplex mode.
Line configuration	Switch(config-line)#	Switch(config)#	Used to configure console and vty parameters and access.

*   The starting prompt is the configuration mode you would use or must be in to access the new configuration mode.

** SVIs = switch virtual interfaces

The Catalyst 3550 also supports a variety of interface types. Each interface type is configured to support a specific feature on the switch. The following section lists and briefly describes the various ports and interface types supported on the Catalyst 3550 switch. You will learn more about configuring each of these interface types in later sections.

Switch Ports

A *switch port* is a Layer 2 interface associated with a physical port. The Catalyst 3550 has three primary types of switch ports: *access ports*, *trunk ports*, and *tunnel ports*. The default mode of a port on a 3550 is simply *switchport*. This differs slightly from switches such as the Catalyst 3548XL, where the default mode is *switchport access*. The **switchport** command enables you to put the port either in a routed mode or a switched mode. When a port is in switch mode, it can be configured as an access port, trunk, or tunnel port.

- **Access ports**—Access ports are ports that belong to only one VLAN and are statically assigned to that VLAN. They carry traffic that is not tagged, and traffic from that port is assumed to belong to the VLAN assigned to the port. If an access port receives tagged traffic (ISL or 802.1Q), that traffic is dropped.

- **Trunk ports**—Trunk ports are configured as 802.1Q or ISL trunks. An ISL trunk port expects to receive only ISL tagged frames on this port. An 802.1Q trunk has a native VLAN. All untagged frames use the native VLAN, which is 1 by default. All tagged and untagged traffic with a null VLN ID is assumed to belong to the native VLAN. A frame with a VLAN ID equal to the native VLAN is sent untagged; all other frames are sent with a VLAN tag.

- **802.1Q tunnel ports**—802.1Q tunnel ports transport information and data of a VLAN within another VLAN across the LAN. Edge switches are able to tag frames with the appropriate VLAN information and then pass that tagged frame on to a core/distribution switch via the 802.1Q tunnel. The core/distribution switch adds yet another tag to the frame and forwards it across the LAN. Switches with ports configured as tunnel ports can recognize these frames and handle them appropriately. 802.1Q tunnels are used in very large enterprise networks, where the VLAN capacity has exceeded the limit of 4096 VLANs. Because of the number of switches involved in modeling 802.1Q tunnels and the fact that their application is targeted toward large enterprise customers, 802.1Q tunnels are beyond the scope of this chapter.

EtherChannel Port Groups

An EtherChannel port group combines multiple physical switch ports into a single logical port. EtherChannel port groups bind the physical port features to the new logical port. If the ports in the group are configured as 802.1Q trunks, for example, the logical EtherChannel port is an 802.1Q trunk. The switch load shares over all physical ports in the EtherChannel port group. Very definite rules, which are switch architecture-specific, apply to switch ports and how many can be put into an EtherChannel port group.

Switch Virtual Interface (SVI)

A *switch virtual interface* (SVI) is a logical interface that ties Layer 3 functionality, such as IP information, to a VLAN. The SVI, in turn, can be used for inter-VLAN routing, to fallback-bridge nonroutable protocols between VLANs, and to represent the VLAN to a routing domain. By default, an SVI is created for VLAN 1 for management. If you are familiar with the Cisco 2900XL/3500XL series switches from *CCIE PSV1*, an SVI is very much like the "interface VLAN 1" used for management. Unlike the previous switches, you can configure multiple SVIs and a routing protocol to provide connectivity between the VLANs. To configure an SVI, aside from the single default, you must have the EMI software image installed on the switch.

Routed Ports

A routed port acts very much like its name implies. It is a physical port on the switch that has no VLAN information. In place of VLAN information, it has Layer 3 information, such as IP addresses. A routed port functions just like an interface on a router. A routed port cannot contain VLAN subinterfaces and requires the EMI software to be installed on the switch. To become a routed port, switching must be disabled for the port (which you can accomplish by using the **no switchport** command). Router ports also use an internal VLAN ID.

The various ports and interfaces can be used in a number of different ways. Figure 1-15 illustrates how they can be used in a common network.

Configuring Catalyst 3550 Ethernet Switches

The Catalyst 3550 is an extremely versatile switch. With the EMI image installed, the switch essentially has most of the configuration options of the Cisco IOS Software found on a router. General management and security functions are configured just like they are on a router. For instance, the host name, enable passwords, routing protocols, and IP addresses are all configured just as you would configure them on a router. If you are experienced with configuring Catalyst 2900XL/35*xx* series switches and Cisco routers, you'll find configuring the Catalyst 3550 a familiar environment. The remaining sections of this chapter focus primarily on configuring the switching aspects of the Catalyst 3550.

Figure 1-15 *Various Ports and Interfaces on the Catalyst 3550*

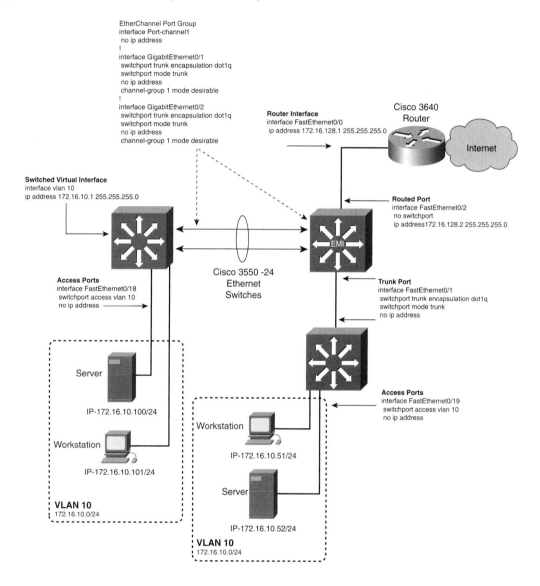

LAN switches were designed to be easy to install and configure. On smaller networks, little to no configuration might be required. On large redundant networks, with multiple VLANs and trunks, switching becomes quite a task. Configuring Ethernet switching on the Catalyst 3550 requires a seven-step process, as follows:

Step 1   Configure switch management.

Step 2   Configure VTP and VLANs and assign ports/interfaces to VLANs.

Step 3   Configure connections between switches using EtherChannel, 802.1Q, or ISL encapsulations.

Step 4   Optional: Control STP and VLAN propagation.

Step 5   Optional: Configure SVIs.

Step 6   Optional: Configure routed ports.

Step 7   Optional: Configure Layer 3 switching.

Step 1 involves configuring the management VLAN, IP addresses, and default gateways on the switch so that it can be accessed in-band from the internetwork.

Step 2 is where you define the VTP domain and the VLANs on the VTP servers or transparent mode switches. During this step, you also assign ports to VLANs.

Step 3 involves configuring VLAN trunks, if there are any on the network.

Step 4 is optional but critical to large networks. It involves controlling STP through the setting of root bridges, clearing VLANs from trunks, and using VLAN prune eligibility.

Whereas Steps 1 through 4 can be performed for most Catalyst series switches, Steps 5 and 6 apply only to the Catalyst 3550. Step 5 involves configuring SVIs, which can be for inter-VLAN connectivity.

Step 6 calls for you to configure routed ports. Routed ports are used when you want to put a static Layer 3 address on an interface, and you want the interface to behave like a *normal* router interface; that is, no frame tagging will occur on the interface and no VLAN information will be sent. A routed interface will, of course, be routable. The EMI software needs to be installed for routed interfaces.

Step 7 also applies only to switches with the EMI software installed. Layer 3 switching for all intents and purposes means enabling a routing protocol on the switch.

Step 1: Configuring Switch Management

All Catalyst switches have the capability to be managed remotely by an IP address. The Catalyst 3550, by default, uses Dynamic Host Configuration Protocol (DHCP) to resolve a default gateway on virtual interface one. If a DHCP server is not available, an IP address and default gateway can be assigned manually. To accomplish this, you must assign an IP address to the switch, along with a default gateway or default route for IP traffic to forward on. The default management VLAN is VLAN 1; you can specify another VLAN.

The Cisco IOS Software on Catalyst 3550 resembles a router with a special *VLAN database* added to it and the capability to create multiple VLAN interfaces (SVIs). The commands for assigning ports, trunks, and the management are all performed from within the global configuration mode on the switch. VLAN information for VLANs 1 through 1001, and VTP information, is configured from either the global configuration mode or the *VLAN configuration mode*, sometimes referred to as the *VLAN database*. Keying in **vlan database** from the enable/privileged mode accesses the VLAN configuration mode, or VLAN database.

The 3550 switch has a default virtual interface called interface VLAN 1. This is the default VLAN for the switch and is in an administratively Down state. To assign a management IP address, enter an IP address from the VLAN interface mode and activate the virtual interface with the **no shutdown** command. If VLAN 1 is being used for management, the interface becomes active and no further configuration is necessary. Example 1-1 demonstrates how to configure the management interface on VLAN 1.

Example 1-1 *Configuring the Management Interface on a Catalyst 3550 Switch*

```
3550_switch(config)#interface vlan 1
3550_switch(config-if)#ip address 172.16.100.10 255.255.255.0
3550_switch(config-if)#no shut
3550_switch(config-if)#
00:07:25: %LINK-3-UPDOWN: Interface Vlan1, changed state to up
00:07:26: %LINEPROTO-5-UPDOWN: Line protocol on Interface Vlan1, changed state up
```

If configuring a management address on a VLAN other than VLAN 1, you must ensure the following happens before the interface will become up and active.

1   The VLAN matching the interface must be in the VLAN database.

2   An interface with that VLAN must be up, or a trunk line must be up.

In Example 1-2, the management interface is on VLAN 128. For this interface to become active, you must create VLAN 128 on the switch, create the virtual interface called interface VLAN 128, and have an active interface for VLAN 128. If a trunk is configured on the switch, the virtual interface also becomes active. Example 1-2 demonstrates the configuration of a management interface on VLAN 128. Notice how VLAN 128 does not become active until the physical interface FAST 0/10 becomes active.

Example 1-2 *Configuring the Management Interface on VLAN 2*

```
3550_switch#conf t
Enter configuration commands, one per line.  End with CNTL/Z.
3550_switch(config)#vlan 128
3550_switch(config-vlan)#exit
3550_switch(config)#interface vlan 128
3550_switch(config-if)#ip address 172.16.128.16 255.255.255.0
3550_switch(config-if)#exit
```

continues

Example 1-2 *Configuring the Management Interface on VLAN 2 (Continued)*

```
3550_switch(config)#interface fast 0/10
3550_switch(config-if)#switchport access vlan 128
3550_switch(config-if)#no shut
3550_switch(config-if)#
00:52:36: %LINK-3-UPDOWN: Interface FastEthernet0/10, changed state to down
00:52:37: %LINEPROTO-5-UPDOWN: Line protocol on Interface FastEthernet0/10, changed
state to down
00:52:40: %LINEPROTO-5-UPDOWN: Line protocol on Interface FastEthernet0/10, changed
state to up
00:53:10: %LINEPROTO-5-UPDOWN: Line protocol on Interface Vlan128, changed state to up
```

The management interface can be viewed just like a physical interface, with the **show interface vlan** *x* command.

To configure a default gateway, use the **ip default-gateway** *ip_address* command, the same as it appears on a router. Example 1-3 shows how to configure the default gateway followed by the **show ip route** command verifying the new default gateway/route. Here the default gateway points at the router 172.16.128.5.

Example 1-3 *Configuring Default Routing on Catalyst 3550*

```
3550_switch(config)#ip default-gateway 172.16.128.5
3550_switch(config)#exit
3550_switch#
3550_switch#show ip route
Default gateway is 172.16.128.5
Host              Gateway          Last Use    Total Uses   Interface
ICMP redirect cache is empty
3550_switch#
```

NOTE

VLAN 1 - "Just Say No"

CCIE PSV1 stressed avoiding use of VLAN 1 for user traffic. A personal design rule I use in the field is to avoid VLAN 1 if at all possible. There are numerous reasons for this. VLAN 1 is the default VLAN for all Catalyst switches and the native VLAN. Any switch added to the network will, by default, be in VLAN 1. This leaves the network vulnerable to potential VTP, VLAN, and data corruption. Mono Spanning Tree on 802.1Q uses VLAN 1 for its entire spanning-tree domain. The switch will also tag frames differently on VLAN 1 depending on the encapsulation used. Some Catalyst switches enable you to clear VLAN 1 from a trunk, whereas some will not; this could force VLAN 1 to span the entire switched network. For these reasons and more that aren't listed, I personally don't run production traffic or management traffic on VLAN 1. When designing LANs and VLAN 1 comes up, just say no!

Controlling IP and Console Access on Catalyst 3550

Controlling access on the Catalyst 3550 switch is identical to controlling access on the router. An enable password might be set, and an enable secret password might also be set. All the rules that apply to the enable and enable secret passwords on routers apply to the switch. The syntax to accomplish this is as follows:

```
3550_switch(config)#enable password cisco
```

The enable password is not encrypted and can be viewed in the configuration. The enable password can be encrypted with the global command:

```
3550_switch(config)#service password-encryption
```

The **service password-encryption** command encrypts all passwords on the switch with Cisco proprietary encryption, simply called *type-5*:

```
3550_switch(config)#enable secret ccie
```

The enable secret password is always encrypted with a very strong Cisco proprietary encryption called type-7. The enable secret password takes precedence over the enable password if both are configured. The password is not in a readable form in the configuration. The full syntax for the enable secret password is as follows:

```
3550_switch(config)#enable secret [level level] {password | [encryption-type] encrypted-
password}
```

You can use the full syntax to cut and paste encrypted passwords from one source to another. Be very careful when setting the level or encryption type with this command, because it is very easy to enter a password incorrectly. A highly recommended practice is that you encrypt all passwords after they have been entered with the **service password-encryption** command. This avoids typos and many syntactical issues that can happen.

Access to the 3550 switch is controlled by configuring passwords and access control lists (ACLs) on the console (cty) and virtual terminal (vty) lines. Recall from *CCIE PSV1* that the cty is the console port on the switch/router and the vty lines are virtual Telnet sessions. You can view the absolute line values on the switch with the **show line** command, as demonstrated in Example 1-4. Line 0 is the vty or console port, whereas lines 1 through 16 are vty or virtual Telnet sessions.

Telnet access can be controlled through creating ACLs and applying them to the vty lines on the switch with the **access-class** line configuration command. ACLs can also be called on the SNMP community strings for SNMP control.

Example 1-4   *Absolute Line Values on the Catalyst 3550*

```
3550_switch#show line
    Tty Typ      Tx/Rx      A Modem  Roty AccO AccI   Uses   Noise  Overruns   Int
*     0 CTY                 -   -     -    -    -       0      0      0/0        -
      1 vty                 -   -     -    -    -       0      0      0/0        -
      2 vty                 -   -     -    -    -       0      0      0/0        -
```

continues

Example 1-4 *Absolute Line Values on the Catalyst 3550 (Continued)*

```
...text omitted
     15 vty            -   -        -   -    -    0      0    0/0      -
     16 vty            -   -        -   -    -    0      0    0/0      -
```

Example 1-5 demonstrates the configuring of a username and password that will be used to control console access and Telnet access. The example shows **login local** being entered on the console port and the 16 vty ports. This forces the switch to use the locally entered username password command for authentication. An ACL, ACL 10, is also being applied to the vty sessions. In this example, the ACL will only allow users to Telnet to the switch from networks in the range of 172.16.0.0. For more information on configuring CTY and vty lines and absolute line numbers, refer to *CCIE PSV1* Chapter 1, "The Key Components for Modeling an Internetwork."

Example 1-5 *Configuring Default Routing on Catalyst 3550*

```
3550_switch(config)#username solie password cisco
3550_switch(config)#line 0
3550_switch(config-line)#login local
3550_switch(config-line)#exit
3550_switch(config)
3550_switch(config)#line 1 16
3550_switch(config-line)#login local
3550_switch(config-line)#access-class 10 in
3550_switch(config-line)#exit
3550_switch(config)
3550_switch(config)#username ksolie password cisco
3550_switch(config)#access-list 10 permit 172.16.0.0 0.0.255.255
```

Step 2: Configuring VTP and VLANs on Catalyst 3550 Switches

Configuring VTP and VLANs on the 3550 series switches requires a three-substep process, as follows:

Step 1 Configure a VTP domain and mode.

Step 2 Configure VLANs, if the switch is operating in VTP server or transparent mode.

Step 3 Configure physical port properties and assign ports to VLANs.

Configuring VTP Domain and Mode on Catalyst 3550 Switches

You can configure VLANs on the Catalyst 3550 from the VLAN database or VLAN configuration mode, or from the traditional router-like global configuration mode. For the most part, the syntax is identical. If you have a lot of experience configuring Catalyst 2900XL/35*xx* switches, the VLAN configuration mode might be more familiar to you. This mode is entered by the privileged-mode command **vlan database**. When in the VLAN database, any VLAN changes that are made must be applied. After making changes in the VLAN database, you may enter one of the following commands:

- **abort**—Exits the VLAN database and undoes any VLAN changes you have made since you entered the VLAN database. VTP changes are not aborted.

- **exit**—Exits the VLAN database and applies all VLAN changes; also increments the VTP revision number.

- **apply**—Applies current VLAN changes and increments the VTP revision number but does not exit the VLAN database.

- **reset**—Clears any current VLAN changes and rereads the VLAN databases.

A VTP domain should always be configured for security reasons. This prevents a new switch from inadvertently corrupting your network. The default VTP name is Null and the mode is server. To configure the VTP domain, use the following syntax in the VLAN configuration mode:

```
3550_switch#vlan database
3550_switch(vlan)#vtp domain domain_name [password]
```

If you add a password behind the domain name, VTP updates will use a Message Digest Algorithm 5 (MD5) hash to encrypt the password. Using VTP passwords is a very effective way to add a layer of security and stability to your switching domain. In the current Cisco IOS Software release, you can only configure a VTP password in the VLAN configuration mode. You cannot enter a VTP password from the global configuration mode. To change the VTP mode, use the following command from the VLAN configuration mode:

```
3550_switch(vlan)#vtp [server | client | transparent]
```

To configure the VTP domain and mode from the global configuration mode, use the following syntax:

```
3550_switch(config)#vtp domain domain_name
3550_switch(config)#vtp [server | client | transparent]
```

You can view the VTP domain by using the **show vtp status** command. This command displays information about the VTP domain, such as configuration revision, domain name, operating mode, and so on. Notice at the bottom of the display the new information that appears on Catalyst 3550. It shows the IP address that will be used by VTP to identify which specific switch you are synchronizing VTP information with. If no trunk lines are configured, or improperly configured with an all-0s address, 0.0.0.0 appears. If the switch is a VTP server and has not received updates via its trunk lines, its own address displays. Example 1-6 lists the output of the **show vtp status** command.

Example 1-6 *Viewing the VTP Domain Information*

```
3550_switch# show vtp status
VTP Version                       : 2
Configuration Revision            : 1
Maximum VLANs supported locally   : 1005
Number of existing VLANs          : 6
VTP Operating Mode                : Server
VTP Domain Name                   : psv2
VTP Pruning Mode                  : Disabled
VTP V2 Mode                       : Disabled
VTP Traps Generation              : Disabled
MD5 digest                        : 0x03 0xE2 0xB2 0x25 0x2B 0xF1 0xBE 0x19
Configuration last modified by 172.16.128.16 at 3-1-93 03:16:46
Local updater ID is 172.16.128.16 on interface Vl128 (lowest numbered VLAN interface
  found)
Preferred interface name is 3550
3550_switch#
```

You can configure the interface or IP address VTP uses to identify the switch to other switches in the VTP domain with the following global configuration command:

```
3550_switch(config)#vtp interface [ VTP_updater_name | ip_address ]
```

NOTE   VLAN information is propagated only if the VTP revision number of the server is *higher* than the client's VTP revision number. If the VTP client's revision number is equal to or higher than the server's, it will not accept VLAN information. To view the current VTP revision numbers, use the commands **show vtp domain** on Catalyst 4000/5500/6500 series switches and **show vtp status** on Catalyst 2900/3500 series switches.

Configuring Normal and Extended-Range VLANs on Catalyst 3550 Switches

The second step involves VLAN configuration if the VTP mode is set as a *server* or *transparent*. If the switch is configured as a VTP *client*, VLANs appear when the trunk line comes up and the VLAN databases are synchronized. VLANs are configured in the VLAN database, just by entering **vlan** [*1-1001*] **options**. As mentioned previously, VLANs 1002 through 1005 and VLAN 1009 are default and special VLANs that should not be used in Ethernet switching. VLANs may also be configured from the global configuration mode with the syntax **vlan** [*1-4094*]. VLANs 1006 through 4094 are extended-range VLANs that are configured from the global configuration mode. The switch must also be in VTP transparent mode to configure extended range VLANs.

Configuring Normal-Range VLANs   You can configure normal-range VLANs, VLANs 1 through 1001, in the global configuration mode or from the VLAN database. If VLANs are configured from the VLAN database, changes in VLANs must be committed with the **apply** command. All changes are also applied when the VLAN database is exited. If a mistake is made, you can cancel VLAN changes with the **abort** or **reset** command as mentioned previously. The VLAN database is saved in the file VLAN.DAT in Flash memory. You can copy the VLAN.DAT file to a TFTP server just as you can any Flash memory file for backup purposes. Example 1-7 demonstrates two ways to configure a VLAN on the Catalyst 3550 switch. The first way uses the VLAN database, and the second way demonstrates using the global configuration mode. In the example, two VLANs are created: VLAN 128 with the name psv2_vlan128, and VLAN 10 with the name psv2_vlan10.

Example 1-7 *Configuration of VLAN 128 and VLAN 10*

```
3550_switch#vlan database
3550_switch(vlan)#vlan 128 name psv2_vlan128
VLAN 128 added:
    Name: psv2_vlan128
3550_switch(vlan)#apply
APPLY completed.
3550_switch(vlan)#exit
! The preceding command automatically applies updates
APPLY completed.
Exiting....
Global Configuration mode---------->
3550_switch#conf t
3550_switch(config)#vlan 10
3550_switch(config-vlan)#name psv2_vlan10
```

Some common options that may be configured on the VLAN from the VLAN configuration mode include the following:

```
Switch(vlan)# vlan vlan_num [name vlan_name] [state {active | suspend}] [said said_value]
  [mtu mtu] [bridge bridge_number] [stp type {ieee | ibm | auto}]
```

- **name**—Enables you to attach a 32-character name to the VLAN.

- **state**—Enables you to suspend the VLAN. A suspended VLAN is propagated via VTP, but no user traffic is carried on the VLAN.

- **said**—Enables you to change the SAID value of the VLAN; the SAID value is used primarily in 802.10.

- **mtu, bridge, and stp**—Enables you to change the default MTU value, bridge number, and STP type.

- **No vlan** [*vlan_num*]—Deletes a VLAN from the VLAN database. When you delete a VLAN, any interfaces assigned to that VLAN become inactive, including the management interface.

If you are configuring the VLAN options from the global configuration mode, the VLAN options are configured from the VLAN interface mode.

For the default VLAN values, see Table 1-2 earlier in this chapter.

To view the status the VLANs, use the **show vlan** command, which displays all the VLANs on the switch, the state, and which ports are assigned to each VLAN. To display specific physical and logical information about a single VLAN, use the **show vlan id** [*vlan_number*] command. Example 1-8 lists the output of the **show vlan** command, followed by the more specific version of the command. Notice how the VLAN logical names help immediately identify the port purpose.

Example 1-8 show vlan *Command Output*

```
3550_switch#show vlan
VLAN Name                             Status    Ports
---- -------------------------------- --------- -------------------------------
1    default                          active    Fa0/1, Fa0/2, Fa0/3, Fa0/4
                                                Fa0/5, Fa0/6, Fa0/7, Fa0/8
                                                Fa0/9, Fa0/11, Fa0/12, Fa0/13
                                                Fa0/14, Fa0/15, Fa0/16, Fa0/17
                                                Fa0/18, Fa0/19, Fa0/20, Fa0/21
                                                Fa0/22, Fa0/23, Fa0/24, Gi0/1
                                                Gi0/2
10   psv2_vlan10                      active
128  psv2_vlan128                     active    Fa0/10
1002 fddi-default                     active
1003 token-ring-default               active
1004 fddinet-default                  active
1005 trnet-default                    active
VLAN Type  SAID       MTU   Parent RingNo BridgeNo Stp  BrdgMode Trans1 Trans2
---- ----- ---------- ----- ------ ------ -------- ---- -------- ------ ------
1    enet  100001     1500  -      -      -        -    -        0      0
10   enet  100010     1500  -      -      -        -    -        0      0
128  enet  100128     1500  -      -      -        -    -        0      0
1002 fddi  101002     1500  -      -      -        -    -        0      0
1003 tr    101003     1500  -      -      -        -    -        0      0
1004 fdnet 101004     1500  -      -      -        ieee -        0      0
1005 trnet 101005     1500  -      -      -        ibm  -        0      0
3550_switch#
-------------------------------------------------------------------------------
-
3550_switch#show vlan id 128
VLAN Name                             Status    Ports
---- -------------------------------- --------- -------------------------------
128  psv2_vlan128                     active    Fa0/10
VLAN Type  SAID       MTU   Parent RingNo BridgeNo Stp  BrdgMode Trans1 Trans2
---- ----- ---------- ----- ------ ------ -------- ---- -------- ------ ------
128  enet  100128     1500  -      -      -        -    -        0      0
3550_switch#
```

CAUTION   The Catalyst 3550 switch supports 128 STP instances. Each VLAN runs a single instance of STP. If a switch has more active VLANs than supported 128 STP instances, STP is disabled on the remaining VLANs. If you have already used up all available 128 STP instances on a switch, adding another VLAN anywhere in the VTP domain creates a VLAN on that switch that is not running STP. If you have the "default allowed list" on the trunk ports of that switch (which is to allow all VLANs), the new VLAN is carried on all trunk ports. Depending on the topology of the network, this could create a loop. This is because the new VLAN could be partitioned, particularly if there are several adjacent switches that all have more than 128 STP instances. You can prevent this by setting allowed lists on the trunk ports of switches so that they will not propagate STP for all VLANs. This is the same as clearing the trunk on the Catalyst 5500/6500 series switches.

Configuring Extended-Range VLANs   The Catalyst 3550 switch enables you to configure extended VLANs. *Extended VLANs* are VLANs in the range of 1006 to 4094. However, the 3550 switch uses an extended VLAN ID for each routed port. Therefore, the practical range, and safe range, for extended VLANs is roughly 1027 through 4094. When configuring extended VLANs, you must follow certain guidelines. Those guidelines are as follows:

- The switch must be in VTP transparent mode prior to any extended VLAN configuration.

- Routed ports use an extended VLAN starting at the lower ranges 1006 through 1026. Always select an extended VLAN ID starting at 4094 and go backward. For caution, use the command **show vlan internal usage** to verify what internal VLANs are in use and the interface that is using them. Example 1-9 demonstrates the use of this command prior to configuring an extended VLAN.

- Extended VLANs can only be created from the configuration mode. They cannot be created from the VLAN configuration mode.

- Extended VLANs are not saved in the VLAN database and are not advertised via VTP.

- Extended VLANs are not supported by VLAN Query Protocol (VQP) or VLAN Membership Policy Server (VMPS).

- STP is enabled by default on extended VLANs.

- At this time, you cannot name an extended VLAN; you can only change the MTU value.

The configuration to configure extended VLANs is identical to configuring a normal-range VLAN, except that you must adhere to the guidelines previously listed. Example 1-9 demonstrates the configuration of an extended VLAN 4094. Prior to configuring the extended VLAN, the switch is put into VTP transparent mode, and the **show vlan internal usage** command is executed to avoid a VLAN conflict.

Example 1-9 *Creating an Extended VLAN*

```
3550_switch#show vlan internal usage  ←Verify internal VLANs
VLAN Usage
---- ------------
1017 -
1025 FastEthernet0/11
! VLAN 1025 in use by INT FAST 0/11
1026 GigabitEthernet0/2
! VLAN 1026 in use by INT GIG 0/2
3550_switch#
3550_switch#conf t
 3550_switch(config)#vtp mode transparent
! VTP transparent mode set
Setting device to VTP TRANSPARENT mode.
3550_switch(config)#vlan 4094
! VLAN 4094 created
```

You can view an extended VLAN with the **show vlan** command. Example 1-10 lists the output of the **show vlan** command after the extended VLAN 4094 has been created.

Example 1-10 *Viewing an Extended VLAN*

```
3550_switch#show vlan
VLAN Name                             Status    Ports
---- -------------------------------- --------- -------------------------------
1    default                          active    Fa0/1, Fa0/2, Fa0/3, Fa0/4
                                                Fa0/5, Fa0/6, Fa0/7, Fa0/8
                                                Fa0/9, Fa0/12, Fa0/13, Fa0/14
                                                Fa0/15, Fa0/16, Fa0/17, Fa0/18
                                                Fa0/19, Fa0/20, Fa0/21, Fa0/22
                                                Fa0/23, Fa0/24, Gi0/1
10   psv2_vlan10                      active
128  psv2_vlan128                     active    Fa0/10
1002 fddi-default                     active
1003 token-ring-default               active
1004 fddinet-default                  active
1005 trnet-default                    active
4094 VLAN4094                         active
VLAN Type  SAID    MTU   Parent RingNo BridgeNo Stp  BrdgMode Trans1 Trans2
---- ----- ------- ----- ------ ------ -------- ---- -------- ------ ------
1    enet  100001  1500  -      -      -        -    -        0      0
10   enet  100010  1500  -      -      -        -    -        0      0
128  enet  100128  1500  -      -      -        -    -        0      0
1002 fddi  101002  1500  -      -      -        -    -        0      0
1003 tr    101003  1500  -      -      -        -    -        0      0
1004 fdnet 101004  1500  -      -      -        ieee -        0      0
1005 trnet 101005  1500  -      -      -        ibm  -        0      0
4094 enet  104094  1500  -      -      -        -    -        0      0
3550_switch
```

TIP   The Catalyst 3550 enables you to configure a range of interfaces at a single time. This can be quite a timesaver if you have to configure many ports on a switch with the same characteristics. To configure a range of interfaces, use the following global configuration command:

```
Switch(config)#interface range interface_type staring_int - ending interface
```

To configure the range of interfaces 0/1 through 0/10, for example, use the following command:

```
3550_switch#(config)interface range fastethernet 0/1 - 10
```

Configuring Physical Port Properties and Assigning Ports to VLANs on Catalyst 3550 Switches

The next step for VTP and VLAN configuration is to configure any physical port properties, along with assigning the port to a VLAN. Physical port properties are changed from the interface configuration mode. Table 1-11 lists the default Layer 2 interface settings on the Catalyst 3550 switch.

Table 1-11   *Default Layer 2 Ethernet Settings on Catalyst 3550*

Feature	Default Setting
Operating mode	Layer 2 switching (**switchport**).
Allowed VLAN range	VLANs 1–4094.
Default VLAN	VLAN 1.
Native VLAN	VLAN 1.
VLAN trunking	DTP.
All ports enabled	
Speed	Autonegotiate.
Duplex mode	Autonegotiate.
Flow control	Off for receive and desired for send for 10/100/100 Mbps (Send is always off for 10/100 Mbps.).
EtherChannel (PAgP)	Disabled.
Port blocking of unknown multicast and unicast traffic and storm control	Disabled.
Protected port	Disabled.
Port security	Disabled.
PortFast	Disabled.

Example 1-11 demonstrates configuring an Ethernet port to 100 Mbps half duplex on a 3550 series switch. This example also assigns the logical name management_vlan_128 to the interface.

Example 1-11 *Configuring Physical Port Properties*

```
3550_switch(config)#interface fast 0/10
3550_switch(config-if)#speed 100
3550_switch(config-if)#duplex half
3550_switch(config-if)#description management_vlan_128
```

NOTE   To change the duplex setting of a port, you first must change the speed from auto to 100 or 10. The switch does not allow you to change duplex when the port is configured for autonegotiation.

Some common physical properties of Ethernet that you can change in the interface configuration mode are as follows:

- **duplex [full | half | auto]**—Sets the port duplex mode.

- **speed [10 | 100 | auto]**—Sets the port speed.

- **mtu** [*1500bytes-2018bytes*]—Configures the MTU of the interface. Ensure that the MTU of the physical interface matches that of VLAN, if you change this value.

- **description** *interface_description*—Enables you to set a description for the interface.

- **shutdown | no shutdown**—Disables and enables the interface.

The interface command **switchport** is used with no options to put the port into a Layer 2 switching mode. The port can be an access port, trunk port, 802.1Q tunnel port, voice port, or protect port. The following are subcommands of the **switchport** command:

- **access**—Assigns the interface to a single VLAN.

- **trunk**—Used to configure the port as an 802.1Q or ISL trunk. The next section discusses this option in more detail.

- **802.1q tunnel ports**—802.1Q tunnel ports transport information and data of a VLAN within another VLAN across the LAN.

- **voice vlan**—The port can use 802.1Q and 802.1p for QoS.

- **protected ports**—Protected ports prevent unicast, multicast, and broadcast traffic between protected ports on the same switch.

Upcoming sections discuss the various modes in greater detail; at this time, however, the focus is on assigning a port to a single VLAN. To accomplish this, first you configure the port to be in access mode, and then you attach a VLAN to the port. The syntax used to accomplish this is as follows:

```
(config-if)#switchport access vlan [1-4094 | dynamic]
```

The **dynamic** keyword is used in VLAN Membership Policy Server (VMPS) configurations. VMPS is not covered in this text. For more information on VMPS, refer to *Cisco LAN Switching* (Cisco Press, 1999).

Example 1-12 demonstrates the configuration of Fast Ethernet 0/5 for VLAN 2.

Example 1-12 *Assigning VLAN 2 to Interface fast 0/5*

```
Switch(config)#int fastEthernet 0/5
Switch(config-if)#switchport mode access
Switch(config-if)#switchport access vlan 2
```

When the VTP mode is set to *transparent*, VLANs are automatically created with the **switchport access vlan** command; you do not need to statically configure them in the VLAN database. If the VTP mode is set as a *client*, you cannot configure VLANs on this switch. The VLANs must be configured on the server switch and propagated via VTP over a trunk to the client switch.

Step 3: Configuring Trunks Between Switches Using EtherChannel, 802.1Q, and ISL Encapsulations

Step 3 involves configuring trunk lines between Ethernet switches. A trunk line can be a normal trunk with ISL or 802.1Q encapsulation, or it can be an EtherChannel trunk, which could also be using 802.1Q or ISL encapsulation. This discussion first focuses on configuring a normal trunk line, and then turns to configuring an EtherChannel trunk.

Configuring trunks on the Catalyst 3550 is a two-step process. Depending on the state of the port prior to configuration, you may have to disable autonegotiation mode. By default, a port is set to negotiate the encapsulation and to be in the dynamic and desirable mode.

Step 1   Configure the trunk encapsulation as ISL or 802.1Q.

Step 2   Configure the port as a normal trunk or EtherChannel trunk.

These steps are accomplished with the following commands from the interface configuration mode:

```
Switch#(config-if)#switchport trunk encapsulation [isl | dot1q | negotiate ]
Switch#(config-if)#switchport mode [trunk | dynamic {auto | desirable}]
```

The different encapsulation types and subcommands mean the following:

- **switchport trunk encapsulation isl**—Specifies ISL encapsulation on the trunk link.

- **switchport trunk encapsulation dot1q**—Specifies 802.1Q encapsulation on the trunk link.

- **switchport trunk encapsulation negotiate**—Specifies that the interface negotiate with the neighboring interface to become an ISL (preferred) or 802.1Q trunk, depending on the configuration and capabilities of the neighboring interface. This is the default encapsulation type.

The port, as a trunk, may be statically configured or dynamically configured. The different trunk configuration modes are as follows:

- **dynamic auto**—Sets the interface to a trunk link if the neighboring interface is set to trunk or desirable mode.

- **dynamic desirable**—Sets the interface to a trunk link if the neighboring interface is set to trunk, desirable, or auto mode. This is the default trunking mode.

- **trunk**—Sets the interface in permanent trunking mode and negotiates to convert the link to a trunk link even if the neighboring interface is not a trunk interface.

You might find that configuring the auto-negotiation, or DTP, is more difficult than just statically defining the trunk. This is mainly due to some of the differences in the default trunks for the various Catalysts switches. Most Catalysts default to ISL; however, the Catalyst 4000 without the Layer 3 module or the latest Cisco IOS Software doesn't support ISL. Another example is that 802.1Q autonegotiation is only supported in CAT OS software Release 4.2. These little things can make DTP unreliable in large heterogeneous networks.

NOTE   Another autoconfiguration issue may arise with VTP and DISL. When DISL negotiates an ISL trunk, it includes the VTP name in the message. If the VTP domain names differ on the switches, the trunk will not become active. Again, to circumvent this, just statically configure the trunk and configure the encapsulation type. For VTP to work, you still need to match VTP names.

Example 1-13 demonstrates the configuration of an 802.1Q trunk on the Gigabit Ethernet interface 0/1.

Example 1-13 *Configuring an ISL Trunk*

```
3550_switch(config)#interface gigabitEthernet 0/1
3550_switch(config-if)#switchport trunk encapsulation dot1q
3550_switch(config-if)#switchport mode trunk
```

To verify whether the trunk is working, be sure to status both sides of the link. The output of the **show interface** *interface_name* **switchport** command and the output of the **show interface** *interface_name* **trunk** command present a general status of the trunk. The information presented here is very similar to the **show trunk** command on the Catalyst 4000/5500/6500 series switches.

This command shows the status of the trunk and the encapsulation. VLAN information, such as the default VLAN, the active VLANs on the links, and any prune-eligible VLANs, will also be listed. Furthermore, protected VLANs and voice VLANs are listed with this command. Example 1-14 lists the output of the **show interface interface_name switchport** command. If the trunk is not listed, some configuration areas to note include the following:

- Mode

- Encapsulation

- Native VLANs for 802.1Q trunks

Set the status of the trunk to be trunking and the mode to be on, or match a valid setting for DTP as listed previously. The encapsulation must match on both sides of the trunk. The native VLAN ID is the VLAN 802.1Q will use for its single instance of spanning tree (MST). This VLAN must be the same throughout the VTP domain.

Example 1-14 *Status of a Trunk Line*

```
3550_switch#show interface gigabitEthernet 0/1 switchport
Name: Gi0/1
Switchport: Enabled
Administrative Mode: trunk
Operational Mode: trunk
Administrative Trunking Encapsulation: dot1q
Operational Trunking Encapsulation: dot1q
Negotiation of Trunking: On
Access Mode VLAN: 1 (default)
Trunking Native Mode VLAN: 1 (default)
Trunking VLANs Enabled: ALL
Pruning VLANs Enabled: 2-1001
Protected: false
Unknown unicast blocked: disabled
Unknown multicast blocked: disabled

Voice VLAN: none (Inactive)
Appliance trust: none
3550_switch#
```

In 802.1Q networks, it is critical to ensure that the native VLAN is the same throughout the entire VTP domain. This is because 802.1Q uses Mono Spanning Tree. Mono Spanning Tree makes the entire VTP domain appear as a single-bridged domain to all third-party 802.1Q switches. Cisco ensures compatibility with MST domains by implementing PVST+ along with MST. This is an extended version of Per VLAN Spanning Tree Plus (PVST+), which provides seamless transparent integration for 802.1Q networks. Mono Spanning Tree runs on the native VLAN. For this reason, it is important to have the same native VLAN throughout the entire internetwork. The default VLAN is 1, which is also the default native VLAN. To change the native VLAN, use the following interface command on the trunk:

```
Switch#(config-if)#switchport trunk native vlan vlan-id
```

The **show interface** with the **trunk** keyword command will also list the VLANs that are *prune eligible*. Do not confuse *prune eligible* VLANs with VLAN propagation. *Prune eligible* means that unnecessary broadcast, multicast, and unknown unicast traffic will not be forwarded over trunk lines to switches that do not have an active port in that particular VLAN. By default, all VLAN information and spanning-tree frames for each VLAN are advertised out all trunking interfaces. VLANs and STP can only be removed from a trunk by using the **clear trunk** command on the Cisco Catalyst 5500/6500 series or by changing the VLANs allowed on a trunk on the Cisco 3550 series switch. You will learn more about these functions in the upcoming section "Step 4: Controlling STP and VLAN Propagation."

Example 1-15 lists the output of the **show trunk** command. The **trunk** keyword displays similar information to the **switchport** keyword. This command, however, focuses more on the VLAN information of the trunk.

Example 1-15 *Status of a Trunk Line with the* **trunk** *Keyword*

```
3550_switch#show interface gigabitEthernet 0/1 trunk
Port        Mode          Encapsulation  Status       Native vlan
Gi0/1       on            802.1q         trunking     1
Port        Vlans allowed on trunk
Gi0/1       1-4094
Port        Vlans allowed and active in management domain
Gi0/1       1,10,20,128
Port        Vlans in spanning tree forwarding state and not pruned
Gi0/1       1,10,20,128
3550_switch#
```

At times, it might be hard to determine whether a trunk line is functioning. The trunk can report a status of trunking but not be fully exchanging VTP updates. You should view the trunk status on each side of the link to ensure it is functioning properly.

As VTP synchronizes within the domain the VLAN database from server to server and server to client, all switches will have the same VLANs listed in their VLAN database. Only switches in the VTP transparent mode or trunks that have VLANs *cleared* or *removed* will have different VLAN databases. Comparing the VLAN databases of the two switches connected together by a trunk is another way to verify that the trunk is working.

When the trunk becomes active, VTP advertisements are sent and received. The following three types of VTP advertisements occur on the trunk.

- **Subset advertisements**—Subset advertisements are issued when you create, delete, or modify a VLAN.

- **Request advertisements**—Request advertisements are issued from the switch whenever the Catalyst is reset or a change in the local VTP domain occurs, such as a name change, or when the switch hears a VTP summary advertisement with a higher configuration revision number than its own.

- **Summary advertisements**—Summary advertisements are issued every 5 minutes by the switch. The main purpose of the summary advertisement is for the switch to verify the VTP revision number, and thereby ensure that the VLAN databases are current. If it has a lower revision number, it issues a request for new VLAN information.

You can observe VTP statistics with the **show vtp status** and the **show vtp counters** command. These commands tell you what advertisements are received and transmitted by the switch. These should be used as another indicator that the trunk line is functioning properly. After you verify the trunk is up, you still must verify that the VTP updates are being exchanged. Remember that the goal of trunking is to pass VLAN information, which requires VTP. Along with the trunk lines, you should also examine the VTP domain counters using the **show vtp counters** command. Example 1-16 lists the output of the **show vtp counters** command.

Example 1-16 *Statusing a Trunk by Viewing VTP Counters*

```
3550_switch#show vtp counters
VTP statistics:
Summary advertisements received   : 101
Subset advertisements received    : 4
Request advertisements received   : 1
Summary advertisements transmitted : 116
Subset advertisements transmitted : 3
Request advertisements transmitted : 0
Number of config revision errors  : 0
Number of config digest errors    : 0
Number of V1 summary errors       : 0

VTP pruning statistics:
Trunk           Join Transmitted Join Received    Summary advts received from
                                                  non-pruning-capable device
--------------- ---------------- ---------------- ---------------------------
Gi0/1                0                0                0
3550_switch#
```

The **show vtp status** command lists very useful VTP information. The VTP version, VTP revision, operating mode, and domain name are listed along with VLAN information. When the VLAN databases are synchronized, each switch should have the same number of VLANs.

Example 1-17 demonstrates the **show vtp status** command.

Example 1-17 *Statusing a Trunk by Viewing VTP Status*

```
3550_switch#show vtp status
VTP Version                    : 2
Configuration Revision         : 3
Maximum VLANs supported locally : 1005
Number of existing VLANs       : 12
VTP Operating Mode             : Server
VTP Domain Name                : psv2
```

continues

Example 1-17 *Statusing a Trunk by Viewing VTP Status (Continued)*

```
VTP Pruning Mode            : Disabled
VTP V2 Mode                 : Disabled
VTP Traps Generation        : Disabled
MD5 digest                  : 0x40 0x2B 0xD9 0xD1 0x05 0xA4 0x98 0xF8
Configuration last modified by 206.191.241.43 at 3-1-93 18:06:59
Local updater ID is 172.16.128.16 on interface Vl128 (lowest numbered VLAN interface
found)
Preferred interface name is 3550
3550_switch#
```

Configuring Layer 2 and Layer 3 EtherChannel

EtherChannel is yet another form of trunk line you can configure. The common way to configure EtherChannel is as Layer 2 between two switches. Usually ISL or 802.1Q is also configured. On the Catalyst 3550 with the EMI software installed, you can also configure Layer 3 EtherChannel.

EtherChannel has some limitations you should be aware of when configuring it. Some of these limitations are hardware specific; therefore, it is a good idea to look up the specific EtherChannel limitations for the platform you are configuring.

The following list applies to the configuration guidelines of the Catalyst 3550 Ethernet switch:

- Each EtherChannel can have up to eight compatibly configured Fast Ethernet interfaces and up to eight Gigabit Ethernet interfaces.

- Do not configure a GigaStack GBIC port as part of an EtherChannel.

- Configure all interfaces in an EtherChannel to operate at the same speeds and duplex modes.

- Enable all interfaces in an EtherChannel. An interface in an EtherChannel disabled by using the **shutdown interface** configuration command is treated as a link failure, and its traffic is transferred to one of the remaining interfaces in the EtherChannel.

- When a group is first created, all ports follow the parameters set for the first port to be added to the group. If you change the configuration of one of these parameters, you must also make the changes to all ports in the group.

- An EtherChannel does not form if one of the interfaces is a Switch Port Analyzer (SPAN) destination port. You may use the EtherChannel group as a source of SPAN to monitor the entire group.

- A port that belongs to an EtherChannel port group cannot be configured as a secure port.

- Assign all interfaces in the EtherChannel to the same VLAN, or configure them as trunks. Interfaces with different native VLANs cannot form an EtherChannel.

- If you configure an EtherChannel from trunk interfaces, verify that the trunking mode (ISL or 802.1Q) is the same on all the trunks.

- An EtherChannel supports the same allowed range of VLANs on all the interfaces in a trunking Layer 2 EtherChannel. If the allowed range of VLANs is not the same, the interfaces do not form an EtherChannel even when PAgP is set to the auto or desirable mode.

- Before enabling 802.1X on the port, you must first remove it from the EtherChannel. If you enable 802.1X on a not-yet-active port of an EtherChannel, the port does not join the EtherChannel.

- Interfaces with different STP path costs can form an EtherChannel as long they are otherwise compatibly configured. Setting different STP path costs does not, by itself, make interfaces incompatible for the formation of an EtherChannel.

- For Layer 3 EtherChannels, assign the Layer 3 address to the port-channel logical interface, not to the physical interfaces in the channel.

- By default, PAgP will have no Layer 2 or Layer 3 Channel groups assigned or defined. The EtherChannel configuration for PAgP is auto and silent; the interface will respond to PAgP packets but will not start PAgP negotiation. PAgP is configured as an aggregate-port learner with a PAgP priority of 128 on all interfaces.

Configuring Layer 2 EtherChannel ISL/802.1Q trunks on the Catalyst 3550 is a three-step process. Depending on the state of the port prior to configuration, you may have to disable autonegotiation mode. By default, a port is set to negotiate the encapsulation and to be in the dynamic and desirable mode.

Step 1   Configure the trunk encapsulation as ISL or 802.1Q.

Step 2   Configure the port as a trunk.

Step 3   Configure EtherChannel port groups.

These steps are accomplished with the following commands from the interface configuration mode:

```
Switch#(config-if)#switchport trunk encapsulation [isl | dot1q / negotiate]
Switch#(config-if)#switchport mode [trunk | dynamic {auto | desirable}]
Switch#(config-if)#channel-group [1-64] mode {auto [non-silent] | desirable [non-silent]
| on}
```

The first two commands are identical to configuring a normal ISL or 802.1Q trunk. The **channel-group** command creates a virtual interface called interface port channel *x*, where *x* is the channel group number. The virtual interface lists all the common properties that must be associated with any link joining the port group. This virtual interface is also where you assign an IP address for Layer 3 EtherChannel. The channel group number can range from 1 to 64. The **mode** keyword enables or disables PAgP. PAgP works rather reliably, but be sure that when you choose the mode in which to run PAgP that you use the same mode on all interfaces in the channel group. The **mode** keyword has the following parameters:

- **auto**—Enables PAgP only if another PAgP device is detected. It places the interface into a passive negotiating state, in which the interface responds to PAgP frames it receives but does not start PAgP negotiation.

- **desirable**—Unconditionally enables PAgP. This keyword places the interface into an active negotiating state, in which the interface starts negotiations with other interfaces by sending PAgP frames.

- **on**—Forces the interface to channel without PAgP. With the on mode, a usable EtherChannel exists only when an interface group in the on mode is connected to another interface group in the on mode.

- **active** (LACP)—Sets the interface into an active negotiating state, in which the interface starts negotiations with other interfaces by sending LACP packets.

- **passive** (LACP)—Sets the interface into a passive negotiating state. In this mode, the interface responds to LACP packets that it receives but does not start LACP packet negotiation. This setting uses minimal LACP packets.

An EtherChannel can also be assigned to a specific VLAN, although this is less common. To accomplish this, assign all interfaces as static-access ports in the same VLAN.

When configuring EtherChannel, you will notice the link drops and initializes quite a bit—once for an encapsulation change, and at least one other time when it joins the channel group. To prevent this from happening, just shut down the link before configuring any trunking or EtherChannel parameters. To remove an interface from the EtherChannel group, use the **no channel-group** interface configuration command.

Figure 1-16 represents a common network. In this LAN, the core switches are connected to each other and to another edge switch. The core switches are going to use Gigabit EtherChannel to trunk the two switches together. 802.1Q will be the VLAN trunking protocol and will eventually allow VLAN 192 full connectivity.

Figure 1-16 *Gigabit EtherChannel on the Catalyst 3550*

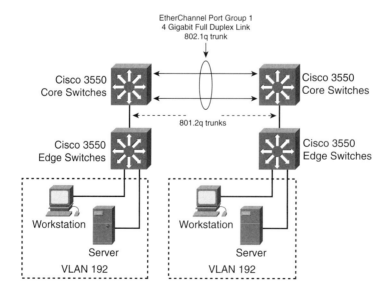

Example 1-18 demonstrates the configuration of the EtherChannel between the core switches in Figure 1-16.

Example 1-18 *Configuring Gigabit EtherChannel with 802.1Q Encapsulation*

```
3550_switch(config)#interface gigabitEthernet 0/1
3550_switch(config-if)#switch trunk encapsulation dot1q
3550_switch(config-if)#switchport mode trunk
3550_switch(config-if)#channel-group 1 mode on
Creating a port-channel interface Port-channel1
3550_switch(config-if)#exit
00:23:18: %LINK-3-UPDOWN: Interface Port-channel1, changed state to up
00:23:19: %LINEPROTO-5-UPDOWN: Line protocol on Interface Port-channel1, changed state
to up
3550_switch(config)#interface gigabitEthernet 0/2
3550_switch(config-if)#switchport trunk encapsulation dot1q
3550_switch(config-if)#switchport mode trunk
3550_switch(config-if)#channel-group 1 mode on
00:24:29: %LINK-3-UPDOWN: Interface GigabitEthernet0/2, changed state to up
00:24:31: %LINEPROTO-5-UPDOWN: Line protocol on Interface GigabitEthernet0/2, changed
state top
3550_switch(config-if)#exit
```

Cisco offers some useful commands to verify the operation status of an EtherChannel:

```
show etherchannel [channel-group-number] {brief | detail | load-balance | port | port-
channel | summary}
show interface etherchannel
```

The **show etherchannel** command displays the number of ports and the mode that they are in along with other information on the EtherChannel port group. You should see the port state as up, and all the interfaces that belong to the channel should be listed. The command also displays information about the load-balance or frame-distribution scheme, port, and port channel. The L2 in the group state defines the EtherChannel as a Layer 2 EtherChannel. Example 1-19 demonstrates the **show etherchannel** command.

Example 1-19 *Output of the* **show etherchannel** *Command*

```
3550_switch#show etherchannel 1 detail
Group state = L2
Ports: 2   Maxports = 8
Port-channels: 1 Max Port-channels = 1
                Ports in the group:
                -------------------
Port: Gi0/1
-----------
Port state    = Up Mstr In-Bndl
Channel group = 1            Mode = On/FEC      Gcchange = 0
Port-channel  = Po1          GC   = 0x00010001     Pseudo port-channel = Po1
Port index    = 0            Load = 0x00
Age of the port in the current state: 00d:03h:04m:31s
```

continues

Example 1-19 *Output of the* **show etherchannel** *Command (Continued)*

```
Port: Gi0/2
------------
Port state      = Up Mstr In-Bndl
Channel group = 1            Mode = On/FEC     Gcchange = 0
Port-channel  = Po1          GC   = 0x00010001    Pseudo port-channel = Po1
Port index    = 0            Load = 0x00
Age of the port in the current state: 00d:03h:03m:17s
                   Port-channels in the group:
                   ----------------------
Port-channel: Po1
------------
Age of the Port-channel   = 00d:03h:04m:33s
Logical slot/port    = 1/0          Number of ports = 2
GC                   = 0x00010001      HotStandBy port = null
Port state           = Port-channel Ag-Inuse
Ports in the Port-channel:
Index   Load   Port    EC state
------+------+------+------------
  0     00    Gi0/1    on
  0     00    Gi0/2    on
Time since last port bundled:    00d:03h:03m:19s    Gi0/2
3550_switch#
```

To verify the PAgP status of a EtherChannel group, use the following command:

show pagp [*channel-group-number*] {**counters** | **internal** | **neighbor**}

This command displays PAgP information such as traffic information, the internal PAgP configuration, and neighbor information.

Configuring Layer 3 EtherChannel

To configure Layer 3 EtherChannel, you create the port-channel logical interface and then put the Ethernet interfaces into the port channel. The **no switchport** command must be used on the port channel and on the physical interface. The steps and syntax used to create a Layer 3 EtherChannel are as follows:

Step 1   Configure the port channel, disable Layer 2 switching, and assign an IP address to the port channel, as follows:

```
3550_switch(config)#interface port-channel [1-64]
3550_switch(config-if)#no switchport
3550_switch(config-if)#ip address address subnet_mask
```

Step 2   Configure the physical interfaces that will reside in the EtherChannel group and assign them to the port channel, as follows:

```
3550_switch(config)#interface interface_name
3550_switch(config-if)#no switchport
3550_switch(config-if)#channel-group [1-64] mode {auto [non-silent] | desirable
[non-silent] | on}
```

Example 1-20 demonstrates the configuration of a Layer 3 EtherChannel with an IP address of 172.16.50.1/24.

Example 1-20 *Configuring Layer 3 EtherChannel*

```
3550_switch(config)#interface port-channel 2
3550_switch(config-if)#no switchport
3550_switch(config-if)#ip address 172.16.50.1 255.255.255.0
3550_switch(config-if)#exit
3550_switch(config)#interface fast 0/17
3550_switch(config-if)#channel-group 2 mode auto
3550_switch(config-if)#interface fast 0/18
3550_switch(config-if)#no switchport
3550_switch(config-if)#channel-group 2 mode auto
```

Configuring EtherChannel Load Balancing

You can configure EtherChannel for different types of load balancing. Two types of load balancing may be used: source-based and destination-based forwarding methods. The default load balancing type is src-mac. EtherChannel balances the traffic load across the links in a channel by reducing part of the binary pattern formed from the addresses in the frame to a numeric value that selects one of the links in the channel.

With source MAC address forwarding, when packets are forwarded to an EtherChannel, they are distributed across the ports in the channel based on the source MAC address of the incoming packet. Therefore, to provide load balancing, packets from different hosts use different ports in the channel, but packets from the same host use the same port in the channel (and the same MAC address learned by the switch does not change).

When the source MAC address forwarding method is used, load distribution based on the source and destination IP address is also enabled for routed IP traffic. All routed IP traffic chooses a port based on the source and destination IP address. Packets between two IP hosts always use the same port in the channel, and traffic between any other pair of hosts can use a different port in the channel.

With destination MAC address forwarding, when packets are forwarded to an EtherChannel, they are distributed across the ports in the channel based on the destination host's MAC address of the incoming packet. Therefore, packets to the same destination are forwarded over the same port, and packets to a different destination are sent on a different port in the channel.

To configure load balancing across EtherChannel, use the following global configuration command:

```
3550_switch(config)#port-channel load-balance {dst-mac | src-mac}
```

To verify the type of load balancing in effect, use the **show etherchannel load-balance** command. This command shows whether dst-mac or src-mac load balancing is being used.

To return EtherChannel load balancing to the default configuration, use the **no port-channel load-balance** global configuration command.

Step 4: Controlling STP and VLAN Propagation

The next step is optional but can be imperative in large networks. Cisco implements a couple of features that allow for switches to be plug and play in small networks but can have the negative effect of generating significant amounts of traffic in large networks. Features such as Per VLAN Spanning Tree (PVST), coupled with the default setting that every VLAN is communicated on every trunk port, can cause the edge switches to be overrun processing spanning-tree requests and other broadcasts.

In the network in Figure 1-17, for example, the crane switch has only a single VLAN, VLAN 2. Because this switch is in the same VTP domain as the other switches, however, it will participate in spanning tree for VLAN 3 and VLAN 4. There is really no need for this switch to waste resources processing spanning-tree requests for a VLAN that is not even on the switch. The larger and more redundant the network, the worse the problem gets. Suppose, for instance, that you have 75 edge switches; there would be 75 separate spanning-tree topologies on one trunk per edge switch! In addition, all of this happens before any user traffic can use the switch.

It is a common misconception that *VLAN pruning* will solve STP issues. However, VLAN pruning affects only broadcast, multicast, and unknown/flooded unicast traffic. Basically, STP constructs the path the data will take, or "road" that the data can flow on, and pruning controls the broadcast data or "traffic" that flows on that path.

There are two very effective ways Cisco offers for dealing with excessive broadcasts and STP:

- **VLAN pruning**—VLAN pruning states that if VTP pruning is enabled, and if a downstream switch does not have an active port in that VLAN being pruned, the switch prevents the forwarding of flooded traffic to that prune-eligible downstream VLAN. VTP pruning is a method of traffic control that reduces unnecessary broadcast, multicast, and unknown unicast traffic. VTP pruning blocks flooded traffic to VLANs on trunk ports that are included in the pruning-eligible list. If the VLANs are configured as "pruning ineligible," the flooding continues.

- **Clearing VLANs from trunks**—Clearing VLANs off of a trunk essentially removes that spanning-tree instance from the trunk. The downstream switch will no longer receive BPDUs for the VLAN cleared. No user traffic for that VLAN will be able to pass down this trunk.

Figure 1-17 *VLAN Trunking and STP*

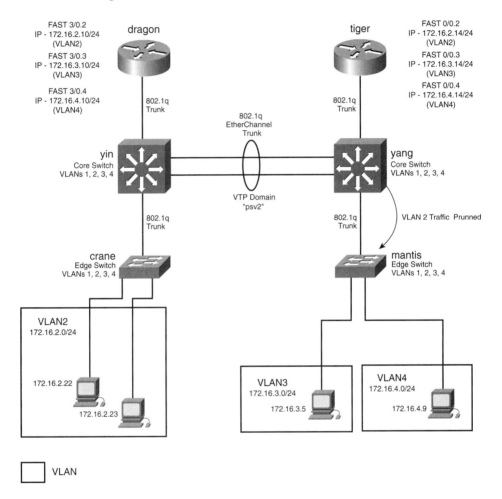

Configuring VTP Pruning

In Figure 1-17, a port is active on VLAN 2 on the crane, yin, and yang switches, but not on the mantis switch. If VTP pruning is enabled for VLAN 2 on the yang switch, the mantis switch will not receive broadcast, multicast, and unknown/flooded unicast traffic for VLAN 2. Likewise, the crane switch will not receive the same type of traffic from VLAN 3 and VLAN 4, assuming pruning is enabled on the yin switch. By default, VTP pruning is disabled; therefore, global VTP pruning must be enabled. Enabling VTP pruning is a two-step process, with the second step optional:

Step 1 Enable VTP pruning from the VLAN configuration mode or the VLAN database with the **vtp pruning** command. This command enables pruning for VLANs, and no further configuration is necessary unless you only want to prune specific VLANs.

```
3550_switch(vlan)#vtp pruning
```

Step 2 (Optional) Add VLANs to the prune-eligible list. By default, all VLANs are prune eligible, and this step may be bypassed. You may mark only certain VLANs prune eligible by using the following interface command:

```
3550_switch(config-if)#switchport trunk pruning vlan {add | except | none |
remove} vlan_range
```

You may add multiple VLANs, separated by a comma, or a range of VLANs, using a hyphen (-). For example, the interface command **switchport trunk pruning vlan add 2-10** makes only the VLANs 2 through 10 prune eligible. You can control VTP pruning on a trunk-by-trunk basis with this command.

Global VTP pruning, whether it is enabled or not, can be verified by the **show vtp status** command. You can verify VTP pruning for individual VLANs by using the **show interface** command with the **switchport** keyword or by viewing the VTP status. Example 1-21 demonstrates how to verify whether VTP pruning is enabled with the **show vtp status command**.

Example 1-21 *Verifying Global VTP Status*

```
yin#show vtp status
VTP Version                    : 2
Configuration Revision         : 6
Maximum VLANs supported locally : 1005

Number of existing VLANs       : 14
VTP Operating Mode             : Server
VTP Domain Name                : psv2
VTP Pruning Mode               : Enabled
VTP V2 Mode                    : Disabled
VTP Traps Generation           : Disabled
MD5 digest                     : 0x13 0xF9 0xA7 0x89 0x56 0x56 0x8D 0x54
Configuration last modified by 172.16.192.16 at 3-1-93 02:35:01
Local updater ID is 172.16.192.16 on interface Vl192 (lowest numbered VLAN interface
found)
```

Example 1-22 demonstrates the use of the **show interface** command in verifying VLAN prune eligibility. The **show interface** command was executed after the interface command **switchport trunk pruning vlan 2-1001** was entered on the yin switch.

Example 1-22 *Verifying VLAN Prune Eligibility*

```
yin#show interfaces fast 0/20 switchport
Name: Fa0/20
Switchport: Enabled
Administrative Mode: trunk
Operational Mode: trunk
Administrative Trunking Encapsulation: dot1q
Operational Trunking Encapsulation: dot1q
Negotiation of Trunking: On
Access Mode VLAN: 1 (default)
Trunking Native Mode VLAN: 1 (default)
Trunking VLANs Enabled: ALL
Pruning VLANs Enabled: 2-1001
Protected: false
Unknown unicast blocked: disabled
Unknown multicast blocked: disabled
```

Controlling STP by Removing It from Trunk Lines

In medium to large networks, it becomes crucial to control how many instances of STP there are on each switch and how many traverse the trunks. Recall that by default every VLAN will have an instance of STP, which Cisco calls PVST+. Switches will run an instance of STP on all trunks for every VLAN they are aware of. If a network has five VLANs, there are five instances of STP, and each instance has a single root switch, and so on. The Catalyst 3550 supports 128 instances of STP per switch. Other switches, such as Catalyst 3548XL and 2900XL, can support 64 STP instances, and this varies on a switch-by-switch basis. To find out how many instances of STP your switch supports, refer to www.cisco.com. If more VLANs are added, STP is disabled for that on some VLANs on that switch. A more common problem is the amount of strain many STP instances put on smaller edge or wiring-closet switches. Unfortunately, VTP pruning does not affect spanning tree. To remove an instance of STP from a trunk, use the following interface command:

```
Switch(config-if)#switchport trunk allowed vlan [add | all | except | remove] vlans_2-1001
```

- **add**—Adds the following VLANs to the trunk
- **all**—Includes all VLANs on the trunk
- **except**—Includes all VLANs except those specified
- **remove**—Removes the following VLANs from the trunk

To remove VLAN 3 through VLAN 6, you would use the following cryptic-looking command:

```
Switch(config-if)#switchport trunk allowed vlan remove 3-6
```

Figure 1-18 shows the same network as Figure 1-17, with updated interfaces names. In this example, on the yin switch, all VLANs are cleared, except 1 and 2, on the trunk to the crane switch.

Figure 1-18 *VLAN Trunking and STP*

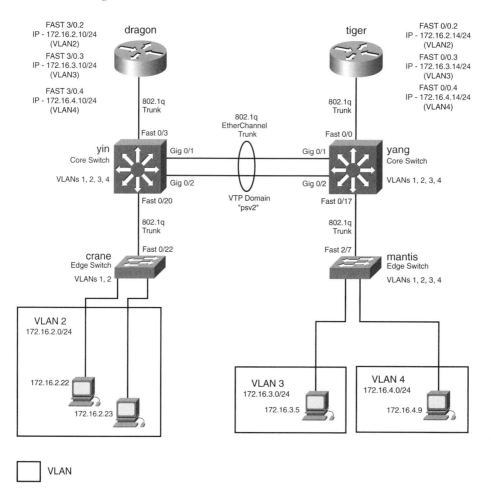

In this particular example, to remove STP from the trunk, you use the **switchport** command. Prior to clearing the trunks, you examine the STP state of VLAN 3. Example 1-23 shows the **show spanning-tree** command on the yin switch. Notice at the bottom that STP is forwarding VLAN 3 information out fast 0/3, the dragon router; fast 0/20 the crane switch; and po1, the EtherChannel port.

Example 1-23 **show spanning-tree** *Command on the Yin Switch*

```
yin#show spanning-tree vlan 3
VLAN0003
  Spanning tree enabled protocol ieee
  Root ID    Priority    32768
```

Example 1-23 **show spanning-tree** *Command on the Yin Switch (Continued)*

```
                        Address      0004.275e.f0c8
                        Cost         3
                        Port         65 (Port-channel1)
                        Hello Time   2 sec  Max Age 20 sec  Forward Delay 15 sec
          Bridge ID  Priority     32771  (priority 32768 sys-id-ext 3)
                        Address      000a.8a0e.ba80
                        Hello Time   2 sec  Max Age 20 sec  Forward Delay 15 sec
                        Aging Time 300
   Interface       Port ID                      Designated            Port ID
   Name            Prio.Nbr      Cost Sts      Cost Bridge ID          Prio.Nbr
   --------------- -------- --------- --- --------- ------------------- --------
   Fa0/3            128.3         19 FWD         3 32771 000a.8a0e.ba80 128.3
   Fa0/20           128.16        19 FWD         3 32771 000a.8a0e.ba80 128.16
   Po1              128.65         3 FWD         0 32768 0004.275e.f0c8 128.1
   yin#
```

Example 1-24 demonstrates the clearing of VLANs 3 through 1001 on the trunk between the yin and crane switches. The second portion of the example shows the spanning tree for VLAN 3. Notice that VLAN 3 is no longer forwarding out the trunk Fa0/20, the trunk line to the crane switch.

Example 1-24 *Clearing/Removing a VLAN from a Trunk*

```
   yin(config)#int fastEthernet 0/20
   yin(config-if)#switchport trunk allowed vlan remove 3-1001
   yin(config-if)#^Z
   yin#show spanning-tree vlan 3
   11:55:53: %SYS-5-CONFIG_I: Configured from console by console
   VLAN0003
     Spanning tree enabled protocol ieee
     Root ID    Priority     32768
                Address      0004.275e.f0c8
                Cost         3
                Port         65 (Port-channel1)
                Hello Time   2 sec  Max Age 20 sec  Forward Delay 15 sec
     Bridge ID  Priority     32771  (priority 32768 sys-id-ext 3)
                Address      000a.8a0e.ba80
                Hello Time   2 sec  Max Age 20 sec  Forward Delay 15 sec
                Aging Time 15
   Interface       Port ID                      Designated            Port ID
   Name            Prio.Nbr      Cost Sts      Cost Bridge ID          Prio.Nbr
   --------------- -------- --------- --- --------- ------------------- --------
   Fa0/3            128.3         19 FWD         3 32771 000a.8a0e.ba80 128.3
   Po1              128.65         3 FWD         0 32768 0004.275e.f0c8 128.1
   yin#
```

The command **show interface** *interface_name* **switchport** also shows which VLANs are carried on the trunk.

The **show interface trunk** command is a very useful command to determine the trunking status of a link and VLAN status. The **show interface trunk** command lists port, its mode and encapsulation, and whether it is trunking. It also lists the VLANs allowed on each trunk and STP status of those VLANs. Example 1-25 lists the output of the **show interface trunk** command, showing that VLANs 3 through 1001 no longer appear on the trunk fast 0/20. VLANs 1002 through 4094 are other default and extended-range VLANs.

Example 1-25 *Showing the Allowed VLANs on a Trunk*

```
yin#show interface trunk
Port      Mode       Encapsulation  Status        Native vlan
Fa0/3     on         802.1q         trunking      1
Fa0/20    on         802.1q         trunking      1
Po1       on         802.1q         trunking      1
Port      Vlans allowed on trunk
Fa0/3     1-4094
Fa0/20    1-2,1002-4094
Po1       1-4094
Port      Vlans allowed and active in management domain
Fa0/3     1-4,10,20,30,40,50,192
Fa0/20    1-2
Po1       1-4,10,20,30,40,50,192
Port      Vlans in spanning tree forwarding state and not pruned
Fa0/3     1-4,10,20,30,40,50,192
Fa0/20    1-2
Po1       1,192
yin#
```

Removing VLANs from the trunks is one way to control STP; for the switches that need redundancy, however, you must use additional methods to control STP.

NOTE   Newer versions of Catalyst software allow for the clearing/removing of VLAN 1. However, most switches still will not allow you to clear/remove VLAN 1. Always exercise caution if removing VLAN from any trunk lines. Remember, this is the native VLAN for 802.1Q by default, and other protocols may be using untagged frames on VLAN 1.

Configuring STP Load Balancing and Root Placement

Redundant switched networks do not perform automatic load balancing. Because the STP forwarding/blocking decision is based, in part, on static MAC addresses, all traffic tends to follow the same direction and the same path for all VLANs. This leads to some links being overused, while others remain idle. Figure 1-19 illustrates a network that has all converged on a single switch. The yang switch is the root of STP for VLANs 2, 3, 4, and 5.

Figure 1-19 *STP Root*

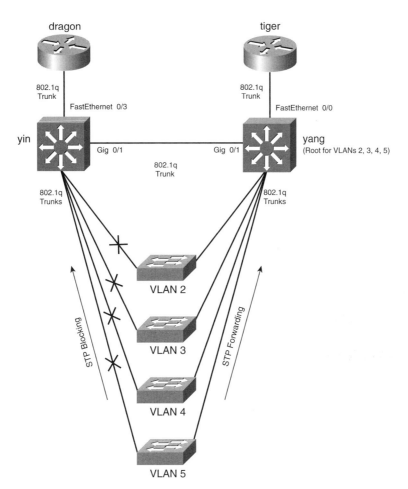

If you wanted to load balance between the yin and yang switches or if you were using HSRP on the dragon and tiger routers, you would want to control STP root placement. If the dragon router were the HSRP primary for VLAN 2, for instance, you would want traffic to go through the yin switch rather than the yang switch. To control and distribute traffic in a switched network, you must manually configure the root for STP.

You can configure the root of spanning tree for Catalyst switches in many ways. The methods you use to set the root depend mostly on the environment you are trying to control. When setting the root bridge, you are essentially telling STP which ports to put into blocking and which ports to put into forwarding. Because STP runs on a PVST basis, each VLAN has a different root bridge. In Figure 1-20, the yin switch is set to be the STP root for VLAN 4 and VLAN 5, and the yang switch is the STP root for VLAN 2 and VLAN 3. This causes the edge switches to balance their load more evenly over the trunk's lines. VLANs 4 and 5 forward to yin, and VLANs 2 and 3 forward to yang.

Figure 1-20 *STP Root*

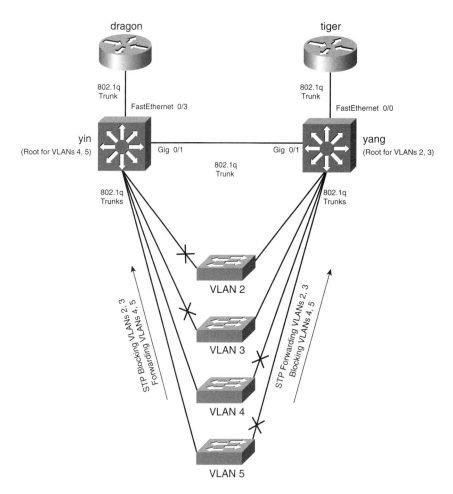

Before further exploring how to set the STP root, you must first learn how to determine where the root bridge is located. The **show spanning-tree root** command displays a quick overview of the root of each VLAN. It shows the MAC address of the root, the root port, the priority, the cost, and the STP timers for that VLAN. Example 1-26 lists the output of the **show span** command.

Example 1-26 *Viewing Spanning Tree for VLAN 2*

```
yin#show spanning-tree root
                                 Root   Hello Max Fwd
Vlan                Root ID      Cost   Time  Age Dly  Root Port
---------------- -------------------- --------- ----- --- ---  ------------
VLAN0001         32768 0004.275e.f0c0     3      2   20  15   Po1
VLAN0002         32768 0004.275e.f0c7     3      2   20  15   Po1
VLAN0003         32768 0004.275e.f0c8     3      2   20  15   Po1
VLAN0004         32768 0004.275e.f0c9     3      2   20  15   Po1
VLAN0005         32768 0004.275e.f0c1     3      2   20  15   Po1
yin#
```

The **show spanning-tree** command and its subcommand, **show spanning-tree vlan**, display detailed and valuable information about spanning tree. There are a few variations of this command depending on how much information you may want. Example 1-27 lists a portion of VLAN 2 output from the **show spanning-tree** command on the yin switch.

Example 1-27 *Viewing Spanning Tree for VLAN 2*

```
yin#show spanning-tree
VLAN0001
  Spanning tree enabled protocol ieee
  Root ID     Priority    32768
<<<text omitted>>>
VLAN0002
  Spanning tree enabled protocol ieee
  Root ID     Priority    100
              Address     0004.275e.f0c7
              Cost        3
              Port        65 (Port-channel1)
              Hello Time   2 sec  Max Age 20 sec  Forward Delay 15 sec
  Bridge ID   Priority    32770  (priority 32768 sys-id-ext 2)
              Address     000a.8a0e.ba80
              Hello Time   2 sec  Max Age 20 sec  Forward Delay 15 sec
              Aging Time 300
Interface     Port ID                    Designated              Port ID
Name          Prio.Nbr    Cost Sts    Cost Bridge ID             Prio.Nbr
---------------- -------- --------- --- --------- -------------------- --------
Fa0/3          128.3         19 FWD     3 32770 000a.8a0e.ba80 128.3
Fa0/20         128.16        19 FWD     3 32770 000a.8a0e.ba80 128.16
Po1            128.65         3 FWD     0   100 0004.275e.f0c7 128.1
<<<text omitted>>>
```

Every bit of information provided by this command is useful. The fields are defined as follows:

- **Spanning tree type**—The type of Spanning Tree Protocol in use: IBM, DEC, or IEEE.
- **Root ID**—The MAC address of the root bridge.

- **Root ID Priority**—The bridge priority that was received from the root bridge. The values of the bridge priority range from 0 to 65,535, with 32,768 as the default.

- **Root ID Cost**—The cumulative cost to the root bridge.

- **Root ID Port**—The root port for that segment.

- **Root Max Age, Hello Time, Forward Delay**—The three STP timers as sent by the root bridge.

- **Bridge ID MAC ADDR**—The MAC address that is being used for this VLAN by this local bridge.

- **Bridge ID Priority**—The priority of the local bridge.

- **Bridge Max Age, Hello Time, Forward Delay**—The three STP timers on the local bridge.

The final rows show each port that is participating in STP within the VLAN and lists whether the port is forwarding or blocking, as well as the cost and service priority of the port. Do not confuse this priority with spanning-tree bridge priority. The values of the port priority range from 0 to 63, with 32 as the default.

Another command that is useful in presenting a general operational picture of spanning tree is the **show spantree summary** command. This command provides an overview of the VLANs and the state of the port from an STP perspective. Example 1-28 lists the output for this command.

Example 1-28 *Viewing Spanning Tree for VLAN 2*

```
3550_switch#show spanning-tree summary
Root Bridge for: none.
Extended system ID is enabled.
PortFast BPDU Guard is disabled
EtherChannel misconfiguration guard is enabled
UplinkFast is disabled
BackboneFast is disabled
Default pathcost method used is short
Name                    Blocking Listening Learning Forwarding STP Active
---------------------- -------- --------- -------- ---------- ----------
VLAN0001                    0        0        0         5          5
VLAN0002                    0        0        0         3          3
VLAN0003                    0        0        0         2          2
VLAN0004                    0        0        0         2          2
VLAN0005                    0        0        0         2          2
---------------------- -------- --------- -------- ---------- ----------
5 vlans                     0        0        0        14         14
yin#
```

To properly set the STP root, it helps to recall the four-step decision process of STP and how spanning tree determines root. The root is selected by the lowest-cost BID. The BID is composed of priority followed by MAC address.

1 Lowest root BID (priority followed by MAC address, adjacent to root bridge)

2 Lowest-path cost to root bridge; the cumulative cost of all paths to root

3 Lowest sender BID

4 Lowest port ID

From this process, you can influence the decision of the root at multiple levels. At times, you may want every port to have the same STP priority; at other times, however, you may want a specific port to have a higher priority, such as in a load-sharing environment. Table 1-12 lists the four primary STP election states, and the Catalyst 3550 global configuration command.

Table 1-12 *Ethernet STP Configuration Outcomes*

STP Election State	Catalyst 3550 Configuration Command
1. Lowest BID	+**spanning-tree** [**vlan** *vlan_id*] [**priority** *0-65535*] +**spanning-tree vlan** *vlan_id* **root** [**primary**|**secondary**] [**diameter** *2-7* [**hello-time** *seconds*]]
2. Lowest path cost to root	*****spanning-tree** [**vlan** *vlan_id*] [**cost** *1-200000000*]
3. Lowest sender BID	+**spanning-tree** [**vlan** *vlan_id*] [**priority** *0-65535*]
4. Lowest port ID	*****spanning-tree** [**vlan** *vlan_id*] [**port-priority** *0-255*]

*Interface configuration commands

+Global configuration commands

You can influence the root bridge selection process in many ways. The way you choose depends on what you are trying to accomplish by setting root. The higher up in the election process you use to influence root, the more it will help safeguards against possible ties or other STP configurations present on other switches that you may not have control over.

- The global **spanning-tree** [**vlan** *vlan_id*] [**priority** *0-65535*] command can influence the Priority field of the BID; the lower the priority, the more likely the switch will become root. It can be set on a per-VLAN level or globally for the entire switch. The valid values for the VLAN ID are 1 through 4094. Valid priority values are 4096, 8192, 12,288, 16,384, 20,480, 24,576, 28,672, 32,768, 36,864, 40,960, 45,056, 49,152, 53,248, 57,344, and 61,440. All other values are rejected.

- The global command **spanning-tree vlan** *vlan_id* **root** [**primary**|**secondary**] [**diameter** *2-7* [**hello-time** *seconds*]] is a macro much like the **set root** macro on CAT OS. When the command is entered with the **primary** keyword, it examines the VLAN(s) on the switch for the highest priority, the root, and sets its priority less than that. The command may also adjust the max age, hello, and forwarding delay timers. This command also uses the extended system ID. The optional **diameter** keyword specifies the maximum number of switches between any two end stations. The valid range is 2 to 7. The optional **hello-time** specifies the interval, in seconds, between the generation of configuration messages by the root switch. The range is 1 to 10 seconds; the default value is 2 seconds. Example 1-29 demonstrates the use of the **root** macro command.

Example 1-29 *Using the Spanning-Tree* **root** *Macro Command*

```
3550_switch(config)#spanning-tree vlan 192 root primary
 vlan 192 bridge priority set to 24576
 vlan 192 bridge max aging time unchanged at 20
 vlan 192 bridge hello time unchanged at 2
 vlan 192 bridge forward delay unchanged at 15
3550_switch(config)#
```

- When this command was entered, the default priority found on VLAN 192 was 32,768; therefore, the switch set the priority less than that (in this case, 24,576). The value of 24,576 is a unique value that states the extended system ID is in use. If the value of the priority were changed to 8192, extended system ID would not be in use.

- The interface command **spanning-tree** [**vlan** *vlan_id*] [**cost** *1-200000000*] influences the STP cost of an interface. The valid VLAN ID is 1 to 4094, and the valid cost ranges from 1 to 200,000,000. Table 1-13 lists the default STP cost.

Table 1-13 *STP Cost Values for LAN Links*

Bandwidth	Revised IEEE STP Cost
4 Mbps	250
10 Mbps	100
16 Mbps	62
45 Mbps	39
100 Mbps	19
155 Mbps	14
622 Mbps	6
1 Gbps	4
10 Gbps	2

- The interface command **spanning-tree** [**vlan** *vlan_id*] [**port-priority** *0-255*] configures the port priority of the interface. The default port priority is 128, and the valid ranges are 0 to 255. The lower the number, the better the priority. Table 1-14 lists the default STP configuration.

Table 1-14   *Default STP Configuration*

Feature	Default Setting
Enable state	Enabled on VLAN 1
	128 STP instances /switch
Switch/bridge priority	32768
STP port priority	128
STP port cost	See Table 1-12
Hello timer	2 seconds
Forward delay time	15 seconds
Maximum aging time	20 seconds

STP hello, forward delay, and max age timers can be configured and tuned with the following global configuration commands. Exercise caution anytime you are configuring STP timers. PVST+ runs one instance of STP per VLAN. If you change the timers on one switch for this VLAN, you must change the timers on all switches for that particular VLAN.

- **spanning-tree vlan** *vlan-id* **hello-time** [*1-10*]
- **spanning-tree vlan** *vlan-id* **forward-time** [*4-30*]
- **spanning-tree vlan** *vlan-id* **max-age** [*6-40*]

For the most part, configuring STP on the Catalyst 3550 is fairly similar to configuring STP on the Catalyst 3500XL/2900XL series switches. For detailed walkthroughs of STP and general switch configuration, refer back to Chapter 2 of *CCIE PSV1*.

Step 5: Configuring Switch Virtual Interfaces (SVIs)

The last three steps of the process are optional. They call for the configuration of the SVIs, routed ports, and Layer 3 switching.

1 Configure switch management.

2 Configure VTP and VLANs and assign ports/interfaces to VLANs.

3 Configure connections between switches using EtherChannel, 802.1Q, and ISL encapsulations.

4 (Optional) Control STP and VLAN propagation.

    5 (Optional) Configure SVIs.

    6 (Optional) Configure routed ports.

    7 (Optional) Configure Layer 3 switching.

Recollect that an SVI is a logical/virtual interface on the switch much like the management interface. An SVI represents a VLAN as one interface to the routing or bridging functions of the switch. Only one SVI can be associated with a VLAN. An SVI can be used to route between VLANs, as a fallback-bridge nonroutable protocol between VLANs, or to provide IP host connectivity to the switch for management.

By default, an SVI is created for the default VLAN (INT VLAN 1) for management. Other SVIs are created with the following global configuration command:

```
3550_switch(config)#interface vlan [1-4094]
3550_switch(config-if)# ip address IP_address subnet_mask
```

After creating the SVI, you can add an IP address to the interface and define features such as HSRP or ACLs. Treat the SVI much like you would a Layer 3 interface on a router. The most common use of an SVI is for management and inter-VLAN routing.

NOTE   To use SVIs in Layer 3 mode or to "route" across SVIs, you must have the EMI image installed on your switch.

In Figure 1-21, there exists a Cisco 3550 with the EMI software installed. Two VLANs exist on the switch: VLAN 2 and VLAN 10. VLAN 10 has workstations in the IP subnet of 172.16.10.0/24, and VLAN 2 has workstations in the IP subnet of 172.16.2.0/24. In this example, two SVIs are created (interface VLAN 2 and interface VLAN 10) and assigned IP addresses within the appropriate VLAN range.

Example 1-30 demonstrates how to configure two SVIs and assign IP addresses.

Example 1-30 *Configuring an SVI*

```
3550_switch(config)#interface vlan 2
02:05:42: %LINEPROTO-5-UPDOWN: Line protocol on Interface Vlan2, changed state to up
3550_switch(config-if)#ip address 172.16.2.1  255.255.255.0
3550_switch(config-if)#exit
3550_switch(config)#interface vlan 10
02:06:17: %LINEPROTO-5-UPDOWN: Line protocol on Interface Vlan10, changed state to up
3550_switch(config-if)#ip address 172.16.10.1  255.255.255.0
```

Figure 1-21 *SVI Configuration*

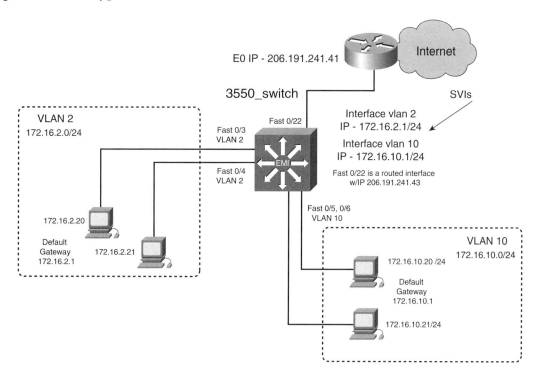

If there is an interface in VLAN 2 or VLAN 10, or if a trunk is active, you will be able to ping the interface. You can also view the interface with the standard **show interface** command and subcommands.

Although the SVI is up and you can ping it, you do not have Internet and IP connectivity yet. For the workstations on the VLANs to be able to have Internet access, and access to one another, Layer 3 switching has to be enabled. Enabling Layer 3 switching on a switch is accomplished through the global command **ip routing**. When routing is enabled, a routing protocol must still be configured for IP connectivity. Example 1-31 represents the configuration that is needed for full IP reachability.

Example 1-31 *Enabling Routing/Layer 3 Switching*

```
3550_switch(config)#ip routing
3550_switch(config)#router eigrp 2003
3550_switch(config-router)#network 172.16.0.0
3550_switch(config-router)#network 206.191.241.0
3550_switch(config-router)#no auto-summary
```

Using the **show ip route** command, you can verify the status of the SVIs. The administrative distance of an SVI is 0, appearing as a connected route. Example 1-32 shows the route/ forwarding table of the 3550 switch.

Example 1-32 *Viewing SVI in the Route/Forwarding Table*

```
3550_switch#show ip route
<<<text omitted>>>
Gateway of last resort is 206.191.241.41 to network 0.0.0.0
172.16.0.0/24 is subnetted, 4 subnets
C       172.16.10.0 is directly connected, Vlan10
C       172.16.2.0 is directly connected, Vlan2
C       206.191.241.43 is directly connected, FastEthernet0/22
D*EX 0.0.0.0/0 [170/537600] via 206.191.241.41, 1d04h, FastEthernet0/22
3550_switch#
```

Step 6: (Optional) Configuring Routed Ports

A *routed port* is a physical port on the Catalyst 3550 switch that functions just like a physical interface on a Cisco router. This is the simplest way to view it. You can configure many of the same features on a routed port as you can on a router's physical interface, including IP address, ACL, and membership of an HSRP group. A routed port cannot have VLAN subinterfaces, however, or be configured as a trunk of any type. Configuring routed ports requires the EMI software image.

Figure 1-22 illustrates two identical networks. The top network has three Catalyst 3550s with Fast Ethernet–routed ports connecting all three switches. The bottom network has three Cisco 2620 routers connected through the routers' Fast Ethernet interfaces.

A routed port is enabled by using the interface command **no switchport**. The **no switchport** command effectively disables switching functions for that interface.

The switch will use an internal VLAN to map the routed port. This internal VLAN will also be used for extended VLANs; be careful that they do not conflict. The internal VLAN ID the switch chooses can be viewed with the **show vlan internal usage** command. Example 1-33 demonstrates the configuration of two routed ports, followed by the **show vlan internal usage** command showing to which VLAN the switch will assign the routed port.

Figure 1-22 *Routed Port Comparison*

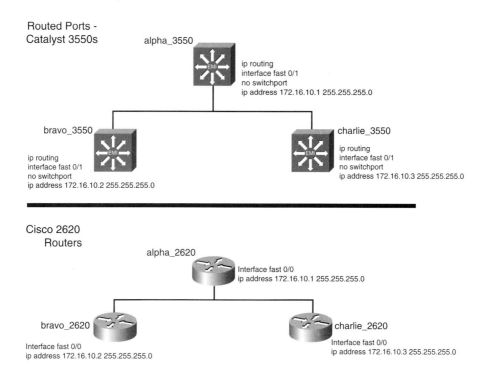

Routed Ports -
Catalyst 3550s

alpha_3550

ip routing
interface fast 0/1
no switchport
ip address 172.16.10.1 255.255.255.0

bravo_3550

ip routing
interface fast 0/1
no switchport
ip address 172.16.10.2 255.255.255.0

charlie_3550

ip routing
interface fast 0/1
no switchport
ip address 172.16.10.3 255.255.255.0

Cisco 2620
Routers

alpha_2620

Interface fast 0/0
ip address 172.16.10.1 255.255.255.0

bravo_2620

Interface fast 0/0
ip address 172.16.10.2 255.255.255.0

charlie_2620

Interface fast 0/0
ip address 172.16.10.3 255.255.255.0

Example 1-33 *Configuring a Routed Port*

```
3550_switch(config)#interface fast 0/7
3550_switch(config-if)#no switchport
02:06:22: %LINEPROTO-5-UPDOWN: Line protocol on Interface FastEthernet0/7, changed to
down
02:06:23: %LINK-3-UPDOWN: Interface FastEthernet0/7, changed state to down
02:06:26: %LINEPROTO-5-UPDOWN: Line protocol on Interface FastEthernet0/7, changed to
up
3550_switch(config-if)#ip address 172.16.200.16 255.255.255.0
3550_switch(config-if)#interface fast 0/8
3550_switch(config-if)#no switchport
3550_switch(config-if)#
02:06:53: %LINEPROTO-5-UPDOWN: Line protocol on Interface FastEthernet0/8, changed to
down
```

continues

Example 1-33 *Configuring a Routed Port (Continued)*

```
02:06:23: %LINK-3-UPDOWN: Interface FastEthernet0/8, changed state to down
02:06:26: %LINEPROTO-5-UPDOWN: Line protocol on Interface FastEthernet0/8, changed to
up
3550_switch(config-if)#ip address 172.16.201.16 255.255.255.0
3550_switch(config-if)#^Z
3550_switch
3550_switch#show vlan internal usage
VLAN Usage
---- -------------
1017 -
1025 FastEthernet0/7
! Internal VLANs used
1026 FastEthernet0/8
```

If you switch a port/interface from a *switch* port to a *routed* port by using the **no switchport** interface command, and you want to change the interface back to a *switched* interface, you must enter the interface command **switchport** without subcommands.

Step 7: (Optional) Configuring Layer 3 Switching

Layer 3 switching is the capability to make Layer 3 decisions and forward Layer 3 packets at Layer 2 speeds. Layer 3 switching is, in actuality, *routing*. Another, and easier, way to define Layer 3 switching is the capability to rapidly *route* and *switch* on the same hardware platform. When IP routing is enabled, the Catalyst 3550 effectively becomes a fast and sleek multiport router. Many of the IP features that are available in the IP routing suite are available when IP routing is enabled. Cisco has preserved the syntax of all IP configuration and related commands and smoothly integrated the traditional Cisco IOS Software. If you know how to configure a Cisco router, which you should at this point, configuring the Layer 3 or routing portion of the 3550 is just like configuring the router. Because of the extensive IOS feature sets, not all IP features, such as data-link switching (DLSw), are supported on the 3550. See Appendix A, "Cisco IOS Software Limitations and Restrictions," for a list of unsupported 3550 commands.

Seeing Isn't Always Believing

I'm a firm believer in using the question mark (?) for help. It has always helped guide me in syntax and show me some new available features. Be careful with the help on the 3550; many of the items that appear in the help cannot be configured. On IOS 12.1(9)EA1c, for example, you will see features such as Border Gateway Protocol (BGP) and On Demand Routing (ODR), but you will get an error if you try to configure them.

Appendix A includes a list of limitations and restrictions. For the most current list of new features, limitations, and restrictions, go to www.cisco.com.

To configure Layer 3 switching, follow these three steps:

Step 1   Configure one of the three supported Layer 3 interfaces and assign an IP address to it. The Catalyst 3550 routing fabric recognizes three types of Layer 3 interfaces.

A routed port

An SVI

Layer 3 EtherChannel

Step 2   Enable IP routing with the global configuration command **ip routing**.

Step 3   Configure Interior Gateway Protocols (IGPs) and other IP functionality. The IGPs supported are RIP v1 and v2, Interior Gateway Routing Protocol (IGRP), Enhanced IGRP, and Open Shortest Path First (OSPF). Interior routing protocols on the switch are configured in the same manner as they would be on a router. For that reason, routing protocol specifics are not discussed here. For more information on configuring IGPs, refer to *CCIE PSV1*.

Practical Example: Configuring SVIs, Routed Ports, and Layer 3 Switching

The network model in Figure 1-23 represents a Catalyst 3550, the dragon switch, serving as the core router and switch for the network. The dragon switch is using two SVIs for VLAN 10 and VLAN 100 for inter-VLAN routing. The workstation ports such as Fast 0/7 port are configured as *access ports* in a single VLAN. The Fast 0/8 interface is serving as a routed port and attaches to the dragon router. The routed port has an IP address of 172.16.200.1/24. IP routing is enabled on the dragon switch with EIGRP, in autonomous system 2003, as the routing protocol.

Figure 1-23   *Routed Port and SVI Configuration*

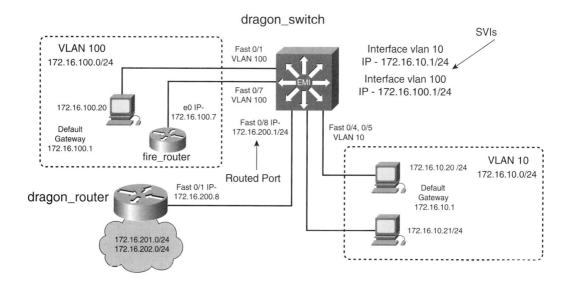

Example 1-34 lists the relevant portions of the dragon switch.

Example 1-34 *Dragon Switch Configuration*

```
hostname dragon_switch
!
ip subnet-zero
ip routing
! Routing enabled
!
spanning-tree extend system-id
! Extended System ID in use
!
interface FastEthernet0/1
 switchport access vlan 100
! VLAN 100
 no ip address
!
<<<text omitted>>>
!
interface FastEthernet0/4
 switchport access vlan 10
! VLAN 10
 no ip address
!
interface FastEthernet0/5
 switchport access vlan 10
! VLAN 10
 no ip address
!
interface FastEthernet0/6
 no ip address
!
interface FastEthernet0/7
 switchport access vlan 100
! VLAN 100
 no ip address
!
interface FastEthernet0/8
 no switchport
! Routed Port/interface
 ip address 172.16.200.1 255.255.255.0
! IP address
!
<<<text omitted>>>
!
interface Vlan1
! Default VLAN
 no ip address
! not used!
 shutdown
!
interface Vlan10
```

Example 1-34 *Dragon Switch Configuration (Continued)*

```
! SVI 10
 ip address 172.16.10.1 255.255.255.0
! IP address
!
interface Vlan100
! SVI 100
 ip address 172.16.100.1 255.255.255.0
! IP address
!
router eigrp 2003
! Routing Protocol
 network 172.16.0.0
! EIGRP on networks 172.16.0.0/16
 no auto-summary
 no eigrp log-neighbor-changes
!
```

In this network, the dragon switch is routing for all VLANs via EIGRP. VLAN 10, VLAN 100, and IP subnets 172.16.200.0/24, 172.16.201.0/24, and 172.16.202.0/24 have full IP reachability to each other. The dragon switch will have two EIGRP neighbors. One neighbor, the fire router, is formed via the access port on Fast 0/7 using SVI VLAN 100. The other neighbor, the dragon router, is formed via the routed port Fast 0/8.

Example 1-35 lists the route/forwarding table of the dragon switch, followed by the **show ip eigrp neighbor** command.

Example 1-35 *Dragon Switch Configuration*

```
dragon_switch#show ip route
Codes: C - connected, S - static, I - IGRP, R - RIP, M - mobile, B - BGP
       D - EIGRP, EX - EIGRP external, O - OSPF, IA - OSPF inter area
       N1 - OSPF NSSA external type 1, N2 - OSPF NSSA external type 2
       E1 - OSPF external type 1, E2 - OSPF external type 2, E - EGP
       i - IS-IS, L1 - IS-IS level-1, L2 - IS-IS level-2, ia - IS-IS inter area
       * - candidate default, U - per-user static route, o - ODR
       P - periodic downloaded static route
Gateway of last resort is not set
     172.16.0.0/24 is subnetted, 5 subnets
C       172.16.200.0 is directly connected, FastEthernet0/8
D       172.16.201.0 [90/156160] via 172.16.200.8, 00:00:16, FastEthernet0/8
D       172.16.202.0 [90/156160] via 172.16.200.8, 00:00:09, FastEthernet0/8
C       172.16.10.0 is directly connected, Vlan10
C       172.16.100.0 is directly connected, Vlan100
dragon_switch#
dragon_switch#show ip eigrp neighbors
IP-EIGRP neighbors for process 2003
H    Address                 Interface     Hold Uptime   SRTT   RTO  Q  Seq Type
                                           (sec)         (ms)       Cnt Num
```

continues

Example 1-35 *Dragon Switch Configuration (Continued)*

```
2   172.16.100.7        Vl100       12 00:03:06   1   200  0  11
1   172.16.200.8        Fa0/8       14 00:03:40   1   200  0  9
dragon_switch#
!
```

By now, you can see what a powerful and versatile platform the Catalyst 3550 Intelligent Ethernet Switch can be and why Cisco chooses to call it an intelligent switch. Because of the diversity of the Catalyst 3550 and all the possible software configurations it can perform, one chapter could not possibly cover them. Instead of writing a mini-novel on the 3550, this chapter has laid the necessary groundwork for configuring some basic and advanced features of the 3550. Layer 3 functionality—such as routing protocols, HSRP, IP ACL, and so on—is nearly identical in terms of configuration as on a Cisco router. The knowledge of routing protocols you have learned from other sources, such as *CCIE PSV1* and other references, can easily be transferred and applied to the Catalyst 3550.

The remaining portion of this chapter covers some of the additional and optional features of the Catalyst 3550. Once again, due the vast array of configuration options available on the Catalyst 3550, it is impossible to cover them in a single chapter. To cover some topics, such as multicast, the way they deserve and should be covered, would require 100 pages, which is simply beyond the scope of this text. (However, they are important and worthy of study.) The following topic list includes other features on the Catalyst 3550 that make it one of the most versatile and powerful platforms available:

- Multicast Layer 2 and Layer 3, IGMPv2, Cisco Group Management Protocol (CGMP), and Multicast VLAN Registration (MVR)
- 802.1X port-based authentication
- Voice VLANs with 802.1Q and 802.1p
- SPAN and Remote SPAN (RSPAN)
- SNMP and RMON
- 802.1Q tunneling
- QoS

Configuring Advanced Features on a Catalyst 3550 Ethernet Switch

Spanning tree, after years of remaining the hidden backbone in many networks, finally has outgrown its role. As critical of a role as STP plays, the 50-second convergence time—20 seconds of max age expiring followed by a 15-second listening and a 15-second learning state—is simply too long for convergence in many modern networks. Cisco provides many workarounds, some of which are discussed here, to help alleviate the long convergence issues and stabilize STP. Some advanced features of the Catalyst 3550 include the following:

- PortFast and BPDU guard and BPDU filtering
- UplinkFast
- BackboneFast
- Root guard
- IEEE 802.1w Rapid Spanning Tree (RSTP)
- IEEE 802.1s Multiple Spanning Tree (MST)
- VLAN maps
- VLAN protected ports with unicast and multicast blocking

Examine these features in greater detail.

Configuring PortFast Spanning Tree and BPDU Guard

PortFast Spanning Tree should only be configured on edge switches. In this state, upon a local failure or during initialization, the 15-second listening state and the 15-second learning state are skipped. All ports are put into a permanent forwarding mode. For this reason, PortFast should only be used on end stations such as workstations and servers. By default, STP PortFast is disabled; it can be enabled with the following interface command:

```
3550_switch(config-if)#spanning-tree portfast [disable]
```

The keyword **disable** removes the PortFast configuration or disables it.

PortFast can also be enabled for all nontrunking ports with the following global configuration command:

```
3550_switch(config)#spanning-tree portfast default
```

Exercise extra caution that the proper end stations are connected to all ports before enabling PortFast on a global level. You can verify PortFast configurations with the **show spanning-tree interface** *interface_name* **portfast** command.

CAUTION   PortFast should be used only when connecting a single end station to a switch port. If PortFast is enabled on a port connected to another networking device, such as a switch, you can create STP loops. When you enable PortFast on the Catalyst 3550, you will get the following message:

```
%Warning: PortFast should only be enabled on ports connected to a single host.
Connecting hubs, concentrators, switches, bridges, etc. to this interface when
PortFast is enabled can cause temporary bridging loops.
Use with CAUTION
%Portfast has been configured on FastEthernet0/7 but will only have effect when
the interface is in a nontrunking mode.
```

PortFast-enabled ports are still able to participate in STP and are still able to send and receive BPDUs. If a PortFast port is indivertibly connected to another switch, an STP loop could result. Cisco implements two features that go hand in hand with PortFast to help prevent situations such as this: BPDU guard and BPDU filtering.

- **BPDU guard**—BPDU guard enforces the rule that PortFast-enabled ports should not receive any BPDUs. If a BPDU is received, that could indicate the port is connected to a switch and a possible STP loop could result. A BPDU guard-enabled port puts the port in an error-disabled state if it receives a BPDU. By default, BPDU guard is disabled on all interfaces and should be enabled if PortFast is enabled. It can be enabled globally, or on a single interface, with the following command:

  ```
  3550_switch(config)#spanning-tree portfast bpduguard default
  ```

  To enable or disable BDPU guard on an interface, use the following interface command:

  ```
  3550_switch(config-if)#spanning-tree bpduguard [enable | disable]
  ```

  You can verify BPDU guard with the **show spanning-tree summary** command.

- **BPDU filtering**—BPDU filtering prevents PortFast-enabled ports from sending *or* receiving BPDUs, with one minor exception. During the link's initialization, a small number of BPDUs are sent before they are filtered by the BPDU filtering. Once again, exercise *extreme caution* with this feature: By disabling the sending and receiving of BPDUs, you effectively are disabling STP for that interface. Therefore, the same warning stands as previously mentioned; be sure that no switches, hubs, bridges, and so on are connected to the interface. By default, BPDU filtering is disabled on all interfaces and should be enabled if PortFast is enabled. It can be enabled globally, or on a single interface, with the following command:

  ```
  3550_switch(config)#spanning-tree portfast bpdufilter default
  ```

  To enable or disable BDPU filtering on an interface, use the following interface command:

  ```
  3550_switch(config-if)# spanning-tree bpdufilter [enable | disable]
  ```

You can verify BPDU filtering by using the **show spanning-tree detail** command. At the end of the output, you will see the number of BPDUs sent and received. The number received should always be 0, and the number sent should be small and not increment if BPDU filtering is enabled. Example 1-36 lists the output of the **show spanning-tree detail** command after enabling PortFast with BPDU guard and BPDU filtering on interface FastEthernet 0/7.

Example 1-36 *Examining Spanning-Tree Details*

```
3550_switch#show spanning-tree detail
<<<text omitted>>>
VLAN0100 is executing the ieee compatible Spanning Tree protocol
  Bridge Identifier has priority 32768, sysid 100, address 000a.8a0e.ba80
  Configured hello time 2, max age 20, forward delay 15
  We are the root of the spanning tree
  Topology change flag not set, detected flag not set
  Number of topology changes 0 last change occurred 03:01:07 ago
  Times:  hold 1, topology change 35, notification 2
          hello 2, max age 20, forward delay 15
```

Example 1-36 *Examining Spanning-Tree Details (Continued)*

```
   Timers: hello 0, topology change 0, notification 0, aging 300
 Port 7 (FastEthernet0/7) of VLAN0100 is forwarding
   Port path cost 100, Port priority 128, Port Identifier 128.7.
   Designated root has priority 32868, address 000a.8a0e.ba80
   Designated bridge has priority 32868, address 000a.8a0e.ba80
   Designated Port id is 128.7, designated path cost 0
   Timers: message age 0, forward delay 0, hold 0
   Number of transitions to forwarding state: 1
   BPDU: sent 11, received 0
! no BPDUs received
   The port is in the portfast mode
! PortFast Enabled
3550_switch#
```

NOTE   PortFast, BPDU guard, and BPDU filtering can be used in a PVST+ or MST environment.

Configuring UplinkFast

Once again, spanning tree's Achilles' heel, the 50-second convergence time, plagues the modern LAN. UplinkFast is another enhancement Cisco has performed with STP designed primarily for use in the wiring closet and on edge switches. It is designed to speed up the convergence speed between the edge and the core switch. Figure 1-24 illustrates where you would use PortFast along with UplinkFast and BackboneFast in a common LAN.

UplinkFast works in the following manner. UplinkFast is enabled globally on the switch and affects all VLANs on the switch. When this happens, the VLAN priority is set to 49,152 for all VLANs on the switch. The VLAN cost of all ports is increased by 3000 on interfaces with a path cost below 3000 to aid in preventing the switch from becoming root. The root port then immediately goes into forwarding state, bypassing the two 15-second listening and learning states. Ports within the VLAN create an uplink group. The uplink group consists of a single port in forwarding state, the root port, and the rest of the ports in blocking state, called *alternate ports*. When a port with UplinkFast detects a local failure, it unblocks the blocked ports in the uplink group with the lowest root path cost (next to the original root port), bypassing the two 15-second listening and learning states. As soon as the switch transitions the alternate port to the forwarding state, the switch begins transmitting dummy multicast frames on all forwarding ports, one for each entry in the local Encoded Address Recognition Logic (EARL) table (except those entries associated with the failed root port). EARL is a centralized processing engine for learning and forwarding packets based on MAC address. By default, approximately 15 dummy multicast frames are transmitted every 100 milliseconds. Each dummy multicast frame uses the station address in the EARL table entry as its source MAC address and a dummy multicast address (01-00-0C-CD-CD-CD) as the destination MAC address. Switches receiving these dummy multicast frames immediately update their EARL table entries for each source MAC address to use the new port, allowing the switches to begin using the new path virtually immediately.

Figure 1-24   *PortFast, UplinkFast, and BackboneFast Locations*

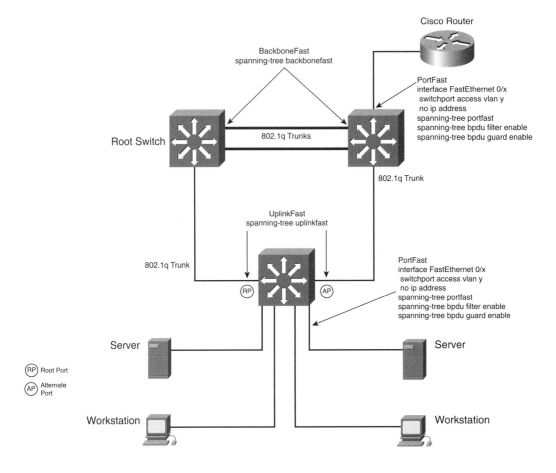

If connectivity through the original root port is restored, the switch waits for a period equal to twice the forward delay time plus 5 seconds before transitioning the port to the forwarding state. This allows time for the neighbor port to transition through the listening and learning states.

To configure UplinkFast, use the following global configuration command:

```
3550_switch(config)#spanning-tree uplinkfast [max-update-rate pkts/seconds]
```

Before using the **uplinkfast** command, set the spanning-tree priority to the default value 32,768. If the STP priority has been modified, change it back to the default; otherwise, the **uplinkfast** command will fail. The **uplinkfast** command is a global command that will affect all VLANs on the switch. You cannot configure UplinkFast for an individual VLAN. The optional **max-update-rate** keyword is the rate at which station address updates are sent. The default rate is 150 packets per second.

NOTE	UplinkFast can only be used in a PVST+.

You can verify UplinkFast operation with the **show spanning-tree uplinkfast** command. This command shows whether UplinkFast is enabled on the interface. It also lists the default timers and statistics.

Configuring BackboneFast

BackboneFast is another Cisco innovation that continues to improve on the amount of time STP takes to converge. BackboneFast allows STP to detect an indirect link failure and use its alternative paths in 30 seconds. This time is significantly shorter than the default 50 seconds it takes STP to converge. BackboneFast accomplishes this by the use of inferior BPDUs and some intelligent and logical deductions based on them. BackboneFast operates in the following manner.

A switch detects an indirect link failure when the switch receives inferior BPDUs from its designated bridge on its root port or blocked ports. The previous four-step BPDU evaluation process determines whether BPDUs are inferior. Inferior BPDUs could indicate that the designated bridge has lost its connection to the root bridge. An inferior BPDU identifies a single switch as both the root bridge and the designated bridge. Under normal spanning-tree rules, the switch ignores inferior BPDUs until the configured maximum aging time expires.

The switch also tries to determine whether it has an alternate path to the root bridge. If the inferior BPDU arrives on a blocked-port, root port, the switch deduces that it has alternative paths to the root bridge. If the inferior BPDU arrives on the root port, all blocked ports become alternative paths to the root bridge. If the switch has alternate paths to the root bridge, it uses these alternate paths to transmit a new kind of PDU called the Root Link Query PDU. The switch sends the Root Link Query PDU out all alternate paths to the root bridge. If the inferior BPDU arrives on the root port and there are no blocked ports, the switch assumes that it has lost connectivity to the root bridge; this causes the max age timers to expire, and the switch becomes the root switch accordingly under normal spanning-tree standards.

If the switch has alternative paths to the root bridge, it transmits root link query (RLQ) PDUs out all alternative paths to the root bridge. If the switch determines that it still has an alternative path to the root, it causes the maximum aging time on the ports on which it received the inferior BPDU to expire. If all the alternative paths to the root bridge indicate that the switch has lost connectivity to the root bridge, the switch causes the maximum aging times on the ports on which it received an inferior BPDU to expire. If one or more alternative paths can still connect to the root bridge, the switch makes all ports on which it received an inferior BPDU its designated ports and moves them out of the blocking state, if they were in blocking state, through the listening and learning states, and into the forwarding state.

NOTE   BackboneFast can only be used in a PVST+ and is not supported for Token Ring VLANs or third-party switches.

BackboneFast is enabled with the following global configuration command:

```
3550_switch(config)#spanning-tree backbonefast
```

You can verify BackboneFast operation with the **show spanning-tree summary** command, as demonstrated in Example 1-37.

Example 1-37 *Verifying STP UplinkFast and BackboneFast*

```
3550_switch#show spanning-tree summary
Root Bridge for: VLAN0010, VLAN0100.
Extended system ID is enabled.
PortFast BPDU Guard is disabled
EtherChannel misconfiguration guard is enabled
UplinkFast is enabled
BackboneFast is enabled
Default pathcost method used is short
Name                    Blocking Listening Learning Forwarding STP Active
----------------------- -------- --------- -------- ---------- ----------
VLAN0001                    1        0        0         4          5
VLAN0010                    0        0        0         1          1
VLAN0100                    0        0        0         1          1
----------------------- -------- --------- -------- ---------- ----------
3 vlans                     1        0        0         6          7
Station update rate set to 150 packets/sec.
UplinkFast statistics
-----------------------
Number of transitions via uplinkFast (all VLANs)          : 2
Number of proxy multicast addresses transmitted (all VLANs) : 0
BackboneFast statistics
-----------------------
Number of transition via backboneFast (all VLANs)         : 0
Number of inferior BPDUs received (all VLANs)             : 0
Number of RLQ request PDUs received (all VLANs)           : 0
Number of RLQ response PDUs received (all VLANs)          : 0
Number of RLQ request PDUs sent (all VLANs)               : 0
Number of RLQ response PDUs sent (all VLANs)              : 0
3550_switch#
```

Configuring STP Root Guard

Root guard is a feature available in PVST+ and MST that protects the LAN from an undesired switch becoming root. This feature can prove useful when integrating two LANs or VLANs and you want to preserve the current root switch in one LAN or VLAN from another switch

becoming root of the network. It may also be used in a service provider network for extra
security to prevent a customer's network from becoming root over the service provider.

Figure 1-25 illustrates where STP root guard would be used in VLAN 5. STP root guard will
be applied to all VLANs on the trunk or interface; for the purposes of this discussion, however,
VLAN 5 is covered. In this model, the fire switch is the desired root switch and has a priority
of 32,768 for VLAN 5. The foreign network, which could also be a customer network, is
connected through the dragon switch. The ranger switch has a priority of 8192 and is root for
VLAN 5 in that network. To prevent the ranger switch from becoming root for VLAN 5, the
interface command **spanning-tree guard root** was used on the GigabitEthernet 0/1 interface
of the dragon switch.

Figure 1-25 *Root Guard Placement*

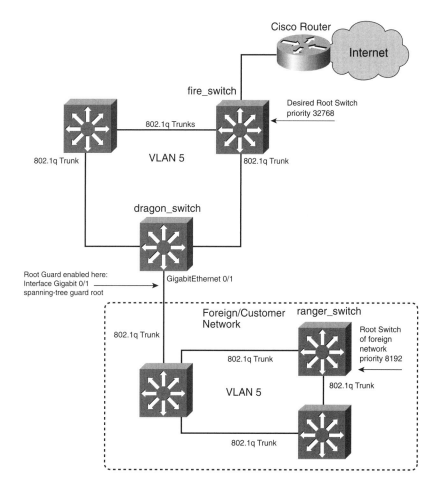

With root guard enabled on the GigabitEthernet 0/1 of the dragon switch, it will perform the following. When it detects a switch with characteristics to become root for VLAN 5 (in this case, the ranger switch), it will put the port into an STP broken state with a reason of "Root Inconsistent." The port will then be put into a blocking state, preventing the ranger switch from becoming root for the entire VLAN and preserving the current root, the fire switch. The following interface command accomplishes this:

```
dragon_switch(config)interface  gigabitethernet 0/1
dragon_switch(config-if)spanning-tree guard root
```

By default, root guard is disabled on all ports. Root guard should not be used with UplinkFast or loop guard. You can verify root guard status with the **show spanning-tree detail** command, as listed in Example 1-38. The following example shows the STP detail of the dragon switch after the ranger switch attempts to take over root for VLAN 5.

Example 1-38 *Root Guard Enabled and Active*

```
3550_switch#show spanning-tree detail
<<<text omitted>>>
Port 25 (GigabitEthernet0/1) of VLAN0005 is broken (Root Inconsistent)
   Port path cost 4, Port priority 128, Port Identifier 128.25.
   Designated root has priority 32768, address 0004.275e.f5c4
   Designated bridge has priority 32773, address 000a.8a0e.ba80
   Designated Port id is 128.25, designated path cost 19
   Timers: message age 1, forward delay 0, hold 0
   Number of transitions to forwarding state: 1
   BPDU: sent 2077, received 3078
   Root guard is enabled
<<<text omitted>>
```

Rapid Spanning Tree (802.1w) and Multiple Spanning Tree (802.1s)

802.1d spanning tree performed its job very well over the years. When 802.1d was conceived, it was designed primarily around bridges. In 802.1d, BPDUs are relayed from bridge to bridge with the sole intent being to build a loop-free topology with a single root bridge. Switches did not exist at the time and obviously neither did VLANs. LANs continued to evolve at a blistering pace, and switching was introduced along with the concept of VLANs and VLAN trunks. For the most part, STP still continued to perform its role rather well.

Spanning tree's Achilles' heel has always been its long convergence time. The 50 seconds it requires to recover from link failure is simply too long in today's Fast Ethernet and Gigabit Ethernet networks.

The IEEE has been very busy addressing many of the needs of the ever-changing Ethernet protocol. Cisco Systems once again pioneered the way by offering technologies such as PortFast and UplinkFast, among others, to the IEEE committee to use in 802.1w RSTP. Two standards developed by the IEEE will play an increasing role in large redundant Ethernet networks: IEEE 802.1w, called Rapid Spanning Tree Protocol (RSTP); and IEEE 802.1s, Multiple Spanning Tree (MST).

NOTE   RSTP was first implemented as part of MST in CAT OS 7.1 and native IOS 12.1.(11)EX and later. It will be available as a standalone protocol, Rapid PVST mode, in Cisco IOS 12.1(13)E and in CAT OS 7.4. At the time of this writing, you must configure MST for RSTP to work.

Quick Convergence with 802.1w Rapid Spanning Tree Protocol

IEEE 802.1w is called *Rapid Spanning Tree Protocol* (RSTP). RSTP could really be called *intelligent spanning tree*. RSTP operates identically to STP in terms of root selection, STP cost, and STP priority. What makes RSTP different is that it can recognize a port's physical status and make logical deductions about spanning-tree topology based on the BPDUs received on that port. The *port type* or *port role* plays an important part in RSTP. Because the bridging functions of the switch are now intelligent, RSTP can converge in a few hundred milliseconds rather than the 50 seconds of 802.1d. Now that's more like it! RSTP uses technologies such as PortFast, and some concepts from UplinkFast and BackboneFast. It can coexist with PVST+ and is fully backward compatible with 802.1d. The election of the root bridge/switch is identical to 802.1d.

Topology changes are marked with the same topology change (TC) flag but are handled differently than they are in 802.1d. Topology changes in 802.1w occur only when a port transitions from the blocking to the forwarding state. Edge-port transitions do not generate topology changes. In 802.1d, TCs flow from where they occurred to the root switch/bridge; from there, the root propagates the TC to all the leaves of the spanning tree. In some ways, it works like a designated router is OSPF. In 802.1w networks, TCs are flooded out all ports where the change occurred, saving the time of having to go to the root switch first. This method aids in quick convergence for 802.1w networks and prevents unnecessary port transitions and BPDU flooding.

In addition to using *port roles*, RSTP uses a new BPDU format.

Updated and Improved BPDU Handling

IEEE 802.1w bridges/switches ensure backward compatibility with legacy 802.1d bridges/ switches by using the same 802.1d BPDU and following the same spanning-tree rules for root, designated port, and nondesignated port election. 802.1w uses the same BPDU as 802.1d, but it is how it uses that BPDU that is different. 802.1w takes full advantage of the Flags field, using all 8 bits to aid in making intelligent forwarding decisions.

Figure 1-26 shows the traditional IEEE 802.1d BPDU frame format compared to the new IEEE 802.1w Rapid Spanning Tree frame. 802.1d BPDUs only use two flags, one of which is for TC, and the other for TC acknowledgments. The remaining 6 bits, bits 2 through 7, are not used in 802.1d.

Figure 1-26 *802.1d and 802.1w Frame Comparison*

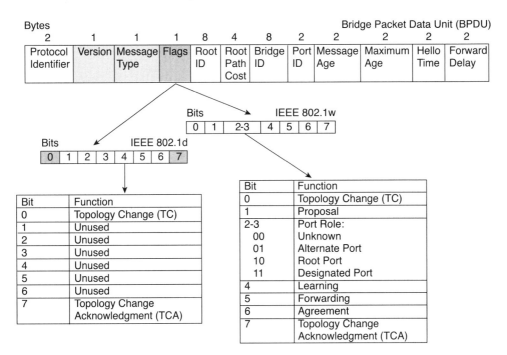

802.1w BPDUs distinguish themselves by setting the BPDU type and version to 2. By setting the versions and type to 2, 802.1w can recognize legacy bridges easily on any link. Likewise, a legacy 802.1d bridge does not recognize the version 2 BPDUs and will drop them. When an 802.1w port detects an 802.1d BPDU on a port, it automatically configures that port for PVST+ and sends normal 802.1d frames on that port. 802.1w sends BPDU every 2 seconds, equal to the hello timer. With 802.1d, a nonroot bridge only generates BPDUs when it receives one on its root port. An 802.1w bridge is actually generating the BPDUs rather than relaying them as in an 802.1d environment. A bridge now sends a BPDU with its current information every hello-timer seconds (2 by default), even if it does not receive any from the root bridge.

If hellos are not received for three consecutive times, BPDU information is immediately aged out; this also occurs if the max age timer expires. BPDUs are now used as a keepalive mechanism between bridges. A bridge considers that it has lost connectivity to its direct neighboring root or designated bridge if it misses three BPDUs in a row. This is referred to as *fast aging* and allows for quick failure detection.

802.1w bridges also accept inferior BPDUs, much like backbone fast ports. 802.1w bridges will accept this inferior BPDU information and replace the old information with it.

As shown in Figure 1-26, other bits are now used in the 802.1w frame. Some of the more significant bits are the proposal bit and the port type.

- The *proposal bit* is just one method RSTP uses for rapid convergence. The proposal mechanism is not bound by timers; therefore, it allows STP to converge very quickly. A proposal message is sent to help synchronize switches. The proposal is sent when a switch detects a change in root. Either the switch becomes root, or a new root port is selected from receiving a more desirable BPDU. When this happens, the switch sends out a proposal message to adjacent switches on designated point-to-point ports. When the downstream switch receives the proposal, it sends an acknowledgment back to the switch that sent it. When it does this, it puts the port that received the proposal into forwarding mode. At the same time, all designated ports are put into the blocking/discarding state; this helps prevent loops on the network. The designated ports then generate a proposal message to any downstream switches. When the proposal is acknowledged, the designated port is put into the forwarding state. This synchronization process works its way out to the edge switch, where it stops. The synchronization process does not happen if the port's prior state is blocking or it is defined as an edge port. In Figures 1-27 and 1-28, an 802.1w network goes through the synchronization process described.

Figure 1-27 *IEEE 802.1w Synchronization*

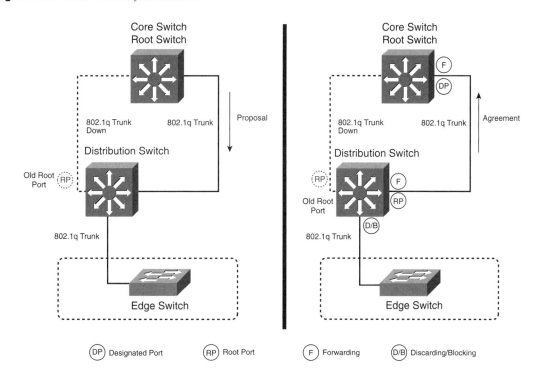

Figure 1-28 *IEEE 802.1w Synchronization*

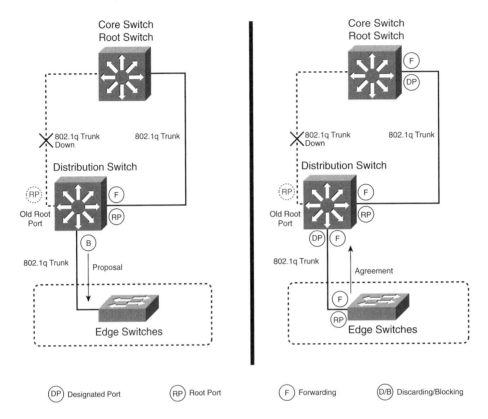

Port Status in RSTP/802.1w

Another way 802.1w dramatically increases the convergence rate is by assigning every port a specific role in the network. From Figure 1-26, you see that 802.1w incorporates room in the BPDU for port status in the Flags field. 802.1w not only classifies the port type, but it also classifies the link type. Figure 1-29 shows the port status and roles in an 802.1w network.

- **Link type (point-to-point versus shared)**—802.1w or RSTP assumes that a link operating at full duplex is a point-to-point link. Convergence happens on a point-to-point link with the proposal/agreement mechanism previously mentioned. If a link is operating in half duplex, RSTP considers it a shared link. You can override both of these settings with the **spanning-tree link-type** command.

- **Edge ports**—RSTP uses the same command, **spanning-tree portfast**, to define edge ports. This smoothes the STP transition from 802.1d to 802.1w. All edge ports operate the same way that they do in 802.1d; they skip the listening and learning states and are immediately put into permanent forwarding mode. In RSTP networks, if a BPDU is received on an edge port, it becomes a normal STP port, losing its edge and PortFast status.

- **Root ports**—Root ports operate and are elected in the same manner as 802.1d STP. The root ports provide the best, lowest-cost path to the root switch. Think of the root port as the port that leads toward root. If RSTP selects a new root port, it blocks the old root port and immediately transitions the new root port to forwarding.

- **Designated ports**—A designated port can be defined as the port that leads away from the root switch, or as the port that a LAN must go through to reach the root switch. There can only be one designated port per segment, and it is elected in the same way that it is in 802.1d: by the bridge sending the best BPDU for that segment. Designated ports also use the proposal/agreement procedure for rapid convergence in RSTP and are placed in the forwarding state.

- **Alternate ports**—Alternate ports are a new RSTP classification. Alternate ports are ports that receive a more useful BPDU from *another* bridge/switch on the same segment. These more useful BPDUs usually come from the designated port. Alternate ports are put into a new RSTP state called discarding, which is discussed in the next section. Discarding is basically equivalent to the blocking state.

- **Backup ports**—Backup ports are ports that have received more useful BPDUs from the *same* bridge/switch they are on. A backup port is really an UplinkFast port and functions in the same manner. It can also be thought of as a backup for the designated port on the same switch. Backup ports are in discarding state. By having explicit alternate ports and backup ports, RSTP is able to make intelligent convergence decisions when it loses BPDUs or loses the root port. This is yet another way RSTP offers quick convergence.

Figure 1-29 illustrates the new RSTP port status on a common network.

802.1w RSTP also uses a slightly different port state than 802.1d. Instead of blocking, a RSTP protocol uses the state of discarding. Table 1-15 compares the old 802.1d STP state to the new 802.1Q RSTP state.

Configuring 802.1w RSTP on the Catalyst 3550, at this time, requires you to configure 802.1s MST. On platforms such as the Catalyst 4000, 6500, and other CAT OS systems, RSTP can be enabled separately from MST with the **set spantree mode** command.

Figure 1-29 *IEEE 802.1w RSTP Port Status*

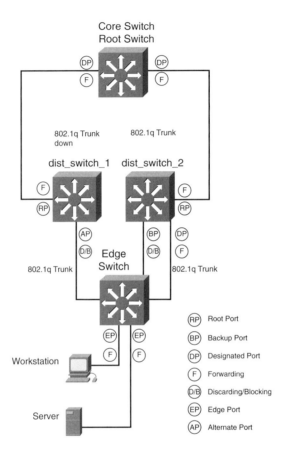

Table 1-15 *STP and RSTP Port State Comparison*

802.1d STP State	802.1w RSTP State	Port Included in Active Topology?
Blocking	Discarding	No
Listening	Discarding	No
Learning	Learning	Yes
Forwarding	Forwarding	Yes

Multiple Spanning Tree (802.1s)

Multiple Spanning Tree 802.1s enables you to group VLANs and their associated STP tree into common groups or instances. Members of the same STP instance have the same STP topology, such as root and which ports are forwarding and so on. The VLANs that are members of one STP instance operate independently of VLANs in another STP instance. MST enables network administrators to quickly configure load balancing across the network, without having to set an individual root or priority for each VLAN on the switch. MST accomplishes this, in part, by the use of MST regions.

MST regions are interconnected bridges that have the same MST configuration. The configuration includes the following:

- MST instance number and name
- Configuration revision
- 4096 element table used for VLAN association

The instance number, name, and configuration revision must match for the switches to be in the same MST region.

This chapter previously covered VLAN load sharing. (Refer to Figure 1-30.) With traditional 802.1d STP, you needed to define the root for VLANs 2 and 3 on the yang switch. You also had to manually assign the root for VLANs 4 and 5 on the yin switch. This procedure was necessary to load share over the links between the yin and yang switches. In large networks, this can lead to a lot of configuration (requiring you to manually set root and priorities for each VLAN).

If you were running MST 802.1s on this network, you would make just two MST instances. One instance would have VLANs 2 and 3 assigned to it, and the root would be the yang switch. The second MST instance would have VLANs 4 and 5 assigned to it, and the root would be the yin switch. If you needed to add more VLANs to the network, the new VLANs would just become a member of one of the two MST instances. With MST, you need only to configure STP for two instances, instead of configuring STP and its associated parameters for every VLAN. Figure 1-31 illustrates the network with 802.1s configured.

Figure 1-30 *STP Load Sharing with 802.1d*

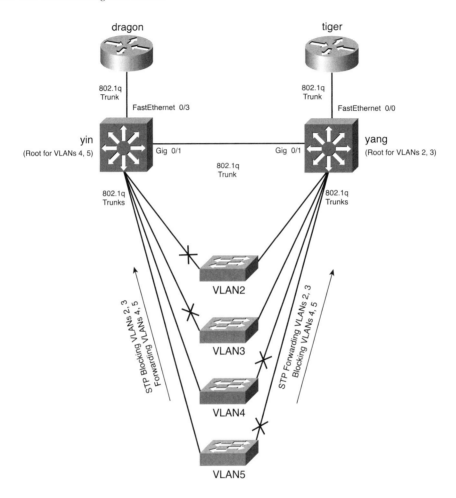

Figure 1-31 *STP Load Sharing with 802.1s*

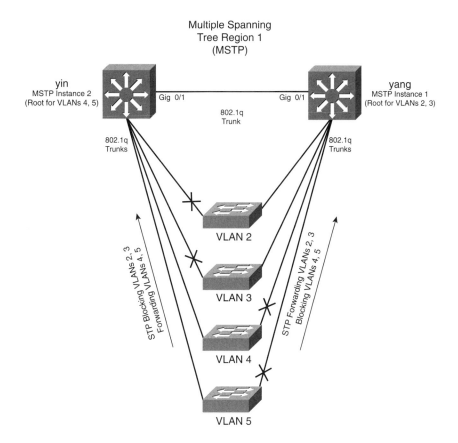

The Cisco implementation of MST defines the following characteristics:

- MST runs a variation of spanning tree called *Internal Spanning Tree* (IST). IST comple-
  ments Common Spanning Tree (CST) information with internal information about the
  MST region. The MST region appears as a single bridge to adjacent 802.1d, or Single
  Spanning Tree (SST), and other MST regions. See Figures 1-32 and 1-33.

- The *Common Internal Spanning Tree* (CIST) is the collection of the following: ISTs in
  each MST region, the CST that interconnects the MST regions, and the legacy 802.1d or
  SST bridges. CIST is identical to an IST inside an MST region and identical to a CST outside an MST region. The STP, RSTP, and MST together elect a single bridge as the root
  of the CIST. The CIST can be thought of like the Mono Spanning Tree that is needed for
  802.1Q.

- MST establishes and maintains additional spanning trees within each MST region. These spanning trees are termed *MST instances* (MSTIs). The IST is numbered 0, and the MSTIs are numbered 1, 2, 3, and so on. The MSTI is local to the MST region and is independent of MSTIs in another region, even if the MST regions are interconnected.

- Spanning tree information for an MSTI is contained in an MST record (M-record). M-records are always encapsulated within MST BPDUs. The original spanning trees computed by MST are called M-trees, which are active only within the MST.

- MST provides interoperability with PVST+ by generating PVST+ BPDUs for the non-CST VLANs.

- MST supports the following PVST+ extensions:
  - UplinkFast and BackboneFast are not configurable in MST mode; they are part of RSTP, which is enabled by default when MST is enabled.
  - PortFast is supported and required for RSTP edge ports.
  - BPDU filter and BPDU guard are supported.
  - Loop guard and root guard are supported.
  - MST switches operate with an extended system ID.

Figures 1-32 and 1-33 illustrate the relationship between the MST, IST, and CST functions. The two diagrams are different views of the same topology. The MST region is represented to the CST as a single bridge. The CST does not know or care about how many bridges or STP paths are in the MST region.

Figure 1-32 *CST IST Relationship with 802.1s*

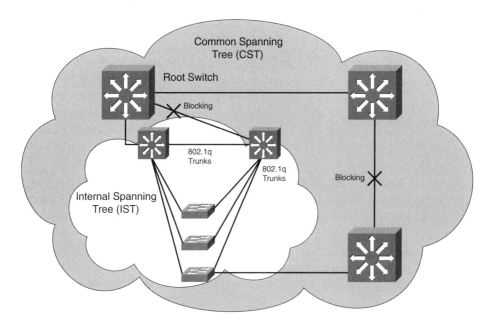

Figure 1-33 *CST MST Relationship with 802.1s*

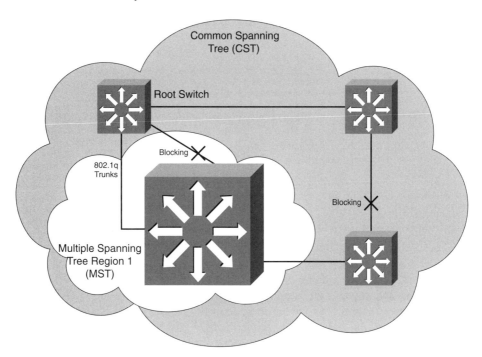

Cisco defines the IST and CST relationship as follows:

> IST connects all the MST bridges in the region and appears as an STP subtree in the CST domain. The MST region appears as a virtual bridge to adjacent 802.1d SST bridges and MST regions. The IST master of an MST region is the bridge with the lowest BID and the lowest-cost path to the CST root. If an MST bridge is the root bridge for the CST, it is the IST master of that MST region. If the CST root is outside the MST region, one of the MST bridges at the boundary is selected as the IST master. This port is referred to as a *boundary port*. Other bridges on the boundary that belong to the same region eventually block boundary ports that lead to the root bridge.

Special port statuses for 802.1s are as follows:

- **Boundary ports** are the port(s) that connect to a legacy 802.1d LAN, or a bridge/switch in a different MST region. Boundary ports can automatically configure themselves by examining an agreement message from another MST or SST legacy 802.1d bridge.

- **IST master** is the bridge/switch with the lowest BID and the least-cost path to the CST root. If the MST bridge/switch is the root bridge for the CST, it is the IST master of that particular MST region. If the CST root is outside the MST region, one of the MST bridges that is a boundary port is selected as the IST master.

NOTE   IST BPDUs for the IST are sent on MST instance 0. Only the first instance of MST actually sends BPDUs. The first instance in Cisco switches is instance 0; therefore, you should avoid mapping VLANs to this instance. Treat it much as you would VLAN 1. It runs everywhere and is needed for the IST.

The previous information was meant to be a comprehensive overview of IEEE 802.1w and IEEE 802.1s. As with many protocols, the technical details can be rather complex. For more detailed information on 802.1w and 802.1s, consult www.ieee.org, standards.ieee.org, and, of course, www.cisco.com.

Configuring IEEE 802.1w Rapid Spanning Tree (RSTP) and IEEE 802.1s Multiple Spanning Tree (MST)

Cisco has made the migration to 802.1s MST and 802.1w RSTP seamless. As a matter of fact, RSTP is automatically enabled when you select MST as the spanning-tree mode. On CAT OS platforms, you may configure the two separately, but on the Catalyst 3550, the two are tightly integrated, and why not? The benefits from RSTP convergence are enormous, and they multiply themselves with the size of the network. You will find that like its predecessor 802.1d STP, configuring 802.1w and 802.1s is simpler than the concepts behind them.

To configure 802.1w RSTP, you need to configure 802.1s MST and enable spanning-tree Port-Fast on all edge ports. RSTP will automatically be enabled when MST is configured. Use the following process to configure RSTP and MST on the Catalyst 3550. This configuration process assumes you have VLANs, VTP, and VLAN trunks up and running.

Step 1   Configure spanning-tree PortFast on all edge ports. Use the interface command **spanning-tree portfast**.

Step 2   Configure the MST name and revision number. All switches within an MST region must have the same MST name and MST revision number. To configure MST, first enter the MST configuration mode with the following global configuration command:

```
3550_switch(config)#spanning-tree mst configuration
```

From this mode, you can configure the MST instance, name, and revision and show the current MST configuration. This mode works like the VLAN database, in that it has to be committed before changes are put into effect. Use the keyword **exit** to commit the changes or the keyword **abort** to clear any configurations entered in this period. To display pending configuration settings, use the MST configuration command **show pending**. Use the following MST configuration commands to configure MST parameters:

```
3550_switch(config-mst)#name MST_region_name
3550_switch(config-mst)#revision  revision_number_<0-65535>
3550_switch(config-mst)#exit
! Must commit changes for MST
3550_switch(config-mst)#abort
! optional Aborts MST config
```

Step 3   Divide the MST region into MST instances and assign VLANs to those instances. Remember, all the VLANs in a single instance will follow the same path to root. Any VLANs not assigned to a specific instance will default to instance 0. All VLANs in use should be assigned to an instance. If you just want to enable RSTP, assign all VLANs to instance 1. If you want to load share, assign half the VLANs to one instance and half to the other. Use the following MST configuration command to assign MST instances and associated VLANs:

```
3550_switch(config-mst)#instance <0-15> vlan vlan,vlan-range
```

Step 4   Enable MST mode. Use the following global configuration command to enable MST mode over the default mode of PVST. This command also enables RSTP 802.1w.

```
3550_switch(config)#spanning-tree mode mst
```

NOTE   The MST instance of 0 is used for the IST. As a design rule, assign VLAN 1 to MST instance 0 and other VLANs not in use. This is a design option more than a functional requirement.

Practical Example: Configuring RSTP and MST Load Sharing

Figure 1-34 shows a LAN network in which you want to configure MST load sharing between the yin and the yang switch. In this model, you configure RSTP and MST. You will make one MST instance, instance 1, for VLANs 2 through 100. The root for VLANs 2 through 100 will be the yang switch. MST instance 2 will contain VLANs 101 through 1005, and the yin switch will be the root for those VLANs. The MST name will be cisco, and the MST revision number will be 1.

Figure 1-34 *RSTP and MST Configuration*

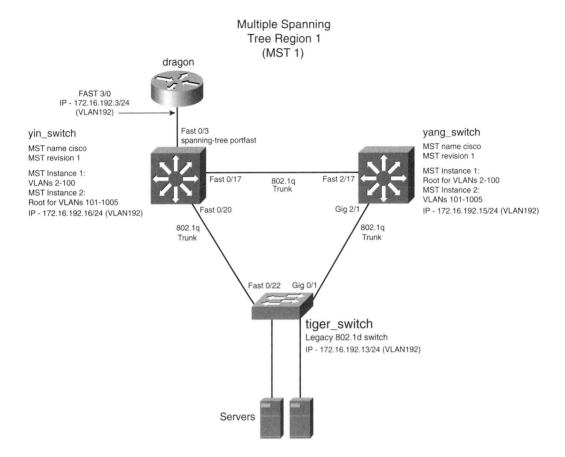

Example 1-39 demonstrates the configuration of RSTP and MST on the yin switch.

Example 1-39 *Configuration of RSTP and MST on the Yin Switch*

```
yin_switch(config)#interface fast 0/3
yin_switch(config-if)#spanning-tree portfast
! enable portfast on the router port
yin_switch(config)#spanning-tree mst configuration
! Enter the MST configuration mode
yin_switch(config-mst)#name cisco
! MST region name
yin_switch(config-mst)#revision 1
! MST region revision
yin_switch(config-mst)#instance 1 vlan 2-100
! VLANs 2-100 assigned to Instance 1
```

Example 1-39 *Configuration of RSTP and MST on the Yin Switch (Continued)*

```
yin_switch(config-mst)#instance 2 vlan 101-1005
! VLANs 2-100 assigned to Instance 2
yin_switch(config-mst)#show current
! view current MST changes
Current MST configuration
Name      [cisco]
Revision  1
Instance  Vlans mapped
--------  --------------------------------------------------------------------
0         1,1006-4094
1         2-100
2         101-1005
yin_switch(config-mst)#exit
! commit current MST changes
yin_switch(config)#spanning-tree mode mst
! enable MST mode
yin_switch(config)#spanning-tree mst 2 root primary
! set MST instance 2 to root
% This switch is already the root bridge of the MST02 spanning tree
  mst 2 bridge priority set to 24576
```

You can view and verify the MST status with the **show spanning-tree mst** *0-15* [**configuration** | **detail** | **interface**] command. This command displays detailed information about the MST instance, such as the root, the root priority, the MST interfaces, and the interface role; state and type are also listed. Example 1-40 demonstrates the **show spanning-tree mst** command on the yin switch.

Example 1-40 show spanning-tree mst *Command*

```
yin_switch#show spanning-tree mst 2
###### MST02      vlans mapped:  101-1005
Bridge    address 000a.8a0e.ba80  priority  24578 (24576 sysid 2)
Root      this switch for MST02
Interface       role state cost      prio type
--------------- ---- ----- --------- ---- --------------------------------
Fa0/3           desg FWD   200000    128  edge P2P
Fa0/17          desg FWD   200000    128  P2P
Fa0/20          boun BLK   200000    128  P2P bound(PVST)
```

Notice that the port Fast 0/17 is a designated point-to-point port to a switch in the same region, whereas port Fast 0/20 is a boundary point-to-point link to a PVST (802.1d) domain. Interface Fast 0/3 goes to the router and is an edge port; because it is in full duplex, it is also a point-to-point link.

To demonstrate how quickly MST and RSTP converge, Example 1-41 issues an extended ping from the yin switch to the tiger switch. Notice that in Example 1-40, the Fast 0/17 port to the yang switch is forwarding. During the ping, the interface 0/17 will be disconnected; as you will see, there is virtually no loss at all in the pings. This is really an incredible convergence improvement over 802.1d. Recall that an 802.1d network would take at least 50 seconds to converge!

Example 1-41 *Rapid Spanning Tree in Action!*

```
yin_switch#ping
Protocol [ip]: ip
Target IP address: 172.16.192.13
Repeat count [5]: 5000
Datagram size [100]:
Timeout in seconds [2]:
Extended commands [n]:
Sweep range of sizes [n]:
Type escape sequence to abort.
Sending 5000, 100-byte ICMP Echos to 172.16.192.13, timeout is 2 seconds:
!!!!!!!!!!!!!!!!!!!!!!!!!!!!!!!!!!!!!!!!!!!!!!!!!!!!!!!!!!!!!!!!!!!!!!!!!!
!!!!!!!!!!!!!!!!!!!!!!!!!!!!!!!!!!!!!!!!!!!!!!!!!!!!!!!!!!!!!!!!!!!!!!!!!!
<<<text omitted>>>
!!
00:53:53: %LINEPROTO-5-UPDOWN: Line protocol on Interface FastEthernet0/17, change to
down
.!!
!!!!!!!!!!!!!!!!!!!!!!!!!!!!!!!!!!!!!!!!!!!!!!!!!!!!!!!!!!!!!!!!!!!!!!!!!!
!!!!!!!!!!!!!!!!!!!!!!!!!!!!!!!!!!!!!!!!!!!!!!!!!!!!!!!!!!!!!!!!!!!!!!!!!!
<<<text omitted>>>
Success rate is 99 percent (4999/5000), round-trip min/avg/max = 1/14/72 ms
yin_switch#
yin_switch#show spanning-tree mst 2
###### MST02       vlans mapped:   101-1005
Bridge     address 000a.8a0e.ba80  priority  24578 (24576 sysid 2)
Root       this switch for MST02
Interface       role state cost       prio type
--------------- ---- ----- ---------- ---- --------------------------------
Fa0/3           desg FWD   200000     128  edge P2P
Fa0/20          boun FWD   200000     128  P2P bound(PVST)   ←Fast 0/17 is gone!!
```

Variations of the same 802.1d spanning-tree commands are available in MST for setting STP root primary, root secondary, port priority, port cost, and STP priority. Functionally, they are identical to 802.1d commands. The syntax for changing these various values is as follows:

```
3550_switch(config)#spanning-tree  mst instance_id [root {primary\secondary }|cost 1-
200000000|priority  0-61440|port-priority  0-255]
```

To adjust the MST timers, use the following syntax:

```
3550_switch(config)#spanning-tree mst instance_id [hello-time 1-10 | max-age  6-40 |
forward-time 6-40 | max-hops 1-40]
```

To change the MST link type to a point to point, use the following interface command:

```
3550_switch(config-if)#spanning-tree  link-type point-to-point
```

You can verify the MST configuration with the following command:

```
show spanning-tree mst instance_id [configuration | detail | interface]
```

The **show spanning-tree mst detail** command shows all the MST instances and the associated STP ports, STP status, and timers. Example 1-42 lists the partial output of the **show spanning-tree mst detail** command on the yin switch. For more detailed information on various **show** commands, refer to the Cisco IOS documentation.

Example 1-42 show mst detail *Command Output*

```
yin_switch#show spanning-tree mst detail
 ###### MST00        vlans mapped:  1,1006-4094
 Bridge     address 000a.8a0e.ba80  priority  32768 (32768 sysid 0)
 Root       address 0004.275e.f0c0  priority  32768 (32768 sysid 0)
            port    Fa0/17          path cost 20019
 IST master address 0030.1976.4d00  priority  32768 (32768 sysid 0)
                                    path cost 200000   rem hops 19
 Operational hello time 2, forward delay 15, max age 20, max hops 20
 Configured  hello time 2, forward delay 15, max age 20, max hops 20
 FastEthernet0/3 of MST00 is designated forwarding
 Port info               port id         128.3  priority    128  cost      200000
 Designated root         address 0004.275e.f0c0  priority  32768  cost       20019
 Designated ist master address 0030.1976.4d00  priority  32768  cost      200000
 Designated bridge      address 000a.8a0e.ba80  priority  32768  port id    128.3
 Timers: message age 0, forward delay 0, transition to forwarding 0
 Bpdus sent 5250, received 0
 FastEthernet0/17 of MST00 is root forwarding
 Port info               port id        128.13  priority    128  cost      200000
 Designated root         address 0004.275e.f0c0  priority  32768  cost       20019
 Designated ist master address 0030.1976.4d00  priority  32768  cost           0
 Designated bridge      address 0030.1976.4d00  priority  32768  port id    32.81
 <<<text omitted>>>
```

Controlling Traffic and Security with VLAN Maps

The Catalyst 3550 enables you to control all traffic within a VLAN with a specific route map type of filter called a *VLAN map*. This section briefly discusses how to configure and apply VLAN maps.

VLAN maps enable you to control all traffic within a VLAN that is local to the switch. VLAN maps apply to all packets that are routed into or out of the VLAN, or are bridged within a VLAN that is local to the switch. A VLAN map does not have a direction (in or out) associated with it.

You can configure VLAN maps to work with a standard, extended, or named ACL. The Catalyst 3550 switch also supports IP standard and IP extended ACLs, numbers 1 to 199 and 1300 to 2699. All non-IP protocols are controlled through MAC addresses and by using MAC VLAN maps. It is important to note that you cannot filter IP traffic based on MAC. The MAC filters only apply to nonrouted traffic such as NetBIOS. You must configure an IP standard or extended ACL to forward IP traffic.

A VLAN map works must like a route map. You may want to skip ahead to Chapter 2, "Configuring Route Maps and Policy-Based Routing," for more information about route maps if you are not already familiar with them.

To configure VLAN maps to control IP traffic, first configure the VLAN map, and then assign a sequence number to the map. VLAN maps are executed from the lowest instance to the highest. Use the global configuration command **vlan access-map** *map_name sequence_number*. Next, add a **match ip** statement, where you can call a named ACL for your match criteria. You then assign an action to the VLAN map; the valid actions are **action forward** and **action drop**. Based on the result of the ACL, the switch forwards or drops the traffic. A MAC filter may also be applied to filter nonroutable traffic. To apply the VLAN map, use the **vlan filter** *map_name* **vlan-list** *vlans* command.

In Figure 1-35, three IP hosts are connected to the switch. In this example, IP traffic needs to be controlled in VLAN 100 such that only 172.16.128.7 and 172.16.128.3 hosts can talk to each other. The IP host 172.16.128.8 will not be able to ping 172.16.128.7 or 172.16.128.3.

Figure 1-35 *VLAN Maps*

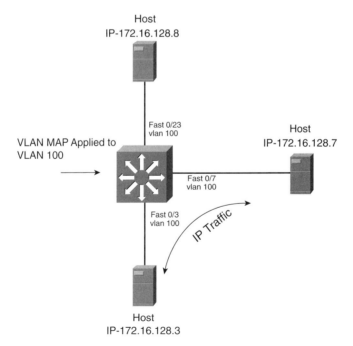

Example 1-43 demonstrates the configuration needed to control IP access with a VLAN map.

Example 1-43 *Configuring a VLAN Map*

```
3550_switch(config)#vlan access-map allow_ip 10
! Define the VLAN map 'allowip'
3550_s(config-access-map)#action forward
! Forward ACL permitip
3550_s(config-access-map)#match ip address permitip
! Call ACL permitip
3550_s(config-access-map)#exit
3550_switch(config)#
3550_switch(config)#ip access-list extended permitip
! ACL permitip
3550_swi(config-ext-nacl)#permit ip host 172.16.100.7 host 172.16.100.3
3550_swi(config-ext-nacl)#permit ip host 172.16.100.3 host 172.16.100.7
3550_swi(config-ext-nacl)#exit
3550_switch(config)#
3550_switch(config)#vlan filter allow_ip vlan-list 100
! Apply VLAN map to VLAN 100
3550_switch(config)#
```

To verify the VLAN map, use the **show vlan access-map** and the **show access-list** commands to verify your configuration.

MAC filters can use VLAN maps to control nonroutable traffic such as NetBIOS or Systems Network Architecture (SNA). Example 1-44 lists the configuration used to prevent nonsecure hosts from communicating with each other via nonroutable protocols. Note that this only controls nonrouted traffic and will have no impact on IP. This example allows nonroutable traffic between the two MAC addresses 00e0.1e58.e792 and 00e0.1e58.c112 and the rest of the network, but the two hosts cannot talk to each other.

Example 1-44 *VLAN Map for MAC Addresses*

```
vlan access-map allowed_macs 10
! define VLAN map 'allowed_macs'
 action forward
! forward ACL valid_macs
 match mac address valid_macs
! call mac ACL 'valid_macs'
!
 vlan filter allowed_macs vlan-list 100
! Apply VLAN map to VLAN 100
!
mac access-list extended valid_macs
! MAC ACL 'valid_macs'
 permit   host 00e0.1e58.e792 any
! Allow these two MAC addresses
 permit   host 00e0.1e58.c112 any
```

Controlling VLAN Access and Security with Protected Ports

Yet another way you can control access or enhance security on the Catalyst 3550 is by using VLAN-protected ports. VLAN-protected ports can only talk to nonprotected ports. Traffic from one VLAN-protected port cannot reach another VLAN-protected port. In Figure 1-36, Fast Ethernet 0/8 and 0/7 are VLAN-protected ports. The IP host 172.16.128.7 cannot ping 172.16.128.8, but it can ping 172.16.128.3. The host 172.16.128.3 can ping both 172.16.128.8 and 172.16.128.7.

Figure 1-36 *VLAN-Protected Ports*

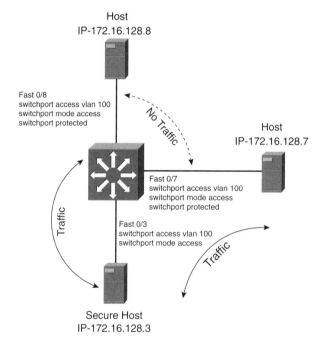

To configure a port as a protected port, use the interface command **switchport protected**. You can verify protected ports with the **show interface fast 0/7 switchport** command, as in Example 1-45.

Example 1-45 *Verifying Protected Ports*

```
3550_switch#show interfaces fast 0/7 switchport
Name: Fa0/7
Switchport: Enabled
Administrative Mode: static access
Operational Mode: static access
Administrative Trunking Encapsulation: negotiate
Operational Trunking Encapsulation: native
Negotiation of Trunking: Off
Access Mode VLAN: 100 (psv2_vlan100)
Trunking Native Mode VLAN: 1 (default)
Trunking VLANs Enabled: ALL
Pruning VLANs Enabled: 2-1001
Protected: true
Unknown unicast blocked: disabled
Unknown multicast blocked: disabled

Voice VLAN: none (Inactive)
Appliance trust: none
```

The Catalyst 3550 switch floods packets with unknown destination MAC addresses to all ports by default. If unknown unicast and multicast traffic is forwarded to a protected port, there could be security issues. To prevent unknown unicast or multicast traffic from being forwarded from one port to another, you can configure a port (protected or nonprotected) to block unknown unicast or multicast packets. Use the following interface commands to block unknown unicast and multicast traffic:

```
3550_switch(config-if)#switchport block unicast
3550_switch(config-if)#switchport block multicast
```

If unicast or multicast blocking is enabled, it would appear in the **show** switchport command as enabled, as listed in the preceding example.

Lab 1: Configuring EtherChannel, Layer 3 Switching, Routed Ports, and SVIs—Part I

Practical Scenario

The world of Ethernet switching continues to evolve at a rapid pace. In the field, you will encounter many types of switches, and the Catalyst 3550 might be one of them. The Catalyst 3550 has many types of configurable interfaces. It is important to be able to configure these different types of interfaces because it gives you more flexibility in your design. Capabilities such as Fast/Gigabit EtherChannel provide enormous bandwidth and excellent redundancy for core switches.

Lab Exercise

FrozenTundra.com is one of the few surviving dot.coms. It makes outdoor clothing and other products to use in the great wilderness of the Northwest and Canada. FrozenTundra.com is upgrading its backbone to Gigabit Ethernet and would like to use the two gigabit interface converter (GBIC) interfaces that come on the Catalyst 3550-24 Ethernet switches. It also wants to perform Layer 3 switching on the 3550 switch, rather than on the routers.

Your task is to configure a working IP network and configure the Ethernet 3550 switch using the following strict design guidelines:

- Configure the FrozenTundra.com IP network as depicted in Figure 1-37. Use EIGRP as the routing protocol and 2003 as the autonomous system ID on all routers.

- Configure all IP addresses as depicted in Figure 1-37. All labeled interfaces should be able to ping each other.

- See the "Lab Objectives" section for configuration specifics.

Lab Objectives

- Configure the EIGRP as the routing protocol, as depicted in Figure 1-37. Use 2003 as the autonomous system ID.

- Configure the management interface of 172.16.2.16/24 on tundra_switch1, and 172.16.2.15/24 on tundra_switch2. These addresses should be reachable, and Telnet login should be supported for four sessions on both switches. Use cisco as the login and enable password.

- Configure the two Gigabit Ethernet interfaces as a single Gigabit EtherChannel. You may use Fast Ethernet for this if you do not have Gigabit Ethernet.

- Configure the tundra_switch1 as the VTP server and the tundra_switch2 as the VTP client. Use the VTP domain of tundra and a VTP password of psv2.

- Configure the tundra_switch1 Fast 0/10, the port that goes to the frozen router, as a routed port. Use the IP address of 10.16.128.16 on this interface.

- Configure the other interfaces as access ports and assign VLANs as depicted in Figure 1-37.

- Configure any SVIs needed for the tundra_switch1 to provide routing for all VLANs in the network.

- Configure HSRP between the tundra_prime router, tundra_switch1, and the tundra_bak router for VLAN 200. The primary IP address should be 172.16.200.1/24, and the tundra_switch1 should be HSRP primary. The tundra_prime router should be HSRP secondary.

- Configure tundra_switch1 as the STP root for VLANs 100 and 200.

- Enable VTP pruning on the EtherChannel link between the two switches.

Equipment Needed

- Five Cisco routers, one Catalyst 3550 with the EMI software image installed, and one other Catalyst 35*xx* switch. Only one switch needs to be a Catalyst 3550 with the EMI installed. You may simulate the other switch with another Catalyst as long as it supports 802.1Q and EtherChannel.

- The switches need two back-to-back 100BASE-T links or a Gigabit Ethernet for the EtherChannel connection. The other routers should be set up with a Category 5 connection to the appropriate switch, as depicted in Figure 1-37.

Physical Layout and Prestaging

- Connect the switches to the routers, as shown in Figure 1-37.

- This lab focuses on the configuration of the Ethernet switches.

Figure 1-37   *Tundra.Net*

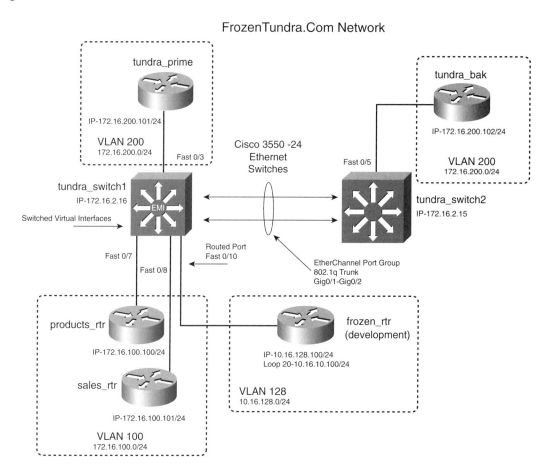

FrozenTundra.Com Network

Lab 1: Configuring EtherChannel, Layer 3 Switching, Routed Ports, and SVIs—Part II

Lab Walkthrough

Attach all the routers to the switch, as illustrated in Figure 1-37. You can use either two Gigabit Ethernet connections between the two switches or 100-Mbps links. Your choice will not affect the operational ability of the lab.

Recall from earlier the seven-step process for configuring the 3550 Ethernet switch.

Step 1 Configure switch management.

Step 2 Configure VTP and VLANs and assign ports/interfaces to VLANs.

Step 3 Configure connections between switches using EtherChannel, 802.1Q, and ISL encapsulations.

Step 4 (Optional) Control STP and VLAN propagation.

Step 5 (Optional) Configure SVIs.

Step 6 (Optional) Configure routed ports.

Step 7 (Optional) Configure Layer 3 switching.

The first step is to configure switch management. This includes setting a host name, a password, and a management address on the switch. In this lab, you also make Telnet available by assigning a login on vty lines 0 through 4. Example 1-46 lists the management portion of the tundra_switch1.

Example 1-46 *Management Portion of tundras_switch1 Thus Far*

```
hostname tundra_switch1
!
enable secret 5 $1$nt35$131XBSgKT6BmA1KHMqj1V1
! Enable Secret=cisco
!
<<<text omitted>>>
!
interface Vlan1
 no ip address
 shutdown
!
interface Vlan2
! MNGT VLAN and IP
 ip address 172.16.2.16 255.255.255.0
<<text omitted>>>
!
line con 0
line vty 0 4
 password cisco
! Telnet access allowed
 login
line vty 5 7
 login
```

The second step calls for you to configure VTP and VLANs. You need to configure a VLAN for any SVIs, access ports, and management VLANs. In this model, you need to configure four VLANs: VLANs 2, 100, 128, and 200. On the 3550, you can do this from the global configuration mode with the command **vlan** *x*. A name can be entered, as well, after entering the VLAN number. The VTP mode of the tundra_switch1 is server, and the tundra_switch2 will be the client. The VTP domain is called tundra, and the password is psv2. Ensure that the VTP domains are in the same case, along with the password. Domain name and password are case sensitive. Be sure that the VTP server's revision number is also higher than the VTP client's; otherwise, the two will not synchronize. The VTP domain and mode can be configured from the VLAN database or the VLAN configuration mode. Example 1-47 demonstrates this being done on the tundra_switch1.

Example 1-47 *Configuring VTP on tundra_switch1*

```
tundra_switch1#vlan database
tundra_switch1(vlan)#vtp domain tundra
tundra_switch1(vlan)#vtp server
tundra_switch1(vlan)#vtp password psv2
```

This step also calls for you to configure the physical port properties and assign the ports to VLANs. Example 1-48 illustrates the VLAN and port configuration of the tundra_switch1 to this point.

Example 1-48 *Configuring VLAN Port Membership*

```
hostname tundra_switch1
!
<<<text omitted>>>
!
interface FastEthernet0/3
 switchport access vlan 200
! assigned to VLAN 200
 switchport mode access
 no ip address
!
interface FastEthernet0/4
 no ip address
!
interface FastEthernet0/5
 no ip address
!
interface FastEthernet0/6
 no ip address
!
interface FastEthernet0/7
 switchport access vlan 100
! assigned to VLAN 100
 switchport mode access
 no ip address
!
interface FastEthernet0/8
 switchport access vlan 100
```

Example 1-48 *Configuring VLAN Port Membership (Continued)*

```
! assigned to VLAN 100
 switchport mode access
 no ip address
!
```

You can verify the VLANs and VTP with the **show vlan** command and the **show vtp status** command, as demonstrated in Example 1-49.

Example 1-49 *Verifying VTP and VLAN Status*

```
tundra_switch1#show vlan
VLAN Name                             Status    Ports
---- -------------------------------- --------- -------------------------------
1    default                          active    Fa0/1, Fa0/2, Fa0/4, Fa0/5
                                                Fa0/6, Fa0/9, Fa0/11, Fa0/12
                                                Fa0/13, Fa0/14, Fa0/15, Fa0/16
                                                Fa0/17, Fa0/18, Fa0/19, Fa0/20
                                                Fa0/21, Fa0/22, Fa0/23, Fa0/24
2    psv2_vlan2                       active
100  psv2_vlan100                     active    Fa0/7, Fa0/8
200  psv2_vlan200                     active    Fa0/3
1002 fddi-default                     active
1003 token-ring-default               active
1004 fddinet-default                  active
1005 trnet-default                    active
VLAN Type  SAID       MTU   Parent RingNo BridgeNo Stp  BrdgMode Trans1 Trans2
---- ----- ---------- ----- ------ ------ -------- ---- -------- ------ ------
1    enet  100001     1500  -      -      -        -    -        0      0
2    enet  100002     1500  -      -      -        -    -        0      0
100  enet  100100     1500  -      -      -        -    -        0      0
128  enet  100128     1500  -      -      -        -    -        0      0
200  enet  100200     1500  -      -      -        -    -        0      0
1002 fddi  101002     1500  -      -      -        -    -        0      0
1003 tr    101003     1500  -      -      -        -    srb      0      0
1004 fdnet 101004     1500  -      -      1        ieee -        0      0
1005 trnet 101005     1500  -      -      1        ibm  -        0      0
tundra_switch1#
tundra_switch1#show vtp status
VTP Version                     : 2
Configuration Revision          : 15
Maximum VLANs supported locally : 1005
Number of existing VLANs        : 8
VTP Operating Mode              : Server
VTP Domain Name                 : tundra
VTP Pruning Mode                : Disabled
VTP V2 Mode                     : Disabled
VTP Traps Generation            : Disabled
MD5 digest                      : 0xE6 0x6C 0xFD 0xDA 0x1B 0xCC 0x7B 0x8A
Configuration last modified by 172.16.2.16 at 3-1-93 04:03:13
Local updater ID is 172.16.2.16 on interface Vl2 (lowest numbered VLAN interface)
tundra_switch1#
```

Step 3 calls for you to configure EtherChannel and 802.1Q trunking between the switches. The configuration on both switches will be identical for the EtherChannel, as long as both are Catalyst 3550s. Example 1-50 demonstrates the Gigabit EtherChannel configuration on the tundra_switch1.

Example 1-50 *Configuring Gigabit EtherChannel with 802.1Q Encapsulation*

```
tundra_switch(config)#interface gigabitEthernet 0/1
tundra_switch(config-if)#switchport trunk encapsulation dot1q
! 802.1q trunking
tundra switch(config-if)#switchport mode trunk
tundra switch(config-if)#channel-group 1 mode on
! EtherChannel Configuration
Creating a port-channel interface Port-channel1
tundra (config-if)#exit
00:23:18: %LINK-3-UPDOWN: Interface Port-channel1, changed state to up
00:23:19: %LINEPROTO-5-UPDOWN: Line protocol on Interface Port-channel1, changed state
to up
tundra switch(config)#interface gigabitEthernet 0/2
tundra switch(config-if)#switchport trunk encapsulation dot1q
tundra switch(config-if)#switchport mode trunk
tundra switch(config-if)#channel-group 1 mode on
```

At this point of the configuration, VTP should be working between switches, and you should be able to ping all local devices. You need to configure the SVIs and routing protocols for inter-VLAN connectivity. In this model, you were to set the root of spanning tree for VLANs 100 and 200 to the tundra_switch1. You can do so with the global configuration command **spanning-tree vlan 100 root** and **spanning-tree vlan 200 root** commands. This macro uses the extended system ID to set the priority of the VLANs to 24,576, which makes them root. VTP pruning should also be enabled for VLAN 200. VTP pruning is enabled with the VLAN configuration command **vtp pruning**. You can verify the status of STP with the **show spanning-tree root** command, as demonstrated in Example 1-51. At the bottom of this example is the **show interface** command, verifying that VTP pruning is enabled on the EtherChannel between the two switches.

Example 1-51 *Verifying STP and VTP Pruning on the tundra_switch1*

```
tundra_switch1#show spanning-tree root
                              Root    Hello Max Fwd
Vlan               Root ID    Cost    Time  Age Dly  Root Port
---------------    -------------------- ---------- ----- --- --- -------------
VLAN0001           32768 0004.275e.f0c0       3     2   20  15  Po1
VLAN0002           32768 0004.275e.f0c1       3     2   20  15  Po1
VLAN0100           24676 000a.8a0e.ba80       0     2   20  15
VLAN0200           24776 000a.8a0e.ba80       0     2   20  15
tundra_switch1#
tundra_switch1#show int port-channel 1 switchport
Name: Po1
Switchport: Enabled
```

Example 1-51 *Verifying STP and VTP Pruning on the tundra_switch1 (Continued)*

```
Administrative Mode: trunk
Operational Mode: trunk
Administrative Trunking Encapsulation: dot1q
Operational Trunking Encapsulation: dot1q
Negotiation of Trunking: On
Access Mode VLAN: 1 (default)
Trunking Native Mode VLAN: 1 (default)
Trunking VLANs Enabled: ALL
Pruning VLANs Enabled: 2,100,200
<<<text omitted>>>
```

In the next two steps, you configure SVIs and the routed interface on the switch. You need three SVIs and a routed port for full IP connectivity on the tundra_switch1. One SVI, interface VLAN 2 is needed for the management VLAN, whereas two more SVIs—interface VLAN 100 and interface VLAN 200—are needed for the other routers. The routed interface is configured by first enabling routing and then using the **no switchport** interface command on the port you want to be a routed interface. Example 1-52 shows the necessary configuration of the tundra_switch1.

Example 1-52 *SVI and Routed Interface Configuration*

```
!
ip routing
! IP routing must be enabled for routed INTs
!
interface FastEthernet0/10
 no switchport
! Disable switching
 ip address 10.16.128.16 255.255.255.0
! Assign an IP address
!
-------------------------------------SVI CONFIG--------→
interface Vlan2
 ip address 172.16.2.16 255.255.255.0
!
interface Vlan100
 ip address 172.16.100.16 255.255.255.0
!
interface Vlan200
 ip address 172.16.200.16 255.255.255.0
 no ip redirects
```

The final portion of the lab is to configure EIGRP as the routing protocol. IP was enabled during the preceding step, so that is not necessary here. To configure the Layer 3 switching portion of the lab, you just need to configure EIGRP on the routers and the Ethernet switch. This is done identically as it would be on a router. The HSRP can also be configured at this time. Once again, the syntax to configure HSRP on a switch is the same as a router. *CCIE PSV1* has in-depth configurations of EIGRP and HSRP; therefore, they are listed here only in the configurations. If you have questions on the configuration options used, refer to *CCIE PSV1*. Example 1-53 lists the full configuration of the tundra_switch1 followed by the route table of the switch and the EIGRP neighbors. Notice that the switch has five EIGRP neighbors.

Example 1-53 *Complete Configuration of the tundra_switch1 Switch*

```
hostname tundra_switch1
!
enable secret 5 $1$nt35$131XBSgKT6BmA1KHMqj1V1
!
ip subnet-zero
ip routing
!
spanning-tree extend system-id
spanning-tree vlan 100 priority 24576
spanning-tree vlan 200 priority 24576
!
interface Port-channel1
 switchport trunk encapsulation dot1q
 switchport trunk pruning vlan 2,100,128,200
 switchport mode trunk
 no ip address
!
<<<text omitted>>>
!
interface FastEthernet0/3
 switchport access vlan 200
 switchport mode access
 no ip address
!
<<<text omitted>>>
!
interface FastEthernet0/7
 switchport access vlan 100
 switchport mode access
 no ip address
!
interface FastEthernet0/8
 switchport access vlan 100
 switchport mode access
 no ip address
!
interface FastEthernet0/9
 no ip address
!
interface FastEthernet0/10
 no switchport
 ip address 10.16.128.16 255.255.255.0
!
<<<text omitted>>>
 no ip address
```

Example 1-53 *Complete Configuration of the tundra_switch1 Switch (Continued)*

```
!
interface GigabitEthernet0/1
 switchport trunk encapsulation dot1q
 switchport trunk pruning vlan 2,100,128,200
 switchport mode trunk
 no ip address
 channel-group 1 mode on
!
interface GigabitEthernet0/2
 switchport trunk encapsulation dot1q
 switchport trunk pruning vlan 2,100,128,200
 switchport mode trunk
 no ip address
 channel-group 1 mode on
!
interface Vlan1
 no ip address
 shutdown
!
interface Vlan2
 ip address 172.16.2.16 255.255.255.0
!
interface Vlan100
 ip address 172.16.100.16 255.255.255.0
!
interface Vlan200
 ip address 172.16.200.16 255.255.255.0
 no ip redirects
 standby 200 ip 172.16.200.1
 standby 200 priority 101
 standby 200 preempt
!
router eigrp 2003
 network 10.0.0.0
 network 172.16.0.0
 no auto-summary
 no eigrp log-neighbor-changes
!
ip classless
ip http server!
line con 0
line vty 0 4
 password cisco
 login
line vty 5 7
end
tundra_switch1#
tundra_switch1#show ip route
Codes: C - connected, S - static, I - IGRP, R - RIP, M - mobile, B - BGP
       D - EIGRP, EX - EIGRP external, O - OSPF, IA - OSPF inter area
```

continues

Example 1-53 *Complete Configuration of the tundra_switch1 Switch (Continued)*

```
              N1 - OSPF NSSA external type 1, N2 - OSPF NSSA external type 2
              E1 - OSPF external type 1, E2 - OSPF external type 2, E - EGP
              i - IS-IS, L1 - IS-IS level-1, L2 - IS-IS level-2, ia - IS-IS inter area
              * - candidate default, U - per-user static route, o - ODR
              P - periodic downloaded static route
Gateway of last resort is not set
      172.16.0.0/24 is subnetted, 3 subnets
C        172.16.200.0 is directly connected, Vlan200
C        172.16.2.0 is directly connected, Vlan2
C        172.16.100.0 is directly connected, Vlan100
      10.0.0.0/24 is subnetted, 2 subnets
D        10.16.10.0 [90/409600] via 10.16.128.100, 03:25:34, FastEthernet0/10
C        10.16.128.0 is directly connected, FastEthernet0/10
tundra_switch1#
tundra_switch1#show ip eigrp neighbors
IP-EIGRP neighbors for process 2003
H   Address                 Interface   Hold Uptime    SRTT   RTO  Q  Seq Type
                                        (sec)          (ms)        Cnt Num
4   172.16.100.100          Vl100         13 03:22:58  1524   5000 0  6
3   172.16.100.101          Vl100         11 03:23:01  1488   5000 0  7
2   10.16.128.100           Fa0/10        10 03:30:33  1080   5000 0  5
1   172.16.200.102          Vl200         13 03:32:03   419   2514 0  5
0   172.16.200.101          Vl200         14 03:32:06   204   1224 0  8
tundra_switch1#
```

Example 1-54 lists relevant configuration portions of the tundra_bak switch.

Example 1-54 *tundra_bak Switch Configuration*

```
hostname tundra_switch2
!
enable secret 5 $1$nt35$131XBSgKT6BmA1KHMqj1V1
!
spanning-tree extend system-id
!
interface Port-channel1
 switchport trunk encapsulation dot1q
 switchport trunk pruning vlan 2,100,128,200
 switchport mode trunk
 no ip address
!
<<<text omitted>>>
!
interface FastEthernet0/5
switchport access vlan 200
!
interface GigabitEthernet0/1
 switchport trunk encapsulation dot1q
 switchport trunk pruning vlan 2,100,128,200
 switchport mode trunk
```

Example 1-54 *tundra_bak Switch Configuration (Continued)*

```
 no ip address
 channel-group 1 mode on
!
interface GigabitEthernet0/2
 switchport trunk encapsulation dot1q
 switchport trunk pruning vlan 2,100,128,200
 switchport mode trunk
 no ip address
 channel-group 1 mode on
!
interface Vlan1
 no ip address
 shutdown
!
interface VLAN2
 ip address 172.16.2.15 255.255.255.0
 no ip directed-broadcast
 no ip route-cache
!
ip default-gateway 172.16.2.16
!
line con 0
line vty 0 4
 password cisco
 login
line vty 5 7
 end
```

Example 1-55 shows the configuration of the tundra_prime router, the tundra_bak, and the frozen_rtr. The EIGRP and IP configurations on the other routers are nearly identical, save for the IP address; therefore, for the sake of brevity, not all of the configurations are listed here.

Example 1-55 *Configurations of tundra_prime and frozen_rtr Routers*

```
hostname tundra_prime
!
interface FastEthernet3/0
 ip address 172.16.200.101 255.255.255.0
 duplex auto
 speed auto
 standby 200 preempt
 standby 200 ip 172.16.200.1
!
router eigrp 2003
 network 172.16.0.0
 no auto-summary
 no eigrp log-neighbor-changes
!
```

continues

Example 1-55 *Configurations of tundra_prime and frozen_rtr Routers (Continued)*

```
hostname frozen_rtr
!
interface loopback 20
 ip address 10.16.10.100 255.255.255.0
!
interface Ethernet0/0
 ip address 10.16.128.100 255.255.255.0
!
router eigrp 2003
 network 10.0.0.0
 no auto-summary
!
```

```
hostname tundra_bak
!
interface Ethernet0/1
 ip address 172.16.200.102 255.255.255.0
 no ip redirects
 no ip directed-broadcast
 standby priority 95
 standby preempt
 standby 200 ip 172.16.200.1
!
router eigrp 2003
 network 172.16.0.0
 no auto-summary
!
```

```
hostname products
!
!
interface Ethernet0
 ip address 172.16.100.100 255.255.255.0
 no ip directed-broadcast
 media-type 10BASE-T
!
router eigrp 2003
 network 172.16.0.0
 no auto-summary
!
```

Lab 2: Configuring 802.1w RSTP and 802.1s MST, Layer 3 Switching, and VLAN Maps—Part I

Practical Scenario

One area of switching that has made vast improvements is that of redundancy and failover recovery. With IEEE 802.1w RSTP and IEEE 802.1s MST, spanning tree can now converge in hundredths of a second rather than the 50 seconds that 802.1d requires. When configuring large production networks, customers pay thousands for redundancy and backup. Being able to provide excellent recovery times via new techniques helps you and your customer get the most for the money.

Lab Exercise

The famous Dr. Walker has established the Walker Children's Hospital, specializing in the care of young children who have leg and bone problems. The hospital network has been running under 802.1d STP for redundancy, but administrators have found that the recovery time is too long. Critical services between areas such as surgery and recovery need very fast convergence in the event of a link failure.

Your task is to configure a working IP network and configure the Ethernet 3550 switch using the following strict design guidelines:

- Configure the Walker Children's Hospital network as depicted in Figure 1-38. Use EIGRP as the routing protocol and 2003 as the autonomous system ID on all routers.

- Configure all IP addresses as depicted in Figure 1-38. All labeled interfaces should be able to ping each other.

- See the "Lab Objectives" section for configuration specifics.

Lab Objectives

- Configure the EIGRP as the routing protocol, as depicted in Figure 1-38. Use 2003 as the autonomous system ID.

- Configure the management interface of 172.16.192.16/24 on walker1 and 172.16.192.13/24 on walker2. These addresses should be reachable.

- Configure the two interfaces between the walker1 and walker2 switches. Do not configure these interfaces as an EtherChannel group. In this model, you use one Gigabit Ethernet interface and one 100-Mpbs interface for backup.

- Configure the walker1 as the VTP server and the walker2 as the VTP client. Use the VTP domain of walker and a VTP password of psv2.

- Configure the other interfaces as access ports and assign VLANs as depicted in Figure 1-38. Configure six interfaces into VLAN 20; these will be edge ports for the admin VLAN.

- Configure 802.1w RSTP and 802.1s MST. Configure all hosts as edge ports for rapid convergence. Use walker as the MST name.

- Configure the walker1 switch so that it will be the root for all VLANs in the range of 2 through 300.

- Configure any SVIs needed for the walker1 switch to provide routing for all VLANs in the network. There should be full IP connectivity across the LAN. All depicted IP addresses should be pingable.

- There have been problems with people sharing files and using unauthorized applications in the admin VLAN. Configure this VLAN such that users of this VLAN will no longer be able to share files or use network applications within that VLAN.

Equipment Needed

- One IP-based workstation, four Cisco routers, one Catalyst 3550 with the EMI software image installed, and one other Catalyst switch that supports MST and RSTP. Only one switch needs to be a Catalyst 3550 with the EMI installed. One router can be substituted for a workstation on VLAN 20. VLAN 20 should have at least one active IP device for testing.

- The switches need two back-to-back 100BASE-T links or a Gigabit Ethernet link for the connection between the two switches. The other routers should be set up with Category 5 connections to the appropriate switch, as depicted in Figure 1-38.

Physical Layout and Prestaging

- Connect the switches to the routers as shown in Figure 1-38.

- This lab focuses on the configuration of the Ethernet switches.

Figure 1-38 *Walker Children's Hospital*

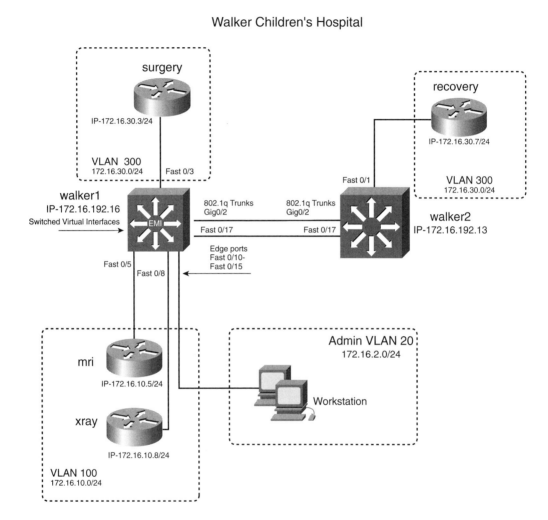

Walker Children's Hospital

Lab 2: Configuring 802.1w RSTP and 802.1s MST, Layer 3 Switching, and VLAN Maps—Part II

Lab Walkthrough

Attach all the routers to the switch as illustrated in Figure 1-38. You can use either two Gigabit Ethernet connections between the two switches or 100-Mbps links. Your choice will not affect the operational ability of the lab.

Recall from earlier the seven-step process for configuring the 3550 Ethernet switch.

Step 1   Configure switch management.

Step 2   Configure VTP and VLANs and assign ports/interfaces to VLANs.

Step 3   Configure connections between switches using EtherChannel, 802.1Q, and ISL encapsulations.

Step 4   (Optional) Control STP and VLAN propagation.

Step 5   (Optional) Configure SVIs.

Step 6   (Optional) Configure routed ports.

Step 7   (Optional) Configure Layer 3 switching.

The first step is to configure switch management. This includes setting a host name, password, and management address on the switch. Example 1-56 lists the management portion of walker1. The configuration of walker2 would be identical except for the IP address, which will be 172.16.192.13.

Example 1-56 *Management Portion of walker1 Thus Far*

```
hostname walker1
! Set the hostname
!
enable secret 5 $1$nt35$131XBSgKT6BmA1KHMqj1V1
! Enable Secret=cisco
!
<<<text omitted>>>
!
interface Vlan1
 no ip address
 shutdown
!
interface Vlan192
! MNGT VLAN and IP
 ip address 172.16.192.16 255.255.255.0
<<<text omitted>>>
!
```

The second step calls for you to configure VTP and VLANs. You need to configure a VLAN for any SVIs, access ports, and management VLANs. In this model, you need to configure five VLANs: VLANs 20, 100, 192, 200, and 300. On the 3550, you can do this from the global configuration mode with the command **vlan** *x*. A name can be entered as well after entering the VLAN number. The VTP mode of walker1 is server, and walker2 will be the VTP client. The VTP domain is called walker, and the password is psv2. Ensure that the VTP domains are in the same case, along with the password. Domain name and password are case sensitive. Be sure that the VTP server's revision number is also higher than the VTP client's; otherwise, the two will not synchronize. The VTP domain and mode can be configured from the VLAN database or the VLAN configuration mode. Example 1-57 demonstrates this being done on the walker1 switch.

Example 1-57 *Configuring VTP on walker1*

```
walker1#vlan database
walker1(vlan)#vtp domain walker
walker1(vlan)#vtp server
walker1(vlan)#vtp password psv2
```

This step also calls for you to configure the physical port properties and assign the ports to VLANs. Example 1-58 illustrates the VLAN and port configuration of walker1 to this point. Because you are configuring RSTP, you must configure edge ports with the interface command **spanning-tree portfast**.

Example 1-58 *Configuring VLAN Port Membership*

```
hostname walker1
!
<<<text omitted>>>
!
interface FastEthernet0/3
 switchport access vlan 300
! assigned to VLAN 300
 switchport mode access
 spanning-tree portfast
! Portfast used in 802.1w
 no ip address
!
interface FastEthernet0/5
 switchport access vlan 100
! assigned to VLAN 100
 switchport mode access
spanning-tree portfast
! Portfast used in 802.1w
 no ip address
!
interface FastEthernet0/8
 switchport access vlan 100
```

continues

Example 1-58 *Configuring VLAN Port Membership (Continued)*

```
! assigned to VLAN 100
 switchport mode access
 spanning-tree portfast
! Portfast used in 802.1w
 no ip address
!
```

When configuring a range of VLANs, it can be easier to use the **range** command. Example 1-59 illustrates the use of the **range** command when configuring the six admin interfaces for VLAN 20.

Example 1-59 *Configuring a VLAN Range*

```
walker1(config)#interface range fastEthernet 0/10 - 15
walker1(config-if-range)#switchport mode access
walker1(config-if-range)#switchport access vlan 20
walker1(config-if-range)#spanning-tree portfast
%Warning: portfast should only be enabled on ports connected to a single
 host. Connecting hubs, concentrators, switches, bridges, etc... to this
 interface  when portfast is enabled, can cause temporary bridging loops.
 Use with CAUTION
%Portfast will be configured in 6 interfaces due to the range command
 but will only have effect when the interfaces are in a non-trunking mode.
walker1(config-if-range)#exit
```

You can verify the VLANs and VTP with the **show vlan** command and the **show vtp status** command, as demonstrated in Example 1-60.

Example 1-60 *Verifying VTP and VLAN Status*

```
walker1#show vlan
VLAN Name                             Status    Ports
---- -------------------------------- --------- -------------------------------
1    default                          active    Fa0/1, Fa0/2, Fa0/4,
                                                Fa0/6, Fa0/9, Fa0/16
                                                Fa0/17, Fa0/18, Fa0/19, Fa0/20
                                                Fa0/21, Fa0/22, Fa0/23, Fa0/24
20   psv2_vlan20                      active    Fa0/10, Fa0/11, Fa0/12, Fa0/13
  Fa0/14, Fa0/15
100  psv2_vlan100                     active    Fa0/5, Fa0/8
192  psv2_vlan192                     active
300  psv2_vlan300                     active    Fa0/3
1002 fddi-default                     active
1003 token-ring-default               active
1004 fddinet-default                  active
1005 trnet-default                    active
```

Example 1-60 *Verifying VTP and VLAN Status (Continued)*

```
VLAN Type  SAID     MTU    Parent RingNo BridgeNo Stp  BrdgMode Trans1 Trans2
---- ----- -------- -----  ------ ------ -------- ---- -------- ------ ------
1    enet  100001   1500   -      -      -        -    -        0      0
20   enet  100020   1500   -      -      -        -    -        0      0
100  enet  100100   1500   -      -      -        -    -        0      0
192  enet  100192   1500   -      -      -        -    -        0      0
300  enet  100300   1500   -      -      -        -    -        0      0
1002 fddi  101002   1500   -      -      -        -    -        0      0
1003 tr    101003   1500   -      -      -        -    srb      0      0
1004 fdnet 101004   1500   -      -      1        ieee -        0      0
1005 trnet 101005   1500   -      -      1        ibm  -        0      0
walker1#
walker1#show vtp status
VTP Version                  : 2
Configuration Revision       : 3
Maximum VLANs supported locally : 1005
Number of existing VLANs     : 9
VTP Operating Mode           : Server
VTP Domain Name              : walker
VTP Pruning Mode             : Enabled
VTP V2 Mode                  : Disabled
VTP Traps Generation         : Disabled
MD5 digest                   : 0xEF 0xD8 0x4D 0x0A 0x57 0x8F 0x7E 0x14
Configuration last modified by 172.16.192.16 at 3-1-93 01:10:51
Local updater ID is 172.16.192.16 on interface Vl192 (lowest numbered VLAN interface)
walker1#
```

Step 3 calls for you to configure 802.1Q trunking between the switches. The configuration on both switches will be identical, as long as both are in the Catalyst 35xx family. Example 1-61 demonstrates the 802.1Q trunk configuration on the walker1 switch for interfaces Gig 0/2 and Fast 0/17.

Example 1-61 *Configuring Gigabit EtherChannel with 802.1Q Encapsulation*

```
walker1(config)#interface gigabit 0/2
walker1(config-if)#switchport trunk encapsulation dot1q
walker1(config-if)#switchport mode trunk
walker1(config-if)#exit
walker1(config)#interface fast 0/17
walker1(config-if)#switchport trunk encapsulation dot1q
walker1(config-if)#switchport mode trunk
walker1(config-if)#exit
```

At this point of the configuration, VTP should be working between switches, and you should be able to ping all local devices. Use the **show vtp status** command to verify VTP and ensure that both switches have the same VTP revision number and the same number of VLANs.

The next portion of the configuration requires you to enable 802.1s and 802.1w spanning tree. RSTP is partially enabled at this point from using the **spanning-tree portfast** command on all nontrunking interfaces. RSTP will be fully enabled when 802.1s or MST is enabled. The MST configuration on the walker1 and walker2 switches will be identical, except that the walker1 switch will use the **spanning-tree mst 1 root primary** command to set root for VLANs 2 through 300. You will define a single STP instance, MST 1, and assign VLANs 2 through 300 to this instance. The MST name will be walker, and the revision will be 1. Example 1-62 demonstrates configuring MST and RSTP on the walker1 switch.

Example 1-62 *Configuring MST and RSTP on the walker1 Switch*

```
walker1(config)#spanning-tree mst config      ←Enter MST configuration mode
walker1(config-mst)#name walker               ←MST name
walker1(config-mst)#revision 1                ←MST revision number
walker1(config-mst)#instance 1 vlan 2-300     ←assign VLANs 2-300 to instance 1
walker1(config-mst)#exit                       ←apply changes !important!
walker1(config)#spanning-tree mst 1 root primary    ←Set root for instance 1
walker1(config)#spanning-tree mode mst        ←enable MST
```

You can verify the status of MST with the **show spanning-tree mst 1** and the **show spanning-tree root** commands, as demonstrated in Example 1-63. You should see VLANs 2 through 300 in MST instance 1, and MST instance 1 should be the root for MST. In this model, the MAC address 000a.8a0e.ba80 is the root.

Example 1-63 *Verifying MST*

```
walker1#show spanning-tree mst 1
###### MST01      vlans mapped:   2-300
Bridge      address 000a.8a0e.ba80  priority  24577 (24576 sysid 1)
Root        this switch for MST01
Interface       role state cost       prio type
--------------- ---- ----- --------- ---- ----------------------------------
Fa0/3           desg FWD   200000     128  edge P2P
Fa0/5           desg FWD   2000000    128  edge SHR
Fa0/8           desg FWD   200000     128  edge P2P
Fa0/10          desg FWD   2000000    128  edge SHR
Fa0/17          desg FWD   200000     128  P2P
Gi0/2           desg FWD   20000      128  P2P
walker1#show spanning-tree root
                                 Root     Hello Max Fwd
MST Instance         Root ID     Cost     Time  Age Dly  Root Port
--------------- -------------------- --------- ----- --- ---  ------------
MST00           32768 0004.275e.f0c0   200000    2   20  15   Gi0/2
MST01           24577 000a.8a0e.ba80        0    2   20  15
walker1#
```

To test the functionality of MST and RSTP, perform the following test. Issue an extended ping from the surgery router to the recovery router. Use a high number of pings, such as 10,000. While you are pinging the interfaces, disconnect the active trunk (in this model, the Gigabit Ethernet). You should see RSTP converge almost instantly, with a 99-percent success rate on the pings! Example 1-64 shows the RSTP test being done.

Example 1-64 *Testing MST and RSTP*

```
surgery#ping
Protocol [ip]:
Target IP address: 172.16.30.7
Repeat count [5]: 10000
Datagram size [100]:
Timeout in seconds [2]:
Extended commands [n]:
Sweep range of sizes [n]:
Type escape sequence to abort.
Sending 10000, 100-byte ICMP Echos to 172.16.30.7, timeout is 2 seconds:
!!!!!!!!!!!!!!!!!!!!!!!!!!!!!!!!!!!!!!!!!!!!!!!!!!!!!!!!!!!!!!!!!!!!!
!!!!!!!!!!!!!!!!!!!!!!!!!!!!!!!!!!!!!!!!!!!!!!!!!!!!!!!!!!!!!!!!!!!!!
!..!   ←Gig 0/2 dropped
!!!!!!!!!!!!!!!!!!!!!!!!!!!!!!!!!!!!!!!!!!!!!!!!!!!!!!!!!!!!!!!!!!!!!
!!!!!!!!!!!!!!!!!!!!!!!!!!!!!!!!!!!!!!!!!!!!!!!!!!!!!!!!!!!!!!!!!!!!!
!!!!!!!!!!!!!!!!!!!!!!!!!!!!!!!!!!!!!!!!!!!!!!!!!!!!!!!!!!!!!!!
Success rate is 99 percent (9998/10000), round-trip min/avg/max = 1/2/20 ms
surgery#
```

In the next two steps, you configure SVIs and enable routing on the walker1 switch. You need four SVIs—one for each VLAN and one for the management VLAN. One SVI, interface VLAN 192, is needed for the management VLAN. You also need three more SVIs: interface VLAN 20 for the admin, and interface VLAN 100 and interface VLAN 300 for the routers. Example 1-65 shows the necessary configuration of the walker1 switch.

Example 1-65 *SVI Interface Configuration*

```
interface Vlan20
 ip address 172.16.2.16 255.255.255.0
!
interface Vlan100
 ip address 172.16.10.16 255.255.255.0
!
interface Vlan192
 ip address 172.16.192.16 255.255.255.0
!
interface Vlan300
 ip address 172.16.30.16 255.255.255.0
```

The final portion of the lab is to configure EIGRP as the routing protocol. IP routing needs to be enabled with the global configuration command **ip routing**. To configure the Layer 3 switching portion of the lab, you just need to configure EIGRP on the routers and the Ethernet switch. This is done identically as it would be on a router. Example 1-66 lists the full configuration of the walker1 switch followed by the EIGRP neighbors. Notice that the switch has four EIGRP neighbors.

Example 1-66 *Complete Configuration of the walker1 Switch*

```
hostname walker1
!
enable secret 5 $1$oTsK$C95mG2YeDzQ4w3ecs0CkS0
!
ip subnet-zero
ip routing
!
spanning-tree mode mst
spanning-tree extend system-id
!
spanning-tree mst configuration
 name walker
 revision 1
 instance 1 vlan 2-300
!
spanning-tree mst 1 priority 24576
!
<<<text omitted>>>
!
interface FastEthernet0/3
 switchport access vlan 300
 switchport mode access
 no ip address
 spanning-tree portfast
!
<<<text omitted>>>
!
interface FastEthernet0/5
 switchport access vlan 100
 switchport mode access
 no ip address
 spanning-tree portfast
!
<<<text omitted>>
!
!
interface FastEthernet0/8
 switchport access vlan 100
 switchport mode access
 no ip address
 spanning-tree portfast
!
<<<text omitted>>>
```

Example 1-66 *Complete Configuration of the walker1 Switch (Continued)*

```
!
interface FastEthernet0/10
 switchport access vlan 20
 switchport mode access
 no ip address
 spanning-tree portfast
!
interface FastEthernet0/11
 switchport access vlan 20
 switchport mode access
 no ip address
 spanning-tree portfast
!
interface FastEthernet0/12
 switchport access vlan 20
 switchport mode access
 no ip address
 spanning-tree portfast
!
interface FastEthernet0/13
 switchport access vlan 20
 switchport mode access
 no ip address
 spanning-tree portfast
!
interface FastEthernet0/14
 switchport access vlan 20
 switchport mode access
 no ip address
 spanning-tree portfast
!
interface FastEthernet0/15
 switchport access vlan 20
 switchport mode access
 no ip address
 spanning-tree portfast
!
<<<text omitted>>>
!
interface FastEthernet0/17
 switchport trunk encapsulation dot1q
 switchport mode trunk
 no ip address
!
interface GigabitEthernet0/2
 switchport trunk encapsulation dot1q
 switchport mode trunk
 no ip address
```

continues

Example 1-66 *Complete Configuration of the walker1 Switch (Continued)*

```
!
interface Vlan1
 no ip address
 shutdown
!
interface Vlan20
 ip address 172.16.2.16 255.255.255.0
!
interface Vlan100
 ip address 172.16.10.16 255.255.255.0
!
interface Vlan192
 ip address 172.16.192.16 255.255.255.0
!
interface Vlan300
 ip address 172.16.30.16 255.255.255.0
!
router eigrp 2003
 network 172.16.0.0
 auto-summary
 no eigrp log-neighbor-changes
!
ip classless
ip http server
!
line con 0
line vty 5 15
!
end
walker1#
walker1#show ip eigrp neighbors
IP-EIGRP neighbors for process 2003
H   Address               Interface   Hold Uptime   SRTT   RTO  Q  Seq Type
                                      (sec)         (ms)        Cnt Num
3   172.16.10.5           Vl100         14 00:03:02 1048   5000 0  5
2   172.16.30.3           Vl300         12 00:03:04    1   3000 0  9
1   172.16.30.7           Vl300         13 00:03:06 1208   5000 0  10
0   172.16.10.8           Vl100         14 00:03:06 1516   5000 0  9
walker1#
```

Example 1-67 lists relevant configuration portions of the walker2 switch.

Example 1-67 *walker2 Switch Configuration*

```
hostname walker2
!
enable secret 5 $1$oTsK$C95mG2YeDzQ4w3ecs0CkS0
!
spanning-tree mode mst
spanning-tree extend system-id
```

Example 1-67 *walker2 Switch Configuration (Continued)*

```
!
spanning-tree mst configuration
 name walker
 revision 1
 instance 1 vlan 2-300
!
interface FastEthernet0/1
 switchport access vlan 300
 switchport mode access
 no ip address
 spanning-tree portfast
!
interface FastEthernet0/17
 switchport trunk encapsulation dot1q
 switchport mode trunk
 no ip address
!
interface GigabitEthernet0/2
 switchport trunk encapsulation dot1q
 switchport mode trunk
 no ip address
!
interface Vlan1
 no ip address
 shutdown
!
interface VLAN192
 ip address 172.16.192.13 255.255.255.0
 no ip directed-broadcast
 no ip route-cache
!
ip default-gateway 172.16.192.16
```

The final portion of the lab requires that you control access on VLAN 20. To prevent the administration workstation from using IP services between them, you can define them as protected ports. Recall that a protected port prevents other ports that are protected from communicating with it. A protected port can still reach other nonprotected ports on the switch. Example 1-68 demonstrates the configuration of the protected ports with the **range** command.

Example 1-68 *Configuring Protected Ports on the walker1 Switch*

```
walker1(config)#interface range fastEthernet 0/10 - 15
walker1(config-if-range)#switchport protected
walker1(config-if-range)#^z
walker1#
walker1#show interfaces fastEthernet 0/10 switchport
Name: Fa0/10
Switchport: Enabled
```

continues

Example 1-68 *Configuring Protected Ports on the walker1 Switch (Continued)*

```
Administrative Mode: static access
Operational Mode: static access
Administrative Trunking Encapsulation: negotiate
Operational Trunking Encapsulation: native
Negotiation of Trunking: Off
Access Mode VLAN: 20 (psv2_vlan20)
Trunking Native Mode VLAN: 1 (default)
Trunking VLANs Enabled: ALL
Pruning VLANs Enabled: 2-1001
Protected: true
Unknown unicast blocked: disabled
Unknown multicast blocked: disabled

Voice VLAN: none (Inactive)
Appliance trust: none
walker1#
```

Example 1-69 shows the configuration of the surgery, mri, xray, and recovery routers.

Example 1-69 *Configurations of surgery, mri, xray, and recovery Routers*

```
hostname surgery
!
interface FastEthernet3/0
 ip address 172.16.30.3 255.255.255.0
 duplex auto
 speed auto
!
router eigrp 2003
 network 172.16.0.0
 no auto-summary
 no eigrp log-neighbor-changes
!

hostname mri
!
interface Ethernet0/1
 ip address 172.16.10.5 255.255.255.0
 !
router eigrp 2003
 network 172.16.0.0
 no auto-summary
 !

hostname xray
!
interface Ethernet0/1
 ip address 172.16.10.8 255.255.255.0
 !
router eigrp 2003
```

Example 1-69 *Configurations of surgery, mri, xray, and recovery Routers (Continued)*

```
 network 172.16.0.0
 no auto-summary
!

hostname recovery
!
interface Ethernet5
 ip address 172.16.30.7 255.255.255.0
 no ip directed-broadcast
 media-type 10BASE-T
!
router eigrp 2003
 network 172.16.0.0
 no auto-summary
!
```

PART II

Controlling Network Propagation and Network Access

CHAPTER 2

Configuring Route Maps and Policy-Based Routing

Perhaps one of the most colorful descriptions for route maps is that route maps are like duct tape for the network—not necessarily because they can be used to fix or mend something broken, but because they can be applied to numerous situations to address many issues. At times, they may not be the most "pretty solutions," but they will be very effective. After you learn to configure and use route maps, you will soon see why some engineers refer to them as *route tape*. In policy-based routing (PBR), for instance, you may use a route map when traffic has to follow a particular path through the internetwork. This path may differ from the path the routing protocol wants to forward traffic on. PBR, along with route maps, enables the network engineer to essentially override the route table and influence which way traffic flows.

You also can apply route maps in a number of ways. The following list contains some of the more common and powerful applications of route maps:

- Route filtering during redistribution between routing protocols
- Route control and attribute modification on BGP neighbors
- Route metric modification or *tagging* during redistribution between routing protocols
- Policy-based routing (PBR)

After you have route maps in your engineering tool kit, you will have one of the most powerful and versatile configuration options available on Cisco routers. This chapter discusses how to configure and use route maps and how to configure PBR.

Route Map Overview

Route maps are much like the "If . . . Then . . ." statements of many programming languages. *If* a certain condition is true, *then* do something. Route maps enable you to define routing policy that will be considered before the router examines its forwarding table; therefore, you can define routing policy that takes precedence over the different route processes. This is why route maps are some of the most powerful commands you can use on a router. Example 2-1 highlights route map logic.

Example 2-1 *Route Map Logic*

```
route-map route_map_name permit 10
 match criteria_1
 set perform_action_1
route-map route-map_name permit 20
 match criteria_2
 set perform_action_2
 set perform_action_3
route-map route-map_name permit 30
 match criteria_3 criteria_4 criteria_5
 set perform_action_2
 set perform_action_4
 set perform_action_5
route-map route-map_name deny 65536        ←implicit deny at the end
 match everything
```

In a nutshell, route maps work in the following manner:

1 Essentially, a process—whether it is a redistribution process, policy routing, or some other process such as Network Address Translation (NAT)—calls a route map by a text-based name.

2 The route map, in turn, has conditions or **match** statements, which are usually, but not always, an access list or extended access list. Border Gateway Protocol (BGP), for instance, can match on an autonomous system number (ASN) or different attributes. The **match** statement(s) can be followed by **set** statements.

If the **match** statement returns a true result, the set statement(s) are executed.

Example 2-2 shows how a route map functions during redistribution.

Example 2-2 *Route Map Function During Redistribution*

```
router ospf 2001
 redistribute eigrp 65001 subnets route-map route_map_name   ←Call the route-map
                                               ←and send EIGRP routes for comparison
 !
route-map route_map_name permit 10        ←Route-map with the lowest sequence number
                                           gets executed first
 match ip address access_list             ←Call access-list, the IF of the route-map
 set condition                            ←If access-list is true, THEN do something
 !
route-map route_map_name permit 20        ←Next highest sequence number
                                           gets executed
 match ip address access_list             ←Call access-list, the IF of the route-map
 set condition                            ←If access-list is true, THEN do something
 !
route-map route_map_name deny 65536       ←Implicit deny at the end all route-maps
 match ip address all_routes              This will not show up in the config
```

The next example is the syntax of an actual route map. Example 2-3 demonstrates how a route map can be applied during redistribution.

Example 2-3   *Route Map Application During Redistribution*

```
router ospf 65
 log-adjacency-changes
 log-adjacency-changes
 redistribute eigrp 65001 subnets route-map set_tag ←Call the route-map "set_tag"
 network 10.10.3.0 0.0.0.255 area 0
 default-metric 10
!
access-list 10 permit 172.16.32.0 0.0.0.255   ←Match the 172.16.32.0/24 subnet
access-list 11 permit 172.16.1.0 0.0.0.255   ← Match the 172.16.1.0/24 subnet
!
route-map set_tag permit 100      ←Route-map "set_tag"
 match ip address 10              ←Call access-list 10, if this is true then…
 set tag 10                       ←If access-list is true set the tag of 10
!
route-map set_tag permit 200      ←If no match above, try and match the following:
 match ip address 11                 ←access list 11
 set metric-type type-1           ←If the ACL is true, set the OSPF metric type to 1
 set tag 11                       ←and set a tag of 11
!
route-map set_tag permit 300
 set tag 300                      ←All other routes get a tag of 300
!
```

In the preceding example, a route map is used to control and tag the routes from Enhanced Interior Gateway Routing Protocol (EIGRP) when they are redistributed into Open Shortest Path First (OSPF). During the OSPF redistribution process, a route map titled set_tag is called. The route map consists of three parts. The first part calls access control list (ACL) 10, which will permit the network 172.16.32.x and set a tag of 10. The second part calls ACL 11, which in turn matches IP address 172.16.1.x. If a match occurs, the metric will be set such that when the route is redistributed, it becomes an OSPF type 1 route; finally, the tag will be set to 11. The last part of the route map doesn't call an ACL, so all routes are matched, and the set condition is applied. In this example, the router is setting the tag to 300. You can set tags in this manner to help document the network, or you can use the tags to identify routes that you may want to filter or perform some other action on.

Route maps have the following common characteristics:

- Route maps are executed in the order of the lowest sequence number to the highest. You can edit or modify maps by using the sequence number.

- If a match is found within a route map instance, execution of further route map instances stops.

- You can use route maps to permit or deny the information found true by the **match** statements.

- If multiple **match** statements are called within a single route map instance, all **match** statements must match for the route map instance to yield a true result.

- If route maps are applied in a policy-routing environment, packets that do not meet the match criteria are then forwarded according to the route table.

- If there is no **match** statement in the route map instance, all routes and packets are matched. The **set** statement will apply to all routes or packets.

- If there is not a corresponding ACL to the **match** statement in the route map instance, all routes are matched. The **set** statement, in turn, applies to all routes.

- As with ACLs, an implicit **deny** is included at the end of the route map policy.

- You can use route maps to create policies based on the following:
  - IP address
  - End-system ID
  - Application
  - Protocol
  - Packet size

Configuring Route Maps

The route map syntax is composed of roughly three separate Cisco commands, depending on what the route map is accomplishing and what type of process is calling it. This discussion covers the following commands in detail as route maps are configured throughout this chapter:

- **route-map** commands
- **match** commands
- **set** commands

When configuring route maps, you can follow a basic five-step configuration process. Depending on the route map application, additional configuration may be needed, such as with BGP communities or PBR.

Step 1 (Optional) Configure any ACLs, AS_PATH list, or any other match criteria that the route map may be using on the **match** commands. This should be done first, so you do not call an empty ACL or AS-PATH list.

Step 2 Configure the route map instance. This is accomplished with the **route-map** *name* **permit** | **deny** *sequence_number* command. Be sure to leave room in between the sequence numbers for future updates or modifications. The route map instance with the lowest sequence number is executed first.

Step 3   Define the match criteria and configure the **match** statements that will be used in this single route map instance. You do this with the route map configuration **match** command. In the absence of any **match** commands, all packets or routes are matched.

Step 4   (Optional) Define the set criteria and configure the **set** statements that will be used in this single route map instance. You can do so with the route map configuration **set** command.

Step 5   (Optional) Configure any ACLs, AS_PATH list, or any other match criteria that the route map may be using on the **match** commands.

Step 6   Apply the route map. Once again, depending on the route map application, it can be applied in many ways. Some of the more common applications include route redistribution, PBR, and BGP.

With this configuration process in mind, we will discuss in more detail the three primary commands used to configure route maps.

route-map Commands

The complete syntax for the **route-map** command is as follows:

```
route-map route_map_name [permit_|_deny][sequence_number_1-65535]
```

The *route_map_name*, also called the *map tag*, is the text-based name of the route map. The name is unique and logically groups and defines the entire route map policy. This is the name that you use to call the route map during redistribution and other processes.

The **permit** and **deny** keywords are optional; the default keyword is **permit**. If the route map is called from a redistribution process, the keyword is set to **permit**, and the match criteria are met for the route map, the route(s) are redistributed. If the keyword were set to **deny**, in the same scenario the route(s) would be denied.

If the route map is called from a policy-routing statement, the match criteria are met for the route map, and the keyword is set to **permit**, the packet would be policy routed. Once again, **permit** is the default keyword. If the **deny** keyword is used, the packet is forwarded according to the normal route process.

The *sequence-number* indicates in what order the route map statements will be executed. When a route map is called, the route map with the lowest sequence number is executed first. If a match is not found in the route map with the lowest sequence number, the route map with the next highest sequence number is executed. This process repeats itself until a match is found or no more route map statements exist. If a match is found, execution for that individual packet or route stops, and the next packet or route begins the process again starting with the **route-map** statement with the lowest sequence number. The default sequence number is 10.

NOTE	When creating route maps, leave room in between sequence numbers for future editing. Begin your first route map with a sequence of 10 or 100, depending on how big you expect the route map to be. By using increments of 10 or 100, you leave room for 65 to 650 route map instances. Starting at a higher sequence number and leaving space in between your sequence numbers will make editing your route maps easier. The maximum route map instance is 65,535.

match Commands

The **match** commands enable you to define the criteria of the route map. For instance, you can use the **match** command to call an ACL to compare routes against. The **match** statement could also match a route tag, a route type, or the length of a packet. BGP offers many exclusive **match** statements that are discussed in Chapters 4 and 5. Table 2-1 lists the **match** parameters available in Cisco IOS Software Release 12.2.

Table 2-1   **match** *Commands in Cisco IOS Software 12.2*

Command	What It Matches
as-path	BGP AS_PATH list
clns	CLNS* information
community	BGP community list
extcommunity	BGP/VPN** extended community list
interface	First-hop interface of a route
ip	IP-specific information
length	Packet length
metric	Route metric
route-type	Route type
tag	Route tag

*   CLNS = Connectionless Network Service

** VPN = virtual private network

The **match ip address** command is by far the most commonly used of the **match** commands. The **match ip address** command enables you to call a standard, extended, or expanded-range ACL. You can use it during redistribution, with BGP, NAT, and during policy routing, as well as for other functions. The syntax for this **match** command is as follows:

```
match ip {address [access_list | prefix-list] | next-hop [access_list] | route-source
[access_list | prefix-list]}
```

In IP networks, this command enables you to match routes that have a network address matching one or more in the specified ACL or prefix list. You can use a standard, extended, or expanded-range ACL.

The **next-hop** keyword enables you to match routes that have a next-hop address matching one or more in the specified ACL. This is primarily used in BGP.

The **route-source** keyword enables you to match the advertising router's IP address of the route/network. You can use a standard, extended, or expanded-range ACL. For BGP, you may also use a prefix list.

NOTE   When using the **match ip address** command in BGP, you can use route maps only to filter outbound updates. The use of a **match ip address** route map is not supported on inbound BGP updates.

The **next-hop** keyword is used primarily in BGP, but it can also be used when redistributing routes based on the next-hop IP address that correlates to the route. In this case, the router will examine the NEXT_HOP attribute for this comparison.

The **route-source** keyword enables you to match a router's advertising IP address. If you view the IP route table, and route 172.16.3.0/24 is advertised from the IP address of 172.16.2.1, for instance, the **route-source** keyword is used to match the advertising router's IP address of 172.16.2.1. In the next sections, these commands are applied to practical examples to show you how they function.

Practical Example: Matching the Route Source and IP Address

In this model, four routers on a common LAN segment are running two routing protocols. The routers earp and holliday are running EIGRP as the routing protocol, and the routers ringo and clanton are running OSPF. The router ringo is functioning as an OSPF autonomous system boundary router (ASBR) by redistributing between EIGRP and OSPF. The ringo router is receiving several routes from the earp and holliday routers, as depicted in Figure 2-1.

In this practical example, a route map is applied during the redistribution of EIGRP into OSPF on the ringo router. The route map named set_tag3 is called on the redistribution process for OSPF on the ringo router. The first route map instance, **route-map set_tag3 permit 100**, will perform a match on **IP route-source**. This statement will match only routes where the advertising IP address is found in ACL 5—in this case, the address 172.16.10.3. Not only will these routes be allowed for redistribution, but the tag of 3 will also be set.

Figure 2-1   *Route Map Practical Example: Matching the Route Source and IP Address*

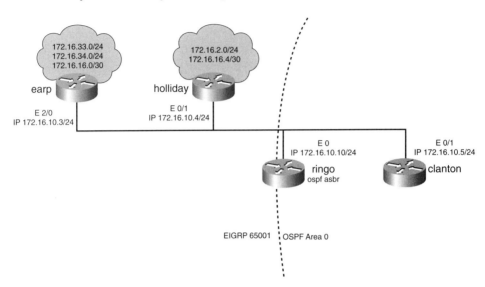

NOTE   When using a route map with OSPF, the advertising OSPF router ID becomes the route source. Use the OSPF router ID for the IP address of the route source when using the **route-source** keyword with OSPF networks.

Example 2-4 lists the forwarding/route table of the ringo router. Notice that routes 172.16.16.0/30, 172.16.33.0/24, and 172.16.34.0/24 are from the earp router, 172.16.10.3. The 172.16.2.0/24 and 172.16.16.4/30 routes are from the holliday router, 172.16.10.4.

Example 2-4   *Forwarding/Route Table of the ringo Router*

```
ringo# show ip route
<<<text omitted>>>>
C    192.168.10.0/24 is directly connected, Loopback20
     172.16.0.0/16 is variably subnetted, 6 subnets, 2 masks
D       172.16.33.0/24 [90/1812992] via 172.16.10.3, 00:07:13, Ethernet0
D       172.16.34.0/24 [90/1812992] via 172.16.10.3, 00:07:13, Ethernet0
D       172.16.16.4/30 [90/2195456] via 172.16.10.4, 00:07:13, Ethernet0
D       172.16.16.0/30 [90/1787392] via 172.16.10.3, 00:07:13, Ethernet0
C       172.16.10.0/24 is directly connected, Ethernet0
D       172.16.2.0/24 [90/307200] via 172.16.10.4, 00:07:14, Ethernet0
ringo#
```

Example 2-5 lists the configuration of the route map on the ringo router.

Example 2-5 *Configuration of the ringo Router*

```
!
interface Loopback20
 ip address 192.168.10.10 255.255.255.0
!
interface Ethernet0
 ip address 172.16.10.10 255.255.255.0
!
<<<text omitted>>>
!
router eigrp 65001
 network 172.16.0.0
 network 192.168.10.0
 no auto-summary
 no eigrp log-neighbor-changes
!
router ospf 7
 log-adjacency-changes
 redistribute eigrp 65001 subnets route-map set_tag3  ←Route-map called
 network 172.16.10.10 0.0.0.0 area 0
 default-metric 10
!
access-list 5 permit 172.16.10.3      ←Match route 172.16.10.3 only
access-list 50 permit any             ←Match all remaining routes
!
route-map set_tag3 permit 100
 match ip route-source 5              ←Match routes from 172.16.10.3 / ACL 5
 set tag 3                            ←set the tag to three
!
route-map set_tag3 permit 200         ←Second Route-map instance
 match ip address 50                  ←Call access-list 50 to match all routes
 set metric-type type-1               ←Set OSPF route type to External Type-1
 set tag 500                          ←Set the tag to 500 for these routes
```

In the preceding example, the second instance of the route map calls ACL 50. Access list 50 will allow the remaining routes to be redistributed and will set a tag of 500 and the metric-type to an OSPF type-1 external.

By viewing the OSPF database, you can clearly see the tags and how redistribution is working. Example 2-6 demonstrates the **show ip ospf database** command on the ringo router.

Example 2-6 **show ip ospf database** *Command*

```
ringo# show ip ospf database
           OSPF Router with ID (192.168.10.10) (Process ID 7)
              Router Link States (Area 0)
 Link ID          ADV Router        Age        Seq#        Checksum Link count
 172.16.10.5      172.16.10.5       1005       0x8000000B 0x18D8    1
```

Example 2-6 show ip ospf database *Command (Continued)*

```
192.168.10.10   192.168.10.10   1027      0x8000000A 0x7017   1
                Net Link States (Area 0)
Link ID         ADV Router      Age       Seq#       Checksum
172.16.10.5     172.16.10.5     1005      0x8000000A 0x75DA
                Type-5 AS External Link States
Link ID         ADV Router      Age       Seq#       Checksum Tag
172.16.2.0      192.168.10.10   1027      0x80000009 0x10E0   500
172.16.16.0     192.168.10.10   1027      0x80000009 0xD285   3
172.16.16.4     192.168.10.10   1027      0x80000009 0x3BA6   500
172.16.33.0     192.168.10.10   1027      0x80000009 0x291B   3
172.16.34.0     192.168.10.10   1027      0x80000009 0x1E25   3
192.168.10.0    192.168.10.10   1027      0x80000009 0x8BB0   500
ringo#
```

Examining the route table of a downstream OSPF router, such as clanton, you can see the effects of the **set metric-type type-1** command. Notice in Example 2-6 that the 172.16.2.0/24, 192.168.10.0/24, and 172.16.16.4/30 routes are OSPF external type 1 routes. Normally, or by default, the routes would be OSPF external type 2 routes. For more information on the different link-state advertisement (LSA) types and their use, refer to *CCIE Practical Studies, Volume I.* You will learn more about the various **set** commands in the upcoming section. Example 2-7 lists the forwarding table of the clanton router.

Example 2-7 *Route Table of the clanton Router*

```
clanton# show ip route
Codes: C - connected, S - static, I - IGRP, R - RIP, M - mobile, B - BGP
       D - EIGRP, EX - EIGRP external, O - OSPF, IA - OSPF inter area
       N1 - OSPF NSSA external type 1, N2 - OSPF NSSA external type 2
       E1 - OSPF external type 1, E2 - OSPF external type 2, E - EGP
       i - IS-IS, L1 - IS-IS level-1, L2 - IS-IS level-2, * - candidate default
       U - per-user static route, o - ODR
Gateway of last resort is not set
O E1 192.168.10.0/24 [110/20] via 172.16.10.10, 04:47:26, Ethernet0/0
     172.16.0.0/16 is variably subnetted, 6 subnets, 2 masks
O E2    172.16.33.0/24 [110/10] via 172.16.10.10, 04:47:27, Ethernet0/0
O E2    172.16.34.0/24 [110/10] via 172.16.10.10, 04:47:27, Ethernet0/0
O E1    172.16.16.4/30 [110/20] via 172.16.10.10, 04:47:27, Ethernet0/0
O E2    172.16.16.0/30 [110/10] via 172.16.10.10, 04:47:27, Ethernet0/0
C       172.16.10.0/24 is directly connected, Ethernet0/0
O E1    172.16.2.0/24 [110/20] via 172.16.10.10, 04:47:27, Ethernet0/0
clanton#
```

BGP uses many specific **match** commands, as the next couple of examples show. BGP can use route maps to call an AS-Path rather than an ACL to control routing information. Table 2-2 lists the syntax for the **match as-path** command.

Table 2-2   match as-path *Command*

Command	Description
match as-path *[1-199]*	Used in BGP to match an autonomous system list. The valid path list is 1–199.

You can use this command in BGP to match the autonomous system path (AS_PATH) attribute.

Another BGP-specific **match** command is **match community**. You can use route maps to match and set the COMMUNITY attribute(s) in BGP.

The syntax for the **match community** command is as follows:

match [community|extcommunity|exactmatch]

The **community** keyword is used in BGP to call an IP community list. The valid range is 1 through 99 for a standard community list, and 100 through 199 for an expanded community list; alternatively, you can use **exact-match** to perform precise matching of communities.

You can use route maps to base the selection of the global address pool on the output interface as well as an ACL match for NAT. The **match interface** command is used in NAT applications. You can also use it to match routes whose next-hop address is an interface, such as a static route pointing at an interface. Table 2-3 shows the syntax for the **match interface** command.

Table 2-3   match interface *Command*

Command	Description
match interface *interface_name*	Used in route maps for NAT to match the output interface, or routes that have an interface as the next-hop address rather than an IP address.

Tags very effectively enable you to control and track routes during redistribution. Cisco routers enable the network engineer to mark certain routes with a numeric value. A tag value is an extra value that is transported along by the routing protocol. The tag value does not influence router forwarding decisions and has no intrinsic value to the routing protocol. The tag is used primarily during redistribution to *tag* or *flag* routes. After a route has been *tagged*, the tag value can be acted on during the redistribution process to control route redistribution. Tags are supported in RIPv2, OSPF, Integrated IS-IS, EIGRP, BGP, and CLNS. IGRP and RIPv1 do not support tags. To view tags, use the **show eigrp topology** *ip_address subnet_mask* and the **show ip ospf database** commands for EIGRP and OSPF, respectively. You can also view the tag value by using the extended **show ip route** command **show ip route** *ip_address*.Table 2-4 shows the syntax for the **match tag** command.

Table 2-4   match tag *Command*

Command	Description
match tag *[0-4294967295]*	Use the **match tag** command to match tag values in routing protocols such as RIPv2, IS-IS, OSPF, EIGRP, BGP, and CLNS.

You can also use route maps to match specific route types in Cisco IOS Software 12.0. For instance, you can match EIGRP external routes or OSPF external type 1 or type 2 routes. The **match route-type** keyword enables you to match the following route types:

- OSPF external type 1 (O E1) and type 2 routes (O E2), NSSA external type 1 (O N1) type 2 (O N2), intra-area routes (O), and interarea routes (O IA)
- EIGRP external routes (D EX)
- IS-IS level 1 routes (L1) and level 2 routes (L2)
- BGP external routes

The syntax for the **match route-type** command is as follows:

```
Match route-type {local|internal|external[type-1|type-2]|level-1|level2|nssa-external}
```

You can use the following keywords with the **match route-type** command:

External—External route (BGP, EIGRP, and OSPF type 1/2)

Internal—Internal route (including OSPF intra/interarea and EIGRP routes)

level-1—IS-IS level 1 route

level-2—IS-IS level 2 route

local—BGP locally generated route

nssa-external—NSSA external route

Although you can use multiple **match** statements in a single line, you should use only one **match** criterion per line. This will make troubleshooting and modifying the route map easier.

Practical Example: Matching Tags

Manipulating the model from the preceding practical example, the following example has the router clanton running OSPF and IGRP as the routing protocols. The clanton router will call a route map on redistribution. This route map will redistribute routes with a tag of 3 and OSPF external type 1 (O E1) routes into IGRP. Figure 2-2 shows the new network model.

Figure 2-2   *Route Map Practical Example: Matching Tags*

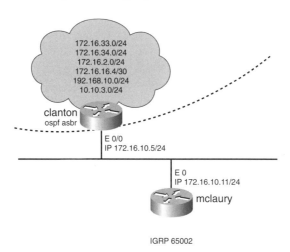

Example 2-8 lists the route table of the clanton router, with the OSPF external type-1 routes highlighted. Example 2-9 lists the OSPF database on the clanton router, highlighting the routes that have a tag of 3.

Example 2-8   *Route Table of the clanton Router*

```
clanton# show ip route
Codes: C - connected, S - static, I - IGRP, R - RIP, M - mobile, B - BGP
       D - EIGRP, EX - EIGRP external, O - OSPF, IA - OSPF inter area
       N1 - OSPF NSSA external type 1, N2 - OSPF NSSA external type 2
       E1 - OSPF external type 1, E2 - OSPF external type 2, E - EGP
       i - IS-IS, L1 - IS-IS level-1, L2 - IS-IS level-2, * - candidate default
       U - per-user static route, o - ODR
Gateway of last resort is not set
O E1 192.168.10.0/24 [110/20] via 172.16.10.10, 01:59:17, Ethernet0/0
     172.16.0.0/16 is variably subnetted, 6 subnets, 2 masks
O E2    172.16.33.0/24 [110/10] via 172.16.10.10, 01:49:44, Ethernet0/0
O E2    172.16.34.0/24 [110/10] via 172.16.10.10, 01:49:44, Ethernet0/0
O E2    172.16.16.0/30 [110/10] via 172.16.10.10, 01:49:44, Ethernet0/0
C       172.16.10.0/24 is directly connected, Ethernet0/0
O E2    172.16.2.0/24 [110/10] via 172.16.10.10, 01:49:44, Ethernet0/0
     10.0.0.0/24 is subnetted, 1 subnets
O E1    10.10.3.0 [110/20] via 172.16.10.10, 01:59:18, Ethernet0/0
clanton#
```

Example 2-9 *OSPF Database of the clanton Router*

```
clanton# show ip ospf database
        OSPF Router with ID (172.16.10.5) (Process ID 7)

                   Router Link States (Area 0)
Link ID          ADV Router      Age       Seq#       Checksum Link count
172.16.10.5      172.16.10.5     557       0x80000006 0x22D3   1
192.168.10.10    192.168.10.10   1642      0x80000005 0x7A12   1
                 Net Link States (Area 0)
Link ID          ADV Router      Age       Seq#       Checksum
172.16.10.5      172.16.10.5     557       0x80000005 0x7FD5
                 Type-5 AS External Link States
Link ID          ADV Router      Age       Seq#       Checksum Tag
10.10.3.0        192.168.10.10   1642      0x80000004 0x9904   500
172.16.2.0       192.168.10.10   1133      0x80000005 0x87DF   3
172.16.16.4      192.168.10.10   1642      0x80000004 0x45A1   500
172.16.33.0      192.168.10.10   1133      0x80000005 0x3117   3
172.16.34.0      192.168.10.10   1133      0x80000005 0x2621   3
192.168.10.0     192.168.10.10   1643      0x80000004 0x95AB   500
clanton#
```

To control redistribution between OSPF and IGRP, use a route map on the redistribution process. The route map to accomplish must have two route map instances. The first route map instance will match all routes in OSPF that have a tag value of 3. The second route map instance will match OSPF external type 1 routes. Example 2-10 lists the significant portions of the configuration on the clanton router.

Example 2-10 *Route Map Configuration on the clanton Router*

```
hostname clanton
!
router ospf 7
 network 172.16.10.5 0.0.0.0 area 0
!
router igrp 65002
 redistribute ospf 7 route-map match_me      ←Redistribute OSPF and call the route-map
 network 172.16.0.0
 default-metric 10000 100 254 1 1500
!
route-map match_match_me permit 10
 match tag 3                                 ←Match routes with a tag 3
!
route-map match_match_me permit 20
 match route-type external type-1            ←Match OSPF external type-1 routes
```

To verify redistribution and that the route maps worked properly, view the route table of the mclaury router. Example 2-11 lists the route table of the mclaury router. Notice that routes with a tag value of 3 are present: 172.16.2.0/24, 172.16.33.0/24, and 172.16.34.0/24. Also, notice that the OSPF external type 1 routes are present: 192.168.10.0/24 and 10.0.0.0/8 as summarized subnets.

Example 2-11 *Route Table of the mclaury Router*

```
mclaury# show ip route
Codes: C - connected, S - static, I - IGRP, R - RIP, M - mobile, B - BGP
       D - EIGRP, EX - EIGRP external, O - OSPF, IA - OSPF inter area
       N1 - OSPF NSSA external type 1, N2 - OSPF NSSA external type 2
       E1 - OSPF external type 1, E2 - OSPF external type 2, E - EGP
       i - IS-IS, L1 - IS-IS level-1, L2 - IS-IS level-2, ia - IS-IS inter area
       * - candidate default, U - per-user static route, o - ODR
       P - periodic downloaded static route
Gateway of last resort is not set
I    192.168.10.0/24 [100/1200] via 172.16.10.5, 00:00:50, Ethernet0
     172.16.0.0/24 is subnetted, 4 subnets
I       172.16.33.0 [100/1200] via 172.16.10.5, 00:00:50, Ethernet0
I       172.16.34.0 [100/1200] via 172.16.10.5, 00:00:50, Ethernet0
C       172.16.10.0 is directly connected, Ethernet0
I       172.16.2.0 [100/1200] via 172.16.10.5, 00:00:50, Ethernet0
I    10.0.0.0/8 [100/1200] via 172.16.10.5, 00:00:50, Ethernet0
mclaury#
```

You can also use route maps to match a route's metric. This is the metric for the route as it appears in the route/forwarding table. If an OSPF route has an associated metric of 20, for instance, **match metric 20** is used to match this route. Table 2-5 lists the syntax used with the **match metric** command.

Table 2-5   **match metric** *Command*

Command	Description
match metric [0-4294967295]	Enter the metric value as it appears in the route/forwarding table of the router.

Using Figure 2-1 as a guide, Example 2-12 lists the route table of the clanton router followed by the route map configuration used to match the OSPF routes with a metric of 20. This example redistributes OSPF routes into EIGRP routes that have a metric of 20.

Example 2-12 *Demonstration of the **match metric** Route Map*

```
clanton# show ip route
Codes: C - connected, S - static, I - IGRP, R - RIP, M - mobile, B - BGP
       D - EIGRP, EX - EIGRP external, O - OSPF, IA - OSPF inter area
       N1 - OSPF NSSA external type 1, N2 - OSPF NSSA external type 2
       E1 - OSPF external type 1, E2 - OSPF external type 2, E - EGP
       i - IS-IS, L1 - IS-IS level-1, L2 - IS-IS level-2, * - candidate default
       U - per-user static route, o - ODR
```

continues

Example 2-12 *Demonstration of the* **match metric** *Route Map (Continued)*

```
Gateway of last resort is not set
O E1 192.168.10.0/24 [110/20] via 172.16.10.10, 00:19:58, Ethernet0/0
        172.16.0.0/16 is variably subnetted, 6 subnets, 2 masks
O E2    172.16.33.0/24 [110/10] via 172.16.10.10, 00:19:59, Ethernet0/0
O E2    172.16.34.0/24 [110/10] via 172.16.10.10, 00:19:59, Ethernet0/0
O E1    172.16.16.4/30 [110/20] via 172.16.10.10, 00:19:59, Ethernet0/0
O E2    172.16.16.0/30 [110/10] via 172.16.10.10, 00:19:59, Ethernet0/0
C       172.16.10.0/24 is directly connected, Ethernet0/0
O E2    172.16.2.0/24 [110/10] via 172.16.10.10, 00:19:59, Ethernet0/0
        10.0.0.0/24 is subnetted, 1 subnets
O E1    10.10.3.0 [110/20] via 172.16.10.10, 00:19:59, Ethernet0/0

hostname clanton
!
<<<text omitted>>>
!
router ospf 7
 network 172.16.10.5 0.0.0.0 area 0
!
router eigrp 65002
 redistribute ospf 7 route-map match_metric_20
 network 172.16.0.0
 default-metric 10000 100 254 1 1500
!
ip classless
!
route-map match_metric_20 permit 10
 match metric 20
!
```

In the preceding example, the routes 10.10.3.0/24, 172.16.16.4/30, and 192.168.10.0/24 were redistributed into EIGRP.

The **match clns address** command is used in ISO CLNS routing much in the same way that it is used in IP routing. The **match clns address** command calls a CLNS address list and compares the address being testing against it. The **next-hop** and **route-source** keywords are used to call an OSI filter set during policy routing. Use the CLNS commands in the same manner as their IP counterparts. The syntax of the **match clns** command is as follows:

```
match clns {address [name]|next-hop [filter set]|route-source [filter set]}
```

Use the **match clns address** command to match routes that have a network address matching one or more in the specified OSI filter set.

The **next-hop** keyword is used to match routes that have a next-hop address matching one or more in the specified OSI filter set.

The **route-source** keyword is used to match routes that have been advertised by routers matching one or more in the specified OSI filter set.

The last **match** command discussed here is the **match length** command. This **match** statement is used primarily in policy routing when ACLs are insufficient for proper traffic distribution. The **match length** command enables you to match the Layer 3 packet length in bytes, including headers and trailers. You can use a route map such as this to send little interactive packets, such as Telnet traffic, one way, and large bulk-data transfers, such as a large FTP transfer, another way. Table 2-6 lists the syntax for the **match length** command.

Table 2-6   match length *Command*

Command	Description
Match length [*min_packet_length_0-2147483647*] [*max_packet_length_0-2147483647*]	Used to match the Layer 3 packet length in bytes with all associated headers and trailers included. You must enter the minimum and maximum packet length.

For an example of the **match length** command, see the later section "Configuring Policy-Based Routing (PBR)."

set Commands

The **set** commands are executed after a successful match has been made in the route map instance. The **set** command is optional and may be omitted. If you are using route maps on redistribution, or just to filter networks, for instance, there is no need to use a **set** command unless you want to *tag* or further influence the route. If no **match** statements are present in the route map instance, all **set** commands are executed for all routes. You may also use multiple **set** commands in each route map instance. The **set** commands discussed here are supported in Cisco IOS Software Release 12.2 and are listed in Table 2-7. The **set** commands have been divided into three categories: BGP-specific **set** commands, routing protocol/redistribution-specific **set** commands, and policy-routing specific **set** commands. The policy-routing specific **set** commands are covered in the upcoming section "Configuring Policy-Based Routing (PBR)."

Table 2-7   set *Commands*

set Command	Description
BGP-specific **set** *commands*	
as-path	Prepend string for a BGP AS_PATH attribute
community|extcommunity	Set BGP COMMUNITY attributes
comm-list	BGP community list for deletion
dampening	Set BGP route flap dampening parameters
local-preference	Set BGP LOCAL_PREF path attribute

continues

Table 2-7 *set Commands (Continued)*

set Command	Description
BGP-specific set commands (Continued)	
origin	Set BGP origin code
weight	Set BGP weight
Routing protocol/redistribution-specific set commands	
metric	Set metric value for destination routing protocol
metric-type	Type of metric for destination routing protocol
tag|automatic-tag	Tag value for destination routing protocol
Policy-routing specific set commands	
default	Set default routing information
interface	Set the Output interface, used in point-to-point links
ip	IP-specific information

BGP-Specific set Commands

The first **set** commands covered here are the ones related to BGP. This section discusses the syntax of the various **set** commands for BGP and their basic application. For more specific and detailed information on the application of the BGP-specific **set** commands, see Chapter 8, "Introduction to BGP-4 Configuration," and Chapter 9, "Advanced BGP Configuration."

The **set as-path** command is used in BGP to prepend one or more autonomous systems to the well-known mandatory transitive AS_PATH attribute. In BGP, this can be used to influence routing decisions. BGP views routes that have one or more autonomous systems prepended to the current AS_PATH attribute as less desirable, which can prove useful in a multihomed BGP network.

CAUTION   The purpose of the **prepend** command is essentially to make the AS_PATH longer—thereby forming a less desirable path—not to completely change it. When using the **set as-path prepend** command in production environments, always use the same ASN that the route is from. If a different ASN is used, and that autonomous system is encountered by the advertised route, the receiving autonomous system/router will not accept the route. Modifying the AS_PATH by prepending a different autonomous system directly affects the inherent loop prevention provided by the AS_PATH attribute. Some Cisco IOS Software levels will not even enable you to enter an AS_PATH different from your own. For educational purposes, some of the examples in this text show the prepending of different autonomous systems; this is done to highlight the placement of the prepended autonomous system only.

Note an important difference in how the **prepend** command works with inbound and outbound route maps. When the **prepend** command is used on outbound route maps, the prepended autonomous system is added after the advertising router's autonomous system. This is because the prepended autonomous system will be in place before the route update is sent. When the update is sent, the advertising router's autonomous system is the first one on the list. If you prepend AS 10 10 to an outbound route map, for instance, and your router's autonomous system is 5, the receiving router/neighbor will have an AS_PATH of 5 10 10.

If you apply the **prepend** command on an inbound route map, the autonomous system that is prepended will actually precede the originating AS_PATH. This is because the autonomous system prepend is happening after the route has been received from its neighbor. If you prepend AS 10 10 on an inbound route map, and the router/neighbor you are receiving the route from has the AS_PATH of 5 500, for example, the AS_PATH to that route will be 10 10 5 500. The syntax for the **set as-path** command is as follows:

```
set as-path {prepend [as_path1|as_path2|as_path3]|[tag]}
```

Use the **set as-path** command in BGP networks to modify the AS_PATH attribute, by prepending one or more autonomous systems to it. You can use this command on inbound and outbound route maps.

The **tag** keyword is used in BGP to recover the AS_PATH information from the tags of Interior Gateway Protocol (IGP)-redistributed routes.

The **set as-path tag** command is used in BGP when doing redistribution to preserve a consistent and correct AS_PATH across an IGP. The Cisco BGP implementation automatically conveys AS_PATH in the form of a tag when redistributing BGP into an IGP. When redistributing IGP routes into BGP, however, AS_PATH information is lost. To recover the AS_PATH information from the tag of a redistributed IGP, use the **set as-path tag** command.

Practical Example: Setting the AS_PATH

The network model shown in Figure 2-3 has two routers running BGP between them. The turkey_creek router is in autonomous system 65001, and the ringo router is in autonomous system 65002. The router turkey_creek will advertise the network 192.168.192.0/24 via BGP. In this example, a route map will be used to prepend the AS_PATH with autonomous system 65001 2001 on outbound updates from the turkey_creek router.

Figure 2-3 *Route Map Practical Example: Setting the AS_PATH*

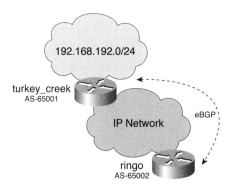

Example 2-13 lists the configuration to manipulate the AS_PATH attribute on the turkey_creek router.

Example 2-13 *BGP Configuration of the turkey_creek Router*

```
hostname turkey_creek
!
<<<text omitted>>>
!
router bgp 65001
 no synchronization
 network 192.168.192.0
 neighbor 172.16.100.10 remote-as 65002
 neighbor 172.16.100.10 ebgp-multihop 10
 neighbor 172.16.100.10 update-source Loopback20
 neighbor 172.16.100.10 route-map set_as out      ←Call route-map "set_as" for
                                                   outbound updates
!
route-map set_as permit 10
 set as-path prepend 65001 2001                    ←prepend AS-PATH with 65001 2001
!
```

You might be tempted to think that the AS_PATH for route 192.168.192.0/24 would read 65001 2001 65001; after all, the command says "prepend." Because this is an outbound route map, however, the prepended autonomous system will occur before the advertisement is sent. Therefore, the "prepended" AS_PATH will appear after the originating autonomous system to the downstream router. The AS_PATH on the downstream router, the ringo router, will read 65001 65001 2001. Example 2-14 demonstrates this by listing the output of the **show ip bgp** command on the ringo router.

Example 2-14 **show ip bgp** *Command on the ringo Router*

```
ringo# show ip bgp 192.168.192.0
BGP routing table entry for 192.168.192.0/24, version 4
Paths: (1 available, best #1, table Default-IP-Routing-Table)
  Not advertised to any peer
  65001 65001 2001
     172.16.200.10 (metric 1915392) from 172.16.200.10 (192.168.192.7)
       Origin IGP, metric 0, localpref 100, valid, external, best
ringo#
```

Example 2-15 applies the route map to inbound updates on the ringo router. The route map will append the AS_PATH 2001 65002 65001 to the routes from the turkey_creek router. Because this is an inbound route map, the final AS_PATH on the ringo router will read 2001 65002 65001 65001. On inbound route maps, the prepend functions like its name implies. Example 2-15 lists the relevant portions of the configuration of the ringo router, followed by the **show ip bgp** command.

Example 2-15 *Configuration of the ringo Router, and the* **show ip bgp** *Command*

```
Hostname ringo
!
<<<text omitted>>>
!
router bgp 65002
 no synchronization
 bgp log-neighbor-changes
 neighbor 172.16.200.10 remote-as 65001
 neighbor 172.16.200.10 ebgp-multihop 10
 neighbor 172.16.200.10 update-source Loopback20
 neighbor 172.16.200.10 route-map modify_as in      ←Route-map "modify_as" is called
!
route-map modify_as permit 10
 set as-path prepend 2001 65002 65001              ←Prepended AS
!

ringo# show ip bgp 192.168.192.0
BGP routing table entry for 192.168.192.0/24, version 2
Paths: (1 available, best #1, table Default-IP-Routing-Table)
  Not advertised to any peer
  2001 65002 65001 65001
     172.16.200.10 (metric 1915392) from 172.16.200.10 (192.168.192.7)
       Origin IGP, metric 0, localpref 100, valid, external, best
ringo#
```

The **set community** command is used in BGP to set various community attributes. As discussed in the later chapters on BGP, communities can be a powerful and efficient way to apply policies to a group of routes. The community is an optional transitive route attribute and communicated among BGP peers. The **set community** command enables you to form community membership. After routes become members of a community, they can be assigned policies, such as "do not export this route to any E-BGP neighbors or advertise this route the Internet community." To send the community attribute in BGP, the **neighbor a.b.c.d send-community** command must be used.

The syntax for the **set community** command in Cisco IOS Software Release 12.2 is as follows:

```
set community {community-number_1-4294967200|AA|NN|no-export|no-advertise |internet
|local-AS [additive]}|none
```

Use the **set community** command to designate or form communities from routes and to apply specific policies to those routes. The valid parameters and values are as follows:

- *Community number*—A valid number from 1 to 4,294,967,200; the routes will be designated to this community number.

- *AA:NN*—This format can also be used to designate communities. The *AA* is a 16-bit ASN between 1 and 65,535. *NN* is an arbitrary 16-bit number between 1 and 65,440.

- **Internet**—The Internet community. Advertise these routes to the Internet community and any router belonging to it.

- **no-export**—Do not advertise these routes to an E-BGP peer. Routes with this community are sent to peers in other subautonomous systems within a confederation.

- **local-as**—Do not advertise these routes to peers outside the local autonomous system. These routes will not be advertised to other autonomous systems or subautonomous systems if confederations are in place.

- **no-advertise**—Do not advertise these routes to any peer (internal or external). Used for I-BGP peers.

- **Additive**—(Optional) Adds the community to the already existing communities.

- **None**—Removes the COMMUNITY attribute from the prefixes that pass the route map.

Practical Example: Setting BGP Community Attributes

Consider the same network model from the preceding example, with the turkey_creek and the ringo routers running BGP between them. (See Figure 2-4.) The turkey_creek router is in AS 65001, and the ringo router is in AS 65002. The router turkey_creek will advertise the network 192.168.192.0/24 via BGP and place it in community 7. The turkey_creek router will also advertise another route, 128.168.192.0/24. The turkey_creek router will put this route in community 8 and set the COMMUNITY attribute to **no-export**. The **no-export** COMMUNITY attribute will instruct the ringo router not to advertise this route to E-BGP neighbors.

Figure 2-4   *Route Map Practical Example: Setting Communities*

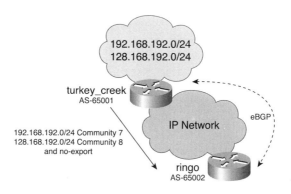

Example 2-16 lists the route map used to accomplish this.

Example 2-16 *Route Map for Communities on turkey_creek*

```
Hostname turkey_creek
!
<<<text omitted>>>
!
router bgp 65001
 no synchronization
 network 128.168.192.0 mask 255.255.255.0
 network 192.168.192.0
 neighbor 172.16.100.10 remote-as 65002
 neighbor 172.16.100.10 ebgp-multihop 10
 neighbor 172.16.100.10 update-source Loopback20
 neighbor 172.16.100.10 send-community        ←send-community must be enabled
 neighbor 172.16.100.10 route-map set_communities out ←route-map "set_communities"
called
!
<<<text omitted>>>
!
access-list 10 permit 192.168.192.0 0.0.0.255      ←allow network 192.168.192.0/24 only
access-list 11 permit 128.168.192.0 0.0.0.255      ←allow network 128.168.192.0/24 only
!
route-map set_communities permit 100
 match ip address 10                      ←Match ip access-list 10 or 192.168.192.0/24
 set community 7                            ←set the community to 7
!
route-map set_communities permit 200
 match ip address 11                      ←Match ip access-list 11 or 128.168.192.0/24
 set community 8 no-export               ←set the community to 8 and don't export to
                                          future E-BGP peers
```

By observing the routes on the ringo router, you can see that route 192.168.192.0/24 is in community 7. Route 128.168.192.0/24 is in community 8 with the **no-export** option set. Example 2-17 lists the output of the **show ip bgp** command on the ringo router.

Example 2-17 *Routes with Communities Set on the ring Router*

```
ringo# show ip bgp 192.168.192.0
BGP routing table entry for 192.168.192.0/24, version 3
Paths: (1 available, best #1, table Default-IP-Routing-Table)
  Not advertised to any peer
  65001
    172.16.200.10 (metric 1915392) from 172.16.200.10 (192.168.192.7)
      Origin IGP, metric 0, localpref 100, valid, external, best
      Community: 7
ringo#
ringo#show ip bgp 128.168.192.0
BGP routing table entry for 128.168.192.0/24, version 2
Paths: (1 available, best #1, table Default-IP-Routing-Table, not advertised to
EBGP peer)
  Not advertised to any peer
  65001
    172.16.200.10 (metric 1915392) from 172.16.200.10 (192.168.192.7)
      Origin IGP, metric 0, localpref 100, valid, external, best
      Community: 8 no-export
ringo#
```

Use the **set comm-list delete** command to remove the COMMUNITY attribute of an inbound or outbound route update. The syntax is as follows:

```
set comm-list {[standard | extended community list]} delete
```

For more examples of the various **set communities** commands and how they function in BGP, see Chapters 7 through 9 on configuring BGP.

Another BGP-specific feature that you can set is dampening. Because of the long time it takes BGP networks to converge, an unstable route, or "route flapping," can have significant and detrimental impacts on large BGP networks. If a route goes down, a WITHDRAWN message is sent via BGP requesting all peers to remove that route from their tables. An instable route in your autonomous system will cause constant sending and withdrawing of messages to other autonomous systems. This effect multiplied by the hundreds or thousands of routes that may be in an autonomous system can negatively affect BGP.

Dampening allows routers to categorize routes as either well behaved or ill behaved. Obviously, a *well-behaved* route should be very stable over an extended period of time. On the other end of the spectrum, an *ill-behaved* route could be a route that is unstable, or flapping. When route dampening is enabled in BGP, with the BGP router command **bgp dampening**, the router will start a history file on how many times each route flaps. The route dampening feature will start to assign a penalty to a route each time it flaps. The penalties start to accumulate for each route, and when the penalty is greater than an arbitrary number called the *suppress value*, the route will no longer be advertised. The route will remain suppressed until either the penalty falls below the reuse-limit or the max_suppress timer is exceeded. The penalty for a route can be decreased over time. The half-life timer is a timer, expressed in minutes, that must elapse before the penalty will be reduced by one-half. If the route remains stable, over time the penalty for that route will decrease. When the penalty is below another arbitrary timer called the reuse-limit, the route will be unsuppressed and advertised once again. Figure 2-5 illustrates the time and penalty relationship in route dampening.

Figure 2-5   *Route Dampening Timer Relationship*

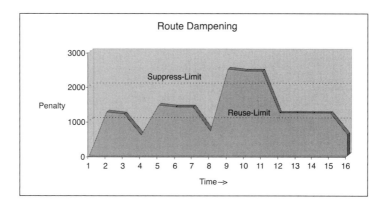

Note that this type of route map is called from the BGP router command **bgp dampening** [**route-map** *route-map_name*]. A route map called on the **neighbor** statement will not work for route dampening.

The **set dampening** command in Cisco IOS Software Release 12.2 is as follows:

```
set dampening {half-life_1-45 reuse_1-20000 suppress_1-20000 max_suppress_time_1-255}
```

Use the **set dampening** command to influence how the router will react when it encounters unstable routes. The **half-life** parameter represents a time (in minutes) that must pass with a route being stable, after which the penalty value is reduced by half. The default is 15 minutes, and the valid range is 1 to 45 minutes.

The **reuse** parameter enables you to mark a point, or a reuse, point that allows the route to be advertised. When the penalty value falls below the reuse point, the route is unsuppressed and re-advertised. The default value is 750, and the valid ranges are 1 to 20,000.

When the penalty exceeds the **suppress** parameter, the route is suppressed and no longer advertised. The valid range is from 1 to 20,000; the default is 2000.

The **max_suppress_time** is a value expressed in minutes that specifies how long a route should be suppressed by the dampening feature. The default value of this is 4 times the half-life timer, or 60 minutes. The valid range is from 1 to 255 minutes.

When a prefix is withdrawn, BGP considers the withdrawn prefix as a flap and increases the penalty by 1000. When BGP receives an attribute change, the penalty is increased by 500.

In Figure 2-6, the router ringo is advertising 129.168.192.0/24 to the turkey_creek router via BGP.

Figure 2-6 *Route Dampening*

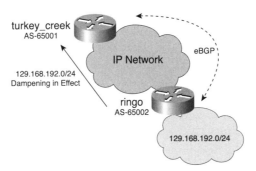

The turkey_creek router has route dampening enabled, with a route map to apply the dampening to route 129.168.192.0/24. Use the **show ip bgp dampened-paths** command and the **show ip bgp a.b.c.d** command to view whether route dampening has occurred and to view what the current penalty count. Note that information related to the dampening does not appear until the route has actually flapped. Example 2-18 shows the penalty and dampening occurring on the turkey_creek router for route 129.168.192.0/24.

Example 2-18 *Verifying Dampening*

```
turkey_creek# show ip bgp dampened-paths
BGP table version is 9, local router ID is 192.168.192.7
Status codes: s suppressed, d damped, h history, * valid, > best, i - internal
Origin codes: i - IGP, e - EGP, ? - incomplete
   Network          From          Reuse    Path
*d 129.168.192.0/24 172.16.100.10   00:38:00 65002 i
turkey_creek#
turkey_creek# show ip bgp
BGP table version is 9, local router ID is 192.168.192.7
Status codes: s suppressed, d damped, h history, * valid, > best, i - internal
Origin codes: i - IGP, e - EGP, ? - incomplete
   Network          Next Hop          Metric LocPrf Weight Path
*> 128.168.192.0/24 0.0.0.0                0          32768 i
*d 129.168.192.0/24 172.16.100.10          0              0 65002 i
*> 192.168.192.0    0.0.0.0                0          32768 i
turkey_creek#
turkey_creek# show ip bgp 129.168.192.0
BGP routing table entry for 129.168.192.0/24, version 9
```

Example 2-18 *Verifying Dampening (Continued)*

```
Paths: (1 available, no best path)
  Not advertised to any peer
  65002, (suppressed due to dampening)
    172.16.100.10 (metric 2323456) from 172.16.100.10 (172.16.100.10)
      Origin IGP, metric 0, localpref 100, valid, external, ref 2
      Dampinfo: penalty 3717, flapped 4 times in 00:04:36, reuse in 00:37:50
turkey_creek#
```

Example 2-19 lists the BGP configuration for the preceding example and the associated route maps of the turkey_creek router.

Example 2-19 *Configuration of the turkey_creek Router*

```
hostname turkey_creek
!
<<<text omitted>>>
!
router bgp 65001
 no synchronization
 bgp dampening route-map set_dampening      ←Dampening enabled with route-map
 network 128.168.192.0 mask 255.255.255.0
 network 192.168.192.0
 neighbor 172.16.100.10 remote-as 65002
 neighbor 172.16.100.10 ebgp-multihop 10
 neighbor 172.16.100.10 update-source Loopback20
!
access-list 11 permit 129.168.192.0 0.0.0.255
!
route-map set_dampening permit 100
 match ip address 11                        ←Match network 129.168.192.0/24
 set dampening 20 1000 2000 80              ←Set dampening parameters
```

For more information and examples on route dampening, see BGP Chapters 7 through 9.

You can also use route maps in BGP to set the well-known discretionary LOCAL_PREF attribute. The LOCAL_PREF attribute is a numeric value ranging from 0 to 4,294,967,295, where the higher the value, the more preferred the route is. The default LOCAL_PREF value is 100. Table 2-8 lists the syntax used in setting the LOCAL_PREF attribute.

Table 2-8   **set local-preference** *Command in Cisco IOS Software Release 12.2*

Command	Description
set local-preference {0-4294967295}	Use the **set local-preference** command to set the LOCAL_PREF of a route. The valid range is from 0 to 4,294,967,295. The default value is 100.

Another BGP attribute that you can set with route maps is the well known mandatory transitive ORIGIN attribute. The ORIGIN attribute is a well-known mandatory attribute. The ORIGIN attribute, as the name states, specifies the origin of the route with respect to the autonomous system that originated it. BGP supports three different types of origin:

- **IGP(i)**—The network layer reachability information (NLRI) is internal to the originating autonomous system. This is a remote IGP system. The route originates from the network command.

- **EGP(e)**—The NLRI is learned via the EGP. This is a local EGP system. The route is redistributed from EGP.

- **Incomplete(?)**—The NLRI is learned from some other means. The route is redistributed from an IGP or static.

Table 2-9 lists the syntax used in setting the origin.

Table 2-9   **set origin** *Command in Cisco IOS Software Release 12.2*

Command	Description
set origin {**igp** | **egp** [*as_number*] | **incomplete**}	Use the **set origin** command to set the ORIGIN attribute of a route/routes. The valid origin types are IGP, EGP, and incomplete.

The final BGP-specific set command discussed here is the **set weight** command. The WEIGHT attribute is a Cisco proprietary feature used to measure a route's preference. The WEIGHT attribute is local to the router and does not get exchanged between routers; therefore it is only effective on inbound route maps. Use the WEIGHT attribute to influence routes from multiple service providers to a central location. Like LOCAL_PREF, assigning a higher weight to a route makes that route more preferred. The WEIGHT attribute also has the highest precedence of any BGP attribute. For more information on BGP, see Chapters 7 through 9. Table 2-10 lists the syntax used in setting the WEIGHT attribute.

Table 2-10   **set weight** *Command in Cisco IOS Software Release 12.2*

Command	Description
set weight {*0-65535*]	Use the **set weight** command to set the weight of a route/routes. The valid weight range is from 0 to 65,535, and the default weight of a route is 32,768.

Practical Example: Configuring BGP Attributes

This practical example uses the same network model as in the previous examples and sets the BGP attributes of LOCAL_PREF, WEIGHT, and ORIGIN. Figure 2-7 is the same network shown earlier. This example calls an inbound route map on the turkey_creek router. The route map set_attributes will set the following attributes: WEIGHT to 1000, LOCAL_PREF to 5000, and ORIGIN to be EGP from autonomous system 65002. In this example, the setting **local-**

preference is for education purposes only. Normally, **local-preference** would not be used or effective on E-BGP peers.

Figure 2-7   *Configuring BGP Attributes*

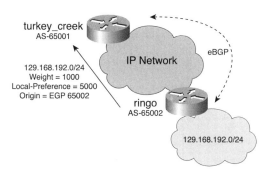

Example 2-20 lists the BGP and route map configuration to accomplish this on the turkey_creek router.

Example 2-20 *BGP Attribute Configuration*

```
hostname turkey_creek
!
<<<text omitted>>>
!
router bgp 65001
 no synchronization
 network 128.168.192.0 mask 255.255.255.0
 network 192.168.192.0
 neighbor 172.16.100.10 remote-as 65002
 neighbor 172.16.100.10 ebgp-multihop 10
 neighbor 172.16.100.10 update-source Loopback20
 neighbor 172.16.100.10 route-map set_attributes in ←call route-map "set_attributes"
!
route-map set_attributes permit 100
 set local-preference 5000      ←Set local-preference to 5000
 set weight 1000                ←Set weight to 1000
 set origin egp 65002           ←Set the ORIGIN to EGP in AS 65002
 !                              ←*note with no match parameter all routes are
                                matched from the neighbor 172.16.100.10
```

To verify the effectiveness of the route map, use the **show ip bgp** command, as demonstrated in Example 2-21.

Example 2-21 *Verifying the Attributes*

```
turkey_creek# show ip bgp
BGP table version is 4, local router ID is 192.168.192.7
Status codes: s suppressed, d damped, h history, * valid, > best, i - internal
Origin codes: i - IGP, e - EGP, ? - incomplete
   Network          Next Hop            Metric LocPrf Weight Path
*> 128.168.192.0/24 0.0.0.0                  0             32768 i
*> 129.168.192.0/24 172.16.100.10            0    5000   1000 65002 e
*> 192.168.192.0    0.0.0.0                  0             32768 i
turkey_creek#
turkey_creek#
turkey_creek# show ip bgp 129.168.192.0
BGP routing table entry for 129.168.192.0/24, version 2
Paths: (1 available, best #1)
  Not advertised to any peer
  65002
    172.16.100.10 (metric 2323456) from 172.16.100.10 (172.16.100.10)
      Origin EGP, metric 0, localpref 5000, weight 1000, valid, external, best,
ref 2
turkey_creek#
```

Configuring Routing Protocol/Redistribution-Specific **set** Commands

The **set** commands covered next relate primarily to IGP routing protocols and are used mostly during route redistribution. The **set metric**, **set metric-type** and **set tag** commands can all be used to change the metric or the tag of a route during redistribution. As mentioned previously, the metrics and tags can also be matched and used for further route control during redistribution.

The most common use of the **set metric** command is to set the metric of the route for the destination routing protocol. If you are redistributing EIGRP routes into OSPF, for example, you can use a route map in conjunction with the **set metric** command to set the new OSPF metric. If you are redistributing into IGRP or EIGRP, the metric value you enter is the composite metric only. This differs slightly from setting the default metric or the metric on redistribution without a route map, where you would set all five submetrics. Another use of the **set metric** command is to set the BGP optional nontransitive MULTI_EXIT_DISC (MED) attribute. The syntax for the **set metric** command in Cisco IOS Software Release 12.2 is as follows:

set metric {[-/+<*0-4294967295*>]|*1-4294967295*]

The + and – keywords enable you to increase or decrease the current metric. To increase the metric by 10, for example, the command would be **set metric +10**. To set just the composite metric for EIGRP, the command is **set metric 4295**. For more information on IGP routing protocol metrics, refer to *CCIE Practical Studies, Volume I*. You can find more information on the BGP MED attribute in Chapters 7 through 9 of this book.

The **set metric-type** command is rather limited. It is used primarily in BGP, OSPF, and IS-IS. You can use it to set IS-IS external and internal metrics and OSPF type 1 and type 2 external metrics. The **set metric-type** command can also be used in BGP to use the IGP metric as the MED for BGP. The syntax for the **set metric-type** command in Cisco IOS Software Release 12.2 is as follows:

```
set metric-type [internal|external|type-1|type-2]
```

- **external**—IS-IS external metric.
- **internal**—Use the metric of the IGP as the MED for BGP. Also used for setting IS-IS internal metric.
- **type-1**—Use to match the OSPF type 1 metric.
- **type-2**—Use to match the OSPF external type 2 metric.

The final **set** command discussed in this section is the **set tag** command. The **set tag** command enables you to set the administrative tag of route. For IGPs, the tag value is usually set with a route map and the **set tag** command. In BGP, when you redistribute BGP into an IGP, the ASN of BGP is automatically put into the tag value. BGP does this to preserve the AS_PATH attribute across an IGP domain. For IGPs, the tag is an administrative value that certain routing protocols carry within the routing update. The tag value has no impact on routing decisions. Instead, it is used to mark routes or flag routes or to track the AS_PATH for BGP. The tag value may also be acted upon during a redistribution process. When the **automatic-tag** command is used with the BGP **table-map** command, the tag value includes the ASN and the origin. The syntax used to manipulate the tag value in Cisco IOS Software Release 12.2 is as follows:

```
set {tag [0-4294967295]|automatic-tag}
```

Use the **set tag** *value* command to set the tag value. Use the **set automatic-tag** command when redistributing an IGP into BGP to recover the tag value as an AS_PATH attribute.

NOTE   You can also use the tag value strictly for documentation purposes in an internetwork. If you have an OSPF domain, where RIP routes and EIGRP routes are redistributed, for example, you may want to tag the routes from EIGRP with a value of 100 and tag the routes from IGRP with a value of 110. When the OSPF database is viewed, it will be easy to determine the origin of specific routes. This can prove a handy documentation tool for troubleshooting route redistribution.

Tags are supported in RIPv2, OSPF, Integrated IS-IS, EIGRP, BGP, and CLNS. IGRP and RIPv1 do not support tags. To view tags, use the **show ip eigrp topology** *ip_address subnet_mask* command and the **show ip ospf database** command for EIGRP and OSPF, respectively. You can also view the tag value in other routing protocols by using the extended **show ip route** command, **show ip route** *ip_address*.

Practical Example: Setting Route Tags and Metric Types

In the internetwork model in Figure 2-8, the routers turkey_creek, earp, holliday, and ringo are running EIGRP. The ringo router also has a BGP peer to the turkey_creek router and is running OSPF and to the clanton router.

Figure 2-8 *Route Tagging and Metric Setting*

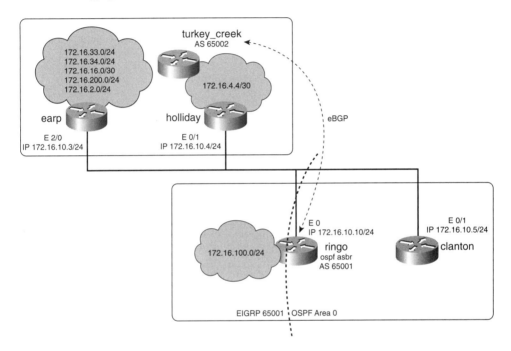

To demonstrate route tagging and metric setting, the following example writes a route map on the ringo router. The route map will be used on the ringo router when redistributing EIGRP routes into OSPF. The route map will first tag the routes from the earp router, 172.16.10.3, with a tag of 3. Next, the route map will tag all other routes with a tag of 500 while making these routes OSPF external type 1 routes. Example 2-22 lists the configuration to accomplish this on the ringo router.

Example 2-22 *Configuration of the ringo Router*

```
hostname ringo
!
<<<text omitted>>>
!
router eigrp 65001
 redistribute bgp 65002
 network 172.16.0.0
```

Example 2-22 *Configuration of the ringo Router (Continued)*

```
 network 192.168.10.0
 default-metric 10000 1000 254 1 1500
 no auto-summary
 eigrp log-neighbor-changes
!
router ospf 7
 log-adjacency-changes
 redistribute eigrp 65001 subnets route-map set_tag3  ←Redistribute and call route-map
 redistribute bgp 65002
 network 172.16.10.10 0.0.0.0 area 0
 default-metric 10
!
router bgp 65002
 no synchronization
 bgp log-neighbor-changes
 neighbor 172.16.200.10 remote-as 65001
 neighbor 172.16.200.10 ebgp-multihop 10
 neighbor 172.16.200.10 update-source Loopback20
!
access-list 5 permit 172.16.10.3      ←Match routes from 172.16.10.3
access-list 50 permit any             ←Match all routes
!
route-map set_tag3 permit 100
 match ip route-source 5              ←Match routes from 172.16.10.3
 set tag 3                            ←Set the TAG value to 3
!
route-map set_tag3 permit 200
 match ip address 50                  ←Match all other routes
 set metric-type type-1               ←Set the OSPF metric to External Type-1
 set tag 500                          ←Set the TAG value to 500
!
```

By observing the route table of the ringo router followed by the OSPF database, you can see the effects of the route maps, as shown in Example 2-23.

Example 2-23 *Route Map Effects on the ringo Router*

```
ringo# show ip route
Codes: C - connected, S - static, I - IGRP, R - RIP, M - mobile, B - BGP
       D - EIGRP, EX - EIGRP external, O - OSPF, IA - OSPF inter area
       N1 - OSPF NSSA external type 1, N2 - OSPF NSSA external type 2
       E1 - OSPF external type 1, E2 - OSPF external type 2, E - EGP
       i - IS-IS, L1 - IS-IS level-1, L2 - IS-IS level-2, ia - IS-IS inter area
       * - candidate default, U - per-user static route, o - ODR
       P - periodic downloaded static route
Gateway of last resort is not set
B    192.168.192.0/24 [20/0] via 172.16.200.10, 01:07:04
     172.16.0.0/16 is variably subnetted, 8 subnets, 2 masks
D       172.16.200.0/24 [90/1915392] via 172.16.10.3, 01:07:08, Ethernet0
```

continues

Example 2-23 *Route Map Effects on the ringo Router (Continued)*

```
D       172.16.33.0/24 [90/1812992] via 172.16.10.3, 01:07:08, Ethernet0
D       172.16.34.0/24 [90/1812992] via 172.16.10.3, 01:07:08, Ethernet0
D       172.16.16.4/30 [90/2195456] via 172.16.10.4, 01:07:08, Ethernet0
D       172.16.16.0/30 [90/1787392] via 172.16.10.3, 01:07:08, Ethernet0
C       172.16.10.0/24 is directly connected, Ethernet0
D       172.16.2.0/24 [90/284160] via 172.16.10.3, 01:07:09, Ethernet0
C       172.16.100.0/24 is directly connected, Loopback20
ringo#
ringo# show ip ospf database
            OSPF Router with ID (172.16.100.10) (Process ID 7)
                Router Link States (Area 0)
Link ID         ADV Router      Age       Seq#        Checksum Link count
172.16.10.5     172.16.10.5     1151      0x80000015 0x4E2     1
172.16.100.10   172.16.100.10   1875      0x80000003 0xC969    1
                Net Link States (Area 0)
Link ID         ADV Router      Age       Seq#        Checksum
172.16.10.5     172.16.10.5     1151      0x80000003 0x1693
                Type-5 AS External Link States
Link ID         ADV Router      Age       Seq#        Checksum Tag
172.16.2.0      172.16.100.10   1875      0x80000002 0x8E2E    3
172.16.16.0     172.16.100.10   1875      0x80000002 0xE1CF    3
172.16.16.4     172.16.100.10   1875      0x80000002 0x4AF0    500
172.16.33.0     172.16.100.10   1875      0x80000002 0x3865    3
172.16.34.0     172.16.100.10   1875      0x80000002 0x2D6F    3
172.16.100.0    172.16.100.10   1875      0x80000002 0xE403    500
172.16.200.0    172.16.100.10   1875      0x80000002 0x4F1     3
192.168.192.0   172.16.100.10   1876      0x80000002 0x4A22    65001
ringo#
```

Notice that at the end of the OSPF database is the BGP route 192.168.192.0/24. This route has a tag of 65001 because BGP will try to preserve the AS_PATH attribute when redistributing BGP into an IGP that supports tags. BGP will use a tag value equal to its autonomous system ID.

You can also see the effects of the route map on the clanton router. Example 2-24 lists the route table of the clanton router, highlighting the different OSPF route types. Notice how the 172.16.16.4/30 and 172.16.100.0/24 routes are not set as default OSPF external type 2 routes, but are external type 1 routes. This is due to the **set route-type type-1** command in the route map on the ringo router.

Example 2-24 *Route Table of the clanton Router*

```
clanton# show ip route
Codes: C - connected, S - static, I - IGRP, R - RIP, M - mobile, B - BGP
       D - EIGRP, EX - EIGRP external, O - OSPF, IA - OSPF inter area
       N1 - OSPF NSSA external type 1, N2 - OSPF NSSA external type 2
       E1 - OSPF external type 1, E2 - OSPF external type 2, E - EGP
       i - IS-IS, L1 - IS-IS level-1, L2 - IS-IS level-2, * - candidate default
       U - per-user static route, o - ODR
```

Example 2-24 *Route Table of the clanton Router (Continued)*

```
Gateway of last resort is not set
O E2 192.168.192.0/24 [110/10] via 172.16.10.10, 01:00:14, Ethernet0/0
       172.16.0.0/16 is variably subnetted, 8 subnets, 2 masks
O E2    172.16.200.0/24 [110/10] via 172.16.10.10, 01:00:14, Ethernet0/0
O E2    172.16.33.0/24 [110/10] via 172.16.10.10, 01:00:14, Ethernet0/0
O E2    172.16.34.0/24 [110/10] via 172.16.10.10, 01:00:14, Ethernet0/0
O E1    172.16.16.4/30 [110/20] via 172.16.10.10, 01:00:14, Ethernet0/0
O E2    172.16.16.0/30 [110/10] via 172.16.10.10, 01:00:14, Ethernet0/0
C       172.16.10.0/24 is directly connected, Ethernet0/0
O E2    172.16.2.0/24 [110/10] via 172.16.10.10, 01:00:15, Ethernet0/0
O E1    172.16.100.0/24 [110/20] via 172.16.10.10, 01:00:15, Ethernet0/0
clanton#
```

Route Maps and Policy-Based Routing

Sometimes in the modern internetwork, the forwarding decisions of a router need to be more complex than the decision information offered by the routing protocols and route table. Routers for the most part base their forwarding decisions on the destination address of packet. Policy-based routing enables the network engineer to configure policies that selectively cause packets to take paths that differ from the next-hop path specified by the route table. This section discusses the benefits and configuration of policy-based routing.

Policy-based routing offers the following benefits:

- **Forwarding decision not based on the destination address**—Policy routing enables the network engineer to define a path based on attributes of a packet, source/destination IP address, application port, and packet lengths, and to forward them according to a different policy. Policy routing can be configured to set the packet's next hop or the packet's default next hop/interface. Policy routing may also be used to route the packet to the null interface, essentially discarding them.

- **Quality of service (QoS)**—Route maps and PBR can provide QoS by enabling you to set the type of service (ToS) values and the IP precedence values in the IP header. QoS configuration is performed on the edge routers. This improves performance by preventing additional configuration on the core devices.

- **Cost saving by using alternative paths**—IP traffic can be manipulated with PBR, for instance, traffic such as large bulky batch file transfers can be sent over low-cost, low-bandwidth links, whereas more time-sensitive, user-interactive traffic is sent over higher-cost and higher-speed links.

- **Multiple and unequal path load sharing based on traffic characteristics**—Policy routing can be used to load balance traffic across multiple and unequal paths based on traffic characteristics versus the route cost.

Assuming that PBR is enabled and configured on the router and interface, PBR operates in the following manner:

Step 1   All packets *received* on a PBR-enabled interface are considered for policy routing. Each packet *received* on that interface is passed through an associated route map.

Step 2   The **match** commands are called by the route map; if all **match** commands are met, the route map is marked as a **permit** or **deny**, and no further route maps instances are executed. If a **match** statement is not present, the route map and any **set** commands apply to all packets.

Step 3   If the route map has a **permit** statement, all **set** commands are applied and the packet is forwarded according to the new policy. You can use multiple **set** commands in a single route map instance. Table 2-7 lists the **set** commands that are specific to PBR. If you use multiple **set** commands in conjunction with one another, they are applied in the same order as follows:

```
set ip {precedence [value_0-7 | name] | tos [value_0-8 | name]}
set ip next-hop ip_address
set interface interface_name
set ip default next-hop ip_address
set default interface interface_name
```

Each of these commands is covered in further detail later in this section.

Step 4   If the route map has a **deny** statement, normal forwarding is used, as specified in the route/forwarding table. The **set** statements will not be applied to the packet.

Step 5   At the end of all the route map instances, an implicit route map will deny all packets. If the packet has not found a match in the previous route map instances, the packet will hit the implicit deny route map instance. When this occurs, the packet will be forwarded by the router following the normal route table.

NOTE   Policy routing only works on inbound packets; therefore, it must be applied to the incoming traffic or to the interface receiving the traffic to be policy routed. To policy route local traffic, you must have local policy routing enabled.

Practical Example: Policy-Based Routing

This section examines how you may use policy routing to control traffic in the internetwork. In the network model depicted in Figure 2-9, a policy route exists on the tombstone router to control traffic from the ringo and curly_bill routers. The policy states that all IP traffic from the ringo router will be forwarded to holliday, whereas all IP traffic from the curly_bill router will be forwarded to earp. All other IP traffic will be handled by the normal routing procedure.

Figure 2-9   *Policy-Based Routing*

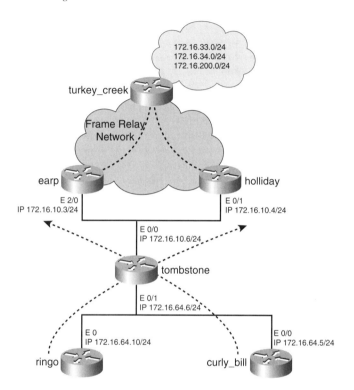

To control the traffic from the ringo and curly_bill routers, this example uses policy routing and route maps on the tombstone router. Policy routing will be enabled on the E0/1 interface of the tombstone router. This is the inbound interface, or the interface that will be receiving traffic from the ringo and curly_bill routers. The route map used in this model, policy_1, will have two route map instances. One will match packets from the ringo router, 172.16.64.10, and set the next hop to be 172.16.10.4, the holliday router. The other route map instance will match packets from the curly_bill router, 172.16.64.5, and set the next hop to be 172.16.10.3, the earp router.

The route/forwarding table on the tombstone router shows that there are two paths to the routes 172.16.33.0/24, 172.16.34.0/24, and 172.16.200.0/24 that reside on the turkey_creek router. One path passes through the earp router, whereas the other one passes through the holliday router. Example 2-25 lists the route table of the tombstone router.

Example 2-25 *Route Table of the tombstone Router*

```
tombstone# show ip route
Codes: C - connected, S - static, I - IGRP, R - RIP, M - mobile, B - BGP
       D - EIGRP, EX - EIGRP external, O - OSPF, IA - OSPF inter area
       N1 - OSPF NSSA external type 1, N2 - OSPF NSSA external type 2
       E1 - OSPF external type 1, E2 - OSPF external type 2, E - EGP
       i - IS-IS, L1 - IS-IS level-1, L2 - IS-IS level-2, ia - IS-IS inter area
       * - candidate default, U - per-user static route, o - ODR
       P - periodic downloaded static route
Gateway of last resort is not set
     172.16.0.0/16 is variably subnetted, 9 subnets, 2 masks
D       172.16.200.0/24 [90/40665600] via 172.16.10.3, 03:58:24, Ethernet0/0
                        [90/40665600] via 172.16.10.4, 03:58:24, Ethernet0/0
D       172.16.33.0/24 [90/40563200] via 172.16.10.3, 03:58:24, Ethernet0/0
                       [90/40563200] via 172.16.10.4, 03:58:24, Ethernet0/0
D       172.16.34.0/24 [90/40563200] via 172.16.10.3, 03:58:24, Ethernet0/0
                       [90/40563200] via 172.16.10.4, 03:58:24, Ethernet0/0
D       172.16.16.4/30 [90/40537600] via 172.16.10.4, 03:59:03, Ethernet0/0
D       172.16.16.0/30 [90/40537600] via 172.16.10.3, 04:56:26, Ethernet0/0
C       172.16.10.0/24 is directly connected, Ethernet0/0
D       172.16.2.0/24 [90/284160] via 172.16.10.3, 03:59:03, Ethernet0/0
D       172.16.100.0/24 [90/409600] via 172.16.64.10, 03:49:42, Ethernet0/1
C       172.16.64.0/24 is directly connected, Ethernet0/1
tombstone#
```

By issuing an extended **traceroute** command on the tombstone router from the address 172.16.64.6 to 172.16.200.10, you can see that EIGRP is using load sharing between the earp and holliday routers. Policy routing will override this process by sending IP traffic from the ringo router to holliday, and IP traffic from curly_bill to earp, as shown in Example 2-26.

Example 2-26 *Extended Trace on the tombstone Router*

```
tombstone# traceroute
Protocol [ip]:
Target IP address: 172.16.200.10
Source address: 172.16.64.6
Numeric display [n]:
Timeout in seconds [3]:
Probe count [3]: 4
Minimum Time to Live [1]:
Maximum Time to Live [30]:
Port Number [33434]:
Loose, Strict, Record, Timestamp, Verbose[none]:
Type escape sequence to abort.
Tracing the route to 172.16.200.10
  1 172.16.10.4 0 msec
    172.16.10.3 0 msec
```

Example 2-26 *Extended Trace on the tombstone Router (Continued)*

```
      172.16.10.4 0 msec
      172.16.10.3 0 msec
    2 172.16.16.5 8 msec
      172.16.16.1 12 msec
      172.16.16.5 8 msec
      172.16.16.1 12 msec
tombstone#
```

The configuration needed for PBR on the tombstone router is listed in the next example, Example 2-27.

Example 2-27 *Policy-Based Routing Configuration on tombstone*

```
hostname tombstone
!
interface Ethernet0/0
 ip address 172.16.10.6 255.255.255.0
!
interface Ethernet0/1
 ip address 172.16.64.6 255.255.255.0
 ip route-cache policy          ←Optional fast switching for policy routing
 ip policy route-map policy_1   ←Call route-map "policy_1" for policy routing
!
router eigrp 65001
 network 172.16.0.0
 no auto-summary
!
access-list 100 permit ip host 172.16.64.10 any    ←match packets from 172.16.64.10
access-list 101 permit ip host 172.16.64.5 any     ←match packets from 172.16.64.5
!
route-map policy_1 permit 100                      ←route-map "policy_1"
 match ip address 100                              ←call ACL 100 for match criteria
 set ip next-hop 172.16.10.4                       ←set IP next hop to holliday
!
route-map policy_1 permit 200                      ←next route map instance
 match ip address 101                              ←call ACL 101 for match criteria
 set ip next-hop 172.16.10.3                       ←set IP next hop to the earp router
!
```

To test the new policy, issue the **traceroute** commands on the ringo and curly_bill routers to the IP address of 172.16.200.10, which resides on the turkey_creek router. The **traceroute** from the ringo router will show that packets pass to the tombstone router, and then to holliday, and finally to turkey_creek. Example 2-28 demonstrates the **traceroute** command on the ringo router with PBR enabled.

Example 2-28 traceroute *Performed on the ringo Router*

```
ringo# traceroute 172.16.200.10
Type escape sequence to abort.
Tracing the route to 172.16.200.10
  1 172.16.64.6 4 msec 4 msec 4 msec
  2 172.16.10.4 8 msec 4 msec 4 msec
  3 172.16.16.5 20 msec 8 msec *
ringo#
```

To test the new policy for the curly_bill router, issue the **traceroute** command on the curly_bill router to the IP address of 172.16.200.10. The packets will pass to the tombstone router, and then to earp, and finally to turkey_creek. Example 2-29 demonstrates the **traceroute** command on the curly_bill router.

Example 2-29 traceroute *Performed on the curly_bill Router*

```
curly_bill# traceroute 172.16.200.10
Type escape sequence to abort.
Tracing the route to 172.16.200.10
  1 172.16.64.6 4 msec 4 msec 4 msec
  2 172.16.10.3 4 msec 4 msec 0 msec
  3 172.16.16.1 12 msec 9 msec *
curly_bill#
```

CAUTION   Whenever implementing policy routing, take care to consider the applications running on the network and the forward and return paths of the network traffic. In models such as this preceding example, you could implement policy routing on the turkey_creek router to avoid asymmetrical routing. *Asymmetrical routing* refers to when IP packets are forwarded along one path toward a destination, but follow a different path back, which can lead to problems with some applications, such as multicast.

Configuring Policy-Based Routing (PBR)

You can configure PBR by following these steps. Some of the steps may be omitted depending on your application for PBR.

Step 1   Define and configure the route map needed for the policy. This is accomplished with the **route-map** command, as discussed previously.

Step 2   Define and configure the **match** statements the route map will use. The most common **match** statements used are the following:

```
match ip address [access-list number]
```

The **match ip address** is used to call a standard, extended, or expanded-range ACL.

```
match length [min_packet_length_0-2147483647] [max_packet_length_0-2147483647]
```

The **match length** is used to match the Layer 3 packet length, in bytes, with all associated headers and trailers included. You must enter the minimum and maximum packet length. Use the **match length** command to policy route traffic based on packet size. You can deploy this to route traffic with large or small packet sizes to specific areas of the network.

Step 3   Configure and define the new routing policy with **set** commands. Multiple **set** commands may be used; if multiple commands are used, they are executed in the following order:

```
set ip {precedence [value_0-7 | name] | tos [value_0-8 | name]}
set ip next-hop ip_address
set interface interface_name
set ip default next-hop ip_address
set default interface interface_name
Set ip precedence {[1-7]|[routine|critical|flash|flash-
override|immediate|internet|network|priority]}
```

By setting the precedence, you are manipulating the first 3 bits, bits 0 through 2, of the 8-bit ToS field in the IP header. Earlier texts on TCP/IP state that this field is unused and ignored by routers, except for some routing protocols. This may have been true in the past; however, with the advent of Voice over IP and newer QoS features, the Precedence field is finding new life and meaning. IP precedence becomes a factor during periods of congestion on an interface. By default, Cisco routers do not manipulate the precedence value in the IP header; it remains at its original setting as when it arrived at the router. When Weighted Fair Queuing (WFQ) is enabled and the precedence bits are set, the packets are ordered for transmission according to the precedence value. The higher the precedence value, the higher its place in the queue for transmission. For the router to act on precedence, the link must be congested, and queuing must be enabled; otherwise, the packets are transmitted in first in, first out (FIFO) order. When setting precedence, you may use the numeric value of the precedence or the name of the precedence. Precedence should be set such that downstream IP devices can take advantage of the settings you use. Table 2-11 lists the valid names values for the **set precedence** command.

For detailed information about the **set precedence** command, see Chapter 5, "Integrated and Differentiated Services," and Chapter 6, "QoS – Rate Limiting and Queuing Traffic."

Table 2-11   **set precedence** *Commands in CISCO IOS Software Release 12.2*

Command	Function
routine	Set routine precedence (value = 0)
priority	Set priority precedence (value = 1)
immediate	Set immediate precedence (value = 2)
flash	Set Flash precedence (value = 3)
flash-override	Set Flash override precedence (value = 4)
critical	Set critical precedence (value = 5)
internet	Set internetwork control precedence (value = 6)
network	Set network control precedence (value = 7)

NOTE   For a router's queuing mechanisms to act on the precedence bits, the following two conditions must be met:

- The outbound link must be congested.
- The outbound link must be configured for WFQ or Weighted Random Early Detection (WRED).

```
Set ip tos {[1-15]|[normal|min-delay|max-throughput|max-reliability|min-monetary-
cost|priority]}
```

The **set ip tos** command enables you to set bits 3 through 6 in the IP header's 8-bit ToS field. The ToS bits are composed of 4 bits. These bits are referred to as the following:

- **D bit (bit 3)**—Normal = off, low delay = on
- **T bit (bit 4)**—Normal = off, high throughput = on
- **R bit (bit 5)**—Normal = off, high reliability = on
- **C bit (bit 6)**—Unused in Cisco Routers. RFC 1349 calls it the *minimize monetary cost*. Some TCP/IP implementations ignore this bit or implement it differently.

Bit 7 in the ToS field is currently unused and is set to 0. If all 4 bits are set to 0, it implies normal service.

Table 2-12 lists the recommended guidelines for setting ToS by protocol type.

Table 2-12   *Recommended ToS Values by Protocol*

Protocol	min-delay	max-throughput	max-reliability	min-monetary-cost
Telnet/Rlogin	1	0	0	0
HTTP	1	0	0	0
FTP control	1	0	0	0
FTP data	0	1	0	0
Any bulk data	0	1	0	0
TFTP	1	0	0	0
SMTP commands	1	0	0	0
SMTP data phase	0	1	0	0
DNS UDP query	1	0	0	0
DNS TCP query	0	0	0	0
DNS zone xfer	0	1	0	0
ICMP	0	0	0	0
IGPs	0	0	1	0
SNMP	0	0	1	0
BOOTP	0	0	0	0
NNTP	0	0	0	1

NOTE   Cisco IOS Software considers the precedence bits of the ToS field if there is traffic that is queued in WFQ, WRED, or Weighted Round Robin (WRR). The precedence bits are not considered when policy routing, Priority Queuing (PQ), Custom Queuing (CQ), or Class-Based Weighted Fair Queuing (CBWFQ) are configured.

`set ip next-hop {ip_address}`

Use this command to set IP address of the next-hop router to which the packet will be forwarded. The IP address used must be an adjacent router.

`set interface {interface_name}`

Use this command to set the output interface for the matched packet.

```
set ip default next-hop {ip_address}
```

This command is used like the **ip next-hop** command. It specifies which IP address to forward packets to if there is not an explicit route to the destination in the route table. Think of this command as a default route to use for policy routing. The next-hop address must be an adjacent router.

```
set default interface {interface_name}
```

This command functions much like the **ip default next-hop** command; it specifies which interface to forward a matched packet to if there is not an explicit route to the destination. Used on point-to-point links.

NOTE   The **set ip next-hop** and **set ip default next-hop** commands are similar but function differently. The **set ip next-hop** command causes the router to use policy routing first and then use the route table. The **set ip default next-hop** command causes the router to use the route table first and then policy route to the specified default next hop.

Step 4   (Optional) Define and configure any ACLs that will be used with the new routing policy. With extended ACLs, for example, you can use policy to forward traffic based on traffic type (for instance, traffic one way, and FTP traffic another). You can also use ACLs to route traffic from specific addresses. When you use standard ACLs, policy routing compares the source IP address in the packet to the ACL.

Step 5   Configure policy routing on the inbound interface. To configure policy routing for an interface, use the following interface command:

```
router(config-if)# ip policy route-map route-map_name
```

Step 6   (Optional) Enable fast switching for PBR. In Cisco IOS Software Release 12.0, PBR can be fast switched. Prior to Cisco IOS Software Release 12.0, PBR could only be processed switched. In a process-switched environment, the switching rate is approximately 1000 to 10,000 packets per second. This speed was not considered fast enough for many applications. You can enable fast switching of PBR with the following interface command:

```
router(config-if)# ip route-cache policy
```

PBR must be configured before you configure fast-switched PBR. Fast-switched PBR does not support the **set ip default next-hop** and **set default interface** commands. The **set interface** command is supported over point-to-point links or with a static route cache entry equal to the interface specified in the **set interface** command.

Step 7   (Optional) Configure local PBR. Packets generated by the router are not policy routed. If you want to policy route traffic generated by the router, you must enable it. To enable local PBR, use the following global configuration command.

```
router(config)# ip local policy route-map route-map_name
```

Practical Example: Configuring PBR and Setting ToS

In this section, you apply a couple of these concepts to a practical example in policy routing. For the network depicted in Figure 2-10, create a policy route that will forward Telnet traffic to the earp router, 172.16.10.3, while setting the ToS bit to minimum delay. All other IP traffic will be forwarded to the holliday router, 172.16.10.4.

Figure 2-10   *Policy-Based Routing*

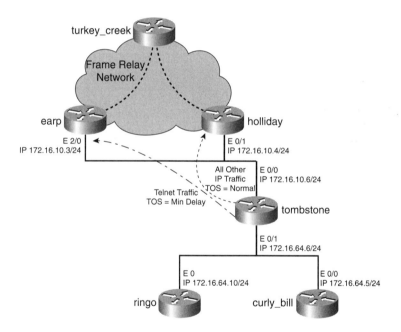

Following the multistep process for configuring PBR, Steps 1 through 3 call for you to first configure the route map with the necessary **match** and **set** commands. The route map will call an ACL that matches Telnet traffic, and the **set** command will set the IP next hop to be the IP address of the earp router. Table 2-12 specifies that Telnet traffic should have the ToS set to **min-delay**; therefore, the route map will set this bit for Telnet traffic in the ToS value to **min-delay**. Another route map instance will be used to match all other traffic and forward it to the holliday router. Because the route map instance will match all traffic, there is no need to include a **match** command. Example 2-30 lists the route map configuration on the tombstone router to accomplish this.

Example 2-30 *Route Map Configuration on the tombstone Router*

```
route-map policy_2 permit 100
 match ip address 101              ←Call access-list 101
 set ip next-hop 172.16.10.3      ←Set the next hop to 172.16.10.3/earp
 set ip tos min-delay             ←Set the TOS to min-delay
 !
route-map policy_2 permit 200
 set ip next-hop 172.16.10.4      ←Match all routes and set the next hop
                                  ←to 172.16.10.4/holliday
```

Now you must configure any ACLs the route map will need. In this case, configure a single ACL to match TCP telnet traffic from any IP address. The ACL you will use resembles the following:

```
access-list 101 permit tcp any any eq telnet
```

There is no need to write an ACL to catch all the regular traffic. As discussed earlier, the absence of a **match** statement, such as in the second route map instance, will match all routes or all packets.

The last two steps call for you to apply the policy route to an interface and to enable fast switching for PBR. This is accomplished with the **interface** commands **ip policy route-map** and **ip route-cache policy**. In this model, you will enable PBR on the E0/1 interface of the tombstone router. With PBR enabled on the E0/1 interface, all Telnet traffic will be forwarded to the earp router, whereas all other IP traffic will be forwarded to the holliday router. Example 2-31 lists the complete PBR configuration of the tombstone router.

Example 2-31 *PBR Configuration on the tombstone Router*

```
hostname tombstone
!
interface Ethernet0/0
 ip address 172.16.10.6 255.255.255.0
!
interface Ethernet0/1
 ip address 172.16.64.6 255.255.255.0
 ip route-cache policy              ←enable PBR fast-switching
 ip policy route-map policy_2       ←Call route-map "policy_2" for PBR
!
router eigrp 65001
 network 172.16.0.0
 no auto-summary
 no eigrp log-neighbor-changes
```

Example 2-31 *PBR Configuration on the tombstone Router (Continued)*

```
!
access-list 101 permit tcp any any eq telnet    ←Match Telnet traffic
!
priority-list 1 protocol ip high              ←Priority queuing for TOS enforcement
priority-list 1 default low
!
route-map policy_2 permit 100
 match ip address 101                          ←call access-list 101 and match Telnet
 set ip next-hop 172.16.10.3                   ←Set the next hop to earp/172.16.10.3
 set ip tos min-delay                          ←Set TOS min-delay bit
!
route-map policy_2 permit 200                  ←Match all other traffic
 set ip next-hop 172.16.10.4                   ←Set the next hop to holliday/172.16.10.4
!
```

In this model, because you are setting ToS values, you need to configure WRED or WFQ on the outbound interface. WFQ is not the default queuing method on Ethernet interfaces. It is the default queuing method on serial interfaces with 2.048 Mbps or less of bandwidth. This portion of the configuration is not present in this example. For more information on configuring WRED and WFQ, see Chapters 5 and 6.

Big Show for Route Maps

CCIE Practical Studies, Volume I introduced what was called the *Big Show* and *Big D*. These terms were used because the discussion focused on only a select few **show** and **debug** commands considered most useful.

The Big Show and Big D commands for route maps are rather limited in their use. The best way to test the functionality of route maps and policy routing is to actually see how they are performing by viewing the route table and using **traceroute** commands. The **show** commands offered by Cisco are very good at showing where the route map is applied and the logical order in which it is operated. The Big Show commands discussed here are as follows:

* **show route-map**
* **show ip policy**
* **show ip cache policy**

The **show route-map** command enables you to determine the logical order and execution of the route map. If PBR is enabled, the command also shows the number of matches and the number of bytes that were policy routed. Working from the previous network models, Example 2-32 demonstrates the **show route-map** command on the tombstone router.

Example 2-32 show route-map *Command on the tombstone Router*

```
tombstone# show route-map
route-map policy_2, permit, sequence 100
  Match clauses:
    ip address (access-lists): 101
  Set clauses:
    ip next-hop 172.16.10.3
    ip tos min-delay
  Policy routing matches: 264 packets, 15852 bytes
route-map policy_2, permit, sequence 200
  Match clauses:
  Set clauses:
    ip next-hop 172.16.10.4
  Policy routing matches: 60 packets, 4478 bytes
route-map policy_1, permit, sequence 100
  Match clauses:
    ip address (access-lists): 100
  Set clauses:
    ip next-hop 172.16.10.4
    ip tos max-throughput
  Policy routing matches: 85 packets, 6880 bytes
route-map policy_1, permit, sequence 200
  Match clauses:
    ip address (access-lists): 101
  Set clauses:
    ip next-hop 172.16.10.3
  Policy routing matches: 43 packets, 3318 bytes
tombstone#
```

Use the **show ip policy** command to verify which interfaces have PBR enabled and which route map they are currently using for PBR. Example 2-33 demonstrates the **show ip policy** command on the tombstone router.

Example 2-33 show ip policy *Command on the tombstone Router*

```
tombstone# show ip policy
Interface      Route map
Ethernet0/1    policy_2
```

You can use the **show ip cache policy** command to verify whether fast switching is enabled for policy routing. This command shows the policy type, the route map in use, and the age of the cache entries. If the policy is a next-hop policy, the next hop also displays. Example 2-34 lists the output of the **show ip cache policy** command on the tombstone router.

Example 2-34 show ip cache policy *Command on the tombstone Router*

```
tombstone# show ip cache policy
Total adds 4, total deletes 2
Type Routemap/sequence    Age        Interface          Next Hop
NH   policy_2/100         00:38:27   Ethernet0/0        172.16.10.3
NH   policy_2/200         00:43:56   Ethernet0/0        172.16.10.4
tombstone#
```

Lab 3: Configuring Complex Route Maps and Using Tags—Part I

Practical Scenario

Route maps are one of most powerful features you can use on a router. You can use them during redistribution, in PBR, in BGP, and in many other scenarios. This lab gives you practice in configuring complex route maps that will be used during redistribution. You then practice setting and using route tags.

Lab Exercise

GameNetworks.com is an upstart company focusing on providing WAN and LAN connectivity for console games. GameNetworks.com enables its customers to play the latest and greatest console games online through its private network. GameNetworks.com has two new locations in Wisconsin and California. Your task is to configure an IP network using the following strict design guidelines:

- Configure the GameNetworks.com IP network as depicted in Figure 2-11. Use EIGRP as the routing protocol and 2002 as the autonomous system ID on the wisconsin_x, unreal, and halo routers. Use EIGRP as the routing protocol on the california_x router and the gamenet router; the autonomous system of this router will be 65001.

- Join the EIGRP routing domains with OSPF on the gamenet and wisconsin_x routers.

- Configure the Frame Relay network as depicted in Figure 2-11.

- Configure all IP addresses as depicted in Figure 2-11.

- Use the "Lab Objectives" section for configuration specifics.

Figure 2-11 *GameNetworks.com*

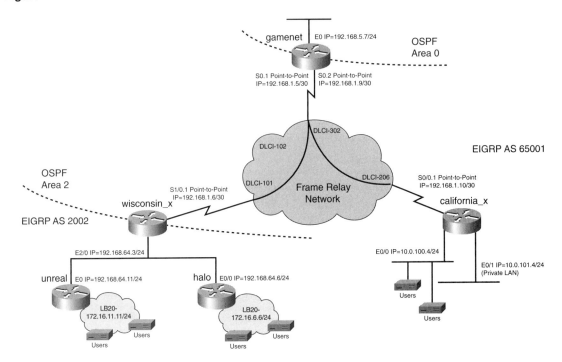

Lab Objectives

- Configure the routing protocols as depicted in Figure 2-11. The only interface on wisconsin_x broadcasting EIGRP updates should be the LAN interface.

- Configure OSPF on the wisconsin_x and gamenet routers. The serial interface of wisconsin_x will be in OSPF area 2. The serial s0.1 interface of the gamenet router is in OSPF area 2, and the LAN interface is in OSPF area 0.

- The s0.2 interface of the gamenet router will be configured for EIGRP, using AS 65001. All interfaces of the california_x router will be in the EIGRP domain.

- Configure a loopback interface on the unreal router with an IP address of 172.16.11.11/24, and on the halo router with an address of 172.16.6.6/24. Advertise these networks via EIGRP.

- Assign a tag value of 100 to all routes future and present advertised by the halo router. This includes all locally connected and LAN networks. In the future, other networks may be added to the halo router; ensure that these networks get a tag of 100, too.

- After a route is tagged with the value of 100, ensure that the tag value is preserved in the routing domain for EIGRP 65001.

- Routes advertised only by the halo router, and no other router, should appear as OSPF type 1 routes when they arrive on the gamenet router.

- Assign an OSPF tag value of 10 to the network 172.16.11.0/24 from the unreal router.

- When redistributing OSPF into EIGRP 65001 on the gamenet router, only redistribute those routes with a tag value of 100. The california_x router should be able to ping the halo network of 172.16.6.0/24, but not the network 172.16.11.0/24 on the unreal router.

- Do not allow the private LAN 10.0.101.0/24, on california_x, to be redistributed into the OSPF routing domain.

Equipment Needed

- Six Cisco routers; three will be connected via V.35 back-to-back cable or similar fashion to a single router serving as the Frame Relay switch.

- Four LAN segments, provided via hubs or switches. The figure shows the california_x router with two LAN interfaces; one of these interfaces may be substituted with a loopback interface.

Physical Layout and Prestaging

- Connect the hubs and serial cables to the routers as shown in Figure 2-11.

- A Frame Relay switch with two PVCs is also required. Example 2-35 lists the Frame Relay configuration used in this lab.

Example 2-35 *Frame Relay Switch Configuration*

```
hostname frame_switch
!
frame-relay switching
!
interface Serial0
 no ip address
 encapsulation frame-relay
 no fair-queue
 clockrate 2000000
 frame-relay intf-type dce
 frame-relay route 102 interface Serial1 101
 frame-relay route 302 interface Serial4 206
!
interface Serial1
 no ip address
 encapsulation frame-relay
```

continues

Example 2-35 *Frame Relay Switch Configuration (Continued)*

```
 clockrate 2000000
 frame-relay intf-type dce
 frame-relay route 101 interface Serial0 102
!
<<<text omitted>>>
!
interface Serial4
 no ip address
 encapsulation frame-relay
 clockrate 64000
 frame-relay intf-type dce
 frame-relay route 206 interface Serial0 302
```

Lab 3: Configuring Complex Route Maps and Using Tags—Part II

Lab Walkthrough

Configure the Frame Relay switch and attach the three routers in a back-to-back fashion to the frame switch. Use V.35 cables to connect the routers. Create the four Ethernet LANs by the use of switches or hubs, as illustrated in Figure 2-11.

After the physical connections are complete, assign IP addresses to all LAN and WAN interfaces as depicted in Figure 2-11. Configure a Frame Relay point-to-point network between the gamenet and wisconsin_x routers and between the gamenet and california_x routers. Use the data-link connection identifiers (DLCIs) from the diagram. Example 2-36 lists the Frame Relay configuration of the gamenet, wisonsin_x, and california_x routers.

Example 2-36 *Frame Relay Configurations for gamenet, wisonsin_x and california_x*

```
hostname gamenet
!
interface Serial0
 no ip address
 no ip directed-broadcast
 encapsulation frame-relay
 no ip mroute-cache
 frame-relay lmi-type cisco
!
interface Serial0.1 point-to-point
 ip address 192.168.1.5 255.255.255.252
 no ip directed-broadcast
 frame-relay interface-dlci 102
```

Example 2-36 *Frame Relay Configurations for gamenet, wisonsin_x and california_x (Continued)*

```
!
interface Serial0.2 point-to-point
 ip address 192.168.1.9 255.255.255.252
 no ip directed-broadcast
 frame-relay interface-dlci 302

hostname wisconsin_x
!
interface Serial1/0
 no ip address
 encapsulation frame-relay
 frame-relay lmi-type cisco
!
interface Serial1/0.1 point-to-point
 ip address 192.168.1.6 255.255.255.252
 frame-relay interface-dlci 101


-------------------------------------------------

hostname california_x
!
interface Serial0/0
 no ip address
 no ip directed-broadcast
 encapsulation frame-relay
!
interface Serial0/0.1 point-to-point
 ip address 192.168.1.10 255.255.255.252
 frame-relay interface-dlci 206
```

After configuring all the LAN and WAN interfaces, assign IP addresses and verify local connectivity. All routers should be able to ping their adjacent routers. For instance, unreal, wisconsin_x, and halo should all be able to ping the others' Ethernet address. When local connectivity is verified, you can begin to configure routing protocols.

Before attempting to control routing updates and writing route maps, confirm that you have IP connectivity across the network, redistributing all routes freely without filters. By so confirming, you can avoid troubleshooting route maps when the problem may be related to route redistribution or other problems with the routing protocols.

Begin by configuring the EIGRP domain between the wisconsin_x, unreal, and halo routers. The configuration of EIGRP on these three routers is rather straightforward. On the wisconsin_x router, you need a **network** statement and a **default-metric** because you need to redistribute OSPF into EIGRP. Example 2-37 lists the EIGRP configuration of the wisconsin_x router.

Example 2-37 *EIGRP Configuration for wisonsin_x*

```
hostname wisconsin_x
!
router eigrp 2002
 redistribute ospf 2002
 network 192.168.64.0
 default-metric 1000 100 254 1 1500
 no auto-summary
```

The EIGRP configuration on the unreal and halo routers will be identical. In Example 2-38, the EIGRP configuration demonstrates the two ways to configure the network for EIGRP. In Cisco IOS Software Release 12.1, EIGRP supports a wildcard mask with the **network** statement. Network 172.16.11.0 is using this method of configuration, and this example is following the standard way to configure EIGRP for the 192 networks. This is done purely for educational proposes.

Example 2-38 *EIGRP Configuration of the unreal and halo Routers*

```
!
hostname unreal
!
router eigrp 2002
 network 172.16.11.0 0.0.0.255
 network 192.168.64.0
 no auto-summary
 eigrp log-neighbor-changes
!
─────────────────────────────────────────────
hostname halo
!
router eigrp 2002
 network 172.16.6.0 0.0.0.255
 network 192.168.64.0
 no auto-summary
 eigrp log-neighbor-changes
```

Then you configure OSPF and EIGRP on the gamenet router. The autonomous system ID used for EIGRP is 65001. The only interface sending EIGRP updates is interface s0.2, 192.168.1.9. The interface S0.1 is in OSPF area 2, and interface E0 is in OSPF area 0. Example 2-39 lists the OSPF and EIGRP configuration on the gamenet router. At this time, no route maps have been configured on any routers.

Example 2-39 *EIGRP and OSPF Configuration of gamenet*

```
hostname gamenet
!
router eigrp 65001
 redistribute ospf 2002
 passive-interface Ethernet0
 passive-interface Serial0.1
 network 192.168.1.0
 default-metric 1000 100 254 1 1500
 no auto-summary
!
router ospf 2002
 redistribute eigrp 65001 subnets
 network 192.168.1.5 0.0.0.0 area 2
 network 192.168.5.0 0.0.0.255 area 0
 default-metric 100
!
```

The california_x router will be configured for EIGRP with an autonomous system ID of 65001. Example 2-40 lists the EIGRP configuration of the california_x router.

Example 2-40 *EIGRP Configuration of the california_x Router*

```
hostname california_x
!
router eigrp 65001
 network 10.0.0.0
 network 192.168.1.0
 no auto-summary
!
```

After configuring routing protocols on all the routers, verify IP connectivity with standard ping tests. Be sure the california_x router can ping the gamenet LAN and the halo and unreal routers. Ensure that the loopback networks are advertised and reachable by the unreal and halo routers. Do not attempt to write route maps for filters and such without first verifying IP reachability.

The lab instructions call for you to write a route map to tag the routes from the halo router with a tag of 100, and to tag the routes from the unreal router with a tag of 10. You will also tag route 192.168.64.0/24 with a tag of 100. Therefore, on the wisconsin_x router, you will write a route map to accomplish this during redistribution.

Following the five-step process for configuring route maps, you will begin by first configuring the route map with its associated **match** and **set** commands. The route map, called set_tag, will match routes using the **match ip route-source** command. Routes from the source IP address of 192.168.64.11, the unreal router, will have the tag set to 10. Routes from the source IP address of 192.168.64.6, the halo router, will have the tag set to 100. Routes from this source will also have the metric set to be an OSPF type 1 metric. Example 2-41 lists the syntax for the route map on the wisconsin_x router.

Example 2-41 *Route-map set_tag Configuration on the wisconsin_x Router*

```
hostname wisconsin_x
!
route-map set_tag permit 10    ←First route-map instance
 match ip route-source 1       ←Match ACL 1, 192.168.64.11
 set tag 10                    ←Set tag to 10
!
route-map set_tag permit 20    ←Second route-map instance
 match ip route-source 2       ←Match ACL 2, 192.168.64.6
 set metric-type type-1        ←Set route type to Ext OSPF type-1
 set tag 100                   ←Set tag to 100
!
route-map set_tag permit 30    ←Third route-map instance
 match ip address 10           ←Match ACL 10, all other routes
 set tag 100                   ←Set tag to 100
!
```

This now completes Steps 1 through 3 required to configure route maps. Now you apply the route maps. In this model, you apply the route map during redistribution of EIGRP into OSPF on the wisconsin_x router. Example 2-42 lists the complete configuration of the wisconsin_x router, including the ACLs.

Example 2-42 *Configuration of the wisconsin_x Router*

```
hostname wisconsin_x
!
<<<text omitted>>>
!
interface Serial0
 no ip address
 no ip directed-broadcast
 encapsulation frame-relay
 no ip mroute-cache
 frame-relay lmi-type cisco
!
interface Serial1/0.1 point-to-point
 ip address 192.168.1.6 255.255.255.252
 frame-relay interface-dlci 101
!
```

Example 2-42 *Configuration of the wisconsin_x Router (Continued)*

```
<<<text omitted>>>
!
interface Ethernet2/0
 ip address 192.168.64.3 255.255.255.0
!
router eigrp 2002
 redistribute ospf 2002             ←redistribute OSPF
 network 192.168.64.0
 default-metric 1000 100 254 1 1500  ←default metric
 no auto-summary
!
router ospf 2002
 redistribute eigrp 2002 subnets route-map set_tag  ←Redistribute and call route-map
 network 192.168.1.6 0.0.0.0 area 2
 default-metric 10                             ←default metric
!
access-list 1 permit 192.168.64.11            ←match routes from 192.168.64.11
access-list 2 permit 192.168.64.6             ←match routes from 192.168.64.6
access-list 10 permit any                     ←match all other routes/192.168.64.0
!
route-map set_tag permit 10                   ←route-map "set_tag" begins
 match ip route-source 1
 set tag 10
!
route-map set_tag permit 20
 match ip route-source 2
 set metric-type type-1
 set tag 100
!
route-map set_tag permit 30
 match ip address 10
 set tag 100
```

Another requirement of this model is to only redistribute routes, on the gamenet router, into EGIRP 65001 from OSPF with a tag value of 100, and to preserve this tag. You can do this by creating and applying a route map to the redistribution process that matches only routes with a tag of 100. You can use the **match tag** command for this purpose. Example 2-43 lists the required route map.

Example 2-43 *Route Map match_tag100 on the gamenet Router*

```
hostname gamenet
!
route-map match_tag100 permit 10    ←begin route-map "match_tag100"
 match tag 100                      ←match the tag value of 100
 set tag 100                        ←set the tag for EIGRP.
!
```

The route map will be applied during redistribution from OSPF into EIGRP. Before you apply this route map, however, configure the last route map needed in the model.

The last requirement is to also prevent the private LAN, 10.0.101.0/24, from the california_x router, to be redistributed into OSPF from EIGRP on the gamenet router. You can prevent this with a route map applied during redistribution. The route map used to filter this subnet will call an ACL that matches only network 10.0.101.0/24. Example 2-44 lists the route map, called filter_net, used to filter network 10.0.101.0/24 and the associated ACL.

Example 2-44 *Route Map filter_net on the gamenet Router*

```
hostname gamenet
!
access-list 10 deny    10.0.101.0 0.0.0.255  ←deny network 10.0.101.0/24
access-list 10 permit any                    ←Allow other networks to be redistributed
route-map filter_net permit 10               ←begin route-map "filter_net"
 match ip address 10                          ←Match ACL 10
```

At this time, you can apply both route maps during the redistribution process. Example 2-45 lists the final configuration of the gamenet router.

Example 2-45 *Final Configuration of the gamenet Router*

```
hostname gamenet
!
 interface Ethernet0
 ip address 192.168.5.7 255.255.255.0
 no ip directed-broadcast
 media-type 10BaseT
!
<<<text omitted>>>
!
interface Serial0
 no ip address
 no ip directed-broadcast
 encapsulation frame-relay
 no ip mroute-cache
 frame-relay lmi-type cisco
!
interface Serial0.1 point-to-point
 ip address 192.168.1.5 255.255.255.252
 no ip directed-broadcast
 frame-relay interface-dlci 102
!
interface Serial0.2 point-to-point
 ip address 192.168.1.9 255.255.255.252
 no ip directed-broadcast
 frame-relay interface-dlci 302
!
router eigrp 65001
 redistribute ospf 2002 route-map match_tag100        ←call route-map "match_tag100"
```

Example 2-45 *Final Configuration of the gamenet Router (Continued)*

```
 passive-interface Ethernet0
 passive-interface Serial0.1
 network 192.168.1.0
 default-metric 1000 100 254 1 1500                  ←set default metric
 no auto-summary
 !
 router ospf 2002
  redistribute eigrp 65001 subnets route-map filter_net  ←call route-map "filter_net"
  network 192.168.1.5 0.0.0.0 area 2
  network 192.168.5.0 0.0.0.255 area 0
  default-metric 100                                 ←set default metric
 !
 access-list 10 deny   10.0.101.0 0.0.0.255
 access-list 10 permit any
 route-map filter_net permit 10
  match ip address 10
 !
 route-map match_tag100 permit 10
  match tag 100
  set tag 100
```

To verify the configuration, ensure that the california_x router sees only the routes with a tag of 100, and that it can ping the 172.16.6.0/24 subnet but not the 172.16.11.0/24 subnet. Example 2-46 demonstrates the route table and the ping test on the california_x router.

Example 2-46 *Verifying the Configuration on california_x*

```
california_x# show ip route
Codes: C - connected, S - static, I - IGRP, R - RIP, M - mobile, B - BGP
       D - EIGRP, EX - EIGRP external, O - OSPF, IA - OSPF inter area
       N1 - OSPF NSSA external type 1, N2 - OSPF NSSA external type 2
       E1 - OSPF external type 1, E2 - OSPF external type 2, E - EGP
       i - IS-IS, L1 - IS-IS level-1, L2 - IS-IS level-2, * - candidate default
       U - per-user static route, o - ODR
Gateway of last resort is not set
     172.16.0.0/24 is subnetted, 1 subnets
D EX   172.16.6.0 [170/3097600] via 192.168.1.9, 02:47:46, Serial0/0.1
D EX 192.168.64.0/24 [170/3097600] via 192.168.1.9, 02:48:50, Serial0/0.1
     10.0.0.0/24 is subnetted, 2 subnets
C       10.0.100.0 is directly connected, Ethernet0/0
C       10.0.101.0 is directly connected, Ethernet0/1
     192.168.1.0/30 is subnetted, 2 subnets
C       192.168.1.8 is directly connected, Serial0/0.1
D       192.168.1.4 [90/2681856] via 192.168.1.9, 02:58:26, Serial0/0.1
california_x#
california_x# show ip route 172.16.6.0
Routing entry for 172.16.6.0/24
  Known via "eigrp 65001", distance 170, metric 3097600
```

continues

Example 2-46 *Verifying the Configuration on california_x (Continued)*

```
    Tag 100, type external
    Redistributing via eigrp 65001
    Last update from 192.168.1.9 on Serial0/0.1, 02:48:18 ago
    Routing Descriptor Blocks:
    * 192.168.1.9, from 192.168.1.9, 02:48:18 ago, via Serial0/0.1
        Route metric is 3097600, traffic share count is 1
        Total delay is 21000 microseconds, minimum bandwidth is 1000 Kbit
        Reliability 254/255, minimum MTU 1500 bytes
        Loading 1/255, Hops 1
california_x#
california_x# ping 172.16.6.6
Type escape sequence to abort.
Sending 5, 100-byte ICMP Echos to 172.16.6.6, timeout is 2 seconds:
!!!!!
Success rate is 100 percent (5/5), round-trip min/avg/max = 32/34/36 ms
california_x# ping 172.16.11.11
Type escape sequence to abort.
Sending 5, 100-byte ICMP Echos to 172.16.11.11, timeout is 2 seconds:
.....
Success rate is 0 percent (0/5)
california_x#
```

To verify that the private subnet, 10.0.101.0/24, is filtered from OSPF, you can view the route table of the wisconsin_x router, as demonstrated in Example 2-47.

Example 2-47 *Final Route Table of the wisconsin_x Router*

```
wisconsin_x# show ip route
Codes: C - connected, S - static, I - IGRP, R - RIP, M - mobile, B - BGP
       D - EIGRP, EX - EIGRP external, O - OSPF, IA - OSPF inter area
       N1 - OSPF NSSA external type 1, N2 - OSPF NSSA external type 2
       E1 - OSPF external type 1, E2 - OSPF external type 2, E - EGP
       i - IS-IS, L1 - IS-IS level-1, L2 - IS-IS level-2, ia - IS-IS inter area
       * - candidate default, U - per-user static route, o - ODR
       P - periodic downloaded static route
Gateway of last resort is not set
     172.16.0.0/24 is subnetted, 2 subnets
D       172.16.11.0 [90/409600] via 192.168.64.11, 03:00:27, Ethernet2/0
D       172.16.6.0 [90/409600] via 192.168.64.6, 03:00:27, Ethernet2/0
C    192.168.64.0/24 is directly connected, Ethernet2/0
O IA 192.168.5.0/24 [110/58] via 192.168.1.5, 03:01:39, Serial1/0.1
     10.0.0.0/24 is subnetted, 1 subnets
O E2    10.0.100.0 [110/100] via 192.168.1.5, 03:01:03, Serial1/0.1
     192.168.1.0/30 is subnetted, 2 subnets
O E2    192.168.1.8 [110/100] via 192.168.1.5, 03:01:44, Serial1/0.1
C       192.168.1.4 is directly connected, Serial1/0.1
wisconsin_x#
```

Lab 4: Configuring Policy-Based Routing—Part I

Practical Scenario

Route maps are also used for PBR. You can use PBR to force traffic to paths that are different from the ones in the normal forwarding/route table. You can use PBR to control traffic based on ToS, packet size and type, and source address, among others. This lab gives you practice in configuring complex PBR route maps using packet size and in controlling default routes.

Lab Exercise

Wizards of the Woods is the leading manufacturer of fantasy card games, fantasy role-playing games, and computer games. Wizards of the Woods has organized its divisions by geographic locations. To each division, there are two Frame Relay PVCs from the headquarters router, called the wow router. One PVC operates at T1 speeds; this runs between the wow and plains router. The other is a low-speed PVC, 64 kbps, between the wow and swamp router. The wow router also provides Internet service to the division. Wizards want to control and streamline traffic through the WAN and to the wow servers by using PBR. Your task is to configure an IP network and PBR using the following strict design guidelines:

- Configure the Wizards of the Woods IP network as depicted in Figure 2-12. Use EIGRP as the routing protocol and 65002 as the autonomous system ID on all routers.

- Configure the Frame Relay network as depicted in Figure 2-12.

- Configure all IP addresses as depicted in Figure 2-12.

- Use the "Lab Objectives" section for configuration specifics.

Lab Objectives

- Configure EIGRP as the routing protocol, as depicted in Figure 2-12. Use 65002 as the autonomous system ID.

- Configure EIGRP such that the routing protocol will prefer the higher-bandwidth link between the plains and wow routers over the swamp and wow routers for traffic that comes from the forest router. EIGRP should prefer this path when routing traffic for the forest, mountain, and island routers. (Hint: Set the bandwidth properly on the serial interfaces.)

- The testing and functionality of this lab will be greatly enhanced if there is an available connection to the Internet. The wow router will be configured to advertise a default route for Internet traffic. If an Internet connection is not available, you may simulate it with a loopback address or another router.

Figure 2-12 *Wizards of the Woods*

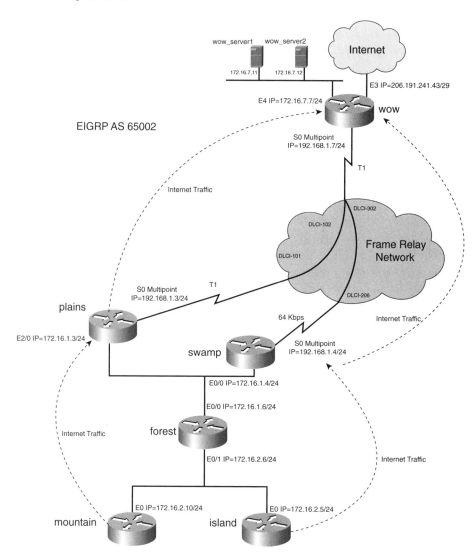

- Configure PBR using the following guidelines:
  - IP traffic from the mountain and island routers with a small packet size, 0 to 1199 bytes, destined for the wow servers should use the high-speed link between the plains and the wow routers.

— IP traffic from the mountain and island routers with a large packet size, 1200 to 1544 bytes, destined for the wow servers should use the low-speed link between the swamp and wow routers.

— Internet traffic from the mountain router should use the high-speed link through the plains router.

— Internet traffic from the island router should use the low-speed link through the swamp router.

— Configure fast switching for PBR.

— For the purposes of the lab, do not worry about the return route of the traffic. EIGRP will load share for return traffic.

● (Optional) If you have access to the Internet, enhance the lab and your practice by making this model as close as you can to the real thing. Configure NAT on the wow router, such that all routers including the mountain and island routers can reach the Internet.

Equipment Needed

● Seven Cisco routers; three will be connected via V.35 back-to-back cable or a similar fashion to a single router serving as the Frame Relay switch.

● Four LAN segments, provided via hubs or switches. Figure 2-12 shows the wow router with two LAN interfaces; one of these interfaces may be substituted with a loopback interface or another router to simulate the Internet, if a real Internet connection is not available.

● You may want to use IP workstations or servers to simulate response for the wow servers.

Physical Layout and Prestaging

● Connect the hubs and serial cables to the routers as shown in Figure 2-12.

● A Frame Relay switch with two PVCs is also required. Example 2-48 lists the Frame Relay configuration used in this lab.

Example 2-48 *Frame Relay Switch Configuration*

```
hostname frame_switch
!
frame-relay switching
!
interface Serial0
 no ip address
 encapsulation frame-relay
 no fair-queue
 clockrate 2000000
```

continues

Example 2-48 *Frame Relay Switch Configuration (Continued)*

```
   frame-relay intf-type dce
   frame-relay route 102 interface Serial1 101
   frame-relay route 302 interface Serial4 206
 !
interface Serial1
 no ip address
 encapsulation frame-relay
 clockrate 2000000
 frame-relay intf-type dce
 frame-relay route 101 interface Serial0 102
 !
<<<text omitted>>>
 !
interface Serial4
 no ip address
 encapsulation frame-relay
 clockrate 64000
 frame-relay intf-type dce
 frame-relay route 206 interface Serial0 302
```

Lab 4: Configuring Policy-Based Routing—Part II

Lab Walkthrough

Configure the Frame Relay switch and attach the three routers in a back-to-back fashion to the frame switch. Use V.35 cables to connect the routers. Create the four Ethernet LANs by the use of switches or hubs, as illustrated in Figure 2-12.

After the physical connections are complete, assign IP addresses to all LAN and WAN interfaces as depicted in Figure 2-12. Configure a Frame Relay network as a single multipoint network between all routers on the WAN. Use the DLCIs from the diagram. Because the Frame Relay network is a multipoint, keep in mind that you will need to disable EIGRP split horizon at some point. At this time, you will also want to set the bandwidth statements so that EIGRP chooses the best possible path through the network. Example 2-49 lists the Frame Relay configuration of all the routers.

Example 2-49 *Frame Relay Configurations for the wow, plains, and swamp Routers*

```
hostname wow
!
interface Serial0
 bandwidth 1544                              ←BW for EIGRP
 ip address 192.168.1.7 255.255.255.0
 encapsulation frame-relay
 no ip split-horizon eigrp 65002            ←used to disable split-horizons
 no ip mroute-cache
```

Example 2-49 *Frame Relay Configurations for the wow, plains, and swamp Routers (Continued)*

```
   frame-relay map ip 192.168.1.3 102 broadcast      ←Map statement to plains
   frame-relay map ip 192.168.1.4 302 broadcast      ←Map statement to swamp
   frame-relay lmi-type cisco
 !

hostname plains
 !
interface Serial1/0
  bandwidth 1544                                      ←BW for EIGRP
  ip address 192.168.1.3 255.255.255.0
  encapsulation frame-relay
  frame-relay map ip 192.168.1.4 101 broadcast       ←Map statement to swamp
  frame-relay map ip 192.168.1.7 101 broadcast       ←Map statement to wow
  frame-relay lmi-type cisco
 !

hostname swamp
 !
interface Serial0/0
  bandwidth 64                                        ←BW for EIGRP
  ip address 192.168.1.4 255.255.255.0
  encapsulation frame-relay
  no ip mroute-cache
  frame-relay map ip 192.168.1.3 206 broadcast       ←Map statement to plains
  frame-relay map ip 192.168.1.7 206 broadcast       ←Map statement to wow
  frame-relay lmi-type cisco
 !
```

After configuring all the LAN and WAN interfaces, assign IP addresses and verify local connectivity. All routers should be able to ping their adjacent routers. For instance, plains, swamp, and forest should all be able to ping the others' Ethernet address. When local connectivity is verified, you can begin to configure routing protocols.

Begin by configuring the EIGRP domain between all the routers, starting with the wow router. On the wow router, you need two **network** statements, one for network 172.16.0.0 and one for 192.168.1.0. This router also needs to generate a default route for Internet traffic. To generate a default route, configure a default static route to the address 206.191.241.41 with the command **ip route 0.0.0.0 0.0.0.0 206.191.241.41**. For the wow router to advertise this route, it needs to be redistributed into EIGRP. Example 2-50 lists the configuration of EIGRP on the wow router.

Example 2-50 *EIGRP Configuration for wisonsin_x*

```
hostname wow
 !
router eigrp 65002
  redistribute static                           ←redistribute the default route
  network 172.16.0.0
```

continues

Example 2-50 *EIGRP Configuration for wisonsin_x (Continued)*

```
network 192.168.1.0
default-metric 10000 100 254 1 1500       ←default metric
no auto-summary
!
ip classless
ip route 0.0.0.0 0.0.0.0 206.191.241.41     ←default route
```

NOTE   Packets will only follow a default route when **ip classless** is enabled.

Because the Frame Relay network is a multipoint, you should disable split horizon for EIGRP on the serial interface with the command **no ip split-horizon eigrp 65002**. Without disabling EIGRP split horizon, if the Ethernet link between the plains and swamp routers were broken, routes from the swamp router would not reach the plains router, and routing would be broken. Another important part of the EIGRP configuration, listed in the preceding example, is the configuration of the **bandwidth** statements on the serial interface. The configuration of the **bandwidth** statements will allow EIGRP to pick the best possible path for routing.

The EIGRP configurations on the plains and swamp routers resemble that of the wow router. Example 2-51 lists the configurations.

Example 2-51 *EIGRP Configuration of the plains and swamp Routers*

```
hostname plains
!
router eigrp 65002
 network 172.16.0.0
 network 192.168.1.0
 no auto-summary
!

hostname swamp
!
router eigrp 65002
 network 172.16.0.0
 network 192.168.1.0
 no auto-summary
```

The EIGRP configurations on the forest, mountain, and island routers are pretty straightforward, as shown in Example 2-52.

Example 2-52 *EIGRP Configuration of the forest, mountain, and island Routers*

```
hostname forest
!
router eigrp 65002
 network 172.16.0.0
 no auto-summary
!

hostname mountain
!
router eigrp 65002
 network 172.16.0.0
 no auto-summary
!

hostname island
!
router eigrp 65002
 network 172.16.0.0
 no auto-summary
```

After configuring all the routers for EIGRP, you should have IP end-to-end connectivity. The island and mountain routers should be able to reach the wow servers. A default route should also be advertised by EIGRP. Example 2-53 lists the route table of the island router.

Example 2-53 *Route Table of the island Router*

```
island# show ip route
Codes: C - connected, S - static, I - IGRP, R - RIP, M - mobile, B - BGP
       D - EIGRP, EX - EIGRP external, O - OSPF, IA - OSPF inter area
       N1 - OSPF NSSA external type 1, N2 - OSPF NSSA external type 2
       E1 - OSPF external type 1, E2 - OSPF external type 2, E - EGP
       i - IS-IS, L1 - IS-IS level-1, L2 - IS-IS level-2, * - candidate default
       U - per-user static route, o - ODR
Gateway of last resort is 172.16.2.6 to network 0.0.0.0
       172.16.0.0/24 is subnetted, 3 subnets
D        172.16.7.0 [90/2246656] via 172.16.2.6, 01:07:24, Ethernet0/0
D        172.16.1.0 [90/307200] via 172.16.2.6, 02:10:57, Ethernet0/0
C        172.16.2.0 is directly connected, Ethernet0/0
D     192.168.1.0/24 [90/2221056] via 172.16.2.6, 02:10:57, Ethernet0/0
D*EX 0.0.0.0/0 [170/2246656] via 172.16.2.6, 01:07:24, Ethernet0/0
island#
```

The *optional* portion of this lab calls for you to configure NAT on the wow router for reachability to the Internet. Having actual IP hosts for testing will help you verify whether the route maps and policy routing are working properly. Actual IP hosts may be substituted by loopback interfaces and by enabling local policy routing. When configuring NAT, configure the serial 0 and E4 interfaces of the wow router as NAT inside interfaces. The E3 interface will be the NAT outside interface. Because you have only a single IP address, you will be using Port Address Translation (PAT), sometimes referred to as the Overload feature. The NAT/PAT configuration used in this model is listed in Example 2-54. For more detailed information on configuring NAT, refer to *CCIE Practical Studies, Volume 1*.

Example 2-54 *NAT/PAT Configuration on the wow Router*

```
hostname wow
!
interface Ethernet3
 ip address 206.191.241.43 255.255.255.248
 no ip directed-broadcast
 ip nat outside                              ←NAT outside interface/Internet
 media-type 10BaseT
!
interface Ethernet4
 ip address 172.16.7.7 255.255.255.0
 no ip directed-broadcast
 ip nat inside                               ←NAT inside interface
 media-type 10BaseT
!
interface Serial0
 bandwidth 1544
 ip address 192.168.1.7 255.255.255.0
 no ip directed-broadcast
 ip nat inside                               ←NAT inside interface
 encapsulation frame-relay
 no ip split-horizon eigrp 65002
 no ip mroute-cache
 frame-relay map ip 192.168.1.3 102 broadcast
 frame-relay map ip 192.168.1.4 302 broadcast
 frame-relay lmi-type cisco
!
ip nat inside source list 101 interface Ethernet3 overload  ←PAT enabled for E3
!
access-list 101 permit ip any any           ←translate all traffic
```

To configure the routing policy specified by the lab, you need to configure policy routing on the forest routers. This lab does not require traffic to take the same return path as which it originated, however, for extra practice, you may want to configure PBR on the wow router, such that traffic does follow the same return path.

The lab objectives call for you to configure PBR with the following guidelines:

* IP traffic from the mountain and island routers with a small packet size, 0 to 1199 bytes, destined for the wow servers should use the high-speed link between the plains and wow routers.

* IP traffic from the mountain and island routers with a large packet size, 1200 to 1544 bytes, destined for the wow servers should use the low-speed link between the swamp and wow routers.

* Internet traffic from the mountain router should use the high-speed link through the plains router.

* Internet traffic from the island router should use the low-speed link through the swamp router.

* Configure fast switching for PBR.

The route map for policy routing on the forest router will have four route map instances. The first instance will match traffic from the router mountain, 172.16.2.10, and island, 172.16.2.5. After traffic is verified from these sources, a match on small packet length, 0 to 1199, will be performed. Traffic that passes both of these criteria will have a next hop set to 172.16.1.3, to use the high-speed link of the plains router. The second route map instance will match the same addresses, but this instance will match large packet lengths, 1200 to 1544. Traffic that passes both of these matches will be forwarded to the next hop of 172.16.1.4, to the lower-speed link of the swamp router.

The final two route map instances are for Internet traffic. One instance will match traffic from the mountain router, 172.16.2.10, and set the IP default next hop to the plains router, 172.16.1.3. The other instance will match traffic from the island router, 172.16.2.5, and set the IP default next hop to the swamp router, 172.16.1.4. Recall that the IP default next-hop address will be used when the router does not have the destination address of the packet in its forwarding/route table.

Recalling the steps to configure PBR, you have the following:

Step 1   Configure ACLs.

Step 2   Configure route map instances.

Step 3   Configure **match** commands.

Step 4   Configure **set** commands.

Step 5   Configure PBR on the interface.

Step 6   Configure fast switching.

Step 7   (Optional) Configure local PBR.

Example 2-55 covers the configuration of Steps 1 through 4 on the forest router.

Example 2-55 *Route Map and ACL Configuration on the forest Router*

```
Hostname forest
!
access-list 110 permit ip host 172.16.2.10 172.16.7.0 0.0.0.255
access-list 110 permit ip host 172.16.2.5 172.16.7.0 0.0.0.255
!
access-list 130 deny   ip any 172.16.0.0 0.0.255.255
access-list 130 deny   ip any 192.168.1.0 0.0.0.255
access-list 130 permit ip host 172.16.2.10 any
!
access-list 140 deny   ip any 172.16.0.0 0.0.255.255
access-list 140 deny   ip any 192.168.1.0 0.0.0.255
access-list 140 permit ip host 172.16.2.5 any
!
route-map policy_1 permit 10          ←PBR small packets
 match ip address 110
 match length 0 1199
 set ip next-hop 172.16.1.3
!
route-map policy_1 permit 20          ←PBR large packets
 match ip address 110
 match length 1200 1544
 set ip next-hop 172.16.1.4
!
route-map policy_1 permit 30          ←PBR for default routing
 match ip address 130
 set ip default next-hop 172.16.1.3
!
route-map policy_1 permit 40          ←PBR for default routing
 match ip address 140
 set ip default next-hop 172.16.1.4
!
```

The last part of the configuration, Steps 5 and 6, calls for you to apply the PBR and to enable fast switching for PBR. This is accomplished with the interface commands **ip policy route-map** and **ip route-cache policy**. Example 2-56 lists the entire configuration of the forest router.

Example 2-56 *Configuration of the forest Router*

```
hostname forest
!
<<<text omitted>>>
!
interface Ethernet0/0
 ip address 172.16.1.6 255.255.255.0
!
interface Ethernet0/1
 ip address 172.16.2.6 255.255.255.0
```

Example 2-56 *Configuration of the forest Router (Continued)*

```
ip route-cache policy
ip policy route-map policy_1
!
router eigrp 65002
 network 172.16.0.0
 no auto-summary
 no eigrp log-neighbor-changes
!
ip classless
no ip http server
!
access-list 110 permit ip host 172.16.2.10 172.16.7.0 0.0.0.255
access-list 110 permit ip host 172.16.2.5 172.16.7.0 0.0.0.255
access-list 130 deny    ip any 172.16.0.0 0.0.255.255
access-list 130 deny    ip any 192.168.1.0 0.0.0.255
access-list 130 permit ip host 172.16.2.10 any
access-list 140 deny    ip any 172.16.0.0 0.0.255.255
access-list 140 deny    ip any 192.168.1.0 0.0.0.255
access-list 140 permit ip host 172.16.2.5 any
route-map policy_1 permit 10
 match ip address 110
 match length 0 1199
 set ip next-hop 172.16.1.3
!
route-map policy_1 permit 20
 match ip address 110
 match length 1200 1544
 set ip next-hop 172.16.1.4
!
route-map policy_1 permit 30
 match ip address 130
 set ip default next-hop 172.16.1.3
!
route-map policy_1 permit 40
 match ip address 140
 set ip default next-hop 172.16.1.4
```

Example 2-57 lists the PBR configuration of the wow router.

Example 2-57 *PBR Configuration of the wow Router*

```
hostname wow
!
ip subnet-zero
ip name-server 206.191.193.1
!
<<<text omitted>>>
```

continues

Example 2-57 *PBR Configuration of the wow Router (Continued)*

```
!
interface Ethernet3
 ip address 206.191.241.43 255.255.255.248
 no ip directed-broadcast
 ip nat outside
 media-type 10BaseT
!
interface Ethernet4
 ip address 172.16.7.7 255.255.255.0
 no ip directed-broadcast
 ip nat inside
 media-type 10BaseT
!
interface Serial0
 bandwidth 1544
 ip address 192.168.1.7 255.255.255.0
 no ip directed-broadcast
 ip nat inside
 encapsulation frame-relay
 no ip split-horizon eigrp 65002
 no ip mroute-cache
 frame-relay map ip 192.168.1.3 102 broadcast
 frame-relay map ip 192.168.1.4 302 broadcast
 frame-relay lmi-type cisco
!
router eigrp 65002
 redistribute static
 network 172.16.0.0
 network 192.168.1.0
 default-metric 10000 100 254 1 1500
 no auto-summary
!
ip nat inside source list 101 interface Ethernet3 overload
ip classless
ip route 0.0.0.0 0.0.0.0 206.191.241.41
no ip http server
!
access-list 101 permit ip any any
```

To test the policy, issue several extended pings from the mountain and island routers. By using the **show route-map** command on the forest router, you will be able to determine whether packets are being policy routed. Example 2-58 demonstrates two pings on the mountain router—one ping to the wow server and one to www.cisco.com (on the Internet).

Example 2-58 *Testing and Verifying PBR*

```
mountain# ping
Protocol [ip]:
Target IP address: 172.16.7.11
Repeat count [5]: 50
```

Example 2-58 *Testing and Verifying PBR (Continued)*

```
Datagram size [100]: 100
Timeout in seconds [2]:
Extended commands [n]:
Sweep range of sizes [n]:
Type escape sequence to abort.
Sending 50, 100-byte ICMP Echos to 172.16.7.11, timeout is 2 seconds:
!!!!!!!!!!!!!!!!!!!!!!!!!!!!!!!!!!!!!!!!!!!!!!!!!!!
Success rate is 100 percent (50/50), round-trip min/avg/max = 8/8/12 ms
mountain#
mountain# ping www.cisco.com
Type escape sequence to abort.
Sending 5, 100-byte ICMP Echos to 198.133.219.25, timeout is 2 seconds:
!!!!!
Success rate is 100 percent (5/5), round-trip min/avg/max = 136/700/1116 ms
mountain#

forest# show route-map
route-map policy_1, permit, sequence 10          ←small packets matched
  Match clauses:
    ip address (access-lists): 110
    length 0 1199
  Set clauses:
    ip next-hop 172.16.1.3
    Policy routing matches: 51 packets, 5814 bytes
route-map policy_1, permit, sequence 20
  Match clauses:
    ip address (access-lists): 110
    length 1200 1544
  Set clauses:
    ip next-hop 172.16.1.4
  Policy routing matches: 0 packets, 0 bytes
route-map policy_1, permit, sequence 30          ←Internet traffic
  Match clauses:
    ip address (access-lists): 130
  Set clauses:
    ip default next-hop 172.16.1.3
    Policy routing matches: 10 packets, 1140 bytes
route-map policy_1, permit, sequence 40
  Match clauses:
    ip address (access-lists): 140
  Set clauses:
    ip default next-hop 172.16.1.4
  Policy routing matches: 0 packets, 0 bytes
forest#
```

By performing the same test on the island router, with the exception of making the ping packet size of 1500 bytes, you can observe the policy routing working on the forest router. Example 2-59 lists the output of the **show route-map** command performed on the forest router, after running the test from the island router.

Example 2-59 **show route-map** *Command on the wow and forest Routers*

```
forest# show route-map
route-map policy_1, permit, sequence 10
  Match clauses:
    ip address (access-lists): 110
    length 0 1199
  Set clauses:
    ip next-hop 172.16.1.3
  Policy routing matches: 51 packets, 5814 bytes
route-map policy_1, permit, sequence 20          ←Large packets matched
  Match clauses:
    ip address (access-lists): 110
    length 1200 1544
  Set clauses:
    ip next-hop 172.16.1.4
  Policy routing matches: 101 packets, 152914 bytes
route-map policy_1, permit, sequence 30
  Match clauses:
    ip address (access-lists): 130
  Set clauses:
    ip default next-hop 172.16.1.3
  Policy routing matches: 10 packets, 1140 bytes
route-map policy_1, permit, sequence 40          ←Internet traffic
  Match clauses:
    ip address (access-lists): 140
  Set clauses:
    ip default next-hop 172.16.1.4
  Policy routing matches: 12 packets, 1286 bytes
forest#
```

PART III

Multicast Routing

CHAPTER 3

Configuring Multicast Routing

Multicast has been used for different purposes for many years. Saying "multicast" these days typically conjures up the idea of streaming video or audio from a particular event. At a much more basic level, however, multicast is a technology that allows one host to send a single stream of traffic to reach any number of destination hosts.

Without multicast, the only options available are

- **Unicast streams**—A number of specific copies equal to the number of destination hosts.
- **Broadcast streams**—Although only one stream from the source, this replicates to all stations regardless of their intent to receive.

In the early days of media streaming, unicast was actually the method used to receive the streams over the Internet. This led to a huge amount of wasted bandwidth on the senders' part, the receivers' networks, and virtually everything in between.

As with many things in the real world, changes, fixes, and new RFCs quickly emerged as a way to deal with the growing demand for online multimedia of this nature. Multicast Backbone (MBONE) was one of the original methods of distributing multicast transmissions across the Internet and between providers.

The purpose of this chapter is not to educate you on all the nuances of multicast network design and maintenance. It is to serve as a refresher—and then as a series of examples on how to configure things, particularly in reference to the CCIE lab exam!

Multicast Basics

Thinking about the idea of a single stream sent out to multiple destinations, but not all destinations, leads you to the concept of multicast groups. Destination stations must maintain membership in a particular multicast group to receive the information. Without the membership, the multicast stream cannot be delivered to stations on the network.

To understand the efficiency of multicasting, consider a video server offering a single channel of content, as shown in Figure 3-1. For full-motion, full-screen viewing, a video stream requires approximately 1.5 Mbps of server-to-client bandwidth. In a unicast environment, the server must send a separate video stream to the network for each client. (This consumes 1.5 * n Mbps of link bandwidth, where n = number of client viewers.) With a 10-Mbps Ethernet interface on the server, it takes only six or seven server-to-client streams to completely saturate the network interface. Even with a highly intelligent Gigabit Ethernet interface on a high-performance server, the practical limit would be from 250 to 300 1.5-Mbps video streams. Therefore, the server interface capacity can be a significant bottleneck, limiting the number of unicast video streams per video server. Replicated unicast transmissions consume a lot of bandwidth within the network, which is another significant limitation. If the path between server and client traverses h3 router hops and h2 switch hops, the "multi-unicast" video consumes 1.5 * n * h3 Mbps of router bandwidth, plus 1.5 * n * h2 Mbps of switch bandwidth. With 100 clients separated from the server by 2 router hops, and 2 switch hops (as shown in Figure 3-2), a single multi-unicast channel consumes 300 Mbps of router bandwidth and 300 Mbps of switch bandwidth. Even if you scale back the video stream bandwidth to 100 kbps (which provides acceptable quality in smaller windows on the screen), the multiple unicast streams consume 20 Mbps of both router and switch bandwidth.

Figure 3-1   *Object of Multicast: One-to-Many Routing*

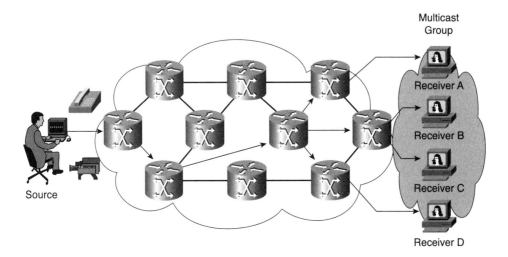

Multicast packets are replicated down appropriate paths in the network with Protocol Independent Multicast (PIM), Internet Group Management Protocol (IGMP), and other associated protocols to create the most efficient routing mechanism possible.

Figure 3-2   *Multicast Versus Unicast Efficiency*

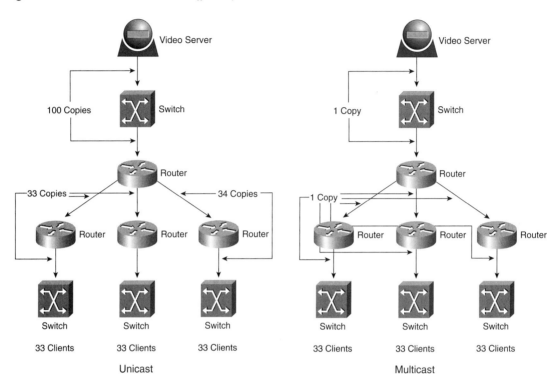

Multicast provides a tremendous advantage: the potential to save overall bandwidth and conserve processing power. However, there are disadvantages as well. Multicast traffic is mostly UDP in nature. Although this makes perfect sense for how to treat a video stream, or audio stream, consider what this actually means. UDP traffic, by definition, is "best delivery," which, of course, means "if you get it, you get it. If you don't, it's okay."

UDP inherently has more dropped packets throughout a transmission. UDP offers no congestion control mechanisms, such as windowing or retransmission. Sequencing is another possible problem with UDP-based transmissions. You can expect to see degradation of the video or sound quality as packets are missed. Playing them back out of order would make no sense. The same holds true for duplicate packets.

IP Multicast Addressing

IP addresses represent a specific set of the IPv4 address space known as *Class D addresses*. In a specific binary method, all the class addresses are laid out. Table 3-1 shows a listing of IPv4 class addressing.

Table 3-1   *IPv4 Class Addressing*

Address Class	Binary Representation	Decimal Notation
A	0*xxxxxxx*	First octet 1–126
B	10*xxxxxx*	First octet 128–191
C	110*xxxxx*	First octet 192–223
D	1110*xxxx*	First octet 224–239
E	1111*xxxx*	First octet 240–255

Note that certain restrictions apply to the address values listed in Table 3-1. For instance, the 127.0.0.0/8 address is reserved for loopback testing of various sorts. In addition, the Class E addresses are reserved for future or research purposes. The Class D address space, as it relates to multicast, is the focus here.

Class D addresses differ from any other preceding class. Typically, an IP address is thought of as a value representing a single, particular host that resides on the network (source address). In Class D addresses, the address denotes the recipient group, wherever it is. The multicast group has no geographic or location boundaries in most cases. The source for multicast packets is always noted as the unicast source address (Class A, B, or C).

Class D addresses are further broken down into some manageable segments along the way. The Internet Assigned Numbers Authority (IANA) controls the assignment of IPv4 address space, including multicast addresses. IANA has broken the Class D space down into some specific groups for easy assignment.

Note that addresses are assigned globally and given out one at a time, instead of in binary ranges like other IPv4 addresses. Table 3-2 shows a breakdown of the Class D address space.

Table 3-2   *Class D Multicast Address Allocations*

Description	IPv4 Address Range
Local-link address (reserved)	224.0.0.0/24
Globally scoped address (Assigned)	224.0.1.0 to 238.255.255.255
(Subset) Source-specific multicast	232.0.0.0/8
(Subset) GLOP addresses	233.0.0.0/8
Administratively scoped addresses (local)	239.0.0.0/8

Local-Link Addresses

The range of 224.0.0.0 through 224.0.0.255 has been reserved by IANA for use by network protocols on local network segments (subnets). Local-link address multicast packets have a Time-To-Live (TTL) of 1, so they are not forwarded by other routers onto different segments.

Many routing protocols use multicast addresses to maximize their efficiency. Table 3-3 lists some examples of local addresses.

Table 3-3   *Well-Known Multicast Groups*

IP Multicast Address	Protocol Usage
224.0.0.1	All systems
224.0.0.2	All routers
224.0.0.5	All OSPF routers
224.0.0.6	All OSPF designated routers
224.0.0.9	All RIPv2 routers
224.0.0.10	All Cisco Enhanced IGRP routers
224.0.0.12	DHCP server and relay agent
224.0.0.13	All multicast PIM routers

This is not an exhaustive list of the local multicast addresses that have been assigned but more of a common representation thereof.

Globally Scoped Addresses

The majority of the Class D multicast address space is known as the *globally scoped addresses*. IANA controls and assigns these addresses for specific multicast applications and uses. These addresses again represent the groups listening to a particular packet flow and do not represent the source of the information.

These addresses are also individually assigned without the concept of ranges or subnets. Table 3-4 shows some examples.

Table 3-4   *Globally Scoped Addresses for Common Applications*

IP Multicast Address	Protocol Usage
224.0.1.1	All systems (Network Time Protocol)
224.0.1.39	Cisco RP announce (auto-RP)
224.0.1.40	Cisco RP discovery (auto-RP)

This range of multicast address assignment is further defined in RFC 1112, *Host Extensions for IP Multicasting*. In addition, you can research all current assignments at http://www.iana.org/assignments/multicast-addresses. Some further addresses are reserved in RFC 1112.

Source-Specific Addresses

The addresses that fall within the 232.0.0.0/8 range are reserved for source-specific multicast. This is a type of multicast that allows some features of the multicast network, such as a rendezvous point (RP)— discussed later—to be bypassed after learning specific source information through a directory service.

Source-specific multicast might also remove the requirement of Multicast Source Discovery Protocol (MSDP) or other inter–autonomous system multicast shared tree arrangements. As an extension of the PIM protocol, other machines than the RP can provide "out-of-band" multicast services.

Typically, a receiver must issue a **join** command to a multicast group address. If multiple recipients join the same multicast group, even if information is sent from different source servers, both applications receive traffic from both sending servers. This solution yields extra traffic throughout the network.

In a source-specific multicast implementation, the router sees the join message specific to a particular multicast source. This is accomplished through the "include" mode within IGMP version 3. The router then sends the request directly to the source instead of sending it to the RP typically used.

There are no shared trees when dealing with source-specific multicast; everything is handled through source trees.

GLOP Addresses

Multicast addresses falling in the 233.0.0.0/8 range are reserved by RFC 2770 for GLOP. As an interesting note, GLOP does not stand for anything as an acronym; however, it is an interesting word! This is where any holder of an autonomous system number is automatically granted multicast addresses that route throughout the Internet.

An autonomous system number is a 16-bit number (1–65,535) used to signify separate systems of Border Gateway Protocol (BGP) speakers on the Internet. Fitting nicely into the equation here, taking those 16 bits and fitting them into the two middle octets yields 256 multicast addresses per octet.

For example, AS 22222 is represented by 01010110 11001110 in binary—or 86.206 split into two octets and converted back to decimal. So AS 22222 is automatically granted 233.86.206.0/24 multicast addresses to use as it sees fit throughout the Internet.

Administratively Scoped Addresses

Also known as *limited-scope addresses*, administratively scoped addresses fall within the range of 239.0.0.0/8. RFC 2365 sets these addresses aside to be used within a company or organization. Private companies, campuses, or other networks can use these addresses to run multicast applications that will not be forwarded outside their autonomous system.

Service provider routers are typically configured to filter this type of multicast traffic to be sure applications do not flow outside the appropriate multicast domain. Large organizations might also separate these into scopes (the multicast theory of subnetting) to separate them across smaller multicast domains.

Layer 2 Multicast Addresses

Typically, a network interface card (NIC) on a system is capable of recognizing only frames destined for their burned-in MAC address (BIA) or the broadcast MAC address (all Fs). In the networks using IP multicast, multiple hosts need to be able to receive a single data stream with a common address. The 802.3 standards actually allowed this to occur by using the least significant bit (bit 0) of the most significant byte (far-left byte). When this bit is set to 0, it represents an individual address to which the NIC registers only its BIA. When this bit is set to a 1, it represents a group address encompassing broadcasts and multicasts.

For those who remember back to their CCIE written exam, this is the bit that was referred to as the I/G bit in an Ethernet MAC address.

As an example of Layer 2 multicast addresses, consider the Intermediate System-to-Intermediate System (IS-IS) routing protocol. A derivation of the OSI Connectionless Network Service (CLNS) protocol suite, IP IS-IS uses a Layer 2 multicast address when it talks to neighbors:

Level 1 IS-IS routers talk with 01-80-C2-00-00-14.

Level 2 IS-IS routers talk with 01-80-C2-00-00-15.

As a side note, the next least significant bit (bit 1) of that same byte represents a locally assigned MAC address (LAA), which allows multiple individual addresses to be received. This is a common occurrence on Token Ring networks where "functional addresses" are used for devices assuming necessary roles in network operation. Figure 3-3 shows a MAC address bit layout.

Figure 3-3 *MAC Address Bit Layout*

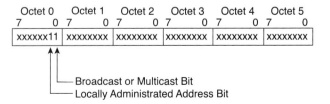

Again, as you might remember from those days of the CCIE written exam and other Ethernet-related trivia, the first three octets in a MAC address represent the OUI code. The IANA has been allocated an organizational unique identifier (OUI) code for Ethernet multicast MAC addresses. This OUI code is 01:00:5E. One additional bit is allocated and forced to be a 0 value. This adds up to 25 bits out of 48 total pre-allocated, leaving 23 bits to vary, as shown in Figure 3-4..

Figure 3-4   *IP Multicast-to-MAC Addressing*

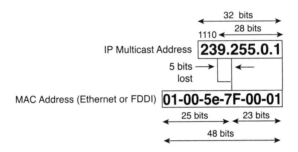

Now, for some interesting trivia to go with the mapping values, look at the binary values shown here by the OUI allocation code—the E value in particular. E in hexadecimal is 1110 in binary. All Class D IP addresses begin with binary values of 11100000 (224) through 11101111 (239). The first nibble of all multicast addresses is 1110 (E in hex).

This means that out of the 32 binary bits in all multicast addresses, at least 4 of them are always the same and statically represented in the OUI allocation representing multicast IP on an Ethernet network.

Regarding the mapping of IP multicast addresses into MAC addresses, however, you can see that this still leaves you with 23 bits to remap. The lower 23 bits of a 32-bit multicast IP address are mapped in here. Because the leading 4 bits are already represented by the E, this leaves 5 bits unmapped as shown in Figure 3-5.

Figure 3-5   *Overlap of Multicast MAC Addresses*

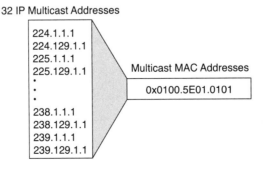

An Ethernet multicast MAC address has some overlap—the same MAC address is assigned to 32 different multicast groups. If one user on an Ethernet segment subscribes to multicast group 225.1.1.1, and another user subscribes to 225.129.1.1, both users receive both multicast streams. In engineering multicast networks on LAN segments, this overlap needs to be specifically watched for and engineered to avoid the problem.

With Token Ring networks, the overlap is even greater. As mentioned earlier, Token Ring uses the concept of functional addresses. Also, remember that Token Ring uses noncanonical addressing, so the bits are swapped on a byte level. Layer 3 IP multicast addresses are mapped to a single functional address, leaving just a little bit of overlap. Subtracting the first 4 bits that all IP multicast addresses have in common leaves 28 bits of overlap, or approximately 268,435,200 multicast addresses mapped into a single MAC address.

Needless to say, the best way to engineer multicast on Layer 2 is to *not use* Token Ring. Within Cisco configuration, the default mechanism is to map multicast packets into broadcast frames (FFFF.FFFF.FFFF).

If you want to use the Token Ring functional address, use the **ip multicast use-functional** command on the Token Ring interface. This uses C000.0004.0000 to map the multicast IP packets.

Multicast Distribution Trees

Multicast routers create distribution trees to control the path that multicast traffic takes throughout a network infrastructure to deliver traffic. Distribution trees consist of two basic types: source trees and shared trees.

Source Trees

The *source distribution tree* is also known as the shortest-path tree, and just like it sounds, it is a small spanning tree with the shortest path from the root (source) of the tree to each of the leaves (recipients). Figure 3-6 shows an example of a multicast source tree.

The notation of S,G represents a pairing of the source (unicast) address and the group (multicast) address; this pair discovers the shortest-path tree. In Figure 3-6, the S,G noted is (192.168.1.1, 224.1.1.1).

This S,G notation is used for each source tree. Every individual source sending to each specific group results in a separate S,G tree being noted. In large networks, this can lead to an inordinate number of S,G trees being planted in a network. This inefficiency necessitated shared trees and encouraged their use.

Figure 3-6   *Multicast Source Tree*

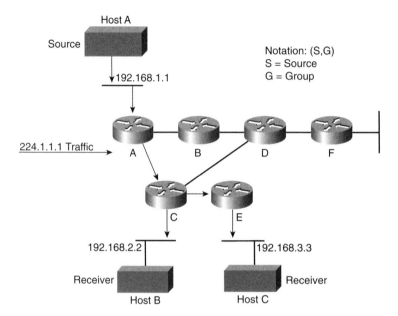

Shared Trees

Unlike source trees, all multicast groups have a common root, regardless of source. The shared root in all these trees is known as the *rendezvous point (RP)*. Unlike the S,G mappings that you see with source trees, with shared trees, you see *,G mappings because the source is not specifically noted; therefore, the asterisk (*) represents any source.

The shared tree is unidirectional in nature; all traffic is sent from the source to the RP. Traffic is then forwarded down from the shared tree and RP to reach each of the receivers; however, exceptions to this rule do apply. If the receiver is located between the source and RP, for instance, the receiver is handled through a source tree directly.

After working within the shared tree and communicating with the RP, any intermediate multicast router might determine that it is a shorter path to the multicast source rather than through the RP shared tree. In this instance, a multicast router joins a source tree (S,G) and prunes from the shared tree. The shortest path is determined by the routing tables.

Figure 3-7 shows a multicast network with an RP. Because all sources in the multicast group use the same tree, the multicast *,G tree maps as (*,224.2.2.2). One of the difficulties with this shared tree concept is that all multicast routers do not automatically learn of new multicast groups. With PIM spare mode, all sources register with a registration message to the RP indicating a new multicast source. All other multicast routers know to inquire of the RP as clients join various multicast groups.

Figure 3-7   *Rendezvous Point in Multicast Network*

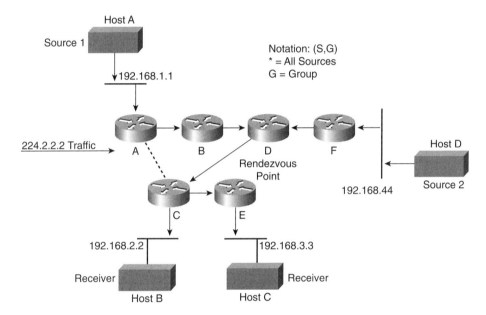

Both shared trees and source trees are loop free. Throughout the topology, multicast packets are sent only down active tree branches, as client systems join or leave multicast groups. When all receivers on a branch leave a group, the routers prune back the tree. If more clients join, the routers dynamically modify the tree.

Routers keep path information for each source. In large networks, with hundreds or thousands of groups being monitored, you need to consider the memory consumption on the router and the size of the multicast routing table in the multicast design. Shared trees inherently require less memory because of the common path to the RP. Similarly, in network design, consider the placement of the RP with respect to the position of multicast sources and the size of the share tree.

Multicast Forwarding

In a normal unicast network, all decisions are based on the destination address of a packet. In a multicast network, paths are determined in a more arbitrary fashion that varies based on which branches within a tree have active clients and which ones do not.

In source trees, traffic is forwarded based on the source address among other factors. In general, traffic is viewed as moving away from the source rather than toward the receivers.

Reverse Path Forwarding

The unicast routing database creates a multicast distribution tree. PIM selects the reverse path from the receivers toward the source to set this up. PIM uses the routing table to determine both the upstream and downstream interface. Depending on which PIM mode you use (sparse or dense), the reverse path forward (RPF) check might be based on a distribution tree toward the RP or toward the multicast source. The following section discusses PIM trees in more detail. The RPF check helps guarantee that a multicast distribution tree is loop free.

When a multicast packet comes through a router, as Figure 3-8 shows, the router performs an RPF check on the packet. If the RPF check succeeds, the packet is forwarded. If the RPF check fails, the packet is dropped.

Figure 3-8 *Reverse Path Forwarding Decision*

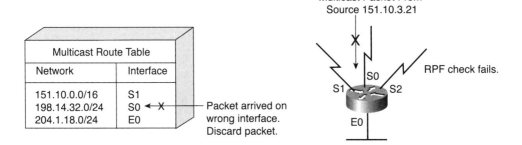

The router first looks up the source address in the unicast routing table to see whether the packet that arrived on the same interface would be the reverse path back to the source. If the packet arrives on the correct interface leading back to the source, the check succeeds and the packet is forwarded. As Figure 3-8 shows, if it arrives on any other interface, the RPF check fails and the packet is dropped.

Protocol Independent Multicasting

Protocol Independent Multicasting (PIM) is a routing protocol-independent method of moving multicast packets throughout an internetwork. Regardless of which routing protocol you use, including everything from static routes to OSPF and BGP, PIM uses the information from the Routing Information Base (RIB) to perform multicast routing. Although PIM uses the unicast routing table for the RPF check, it does not send and receive routing updates like other routing protocols do. All PIM modes are configured on a per-interface basis.

For the CCIE exam, you need to know about the following three PIM forwarding modes:

- PIM dense mode
- PIM sparse mode
- Bidirectional PIM

PIM Dense Mode

PIM dense mode uses a push method to move multicast packets through a network. In simple terms, a multicast router sends all multicast traffic out on all interfaces until another device tells it to be quiet (pruning).

Dense mode is persistent, however. It resets this flooding behavior every 3 minutes and must be repruned. PIM dense mode supports only source trees and cannot be used to build a shared multicast tree. (Note the importance of the wording here regarding tree types.)

To configure PIM dense mode, use the following command in interface configuration mode:

```
Router(config-if)# ip pim dense-mode
```

PIM Sparse Mode

PIM sparse mode uses a pull method to move multicast packets through the network. Network branches with active receivers are the only segments to receive multicast traffic. The various multicast routers paying attention to joins and leaves of a multicast group activate or prune traffic as necessary.

PIM sparse mode requires an RP. After receivers register, the data is sent down the shared tree toward the receivers. Each multicast router compares the metric of the RP address to the metric of the source address of the multicast group. If the metric for the source is better (highlighting the location of the RP in the network), the S,G tree is built. The trees might take the same path for a short time and , therefore, are considered congruent paths, as demonstrated in Figure 3-9.

Figure 3-10 *Multicast Lab Network Diagram*

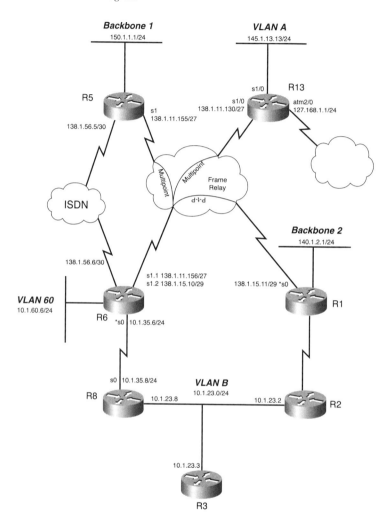

Lab 5: Solution

The wording is key when considering this type of scenario. The fact that the scenario did not want unnecessary traffic to be exchanged indicates that you should not use the PIM dense mode.

The next issue in the configuration is where you should place the **pim** statements and who should be the RP. Obviously, all routers need the **ip multicast-routing** command configured in global mode. In addition, all interfaces between the most distant endpoints participating in multicast groups must be configured with the **ip pim sparse-mode interface** command.

Which router chosen to be the RP in this example is negligible? No preference is indicated by the scenario question, and the topology is not large enough to make any difference as to which router is chosen. In live multicast networks, the placement of the RP can prove critical when viewing functional choices such as the SPT algorithm and designing overall traffic flow.

The next step is to configure all other routers with the **ip pim rp-address** command. A common question arising from this is whether the **rp-address** command must be placed on the actual router that is the RP. The answer is that it does not matter. If explicitly configured, the router knows. If not configured, as other routers send PIM join and prune messages, the router knows to assume the RP role automatically.

NOTE   Check the Cisco IOS Software release notes regarding this concept. Newer versions of Cisco IOS Software actually require you to configure the **rp-address** command on the RP itself.

To test the scenario and complete the joins, you must select some interfaces in both VLANs and issue the **ip igmp join-group 239.42.42.42 interface** command. After issuing these commands, you can ping the multicast group and receive responses from each joining router.

Lab 5: Configurations

Example 3-1   *Command Entries Edited from* **show running-configuration** *on Routers*

```
R2
ip multicast-routing
!
interface ethernet 0
 ip pim sparse-mode
 ip igmp join-group 239.42.42.42
!
ip pim rp-address 10.1.23.3

R3
ip multicast-routing
!
interface ethernet 0
 ip pim sparse-mode

R6
ip multicast-routing
```

continues

Example 3-1 *Command Entries Edited from* **show running-configuration** *on Routers (Continued)*

```
!
interface ethernet 0
 ip pim sparse-mode
 ip igmp join-group 239.42.42.42
!
interface serial 0
 ip pim sparse-mode
!
ip pim rp-address 10.1.23.3

R8
ip multicast-routing
!
interface ethernet 0
 ip pim sparse-mode
 ip igmp join-group 239.42.42.42
!
interface serial 0
 ip pim sparse-mode
!
ip pim rp-address 10.1.23.3
```

Multicast Frame Relay

Running multicast over Frame Relay networks is similar to running it over any other network, except for some distinct differences that you might actually notice in real-life networks. With point-to-point Frame Relay interfaces, things such as routing protocols and other options tend to work "normally."

In multipoint interfaces, consider the differences. Frame Relay is a nonbroadcast multiaccess network. The word "broadcast," much like in Ethernet MAC marking, indicates multicast packets as well. To make routing protocols work, you use **frame-relay map** commands with the **broadcast** parameter.

You also need to also consider how the Frame Relay interface handles multicast traffic. On a physical interface, there are two interface queues—one handles normal traffic, and the other handles broadcast traffic. The broadcast queue is a strict-priority queue and is typically used for important items, such as routing protocol updates. The Frame Relay interface does not have a way to differentiate multicast traffic flows such as video or audio streaming from other multicast items such as OSPF routing protocols.

Traffic traversing the broadcast queue is also process switched by default, not fast switched.

In the lab networks, nobody cares. In real life, having a bandwidth-intensive video stream monopolize a strict-priority queue and starving out other "normal" traffic is a much more important event. To remedy this problem, you must instruct the router to deal with nonrouting multicast traffic, just as it would with any other "normal" traffic on the interface.

Frame Relay handling of multicast might raise other issues, too. Typically, PIM works on an interface basis. In a normal multipoint Frame Relay environment, there might be many paths out the same actual interface. When it comes to properly processing join and prune messages, this can lead to difficulties where one router's prune message cuts off traffic for every other router.

Much of the technical differences involved are beyond the scope of this book. (You can consult some of the reference material listed at the end of this chapter for further reading.)

For lab-based scenarios as well as most real-life scenarios, you need to address the different handling of Frame Relay interfaces with regard to multicast traffic.

The **ip pim nbma-mode** interface command enables you to do this. This command works only with PIM sparse mode because it relies on PIM join messages to indicate traffic types. This command is issued in addition to the **ip pim sparse-mode** command. This command, among other functions, allows multicast traffic to be fast switched over Frame Relay network interfaces. Watch the wording and topology within your CCIE lab scenarios.

Multicast TTL

As multicast packets traverse a router, the TTL is decremented. If the TTL is less than or equal to 0, the packet is dropped. If the TTL is greater than 0, it might be compared to the TTL threshold manually configured on the router. If the packet's TTL is greater than the threshold, it is forwarded.

Typically, TTL thresholds are set only on multicast or autonomous system boundary routers to make sure traffic does not cross where it should not.

To set a TTL threshold, use the **ip multicast ttl-threshold** *ttl-value* interface command.

Multicast Boundary

As a more stringent control, if multicast traffic is not desired to cross an imaginary line in a router, you can set up a multicast boundary. You can restrict this to certain multicast groups through a standard IP access list.

The **ip multicast boundary (acl#)** interface command enables you to create multicast boundaries. Multicast boundaries are bidirectional in nature. You can also add a parameter of **filter-autorp** to the command to filter multicast range announcements within the auto-RP messages. Auto-RP is discussed next.

```
Router(config-if)# ip multicast boundary 1
Router(config)# access-list 1 deny 239.0.0.0 0.255.255.255
Router(config)# access-list 1 permit 224.0.0.0 15.255.255.255
```

PIM Auto-RP

Instead of manually configuring the RP to each multicast router, the RP can announce itself. This proves especially useful in large network environments.

Auto-RP uses 224.0.1.39 and 224.0.1.40 multicast groups to send information. Auto-RP floods this information through PIM dense mode. For auto-RP to work properly, the routers must use the **ip pim sparse-dense-mode** interface command. Without the dense mode capability, the RP will never be learned.

The auto-RP functionality also includes mapping agents. Mapping agents hear about RPs (via the 224.0.1.39 multicast group) and send RP-to-group mappings in a discovery statement via 224.0.1.40.

The mapping agents receive messages from candidate RPs throughout the network. The mapping agent is responsible for creating consistent multicast group-to-RP mappings and sending these announcements to all multicast routers by dense mode flooding.

In a Frame Relay environment using auto-RP, you must address a few considerations. All candidate RPs must have a **map** statement or otherwise connect to the mapping agents. All mapping agents must connect to all multicast routers.

To configure the router as the RP and announce so that other multicast routers can automatically learn, use the **ip pim send-rp-announce** *source intf* **scope** *ttl-value* global command.

To function as a mapping agent, use the **ip pim send-rp-discovery scope** *ttl-value* global command.

Typically, loopbacks are used for the RP addresses (source interface). The loopback interface must be reachable with an Interior Gateway Protocol (IGP) and must have PIM enabled on the interface. Select loopback interfaces because they will be an "always up" interface, and, therefore, are reachable through any other "up" interface.

Anycast RP

A newer method of controlling multicast RP stability throughout an internetwork is called *anycast RP*. Some new concepts and protocols relate to this approach. The gist behind anycast RP is that a single IP address is statically configured as the RP throughout a network. (See Example 3-2.)

This IP address can exist on multiple routers simultaneously. (This concept is one that causes many people to have a puzzled expression.) Yes, you can configure the same IP address on multiple routers. One of the interesting things about IP addresses, particularly for a /32 route, is that routing tables all across a network could care less where an IP exists. All routing tables pull information from RIBs, which are exchanged through routing protocols. Routing protocols differentiate IP reachability based on metrics. If multiple routers advertise the same IP network, the best path is chosen based on metric value. No router actually knows where a route exists or compares information beyond that. Multicast senders and receivers join their closest RP based on routing metrics.

Working with this general concept, you need to understand how basic routing functionality and multiple IP address existence can help. You need to consider an additional protocol.

Typically designed for service provider types of interdomain multicast, the Multicast Source Discovery Protocol (MSDP) is in this scenario to make sure that all the configured RPs contain the same basic information about multicast sources and multicast groups.

MSDP sessions run between all RP routers. As shown in Figure 3-11, an IP network can have multiple RPs present. Each multicast router throughout the network has the RP address statically configured.

Each of the RP routers has a loopback configured with the IP address that is considered the RP. In addition, each router has some other IP address to uniquely identify it. This second IP address peers with MSDP. In larger environments, you can configure MSDP as a full mesh between peers.

Figure 3-11 *Anycast RP Diagram*

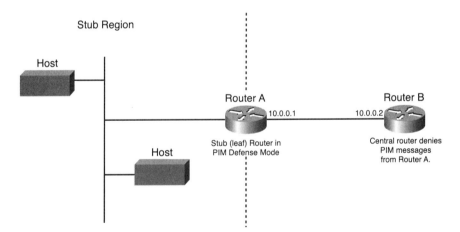

Example 3-2 *Configuration of MSDP on Anycast RP Routers*

```
RP1
interface loopback 0
  ip address 10.1.1.1 255.255.255.255
!
interface loopback 1
  ip address 10.0.0.101 255.255.255.255
!
ip msdp peer 10.0.0.102 connect-source loopback 1
ip msdp originator-id loopback 1

RP2
interface loopback 0
  ip address 10.1.1.1 255.255.255.255
!
interface loopback 1
  ip address 10.0.0.102 255.255.255.255
!
ip msdp peer 10.0.0.101 connect-source loopback 1
ip msdp originator-id loopback 1
```

MSDP peers with a TCP session and exchanges any new source active (SA) messages with all other peers. The commands listed are the minimum necessary to make MSDP operational. This minimum is listed here not to belittle the technology but because this theory is commonly oriented toward service providers and not toward typical enterprises. This topic, however, has come under increasing scrutiny to those preparing for the CCIE Routing and Switching lab.

The commands listed in Example 3-2 establish a shared (10.1.1.1) and unique (10.0.0.101 and 10.0.0.102) IP address on each RP. The **ip msdp** commands specify the peering RP, as well as which interface is the connect source and originator ID for all messages. This avoids confusion and obvious difference in each router's routing table.

Lab 6: Set Up Frame Relay Multicast Routing

Using the same network from Figure 3-10, configure VLAN A and Backbone 1 to participate in multicast group 225.3.3.3. R13 needs to be the RP for all multicast groups, except administratively scoped addresses, but should not be explicitly configured on any other routers. R5 needs to be the RP for the administratively scoped addresses.

Make sure that multicast packets do not cross back into VLAN B or other networks. These other networks might be running separate multicast groups.

Lab 6 Solution

For all CCIE scenarios, everything is in the wording. Running multicast on VLAN A and Backbone 1 tells you that R5, R6, and R13 must be involved in the multicast network, which, of course, is a Frame Relay multipoint network interface.

Therefore, in addition to the **ip multicast-routing** commands on these three routers, the Frame Relay interfaces must also run the **ip pim nbma-mode** command.

Next, you realize PIM sparse mode will be used because there is an RP. Because you must use auto-RP commands, however, PIM dense mode is needed, too. Each Frame Relay interface (the links between each of the multicast routers) will be configured with IP PIM sparse dense mode.

You must create access lists to filter certain multicast networks. On R13, administratively scoped addresses are not served as RP.

```
access-list 13 deny 239.0.0.0 0.255.255.255
access-list 13 permit 224.0.0.0 15.255.255.255
```

That access list denies administratively scoped addresses but permits all the other addresses. On R5, just the opposite takes place:

```
access-list 5 permit 239.0.0.0 0.255.255.255
```

The access list implicitly denies all other multicast addresses.

Each router then uses the **ip pim send-rp-announce** *src-intf* **scope 16 group-list** *acl#* global command to begin advertising itself as the RP for the multicast groups in the access lists.

R6 is the multipoint Frame Relay interface that all traffic between R5 and R13 must join. With that in mind, it is the best choice for the mapping agent (multicast RP relay). Use the **ip pim send-rp-discovery scope 16** global command to make it the mapping agent.

Finally, the scenario requires that you set up a boundary between the Frame Relay cloud multicast network and any other network below.

```
access-list 6 deny any
ip multicast boundary 6
```

The question is, where do you place the **multicast boundary**? The answer is wherever you need to, ensuring that no line will be crossed. Three other interfaces on R6 serve other networks: the Ethernet interface, the serial link to R8, and another Frame Relay subinterface to R1. You need to place the **multicast boundary** command on each of these interfaces.

Lab 6: Configurations

To configure a router with command entries, refer to Example 3-3 to see how the **show running-configuration** works on a router.

Example 3-3 *Command Entries Edited from* **show running-configuration** *on Routers*

```
R5
ip multicast-routing
!
access-list 5 permit 239.0.0.0 0.255.255.255
!
ip pim send-rp-announce ethernet 0 scope 16 group-list 5
!
interface ethernet 0
 ip pim spare-dense-mode
 ip igmp join-group 225.3.3.3
!
interface serial 1
 ip pim sparse-dense-mode
 ip pim nbma-mode
!
```

```
R6
ip multicast-routing
!
ip pim send-rp-discovery scope 16
!
access-list 6 deny any
!
interface serial 1.1 multipoint
 ip pim sparse-dense-mode
 ip pim nbma-mode
!
interface serial 1.2 point-to-point
 ip multicast boundary 6
!
interface ethernet 0
 ip multicast boundary 6
!
interface serial 0
 ip multicast boundary 6
```

```
R13
ip multicast-routing
!
access-list 13 deny 239.0.0.0 0.255.255.255
access-list 13 permit 224.0.0.0 15.255.255.255
!
ip pim send-rp-announce ethernet 1/0 scope 16 group-list 13
!
interface ethernet 1/0
```

Example 3-3 *Command Entries Edited from* **show running-configuration** *on Routers (Continued)*

```
 ip pim sparse-dense-mode
 ip igmp join-group 225.3.3.3
 !
interface serial 1/0
 ip pim sparse-dense-mode
 ip pim nbma-mode
```

Multicast Joining

From the solution for Lab 5 (and from the implications of Lab 6), you are aware of the **ip igmp join-group** *mcast#* interface command. To make your router (lab) actually respond to multicast and join the group, you must type in an **igmp** command like this. What else is it used for, however?

In real life, you can use it to supply multicast groups to a LAN segment, enabling clients to interpret multicast but not enabling them to initiate group membership through IGMP. With the interface participating in the group, multicast traffic *is* forwarded to that LAN segment. Be aware of this functionality when it comes to paying attention to the wording of a CCIE lab scenario.

There is a downside—in real life—to this. Because the packets are processed by the router before being sent out, they are only process switched. This can degrade the performance of your router overall and is not necessarily a good thing to do. In the lab, however, you do not have those same concerns.

But wait—there's a better way to accomplish this! As you consider the wording of a CCIE lab scenario, look for the concept wording about forwarding multicast traffic on to a LAN segment without receiving IGMP messages from clients. In addition, watch for references to ensure that the router does not process the multicast packets; optimize the processing speed of the router while doing this.

What does this mean?

If you use the **ip igmp static-group** *mcast#* interface command, it accomplishes exactly that. Therefore, watch for the wording in the lab scenario to tell you what you need to know.

With the **ip igmp static-group** command, multicast packets are automatically fast switched without interaction with the RP.

Another scenario to watch out for deals with converting incoming multicast traffic into some other type of packet, such as broadcasts. This is used for clients who are not properly capable of receiving multicasts. The downside, of course, is that when converting to broadcast packets, many more stations might receive (and process) the multicast traffic than actually want it.

This conversion process uses multicast helper addresses and "bouncing" through a UDP port. The whole operation is similar to how Dynamic Host Configuration Protocol (DHCP) relay works. First, the unique, high UDP port is selected and a filtering access list is created, using the following commands:

```
Router(config)# ip forward-protocol udp 4400
Router(config)# access-list 101 permit udp any any eq 4400
Router(config)# access-list 101 deny udp any any
```

Next, these are bound to the conversion process on a LAN segment interface. To flood things out, you must use PIM dense mode as specified in the following commands:

```
Router(config-if)# ip pim dense-mode
Router(config-if)# ip directed-broadcast
Router(config-if)# ip multicast helper-map broadcast 225.4.4.4 101
```

These commands bind multicast group 225.4.4.4 to the UDP port specified in access list 101 and handle the conversion process of that group into broadcast packets for the interface. Note the **ip directed-broadcast** command here. The default in Cisco IOS Software 12.0 or later is to not allow subnet-level broadcasts to come in to the interface.

You might potentially open up a security flaw by working this scenario. But again, in the CCIE lab, you are not always concerned with these things.

Lab 7: Multicast Joining

Consider the network topology from Figure 3-10 again. Clients on Backbone 2 cannot send IGMP join messages but need to listen to a multicast stream 225.9.13.5 from source 10.1.60.6. No multicast traffic should run over the Frame Relay cloud. R1 should be optimized to handle the multicast traffic because it is already an overtaxed router.

Lab 7: Solution

A few things going on here are important. Isolate the provided information. The source is 10.1.60.66 (VLAN 60 from R6) running over multicast group 225.9.13.5. The destination is clients on Backbone 2 (off of R1).

Remember that multicast trees follow the unicast best-route mentality when traversing a network. This tells you that the Frame Relay line between R6 and R1 is the preferred path. However, it is not allowed to work that way. Who said the CCIE lab was easy?

All routers run the **ip multicast-routing** global command.

Handle the scenario one step at a time. You can set up R6 as the RP, and E0/0 can join the IGMP group 225.9.13.5 at this point. In a scenario such as this, where no preference is given to sparse-only versus sparse-dense PIM, the latter is typically chosen. (See Example 3-4.)

Example 3-4   *Command Entries Edited from* **show running-configuration** *on Routers*

```
R6(config-if)# ip pim sparse-dense-mode
R6(config-if)# ip igmp join-group 225.9.13.5
```

Globally, you need to define the RP on each router:

```
R6(config)# ip pim rp-address 10.1.60.6
```

All routers between R6 and R1 (not through the Frame Relay cloud) need to have multicast and PIM enabled to forward the traffic.

R1 needs to join the multicast group on its Ethernet segment but needs to be optimized as well. A nonoptimized router spends a lot of time processing packets and using memory that it should not use. This leads you to using the **static-group** rather than the **join-group** command. The fact that clients were unable to use IGMP joins should have also told you this. (See Example 3-5.)

Example 3-5   *Command Entries Edited from* **show running-configuration** *on Routers*

```
R1(config-if)# ip pim dense-mode
R1(config-if)# ip igmp static-group 225.9.13.5
```

The final thing you must consider is the routing of the multicast packets. This chapter has not yet addressed the concept of overriding the multicast routes; however, you need to think of these things and consider how to address issues that you might not have faced prior to seeing them on the CCIE lab!

Multicast packets are automatically checked for RPF based on the anticipated interface back to the IP source of the multicast sender. If a multicast packet arrives on an interface that is not the direction back to the sender's IP, the packet is dropped. Because you move multicast packets around, all these interfaces need to be multicast-capable in this scenario, too.

You definitely need to "adjust" R1 for routing. Whether you need to do so with other routers depends on what the IP routing table demands for next hop. On R1, you can adjust the choice manually with a static multicast route as follows:

```
R6(config)# ip mroute 10.1.60.6 255.255.255.255 [protocol as-number] {rpf IP# | intf}
[(admin. Distance)]
```

On R1, the RPF IP is the address on R2; or like IP static routes, you can route to the interface itself. The **ip mroute** command enables you to denote multicast source IP addresses in the address portion of the command.

Lab 7: Configuration

This section presents the router configuration for this lab solution. (See Example 3-6.)

Example 3-6 *Command Entries Edited from* **show running-configuration** *on Routers*

```
R6
ip multicast-routing
!
interface ethernet 0
 ip pim sparse-dense-mode
!
interface serial 0
 ip pim sparse-dense-mode
!
!


R8
ip multicast-routing
ip pim rp-address 10.1.60.6
!
interface serial 0
 ip pim sparse-dense-mode
!
interface ethernet 0
 ip pim sparse-dense-mode
!


R2
ip multicast-routing
ip pim rp-address 10.1.60.6
!
interface ethernet 0
 ip pim sparse-dense-mode
!
interface serial 1
 ip pim sparse-dense-mode
!


R1
ip multicast-routing
ip pim rp-address 10.1.60.6
!
interface serial 1
 ip pim sparse-dense-mode
!
interface ethernet 0
 ip pim dense-mode
```

Example 3-6   *Command Entries Edited from* **show running-configuration** *on Routers (Continued)*

```
 ip igmp static-group 225.9.13.5
 !
ip mroute 225.9.13.5 255.255.255.255 serial 1
 !
```

Controlling Multicast

When it comes to controlling multicast in networks, you face several issues and have several points at which you can control it. Such control is of particular concern when it comes to rate limiting. How can you rate limit multicast traffic? The short answer is, in several ways depending on the device performing the rate limiting.

On the Catalyst 3550, you can rate limit on a per-port basis with a function known as *storm control*. To make sure that multicast traffic occupies no more than 10 percent of a particular port (or EtherChannel group), issue the following command:

```
Cat3550(config-if)# storm-control multicast level 10
```

On a router, inclusive of WAN links, you can rate limit by issuing the **ip multicast rate-limit** (**in** | **out**) [**group-list** (*acl#*)] [**source-list** (*acl#*)] **interface** *kbps* command. If this command is not present, no rate limiting is being performed. If this command is present but no bandwidth is set, the default is 0, meaning no multicast is allowed.

Fast Switching

As you might recall, special care was taken with the **ip igmp static-group** command to ensure that multicast packets would be fast switched through a router. Now, consider what you need to do if the scenario calls for the disabling of fast switching.

The process is similar to what you use for unicast forwarding. Fast switching involves the use of a route cache to store recently used route choices and speed up subsequent path selection. To disable this in unicast, use the **no ip route-cache interface** command. In multicast, the logic is the same. The **no ip mroute-cache interface** command handles this.

Multicast Stub

When building a PIM tree, you can have branches (segments) with only one possible way to go in each direction. Similar to a stub network in the unicast world, you can limit the amount of control traffic in and out of the stub area because there is actually no path choice to be made. Figure 3-12 shows a multicast stub network.

Figure 3-12 *Multicast Stub Network*

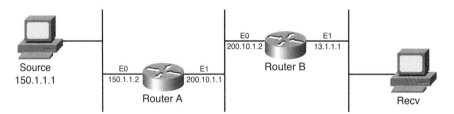

On the stub router (Router A), the outward-facing link uses the **ip igmp helper-address 10.0.0.2 interface** command. This forwards all IGMP messages to the central router, without processing the typical IGMP report and query messages necessary itself, to make PIM work.

On the central router (Router B), the link facing the stub would have a **filter** command calling an access list to stop the PIM mechanism between Router A and Router B.

```
RouterB(config)# access-list 11 deny host 10.0.0.1
RouterB(config-if)# ip pim neighbor-filter 11
```

After these configuration steps, the IGMP messages from any hosts behind Router A forward on to Router B. Router A does participate in any PIM trees and does not participate based on the **filter** command.

Load Balancing or Disconnected Multicast Networks

Multicast does not offer load balancing or load sharing (in any sense). It performs an RPF check, and the answer is either yes or no, with no gray area. How do you share between equal-cost paths? How do you run multicast between two routers when the network in the middle does not support multicast? Like many things in the CCIE world, you need to think outside the box.

One simple word: *tunnel.* Do not forget about tunnels as part of the solution. Tunnels provide a simple way to encapsulate otherwise nonroutable traffic and deliver it from point A to point B. By encapsulating multicast (or any other) traffic into an IP unicast generic routing encapsulation (GRE) packet, the encapsulated packet takes on unicast properties. With that, the routers in the middle see only an IP packet destined for some place. The unicast IP packet can be load balanced because the router is concerned only with destination now and not source or group information as in the multicast world.

Lab 8: Advanced Multicast Delivery

Working from the network shown in Figure 3-10, enable multicast traffic for group 226.7.6.5 between VLAN A, VLAN B, and source on VLAN 60. The WAN cannot directly carry multicast traffic. Make sure that VLAN B does not use more than 2 Mbps of traffic for multicast.

Lab 8: Solution

As with any other configuration, you must issue the **ip multicast-routing global** command on all appropriate routers. All Ethernet interfaces need the appropriate **ip pim sparse-dense-mode** command, too.

To allow multicast through the Frame Relay cloud indirectly, create a tunnel on both R13 and R6, using the following commands:

```
R13(config)# interface Tunnel 0
R13(config-if)# ip unnumbered Serial 1/0
R13(config-if)# ip pim sparse-dense-mode
R13(config-if)# tunnel source Serial 1/0
R13(config-if)# tunnel destination 138.1.11.156
```

This creates the tunnel and allows the encapsulation of multicast packets.

You must complete another step, however, to override the typical RPF check (which looks to Serial 1/0 directly as the path), as follows:

```
R13(config)# ip mroute 10.1.60.0 255.255.255.0 Tunnel 0
```

With the source on VLAN 60, it is not necessary to override multicast routing (RPF) on R6.

For VLAN B's limiting, you must make configuration changes on the Catalyst 3550. Of course, the numbers you pick depend on whether the interface is 10 Mbps or 100 Mbps! Remember that storm control is a percentage-based algorithm.

```
Cat3550(config)# interface intf
! Note:  10 megabit Ethernet interface
Cat3550(config-if)# storm-control multicast level 2
```

Or

```
Cat3550(config)# interface intf
! Note:  100 megabit Ethernet interface
Cat3550(config-if)# storm-control multicast level 20
```

If your lab scenario specifies a multicast source, you can place rate limiting on a router with a specific source IP listing instead. The semantics of your lab scenario dictate which way to configure.

Lab 8: Configurations

This lab also demonstrates how to use command entries edited from the **show running-configuration** on routers. (See Example 3-7.)

Example 3-7 *Command Entries Edited from* **show running-configuration** *on Routers*

```
R8
ip multicast-routing
!
interface ethernet 0
 ip pim sparse-dense-mode
 ip igmp join-group 226.7.6.5
!
interface serial 0
 ip pim sparse-dense-mode


R6
ip multicast-routing
!
interface ethernet 0
 ip pim sparse-dense-mode
 ip igmp join-group 226.7.6.5
!
interface serial 0
 ip pim sparse-dense-mode
!
interface tunnel 0
 ip unnumbered serial 1.1
 ip pim sparse-dense-mode
 tunnel source serial 1
 tunnel destination 138.1.11.130
!


R13
ip multicast-routing
!
interface ethernet 1/0
 ip pim sparse-dense-mode
 ip igmp join-group 226.7.6.5
!
interface tunnel 0
 ip unnumbered serial 1/0
 ip pim sparse-dense-mode
 tunnel source serial 1/0
 tunnel destination 138.1.11.156
!
ip mroute 10.1.60.0 255.255.255.0 tunnel 0

Cat3550
```

Example 3-7 *Command Entries Edited from* **show running-configuration** *on Routers (Continued)*

```
interface 0/8
 description Link to R8-VLAN B
 storm-control multicast level 20
```

NOTE   You do not need to add other VLAN B routers because they will not route multicast traffic
anywhere according to the diagram.

DVMRP Multicast Routing

Because multicast routing and unicast routing deal with separate topologies, policy requires
that PIM follow the multicast topology to build loop-free distribution trees. PIM can use any
unicast routing protocol to reference for RPF checks, but multicast-specific protocols might be
better for tree building.

Using Distance Vector Multicast Routing Protocol (DVMRP), Cisco routers can exchange
DVMRP unicast routes with other routers or mrouted-based machines. PIM can also use this
for RPF information. The important note here is that DVMRP is a routing protocol for unicast
routes that are used within the multicast routing topology. It is not a method for routing
multicast through a network directly, nor is it a better path mechanism for normal unicast
routing.

Cisco routers can exchange DVMRP routes but will not actually route multicast via decisions
reached through DVMRP. Running DVMRP allows PIM to use the multicast topology, however,
which allows sparse mode PIM throughout the Internet topology. MBONE is another application of this type, where participants use a multicast routing protocol to build efficient multicast
topologies over otherwise discontiguous networks.

After DVMRP unicast routing is engaged, learned routes are cached in a separate RIB for
DVMRP. PIM prefers routes in the DVMRP RIB to routes in other RIBs learned by other
unicast routing protocols.

The DVMRP unicast routing can run on any interface type. With GRE tunnels, a special
operating mode exists to dictate the tunnel be used for PIM topology building. Under the tunnel
interface, issue the following command:

```
Router(config)# interface tunnel 0
Router(config-if)# tunnel mode dvmrp
```

As noted earlier, this does not enable true multicast routing decisions but allows PIM to make
tree-building decisions based on a more streamlined multicast topology. Overall, the router

must know which interfaces to cache DVMRP information for to build a multicast topology. You can accomplish this by issuing the following command:

```
Router(config)# interface intf
! Any interface
Router(config-if)# ip dvmrp unicast-routing
```

By default, only 7000 DVMRP routes are exchanged over any single interface. These interfaces are ones where DVMRP is specifically enabled, or DVMRP tunnels where DVMRP neighbors are discovered. You can change this default number by using the **ip dvmrp route-limit** *limit-value* global command. In addition, you can enhance the routing topology by summarizing the address. This is an interface-specific command:

```
Router(config)# interface intf
! Any interface
Router(config-if)# ip dvmrp summary-address net-addr net-mask [metric value]
```

DVMRP automatically summarizes to classful boundaries; however, the **ip dvmrp summary-address** (*mcast-net#*) **(mask) interface** command enables you to override this. Alternatively, the **no ip dvmrp auto-summary interface** command enables you to turn it off.

Remember about potentially needing to use the **multicast static route** command to override and further manipulate this routing table. Like other routing protocols, you can also apply offset lists to the metric values in more complicated scenarios with the **ip dvmrp metric-offset [in | out]** *increment* command.

You might run into increasingly complicated scenarios on the CCIE lab. Just remember unicast routing and processing concepts. After all, multicast routing and processing mirrors unicast to a great extent. Other important points to remember include that you can allow a default route into the PIM unicast topology with the **ip dvmrp default-information originate** command, and you can specifically filter or change routes with the **ip dvmrp accept-filter** *access-list* [*distance* | **ip neighbor-list** *access-list*] command.

PIM Version 2

Much of the basic multicast operation discussed so far, particularly with the RP, worked with PIM version 1. PIM version 1 had an interesting way of building trees and routing multicast through the unicast routing structure. PIM version 2 made some enhancements to this. Remember the auto-RP feature discussed earlier? That is a Cisco proprietary feature. It is a nice feature, and everyone likes it, but Cisco devices are the only ones that understand it. PIMv2 has a bootstrap router (BSR) that provides the same type of functionality and announcement features. PIMv2 and PIMv1 are not automatically compatible with each other.

PIMv1 worked with RPs in an active mode. In the topology, there could be one or more RPs, but all of them were in an active state and processing messages and tree and routing information. With PIMv2, there is now a concept of backup BSR (RP). With the presence of a backup, the messages that are needed to keep the topology running are fewer than before. Much of the detail, although nice to know, is beyond the scope of this chapter.

If you have PIMv1 routers, do not use a BSR. Use the auto-RP (if all Cisco) feature or manual RP assignments instead. With the BSRs, you can configure multiple BSR candidates within a multicast domain. The one with the highest priority takes over, but this design allows failover concepts within the network.

The BSR handles the announcement features that auto-RP did. A discovery-like feature is also present, in that the BSR does not necessarily need to be the RP within a network.

To configure the PIM version on a router, use the **ip pim version (1 | 2)** global command.

When selecting the BSR, use the **ip pim bsr-candidate** *src intf hash-length# priority#* global command. The hash-length value relates to the length used in the hash of exchanged messages. Although not required, it is recommended that this value be the same between all BSR candidates. The higher priority value becomes the BSR.

To make sure PIMv1 and PIMv2 networks do not interfere with one another, or to have two separate PIMv2 domains, set up multicast boundaries. This works both ways. For PIMv2, use the **ip pim border interface** command so that BSR messages do not cross. For PIMv1, use the **ip multicast boundary interface** command and associate it to an access list matching 224.0.1.39 and 224.0.1.40 to prevent the auto-RP multicast groups from traversing that interface.

Beyond that, set up routers to become candidates for acting as RP to some or all multicast groups. Use the **ip pim rp-candidate (src intf) (ttl#) [group-list (acl#)]** global command to set up a router as an RP candidate.

Lab 9: PIM

Again, using the network described in Figure 3-10, set up Backbone 1 and VLAN A to use PIMv1. R5 needs to automatically announce itself as the RP. Set up VLAN 60 and VLAN B to use PIMv2. All PIMv2 routers need to be BSR candidates, although R3 should win this election. R2 should be RP for the first half of the multicast group range, and R8 should be RP for the second half.

Lab 9: Solution

More complicated labs take some more time to set up. This lab requires a little thinking and tweaking along the way.

VLAN A and Backbone 1 are represented by R5 and R13. To talk to each other, however, Serial 1.1 of R6 must also participate in this version of multicast routing. All routers need IP multicast routing enabled. With this half of the multicast network, working in the Frame Relay cloud, R5 needs to be the RP and announce itself.

This alerts you to a few different requirements. First, PIM sparse dense mode is necessary. Second, because the Frame Relay between R5 and R13 is a multipoint interface on R6, you also need to set up a mapping agent to forward the RP announcements on to R13.

Being a Frame Relay cloud as well, you should have the **ip pim nbma-mode** command on serial interfaces, too.

Although not required, you can also specify IP PIMv1 on R5 and R13. R6 should not have this command because the second portion of this scenario specifically requires version 2.

Looking at the second half of this network and scenario, you can see that multicast is called for on VLAN 60 and VLAN B. There are a number of routers therein. Obviously, each needs IP multicast routing enabled.

The scenario states that all routers here should be BSR candidates; therefore, each needs the **ip pim bsr-candidate** commands, although R3 should have a higher weight than the others to actually be elected the bootstrap router.

After you take care of the BSR, it is time to look at the RPs in this part of the network. R2 and R8 both need to be RPs, although for different groups. Therefore, use the **ip pim rp-candidate** command with a group list calling an access control list on each router.

This exercise calls for a little knowledge of binary to create an access list covering half of the multicast range. Remember that the overall range is 224.0.0.0/4. Therefore, 224.0.0.0/5 is needed for one, and the rest (232.0.0.0/5) goes to the other side. Binary—it makes life exciting!

Lab 9: Configurations

This lab demonstrates another use of command entries and how you can edit them from the **show running-configuration** on routers. (See Example 3-8.)

Example 3-8 *Command Entries Edited from* **show running-configuration** *on Routers*

```
R13
ip multicast-routing
ip pim version 1
!
interface ethernet 1/0
 ip pim sparse-dense-mode
!
interface serial 1/0
 ip pim sparse-dense-mode
 ip pim nbma-mode
!


R5
ip multicast-routing
ip pim version 1
!
```

Example 3-8 *Command Entries Edited from* **show running-configuration** *on Routers (Continued)*

```
interface ethernet 0
 ip pim sparse-dense-mode
!
interface serial 1
 ip pim sparse-dense-mode
 ip pim nbma-mode
!
ip pim send-rp-announce ethernet 0 scope 16
```

```
R6
ip multicast-routing
ip pim bsr-candidate ethernet 0 30 10
ip pim send-rp-discovery scope 16
!
interface serial 1.1
 ip pim sparse-dense-mode
 ip pim nbma-mode
!
interface ethernet 0
 ip pim sparse-dense-mode
!
interface serial 0
 ip pim sparse-dense-mode
!
```

```
R8
ip multicast-routing
ip pim bsr-candidate ethernet 0 30 10
!
interface serial 0
 ip pim sparse-dense-mode
!
interface ethernet 0
 ip pim sparse-dense-mode
!
access-list 8 permit 232.0.0.0 7.255.255.255
ip pim rp-candidate ethernet 0 group-list 2
```

```
R3
ip multicast-routing
ip pim bsr-candidate ethernet 0 30 20
!
interface ethernet 0
 ip pim sparse-dense-mode
!
```

continues

Example 3-8 *Command Entries Edited from* **show running-configuration** *on Routers (Continued)*

```
R2
ip multicast-routing
ip pim bsr-candidate ethernet 0 30 10
!
interface ethernet 0
 ip pim sparse-dense-mode
!
access-list 2 permit 224.0.0.0 7.255.255.255
ip pim rp-candidate ethernet 0 group-list 2
```

Monitoring and Testing

After you configure multicast routing on devices throughout your network topology, it is always good to test the full functionality. In the CCIE lab, the object in any scenario is to think like the router—be the router.

To that end, a number of commands enable you to "see" what the router sees and attempt to think like the router thinks.

show and debug Commands

A variety of **show** and **debug** commands enable you to troubleshoot and monitor a multicast network. The basics of troubleshooting multicast networks are similar to those for troubleshooting unicast networks because of the reliance of multicast on the unicast routing table for its decisions.

When troubleshooting multicast, you must consider two primary areas:

- The flow of the packets themselves (for example, comparing the unicast routing table to the configuration commands used)
- The signaling of multicast, RP selection and use, and associated configurations there

Some commands to use are as follows:

> **show ip pim neighbor**
>
> **show ip pim interface**
>
> **show ip pim rp**
>
> **show ip mroute**
>
> **show ip mroute summary**

show ip igmp groups

show ip igmp interface

show ip rpf (*ip#*)

debug ip pim (*multicast#*)

debug ip igmp

debug ip mroute (*multicast#*)

debug ip mpacket

mtrace, mrinfo, and mstat Commands

The **mtrace**, **mrinfo**, and **mstat** commands are built in to Cisco IOS Software and provide some useful features.

The **mtrace** command enables you to perform an RPF check and trace from the multicast source through a multicast tree to a particular destination or what a group might see. The basic command syntax for this command is as follows:

```
mtrace source-addr [destination-addr] [group-addr]
```

Example 3-9 shows some sample output from this command.

Example 3-9 **mtrace** *Command Output*

```
Router> mtrace 172.16.0.0 172.16.0.10 239.254.254.254
Type escape sequence to abort.
Mtrace from 172.16.0.0 to 172.16.0.10 via group 239.254.254.254
From source (?) to destination (?)
Querying full reverse path...
0 172.16.0.10
-1 172.16.0.8 PIM thresh^ 0 0 ms
-2 172.16.0.6 PIM thresh^ 0 2 ms
-3 172.16.0.5 PIM thresh^ 0 894 ms
-4 172.16.0.3 PIM thresh^ 0 893 ms
-5 172.16.0.2 PIM thresh^ 0 894 ms
-6 172.16.0.1 PIM thresh^ 0 893 ms
```

The **mrinfo** command enables you to determine which other routers exchange PIM information with the router currently tested. Use flags to discuss particular capabilities of the multicast routers, too. The basic command syntax for this command is as follows:

```
mrinfo [mcast-neighbor#] [interface]
```

Example 3-10 shows some sample output from this command.

Example 3-10 **mrinfo** *Command Output*

```
Router# mrinfo
172.31.7.37 (r8.lab.emanon.com) [version cisco 12.1] [flags: PMSA]:
172.31.7.37 -> 172.31.7.34 (r4.lab.emanon.com) [1/0/pim]
172.31.7.37 -> 172.31.7.47 (r7.lab.emanon.com) [1/0/pim]
172.31.7.37 -> 172.31.7.44 (r14.lab.emanon.com) [1/0/pim]
10.11.26.10 -> 10.11.26.9 (routera.lab.emanon.com) [1/32/pim]
```

The flags included in this output indicate the following:

- **P**—Prune capable
- **M**—Mtrace capable
- **S**—SNMP capable
- **A**—Auto-RP capable

The **mstat** EXEC command enables you to view the IP multicast packet rates and loss information for a multicast source, destination, or group address. The basic command syntax for this command is as follows:

```
mstat source-addr [destination-addr] [group-addr]
```

Multicast Troubleshooting Example

As you can see from the multicast network in Figure 3-13, multicast packets come into E0 of Router A from source 150.1.1.1 and send to group 225.3.3.3. This yields an S,G of (150.1.1.1, 225.3.3.3).

Figure 3-13 *Troubleshooting Multicast Networks*

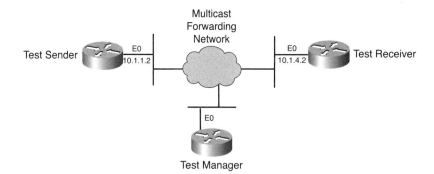

Hosts connected to Router A correctly receive the multicast feed, but those connected to Router B do not. Your first step should be to look at the multicast routing table on both routers. Example 3-11 shows the configuration for Router A.

Example 3-11 *Configuration for Router A*

```
RouterA# show ip mroute 225.3.3.3
IP Multicast Routing table
Flags: D - Dense, S - Sparse, C - Connected, L - Local, P - Pruned
       R - RP-bit set, F - Register flag, T - SPT-bit set, J - Join SPT
       M - MSDP created entry, X - Proxy Join Timer Running
       A - Advertised via MSDP
Timers: Uptime/Expires
Interface state: Interface, Next-Hop or VCD, State/Mode
(*, 225.3.3.3), 00:01:23/00:02:59, RP 0.0.0.0, flags: D
  Incoming interface: Null, RPF nbr 0.0.0.0
  Outgoing interface list:
    Ethernet1, Forward/Sparse-Dense, 00:01:23/00:00:00
(150.1.1.1, 225.3.3.3), 00:01:23/00:03:00, flags: TA
  Incoming interface: Ethernet0, RPF nbr 0.0.0.0
  Outgoing interface list:
    Ethernet1, Forward/Sparse-Dense, 00:01:23/00:00:00
```

Because the router runs in PIM dense mode, the *,G route is not important. The flag showing D denotes dense mode. The S,G route indicates incoming and outgoing interfaces that should be expected. Router A appears to be working correctly. Example 3-12 shows the configuration for Router B.

Example 3-12 *Multicast* **show** *Commands for Validation*

```
RouterB# show ip mroute 225.3.3.3
IP Multicast Routing table
Flags: D - Dense, S - Sparse, C - Connected, L - Local, P - Pruned
       R - RP-bit set, F - Register flag, T - SPT-bit set, J - Join SPT
       M - MSDP created entry, X - Proxy Join Timer Running
       A - Advertised via MSDP
Timers: Uptime/Expires
Interface state: Interface, Next-Hop or VCD, State/Mode
(*, 225.3.3.3), 00:05:36/00:02:19, RP 0.0.0.0, flags: DJC
  Incoming interface: Null, RPF nbr 0.0.0.0
  Outgoing interface list:
    Ethernet0, Forward/Sparse-Dense, 00:05:36/00:00:00
    Ethernet1, Forward/Sparse-Dense, 00:05:37/00:00:00
```

The multicast routing table in Example 3-12 does not show the S,G group, which means that Router B is not forwarding the multicast packets. Refer to Example 3-13 to see the **show ip pim neighbor** command used in validation work.

Example 3-13 *Multicast* **show** *Commands for Validation*

```
RouterB# show ip pim neighbor
PIM Neighbor Table
Neighbor Address  Interface        Uptime    Expires   Ver  Mode
200.10.1.1              Ethernet0        2d00h    00:01:15  v2
```

Router A is shown as a PIM neighbor, as expected. Example 3-14 shows the **show ip rpf 150.1.1** command used to provide validation.

Example 3-14 *Multicast* **show** *Commands for Validation*

```
RouterB# show ip rpf 150.1.1.1
RPF information for ? (150.1.1.1)
  RPF interface: Ethernet2
  RPF neighbor: ? (4.1.1.2)
  RPF route/mask: 150.1.1.1/32
  RPF type: unicast (static)
  RPF recursion count: 1
  Doing distance-preferred lookups across tables
```

This shows the IP route to 150.1.1.1 comes up as the Ethernet2 interface of Router B as expected. Based on the figure, E0 should be expected, but you never knows what else in a scenario affects the IP routing table. Example 3-15 shows how the multicast **debug** output for validation works.

Example 3-15 *Multicast* **debug** *Output for Validation*

```
RouterB# debug ip mpacket
*Jan 14 09:45:32.972: IP: s=150.1.1.1 (Ethernet0)
d=225.3.3.3 len 60, not RPF interface
*Jan 14 09:45:33.020: IP: s=150.1.1.1 (Ethernet0)
d=225.3.3.3 len 60, not RPF interface
*Jan 14 09:45:33.072: IP: s=150.1.1.1 (Ethernet0)
d=225.3.3.3 len 60, not RPF interface
*Jan 14 09:45:33.120: IP: s=150.1.1.1 (Ethernet0)
d=225.3.3.3 len 60, not RPF interface
```

Based on the **debug**, you see what was determined with the RPF check. The multicast packets arrive on an interface that is not associated with the RPF check; therefore, the interface drops the multicast packets.

The simplest fix to this problem, assuming that the unicast routing table is the way that it is based on other scenario questions or good reasons, is to set a static multicast route for the 225.3.3.3 group's source to reset the expected interface to Ethernet0. The following **ip mroute** command might assist in fixing this dilemma.

```
Router(config)# ip mroute 150.1.1.1 255.255.255.255 ethernet0
```

Multicast Routing Manager (MRM)

The MRM is a great tool to use on multicast networks and on any routers therein. Three pieces are necessary to perform a "live" multicast test: a test sender (multicast source), test receiver (multicast receiver), and test manager.

The network in Figure 3-14 shows how an MRM test can be laid out.

Figure 3-14 *Multicast Testing*

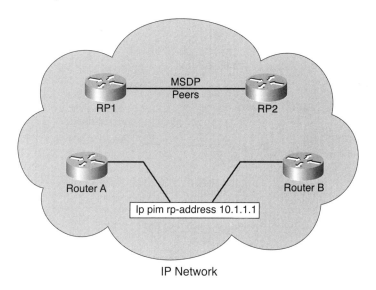

The number of multicast routers within the Multicast Forwarding Network is irrelevant. Place the test sender and test receiver appropriately to test and troubleshoot different parts of the network.

The test sender, on its Ethernet0 interface, will use the **ip mrm test-sender interface** command. Likewise, the test receiver, on its Ethernet0 interface, will use the **ip mrm test-receiver interface** command.

The test manager will require more configuration steps. First, you must configure access lists delineating the senders and receivers on a network. A standard access list delineates specific hosts. ACL 1 is the sender list and ACL 2 is the receiver list:

```
Manager(config)# access-list 1 permit 10.1.1.2
Manager(config)# access-list 2 permit 10.1.4.2
```

Next, configure an MRM test and denote the senders and receiver within that test. Notice that the senders' and receivers' lines call the access lists to specify the senders and receivers. You can set more than one concurrent test on the manager:

```
Manager(config)# ip mrm manager mynettest
Manager(config-mrm)# manager ethernet0 group 239.2.3.4
Manager(config-mrm)# senders 1
Manager(config-mrm)# receivers 2 sender-list 1
```

After completing configuration, you can start the test from the EXEC mode using the **mrm** *test-name* **start** command.

MRM is a complete test of the multicast network. Senders and receivers must join a specific multicast group (224.0.1.111) to talk with the manager. Control messages are passed through this multicast group. Also, a series of UDP messages and RTP messages test procedures (in addition to the desired group).

After a test begins, the MRM sends unicast control messages to the sender and receivers, after which the manager begins to send test beacons. The sender and receivers send acknowledgments to the beacons and initiate the testing of the configured multicast group. Report information is sent to the manager to determine the success or failure throughout the test.

While the test is in progress, the sender sends RTP packets to the configured multicast group address every 200 milliseconds (default). The receivers expect to receive packets within the same window, thus giving reportable statistics to the manager. If the receivers detect packet loss within a 5-second window, a report is sent to the manager:

```
Manager# mrm mynettest start
  *Mar 20 10:29:51.798: IP MRM test mynettest starts ......
Manager#
```

No updates automatically appear on the screen. To display a status report at the manager router, enter the following command:

```
Manager# show ip mrm status
IP MRM status report cache:
Timestamp       Manager        Test Receiver   Pkt Loss/Dup (%)    Ehsr
*Mar 20 14:12:46 10.1.2.2      10.1.4.2        1         (4%)      29
*Mar 20 18:29:54 10.1.2.2      10.1.4.2        1         (4%)      15
Manager#
```

The report shows that the receiver (10.1.4.2) sent two separate status reports (one line each). Each report contains one packet loss during the interval window (default of 1 second). The Ehsr value shows the estimated next sequence number value from the MRM sender. If the MRM receiver sees duplicate packets, it shows a negative number in the Pkt Loss/Dup column.

To stop the test, enter the following command:

```
Manager# mrm mynettest stop
  *Mar 20 10:31:32.018: IP MRM test mynettest stops
Manager#
```

CCIE Multicast Lab Scenario

When studying multicast for the CCIE lab, think about the wording of things. This chapter provided a number of examples from which you can understand the importance of isolating the key words. You must ascertain exactly how the CCIE lab wants you to perform the work.

When comparing the multicast routing table with the unicast routing table, you might encounter "gotchas," as outlined previously in the "Multicast Troubleshooting Example" section. You might encounter other unforeseen difficulties. Know where the "IP Multicast" section is on the "Configuration Guide" section of the Documentation CD-ROM. This section is crucial to your research of unknown or unforeseen difficulties. In it, you might also come across small hints that jog your memory.

Further Reading

RFC 2362, *Protocol Independent Multicast-Sparse Mode*

RFC 1075, *Distance Vector Multicast Routing Protocol*

Developing IP Multicast Networks: The Definitive Guide to Designing and Deploying Cisco IP Multicast Networks, Volume I, by Beau Williamson (Cisco Press, 2000)

Cisco Connection Online—Documentation CD—*Configuring IP Multicast Guides*

PART IV

Performance Management and Quality of Service

CHAPTER 4

Router Performance Management

At some point in the life cycle of almost every network, some type of quality mechanism must be implemented to provide a level of service. With some networks, it may only be necessary to perform simple hardware or software upgrades every few years. Other networks may require the use of *Service Level Agreements (SLAs)*, either as customer or as service provider, to guarantee a certain level of service. A number of methods can be used to establish a certain level of quality of service (QoS); the method that you choose will be determined by the availability of the solution, the cost, and the value that it presents to your organization. When determining your required level of service, you must decide whether you require a "best effort" level of quality, or whether you require a certain level of guaranteed QoS. For instance, your network may only require a guaranteed amount of bandwidth availability during certain peak hours of operation, a certain data transfer rate over the transmission medium, or you may have applications on your network that have very specific requirements that must be met. In each of these situations, you can use a QoS method to ensure that your network is performing within the established limits. You must also consider that to achieve guaranteed levels of service, redundant links and hardware may be required, costing more money to implement and support.

In many cases, network quality issues result from issues that cannot be fixed using QoS. Before designing or applying Cisco IOS QoS techniques, verify that your network is already operating at its best. For instance, I am sure everyone has seen at least one instance where a certain router is constantly causing network delays. Users on the network commonly complain that the network is slow, but no one can determine why until someone takes a good look at the router's Ethernet interface and notices a high number of errors. The type of errors found on the interface indicates a bad Ethernet cable, and after the cable is replaced, everything works great. The following simple quality-control issues are not addressed with Cisco IOS QoS:

- **Router resource limitations**—Routers dropping packets because their resources are exhausted
- **Router hardware problems**—Bad interfaces causing performance problems
- **Layer 1 network problems**—Bad cabling or cables that exceed specifications

Router resource limitations generally occur when routers are no longer able to support traffic characteristics, or features that are currently used in today's networks are still in use. These issues can usually be fixed by adding memory or replacing outdated equipment. Router hardware problems, which tend to be harder to find, but easiest to fix, tend to disappear when you start taking a good look at your network. And Layer 1 cabling problems can cause myriad strange and complicated problems that are difficult to trace.

The beginning of this chapter covers quality-control issues, and includes several quick troubleshooting exercises that lead to a speedy problem diagnosis and resolution. An entire book could be dedicated to quality-control issues; this chapter just identifies tools that already exist within Cisco IOS Software, and shows how the output from these tools can provide valuable troubleshooting data. The output from the commands covered in this section is referred to throughout the rest of this book.

After this discussion, the chapter takes over where the first edition left off by exploring ATM QoS technologies. The ATM section begins by providing a quick ATM review before diving directly into ATM QoS. This chapter then explores the different Cisco IOS switching methods, and how they can be used to improve network interface performance. This chapter ends with an in-depth look at interface compression, exploring how you can use it to improve network performance by sending more packets over existing interfaces without costly network bandwidth upgrades.

Determining Router Performance

Before attempting to determine the types of QoS that are required on your network, accomplish the following few tasks first:

- Verify that your network hardware is properly configured and in good working order.

- Perform a network baseline to determine whether your hardware is adequate to support your requirements, and whether you have sufficient bandwidth to support your network applications. The baseline also shows whether any of the applications on your network have certain link speed or quality requirements.

- Interview key network stakeholders. Determine who needs to be involved in network planning activities, and make sure that you know their current and future network requirements.

Verifying Cisco IOS Software and Memory Configuration

A number of key commands help you determine whether a router running Cisco IOS Software is working properly. Gather and record information over a period of time, taking into consideration how your network performs under peak- and low-utilization periods. How long you gather and record information depends on the size and scale of your network. To begin, determine which version of Cisco IOS Software your routers are currently running and check the amounts of Flash memory and DRAM on your router. Verify that the version of software and amount of memory are adequate to support the features that you currently have and will require in the near future. On a Cisco router, to find the version of Cisco IOS Software and the amount of installed memory, use the **show version** command, as shown in Example 4-1.

Example 4-1   **show version** *Command*

```
Router# show version
Cisco Internetwork Operating System Software
IOS (tm) C2600 Software (C2600-JS-M), Version 12.0(3)T3,  RELEASE SOFTWARE (fc1)
Copyright (c) 1986-1999 by cisco Systems, Inc.
Compiled Thu 15-Apr-99 17:05 by kpma
Image text-base: 0x80008088, data-base: 0x80C2D514
ROM: System Bootstrap, Version 11.3(2)XA4, RELEASE SOFTWARE (fc1)
2610 uptime is 2 hours, 21 minutes
System restarted by reload
System image file is "flash:c2600-js-mz.120-3.T3.bin"
cisco 2610 (MPC860) processor (revision 0x203) with 24576K/8192K bytes of memory.
Processor board ID JAD04180ETY (2670216847)
M860 processor: part number 0, mask 49
Bridging software.
X.25 software, Version 3.0.0.
SuperLAT software copyright 1990 by Meridian Technology Corp).
TN3270 Emulation software.
1 Ethernet/IEEE 802.3 interface(s)
2 Serial network interface(s)
16 terminal line(s)
32K bytes of non-volatile configuration memory.
8192K bytes of processor board System flash (Read/Write)
Configuration register is 0x2102
Router#
```

In this example, the router is running Cisco IOS Release 12.0(3), image name c2600-js-mz. 120-3.T3.bin stored in 8 MB of Flash memory; this router also has 32 MB of DRAM, 25 MB of system memory, and 8 MB shared packet memory. Cisco IOS Software versions and quantities of Flash memory and random-access memory should be tracked and recorded for reference purposes. You can use this information to track software bugs, track features, and prepare for upgrades. At this time, it is also useful to note how the router was started; in the example, this router was restarted by **reload**. It is always good to note when the router has an error, and if so, remember the error and watch for future recurrences:

```
System restarted by error - a SegV exception, PC 0x808da564
```

Logging unexpected system restarts can save troubleshooting time and provide valuable information that you can use to find the source of the router restarts. You can find this information by searching for the error at Cisco.com, or opening a case with the Cisco Technical Assistance Center (TAC). You may find the following tools useful when diagnosing router restarts:

- Bug Tracker
- Searching the TAC website
- Error Message Decoder

If you find that your routers frequently experience real hardware or software problems, concentrate on fixing the problems first; after you have fixed the problems, you can approach your network application's requirements and find solutions to enhance application performance.

Determining Network Application Requirements

If possible, try to obtain information on new network applications that will be deployed in your network. Try to find out what their network use requirements will be, how many computers will use the new applications, where they are located, and whether there are any bandwidth or link quality requirements. If you cannot increase the amount of bandwidth on your network, you may still be able to increase network performance by the use of Cisco IOS Software QoS features, including the following:

- Simple queuing and traffic prioritization
- Advanced switching methods
- Compression
- Congestion avoidance
- Advanced queuing and congestion management
- Traffic shaping
- Traffic policing
- Applying ATM QoS
- Low Latency Queuing
- Classifying traffic to provide QoS at various network points

The battle to learn and understand the effects of new applications and technologies will always drive the need for network quality enhancements. For instance, you may find that branch routers with smaller WAN links require compression to support the network applications that have been or are going to be deployed. After determining that the router will require the applications of compression techniques, you may find that the compression algorithm is very demanding on the router's processor or memory. After you have decided to move forward with the plan to implement compression, you may have to increase the amount of memory or, in some cases, replace older equipment to support other technologies.

To check the processor use and process CPU allocation, use the **show processes cpu** command, as shown in Example 4-2.

Example 4-2   **show processes cpu** *Command*

```
Router# show processes cpu
CPU utilization for five seconds: 1%/0%; one minute: 0%; five minutes: 0%
 PID  Runtime(ms)  Invoked  uSecs   5Sec   1Min   5Min TTY Process
   1            4     1650      2  0.00%  0.00%  0.00%   0 Load Meter
   2         1573     2653    592  1.31%  0.49%  0.34%   0 Exec
   3         5701      990   5758  0.00%  0.04%  0.05%   0 Check heaps
   4            0        1      0  0.00%  0.00%  0.00%   0 Pool Manager
   5            0        2      0  0.00%  0.00%  0.00%   0 Timers
   6            4       61     65  0.00%  0.00%  0.00%   0 Serial Backgroun
   7            0      276      0  0.00%  0.00%  0.00%   0 Environmental mo
   8            0      143      0  0.00%  0.00%  0.00%   0 ARP Input
   9            5        6    833  0.00%  0.00%  0.00%   0 DDR Timers
  10            0        2      0  0.00%  0.00%  0.00%   0 Dialer event
  11            8        2   4000  0.00%  0.00%  0.00%   0 Entity MIB API
  12            0        1      0  0.00%  0.00%  0.00%   0 SERIAL A'detect
  13            0        1      0  0.00%  0.00%  0.00%   0 Critical Bkgnd
  14           52      992     52  0.00%  0.00%  0.00%   0 Net Background
  15            4       59     67  0.00%  0.00%  0.00%   0 Logger
  16           48     8228      5  0.00%  0.00%  0.00%   0 TTY Background
  17            8     8380      0  0.00%  0.00%  0.00%   0 Per-Second Jobs
  18           16     8312      1  0.00%  0.00%  0.00%   0 Partition Check
  19           88      725    121  0.00%  0.00%  0.00%   0 Net Input
  20           12     1651      7  0.00%  0.00%  0.00%   0 Compute load avg
  21         3915      141  27765  0.00%  0.05%  0.00%   0 Per-minute Jobs
```

The first line is often the most important part of the **show processes cpu** command: **CPU utilization for five seconds: 1%/0%; one minute: 0%; five minutes: 0%**. This one line displays the CPU utilization in 5-second, 1–minute, and 5-minute increments. This data can be displayed locally on the router by repeatedly issuing the command for immediate use, or you can use data collection software to collect data over a period of time and use it to find network trends, and determine future network requirements. The router shown in the preceding example is running at 0-percent utilization. If you notice a router that constantly runs at or more than 75-percent utilization, you may have to consider a router upgrade, or, in the case of the previous compression example, you may consider upgrading the smaller WAN circuit and disabling compression.

To gather performance trend information from a router, the output of the **show processes cpu** command is most valuable when gathered over a period of time, including peak- and low-traffic times. If processor utilization is high, log the process IDs from the PID column that are consuming the most time. You might be able to disable some processes to save resources.

While gathering processor utilization, you can gather memory utilization as well. Although sometimes difficult to read or understand, the **show memory** commands display quite a bit of information about the system utilization. There are many variations of the **show memory** command, one of the most useful of which is the **show memory dead** command.

As shown in Example 4-3, the **show memory dead** command displays a summary of the memory use, total, used, and free memory statistics, and then goes on to display all the dead processes that still have memory allocated for their use. If this number is large, you may need to find the dead process and work with the Cisco TAC and fix the problem.

Example 4-3 **show memory dead** *Command*

```
Router# show memory dead
                Head    Total(b)    Used(b)    Free(b)   Lowest(b)  Largest(b)
Processor   811E15FC    6416900    3884876    2532024    2495784    2508960
      I/O   1800000     8388608    1566808    6821800    6819308    6821756
            Processor memory
  Address  Bytes Prev.    Next     Ref  PrevF    NextF    Alloc PC   What
  8120E740    64 8120E6E8 8120E7AC   1                    808AF3AC   CEF process
  812A3F44    92 812A3EB0 812A3FCC   1                    801D4870   TTY timer block
  812A8C00    24 812A8BBC 812A8C44   1                    808AF3AC   CEF process
  812A8DDC    24 812A8D98 812A8E20   1                    808AF3A0   CEF process
```

In addition to displaying the memory summary and memory allocated for dead processes, it is also helpful to check for memory allocation failures, using the **show memory failures alloc** command. This command displays any memory allocation failures, which, when gathered over a period of time, might indicate a need to increase the amount of memory. Under normal circumstances, this command should not have any output.

As a rule, routers should never run at a constant high processor or memory load. There are a number of beliefs about how one should judge the processor and memory utilization of their routers. Generally, as a precautionary method, before performing any QoS feature additions, make sure that your routers can handle the additional load added by the new QoS techniques. If your router's memory utilization is already high, adding new features, even those as simple as a change in switching modes, such as Cisco Express Forwarding (CEF) switching, may push the router over its limits. After you have verified that the router has the basic capabilities to perform the functions that you require, using the **processor** and **memory** commands just shown, or you have identified the need for a router upgrade or replacement, next verify that the router has enough interface capacity to handle the proposed traffic load. The next section covers router interface performance evaluation. This section shows you how to identify interface hardware and cable faults, traffic bottlenecks, and the efficiency of the route switch-mode selection.

Verifying Router Interface Performance

One of the most useful performance management **show** commands is the **show interface** command. The **show interface** commands display information about interface hardware, configuration, utilization, errors, and queuing. Example 4-4 shows the output for the **show interface serial** command, and Table 4-1 shows the **show interface serial** command output descriptions.

Example 4-4   **show interface** *Output*

```
Router# show interface serial s 0/1
Serial0/1 is up, line protocol is up
  Hardware is PowerQUICC Serial
  Internet address is 175.25.33.98/24
  MTU 1500 bytes, BW 1544 Kbit, DLY 20000 usec,
     reliability 255/255, txload 1/255, rxload 1/255
  Encapsulation HDLC, loopback not set
  Keepalive set (10 sec)
  Last input 00:00:02, output 00:00:03, output hang never
  Last clearing of "show interface" counters never
  Input queue: 0/75/0 (size/max/drops); Total output drops: 0
  Queueing strategy: weighted fair
  Output queue: 0/1000/64/0 (size/max total/threshold/drops)
     Conversations  0/2/256 (active/max active/max total)
     Reserved Conversations 0/0 (allocated/max allocated)
  5 minute input rate 0 bits/sec, 0 packets/sec
  5 minute output rate 0 bits/sec, 0 packets/sec
     179 packets input, 12647 bytes, 0 no buffer
     Received 70 broadcasts, 0 runts, 0 giants, 0 throttles
     1 input errors, 0 CRC, 1 frame, 0 overrun, 0 ignored, 0 abort
     173 packets output, 17321 bytes, 0 underruns
     0 output errors, 0 collisions, 78 interface resets
     0 output buffer failures, 0 output buffers swapped out
     106 carrier transitions
     DCD=up  DSR=up  DTR=up  RTS=up  CTS=up
```

Table 4-1 **show interface serial** *Output Description*

Item	Description
Hardware is PowerQUICC Serial	Describes the hardware name for the interface specified. In this case, the hardware is a PowerQUICC WIC-1T Serial module. A more detailed hardware type description and interface specific troubleshooting counters can be found using the **show controllers** command.
Internet address is 175.25.33.98/24	The IP address assigned to the interface. This information only appears on IP interfaces.
MTU 1500 bytes	MTU size for this interface. You can change the MTU size for an interface by using the **mtu** command in interface configuration mode. The **no mtu** command sets the MTU size to default.
BW 1544 Kbit	Displays the bandwidth for this interface. The bandwidth value does not actually change the bandwidth available for the interface. This command just provides a metric that is used to limit Hello traffic for the EIGRP or IGRP routing protocols. The default bandwidth value will be that of the interface, or another more precise value that can be manually entered using the **bandwidth** command in interface configuration mode.
DLY 20000 usec	The average interface delay of the interface in microseconds. Also, note that the Delay value shown here is only a metric that is to be used for EIGRP or IGRP routing protocols. You can change the delay for an interface by using the **delay** command in interface configuration mode.
reliability 255/255	The average reliability of the link over a period of 5 minutes. 255/255 refers to 100 percent. 127/255 would be 50 percent. 1/255 would be 0 percent.
txload 1/255	The transmit load for the interface over a 5-minute period. A load of 255/255 is 100-percent interface utilization.
rxload 1/255	The receive load for the interface over a 5-minute period. A load of 255/255 is 100-percent interface utilization.
Encapsulation HDLC	The interface encapsulation type.
loopback not set	Shows whether a loopback has been configured. Interface loopbacks can be used to test physical connectivity problems by transmitting a signal to a remote destination, sometimes referred to as "looping an interface" to a service provider. To configure an interface loopback, use the **loopback** command in interface configuration mode.

Table 4-1   **show interface serial** *Output Description (Continued)*

Item	Description
Keepalive set (10 sec)	Displays the keepalive for the interface. The standard keepalive for a serial interface is 10 seconds. To change the interface keepalive, use the **keepalive** command under interface configuration mode.
Last input 00:00:02	Displays the last time input was received on this interface.
output 00:00:03	Displays the last time output was transmitted on this interface.
output hang never	Displays the last time the interface was reset because a transmission took too long.
Last clearing of **show interface** counters never	Displays the last time the counters for this interface were cleared. You can clear the interface counters by using the **clear interface** command from enable mode.
Input queue: 0/75/0 (size/max/drops)	Displays the input queue size for the interface. **size** shows the current input queue size. **max** shows the maximum size of the queue. **drops** displays the number of packets dropped when the maximum queue size is exceeded.
Total output drops: 0	Displays the total number of output drops. Output drops occur when the router is attempting to transmit data and has no available buffers and so the packet is dropped.
Queuing strategy: weighted fair	Displays the queuing strategy for the interface. The default queuing type for a serial interface under 2 Mb (E1) is Weighted Fair. If no queuing type has been configured, or Weighted Fair Queuing has been disabled, the default queuing type is FIFO.
Output queue: 0/1000/64/0 (size/max total/threshold/drops)	Displays the output queue size for the interface. **size** shows the current size of the queue. **max total** shows the maximum size of the queue. **threshold** shows the number of packets that can be stored in the queue before new packets are discarded. **drops** shows the number of dropped packets.

continues

Table 4-1   **show interface serial** *Output Description (Continued)*

Item	Description
Conversations 0/2/256 (active/max active/max total)	Displays the Weighted Fair Queuing settings for the interface. Weighted Fair Queuing is covered in detail in the next chapter.
	active displays the current number of Weighted Fair Queuing conversation queues.
	max active displays the maximum number of Weighted Fair Queuing queues that can concurrently be active.
	max total displays the total number of dynamic Weighted Fair Queuing queues.
Reserved Conversations 0/0 (allocated/max allocated)	When RSVP has been enabled, the current number of RSVP resource allocations and maximum number of RSVP resource allocations are displayed.
5 minute input rate 0 bits/sec, 0 packets/sec	Displays the 5-minute average input rate for the interface.
5 minute output rate 0 bits/sec, 0 packets/sec	Displays the 5-minute average output rate for the interface.
235 packets input	These counters display the following:
15967 bytes	The number of packets received.
0 no buffer	The number of bytes received on the interface.
	The number of times the router ran out of buffer space.
Received 126 broadcasts	These counters display the following:
	The number of broadcasts received.
0 runts	The number of runts received. A runt is a packet that is smaller than the minimum packet size for the interface.
	The number of giants received. A giant is a packet that exceeds the MTU size for the interface.
0 giants	The number of throttles received. A throttle occurs when the router runs out of buffer or processor resources, and as a result, the interface's receiver is disabled.
0 throttles	

Table 4-1   **show interface serial** *Output Description (Continued)*

Item	Description
2 input errors	These counters display the following:
	The combined number of all input errors. An input error is any packet that arrives at the interface with any error type. Packets with more than one error type are only counted once.
0 CRC	The number of CRC errors received.
	This number should be less than 0.0001 percent of the total bytes received on the interface using the formula (CRC errors/total bytes) × 100 = Percentage CRC errors. High errors could indicate Layer 1 problems.
	The number of incoming framing errors received.
2 frame	The number of buffer overruns occurring on incoming packets. An overrun occurs when the interface is receiving data faster than the system buffers can process it.
0 overrun	
0 ignored	The number of ignored packets. Packets are ignored when the interface runs out of buffer space and has to ignore new packets until resources become available.
0 abort	
	The abort counter indicates the number of times the interface received an illegal series of 1s. Interface aborts usually indicate a clocking error.
236 packets output	These counters display the following:
	The number of packets transmitted.
22838 bytes	The number of bytes transmitted.
0 underruns	The number of times that the router detects that the data sender is sending faster than the router can receive.
0 output errors	These counters display the following:
0 collisions	The number of output errors.
	The number of packets retransmitted because of collisions—serial interfaces should not have collisions.
80 interface resets	
	The number of times the interface has reset itself.

continues

Table 4-1 **show interface serial** *Output Description (Continued)*

Item	Description
0 output buffer failures	These counters display the following: The number of times the router received a no resource error upon output.
0 output buffers swapped out	The number of times the router swapped packets to DRAM.
106 carrier transitions	The number of carrier transitions sensed on this interface. A carrier transition occurs when the carrier detect signal changes state.
DCD=up	**DCD** (Data Carrier Detect)—Signal sent by DCE indicating that the carrier detect signal has been received from the DTE.
DSR=up	**DSR** (Data Set Ready)—Signal sent by the DCE to notify the DTE that the DCE is ready.
DTR=up	**DTR** (Data Terminal Ready)—Signal sent by the DTE to the DCE for new connections or to maintain an existing connection.
RTS=up	**RTS** (Request to Send)—Signal sent by the DTE to notify the DCE that the DTE is ready to transmit.
CTS=up	**CTS** (Clear to Send)—Sent by the DCE indicating that the DCE is ready to receive data from the DTE.

Example 4-5 shows the output from the **show interface fastethernet** command, and Table 4-2 shows the command output descriptions.

Example 4-5 **show interface fastethernet** *Command*

```
1750a>show interface fastethernet 0
FastEthernet0 is administratively down, line protocol is down
  Hardware is PQUICC_FEC, address is 0004.2722.81d8 (bia 0004.2722.81d8)
  MTU 1500 bytes, BW 100000 Kbit, DLY 100 usec,
     reliability 255/255, txload 1/255, rxload 1/255
  Encapsulation ARPA, loopback not set
  Keepalive set (10 sec)
  Auto-duplex, 10Mb/s, 100BaseTX/FX
  ARP type: ARPA, ARP Timeout 04:00:00
  Last input never, output 01:03:50, output hang never
  Last clearing of "show interface" counters never
  Queueing strategy: fifo
  Output queue 0/40, 0 drops; input queue 0/75, 0 drops
```

Example 4-5 show interface fastethernet *Command (Continued)*

```
5 minute input rate 0 bits/sec, 0 packets/sec
5 minute output rate 0 bits/sec, 0 packets/sec
   0 packets input, 0 bytes
   Received 0 broadcasts, 0 runts, 0 giants, 0 throttles
   0 input errors, 0 CRC, 0 frame, 0 overrun, 0 ignored
   0 watchdog
   0 input packets with dribble condition detected
   177 packets output, 35436 bytes, 0 underruns
   0 output errors, 0 collisions, 0 interface resets
   0 babbles, 0 late collision, 0 deferred
   0 lost carrier, 0 no carrier
   0 output buffer failures, 0 output buffers swapped out
```

Table 4-2   *Ethernet-Specific* show interface *Output*

Item	Description
FastEthernet0 is administratively down, line protocol is down.	Displays the current interface and line protocol states; the possible states for Fast Ethernet interfaces are administratively up or down. up down administratively down For an interface to be in an up state, it must have received a keepalive within the amount of time configured.
Hardware is PQUICC_FEC	Displays the type of hardware installed.
address is 0004.2722.81d8 (bia 0004.2722.81d8)	Displays the current MAC address and the burned-in address (BIA). You can change the MAC address by using the **mac-address** command in interface configuration mode.
MTU 1500 bytes	MTU.
BW 100000 Kbit	Bandwidth.
DLY 100 usec	Delay of the interface in microseconds. These values are usually best left at their intended values; changing the bandwidth or delay of an interface delay or bandwidth does not change the actual value; however, MTU values are sometimes changed to provide interoperability between different vendors' hardware. These values do not change on a dynamic basis.
Auto-duplex	Duplex mode for the interface. The duplex mode for the interface can be changed using either the **full-duplex** or **half-duplex** commands in interface configuration mode.

continues

Table 4-2 *Ethernet-Specific* **show interface** *Output (Continued)*

Item	Description
10Mb/s	Displays the speed of the interface.
	For Fast Ethernet interfaces or greater, you can change the interface speed by using the **speed** command in interface configuration mode.
	The speed can either be forced to a specific speed, or if the speed has been changed, it can be set back to automatic by specifying **auto**.
100BaseTX/FX	Displays the Ethernet media type.
ARP type: ARPA	Displays the ARP type.
	You can change the ARP type by using the **arp type** command in interface configuration mode. The default ARP type is ARPA.
ARP Timeout 04:00:00	Displays the ARP timeout [more].
	You can change the ARP timeout by using the **arp timeout** command in interface configuration mode.
Queuing strategy: fifo	Displays the queuing strategy for the interface; on Ethernet interfaces, the default queuing type is FIFO.
0 watchdog	Displays the number of times the watchdog timer has expired. The watchdog timer usually expires when packet sizes exceed 2048 bytes.
0 input packets with dribble condition detected	Displays the number of frames that are oversized but still forwarded.
0 interface resets	Displays the number of times the interface has reset itself.
0 collisions	Indicates the number of collisions received on an interface.
	Collisions do not typically occur on Fast Ethernet interfaces.
0 babbles	These counters display the following:
	The number of times the transmit jabber timer expired.
0 late collision	The number of late collisions, when a collision occurs after the frame preamble has been transmitted.
0 deferred	The number of packets that have been deferred because the carrier was asserted.
0 lost carrier	Displays the number of times the interface lost the carrier during transmission.
0 no carrier	Displays the number of times the interface found no carrier during transmission.

After verifying the state of the interface over a period of time, you will be able to determine the type of problem that the router in question is displaying. At this point, you should see a clear trend pointing you in one of three directions. Perhaps the router is out of resources and dropping packets. Or, the router has a physical layer quality problem. Neither of these problems can be fixed with QoS. Alternatively, perhaps the router is under a load of traffic that requires additional tuning, and the network quality may be improved using QoS:

- **A router resource problem**—Indicated by a large number of throttles or buffer failures. This may be fixed with buffer tuning, but will, most likely, eventually require a router or memory upgrade depending on the situation.

- **A physical layer problem**—Indicated by a large number of errors, which can be fixed using good old-fashioned troubleshooting.

- **A high traffic load on the router**—Indicated by a high txload, rxload, a high number of dropped packets, underruns, and buffer errors.

To further isolate a problem with the quality of interface performance, you can take a few more steps. You can take a more detailed look at the interface controllers or, if the interface has an integrated channel service unit/data service unit (CSU/DSU), you can monitor any alarm conditions. When troubleshooting link-quality problems, one of the first places to look is the **show controllers** command. The **show controllers** command displays information about the interface hardware, as well as cable type and clocking information. The last few lines of the **show controllers** command also display hardware-specific errors. Example 4-6 shows the **show controllers serial** command.

Example 4-6 **show controllers serial** Command *Output*

```
Router# show controller s 0/1
Interface Serial0/1
Hardware is PowerQUICC MPC860
DTE V.35 TX and RX clocks detected.
idb at 0x8129D3E8, driver data structure at 0x812A2958
SCC Registers:
General [GSMR]=0x2:0x00000030, Protocol-specific [PSMR]=0x8
Events [SCCE]=0x0000, Mask [SCCM]=0x001F, Status [SCCS]=0x06
Transmit on Demand [TODR]=0x0, Data Sync [DSR]=0x7E7E
Interrupt Registers:
Config [CICR]=0x00367F80, Pending [CIPR]=0x00000800
Mask   [CIMR]=0x20200400, In-srv  [CISR]=0x00000000
Command register [CR]=0x640
Port A [PADIR]=0x0000, [PAPAR]=0xFFFF
       [PAODR]=0x0000, [PADAT]=0xF0F7
Port B [PBDIR]=0x03A0F, [PBPAR]=0x0C00E
       [PBODR]=0x0000E, [PBDAT]=0x31DDD
Port C [PCDIR]=0x00C, [PCPAR]=0x000
       [PCSO]=0x0A0,   [PCDAT]=0xF30, [PCINT]=0x00F
Receive Ring
        rmd(68012330): status 9000 length 18 address 1935788
        rmd(68012338): status 9000 length 11D address 1932388
        rmd(68012340): status 9000 length 18 address 1938508
        rmd(68012348): status 9000 length 18 address 1937E88
        rmd(68012350): status 9000 length 18 address 1933D88
```

continues

Example 4-6 show controllers serial **Command** *Output (Continued)*

```
                rmd(68012358): status 9000 length 18 address 1937808
                rmd(68012360): status 9000 length 18 address 1937188
                rmd(68012368): status 9000 length 18 address 1934A88
                rmd(68012370): status 9000 length 11D address 1936488
                rmd(68012378): status 9000 length 18 address 1935E08
                rmd(68012380): status 9000 length 11D address 1934408
                rmd(68012388): status 9000 length 18 address 1933088
                rmd(68012390): status 9000 length 18 address 1936B08
                rmd(68012398): status 9000 length 18 address 1933708
                rmd(680123A0): status 9000 length 18 address 1932A08
                rmd(680123A8): status B000 length 18 address 1938B88
Transmit Ring
                tmd(680123B0): status 5C00 length 18 address 193A158
                tmd(680123B8): status 5C00 length 18 address 193A158
                tmd(680123C0): status 5C00 length 18 address 193A158
                tmd(680123C8): status 5C00 length 18 address 193A158
                tmd(680123D0): status 5C00 length 18 address 193A158
                tmd(680123D8): status 5C00 length 123 address 1950098
                tmd(680123E0): status 5C00 length 123 address 194DE38
                tmd(680123E8): status 5C00 length 18 address 193A158
                tmd(680123F0): status 5C00 length 18 address 193A158
                tmd(680123F8): status 5C00 length 18 address 193A158
                tmd(68012400): status 5C00 length 18 address 193A158
                tmd(68012408): status 5C00 length 18 address 193A158
                tmd(68012410): status 5C00 length 18 address 193A158
                tmd(68012418): status 5C00 length 123 address 194F2D8
                tmd(68012420): status 5C00 length 123 address 1950098
                tmd(68012428): status 7C00 length 18 address 193A158
SCC GENERAL PARAMETER RAM (at 0x68013D00)
Rx BD Base [RBASE]=0x2330, Fn Code [RFCR]=0x18
Tx BD Base [TBASE]=0x23B0, Fn Code [TFCR]=0x18
Max Rx Buff Len [MRBLR]=1548
Rx State [RSTATE]=0x18008440, BD Ptr [RBPTR]=0x2380
Tx State [TSTATE]=0x18000548, BD Ptr [TBPTR]=0x23B8
SCC HDLC PARAMETER RAM (at 0x68013D38)
CRC Preset [C_PRES]=0xFFFF, Mask [C_MASK]=0xF0B8
Errors: CRC [CRCEC]=0, Aborts [ABTSC]=0, Discards [DISFC]=0
Nonmatch Addr Cntr [NMARC]=0
Retry Count [RETRC]=0
Max Frame Length [MFLR]=1608
Rx Int Threshold [RFTHR]=0, Frame Cnt [RFCNT]=65046
User-defined Address 0000/0000/0000/0000
User-defined Address Mask 0x0000

buffer size 1524
PowerQUICC SCC specific errors:
0 input aborts on receiving flag sequence
0 throttles, 0 enables
0 overruns
0 transmitter underruns
0 transmitter CTS losts
```

Another command that comes in handy when troubleshooting WAN interface card (WIC) modules with integrated CSU/DSU controller's link quality is the **show service-module serial** command. As shown in Example 4-7, this command displays information about the internal CSU/DSU, such as the alarm status and self-test information. You should note and track CSU/DSU alarms over time. Example 4-7 shows the **show service-module serial** command output, and Table 4-3 describes the output.

Example 4-7   **show service module serial** *Command Output*

```
Router# show service-module serial 0/0
Module type is 4-wire Switched 56
    Hardware revision is B, Software revision is 1.00,
    Image checksum is 0x42364436, Protocol revision is 1.0
Receiver has no alarms.
CSU/DSU Alarm mask is 0
Current line rate is 56 Kbits/sec
Last module self-test (done at startup): Passed
Last clearing of alarm counters 02:13:56
    oos/oof             :    0,
    loss of signal      :    0,
    loss of frame       :    0,
    rate adaptation attemp:    0,
```

Table 4-3   **show service-module serial** *Command Output*

Item	Description
Module type is 4-wire Switched 56 Hardware revision is B, Software revision is 1.00 Image checksum is 0x42364436, Protocol revision is 1.0	Type of CSU/DSU module.
Receiver has no alarms, CSU/DSU Alarm mask is 0	This area shows any alarms that are currently being detected by the CSU/DSU.
Current line rate is 56 Kbits/sec	Displays the current rate of line.
Last module self-test (done at startup): Passed	Displays the status of the last module self-test.
Last clearing of alarm counters 02:13:56	Displays the last time the CSU/DSU alarm counters were cleared.
oos/oof: 0,	The out-of-synchronization (OOS) alarm indicates a clocking synchronization problem. An out-of-frame (OOF) alarm indicates about one-fourth of the framing bits have been missed.

continues

Table 4-3   **show service-module serial** *Command Output (Continued)*

Item	Description
Loss of signal: 0,	A loss-of-signal (LOS) alarm indicates that no physical signal is detected.
Loss of frame: 0,	A loss-of-frame (LOF) alarm indicates missing framing bits.
Rate adaptation attempt: 0,	Indicates that the receiver attempted rate adaptation.

After you have either fixed a router interface problem, or verified that the router does not have any hardware or software problems that may be causing link-quality issues, you can address two more issues before moving on to QoS configuration. First, you can verify that the router is using the most efficient switching mode possible; and then, if the interface is still too congested, you may need to consider compression or QoS.

ATM: The Other WAN Technology

One of the obstacles network professionals encounter on a regular basis is the introduction of new technologies. Although Asynchronous Transfer Mode (ATM) is not a new technology—the first ATM specifications were developed in the early 1990s, and ATM hardware appeared soon after—and although most network professionals have plenty of experience with other WAN protocols such as High-Level Data Link Controller (HDLC), PPP, Frame Relay, and X.25, many people are not as familiar with the newer ATM technologies. The goal of this section is not to repeat the ATM information from Volume I of this series; this section is designed to provide a basic understanding of ATM router performance and QoS technologies. This section explores the following ATM-specific topics:

- Understanding basic ATM concepts
- Comparing ATM and Frame Relay technologies
- ATM performance management (displaying interface data, and basic troubleshooting of ATM)
- Basic ATM QoS on Cisco routers (concepts, application, and troubleshooting)

The Similarities and Differences of ATM and Frame Relay

All the Layer 2 WAN technologies mentioned earlier in this section share several similarities. For instance, as Table 4-4 shows, HDLC, PPP, ISDN, X.25, and Frame Relay all have similar Layer 2 frame formats and are based on similar framing Layer 2 standards. Link Access Procedure, Balanced (LAPB); Link Access Procedure on the D channel (LAPD); Link Access Procedure for Frame Relay (LAPF), and Synchronous Data Link Control (SDLC)—all these use similar frame formats containing Flag, Address, Control, Information, FCS, and Flag fields. However, each of these technologies was originally intended for use with low-bandwidth interfaces, such as T1, ISDN BRI, PRI, or DS3. The frames that these technologies use were designed to handle variable-length packets, because the protocols were designed to work primarily with variable-length Layer 3 data units.

Table 4-4   *Layer 2 WAN Protocols*

Layer 2 Protocol	Interface Encapsulation Type
LAPB	X.25
LAPF, LAPD	Frame Relay
SDLC	HDLC
LAPD	ISDN
B-ISDN*	ATM

* B-ISDN = broadband ISDN

ATM was created to use much-higher-bandwidth interfaces, at consistent data rates. From the beginning, the ATM protocol was designed to be able to support voice, data, and video traffic, commonly referred to as *multiservice traffic*. This is accomplished by the use of fixed-length ATM cells. ATM switches provide a network core, similar to the core provided by Frame Relay switches that provides CPE devices, such as routers' virtual circuits using virtual paths and virtual channels. In fact, when you lease a Frame Relay circuit from a service provider, they will, most likely, provision your Frame Relay circuit on an ATM switch, such as a Cisco MGX switch. When you document your network, you will show routers connected to a Frame Relay cloud like that shown in Figure 4-1, because your service provider will probably not provide detailed network information about their network. The Frame Relay traffic is encapsulated in ATM cells, sent through the ATM core network as ATM traffic, and translated back into Frame Relay at the edge ATM switch, as shown in Figure 4-2. Because this book is primarily focused on routing and switching technologies, ATM switching is not covered in any detail.

Figure 4-1   *Customer Perception of Frame Relay Networks*

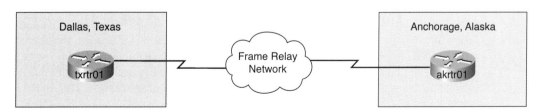

Figure 4-2 *Frame Relay over ATM Networks*

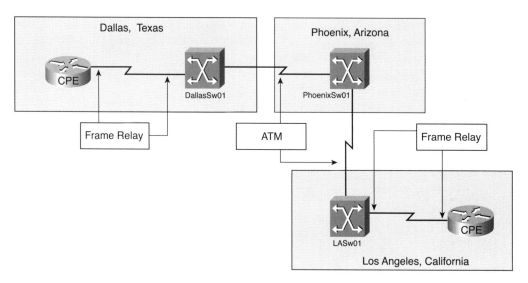

What makes the two technologies so similar is the fact that they both use virtual circuits to provide certain levels of service. Frame Relay virtual circuits are identified using locally significant *Data-Link Connection Identifiers (DLCIs)*. Generally speaking, Frame Relay circuits are provisioned with certain levels of service; a *Committed Information Rate (CIR)*, which dictates the guaranteed access rate. It is possible to order less-expensive, best-effort Frame Relay service. With Zero CIR service, the switch only forwards Frame Relay traffic during periods of no congestion; the term is not necessarily referring to the connection between your routers. At some point, congestion within your service provider's network may affect traffic that you cannot see from your routers. Frame Relay also supports bursting, or the transmission of excess frames during periods of low utilization. Frame Relay traffic can be controlled, or shaped, using the *Sustained Burst Rate (Bc)* and *Excess Burst Rate (Be)* to perform traffic shaping on the edge router.

With Frame Relay, low-priority traffic is marked for discard eligibility using the *Discard Eligible (DE)* bit. When a Frame Relay switch receives a frame containing a DE=1 bit during a period of congestion, it considers the DE frame low priority and it is discarded. Unfortunately, in most cases, when the DE bit is not changed from 0, the default value, and the network is congested, all frames leaving the router are considered discard eligible. Any of the Frame Relay switches in a congested network path may indiscriminately drop any of those frames. Because Frame Relay is a connectionless protocol, it relies on upper-layer protocols, such as TCP, to retransmit the data from those lost frames.

Frame Relay networks also have a QoS congestion notification system. This system uses forward *explicit congestion notification (FECN)* and backward *explicit congestion notification (BECN)* frames to notify up- or downstream neighbors of congested network paths. Because the use of the FECN and BECN frames must explicitly be configured throughout the network on customer and service provider equipment, however, if congestion notification is not configured, it does not offer much value. When devices are not configured to act upon congestion notification frames, the only benefit they provide is a historical reference of network reliability by means of the Frame Relay counters. So, during periods of congestion, Frame Relay networks that are not configured to use traffic shaping and congestion notification may prove to be very unreliable.

ATM was designed to support many of the same technologies that were originally created for Frame Relay networks. When Frame Relay was originally designed, most of the QoS features were left for vendor implementation, so the use of these features depends on the Frame Relay hardware/software vendor's Frame Relay implementation, and the service provider's Frame Relay network design and configuration. Because ATM is a newer technology and it was designed after the technical community had experience with older X.25 and Frame Relay technologies, however, ATM networks inherently support QoS by use of the ATM Adoption Layer (AAL) types and ATM classes of service, shown in Table 4-5.

Table 4-5   *AAL Types and Their Intended Uses*

AAL Type	AAL Description	Intended Use
AAL-1	*Constant bit rate (CBR)*—Designed to support applications requiring a low cell loss requirement and minimal *cell delay variation (CDV)*. CBR circuits are designed to mimic classic circuits by providing and enforcing a hard limit on cell rates like a real TDM circuit.	Voice and video traffic, not intended for bursty traffic such as data
AAL-2	This AAL type is designed to support connection-oriented applications with variable-rate, delay-sensitive traffic.	Voice and video traffic
AAL-3/4	AAL-3/4 was originally intended to support *Switched Multimegabit Data Service (SMDS)* traffic.	Legacy SMDS data traffic
AAL-5	AAL-5 was specifically designed to support bursty, variable-rate data traffic. AAL-5 does not work well with delay-sensitive applications.	Data traffic

Unlike Frame Relay, which was originally designed as a baseband technology, ATM was designed as a broadband technology and was designed to run over high-speed networks. Most ATM interfaces have built-in ATM logic, and are designed specifically for ATM networks that are not interchangeable with other serial interfaces. Therefore, it is very important to plan ATM networks carefully. Because the ATM specification was designed for broadband networks, ATM interfaces are usually available in DS3 or greater data rates, and for this reason, the location and use of ATM interfaces should be planned in advance.

NOTE   There are a few types of interfaces (ATM-Data Exchange Interface [ATM-DXI], Digital
Subscriber Line [DSL], and inverse multiplexing over ATM [IMA]) that support ATM at rates
lower than DS3. These type of networks are not covered in this book.

When configuring an ATM subinterface, you also have different AAL-5 encapsulation types
from which to choose. AAL-5 *Subnetwork Access Protocol (SNAP)* encapsulation is the default
encapsulation type for ATM interfaces, and is appropriate for most data traffic. Table 4-6 shows
the AAL encapsulation types, their description, and the recommended traffic type.

Table 4-6   *AAL-5 Encapsulation Types*

AAL-5 Encapsulation Type	Description	Recommended Traffic Type
aal5ciscoppp	Cisco PPP over AAL-5 encapsulation	PPP traffic over ATM
aal5mux	AAL-5 MUX encapsulation for multiplexing different AAL types on different permanent virtual circuits (PVCs) running on a single physical circuit	IP or voice traffic
aal5nlpid	AAL-5 network layer protocol identification (NLPID) encapsulation	RFC 1483 multiprotocol data traffic
aal5snap	AAL-5 *logical link control* (LLC)/SNAP encapsulation	The default, RFC 1490 data multiprotocol traffic

Cisco IOS Software's atm commands have greatly matured over the past few major releases.
Currently, you may encounter three different ATM configuration types. In later Cisco IOS
Software releases, ATM AAL types are referred to as encapsulation types on Cisco routers,
and can be configured in VC configuration mode.

As a quick review, let's go over the steps required for building a standard ATM PVC on a Cisco
router and compare ATM to Frame Relay configuration. In this example, we will use the latest
Cisco IOS Software configuration commands.

Step 1   Enable the physical interface and configure global interface properties.

Frame Relay	ATM
Enable the serial interface. ``` interface Serial0/0 no shutdown ``` Configure Frame Relay encapsulation type. ``` encapsulation frame-relay IETF ``` Optionally, configure Local Management Interface (LMI) type. ``` frame-relay lmi-type ansi ``` Optionally, configure interface clocking or CSU/DSU. ``` clockrate 1300000 ```	Enable the physical ATM interface. ``` interface ATM0 no shutdown ```

Step 2   Create a multipoint subinterface.

Frame Relay	ATM
Create a multipoint subinterface; as a best practice, you may consider using a subinterface number that relates to the PVC's DLCI number. ``` interface Serial0/0.651 multipoint ```	Create a multipoint subinterface; as a best practice, you may consider using a subinterface number that relates to the PVC's virtual path identifier/virtual channel identifier (VPI/VCI) numbers. ``` interface ATM0.4 multipoint ```

Step 3   Assign an IP address to the subinterface.

```
interface Serial0/0.651 multipoint
 ip address 192.168.26.1 255.255.255.252
```

or

```
interface ATM0.4 multipoint
 ip address 192.168.25.2 255.255.255.252
```

Step 4 Assign a Layer 2 address to the subinterface.

Frame Relay	ATM
Assign a DLCI to the Frame Relay subinterface. ``` interface Serial0/0.651 multipoint ip address 192.168.26.1 255.255.255.252 frame-relay map ip 192.168.26.2 651 broadcast ``` or on a physical interface ``` interface Serial0/0 ip address 192.168.26.1 255.255.255.252 frame-relay interface-dlci 651 ```	Assign a VPI/VCI pair and an optional Virtual Circuit Descriptor (VCD) name or number to the subinterface using the **pvc** [*vcd-name*] **vpi/vci** command. ``` interface ATM0.4 multipoint ip address 192.168.25.2 255.255.255.252 pvc 4/482 ```

NOTE   With Frame Relay networks, you can either use the **frame relay map** command or the **frame-relay interface dlci** command, but not both.

Step 5 With ATM only, choose an ATM encapsulation type based on the ATM AAL provisioned by the service provider:

```
interface ATM0.4 multipoint
ip address 192.168.25.2 255.255.255.252
pvc 4/482
  encapsulation aal5snap
```

Map the Layer 2 identifier to the Layer 3 IP address of the remote nonbroadcast multiaccess (NBMA) neighbor and, optionally, enable pseudo-broadcast replication.

Frame Relay	ATM

If you have not already done so, map the DLCI to an IP address and enable broadcast replication.
 	
``
interface Serial0/0.651 multipoint
ip address 192.168.26.1 255.255.255.252
frame-relay map ip 192.168.26.2 651 broadcast
``
	Map the VCD and VPI/VCI pair to an IP address and enable broadcast replication.
	
	``
	interface ATM0.4 multipoint
	ip address 192.168.25.2
	255.255.255.252
	pvc 4/482
	  protocol ip 192.168.25.1 broadcast
	  encapsulation aal5snap
	``

Step 6 Optionally, configure ATM QoS parameters. This is covered later in this section.

Look at the complete ATM and Frame Relay network that was used for the examples shown in the previous configuration steps. Figure 4-3 shows the complete ATM/Frame Relay networks, including all Layer-2 and Layer-3 addressing.

Figure 4-3   *The Complete ATM/Frame Relay Networks*

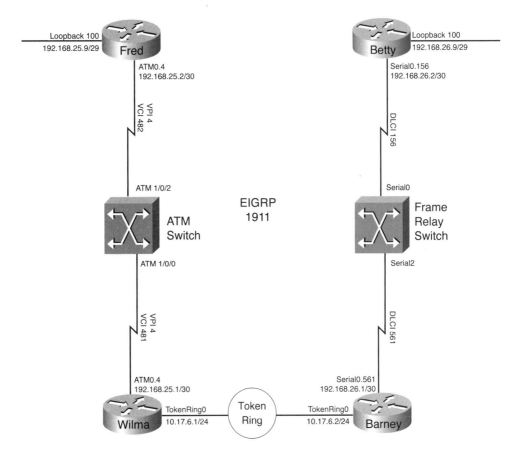

In this example, the Fred and Wilma routers belong to the ATM network, and the Betty and Barney routers belong to the Frame Relay network, and a Token Ring LAN interconnects both networks. This example illustrates the similarities and differences between Frame Relay and ATM networks. Example 4-8 shows the configuration for the Fred router.

Example 4-8   *Configuration for the Fred ATM Router*

```
hostname Fred
!
interface Loopback100
 ip address 192.168.25.9 255.255.255.248
!
interface ATM0
```

continues

Example 4-8 *Configuration for the Fred ATM Router (Continued)*

```
 no ip address
 no atm ilmi-keepalive
 !
interface ATM0.4 multipoint
 ip address 192.168.25.2 255.255.255.252
 pvc 4/482
  protocol ip 192.168.25.1 broadcast
  encapsulation aal5snap
 !
router eigrp 1911
 network 192.168.25.0 0.0.0.3
 network 192.168.25.8 0.0.0.7
 no auto-summary
 no eigrp log-neighbor-changes
```

Three commands were used to configure and enable the ATM interface and then configure Enhanced Interior Gateway Routing Protocol (EIGRP) routing over the ATM interface in this preceding example. First, the **pvc 4/482** command was used to create a PVC on the ATM0.4 multipoint ATM interface. This PVC was mapped to the IP address on the subinterface using the **protocol ip 192.168.25.1 broadcast** command. The addition of the **broadcast** option allows EIGRP to function over the NBMA network ATM network. And the **encapsulation aal5snap command** enables AAL-5 SNAP adaptation on the subinterface. Example 4-9 shows the opposite side of the ATM circuit configuration on the Wilma router.

Example 4-9 *Configuration for the Wilma Router*

```
hostname Wilma
 !
interface TokenRing0
 ip address 10.17.6.1 255.255.255.0
 ring-speed 16
 !
interface ATM0
 no ip address
 no atm ilmi-keepalive
 !
interface ATM0.4 multipoint
 ip address 192.168.25.1 255.255.255.252
 pvc 4/481
  protocol ip 192.168.25.2 broadcast
  encapsulation aal5snap
 !
router eigrp 1911
 network 10.17.6.0 0.0.0.255
 network 192.168.25.0 0.0.0.3
 no auto-summary
```

As you can see, the Fred and Wilma routers both have very similar ATM configurations. These configurations can also be tested using one of several atm show commands. For instance, the **show atm interface atm0.4** command displays information about the type and number of packets that have been transmitted on an ATM interface, as shown in Example 4-10.

Example 4-10 show atm interface atm0.4 *Command on the Fred Router*

```
Fred# show atm interface atm 0.4
Interface ATM0.4:
AAL enabled:  AAL5  AAL3/4, Maximum VCs: 1023, Current VCCs: 1
Maximum Transmit Channels: 0
Max. Datagram Size: 4528, MIDs/VC: 1024
PLIM Type: SONET - 155000Kbps, TX clocking: LINE
1981 input, 1986 output, 0 IN fast, 0 OUT fastUBR+ : 4
 Avail bw = 154996
Rate-Queue 0 set to 56Kbps, reg=0x0 DYNAMIC, 1 VCC
Config. is ACTIVE
```

When troubleshooting an ATM interface, it is helpful to be able to see the protocol mappings. The **show atm map** command displays the Layer 2–to–Layer 3 protocol mapping information for all VCs on a router, like the **show frame-relay map** command on Frame Relay networks. Example 4-11 shows the **show atm map** command output from the Fred router.

Example 4-11 show atm map *Command on the Fred Router*

```
Fred# show atm map
Map list ATM0.4pvc1 : PERMANENT
ip 192.168.25.1 maps to VC 1, VPI 4, VCI 482, ATM0.4
        , broadcast
```

The preceding example shows that ATM interface 0.4 has a permanent PVC mapping for the IP address 192.168.25.1 to VPI 4 and VCI 482. VPI/VCI 4/482 belongs to VC 1, and this VC supports pseudo-broadcasts, which was configured earlier using the **protocol ip 192.168.25.2 broadcast** command under the ATM subinterface. The **show atm vc** command shows the VC configuration for an ATM router, similar to the **show frame-relay pvc** command on Frame Relay networks, as shown in Example 4-12.

Example 4-12 show atm vc *Command on the Fred Router*

```
Fred# show atm vc
              VCD /                                Peak  Avg/Min Burst
Interface  Name      VPI  VCI  Type  Encaps  SC  Kbps  Kbps  Cells  Sts
0.4        1           4  482  PVC   SNAP    UBR 155000              UP
```

The **show atm vc** command displays the interface the VC exists under, the VCD name, VPI and VCI numbers, the VC type, encapsulation, ATM class of service, the peak cell rate, the average cell rate (both in kilobits/second), the burst rate in cells, and the VC status. Each of these parameters should match the information provided by the service provider or ATM switch configuration. Therefore, in this example, the Fred router's ATM 0.4 interface is an unspecified bit rate (UBR) circuit with a peak cell rate of 155,000 kbps, the full line rate, and the circuit is up. Example 4-13 shows the configuration from the ATM switch.

Example 4-13 *Configuration for the ATM Switch*

```
interface ATM1/0/0
 no ip address
 logging event subif-link-status
 no atm ilmi-keepalive
!
interface ATM1/0/2
 no ip address
 logging event subif-link-status
 no atm ilmi-keepalive
 atm pvc 4 482  interface  ATM1/0/0 4 481
```

Example 4-14 shows the configuration for the Barney and Betty Frame Relay routers, highlighting the Frame Relay configuration. You can compare this information to the ATM configuration shown earlier in Examples 4-10 through 4-13 to determine the differences and similarities between the ATM and Frame Relay configuration methods.

Example 4-14 *Configuration for the Barney and Betty Router*

```
hostname Barney
!
interface Serial0/0
 no ip address
 encapsulation frame-relay IETF
 clockrate 1300000
 frame-relay lmi-type ansi
!
interface Serial0/0.651 multipoint
 ip address 192.168.26.1 255.255.255.252
 frame-relay map ip 192.168.26.2 651 broadcast
!
interface TokenRing0/0
 ip address 10.17.6.2 255.255.255.0
 ring-speed 16
 ip rsvp bandwidth 822 24
!
router eigrp 1911
 network 10.17.6.0 0.0.0.255
 network 192.168.26.0 0.0.0.3
 no auto-summary
 no eigrp log-neighbor-changes
```

Example 4-14 *Configuration for the Barney and Betty Router (Continued)*

```
hostname Betty
!
interface Loopback100
 ip address 192.168.26.9 255.255.255.252
 no ip directed-broadcast
!
interface Serial0/1
 no ip address
 encapsulation frame-relay IETF
 clockrate 1300000
 frame-relay lmi-type ansi
!
interface Serial0/1.156 multipoint
 ip address 192.168.26.2 255.255.255.252
 frame-relay map ip 192.168.26.1 156 broadcast
!
router eigrp 1911
 network 192.168.26.8 0.0.0.3
 network 192.168.26.0 0.0.0.3
 no auto-summary
```

Table 4-7 lists some of the ATM and Frame Relay similarities and differences.

Table 4-7   *ATM and Frame Relay Comparison*

Frame Relay Technology	Technology Description	ATM Technology	Technology Description
DLCI	Identifies Frame Relay VCs.	VPI/VCI	Identifies ATM VCs.
LMI	Used to communicate Layer 2 signaling information from Frame Relay switch to FRAD.	ILMI	Communicates ATM signaling information between ATM switch and ATM CPE interface on router.
Serial sub-interfaces	Used to create logical point-to-point or point-to-multipoint Frame Relay circuit interfaces.	ATM subinterfaces	Used to create logical point-to-point or point-to-multipoint ATM circuit interfaces.
Frame Relay Map Statements	Maps Frame Relay DLCI to Layer 3 IP address and, optionally, enables the use of NBMA pseudo-broadcast.	Map lists or protocol mappings (depending on Cisco IOS Software version or configuration preference)	Maps ATM VCD, and VPI/VCI to Layer 3 IP address, and optionally enables the use of NBMA pseudo-broadcast.

continues

Table 4-7 *ATM and Frame Relay Comparison (Continued)*

Frame Relay Technology	Technology Description	ATM Technology	Technology Description
Frame Relay encapsulation on a serial interface	One of the 11 encapsulation types available on a serial interface.	ATM interface encapsulation	The only type of encapsulation available on an ATM interface. ATM interfaces have ATM hardware support built in. Other ATM encapsulation types can be selected and applied on a VC-by-VC basis.
CIR and optionally Be, Bc	The Frame Relay QoS SLA for a virtual circuit.	CBR, ABR, UBR, VBR.	The ATM circuit QoS type. On ATM switches, VCs are built for one of the following ATM classes of service: CBR ABR UBR VBR-rt VBR-nrt
DE	Frame Relay DE bit—Used to mark frames as discard eligible, or low priority. DE=0 priority DE=1 low priority	CLP	ATM cell loss priority (CLP) bit—Used to mark cells with a priority for use to determine discard eligibility on congested interfaces. CLP=0 priority CLP=1 low priority

Table 4-7   *ATM and Frame Relay Comparison (Continued)*

Frame Relay Technology	Technology Description	ATM Technology	Technology Description
FECN/BECN	Forward and backward congestion notification frames, sent by Frame Relay switches to indicate congestion.	EFCI and ER	A mode of congestion notification used with the ATM ABR class of service. Explicit forward congestion indication (EFCI) is a mode for forward notification, and explicit rate (ER) mode is used for backward congestion notification.
FRTS	Frame Relay traffic shaping (FRTS) uses Frame Relay CIR, Be, and Bc to shape Frame Relay traffic on a Frame Relay egress interface to control Frame Relay frame loss during times of congestion.	Inherent ATM QoS	ATM circuits inherently support some mode of ATM QoS. The ATM circuit type determines the type of QoS supported, and the type of QoS provided by the ATM router interface is partially determined by configuration.

Now that you have seen some of the ways that ATM and Frame Relay technologies contrast, the next section introduces you to the ATM QoS mechanisms and how they are implemented using Cisco IOS Software.

ATM QoS

Unlike Frame Relay networks that either forward or drop frames based on discard eligibility, ATM networks have four main classes of service that can be provisioned on ATM switches: constant bit rate (CBR), variable bit rate (VBR), unspecified bit rate (UBR), and available bit rate (ABR). Two of these main classes also have subclasses; there are two forms of VBR circuits: VBR real-time (VBR-rt) and VBR non-real-time (VBR-nrt), and UBR and UBR+. All of these choices are usually provisioned at the ATM switch and the CPE devices. The routers have matching QoS parameters that allow the routers to comply with the switch configurations. The type of circuit provisioned will depend on the SLA, and the pricing for the circuit will depend on the required level of service. Each class of service has different behaviors during periods of congestion, and will provide very distinct levels of service, so it is always best to plan ATM networks for the type of traffic that the network will support. Table 4-8 shows the ATM classes of service and traffic types that they support.

Table 4-8 *ATM Classes of Service*

ATM Class of Service	Service Level Traffic Characteristics
CBR	Provides a constant bit rate similar to that of a physical circuit. Like physical circuits, CBR circuits do not allow for traffic bursts; when the bit rate has been exceeded, any excess traffic is dropped.
	CBR circuits are best suited for traffic that requires a constant bit rate and does not tolerate delay—such as constant-use voice or video traffic on service provider networks. For this reason, CBR circuits are usually not provisioned for data networks.
VBR-rt	VBR real-time is recommended for traffic that has real-time data requirements and does not tolerate delay or jitter.
	VBR-rt circuits are usually provisioned for voice or video networks that do not require full line bandwidth all the time, and are more suitable for VoIP networks or videoconferencing systems that are not used on a constant basis.
VBR-nrt	VBR non-real-time circuits provide varying rates of service that support traffic bursts like those seen on data networks.
	VBR-nrt is frequently deployed in enterprise networks for use by bursty data applications that can tolerate varying rates of delay, either by protocol retransmission or network application support for retransmission.
UBR	UBR circuits are usually provisioned for networks that require only a "best-effort" class of service.
	UBR circuits can be thought of more like Frame Relay 0-CIR circuits; they provide the best level of service depending on network congestion. UBR circuits are suitable for WAN circuits between data networks running applications that support delay and retransmission or Internet traffic.
UBR+	UBR+ circuits are not provisioned as UBR+ on ATM switches; UBR+ is specific to UBR service configured as UBR+ on a Cisco router.
	UBR+ configuration enables you to configure a router with a minimum cell rate (MCR), which is communicated to the ATM switch. The ATM network does not necessarily guarantee UBR+ service levels; they still must be negotiated with an ATM service provider and agreed to in an SLA.
ABR	ABR circuits provide a negotiated level of quality in ATM networks providing an MCR, and allow for burst when the network is not congested. With ABR circuits, the ATM network provides a base level of service, and communicates network status information to routers by setting information contained in resource management (RM) cells that allows the routers' ATM interfaces to use extra network resources during periods of low traffic.

To gain the full benefit of the ATM classes of service, certain ATM QoS parameters must be configured on the router's ATM interface. Each ATM class of service has its own parameters; these parameters are configured in PVC configuration mode using the ATM class of service commands. The exact configuration values and availability will depend on the ATM interface type and ATM switch configuration. Before ordering an ATM circuit, make sure that you are prepared to have the proper ATM hardware to use the circuit; some platforms support only certain ATM circuit types. The remainder of this section focuses mainly on router configuration using Cisco 4500 and 4700 series NP-1A-OC3 interfaces. Most of the commands that apply to the 4500 series apply to other, newer routers.

Configuring VBR-nrt Circuits

As the name implies, VBR-nrt circuits are designed to support traffic that does not require real-time characteristics and can tolerate jitter and delay. Although ATM service level configuration is not required, the router must be configured to support the proper ATM traffic-shaping values in order to provide the level of service provisioned by the ATM service provider. VBR-nrt VCs require three parameters to properly shape traffic. These include the following:

- Sustained cell rate (SCR)
- Peak cell rate (PCR)
- Maximum burst size (MBS)

Each of these parameters is configured under PVC configuration mode using the following command:

```
vbr-nrt pcr scr [mbs]
```

The PCR, described in kbps, is the absolute peak rate that the ATM network will accept. The interface uses this value to throttle traffic peaks and smooth traffic so that traffic bursts will not be discarded in the ATM network. The SCR is the sustained rate that the ATM network will allow traffic to be transited at. The MBS, measured in cells, is the maximum burst size that will be accepted.

NOTE   When calculating your bandwidth requirements, always order circuits with room to grow, and your ATM VCs should always be provisioned at the sustained rate. Never design networks to use the peak rate; otherwise, you may end up with an unusable or unstable network.

Examples 4-15 and 4-16 show how an ATM VBR-nrt circuit is created between the Wilma and Fred routers.

Example 4-15 *Using VBR-nrt on the Wilma Router*

```
interface ATM0
 no ip address
 no atm ilmi-keepalive
!
interface ATM0.4 multipoint
 ip address 192.168.25.1 255.255.255.252
 pvc 4/481
  protocol ip 192.168.25.2 broadcast
  vbr-nrt 44209 9000
  encapsulation aal5snap
```

Example 4-16 *Using VBR-nrt on the Fred Router*

```
interface ATM0
 no ip address
 no atm ilmi-keepalive
!
interface ATM0.4 multipoint
 ip address 192.168.25.2 255.255.255.252
 pvc 4/482
  protocol ip 192.168.25.1 broadcast
  vbr-nrt 44209 9000
  encapsulation aal5snap
```

NOTE   If the MBS is not specified during configuration, as in the preceding example, the router uses a default value.

You can test this configuration by using extended pings with the **show atm pvc**, **show atm vc detail**, and **show controller atm 0.4 | begin Packet switching** commands, as shown on the Fred router in Example 4-17.

Example 4-17 *Verifying the ATM Configuration Using* **atm show** *Commands on the Fred Router*

```
Fred# show atm pvc
            VCD /                                  Peak  Avg/Min Burst
Interface   Name       VPI  VCI  Type  Encaps  SC  Kbps   Kbps   Cells  Sts
0.4         1           4   482  PVC   SNAP    VBR 44209  9000    95    UP
Fred# show atm vc detail
ATM0.4: VCD: 1, VPI: 4, VCI: 482
VBR-NRT, PeakRate: 44209, Average Rate: 9000, Burst Cells: 95
AAL5-LLC/SNAP, etype:0x0, Flags: 0x20, VCmode: 0x401
OAM frequency: 0 second(s)
InARP frequency: 15 minutes(s)
```

Example 4-17 *Verifying the ATM Configuration Using* **atm show** *Commands on the Fred Router (Continued)*

```
InPkts: 329444, OutPkts: 329722, InBytes: 1169546091, OutBytes: 1169566161
InPRoc: 329444, OutPRoc: 328129, Broadcasts: 1593
InFast: 0, OutFast: 0, InAS: 0, OutAS: 0
OAM cells received: 0
OAM cells sent: 0
Status: UP
Fred# show controllers atm 0.4 | begin Packet switching
Packet switching
  Fastswitched  0
  To-process    329564
  Bridged       0
Transmit errors
  Restarts      0
  Pktid misses  0
  Bad pktid     0
  Wrong queue   0
  No pkt        0
  Tx errors     0
  Bad VC        0
Receive errors
  Bad pktid     0
  Wrong queue   0
  No pkt        0
  CRC           0
  Length        0
  Giant         0
  Reas tout     0
  AAL5 format   0
```

In the preceding example, the **show atm pvc** command shows the VC configuration for the ATM PVC between the Fred and Wilma routers, and the **show atm vc detail** and **show controller atm 0.4 | begin Packet switching** commands verify that packets were successfully transmitted without errors.

Configuring UBR and UBR+ Circuits

UBR circuits do not guarantee that all traffic sent out on an interface will necessarily be transmitted across an ATM network. These circuits are generally used under two circumstances: The traffic sent across the network is tolerant of delay and jitter and only requires best-effort service, or there is a cost limitation preventing a better level of service. Standard UBR circuits require only one configuration parameter, the *PCR*, and are configured in PVC configuration mode using the **ubr** *pcr* command (where pcr is measured in kbps).

UBR+ circuits also allow for an MCR value, measured in kbps that allows for the support of peak and minimum cell rates. UBR+ is configured under PVC configuration mode using the **ubr+** *pcr mcr* command. Example 4-18 shows how the ATM UBR+ service level is used after

configuring an additional 100-Mbps PVC between the Fred and Wilma routers. This example
shows the PVC configuration from the Fred router.

Example 4-18 *Adding a* **UBR+ PVC** *to the Mix*

```
interface ATM0.5 multipoint
  ip address 192.168.25.5 255.255.255.252
  pvc 5/582
    protocol ip 192.168.25.6 broadcast
    ubr+ 106000 100000
  encapsulation aal5snap
```

You can verify this configuration by using **atm show** commands. Example 4-19 shows the
output of **show atm pvc** and **show atm vc vcd** commands from the Fred router.

Example 4-19 *Verifying the Configuration on the Fred Router*

```
Fred# show atm pvc
             VCD /                                 Peak  Avg/Min Burst
Interface  Name       VPI  VCI  Type  Encaps  SC   Kbps  Kbps    Cells Sts
0.4        1            4  482  PVC   SNAP    VBR   44209    9000    95 UP
0.5        4            5  582  PVC   SNAP    UBR+ 106000  100000      UP
Fred# show atm vc 4
ATM0.5: VCD: 4, VPI: 5, VCI: 582
UBR+, PeakRate: 106000, Minimum Guaranteed Rate: 100000
AAL5-LLC/SNAP, etype:0x0, Flags: 0x20, VCmode: 0x1
OAM frequency: 0 second(s)
InARP frequency: 15 minutes(s)
InPkts: 9877, OutPkts: 9969, InBytes: 25996105, OutBytes: 26002689
InPRoc: 9877, OutPRoc: 9878, Broadcasts: 91
InFast: 0, OutFast: 0, InAS: 0, OutAS: 0
OAM cells received: 0
OAM cells sent: 0
Status: UP
```

Switching Modes

Routers use two modes to determine the paths and forward traffic, routing, and switching. Each
protocol uses a routing method to determine the destination location for data unit packets,
frames, or cells. Layer 3 and Layer 2 addresses are mapped to each other, and then, if route
caching is configured, this information is stored in a route cache. When route caching is enabled
after the destination for a packet is known and has been stored in the route cache, any future
packets belonging to the same flow, containing the same destination address information, are
forwarded to their destination interface using the information from the route cache; otherwise,
the destination mapping is done on a per-packet basis. The process of mapping Layer 2 to
Layer 3 addresses and forwarding to a destination interface is referred to as *switching*. Each
interface has a default switching method; even if you do not explicitly configure a particular

type of switching, the router will switch packets using its default method. The effectiveness of the switching method depends on the features you have enabled and the switching mode that is in use. Before discussing how QoS can be configured to improve existing network performance, it is important to verify that the router interfaces are using the most efficient switching method.

NOTE   Some QoS and security techniques have certain switching method requirements. When selecting a QoS method, always remember to plan for the required switching method.

Process Switching

Depending on the type of hardware and software installed, different router models use different switching modes. The most basic switching mode is *process switching*. Process switching copies the first packet in a flow to the system buffer. The destination is looked up in the routing table. The cyclic redundancy check (CRC) is computed using the route processor. Then the Layer 2 information for the packet is rewritten and sent to the destination interface. Any subsequent packets belonging to the same flow are switched using the same switching Layer 3–to–Layer 2 path. Process switching has the highest latency of all the switching types because it uses the system buffers and processor to process and store each packet as it is received. Process switching is enabled by disabling the default of either fast or optimum switching using the command **no ip route-cache** to disable fast switching and adding the **optimum** argument to disable optimum switching. Process switching is sometimes required for certain processor-intensive packet-processing processes, such as debugging IP packets.

Fast Switching

Fast switching uses the route cache to store information about packet flows. When fast switching is enabled, the first packet in a flow is stored in packet memory, a separate area in the system buffer, the system processor is used to perform the Layer 3–to–Layer 2 mapping, and then the path information is stored in the route cache so that any subsequent packets from the same flow can be fast switched. The next packet and any further packets from the same flow are fast switched. Because the destination of the packet flow is already known, with fast switching, the route cache is consulted to find the destination interface. After the destination has been found and stored in the cache, the packet is rewritten with the proper Layer 2 header, and the CRC is computed using the interface's processor. The packet never interrupts the system processor, and because the destination interface information is known, the system buffer is not used to store the packet information. Fast switching is the default switching mode for many Cisco routers, including the 1600, 1700, 2500, and 2600 on Ethernet, Fast Ethernet, and serial interfaces. If fast switching has been disabled, it can easily be re-enabled using the **ip route-cache** command on the interface. You can monitor fast switching information by using the **show ip cache** command.

Optimum and Distributed Switching

Two other switching methods—not available to the 1600, 1700, 2500, or 2600 platforms—are optimum switching and distributed switching. With optimum switching, the same process used in fast switching is followed; the difference is that after the first packet has been processed, the path information for each subsequent packet from the flow is stored in the optimum switching cache, which is faster. Distributed switching requires the use of a Versatile Interface Processor (VIP) card to process switching information. The optimum switching method also uses a more efficient search algorithm that decreases the amount of lookups that must be performed by the VIP card. The VIP card retains a copy of the route cache and performs all switching locally so that the interface does not need to wait for the use of the shared packet memory in the system buffers or the system processor. Multiple VIP cards can also be installed to further increase switching performance. This makes distributed switching even faster than fast or optimized switching. Optimum switching mode is available only on high-end Cisco routers, such as the 7200. To enable optimum switching, use the **ip route-cache optimum** command on each interface where it is required. To monitor or troubleshoot optimum switching, use the **show ip cache optimum** command.

NetFlow Switching

NetFlow switching enables you to collect and store accounting IP traffic data that you can use for billing of network utilization. NetFlow switching uses the default fast or optimum switching mode for forwarding IP traffic; and in addition to route caching, NetFlow switching tracks information about IP network traffic flows. Flows are tracked by user, protocol, port, and type of service; this information can then be exported to a network management station. NetFlow switching operates by first performing standard fast, optimum, or CEF switching, as mentioned earlier; however, after a flow has been established, all new packets belonging to the same flow bypass access lists for the NetFlow interface, and statistics for that flow are collected. Because NetFlow accounting data is stored in the routing cache, the NetFlow switching data collection processes are transparent to all other network devices. NetFlow switching does, however, increase the load on the process or memory for the router, so it is a good idea to be aware of how much memory is required before implementing this switching method. By default, the NetFlow cache uses 64 bytes of memory per flow. If the default 65,536 flows are used, 4 MB of DRAM are required to support the NetFlow process for one interface.

NOTE   If a route caching method has not been configured and NetFlow switching is enabled, the default switching method (CEF, fast, or optimum) is enabled by default.

NetFlow switching is enabled using the **ip route-cache flow** command in interface configuration mode and monitored using the **show ip cache flow** command. This command shows the percentage of packets received at different packet sizes, the size of the NetFlow cache in bytes, the number of active and inactive flows, flow allocation problems, and detailed flow information, including source and destination interfaces. To export NetFlow cache entries to a network management station, use the **ip flow-export** command to specify the address of the station and the UDP port that will be used to send the data.

Cisco Express Forwarding

Cisco Express Forwarding (CEF) is the most efficient way to switch Layer 3 traffic. The reason why CEF switching is more advanced than fast or optimum switching is that CEF switching is less CPU intensive with the use of the *Forwarding Information Base (FIB)* and adjacency table. The FIB lookup table is used to store all known routes from the routing table using a more advanced search algorithm and data structure, bypassing the need for process switching. Unlike the other route caching switching methods, CEF uses the FIB, which adjusts to network topology changes as they happen. The adjacency table is used to store information about CEF neighbors. CEF nodes are considered to be neighbors if they are only one hop away from each other. The adjacency table stores Layer 2 next-hop addressing information for each of the FIB entries. Routes might have more than one path per entry, making it possible to use CEF to switch packets while load balancing across multiple paths. Each time a packet is received on a CEF-enabled interface, the FIB is consulted to look up the route, encapsulate the Layer 2 data, and switch the packet.

CEF switching is enabled globally using the **ip cef** command. After the **ip cef** command has been entered in global configuration mode, CEF switching is enabled on all CEF-capable interfaces by default. If CEF has been disabled on an interface, it can be re-enabled by issuing the **ip route-cache cef** command in interface configuration mode, and disabled using the **no** version of the same command. There is also a distributed version of CEF available for high-end Cisco routers, which is enabled by default after the **ip cef** command has been issued. You can monitor CEF by using the **show ip cef** command, and you can learn detailed CEF information by using the **show ip cef detail** routing command, as shown in Example 4-20.

Example 4-20 show ip cef detail *Command Output*

```
Router# show ip cef detail
IP CEF with switching (Table Version 10), flags=0x0
  10 routes, 0 reresolve, 0 unresolved (0 old, 0 new)
  13 leaves, 17 nodes, 19240 bytes, 13 inserts, 0 invalidations
  0 load sharing elements, 0 bytes, 0 references
  2 CEF resets, 0 revisions of existing leaves
  refcounts:  1061 leaf, 1058 node
Adjacency Table has 2 adjacencies
0.0.0.0/32, version 0, receive
1.1.1.1/32, version 6, connected, receive
35.132.253.0/24, version 7, attached, connected, cached adjacency to Serial0/2
0 packets, 0 bytes
```

continues

Example 4-20 show ip cef detail *Command Output (Continued)*

```
        via Serial0/2, 0 dependencies
          valid cached adjacency
      35.132.253.0/32, version 4, receive
      35.132.253.1/32, version 3, receive
      35.132.253.255/32, version 5, receive
      167.56.24.0/24, version 8, attached, connected, cached adjacency to Serial0/1
      0 packets, 0 bytes
        via Serial0/1, 0 dependencies
          valid cached adjacency
      167.56.24.0/32, version 1, receive
      167.56.24.31/32, version 0, receive
      167.56.24.255/32, version 2, receive
      224.0.0.0/4, version 9
      0 packets, 0 bytes, Precedence routine (0)
        via 0.0.0.0, 0 dependencies
          next hop 0.0.0.0
          valid drop adjacency
      224.0.0.0/24, version 2, receive
      255.255.255.255/32, version 1, receive
```

CEF Load Balancing

As mentioned earlier, you can use CEF to load balance packet switching over multiple paths. CEF can be configured to load balance either per destination or per packet, depending on network requirements. Balancing traffic on a per-destination basis sends packets with the same source and destination over the same path, distributing the traffic load of same-source destination traffic over the same path. If you use per-destination load balancing, packets with the same source and destination take the same path in each direction, not always the same return path, depending on routers in the reverse path. Because per-destination load balancing guarantees that packets follow the same path, packets arrive at their destination in the order that they were sent. This type of load balancing is best for traffic that requires packets to arrive in a certain sequence and is enabled by default when using CEF switching. If you will be requiring load distribution of traffic equally over multiple paths, consider using per-packet load balancing; however, it is important to remember that per-packet load balancing does not guarantee that packets will take the same path, which may cause packets to arrive out of order. Per-packet load balancing works best in situations where traffic must be evenly distributed over multiple paths due to uneven traffic loads. To change from per-destination to per-packet load balancing, disable per-destination load balancing on each required interface using the **ip load-sharing per-destination** command, and per-packet balancing is enabled using the **ip load-sharing per-packet** command, as shown in Example 4-21.

Example 4-21 *Changing to Per-Packet Load Balancing*

```
Router(config)8 int serial 0/1
Router(config-if)# no ip load-sharing per-destination
Router(config-if)# ip load-sharing per-packet
Router(config)# int serial 0/2
Router(config-if)# no ip load-sharing per-destination
Router(config-if)# ip load-sharing per-packet
```

Verifying CEF Configuration

To determine the current configured switching mode for an interface, use the **show ip interface** command. Example 4-22 shows how this command was used to display the current switching mode for interface serial 0/1. According to the **show ip interface** command output, serial 0/1 is currently using the default fast switching mode with fast switching on the same interface and multicast fast switching enabled. Flow switching and distributed fast switching are currently not enabled.

Example 4-22 *Viewing the Current Route Switch Configuration*

```
Router# show ip interface serial 0/1
Serial0/1 is up, line protocol is up
  Internet address is 167.56.24.31/24
  Broadcast address is 255.255.255.255
  Address determined by setup command
  MTU is 1500 bytes
  Helper address is not set
  Directed broadcast forwarding is disabled
  Outgoing access list is not set
  Inbound  access list is not set
  Proxy ARP is enabled
  Security level is default
  Split horizon is enabled
  ICMP redirects are always sent
  ICMP unreachables are always sent
  ICMP mask replies are never sent
  IP fast switching is enabled
  IP fast switching on the same interface is enabled
  IP Flow switching is disabled
  IP Fast switching turbo vector
  IP multicast fast switching is enabled
  IP multicast distributed fast switching is disabled
  Router Discovery is disabled
  IP output packet accounting is disabled
  IP access violation accounting is disabled
  TCP/IP header compression is disabled
```

continues

Example 4-22 *Viewing the Current Route Switch Configuration (Continued)*

```
RTP/IP header compression is disabled
Probe proxy name replies are disabled
Policy routing is disabled
Network address translation is disabled
WCCP Redirect outbound is disabled
WCCP Redirect exclude is disabled
BGP Policy Mapping is disabled
```

To enable NetFlow switching and disable multicast route caching, use the **ip route-cache flow** commands on the interface, as shown in Example 4-23.

Example 4-23 *Changing the Route Switch Configuration*

```
Router(config-if)#ip route-cache ?
  cef            Enable Cisco Express Forwarding
  flow           Enable Flow fast-switching cache
  policy         Enable fast-switching policy cache for outgoing packets
  same-interface Enable fast-switching on the same interface
  <cr>
Router(config-if)#ip route-cache flow
Router(config-if)#^Z
Router# show ip int s 0/1
Serial0/1 is up, line protocol is up
  Internet address is 167.56.24.31/24
  Broadcast address is 255.255.255.255
  Address determined by setup command
  MTU is 1500 bytes
  Helper address is not set
  Directed broadcast forwarding is disabled
  Outgoing access list is not set
  Inbound  access list is not set
  Proxy ARP is enabled
  Security level is default
  Split horizon is enabled
  ICMP redirects are always sent
  ICMP unreachables are always sent
  ICMP mask replies are never sent
  IP fast switching is enabled
  IP fast switching on the same interface is enabled
  IP Flow switching is enabled
  IP Flow switching turbo vector
  IP multicast fast switching is disabled
  IP multicast distributed fast switching is disabled
  Router Discovery is disabled
  IP output packet accounting is disabled
  IP access violation accounting is disabled
  TCP/IP header compression is disabled
  RTP/IP header compression is disabled
  Probe proxy name replies are disabled
  Policy routing is disabled
```

Example 4-23 *Changing the Route Switch Configuration (Continued)*

```
Network address translation is disabled
WCCP Redirect outbound is disabled
WCCP Redirect exclude is disabled
BGP Policy Mapping is disabled
```

Table 4-9 briefly describes each of the switching modes available in Cisco IOS Software and lists the commands used to activate them.

Table 4-9   *Switching Modes*

Switching Mode	Description	IP Switching Command
Process switching	Each packet is processed one at a time by the system processor and buffers; address information is processed for each packet as well.	**no ip route-cache**
Fast switching	The first packet in a flow is process switched; each subsequent packet in a flow is fast switched using the route cache.	**ip route-cache**
Optimum switching	The first packet in a flow is process switched; each subsequent packet in a flow is fast switched using the optimum switching route cache.	**ip route-cache optimum**
Distributed switching	Packet processing is performed locally using a VIP card, preventing packets from the need to use the system processor, route cache, or buffers.	**ip route-cache distributed**
NetFlow switching	Store accounting data that can be used for network utilization collection and billing.	**ip route-cache flow**
CEF switching	Stores Layer 3 routing information in an FIB table and Layer 2 neighbor information in an adjacency table. Topology information stored in the FIB changes dynamically with the routing table. This makes CEF the most efficient switching method because no process switching is involved in the switching process.	To enable CEF globally: **ip cef** Per interface: **ip route-cache cef**

Compression

Another way to increase the number of packets that can be transmitted is to reduce the size of frames by enabling compression. Because compressed frames are smaller in size, more compressed frames can be sent across the media, improving transmission times. Compression is implemented either in hardware or in software, depending on the Cisco IOS Software version installed, the type of interface and encapsulation in use, and the hardware platform that it is installed onto. This chapter covers only software compression techniques, in particular the STAC and Predictor compression algorithms.

Before enabling compression on any router, it is very important to check the processor and memory utilization. If a router's memory utilization exceeds 40 percent, compression will not be a helpful solution. It is also important to note that STAC and Predictor both support different encapsulation protocols and have different memory and CPU requirements. Table 4-10 outlines these issues.

Table 4-10 *Compression Issues*

Compression Method	Protocol	System Requirements
STAC	HDLC, PPP, LAPB, X.25	Higher CPU requirements
Predictor	PPP, LAPB	Higher memory Requirements

The amount of traffic being transmitted, the type of packets being sent, and the amount of available bandwidth also affect the impact that compression has on a router. If you are considering implementing compression on an interface that is mainly used to download data that has already been compressed, for example, enabling compression will not be beneficial because data cannot be compressed twice. If an interface has a large amount of bandwidth, and large amounts of data are being transmitted, the dictionaries in memory are likely to be very large. To check memory utilization, use the **show memory summary** command and compare the total memory to the free memory. If you do not have much free memory, your router will probably not be able to handle compression. To verify CPU utilization, use the **show process cpu command**; note the average processor utilization over a period of time. If it consistently reaches 40 percent, compression is probably not a performance solution. Example 4-24 shows the processor utilization for a router before and after STAC compression was enabled.

Example 4-24 *How Compression Affects Utilization*

```
Before STAC Compression
Lilo# show proc cpu
CPU utilization for five seconds: 2%/0%; one minute: 0%; five minutes: 4%
After STAC Compression
Lilo# show proc cpu
CPU utilization for five seconds: 44%/36%; one minute: 47%; five minutes: 25%
```

The Stacker Compression Algorithm

The *stacker algorithm*, referred to as STAC LZS, is a compression algorithm based on the Lemple-Ziv standard algorithm, which replaces characters in a data stream with codes. These codes are stored in a dictionary containing definitions matching the symbolic code used to compress the data to the actual data characters. The dictionary is constantly changing based on the types of traffic being compressed.

Cisco IOS Software supports the STAC compression method for PPP, LAPB, HDLC, Frame Relay, and X.25 interface encapsulations. Because the dynamic STAC compression dictionary stored in memory is constantly changing, it is very important to monitor the memory utilization on routers running the STAC algorithm. Due to the constant examination of packets, interfaces that use the STAC compression algorithm require large amounts of available processor time.

To configure STAC compression on either a PPP- or HDLC-encapsulated point-to-point interface, you just use the command compress stac on both sides of the connection. Example 4-25 shows how STAC was used on an HDLC connection between the Lilo and Stitch routers.

Example 4-25 *STAC Compression Example*

```
hostname Lilo
!
interface Serial0/2
 ip address 175.25.25.1 255.255.255.0
 no ip directed-broadcast
 clockrate 1300000
 compress stac

hostname Stitch
!
interface Serial0
 ip address 175.25.25.2 255.255.255.0
 no ip mroute-cache
 compress stac
```

To verify the operation of STAC compression, use the **show compress** command, as shown in Example 4-26. This command displays information about compression-enabled interfaces; the number of bytes compressed on 1-, 5-, and 10-minute intervals; and the statistics for the number of uncompressed and compressed bytes that were sent and received.

Example 4-26 *Using the* **show compress** *Command*

```
Router# show compress
 Serial0/2
     Software compression enabled
     uncompressed bytes xmt/rcv 7313/6614
     1  min avg ratio xmt/rcv 0.000/0.992
     5  min avg ratio xmt/rcv 0.000/0.993
     10 min avg ratio xmt/rcv 0.000/0.926
     no bufs xmt 0 no bufs rcv 0
     resyncs 0
       Additional Stacker Stats:
       Transmit bytes:  Uncompressed = 18653960 Compressed = 6053
       Received bytes:  Compressed =        5604 Uncompressed = 0
```

The Predictor Compression Algorithm

The *Predictor compression algorithm* is also a dictionary-based compression algorithm. While processing data, however, Predictor tries to predict the next series of characters in a data stream, using an index in the compression dictionary, which stores these sequences. If the next stream of data matches the first, the data sequence stored in the dictionary replaces the data sequence in the data stream. This prediction makes Predictor more efficient with its CPU use, but it also uses more memory than STAC.

To enable the Predictor compression method on a PPP- or LAPB-encapsulated interface, use the **compress predictor** command. Example 4-27 shows how the Predictor compression method was used between the Lilo and Stitch routers.

Example 4-27 *Using the Predictor Compression Method*

```
hostname Lilo
!
interface Serial0/2
 ip address 175.25.25.1 255.255.255.0
 no ip directed-broadcast
 encapsulation ppp
 no ip mroute-cache
 clockrate 1300000
 compress predictor
!
```
```
hostname Stitch
!
interface Serial0
 ip address 175.25.25.2 255.255.255.0
 encapsulation ppp
 no ip mroute-cache
 compress predictor
```

To check the status of Predictor compression in Cisco IOS Software, use the **show compress** command. Example 4-28 shows how the **show compress** command was used with Predictor to display information about the Predictor-enabled interface. The **show compress** command displays information about the number of compressed/uncompressed bytes that were sent out; the 1-, 5-, and 10-minute compression ratios; and displays troubleshooting information about memory issues in the **no bufs** area. When the two ends of a connection lose synchronization between their dictionaries, time must be spent resynchronizing, which adds latency to the connection. Information about dictionary resyncs is displayed in the dictionary **resyncs** area.

Example 4-28 *Using the* **show compress** *Command with Predictor*

```
Lilo# show compress
 Serial0/2
     Software compression enabled
     uncompressed bytes xmt/rcv 681/544
```

Example 4-28 *Using the* **show compress** *Command with Predictor (Continued)*

```
1  min avg ratio xmt/rcv 0.414/0.328
5  min avg ratio xmt/rcv 0.211/0.118
10 min avg ratio xmt/rcv 0.211/0.118
no bufs xmt 0 no bufs rcv 0
resyncs 0
```

When running either of the compression algorithms, it is a good idea to monitor the processor and memory utilization for each router. Example 4-29 shows the processor and memory utilization differences between the Lilo and Stitch routers. Notice that both routers experienced an increase in memory utilization, but not much of a change in processor utilization.

Example 4-29 *Memory and CPU Use with Predictor*

```
Lilo Before Predictor
Lilo# show process cpu
CPU utilization for five seconds: 0%/0%; one minute: 0%; five minutes: 0%
Lilo# show mem sum
             Head    Total(b)   Used(b)    Free(b)   Lowest(b) Largest(b)
Processor  8148D770   5712016   3997864    1714152    1504420   1637856
     I/O   1A00000    6291456   1909112    4382344    4382344   4382300
Lilo After Predictor
Lilo# show proc cpu
CPU utilization for five seconds: 1%/0%; one minute: 2%; five minutes: 0%
Lilo# show memory sum
             Head    Total(b)   Used(b)    Free(b)   Lowest(b) Largest(b)
Processor  8148D770   5712016   4132576    1579440    1504420   1506656
     I/O   1A00000    6291456   1909112    4382344    4382344   4382300
Stitch Before Predictor
Stitch# show process cpu
CPU utilization for five seconds: 11%/11%; one minute: 2%; five minutes: 2%
Stitch# show memory sum
             Head    Total(b)   Used(b)    Free(b)   Lowest(b) Largest(b)
Processor  81257BA0   5932128   3578052    2354076    2149660   2228244
     I/O   1800000    8388616   1746452    6642164    6642164   6642108
Stitch After Predictor
Stitch# show process cpu
CPU utilization for five seconds: 1%/0%; one minute: 2%; five minutes: 1%
Stitch# show memory sum
             Head    Total(b)   Used(b)    Free(b)   Lowest(b) Largest(b)
Processor  81257BA0   5932128   3711024    2221104    2149660   2097044
     I/O   1800000    8388616   1746452    6642164    6642164   6642108
```

After you have verified that the router can run the intended software, there are no Layer 1 problems, the router is using the most efficient switching mode, and you possibly considered using compression, you have addressed all the basic issues that could be affecting router performance. Another, more advanced way to improve router performance is to configure a QoS mechanism.

The next two chapters explain how various QoS types differ, how they are configured and monitored, and where each QoS feature works best.

Lab 10: ATM QoS

This chapter focused on a number of quality-troubleshooting and -refining practices that you can use in the field or in a laboratory environment to provide better levels of quality for network applications. The lab for this chapter focuses on ATM QoS techniques and their applications.

Lab Objectives

The primary focus of this lab is ATM technologies and QoS techniques; however, this lab also provides practice with the following technologies:

- EIGRP routing over NBMA networks
- Policy routing
- Voice over IP

Equipment Needed

- One Cisco LightStream 1010 ATM switch with two ATM OC-3 interfaces
- Two Cisco routers with ATM OC-3 interfaces; one with one Token Ring interface, and one with one serial interface
- One Cisco router with one Token Ring and one Ethernet interface
- One Cisco router with one Ethernet interface and one FXS voice module
- One Cisco router with one serial interface and one FXS voice module
- One multistation access unit (MSAU) and Ethernet switch or hub

Physical Layout and Prestaging

For this lab, you use the network layout shown in Figure 4-4. The City VetNet router will reach the Tom's Barn (TomsBarn) router via the OC-3 connection running from the City router and the Country Store (CntryStr) router. The CntryStr router connects to the Feed Store (FeedStore) router via a Token Ring network. VoIP is used between the FeedStore router and the TomsBarn router, and between the TomsBarn router and the rest of the network over an Ethernet connection.

Figure 4-4   *Emergency Veterinarian Network (VetNet)*

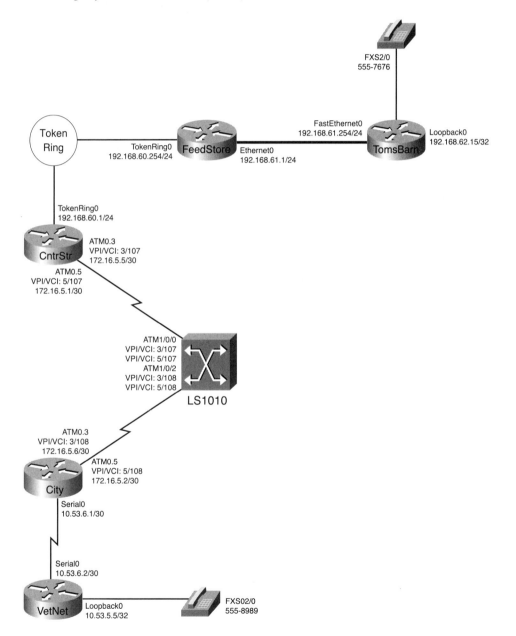

Step 1 Cable the routers as shown in Figure 4-4. Verify that all Layer 1 connections are working properly before continuing with the rest of the lab.

Step 2 Configure the ATM switch using the interfaces and VPI/VCI pairs shown in Table 4-11.

Table 4-11 *ATM Switch Configuration*

Switch ATM Interface	VPI	VCI	Router Name and Interface
ATM 1/0/0	3	107	CntryStr—ATM0.3
ATM 1/0/0	5	107	CntryStr—ATM0.5
ATM 1/0/2	3	108	City—ATM0.3
ATM 1/0/2	5	108	City—ATM0.5

Example 4-30 shows the ATM configuration and the **show atm vc** command output from the ATM switch.

Example 4-30 *ATM VC Configuration*

```
ATM-Switch# show atm vc interface atm 1/0/0
hostname ATM-Switch
!
interface ATM1/0/0
 no ip address
!
interface ATM1/0/1
 no ip address
!
interface ATM1/0/2
 no ip address
 atm pvc 3 108  interface  ATM1/0/0 3 107
 atm pvc 5 108  interface  ATM1/0/0 5 107
!
CRLF
ATM-Switch# show atm vc interface atm 1/0/0
Interface       VPI  VCI   Type   X-Interface     X-VPI X-VCI Encap  Status
ATM1/0/0        0    5     PVC    ATM2/0/0        0     39    QSAAL  UP
ATM1/0/0        0    16    PVC    ATM2/0/0        0     35    ILMI   UP
ATM1/0/0        3    107   PVC    ATM1/0/2        3     108          UP
ATM1/0/0        5    107   PVC    ATM1/0/2        5     108          UP
ATM-Switch# show atm vc interface atm 1/0/2
Interface       VPI  VCI   Type   X-Interface     X-VPI X-VCI Encap  Status
ATM1/0/2        0    5     PVC    ATM2/0/0        0     41    QSAAL  UP
ATM1/0/2        0    16    PVC    ATM2/0/0        0     37    ILMI   UP
ATM1/0/2        3    108   PVC    ATM1/0/0        3     107          UP
ATM1/0/2        5    108   PVC    ATM1/0/0        5     107          UP
```

Lab Exercise

Step 1   Configure all IP addresses as shown in Table 4-12. Make sure that all routers are able to ping their directly connected neighbor's interface before you move to Step 2. Configure the ATM interfaces to use the ATM encapsulation type most suited to burst data traffic.

Table 4-12   *IP Addressing for This Network Model*

Router Name	RouterInterface	IP Address
TomsBarn	FastEthernet0	192.168.61.254/24
	Loopback0	192.168.62.15/32
FeedStore	Ethernet0/0	192.168.61.1/24
	TokenRing0/0	192.168.60.254/24
CntryStr	ATM0.3	172.16.5.5/30
	ATM0.5	172.16.5.1/30
	TokenRing0	192.168.60.1/24
City	ATM0.3	172.16.5.6/30
	ATM0.5	172.16.5.2/30
	Serial2	10.53.6.1/30
VetNet	Serial1	10.53.6.2/30
	Loopback0	10.53.5.5/32

Step 2   Configure EIGRP routing for all routers, and put all router interfaces in EIGRP AS 62. Make sure that EIGRP routers only advertise the most specific routes; do not allow auto-summarization. Verify that all routers are able to ping the loopback interfaces on the TomsBarn and VetNet routers before proceeding to Step 3.

Step 3   Configure the ATM PVCs on the City and CntryStr routers so that the PVC on interface ATM 0.3 will have an unspecified bit rate with a maximum burst rate of 149,344 Mbps, and a minimum cell rate of 44,209 Mbps, and interface 0.5 will have a non-real-time variable bit rate with a maximum burst rate of 6.176 Mbps, and a minimum guaranteed rate of 1.544 Mbps.

Step 4   Configure Voice over IP between the TomsBarn and VetNet routers. Use the loopback0 IP addresses for the session targets, and use FXS voice port 2/0 for the phones. Test the configuration by issuing test calls between the phones connected to the two routers.

Step 5   Configure policy routing on the CntryStr and City routers so that all voice, and only voice traffic (including call setup), will be sent through the 1.5-Mbps ATM interface. Verify that the voice traffic takes the path through the proper interface.

Step 6   The new OC-3 has caused a bottleneck to form on the serial line between the VetNet and City routers. Enable compression on these routers using the compression method with the most efficient CPU utilization. This lab is complete when you have successfully placed test calls from the TomsBarn and VetNet phones.

Lab Walkthrough

Step 1   Configure all IP addresses as shown in Table 4-12. Make sure that all routers are able to ping their directly connected neighbor's interface before you move on to Step 2. Configure the ATM interfaces to use the ATM encapsulation type most suited to burst data traffic.

AAL5Snap is the ATM encapsulation type that was created specifically for today's burstier data traffic needs. AAL5Snap encapsulation is configured using the **encapsulation aal5snap** command under PVC configuration mode, as shown on the CntryStr router in Example 4-31.

Example 4-31 *Using AAL5Snap Encapsulation*

```
interface ATM0
 no ip address
 no atm ilmi-keepalive
 !
interface ATM0.3 multipoint
 ip address 172.16.5.5 255.255.255.252
 pvc 3/107
  protocol ip 172.16.5.6 broadcast
  encapsulation aal5snap
 !
 !
interface ATM0.5 multipoint
 ip address 172.16.5.1 255.255.255.252
 pvc 5/107
  protocol ip 172.16.5.2 broadcast
  encapsulation aal5snap
```

Step 2   Configure EIGRP routing for all routers, and put all router interfaces in EIGRP AS 62. Make sure that EIGRP routers only advertise the most specific routes; do not allow auto-summarization. You may not use EIGPR neighbor statements in this laboratory. Verify that all routers are able to ping the loopback interfaces on the TomsBarn and VetNet routers before you proceed to Step 3.

There are two ways to make EIGRP neighbors converge over an NMBA network. The first way is to use EIGRP neighbor statements to configure static neighbor relationships between the peers, which is not allowed in this lab. The second way is to use a Layer 2–to–Layer 3 protocol mapping with pseudo-broadcast support to allow the ATM interfaces to create pseudo-broadcasts, allowing EIGRP to converge over the NMBA network. This step requires an accurate ATM configuration to work properly. If you remember back to the ATM review section of this chapter, in newer versions of Cisco IOS Software, Layer 2–to–Layer 3 protocol mappings on ATM networks are created using the **protocol ip** *ip address* **broadcast** statement in PVC configuration mode under the ATM subinterface. Example 4-32 shows the ATM configuration for the City router.

Example 4-32 *The City Router's ATM Configuration*

```
interface ATM0
 no ip address
 no atm ilmi-keepalive
!
interface ATM0.3 multipoint
 ip address 172.16.5.6 255.255.255.252
 pvc 3/108
  protocol ip 172.16.5.5 broadcast
  encapsulation aal5snap
 !
!
interface ATM0.5 multipoint
 ip address 172.16.5.2 255.255.255.252
 pvc 5/108
  protocol ip 172.16.5.1 broadcast
  encapsulation aal5snap
```

After verifying the ATM configuration, you can check the NMBA broadcast support by issuing a **show atm map** command and verifying that each PVC has an associated broadcast statement as shown, on the City router, in Example 4-33.

Example 4-33 *show atm map on the City Router*

```
City# show atm map
Map list ATM0.3pvc1 : PERMANENT
ip 172.16.5.5 maps to VC 1, VPI 3, VCI 108, ATM0.3
        , broadcast
Map list ATM0.5pvc2 : PERMANENT
ip 172.16.5.1 maps to VC 2, VPI 5, VCI 108, ATM0.5
        , broadcast
```

You can verify that the EIGRP configuration is working properly by pinging the loopback interfaces from the TomsBarn and VetNet routers. Example 4-34 shows the EIGRP configuration from the CntryStr router and the pings from the TomsBarn and VetNet routers.

Example 4-34 *EIGRP Configuration from the CntryStr Router*

```
router eigrp 62
 network 172.16.5.0 0.0.0.3
 network 172.16.5.4 0.0.0.3
 network 192.168.60.0
 no auto-summary
TomsBarn# ping 10.53.5.5

Type escape sequence to abort.
Sending 5, 100-byte ICMP Echos to 10.53.5.5, timeout is 2 seconds:
!!!!!
Success rate is 100 percent (5/5), round-trip min/avg/max = 4/6/8 ms
VetNet# ping 192.168.62.15

Type escape sequence to abort.
Sending 5, 100-byte ICMP Echos to 192.168.62.15, timeout is 2 seconds:
!!!!!
Success rate is 100 percent (5/5), round-trip min/avg/max = 4/6/8 ms
```

NOTE   Earlier versions of Cisco IOS Software required PVC-independent map lists to map Layer 2–to–Layer 3 protocols. These commands still exist in newer versions of the software if you want to use them.

Step 3   Configure the ATM PVCs on the City and CntryStr routers so that the PVC on interface ATM 0.3 will have an unspecified bit rate, with a maximum burst rate of 149,344 Mbps, and a minimum cell rate of 44,209 Mbps, and interface 0.5 will have a non-real-time variable bit rate, with a maximum burst rate of 6.176 Mbps, and a minimum guaranteed rate of 1.544 Mbps.

The ATM traffic-shaping exercise for this lab requires you to configure each PVC on the City and CntryStr routers with a separate level of ATM service. The first, bigger PVC is set to use a sustained rate of 45 Mbps (DS3), and it is also able to burst to 150 Mbps; this is accomplished using the UBR+ ATM service level on the ATM 3/107 and 3/108 PVCs. This configuration can be verified by using the **show atm vc** command. Example 4-35 shows the UBR+ configuration for the City router.

Example 4-35 *The City Router's UBR+ Configuration*

```
interface ATM0.3 multipoint
 ip address 172.16.5.6 255.255.255.252
 pvc 3/108
  protocol ip 172.16.5.5 broadcast
  ubr+ 149344 44209
  encapsulation aal5snap
City# show atm vc
             VCD /                                     Peak  Avg/Min Burst
Interface   Name        VPI  VCI  Type  Encaps  SC    Kbps  Kbps    Cells  Sts
0.3          1           3    108  PVC   SNAP    UBR+  149344 44209         UP
```

The second, smaller, T1-sized PVC should be configured to use the VBR-nrt service level with a PCR of 6,176 kbps, and an SCR of 1,544 kbps, as shown on the CntryStr router in Example 4-36.

Example 4-36 *The CntryStr's VBR-nrt Configuration*

```
interface ATM0.5 multipoint
 ip address 172.16.5.1 255.255.255.252
 pvc 5/107
  protocol ip 172.16.5.2 broadcast
  vbr-nrt 6176 1544
  encapsulation aal5snap
```

NOTE   Even when you change the ATM service class for an ATM interface, the bandwidth parameter shown when the **show interface** command is issued will not be changed. Remember, the bandwidth shown using the **show interface** command is only the EIGRP bandwidth metric for the interface.

Step 4   Configure Voice over IP between the TomsBarn and VetNet routers. Use the loopback0 IP addresses for the session targets, and use FXS voice port 2/0 for the phones. Test the configuration by issuing test calls between the phones connected to the two routers.

This step is very straightforward, assuming the rest of the configuration up to this point is working properly. All you have to do is set up two dial peers on each router, and set a session target and port to the local and remote dial peers. Example 4-37 shows the voice configuration for the TomsBarn router.

Example 4-37 *TomsBarn Voice over IP Configuration*

```
dial-peer voice 5557676 pots
 destination-pattern 5557676
 port 2/0
 !
dial-peer voice 5558989 voip
 destination-pattern 5558989
 session target ipv4:10.53.5.5
```

Step 5   Configure policy routing on the CntryStr and City routers so that all voice, and only voice traffic (including call setup), will be sent through the 1.5-Mbps ATM interface. Verify that the voice traffic takes the path through the proper interface.

This step requires a few tasks to work properly. First, on one of the routers, in this example you use the CntryStr router, create an access list that matches voice traffic coming from the TomsBarn router. Next, create a route map that matches that traffic and sends it to interface ATM 0.5. Then, test and, if necessary, fine-tune that configuration using the **debug ip policy** command and test calls initiated from the phone in TomsBarn. Then, after you have the configuration correct, repeat the same steps on the City router. Example 4-38 shows the policy routing configuration from the CntryStr router.

Example 4-38 *The Policy Routing Configuration for the CntryStr Router*

```
interface TokenRing0
 ip address 192.168.60.1 255.255.255.0
 no ip route-cache
 no ip mroute-cache
 ip policy route-map voice-traffic
 ring-speed 16
!
access-list 150 permit tcp host 192.168.61.254 host 10.53.6.2 eq 1720
access-list 150 permit tcp host 192.168.61.254 eq 1720 host 10.53.6.2
access-list 150 permit tcp host 192.168.61.254 host 10.53.5.5 eq 1720
access-list 150 permit udp host 192.168.61.254 host 10.53.6.2 range 16384 32767
route-map voice-traffic permit 10
 match ip address 150
 set interface ATM0.5
```

In the preceding example, the first three lines specify H.323 call setup traffic between the two routers, and the last line specifies the RTP voice traffic. Route mapped voice traffic is used to configure the policy that sends the access list 150 traffic to interface ATM 0.5. You can verify this by making test calls from the TomsBarn router to the VetNet router, and by using **show route-map** and **debug ip policy** to show policy matches, as shown in Example 4-39.

Example 4-39 *show route-map and debug ip policy*

```
CntryStr#show route-map voice-traffic
route-map voice-traffic, permit, sequence 10
  Match clauses:
    ip address (access-lists): 150
  Set clauses:
    interface ATM0.5
  Policy routing matches: 3942 packets, 328996 bytes
02:24:57: IP: s=192.168.61.254 (TokenRing0), d=10.53.5.5, len 346, policy match
02:24:57: IP: route map voice-traffic, item 10, permit
02:24:57: IP: s=192.168.61.254 (TokenRing0), d=10.53.5.5 (ATM0.5), len 346, policy
routed
02:24:57: IP: TokenRing0 to ATM0.5 172.16.5.2
02:24:58: IP: s=192.168.61.254 (TokenRing0), d=10.53.5.5, len 40, policy match
02:24:58: IP: route map voice-traffic, item 10, permit
02:24:58: IP: s=192.168.61.254 (TokenRing0), d=10.53.5.5 (ATM0.5), len 40, policy
routed
02:24:58: IP: TokenRing0 to ATM0.5 172.16.5.2
02:24:58: IP: s=192.168.61.254 (TokenRing0), d=10.53.6.2, len 60, policy match
02:24:58: IP: route map voice-traffic, item 10, permit
02:24:58: IP: s=192.168.61.254 (TokenRing0), d=10.53.6.2 (ATM0.5), len 60, policy
routed
```

Step 6 The new OC-3 has caused a bottleneck to form on the serial line between the VetNet and City routers. Enable compression on these routers using the compression method with the most efficient CPU utilization. This lab is complete when you have successfully placed test calls from the TomsBarn and VetNet phones.

The Predictor compression algorithm makes the most efficient use of the router's CPU resources. Before you can use Predictor compression, however, you must use PPP encapsulation. After you have configured PPP and Predictor on the City and VetNet routers, you should be able to make successful test calls between the TomsBarn and VetNet routers. Example 4-40 shows the compression configuration for the VetNet router.

Example 4-40 *The VetNet Compression Configuration*

```
interface Serial1
  ip address 10.53.6.2 255.255.255.252
  encapsulation ppp
  clockrate 1300000
  compress predictor
```

After you complete the test calls, this lab is finished. Compare your router configuration to those shown in Example 4-41.

Example 4-41 *Complete Router Configurations for This Lab*

```
hostname TomsBarn
!
ip cef
!
interface Loopback0
  ip address 192.168.62.15 255.255.255.255
!
interface FastEthernet0
  ip address 192.168.61.254 255.255.255.0
!
router eigrp 62
  network 192.168.61.0
  network 192.168.62.15 0.0.0.0
  no auto-summary
!
ip classless
!
dial-peer voice 5557676 pots
  destination-pattern 5557676
  port 2/0
!
dial-peer voice 5558989 voip
  destination-pattern 5558989
  session target ipv4:10.53.5.5
```

```
hostname FeedStore
!
ip cef
!
interface Ethernet0/0
  ip address 192.168.61.1 255.255.255.0
!
interface TokenRing0/0
  ip address 192.168.60.254 255.255.255.0
  ring-speed 16
!
router eigrp 62
  network 192.168.60.0
  network 192.168.61.0
```

Example 4-41 *Complete Router Configurations for This Lab (Continued)*

```
 no auto-summary
hostname CntryStr
!
ip cef
!
interface TokenRing0
 ip address 192.168.60.1 255.255.255.0
 ip route-cache policy
 no ip route-cache cef
 ip policy route-map voice-traffic
 ring-speed 16
!
interface ATM0
 no ip address
 no atm ilmi-keepalive
!
interface ATM0.3 multipoint
 ip address 172.16.5.5 255.255.255.252
 pvc 3/107
  protocol ip 172.16.5.6 broadcast
  ubr+ 149344 44209
  encapsulation aal5snap
!
interface ATM0.5 multipoint
 ip address 172.16.5.1 255.255.255.252
 pvc 5/107
  protocol ip 172.16.5.2 broadcast
  vbr-nrt 6176 1544
  encapsulation aal5snap
!
router eigrp 62
network 172.16.5.0 0.0.0.3
 network 172.16.5.4 0.0.0.3
 network 192.168.60.0
 no auto-summary
!
ip classless
!
access-list 150 permit tcp host 192.168.61.254 host 10.53.6.2 eq 1720
access-list 150 permit tcp host 192.168.61.254 eq 1720 host 10.53.6.2
access-list 150 permit tcp host 192.168.61.254 host 10.53.5.5 eq 1720
access-list 150 permit udp host 192.168.61.254 host 10.53.6.2 range 16384 32767
route-map voice-traffic permit 10
 match ip address 150
 set interface ATM0.5

hostname City
!
ip cef
```

continues

Example 4-41 *Complete Router Configurations for This Lab (Continued)*

```
!
interface Serial0
 ip address 10.53.6.1 255.255.255.252
 encapsulation ppp
 no ip route-cache cef
 ip policy route-map voice-traffic
 compress predictor
!
interface ATM0
 no ip address
 no atm ilmi-keepalive
!
interface ATM0.3 multipoint
 ip address 172.16.5.6 255.255.255.252
 pvc 3/108
  protocol ip 172.16.5.5 broadcast
  ubr+ 149344 44209
  encapsulation aal5snap
!
interface ATM0.5 multipoint
 ip address 172.16.5.2 255.255.255.252
 pvc 5/108
  protocol ip 172.16.5.1 broadcast
  vbr-nrt 6176 1544
  encapsulation aal5snap
!
router eigrp 62
 network 10.53.6.0 0.0.0.3
 network 172.16.5.0 0.0.0.3
 network 172.16.5.4 0.0.0.3
 no auto-summary
!
ip classless
!
access-list 1 deny   172.16.5.4 0.0.0.3
access-list 1 permit any
access-list 150 permit tcp host 10.53.6.2 host 192.168.61.254 eq 1720
access-list 150 permit tcp host 10.53.6.2 eq 1720 host 192.168.61.254
access-list 150 permit tcp host 10.53.6.2 host 192.168.62.15 eq 1720
access-list 150 permit udp host 10.53.6.2 host 192.168.61.254 range 16384 32767
route-map voice-traffic permit 10
 match ip address 150
 set interface ATM0.5
```

```
hostname VetNet
!
interface Loopback0
 ip address 10.53.5.5 255.255.255.255
!
interface Serial0
 ip address 10.53.6.2 255.255.255.252
 encapsulation ppp
```

Example 4-41 *Complete Router Configurations for This Lab (Continued)*

```
 clockrate 1300000
 compress predictor
 !
router eigrp 62
 network 10.53.5.5 0.0.0.0
 network 10.53.6.0 0.0.0.3
 no auto-summary
 !
ip classless
 !
dial-peer voice 5558989 pots
 destination-pattern 5558989
 port 2/0
 !
dial-peer voice 5557676 voip
 destination-pattern 5557676
 session target ipv4:192.168.62.15
```

Further Reading

RFC 2330, *Framework for IP Performance Metrics*, by Paul L. Della Maggiora, Christopher E. Elliott, Robert L. Pavone, Jr., Kent J. Phelps, and James M. Thompson.

Network Consultants Handbook, by Matthew J. Castelli.

Internetworking Troubleshooting Handbook, Second Edition, by Cisco Systems.

CHAPTER 5

Integrated and Differentiated Services

The preceding chapter explored router performance and examined several route-switching mechanisms that you can use to provide certain levels of Quality of Service (QoS) by reducing latency and jitter caused by errors and device resource utilization. This chapter focuses on more granular QoS techniques provided by integrated and differentiated services. This chapter covers the following topics:

- How to provide a guaranteed level of service using Resource Reservation Protocol (RSVP)

- How to mark traffic with priority levels using the built-in Internet Protocol (IP) Type of Service (TOS) bits

- How to prioritize traffic using IP precedence bits

- How to use the new differentiated services codepoint bits for advanced traffic classification and marking

While analyzing these topics, this chapter also applies these technologies using practical examples and gives you the opportunity to gain real hands-on experience with the protocols with practical laboratory experiments.

Integrated Services

Integrated services, commonly referred to as IntServ, is an architecture for providing end-to-end QoS. IntServ solutions allow end stations to make quality requests upon the network; the network participates in this QoS scheme by either reserving or not reserving network resources for the requesting end stations. The integrated services architecture provides a way of guaranteeing network quality levels by specifically reserving services and controlling the load of the traffic on devices to provide the guaranteed service requirements. The most common implementation of the integrated services architecture is the RSVP signaling protocol.

Bandwidth Reservation Using RSVP

RSVP, also known as Resource Reservation Setup Protocol, is defined in RFC 2205 as a signaling protocol used for resource reservation, provides an end-to-end QoS reservation that is initiated by a requesting host or application. RSVP supports multicast or unicast IP traffic in flows. A *flow* is basically defined as traffic from a particular IP address, protocol type, and port number that is destined to a specific IP address or multicast group on a specific port using a specific protocol type. Because flows are defined by source and destination protocol information, each flow provides a unidirectional description of a conversation between end stations. Using RSVP, real-time applications can specify the network quality parameters required for the application to function as designed. In RSVP, hosts usually request specific QoS features and routers along the path between the hosts providing the services. It is also important to note that RSVP requests are unidirectional flowing from the requesting host to the destination, with each device in between participating in the RSVP session. RSVP uses the information from the routing tables to find routes to the destination. With the information provided by the routing tables and the different message types, RSVP dynamically adjusts to changing network conditions.

RSVP also sends periodic refresh messages that are used to maintain the RSVP state. If the messages are not received within the specified period of time, defined in RSVP request messages, the RSVP state times out and the reservation is deleted.

RSVP requests use flow specifications referred to as flowspecs and filter specs to form a flow descriptor; the *flow descriptor* is used to describe the characteristics of a flow. The *flowspec* defines the requesting host's quality requirements; the packet scheduler uses the information provided by the flowspec to determine the scheduling requirements for the flow, and the *filter spec* is used to define the requirements for the host's packet classifier. The *packet scheduler* determines when packets are to be forwarded, and the *packet classifier* determines the QoS characteristics for the packets in the flow.

Two types of flow reservations are classified in RSVP: distinct reservations and shared reservations. *Distinct reservations* are defined by a flow that has been initiated by one sender with one reservation created for each sender, whereas *shared reservation* flows may have originated from one or more sender. A separate reservation is created for each sender that requests a distinct reservation; only one reservation is created and shared for senders utilizing shared reservations. The shared reservation type is typically used by applications. Table 5-1 summarizes the RSVP reservation types and briefly describes their application.

Table 5-1   *RSVP Reservation Types*

Reservation Type	Description
Distinct reservation	One sender originates traffic flow.
Shared reservation	At least one sender originates flow(s). These flows are generally not operating at the same time; therefore, they can share the same reservation.

RSVP reservations use two types of lists to define groups of senders. *Explicit sender-selection lists* specify senders using a filter spec that defines single senders, and *wildcard lists* specify senders that use the same filter spec using the same QoS characteristics. Explicit senders use the fixed-filter (FF) style for distinct reservations or the shared-explicit (SE) style for shared reservations. Wildcard senders use the wildcard-filter (WF) style for shared reservations and do not have a definition for distinct reservations. Table 5-2 shows how filter types are matched to sender selections and the characteristics that belong to each of the styles.

Table 5-2   *RSVP Reservation Styles*

Filter Style	Description	Reservation Type	Sender Selection
Wildcard-filter style (WF)	Uses a single reservation that is shared by multiple flows	Shared	Wildcard
Fixed-filter style (FF)	Uses a single reservation for packets from one particular flow	Distinct	Explicit
Shared-explicit style (SE)	Used by multicast applications with flows from multiple sources	Shared	Explicit

As mentioned earlier, RSVP is an end-to-end QoS model, which means that each device in an RSVP path must request resources from another device. Each RSVP-enabled router in the path must make two decisions before granting a request: whether the router itself has adequate resource to provide the requested resources, and whether the requesting host has permission to make a reservation. These decisions are made by the Admission Control Module and the Policy Control Module. The *Admission Control Module* determines whether the router has the resources to grant, and the *Policy Control Module* determines whether the requesting host has the right to request the service. If both conditions are met, a resource reservation is made. If either condition fails, the router refuses the reservation request, but the traffic is still sent using regular service. RSVP uses several message types to pass reservation requests and reservation request parameters. These message types are covered shortly, after this chapter describes the steps required to set up an RSVP path. To set up an RSVP path, follow these steps:

Step 1   The RSVP sender, the host requesting services, sends an RSVP PATH message that describes the data it intends to send.

Step 2   Each RSVP router in the path to the destination reads the PATH message, saves the information about the previous-hop IP address, adds its IP address to the message as the previous hop, and then sends the message on to the next router.

Step 3   The receiving host receives the PATH information.

Step 4   After reading the PATH message, the RSVP receiver requests a resource reservation back to the sending host, using the exact reverse path and using the RSVP RESV message.

Step 5   The RSVP-enabled routers either refuse the RSVP requests, if they do not
have adequate resources, or they merge the request and request a reservation
from the next router (in the reverse path).

Step 6   The original sending host receives the request from the closest next-hop
router (the router that reserved the resources) and uses the reserved path.

Figure 5-1 shows a diagram of how RSVP sessions are created using RSVP PATH and
RESV messages.

Figure 5-1   *RSVP Session Setup Diagram*

Remember a few key terms when using the RSVP protocol. An *RSVP sender* is the host who
initiated the RSVP reservation. The *RSVP receiver* is the host who the resources are reserved
to. Any routers that have been configured to run the RSVP protocol in between the sender and
receiver are referred to as *RSVP-enabled routers*.

The *resource reservation path* (RSVP PATH) message, the message initially sent by the RSVP
sender to request a reservation, lists all the hops along the RSVP path that are used to reach the
RSVP receiver. The RSVP PATH message also makes it possible for each RSVP-enabled router
to store an RSVP state for each reservation request. The *resource reservation request* (RSVP
RESV) message is sent by the receiving host and processed by each RSVP-enabled router in
the path until it arrives at the destination host, the RSVP sender. The sender receives and replies
to RESV messages, sending them back to the receiving host using the exact reverse path that
was originally used to send the request.

NOTE   The original RSVP RESV message sent by the RSVP receiver may not always be sent all the
way back to the sending host in all situations. If multiple receivers send an RSVP RESV
message, and there is a point where the flowspecs for these reservations merge, only the largest
flowspec is forwarded all the way back to the sender. The RSVP RESV message may also
include a request for a confirmation of the resource reservation. When that is the case, either the
sender or the RSVP router (at the flowspec merge point) sends a confirmation to the receiver.

RSVP uses the IP protocol for all of its communication. Because IP is not a reliable protocol,
sometimes RSVP messages will not be received by all required devices. To solve this problem,
RSVP sends periodic refresh messages using the hello interval specified in the original PATH

message. These messages are sent using RSVP PATH and RESV messages. When a sending host application is finished using the resources, it should send an RSVP TEARDOWN message. The next hop router receives the TEARDOWN message, removes the reservation, and sends a TEARDOWN message to the next-hop router along the path. The use of RSVP TEARDOWN messages is not limited to the RSVP sending host; the RSVP receiver may also send a TEARDOWN message, at any time, if it decides to end the RSVP session. In the event that a TEARDOWN message is lost, there is no need for concern, because RSVP sessions automatically time out when an interval called the *cleanup timeout interval* has been exceeded.

RSVP uses a number of message types to set up, maintain, and tear down RSVP sessions. In the event of a problem, these messages can be used to troubleshoot an RSVP session. Table 5-3 describes these messages in detail.

Table 5-3   *RSVP Message Types*

Message Type	Message Details	Message Description
PATH	A required message used to set up an RSVP session	PATH messages store information about the RSVP path state, including the IP address of the previous hop; this information is to be used by the receiving host as the reverse path to reach the sender.
		The PATH message includes the following fields:
		SESSION—Describes the receiver's destination IP address (unicast or multicast), protocol type, and port number
		RSVP_HOP—The IP address and *logical outgoing interface* (*LIH*) of each RSVP-enabled device in the path, specifying each *previous hop* (*PHOP*) and *next hop* (*NHOP*) in the path
		TIME_VALUES—The refresh period for the RSVP session
		The PATH message also contains a *Sender Descriptor*, which is used to describe the sending host's characteristics, using the SENDER_TEMPLATE and SENDER_TSPEC. The SENDER_TEMPLATE contains the sending station's IP address, protocol type, and port number. The SENDER_TSPEC defines the required characteristics for the flow, such as the source and destination IP address, protocol types, and port numbers.
		PATH messages are also used as periodic hello messages to keep RSVP sessions alive. The default hello interval is 30 seconds.

continues

Table 5-3 *RSVP Message Types (Continued)*

Message Type	Message Details	Message Description
PATH ERROR	An optional error message sent out when there is an error found in a PATH message	This message is sent to the sender as error notification when an error has been found in PATH messages.
PATH TEARDOWN	An optional error message sent out notifying the next hop router that the PATH is no longer valid and should be deleted	PATH TEARDOWN messages are sent out when a path is to be removed immediately. They can either be sent by an RSVP sender or RSVP-enabled router. The messages are sent to all RSVP-enabled routers along the reservation path and are forwarded to all RSVP receivers.
RESV	A required message sent out by RSVP receivers to share flow specifications	RESV messages are used to transmit RSVP reservation requests and request data between RSVP-enabled devices. RESV messages contain the following data: The SESSION, RSVP_HOP, and TIME_VALUES fields as specified previously in the RSVP PATH message RESV_CONFIRM—Contains the IP address of a receiver requesting RSVP session confirmation SCOPE—Contains an explicit list of senders that this message applies to STYLE—The reservation style for the message *Flow Descriptor List*—The list of flow descriptors *Flow Descriptor*—The flow descriptor for this message, which includes the flowspec, the filter spec, and the reservation style (FF, WF, SE)
RESV ERROR	An optional error message sent out when an RESV message error has been found	This message is sent to the receiver as error notification when an error has been found in an RESV message.
RESV CONFIRM	An optional message sent by the sender to the receiver as a notification that the message applies end to end	This message is sent out to the receiver to notify the receiver of an end-to-end RSVP session.

Table 5-3   *RSVP Message Types (Continued)*

Message Type	Message Details	Message Description
RESV TEARDOWN	An optional message sent by RSVP receivers and intermediate RSVP-enabled routers to indicate that an RSVP resource should be deleted	TEARDOWN messages are sent out when a path is to be removed immediately. These messages can be sent either by RSVP-enabled routers or by RSVP receivers and should be forwarded upstream to all RSVP-enabled routers and RSVP senders.

Two types of reservations can be requested using RSVP: controlled load services and guaranteed bit rate services. *Controlled load services* allow an RSVP session to flow through the network with the least possible interruption from other traffic flows, somewhat like an emulated circuit. *Guaranteed bit rate services* try to guarantee the worst-case delay that will be incurred by the flow when traveling across the network. Guaranteed bit rate services compute the delay taken from PATH messages along the RSVP path of a flow and provide this information to the receiver during resource reservation requests. Now that you have seen how RSVP uses the various message types to set up, maintain, and tear down RSVP reservations, it's time to look at how RSVP is configured on Cisco routers.

RSVP Configuration

The configuration of RSVP requires two steps. First, all router interfaces along the RSVP path must be configured to use Weighted Fair Queuing (WFQ). WFQ is required to provide flow support and queuing to RSVP on a per-interface basis. RSVP bandwidth must be reserved on each interface. By default, RSVP may reserve up to 75 percent of an interface's bandwidth.

NOTE   Low Latency Queuing (LLQ) can also be used to provide RSVP support. LLQ is covered in Chapter 6, "QoS—Rate Limiting and Queuing Traffic."

Step 1   Enable WFQ along the RSVP path. For each router that is to have an interface participating in the RSVP reservation process, WFQ must be enabled. By default, WFQ is enabled on interfaces with less than E1 speeds. To enable WFQ, use the **fair-queue** command on each interface.

```
fair-queue [discard-threshold] [dynamic-queues] [reservable-queues]
```

With the exception of the *reservable-queues* value, the default WFQ settings will generally be sufficient for any low-bandwidth interface. The WFQ *discard-threshold* is a value ranging from 1 to 4096. This value specifies how many packets a congested interface should queue before discarding any new packets; the default value is 64. The *dynamic-queues* parameter enables you to specify the number of dynamic flows that should be allowed on a congested interface; the range for the *dynamic-queues* parameter is 16 to 4096 queues. By default, WFQ supports 256 dynamic queues. The *reservable-queues* parameter enables you to configure a limit on the number of RSVP reservable queues that WFQ will support; you can configure any number of queues ranging from 0 to 1000. By default, WFQ does not support reservable queues. WFQ is covered in detail in the next chapter.

Step 2 Configure RSVP bandwidth reservation limitations per interface using the **ip rsvp bandwidth** command. Table 5-4 shows the optional RSVP bandwidth arguments and their descriptions:

```
ip rsvp bandwidth [reservable-bandwidth] [largest-flow]
```

Table 5-4 *RSVP Bandwidth Arguments*

Command	Description
reservable-bandwidth	(Optional) This command parameter enables you to configure the total amount of bandwidth that can be configured on an interface in kbps. The default setting is 75 percent of the available bandwidth in kilobits.
largest-flow	(Optional) This command parameter enables you to specify the size of the largest flow size in kbps. By default, the largest flow is limited to 75 percent of the available bandwidth in kilobits per second.

In addition to the RSVP bandwidth allocation configuration, you can use a number of other optional RSVP commands to customize the performance and security of RSVP. To configure RSVP with a static neighbor assignment, use the command **ip rsvp neighbor** and specify either a standard or extended numbered access-list (lists 1 through 199):

```
ip rsvp neighbor [access-list]
```

If you are using NetFlow switching with RSVP, the **ip rsvp flow-assist** command enables RSVP to use NetFlow support for RSVP:

```
ip rsvp flow-assist
```

You can also configure RSVP to change the IP precedence or DSCP value of packets by using either the **ip rsvp precedence** or **ip rsvp signalling** commands. Using the **ip rsvp precedence** command, you can change the IP precedence to a value between 0 and 7. With the **ip rsvp signalling dscp** command, you can change the DSCP value to a value between 0 and 63. You can use the **ip rsvp tos** command to change the type of service (ToS) value to a value between 0 and 31. With each of these commands, you can either change packets that conform to the flow size, packets that exceed the flow size, or both. IP precedence, ToS, and DSCP packet marking are covered later in this chapter:

```
ip rsvp precedence [conform | exceed] precedence-value [conform | exceed]
precedence-value
ip rsvp signalling dscp dscp-value
ip rsvp tos [conform | exceed] tos-value [conform | exceed] tos-value
```

Simulating RSVP Messages

In a lab environment, it is possible to simulate static RSVP senders and receivers using the **ip rsvp sender-host** and **ip rsvp reservation-host** commands. The **ip rsvp reservation-host** command simulates an RSVP RESV message, and the **ip rsvp sender-host** command simulates an RSVP PATH message. Table 5-5 shows the RSVP sender and reservation command parameters and their descriptions:

```
ip rsvp reservation-host destination-address source-address [IP-protocol-number
 | tcp | udp] destination-port source-port next-hop-address interface-name
interface-number [ff | se | wf] [load | rate] average-bit-rate maximum-burst
ip rsvp sender-host destination-address source-address [IP-protocol-number | tcp
 | udp] destination-port source-port next-hop-address interface-name interface
-number [ff | se | wf] [load | rate] average-bit-rate maximum-burst
```

NOTE   The **ip-rsvp reservation-host** and **ip rsvp sender-host** commands may have different options available on different router platforms. You may need to issue a test run of the command to find which options are available on your router platform before deciding which options you will use.

Table 5-5   **rsvp simulation** *Command Parameters*

Command Parameter	Parameter Description
destination-address	The destination IP address of the RSVP session.
source-address	The source IP address of the RSVP session.
[*IP-protocol-number*	tcp	udp]	The port number associated with the RSVP flow. This port can be TCP, UDP, or a specific IP protocol number ranging from 0 to 255.
destination-port	The destination port number, ranging from 0 to 65,535. For unspecified ports, use 0 as both the source and destination port numbers.
source-port	The source port number, ranging from 0 to 65,535. For unspecified ports, use 0 as both the source and destination port numbers.
[ff	se	wf]	(**ip rsvp reservation-host** command only) Specifies the reservation style: FF (Fixed-Filter style)—Single reservation shared by multiple flows SE (Shared-Explicit style)—Single reservation for one flow WF (Wildcard-Filter style)—Multicast application support for multiple flows

continues

Table 5-5   **rsvp simulation** *Command Parameters (Continued)*

Command Parameter	Parameter Description
[load | rate]	The bandwidth reservation type, either load or rate. The load parameter is used to specify controlled load service, and the rate parameters specify a guaranteed bit rate.
average-bit-rate	The reserved average bit rate, in kbps. This value can range from 0 to 10,000,000.
maximum-burst	The maximum burst size in kilobytes. This value can range from 0 to 65,535.

Example 5-1 shows how two hosts shown in Figure 5-2, a sender and a receiver, are set up using the **ip rsvp sender-host** and **reservation-host** commands. To simulate RSVP senders or receivers, you must enable RSVP on an interface, and the address for the source address of the RSVP sender/receiver must exist locally on the router.

Figure 5-2   *Simulating RSVP RESV and PATH Messages*

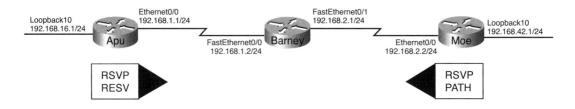

Example 5-1   *RSVP Simulation on the Apu Router*

```
Apu# show run | begin Loopback
interface Loopback10
 ip address 192.168.16.1 255.255.255.0
 ip rsvp bandwidth 7000 7000
!
interface Ethernet0/0
 ip address 192.168.1.1 255.255.255.0
 ip rsvp bandwidth 7000 7000
!
router eigrp 170
 network 192.168.1.0
 network 192.168.16.0
 no auto-summary
 eigrp log-neighbor-changes
!
ip rsvp reservation-host 192.168.16.1 192.168.42.1 TCP 0 0 FF RATE 128 8
```

In this example, the Apu router is simulating an RSVP session with the Moe router. The **ip rsvp reservation-host** command is used to simulate RSVP RESV messages from the Loopback10 interface on the Apu router to the Loopback10 interface on the Moe router. Example 5-2 shows the detailed RSVP reservation information from the Apu router.

Example 5-2   **show ip rsvp reservation** *Information from the Apu Router*

```
Apu# show ip rsvp reservation detail
RSVP Reservation. Destination is 192.168.16.1, Source is 192.168.42.1,
  Protocol is TCP, Destination port is 0, Source port is 0
  Reservation Style is Fixed-Filter, QoS Service is Guaranteed-Rate
  Average Bitrate is 128K bits/sec, Maximum Burst is 8K bytes
  Min Policed Unit: 0 bytes, Max Pkt Size: 65535 bytes
  Resv ID handle: 00001301.
  Policy: Forwarding. Policy source(s): Default
```

As you can see, the Apu router created a reservation from the Moe router's 192.168.42.1 IP address. This reservation will apply to any IP traffic. The Apu router reserves a guaranteed 128-kbps average bit rate, allowing a maximum burst of 8 kilobytes; therefore, the maximum amount of data that can be supported is 192 kbps during bursts. To continue verifying this RSVP session from end to end, you can use the **show ip rsvp senders** command on the Barney router to verify that it received the RSVP PATH message from the Moe router, as shown in Example 5-3.

NOTE   The formula used to find the burst rate for RSVP is as follows:

```
R = Bit-rate (in kbps)
T = Time interval (always 1 second)
B = Burst (converted from kilobytes to kilobits)
BR = Burst Rate
R(T) + B = BR
So, if you use the information from the previous example, this is how you find
the burst rate.
128kbps(1s) + 64kbit = 192 kilobit
```

To convert from kilobytes to kilobits, use the following formula (where B is equal to the burst value in kilobytes):

```
B * 8 = burst value in kilobits
```

Example 5-3   *Using the* **show ip rsvp sender** *Command to Verify End-to-End Reservations on the Barney Router*

```
Barney# show ip rsvp sender
To              From           Pro DPort Sport Prev Hop      I/F  BPS  Bytes
192.168.16.1    192.168.42.1   TCP 0     0     192.168.2.2   Fa0/1 128K  8K
```

As you can see, the Barney router received the RSVP PATH message from the Moe router showing a previous hop of 192.168.2.2, the Moe router's Ethernet0/0 interface, and a destination host IP address of 192.168.16.1, the Apu router's Loopback10 interface. As a final end-to-end verification, Example 5-4 shows the configuration and **show ip rsvp sender detail** information on the Moe router.

Example 5-4 *RSVP Simulation on the Moe Router*

```
Moe# show run | begin Loopback10
interface Loopback10
 ip address 192.168.42.1 255.255.255.0
 ip rsvp bandwidth 7000 7000
!
interface Ethernet0/0
 ip address 192.168.2.2 255.255.255.0
 ip rsvp bandwidth 7000 7000
!
router eigrp 170
 network 192.168.2.0
 network 192.168.42.0
 no auto-summary
 no eigrp log-neighbor-changes
ip rsvp sender-host 192.168.16.1 192.168.42.1 tcp 0 0 128 8
Moe# show ip rsvp sender detail
PATH Session address: 192.168.16.1, port: 0. Protocol: TCP
  Sender address: 192.168.42.1, port: 0
  Traffic params - Rate: 128K bits/sec, Max. burst: 8K bytes
                   Min Policed Unit: 0 bytes, Max Pkt Size 65535 bytes
  Path ID handle: 00000601.
  Incoming policy: Accepted. Policy source(s): Default
  Output on Ethernet0/0. Policy status: Forwarding. Handle: 00000601
```

In the preceding example, an RSVP sender, host 192.168.42.1, the IP address of loopback interface 10, is set up to create an RSVP reservation to host 192.168.16.1 on TCP port 0. The **ip rsvp sender-host 192.168.16.1 192.168.42.1 tcp 0 0 128 64** command was used to create the RSVP PATH simulation message from the Moe router. This command does not appear in the running configuration.

Creating Static RSVP Reservations

RSVP reservations can also be statically configured using the **ip rsvp reservation** and **ip rsvp sender** commands. The **ip rsvp reservation** command, shown next, creates a static reservation for an RSVP receiver, and the **ip rsvp sender** command creates a static reservation for an RSVP sender. These two commands enable you to configure both sides of an RSVP session reservation:

```
ip rsvp reservation destination-address source-address [IP-protocol-number | tcp
 | udp] destination-port source-port next-hop-address interface-name interface-
number [ff | se | wf] [load | rate] average-bit-rate maximum-burst
ip rsvp sender destination-address source-address [IP-protocol-number | tcp |
udp] destination-port source-port previous-hop-address interface-name
interface-number average-bit-rate maximum-burst
```

Both the **ip rsvp reservation** and **ip rsvp sender** commands have several required parameters. Table 5-6 lists these **rsvp** command arguments and their descriptions.

Table 5-6   **static rsvp** *Commands and Descriptions*

RSVP Command Argument	Description
destination-address	The IP address or host name of the RSVP receiver.
source-address	The IP address or host name of the RSVP sender.
[*IP-protocol-number*	tcp	udp]	*IP-protocol-number* is an IP protocol ranging from 0 to 255, or the TCP or UDP protocol.
destination-port	The destination port number, ranging from 0 to 65,535.
source-port	The source port number, ranging from 0 to 65,535.
next-hop-address or *previous-hop-address*	The **ip rsvp reservation** command requires the IP address or host name of the next hop. The **ip rsvp sender** command requires the IP address or name of the previous hop.
[ff	se	wf]	FF—Fixed-Filter reservations provide a single reservation for one flow. SE—Shared-Explicit reservations provide shared reservations for specified flows. WF—Wildcard-Filter reservations provide shared reservations for all senders.
[load	rate]	Load—Represents controlled load service. Used to provide controlled load services by isolating flow with minimal interference from other flows by specifying an average bit rate and a maximum burst rate. Rate—Represents guaranteed bit rate. Used to provide a guaranteed bit rate by specifying an average bit rate and a maximum burst rate.
average-bit-rate	This value, ranging from 1 to 10,000,000, specifies the average bit rate to reserve in kbps.
maximum-burst	This value, ranging from 1 to 65,535, specifies the maximum amount that the reserved flow can burst in kilobits.

Example 5-5 shows how the **ip rsvp reservation** command was used to set up a reservation from sender 152.148.89.91 to receiver 10.1.1.11 for TFTP traffic that is being sent to the next hop of 10.2.2.2 using an FF reservation with a 64-kbps average bit rate and a 4-kb maximum burst. The output of the **show ip rsvp host receivers** is also shown.

Example 5-5 *Using Static Reservations*

```
RSVP-Example# show run | begin Serial0
interface FastEthernet0/0
 ip address 10.1.1.1 255.255.255.0
ip rsvp bandwidth 75000 75000
 !
interface Serial0/0
 ip address 10.2.2.1 255.255.255.0
 ip rsvp bandwidth 1158 1158
 !
ip rsvp reservation 10.1.1.11 152.148.89.91 UDP 69 0 10.2.2.2 Serial0/0 FF
RATE 64 4
RSVP-Example# show ip rsvp host receivers
To           From         Pro DPort Sport Next Hop   I/F   Fi Serv BPS Bytes
10.1.1.11    152.148.89.91 UDP 69    0     10.2.2.2   Se0/0 FF RATE 64K  4K
```

In the preceding example, a static RSVP session is configured between hosts 10.1.1.11 and 152.148.89.91. Host 152.148.89.91 will request the RSVP session using an RSVP PATH message, and host 10.1.1.11 will respond to the message using an RSVP RESV message. This RSVP session is reserved for any TFTP traffic sent by host 152.148.89.91.

Now that you have seen examples of how RSVP can be used for simulated RSVP sessions, dynamic RSVP sessions, or static RSVP reservations, it's time to look at other ways you can use RSVP for multiservice voice applications.

Reserving the Proper Amount of Bandwidth for Voice

When configuring voice over IP for use with RSVP, it is very important to remember that there are many different voice codecs that are available to choose from, and each of these codecs will have different QoS requirements from the network. The codec used to sample and encode packets will affect the performance and quality of the calls. Complex codecs that sample data more often have a greater packetization delay; however, they also have lower required transmission rates because they compress the data and send fewer packets. To select a voice codec, use the **codec** *codec-name* command under the remote voice over IP dial-peer to select a codec rate; the default codec is g729r8.

NOTE   *Packetization* delay is a measurement of the time it takes to sample raw voice data and encode that sampled data into a packet for transmission.

Table 5-7 shows the various voice codecs rates available on a Cisco 1750 series router, the codec name, the codec rate in bits per second, the packetization delay, and the actual RSVP rate that the codec will request. Make sure you select a codec that will require a reasonable amount of bandwidth from the network. If you do not configure RSVP with enough bandwidth to create a reservation, and you configure dial-peers to request or accept RSVP settings, the calls will not be accepted.

Table 5-7   Voice Over IP Codecs

Codec Rate	Codec Name	Codec Rate in bps	Packetization Delay	Actual RSVP Rate Requested
g711alaw	G.711 A Law	64,000 bps	10 to 30 ms	80 k
g711ulaw	G.711 u Law	64,000 bps	10 to 30 ms	80 k
g723ar53	G.723.1 ANNEX-A	5300 bps	30 ms	18 k
g723ar63	G.723.1 ANNEX-A	6300 bps	30 ms	18 k
g723r53	G.723.1	5300 bps	30 ms	18 k
g723r63	G.723.1	6300 bps	30 ms	18 k
g726r16	G.726	16,000 bps	10 to 30 ms	32 k
g726r24	G.726	24,000 bps	10 to 30 ms	40 k
g726r32	G.726	32,000 bps	10 to 30 ms	48 k
g728	G.728	16,000 bps	10 to 30 ms	32 k
g729br8	G.729 ANNEX-B	8000 bps	10 to 30 ms	24 k
g729r8	G.729	8000 bps	10 to 30 ms	24 k

The **show dialer-peer voice | include codec** command displays the current codec configuration; you can use this information to calculate the RSVP reservation information for voice traffic as shown in Example 5-6. The full version of the **show dial-peer voice** command displays detailed information for each of the dial-peers.

Example 5-6   *Using Show Commands to Find the Codec*

```
Show-me-the-codec# show dial-peer voice | include codec
        codec = g729r8,   payload size =  20 bytes,
```

Using RSVP for Voice Traffic

To configure Voice over IP (VoIP) to request RSVP service, use the **req-qos** command under the dial peer for the VoIP session. The **req-qos** command, which is short for request qos, is used to request a certain QoS level from the network and can request three different types of service: **best-effort**, **controlled-load**, or **guaranteed-delay**. The **acc-qos** command defines the minimum amount of acceptable types of service that will be accepted from the network. The **controlled-load** command is used to request or accept traffic. The **best-effort** command is used to remove a preexisting RSVP reservation from a dial-peer connection. Table 5-8 summarizes the dial peer qos command parameters and gives a brief description of their usage.

Table 5-8   **rsvp voice qos** *Command Summary*

RSVP Voice Command	Command Description
best-effort	Best-effort service is, like its name implies, a best effort. Devices in the path between best-effort devices attempt to deliver packets to the best of their capability, but no special effort is made to prioritize best-effort traffic. This command is used to remove a **controlled-load** or **guaranteed-delay** command from a dial peer.
controlled-load	Provides a reservation that provides a limited amount of delay and packet drop for real-time delay-sensitive applications. Similar to ATM VBR-rt PVCs, controlled-load reservations provide bandwidth reservations that limit the amount of delay and packet loss that real-time network applications will experience when traversing a loaded network.
guaranteed-delay	Provides a guaranteed rate, similar to ATM CBR PVCs, by gathering data from RSVP PATH messages.

The following four steps are required to enable VoIP reservation requests using the **req-qos** or **acc-qos** commands:

Step 1   Configure the local and remote VoIP dial peers using the **dial-peer** command.

Step 2   From dial-peer configuration mode, add the **acc-qos** or **req-qos** commands to the VoIP dial peer.

Step 3   Each interface that will be forwarding voice traffic will have to have WFQ configured before the RSVP configuration can be applied. Prior to enabling RSVP, enable WFQ on the interface level using the **fair-queue** command.

Step 4   Configure RSVP for each interface. Before configuring RSVP, make sure you know how much bandwidth and delay that voice codec will require. After you know how much bandwidth to reserve, configure RSVP for each RSVP-enabled interface using the **ip rsvp bandwidth** *bandwidth* command.

NOTE   If you did not explicitly configure your voice codec and you need to find the codec type in use, you can do this using the **show voice | include codec** command mentioned earlier in this chapter.

The following example shows how the previously outlined steps are used to enable RSVP for VoIP calls on the Bender router. Figure 5-3 shows the voice connection between the Bender router and its VoIP dial peer on the Frye router.

Figure 5-3   *Bender and Frye Network*

Step 1   Configure the local and remote VoIP dial peers using the **dial-peer** command. The following example shows the dial-peer configuration for the Bender router. In this example, dial-peer 5555678 specifies the local destination pattern, 5555678, and the local FXS port, port 2/1. Dial-peer 5558765 specifies the remote peer that resides on the 129.44.85.1 router and is assigned the 5558765 destination pattern. The g726r16 voice codec is used · for calls to this dial peer:

```
Bender(config)# dial-peer voice 5555678 pots
Bender (config-dial-peer)# destination-pattern 5555678
Bender (config-dial-peer)# port 2/1
Bender (config)# dial-peer voice 5558765 voip
Bender (config-dial-peer)# destination-pattern 5558765
Bender (config-dial-peer)# session target ipv4:129.44.85.1
Bender (config-dial-peer)# codec g726r16
```

Step 2   From dial-peer configuration mode, add the **acc-qos** or **req-qos** commands to the VoIP dial peer. In this example, the Bender router is configured to request and accept controlled load service from the network:

```
Bender(config-dial-peer)# dial-peer voice 5558765 voip
Bender(config-dial-peer)# req-qos controlled-load
Bender(config-dial-peer)# acc-qos controlled-load
```

Step 3   Each interface that will be forwarding voice traffic will have to have WFQ configured before the RSVP configuration can be applied. Therefore, prior to enabling RSVP, enable WFQ on the interface level using the **fair-queue** command.

One quick way to find the queuing strategy that is currently being used on an interface is to use the **show queueing interface** *interface-name interface-number* | **include strategy** command. You will see a queuing strategy of none if FIFO queuing is enabled; in this case, WFQ should be enabled before configuring RSVP:

```
Bender# show queueing interface fastEthernet 0 | include strategy
Interface FastEthernet0 queueing strategy: none
```

In the following example, the Bender router connects to the Frye router using its FastEthernet0 interface, so WFQ must be enabled here:

```
Bender(config)# interface FastEthernet0
Bender(config-if)# ip address 129.44.85.5 255.255.255.0
Bender(config-if)# fair-queue
```

Step 4 Configure RSVP for each interface. Before configuring RSVP, make sure you know how much bandwidth and delay that voice codec will require. Because the Bender router has already been configured to use the g726r16 codec, you know that RSVP requires at least a 32-kbps bandwidth reservation. To make sure that the RSVP configuration will allow reservations for that amount of bandwidth, use the **ip rsvp bandwidth 32** command, as shown here:

```
Bender(config)# interface FastEthernet0
Bender(config-if)# ip rsvp bandwidth 32
```

To verify the connection, place a test call from one of the routers and, while the test call is in progress, use the **show ip rsvp installed** and **show ip rsvp reservation detail** commands to display the current RSVP reservations. The **show ip rsvp installed** command displays a quick summary of the current RSVP sessions. The **show ip rsvp reservation detail** command displays all the characteristics that apply to each RSVP reservation, as shown in Example 5-7.

Example 5-7 *Using the* **show ip rsvp reservation detail** *Command to Verify VoIP*

```
Bender# show ip rsvp installed
RSVP: FastEthernet0
BPS     To               From              Protoc DPort  Sport  Weight Conversation
32K     129.44.85.1      129.44.85.5       UDP    17176  18930  0      264
Bender# show ip rsvp reservation detail
RSVP Reservation. Destination is 129.44.85.1, Source is 129.44.85.5,
  Protocol is UDP, Destination port is 17176, Source port is 18930
  Next Hop is 129.44.85.1, Interface is FastEthernet0
  Reservation Style is Fixed-Filter, QoS Service is Controlled-Load
  Average Bitrate is 32K bits/sec, Maximum Burst is 160 bytes
  Min Policed Unit: 80 bytes, Max Pkt Size: 80 bytes
  Resv ID handle: 00000E01.
  Policy: Forwarding. Policy source(s): Default
RSVP Reservation. Destination is 129.44.85.5, Source is 129.44.85.1,
  Protocol is UDP, Destination port is 18930, Source port is 17176
  Reservation Style is Fixed-Filter, QoS Service is Controlled-Load
  Average Bitrate is 32K bits/sec, Maximum Burst is 160 bytes
  Min Policed Unit: 80 bytes, Max Pkt Size: 80 bytes
  Resv ID handle: 00000C01.
  Policy: Forwarding. Policy source(s): Default
```

In this example, each time a phone call is made between the 555-5678 and 555-8765 phones, two RSVP reservations are made, one from 129.44.85.1 to 129.44.85.5, and one from 129.44.85.5 to 129.44.85.1. Each reservation uses a controlled-load service to provide a 32-kbps average bit rate to each call. As soon as the call has ended, the reservation is removed and the bandwidth is released for other purposes.

Example 5-8 shows the full configurations for the RSVP controlled rate service for the VoIP session from the Bender and Frye routers used in the preceding example.

Example 5-8   *Using VoIP and RSVP*

```
Bender# show run | begin FastEthernet
interface FastEthernet0
 ip address 129.44.85.5 255.255.255.0
 fair-queue 64 256 1
 ip rsvp bandwidth 32 32
!
interface Serial1
dial-peer voice 5555678 pots
 destination-pattern 5555678
 port 2/1
!
dial-peer voice 5558765 voip
 destination-pattern 5558765
 session target ipv4:129.44.85.1
 req-qos controlled-load
 acc-qos controlled-load
 codec g726r16

Frye# show run | begin FastEthernet
interface FastEthernet0
 ip address 129.44.85.1 255.255.255.0
 fair-queue 64 256 1
 ip rsvp bandwidth 32 32
!
dial-peer voice 5558765 pots
 destination-pattern 5558765
 port 2/0
!
dial-peer voice 5555678 voip
 destination-pattern 5555678
 session target ipv4:129.44.85.5
 req-qos controlled-load
 acc-qos controlled-load
 codec g726r16
```

NOTE   If voice RSVP QoS parameters are only specified on one side of a connection, the call will never complete successfully. To successfully allow a voice call using RSVP, one side of the connection must request a level of service, and the other side must be willing to accept that level of service.

Troubleshooting RSVP

You can use a number of commands for RSVP troubleshooting. Before beginning the RSVP troubleshooting process, however, you should check a couple of items. First, verify that WFQ has been enabled for the RSVP interface. If it has not, enable WFQ using the **fair-queue** command. Second, when using RSVP on fractional circuits, such as Frame Relay DS0s, remember to configure the interface bandwidth because serial interfaces default to 1158 kbps, or 75 percent of the interface's bandwidth.

The **show ip rsvp neighbor** command displays interfaces that have RSVP-attached neighbors and the IP address of the neighbor, as demonstrated in Example 5-9.

Example 5-9 *Showing* **RSVP Neighbors**

```
Silly# show ip rsvp neighbor
Interfac Neighbor        Encapsulation
Se1.1    192.168.1.2     RSVP
Se1.2    192.168.2.2     RSVP
```

The **show ip rsvp sender** and **show ip rsvp request** commands provide a summarization of RSVP sender and other related information about the RSVP requests. To view detailed information about RSVP requests, use the **detail** version of the **show ip rsvp request** of the command. Examples of these commands are shown in Example 5-10.

Example 5-10 *RSVP* **show rsvp sender** *and* **request** *Commands*

```
Smiley# show ip rsvp sender
To              From            Pro DPort Sport Prev Hop      I/F  BPS  Bytes
192.168.1.2     192.168.2.2     UDP 18182 18050 192.168.2.2   Se1.2 24K   1K
192.168.2.2     192.168.1.2     UDP 18050 18182 192.168.1.2   Se1.1 24K   1K
Smiley# show ip rsvp request
To          From        Pro DPort Sport Next Hop      I/F   Fi Serv BPS Bytes
192.168.1.2 192.168.2.2 UDP 18182 18050 192.168.2.2   Se1.2 FF RATE 24K  1K
192.168.2.2 192.168.1.2 UDP 18050 18182 192.168.1.2   Se1.1 FF RATE 24K  1K
Grumpy# show ip rsvp request detail
RSVP Reservation. Destination is 192.168.2.2, Source is 192.168.1.2,
  Protocol is UDP, Destination port is 18634, Source port is 18540
  Next Hop is 192.168.2.1, Interface is Serial0
  Reservation Style is Fixed-Filter, QoS Service is Guaranteed-Rate
  Average Bitrate is 24K bits/sec, Maximum Burst is 1K bytes
```

The **show ip rsvp installed** command, shown in Example 5-11, gives information about current RSVP reservations, such as the RSVP interface, the size of the reservation in bps, the source and destination IP addresses, the protocol, the source and destination ports, the weight of the RSVP flow, and the conversation number. The **show ip rsvp interfaces** command, also shown in Example 5-11, displays information about each of the router's RSVP interfaces.

Example 5-11 show ip rsvp installed *Command*

```
Grumpy# show ip rsvp installed
RSVP: Serial1
BPS    To                 From              Protoc DPort  Sport  Weight Conversation
RSVP: Serial1.1
BPS    To                 From              Protoc DPort  Sport  Weight Conversation
24K    192.168.1.2        192.168.2.2       UDP    18182  18050  6      265
RSVP: Serial1.2
BPS    To                 From              Protoc DPort  Sport  Weight Conversation
24K    192.168.2.2        192.168.1.2       UDP    18050  18182  6      266
Grumpy# show ip rsvp interfaces
interface    allocated   i/f max  flow max  pct UDP  IP   UDP_IP  UDP M/C
Se1          48K         1158K    1158K     4   0    0    0       0
Se1.1        24K         128K     128K      18  0    1    0       0
Se1.2        24K         128K     128K      18  0    1    0       0
```

To view information about all the current RSVP reservations, use the **show ip rsvp reservation** command. This command shows you the source and destination IP addresses for each reservation, the protocol and source and destination port number, the next-hop IP address and interface used to reach each of the senders, the reservation filter type (FF, SE, or WF), the reservation type (RATE or LOAD), the reservation size in bps, and the burst size in bytes, as shown in Example 5-12.

Example 5-12 show ip rsvp reservation *Command*

```
Grumpy# show ip rsvp reservation
To             From          Pro DPort Sport Next Hop       I/F    Fi Serv BPS Bytes
192.168.1.2    192.168.2.2   UDP 18182 18050 192.168.1.2    Se1.1  FF RATE 24K  1K
192.168.2.2    192.168.1.2   UDP 18050 18182 192.168.2.2    Se1.2  FF RATE 24K  1K
192.168.2.3    192.168.1.2   UDP 18502 16808 192.168.2.2           FF LOAD 24K  1K
```

Practical Example: RSVP and VoIP

VoIP requires a certain level of QoS to function properly. When using VoIP in a WAN environment over small, congested links, in most cases, some form of QoS will have to be implemented. Fortunately, VoIP has built-in support for RSVP, making it simple to configure. In the following lab, you practice your VoIP configuration and use RSVP to support the voice.

Lab Exercise

Dan's Pizza has more than 4000 locations nationwide. Each store has a Frame Relay connection to its local hub site. The hub sites provide each district with access to the corporate network, support for all network applications, and one phone line for internal calls. In the past few months, several new applications have been deployed, making voice traffic somewhat jittery and causing conversation to be difficult to understand. RSVP will be implemented to reserve enough bandwidth to smooth out the voice calls. In this lab, you configure part of the subnetwork, area 140, to provide quality service for voice traffic.

Lab Objective

The objective of this lab is to use RSVP to reserve bandwidth for voice traffic between two store locations. For this network model, you use the portion of the Dan's Pizza network shown in Figure 5-4. This exercise demonstrates how RSVP is configured, using VoIP as the test application. The RSVP configuration is verified using RSVP **show** and **debug** commands.

Figure 5-4 *Dan's Pizza Subnetwork 140*

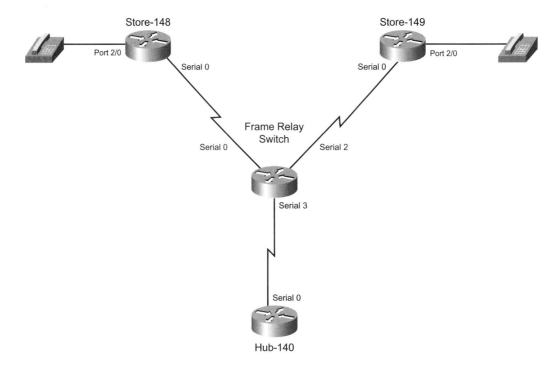

Equipment Needed

To use RSVP and reserve bandwidth for voice traffic between the two store locations, the following equipment is needed:

- Two Cisco routers with at least one voice port and one serial port

- One Cisco router with one serial port
- One Cisco router with three serial ports to act as a Frame Relay switch
- Two telephones for testing purposes

Physical Layout and Prestaging

To complete the physical layout and prestaging, perform the following:

- Cable the routers as shown in Figure 5-4.
- Attach one phone to a voice port on each of the voice routers.
- Configure the Frame Relay switch to use the PVC information in Table 5-9.
- Verify that all interfaces are in an up/up state.

Table 5-9   *Frame Switch Configurations for the Example*

Local Interface	Local DLCI	Remote Interface	Remote DLCI
Serial 0	148	Serial 3	841
Serial 2	149	Serial 3	941
Serial 3	841	Serial 0	148
Serial 3	941	Serial 2	149

Lab Tasks

To complete this lab exercise, you need to complete the following tasks:

- Configure the IP network as shown in Figure 5-5, applying IP addressing and Frame Relay configuration using subinterfaces on the Hub 140 router and physical interfaces on the Store routers.
- Configure OSFP on all routers; all serial interfaces should belong to OSPF area 0. Verify that all routers are reachable.
- Configure Store 148 and Store 149 to be able to call each other using the phone numbers from Figure 5-5. Test phone connections.
- Configure the required RSVP support to allow Store 148 to call Store 149, and vice versa, with RSVP guaranteed bit rate service. Each flow should receive and average a bit rate of at least 24 kbps, and should be allowed to burst to a full 75 percent of the interface bandwidth. Test and verify that the RSVP sessions work properly.

To do so, perform the steps in the following section.

Figure 5-5   *Physical Layout for This Lab*

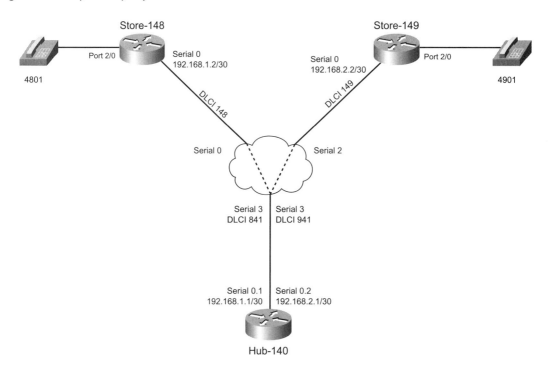

Lab Walkthrough

Step 1   Attach each router to the Frame Relay switch; Hub 140, Store 148, and
Store 149 should connect to the Frame Relay switch using serial data
terminal equipment/data circuit-terminating equipment (DTE/DCE)
connections. Note each serial connection and use this information to
configure the Frame Relay switch. Store 148 should use DLCI 148 on
its serial interface, Store 149 should be configured to use DLCI 149, and
Hub 140 should be assigned DLCIs 841 and 941. Configure each of the
routers to support their Frame Relay connections. Because Store 148 and
Store 149 use physical interfaces for their Frame Relay connections, they
should be configured with a Frame Relay map pointing to Hub 140. Hub 140
uses multipoint subinterfaces, so it can also use Frame Relay map commands
on each subinterface. Example 5-13 shows the Frame Relay switch
configuration and the Frame Relay routes.

Example 5-13 *Frame Relay Switch Configuration*

```
frame-relay-switch# show run | begin frame
frame-relay switching
!
interface Serial0
 no ip address
 encapsulation frame-relay IETF
 clockrate 1300000
 frame-relay lmi-type ansi
 frame-relay intf-type dce
 frame-relay route 148 interface Serial3 841
!
interface Serial2
 no ip address
 encapsulation frame-relay IETF
 frame-relay lmi-type ansi
 frame-relay intf-type dce
 frame-relay route 149 interface Serial3 941
!
interface Serial3
 no ip address
 encapsulation frame-relay IETF
 clockrate 1300000
 frame-relay lmi-type ansi
 frame-relay intf-type dce
 frame-relay route 841 interface Serial0 148
 frame-relay route 941 interface Serial2 149
frame-relay-switch# show frame-relay route
Input Intf     Input Dlci     Output Intf     Output Dlci     Status
Serial0        148            Serial3         841             active
Serial2        149            Serial3         941             active
Serial3        841            Serial0         148             active
Serial3        941            Serial2         149             active
```

Step 2   After you have verified Frame Relay connectivity between routers, assign the IP addresses. Store 148 interface Serial 0 should use IP address 192.168.1.2/30. Store 149's serial interface should be assigned IP address 192.168.2.2/30, Hub 140 interface's Serial 0.1 should use 192.168.1.1/30, and 0.2 should use 192.168.2.1/30. Before moving on, you should verify that all Store router interfaces can ping their directly connected hub subinterface.

Step 3   Configure OSFP on each router so that each router can ping its neighbor and each of the store routers can ping each other. Use a nonbroadcast Open Shortest Path First (OSPF) configuration for this example.

       To configure OSPF for the nonbroadcast connections between the hub router and the two stores, you must configure OSPF for a nonbroadcast network. In this case, this requires the use of the **ip ospf network non-broadcast** command and static neighbor configurations. Example 5-14 shows how the **ip ospf network** command is used on the Hub 140 router. Before moving on to Step 4, verify the OSPF configuration by pinging from one store router to the other using the IP addresses on their serial interfaces.

Example 5-14 *Hub 140 Router's OSPF Configuration*

```
Hub-140#show run | begin Serial0/0.1
interface Serial0/0.1 multipoint
 ip address 192.168.1.1 255.255.255.252
 ip ospf network non-broadcast
 frame-relay map ip 192.168.1.2 841 broadcast
!
interface Serial0/0.2 multipoint
 ip address 192.168.2.1 255.255.255.252
 ip ospf network non-broadcast
 frame-relay map ip 192.168.2.2 941 broadcast
!
router ospf 1
 log-adjacency-changes
 network 192.168.1.0 0.0.0.3 area 0
 network 192.168.2.0 0.0.0.3 area 0
 neighbor 192.168.2.2
 neighbor 192.168.1.2
```

Step 4 After all routers can ping each other, configure VoIP on Store 148 as follows: Create one dial peer. (In this example, I used peer number 4801 to keep things simple.) Assign dial-peer 4801 the destination dial pattern 4801. Dial peer 4801 must also be assigned to a port. (In this case, I used port 2/0.) To dial the 4901 extension from the Store 149 router, you must create a VoIP dial peer that specifies Store 149's serial IP address and assign it the destination pattern 4901. Store 149 should be configured similarly to store 148. After each router's voice configuration is complete, you should be able to call the 4801 extension from Store 149's phone and the 4901 extension from Store 148's phone. Example 5-15 shows the VoIP configuration for the Store 148 router.

Example 5-15 *The Store-148 Router's Voice Over IP Configuration*

```
Store-148# sho run | begin dial-peer
dial-peer voice 4801 pots
 destination-pattern 4801
 port 2/0
!
dial-peer voice 4901 voip
 destination-pattern 4901
 session target ipv4:192.168.2.2
```

Step 5 After you have tested the voice connectivity, it is time to configure RSVP.
The first step in the RSVP configuration is to enable WFQ, if it is not already
configured. WFQ is enabled using the **fair-queue** command. Because this is
a simple WFQ configuration, you can just type the **fair-queue** command and
accept the defaults. After configuring WFQ, enable RSVP on the interface by
using the **ip rsvp bandwidth** command. Make sure to reserve at least 24 kbps
and allow bursting to 75 percent of the interface's bandwidth, in this case
1158 kbps. Next, enable voice over **ip rsvp bandwidth** requests using the
req-qos command to request a guaranteed bit rate. Example 5-16 shows the
VoIP and RSVP configuration for the Store 149 router, and Example 5-17
shows the output from the **show ip rsvp reservation detail** command from
the Store 148 router.

Example 5-16 *RSVP and Voice Configuration for Store 149*

```
Store-149# show run | begin Serial
interface Serial0
 ip address 192.168.2.2 255.255.255.252
 ip ospf network non-broadcast
 ip ospf priority 0
 frame-relay map ip 192.168.2.1 149 broadcast
 ip rsvp bandwidth 1158 24
!
dial-peer voice 4901 pots
 destination-pattern 4901
 port 2/0
!
dial-peer voice 4801 voip
 destination-pattern 4801
 session target ipv4:192.168.1.2
 req-qos guaranteed-delay
```

Example 5-17 *Reservation Information from the Store 148 Router*

```
Store-148# show ip rsvp reservation detail
RSVP Reservation. Destination is 192.168.1.2, Source is 192.168.2.2,
  Protocol is UDP, Destination port is 17188, Source port is 19346
  Next Hop is 192.168.2.1, Interface is Serial0
  Reservation Style is Fixed-Filter, QoS Service is Guaranteed-Rate
  Average Bitrate is 24K bits/sec, Maximum Burst is 120 bytes
  Min Policed Unit: 60 bytes, Max Pkt Size: 60 bytes
  Resv ID handle: 00007601.
  Policy: Forwarding. Policy source(s): Default
RSVP Reservation. Destination is 192.168.2.2, Source is 192.168.1.2,
  Protocol is UDP, Destination port is 19346, Source port is 17188
  Reservation Style is Fixed-Filter, QoS Service is Guaranteed-Rate
  Average Bitrate is 24K bits/sec, Maximum Burst is 120 bytes
  Min Policed Unit: 60 bytes, Max Pkt Size: 60 bytes
  Resv ID handle: 00007201.
  Policy: Forwarding. Policy source(s): Default
```

As you can see, in the preceding example, the Store 148 router reserved an average bit rate of 24 kbps, with a maximum burst rate of 120 bytes; this RSVP reservation is a guaranteed rate.

Another way to test the configuration is to enable detailed RSVP debugging using the **debug ip rsvp detail** command and then dial 4901 from the Store 148 router. When you pick up the 4901 phone, you should receive output similar to that shown in Example 5-18.

Example 5-18 *Sample* **debug ip rsvp detail** *Output*

```
*Mar  1 05:28:57.294: RSVP 192.168.1.2_17598-192.168.2.2_18180: Static
reservation is new
Comment: New reservation requested
*Mar 1 05:28:57.294: RSVP-RESV: Locally created reservation. No admission/traffic
control needed
*Mar  1 05:28:57.298: RSVP session 192.168.1.2_17598: Sending PATH message for
192.168.1.2 on interface Serial0
Comment: RSVP PATH information from 192.168.1.2
Comment: Reservation information - IP addresses and port numbers
*Mar  1 05:28:57.298: RSVP:     version:1 flags:0000 type:PATH cksum:31D8 ttl:255
reserved:0 length:136
*Mar  1 05:28:57.298:  SESSION             type 1 length 12:
*Mar  1 05:28:57.298:    Destination 192.168.1.2, Protocol_Id 17, Don't Police ,
DstPort 17598
Comment: RSVP Destination Information
*Mar  1 05:28:57.298:  HOP                 type 1 length 12: C0A80202
*Mar  1 05:28:57.298:                                     : 00000000
*Mar  1 05:28:57.302:  TIME_VALUES        type 1 length 8 : 00007530
*Mar  1 05:28:57.302:  SENDER_TEMPLATE    type 1 length 12:
*Mar  1 05:28:57.302:    Source 192.168.2.2, udp_source_port 18180
Comment: RSVP Sender information
*Mar  1 05:28:57.302:  SENDER_TSPEC       type 2 length 36:
*Mar  1 05:28:57.302:    version=0, length in words=7
*Mar  1 05:28:57.302:    Token bucket fragment (service_id=1, length=6 words
*Mar  1 05:28:57.302:      parameter id=127, flags=0, parameter length=5
*Mar  1 05:28:57.302:      average rate=3000 bytes/sec, burst depth=120 bytes
*Mar  1 05:28:57.302:      peak rate   =3000 bytes/sec
*Mar  1 05:28:57.306:      min unit=60 bytes, max pkt size=60 bytes
Comment: Reservation parameters contained in TSPEC
*Mar  1 05:28:57.306:  ADSPEC             type 2 length 48:
*Mar  1 05:28:57.306:  version=0  length in words=10
*Mar  1 05:28:57.306:  General Parameters  break bit=0  service length=8
*Mar  1 05:28:57.306:                                     IS Hops:1
*Mar  1 05:28:57.306:          Minimum Path Bandwidth (bytes/sec):193000
*Mar  1 05:28:57.306:                 Path Latency (microseconds):0
*Mar  1 05:28:57.306:                             Path MTU:1500
*Mar  1 05:28:57.306:  Controlled Load Service  break bit=0  service length=0
Comment: Minimum bandwidth, latency, and MTU requirements
*Mar  1 05:28:57.306:
*Mar  1 05:28:57.346: RSVP:     version:1 flags:0000 type:PATH cksum:0000 ttl:254
reserved:0 length:136
*Mar  1 05:28:57.346:  SESSION             type 1 length 12:
*Mar  1 05:28:57.350:    Destination 192.168.2.2, Protocol_Id 17, Don't Police ,
DstPort 18180
```

Example 5-18 *Sample* **debug ip rsvp detail** *Output (Continued)*

```
Comment: RSVP PATH information from 192.168.2.2
Comment: Reservation information - IP addresses and port numbers
*Mar  1 05:28:57.350:  HOP                    type 1 length 12: C0A80201
*Mar  1 05:28:57.350:                                       : 00000000
*Mar  1 05:28:57.350:  TIME_VALUES            type 1 length 8 : 00007530
*Mar  1 05:28:57.350:  SENDER_TEMPLATE        type 1 length 12:
*Mar  1 05:28:57.350:   Source 192.168.1.2, udp_source_port 17598
*Mar  1 05:28:57.350:  SENDER_TSPEC           type 2 length 36:
*Mar  1 05:28:57.354:   version=0, length in words=7
*Mar  1 05:28:57.354:   Token bucket fragment (service_id=1, length=6 words
*Mar  1 05:28:57.354:       parameter id=127, flags=0, parameter length=5
*Mar  1 05:28:57.354:       average rate=3000 bytes/sec, burst depth=120 bytes
*Mar  1 05:28:57.354:       peak rate   =3000 bytes/sec
*Mar  1 05:28:57.354:       min unit=60 bytes, max pkt size=60 bytes
*Mar  1 05:28:57.354:  ADSPEC                 type 2 length 48:
*Mar  1 05:28:57.354:   version=0  length in words=10
*Mar  1 05:28:57.354:   General Parameters  break bit=0  service length=8
*Mar  1 05:28:57.354:                                  IS Hops:2
*Mar  1 05:28:57.354:             Minimum Path Bandwidth (bytes/sec):193000
*Mar  1 05:28:57.358:                  Path Latency (microseconds):0
*Mar  1 05:28:57.358:                           Path MTU:1500
*Mar  1 05:28:57.358:   Controlled Load Service  break bit=0  service length=0
*Mar  1 05:28:57.358:
*Mar  1 05:28:57.358: RSVP 192.168.1.2_17598-192.168.2.2_18180: Received PATH
 Message for 192.168.2.2(Serial0) from 192.168.2.1, rcv IP ttl=253
*Mar  1 05:28:57.358: RSVP 192.168.1.2_17598-192.168.2.2_18180: start requesting
 24 kbps FF reservation for 192.168.1.2(17598) UDP-> 192.168.2.2(18180) on
Serial0 neighbor 192.168.2.1
*Mar  1 05:28:57.366: RSVP 192.168.1.2_17598-192.168.2.2_18180: Sending RESV
message 192.168.2.2(18180) <- 192.168.1.2(17:17598)
*Mar  1 05:28:57.366: RSVP session 192.168.2.2_18180: send reservation to
192.168.2.1 about 192.168.2.2
<text omitted>
Comment: Exchanging RSVP PATH and RSVP messages to create reservations
*Mar  1 05:28:57.450: RSVP 192.168.1.2_17598-192.168.2.2_18180: RESV CONFIRM
message for 192.168.2.2 (Serial0) from 192.168.2.1
Comment: RSVP CONFIRM message
*Mar  1 05:29:08.662: RSVP 192.168.2.2_18180-192.168.1.2_17598: remove sender
host PATH 192.168.1.2(17598) <- 192.168.2.2(17:18180)
*Mar  1 05:29:08.662: RSVP 192.168.2.2_18180-192.168.1.2_17598: remove Serial0
RESV 192.168.1.2(17598) <- 192.168.2.2(17:18180)
*Mar  1 05:29:08.662: RSVP 192.168.2.2_18180-192.168.1.2_17598: remove sender
host PATH 192.168.1.2(17598) <- 192.168.2.2(17:18180)
*Mar  1 05:29:08.666: RSVP session 192.168.1.2_17598: send path teardown
multicast about 192.168.1.2 on Serial0
Comment: Teardown session, remove sender 192.168.1.2
<packet data omitted>
*Mar  1 05:29:08.678: RSVP 192.168.1.2_17598-192.168.2.2_18180: remove receiver
host RESV 192.168.2.2(18180) <- 192.168.1.2(17:17598)
```

continues

Example 5-18 *Sample* **debug ip rsvp detail** *Output (Continued)*

```
*Mar  1 05:29:08.678: RSVP 192.168.1.2_17598-192.168.2.2_18180: remove Serial0
 RESV request 192.168.2.2(18180) <- 192.168.1.2(17:17598)
*Mar  1 05:29:08.678: RSVP session 192.168.2.2_18180: send reservation teardown
to 192.168.2.1 about 192.168.2.2
Comment: Teardown session, remove receiver 192.168.2.2
*Mar  1 05:29:08.682: RSVP:     version:1 flags:0000 type:RTEAR cksum:572F ttl:255
reserved:0 length:100
<packet data omitted>
*Mar  1 05:29:08.702: RSVP 192.168.1.2_17598-192.168.2.2_18180: PATH TEAR message
 for 192.168.2.2 (Serial0) from 192.168.1.2
Comment: RSVP TEAR message from 192.168.1.2
*Mar  1 05:29:08.706: RSVP 192.168.1.2_17598-192.168.2.2_18180: remove Serial0
 PATH 192.168.2.2(18180) <- 192.168.1.2(17:17598)
*Mar  1 05:29:08.714: RSVP:     version:1 flags:0000 type:RTEAR cksum:0000
ttl:255
<packet data omitted>
*Mar  1 05:29:08.726: RSVP 192.168.2.2_18180-192.168.1.2_17598: RESV TEAR message
 for 192.168.1.2 (Serial0) from 192.168.2.1
Comment: RSVP TEAR message from 192.168.2.2
```

When the call is first initiated, you should see RSVP PATH and RESV messages creating the RSVP session. During the call, you should see further RSVP PATH and RESV messages as hello messages are sent to maintain the RSVP session through the call. The RSVP PATH messages should contain the RSVP reservation parameters for the call, including average rate, bytes per second, burst depth, peak rate, and packet sizes. After you hang up the call, you should see RSVP TEARDOWN messages. In addition to the RSVP **debug** output, you can display the RSVP configuration using the **show** commands listed earlier in the chapter.

Example 5-19 shows the complete configuration for all the routers in this lab.

Example 5-19 *Complete Router Configurations for This Lab*

```
The Hub-140 Router
interface Serial0
 encapsulation frame-relay
 fair-queue 64 256 48
 frame-relay lmi-type ansi
 ip rsvp bandwidth 1536 1536
!
interface Serial0.1 multipoint
 ip address 192.168.1.1 255.255.255.252
 ip ospf network non-broadcast
 frame-relay map ip 192.168.1.2 841 broadcast
 ip rsvp bandwidth 1158 24
!
interface Serial0/0.2 multipoint
 ip address 192.168.2.1 255.255.255.252
 ip ospf network non-broadcast
```

Example 5-19 *Complete Router Configurations for This Lab (Continued)*

```
 frame-relay map ip 192.168.2.2 941 broadcast
 ip rsvp bandwidth 1158 24
 !
router ospf 1
 network 192.168.1.0 0.0.0.3 area 0
 network 192.168.2.0 0.0.0.3 area 0
 neighbor 192.168.2.2
 neighbor 192.168.1.2 priority 1

The Store-148 Router
 !
interface Serial0
 ip address 192.168.1.2 255.255.255.252
 encapsulation frame-relay
 fair-queue 64 256 37
 frame-relay lmi-type ansi
 ip ospf network non-broadcast
 ip ospf priority 0
 frame-relay map ip 192.168.1.1 148 broadcast
 ip rsvp bandwidth 1158 24
 !
router ospf 1
 log-adjacency-changes
 network 192.168.1.0 0.0.0.3 area 0
 neighbor 192.168.1.1 priority 1
 !
voice-port 2/0
 !
voice-port 2/1
 !
dial-peer voice 4801 pots
 destination-pattern 4801
 port 2/0
 !
dial-peer voice 4901 voip
 destination-pattern 4901
 session target ipv4:192.168.2.2
 req-qos guaranteed-delay

The Store-149 Router
interface Serial0
 ip address 192.168.2.2 255.255.255.252
 encapsulation frame-relay IETF
 fair-queue 64 256 37
 frame-relay lmi-type ansi
 ip ospf network non-broadcast
 ip ospf priority 0
 clockrate 1300000
 frame-relay map ip 192.168.2.1 149 broadcast
 ip rsvp bandwidth 1158 24
 !
```

continues

Example 5-19 *Complete Router Configurations for This Lab (Continued)*

```
!
router ospf 1
 network 192.168.2.0 0.0.0.3 area 0
 neighbor 192.168.2.1 priority 1
 !
voice-port 2/0
 !
voice-port 2/1
 !
dial-peer voice 4901 pots
 destination-pattern 4901
 port 2/0
 !
dial-peer voice 4801 voip
 destination-pattern 4801
 session target ipv4:192.168.1.2
 req-qos guaranteed-delay
```

Now that you have seen how IntServ can be applied to provide end-to-end QoS, it's time to explore how differentiated services classify packets for specific levels of QoS.

Differentiated Services

Differentiated services, commonly referred to as DiffServ, provide a method of classifying packets into classes or classes of service (COS). Classes of service are defined by the values defined in the type of service (TOS) field of the IP header. The contents of this field were originally defined in RFCs 1122 and 1349, as the Precedence and Type of Service fields. Several working groups made many valiant attempts at packet classification methods, but most of these efforts were not realized until recently, when newer multiservice applications began to require more quality control and fine-tuning from the network. RFC 1349 defined bits 3 through 6 of the ToS byte as the Type of Service field with ToS definitions shown in Table 5-10. The ToS field was originally intended as a mechanism to classify packets into different service types by marking the application's network requirements for delay, throughput, reliability, and cost.

NOTE	DiffServ classes of service are not be confused with Layer 2 classes of service for Inter-Switch Link (ISL), or 802.1Q frame-marking services on local-area networks. This chapter only uses the term *class of service* to refer to Layer 3 packet marking.

Table 5-10   *Type of Service Values*

Hexadecimal Bits	Decimal Value	Type of Service	Cisco IOS Software ToS Values
0000	0	Normal	normal
1000	8	Minimize delay	min-delay
0100	4	Maximize throughput	max-throughput
0010	2	Maximize reliability	max-reliability
0001	1	Minimize cost	min-monetary-cost

Using the ToS values, it is possible to mark packets from certain applications and use that classification information later in the network when congestion is encountered to provide these applications with higher levels of service. By default, all IP packets have a ToS value of 0000, specifying that they should be delivered with a normal "best-effort" service level. With Cisco IOS Software, it is possible to change the ToS values to define application traffic using access lists, as shown in Example 5-20. Using access lists, you can classify the ToS value for packets using the ToS value name or a decimal value ranging from 0 to 15.

Example 5-20   *Using the ToS Values with Access Lists*

```
interface Serial1
 ip address 192.168.1.2 255.255.255.252
 ip ospf network non-broadcast
 ip ospf priority 0
 ip policy route-map throughput
 frame-relay map ip 192.168.1.1 148 broadcast
!
ip local policy route-map throughput
!
access-list 150 permit udp host 192.168.1.2 range 16384 32767 host 192.168.2.2
range 16384 32767
access-list 150 permit udp host 192.168.2.2 range 16384 32767 host 192.168.1.2
 range 16384 32767
access-list 150 permit tcp host 192.168.1.2 eq 1720 host 192.168.2.2
access-list 150 permit tcp host 192.168.1.2 host 192.168.2.2 eq 1720
!
route-map throughput permit 10
 match ip address 150
 set ip tos max-throughput
!
dial-peer voice 4801 pots
 destination-pattern 4801
 port 2/0
!
dial-peer voice 4901 voip
 destination-pattern 4901
 session target ipv4:192.168.2.2
```

In the preceding example, **route-map throughput** is used to mark all voice and signaling traffic specified in access list 150 (UDP traffic ranging from ports 16,384 to 32,767 and TCP traffic on port 1720) with the maximum throughput ToS. This information can be used later in the network to provide the voice traffic with better levels of service using DiffServ applications such as packet classifying, metering, marking, shaping, and policing.

The remainder of this chapter focuses on DiffServ technologies, exploring packet marking using IP precedence, differentiated services codepoint (DSCP) values, and congestion control using Weighted Random Early Detection (WRED). The next chapter covers advanced traffic shaping and policing features, such as using generic traffic shaping and class-based shaping, traffic policing, and traffic classification using committed access rate (CAR).

Setting IP Precedence

IP Precedence is a field in the ToS area of the IP header. Eight levels of precedence are possible, ranging from 0 to 7, as shown in Table 5-11. Like the ToS values, IP precedence values can also be set to specify classifications for traffic.

Table 5-11   *IP Precedence Values*

Value	Description
Routine (0)	The default setting for IP packets.
Priority (1)	Sets priority precedence.
Immediate (2)	Sets immediate precedence.
Flash (3)	Sets Flash precedence.
Flash-Override (4)	Sets Flash-override precedence.
Critical (5)	Highest setting for nonrouter IP traffic.
Internet (6)	Sets Internet control precedence. Reserved for router traffic, such as routing updates.
Network Control (7)	Sets network control precedence. Reserved for router traffic and network control traffic.

When changing the precedence of IP packets, it is important to note two things. First, by default, all IP traffic except router-generated control and routing traffic uses the routine precedence value. If you do not make changes, all IP packets use this setting. Second, although it is possible to use the Internet and Network Control values when changing IP precedence, these values are generally reserved for router and network control traffic; using them for other types of traffic may disrupt router operation, interrupting network service.

On Cisco routers, one of the simplest ways to set IP precedence is by using route maps. For more information on the configuration of route maps, refer to Chapter 2, "Configuring Route

Maps and Policy-Based Routing." Two basic steps are required for using route maps to set IP precedence: defining the packets to be set, and creating the route map to specify the change.

Step 1   Define the packets that are to be set using a standard or extended access list to specify the traffic that is to have its precedence value changed. The following access list specifies all traffic from host 10.1.1.4:

```
Router(config)# access-list 15 permit host 10.1.1.4
```

Step 2   Create a route map to specify the packets to be modified and the change to be made:

```
Router(config)# route-map precedence
Router(config-route-map)# match ip address 15
Router(config-route-map)# set ip precedence ?
  <0-7>             Precedence value
  critical          Set critical precedence (5)
  flash             Set flash precedence (3)
  flash-override    Set flash override precedence (4)
  immediate         Set immediate precedence (2)
  internet          Set internetwork control precedence (6)
  network           Set network control precedence (7)
  priority          Set priority precedence (1)
  routine           Set routine precedence (0)
  <cr>
Router(config-route-map)# set ip precedence 5
Router(config-route-map)# exit
```

Step 3   Apply the route map to an interface using the **ip policy route-map** command:

```
Router(config)# interface ethernet 0/0
Router(config-if)# ip policy route-map precedence
```

To monitor the status of the policy, you can use the **show route-map** command or **debug ip policy**. The **show route-map** command displays configuration and statistical information about the route map, and **debug ip policy** shows policy matches and misses. Be extremely cautious using the **debug ip policy** command on production routers; if the policy is working properly and you have too many matches, you may either overload the router or be unable to see your debugging information. Example 5-21 shows output from the **show route-map** command.

NOTE   The **ip policy route-map** *route-map-name* command is used to apply policy routing on an interface-by-interface basis. This does not include locally router-generated packets. To apply policy routing to router-generated traffic, use the **ip local policy route-map** *route-map-name* in global configuration mode.

Example 5-21 show route-map *Command*

```
Router# show route-map precedence
route-map precedence, permit, sequence 10
  Match clauses:
    ip address (access-lists): 15
  Set clauses:
    ip precedence critical
  Policy routing matches: 5 packets, 766 bytes
Router# debug ip policy
00:38:09: IP: s=10.1.1.1 (local), d=10.1.1.4, len 100, policy match
00:38:09: IP: route map precedence, item 15, permit
00:38:09: IP: s=10.1.1.1 (local), d=10.1.1.4, len 100, policy rejected -- normal
forwarding
00:38:09: IP: s=10.1.1.1 (local), d=10.1.1.4, len 100, policy match
00:38:09: IP: route map precedence, item 15, permit
```

As internetwork standards evolve, newer packet classification methods are constantly being added to Cisco IOS Software. At the time of this writing, there are several new ways to use the IP precedence values to classify and react to marked packets. These include the following:

- Marking packets with access lists
- Marking packets with route maps or policy routing
- Using packet classification with RSVP
- Classifying packets for queuing prioritization using WFQ, Priority Queuing (PQ), Custom Queuing (CQ), and Class-Based WFQ (CBWFQ)
- Advanced packet classification with CAR and traffic policing
- Shaping classified traffic using generic traffic shaping (GTS), class-based shaping, and Frame Relay traffic shaping (FRTS)
- Prioritizing Real Time Protocol (RTP) traffic by setting IP RTP Priority
- Prioritizing real-time traffic using Low Latency Queuing (LLQ)
- Congestion control using WRED
- Marking voice traffic using DiffServ values

With the exception of FRTS, which was covered in the first edition of the *CCIE Practical Studies* series, these technologies are covered in Chapter 6. Unfortunately, because this book must fit within a hard cover, they say that we must limit its size to a certain number of pages and eventually stop writing so that it can be published. Therefore, we cannot go into detail on each type of packet classification.

Marking Traffic with DSCP

In the past few years, the ToS field in the IP header has been redefined to support newer DiffServ features. The new Differentiated Service (DS) field contains two subfields that are broken down into what is referred to as codepoints. *Codepoints* are basically subclassification of the values within the DS field of an IP packet that contain the same value in the DSCP field. The DS field contains two codepoints: the *Class Selector Codepoints*, formerly known as the IP Precedence field; and the *Assured Forwarding (AF) Codepoints*. To remain compatible with IP precedence, the class selector codepoints are bits 0, 1, and 2 (the first 3 bits in the DS field XXX000). The first 6 bits of the DS field belong to the DSCP field, which creates 64 possible classes to be used for packet marking. The AF codepoints are covered later in this section.

RFC 2474 and RFC 2475 describe the definition and architecture for DiffServ applications by using the DSCP field for packet marking. Packet marking is basically the process of reading, using, or changing the value of the DSCP field to provide a *per-hop behavior (PHB)* for traffic conditioning, metering, shaping, or policing. A PHB is defined as a behavior or forwarding treatment that is applied to a *Behavior Aggregate (BA)* on a DiffServ-compliant device. BAs are packets with the same codepoint going in the same direction.

NOTE   The use of the DSCP field is defined in RFCs 2474, 2475, 2597, 2598, and 2697, and later updated in RFCs 3168 and 3260.

Within these 64 DSCP classes, the IETF has specified three class pools, as shown in Table 5-12. The first pool, which uses the first 5 bits of the DSCP field ending with a 0, is reserved for standard class assignments that are administered by IANA. For example, the prefixes 000, 001, 010, 011, 100, 101, 110, and 111 are set aside to remain compatible with IP precedence. 000000 is reserved for best-effort traffic, and any traffic that does not match any other class is sent to the 00000 codepoint.

Table 5-12   *DSCP Pools*

Pool Number	Codepoint Value	Reservation
1	Bits 0,1,2,3,4 xxxxx0	Reserved for standards administered by IANA
2	Bits 0,1,2,3 xxxx11	Reserved for experimental or local use
3	Bits 0,1,2,3 xxxx01	Reserved for experimental or local use and future standards expansion

Using the DSCP field for packet marking allows for the creation of many classes for traffic prioritization, which is valuable when you are working with traffic that requires a guaranteed amount of bandwidth with low jitter and latency, such as voice or video. For this reason, RFC 2598 describes the use of *Expedited Forwarding (EF)* PHB. EF PHB provides the highest QoS defined for use with DiffServ. EF PHB provides AF classes for high-priority traffic, with the class 101110 being the highest priority with the greatest quality provisions.

You can also use DSCP values with WRED to control the proactive drop of TCP packets by specifying AF classes. RFC 2597 defines AF classes for specification of packet-drop priority. To illustrate the use of AF classes in a network environment, suppose you have defined three types of traffic as high priority; however, when network congestion reaches the point where packets must be dropped, with AF classes you can specify the order in which packets are dropped. Table 5-13 shows the AF classes and their drop priority. All bits in Class 1 begin with the standard IP Precedence value of 001, which is priority precedence. Class 2 begins with the value 010, which is immediate precedence, Class 3 begins with the value 011, which is Flash precedence, and Class 4 begins with the value 100, which is Flash-override precedence.

NOTE   The use of WRED is covered in detail later in this chapter.

Table 5-13   *AF Classes and Drop Priority*

Drop Precedence	Class 1	Class 2	Class 3	Class 4
Low drop	AF11	AF21	AF31	AF41
	DSCP 10	DSCP 18	DSCP 26	DSCP 34
	001010	010010	011010	100010
Medium drop	AF12	AF22	AF32	AF42
	DSCP 12	DSCP 20	DSCP 28	DSCP 36
	001100	010100	011100	100100
High drop	AF13	AF23	AF33	AF43
	DSCP 14	DSCP 22	DSCP 30	DSCP 38
	001110	010110	011110	100110

The DSCP value can be used with Cisco IOS Software in a number of ways. It can be used with access lists to specify DSCP values in IP packets. It can be used with class maps and policy maps to mark packets. The DSCP bit can also be used with CAR to specify actions to perform on packets based on their DSCP values. DSCP can be used with WRED to specify which traffic to drop first in a proactive packet-drop scenario. Table 5-14 shows the DSCP values that can be set, either by name or by decimal number, and their descriptions.

Table 5-14 *Cisco IOS Software's DSCP Values*

DSCP Value Name	DSCP Value Decimal and Hexadecimal	Description
af11	10 001010	AF11—Assured forwarding, low drop probability, Class 1 DSCP, and priority precedence
af12	12 001100	AF12—Assured forwarding, medium drop probability, Class 1 DSCP, and priority precedence
af13	14 001110	AF13—Assured forwarding, high drop probability, Class 1 DSCP, and priority precedence
af21	18 010010	AF21—Assured forwarding, low drop probability, Class 2 DSCP, and immediate precedence
af22	20 010100	AF22—Assured forwarding, medium drop probability, Class 2 DSCP, and immediate precedence
af23	22 010110	AF23—Assured forwarding, high drop probability, Class 2 DSCP, and immediate precedence
af31	26 011010	AF31—Assured forwarding, low drop probability, Class 3 DSCP, and Flash precedence
af32	28 011100	AF32—Assured forwarding, medium drop probability, Class 3 DSCP, and Flash precedence
af33	30 011110	AF33—Assured forwarding, high drop probability, Class 3 DSCP, and Flash precedence
af41	34 100010	AF41—Assured forwarding, low drop probability, Class 4 DSCP, and Flash-override precedence
af42	36 100100	AF42—Assured forwarding, medium drop probability, Class 4 DSCP, and Flash-override precedence
af43	38 100110	AF43—Assured forwarding, high drop probability, Class 4 DSCP, and Flash-override precedence
cs1	1 001000	CS1 or Priority IP precedence 1
cs2	2 010000	CS2 or Immediate IP precedence 2

continues

Table 5-14 *Cisco IOS Software's DSCP Values (Continued)*

DSCP Value Name	DSCP Value Decimal and Hexadecimal	Description
cs3	3 011000	CS3 or Flash IP precedence 3
cs4	4 100000	CS4 or Flash-override IP precedence 4
cs5	5 101000	CS5 or Critical IP precedence 5
cs6	6 110000	CS6 or Internet IP precedence 6
cs7	7 111000	CS7 or Network Control IP precedence 7
default	0 000000	The default "best-effort" value for all traffic
ef	46 101110	EF-PHB—Expedited forwarding, highest service level

The most standard application of DSCP classification is with access lists. Example 5-22 shows two ways to use the AF DSCP value to mark all UDP voice traffic with the lowest drop probability and high precedence. The recommended DSCP value for voice signaling traffic is DSCP 26 or AF31. This is essentially the same as marking the traffic with the Flash IP precedence value. By marking the packets with the AF31 DSCP value, you can ensure that queuing or congestion control mechanisms, such as WFQ or WRED, will give these packets high priority, recommended for voice signaling traffic, least drop probability, and you can also use other more advanced methods to control the quality levels provided to these applications.

Example 5-22 *Using DSCP Classification to Prioritize Voice Traffic*

```
interface Serial1
 ip address 192.168.1.2 255.255.255.252
 frame-relay map ip 192.168.1.1 148 broadcast
 ip rsvp bandwidth 1158 24
 ip rsvp signalling dscp 26
!
dial-peer voice 4801 pots
 destination-pattern 4801
 port 2/0
!
dial-peer voice 4901 voip
 destination-pattern 4901
```

Example 5-22 *Using DSCP Classification to Prioritize Voice Traffic (Continued)*

```
session target ipv4:192.168.2.2
req-qos guaranteed-delay
ip qos dscp af31 signalling
```

In the preceding example, the **ip rsvp signalling dscp 26** command is used to assign RSVP signaling traffic the AF DSCP value of af31 (low drop/Flash). The second highlighted command, **ip qos dscp af31 signalling**, provides prioritized classification for voice signaling traffic, which can be used to prioritize this traffic in other parts of the network. Each of these commands allows for the two separate protocols to receive higher priorities for weighted queuing or congestion strategies during periods of congestion.

NOTE   The act of marking traffic with DSCP values by itself does not guarantee that the traffic will receive better treatment in a network. Packet marking just identifies the traffic so that you can apply QoS techniques to that traffic at other places in the network.

Now that you have learned ways to use the DSCP values to classify traffic for congestion control, it is time to examine how congestion control itself works and how it is configured.

Avoiding Congestion with WRED

When no congestion avoidance mechanism is in place, interfaces drop packets based on tail drop. *Tail drop* basically means that when the queue for an interface is full, any new packets arriving for transmission on that interface are dropped until the interface has enough queue space to service new packets. Another way to manage network congestion is by avoiding it altogether; Weighed Random Early Detection (WRED) is designed to do just that. Based on the Random Early Detection (RED) algorithm, developed by Sally Floyd and others, WRED proactively drops packets based on the estimated average queue size, minimum queue size, where no packets are dropped, and a maximum queue size, where all packets are dropped. WRED drops packets when congestion is encountered on a queue to prevent a scenario called *global synchronization*.

NOTE   For more information on RED, check out RFC 2309 and the RED research papers at http://ftp.ee.lbl.gov/floyd/red.html or Sally Floyd's website at http://www.icir.org/floyd/.

Global synchronization occurs when a network is congested and packets are dropped, causing all TCP end stations to simultaneously back off and then retransmit the dropped packets, which wastes network resources. During incidents of global synchronization, network traffic will continuously frequently peak and then drop off because the end stations running TCP applications have synchronized. WRED is designed to prevent global synchronization by proactively dropping packets from larger traffic flows, causing some of the dominant network end stations to decrease their TCP window size and send fewer packets between acknowledgments, reducing their network utilization, making more room for smaller traffic flows and preventing further packet loss.

NOTE   The major difference between WRED and RED is that WRED weighs traffic flows based on the value of the IP Precedence field in the IP header and RED does not. With WRED, higher-priority traffic has a higher weight and is less likely to be dropped during periods of network congestion.

It is important to note that WRED works only with TCP traffic, because TCP is connection oriented, requiring flow control using windowing and acknowledgments. Because UDP, IP, and other non-IP protocols such as Internetwork Packet Exchange (IPX) and AppleTalk are connectionless and do not provide a windowing mechanism like TCP, they may be adversely affected by WRED. If interface congestion consists mostly of connectionless, or non-IP traffic, the WRED congestion avoidance method will not provide a benefit.

In Cisco IOS Software, you can configure an interface using WRED in two ways. The simplest way to configure WRED is by enabling it on an interface using the **random-detect** command. After enabling WRED, you may also configure the weight for the mean queue depth calculation by using the **random-detect exponential-weighting-constant** command. This command specifies a weight to be used by WRED when calculating the average queue length; the default weight factor is 9:

```
random-detect exponential-weighting-constant exponent
```

Acceptable exponent values range from 1 to 16 and are in the format 2^n. To configure the IP precedence, the values used to weigh the packets use the **random-detect precedence** command, which specifies the minimum and maximum WRED packet thresholds and the mark probability denominator. By default, the minimum threshold for an IP precedence of 0 is set to half maximum threshold for the interface. Table 5-15 explains the minimum and maximum thresholds and the mark probability denominator in more detail:

```
random-detect precedence precedence-value minimum-threshold maximum threshold
  [mark-probability-denominator]
```

Table 5-15   *WRED and IP Precedence Values*

Command Argument	Description
precedence-value	The specific IP precedence-value to be matched, ranging from 0 to 7.
minimum-threshold	The minimum number of packets that will be queued before packets with the specified precedence value will be randomly dropped.
maximum-threshold	The maximum number of packets that will be queued before all packets of the specified precedence value will be tail dropped.
[*mark-probability-denominator*]	(Optional) This value represents the fraction for the amount of packets that will be dropped during periods of congestion when the average queue size is at maximum capacity. In other words, before the maximum threshold has been met, one out of every 10 mark probability denominator packets will be dropped.

You can customize WRED configurations for network applications by setting individual precedence thresholds. The minimum and maximum packet queue sizes can be defined for each of the eight IP precedence values. You can use the **mark-probability-denominator** argument to change the rate at which packets are dropped. For example, the default **mark-probability-denominator** for a WRED interface is 10, so when the packet level is between the minimum and maximum threshold values, one out of every 10 packets will be dropped. After the maximum threshold is met, packets of this precedence value will be tail dropped. Example 5-23 shows how WRED has been configured to limit the size of the lower-priority queues, queues 0 to 4, and increase the minimum average queue size for critical (precedence 5) traffic to 35 packets.

Example 5-23 *Using WRED and IP Precedence*

```
Sally-1# show run | begin Serial0
interface Serial0
 ip address 289.22.78.1 255.255.255.0
 ip ospf network point-to-point
 no ip mroute-cache
 random-detect
 random-detect precedence 0 17 40
 random-detect precedence 1 19 40
 random-detect precedence 2 21 40
 random-detect precedence 3 23 40
 random-detect precedence 4 25 40
 random-detect precedence 5 35 40 20
```

Example 5-24 shows a before and after snapshot of the WRED parameters as seen using the **show queueing random-detect command** on a serial interface.

Example 5-24 *Before and After the WRED Configuration Change*

```
Sally-1# show queueing random-detect
Current random-detect configuration:
  Serial0
    Queueing strategy: random early detection (WRED)
    Exp-weight-constant: 9 (1/512)
    Mean queue depth: 0
    Class    Random    Tail   Minimum    Maximum     Mark
             drop      drop   threshold  threshold   probability
      0        0        0        20         40        1/10
      1        0        0        22         40        1/10
      2        0        0        24         40        1/10
      3        0        0        26         40        1/10
      4        0        0        28         40        1/10
      5        0        0        31         40        1/10
      6        0        0        33         40        1/10
      7        0        0        35         40        1/10
    rsvp       0        0        37         40        1/10
Sally-1# show queueing random-detect
Current random-detect configuration:
  Serial0
    Queueing strategy: random early detection (WRED)
    Exp-weight-constant: 9 (1/512)
    Mean queue depth: 0
    Class    Random    Tail   Minimum    Maximum     Mark
             drop      drop   threshold  threshold   probability
      0        0        0        17         40        1/10
      1        0        0        19         40        1/10
      2        0        0        21         40        1/10
      3        0        0        23         40        1/10
      4        0        0        25         40        1/10
      5        0        0        35         40        1/20
      6        0        0        33         40        1/10
      7        0        0        35         40        1/10
    rsvp       0        0        37         40        1/10
```

As seen in the preceding example, the **show queueing random-detect** command displays the WRED configuration for each WRED-enabled interface, including the exponent weight constant, the number of packets dropped for each precedence value, and the minimum and maximum values for each of the eight IP precedence values and RSVP.

As previously mentioned, by default WRED works with the IP precedence values to prevent high-priority packets from being dropped during periods of congestion. If the volume of traffic is high enough that an interface still becomes congested, and the packet levels are between the minimum and maximum thresholds, packets of a certain precedence value will be dropped according to the configured thresholds. WRED can also be leveraged to work with DSCP values using the **random-detect dscp-based** command, as shown in Example 5-25.

NOTE   In the event that an interface receives a high volume of non-TCP traffic, high-priority traffic, marked with IP precedence or DSCP values, may exceed the maximum thresholds, causing prioritized packets to be tail dropped.

Example 5-25 *Using DSCP Values with WRED*

```
Store-148#sho run | begin Serial1
interface Serial1
 no ip address
 encapsulation frame-relay
 random-detect dscp-based
 frame-relay lmi-type ansi
```

In the preceding example, WRED was configured so that the weight will be calculated using DSCP values rather than IP precedence. WRED's capabilities are greatly enhanced when it is used in combination with DSCP classification. Instead of supporting the eight IP precedence queues supported by precedence-based WRED, DSCP-based WRED supports all the AF- and CS-based DSCP values, and each of these queues can be altered using the **random-detect dscp-based** *dscp-value minimum-threshold, maximum-threshold mark-probability-denominator* command. Example 5-26 shows the output from the **show queueing** command after configuring DSCP-based WRED.

Example 5-26 **show queueing** *and DSCP-Based WRED*

```
Sally-1# show queueing
Current fair queue configuration:
  Interface          Discard   Dynamic  Reserved  Link    Priority
                     threshold queues   queues    queues  queues
  Serial0            64        256      37        8       1
Current DLCI priority queue configuration:
Current priority queue configuration:
Current custom queue configuration:
Current random-detect configuration:
  Serial1
    Queueing strategy: random early detection (WRED)
    Exp-weight-constant: 9 (1/512)
    Mean queue depth: 0
dscp           Random drop      Tail drop      Minimum Maximum  Mark
               pkts/bytes       pkts/bytes     thresh  thresh   prob
  af11         0/0              0/0            33      40       1/10
  af12         0/0              0/0            28      40       1/10
  af13         0/0              0/0            24      40       1/10
  af21         0/0              0/0            33      40       1/10
  af22         0/0              0/0            28      40       1/10
```

continues

Example 5-26 show queueing *and DSCP-Based WRED (Continued)*

```
     af23       0/0             0/0          24   40  1/10
     af31       0/0             0/0          33   40  1/10
     af32       0/0             0/0          28   40  1/10
     af33       0/0             0/0          24   40  1/10
     af41       0/0             0/0          33   40  1/10
     af42       0/0             0/0          28   40  1/10
     af43       0/0             0/0          24   40  1/10
     cs1        0/0             0/0          22   40  1/10
     cs2        0/0             0/0          24   40  1/10
     cs3        0/0             0/0          26   40  1/10
     cs4        0/0             0/0          28   40  1/10
     cs5        0/0             0/0          31   40  1/10
     cs6        0/0             0/0          33   40  1/10
     cs7        0/0             0/0          35   40  1/10
     ef         0/0             0/0          37   40  1/10
     rsvp       0/0             0/0          37   40  1/10
     default   0/0             0/0           20   40  1/10
     Current per-SID queue configuration:
```

WRED information is also summarized with the **show interface** command, which displays the number of dropped packets, as shown in Example 5-27.

Example 5-27 show interface *Command and WRED*

```
Sally-1# show interface serial 0
Serial0 is up, line protocol is up
  Hardware is PQUICC with 56k 4-wire CSU/DSU
  Internet address is 2.2.2.1/24
  MTU 1500 bytes, BW 1544 Kbit, DLY 20000 usec,
      reliability 255/255, txload 1/255, rxload 1/255
  Encapsulation HDLC, loopback not set
  Keepalive set (10 sec)
  Last input 00:00:17, output 00:00:02, output hang never
  Last clearing of "show interface" counters never
  Input queue: 0/75/0/0 (size/max/drops/flushes); Total output drops: 0
  Queueing strategy: random early detection(RED)
  5 minute input rate 0 bits/sec, 0 packets/sec
  5 minute output rate 0 bits/sec, 0 packets/sec
     2826 packets input, 201606 bytes, 0 no buffer
     Received 2821 broadcasts, 0 runts, 0 giants, 0 throttles
     1427 input errors, 99 CRC, 479 frame, 0 overrun, 0 ignored, 841 abort
     3934 packets output, 274630 bytes, 0 underruns
     0 output errors, 0 collisions, 243 interface resets
     0 output buffer failures, 0 output buffers swapped out
     175 carrier transitions
     DCD=up  DSR=up  DTR=up  RTS=up  CTS=up
```

WRED also includes support for RSVP. By default WRED has a 37-packet minimum average queue size for RSVP traffic, the largest of all average queue sizes. You can customize the RSVP WRED configuration by using the **random-detect precedence rsvp** or **random-detect dscp rsvp** commands to configure minimum and maximum average queue sizes.

NOTE   If you are planning to use FIFO queuing on an interface running WRED and you are considering another queuing method, such as WFQ, CQ, or PQ, in the future, you should be aware that WRED and WFQ, CQ, and PQ are all mutually exclusive technologies. After WRED has been configured, it must be removed before any other queuing method can be enabled.

WRED can also be configured to support individual traffic flows. Flow-Based RED is commonly referred to as FRED. Each flow consists of a source and destination IP address and port number. FRED monitors the state information for each flow and prevents any resource-intensive flows from monopolizing the resources by allocating buffers to each flow.

To enable FRED, you must first enable WRED using the **random-detect** command, and then enable FRED using the **random-detect flow** command, and then, if necessary, configure the average queue depth and the number of dynamic queues allowed. By default, FRED is limited to 256 flows with an average queue depth factor of 4. The average depth factor is used to scale the number of buffers available to each flow, which determines how many packets permitted per queue, and is configurable using the **random-detect flow average-depth-factor** command. The depth factor can be 1, 2, 4, 8, or 16; the default average depth factor is 4.

```
random-detect flow average-depth-factor depth-factor
```

The maximum number of active flows is set using the **random-detect flow count** command. The flow count can range from 16 to 32,768, with the default value of 256 flows.

```
random-detect flow count flow-count
```

These FRED flow configuration tools enable you to create more granular congestion control configurations so that you can apply different congestion control actions to traffic based on DSCP values, limit the number of flows, and define the size of the queues, as shown in Example 5-28.

Example 5-28 *Creating Custom WRED Configurations*

```
Store-148#sho run | begin Serial1
interface Serial1
 no ip address
 encapsulation frame-relay
 random-detect dscp-based
 random-detect flow
 random-detect flow average-depth-factor 2
 frame-relay lmi-type ansi
```

The preceding example created three new fields in the output of the **show queueing random-detect** command. The *mean queue depth*, which is also shown when WRED is enabled, displays the average queue depth by taking an average of the minimum and maximum queue depth sizes for each queue. The *Max flow* count field displays the maximum number of flows that will be permitted with the current configuration. The *Average depth factor* field displays the current average depth factor configuration, and the *flows* field shows the number of active flows, the maximum number of active flows, and the maximum number of possible active flows given the current configuration. Example 5-29 shows the output of the **show queueing random-detect** command after the application of the configuration shown earlier in Example 5-28.

Example 5-29 **show queueing** *Command Output After Flow Configuration*

```
Sally-1# show queueing random-detect interface Serial 1
Current random-detect configuration:
  Serial1
    Queueing strategy: random early detection (WRED)
    Exp-weight-constant: 9 (1/512)
    Mean queue depth: 0
    Max flow count: 256       Average depth factor: 2
    Flows (active/max active/max): 0/0/256
    dscp       Random drop      Tail drop      Minimum Maximum  Mark
               pkts/bytes       pkts/bytes     thresh  thresh   prob
    af11       0/0              0/0            33      40       1/10
    af12       0/0              0/0            28      40       1/10
    af13       0/0              0/0            24      40       1/10
    af21       0/0              0/0            33      40       1/10
    af22       0/0              0/0            28      40       1/10
    af23       0/0              0/0            24      40       1/10
    af31       0/0              0/0            33      40       1/10
    af32       0/0              0/0            28      40       1/10
    af33       0/0              0/0            24      40       1/10
    af41       0/0              0/0            33      40       1/10
    af42       0/0              0/0            28      40       1/10
    af43       0/0              0/0            24      40       1/10
    cs1        0/0              0/0            22      40       1/10
    cs2        0/0              0/0            24      40       1/10
    cs3        0/0              0/0            26      40       1/10
    cs4        0/0              0/0            28      40       1/10
    cs5        0/0              0/0            31      40       1/10
    cs6        0/0              0/0            33      40       1/10
    cs7        0/0              0/0            35      40       1/10
    ef         0/0              0/0            37      40       1/10
    rsvp       0/0              0/0            37      40       1/10
    default    0/0              0/0            20      40       1/10
```

This chapter covered several ways to provide QoS to applications using integrated and differentiated services. Many of the technologies are difficult to understand without the application of a queuing, shaping, or policing mechanism to apply an actual action upon receiving a marked packet. The full benefits of a good DiffServ design will not be seen until advanced queuing, shaping, and policing techniques are applied. The next chapter explores how DiffServ technologies can be extended and added to by applying more advanced queuing, shaping, policing, and classification techniques.

Practice Scenario

The following practical scenario is provided to help reinforce some of the concepts that have been discussed in this chapter.

Lab 11: The Jetsons Meet IntServ and DiffServ

Integrated and differentiated services provide several enhancements to today's congested networks. In this practical scenario, you explore the various ways that these technologies can be used together to provide more efficient networks.

Lab Exercise

In this lab scenario, you configure integrated and differentiated service to provide better VoIP quality for the users in the Jetsons network. The network used in this scenario will make use of many of the technologies in this chapter, including RSVP with DSCP classification and WRED for congestion control through the ATM WAN.

Lab Objectives

In this lab, you complete the following objectives:

- Use RSVP to reserve resources for VoIP traffic.
- Apply DSCP marking for certain types of RSVP and voice signaling traffic.
- Use WRED to control congestion across the wide-area network.
- Apply voice codecs to provide the best compression, quality, and reliability.
- Refresh ATM skills by applying WRED and RSVP to ATM WAN interfaces.
- Configure a LightStream 1010 ATM switch for PVC connections between ATM router interfaces.

Equipment Needed

The following equipment is needed:

- One LightStream ATM switch with two OC-3 modules

- Two Cisco routers with ATM OC-3 interfaces; one router with at least one serial interface, and the other router with one Token Ring interface
- One router with one Ethernet and one Token Ring interface
- One router with one serial and one FXS voice interface and a phone for testing
- One router with one Fast Ethernet and one FXS voice interface and a phone for testing
- One hub or switch for Ethernet connectivity, and one multistation access unit (MSAU) for Token Ring connections

---

NOTE   This lab makes use of ATM equipment as the wide-area core network. If you do not have ATM equipment, simulate these connections with Frame Relay. This lab also uses Token Ring interfaces; because Token Ring is not one of the key components for this experiment, however, you can use Ethernet in its place.

Physical Layout and Prestaging

The following physical layout and prestaging needs to be completed:

- Cable the routers as shown in Figure 5-6, and connect the ATM OC-3 interfaces to the ATM switch.

Figure 5-6   *The Jetsons Network*

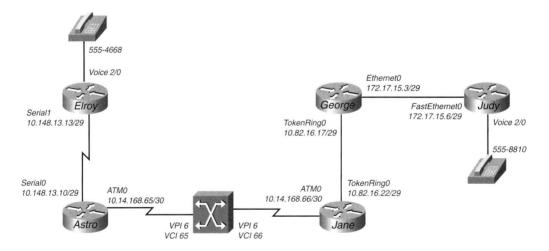

- Connect the Elroy and Astro serial interfaces using back-to-back cables.
- Connect the Jane and George routers to an MSAU.
- Connect the Judy and George routers using an Ethernet switch or hub.
- Connect telephones to the FXS ports on the Elroy and Judy routers.
- Configure the ATM switch using the information from Table 5-16.

Table 5-16 *ATM PVC Configuration*

Router Interface	VPI	VCI	Switch Interface	VPI	VCI
Astro ATM0	6	65	ATM1/0/2	6	65
Jane ATM0	6	66	ATM1/0/0	6	66

Configuring ATM switching for two PVCs is a very simple process. Just create one ATM PVC statement on one of the interfaces specifying that ATM traffic on that PVC should go to the other ATM interface connected to the remote network. Example 5-30 shows the configuration for the ATM switch.

Example 5-30 *ATM Switch Configuration*

```
interface ATM1/0/2
 no ip address
atm pvc 6 65  interface  ATM1/0/0 6 66
```

- Configure all IP addresses on the serial, ATM, Token Ring, and Ethernet interfaces as shown in the preceding figure. Verify that all routers are able to reach their directly connected neighbor using pings.

Lab Tasks

Follow these steps to complete this lab:

Step 1   Enable Enhanced Interior Gateway Routing Protocol (EIGRP) process 32074 on all routers, and make sure that they do not classfully summarize networks. Verify IP connectivity before proceeding to Step 2.

Step 2   Configure VoIP for the phones connected to the FXS interfaces on the Elroy and Judy routers using the phone numbers shown in Figure 5-5. The phones should automatically dial each other when taken off the hook. Use one of the voice codecs that consumes the least amount of bandwidth. Verify this configuration by test calls in both directions.

Step 3 Configure RSVP request and acceptance for guaranteed delay service on all VoIP traffic. Make sure all RSVP and voice signaling traffic is classified as the highest priority using DSCP marking. Do not allow an interface to use more bandwidth that 50 percent of the smallest Jetsons network interface. The largest flow should not be any larger than the flow size required for the voice codec in use. Test the configuration on both phones before continuing to Step 4. This step requires quite a few tasks to work properly.

Step 4 Enable WRED to control congestion on the serial interfaces of the Astro and Elroy routers. Each router should weigh the priority of packets based on their DSCP values; packets marked with the 000000 DSCP value should be discarded after 20 bytes, and there should be no more than default DSCP packets before WRED begins to discard them as well.

After all routers have been cabled, verify connectivity using the **show cdp neighbors** and **show ip interface brief** commands. This will save a lot of time troubleshooting cabling and clock rate problems. After verifying Layer 2 connectivity, assign IP addresses to each of the routers using the information from Figure 5-6. After you have assigned all IP addresses, verify Layer 3 connectivity between directly connected networks using the **ping** command. Then, after you have verified that all directly connected router interfaces are reachable, you are ready to proceed with the rest of this lab.

Lab Walkthrough

The following walkthrough shows the steps that were followed to successfully complete this practical scenario:

Step 1 Enable EIGRP process 32074 on all routers, and make sure that they do not classfully summarize networks. Verify IP connectivity before proceeding to Step 2.

This step sounds a little easier than it is. In the beginning as you are enabling EIGRP routing, you may begin to notice that the Astro and Jane routers do not automatically become neighbors. This is because they are connecting over a nonbroadcast multiaccess (NBMA) ATM network. Two tasks must be completed before these two peers will become EIGRP neighbors.

— Create an ATM map list to map the Layer 2 to Layer 3 addresses and enable broadcasts, just like a Frame Relay **map** statement, and apply the map list to the ATM subinterface using the **map-group** *map-list-name* command as shown in Example 5-31.

Example 5-31 *ATM Configuration for the Astro Router*

```
Astro# show run | begin ATM
interface ATM0
 no ip address
 no atm ilmi-keepalive
!
interface ATM0.20 multipoint
 ip address 10.14.168.65 255.255.255.252
 map-group atm
 atm pvc 20 6 65 aal5snap
!
map-list atm
 ip 10.14.168.66 atm-vc 20 broadcast
```

The **atm map-group** maps the IP address to the ATM address of the interface. After you have applied the map group to the ATM subinterface, you should be able to verify the ATM configuration using the **show atm map** and **show atm vc** commands, as shown in Example 5-32.

Example 5-32 *Verifying the ATM Configuration on the Astro Router*

```
Astro# show atm map
Map list atm : PERMANENT
ip 10.14.168.66 maps to VC 20
        , broadcast
Astro# show atm vc
          VCD /                                 Peak  Avg/Min Burst
Interface Name      VPI  VCI Type  Encaps  SC  Kbps  Kbps  Cells  Sts
0.20      20          6   65 PVC   SNAP    UBR 155000                UP
```

— Optionally, create a static EIGRP neighbor assignment using the EIGRP **neighbor** *IP-address interface-name interface-number* command. Example 5-33 shows the EIGRP configuration from the Astro router and the resulting **show ip eigrp neighbors** command output.

Example 5-33 *The EIGRP Configuration for the Astro Router*

```
Astro# show run | begin eigrp
router eigrp 32074
 network 10.14.168.64 0.0.0.3
 network 10.148.13.8 0.0.0.7
 neighbor 10.14.168.66 ATM0.20
 no auto-summary
Astro# show ip eigrp neighbors
IP-EIGRP neighbors for process 32074
H   Address            Interface    Hold Uptime   SRTT   RTO  Q  Seq Type
                                    (sec)         (ms)        Cnt Num
1   10.14.168.66       AT0.20        13 00:18:05 1264   5000  0  7   S
0   10.148.13.13       Se0           13 00:19:28    1    200  0  8
```

Step 2   Configure VoIP for the phones connected to the FXS interfaces on the Elroy
and Judy routers using the phone numbers shown in Figure 5-6. The phones
should automatically dial each other when taken off the hook. Use one of the
voice codecs that consumes the least amount of bandwidth. Verify this
configuration by test calls in both directions.

This step requires most of the same principles applied in all the other VoIP
examples so far: configuring two dial peers; and setting destination patterns,
session targets, ports, and codecs. The least resource-intensive voice codec
is one of the g.723 codecs. The only difference in this configuration is
the automatic dial configuration. This is easily accomplished using the
connection plar *dial-string* command under the voice port. Example 5-34
shows the VoIP configuration for the Judy router. This example also shows
that two calls were successfully placed. You can display active call summary
information by using the **show call active voice** command on both routers.

Example 5-34 *VoIP Configuration and Test Data for the Judy Router*

```
Judy# show run | begin voice-port
voice-port 2/0
 connection plar 5554668
!
voice-port 2/1
!
dial-peer voice 5558810 pots
 destination-pattern 5558810
 port 2/0
!
dial-peer voice 5554668 voip
 destination-pattern 5554668
 session target ipv4:10.148.13.13
 codec g723ar63
Astro# show call active voice
Telephony call-legs: 1
SIP call-legs: 0
H323 call-legs: 1
Judy# show call active voice
Telephony call-legs: 1
SIP call-legs: 0
H323 call-legs: 1
```

Step 3   Configure RSVP request and acceptance for guaranteed delay service on all
VoIP traffic. Make sure all RSVP and voice signaling traffic is classified as
the highest priority using DSCP marking. Do not allow any interface to use
more bandwidth that 50 percent of the smallest Jetsons network interface.
The largest flow should be no larger than the flow size required for the voice
codec in use. Test the configuration on both phones before continuing to Step 4.
This step requires quite a few tasks to work properly.

— First enable RSVP on all interfaces using the reserved bandwidth of 772 bps, which is 50 percent of the smallest interface bandwidth of a serial interface. The largest reservable flow should not be greater than 18 bps, the rate of the voice codec. And all RSVP signaling traffic should be marked with the EF DSCP value. This can all be accomplished using two commands: **ip rsvp bandwidth 772 18**, and **ip rsvp signalling dscp 46**.

— Next, you need to configure all voice traffic to request and accept guaranteed delay service from the network. This requires only two configuration tasks: entering the **req-qos guaranteed-delay**, **acc-qos guaranteed-delay**, and **ip qos dscp ef signalling** commands in the dial-peer configuration for the remote peer on both the Elroy and Judy routers. Example 5-35 shows the RSVP configuration for the Elroy router.

Example 5-35 *Elroy VoIP RSVP Configuration*

```
Elroy# show run | begin Serial1
interface Serial1
 ip address 10.148.13.13 255.255.255.248
 fair-queue 64 256 26
 ip rsvp bandwidth 772 18
 ip rsvp signalling dscp 46
!
voice-port 2/0
 connection plar 5558810
!
voice-port 2/1
!
dial-peer voice 5554668 pots
 destination-pattern 5554668
 port 2/0
!
dial-peer voice 5558810 voip
 destination-pattern 5558810
 session target ipv4:172.17.15.6
 req-qos guaranteed-delay
 acc-qos controlled-load
 codec g723ar63
 ip qos dscp ef signalling
```

You can verify this step by using the **show ip rsvp reservation detail** command on the Elroy router. This command should display data similar to that shown in Example 5-36.

Example 5-36 *show ip rsvp reservation detail Command Output from the Elroy Router*

```
Elroy# show ip rsvp reservation detail
RSVP Reservation. Destination is 10.148.13.13, Source is 172.17.15.6,
  Protocol is UDP, Destination port is 16394, Source port is 19344
  Reservation Style is Fixed-Filter, QoS Service is Guaranteed-Rate
  Average Bitrate is 18K bits/sec, Maximum Burst is 80 bytes
  Min Policed Unit: 40 bytes, Max Pkt Size: 40 bytes
  Resv ID handle: 0000B801.
  Policy: Forwarding. Policy source(s): Default
RSVP Reservation. Destination is 172.17.15.6, Source is 10.148.13.13,
  Protocol is UDP, Destination port is 19344, Source port is 16394
  Next Hop is 10.148.13.10, Interface is Serial1
  Reservation Style is Fixed-Filter, QoS Service is Guaranteed-Rate
  Average Bitrate is 18K bits/sec, Maximum Burst is 80 bytes
  Min Policed Unit: 40 bytes, Max Pkt Size: 40 bytes
  Resv ID handle: 0000BA01.
  Policy: Forwarding. Policy source(s): Default
```

Step 4   Next, enable WRED to control congestion on the serial interfaces of the Astro and Elroy routers. Each router should weigh the priority of packets based on their DSCP values; packets marked with the 000000 DSCP value should be discarded after 20 bytes, and there should be no more than default DSCP packets before WRED begins to discard them as well.

This command only requires two tasks: enabling DSCP-based WRED and creating a limit for packets with the default DSCP value. The WRED configuration for the Elroy router is shown in Example 5-37.

Example 5-37 *WRED Configuration for the Elroy Router*

```
Elroy# show run | begin Serial1
interface Serial1
 ip address 10.148.13.13 255.255.255.248
 random-detect dscp-based
 random-detect dscp 0 20 30
 ip rsvp bandwidth 772 18
 ip rsvp signalling dscp 46
```

As a final WRED configuration step, you can verify the WRED default DSCP values using the **show queueing random-detect | begin default** command, as shown in Example 5-38.

Example 5-38 *Verifying the WRED Configuration on the Elroy Router*

```
Elroy# show queueing random-detect | begin default
default        0/0             0/0            20      30  1/10
```

Example 5-39 shows the complete configurations for this lab.

Example 5-39 *The Complete Configurations for Lab 5*

```
Elroy Router Configuration
interface Serial1
 ip address 10.148.13.13 255.255.255.248
 random-detect dscp-based
 random-detect dscp 0 20 30
 ip rsvp bandwidth 772 18
 ip rsvp signalling dscp 46
!
router eigrp 32074
 network 10.148.13.8 0.0.0.7
 no auto-summary
 no eigrp log-neighbor-changes
!
voice-port 2/0
 connection plar 5558810
!
voice-port 2/1
!
dial-peer voice 5554668 pots
 destination-pattern 5554668
 port 2/0
!
dial-peer voice 5558810 voip
 destination-pattern 5558810
 session target ipv4:172.17.15.6
 req-qos guaranteed-delay
 acc-qos controlled-load
 codec g723ar63
 ip qos dscp ef signalling
```

```
Astro Router Configuration
interface Serial0
 ip address 10.148.13.10 255.255.255.248
 random-detect dscp-based
 random-detect dscp 0 20 30
 clockrate 1300000
 ip rsvp bandwidth 772 18
!
interface ATM0
 no ip address
 no atm ilmi-keepalive
 ip rsvp bandwidth 772 18
!
interface ATM0.20 multipoint
 ip address 10.14.168.65 255.255.255.252
 map-group atm
 atm pvc 20 6 65 aal5snap
 ip rsvp bandwidth 772 18
```

continues

Example 5-39 *The Complete Configurations for Lab 5 (Continued)*

```
!
router eigrp 32074
 network 10.14.168.64 0.0.0.3
 network 10.148.13.8 0.0.0.7
 neighbor 10.14.168.66 ATM0.20
 no auto-summary
!
map-list atm
 ip 10.14.168.66 atm-vc 20 broadcast
```

```
Jane Router Configuration
interface TokenRing0
 ip address 10.82.16.22 255.255.255.248
 ring-speed 16
 ip rsvp bandwidth 772 18
!
interface ATM0
 no ip address
 no atm ilmi-keepalive
 ip rsvp bandwidth 772 18
!
interface ATM0.20 multipoint
 ip address 10.14.168.66 255.255.255.252
 map-group atm
 atm pvc 20 6 66 aal5snap
 ip rsvp bandwidth 772 18
!
router eigrp 32074
 network 10.14.168.64 0.0.0.3
 network 10.82.16.16 0.0.0.7
 neighbor 10.14.168.65 ATM0.20
 no auto-summary
!
map-list atm
 ip 10.14.168.65 atm-vc 20 broadcast
```

```
George Router Configuration
interface Ethernet0/0
 ip address 172.17.15.3 255.255.255.248
 ip rsvp bandwidth 772 18
!
interface TokenRing0/0
 ip address 10.82.16.17 255.255.255.248
 ring-speed 16
 ip rsvp bandwidth 772 18
!
router eigrp 32074
 network 10.82.16.16 0.0.0.7
 network 172.17.15.0 0.0.0.7
 no auto-summary
```

Example 5-39 *The Complete Configurations for Lab 5 (Continued)*

```
Judy Router Configuration
interface FastEthernet0
 ip address 172.17.15.6 255.255.255.248
 ip rsvp bandwidth 772 18
 ip rsvp signalling dscp 46
!
router eigrp 32074
 network 172.17.15.0 0.0.0.7
 no auto-summary
!
voice-port 2/0
 connection plar 5554668
!
voice-port 2/1
!
dial-peer voice 5558810 pots
 destination-pattern 5558810
 port 2/0
!
dial-peer voice 5554668 voip
 destination-pattern 5554668
 session target ipv4:10.148.13.13
 req-qos guaranteed-delay
 acc-qos controlled-load
 codec g723ar63
 ip qos dscp ef signalling
```

Further Reading

RFC 1122, *Requirements for Internet Hosts—Communication Layers*, by Robert Braden.

RFC 1349, *Type of Service in the Internet Protocol Suite*, by Philip Almquist.

RFC 2205, *Resource ReSerVation Protocol (RSVP)—Version 1 Functional Specification*, by Bob Braden, Lixia Zhang, Steve Berson, Shai Herzog, and Sugih Jamin.

RFC 2309, *Recommendations on Queue Management and Congestion Avoidance in the Internet*, by Craig Partridge, Larry Peterson, K. K. Ramakrishna, Scott Shaker, John Wroclawski, and Lixia Zhang.

RFC 2474, *Definition of the Differentiated Services Field (DS Field) in the IPv4 and IPv6 Headers*, by Kathleen Nichols, Steven Blake, Fred Baker, and David L. Black.

RFC 2475, *An Architecture for Differentiated Services,* by Steven Blake, David L. Black, Mark A. Carlson, Elwyn Davies, Zheng Wang, and Walter Weiss.

RFC 2597, *Assured Forwarding PHB Group*, by Juha Heinanen, Fred Baker, Walter Weiss, and John Wroclawski.

RFC 2598, *An Expedited Forwarding PHB*, by Van Jacobson, Kathleen Nichols, and Kedarnath Poduri.

RFC 2697, *A Single Rate Three Color Marker*, by Juha Heinanen and Roch Guerin.

Douskalis, Bill. *Putting VoIP to Work, Softswitch Network Design and Testing*.

Douskalis, Bill. *IP Telephony*.

Huston, Geoff. *Internet Performance Survival Guide*.

Ibe, Oliver C. *Converged Network Architectures*.

CHAPTER 6

QoS — Rate Limiting and Queuing Traffic

The preceding two chapters discussed router performance management, equipment-quality management, ATM quality of service (QoS), Layer 3 switching methods, compression, applying end-to-end QoS with integrated services, and marking traffic priority with differentiated services. After you have applied these QoS methods, you then need to consider the most effective queuing mechanism for each specific traffic type. Each interface uses some type of queuing; the type you decide to use will depend on the amount of control over traffic your service policies require, the link bandwidth, and the traffic-quality requirements. This chapter discusses various queuing methods and their application, including the following:

- First-In, First-Out Queuing
- Weighted Fair Queuing
- Priority Queuing
- Custom Queuing

After covering "the basic four" queuing types, this chapter explores more advanced traffic shaping, queuing, policing, and marking technologies, such as the following:

- Generic traffic shaping
- Class-Based Weighted Fair Queuing
- Class-based shaping
- Traffic policing
- Low Latency Queuing
- Setting IP RTP Priority
- Using committed access rate to enforce traffic policy

The Basics: FIFO Queuing

First-in, first-out (FIFO) queuing is the default queuing strategy that applies to all interfaces with more than 2 Mbps, or, in other words, E1 size or greater interfaces. With the FIFO Queuing strategy, packets are forwarded through the interface in the order that they are received. For example, Figure 6-1 shows three traffic conversations, or flows. Conversation A consists of Telnet packets that are approximately 64 bytes; packets in conversation B are from a network application, and range from 750 and 1020 bytes; and packets from conversation C are HTTP web traffic packets, which are approximately 1500 bytes. When these three host stations send packets during periods of low network traffic utilization, all three conversations should be successful; if these same three conversations take place during a period of high network utilization, however, packets from conversation C will be interspersed between the much smaller packets from the A and B conversations, which could potentially cause jittery behavior from the Telnet session.

In most situations, when network application traffic is within the line interface limits, there are usually no problems running FIFO Queuing; when an interface begins to encounter periods of high congestion, or has a high concentration of larger-sized packets, however, FIFO Queuing might pose problems to protocols that use smaller packet sizes or applications that are not tolerant of network delay. Real-time applications, such as voice and video applications, are also highly sensitive to *serialization delay*, the time it takes an interface to serialize packets; these applications typically do not run well when interspersed with other data traffic on low-speed serial interfaces.

Figure 6-1   *Example of FIFO Queuing*

Therefore, when an interface is consistently meeting or exceeding its bandwidth limitations, or in environments where networks experience frequent traffic bursts, a more advanced queuing mechanism might be required.

Weighed Fair Queuing

Based on the min-max fair-share algorithm, *Weighed Fair Queuing (WFQ)* is the default queuing method for interfaces with bandwidth less than E1 speed (2048 kbps).

The min-max fair-share algorithm allocates resources based on demand in a round-robin queuing system. With the min-max fair-share algorithm, smaller packets are transmitted before larger packets. Packets waiting to be transmitted are queued, based on an equation that takes the capacity of available resource bandwidth and divides it by the number of packets waiting to be queued:

$$\text{Fair allocation} = \frac{\text{(resource capability} - \text{resource already allocated)}}{\text{Number of packets}}$$

One thing that sets the Cisco WFQ algorithm apart from the min-max fair-share algorithm is that WFQ bases its weight measurement on the value of the IP Precedence field from the IP header. The WFQ algorithm attempts to use this to fairly balance the load between large and small packets by weighing the packet size and considering the precedence of the packet. For a packet with an IP precedence value of 0, the default routine precedence, the weight is found using the following formula:

$$Weight = \frac{32768}{(IP\ Precedence + 1)}$$

Table 6-1 shows the values used to generate weight values based on IP precedence values.

Table 6-1   *Weight Table*

IP Precedence Value	Weight
0	32,768
1	16,384
2	10,923
3	8192
4	6554
5	5461
6	4681
7	4096

NOTE   In earlier versions of Cisco IOS Software, prior to IOS Release 12.0(5)T, weight was calculated using a different base value. To find the weight value for older Cisco IOS versions, replace the 32768 value with 4096, as shown here:

```
Weight = 4096 ( IP Precedence + 1)
```

When stations communicate using source and destination IP addresses, IP protocols, and TCP or UDP port numbers, this is considered a *flow*. WFQ uses two flow types: active flows, which are active conversations with packets waiting to be transmitted; and inactive flows, which are new conversations that have not been seen before, or idle flows from completed conversations. During the WFQ process, packet size is noted when new packets arrive. If the IP flow that they belong to is new, a rounded packet size is also used. Together, the packet size, the rounded packet size, and the value of the IP Precedence field are used to generate a sequence number. Lower sequence numbers are transmitted first. After the weight has been found, a sequence number is generated for each packet waiting to be queued. Note that the IP precedence value for a flow is considered only for the first packet in a flow; subsequent packets use the weight of the first packet:

Sequence number for inactive flow	SN = (P * W) + R
Sequence number for active flow	SN = W + RN

SN = Sequence Number

P = Packet size (bytes)

W = Weight

R = Rounded packet size

RN = Sequence number of last packet in an active flow

Figure 6-2 shows how the packets from different flows are queued and forwarded using WFQ. In this example, there are flows from four conversations: conversation A, with two 1024-byte packets with an IP precedence value of one, labeled A1 and A2; conversation B, with three 64-byte packets with the default IP precedence value of 0; conversation C, with four 64-byte packets with an IP precedence of 5; and conversation D, with one 768-byte packet with an IP precedence value of 0. The packets arrive at the WFQ router in the order shown on the right side of the figure: C-1, A-1, B-1, B-2, C-2, C-3, C-4, A-2, B-3, and D-1. Because packet C-1 arrives at the WFQ router first, it is the first packet for which the sequence number needs to be calculated. Packet C-1 is assigned a sequence number of 35,010, by applying the inactive flow formula shown in Example 6-1.

Figure 6-2 *Weighted Fair Queuing Diagram*

Example 6-1 *Math Behind WFQ and the C Packets*

```
Packets C-1 is 64 bytes with IP Precedence = 5

        Weight = 32768/5+1
        Weight = 5461
        SN = (64 x 5461) + 60
        SN = 349504 + 60
        SN = 349564
Packet C-2 is 64 bytes
```

Example 6-1 *Math Behind WFQ and the C Packets (Continued)*

```
              SN = 5461 + 349564
              SN = 355025

Packet C-3 is 64 bytes:

              SN = 5461 + 355025
              SN = 360486

Packet C-4 is 64 bytes:

              SN = 5461 + 360486
              SN = 365947
```

In this example, packet C-1, a 64-byte packet with an IP precedence value of 5, is assigned a weight of 5461. The weight for this example is found by applying the Weight = 32,768 / (Precedence + 1) formula, and the sequence number is found by using the SN = (P * W) + R formula for inactive flows mentioned earlier in this chapter. Any new packets that arrive for the C conversation will use the SN = W + RN formula to calculate the sequence number for an active flow. The sequence numbers for packets C-2, C-3, and C-4 are found using the active flow formula just mentioned. The next packet, packet C-2, uses the weight and sequence number from packet C-1, W = 5461 and RN = 349,564 to yield a new sequence number of 355,025 for packet C-2. Example 6-2 shows how the sequence number is found for packet A-1 and A-2.

Example 6-2 *Calculating the Sequence Number for Packets A-1 and A-2*

```
Packet A-1 is 1024 bytes with IP Precedence =  0
        Weight = 32768/0+1
        Weight = 32768
        SN = (1024 x 32768) + 1000
        SN = 33554432 + 1000
        SN = 33555432

Packet A-2 is 1024:

        SN = 32768 + 33555432
        SN = 33588200
```

Because the A conversation is a new flow, the WFQ router calculates the sequence number for packet A-1 using the inactive flow formula, which yields a weight of 32,768, and a sequence number of 33,555,432. The weight and sequence number from packet A-1 is used to help find the sequence number for packet A-2, using the active flow formula, SN = W + RN, or 32,768 + 33,555,432 = 33,588,200. Packet B-1, a new flow, uses the inactive flow formula, and packets B-2 and B-3 use the active flow formula shown in Example 6-3.

Example 6-3   *Finding the Sequence Number for Packets B-1, B-2, and B-3*

```
Packets B-1 is 64 bytes with IP Precedence = 0

        Weight = 32768
        SN = (64 x 32768) + 60
        SN = 2097152 + 60
        SN = 2097212

Packet B-2 is 64 bytes

        SN = 32768 + 2097212
        SN = 2129980
Packet B-3 is 64 bytes:

        SN = 32768 + 2129980
        SN = 2162748
```

The sequence number for packet D is shown next, in Example 6-4.

Example 6-4   *Sequence Number for Packet D-1*

```
Packet D-1 is 768 bytes with IP Precedence = 0

        Weight = 32768
        SN = (768 x 32768) + 700
        SN = 25165824 + 700
        SN = 25166524
```

When all the information from the last few packets is put together, you end up with the outcome shown in Table 6-2.

Table 6-2   *Order in Which Packets Are Transmitted*

Packet Name	Sequence Number
C-1	349,564
C-2	355,025
C-3	360,486
C-4	365,947
B-1	2,097,212
B-2	2,129,980
B-3	2,162,748
D-1	25,166,524
A-1	33,555,432
A-2	33,588,200

The sequence numbers in the preceding table are applied to each packet as it is scheduled for transmission on the WFQ interface, and packets are transmitted in order of smallest to greatest sequence number, as shown in Figure 6-3. The smaller packets with higher priority and smaller sequence number are transmitted first, whereas larger packets with routine priority and larger sequence number must wait for smaller packets to be transmitted. WFQ excels in environments where there are conversations consisting of smaller packets or packets of high IP precedence requiring real-time transmission speeds (Telnet packets, for instance).

Figure 6-3   *Transmit Order for WFQ Packets*

As mentioned earlier, WFQ is the default queuing method on interfaces E1 size or smaller. If WFQ has been disabled, you can easily re-enable it by using the **fair-queue** command. Table 6-3 shows the **fair-queue** command arguments and their descriptions.

```
fair-queue [congestive-discard-threshold] [dynamic-queues] [reservable-queues]
```

Table 6-3   **fair-queue** *Command Arguments*

Argument	Description
congestive-discard-threshold	(Optional) The number of packets allowed in each queue. Range from 1 to 4096. Default congestive discard threshold is 64.
dynamic-queues	(Optional) The number of dynamic queues that can be created. Values range from 0 to 4096 in powers of 2 beginning with 16 (16, 32, 64, 128, 256, 512, 1024, 2048, and 4096). The default number of dynamic queues is 256.
reservable-queues	(Optional) When RSVP has been enabled, the number of reservable queues can be configured. Range from 0 to 1000. By default, there are no reservable queues.

To enable WFQ with the default queue sizes, you can just type the **fair-queue** command with no arguments, and WFQ will be enabled with the default queue size of packets and 256 dynamic queues. To remove WFQ, which changes the queuing method to FIFO, type **no fair-queue**. To view the current queuing method in use on an interface, use the **show interface** command. The individual queuing values were shown earlier in Table 6-3 and are highlighted in Example 6-5.

Example 6-5   *Display Queuing Configuration*

```
Vacation# show interface serial 0/1
Serial0/1 is up, line protocol is up
  Hardware is PowerQUICC Serial
  MTU 1500 bytes, BW 1544 Kbit, DLY 20000 usec,
     reliability 255/255, txload 1/255, rxload 1/255
  Encapsulation HDLC, loopback not set
  Keepalive set (10 sec)
  Last input 00:00:09, output 00:00:03, output hang never
  Last clearing of "show interface" counters never
  Input queue: 0/75/0 (size/max/drops); Total output drops: 0
  Queueing strategy: weighted fair
  Output queue: 0/1000/64/0 (size/max total/threshold/drops)
     Conversations  0/1/256 (active/max active/max total)
     Reserved Conversations 0/0 (allocated/max allocated)
```

To limit the display of queuing information, you can also use the **show queueing interface**
command, which shows queuing information for a particular interface. As shown in Example 6-6,
this command displays the same queuing information as is available using the **show interface**
command.

Example 6-6   **show queueing interface** *Command*

```
Vacation# show queueing interface serial 0/1
  Input queue: 0/75/0 (size/max/drops); Total output drops: 0
  Queueing strategy: weighted fair
  Output queue: 0/1000/64/0 (size/max total/threshold/drops)
     Conversations  0/1/256 (active/max active/max total)
     Reserved Conversations 0/0 (allocated/max allocated)
```

When the **show queueing** command is used without any arguments, it displays all the queuing
methods in use on each interface in a router and the queuing configurations. When the **fair**
argument is used with this command, the output displays only information about WFQ, as show
in Example 6-7.

NOTE   The **show queueing** command does not display all queuing information for FIFO Queuing; this
information is shown using the **show interface** command.

Example 6-7   **show queueing** *Command*

```
Vacation# show queueing
Current fair queue configuration:
  Interface          Discard     Dynamic     Reserved
```

Example 6-7 show queueing *Command (Continued)*

```
                       threshold    queue count  queue count
  Serial0/0            64           256          0
  Serial0/1            64           256          0
  Serial0/2            64           256          0
Current priority queue configuration:
Current custom queue configuration:
Current random-detect configuration:
Router#show queueing fair
Current fair queue configuration:
  Interface            Discard      Dynamic      Reserved
                       threshold    queue count  queue count
  Serial0/0            64           256          0
  Serial0/1            64           256          0
  Serial0/2            64           256          0
```

Sometimes, certain applications require real-time transmission speeds or are intolerant of the delays incurred by queuing traffic. If this is the case, you might need to remove WFQ or tune the queue sizes. Example 6-8 shows how the queue size on the Boston router is changed so that there are only 32 possible dynamic queues, and each queue will only hold 48 packets.

Example 6-8 *Boston Router Queuing Configuration*

```
Boston(config)# interface serial 0/1
Boston(config-if)# fair-queue 48 32
Boston(config-if)#^Z
Boston# show interface serial 0/1
Serial0/1 is up, line protocol is up
  Hardware is PowerQUICC Serial
  MTU 1500 bytes, BW 1544 Kbit, DLY 20000 usec,
      reliability 255/255, txload 1/255, rxload 1/255
  Encapsulation HDLC, loopback not set
  Keepalive set (10 sec)
  Last input 00:00:05, output 00:00:07, output hang never
  Last clearing of "show interface" counters never
  Input queue: 0/75/0 (size/max/drops); Total output drops: 0
  Queueing strategy: weighted fair
  Output queue: 0/1000/48/0 (size/max total/threshold/drops)
     Conversations  0/0/32 (active/max active/max total)
     Reserved Conversations 0/0 (allocated/max allocated)
  5 minute input rate 0 bits/sec, 0 packets/sec
  5 minute output rate 0 bits/sec, 0 packets/sec
     455 packets input, 26845 bytes, 0 no buffer
     Received 455 broadcasts, 0 runts, 0 giants, 0 throttles
     3 input errors, 0 CRC, 3 frame, 0 overrun, 0 ignored, 0 abort
     457 packets output, 31892 bytes, 0 underruns
     0 output errors, 0 collisions, 7 interface resets
     0 output buffer failures, 0 output buffers swapped out
     2 carrier transitions
     DCD=up  DSR=up  DTR=up  RTS=up  CTS=up
```

NOTE	Before changing queue sizes, always perform a detailed traffic analysis and test the configuration to avoid causing production-network problems.

As you learned in the preceding chapter, WFQ is required to run other QoS features, such as WRED and Resource Reservation Protocol (RSVP). WFQ is also the foundation of Low Latency Queuing (LLQ) and Class-Based Weighted Fair queuing (CBWFQ), so it is important to understand how WFQ and traffic-classification and marking technologies work.

Priority Queuing

When situations call for a queuing scheme that allows certain applications to have priority over all others, Priority Queuing (PQ) should be considered. PQ has four queues, each with a different priority; packets from each queue are forwarded after the queue with the highest priority has emptied. With PQ, you have four queue priorities: High, Medium, Normal, and Low. Within each queue, packets are forwarded on a first-in, first-out basis. Keep in mind a few things when using PQ:

- The queue size does not necessarily affect the amount of forwarding time that packets in that queue receive. The limit of the queue size for PQ is configured in packets. Each queue is served in order of priority. The High priority queue is always served first; then, if the High priority queue is empty, the Medium queue is emptied. Anytime a packet is received in the High queue, that queue is emptied before processing any other queues. After the Medium priority queue is emptied, if there are not any packets in the High priority queue, the Normal queue is emptied. Finally, if the High, Medium, and Normal queues are empty, the Low priority queue is emptied. So, there is a possibility that when PQ is in use, packets in lower-priority queues will not be forwarded in a timely manner, adding delay for applications with packets that use the lower-priority protocols, causing network applications to time out.

- If a packet does not match any of the configured queues, that packet goes to the default queue, which is the Normal queue. You can change the default queue, as shown later in this chapter.

- PQ is not dynamic; it does not adjust to network patterns. When PQ is in use, it is a good idea to periodically perform network baselines and analyze traffic to make sure that the queue sizes and protocol distributions are configured correctly to handle traffic at peak times.

Table 6-4 shows how each of the four priority queues is serviced.

Table 6-4   *Priority Queues*

Queue	Description
High	Packets arriving in the High priority queue are serviced immediately. After the High priority queue has been emptied, the Medium, Normal, and Low priority queues are serviced. If at any time packets arrive for the High priority queue, they are forwarded before any other queue receives service, until the High priority queue has been emptied. The default size of the High priority queue is 20 packets.
Medium	After the High priority queue has been emptied, the Medium queue is serviced. If any packets arrive for the High priority queue while the Medium priority queue is forwarding, the packets in the High priority queue are forwarded first, until the queue is empty, and then the Medium queue receives attention again. The default size of the Medium priority queue is 40 packets.
Normal	If there are no packets in the High or Medium queues, the Normal queue is serviced. If packets arrive in the High or Medium queues, they are forwarded in order of High to Medium, and after those queues have emptied, packets in the Normal queue are forwarded. The default size of the Normal priority queue is 60 packets. By default, all unspecified traffic is assigned to the Normal priority queue; however, you can change this behavior by using the **default** argument.
Low	Packets in the Low priority queue are forwarded if all the other queues are empty. If a packet arrives in any of the other queues, those queues are cleared first in order of priority, until they are empty, and then the Low priority queue is serviced again. The default size of the Low priority queue is 80 packets.

Figure 6-4 shows how packets are queued when PQ is in effect.

Figure 6-4 *Priority Queuing Diagram*

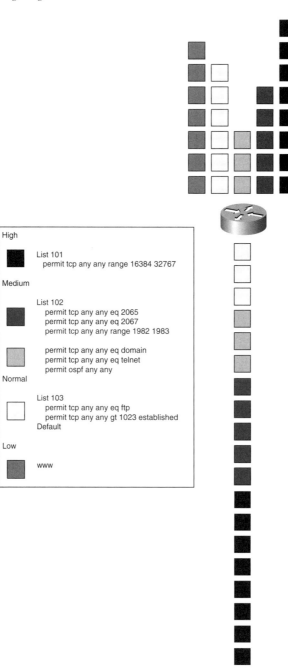

To configure PQ, you use the **priority-list** command to create a priority list. You can configure up to 16 different priority lists. Each list contains the four queues: High, Medium, Normal, and Low. Packets are assigned to one of the four queues based on their characteristics: protocol, ingress interface, packet size, and so on. Traffic that has not been defined in one of the four queues is sent to the default queue, which, unless explicitly configured otherwise, is the Normal queue. Table 6-5 shows the **priority-list** command, its arguments, keywords, and their descriptions.

Table 6-5   **priority-list** *Command and Descriptions*

Command	Argument	Description
`priority-list list-number default {high I medium normal I low}`	None	Defines the default queue for the specified priority queue list number. The default queue is where packets that do not match any other statement are sent. If unspecified, the default queue is the Normal queue.
`priority-list list-number interface interface-number {high I medium I normal I low}`	None	Specifies that any traffic from the particular ingress interface is the traffic to be prioritized and the queue that those packets should be assigned to.
`priority-list list-number protocol argument`	`arp {high I medium I normal I low} [gt frame-size I lt frame-size]`	Specifies the ARP protocol. Specifies High, Medium, Normal, or Low queue. (Optional) **gt** specifies a frame size greater than the specified ARP frame size, ranging from 0 to 65,535. (Optional) **lt** specifies a frame size less than the specified ARP frame size, ranging from 0 to 65,535.
	`bridge {high I medium I normal I low} [gt frame-size I list access-list-number I lt frame-size]`	Specifies transparent bridging protocols. Specifies High, Medium, Normal, or Low queue. (Optional) **gt** specifies a frame size greater than the specified frame size, ranging from 0 to 65,535. (Optional) **list** specifies an associated access list (200-299) should be used for traffic designations. (Optional) **lt** specifies a frame size less than the specified frame size, ranging from 0 to 65,535.

continues

Table 6-5   **priority-list** *Command and Descriptions (Continued)*

Command	Argument	Description
priority-list *list-number* **protocol** *argument* (*Continued*)	**bstun** {high I medium I normal I low} [address *BSTUN-group-number hex-address* I gt *frame-size* I lt *frame-size*]	Specifies the Block Serial Tunnel (BSTUN) protocol.
		Specifies High, Medium, Normal, or Low queue.
		(Optional) **address** specifies a particular BSTUN group number, ranging from 1 to 255, and an address in hexadecimal.
		(Optional) **gt** specifies a frame size greater than the specified BSTUN frame size, ranging from 0 to 65,535.
		(Optional) **lt** specifies a frame size less than the specified BSTUN frame size, ranging from 0 to 65,535.
	cdp {high I medium I normal I low} [gt *frame-size* I lt *frame-size*]	Specifies the Cisco Discovery Protocol (CDP).
		Specifies High, Medium, Normal, or Low queue.
		(Optional) **gt** specifies a frame size greater than the specified CDP frame size, ranging from 0 to 65,535.
		(Optional) **lt** specifies a frame size less than the specified CDP frame size, ranging from 0 to 65,535.
	compressedtcp high I medium I normal I low} [gt *frame-size* I lt *frame-size*]	Specifies compressed TCP traffic as the protocol.
		Specifies High, Medium, Normal, or Low queue.
		(Optional) **gt** specifies a frame size greater than the specified frame size, ranging from 0 to 65,535.
		(Optional) **lt** specifies a frame size less than the specified frame size, ranging from 0 to 65,535.
	dlsw {high I medium I normal I low} [gt *frame-size*] [lt *frame-size*]	Specifies DLSw as the protocol.
		Specifies High, Medium, Normal, or Low queue.
		(Optional) **gt** specifies a frame size greater than the specified frame size, ranging from 0 to 65,535.
		(Optional) **lt** specifies a frame size less than the specified frame size, ranging from 0 to 65,535.

Table 6-5   **priority-list** *Command and Descriptions (Continued)*

Command	Argument	Description
`priority-list` *`list-number`* `protocol` *`argument`* (*Continued*)	`ip` {high | medium | normal | low} [fragments | gt *frame-size* | list *access-list-number* | lt *frame-size* | tcp *port-number* | udp *port-number*]	Specifies a protocol from the TCP/IP suite as the protocol.
		Specifies High, Medium, Normal, or Low queue.
		(Optional) **fragment** specifies the prioritization of IP packet fragments, that is, IP packets with the Fragment Offset field set to 1.
		(Optional) **gt** specifies a frame size greater than the specified frame size, ranging from 0 to 65,535.
		(Optional) **list** specifies an associated access list (1–199) that should be used for traffic designations.
		(Optional) **lt** specifies a frame size less than the specified frame size, ranging from 0 to 65,535.
		(Optional) **tcp** specifies that traffic from or to a particular TCP port as the designated traffic.
		Ranges are port numbers 0 to 65,535 or a keyword from the following list:
		bgp, **chargen**, **cmd**, **daytime**, **discard**, **domain**, **echo**, **exec**, **finger**, **ftp**, **ftp-data**, **gopher**, **hostname**, **ident**, **irc**, **klogin**, **kshell**, **login**, **lpd**, **nntp**, **pim-auto-rp**, **pop2**, **pop3**, **smtp**, **sunrpc**, **syslog**, **tacacs**, **talk**, **telnet**, **time**, **uucp**, **whois**, and **www**
		(Optional) **udp** specifies that traffic from or to a particular UDP port is the designated traffic.
		Ranges are port numbers 0 to 65,535 or a keyword from the following list:
		biff, **bootpc**, **bootps**, **discard**, **dnsix**, **domain**, **echo**, **isakmp**, **mobile-ip**, **nameserver**, **netbios-dgm**, **netbios-ns**, **netbios-ss**, **ntp**, **pim-auto-rp**, **rip**, **snmp**, **snmptrap**, **sunrpc**, **syslog**, **tacacs**, **talk**, **tftp**, **time**, **who**, or **xdmcp**

continues

Table 6-5 **priority-list** *Command and Descriptions (Continued)*

Command	Argument	Description
`priority-list` *`list-number`* `protocol` *`argument`* (*Continued*)	`ipx` {high I medium I normal I low} [gt *frame-size*] [list *list-number*] [lt *frame-size*]	Specifies the IPX protocol. (Optional) **gt** specifies a frame size greater than the specified IPX frame size, ranging from 0 to 65,535. (Optional) **list** specifies an IPX standard or extended access list (800–999). (Optional) **lt** specifies a frame size less than the specified IPX frame size, ranging from 0 to 65,535.
	`llc2` {high I medium I normal I low} [gt *frame-size*] [lt *frame-size*]	Specifies the Logical Link Control, Type-2 (LLC2) protocol. Specifies High, Medium, Normal, or Low queue. (Optional) **gt** specifies a frame size greater than the specified frame size, ranging from 0 to 65,535. (Optional) **lt** specifies a frame size less than the specified frame size, ranging from 0 to 65,535.
	`pad` {high I medium I normal I low}[gt *frame-size*] [lt *frame-size*]	Specifies the X.25 Packet Assembler/Disassembler (PAD) protocol. Specifies High, Medium, Normal, or Low queue. (Optional) **gt** specifies a frame size greater than the specified frame size, ranging from 0 to 65,535. (Optional) **lt** specifies a frame size less than the specified frame size, ranging from 0 to 65,535.
	`qllc` {high I medium I normal I low}[gt *frame-size*] [lt *frame-size*]	Specifies the Qualified Logical Link Control (QLLC) protocol. Specifies High, Medium, Normal, or Low queue. (Optional) **gt** specifies a frame size greater than the specified frame size, ranging from 0 to 65,535. (Optional) **lt** specifies a frame size less than the specified frame size, ranging from 0 to 65,535.
	`rsrb` {high I medium I normal I low}[gt *frame-size*] [lt *frame-size*]	Specifies the Remote Source Route Bridging (RSRB) protocol. Specifies High, Medium, Normal, or Low queue. (Optional) **gt** specifies a frame size greater than the specified frame size, ranging from 0 to 65,535. (Optional) **lt** specifies a frame size less than the specified frame size, ranging from 0 to 65,535.

Table 6-5   **priority-list** *Command and Descriptions (Continued)*

Command	Argument	Description
`priority-list list-number` `protocol argument` (*Continued*)	`snapshot {high	medium	` `normal	low}[gt frame-` `size] [lt frame-size]`	Specifies Snapshot routing traffic. Specifies High, Medium, Normal, or Low queue. (Optional) **gt** specifies a frame size greater than the specified frame size, ranging from 0 to 65,535. (Optional) **lt** specifies a frame size less than the specified frame size, ranging from 0 to 65,535.
	`stun {high	medium |` `normal	low}[address` `STUN-group STUN-address |` `gt frame-size	lt frame-` `size]`	Specifies the Serial Tunneling (STUN) protocol. Specifies High, Medium, Normal, or Low queue. (Optional) **address** specifies the STUN group number, ranging from 0 to 255, and a hexadecimal STUN address, which must be written in hexadecimal form (for example, 0x01). (Optional) **gt** specifies a frame size greater than the specified frame size, ranging from 0 to 65,535. (Optional) **lt** specifies a frame size less than the specified frame size, ranging from 0 to 65,535.

`priority-list list-number`
`queue-limit`
	`high-queue-limit medium-`
	`queue-limit normal-queue-`
	`limit low-queue-limit`
		Changes the individual queue size limits for each of the priorities (High, Medium, Normal, and Low) for the PQ list number.

As just shown, PQ enables you to classify traffic in different ways:

- **Protocol type**—This includes the major protocol type, such as IP or IPX, and any subprotocol information, such as TCP or UDP port numbers.
- **Interface**—The interface from which the traffic is coming.
- **Packet size**—The size of the packet, either greater or less than a specified value, including the MAC encapsulation, in bytes.
- **Fragments**—Fragmented packets.
- **Multiple criteria**—Using an access list to define more than one traffic attribute.

PQ configuration requires three steps: define the queue assignments, customize the queuing configuration, and apply the configuration to an interface:

Step 1   Define the queues. Using the **priority-list** command, specify the protocol attribute or interface for each of the four priority queues. In this example, access-list 188 defines GRE and NTP packets; these packets are assigned to the High priority queue, Telnet packets are assigned to the Medium priority queue, SMTP packets are assigned to the Normal priority queue, and HTTP web packets are considered low priority and sent to the Low priority queue using the **priority-list** command:

```
access-list 188 permit gre any any
access-list 188 permit udp any any eq ntp
priority-list 1  protocol ip high list 188
priority-list 1  protocol ip medium tcp telnet
priority-list 1  protocol ip normal tcp smtp
priority-list 1  protocol ip low tcp www
```

Step 2   Customize queuing configuration. Configure the default queue for unassigned packets. If a default queue is not explicitly defined, all undefined packets are sent to the Normal queue:

```
Bart(config)# priority-list 7 default medium
```

Optionally, you can change sizes for the four queues. The **queue-limit** command enables you to define the sizes, in packets, for each of the queues using the **priority-list** *list-number* queue-limit *high-limit medium-limit normal-limit low-limit* command:

```
Bart(config)# priority-list 7 queue-limit 40 20 30 20
```

Step 3   Assign the priority list to an interface. Tunnels and subinterfaces might not be configured for PQ:

```
interface Serial0/1
 ip address 10.2.1.1 255.255.255.0
 priority-group 7
```

To view the configuration of PQ on an interface, use the **show interface** command:

```
Queueing strategy: priority-list 7
Output queue (queue priority: size/max/drops):
   high: 34/40/54, medium: 0/20/0, normal: 0/30/0, low: 0/20/0
```

Example 6-9 shows how PQ was used to give voice traffic the greatest priority. Data-link switching (DLSw), Domain Name System (DNS), Telnet, and Open Shortest Path First (OSPF) traffic receive medium priority, and FTP and any other unspecified traffic wait in the Normal priority queue. In this example, World Wide Web traffic is of the lowest priority. Example 6-10 shows how this configuration looks using the **show queueing priority** command.

Example 6-9   *Priority Queuing in Action*

```
interface Serial0/1
 ip address 158.42.18.12 255.255.255.0
 priority-group 1
!
access-list 101 remark High Priority Queue - voice traffic
access-list 101 permit udp any any range 16384 32767
access-list 101 permit tcp any any eq 1720
access-list 102 remark Medium Priority Queue - DLSw, DNS, Telnet, OSPF
access-list 102 permit tcp any any eq 2065
access-list 102 permit tcp any any eq 2067
access-list 102 permit tcp any any range 1981 1983
```

Example 6-9 *Priority Queuing in Action (Continued)*

```
access-list 102 permit tcp any any eq domain
access-list 102 permit tcp any any eq telnet
access-list 102 permit ospf any any
access-list 103 remark Normal Priority Queue - FTP and established
access-list 103 permit tcp any any eq ftp
access-list 103 permit tcp any any gt 1023 established
priority-list 1 protocol ip high list 101
priority-list 1 protocol ip medium list 102
priority-list 1 protocol ip normal list 103
priority-list 1 protocol ip low tcp www
```

Example 6-10 *Displaying Priority Queuing Configuration Data*

```
Bart# show queueing priority
Current DLCI priority queue configuration:
Current priority queue configuration:
List   Queue  Args
1      high   protocol ip          list 101
1      medium protocol ip          list 102
1      normal protocol ip          list 103
1      low    protocol ip          tcp port www
```

After applying this configuration and waiting for data transmissions, Example 6-11 shows that the High priority queue currently has 34 packets in the queue; the maximum size of the queue in packets is 20, and the High priority queue has dropped 54 packets. However, the Medium, Normal, and Low priority queues are empty and have not dropped any packets. In this case, you might want to obtain further packet analysis to re-adjust the queue sizes for a more even distribution of packets.

Example 6-11 *Showing Priority Queuing with Test Traffic*

```
Bart# show interfaces serial 0/1
Serial0/1 is up, line protocol is up
  Hardware is PowerQUICC Serial
  Internet address is 158.42.18.12/24
  MTU 1500 bytes, BW 1544 Kbit, DLY 20000 usec,
     reliability 255/255, txload 1/255, rxload 1/255
  Encapsulation HDLC, loopback not set
  Keepalive set (10 sec)
  Last input never, output never, output hang never
  Last clearing of "show interface" counters never
  Input queue: 0/75/0/0 (size/max/drops/flushes); Total output drops: 0
  Queueing strategy: priority-list 1
  Output queue (queue priority: size/max/drops):
     high: 34/20/54, medium: 0/40/0, normal: 0/60/0, low: 0/80/0
  5 minute input rate 139000 bits/sec, 7 packets/sec
```

continues

Example 6-11 *Showing Priority Queuing with Test Traffic (Continued)*

```
   5 minute output rate 308000 bits/sec, 33 packets/sec
      4 packets input, 240 bytes, 0 no buffer
      Received 0 broadcasts, 0 runts, 0 giants, 0 throttles
      0 input errors, 0 CRC, 0 frame, 0 overrun, 0 ignored, 0 abort
      228 packets output, 341544 bytes, 0 underruns
      0 output errors, 0 collisions, 0 interface resets
      0 output buffer failures, 0 output buffers swapped out
      0 carrier transitions
      DCD=up  DSR=up  DTR=up  RTS=up  CTS=up
```

Practical Example: Applying Priority Queuing

This lab tests PQ in a real network model using traffic generated by a Windows PC and another Windows server. To test the PQ configuration, you configure the PC and server to send and receive typical TCP/IP network messages by setting up Dynamic Host Configuration Protocol (DHCP), Microsoft Windows Internet Naming Service (WINS), and DNS services on the workstation, and queuing this traffic on the routers between the client workstation and the server.

Lab Exercise

This lab requires two routers, each with one Ethernet or Token Ring interface and one serial interface. The two routers should be configured and cabled, as shown in Figure 6-5. This lab also contains two end stations: one Microsoft Windows server running FTP server, WINS, and DNS services, and one Windows client PC configured to use the Windows server for DNS and WINS services. To validate the queuing configuration, the Windows PC and server are required. If you do not have a PC or server, you can still complete the router configuration portion of the lab. Without traffic-generating software, however, queue sizes are unlikely to increase.

Figure 6-5 *North American Network*

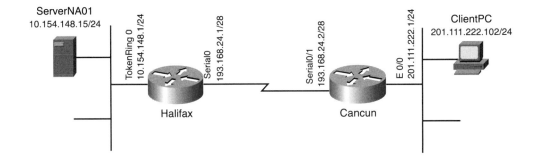

Lab Objectives

In this lab, you learn the following:

- How to configure PQ
- How to test PQ configuration

Equipment Needed

- For this lab, you need two Cisco routers, each with one Ethernet or Token Ring interface and one serial interface.
- One PC running Windows software with a network card running TCP/IP.
- One PC running Windows Server software with a network card running TCP/IP with a DNS, FTP, and WINS server configured.

Physical Layout and Prestaging

- Cable the routers, as shown in Figure 6-5.
- Attach each PC to the network (the router's interface), as shown in Figure 6-5.

Lab Tasks

Step 1   Configure routers, as shown in Figure 6-5. The Halifax router should have an Ethernet or Token Ring interface connected to the server and should connect to the Cancun router over its serial interface. The IP addresses should also be assigned, as shown earlier in Figure 6-5.

Step 2   Configure a Windows server computer to provide DNS, WINS, and FTP services. The server should be configured to use the static IP address of 10.154.148.15/24. FTP clients will connect to the FTP server using passive FTP sessions. Later, a Windows client PC will be configured to use the services of WINS and DNS settings from the server. You can validate TCP/IP services on the client and server computers by using the **ipconfig /all** command at the MS-DOS prompt.

Step 3   Instead of configuring a static IP address, DNS server, and WINS server on the Windows client PC, configure the Cancun router to provide the information using DHCP. Use the following values to configure DHCP:

DHCP scope: 201.111.222.0/24

Default gateway: 201.111.222.1

DHS server: 10.154.148.15

Domain name: cciepsv2.net

WINS Server: 10.154.148.15

Step 4   Configure PQ and any access lists that might be required to support the protocols shown in Table 6-6.

Table 6-6   *Priority Queuing Configuration*

Queue	Protocol
High	DNS WINS
Medium	Windows NetBIOS support NetBIOS session, datagram and name services, and DNS and WINS management SNMP
Normal	Passive-mode FTP
Low	World Wide Web HTTP traffic All unspecified traffic

Step 5   Assign the PQ process to the interface that will queue all client traffic across the WAN connection between the Cancun and Halifax routers. (Remember the rules for efficient traffic queuing on different interface types.)

Step 6   Validate that the client and server computer can ping each other. Using a passive FTP session, copy a file from the client PC to ServerNA01. Try to use FTP to get another file from the server. While copying these files, look at the queuing information from the **show interface** output.

Lab Walkthrough

Step 1   Configure routers, as shown in Figure 6-5. The Halifax router should have an Ethernet interface connected to the server and a serial interface connected to the Cancun router. The IP addresses should also be assigned, as shown earlier in Figure 6-5.

Step 2   Configure a Windows server computer to provide DNS, WINS, and FTP services. The server should be configured to use the static IP address of 10.154.148.15/24. FTP clients will connect to the FTP server using passive FTP sessions. Later, a Windows client PC will be configured to use the services of WINS and DNS settings from the server. You can validate TCP/IP services on the client and server computers by using the **ipconfig /all** command at the MS-DOS prompt.

Example 6-12 shows the output of the **ipconfig /all** command on the server
and PC client computers. If there are any connectivity problems with the
server or client computers, remember to verify that each of the computers is
configured to use the default gateway of the Ethernet interface on the router.
Also, verify that each of the computers can ping its default gateway, each hop
on the way to the other computer, and lastly, the other computer.

Example 6-12 *TCP/IP Configuration for Windows Server and Client Computers*

```
The Server
C:\>ipconfig /all
Windows 2000 IP Configuration
        Host Name . . . . . . . . . . . . : ServerNA01
        Primary DNS Suffix  . . . . . . . : cciepsv2.net
        Node Type . . . . . . . . . . . . : Hybrid
        IP Routing Enabled. . . . . . . . : No
        WINS Proxy Enabled. . . . . . . . : No
Ethernet adapter Local Area Connection:
        Connection-specific DNS Suffix  . :
        Description . . . . . . . . . . . : FEM656C-3Com Global 8-100+56K CardB
us PC Card-(Fast Ethernet) #2
        Physical Address. . . . . . . . . : 00-50-DA-AC-5D-4C
        DHCP Enabled. . . . . . . . . . . : No
        IP Address. . . . . . . . . . . . : 10.154.148.15
        Subnet Mask . . . . . . . . . . . : 255.255.255.0
        Default Gateway . . . . . . . . . : 10.154.148.1
        DNS Servers . . . . . . . . . . . : 10.154.148.15
        Primary WINS Server . . . . . . . : 10.154.148.15
The Client
C:\>ipconfig /all
Windows 98 IP Configuration
        Host Name . . . . . . . . . : clientpc.cciepsv2.net
        DNS Servers . . . . . . . . : 10.154.148.15
        Node Type . . . . . . . . . : Hybrid
        NetBIOS Scope ID. . . . . . :
        IP Routing Enabled. . . . . : No
        WINS Proxy Enabled. . . . . : No
        NetBIOS Resolution Uses DNS : Yes
0 Ethernet adapter :
        Description . . . . . . . . : Xircom Ethernet 10/100 + Modem 56 PC Card
        Physical Address. . . . . . : 00-80-C7-1D-12-A7
        DHCP Enabled. . . . . . . . : Yes
        IP Address. . . . . . . . . : 201.111.222.102
        Subnet Mask . . . . . . . . : 255.255.255.0
        Default Gateway . . . . . . : 201.111.222.1
        DHCP Server . . . . . . . . : 201.111.222.1
        Primary WINS Server . . . . : 10.154.148.15
        Secondary WINS Server . . . :
        Lease Obtained. . . . . . . : 01 07 02 7:23:30 PM
        Lease Expires . . . . . . . : 01 08 02 7:23:30 PM
```

NOTE	In Windows 95, the **ipconfig** command does not exist. To verify the TCP/IP configuration in Windows 95, use the **winipcfg.exe** command from Run on the Start menu. As shown in Figure 6-6, **winipcfg.exe** is a graphical program that displays the same information as **ipconfig** does at the command prompt.

Figure 6-6   **winipcfg.exe** *Program*

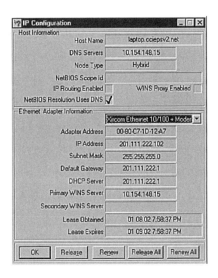

Step 3   Instead of configuring a static IP address, DNS server, and WINS server on the Windows client PC, configure the Cancun router to provide the information using DHCP. Use the following values to configure DHCP:

DHCP scope: 201.111.222.0/24

Default gateway: 201.111.222.1

DHS server: 10.154.148.15

Domain name: cciepsv2.net

WINS server: 10.154.148.15

To configure DHCP for the client PC, on the Cancun router, the following steps were taken:

(a) Create a DHCP pool. In this example, the client-pcs pool was created:

```
ip dhcp pool client-pcs
```

(b) Assign a network, default router, DNS server, WINS server, and domain name to the DHCP pool:

```
network 201.111.222.0 255.255.255.0
default-router 201.111.222.1
dns-server 10.154.148.15
domain-name cciepsv2.net
netbios-name-server 10.154.148.15
```

(c) Set aside any addresses that you do not want to use for DHCP by using the **exclude-address** command. In this example, the range of addresses from 201.111.222.1 to 100 were excluded from the DHCP range:

```
ip dhcp excluded-address 201.111.222.1 201.111.222.100
```

Example 6-13 shows the DHCP configurations for the Cancun router.

Example 6-13 *Cancun Router's DHCP Configuration*

```
ip dhcp excluded-address 201.111.222.1 201.111.222.100
!
ip dhcp pool laptops
   network 201.111.222.0 255.255.255.0
   default-router 201.111.222.1
   dns-server 10.154.148.15
   domain-name cciepsv2.net
   netbios-name-server 10.154.148.15
```

Step 4 Configure PQ and any access lists that might be required to support the protocols shown in Table 6-6.

To configure the PQ, as shown earlier in Table 6-6, three access lists were used. Access list 101 was used to specify DNS and WINS traffic. Access list 102 was used to specify the Windows NetBIOS and Simple Network Management Protocol (SNMP) traffic. Windows uses TCP port 135 for DNS and WINS management traffic, TCP port 139, and UDP ports 137 and 138, or keywords **netbios-ns** and **netbios-ss**, for NetBIOS traffic between Windows computers. And finally, access list 103 was used to specify passive FTP traffic and the use of the random TCP ports greater than 1023 that FTP uses during file copies. Without this specification, the return FTP traffic would have been sent to the Low priority queue rather than the Normal priority queue:

```
access-list 101 permit tcp any host 10.54.148.15 eq domain
access-list 101 permit udp any host 10.54.148.15 netbios-ns
access-list 101 permit udp any any eq snmp
access-list 102 permit tcp any host 10.54.148.15 eq 135
access-list 102 permit udp any host 10.54.148.15 eq netbios-ns
access-list 102 permit udp any host 10.54.148.15 eq netbios-ss
access-list 102 permit tcp any host 10.54.148.15 eq 139
access-list 103 permit tcp any host 10.54.148.15 eq ftp
access-list 103 permit tcp any host 10.54.148.15 gt 1023 established
```

The access list numbers were used with the **priority-list** command to create the four priority queues, and the **default** keyword was used to assign all unspecified traffic to the Low priority queue:

```
priority-list 10 protocol ip high list 101
priority-list 10 protocol ip medium list 102
priority-list 10 protocol ip normal list 103
priority-list 10 protocol ip low
priority-list 10 default low
```

Step 5   Assign the PQ process to the interface that will queue all client traffic across the WAN connection between the Cancun and Halifax routers. (Remember the rules for efficient traffic queuing on different interface types.)

The PQ process was assigned to the serial interface of the Cancun router using the **priority-group** command:

```
interface Serial0/1
 priority-group 10
```

Step 6   Validate that the client and server computer can ping each other. Using a passive FTP session, copy a file from the client PC to ServerNA01. Try to use FTP to get another file from the server. While copying these files, look at the queuing information from the **show interface** output.

Experimenting with the traffic in this lab, a number of different traffic types, TFTP file copies, extended pings, packet generation, file copies in Windows Explorer, and web surfing were tried, which is how the results shown in the Example 6-14 were generated.

Example 6-14 *Viewing the Queuing Information During FTP Sessions*

```
Cancun# show interfaces serial 0/1
Serial0/1 is up, line protocol is up
  Hardware is PowerQUICC Serial
  Internet address is 193.168.24.2/29
  MTU 1500 bytes, BW 1544 Kbit, DLY 20000 usec,
     reliability 255/255, txload 28/255, rxload 1/255
  Encapsulation HDLC, loopback not set
  Keepalive set (10 sec)
  Last input 00:00:01, output 00:00:05, output hang never
  Last clearing of "show interface" counters 00:03:56
  Input queue: 0/75/0 (size/max/drops); Total output drops: 0
  Queueing strategy: priority-list 10
  Output queue (queue priority: size/max/drops):
     high: 0/20/0, medium: 0/40/0, normal: 3/60/0, low: 0/80/0
  5 minute input rate 7000 bits/sec, 10 packets/sec
  5 minute output rate 174000 bits/sec, 18 packets/sec
     2726 packets input, 156448 bytes, 0 no buffer
     Received 28 broadcasts, 0 runts, 0 giants, 0 throttles
     0 input errors, 0 CRC, 0 frame, 0 overrun, 0 ignored, 0 abort
     4983 packets output, 6970545 bytes, 0 underruns
     0 output errors, 0 collisions, 0 interface resets
     0 output buffer failures, 0 output buffers swapped out
     0 carrier transitions
     DCD=up  DSR=up  DTR=up  RTS=up  CTS=up
```

You have completed this practical example when you have sent some test traffic and verified the PQ configuration. Example 6-15 shows the completed configurations for the Halifax and Cancun routers.

Example 6-15 *Complete Configurations for the Practical Example*

```
hostname Cancun
!
ip dhcp excluded-address 201.111.222.1 201.111.222.100
!
ip dhcp pool laptops
   network 201.111.222.0 255.255.255.0
   default-router 201.111.222.1
   dns-server 10.154.148.15
   domain-name cciepsv2.net
   netbios-name-server 10.154.148.15
!
interface Ethernet0/0
 ip address 201.111.222.1 255.255.255.0
!
interface Serial0/1
 ip address 193.168.24.2 255.255.255.248
priority-group 10
 clockrate 1300000
!
router rip
 version 2
network 193.168.24.0
 network 201.111.222.0
!
access-list 101 permit tcp any any host 10.54.148.15 eq domain
access-list 101 permit udp any any host 10.54.148.15 eq netbios-ns
access-list 101 permit udp any any eq snmp
access-list 102 permit tcp any host 10.54.148.15 any eq 135
access-list 102 permit udp any host 10.54.148.15 any eq netbios-ns
access-list 102 permit udp any host 10.54.148.15 any eq netbios-ss
access-list 102 permit tcp any host 10.54.148.15 any eq 139
access-list 103 permit tcp any host 10.54.148.15 any eq ftp
access-list 103 permit tcp any host 10.54.148.15 any gt 1023 established
priority-list 10 protocol ip high list 101
priority-list 10 protocol ip medium list 102
priority-list 10 protocol ip normal list 103
priority-list 10 protocol ip low
priority-list 10 default low

hostname Halifax
!
interface Ethernet0
 ip address 10.154.148.1 255.255.255.0
!
interface Serial0
 ip address 193.168.24.1 255.255.255.248
```

continues

Example 6-15 *Complete Configurations for the Practical Example (Continued)*

```
 !
 router rip
  version 2
  network 10.0.0.0
 network 193.168.24.0
```

Now that you have seen how PQ works, you might have noted one of the reasons why you might not want to enable PQ in your network: Low priority queue starvation. When you must queue traffic, but you do not have a strict-priority requirement, there are several other queuing mechanisms that you can consider as an alternative to strict PQ.

Custom Queuing

Each of the queuing methods discussed so far make a best effort to forward traffic of a certain priority. These queuing methods also have rather static configuration capabilities. WFQ enables you to control only the size and number of the queues and does not allow for much customization, which might be quite a problem if you must sort multiple traffic. PQ enables you to configure only four queues and the number of packets allowed in those queues. PQ also has one major drawback: Lower-priority queues might not receive enough attention; and, in some cases, depending on the amount of high-priority traffic, they might not receive any attention at all. Custom Queuing (CQ) works around many of these issues with its highly customizable configuration properties.

Custom Queuing earns its name by having a total of 17 queues, 16 of which are configurable for user-defined traffic types. The first queue, queue 0, is the system queue and is used by the Cisco IOS Software for system traffic; this queue is not user configurable. Each of the 16 other queues has a queue size limitation in either bytes, or a limit on the number of packets that they are capable of containing. Each queue is serviced until the byte count or packet limit is met. If either of these events occur, the forwarding of the current packet is finished, and then the next queue is emptied (or reaches the byte or packet limit), and so on, in a round-robin approach, ensuring that each queue receives equal attention and that no one queue can prevent other queues from receiving attention. If a queue is full, any new packets destined for that queue are dropped. If a queue is empty, it is skipped and the next queue is serviced. CQ queue content is determined by the following:

- Ingress interface (the interface that they were received by).

- An access list, CQ supports all major protocols including IP, IPX, AppleTalk, and SNA protocols and their access lists.

- Packet size, either greater or less than a specified size.

- Or specific protocol characteristic defined either by an address, port number, or Cisco IOS Software parameter.

In Figure 6-7, for example, you can see that there are six queues. Queue 1 has been allocated to use 50 percent of the available interface bandwidth. Queue 2 is allocated 20 percent of the bandwidth. Queue 3 is allocated 12 percent; Queue 4, 5 percent; Queue 5, 3 percent; and Queue 6 is allotted the remaining 10 percent of the bandwidth. The line with the arrow indicates the order in which the queues are serviced. Each queue is emptied, to its byte or packet limit, and then the next queue is serviced. With this queuing scheme, after Queue 1 has transmitted all of its packets, Queues 2, 3, 4, 5, and 6 are serviced in that order. While the other queues were being serviced, new packets arrived in most of the queues, as shown in Figure 6-8. Again, each of the queues is serviced until their allocated limits are reached, and then the next queue is emptied to its limit. If one of the queues does not contain any packets, as is the case with Queue 4, it is skipped. After a queue's packet or byte size limitation is met, any new packets destined for that queue are dropped.

Figure 6-7   *Custom Queuing Diagram*

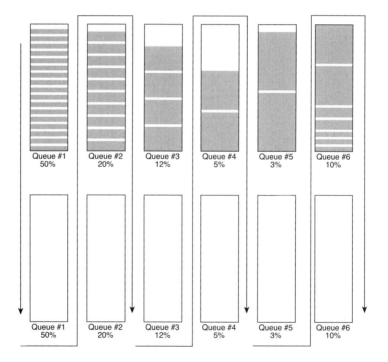

In Figure 6-8, Queue 2 is 100 percent full. A queue is full when the numbers of items in the queue reach the queue limit, or the size of the queue, in bytes, has been reached. With CQ, when a queue is full, the last packet in the queue is transmitted before the next queue is serviced. If a queue fills up while waiting for service, any new packets for the queue are dropped.

Figure 6-8   *Custom Queuing Diagram Revisited*

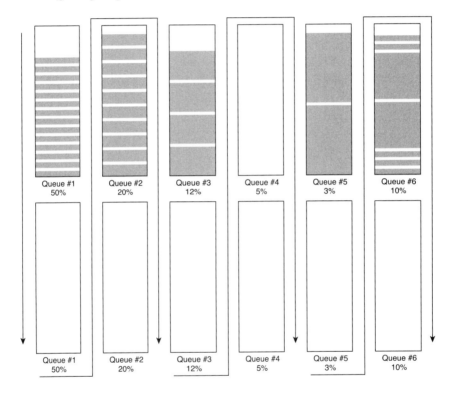

Although there are 17 queues in CQ, only 16 are user configurable. Queue 0 is used by the operating system to forward network control traffic. When you are using the **queue-list** command, the 0 queue will appear to be available for configuration; however, it should not be used for traffic unless the router generates it.

The **queue-list** command defines a set of 16 custom queues and up to 16 of these custom queue access lists can be defined per router. Table 6-7 shows the **queue-list** command, its arguments, parameters, and their descriptions.

Table 6-7   *Custom Queuing Syntax*

Command	Argument	Description
`queue-list `*`list-number`*`  default `*`queue-number`*	None	The **default** command defines the default queue for traffic that has not been specifically assigned to one of queues.
		The *list-number* specifies to which queue list the configuration is to be applied. This number ranges from 1 to 16.
		The *queue-number* specifies to which of the 17 queues the command is being applied. This number ranges from 0 to 16.
`queue-list `*`list-number`*`  interface `*`interface-name`*`  interface-number queue-`*`number`*	None	The **interface** command is used to specify that all traffic from a certain ingress interface, defined by the following interface name and number, is to be assigned to the queue specified by the *queue-number* argument.
`queue-list `*`list-number`*`  lowest-custom `*`queue-number`*	None	The **lowest-custom** command is used to specify the lowest queue number used by the queue list if all 16 queues are not used for CQ.
`queue-list `*`list-number`*`  protocol `*`protocol queue-`*`number`*	Arguments for protocol:	The **protocol** command is used to specify that all traffic from the following protocol is to be sent to the queue number specified.
	`arp [gt `*`frame-size`*`	lt `*`frame-size`*`]`	The **arp** keyword is used to specify the ARP protocol.
		(Optional) **gt** specifies traffic from the ARP protocol with a packet size greater than that specified, ranging from 0 to 65,535.
		(Optional) **lt** specifies traffic from the ARP protocol with a packet size less than that specified, ranging from 0 to 65,535.

continues

Table 6-7 *Custom Queuing Syntax (Continued)*

Command	Argument	Description
`queue-list` *`list-number`* `protocol` *`protocol`* `queue-` *`number`* (*Continued*)	`bridge [gt` *`frame-size`* `|` `list` *`list-number`* `| lt` *`frame-size`*`]`	The **bridge** keyword is used to specify the transparently bridged traffic.
		(Optional) **gt** specifies traffic from a bridged protocol with a packet size greater than that specified, ranging from 0 to 65,535.
		(Optional) **list** specifies traffic belonging to the access list (200–299) specified by the list number.
		(Optional) **lt** specifies traffic from a bridged protocol with a packet size less than that specified, ranging from 0 to 65,535.
	`bstun [address` *`group-`* *`number hex-number`* `| gt` *`frame-size`* `| lt` *`frame-`* *`size`*`]`	The **bstun** keyword is used to specify the BSTUN protocol.
		(Optional) **address** specifies traffic from a particular BSTUN group and address in hexadecimal format. The BSTUN groups range from 1 to 255.
		(Optional) **gt** specifies BSTUN traffic with a packet size greater than that specified, ranging from 0 to 65,535.
		(Optional) **lt** specifies BSTUN traffic with a packet size less than that specified, ranging from 0 to 65,535.
	`cdp [gt` *`frame-size`* `| lt` *`frame-size`*`]`	The **cdp** keyword is used to specify the CDP protocol.
		(Optional) **gt** specifies CDP traffic with a packet size greater than that specified, ranging from 0 to 65,535.
		(Optional) **lt** specifies CDP traffic with a packet size less than that specified, ranging from 0 to 65,535.
	`compressedtcp [gt` *`frame-`* *`size`* `| lt` *`frame-size`*`]`	The **compressedtcp** keyword is used to specify the compressed TCP traffic.
		(Optional) **gt** specifies compressed TCP traffic with a packet size greater than that specified, ranging from 0 to 65,535.
		(Optional) **lt** specifies compressed TCP traffic with a packet size less than that specified, ranging from 0 to 65,535.

Table 6-7   *Custom Queuing Syntax (Continued)*

Command	Argument	Description
`queue-list` *`list-number`* `protocol` *`protocol`* `queue-number` (*Continued*)	`dlsw [gt frame-size	lt frame-size]`	The **dlsw** keyword is used to specify the DLSw+ protocol.
		(Optional) **gt** specifies DLSw+ traffic with a packet size greater than that specified, ranging from 0 to 65,535.
		(Optional) **lt** specifies DLSw+ traffic with a packet size less than that specified, ranging from 0 to 65,535.
	`ip [fragments	gt frame-size	list list-number	lt frame-size tcp tcp-protocol	udp udp-protocol]`	The **ip** keyword is used to specify the TCP/IP suite of protocols.
		(Optional) The **fragments** keyword specifies only fragmented IP packets of the fragmented packet are matched, not the first fragment.
		(Optional) **gt** specifies IP traffic with a packet size greater than that specified, ranging from 0 to 65,535.
		(Optional) **list** specifies traffic belonging to the access list (1–199 or 1300–1399) specified the by the list number.
		(Optional) **lt** specifies IP traffic with a packet size less than that specified, ranging from 0 to 65,535.
		(Optional) **tcp** specifies that traffic from or to a particular TCP port number. Ranges are TCP port numbers 0 to 65,335 or a keyword from the following list:
		bgp, chargen, cmd, daytime, discard, domain, echo, exec, finger, ftp, ftp-data, gopher, hostname, ident, irc, klogin, kshell, login, lpd, nntp, pim-auto-rp, pop2, pop3, smtp, sunrpc, syslog, tacacs, talk, telnet, time, uucp, whois, and **www**
		(Optional) **udp** specifies that traffic from or to a particular UDP port number. Ranges are UDP port numbers 0 to 65,335 or a keyword from the following list:
		biff, bootpc, bootps, discard, dnsix, domain, echo, isakmp, mobile-ip, nameserver, netbios-dgm, netbios-ns, netbios-ss, ntp, pim-auto-rp, rip, snmp, snmptrap, sunrpc, syslog, tacacs, talk, tftp, time, who, and **xdmcp**

continues

Table 6-7   *Custom Queuing Syntax (Continued)*

Command	Argument	Description
`queue-list` *`list-number`* `protocol` *`protocol`* `queue-` *`number`* (*Continued*)	`llc2 [gt` *`frame-size`* `l lt` *`frame-size`*`]`	The **llc2** keyword is used to specify the LLC-2 protocol.
		(Optional) **gt** specifies LLC-2 traffic with a packet size greater than that specified, ranging from 0 to 65,535.
		(Optional) **lt** specifies LLC-2 traffic with a packet size less than that specified, ranging from 0 to 65,535.
	`pad [gt` *`frame-size`* `l lt` *`frame-size`*`]`	The **pad** keyword is used to specify the PAD protocol.
		(Optional) **gt** specifies PAD traffic with a packet size greater than that specified, ranging from 0 to 65,535.
		(Optional) **lt** specifies PAD traffic with a packet size less than that specified, ranging from 0 to 65,535.
	`qllc [gt` *`frame-size`* `l lt` *`frame-size`*`]`	The **qllc** keyword is used to specify the QLLC protocol.
		(Optional) **gt** specifies QLLC traffic with a packet size greater than that specified, ranging from 0 to 65,535.
		(Optional) **lt** specifies QLLC traffic with a packet size less than that specified, ranging from 0 to 65,535.
	`rsrb [gt` *`frame-size`* `l lt` *`frame-size`*`]`	The **rsrb** keyword is used to specify the RSRB protocol.
		(Optional) **gt** specifies RSRB traffic with a packet size greater than that specified, ranging from 0 to 65,535.
		(Optional) **lt** specifies RSRB traffic with a packet size less than that specified, ranging from 0 to 65,535.

Table 6-7   *Custom Queuing Syntax (Continued)*

Command	Argument	Description
`queue-list` *`list-number`* `protocol` *`protocol queue-number`* (*Continued*)	`snapshot [gt` *`frame-size`* ` |` `lt` *`frame-size`*`]`	The **snapshot** keyword is used to specify Snapshot routing traffic. (Optional) **gt** specifies Snapshot routing traffic with a packet size greater than that specified, ranging from 0 to 65,535. (Optional) **lt** specifies Snapshot routing traffic with a packet size less than that specified, ranging from 0 to 65,535.
	`stun [address` *`group-number hex-number`* ` | gt` *`frame-size`* ` | lt` *`frame-size`*`]`	The **stun** keyword is used to specify the STUN protocol. (Optional) **address** specifies traffic from a particular STUN group and address in hexadecimal format. The STUN groups range from 1 to 255. (Optional) **gt** specifies STUN traffic with a packet size greater than that specified, ranging from 0 to 65,535. (Optional) **lt** specifies STUN traffic with a packet size less than that specified, ranging from 0 to 65,535.
`queue-list` *`list-number`* `queue` *`queue-number`* `[byte-count` *`byte-size`*`] [limit` *`queue-entries`*`]`	None	The **byte-count** argument specifies a size limit in bytes for the specified queue. Byte counts range from 1 to 16,777,215. The **limit** argument specifies a limit to the number of entries that may exit in the specified queue. This limit ranges from 0 to 32,767. The use of these arguments is covered later in this section.
`queue-list` *`list-number`* `stun` *`queue-number`* `address` *`group-number hex-number`*	None	The **stun** argument specifies STUN traffic belonging to the STUN group particular with the specific hexadecimal address. The STUN group numbers range from 1 to 255, and the hexadecimal address must be written with the 0x prefix.

CQ configuration requires four steps: define the traffic that is to be queued using access lists, create the queue list by creating queues and assigning traffic types to the queues, customize the queues, and apply the queues to an interface. In the next example, these steps are used to configure a sample network.

Step 1   Create the queue list by assigning traffic types to a queue.

In this example, distribute traffic, as shown in Table 6-8.

Table 6-8   *Protocol Distribution for Custom Queuing Exercise*

Queue Number	Traffic Type
1	OSPF, SNMP
2	GRE
3	DLSw+
4	DNS, SMTP and DHCP
5	Windows NetBIOS support
6	NFS
7	Passive-mode FTP to 192.16.12.8, TFTP
8	WWW
9	Other

To configure these nine queues, use seven IP access lists, as shown in Example 6-16.

Example 6-16 *Access Lists for Custom Queuing*

```
access-list 101 permit ospf any any
access-list 101 permit udp any any eq snmp
access-list 102 permit gre any any
access-list 103 remark DLSw 2065, 2067, 1981, 1982, and 1983
access-list 103 permit tcp any any eq 2065
access-list 103 permit tcp any any eq 2067
access-list 103 permit tcp any any eq 1981
access-list 103 permit tcp any any eq 1982
access-list 103 permit tcp any any eq 1983
access-list 104 permit tcp any any eq domain
access-list 104 permit tcp any any eq smtp
access-list 104 permit udp any any eq bootpc
access-list 105 permit tcp any any eq 139
access-list 105 permit udp any any eq netbios-dgm
access-list 105 permit udp any any eq netbios-ns
access-list 105 permit udp any any eq netbios-ss
access-list 106 permit tcp any any eq 2049
access-list 106 permit udp any any eq 2049
```

Example 6-16 *Access Lists for Custom Queuing (Continued)*

```
access-list 107 permit tcp any 192.16.12.8eq ftp
access-list 107 permit tcp any 192.16.12.8gt 1023 established
access-list 107 permit udp any any eq tftp
```

Step 2   After the access lists have been configured, it is time to configure the queuing assignments. This is accomplished using the **queue-list** command and referencing the access lists with the **queue-list** command, as shown in Example 6-17.

Example 6-17 *Queue List Configuration*

```
queue-list 3 protocol ip 1 list 101
queue-list 3 protocol ip 2 list 102
queue-list 3 protocol ip 3 list 103
queue-list 3 protocol ip 4 list 104
queue-list 3 protocol ip 5 list 105
queue-list 3 protocol ip 6 list 106
queue-list 3 protocol ip 7 list 107
queue-list 3 protocol ip 8 tcp www
```

Step 3   Next, customize the queuing configuration. In this example, default IP traffic should be sent out Queue 9:

```
queue-list 3 default 9
```

Step 4   Assign the queuing scheme to an interface. This is accomplished using the **custom-queue-list** command in interface configuration mode:

```
interface Serial0/2
 ip address 165.11.2.1 255.255.255.0
 custom-queue-list 3
```

After CQ has been enabled for an interface, you can verify its configuration in two ways: the **show queueing** command and the **show interface** command. The **show queueing command** displays the current queuing configuration for the router. If more than one queuing type is in use, you can add the **custom** keyword onto the **show queueing** command to specify only the CQ configuration, as shown in Example 6-18.

Example 6-18 *Verifying CQ Configuration*

```
FS_HQ# show queueing custom
Current custom queue configuration:
List   Queue  Args
3      9      default
3      1      protocol ip       list 101
3      2      protocol ip       list 102
3      3      protocol ip       list 103
3      4      protocol ip       list 104
```

continues

Example 6-18 *Verifying CQ Configuration (Continued)*

```
3     5      protocol ip       list 105
3     6      protocol ip       list 106
3     7      protocol ip       list 107
3     8      protocol ip       tcp port www
3     9      protocol ip
```

To see the queue packet size limits, use the **show interface** command. Example 6-19 shows that
CQ 3 is in use with each of the 16 queues limited to 20 packets, the default.

Example 6-19 *Using the* **show interface** *Command for Custom Queuing*

```
FS_HQ#sh int s0/2
Serial0/2 is up, line protocol is up
  Hardware is PowerQUICC Serial
  Internet address is 165.11.2.1/24
  MTU 1500 bytes, BW 1544 Kbit, DLY 20000 usec,
     reliability 255/255, txload 6/255, rxload 6/255
  Encapsulation HDLC, loopback not set
  Keepalive set (10 sec)
  Last input 00:00:00, output 00:00:02, output hang never
  Last clearing of "show interface" counters never
  Input queue: 0/75/0/0 (size/max/drops/flushes); Total output drops: 0
  Queueing strategy: custom-list 3
  Output queues: (queue #: size/max/drops)
     0: 0/20/0 1: 0/20/0 2: 0/20/0 3: 0/20/0 4: 0/20/0
     5: 0/20/0 6: 0/20/0 7: 0/20/0 8: 0/20/0 9: 0/20/0
     10: 0/20/0 11: 0/20/0 12: 0/20/0 13: 0/20/0 14: 0/20/0
     15: 0/20/0 16: 0/20/0
  5 minute input rate 41000 bits/sec, 4 packets/sec
  5 minute output rate 41000 bits/sec, 4 packets/sec
     1087 packets input, 1437808 bytes, 0 no buffer
     Received 53 broadcasts, 0 runts, 0 giants, 0 throttles
     0 input errors, 0 CRC, 0 frame, 0 overrun, 0 ignored, 0 abort
     1079 packets output, 1435130 bytes, 0 underruns
     0 output errors, 0 collisions, 6 interface resets
     0 output buffer failures, 0 output buffers swapped out
     18 carrier transitions
     DCD=up  DSR=up  DTR=up  RTS=up  CTS=up
```

Notice that each queue is displayed with the current size of the queue, the maximum number of
packets per queue, and the number of packets that have been dropped in each queue. In the
preceding example, each of the queues is currently empty; this is because CQ is used only when
there is congestion on an interface, and in this case, this interface is transmitting less than one
packet per second.

You have control over the size of each of the queues with CQ. Before changing the bandwidth allocation for each of the queues, consider a few things. First, consider the average packet size when adjusting queue size by limiting the size of the queue in bytes. If you set the byte count size of your queue to 2000 bytes, and your average packet size is 1024 bytes, for example, only two packets will be sent from this queue each time it is serviced. Second, if you set a packet size that is too large, the bandwidth might not be properly allocated, resulting in wasted queue space. Therefore, it is better to analyze average packet sizes before allocating bandwidth to the queues, because setting queue sizes that are too small will cause irregular packet transmission, and setting queue sizes too large will underutilize the queue size or cause one protocol to monopolize the interface bandwidth.

Nine basic steps are required to determine the size of bandwidth that should be allocated to each queue. The **byte-count** command enables you to control the size of the individual queues. The **byte-count** command is basically used to allocate bandwidth to particular traffic types based on a percentage of traffic. Before allocating traffic, it is important to determine the average packet sizes per protocol and queue, and the total amount of interface bandwidth. Then determine the percentage of interface bandwidth that each of these queues requires.

For example, the following steps outline how a simple queuing scheme is created, consisting of generic routing encapsulation (GRE), WWW, and passive-mode FTP traffic, using the same protocols defined in the preceding example.

Step 1   Find the average packet size for each protocol. Table 6-9 shows the average packets sizes for the protocols for this example. This table also provides the bandwidth allocation that should be used for this example:

Average packet size (A)

Total amount of traffic in bytes (B)

Total number of packets (P)

A = B/P

Table 6-9   *Packet Sizes for Protocols*

Protocol	Bandwidth Allocation	Average Packet Size
GRE	55	794
WWW	20	746
FTP	25	678

Step 2   Find the ratio of packets that must be sent to accumulate the percentage of bandwidth allocated to the queue in bytes. The percentage of bandwidth should have been found before beginning the bandwidth allocation process. This ratio is found by dividing the percentage of bandwidth by the packet size (in bytes). Table 6-10 displays the results of this equation:

Traffic ratio (R)

Percentage of bandwidth (B)

Packet size (P)

R = B/P

```
55/794 = 0.06926
20/746 = 0.02680
25/678 = 0.03687
```

Table 6-10   *CQ Traffic Rations*

Protocol	Bandwidth Allocation	Average Packet Size	Ratio
GRE	55	794	0.06926
WWW	20	746	0.02680
FTP	25	678	0.03687

Step 3   Normalize the ratio found in Step 2; this is accomplished by dividing each of the ratios by the lowest ratio found in Step 2. Table 6-11 shows the normalized ratios for this example:

Lowest ratio (L)

Ratio (R)

Normalized number (N)

N = R/L

```
0.02680 is the lowest ratio
0.06926/0.02680 = 2.58 rounded to 2.6
0.02680/0.02680 = 1
0.03687/0.02680 = 1.38 rounded to 1.4
```

Table 6-11   *CQ Normalized Rations*

Protocol	Bandwidth Allocation	Average Packet Size	Ratio	Normalized Ratio
GRE	55	794	0.06926	2.6
WWW	20	746	0.02680	1
FTP	25	678	0.03687	1.4

Step 4   Round each ratio with a decimal up to the next highest whole number. The packet ratio should be rounded to a whole number because CQ transmits the last full packet in the queue before moving on to the next queue. Table 6-12 shows the ratios for this example in whole numbers.

Table 6-12   *CQ Whole Ratios*

Protocol	Bandwidth Allocation	Average Packet Size	Ratio	Normalized Ratio	Whole Ratio
GRE	55	794	0.06926	2.6	3
WWW	20	746	0.02680	1	1
FTP	25	678	0.03687	1.4	2

Step 5   To convert the packet ratio to a byte count, the ratio must be multiplied by the average packet size. Table 6-13 displays the byte counts:

Packet ratio (R)

Average packet size (P)

Byte count (B)

$B = R * P$

```
3 x 794 = 2382
1 x 746 = 746
2 x 678 = 1356
```

Table 6-13   *CQ Byte Counts*

Protocol	Bandwidth Allocation	Average Packet Size	Ratio	Normalized Ratio	Whole Ratio	Byte Count
GRE	55	794	0.06926	2.6	3	2382
WWW	20	746	0.02680	1	1	746
FTP	25	678	0.03687	1.4	2	1356

Step 6   To find the bandwidth distribution that this ratio represents, combine the total bandwidth used by all queues:

Bandwidth distribution (D)

Byte count (B)

$D = B + B + B$ (each B)

```
2382 + 746 + 1356 = 4484
```

Step 7   To find the total percentage of bandwidths, in bytes, used by each queue, divide each byte count by the total bandwidth distribution. Table 6-14 shows the percentages of bandwidth for this example:

Percentage of bandwidth (P)

Bandwidth distribution (D)

Byte count (B)

P = B/D

```
4484
2382/4484 = 53
746/4484 = 17
1356/4484 = 30
```

Table 6-14   *CQ Bandwidth Percentages*

Protocol	Bandwidth Allocation	Average Packet Size	Ratio	Normalized Ratio	Whole Ratio	Byte Count	Percentage of Bandwidth
GRE	55	794	0.06926	2.6	3	2382	53
WWW	20	746	0.02680	1	1	746	17
FTP	25	678	0.03687	1.4	2	1356	30

Step 8   If this ratio is not close enough to the original bandwidth allocation percentage, go back to Step 3 and multiply the ratio by another value. In this example, I tried using the numbers 2 and 3. Notice that 2 comes the closest to the required byte count, and 3 goes over the byte count. In this case, I decided to try 2.5, which is the closest to the original required percentage of bandwidth allocation. Table 6-15 shows the final bandwidth percentage allocations and byte count sizes for this example:

```
2.6 x 2 = 5.2 rounded to 6
1 x 2 = 2
1.4 x 2 = 2.8 rounded to 3
6 x 794 = 4764/8288 = 58
2 x 746 = 1492/8288 = 18
3 x 678 = 2032/8288 = 25
          ----
          8288
2.6 x 3 = 7.8 rounded to 8
1 x 3 = 3
1.4 x 3 = 4.2 rounded to 5
8 x 794 = 6352/11980 = 53
3 x 746 = 2238/11980 = 19
5 x 678 = 3390/11980 = 28
          ----
          11980
```

```
2.6 x 2.5 = 6.5 rounded to 7
1 x 2.5 = 2.5 rounded to 3
1.4 x 2.5 = 3.5 rounded to 4
7 x 794 = 5558/10508 = 53%
3 x 746 = 2238/10508 = 21%
4 x 678 = 2712/10508 = 26%
            - - - -
            10508
```

Table 6-15   *Final Bandwidth Allocations per Queue*

Protocol	Bandwidth Allocation	Average Packet Size	Ratio	Normalized Ratio	Whole Ratio	Byte Count	Percentage of Bandwidth
GRE	55	794	0.06926	2.6	7	5558	53
WWW	20	746	0.02680	1	3	2238	21
FTP	25	678	0.03687	1.4	4	2712	26

Step 9   After the byte counts have been found, apply them to the queues using the **queue-list byte-count** command, as shown in Example 6-20.

Example 6-20 *Complete CQ Custom Byte-Count Configuration*

```
interface Serial0/2
 ip address 165.11.2.1 255.255.255.0
 custom-queue-list 5
!
access-list 110 permit gre any any
access-list 120 permit tcp any any eq ftp
access-list 120 permit tcp any any gt 1023 established
queue-list 5 protocol ip 1 list 110
queue-list 5 protocol ip 2 list 120
queue-list 5 protocol ip 3 tcp www
queue-list 5 queue 1 byte-count 5558
queue-list 5 queue 2 byte-count 2238
queue-list 5 queue 3 byte-count 2712
FS_HQ# show queueing custom
Current custom queue configuration:
List   Queue   Args
5      1       protocol ip        list 110
5      2       protocol ip        list 120
5      3       protocol ip        tcp port www
5      1       byte-count 5558
5      2       byte-count 2238
5      3       byte-count 2712
```

This chapter began by discussing the four basic queuing types available in Cisco IOS Software. The remainder of this chapter goes beyond basic queuing techniques and applies technologies from the preceding two chapters, combining and contrasting them with queuing techniques from this chapter, to create customized QoS solutions. The next sections focus on more advanced queuing, shaping, policing, prioritization, and classification techniques, beginning with the next section, which discuses more advanced traffic policy enforcement techniques.

Enforcing Traffic Policy with QoS

Networks generally have basic traffic policy requirements that must be enforced. For instance, service providers provide customers with WAN circuits such as ATM or Frame Relay. These circuits are provisioned with certain service level agreements that the service providers enforce on customers to provide all customers certain service levels. Customers are responsible for making sure that their network's traffic complies with those agreements by shaping, rate limiting, and prioritizing their own traffic with QoS tools supplied in Cisco IOS Software. This section explores these technologies and shows how they can be used to provide QoS to network applications.

Traffic Shaping

Traffic shaping forces traffic to comply with certain bandwidth-allocation limitations by reducing the outbound traffic rate. Unlike traffic policing, which discards traffic that exceeds burst sizes, during traffic, bursts traffic-shaping buffers the additional packets and sends them out when bandwidth is available, or when the number of buffered packets falls below the configured limit, thus smoothing the flow of traffic.

NOTE   Traffic shaping does not replace proper circuit provisioning; it is designed to smooth traffic bursts. Traffic shaping does not supply additional bandwidth to an interface. Interfaces that are continuously congested still discard packets.

Traffic shaping uses a token-bucket system to determine whether to transmit, delay, or drop new packets. With the token-bucket system, each interface has *committed information rate (CIR)*, which is the rate at which the interface can transmit packets for an interval of time, or in token-bucket theory, the rate at which the tokens are added to the bucket. The *sustained burst rate (Bc)* defines the maximum number of tokens that the bucket can contain at a given interval. When a packet arrives at an interface, it takes a token from the bucket. When a packet is transmitted, the token is released; and after the *time interval (Tc)*, the token is returned to the bucket. If the bucket is empty, any new packets arriving at that interface are queued until the time interval has elapsed and the tokens have been replenished. If the CIR is consistently exceeded, tokens are removed from the bucket faster than they are being replenished, filling the queue and causing packets to be dropped. The key to good traffic-shaping design is to create a bucket that will constantly have enough tokens to either queue and forward each packet, and replace tokens after packets have been removed from the buffer and transmitted.

Generic Traffic Shaping

Traffic shaping can be applied to a number of different Layer 2 technologies, such as Ethernet, ATM (variable bit rate [VBR] and available bit rate [ABR]), High-Level Data Link Control (HDLC), PPP (ISDN and dialup interfaces are not supported), and Frame Relay. With the exception of Frame Relay, all these technologies support generic traffic shaping (GTS), introduced in Cisco IOS Software Release 11.2; GTS has the capability to shape outgoing traffic on a per-interface basis. GTS can also shape certain types of traffic defined in an access list by specifying group traffic shaping.

NOTE   For more information on Frame Relay traffic shaping (FRTS), see *CCIE Practical Studies, Volume I*, Chapter 5, "WAN Protocols and Technologies: Frame Relay."

Before enabling GTS, you must know a few things. First, like Frame Relay traffic shaping, to configure GTS, you must know the target bit rate for the interface, commonly referred to as the *committed information rate (CIR)*. This is the rate at which traffic is sent during normal circumstances. It is also helpful, but not necessary, to know the sustained and excess burst rates available for traffic burst. The *sustained burst rate (Bc)* is the rate in bits that traffic is allowed to burst beyond the normal traffic rate per interval. The *excess burst rate (Be)* is the rate at which traffic is allowed to burst beyond the sustained burst rate during the first interval. Tokens are replenished in the traffic-shaping token bucket each time interval *(Tc)*. To properly configure traffic shaping, you must first know the time interval that traffic shaping uses to replenish the token bucket, which is found using the following formula:

$Tc = Bc/CIR$

NOTE   The time interval for traffic shaping cannot be less than 10 ms or greater than 125 ms. The router finds the best time interval based on the $Tc = Bc/CIR$ formula. The default time interval is 125 ms. The time interval is a result of the CIR and Bc configuration and is not user configurable. Cisco recommends that the Bc should be 1/8 the CIR, which will create eight 125-ms time intervals per second.

To configure GTS for all interface traffic, use the **traffic-shaping rate** command on each interface where traffic shaping is required. To define specific traffic that is to be shaped, use the **traffic-shaping group** command and an access list. Table 6-16 shows the GTS command available in Cisco IOS Software Release 12.12(T), the command's arguments, and the argument descriptions:

```
traffic-shape {group | rate access-list} target-bit-rate [sustained] [excess] [buffer-
    limit]
```

Table 6-16   *Generic Traffic Shaping Command Arguments*

Command Argument	Description
group access-list	Specifies that all traffic matching the access list (1–2699) is to be shaped.
rate	Specifies that all traffic on this interface is to be shaped.
target-bit-rate	The normal rate that traffic will be transmitted (CIR) at, ranging from 8000 to the interface's full bit rate in bits per second. For example, a 100-Mbps interface's full CIR will range from 8000 to 100,000,000.
	Some Cisco IOS Software versions have different range values for this command. You must use a value that exists in the range provided by the software version that the router is running.
sustained	(Optional) The sustained bit rate (Bc) that traffic is allowed to burst to, ranging from 0 to 100,000,000 in bits per interval.
	The sustained burst rate that the traffic can burst per interval can be found using the following formula:
	Bc = Tc * CIR
excess	(Optional) The excess bit rate (Be) that traffic is allowed to burst to beyond the sustained bit rate during the first interval, ranging from 0 to 100,000,000 in bits per interval.
	The Be is an optional parameter that assumes that the token bucket will be completely full:
	Be = Bc * 2
buffer	(Optional) Used to specify a buffer limit, ranging from 1 to 4096.

GTS configuration requires two steps: find the traffic-shaping values, and configure an interface for traffic shaping.

Step 1   Find the correct traffic-shaping values. To find the traffic-shaping values for your particular traffic-shaping configuration, you need the following information:

      — CIR

      — Bc

      — Be

If you will be configuring only traffic shaping to the interface's CIR limitations, you need to know only the CIR for the particular interface. For a more granular configuration, you can also provide the Bc. The Bc specifies the number of bits that the interface can transmit within a given interval. If you do not know your Bc, you can find it using the following formula:

Bc = CIR * Tc

And the final, optional, item that you must have before configuring GTS is the Be. The Be specifies the amount of traffic that can burst when the interface has replenished enough tokens to support a burst; this will generally be considered the first interval. The Be is found using the following formula:

Be = Bc * 2

If the interface will not be supporting burst, you use the following formula:

Be = Bc

Step 2   From interface configuration mode, enable traffic shaping using the **traffic-shaping** command. In the following example, traffic shaping is being used to limit the rate on all traffic on interface serial0/0 to 256 kbps. This limit is imposed by delaying any traffic over 32 kb/interval; the interval of time used to shape traffic is 125 ms. So, in this case, during each 125-ms interval, interface serial0/0 can transmit up to 32 kb. Any amount of traffic that exceeds the 32 kb limit during that interval will be queued until the next interval:

```
interface Serial0/0
 ip address 10.1.1.5 255.255.255.0
 traffic-shape rate 256000 32000 32000 1000

Router# show traffic-shape

Interface   Se0/0
          Access Target   Byte   Sustain   Excess    Interval  Increment Adapt
VC        List   Rate     Limit  bits/int  bits/int  (ms)      (bytes)   Active
-                256000   8000   32000     32000     125       4000      -
```

In Example 6-21, packets from the 136.78.65.0/28 network are transmitted over the WAN interface, as shown in Figure 6-9. Traffic shaping is used to constrain the amount of traffic leaving Ethernet 0, with the source address beginning with 136.78.65.0/28, to 512 kbps, with a 64-kb/interval sustained bit rate. In this case, there is no excess burst rate. This means that traffic from the 136.78.65.0/28 network will be shaped to 64 kb for each of the eight 125-ms intervals, which will amount to 512 kbps. If the interface receives more than 64 kb in any one interval, the excess traffic will be queued until the next interval, preventing the interface from sending more than 512 kbps or 64 kb per 125 ms.

Figure 6-9   *Using GTS to Limit LAN to WAN Traffic*

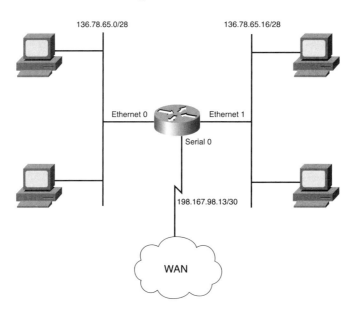

Example 6-21 *Using GTS to Shape Traffic*

```
interface Ethernet0
 ip address 136.78.65.1 255.255.255.240
traffic-shape rate 512000 64000 64000
!
interface Ethernet1
 ip address 136.78.65.17 255.255.255.240
!
interface Serial0
 ip address 198.167.98.14 255.255.255.252
!
access-list 136 permit ip 136.78.65.0 0.0.0.15 any
!
LAN-Router# show traffic-shape
Interface   Et0
        Access Target   Byte    Sustain   Excess    Interval  Increment Adapt
VC      List   Rate     Limit   bits/int  bits/int  (ms)      (bytes)   Active
-       136    512000   8000    64000     0         125       8000      -
LAN-Router# show traffic-shape statistics
                Access Queue   Packets   Bytes    Packets   Bytes    Shaping
I/F             List   Depth                       Delayed   Delayed  Active
Et0             136    0       39        2886     0         0        no
```

To view the GTS configuration, use the **show traffic-shaping** command. The **show traffic-shaping statistics** command enables you to monitor GTS activity. The command displays information about the current queue depth on each of the GTS-enabled interfaces, the number of packets sent with and without traffic-shaping queuing delays, and whether traffic shaping is currently active. As long as the traffic rate is below the traffic-shaping rate, the traffic will not be shaped. When the traffic rate exceeds the configured traffic-shaping parameters—or, in other words, if packets are arriving at the interface faster than tokens are being replenished—the excess traffic will be shaped. Traffic shaping will be active only when an interface is exceeding its CIR, Bc, and Be.

Classifying and Marking Traffic with CAR

Committed access rate (CAR) is a traffic policy classification and marking method used to police IP traffic based on IP precedence, DSCP value, MAC addresses, or access lists.

Traffic policy classification involves defining a traffic policy and using CAR to enforce rate limits. Traffic that conforms to the configured rate limit can be forwarded as is, or it can be marked to provide QoS at different points all the way through the network.

Marking changes the value of the IP precedence or DSCP in the ToS byte from the IP header. The traffic-marking action is defined either when a packet conforms to a value or when a packet exceeds a value. By marking traffic, CAR affects how traffic is treated at points later in the network because WFQ and WRED react to the CAR-assigned ToS values, giving higher-priority traffic a better weight.

CAR uses the token-bucket scheme, similar to that used by traffic shaping to determine whether an interface has resources available to transmit a packet by checking to see whether there are enough tokens in the bucket. If the interface has the resources to forward the packet (tokens are available), the tokens are removed from the bucket, the packet is transmitted, and, after the interval has elapsed, the tokens are added back into the bucket. If the interface does not have resources available, no tokens are available; CAR defines the action to take on the packet. The actions that CAR matches are conform actions, where the packet conforms to a specified traffic trait, or exceed values, where traffic exceeds a certain traffic trait value. CAR uses three rate definitions to define traffic rates:

- **Normal rate**—Like the CIR in traffic shaping, the normal rate in CAR can be described as the average rate of traffic, or the average rate that tokens are added to the bucket.

- **Normal burst**—Like the sustained bit rate (Bc) in traffic shaping, the normal burst is the amount of traffic allowed to exceed the normal traffic rate during an interval of time.

- **Excess burst**—Traffic that exceeds the normal burst. When excess burst is configured, tokens are borrowed and added to the bucket to allow for a certain amount of traffic bursts. After the borrowed tokens have been used, any further traffic received on that interface is dropped. Traffic bursts can occur only for short periods of time, before causing the token bucket to run out of tokens:

  - Cisco recommends that the normal traffic rate be equal to the average traffic rate over a period of time. The normal burst rate should equal the normal rate in bytes (times 8 for bits) * 1.5 seconds. If you are planning to use an extended rate, the extended rate must be greater than the normal burst rate. If the extended burst rate is not greater than the normal burst rate (Bc = Be), the interface will not allow for extended bursts. So the extended rate should be the normal burst rate times 2. If you have a rate of 1.544 Mbps, the normal burst is 2.316 Mbps, and the excess burst is 4.632 Mbps.

NOTE   When determining which shaping or policing method you should deploy on your network, always follow one rule of thumb: Traffic shapers shape traffic using buffers, so shaping should always be done on an egress interface where excess traffic can be buffered. Traffic policing or CAR is more effective when applied to inbound traffic because policing and rate limiting do not buffer traffic.

To configure CAR, use the **rate-limit** command in interface configuration mode as shown here. Table 6-17 shows the **rate-limit** command arguments and their descriptions in Cisco IOS Software Release 12.2(12)T:

```
rate-limit {input | output} {rate | access-group {access-list-number | rate-limit access-
list-number} | dscp dscp-value | qos-group qos-group-index } normal-burst maximum-burst
conform-action {continue | drop | set-dscp-continue dscp-value | set-dscp-transmit dscp-
value | set-mpls-exp-continue mpls-exp-value | set-mpls-exp-transmit mpls-exp-value | set-
prec-continue precedence-value | set-prec-transmit precedence-value | set-qos-continue
qos-group-index | set-qos-transmit qos-group-index | transmit) exceed-action {continue |
drop | set-dscp-continue dscp-value | set-dscp-transmit dscp-value | set-mpls-exp-continue
mpls-exp-value | set-mpls-exp-transmit mpls-exp-value | set-prec-continue precedence-
value | set-pres-transmit precedence-value | set-qos-continue qos-group-index | set-qos-
transmit qos-group-index | transmit)
```

Table 6-17   *CAR Command Arguments and Their Descriptions*

Command Argument	Description
input	output	Specifies the traffic direction.
normal-rate	The average traffic rate, under normal circumstances, for a period of time in bits/second ranging from 8000 to 2,000,000,000.

Table 6-17   *CAR Command Arguments and Their Descriptions (Continued)*

Command Argument	Description
`access-group {access-list-number |` `rate-limit rate-list-number}`	Specifies either a standard or extended access list, ranging from 1 to 2699, or a rate list. Rate lists 0–99 are used to specify IP precedence values, and rate lists 100–199 are used to specify MAC addresses.
`dscp dscp-value`	Specifies a DSCP value ranging from 0 to 63.
`qos-group qos-group-index`	Specifies a QoS group ranging from 0 to 99.

`normal-burst`	Specifies the normal burst size in bytes, ranging from 1000 to 512,000,000.
	
	The normal burst is found using the following formula:
	`Normal burst (Bc) = normal rate (CIR in bytes) *`
	`1.5 seconds`

`maximum-burst`	Specifies the excess burst size in bytes, ranging from 2000 to 1,024,000,000.
	
	If used, you can find the excess burst by using the following formula:
	`Excess Burst (Be) = Normal burst (Bc) * 2`
	Otherwise, excess burst equals normal burst, as shown here:
	`Excess burst (Be) = normal burst (Bc)`

`conform-action`	Any packets conforming to the normal rate will do the activity specified by the next value.
`continue`	Continues processing through the rest of the list.
`drop`	Immediately drops the packet and exits the list.
`set-dscp-continue dscp-value`	Sets the DSCP value to the specified value, ranging from 0 to 63, and continues processing the rest of the list.
`set-dscp-transmit dscp-value`	Sets the DSCP value, ranging from 0 and 63, transmits the packet, and exits the list without further processing.
`set-mpls-exp-continue mpls-exp-value`	Sets the MPLS experimental value, ranging from 0 to 7, and continues processing the rest of the list.
`set-mpls-exp-transmit mpls-exp-value`	Sets the MPLS experimental value, ranging from 0 to 7, immediately transmits the packet, and exits the list without any further processing.
`set-prec-continue precedence-value`	Sets the IP precedence value, ranging from 0 to 7, and continues process the rest of the list.

continues

Table 6-17   *CAR Command Arguments and Their Descriptions (Continued)*

Command Argument	Description
set-prec-transmit *precedence-value*	Sets the IP precedence value, ranging from 0 to 7, transmits the packet, and exits the list without further processing.
set-qos-continue *qos-group-index*	Sets the QoS group number, ranging from 0 to 99, for the packet and continues processing the rest of the list.
set-qos-transmit *qos-group-index*	Sets the QoS group number for the packet, ranging from 0 to 99, transmits the packet, and exits the list without further processing.
transmit	Transmits the packet and stops evaluating the list.
exceed-action	Specifies the action to take if the normal rate has been exceeded.
	The action to take upon an exceeded action.
continue	Continues processing through the rest of the list.
drop	Immediately drops the packet and exits the list.
set-dscp-continue *dscp-value*	Sets the DSCP value to the specified value, ranging from 0 to 63, and continues processing the rest of the list.
set-dscp-transmit *dscp-value*	Sets the DSCP value, ranging from 0 and 63, transmits the packet, and exits the list without further processing.
set-mpls-exp-continue *mpls-exp-value*	Sets the MPLS experimental value, ranging from 0 to 7, and continues processing the rest of the list.
set-mpls-exp-transmit *mpls-exp-value*	Sets the MPLS experimental value, ranging from 0 to 7, immediately transmits the packet, and exits the list without any further processing.
set-prec-continue *precedence-value*	Sets the IP precedence value, ranging from 0 to 7, and continues processing the rest of the list.
set-pres-transmit *precedence-value*	Sets the IP precedence value, ranging from 0 to 7, transmits the packet, and exits the list without further processing.
set-qos-continue *qos-group-index*	Sets the QoS group number for the packet, ranging from 0 to 99, and continues processing the rest of the list.
set-qos-transmit *qos-group-index*	Sets the QoS group number for the packet, ranging from 0 to 99, transmits the packet, and exits the list without further processing.
transmit	Transmits the packet and stops evaluating the list.

In Example 6-22, the **rate-limit** command is used with access list 101 to limit incoming traffic for host 195.42.48.155 to 2 Mbps with a 375,000-byte normal burst and 750,000-byte excess burst. Any traffic conforming to the normal traffic rate will have its IP precedence value set to Flash-override (4) and will by transmitted immediately. Traffic exceeding the normal burst rate will be continue to be processed.

Next, CAR is used to police and mark traffic. First, this **rate-limit** command is used with access list 102 to limit all passive FTP traffic to host 195.42.48.7 to 4 Mbps. Then, it is also used to set the normal burst rate to 75,000 bytes and the extended burst rate to 1,500,000 bytes. Any traffic that conforms to the rate limits should be transmitted, and the router should continue on with CAR list processing. Any FTP traffic that exceeds this rule will be dropped.

NOTE   The following formulas were used to find the CAR parameters for the FTP example:

1. Normal rate in bytes = normal rate in bps * (1 byte / 8 bits = 125)

   4,000,000 bits * 125 = 500,000,000 bits = 500,000 bytes

2. Normal burst = normal rate in bytes * 1.5 seconds

   500,000 bytes * 1.5 = 750,000 bytes

3. Excess burst = normal burst * 2

   750,000 * 2 = 1,500,000 bytes

Example 6-22 *Using CAR to Police and Mark Traffic*

```
interface Ethernet0
 ip address 195.42.48.1 255.255.255.0
 rate-limit input access-group 101 2000000 375000 750000 conform-action set-prec-
continue 4 exceed-action continue
 rate-limit input 2000000 3000 6000 conform-action
  transmit exceed-action drop
 rate-limit input access-group 102 4000000 750000 1500000 conform-action continue
exceed-action drop
 rate-limit output 2000000 3000 6000 conform-action
transmit exceed-action drop
 !
access-list 101 permit ip any host 195.42.48.155
access-list 102 permit tcp any host 195.42.48.7 eq ftp
access-list 102 permit tcp any  host 195.42.48.7 gt 1023 established
```

Another way to specify traffic with CAR is to use the **access-list rate-limit** command, in conjunction with a rate list, to police traffic based on either IP precedence values or MAC addresses. The **access-list rate-limit** command is similar to the **access-list** command. Lists 0 through 99 are IP precedence lists used to either specify an exact IP precedence value (0 through 7) or specify certain precedence values using a mask. Lists 100 through 199 are used to specify MAC addresses:

```
access-list rate-limit list-number {precedence-value | precedence-mask)
access-list rate-limit list-number MAC-address
```

Precedence masks are created by converting the IP precedence values to 8-bit numbers. The routine value, 0, is converted the 8-bit number 00000001, for instance, and the priority bit, 1, is converted to 00000010, as shown in Table 6-18.

Table 6-18   *IP Precedence Mask Values*

Precedence Value	8-Bit Number Value
Routine (0)	00000001
Priority (1)	00000010
Immediate (2)	00000100
Flash (3)	00001000
Flash-override (4)	00010000
Critical (5)	00100000
Internet (6)	01000000
Network (7)	10000000

To find the bitmask value for the IP precedence mask, add the 8-bit number values for each of the precedence values to be matched. This number is then converted to hexadecimal, the format required for the command. For example, to match all high-priority traffic—Network, Internet, and Critical—a binary bitmask of 11100000 is converted to hexadecimal. This equals E0.

Network (7)	10000000
Internet (6)	01000000
Critical (5)	00100000
Bitmask =	11100000

So, to create an access list that matches the IP precedence values 1, 3, 5, and 7, you would create the mask 10101010, and the mask would convert to AA in hexadecimal.

Network (7)	10000000
Critical (5)	00100000
Flash (3)	00001000
Priority (1)	00000010
Bitmask =	10101010

Example 6-23 shows how the rate-limit access list is used to specify the odd IP precedence traffic and limit it to 256 kbps, with 48,000-byte normal burst and 96,000-byte excess burst.

Example 6-23 *Using a Rate-Limit Access List*

```
interface Serial0/0
 ip address 36.128.42.11 255.255.255.0
rate-limit output access-group 1 256000 48000 96000 conform-action continue
exceed-action drop
!
access-list rate-limit 1 mask AA
```

To verify and monitor CAR behavior, use the **show interface rate-limit** command. This command displays information about each of the rate limits that have been configured on a per-interface basis. Example 6-24 shows the **show interface rate-limit** command for the CAR configuration from the Serial 0/0 interface in Example 6-23.

Example 6-24 **show interface rate-limit** *Command*

```
Simpson# show int e 0 rate-limit
Simpson#show interfaces serial 0/0 rate-limit
Serial0/0
  Output
    matches: access-group 1
      params:  256000 bps, 48000 limit, 96000 extended limit
      conformed 2050 packets, 1534364 bytes; action: continue
      exceeded 629 packets, 514122 bytes; action: drop
      last packet: 160ms ago, current burst: 122 bytes
      last cleared 00:21:28 ago, conformed 9000 bps, exceeded 3000 bps
```

Now that you have seen basic ways to control traffic policies by using traffic shaping, and rate limiting, it's time to examine how you can prioritize real-time voice traffic by using IP RTP Priority.

Prioritizing Real-Time Voice Traffic

IP RTP priority allows all outbound Real Time Protocol (RTP) traffic to be strictly prioritized over all other traffic on an interface level; all other traffic is fairly queued using WFQ. IP RTP Priority is useful on links with speeds less than 1.544 Mbps (T1), where voice traffic is more at risk of delay due to fragmentation, congestion, queuing, or serialization. Because voice traffic is real-time traffic, it is extremely sensitive to delay. You enable IP RTP Priority by using the **ip rtp priority** command in interface configuration mode. The priority queue created by the **ip rtp priority** command is a strict-priority queue; after the bandwidth configured with the **ip rtp priority** command has been exceeded, all further packets in that queue are discarded until queue space is available to store packets. Before configuring RTP Priority on any interface, you have some important information to gather: the number of voice calls that will be placed, the voice codec in use, and the call frequency. You must also consider whether you will be prioritizing only voice traffic or whether you will also need to prioritize control traffic. For this reason, it is crucial that the IP RTP Priority bandwidth be correctly allocated. As with LLQ, it is always better to err on the safe side and allow slightly more bandwidth than required than to have packets dropped because of packet headers, network jitter, or control traffic. As with CBWFQ and LLQ, the sum of the bandwidth configured for IP RTP Priority cannot exceed 75 percent of the interface's available bandwidth; the remaining 25 percent is reserved for network control and routing traffic.

To enable IP RTP Priority from interface configuration mode, use the **ip rtp priority** command. Table 6-19 lists the **ip rtp priority** command arguments and their descriptions:

```
ip rtp priority starting-port-number port-range bandwidth
```

Table 6-19 **ip rtp priority** *Command Arguments*

Command Argument	Description
starting-port-number	The first RTP port number to assign to the priority queue. RTP port numbers are UDP ports ranging from 2000 to 65,535.
port-range	The RTP port range that when added to the starting port number equals the full range of RTP ports for prioritization, ranging from 0 to 16,383.
bandwidth	Specifies the maximum bandwidth to be used for the RTP Priority queue, ranging from 0 to 2000 in kbps.

Example 6-25 shows how RTP Priority is used to strictly prioritize all RTP traffic ranging from UDP ports 16,384 to 32,767 (the full range of RTP ports) and limit the priority queue to 64 kbps. All other traffic on this interface is queued fairly using WFQ.

Example 6-25 *Using* **ip rtp priority** *to Prioritize Voice Traffic*

```
interface Serial0
 bandwidth 256
 ip address 85.114.95.1 255.255.255.0
 encapsulation frame-relay
 fair-queue 64 256 0
 frame-relay interface-dlci 110
 ip rtp priority 16384 16383 64
```

To verify RTP configuration, you can either use the **show interface** or **show queue** command. Each command shows the same type of RTP Priority data, the bandwidth reservation. Example 6-26 shows the **show interface** command output for an interface before RTP Priority was applied, and Example 6-27 shows the output from the **show interface** and **show queueing** commands after RTP Priority has been applied.

Example 6-26 *Before Configuring RTP Priority*

```
Simpson#show interfaces serial 0 | begin Queue
  Queueing strategy: weighted fair
  Output queue: 0/1000/64/0 (size/max total/threshold/drops)
     Conversations  0/2/256 (active/max active/max total)
     Reserved Conversations 0/0 (allocated/max allocated)
     Available Bandwidth 1158 kilobits/sec
```

Example 6-27 *Display RTP Priority Bandwidth*

```
Simpson#show queueing interface serial 0
Interface Serial0 queueing strategy: fair
  Input queue: 0/75/0/0 (size/max/drops/flushes); Total output drops: 0
  Queueing strategy: weighted fair
  Output queue: 0/1000/64/0 (size/max total/threshold/drops)
     Conversations  0/2/256 (active/max active/max total)
     Reserved Conversations 0/0 (allocated/max allocated)
     Available Bandwidth 1094 kilobits/sec

Simpson#show interfaces serial 0 | begin Queue
  Queueing strategy: weighted fair
  Output queue: 0/1000/64/0 (size/max total/threshold/drops)
     Conversations  0/2/256 (active/max active/max total)
     Reserved Conversations 0/0 (allocated/max allocated)
     Available Bandwidth 1094 kilobits/sec
```

The first example shows the interface before applying RTP Priority. In this example, the interface has 1158 kbps available for all interface traffic. (1158 kbps is exactly 75 percent of the serial interface's bandwidth; the other 25 percent of the bandwidth is reserved for router control and signaling traffic.) The second example shows the same router interface after RTP Priority has been applied. In this example, RTP Priority was configured to reserve 64 kbps for the IP RTP strict-priority queue, so only 1094 kbps is left available for other all other unspecified traffic. The **debug priority** command displays WFQ output drops for the strict-priority RTP queue.

As you can see, setting RTP Priority for interfaces with smaller amounts of bandwidth can help save resources for time-critical, delay-sensitive RTP traffic. This section has shown how you can apply traffic shaping, rate limiting, and voice traffic prioritization on an interface basis to provide policy enforcement using QoS techniques. The next section explores more powerful and granular QoS techniques that can be applied within Cisco IOS Software's class-based queuing solutions.

Class-Based Queuing Solutions

Class-Based Weighed Fair Queuing (CBWFQ) combines advantages of CQ and WFQ to create an advanced queuing method that provides fair queuing to up to 64 user-defined classes. CBWFQ classes can be defined by protocol type, access list, or input interface; each class has its own queue. Classes are customized using characteristics such as bandwidth, weight, and queue size. After a queue exceeds its maximum size, packets are dropped using tail drop, the default behavior, or WRED if configured to do so. Traffic that does not match any class characteristics, called default class, is sent to the default queue where each flow (traffic sharing the same source and destination address and port number) is fairly queued using WFQ.

Before configuring CBWFQ, you need to be aware of a number of rules, including the following:

- Before CBWFQ can be installed, interfaces must be running their default queuing method. CBWFQ overrides the default method of queuing.

- Unless specified, CBWFQ uses tail drop rather than WRED when dropping packets.

- If you are planning to use CBWFQ with WRED, make sure that the interface is not already running WRED.

- CBWFQ does not support subinterfaces; it must be installed on a physical interface.

- CBWFQ supports only ATM variable bit rate (VBR) and available bit rate (ABR) circuits.

- Policy maps can be used for more than one interface, saving configuration space.

- The CBWFQ-configured bandwidth must not exceed 75 percent of the interface bandwidth. The other 25 percent is used for overhead control and routing traffic. If the bandwidth used by a policy map exceeds that available on the interface, the policy map is denied and removed from all other interfaces.

- CBWFQ, CQ, PQ, WFQ, and WRED are all mutually exclusive, service policies must be removed before any other queuing method can be installed.

- CBWFQ supports queue size limits and WRED, but not both in the same class policy.

As discussed in the following section, CBWFQ is a powerful QoS tool. Using CBWFQ, you can configure extremely granular QoS policies managing different types of traffic in different ways on the same interface.

CBWFQ can also use Network-Based Application Recognition (NBAR) protocol heuristics specified within a policy by protocol name. Although NBAR is not covered in great detail in this book, NBAR CBWFQ configuration is shown and described later in this chapter.

NOTE   NBAR protocol heuristics help identify protocols and applications that previously required long and complicated access lists. NBAR uses packet description language modules (PDLMs) to define protocol characteristics. PDLMs can be found on the Cisco website in the Software Download area under Cisco IOS Software, Other Cisco IOS Extensions, Packet Description Language Modules. PDLMs are loaded into a router, like any other software code or configurations. After you have loaded a PDLM, you can specify its location by using the **ip nbar** *path:filename* command in global configuration mode.

NOTE   CBWFQ NBAR support requires the use of Cisco Express Forwarding (CEF) switching on the interface where the service policy is applied.

CBWFQ classes are defined using class maps. Class maps contain the match criterion, which is used to specify the protocol that belongs to each class. Class maps make uses of the new Cisco IOS Software modular command-line interface (CLI) and are created using the **class-map** command. The **class-map** command differs slightly from Cisco IOS version 12.1 and 12.2. In 12.2, the optional **match-any** or **match-all** statement is added.

In Cisco IOS Software Release 12.2 and higher, you can also specify the type of class map by using the optional **match-all** or **match-any** statements. The **match-all** class map matches all of the criteria (logical AND), and a **match-any** class map matches any of the criteria specified by the class map (logical OR).

Cisco IOS Software Release 12.1:

```
class-map class-name
```
Cisco IOS Software Release 12.2:

```
class-map [match-any | match-all] class-name
```

NOTE   A number of QoS changes were made in Cisco IOS Software Release 12.2. In this chapter, Cisco IOS Software Release 12.2 is used in all examples. To remain compatible with Cisco IOS Software Release 12.1, I tried to use commands that are available in versions 12.1 and 12.2.

After you have created the class map, you enter the class map configuration mode, where you can specify the match criteria. Using the **match** command within the class map configuration mode, you can define class maps to use access lists, input interfaces, protocol types, and many other items as definitions. Table 6-20 shows the class map configuration commands and their definitions as of Cisco IOS Software Release 12.2(7).

Table 6-20   *Class Map* **match** *Command Values*

Match Command	IOS Version	Description
`access-group {access-list-number | name access-list-name}`	12.1	Matches an access list, ranging from 1 to 2699, or a named access list.
`any`	12.2	Matches any packets.
`class-map class-map-name`	12.2	Matches another nested class map.
`cos cos-value`	12.2	Class of service (CoS) matches one of the IEEE 802.1Q/ISL class of service/user priority values, ranging from 0 to 7. Up to 4 CoS value entries may be made using spaces as separators.
`destination-address mac hex-address`	12.2	Matches an destination MAC address in hexadecimal xxxx.xxxx.xxxx format.
`input-interface interface-name interface-number`	12.1	Matches an input interface.
`ip {dscp dscp-value | precedence precedence-value | rtp lower-port-range range}`	12.2	**ip dscp** matches up to 8 DSCP values from 0 to 63, one of the 12 AF classes mentioned in Table 7-14, one of the 7 Class Selector (CS) codepoints corresponding to an IP precedence value, the default DSCP value, or the Expedited Forwarding (EF) PHB value. **ip precedence** matches (up to 4) IP precedence values using either an integer value (0–7), or the IP precedence names from Table 6-14. **ip rtp** matches a RTP UDP port number from 2000 to 65,535, and a RTP UDP port range from 0 to 16,383.
`mpls experimental value`	12.2	Multiprotocol label switching (MPLS). Matches up to 8 MPLS values, ranging from 0 to 7.

Table 6-20 *Class Map* **match** *Command Values (Continued)*

Match Command	IOS Version	Description
not {access-group *access-list-number* | any | class-map *class-map-name* | destination-address mac *hex-address* | input-interface *interface-name interface-number* | ip {dscp *dscp-value* | precedence *precedence-value* | rtp *lower-port-range range*) | mpls *value* | qos-group *qos-group-index* | sources-address mac *hex-address*}	12.2	Does not match an access-group, any, class-map, destination-address, input-interface, ip, mpls, qos-group, or sources-address specified.
protocol *protocol-name*	12.1*	Matches the specified protocol using NBAR heuristics:
		arp—IP ARP
		bgp—BGP protocol
		bridge—Bridging
		bstun—Block Serial Tunnel
		cdp—Cisco Discovery Protocol
		citrix—Citrix traffic
		clns—ISO CLNS
		clns_es—ISO CLNS end system
		clns_is—ISO CLNS intermediate system
		cmns—ISO CMNS
		compressedtcp—Compressed TCP
		cuseeme—CU-SeeMe desktop videoconference
		custom-01—Custom protocol custom-01
		custom-02—Custom protocol custom-02
		custom-03—Custom protocol custom-03
		custom-04—Custom protocol custom-04
		custom-05—Custom protocol custom-05
		custom-06—Custom protocol custom-06
		custom-07—Custom protocol custom-07
		custom-08—Custom protocol custom-08
		custom-09—Custom protocol custom-09

continues

Table 6-20 *Class Map* **match** *Command Values (Continued)*

Match Command	IOS Version	Description
`protocol protocol-name` (*Continued*)		**custom-10**—Custom protocol custom-10
		dhcp—DHCP protocol
		dlsw—Data-link switching
		dns—DNS lookup
		egp—EGP routing protocol
		eigrp—EIGRP routing Protocol
		exchange—MS-RPC for Exchange
		fasttrack—FastTrack traffic (KaZaA, Morpheus, Grokster, and so on)
		finger—Finger
		ftp—FTP protocol
		gnutella—Gnutella traffic (BearShare,LimeWire,Gnotella, and so on)
		gopher—Gopher
		gre—GRE tunneling protocol
		http—HTTP web traffic
		icmp—ICMP protocol
		imap—IMAP Protocol
		ip—IPv4 protocol
		ipinip—IP in IP tunnel encapsulation
		ipsec—IP Security Protocol (ESP/AH)
		ipv6—IPv6
		ipx—Novell IPX
		irc—Internet Relay Chat
		kerberos—Kerberos authentication
		l2tp—L2F/L2TP tunnel
		ldap—LDAP directory protocol
		llc2—LLC-2
		napster—Napster traffic
		netbios—NetBIOS
		netshow—Microsoft NetShow

Table 6-20   *Class Map* **match** *Command Values (Continued)*

Match Command	IOS Version	Description
`protocol protocol-name` (*Continued*)		**nfs**—UNIX Network File System
		nntp—Network News Transfer Protocol
		notes—Lotus Notes
		novadigm—Novadigm EDM
		ntp—Network Time Protocol
		pad—X.25 PAD
		pcanywhere—Symantec pcANYWHERE
		pop3—Post Office Protocol
		pptp—Microsoft PPTP tunneling
		printer—LPD print spooler
		qllc—QLLC protocol
		rcmd—BSD **r** commands (**rsh, rlogin, rexec**)
		realaudio—Real Audio streaming protocol
		rip—RIP routing protocol
		rsrb—RSRB bridging
		rsvp—RSVP protocol
		rtp—Real Time Protocol
		secure-ftp—FTP over TLS/SSL
		secure-http—Secured HTTP
		secure-imap—IMAP over TLS/SSL
		secure-irc—IRC over TLS/SSL
		secure-ldap—LDAP over TLS/SSL
		secure-nntp—NNTP over TLS/SSL
		secure-pop3—POP3 over TLS/SSL
		secure-telnet—Telnet over TLS/SSL
		smtp—SMTP protocol
		snapshot—Snapshot routing protocol
		snmp—SNMP protocol
		socks—SOCKS
		sqlnet—SQL*NET for Oracle

continues

Table 6-20   *Class Map* **match** *Command Values (Continued)*

Match Command	IOS Version	Description
`protocol protocol-name` (*Continued*)		**sqlserver**—MS SQL Server
		ssh—Secured Shell
		streamwork—Xing Technology StreamWorks player
		stun—Serial Tunnel protocol
		sunrpc—Sun RPC
		syslog—System logging utility
		telnet—Telnet
		tftp—TFTP protocol
		vdolive—VDOLive streaming video
		vofr—Voice over Frame Relay
		xwindows—X Windows remote access
		xns—Xerox Network Services
`qos-group qos-group-index`	12.2	Matches a specified QoS group, ranging from 0 to 99.
`source-address mac hex-address`	12.2	Matches a source MAC address in hexadecimal format (xxxx.xxxx.xxxx).

* Not all protocols are available in all versions of Cisco IOS Software.

After you have entered class map configuration mode, you can do a number of things besides entering a **match** command. To configure a description for your class map, use the **description** command. To rename the class map without removing it, use the **rename** command.

After defining the class map, you must then define a policy map to make the policy that will be applied to your class map. Policy maps are defined using the **policy-map** *policy-name* command, which enters you into policy map configuration mode, specified by the **(config-pmap)#** prompt. The policy map is applied to interfaces using a service policy. To enter policy map configuration mode, use the **policy-map** command. In this mode, you can also add a description to the policy map, alter the configuration, or rename the policy map.

NOTE   Using the Cisco Modular QoS command-line interface, you can also embed policies and classes within other policies and classes, by which you can create very granular QoS configurations without the need to retype each class or policy definition.

After you are in policy map configuration mode, you must define the class that the policy will apply to using the **class** *class-name* command, which enters you into policy map class configuration mode specified by the **(config-pmap-c)#** prompt.

After you are in policy map class configuration mode, the mode used to configure the policy for the class previously specified, you can define the parameters for the service policy. Table 6-21 shows the service policy parameters.

Table 6-21   *Service Policy Parameters*

Policy Command	IOS Version	Description
bandwidth {*bandwidth-limit* | percent *percentage* | remaining percent *remaining-percentage*)	12.1	Assigns a bandwidth limit for the class. This limit can be either an amount specified in kbps or a percentage (not to exceed 75% of the interfaces bandwidth). To use a specific amount of bandwidth, enter the amount, ranging from 8 to 2,000,000 in kbps. To specify a percentage of interface bandwidth, use the **percent** or **remaining percent** keywords, followed by a value ranging from 1-100 percent.
police {*rate-bps* {[*normal-burst-*] [*excess-burst*]| [bc *normal-burst*] [bc *excess-burst*] | cir *rate-bps* [*normal-burst*] [*excess-burst*] [bc *normal-burst*] [be *excess-burst* | pir [*peak-rate*] *excess-burst*]} [conform-action *action*] [exceed-action *action*] [violate-action *action*] }	12.2	Enables traffic policing for the traffic defined in this class. Class-Based policing is covered later in this chapter.
priority {*bandwidth burst* | percent *percentage burst*}	12.1	Creates a strict-priority queue within the service policy, referred to as Low Latency Queuing (LLQ), which is covered later in this chapter. **bandwidth** defines a limit for the strict-priority queue, ranging from 8 to 2,000,000 in kbps. **burst** 32 to 2,000,000 in bytes. **percent** defines a percentage of bandwidth, from 1-100 percent. **burst** ranges from 32 to 200000 in bytes.
queue-limit *number-of-packets*	12.1	Defines a maximum queue size. After the queue size has been exceeded, all packets are dropped using tail drop. The range is from 1 to 512 packets. The default value is 64 on all non-VIP-based platforms.

continues

Table 6-21 *Service Policy Parameters (Continued)*

Policy Command	IOS Version	Description
`random-detect [dscp dscp-value minimum-threshold max-threshold mark-probability-denominator	dscp-based	ecn	exponential-weighing-constant weighed-average	prec-based	precedence [precedence-value minimum-threshold max-threshold mark-probability-denominator |rsvp minimum-threshold max-threshold mark-probability-denominator]`	12.1*	Enables WRED for packets that exceed the maximum queue size. **dscp** *value* matches (up to 4 values) a DSCP value from 0 to 63, one of the of the 12 AF classes, one of the 7 Class Selector (CS) code-points corresponding to an IP precedence value (1–7), the default DSCP value, the Expedited Forwarding (EF) PHB value, or RSVP traffic specifying a minimum and maximum threshold in packets and optionally the RSVP mark probability denominator. You can find the AF, CS, and EF value descriptions in Table 7-14. **dscp-based** enables DSCP-based WRED rather than precedence-based WRED. **ecn**—Explicit congestion notification. **exponential-weighting-constant** specifies the weight to be used by WRED when calculating average queue length; the default weight factor is 9. Ranges from 1 to 16 in the format 2^*[number]*. **prec-based** enables precedence-based WRED, the default WRED behavior. **precedence** configures the parameters for the IP precedence values—for each IP precedence value from 0 to 7, the minimum and maximum threshold of a packet that must be reached for packet drop, and the mark probability denominator that defines the fraction of packets that are dropped when the thresholds have been exceeded.
`service-policy`	12.2	Specifies another nested policy map name.
`shape`	12.2	Configures class-based shaping, covered later in this chapter. **average** *CIR [Bc] [Be]*. **max-buffers** configures a maximum buffer limit. **peak** *CIR [Bc] [Be]*.

*DSCP commands do not appear until 12.2

By default, all traffic that has not been defined as belonging to a class is provided with best-effort service; however, a default class can also be defined. Default classes allow for the configuration of any unclassified traffic. In this way, any unclassified traffic in the default class can either be given the same level of service that would achieved on a WFQ-enabled interface, with each unclassified traffic flow receiving a fair share of the remaining bandwidth, or it can be queued on a FIFO basis with a bandwidth restriction.

The default class is defined by creating a class-default class, using the command **class class-default** command from policy map configuration mode, which enters you into policy map class configuration mode for the default class:

```
Router(config-pmap)#class class-default
```

When you are defining the class-default class, the **fair-queue** command becomes available, allowing all previously unclassified traffic to be queued using WFQ. This command is available only for the default class:

```
fair-queue dynamic-queue-limit
```

Using the **fair-queue** command, you can define a dynamic queue limit for all WFQ traffic in the default class. The *dynamic-queue-limit* ranges from 16 to 4096 and can be entered in powers of 2 (2^[number]).

Alternatively, instead of configuring WFQ for the remaining unclassified traffic, you can set a bandwidth limitation using FIFO best-effort queuing with the **bandwidth** command.

NOTE   When configuring the default class, it is important to note that either WFQ or a bandwidth limitation can be configured, but both commands cannot be configured together.

The default class can also have class parameters, such as traffic policing, IP RTP Priority, tail dropping with queue limits, WRED, and class-based shaping, as mentioned previously in Table 6-21.

After the class map has been characterized and the policy map has been defined, you now have a service policy. To apply the service policy to an interface, use the **service-policy** command in interface configuration mode. You can use the **service policy** command on either inbound or outbound interface traffic by using the **input** or **output** command arguments:

```
Interface serial0
  service-policy {input | output} policy-name
```

Using CBWFQ, you can classify traffic types into service groups and apply the appropriate policies to enforce the proper traffic limitations or prioritization. In the following example, two classes are defined. ClassIP provides 25 percent of the interface bandwidth to IP traffic and also uses WRED as a congestion-avoidance mechanism. ClassIPX provides another 25 percent of the interface bandwidth to IPX traffic; because IPX is not supported by WRED, however, during periods of congestion, tail drop is used to discard packets. Any other remaining unclassified traffic is to be queued using 16 WFQ queues:

Step 1   The first step required for CBWFQ configuration is to define the class. In this example, ClassIP is defined to match all IP traffic:

```
Simpson(config)#class-map ClassIP
```

Step 2   After the class has been defined, from within the class map configuration mode, define the class characteristics. The ClassIP class must match all IP packets, so the **match protocol ip** statement is used. After the match criteria has been defined, you can exit class map configuration mode:

```
Simpson(config-cmap)# match protocol ip
Simpson(config-cmap)# exit
```

Step 3   (Optional) Create any other required classes, up to 64. This step is required for each class definition that will be used for the service policy. In this example, ClassIPX is defined to match all IPX traffic:

```
Simpson(config)# class-map ClassIPX
Simpson(config-cmap)# match protocol ipx
Simpson(config-cmap)# exit
```

Step 4   Create a policy map. The policy map is used to define class policies. One policy map can contain multiple classes and their policies. In this example, the myPolicy policy is used for the class policy definitions for ClassIP and ClassIPX:

```
Simpson(config)# policy myPolicy
```

Step 5   Specify the class map to be used with the service policy under the policy map. To create a service policy for the IP traffic, ClassIP is specified under myPolicy:

```
Simpson(config-pmap)# class ClassIP
```

Step 6   Within the policy map class configuration mode, specify the policy parameters. As mentioned earlier, ClassIP is assigned 50 percent of the interface bandwidth. This is accomplished using the **bandwidth percent 50** command. To configure the policy to use WRED for IP congestion avoidance, the **random-detect** command is used without any parameters:

```
Simpson(config-pmap-c)# bandwidth percent 50
Simpson(config-pmap-c)# random-detect
Simpson(config-pmap-c)# exit
```

Step 7   (Optional) If necessary, repeat Steps 5 and 6 for each class definition. Next, ClassIPX is assigned 25 percent of the interface bandwidth:

```
Simpson(config-pmap)# class ClassIPX
Simpson(config-pmap-c)# bandwidth percent 25
Simpson(config-pmap-c)# exit
```

Step 8   (Optional) Create a default class for all unclassified traffic. In this example, a default class is created to queue any unclassified traffic using up to 16 dynamic WFQ queues:

```
Simpson(config-pmap)#class class-default
Simpson(config-pmap-c)# fair-queue 16
Simpson(config-pmap-c)# exit
Simpson(config-pmap)# exit
```

Step 9   After you finish creating the class map and policy, apply the policy to an interface using the **service-policy** command. To activate the service policy, it is applied to an interface. In this example, it is applied to outbound traffic on interface serial 0/1:

```
Simpson(config)# int s 0/1
Simpson(config-if)# service-policy output myPolicy
```

Step 10   Example 6-28 shows the complete configuration for the example from the preceding steps.

Example 6-28 *Final Configuration for the CBWFQ Example*

```
class-map match-all ClassIPX
  match protocol ipx
class-map match-all ClassIP
  match protocol ip
!
 policy-map myPolicy
  class ClassIP
   bandwidth percent 50
   random-detect
  class ClassIPX
   bandwidth percent 25
  class class-default
   fair-queue 16
!
interface Serial0/1
 ip address 192.168.3.1 255.255.255.252
 ipx network 10AB
 service-policy output myPolicy
```

Step 11   Monitor and verify the configuration for the policy using the **show policy-map** or the **show policy-map interface** commands. The **show policy-map myPolicy** command shows how myPolicy was configured. In this example, ClassIP is configured with 50 percent of the interface bandwidth to IP traffic using WFQ, with WRED using the default WRED IP precedence settings. ClassIPX limits all IPX traffic to 25 percent of the interface bandwidth using tail drop in the event of congestion. And all unclassified traffic is assigned to class-default, and class-default is queued using WFQ:

```
Simpson# show policy-map myPolicy
```

```
Policy Map myPolicy
   Class ClassIP
     Bandwidth 50 (%)
           exponential weight 9
           class    min-threshold    max-threshold    mark-probability
           -------------------------------------------------------------

           0         -                -                1/10
           1         -                -                1/10
           2         -                -                1/10
           3         -                -                1/10
           4         -                -                1/10
           5         -                -                1/10
           6         -                -                1/10
           7         -                -                1/10
           rsvp      -                -                1/10

   Class ClassIPX
     Bandwidth 25 (%) Max Threshold 64 (packets)
   Class class-default
     Flow based Fair Queueing
Bandwidth 0 (kbps) Max Threshold 64 (packets)
```

The **show policy-map interface serial 0/1** command displays detailed information on the service policy for serial 0/1, including the number of packets sent, packet transmission rate, number of dropped packets, number of queued packets, and detailed queuing information.

```
Simpson#sh policy-map interface serial 0/1
 Serial0/1

  Service-policy output: myPolicy

    Class-map: ClassIPX (match-all)
      5 packets, 520 bytes
      5 minute offered rate 0 bps, drop rate 0 bps
      Match: protocol ip
      Queueing
        Output Queue: Conversation 25
        Bandwidth 50 (%)
        Bandwidth 772 (kbps)
        (pkts matched/bytes matched) 5/520
        (depth/total drops/no-buffer drops) 0/0/0
         exponential weight: 9
         mean queue depth: 0
```

class	Transmitted pkts/bytes	Random drop pkts/bytes	Tail drop pkts/bytes	Minimum thresh	Maximum thresh	Mark prob
0	5/520	0/0	0/0	20	40	1/10
1	0/0	0/0	0/0	22	40	1/10
2	0/0	0/0	0/0	24	40	1/10
3	0/0	0/0	0/0	26	40	1/10
4	0/0	0/0	0/0	28	40	1/10
5	0/0	0/0	0/0	30	40	1/10
6	0/0	0/0	0/0	32	40	1/10
7	0/0	0/0	0/0	34	40	1/10
rsvp	0/0	0/0	0/0	36	40	1/10

```
    Class-map: ClassIPX (match-all)
      0 packets, 0 bytes
      5 minute offered rate 0 bps, drop rate 0 bps
      Match: protocol ipx
```

```
Queueing
  Output Queue: Conversation 26
  Bandwidth 25 (%)
  Bandwidth 386 (kbps) Max Threshold 64 (packets)
  (pkts matched/bytes matched) 0/0
  (depth/total drops/no-buffer drops) 0/0/0

Class-map: class-default (match-any)
  140 packets, 9840 bytes
  5 minute offered rate 0 bps, drop rate 0 bps
  Match: any
  Queueing
    Flow Based Fair Queueing
    Maximum Number of Hashed Queues 16
    (total queued/total drops/no-buffer drops) 0/0/0
```

When monitoring a CBWFQ-enabled interface, you can use the **show interface** output to display the default class configuration, including the queuing strategy, queuing counters, and whether WFQ is enabled, as well as information about the WFQ queues and RSVP conversations. Before you apply any CBWFQ commands, the bandwidth shown by the **show interfaces** command will be equal to the 75 percent of the interface bandwidth. That is the maximum (default) amount available to be used by CBWFQ; the other 25 percent is reserved for router control traffic and routing traffic. In this example, the available bandwidth prior to the CBWFQ configuration was 1158 kb, 75 percent of the 1544 kb available on the serial interface. After applying the CBWFQ configuration, the interface's available bandwidth should be 0 percent. If the bandwidth configured using the **bandwidth** command within a service policy exceeds the amount available, the policy will be removed from the interface and any other interfaces that it is applied to. You can change the amount of bandwidth available for CBWFQ by using the **max-reserved-bandwidth** *percent* command in interface configuration mode, although using this command may seriously affect router performance. Example 6-29 shows how CBWFQ affects the output from the **show interfaces** command before and after applying CBWFQ.

Example 6-29 *CBWFQ and the* **show interfaces** *Command*

```
Simpson# show interfaces serial 0/1
Serial0/1 is up, line protocol is up
  Hardware is PowerQUICC Serial
  Internet address is 192.168.3.1/24
  MTU 1500 bytes, BW 1544 Kbit, DLY 20000 usec,
    reliability 252/255, txload 1/255, rxload 1/255
  Encapsulation HDLC, loopback not set
  Keepalive set (10 sec)
  Last input 00:00:09, output 00:00:00, output hang never
  Last clearing of "show interface" counters never
  Input queue: 0/75/0/0 (size/max/drops/flushes); Total output drops: 0
  Queueing strategy: weighted fair
  Output queue: 0/1000/64/0 (size/max total/threshold/drops)
    Conversations  0/1/16 (active/max active/max total)
    Reserved Conversations 0/0 (allocated/max allocated)
    Available Bandwidth 1158 kilobits/sec
```

continues

Example 6-29 *CBWFQ and the* **show interfaces** *Command (Continued)*

```
         5 minute input rate 0 bits/sec, 0 packets/sec
         5 minute output rate 0 bits/sec, 0 packets/sec
             74999 packets input, 4663284 bytes, 0 no buffer
             Received 60312 broadcasts, 0 runts, 0 giants, 0 throttles
             7 input errors, 0 CRC, 7 frame, 0 overrun, 0 ignored, 0 abort
             60335 packets output, 4175959 bytes, 0 underruns
             0 output errors, 0 collisions, 15 interface resets
             0 output buffer failures, 0 output buffers swapped out
             13 carrier transitions
             DCD=up  DSR=up  DTR=up  RTS=up  CTS=up

Simpson# show interfaces serial 0/1
Serial0/1 is up, line protocol is up
  Hardware is PowerQUICC Serial
  Internet address is 192.168.3.1/24
  MTU 1500 bytes, BW 1544 Kbit, DLY 20000 usec,
      reliability 255/255, txload 1/255, rxload 1/255
  Encapsulation HDLC, loopback not set
  Keepalive set (10 sec)
  Last input 00:00:06, output 00:00:06, output hang never
  Last clearing of "show interface" counters never
  Input queue: 0/75/0/0 (size/max/drops/flushes); Total output drops: 0
  Queueing strategy: weighted fair
  Output queue: 0/1000/64/0 (size/max total/threshold/drops)
      Conversations  0/1/16 (active/max active/max total)
      Reserved Conversations 2/2 (allocated/max allocated)
      Available Bandwidth 0 kilobits/sec
  5 minute input rate 0 bits/sec, 0 packets/sec
  5 minute output rate 0 bits/sec, 0 packets/sec
      74950 packets input, 4660302 bytes, 0 no buffer
      Received 60263 broadcasts, 0 runts, 0 giants, 0 throttles
      6 input errors, 0 CRC, 6 frame, 0 overrun, 0 ignored, 0 abort
      60284 packets output, 4172143 bytes, 0 underruns
      0 output errors, 0 collisions, 14 interface resets
      0 output buffer failures, 0 output buffers swapped out
      13 carrier transitions
      DCD=up  DSR=up  DTR=up  RTS=up  CTS=up
```

This section introduced CBWFQ and described some ways that you can apply this technology to mark, queue, or drop traffic based on classes. The next section discusses CBWFQ's own traffic-shaping mechanism: class-based shaping.

Class-Based Shaping

As mentioned in the preceding section, as of Cisco IOS Software Release 12.2, it is possible to enable shaping within CBWFQ for service policies using class-based shaping. Class-based shaping enables you to configure shaping on a class-by-class basis within service policies rather than a per-interface basis using GTS. Class-based shaping is enabled from within CBWFQ by using the **shape** command in policy map class configuration mode. Table 6-22 shows the class-based shaping command and its arguments:

```
shape {average target-bit-rate [sustained-bit-rate] [excess-per-interval] | peak target-
    bit-rate [sustained-bit-rate] [excess-per-interval]  | max-buffers buffers }
```

Table 6-22   *Class-Based Shaping Command Arguments and Their Descriptions*

Command	Description
`average target-bit-rate` `[sustained-bit-rate]` `[excess-per-interval]`	The CBS **average** command configures the router to shape traffic to an average rate; with average-rate shaping, the shaper shapes all traffic to the normal burst rate for each interval. Like the GTS CIR, the target bit rate is the normal rate at which traffic will be transmitted (CIR), ranging from 8000 to the interface's full bit rate in bits per second. For example, a 1.544-Mbps interface's full CIR will range from 8000 to 154,400,000.
	(Optional) Like the GTS sustained bit rate (Bc), the CBS sustained bit rate is that traffic is allowed to burst to a multiple of 128 ranging from 256 to 1,544,000 (on a serial interface) in bits per interval. Cisco recommends that instead of manually calculating the value, you let the algorithm configure the sustained bit rate.
	You can find the sustained burst rate that the traffic can burst per interval by using the following formula:
	Bc = Tc * CIR
	(Optional) The excess bit/interval (Be) that traffic is allowed to burst to beyond the sustained bit rate, a multiple of 128 ranging from 0 to 1,544,000 (on a serial interface) in bits per interval. Cisco recommends that instead of manually calculating the value, you let the algorithm configure the sustained bit rate. If the Be is not entered, the software assumes that Be = Bc.
	Excess burst will always be greater than normal bursts, so the recommended formula for finding Be is this:
	Be = Bc * 2
`peak target-bit-rate` `[sustained-bit-rate]` `[excess-per-interval]`	The CBS **peak** command configures the router to shape traffic to the peak rate (Be + Bc) per interval. With peak-rate shaping, if tokens are available, traffic is shaped to the normal burst rate, but the excess burst per interval. Like the GTS CIR, the target bit rate is the normal rate that traffic will be transmitted at (CIR), ranging from 8000 to the interface's full bit rate in bits per second. For example, a 1.544-Mbps interface's full CIR will range from 8000 to 1,544,000.
	(Optional) Like the GTS sustained bit rate (Bc), the CBS sustained bit rate is that traffic is allowed to burst to a multiple of 128 ranging from 256 to 1,544,000 (on a serial interface) in bits per interval. Cisco recommends that instead of manually calculating the value, you let the algorithm configure the sustained bit rate.

continues

Table 6-22 *Class-Based Shaping Command Arguments and Their Descriptions (Continued)*

Command	Description
`peak target-bit-rate [sustained-bit-rate] [excess-per-interval]`	You can find the sustained burst rate that the traffic can burst per interval by using the following formula: Bc = Tc * CIR (Optional) The excess bit/interval (Be) that traffic is allowed to burst to beyond the sustained bit rate, a multiple of 128 ranging from 0 to 1,544,000 (on a serial interface) in bits per interval. Cisco recommends that instead of manually calculating the value you let the algorithm configure the sustained bit rate. If the Be is not entered, the software assumes that Be = Bc. Excess burst will always be greater than normal bursts, so the recommended formula for finding Be is this: Be = Bc * 2
`max-buffers buffers`	(Optional) Used to specify a buffer limit ranging from 1 to 4096.

The **shape** command is similar to the **traffic-shape** command used by GTS, having two choices for shape types: *average* and *peak*. If you use **average**, the shaping type traffic is shaped to the amount specified by the target bit rate (CIR), with the option to configure a sustained bit rate (Bc) and an excess bit rate (Be). The **peak** shaping type allows traffic to burst past the CIR to a peak rate when bandwidth is available using the CIR, Be, and Bc supplied as shown in Example 6-30; however, Cisco does not recommend manual configuration of the normal and excess burst parameters when using CBS.

Example 6-30 *Using Class-Based Shaping with WFQ*

```
class-map match-all Internet-traffic
  match protocol ip
  match access-group 101
!
!
policy-map Internet
  class Internet-traffic
    bandwidth percent 20
    shape peak 768000 19200 38400
!
interface Serial0/1
 ip address 36.128.42.11 255.255.255.0
 service-policy output Internet
!
access-list 101 permit tcp any any eq www
access-list 101 permit tcp any host 192.168.1.1 eq ftp
access-list 101 permit tcp any host 192.168.1.1 gt 1023 established
```

In this example, all web and passive FTP traffic exiting interface serial 0/1 is to be shaped to a 768-Kbit peak and limited to 20 percent of the interface's bandwidth. Under circumstances where there is available bandwidth, traffic might burst up to the 38,400 bits per interval if tokens are available, which is specified with the **peak** command. Example 6-31 verifies the configuration with the **show policy-map** command.

Example 6-31 *Verifying the Class-Based Shaping Configuration*

```
Internet-Router# show policy-map Internet
  Policy Map Internet
    Class Internet-traffic
      Bandwidth 20 (%) Max Threshold 64 (packets)
      Traffic Shaping
        Peak Rate Traffic Shaping
              CIR 768000 (bps) Max. Buffers Limit 1000 (Packets)
Bc 19200                          Be 38400

Internet-Router# show policy-map interface serial 0/1
 Serial0/1

  Service-policy output: Internet

    Class-map: Internet-traffic (match-all)
      0 packets, 0 bytes
      5 minute offered rate 0 bps, drop rate 0 bps
      Match: protocol ip
      Match: access-group 101
      Queueing
        Output Queue: Conversation 265
        Bandwidth 20 (%)
        Bandwidth 308 (kbps) Max Threshold 64 (packets)
        (pkts matched/bytes matched) 0/0
        (depth/total drops/no-buffer drops) 0/0/0
      Traffic Shaping
          Target/Average   Byte    Sustain    Excess    Interval   Increment
            Rate           Limit   bits/int   bits/int  (ms)       (bytes)
          2304000/768000   7200    19200      38400     25         7200

        Adapt  Queue    Packets   Bytes    Packets   Bytes    Shaping
        Active Depth                       Delayed   Delayed  Active
        -      0        0         0        0         0        no

    Class-map: class-default (match-any)
      3 packets, 404 bytes
      5 minute offered rate 0 bps, drop rate 0 bps
      Match: any
```

Now that you can see how easy it is to add traffic shaping policy to traffic classes using CBWFQ, consider how traffic policing applies within CBWFQ.

Class-Based Policing

When traffic policy must be enforced, and actions are to be performed when traffic complies, exceeds, or violates certain rates, you might consider using traffic policing. *Traffic policing* enables you to configure and enforce traffic policies that can limit either inbound or outbound traffic with user-defined criteria. You define the traffic criteria by using class maps and policy maps, and applying the resulting traffic service policies to interfaces. You can use traffic policing to enforce a maximum traffic rate by transmitting, dropping, or marking packets.

Earlier in the chapter, you learned about traffic shaping and rate limiting with CAR. This section examines how you can use traffic policing to enforce traffic rates, the same type of principles that applied to traffic shaping and CAR. With traffic shaping, for instance, when outbound traffic is being shaped, it is being buffered at the egress interface. Traffic shaping and traffic policing both use a token-bucket algorithm; tokens are replenished at the traffic rate. To transmit a packet, there must be enough tokens in the token bucket. Traffic policing applies to incoming and outgoing traffic and does not use buffering to enforce policies. With traffic shaping, tokens are added only to the bucket at each interval; with traffic policing, tokens are always being added back into the bucket. If there are not enough tokens in the bucket, the packet is dropped or classified; traffic policing does not queue packets. Traffic policing does not remove tokens from the bucket when either an exceed or violate action take place.

During traffic bursts, traffic is either dropped or marked. Because traffic policing does not support buffering like traffic shaping, traffic policing drops packets that exceed the interface's bandwidth limits. That is why traffic policing supports the classification of traffic upon actions. You can also use traffic policing to mark packets for later action by altering QoS values, such as the ATM CLP bit, Frame Relay DE bit, IP precedence, or DSCP values. When traffic is marked, usually at an edge device, other QoS methods, such as WFQ, WRED, or traffic shaping, can be applied by downstream devices. So, if the interface has the bandwidth to forward a burst packet, and the traffic policy permits it, the packet is forwarded with the appropriate traffic policy. The traffic policy for the transmitted burst packet should include some type of action; this action should mark the packet as a burst packet by setting a discard bit or marking the ToS. If the normal and excess burst parameters are correctly configured, traffic policing should encourage end stations to shorten their TCP window size when they realize packets have been dropped, preventing global synchronization like WRED does.

Another behavior that differs among traffic shaping, CAR, and traffic policing is the use of the two-bucket policy. In traffic shaping, when you define a violate action, you are actually defining a second bucket that will be used for packets that already exceed the normal and excess burst rate.

Traffic policing is configured using the **police** statement in policy map class configuration mode within a policy map. There are several ways to configure traffic policing in Cisco IOS Software using the **police** command. The first way, shown here, is to enter all the traffic-policing parameters, simultaneously, which can be quite cumbersome:

```
police {rate-bps {[normal-burst] [excess-burst] | [bc normal-burst] [bc excess-burst] |
    cir rate-bps [normal-burst] [excess-burst] [bc normal-burst] [be excess-burst | pir
    [peak-rate] excess-burst]} [conform-action {action | exceed-action} [exceed-action
    action [violate-action action]
```

The other way to configure traffic policing is by entering the policy map police configuration mode by issuing a **police** command, as shown here:

```
police {rate-bps {[normal-burst] [excess-burst] | [bc normal-burst] [bc excess-burst] |
    cir rate-bps [normal-burst] [excess-burst] [bc normal-burst] [be excess-burst | pir
    [peak-rate] excess-burst]}
```

After the **police** command has been issued, you will be transferred into policy map police configuration mode, specified by the **Router(config-pmap-c-police)#** prompt. In this mode, you can issue or remove any conform, exceed, or violate actions, one at a time, without having to type long commands. The conform, exceed, and violate actions are as follows:

```
conform-action {drop | set-clp-transmit | set-dscp-transmit dscp-value | set frde-transmit
    | set-mpls-exp-transmit mpls-experimental-value | set-prec-transmit precedence-value |
    set-qos-group qos-group-index | transmit}
exceed-action {drop | set-clp-transmit | set-dscp-transmit dscp-value | set frde-transmit
    | set-mpls-exp-transmit mpls-experimental-value | set-prec-transmit precedence-value |
    set-qos-group qos-group-index | transmit}
violate-action {drop | set-clp-transmit | set-dscp-transmit dscp-value | set frde-transmit
    | set-mpls-exp-transmit mpls-experimental-value | set-prec-transmit precedence-value |
    set-qos-group qos-group-index | transmit}
```

Table 6-23 shows the **police** command and policy map police configuration mode command arguments and their descriptions.

Table 6-23   *Traffic Policing Commands and Descriptions*

Command Argument	Description
traffic-rate	The average traffic rate, under normal circumstances for a period of time in bits/second, ranging from 8000 to 2,000,000,000: `CIR = Tc/Bc in bps`

normal-burst	(Optional) Specifies the normal burst size in bytes ranging from 1000 to 512,000,000:
	
	`Bc(in bytes) = CIR(in bps) * (1byte)/(8 bits) *`
	`    1.5 seconds`
	
	Note: 1.5 seconds is an average round-trip time. If your average round-trip time is not 1.5 seconds, you should change this value to accurately represent the route trip time.

continues

Table 6-23   *Traffic Policing Commands and Descriptions (Continued)*

Command Argument	Description
`excess-burst`	(Optional) Specifies the excess burst size in bytes ranging from 1000 to 512,000,000: `Be(in bytes) = Bc * 2`
`conform-action`	(Optional) Any packets conforming to the normal rate will do the activity specified by the next value.
	Specifies the conform action to be performed:
`drop`	Immediately drops the packet and exits the list.
`exceed-action`	Skips redundant action configuration and lets you go straight to exceed action. This is used when the conform and exceed actions are the same.
`set-clp-transmit`	Sets the ATM cell loss priority (CLP) bit and transmits the cell.
`set-frde-transmit`	Sets the Frame Relay discard eligible (DE) bit and transmits the packet.
`set-dscp-transmit dscp-value`	Sets the DSCP value (ranging from 0 and 63) and transmits the packet.
`set-mpls-exp-transmit mpls-experimental-value`	Sets the MPLS experimental value (ranging from 0 to 7) and transmits the packet.
`set-prec-transmit precedence-value`	Sets the IP precedence value (ranging from 0 to 7) and transmits the packet.
`set-qos-group gos-group-index`	Sets the QoS group number (ranging from 0 to 99) and transmits the packet.
`transmit`	Transmits the packet.
`[exceed-action {drop |` `  set-clp-transmit |` `  set-frde-transmit |` `  set-dscp-transmit dscp-value |` `  set-mpls-exp-transmit mpls-` `  experimental-value |` `  set-prec-transmit precedence-value` `	set-qos-group gos-group-index |` ` transmit}]`	(Optional) The **exceed-action** command specifies the action to take when traffic is in the normal to exceeded burst range (Bc to Be). The **exceed-action** command is accompanied by an action to perform.
`[violate-action {drop |` `  set-clp-transmit |` `  set-frde-transmit |` `  set-dscp-transmit dscp-value |` `  set-mpls-exp-transmit mpls-` `  experimental-value |` `  set-prec-transmit precedence-value` `	set-qos-group gos-group-index` ` transmit}]`	(Optional) The **violate-action** command specifies the action to take when traffic has surpassed the maximum burst range (Be). The **violate-action** command is accompanied by an action to perform.

There are four or five steps (depending on whether you decide to use the long form of the command or the shorter policy map police mode form of the command) required in traffic policy configuration: defining the service classes to specify traffic characteristics, defining the policies that contain the police actions to take upon traffic classes, assigning the resulting service policy to an interface, and verifying and monitoring the configuration.

Step 1   Define the traffic class using the **class-map** command. The traffic class is used to define the traffic to be matched by the policy. In this example, class IP-traffic is used to match all IP traffic, and ClassIPX-traffic matches all IPX traffic:

```
Simpson(config)# class-map IP-traffic
Simpson(config-cmap)# match protocol ip
Simpson(config-cmap)# exit
Simpson(config)# class-map IPX-traffic
Simpson(config-cmap)# match protocol ipx
Simpson(config-cmap)# exit
```

Step 2   Define a policy to use for service policy configuration, and assign traffic policies to classes. In this example, policy WAN-traffic is used to limit all IP traffic to 512 kbps with a 96,000-byte burst size using the Bc = CIR * (1byte) / (8 bits) * 1.5 seconds formula recommended by Cisco. Packets conforming to this policy are transmitted, and traffic exceeding the policy is dropped. The same type of policy is also configured for IPX traffic using class IPX-traffic:

```
Simpson(config)# policy-map WAN-traffic
Simpson(config-pmap)# class IP-traffic
Simpson(config-pmap-c)# police 512000 96000 conform-action transmit exceed-
   action drop
Simpson(config-pmap-c)# exit
Simpson(config)# policy-map WAN-traffic
Simpson(config-pmap)# class IPX
Simpson(config-pmap-c)# police 512000 96000 conform-action transmit exceed-
   action drop
Simpson(config-pmap-c)# exit
Simpson(config-pmap)# exit
```

Step 3   Or if you used the modular policy map police configuration mode method, you would use the **police 512000 96000** command to enter policy map police configuration mode. You would then enter the conform and exceed actions in that mode, as shown here:

```
Simpson(config-pmap-c)#police 512000 96000
Simpson(config-pmap-c-police)#
Simpson(config-pmap-c-police)# conform-action transmit
Simpson(config-pmap-c-police)#exceed-action drop
Simpson(config-pmap-c-police)#exit
Simpson(config-pmap-c)#class IPX-traffic
Simpson(config-pmap-c)# police 512000 96000
Simpson(config-pmap-c-police)#
Simpson(config-pmap-c-police)# conform-action transmit
Simpson(config-pmap-c-police)#exceed-action drop
Simpson(config-pmap-c-police)#exit
Simpson(config-pmap-c)#exit
```

Step 4   Assign the policy map to an interface as a service policy:

```
Simpson(config)#interface serial 0/1
Simpson(config-if)#service-policy output WAN-traffic
```

Step 5   Verify the configuration. To verify and monitor the traffic-policing configuration, use the **show policy-map** or **show policy-map interface** command. The **show policy-map** command displays information about the current traffic policy configuration, and the **show policy-map interface** command displays detailed information about the state of the current traffic policies:

```
Simpson# show policy-map WAN-traffic
  Policy Map WAN-traffic
    Class IP-traffic
     police cir 512000 bc 96000
       conform-action transmit
       exceed-action drop
    Class IPX-traffic
     police cir 512000 bc 96000
       conform-action transmit
       exceed-action drop
Simpson# show policy-map interface serial 0/1
 Serial0/1

  Service-policy output: WAN-traffic

    Class-map: IP-traffic (match-all)
      6887 packets, 5241646 bytes
      5 minute offered rate 121000 bps, drop rate 75000 bps
                          Match: protocol ip
     police:
         cir 512000 bps, bc 96000 bytes
       conformed 4351 packets, 1857386 bytes; actions:
         transmit
       exceeded 2536 packets, 3384260 bytes; actions:
         drop
       conformed 46000 bps, exceed 75000 bps

    Class-map: IPX-traffic (match-all)
      0 packets, 0 bytes
      5 minute offered rate 0 bps, drop rate 0 bps
     Match: protocol ipx
     police:
         cir 512000 bps, bc 96000 bytes
       conformed 0 packets, 0 bytes; actions:
         transmit
       exceeded 0 packets, 0 bytes; actions:
         drop
       conformed 0 bps, exceed 0 bps

    Class-map: class-default (match-any)
      19 packets, 1428 bytes
      5 minute offered rate 0 bps, drop rate 0 bps
     Match: any
```

Example 6-32 shows how traffic policing is used to assign traffic policies to different types of traffic. Class management uses access list 101 to specify SNMP, DNS, DHCP, syslog, and TFTP traffic. Class user-traffic uses access list 102 to specify NetBIOS and Telnet traffic as user traffic. And class internet uses access list 103 to define HTTP web traffic and passive FTP traffic to host 10.1.1.141 as Internet traffic. These classes are each assigned traffic policies using the **police** command for each class under policy traffic-policy. Class management is assigned a 2-Mbps rate limit with a 375,000-byte normal burst and a 750,000-byte extended burst. Packets that conform to the normal traffic rate are set to an IP precedence value of Flash-override (4) and transmitted. When traffic from class management exceeds the excess burst rate, it is still transmitted, but the IP precedence value for the packet is no longer changed. Traffic from the user-traffic class conforming to the normal traffic rate of 3 Mbps with a normal burst of 562,500 bytes and an extended burst of 1,125,000 bytes has its IP precedence value set to Flash (3) and is still transmitted if the normal burst rate has been exceeded. Traffic from the internet class that conforms to the rate limit of 5 Mbps with a normal burst of 937,500 bytes and an extended burst of 1,875,000 is transmitted; traffic exceeding that rate is dropped.

Example 6-32 *Using Traffic Policing to Regulate Traffic*

```
class-map match-all management
  match access-group 101
class-map match-all internet
  match access-group 103
class-map match-all user-traffic
  match access-group 102
!
policy-map traffic-policy
  class management
    police cir 2000000 bc 375000 be 750000
      conform-action set-prec-transmit 4
      exceed-action transmit
  class user-traffic
    police cir 3000000 bc 562500 be 1125000
      conform-action set-prec-transmit 3
      exceed-action transmit
  class internet
    police cir 5000000 bc 937500 be 1875000
      conform-action transmit
      exceed-action drop
!
interface Ethernet0/0
 ip address 10.1.1.101 255.255.255.0
 service-policy output traffic-policy
!
access-list 101 permit udp any any eq snmp
access-list 101 permit udp any any eq domain
access-list 101 permit tcp any any eq domain
access-list 101 permit udp any any eq bootps
access-list 101 permit udp any any eq bootpc
access-list 101 permit udp any any eq syslog
access-list 101 permit udp any any eq tftp
access-list 102 permit udp any any eq netbios-dgm
access-list 102 permit udp any any eq netbios-ns
access-list 102 permit udp any any eq netbios-ss
```

continues

Example 6-32 *Using Traffic Policing to Regulate Traffic (Continued)*

```
access-list 102 permit tcp any any eq telnet
access-list 103 permit tcp any any eq www
access-list 103 permit tcp any host 10.1.1.141 eq ftp
access-list 103 permit tcp any host 10.1.1.141 gt 1023 established
```

Example 6-33 shows how the **show policy-map** command and the **show policy-map interface** command to display information about the traffic-policy policy.

Example 6-33 *Using the* **show policy-map** *Command*

```
Simpson# show policy-map traffic-policy
  Policy Map traffic-policy
    Class management
     police cir 2000000 bc 375000 be 750000
       conform-action set-prec-transmit 4
       exceed-action transmit
    Class user-traffic
     police cir 3000000 bc 562500 be 1125000
       conform-action set-prec-transmit 3
       exceed-action transmit
    Class internet
     police cir 5000000 bc 937500 be 1875000
       conform-action transmit
       exceed-action drop

Simpson# show policy-map interface ethernet 0/0
 Ethernet0/0

  Service-policy output: traffic-policy

    Class-map: management (match-all)
      0 packets, 0 bytes
      5 minute offered rate 0 bps, drop rate 0 bps
     Match: access-group 101
     police:
         cir 2000000 bps, bc 375000 bytes
       conformed 0 packets, 0 bytes; actions:
         set-prec-transmit 4
       exceeded 0 packets, 0 bytes; actions:
         transmit
       conformed 0 bps, exceed 0 bps

    Class-map: user-traffic (match-all)
      0 packets, 0 bytes
      5 minute offered rate 0 bps, drop rate 0 bps
     Match: access-group 102
     police:
         cir 3000000 bps, bc 562500 bytes
       conformed 0 packets, 0 bytes; actions:
         set-prec-transmit 3
```

Example 6-33 *Using the* **show policy-map** *Command (Continued)*

```
              exceeded 0 packets, 0 bytes; actions:
                transmit
              conformed 0 bps, exceed 0 bps

      Class-map: internet (match-all)
          0 packets, 0 bytes
          5 minute offered rate 0 bps, drop rate 0 bps
          Match: access-group 103
          police:
              cir 5000000 bps, bc 937500 bytes
              conformed 0 packets, 0 bytes; actions:
                transmit
              exceeded 0 packets, 0 bytes; actions:
                drop
              conformed 0 bps, exceed 0 bps

      Class-map: class-default (match-any)
          794 packets, 54247 bytes
          5 minute offered rate 0 bps, drop rate 0 bps
          Match: any
Simpson#
```

The next example, Example 6-34, shows how a two-bucket traffic policy sets the ToS bits for different packets based on traffic type and burst size. Example 6-34 shows how class Servers sets the traffic policy for all traffic destined to the network 209.145.63.0/27. Class apps specifies all traffic using the Telnet, SMTP protocols, or passive FTP to server 209.145.63.8, and class web specifies HTTP web traffic. In the example traffic belonging to the Servers class that conforms to the average bit rate of 4 Mbps with a 750,000-byte normal burst and 1,500,000-byte, extended burst will have its DSCP value changed to cs2. Traffic exceeding the normal burst will have its DSCP value changed to cs4, and any Servers traffic that violates the excess burst rate will be transmitted without a DSCP value change. Class apps specifies that traffic going to the servers on the 209.145.63.0/27 network will have a 3-Mbps average bit rate, a 562,500-byte normal burst, and a 1,125,000-byte extended burst. Traffic conforming to the apps policy will have its DSCP value set to cs3, traffic exceeding the normal burst will have its DSCP changed to cs4, and traffic violating the policy will be transmitted without a DSCP change. And finally, web traffic belonging to class web will have the same traffic-policing configuration parameters as class apps; but the conform, exceed, and violate actions will differ. In this case, traffic conforming to the web policy will be transmitted with the DSCP value unchanged, and traffic that exceeds the excess and normal burst will be dropped. With this type of configuration, devices at the edge of the network can specify ToS settings to alter the QoS treatment for downstream devices running WFQ or WRED. By changing the DSCP value, the drop precedence of the packets is changed to a higher value, lowering the chances of those packets being dropped.

Example 6-34 *Using a Two-Bucket Traffic Policy*

```
class-map match-all apps
  match access-group 102
class-map match-all Servers
  match access-group 101
class-map match-all web
  match access-group 103
!
policy-map policy1
  class Servers
   police cir 4000000 bc 750000 be 1500000
     conform-action set-dscp-transmit cs2
     exceed-action set-dscp-transmit cs4
     violate-action transmit
  class apps
   police cir 3000000 bc 562500 be 1125000
     conform-action set-dscp-transmit cs3
     exceed-action set-dscp-transmit cs4
     violate-action transmit
   class web
    police cir 3000000 bc 562500 be 1125000
     conform-action transmit
     exceed-action drop
!
interface Ethernet0/0
 ip address 10.1.1.111 255.255.255.0
 service-policy output policy1
!
access-list 101 permit ip any 209.145.63.0 0.0.0.31
access-list 102 permit tcp any any eq telnet
access-list 102 permit tcp any any eq smtp
access-list 102 permit tcp any host 209.145.63.8 eq ftp
access-list 102 permit tcp any  host 209.145.63.8 gt 1023 established
access-list 103 permit tcp any any eq www
```

Example 6-35 shows the **show policy-map policy1** and show **policy-map interface** command output.

Example 6-35 *Two-Bucket* **show** *Commands*

```
Simpson# show policy-map policy1
  Policy Map policy1
    Class Servers
      police cir 4000000 bc 750000 be 1500000
        conform-action set-dscp-transmit cs2
        exceed-action set-dscp-transmit cs4
        violate-action transmit
    Class apps
      police cir 3000000 bc 562500 be 1125000
        conform-action set-dscp-transmit cs3
```

Example 6-35 *Two-Bucket* **show** *Commands (Continued)*

```
              exceed-action set-dscp-transmit cs4
              violate-action transmit
      Class web
          police cir 3000000 bc 562500 be 1125000
              conform-action transmit
              exceed-action drop
    Simpson# show policy-map interface ethernet 0/0
     Ethernet0/0

      Service-policy output: policy1

        Class-map: Servers (match-all)
           0 packets, 0 bytes
           5 minute offered rate 0 bps, drop rate 0 bps
           Match: access-group 101
           police:
              cir 4000000 bps, bc 750000 bytes, be 1500000 bytes
              conformed 0 packets, 0 bytes; actions:
                set-dscp-transmit cs2
              exceeded 0 packets, 0 bytes; actions:
                set-dscp-transmit cs4
              violated 0 packets, 0 bytes; actions:
                transmit
              conformed 0 bps, exceed 0 bps, violate 0 bps

        Class-map: apps (match-all)
           0 packets, 0 bytes
           5 minute offered rate 0 bps, drop rate 0 bps
           Match: access-group 102
           police:
              cir 3000000 bps, bc 562500 bytes, be 1125000 bytes
              conformed 0 packets, 0 bytes; actions:
                set-dscp-transmit cs3
              exceeded 0 packets, 0 bytes; actions:
                set-dscp-transmit cs4
              violated 0 packets, 0 bytes; actions:
                transmit
              conformed 0 bps, exceed 0 bps, violate 0 bps

        Class-map: web (match-all)
           0 packets, 0 bytes
           5 minute offered rate 0 bps, drop rate 0 bps
           Match: access-group 103
           police:
              cir 3000000 bps, bc 562500 bytes
              conformed 0 packets, 0 bytes; actions:
                transmit
              exceeded 0 packets, 0 bytes; actions:
                drop
```

continues

Example 6-35 *Two-Bucket* **show** *Commands (Continued)*

```
        conformed 0 bps, exceed 0 bps

    Class-map: class-default (match-any)
      714 packets, 48821 bytes
      5 minute offered rate 0 bps, drop rate 0 bps
      Match: any
```

Sometimes, shaping and policing will not be the best solution to the problem. In some cases, certain traffic requires a strict-priority queue. The next section shows how you can use Low Latency Queuing to provide strict-priority queues, like those created with PQ, within a class-based queuing design.

Low Latency Queuing (LLQ)

Low Latency Queuing (LLQ), also known as Priority-Based Weighted Fair Queuing, makes it possible to strictly prioritize traffic classes from within a class-based policy using CBWFQ and the modular QoS CLI.

LLQ allows traffic from at least one class policy to be sent to one strict-priority queue called a *priority class*. There are two major advantages to using LLQ over PQ or CBWFQ alone. With PQ, as long as the highest priority queue is full, it might be allowed to monopolize the bandwidth, starving out other lower-priority queues. With LLQ, however, the priority queue is limited to a certain user-defined bandwidth. After this limit has been exceeded, any further packets are dropped until sufficient resources have been made available. CBWFQ fairly allocates bandwidth among its classes. This occasionally causes problems for applications that require guaranteed resources with little tolerance for delay and jitter. LLQ solves this problem by creating the one high-priority queue that, when configured properly, helps prevent jitter.

To enable LLQ, use the **priority** command from within the policy class configuration mode. The **policy** command has two arguments: **bandwidth**, and **burst**. The **bandwidth** argument is used to specify the bandwidth limit for the priority queue. The optional **burst** argument specifies the amount of traffic, in bytes, that is allowed to burst above the bandwidth limit:

```
Simpson(config-pmap-c)# priority bandwidth [burst]
```

Under normal conditions, when there is no congestion, the strict-priority traffic is not limited by the bandwidth limitations; during periods of congestion, however, when the bandwidth limit has been reached, any new packets arriving for transmission on the priority queue are dropped. Because LLQ has been designed with voice traffic in mind, the priority class does not support the use of the **random-detect** command because WRED does not provide congestion avoidance with UDP traffic. When used with the **priority** command, the **bandwidth** command is also not supported because the **priority** command has its own bandwidth parameter and because the priority class does not use queue limits for traffic policing. The **queue-limit** command is also not supported in the priority classes. If unsupported commands are issued from within the priority class, an error appears warning that strict priority must be removed before the command can be issued.

Before you configure LLQ, it is important to know how much bandwidth will be required to support the amount of traffic that is specified for the priority class. LLQ has a traffic-metering algorithm that considers the Layer 2 headers when allocating traffic; however, it does not compensate for network jitter from upstream routers, ATM cell headers, or router-generated control or routing traffic. If bandwidth allocations are not large enough to allow this traffic, packets might be dropped during periods of unusually high traffic or bursts. The following list displays the rules to consider when using LLQ with CBWFQ:

- Because LLQ uses its own bandwidth parameter when policing traffic, the **bandwidth** command is not supported in priority classes.

- To properly support connectionless voice traffic, WRED is not supported in priority classes.

- Because LLQ uses bandwidth as its policing limitation, queue limits are not allowed in the priority class.

- LLQ is not supported with VoIP on Frame Relay.

To demonstrate the use of LLQ with CBWFQ for Voice over IP (VoIP) using routers with FXS ports, Figure 6-10 shows how Router Albuquerque and Router Santa Fe are connected over a serial HDLC point-to-point link. The phone connected to Router Albuquerque uses extension 4567, and the phone connected to Router Santa Fe uses extension 7879. Lately, during periods of network congestion, the voice calls from Albuquerque have been very low quality. To fix this problem, LLQ is being implemented on the Albuquerque router. Because Router Albuquerque is using voice codec g729r8, it has been determined that the priority queue on this interface will require only a maximum of 30 kb of bandwidth.

Figure 6-10 *Using LLQ with Voice Traffic*

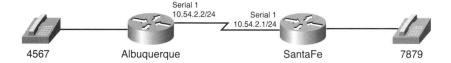

Example 6-36 shows how a service policy is created to prioritize all voice traffic while still providing acceptable data traffic throughput.

Example 6-36 *Using LLQ with Voice over IP*

```
hostname Albuquerque
!
class-map data
  match protocol ip
class-map voice
  match access-group 101
!
policy-map voice-data
  class voice
     priority 30
  class data
    bandwidth 1125
    random-detect
!
dial-peer voice 4567 pots
 destination-pattern 4567
 port 2/0
!
dial-peer voice 7879 voip
 destination-pattern 7879
 session target ipv4:10.54.2.1
!
interface Serial1
 ip address 10.54.2.2 255.255.255.0
 service-policy output voice-data
!
access-list 101 permit udp any any range 16384 32767
access-list 101 permit tcp any any eq 1720
```

The voice class matches all VoIP ports, defined in access list 101, and the data class matches the IP protocol. The policy map voice-data assigns the voice class to a strict-priority class using 30 kb of bandwidth, including room for router jitter and control traffic, and the data class is limited to 1125 kb of bandwidth and will use WRED to proactively discard packets during periods of congestion. Example 6-37 shows the **show policy-map** command output, which displays a summary of the policy configuration and how it works with the traffic sent across this network.

Example 6-37 **show policy-map** *Command Output*

```
Albuquerque# show policy-map voice-data
  Policy Map voice-data
    Weighted Fair Queueing
      Class voice
        Strict Priority
        Bandwidth 30 (kbps)
```

Example 6-37 show policy-map *Command Output (Continued)*

```
    Class data
      Bandwidth 1125 (kbps)
      exponential weight 9
      class    min-threshold    max-threshold    mark-probability
      -------------------------------------------------------------
      0        -                -                1/10
      1        -                -                1/10
      2        -                -                1/10
      3        -                -                1/10
      4        -                -                1/10
      5        -                -                1/10
      6        -                -                1/10
      7        -                -                1/10
      rsvp     -                -                1/10
Albuquerque# show policy-map interface serial 1
 Serial1  output : voice-data
  Weighted Fair Queueing
    Class voice
      Strict Priority
      Output Queue: Conversation 264
        Bandwidth 30 (kbps) Packets Matched 152
        (total drops/bytes drops) 0/0
    Class data
      Output Queue: Conversation 265
        Bandwidth 1125 (kbps) Packets Matched 48
        (depth/total drops/no-buffer drops) 0/0/0
        exponential weight: 9
        mean queue depth: 0
        drops: class  random   tail    min-th   max-th   mark-prob
               0      0        0       20       40       1/10
               1      0        0       22       40       1/10
               2      0        0       24       40       1/10
               3      0        0       26       40       1/10
               4      0        0       28       40       1/10
               5      0        0       30       40       1/10
               6      0        0       32       40       1/10
               7      0        0       34       40       1/10
               rsvp   0        0       36       40       1/10
```

As you can see, CBWFQ can perform a number of QoS techniques. After you have seen some of the ways that CBWFQ can be applied, you will probably imagine all kinds of ways that you can apply this technology in networks, such as the following:

- Marking traffic for policy enforcement
- Classifying traffic into policy groups
- Queuing certain traffic with WFQ or PQ technologies
- Performing tail drop or WRED, depending on traffic type
- Prioritizing traffic to reserve bandwidth

- Shaping traffic
- Enforcing traffic policy by policing traffic

As you might imagine, these three chapters easily could have been expanded into an entire book of 1000+ pages. The best way to test and apply these QoS technologies is in a laboratory environment with test traffic and then to apply the QoS solution in production after completing several tests. With some creativity and knowledge of the skills covered in these QoS chapters, you can create some extremely versatile QoS solutions.

Practice Scenarios

Lab 12: Custom Queuing

The law firm Blackerby, Smith, and Heitz, commonly referred to as BSH, has a network consisting of one headquarters site in Orlando containing all the servers and a PBX. They currently have two branch sites: Columbia and Atlanta. In the next two months, however, they plan to add two other new sites: one in Birmingham, and one in Greensboro, as shown in Figure 6-11.

Figure 6-11 *Blackerby, Smith, and Heitz Network Diagram*

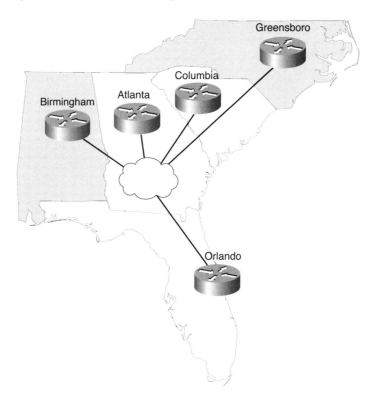

Equipment Needed

This lab requires the following:

- Three routers with one serial interface, one Ethernet interface, and two FXS voice ports
- One router with four serial interfaces to act as a Frame Relay switch
- (Optionally) Two computers with Ethernet interfaces
- (Optionally) One extra router with one Ethernet interface

The core of this lab requires four routers. Three of the routers require one serial interface, and one of the routers, which will act as a Frame Relay switch, requires four serial interfaces. The routers should be attached by their serial interfaces as shown in Figure 6-12.

Figure 6-12 *Physical Lab Configuration*

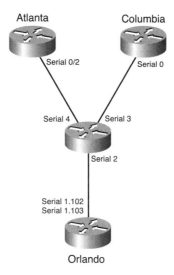

Physical Layout and Prestaging

- Configure the Frame Relay as shown in Figure 6-13 using the IP addressing and DLCI assignments shown in Table 6-24.

Figure 6-13   *Frame Relay DLCI Configuration*

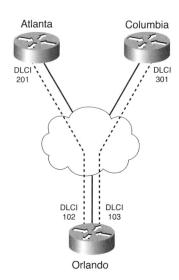

Table 6-24   *IP Address and Frame Relay DLCI Assignments*

Router Interface	DLCI	IP Address
Atlanta Serial 0/2	201	192.168.2.2/30
Columbia Serial 0	301	192.168.3.2/30
Orlando Serial 1.102	102	192.168.2.1/30
Orlando Serial 1.103	103	192.168.3.1/30

- Configure the Frame Relay switch as shown in Figure 6-13 using the DLCI assignments in Table 6-25.

Table 6-25   *Frame Relay Switch DLCI Assignments*

Local Interface	Local DLCI	Remote Interface	Remote DLCI
Serial 4	201	Serial 2	102
Serial 3	301	Serial 2	103
Serial 2	102	Serial 4	201
Serial 2	103	Serial 3	301

Lab Objectives

Each site has several computers that the local office staff uses to access files and applications at the headquarters site in Orlando. Each site also has two telephones that are used to dial the headquarters site. Calls to the Orlando site from the branch offices happen infrequently at various times during the day; both phone lines are rarely used at the same time. All the voice and data traffic between the Orlando and Atlanta sites is carried over Frame Relay circuits with 256-kbps CIR. The headquarters site currently has Frame Relay T1, with a 768-kbps CIR. The current traffic patterns have recently been analyzed, and it has been found that during peak hours, 9:00 to 10:30 a.m., 12:00 to 1:00 p.m., and 3:30 to 5:00 p.m., traffic is very bursty, and some of the applications are intolerant of the delays caused by the bursty periods. While planning the upgrade of the network for the two new sites, it has been decided that the Frame Relay circuit in Orlando will have its CIR increased to 1.544 Mbps. This should ease some of the issues with the bursty traffic. To prevent any new problems, it has been decided that Custom Queuing will be implemented before the upgrade, only at the Orlando site. The objectives for this lab include the following:

- Configure VoIP between the FXS cards on the Orlando and Columbia routers.
- Configure Custom Queuing to support traffic limitations based on byte count.

Lab Tasks

Step 1 Configure the Orlando router to connect to the Atlanta and Columbus routers, without the use of **frame-relay map** statements. Also, configure the Atlanta and Columbia routers to reach the Orlando router. At this point, all routers should have both line and protocol in an up state.

Step 2 Configure the IP addresses for each router, as shown in Figure 6-14. Configure all networks to belong to OSPF area 0 and verify IP connectivity.

Step 3 If possible, configure VoIP between Columbia and Orlando, as shown in Figure 6-14. Configure one of the phones in Columbia to use extension 5301 and the other to use 5302, and configure the Orlando site to have only one phone using extension 5000. Verify that all phones can dial each other.

Step 4 Configure two computers, one on the 192.168.3.144 network and one on the 192.168.100.96 network.

Step 5 Place another router on the 192.168.3.208 network. Configure this router with a default route to the 192.168.3.209 interface on the Atlanta router. Configure this router to allow Telnet access.

Figure 6-14 *Complete Network Diagram*

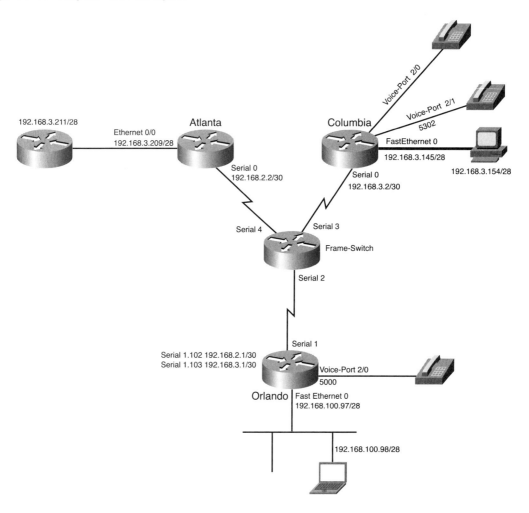

Step 6   Verify that hosts on networks 192.168.3.144 and 192.168.100.96 can Telnet to the router at 192.168.3.211.

Step 7   Using the information from Table 6-26 and the formulas from the "Custom Queuing" section earlier in the chapter, enter the byte-count data in Table 6-27. The information from the Byte Count fields will be used to configure the byte-count queue limits.

Table 6-26 *Bandwidth Percentages for This Lab*

Queue Number	Protocol(s)	Percentage Bandwidth	Average Packet Size
1	Voice	25	64
2	DHCP, DNS, SNMP	5	79
3	Telnet	10	64
4	SMTP	10	625
5	Passive FTP to 192.168.3.211	10	315
6	WWW	5	1024
7	Other	25	1042

Table 6-27 *Byte-Count Limitation Data*

Protocol	Bandwidth Allocation	Average Packet Size	Ratio	Normalized Ratio	Whole Ratio	Byte Count
Voice	25%	64				
DHCP, DNS, SNMP	5%	79				
Telnet	10%	64				
SMTP	10%	625				
Passive FTP to 192.168.3.211	10%	315				
WWW	5%	1024				
Other	25%	1042				

Step 8 Configure CQ for the serial interface on the Orlando router, using the byte-count limitations that you found in Table 6-27, for each of the queues. Configure any access lists necessary to sort the traffic into the queues.

Step 9 Make Queue 7 is the default queue for all unspecified traffic.

Lab Walkthrough

Configure the Frame Relay switch so that the switch has DLCI 201. It should match up with DLCI 102 and DLCI 301, and it should also match up with 103. Example 6-38 shows the complete Frame Relay switch configuration.

Example 6-38 *Frame Relay Switch Configuration*

```
hostname Frame-Relay
!
frame-relay switching
!
interface Serial2
 description Connection to Orlando
 no ip address
 encapsulation frame-relay
 frame-relay lmi-type ansi
 frame-relay intf-type dce
 frame-relay route 102 interface Serial4 201
 frame-relay route 103 interface Serial3 301
!
interface Serial3
 description Connection to Columbia
 no ip address
 encapsulation frame-relay
 frame-relay lmi-type ansi
 frame-relay intf-type dce
 frame-relay route 301 interface Serial2 103
!
interface Serial4
 description Connection to Atlanta
  no ip address
 encapsulation frame-relay
 frame-relay lmi-type ansi
 frame-relay intf-type dce
 frame-relay route 201 interface Serial2 102
!
end
```

In the example, notice that the **frame-relay route** statements for interface serial 2 both have
local DLCI numbers for DLCI 102 and 103. These numbers are matched to the DLCI numbers
assigned to the Orlando router. The other two DLCI numbers, 201 and 203, are assigned to
interfaces 3 and 4, which connect to the Atlanta and Columbus routers. Example 6-39 shows
the Frame Relay routing table from the Frame Relay switch.

Example 6-39 *Frame Relay Routing Table of the Frame Relay Switch*

```
Frame-Switch# show frame route
Input Intf Input Dlci Output Intf Output Dlci Status
Serial2          102 Serial4          201 active
Serial2          103 Serial3          301 active
Serial3          301 Serial2          103 active
Serial4          201 Serial2          102 active
```

Step 1 Configure the Orlando router to connect to the Atlanta and Columbus routers without the use of **frame-relay map** statements. Also, configure the Atlanta and Columbus routers to reach the Orlando router. At this point, all routers should have both line and protocol in an up state.

To configure the Layer 2 connections from the Orlando router to the Atlanta and Columbus routers without the use of **frame-relay map** statements, use subinterfaces on the Orlando router's serial interface:

```
Orlando(config)# interface Serial1
Orlando(config-if)# encapsulation frame-relay
Orlando(config-if)# clockrate 1300000
Orlando(config-if)# interface Serial0.102 point-to-point
Orlando(config-if)# frame-relay interface-dlci 102
Orlando(config-if)# interface Serial0.103 point-to-point
Orlando(config-if)# frame-relay interface-dlci 103
```

The other two routers should just need the **encapsulation frame-relay** command and a clock rate if they are on the data circuit-terminating equipment (DCE) side of the connection:

```
Atlanta(config-if)# int s 0/2
Atlanta(config-if)# encapsulation frame-relay
Atlanta(config-if)# clockrate 1300000
Columbia(config-if)# int s 0
Columbia(config-if)# encapsulation frame-relay
Columbia(config-if)# clockrate 1300000
```

Step 2 Configure the IP addresses for each router, as shown in Figure 6-14. Configure all networks to belong to OSPF area 0 and verify IP connectivity.

To establish IP connectivity from the Atlanta and Columbus routers to the Orlando router, the following addresses are assigned. Make sure to use the **ip ospf network point-to-point** command for the OSPF connections. The following example shows the Frame Relay interface configuration for the Orlando subinterfaces:

```
Orlando(config)# interface Serial1.102 point-to-point
Orlando(config-if)# ip address 192.168.2.1 255.255.255.252
Orlando(config-if)# ip ospf network point-to-point

Orlando(config)# interface Serial1.103 point-to-point
Orlando(config-if)# ip address 192.168.3.1 255.255.255.252
Orlando(config-if)# ip ospf network point-to-point
```

The Atlanta and Columbia routers are allowed to use **frame-relay map** statements. After all IP addresses have been assigned, each router will require OSPF configuration. The following example shows the Frame Relay interface configuration for the Atlanta and Columbia routers:

```
Atlanta(config)# int s 0/2
Atlanta(config-if)# ip address 192.168.2.2 255.255.255.252
Atlanta(config-if)# frame-relay map ip 192.168.2.1 201 broadcast
Atlanta(config-if)# ip ospf network point-to-point
```

```
Columbiaconfig)# int s 0
Columbia(config-if)# ip address 192.168.3.2 255.255.255.252
Columbia(config-if)# frame-relay map ip 192.168.3.1 301 broadcast
Columbia(config-if)# ip ospf network point-to-point
```

Step 3   If possible, configure VoIP between Columbia and Orlando, as shown in
Figure 6-14. Configure one of the phones in Columbia to use extension 5301
and the other to use 5302, and configure the Orlando site to have only one
phone using extension 5000. Verify that all phones can dial each other.

If you have the two voice-capable routers with FXS cards required to complete this step, you need to create two dial peers on each router. One **dial-
peer** statement will be for pots. This statement should specify the destination
pattern, which is the number dialed from the telephone, and the port which is
the locally connected voice port. The other **dial-peer** statement is the **voip**
statement, which specifies the destination pattern for the remote telephone
and the IP address that VoIP will use when that number is dialed:

```
Orlando(config)#dial-peer voice 5000 pots
Orlando (config-dial-peer)# destination-pattern 5000
Orlando (config-dial-peer)# port 2/0
Orlando (config-dial-peer)#dial-peer voice 5301 voip
Orlando (config-dial-peer)# destination-pattern 5301
Orlando (config-dial-peer)# session target ipv4:192.168.3.2
Orlando (config-dial-peer)#dial-peer voice 5302 voip
Orlando (config-dial-peer)# destination-pattern 5302
Orlando (config-dial-peer)# session target ipv4:192.168.3.2
Columbia(config)#dial-peer voice 5301 pots
Columbia (config-dial-peer)# destination-pattern 5301
Columbia (config-dial-peer)# port 2/0
Columbia (config-dial-peer)#dial-peer voice 5302 pots
Columbia (config-dial-peer)# destination-pattern 5302
Columbia (config-dial-peer)# port 2/1
Columbia (config-dial-peer)#dial-peer voice 5000 voip
Columbia (config-dial-peer)# destination-pattern 5000
Columbia (config-dial-peer)# session target ipv4:192.168.3.1
```

Step 4   Configure two computers, one on the 192.168.3.144 network and one on the
192.168.100.96 network.

If you have two extra computers, place one on the 192.168.3.144 network and
one on the 192.168.100.96 network.

Step 5   Place another router on the 192.168.3.208 network. Configure this router
with a default route to the 192.168.3.209 interface on the Atlanta router.
Configure this router to allow Telnet access.

The fourth router should need only an IP address on its Ethernet interface and
a default route to 192.168.3.209:

```
Router(config)# interface Ethernet0
Router(config-if)# ip address 192.168.3.211 255.255.255.240
Router(config)# exit
Router(config)# ip route 0.0.0.0 0.0.0.0 192.168.3.209
Router(config)#line vty 0 4
Router(config-line)#login
Router(config-line)#pass cisco
```

Step 6 Verify that hosts on networks 192.168.3.144 and 192.168.100.96 can Telnet to the router at 192.168.3.211.

If you were able to complete Step 4, you should be able to verify that hosts on the networks 192.168.3.144 and 192.168.100.96 can ping each other. If you completed Step 5 successfully, both of those hosts should also be able to Telnet to the router on the 192.168.3.208 network.

Step 7 Using the information from Table 6-26 and the formulas from earlier in the chapter, enter the byte-count data in Table 6-27. The information from the Byte Count fields will be used to configure the byte-count queue limits. Table 6-28 shows the byte-count sizes for this lab.

Table 6-28 *Byte-Count Sizes for Custom Queuing*

Protocol	Bandwidth Allocation	Average Packet Size	Ratio	Normalized Ratio	Whole Ratio	Byte Count	Actual Bandwidth
Voice	25%	64	0.3906	79.7	80	5120	26.8%
DHCP, DNS, SNMP	5%	79	0.0633	12.9	13	1027	5.3%
Telnet	10%	64	0.1563	31.9	32	2048	10.7%
SMTP	10%	625	0.016	3.3	4	2500	13%
Passive FTP to 192.168.3.211	10%	315	0.0317	6.5	7	2205	11.5%
WWW	5%	1024	0.0049	1	1	1024	5.3%
Other	25%	1042	0.0240	4.9	5	5210	27.2%
						19,134	

Step 8 Configure CQ for the serial interface on the Orlando router, using the byte-count limitations that you found in Table 6-27 for each of the queues. Configure any access lists necessary to sort the traffic into the queues.

For this lab, access list 101 was used to specify voice traffic; access list 102 was used to specify DHCP, DNS, and SNMP traffic; and access list 103 was used to specify FTP traffic. These access lists were used with queue list 1 to specify the traffic and byte counts for each queue. The queue list was applied to interface serial 1 using the **custom-queue-list** command:

```
Orlando(config)#access-list 101 permit tcp any any eq 1720
Orlando(config)#access-list 101 permit udp any any range 16384 32767
Orlando(config)#access-list 101 remark Voice traffic
Orlando(config)#access-list 102 remark DHCP, DNS and SNMP traffic
Orlando(config)#access-list 102 permit udp any any eq bootpc
Orlando(config)#access-list 102 permit udp any any eq domain
Orlando(config)#access-list 102 permit tcp any any eq domain
```

```
Orlando(config)#access-list 102 permit udp any any eq snmp
Orlando(config)#access-list 103 remark FTP and random port for data
Orlando(config)#access-list 103 permit tcp any host 192.168.3.211 eq ftp
Orlando(config)#access-list 103 permit tcp any host 192.168.3.211 gt 1023
established
Orlando(config)#queue-list 1 protocol ip 1 list 101
Orlando(config)#queue-list 1 protocol ip 2 list 102
Orlando(config)#queue-list 1 protocol ip 3 tcp telnet
Orlando(config)#queue-list 1 protocol ip 4 tcp smtp
Orlando(config)#queue-list 1 protocol ip 5 list 103
Orlando(config)#queue-list 1 protocol ip 6 tcp www
Orlando(config)#queue-list 1 protocol ip 7
Orlando(config)#queue-list 1 queue 1 byte-count 5120
Orlando(config)#queue-list 1 queue 2 byte-count 1027
Orlando(config)#queue-list 1 queue 3 byte-count 2048
Orlando(config)#queue-list 1 queue 4 byte-count 2500
Orlando(config)#queue-list 1 queue 5 byte-count 2205
Orlando(config)#queue-list 1 queue 6 byte-count 1024
Orlando(config)#queue-list 1 queue 7 byte-count 5210
Orlando(config)#interface Serial1
Orlando(config-if)#custom-queue-list 1
```

Step 9 Make Queue 1 the default queue for all unspecified traffic.

To make Queue 7 the default queue, you need to use only the default version of the **queue-list** command to specify Queue 7:

```
queue-list 1 default 7
```

Example 6-40 shows the complete configuration for the Orlando router.

Example 6-40 *Orlando Router Configuration*

```
hostname Orlando
!
voice-port 2/0
!
voice-port 2/1
!
dial-peer voice 5000 pots
 destination-pattern 5000
 port 2/0
!
dial-peer voice 5301 voip
 destination-pattern 5301
 session target ipv4:192.168.3.2
 !
dial-peer voice 5302 voip
 destination-pattern 5302
 session target ipv4:192.168.3.2
!
interface Serial1
 no ip address
 encapsulation frame-relay
 custom-queue-list 1
 clockrate 1300000
```

Example 6-40 *Orlando Router Configuration (Continued)*

```
!
interface Serial1.102 point-to-point
 ip address 192.168.2.1 255.255.255.252
 ip ospf network point-to-point
 frame-relay interface-dlci 102
!
interface Serial1.103 point-to-point
 ip address 192.168.3.1 255.255.255.252
 ip ospf network point-to-point
 frame-relay interface-dlci 103
!
interface FastEthernet0
  ip address 192.168.100.97 255.255.255.240
!
router ospf 101
 network 192.168.2.0 0.0.0.3 area 0
 network 192.168.3.0 0.0.0.3 area 0
 network 192.168.100.96 0.0.0.15 area 0
!
access-list 101 permit tcp any any eq 1720
access-list 101 permit udp any any range 16384 32767
access-list 101 remark Voice traffic
access-list 102 remark DHCP, DNS and SNMP traffic
access-list 102 permit udp any any eq bootpc
access-list 102 permit udp any any eq domain
access-list 102 permit tcp any any eq domain
access-list 102 permit udp any any eq snmp
access-list 103 remark FTP and random port for data
access-list 103 permit tcp any host 192.168.3.211 eq ftp
access-list 103 permit tcp any host 192.168.3.211 gt 1023 established
queue-list 1 protocol ip 1 list 101
queue-list 1 protocol ip 2 list 102
queue-list 1 protocol ip 3 tcp telnet
queue-list 1 protocol ip 4 tcp smtp
queue-list 1 protocol ip 5 list 103
queue-list 1 protocol ip 6 tcp www
queue-list 1 protocol ip 7
queue-list 1 default 7
queue-list 1 queue 1 byte-count 5120
queue-list 1 queue 2 byte-count 1027
queue-list 1 queue 3 byte-count 2048
queue-list 1 queue 4 byte-count 2500
queue-list 1 queue 5 byte-count 2205
queue-list 1 queue 6 byte-count 1024
queue-list 1 queue 7 byte-count 5210
!
```

Example 6-41 shows output from the **show interface** and **show queueing** commands. Notice that the **show interface** command shows that CQ is enabled and that there are currently no packets in the queues. The **show queueing** command output was used to display information about the custom queues used in this lab.

Example 6-41 *Output from* **show interface** *and* **show queueing** *on the Orlando Router*

```
Orlando# show interface serial 1
Serial0 is up, line protocol is up
  Hardware is PowerQUICC Serial
  MTU 1500 bytes, BW 1544 Kbit, DLY 20000 usec,
     reliability 255/255, txload 42/255, rxload 1/255
  Encapsulation FRAME-RELAY, loopback not set
  Keepalive set (10 sec)
  LMI enq sent  604, LMI stat recvd 597, LMI upd recvd 0, DTE LMI up
  LMI enq recvd 0, LMI stat sent  0, LMI upd sent  0
  LMI DLCI 0  LMI type is ANSI Annex D  frame relay DTE
  FR SVC disabled, LAPF state down
  Broadcast queue 0/64, broadcasts sent/dropped 1431/3, interface broadcasts 1224
  Last input 00:00:05, output 00:00:05, output hang never
  Last clearing of "show interface" counters 01:47:08
  Input queue: 0/75/2/0 (size/max/drops/flushes); Total output drops: 33540
  Queueing strategy: custom-list 1
  Output queues: (queue #: size/max/drops)
     0: 0/20/0 1: 0/20/0 2: 0/20/0 3: 0/20/0 4: 0/20/0
     5: 0/20/0 6: 0/20/0 7: 0/20/33540 8: 0/20/0 9: 0/20/0
     10: 0/20/0 11: 0/20/0 12: 0/20/0 13: 0/20/0 14: 0/20/0
     15: 0/20/0 16: 0/20/0
  5 minute input rate 4000 bits/sec, 25 packets/sec
  5 minute output rate 259000 bits/sec, 27 packets/sec
     14023 packets input, 884229 bytes, 0 no buffer
     Received 0 broadcasts, 0 runts, 0 giants, 0 throttles
     1 input errors, 0 CRC, 1 frame, 0 overrun, 0 ignored, 0 abort
     14672 packets output, 16220918 bytes, 0 underruns
     0 output errors, 0 collisions, 4 interface resets
     0 output buffer failures, 0 output buffers swapped out
     15 carrier transitions
     DCD=up  DSR=up  DTR=up  RTS=up  CTS=up
Orlando# show queueing
Current fair queue configuration:
Current priority queue configuration:
Current custom queue configuration:
List   Queue  Args
1      7      default
1      1      protocol ip          list 101
1      2      protocol ip          list 102
1      3      protocol ip          tcp port telnet
1      4      protocol ip          tcp port smtp
1      5      protocol ip          list 103
1      6      protocol ip          tcp port www
1      7      protocol ip
1      1      byte-count 5120
1      2      byte-count 1027
```

Example 6-41 *Output from* **show interface** *and* **show queueing** *on the Orlando Router (Continued)*

```
1      3      byte-count 2048
1      4      byte-count 2500
1      5      byte-count 2205
1      6      byte-count 1024
1      7      byte-count 5210
Current random-detect configuration:
```

Example 6-42 shows the complete configuration for the Atlanta router, and Example 6-43 shows the complete configuration for the Columbia router.

Example 6-42 *Atlanta Router Configuration*

```
hostname Atlanta
!
interface Ethernet0/0
 ip address 192.168.2.209 255.255.255.240
!
interface Serial0/2
ip address 192.168.2.2 255.255.255.252
 encapsulation frame-relay
 ip ospf network point-to-point
 clockrate 1300000
 frame-relay map ip 192.168.2.1 201 broadcast
 !
router ospf 101
 network 192.168.2.0 0.0.0.3 area 0
 network 192.168.2.208 0.0.0.15 area 0
 !
```

Example 6-43 *Columbia Router Configuration*

```
hostname Columbia
!
voice-port 2/0
!
voice-port 2/1
!

dial-peer voice 5301 pots
 destination-pattern 5301
 port 2/0
!
dial-peer voice 5302 pots
 destination-pattern 5302
 port 2/1
```

continues

Example 6-43 *Columbia Router Configuration (Continued)*

```
 !
dial-peer voice 5000 voip
 destination-pattern 5000
 session target ipv4:192.168.3.1
 !
interface Serial0
 ip address 192.168.3.2 255.255.255.252
 encapsulation frame-relay
 ip ospf network point-to-point
 clockrate 1300000
 frame-relay map ip 192.168.3.1 301 broadcast
 !
interface FastEthernet0
 ip address 192.168.3.145 255.255.255.240
 !
router ospf 101
 network 192.168.3.0 0.0.0.3 area 0
 network 192.168.3.144 0.0.0.15 area 0
```

Lab 13: Managing Internet Traffic with CBWFQ and NBAR

In this lab, you take the lessons learned up to this point and apply them to a real-world QoS simulation. This simulation applies CBWFQ to solve a common Internet problem: users using enterprise networks for personal entertainment.

Lab Exercise

In this lab, NBAR heuristics specify certain classes of data and apply a service policy to the class enforcing proper Internet usage. This scenario includes the following technologies:

- Classifying traffic with NBAR
- Marking traffic with DSCP bits
- Configuring ATM QoS
- Prioritizing traffic with bandwidth reservations
- Selectively applying tail drop, WRED, and WFQ for certain traffic types
- Selecting the appropriate queuing and switching types

Lab Objective

The objective of this lab is to apply the QoS technologies used up to this point to put together an Internet service policy for the network model shown in Figure 6-15.

Figure 6-15 *Model of an Internet Border*

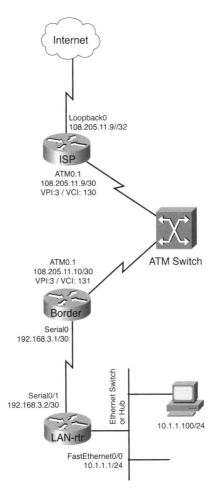

Equipment Needed

- One Cisco router with one OC-3 ATM interface
- One Cisco router with one OC-3 ATM interface and one serial interface
- One LightStream ATM switch with two OC-3 ATM interfaces
- One Cisco router with one serial port and one Ethernet port
- One PC with an Ethernet NIC running TCP/IP
- One Ethernet switch or hub

Physical Layout and Prestaging

- Cable the routers as shown in Figure 6-15.

- Attach the PC to the Ethernet switch or hub and configure it to be on the 10.1.1.0/24 network.

- Configure the ATM switch to use the PVC information from Figure 6-15.

- Apply IP addresses to each router interface, except for the ATM interfaces on the Border and ISP routers, and verify that the routers can ping their directly connected neighbor.

- Verify that all interfaces are in an up/up state.

Lab Tasks

Step 1   Configure the ATM PVCs on the ISP and Border routers. Assign the ISP router's ATM 0.1 interface VPI: 3 and VCI 130, and the Border router's ATM 0.1 interface should be assigned VPI: 3 VCI: 131. Configure these routers to use VBR-nrt for a 45-Mbps sustained cell rate and a 50-Mbps peak cell rate. Verify that each of the routers can ping each other.

Step 2   Configure all routers except the ISP router to belong to EIGRP AS 148. Summarize all routes on their true network boundary; do not use classful summarization. Have the Border router redistribute the default route pointing to the ISP router. Verify that all routers can ping all other routers in the network before moving to Step 3.

Step 3   From the Border router, configure network address translation (NAT) so that all inside networks, 10.1.1.0/24 and 192.168.0.0/16, can get the Internet, beyond the ISP router, without any additional routing. Verify that the host PC can reach the ISP router on its 108.205.11.9/32 interface.

Step 4   Configure a policy for the outbound interface on the LAN-rtr. This policy should match the variables shown in Table 6-29.

Step 5   Enable DSCP WRED on the outbound ATM interface for the Border router. This is where the policies created in Step 4 finish their execution.

Table 6-29   *Policy Configuration*

Class Name	Traffic Type	Policy
High-Pri_Internet	HTTP traffic to cisco.com	Reserve 15% bandwidth. Mark each packet with the EF DSCP value.
Med-Pri-Internet	All other HTTP and SSH traffic	Reserve 55% bandwidth. Mark these packets with the CS3 DSCP value.
Low-Pri-Internet	FTP, Telnet, SFTP, HTTPS, and secure POP3	Reserve 5% bandwidth Apply WRED instead of tail-drop. Mark these packets with the CS1 DSCP value.
No-Pri_Internet	Gnutella, MS NetShow, Napster, NNTP, Real Audio, Streamwork streaming protocol	Limit to 8 bps any packets conforming to this policy. Have their DSCP bits set to the default DSCP value. All packets exceeding this value are to be dropped.
Default	Unclassified	Use WFQ and WRED to queue and drop packets.

Lab Walkthrough

Step 1   Configure the ATM PVCs on the ISP and Border routers. Assign the ISP router's ATM 0.1 interface VPI: 3 and VCI 130, and the Border router's ATM 0.1 interface should be assigned VPI: 3 VCI: 131. Configure these routers to use VBR-nrt for a 45-Mbps sustained cell rate and a 50-Mbps peak cell rate. Verify that each of the routers can ping each other.

This step is relatively straightforward and requires only a few items. Configure an ATM PVC on the ISP and Border routers using VBR-nrt shaping and verify that the routers can reach each other:

```
ISP Router
interface ATM0.1 multipoint
 ip address 108.205.11.9 255.255.255.252
 pvc 3/130
  protocol ip 108.205.11.10 broadcast
  vbr-nrt 50000 45000
  encapsulation aal5snap
```

```
Border Router
interface ATM0.1 multipoint
 ip address 108.205.11.10 255.255.255.252
 pvc 3/131
  protocol ip 108.205.11.9 broadcast
  vbr-nrt 50000 45000
  encapsulation aal5snap
```

Step 2   Configure all routers except the ISP router to belong to EIGRP AS 148.
Summarize all routes on their true network boundary; do not use classful
summarization. Have the Border router redistribute the default route pointing
to the ISP router. Verify that all routers can ping all other routers in the
network before moving on to Step 3.

This step requires only a few items to work properly. First, you must create
the correct network statements so that the entire 108.205.0.0/16 network is
not advertised to the internal network beyond the Border router. Next, you
must turn off auto-summarization to prevent classful summarization, and last
you need to use the **redistribute static** command to redistribute the default
route as shown here on the Border router:

```
router eigrp 148
 redistribute static
 network 108.205.11.8 0.0.0.3
 network 192.168.3.0
 no auto-summary
!
ip route 0.0.0.0 0.0.0.0 108.205.11.9
```

Step 3   From the Border router, configure NAT so that all inside networks,
10.1.1.0/24 and 192.168.0.0/16, can get the Internet, beyond the ISP router,
without any additional routing. Verify that the host PC can reach the ISP
router on its 108.205.11.9/32 interface.

Only three task are required to configure Step 3: create an access list that
specifies the two internal networks, create a NAT statement to NAT the
addresses specified by the access list to the ATM 0.1 interface's IP address,
and apply the NAT configuration to the ATM0.1 and Serial0 interfaces on the
Border router, as shown here:

```
interface Serial0
 ip address 192.168.3.1 255.255.255.252
 ip nat inside
!
interface ATM0.1 multipoint
 ip address 108.205.11.10 255.255.255.252
 ip nat outside
 pvc 3/131
  protocol ip 108.205.11.9 broadcast
  vbr-nrt 50000 45000
  encapsulation aal5snap
!
ip nat inside source list 1 interface ATM0.1 overload
!
access-list 1 permit 192.168.0.0 0.0.255.255
access-list 1 permit 10.1.1.0 0.0.0.255
```

Step 4   Configure a policy for the outbound interface on the LAN-rtr. This policy
should match the variables shown in Table 6-28.

This step requires multiple items to work properly. First, you must define a class map for each of the traffic types defined in the table, assigning each of the protocol types to the class to which it belongs. Next, create a policy map that references each class definition and apply the required policy to each of the classes. Then, create a class-default class to match all undefined traffic and apply the default policy. This policy is then applied to the Serial0/1 interface using the **outbound service-policy** command, as shown here, from the LAN-rtr router:

```
class-map match-all No-Pri_Internet
  match protocol gnutella
  match protocol netshow
  match protocol napster
  match protocol nntp
  match protocol realaudio
  match protocol streamwork
class-map match-all Low-Pri-Internet
  match protocol ftp
  match protocol telnet
  match protocol secure-ftp
  match protocol secure-http
  match protocol secure-pop3
class-map match-all High-Pri_Internet
  match protocol http host "cisco.com"
class-map match-all Med-Pri-Internet
  match protocol http
  match protocol ssh
!
policy-map Internet-Policy
  class High-Pri_Internet
   bandwidth percent 15
   set ip dscp ef
  class Med-Pri-Internet
   bandwidth percent 55
   set ip dscp cs3
  class Low-Pri-Internet
   bandwidth percent 5
   random-detect
   set ip dscp cs1
  class No-Pri_Internet
   police cir 8000
     conform-action set-dscp-transmit default
     exceed-action drop
  class class-default
   fair-queue
   random-detect
!
interface Serial0/1
 ip address 192.168.3.2 255.255.255.252
 service-policy output Internet-Policy
 clockrate 1300000
```

Step 5   Enable DSCP WRED on the outbound ATM interface for the Border router. This is where the policies created in Step 4 finish their execution.

The final step requires only one line of configuration, shown here. After you have completed this part of the configuration, any traffic marked with a DSCP value on the LAN-rtr router will have DSCP-based WRED applied on the outbound ATM interfaces upon exit from the Border router. Remember, the **random-detect** statement is supported only on physical interfaces:

```
interface ATM0
 no ip address
 no atm ilmi-keepalive
 random-detect dscp-based
```

Example 6-44 shows the complete router configurations for this lab.

Example 6-44 *Complete Router Configurations*

```
hostname ISP
!
interface ATM0
 no ip address
 no atm ilmi-keepalive
!
interface ATM0.1 multipoint
 ip address 108.205.11.9 255.255.255.252
 pvc 3/130
  protocol ip 108.205.11.10 broadcast
  vbr-nrt 50000 45000
  encapsulation aal5snap
```

```
hostname Border
!
ip cef
!
interface Serial0
 ip address 192.168.3.1 255.255.255.252
 ip nat inside
!
interface ATM0
 no ip address
 no atm ilmi-keepalive
 random-detect dscp-based
!
interface ATM0.1 multipoint
 ip address 108.205.11.10 255.255.255.252
 ip nat outside
 pvc 3/131
  protocol ip 108.205.11.9 broadcast
  vbr-nrt 50000 45000
  encapsulation aal5snap
!
router eigrp 148
 redistribute static
 network 108.205.11.8 0.0.0.3
 network 192.168.3.0
 no auto-summary
```

Example 6-44 *Complete Router Configurations (Continued)*

```
!
ip nat inside source list 1 interface ATM0.1 overload
ip classless
ip route 0.0.0.0 0.0.0.0 108.205.11.9
!
access-list 1 permit 192.168.0.0 0.0.255.255
access-list 1 permit 10.1.1.0 0.0.0.255
```

```
hostname LAN-rtr
!
ip cef
!
class-map match-all No-Pri-Internet
  match protocol gnutella
  match protocol netshow
  match protocol napster
  match protocol nntp
  match protocol realaudio
  match protocol streamwork
class-map match-all Low-Pri-Internet
  match protocol ftp
  match protocol telnet
  match protocol secure-ftp
  match protocol secure-http
  match protocol secure-pop3
class-map match-all High-Pri-Internet
  match protocol http host "cisco.com"
class-map match-all Med-Pri-Internet
  match protocol http
  match protocol ssh
!
policy-map Internet-Policy
  class High-Pri-Internet
   bandwidth percent 15
   set ip dscp ef
  class Med-Pri-Internet
   bandwidth percent 55
   set ip dscp cs3
  class Low-Pri-Internet
   bandwidth percent 5
   random-detect
   set ip dscp cs1
  class No-Pri-Internet
   police cir 8000
     conform-action set-dscp-transmit default
     exceed-action drop
  class class-default
   fair-queue
   random-detect
!
```

continues

Example 6-44 *Complete Router Configurations (Continued)*

```
!
interface Ethernet0/0
 ip address 10.1.1.1 255.255.255.0
!
interface Serial0/2
 ip address 192.168.3.2 255.255.255.252
service-policy output Internet-Policy
 clockrate 1300000
!
router eigrp 148
 network 10.1.1.0 0.0.0.255
 network 192.168.3.0 0.0.0.3
 no auto-summary
```

Further Reading

IP Quality of Service, by Srinivas Vegesna.

Cisco IOS 12.0 Quality of Service, by Cisco Systems.

Cisco Voice over Frame Relay, ATM, and IP, by Scott McQuerry, Kelly McGrew, and Stephen Foy.

Integrating Voice and Data Networks, by Scott Keagy.

Deploying Cisco Voice over IP Solutions, by Phil Bailey.

RFC 1122, *Requirements for Internet Hosts—Communication Layers*, by Robert Braden.

RFC 1349, *Type of Service in the Internet Protocol Suite*, by Philip Almquist.

RFC 2205, Resource ReSerVation Protocol (RSVP)—Version 1 Functional Specification, by Bob Braden, Lixia Zhang, Steve Berson, Shai Herzog, and Sugih Jamin.

RFC 2474, *Definition of the Differentiated Services Field (DS Field) in the IPv4 and IPv6 Headers*, by Kathleen Nichols, Steven Blake, Fred Baker, and David L. Black.

RFC 2475, *An Architecture for Differentiated Services*, by Steven Blake, David L. Black, Mark A. Carlson, Elwyn Davies, Zheng Wang, and Walter Weiss.

RFC 2597, *Assured Forwarding PHB Group*, by Juha Heinanen, Fred Baker, Walter Weiss, and John Wroclawski.

RFC 2598, *An Expedited Forwarding PHB*, by Van Jacobson, Kathleen Nichols, and Kedarnath Poduri.

RFC 2697, *A Single Rate Three Color Marker*, by Juha Heinanen and Roch Guerin.

BGP Theory and Configuration

CHAPTER 7

BGP-4 Theory

Border Gateway Protocol version 4 (BGP-4), the latest version of BGP, is an extension to BGP versions 3 and 2. BGP-4 is currently the routing protocol used to manage routing for the IPv4 Internet. BGP, originally drafted in RFCs 1105, 1163, and 1267, replaced Exterior Gateway Protocol (EGP) as the Internet routing protocol in the early 1990s. This chapter introduces the BGP protocol, explains BGP terminology, and covers BGP protocol operation. The next chapter focuses on BGP configuration.

BGP Overview

BGP-4, referred to in the rest of this book as BGP, is an interdomain routing protocol used to route IPv4 traffic between autonomous systems. *Autonomous systems* are defined as routing domains that are under the same administrative control and follow the same policies. Figure 7-1 shows the connection of two autonomous systems, AS 1 and AS 2. Each of these autonomous systems contains routers that follow the same policies, and are generally under the same administrative control.

Figure 7-1   *BGP Autonomous Systems*

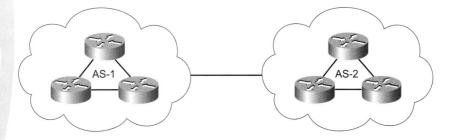

Like IP addresses, public autonomous system numbers (AS numbers) must be unique to each network and are assigned by a Regional Internet Registry (RIR), such as American Registry for Internet Numbers (ARIN) in the United States. Interior Gateway Protocols (IGPs) are used to manage the routing inside of the routing domain (autonomous system), and Exterior Gateway Protocols (EGP), such as BGP, are used to route between the various routing domains (autonomous systems).

There are two BGP session types: internal BGP (I-BGP) and external BGP (E-BGP). I-BGP is used to route traffic within an autonomous system. All traffic in this autonomous system must comply with the same routing policies and present the same view of the autonomous system to E-BGP networks. E-BGP routes traffic between bordering autonomous systems. Each autonomous system maintains its own routing policies, and border routers are used to enforce routing policy control. Each autonomous system that participates in routing with the public Internet requires a unique AS number. AS numbers range from 1 to 65,535, with the range of 64,512 to 65,535 reserved for private autonomous system use. Routers participating in BGP sessions are referred to as *BGP speakers*. BGP speakers form BGP peering sessions over reliable TCP connections using TCP port 179. BGP relies on the TCP protocol to provide session TCP establishment, flow control, retransmission, and session teardown.

NOTE	For two BGP peers to form a BGP session, they must first have an active TCP session. When troubleshooting BGP connectivity problems, it is important to verify that each of the BGP peers are able to reach each other using TCP port number 179.

BGP sessions are initiated, maintained, and closed using different message types. These message types help BGP peers to progress through various connection states. After each of the peers has entered the *Established* state, they will then exchange routing updates. After the initial routing tables have been exchanged, BGP routing updates contain only route changes (additions, modifications, and route removals). If, for any reason, the TCP session between the BGP peers is broken, the BGP process is immediately terminated, and all routes learned through that BGP session are removed from the routing table.

NOTE	BGP messages types are covered in detail in the "BGP Messages" section of this chapter.

When exchanging routing information, each BGP speaker might receive multiple BGP paths but will only use and forward the best path to each destination network. If a BGP speaker cannot verify the reachability of a path using the information from the main IP routing table, BGP will not use the path. It will, however, store all the routes, including those that are not currently chosen as best paths, in one of the other internal BGP tables.

NOTE	The BGP route selection process is covered in detail later in this chapter in the "Route Selection Process" section.

Unlike distance-vector or link-state protocols, BGP makes route determinations based on the AS path that is used to reach a destination network. The *AS path* is a list of autonomous systems that a route passes through to reach its destination. Because BGP was designed to support the entire Internet routing table, BGP is not aware of individual router hops; instead, BGP stores information about the number of AS hops that are used to reach a destination. This is why BGP is referred to as a *path-vector protocol*, because BGP stores information about network paths, rather than distance-vector or link-state routing information. To decrease the number of networks advertised and to increase the believability of the routes, networks are usually aggregated, or summarized, at an AS border router. Aggregation of networks keeps BGP routing tables down in size, decreasing the number of routes that must be sent to neighboring routers and allowing for more controllable network policies.

NOTE   In later versions of Cisco IOS software, the Cisco implementation of BGP supports IPv4 and IPv6 unicast and multicast networks. This book only covers BGP for the unicast IPv4 protocol. When the term IP is used in the chapter, it refers to the IPv4 protocol. For more information on IPv6, see *Cisco Self-Study: Implementing IPv6 Networks (IPv6)*, by Regis Desmeules.

Routing polices are configured using BGP attributes. Attributes are generally assigned to individual network paths, or to an entire autonomous system at the AS border router. BGP speakers use the path attributes to select the best path to each destination network. There are different path selection criteria for interior and exterior BGP sessions. Because exterior BGP speakers must choose from routes that originated in other autonomous systems, these BGP speakers select the paths with the shortest AS path, along with other BGP attributes. I-BGP speakers forward and receive routes that belong to the same AS, so the autonomous system path for these routes is blank; therefore, these BGP speakers must use other BGP attributes to choose the best path. To prevent routing loops, all interior BGP speakers belonging to the same autonomous system do not accept routes that contain their own AS number in the AS path.

NOTE   BGP path attributes are covered in detail later in this chapter in the "BGP Path Attributes" section.

BGP Routing Tables

Routers running the BGP protocol use different routing tables for different purposes. The main IP routing table contains routes obtained through IGP routing processes, such as RIP or Open Shortest Path First (OSPF), static, or directly connected networks. There are also three other conceptual BGP tables, referred to as *Routing Information Bases* (RIBs), which contain only BGP-specific routing information. The BGP tables are used to store information about BGP paths. This information includes the best path to each destination network (used for local routing), the information to send to other BGP peers, and information obtained from other BGP peers. After BGP has selected the best path to a network, that path is added to the main IP routing table.

BGP uses two different routing tables to store incoming and outgoing network advertisements: Adj-RIB-In and Adj-RIB-Out. These tables store information received from other BGP speakers and information to be passed to other BGP peers. Each BGP speaker maintains one Adj-RIB-In and one Adj-RIB-Out per BGP peer relationship. The *Adj-RIB-In* table stores unprocessed BGP information learned from other BGP peers. The information contained in this table is used to determine the best path to the destination network, based on its BGP attributes, using the BGP route selection process. Information from this table is processed by the BGP finite-state machine (the local BGP routing process) and sent to the local BGP table. Information in the *Adj-RIB-Out* table is sent to other BGP peers.

After the local BGP decision process has finished selecting the best path to each destination network, information is stored in the local BGP table, which is known as the *Loc-RIB*. Loc-RIB stores information about paths that conform to the locally configured BGP policies. The BGP speaker learns these routes by means of local BGP configuration, or by learning the route through a BGP session with another BGP speaking router. Unlike the other two BGP routing tables, there is only one Loc-RIB per router (for IPv4 BGP routing). Each path in the Loc-RIB is accompanied by the following routing data: the next-hop IP address used to reach the networks, the metric applied to the network path, the local preference of the path, the weight assigned to the path, the AS path used to reach each of these networks, whether the path was learned through an interior or exterior BGP process or undetermined network origin. If a local router is able to verify that the next hop to the route is reachable—using an IGP route from the local routing table, a static route, or from a directly connected network—the BGP process selects the route and stores it in the main IP routing table. Figure 7-2 illustrates how the BGP routing tables are used during the exchange of BGP routes between two BGP peers, the Apples and Oranges routers, while exchanging routes.

NOTE   The term *RIB* stands for Routing Information Base (database) and refers to a routing table.

Figure 7-2   *BGP Routing Tables*

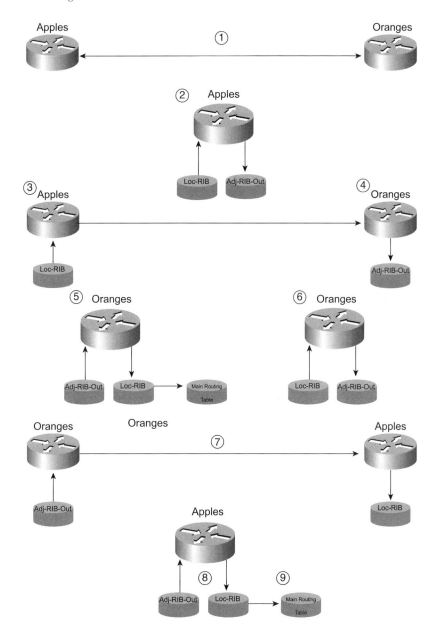

Step 1 BGP speakers, Apples and Oranges, form a BGP peering session.

Step 2 The Apples router takes the routes from its local BGP table, Loc-RIB, processes the routes according to its outgoing BGP policy for the Oranges peer, and sends the routes that comply with the policy to the outgoing BGP table, Adj-RIB-Out.

Step 3 The Apples router sends the Oranges all BGP routes matching the local BGP routing policy conforming to the policies configured for the Oranges router, which the Apples router has stored in the Adj-RIB-Out table for the Apples/Oranges peer session.

Step 4 The Oranges router receives the incoming routes from the Apples router and stores them in the Adj-RIB-In table for the Apples/Oranges peering session, to be processed by the BGP decision process.

Step 5 The Oranges router processes each of the new routes contained in the Adj-RIB-In table, and stores the best path for each network that conforms to the incoming BGP policies for the Apples peer in the Loc-RIB table. Although there is one Adj-RIB-In and one Adj-RIB-Out per BGP session, there is only one main BGP Loc-RIB table per router. After the Oranges router has verified that the next hop to the path is reachable, by searching the main IP routing table for a matching route, and assuming that the main IP routing table does not already have a route to that network via an IGP routing protocol with a lower administrative distance, the path is then stored in the main routing table where it can be used for routing decisions.

Step 6 The Oranges router takes the routes from its local BGP table, Loc-RIB, processes the routes according to the outgoing policy for the Apples router, and sends the routes to be advertised to the outgoing BGP table, Adj-RIB-Out.

Step 7 The Oranges router sends the routes from its outgoing BGP table, Adj-RIB-Out, that conform to the outgoing policy to the Apples router, which stores them in its incoming BGP route table, Adj-RIB-In.

Step 8 The Apples router processes the routes in its Adj-RIB-In table, according to its incoming policy for routes from the Oranges peer, and stores the best path to each destination (that conforms to the incoming policy for the Oranges peer) in the local BGP table, Loc-RIB.

Step 9 The Apples router then verifies that the next hop to each of the network paths contained in the Loc-RIB table is reachable, and, so long as another route to the destination network with a lower administrative distance is not already in the table, stores the reachable best path routes in its main IP routing table.

After the routers have completed the update process and the routes have been processed, only route additions, changes, and removals are sent. As long as the TCP session between the BGP peers is established, the peering routers only send route changes. If the TCP session is lost, all routes learned by means of that session are removed, and when the session is restored, the entire route exchange process takes place again.

BGP speakers do not advertise any networks, unless they are explicitly configured to do so. Before a BGP speaker advertises any network, that network must be explicitly configured as a BGP network. BGP networks can be configured in a number of ways: via the **network** command; as part of an aggregate network; by redistribution; or as a triggered network advertisement, which is created by configuring condition BGP advertisements. BGP network configuration creates the outgoing BGP policy that will apply to each BGP peer. While creating an outgoing BGP policy, you can specify the BGP attributes that will apply to each of the BGP networks you have created. The BGP attributes can be used to influence the way other routers see a particular route, making it more or less desirable.

Before a BGP speaker installs a route to a network in the main IP routing table, the router must know how to reach the next hop that is used to get to that network. Route reachability is verified by searching for a route to the next hop in the main IP routing table. Unlike IGP routing protocols, such as EIGRP and OSPF, which assume that a route is reachable if they learned it through a valid adjacency, BGP does not install routes that it cannot verify as reachable. If a route to the next hop for a BGP network is found in the main IP routing table, BGP assumes that the network is reachable, and that the particular BGP route might be stored in the main IP routing table. If the router receives a route to a network that is not reachable, that route continues to be stored in the incoming BGP table, adj-RIB-In, and might be seen using the **show ip bgp** command, but is not placed in the main IP routing table. If a BGP route that has already been placed in the main IP routing table becomes unreachable (the next hop that is used to reach the network is removed from the main IP routing table), the route is removed. If another reachable route exists, that route is added to the main routing table in the other route's place. When the original route becomes reachable, it might replace the other route, assuming it is the best path to the destination network.

Neighbor Relationships

For two BGP speakers to exchange routing information, they must form a peer relationship, sometimes referred to as a *neighbor relationship*. Each BGP speaker must form a peer relationship with each router with which it is to exchange routes. There are two types of BGP neighbor relationships: internal and external. This section shows how TCP sessions are formed between BGP peers and describes how internal and external BGP peers form neighbor relationships.

Internal and External BGP

As previously mentioned, there are two types of BGP sessions: external BGP sessions, which interconnect AS; and internal BGP sessions, which are used between BGP speakers within the same AS. Both external and internal BGP speakers forward information about BGP paths and rely on IGP routing protocols to maintain a routing table.

External BGP Operation

External BGP is used to exchange routing information between routers belonging to different ASs. Each AS has its own routing policies and is managed independently, usually by people in different organizations or departments. Because E-BGP peers belong to different networks, each E-BGP peer must be configured with policies to control the propagation of internal routes to external networks, filter internal networks that should not be advertised externally, aggregate routes as necessary, and provide session stability. Unless otherwise specified, E-BGP peering routers must be directly connected to each other. Figure 7-3 shows how E-BGP is used to form external BGP sessions between AS 1, AS 2, and AS 3. Notice that only the AS border routers participate in E-BGP, and the E-BGP peers are directly connected to each other at the AS border.

Figure 7-3 *E-BGP Logical Diagram*

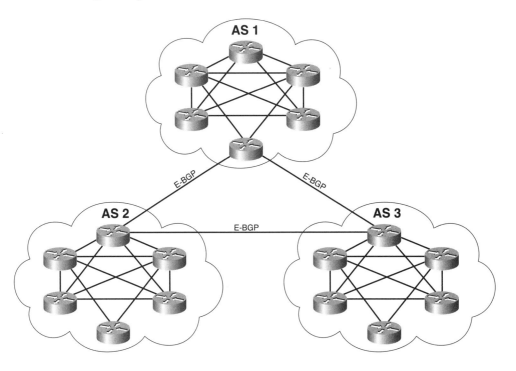

After BGP has been configured, each of the peers negotiates a BGP session and exchanges routes. When you connect a local BGP router to a service provider, you will, most likely, be using a serial, ATM, or Frame Relay connection that goes from your Internet border router directly to your service provider's customer-facing border router. In most cases, this connection is not made across other non-BGP-speaking routers.

NOTE   With the ever-present security threats that must be considered in today's networks, E-BGP connections might need to pass through a firewall or other security device before exiting the network. To overcome the rule that requires E-BGP peers to be directly connected, you can use the **ebgp-multihop** command to specify that the BGP session will be formed over more than one hop. Chapter 8, "Introduction to BGP-4 Configuration," covers the use of the **ebgp-multihop** command.

When designing BGP networks, stable interfaces should be used to prevent route dampening. *Route dampening* occurs when an interface has repeatedly transitioned from an up to down state, and the BGP peering router dampens the route, temporarily suspending route advertisements from the flapping router until a certain period of stability has been exceeded. Most service providers provide their customers with their route-dampening policy and the policy violation penalties. When configuring a multihomed router for E-BGP peering, it is always a good practice to set the BGP router ID to that of a loopback interface, so that the BGP session is least affected by network instabilities and routes are not dampened.

NOTE   Many service providers require that customers that do not have multihomed routers must use the IP addresses of directly connected networks for BGP sessions. To work around this problem, you can set the IP address of the BGP router ID to that of a loopback interface, and change the BGP update source to the IP address of the directly connected interface. Multihoming is covered in detail in Chapter 8.

NOTE   It is generally a good idea to use a loopback interface for the BGP router ID. When OSPF and BGP are both used on the same router, however, you must plan your BGP and OSPF router IDs even more carefully. RFC 1745 states, "The BGP/IDRP identifier *must* be the same as the OSPF router ID at all times that the router is up." If the OSPF and BGP router IDs do not match, BGP cannot synchronize with OSPF, causing BGP not to advertise any unsynchronized routes to any peers.

In most enterprise environments, I-BGP is generally used to connect two or more enterprise border routers to multihome a network to two or more service providers. However, some large enterprise networks might use I-BGP between core routers and E-BGP between the core routers in core sites to provide routing policy. On most enterprise networks, E-BGP sessions are more common than I-BGP connections. This is because E-BGP sessions are used to connect local autonomous systems to the Internet service providers using I-BGP. There are quite a few ways to connect private networks to the public Internet, the most common of which is to use a static route that provides a default route to any unknown network. When this configuration is used, the service provider provides all BGP routing from within their own network and advertises the customer's network from a block of addresses that the service provider has provided the customer. In this case, BGP is not needed on the customer's network. As shown in Figure 7-4, the Internet router provides the only route to the Internet through the service provider's network. The customer's network runs its own IGP for interior routing for all internal traffic between floors on the local network, and the Internet router provides a default route to the Internet using the service provider's network to provide any Internet routing.

Figure 7-4   *Single-Homed Networks*

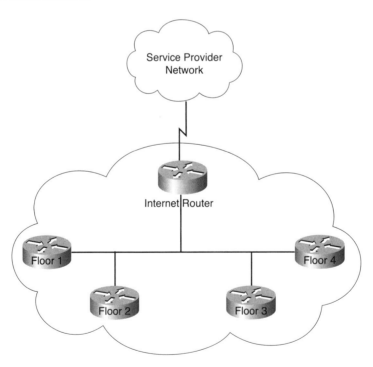

If your network has its own scope of public IP addresses that has been allocated by a public address registry, such as ARIN (American Registry for Internet Numbers), an organization that registers public IP addresses and AS numbers, you must obtain your own unique BGP AS number to advertise your public networks to the Internet.

NOTE   For more information on Internet number registration in the United States, check out the ARIN website at www.arin.net. For European address registration, visit the Réseaux IP Européens Network Coordination Centre (RIPE NCC), www.ripe.net. For Asian network address registration, visit the Asia Pacific Network Information Centre (APNIC) at www.apnic.net. Each of these websites contains a great deal of information about Internet number allocation and assignment, policies for number assignment, and statistical information.

After you have been allocated a range of public IP addresses and have registered an AS number, you must then arrange to advertise this information to an upstream network service provider, following that service provider's policies. You can connect and advertise networks to upstream providers in a number of ways. The two most popular ways are single-homing a network, which usually does not require an AS number or an RIR assigned public IP address allocation, and multihoming networks to more than one provider, which requires AS number and IP address assignments. Figure 7-5 shows how one campus network is multihomed to two different service providers using BGP. In this example, Notebook.com is connected to Service Provider 1 (AS 890) and Service Provider 2 (AS 123). Notebook.com advertises its IP networks using AS 567. In this example, Internet connection redundancy is provided to different service providers connecting to one router; this might be a solution in some cases where budget constraints limit you to one Internet border router; be aware, however, that having only one router does create a single point of failure.

In the next example, shown in Figure 7-6, Quicky Web Title Registration uses Internet Router 1 and Internet Router 2 to advertise its Northwestern, Southwestern, Northeastern, and Southeastern regions' networks to their upstream service provider's network. Quicky's network uses AS 456 to advertise its public networks, and the service provider uses AS 876 to connect to AS 456. In this example, Internet redundancy is provided by connecting two Internet border routers to one service provider, which provides two different routers, WAN interfaces, and circuits for hardware redundancy, but causes a single point of failure with the Internet service provider. In this example, if the service provider has an outage, Quicky's entire Internet connection would be lost.

Figure 7-5 *Single-Homed Campus to Multiple Providers*

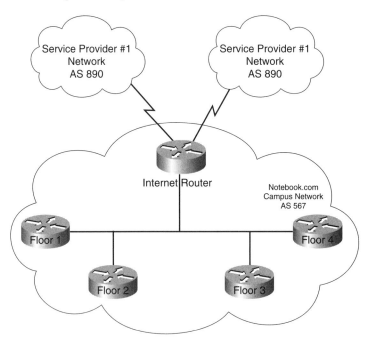

In Figure 7-7, ServiceBank Incorporated uses AS 345 to connect to Service Provider 1 (AS 923) and Service Provider 2 (AS 159). In this example, ServiceBank uses two Internet routers, each connected to a different service provider, to multihome their network to multiple providers. In this case, I-BGP needs to be used to exchange routing information between the two E-BGP Internet routers. This example uses two routers, two circuits, and two service providers; this configuration eliminates any single points of failure. In this example, if ServiceBank has any one failure with any router, circuit, or service provider, they will still be connected to the Internet and able to pass traffic.

Figure 7-8 shows how Mighty Software uses one BGP AS, AS 5655, to connect its European and American networks to the Internet. In this example, Mighty Software's Europe router forms an E-BGP connection, using AS 5655 with the service provider's AS 888. The Europe router is also connected to the Paris, Vienna, London, and Rome routers using a partial mesh of serial E1 WAN connections. The Paris, Vienna, London, and Rome routers are connected via E1 circuits, and they use an IGP routing protocol to route internal networks. The Europe router handles all BGP routing with the service provider for European Internet traffic, and all the other European routers use the Europe router to access the Internet. Likewise, on the American network, the United-States router handles all Internet traffic using an E-BGP connection to the service provider's network, and all U.S. routers form a partial mesh to route to the Internet, the Europe network, and to each other. In this example, there are very few points where a failure can affect Internet connectivity; the only real single point of failure is the single Internet provider.

Figure 7-6   *Multihomed Campus to Single Provider*

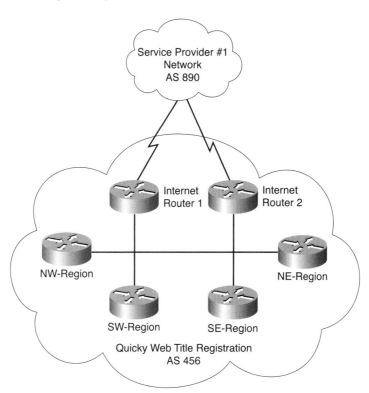

In Figure 7-9, Supernet has two divisions, each having its own AS number. Each AS is multi-homed to a single provider's network for Internet traffic. AS 2522 uses the Portland and New Jersey routers for E-BGP to Service Provider A (AS 5377), and AS 8995 uses the Boise and Detroit routers for E-BGP connections to Service Provider B's network (AS 919). Each of these networks is partially meshed, and they all use an IGP routing protocol for internal routing. The New Jersey and Boise routers are also used to form an E-BGP connection between the two ASs. I-BGP connects are required for communication between the Portland and New Jersey routers and the Boise and Detroit routers. This example is the most redundant of all shown so far. Multiple sites have multiple connections to multiple service providers, limiting the number of failure points. Whenever the resources are available, it is always best to create the most redundant architecture possible, limiting the possible points of failure.

Figure 7-7 *Multihomed Campus to Multiple Providers*

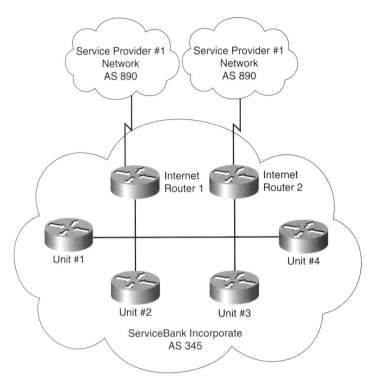

After an E-BGP peer relationship has been formed between an AS border router and an upstream service provider network, Internet border routers must run an internal BGP process to communicate with other BGP speakers within the local AS. The next section discusses I-BGP operation and I-BGP rules.

I-BGP Operation

I-BGP is used between BGP peers within the same AS. As with E-BGP, each I-BGP speaker must be configured to peer with each of its neighboring BGP-speaking routers. BGP does not allow for automatic neighbor discovery. For I-BGP peering routers to provide a consistent view of the network, they must be configured in a full-mesh type of architecture, such as that shown in Figure 7-10. Each router in an I-BGP peering relationship must be connected to all other I-BGP peers via local BGP configuration. Each I-BGP peer must also transition through the various BGP states, and send the same BGP messages and form an Established BGP connection to each of its neighboring peers to exchange routing information.

Figure 7-8   *Multihomed to Single-Provider International*

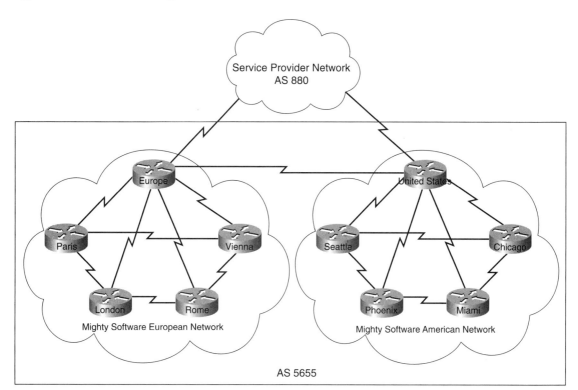

Unlike E-BGP peering routers, I-BGP routers do not have to be directly connected. In Figure 7-11, for example, AS 4589 contains five I-BGP peering routers: Las Vegas, Cleveland, Omaha, D.C., and Tulsa.

Each I-BGP-speaking router in AS 4589 has an I-BGP peering connection with each other router within AS 4589, even if they are not directly connected. The E-BGP-speaking routers—Cleveland and Vancouver, and Tulsa and Juarez—have direct serial connections that are used to form the E-BGP sessions. Notice also that the other I-BGP-speaking routers do not form peer relationships with the E-BGP routers external to their AS. This is because each BGP session, either I-BGP or E-BGP, must be explicitly configured on each of the peering routers. Table 7-1 shows the BGP peer connection types and the BGP peering neighbors.

Figure 7-9 *Multihomed to Multiple-Providers National*

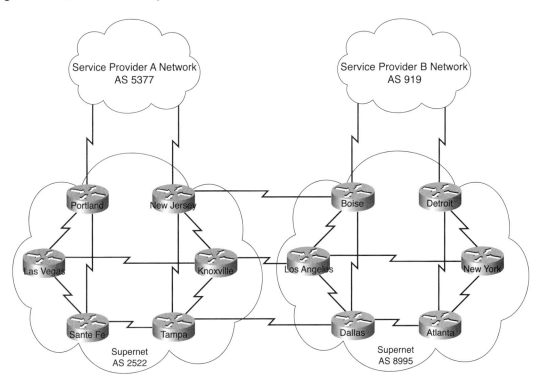

Figure 7-10 *I-BGP Logical Diagram*

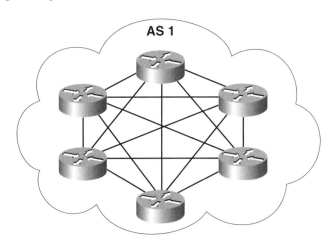

Figure 7-11 *I-BGP Full-Mesh Versus E-BGP*

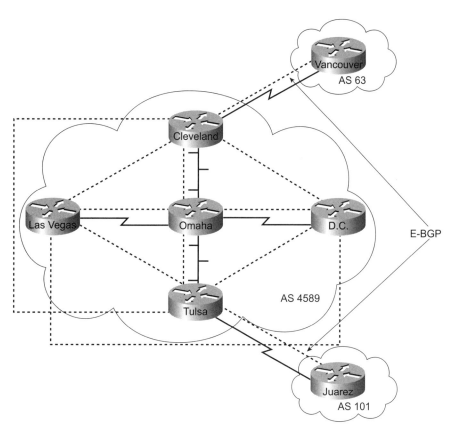

Table 7-1   *BGP Peer Connections*

BGP Router	I-BGP Peers	E-BGP Peers
Las Vegas	Cleveland Omaha Tulsa D.C.	None
Cleveland	Las Vegas Omaha D.C. Tulsa	Vancouver

continues

Table 7-1 *BGP Peer Connections (Continued)*

BGP Router	I-BGP Peers	E-BGP Peers
D.C.	Cleveland Omaha Tulsa Las Vegas	None
Omaha	Cleveland Las Vegas D.C. Tulsa	None
Tulsa	Las Vegas Omaha D.C. Cleveland	Juarez

As mentioned earlier in this chapter, BGP is a path-vector routing protocol, which means that routers that participate in BGP routing processes route traffic based on AS paths, rather than individual router hops like distance-vector algorithms or other link-state metrics such as costs. For BGP to form loop-free paths, it uses an attribute referred to as *AS_PATH*, which contains the path that the BGP route traversed to reach a destination. Each E-BGP-speaking router adds its AS to the AS_PATH on each route it learns, and then forwards that information to downstream BGP routers, which use that information to determine the return path. I-BGP neighbors do not forward (or re-advertise) routes learned from within their own AS (contained in the AS_PATH) to other I-BGP peers, which prevent routing loops from forming within an AS. When two routers in the same AS are each connected to two other E-BGP routers in other autonomous systems, they do not include their internal BGP AS number in the AS_PATH when forwarding routes internally.

NOTE　The AS_PATH attribute is covered in detail later in the "The AS_PATH Attribute" section of this chapter.

As shown in Figure 7-12, Router A is connected to Router C via E-BGP, and Router B is connected to Router D via E-BGP. Routers A and B also have I-BGP connections. When Router A learns of routes through its E-BGP session with Router C, the AS_PATH for each of those routes will include AS 209. When Router A forwards these routes to Router B, it does not include its AS number, AS 400, in the AS_PATH, because Routers A and B have an I-BGP peer relationship. When Router B forwards the routes to Router D, however, it includes its AS number 400, in the path because Router D is an E-BGP peer. Therefore, Router D sees an AS_PATH of 400 and 209 when in the path to Router C, but it is unaware that AS 400 had multiple routes in the path.

In the preceding example, when Router A receives updates from Router C, these updates contain an AS_PATH value of 209. When Router A forwards the updates to Router B to tell it about networks advertised by Router C, the updates still contain an AS_PATH value of 209, because Routers A and B both belong to the same AS. When Routers A and B forward routes from Router C to Router D, however, they add their AS number, 400, to the AS_PATH, so Router D sees that routes from Router C contain an AS_PATH of 400 and 209. Likewise, Router C sees routes from Router D with an AS_PATH value of 400 and 403.

Figure 7-12 *ASm Paths and I-BGP*

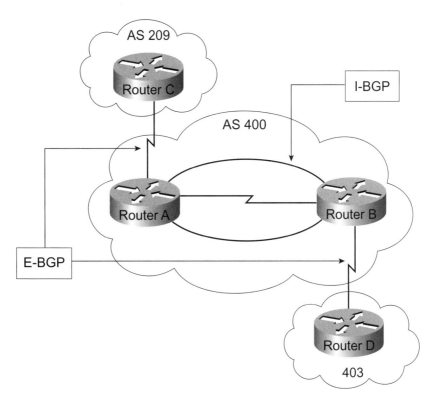

If this topology changes and Router D forms two E-BGP connections, one with Router A and one with Router B, Router D still has one AS path to follow to reach Router C in AS 209. So, routes cannot loop between Routers A and B in AS 400 to reach AS 209. Figure 7-13 illustrates this. Router C uses Router A to reach Router D in AS 403. If the link between Routers A and D goes down, Routers A and D can still reach each other via Router B; and Router D can still reach router C in AS 209, if either of the links between itself and Routers A or B are down.

Figure 7-13 *Adding a New E-BGP Connection to AS 400*

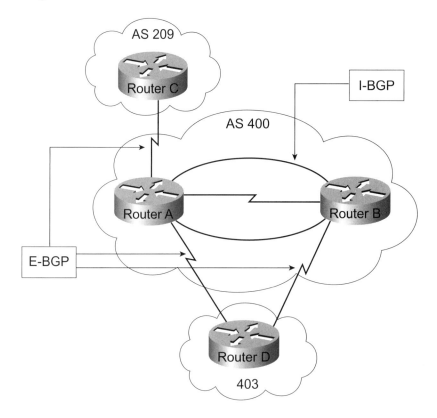

For I-BGP-speaking routers to send internal BGP routes to E-BGP-speaking peers, the I-BGP-speaking router must first have an exact match for the BGP route in its IP routing table. Routes that are not present, or synchronized with the main IP routing table, are not advertised to any BGP peers, because the I-BGP-speaking peer cannot verify reachability for a route that is not found in the main IP routing table. If the router does have an exact match for the route in its main IP routing table, however—learned through an IGP routing process, via a static route, or a directly connected network—that route is advertised to other BGP peers. This is referred to as the *rule of synchronization*; routes in the BGP table must be synchronized with routes in the main IGP routing table (that is, an exact, valid, reachable match for the route must exist) before they can advertise routes to remote peers.

NOTE   One key concept to remember with BGP is the rule of synchronization. Paths in the local BGP table (Loc-RIB) must be synchronized with valid, reachable routes from the IGP routing table before the local BGP process will advertise paths to remote BGP peers or store the BGP routes in the main IP routing table. In other words, routes learned through I-BGP are validated against routes learned via IGP protocols when synchronization is enabled. Synchronization can be, and often is, disabled on BGP-speaking routers that run both I-BGP and E-BGP. If BGP synchronization is not disabled, and an IGP protocol is not providing routing information, the BGP speaker does not use or propagate routes that it does not know how to reach. The use of BGP synchronization is covered in detail in Chapter 8.

To provide a consistent view of an AS to upstream BGP peers, by default, AS bordering routers do not advertise unsynchronized routes learned through I-BGP sessions to E-BGP peers. This is due to the rule of synchronization. BGP synchronization allows I-BGP peers to provide upstream peers with a consistent view of their networks. Because I-BGP-speaking routers that have synchronized BGP and IGP routing tables assume that all other internal peers have the same routing tables, there should not be any unsynchronized routes. As long as all the speakers in an I-BGP network are fully meshed and have a consistent view of the BGP network, IGP to BGP synchronization can be disabled. In Figure 7-13, for example, Router A will not advertise the routes that it has learned from Router B to Routers C or D unless synchronization has been disabled or they are running an IGP routing protocol with synchronized IGP to BGP routes. Likewise, Router B will not advertise any routes it receives from Router A on to Router D unless the IGP and BGP routes are synchronized or BGP synchronization is disabled.

Now that basic BGP operation and terminology have been covered, it is time to move on to more advanced BGP operation. The next few sections cover the following topics in detail:

- BGP messages
- The BGP Finite-State Machine
- BGP attributes
- Route reflectors and confederations
- The BGP decision process

BGP Messages

BGP uses a series of messages to initiate BGP sessions with peering routers, verify that sessions are active, send routing updates, and notify peer routers of error conditions. Each of these messages is used for a particular type of action. Table 7-2 shows a summary of the messages used for all BGP peering sessions.

Table 7-2   *BGP Message Summary*

Message Number	Message Type	Message Description
1	OPEN message	Used to open BGP sessions
2	UPDATE message	Carries route updates for established BGP sessions
3	NOTIFICATION message	Notifies a peer router of an error condition
4	KEEPALIVE message	Sent between BGP peering routers to verify BGP session
5	ROUTE-REFRESH message	An optional message (negotiated during capability advertisement) that is sent to request dynamic BGP route updates from the Adj-RIB-Out table of a remote BGP speaker

NOTE   BGP-4 protocol operation was originally defined in RFC 1771; the IETF Inter-Domain Routing (IDR) working group has been working on a draft that will update that RFC. That Internet draft should reach RFC status by late 2003. For more information about the IETF IDR working group, go to http://www.ietf.org/html.charters/idr-charter.html.

OPEN Message

To establish a BGP session, each BGP peer must send each of its neighboring peers an OPEN message. The OPEN message contains information about the local BGP speaker, and is used after a TCP session has been established. All fields in the OPEN message must be negotiated and accepted before a session can exchange routing information. Table 7-3 describes the information that comprises the OPEN message.

Figure 7-14 shows how Router A and Router B use BGP OPEN messages to form a BGP session. In this example, Router A sends an OPEN message to Router B containing its BGP version of 4, the My AS value of 402, a hold timer of 180 seconds, and the BGP ID of 204.168.75.1. Router B responds with its own OPEN message containing its local BGP version of 4, its My AS of 917, a hold timer of 180 seconds, and the BGP ID of 204.168.75.25. Notice that in this example, each of the BGP speakers are in a different AS, identified by their My AS values; this indicates that they will participate in an E-BGP session.

Table 7-3 *BGP OPEN Message Parameters*

Message Parameter	Description
Version	The version of BGP used by the local BGP speaker.
	The BGP version of the local router is usually the current version, but can be configured to an older version to be compatible with a peering router running an older BGP version.
	If the BGP versions do not match, a BGP session will not be opened. Each of the peering routers try to negotiate a compatible BGP version prior to opening a session.
My AS	The AS number used by the local BGP speaker.
	If the My AS value does not match that configured for the remote peer, a BGP session will not be opened.
	The My AS value also defines whether the BGP peers will be participating in an internal or external BGP session.
Hold Timer	The length of time a BGP speaker expects to wait before receiving either an UPDATE or KEEPALIVE message from its peer.
	BGP peering routers must negotiate and agree on a hold time to establish a BGP session. On Cisco routers, the default hold time for a BGP session is 180 seconds. However, the hold timer is configurable to a value between 0 and 4,294,967,295. If a hold timer of 0 is configured, KEEPALIVE messages will not be used to verify BGP session validity. If a hold time of 0 is not used, the hold timer must be configured to use a value greater than 3 seconds. Hold timers are configured using the **default timers bgp** command, which is covered in Chapter 8.
	It is very important to note that each of the BGP neighbors must agree on an acceptable hold timer before a BGP session can be established, so this value should not be changed unless the peering routers hold timer values will be changed as well.
BGP ID	The local BGP speaker's identification.
	The BGP ID is usually the local router ID that, like OSPF, is the highest IP address of a loopback interface. Loopback interfaces are used to provide the most stable interface for the router ID. The router ID can be changed to another local IP address using the **bgp router-id** command, which is covered in Chapter 8.
	The BGP ID value must match the values configured by both the local and remote BGP peers for each BGP peer relationship, and the remote peer must be reachable by the local BGP peer or the session will not be opened.

continues

Table 7-3 *BGP OPEN Message Parameters (Continued)*

Message Parameter	Description
Optional	Contains optional BGP parameters, such as the Marker field, which contains authentication information; if authentication is not configured, the Marker field will contain all 1s.
	The optional *Capabilities* field contains information that allows for BGP feature negotiation; it is either supported or unsupported between BGP peers. If a Capability option is not supported, it will be ignored by the remote peer, and the session will be renegotiated without the capability.

Figure 7-14 *Opening a BGP Session*

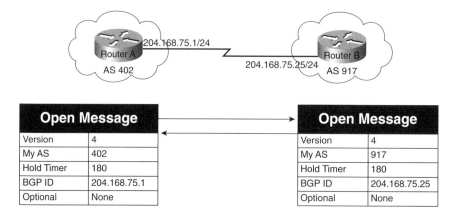

Example 7-1 shows a packet capture that contains a BGP OPEN message. BGP uses the IP precedence value of Internetwork Control, shown as 110000, which is used for high-priority routing traffic. For more detailed information on the type of service (ToS) bits, refer to Chapter 5, "Integrated and Differentiated Services." Notice in this message that the TCP session is using the destination port 179, the BGP destination port. The BGP header for this OPEN message (BGP message type 1) includes a Marker field containing all 1s, which indicates that MD-5 authentication is not in use, with a 45-byte header; the Version field specifies that the sending host is using BGP-4. The host belongs to AS number 1 and the hold time is 180 seconds, and the sending host's BGP ID is 192.168.5.1.

Example 7-1 *BGP OPEN Message*

```
Frame Status Source Address Dest. Address Size Rel. Time Delta Time Abs. Time
Summary
8 [10.50.4.1] [10.50.4.2] 99 0:00:37.326 0.003.216 04/28/2002 03:14:50 PM
BGP: type = Open
DLC: -----
DLC Header -----
```

Example 7-1 *BGP OPEN Message (Continued)*

```
DLC:
DLC: Frame 8 arrived at 15:14:50.2341; frame size is 99 (0063 hex) bytes.
DLC: Destination = Station 000427228197
DLC: Source = Station 0004272281D8
DLC: Ethertype = 0800 (IP)
DLC:
IP: ----- IP Header -----
IP:
IP: Version = 4, header length = 20 bytes
IP: Type of service = C0
IP: 110. .... = internetwork control
IP: ...0 .... = normal delay
IP: .... 0... = normal throughput
IP: .... .0.. = normal reliability
IP: .... ..0. = ECT bit - transport protocol will ignore the CE bit
IP: .... ...0 = CE bit - no congestion
IP: Total length = 85 bytes
IP: Identification = 2
IP: Flags = 0X
IP: .0.. .... = might fragment
IP: ..0. .... = last fragment IP: Fragment offset = 0 bytes
IP: Time to live = 1 seconds/hops
IP: Protocol = 6 (TCP)
IP: Header checksum = 9C7B (correct)
IP: Source address = [10.50.4.1]
IP: Destination address = [10.50.4.2]
IP: No options
IP:
TCP: ----- TCP header -----
TCP:
TCP: Source port = 11002
TCP: Destination port = 179 (BGP)
TCP: Sequence number = 3817488861
TCP: Next expected Seq number= 3817488906
TCP: Acknowledgment number = 3816595146
TCP: Data offset = 20 bytes
TCP: Flags = 18
TCP: ..0. .... = (No urgent pointer)
TCP: ...1 .... = Acknowledgment
TCP: .... 1... = Push
TCP: .... .0.. = (No reset)
TCP: .... ..0. = (No SYN)
TCP: .... ...0 = (No FIN)
TCP: Window = 16384
TCP: Checksum = 97C3 (correct)
TCP: No TCP options
TCP: [45 Bytes of data]
TCP:
BGP: ----- BGP Message -----
BGP: BGP: 16 byte Marker (all 1's)
BGP: Length = 45
```

continues

Example 7-1 *BGP OPEN Message (Continued)*

```
BGP: BGP type = 1 (Open)
BGP:
BGP: Version = 4
BGP: AS number = 1
BGP: Hold Time = 180 Second(s)
BGP:
BGP Identifier = C0A80501, [192.168.5.1]
BGP:
BGP: Optional Parameters Length = 16
BGP: Unknown Option Data
BGP:
ADDR HEX                                            ASCII 0000:
00 04 27 22 81 97 00 04 27 22 81 d8 08 00 45 c0 I ..'"....'"....E.
0010: 00 55 00 02 00 00 01 06 9c 7b 0a 32 04 01 0a 32 I .U.......{.2...2
0020: 04 02 2a fa 00 b3 e3 8a 41 dd e3 7c 9e ca 50 18 I ..*.....A..l..P.
0030: 40 00 97 c3 00 00 ff ff ff ff ff ff ff ff ff ff I @..............
0040: ff ff ff ff ff ff 00 2d 01 04 00 01 00 b4 c0 a8 I .......-........
0050: 05 01 10 02 06 01 04 00 01 00 01 02 02 80 00 02 I ................
0060: 02 02 00 I ...
```

BGP Capabilities Advertisement

Starting with BGP-4, BGP peer capabilities can be negotiated during session BGP initialization, using the Optional Capabilities parameter, which is contained in the OPEN message. BGP capabilities negotiation is described in RFC 2842. This element was added into BGP so that new features could be added into the BGP specification without requiring upgrades to newer versions of the protocol.

Using capabilities advertisement, peers can exchange capabilities and negotiate a session using the most agreed-upon features. If one of the peers does not support an optional parameter, it sends the advertiser a NOTIFICATION message with the error "Unsupported Optional Parameter." After receiving the NOTIFICATION message, the advertising peer resends the message without the unsupported parameter and so on, until both peers agree on a set of parameters. Table 7-4 describes the IANA-defined BGP capabilities codes.

Table 7-4 *BGP Capabilities Codes*

Capabilities Code	Description
0	Reserved
1	Multiprotocol extensions for BGP-4
2	ROUTE-REFRESH capability for BGP-4

Table 7-4   *BGP Capabilities Codes (Continued)*

Capabilities Code	Description
3	Cooperative route filtering capability
4	Multiple routes to a destination capability
5–63	Unassigned
64	Graceful restart capability
65	Support for 4-octet AS number capability
66	Support for dynamic capability
128–255	Vendor specific

UPDATE Message

After a BGP session has been established, the peering routers begin to exchange routing information using UPDATE messages. UPDATE messages contain information about each route advertised to the peering router. In BGP routing, network prefixes are also referred to as *Network Layer Reachability Information (NLRI)*. Table 7-5 shows the information contained in BGP UPDATE messages and descriptions of the BGP UPDATE message fields.

Table 7-5   *BGP UPDATE Message Information*

Message Parameters	Description
Unfeasible Route Length	This field contains the total number of routes that are to be withdrawn from the BGP routing tables. If this value is 0, no routes are to be withdrawn in this message.
Withdrawn Routes	The Withdrawn Routes field contains prefixes that are to be removed from the BGP tables. This information is stored in a *[length, prefix]* format. Each route that is to be removed from an established BGP session is sent to the neighboring router in this format.
Total Path Attribute Length	This field identifies the total length of the Path Attributes field (in octets).

continues

Table 7-5 *BGP UPDATE Message Information (Continued)*

Message Parameters	Description
Path Attributes	BGP path attributes (attribute type codes) are basically the metrics that are to be used by the decision process. There are 19 BGP path attributes defined by IANA, the top 10 of which are as follows:
	1. ORIGIN
	2. AS_PATH
	3. NEXT_HOP
	4. MULTI-EXIT-DISC
	5. LOCAL-PREF
	6. ATOMIC-AGGREGATE
	7. AGGREGATOR
	8. COMMUNITY
	9. ORIGINATOR_ID
	10. CLUSTER_LIST
	The Path Attributes field contains three values:
	• **Attribute Type**—Contains two subsections that describe each attribute type code (listed here) and the flags that apply to those attributes
	• **Attribute Length**—Defines the length of the attribute
	• **Attribute Value**—Contains the value belonging to the attribute type code
Attribute Type (a subsection of the Path Attributes field)	The Attribute Type field contains two items: the Attribute Flags and the Attribute Type Code. Each of the attributes from the Attribute Type Code section of the Path Attributes field has an associated Attribute Type category, which defines how the attribute is to be forwarded by other BGP routers. There are four attribute types:
	1. Well-known mandatory
	2. Well-known discretionary
	3. Optional transitive
	4. Optional nontransitive
	The Attribute Flags field is covered shortly.
NLRI	The NLRI field is the part of the UPDATE message field that contains paths that are to be advertised as reachable (network layer reachability information).
	The NLRI field contains the prefixes for each of the paths to be advertised in a [*length, prefix*] format. This is the information that was taken from the local routers' Adj-RIB-Out database and will be added to the neighboring routers' Adj-RIB-In database.

After two BGP peers have formed an established BGP session, they can exchange routing information in the form of UPDATE messages. The UPDATE messages contain information about new routes that are to be added to the BGP table, routes that are no longer reachable (and are to be removed from the BGP table), and path attributes for the routes.

As shown in the preceding table, the Unfeasible Route Length field contains the number of routes that are to be removed from the BGP table. The Withdrawn Routes field contains the actual routes that are to be removed, in the [*length*, *prefix*] format. The Path Attributes field contains the attribute type codes for the paths sent in the update, and the Attribute Flags field specifies how attributes are to be handled by the routing process. And, finally, the NLRI field contains the new or changed routes that are being advertised.

In BGP, each routing update contains attributes that belong to all the NLRI paths in the message. The 10 basic attribute type codes and attribute values you will most likely encounter when working with BGP-4 in an IP environment are as follows:

1 **ORIGIN**—Specifies the origin of the route: I-BGP, E-BGP, or Incomplete.

2 **AS_PATH**—Contains a list of ASs that the route traversed in its path.

3 **NEXT_HOP**—The next hop taken to reach the destination route.

4 **MULTI-EXIT-DISC**—Multiple Exit Discriminator is a metric used to determine which path to take if there are multiple exit points to an AS.

5 **LOCAL-PREF**—Indicates preference for one path over others within an AS.

6 **ATOMIC-AGGREGATE**—Indicates that the local process chose a less-specific path to a destination over one that is more specific.

7 **AGGREGATOR**—This attribute is used to indicate the IP address of a router that has aggregated a number of routes together.

8 **COMMUNITY**—Specifies the local BGP COMMUNITY value; by default, all community-aware routers belong to the Internet community.

9 **ORIGINATOR_ID**—Specifies a route reflection with a route reflector cluster.

10 **CLUSTER_LIST**—Contains a reflection path that shows through which path a reflected route has passed.

Each of these attribute code types is accompanied by an *attribute flag* that specifies how the attribute is to be treated when it is processed by a peer router. Table 7-6 shows the four attribute flags and their associated flags; these are covered in detail later in this chapter.

Table 7-6   *BGP Attribute Flags*

Attribute Flag	Flag Name	Description
Highest bit	Optional bit	Defines whether an attribute is well known (0) or optional (1).
Second highest bit	Transitive bit	Defines whether an optional attribute is nontransitive (0) or transitive (1).
Third highest bit	Partial bit	Defines whether an optional transitive attribute is complete (0) or partial (1).
Fourth highest bit	Extended Length bit	Defines whether the attribute length is 1 octet (0) or 2 octets (1). This flag is only used (set to 1) when the attribute length is greater than 255 octets.

Example 7-2 shows a protocol analysis of an UPDATE message. Notice in the example that this message is a 68-byte BGP type 2 UPDATE message, with a Marker field of all 1s, indicating no authentication is taking place. This update does not contain any withdrawn routes, indicated by the 0 Unfeasible Routes Length. The first attribute in this message is the well-known transitive type 1 ORIGIN attribute value of 0-IGP, indicating that the message came from an I-BGP session. The next well-known transitive attribute is the type 2 AS_PATH attribute; this attribute lists the ASs through which the route has passed. The Path Segment Type field value of 2 (AS-SEQUENCE) means that this update contains an ordered list of autonomous systems. The Path Segment Length field value of 1 indicates that there is only one AS in the path, and the AS Identifier field value indicates that the packet originated from AS 2. The next well-known transitive attribute is the type 3 NEXT-HOP attribute that contains the next hop of 10.50.4.2. The final optional nontransitive attribute is the type 4 MED attribute. This attribute is used to determine which route to take if there are multiple exit points to an AS. The MED for this update is 0.

The next field in this update contains the NLRI information. The NLRI field contains new or changed routes that are being advertised in this message. This message contains routes to the networks 192.168.11.0/24, 192.168.12.0/24, 192.168.13.0/24, 192.168.14.0/24, and 192.168.15.0/24. Each of these routes is presented in [*prefix length*, *subnet mask*, *IP address*] format.

Example 7-2   *BGP UPDATE Message*

```
Frame Status Source Address Dest. Address Size Rel. Time Delta Time Abs. Time
 Summary
13 [10.50.4.2] [10.50.4.1] 141 0:00:37.537 0.001.028 04/28/2002 03:14:50 PM
 BGP: type = Update
DLC: ----- DLC Header -----
DLC:
DLC: Frame 13 arrived at 15:14:50.4449; frame size is 141 (008D hex) bytes.
DLC: Destination = Station 0004272281D8
DLC: Source = Station 000427228197
DLC: Ethertype = 0800 (IP)
```

Example 7-2 *BGP UPDATE Message (Continued)*

```
DLC:
IP: ----- IP Header -----
IP:
IP: Version = 4, header length = 20 bytes
IP: Type of service = C0
IP: 110. .... = internetwork control
IP: ...0 .... = normal delay
IP: .... 0... = normal throughput
IP: .... .0.. = normal reliability
IP: .... ..0. = ECT bit - transport protocol will ignore the CE bit
IP: .... ...0 = CE bit - no congestion
IP: Total length = 127 bytes
IP: Identification = 3
IP: Flags = 0X
IP: .0.. .... = might fragment
IP: ..0. .... = last fragment
IP: Fragment offset = 0 bytes
IP: Time to live = 1 seconds/hops
IP: Protocol = 6 (TCP)
IP: Header checksum = 9C50 (correct)
IP: Source address = [10.50.4.2]
IP: Destination address = [10.50.4.1]
IP: No options
IP:
TCP: ----- TCP header -----
TCP:
TCP: Source port = 179 (BGP)
TCP: Destination port = 11002
TCP: Sequence number = 3816595210
TCP: Next expected Seq number= 3816595297
TCP: Acknowledgment number = 3817488925
TCP: Data offset = 20 bytes
TCP: Flags = 18
TCP: ..0. .... = (No urgent pointer)
TCP: ...1 .... = Acknowledgment
TCP: .... 1... = Push
TCP: .... .0.. = (No reset)
TCP: .... ..0. = (No SYN)
TCP: .... ...0 = (No FIN)
TCP: Window = 16320
TCP: Checksum = 19F9 (correct)
TCP: No TCP options
TCP: [87 Bytes of data]
TCP:
BGP: ----- BGP Message -----
BGP:

BGP: 16 byte Marker (all 1's)
BGP: Length = 68
BGP:
```

continues

Example 7-2 *BGP UPDATE Message (Continued)*

```
BGP type = 2 (Update)
BGP:
BGP: Unfeasible Routes Length = 0
BGP: No Withdrawn Routes in this Update
BGP: Path Attribute Length = 25 bytes
BGP: Attribute Flags = 4X
BGP: 0... .... = Well-known
BGP: .1.. .... = Transitive
BGP: ..0. .... = Complete
BGP: ...0 .... = 1 byte Length
BGP: Attribute type code = 1 (Origin)
BGP: Attribute Data Length = 1
BGP: Origin type = 0 (IGP)
BGP: Attribute Flags = 4X
BGP: 0... .... = Well-known
BGP: .1.. .... = Transitive
BGP: ..0. .... = Complete
BGP: ...0 .... = 1 byte Length
BGP: Attribute type code = 2 (AS Path)
BGP: Attribute Data Length = 4
BGP: Path segment type = 2 (AS_SEQUENCE)
BGP: Path segment length = 1
BGP: AS Identifier = 2
BGP: Attribute Flags = 4X
BGP: 0... .... = Well-known
BGP: .1.. .... = Transitive
BGP: ..0. .... = Complete
BGP: ...0 .... = 1 byte Length
BGP: Attribute type code = 3 (Next Hop)
BGP: Attribute Data Length = 4
BGP: Next Hop = [10.50.4.2]
BGP: Attribute Flags = 8X
BGP: 1... .... = Optional
BGP: .0.. .... = Non-transitive
BGP: ..0. .... = Complete
BGP: ...0 .... = 1 byte Length
BGP: Attribute type code = 4 (Multi Exit Disc)
BGP: Attribute Data Length = 4
BGP: Multi Exit Disc Attribute = 0
BGP:
BGP: Network Layer Reachability Information:
BGP: IP Prefix Length = 24 bits, IP subnet mask [255.255.255.0]
BGP: IP address [192.168.11.0]
BGP: IP Prefix Length = 24 bits, IP subnet mask [255.255.255.0]
BGP: IP address [192.168.12.0]
BGP: IP Prefix Length = 24 bits, IP subnet mask [255.255.255.0]
```

Example 7-2 *BGP UPDATE Message (Continued)*

```
BGP: IP address [192.168.13.0]
BGP: IP Prefix Length = 24 bits, IP subnet mask [255.255.255.0]
BGP: IP address [192.168.14.0]
BGP: IP Prefix Length = 24 bits, IP subnet mask [255.255.255.0]
BGP: IP address [192.168.15.0]
BGP:
BGP: 16 byte Marker (all 1's)
BGP: Length = 19
BGP:
BGP type = 4 (KEEPALIVE)
BGP:
DLC: --- Frame too short
ADDR HEX                                                    ASCII
0000: 00 04 27 22 81 d8 00 04 27 22 81 97 08 00 45 c0 | ..'"....'"....E.
0010: 00 7f 00 03 00 00 01 06 9c 50 0a 32 04 02 0a 32 | .........P.2...2
0020: 04 01 00 b3 2a fa e3 7c 9f 0a e3 8a 42 1d 50 18 | ....*..|....B.P.
0030: 3f c0 19 f9 00 00 ff ff ff ff ff ff ff ff ff ff | ?..ù...........
0040: ff ff ff ff ff ff 00 44 02 00 00 00 19 40 01 01 | .......D.....@..
0050: 00 40 02 04 02 01 00 02 40 03 04 0a 32 04 02 80 | .@......@...2...
0060: 04 04 00 00 00 00 18 c0 a8 0b 18 c0 a8 0c 18 c0 | ...............
0070: a8 0d 18 c0 a8 0e 18 c0 a8 0f ff ff ff ff ff ff | ...............
0080: ff ff ff ff ff ff ff ff ff ff 00 13 04 | ............
```

In Figure 7-15, for example, Routers A and B have an established BGP session and are now exchanging routing information using UPDATE messages. Router A sends an update removing two routes: one to 50.1.1.0/24, and one to 50.2.2.0/24. This routing update also contains four new routes: 51.3.3.0/24, 51.4.4.0/24, 51.5.5.0/24, and 60.1.1.0/24. These routes are sent out as routes learned through E-BGP, but originating from an I-BGP session (indicated by the Type 1 IGP path attribute), with an AS path of AS 402, AS 10, and AS 30, with a next hop of 51.5.2.4. Router B receives the UPDATE message, removes the routes to 50.1.1.0/24 and 50.2.2.0/24 from its Adj-RIB-In table, and then adds the routes to the 51.3.3.0/24, 51.4.4.0/24, 51.5.5.0/24, and 60.1.1.0 networks to its Adj-RIB-In table to be processed by its BGP decision process.

Router B then takes its routes from the local Adj-RIB-Out table, and sends an update to Router A containing new routes to networks 197.62.59.0/24, 197.63.59.0/24, and 197.64.59.0/24. The new routes all came from an E-BGP session, but originated from an I-BGP session, using an AS path of AS 917, AS 40, and AS 29, and have the next hop of 197.61.1.1. Router A takes these new routes and adds them to its Adj-RIB-In table to be processed by the BGP decision process, and then adds the best routes to its local BGP routing table Loc-RIB. Until there are any route changes, Routers A and B will not send any further routing updates; they will only send KEEPALIVE messages back and forth, notifying each other that the BGP session is still active.

Figure 7-15 *Routers Exchanging BGP Updates*

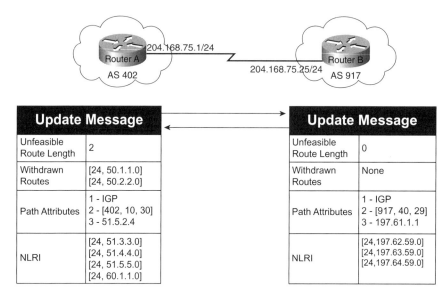

NOTIFICATION Message

BGP NOTIFICATION messages are used to indicate an error condition resulting in BGP session termination. NOTIFICATION messages are always immediately followed by session termination. Upon termination of a BGP connection, the TCP session between the BGP peers is torn down, all resources are released, "route withdrawal" messages are sent to peering BGP peers, and all BGP routes are removed from the table. A BGP session might terminate in an error condition for a number of reasons. Table 7-7 describes the six major NOTIFICATION error messages.

Table 7-7 *BGP NOTIFICATION Messages*

MessageNumber	Message Type	Description
1	Message Header Error	Indicates that an error was found processing a BGP message header. Message header errors include a subcode that indicates the reason for the error.
2	OPEN Message Error	Indicates a message found in an OPEN message. OPEN message errors include an error subcode that indicates the cause of the error.
3	UPDATE Message Error	Indicates a message found in an UPDATE message. UPDATE message errors are accompanied by an error subcode that indicates the cause of the error.

Table 7-7   *BGP NOTIFICATION Messages (Continued)*

MessageNumber	Message Type	Description
4	Hold Timer Expired	This error type indicates that the local system did not receive a KEEPALIVE or UPDATE message within the negotiated time interval.
5	Finite-State Machine Error	When an unexpected error occurs, a finite-state machine error is sent to the peering router, terminating the BGP session.
6	Cease	Indicates the immediately terminated BGP session.

Each NOTIFICATION message contains three fields: Error Code, Error Subcode, and Data. The *Error Code* field specifies the type of NOTIFICATION error. The *Error Subcode*, if provided, gives a more detailed explanation of the error. One or more error subcodes might be included in a NOTIFICATION message. The *Data* field includes any diagnosis information that is related to the error. Not all NOTIFICATION messages include a value in the Data field.

When an error is found while processing a BGP header, a message header error NOTIFICATION message is generated. This message is generated in the event that a BGP header is received with an invalid Marker field, if the value of the length of a message header is greater or less than the required value, or if the type of the message header is unknown. Table 7-8 shows Message Header Error Notification subcodes and their descriptions.

Table 7-8   *Message Header Error NOTIFICATION Subcodes*

Message Number	Message Subcode Type	Description
0	No error subcode	Null field.
1	Connection Not Synchronized	Indicates that the Marker field in a BGP message is not the expected value. **OPEN message**—All 1s, unless TCP MD-5 authentication is in use **All others**—Negotiated in OPEN messages
2	Bad Message Length	The length of a message header is greater or less than the required value. This message contains the bad value in the Data field. **OPEN**—Minimum 29 octets, maximum 4096 octets **UPDATE**—Minimum 23 octets, maximum 4096 octets **KEEPALIVE**—No greater or less than 19 octets (the size of an empty BGP KEEPALIVE message)
3	Bad Message Type	Indicates that an unrecognized message type was received. The value of the Type field is included in the Data field of this message.

BGP OPEN message errors can be caused by failed or misconfigured TCP MD-5 authentication attempts, corrupt TCP packets, or other BGP configuration problems. OPEN message errors include a message subcode that describes the reason for the error message. Table 7-9 shows possible subcode messages and their descriptions.

Table 7-9   *OPEN Message Error NOTIFICATION Subcodes*

Message Number	Message Subcode Type	Description
1	Unsupported Version	The BGP peer is using an unsupported BGP version. The Data field in this message includes the largest locally supported BGP version.
2	Bad Peer AS	The peering router's My AS value is not as expected. This error might be cause by a misconfiguration on one of the peering routers.
3	Bad BGP ID	The peering router's BGP ID value is not as expected. This error might be caused by a misconfiguration on either router. This value must be a valid IP address.
4	Unsupported Optional	The local router received an unsupported Optional value.
5	Authentication Failure	This message is generated upon BGP authentication failure.
6	Unacceptable Hold Time	The hold-timer value is not acceptable to the local system, any hold time might be rejected; hold timers must be negotiated on both BGP peers.

After the OPEN messages have been received and the routers have established a valid BGP session, they begin to send UPDATE messages. A number of different errors might occur when processing UPDATE messages. These errors are generally the result of a misconfiguration on one of the peer routers. Table 7-10 shows the various UPDATE message error NOTIFICATION messages and their descriptions.

Table 7-10   *UPDATE Message Error NOTIFICATION Subcodes*

Message Number	Message Subcode Type	Description
1	Malformed Attribute List	The length of the Unfeasible Route Length and/or Total Attribute Length plus the fixed UPDATE header size (the fixed size of the UPDATE header [19] plus the size of the Total Path Attribute Length field [2] plus the Unfeasible Route Length field [2]) is too large. This message might also be sent if the same attribute appears more than once in the same UPDATE message.

Table 7-10   *UPDATE Message Error NOTIFICATION Subcodes (Continued)*

Message Number	Message Subcode Type	Description
2	Unrecognized Well-Known Attribute	Indicates an unknown well-known mandatory attribute. The value of this attribute is included in the Data field of the message.
3	Missing Well-Known Attribute	Indicates that a well-known mandatory attribute is missing. The Data field includes the missing attribute.
4	Attribute Flag Error	The Attribute Flag field and Attribute Code field do not match. This might be a bad attribute, flag, code, or value. This information is included in the Data field for the message.
5	Attribute Length Error	The actual attribute length does not match the length specified by the Attribute Length field. The attribute data (attribute type, length, and value) is included in the Data field for the message.
6	Invalid Origin Attribute	The ORIGIN value is not defined or is unrecognized. The value of the ORIGIN field is included in the error message.
7	AS Routing Loop	The local AS number has been seen in an UPDATE message—an AS routing loop is assumed.
8	Invalid Next-Hop Attribute	The next-hop value is not a valid IP address; this is a syntax error. The value is included in the message.
9	Optional Attribute Error	Indicates an error in the value of a recognized optional attribute. The value of this error appears in the Data field of this message.
10	Invalid Network Field	Indicates a syntax error in the NLRI field for a message.
11	Malformed AS_PATH	The AS_PATH is syntactically incorrect.

If a BGP session has no errors, you will not see any NOTIFICATION messages unless an interface goes down or the BGP configuration has changed. After two BGP peers have formed a BGP session, they exchange KEEPALIVE messages to verify session BGP integrity. The next section discusses the BGP KEEPALIVE message type.

KEEPALIVE Message

After the BGP session has been successfully established, and BGP updates have been sent and received, the BGP peers send each other periodic KEEPALIVE messages. KEEPALIVE messages are sent by the peering routers every 60 seconds, by default, to notify neighboring peers that the BGP connection is active. The KEEPALIVE message interval can be changed from the default value to any other value between 3 and 4,294,967,295 or set to 0 to signify that KEEPALIVE messages will not be exchanged. KEEPALIVE values of 1 or 2 seconds are not valid. If invalid KEEPALIVE values are used, the BGP session will fail with the NOTIFICATION message "Open failed: Connection refused by remote host." KEEPALIVE timers might also be set to 1/3 the negotiated hold-timer value, which is, by default, 180 seconds. Figure 7-16 shows the process, followed by each of the three BGP messages, including the KEEPALIVE messages sent during a successful BGP session.

The KEEPALIVE message contains no data; it is just a 19-byte BGP header, as shown in the protocol analysis contained in Example 7-3.

Example 7-3 *BGP KEEPALIVE Message*

```
Frame Status Source Address  Dest. Address Size  Rel. Time Delta Time Abs. Time
  Summary
10 [10.50.4.1] [10.50.4.2] 73 0:00:37.336 0.008.155 04/28/2002 03:14:50 PM
 BGP: type =
KEEPALIVE
DLC: ----- DLC Header -----
DLC:
DLC: Frame 10 arrived at 15:14:50.2443; frame size is 73 (0049 hex) bytes.
DLC: Destination = Station 000427228197
DLC: Source = Station 0004272281D8
DLC: Ethertype = 0800 (IP)
DLC:
IP: ----- IP Header -----
IP: IP: Version = 4, header length = 20 bytes
IP: Type of service = C0
IP: 110. .... = internetwork control
IP: ...0 .... = normal delay
IP: .... 0... = normal throughput
IP: .... .0.. = normal reliability
IP: .... ..0. = ECT bit - transport protocol will ignore the CE bit
IP: .... ...0 = CE bit - no congestion
IP: Total length = 59 bytes
IP: Identification = 3 IP: Flags = 0X
IP: .0.. .... = might fragment
IP: ..0. .... = last fragment
IP: Fragment offset = 0 bytes
IP: Time to live = 1 seconds/hops IP: Protocol = 6 (TCP)
IP: Header checksum = 9C94 (correct)
IP: Source address = [10.50.4.1]
IP: Destination address = [10.50.4.2]
IP: No options
IP:
```

Example 7-3   *BGP KEEPALIVE Message (Continued)*

```
TCP: ----- TCP header -----
TCP:
TCP: Source port = 11002
TCP: Destination port = 179 (BGP)
TCP: Sequence number = 3817488906
TCP: Next expected Seq number= 3817488925
TCP: Acknowledgment number = 3816595191
TCP: Data offset = 20 bytes
TCP: Flags = 18 TCP: ..0. .... = (No urgent pointer)
TCP: ...1 .... = Acknowledgment
TCP: .... 1... = Push
TCP: .... .0.. = (No reset)
TCP: .... ..0. = (No SYN)
TCP: .... ...0 = (No FIN)
TCP: Window = 16339
TCP: Checksum = 7BB6 (correct)
TCP: No TCP options
TCP: [19 Bytes of data]
TCP: BGP: ----- BGP Message -----
BGP:
BGP: 16 byte Marker (all 1's)
BGP: Length = 19 BGP: BGP type = 4 (KEEPALIVE)
BGP:
BGP:
ADDR HEX                               ASCII
0000: 00 04 27 22 81 97 00 04 27 22 81 d8 08 00 45 c0 | ..'"....'"....E.
0010: 00 3b 00 03 00 00 01 06 9c 94 0a 32 04 01 0a 32 | .;.........2...2
0020: 04 02 2a fa 00 b3 e3 8a 42 0a e3 7c 9e f7 50 18 | ..*.....B..|..P.
0030: 3f d3 7b b6 00 00 ff ff ff ff ff ff ff ff ff ff | ?.{............
0040: ff ff ff ff ff ff 00 13 04 | .........
```

ROUTE-REFRESH Message

Prior to Cisco IOS Software Release 12.0(6)T, all BGP-speaking routers used to require a manual BGP session reset each time the local routing policy changed. This session reset allowed peers to apply new policies as the routers processed and received the incoming routing updates from their remote peers. In legacy versions of Cisco IOS software, this problem was solved, on a peer-by-peer basis, using BGP *soft reconfiguration*. After BGP soft reconfiguration has been configured on a legacy peer, that router stores the full, unmodified copy of the incoming Adj-RIB-In table that it received from each remote peer in memory. Although this feature promotes network stability by preventing BGP session interruptions, it also consumes large amounts of system resources. Soft configuration is triggered each time a soft-reconfiguration request is issued using the **clear ip bgp** {* | *ip-address* | *peer-group*} **soft** [**in** | **out**] command; the use of this command is covered later in Chapter 9, "Advanced BGP Configuration." When this command is issued, the local BGP peer acts as though it has just received a full routing update from the remote peer by refreshing routes stored in the Loc-RIB table using the Adj-RIB-In information stored in memory.

Figure 7-16 *BGP Messages*

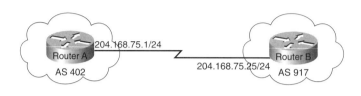

Open Message			Open Message	
Version	4		Version	4
My AS	402		My AS	917
Hold Timer	180		Hold Timer	180
BGP ID	204.168.75.1		BGP ID	204.168.75.25
Optional	None		Optional	None

Update Message			Update Message	
Unfeasible Route Length	2		Unfeasible Route Length	0
Withdrawn Routes	[24, 50.1.1.0] [24, 50.2.2.0]		Withdrawn Routes	None
Path Attributes	1 - IGP 2 - [402, 10, 30] 3 - 51.5.2.4		Path Attributes	1 - IGP 2 - [917, 40, 29] 3 - 197.61.1.1
NLRI	[24, 51.3.3.0] [24, 51.4.4.0] [24, 51.5.5.0] [24, 60.1.1.0]		NLRI	[24,197.62.59.0] [24,197.63.59.0] [24,197.64.59.0]

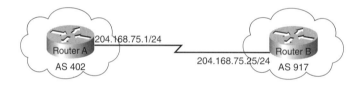

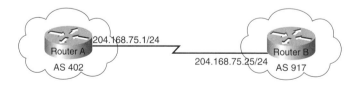

Keepalive Message	Keepalive Message

The BGP ROUTE-REFRESH capability, specified in RFC 2918, also referred to in Cisco IOS Software as the BGP *soft reset enhancement*, which is automatically enabled in later releases of Cisco IOS Software, is negotiated between BGP speakers during the capabilities exchange portion of BGP session initialization. This capability allows BGP peers to either request dynamic inbound updates or send outbound route updates to a peer without the soft reconfiguration. The IANA-assigned ROUTE-REFRESH capability (2) is contained in the Optional Capabilities field of the BGP OPEN messages. For ROUTE-REFRESH messages to be sent and understood, each of the peers negotiating a BGP session must support the capability. If a peer that does not understand this capability receives a ROUTE-REFRESH request message from a remote peer, that peer ignores the message, logging an "Unsupported OPEN Parameter" error, and continues on uninterrupted. When the ROUTE-REFRESH capability is not supported by both peers in a BGP peer relationship, neither of the peers will be able to use the capability, and either soft reconfiguration or manual session re-initialization has to take place to refresh the Adj-RIB-In table. If the ROUTE-REFRESH capability is successfully negotiated during session initialization, and a ROUTE-REFRESH request is, for some reason, unsuccessful, the session can still be manually cleared.

BGP Finite-State Machine Operation

BGP peers transition through several states before becoming adjacent neighbors and exchanging routing information. During each of the states, the peers must send and receive messages, process message data, and initialize resources before proceeding to the next state. This process is known as the BGP *Finite-State Machine (FSM)*. If the process fails at any point, the session is torn down and the peers both transition back to an Idle state and begin the process again. Each time a session is torn down, all routes from the peer who is not up will be removed from the tables, which causes downtime. If configuration issues exist on one of the BGP peers, the peering routers continuously transition between unestablished states until the issue has been resolved. BGP peers transition through all the following states until an established BGP session has been created:

- Idle
- Connect
- Active
- OpenSent
- OpenConfirm
- Established

Each of these states also has accompanying *input events* (IEs). Input events are events occurring during a BGP session that trigger an action. Table 7-11 shows the BGP IEs.

Table 7-11   *BGP Input Events*

Event ID	Event Name	Description
1	BGP Start	Occurring during the Idle state, the BGP start event signals the beginning of a BGP session. It also initializes the resources for the BGP process. The BGP start event is only listened for during the Idle state. If the local speaker receives a start event and it is not in the Idle state, that event is ignored.
2	BGP Stop	The BGP Stop signals the termination of a BGP session.
3	BGP Transport Connection Open	This event notifies the local speaker that the TCP connection is open and the BGP resource initialization is complete.
4	BGP Transport Connection Closed	This event notifies the local speaker that the remote BGP speaker has closed the TCP session. This message also triggers the release of BGP resources and causes the local speaker to return to the Idle state.
5	BGP Transport Connection Failed	This event notifies the local speaker that the TCP session to the remote BGP peer has failed. This message also triggers the release of BGP resources and causes the local speaker to return to the Idle state.
6	BGP Transport Fatal Error	This event notifies the local speaker that the TCP session to the remote BGP peer has resulted in a fatal error. This message also triggers the release of BGP resources and causes the local speaker to return to the Idle state.
7	ConnectRetry Timer Expired	This event occurs when the ConnectRetry timer has expired. When the ConnectRetry timer expires, it is restarted.
8	Hold Timer Expired	This event occurs when the hold timer has expired, meaning that the remote peer has not responded to a message from the local peer.
9	KEEPALIVE Timer Expired	This event indicates that the KEEPALIVE timer expired, signaling that a KEEPALIVE has not been received from the remote peer within the timeout period.
10	Receive Open Message	This event notifies the local system that a BGP OPEN message has been received by the remote peer, and the BGP session can move on to the OpenConfirm state.

Table 7-11 *BGP Input Events (Continued)*

Event ID	Event Name	Description
11	Receive KEEPALIVE Message	This event notifies the local system that a BGP KEEPALIVE message has been received by the remote peer, and the BGP session can move on to the Established state.
12	Receive Update Message	This event notifies the local system that the remote peer has received a BGP UPDATE message.
13	Receive Notification Message	This event notifies the local system that a BGP NOTIFICATION message has been received, and the BGP session should be terminated immediately.

Idle State

According to RFC 1771, at the beginning of each BGP peer session, each of the peer routers must pass through various BGP states. The first state that a router enters when configured for BGP is the Idle state. In the Idle state, the BGP-speaking router refuses incoming BGP session requests. At this point, the router has not allocated any resources to the BGP process and does not do so until a BGP start event has either been initiated by the router's BGP process or by manual user intervention. Table 7-12 summarizes the Idle state behaviors and the reasons for those behaviors.

Table 7-12 *Idle State Behaviors*

Idle State Behavior	Reasons
Refuses incoming sessions	The router has either just been configured and has not established a BGP session with this peer before, or the BGP session has been reset. Incoming sessions are refused until a BGP start event has been issued.
No BGP resource allocation	Newly configured peer session. Reset session. Resources are allocated after a start event has been received.
BGP start event either sent or received	After the start event has been issued, the BGP peer initializes its resources, starts the ConnectRetry timer, attempts to establish a TCP connection with the peer, and listens for incoming TCP connection attempts.
Upon error	TCP sessions will be closed. The router will remain in Idle state and the start event will re-occur; each time a start event is generated, the time between the current and last start event exponentially increases.

continues

Table 7-12 *Idle State Behaviors (Continued)*

Idle State Behavior	Reasons	
Transition from other state to Idle state	Active state	Returns to Idle state upon other undefined error.
	OpenSent state	Returns to Idle state upon: OPEN message error BGP stop event (sent or received) Hold timer expired Other undefined error
	OpenConfirm state	Returns to Idle State upon: Receiving disconnect notification from TCP Hold timer expired NOTIFICATION message received BGP stop event Other undefined error
	Established state	Returns to Idle state upon: UPDATE message error Receiving disconnect notification from TCP NOTIFICATION message received BGP stop event Hold timer expired Other undefined error

BGP start events initially occur after initial BGP configuration, or, if the FSM has recently transitioned from another state to the Idle state, the next start event will occur after 60 seconds. To prevent routers from continuously bringing up and tearing down BGP sessions, each start event is issued at an exponentially increasing interval.

After the start event has been issued, the router initializes its BGP resources and starts the ConnectRetry timer, which controls the frequency between TCP connection attempts. At this point, the router tries to establish a TCP session with its configured BGP peer, and also listens for TCP session requests from that peer. If the TCP connection is closed or fails for any other reason, the FSM remains in the Idle state, and the time between BGP start events increases exponentially, which greatly increases the time between BGP start events. Otherwise, the FSM transitions to the Connect state. Figure 7-17 shows the logical flow between steps that the FSM follows during the BGP Idle state. In this figure, the black text boxes display the actions taking place, the gray text boxes display BGP events that might be associated with the actions taking place, and the white text boxes show the detail for each action that takes place.

Figure 7-17 *BGP Idle State*

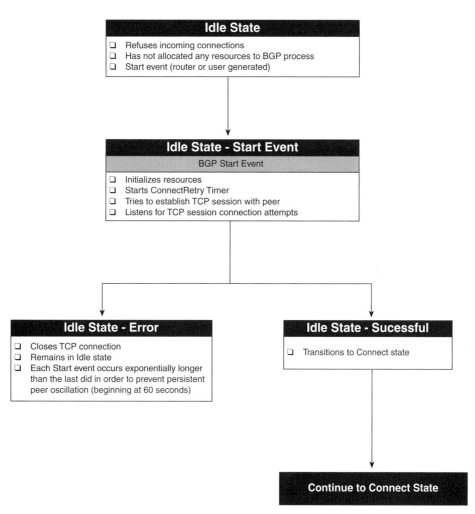

NOTE   *Connection collisions* occur when two BGP peering routers attempt to establish a TCP connection at the same time; or when a BGP session has already started, and the remote peer tries to restart a new connection. When connection collisions occur, the two peers compare BGP IDs, and the connection opened by the peer with the highest BGP ID is opened; the other connection is closed. In the case that the connection collision occurs on a BGP session that has already started, the new BGP session request is closed. Connection collisions can only be detected in the OpenSent, OpenConfirm, or Established state.

If you notice that a router is constantly remaining in the Idle state, you can check the following:

- Verify that the remote peer has the correct IP address and AS number configured for the local peer. You might need to change the BGP update source or the BGP router ID so that the peer will see BGP requests coming from the right IP address. Remember that BGP does not accept connections from unknown BGP peers.

- Verify that you have the correct IP address and AS number configured for the remote peer. Remember, BGP verifies the contents of BGP OPEN messages; if the contents of the OPEN message received from a remote peer do not match the local BGP configuration for that peer, the routers will not form a BGP peer relationship.

- Make sure the routers can reach each other using the configured IP address and TCP port number 179. You might need to add routes or change access lists or firewall rule sets to allow BGP peers to communicate.

Connect State

During the Connect state, the router is waiting for a successful TCP connection with its BGP peer. After a TCP session has successfully been established, the FSM clears the ConnectRetry timer, finishes initializing BGP resources, and sends an OPEN message to its peer. Table 7-13 shows the various Connect state behaviors, their associated events, and the associated state transitions.

Table 7-13   *Connect State Behaviors*

Connect State Behavior	Reasons
Ignores incoming start events	Start events are only received and acknowledged in the Idle state. Any start events received during the Connect state are ignored.
BGP resource allocation is completed	The BGP process begins on the router; however, routing does not occur until the FSM has entered the Established state.
OPEN message is sent to peer	After an OPEN message has been sent to the BGP peer, the router enters OpenSent state.
Upon TCP connection error	The ConnectRetry timer is reset. The router still listens for a TCP session request from its peer, but it transitions from the Connect state to the Active state.
ConnectRetry timer expires	The ConnectRetry timer is reset. The router tries to initialize a TCP session with its peer, listens for connection attempts from its peer, and stays in the Connect state.
An undefined event occurs	If any other event occurs, the router releases its BGP resources and transitions back to the Idle state.

Table 7-13   *Connect State Behaviors (Continued)*

Connect State Behavior	Reasons	
Transition from other state to Connect state	Active state	If the ConnectRetry timer expires while a router is in the Active state, that peer does the following: Resets the ConnectRetry timer Attempts to initialize a TCP connection with its peer Listens for a TCP connection from its remote peer

During successful BGP peer sessions, the peering routers typically do not spend much time in the Connect state before they transition to the OpenSent state. Figure 7-18 shows the BGP Connect state behaviors and the reasons for these behaviors. In this figure, the black text boxes display the actions taking place, the gray text boxes display BGP events that might be associated with the actions taking place, and the white text boxes show the details for each action that takes place.

If the TCP session between two BGP peers in Connect state is closed or fails for any reason, the FSM resets the ConnectRetry timer, continues to listen for a TCP session request from its peer, and enters the Active state.

When BGP peers get stuck in the Connect state, it is usually because of a configuration error:

- Always make sure that you have inbound and outbound TCP connectivity on port 179 (and a random TCP port greater than 1023 on the source side) so that BGP sessions can be formed in each direction. BGP TCP sessions are opened using a random source port, and a TCP destination port of 179.

- Verify the local and remote BGP configurations. Check the IP addresses and AS numbers for typos, and make sure the BGP routing process is numbered correctly.

Active State

If a router has entered the Active state, it is because it was unable to establish a successful TCP connection with one of its BGP peers. While in the Active state, a BGP speaker ignores the start event (remember, it is only listened for during the Idle state), attempts to initiate a TCP session with its peer, and resets the ConnectRetry timer.

If a successful TCP session is established while the BGP speaker is in the Active state, it sends an OPEN message to its peer, sets the hold timer, which is used to determine the time that a peer should wait for a return message from its peer, and transitions to the OpenSent state. The hold timer's initial value is set to 4 minutes, and later, upon a successful BGP session establishment, it is changed to the value negotiated during the OPEN message processing.

Figure 7-18 *BGP Connect State*

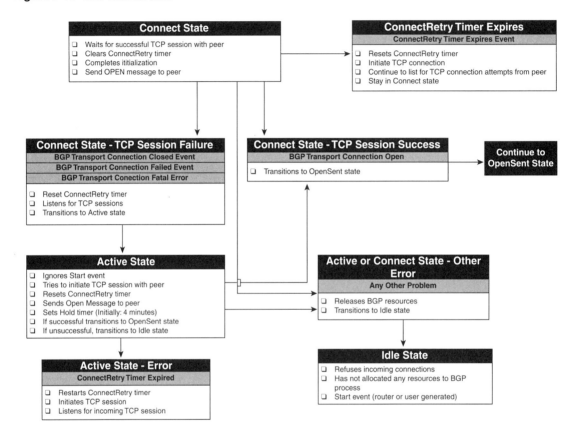

If the TCP session is not successfully established before the ConnectRetry timer expires, the FSM restarts the ConnectRetry timer, attempts to initiate a TCP session, and continues to listen for a TCP session request from its peer while transitioning back to the Connect state.

You might notice routers cycling between the Idle and Active states under the following conditions:

- The BGP peer ID is entered incorrectly during configuration.
- The BGP peer is not reachable via TCP port 179.
- Network congestion is causing the ConnectRetry timer to expire.
- A flapping network interface.

OpenSent State

In the OpenSent state, the BGP peer waits for an OPEN message from its peer. After an OPEN message has been received, it is checked for validity. At this time, all fields in the OPEN message are checked against the local BGP configuration. Any fields that do not match the expected values cause an OPEN message error to occur. At this time, the BGP peer also checks to verify that a connection collision has not occurred. If the message is valid, the peer sends a KEEPALIVE message to its peer, sets the KEEPALIVE timer, sets the hold timer, and transitions to the OpenConfirm state. Table 7-14 shows the OpenSent state behaviors and their descriptions.

Table 7-14   *OpenSent State Behaviors*

OpenSent State Behavior	Reasons
Ignores incoming start events	Start events are only received and acknowledged in the Idle state. Any start events received during the Connect state are ignored.
Waits for OPEN message from peer	The BGP peer remains in the OpenSent state until the following occurs: • A valid OPEN message is received. • A TCP disconnect event occurs. • A NOTIFICATION message is received. • A stop event occurs. • The hold timer expires. • Any other undefined event occurs.

A number of events can cause a BGP speaker to transition from the OpenSent state to the Idle state. As mentioned previously, if the speaker receives an invalid OPEN message from its peer, an OPEN message error will occur. Upon an OPEN message error, the local router sends out a NOTIFICATION message specifying the cause of the error and transitions to the Idle state where the connection process starts again. If a NOTIFICATION message is received from another peer router, the local router closes its TCP connection, resets the ConnectRetry timer, and transitions to the Active state.

Upon receipt of a BGP stop event, hold-timer expiration, or other unexpected event, the local router also sends a NOTIFICATION message and transitions back to the Idle state. From the Idle state, the peering BGP routers once again try to launch a successful BGP session. Figure 7-19 shows the various events that might occur in the OpenSent state.

Figure 7-19 *BGP OpenSent State*

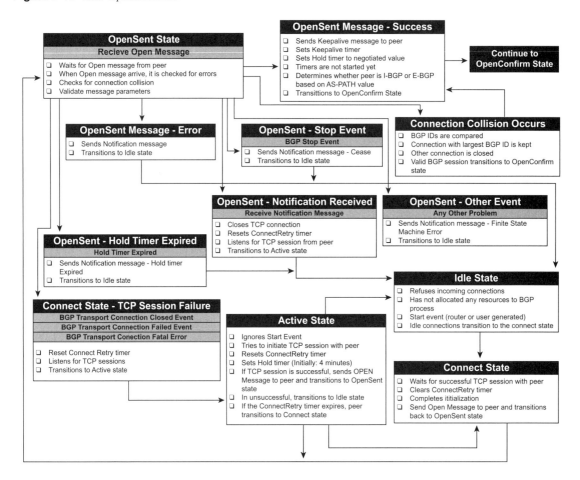

BGP peers rarely appear to wait in the OpenSent state for long amounts of time. After the local router receives an OPEN message from its peer, it sends its peer a KEEPALIVE message and transitions to the OpenConfirm state.

OpenConfirm State

In the OpenConfirm state, the local router is waiting for the receipt of a KEEPALIVE message from its peer. Upon receipt of a KEEPALIVE message, the BGP session transitions to the Established state. As with the OpenSent state, BGP peers might transition to the OpenConfirm state for a number of reasons. Table 7-15 shows these state transitions and other behaviors of the OpenConfirm state.

Table 7-15   *OpenConfirm State Behaviors*

OpenConfirm State Behavior	Reasons
Ignores incoming start events	Start events are only received and acknowledged in the Idle state. Any start events received during the OpenConfirm state are ignored.
Waits for KEEPALIVE message from peer	The BGP peer remains in the OpenConfirm state until the following occurs: • A KEEPALIVE message is received. • A TCP disconnect message is received. • A NOTIFICATION message is received. • A stop event occurs. • The hold timer expires. • Any other undefined event occurs.
If the KEEPALIVE timer expires	The KEEPALIVE timer might be reset up to three times the length of the hold timer before the hold timer will expire, and the local peer will transition to the Idle state.
If a peer returns from the OpenConfirm to Idle state	The BGP connection is closed. All BGP resources for that BGP peering session are released.

Figure 7-20 shows the actions that can occur during the OpenConfirm state. The local router can successfully transition to the Established state, after receiving a KEEPALIVE message or transition back to the Idle state upon a Disconnect, Stop, or Notification event.

BGP peers only stay in the OpenConfirm state long enough to receive a KEEPALIVE message. If the KEEPALIVE is not received within the space of the hold timer, the session transitions back to the Idle state.

Established State

BGP peers reach the Established state after they have successfully exchanged OPEN and KEEPALIVE messages. After the peers reach the Established state, they begin to send UPDATE messages containing routing information and KEEPALIVE messages to verify the TCP Connection state. If an error is encountered at any time while a peer is in the Established state, the local peer sends a NOTIFICATION message with the reason for the error and transitions back to the Idle state. Figure 7-21 shows the various events that might occur while a speaker is in the Established state.

Figure 7-20 *BGP OpenConfirm State*

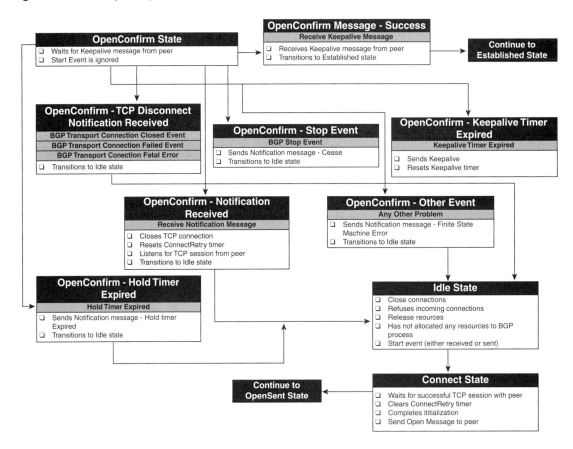

Now that the basic BGP operations have been covered, it is time to discuss the various attributes that are exchanged within BGP UPDATE messages.

Figure 7-21 *BGP Established State*

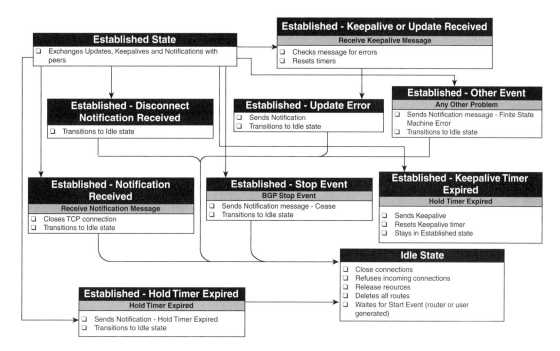

BGP Path Attributes

BGP path attributes describe the values that belong the paths sent in a BGP UPDATE message. All attributes contained in an UPDATE message apply to all paths specified by the NLRI field of the UPDATE.

ORIGIN Attribute

The *ORIGIN* of a route describes the way that the path was introduced into the BGP path. ORIGIN is a well-known mandatory attribute, meaning all BGP implementations must accept and understand the value of the ORIGIN attribute, and it is passed to other BGP peers. Table 7-16 shows three BGP ORIGIN codes. If a route entered BGP from an I-BGP session, the route will have the ORIGIN type 0, IGP. If the route was originally introduced into BGP by an Exterior Gateway Protocol (EGP) session, it is type 1, EGP. If the route entered BGP from an unknown (external to BGP) routing process, then the ORIGIN value is type 3, Incomplete.

Table 7-16   *BGP ORIGIN Codes*

ORIGIN Code	ORIGIN Code Name	Description
0	IGP	The route originated on a BGP router. This route type includes any route that originated from the BGP process on a BGP-speaking router.
		The IGP ORIGIN type is the most preferred ORIGIN for a route and is selected before EGP or Incomplete.
1	EGP	The route originated from an EGP (not E-BGP) session.
		The EGP ORIGIN type is more desirable than the Incomplete ORIGIN type.
2	Incomplete	The route originated from a routing process other than BGP, and entered BGP by means of manual redistribution, such as redistribution from an IGP protocol, static route, or connected route.
		The Incomplete ORIGIN type is not preferred over IGP or EGP.

Figure 7-22 shows a route with the attribute type 1, IGP. This route originated from an I-BGP session. As you can see, Router C originated the routes to networks 10.2.1.0/24 and 10.2.2.0/24, so Router C will assign these routes the IGP ORIGIN attribute as it does in the UPDATE message to Router B.

Figure 7-23 illustrates how the Incomplete ORIGIN type is used to mark paths whose origins are unknown. In this figure, Router R originates the route in AS 6565, but because the router was learned by means of a redistributed OSPF process, the paths are sent out with the Incomplete ORIGIN type. Each downstream router that forwards these paths includes the Incomplete ORIGIN value as well.

Figure 7-22 *BGP ORIGIN Code IGP*

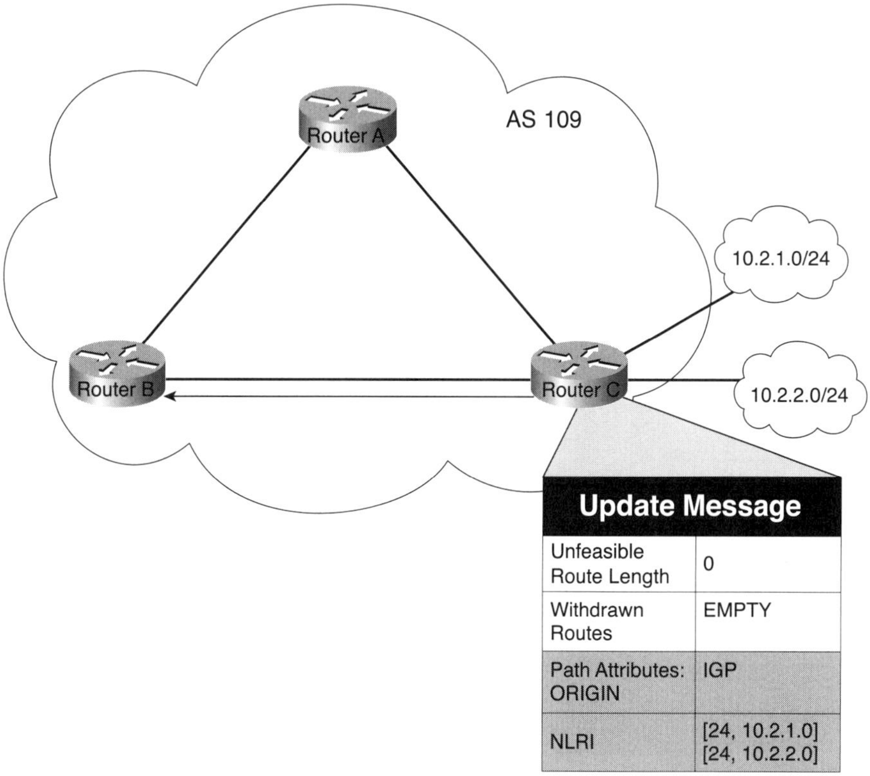

AS_PATH Attribute

The AS_PATH is a well-known mandatory attribute. It describes the path that the route has taken on the way to its destination. The primary reason for the BGP AS_PATH attribute is to prevent routing loops. BGP peers know that they have encountered a routing loop if they receive an UPDATE message that contains their local AS number in the AS_PATH. If a looped update is received, the UPDATE is ignored.

Each AS border router that sends an update for a given path to an E-BGP peer prepends its AS number to the AS_PATH. The AS_PATH field contains three values:

- The *path segment type*, which has two possible values: AS_SET and AS_SEQUENCE.
- The *path segment length* value contains the number of ASs in a segment.
- The *path segment* value contains the list of AS numbers.

Figure 7-23 *BGP ORIGIN Code Incomplete*

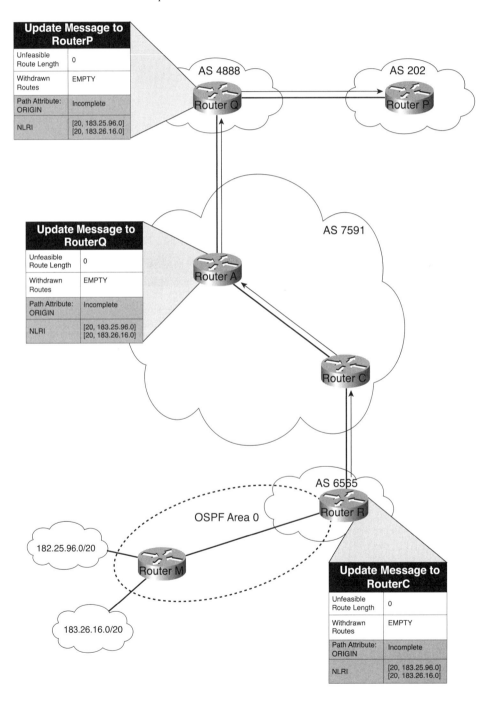

The AS_PATH Path Segment Type is generally of the AS_SEQUENCE type, where each E-BGP router prepends its AS number to the leftmost side of the AS_SEQUENCE field. The AS_PATH contains the path of AS numbers that the path has traversed to reach the current AS. Figure 7-24 shows how the AS_PATH value is used with the AS_SEQUENCE path segment type.

Figure 7-24 *AS_PATH Attribute with an AS_SEQUENCE*

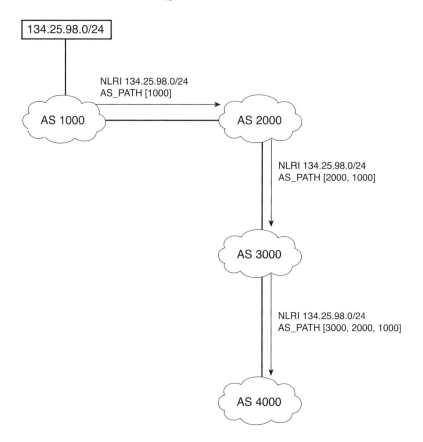

In this example, AS 1000 originates the route to the 134.25.98.0/24 network. Because this route is originated in AS 1000, the AS_PATH value for this NLRI contains only the local AS number of 1000. When AS 2000 receives the UPDATE and its AS 3000 bordering router sends the UPDATE off to its E-BGP peer in AS 3000, it pretends its own AS number to the AS_PATH, and the AS 3000 border router does the same for its E-BGP peer in AS 4000. The AS_PATH contains the sequence of AS numbers that must be traversed to reach the 134.25.98.0/24 network. The leftmost value is the closest AS number, and each number in between the leftmost and rightmost numbers is an AS along the path to the originating AS—the rightmost AS number.

The AS_SET value is used with aggregation. The AS_SET path segment type is used when routes that have differing AS_PATH values have been aggregated. Figure 7-25 shows how the AS_SET value is used within the AS_PATH sequence to show that two paths are required to reach all the networks for the 192.168.0.0/21 aggregate.

Figure 7-25 *AS_PATH Attribute with an AS_SET*

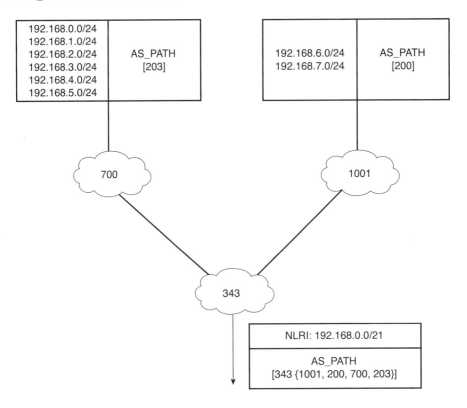

In this example, AS 700 has six routes—192.168.0.0/24, 192.168.1.0/24, 192.168.2.0/24, 192.168.3.0/24, 192.168.4.0/24, and 192.168.5.0/24—which it is advertising to its E-BGP peer in AS 343. Each of these networks originated in AS 203. When the AS 700 border router sends this update to its E-BGP neighbor in AS 343, it prepends its AS number to the AS_PATH, so the full AS_PATH that AS 343 will use to reach the 192.168.0 through 5 networks is [700, 203]. AS 1001 also advertises 192.168.6.0/24 and 192.168.7.0/24 with an AS_PATH of [1001, 200].

To preserve the AS information for the aggregated routes when AS 343 aggregates the 192.168.0.0/21 range of addresses, it must use an AS_SET AS_PATH segment code type to list the unordered path that is used to reach the networks.

Figure 7-26 shows how the AS_PATH attribute is modified for the path to networks 183.25.96.0/20 and 183.25.16.0/20, as they cross various ASs.

Figure 7-26 *Using the ORIGIN and AS_PATH Attributes*

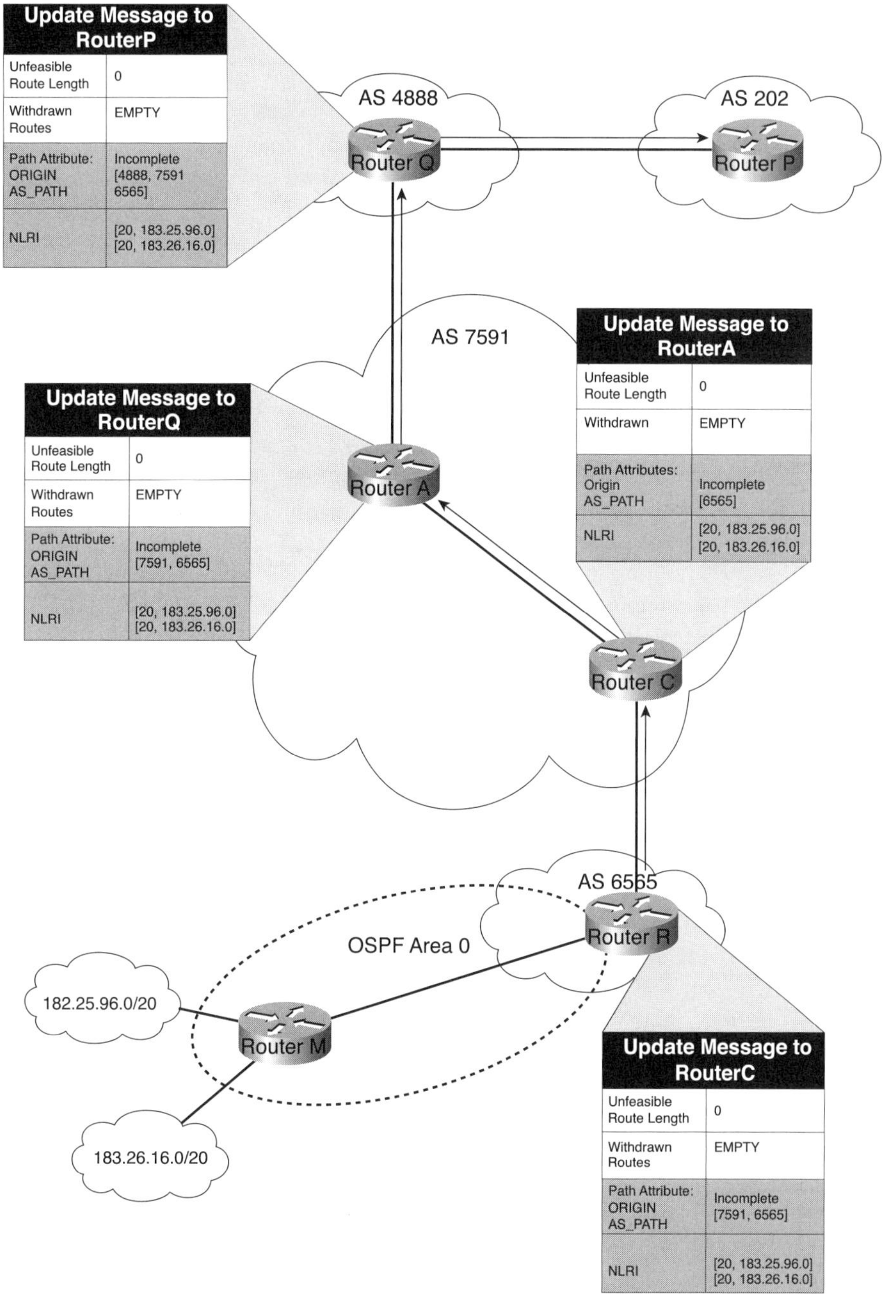

This example shows how Router R originates the route to the 183.25.96.0/20 and 183.26.16.0/20 networks that it learned through its local OSPF routing process, originates the routes as having an Incomplete ORIGIN, and sends them off to AS 7591 with the AS_PATH value 6556, Router R's local AS number. Because Router C and Router A both belong to AS 7591, Router C does not prepend its AS number to the route as it advertises it to Router A. Because Router A is sending the route to its E-BGP peer Router Q, however, it does prepend AS number 7591 to the AS_PATH as it sends it out. Then Router Q receives the route, which still contains the Incomplete ORIGIN code with the AS_PATH of [7591, 6565] and prepends its AS number, 4888, to the AS_PATH and sends it to Router P in AS 202. When a router in AS 202 wants to reach the 183.25.96.0/20 or 183.26.16.0/20 networks, it follows the AS_PATH 4888, 7591, 6565, and its packets arrive at Router R, where the local OSPF process sends them to Router M.

NEXT_HOP Attribute

The NEXT_HOP is a well-known mandatory attribute that specifies the IP address of the next hop that is taken to reach a path. The NEXT_HOP attribute is treated differently in I-BGP and E-BGP. Because of the rule of synchronization, mentioned earlier, I-BGP routers do not modify the NEXT_HOP attribute unless they are specifically told to do so using the **next-hop-self** command. E-BGP neighbors modify the next hop to be the egress interface used to reach their E-BGP peer. In Figure 7-27, for the Santa Fe router to reach any of the networks advertised by the Roswell router, it must use the next-hop address of 192.168.4.5. Likewise, the Roswell router must use the 192.168.4.4 next-hop address to reach networks 207.23.12.0/22 and 207.23.24.0/22.

For an I-BGP peer to reach the next hop advertised by another I-BGP peer, it must be reachable using a route from the main routing table. If, for some reason, the I-BGP peer does not have a route to reach the next-hop address, the **next-hop-self** command can be used to alter the next-hop address specified in the outgoing UPDATE messages to that peer.

Figure 7-28 illustrates how the NEXT_HOP attribute is used between I-BGP peering routers. In this example, the East router peers with the North and West routers in AS 7995, and forms an E-BGP session with the South router in AS 8245. The South router advertises the network 147.50.0.0/18 to the East router, which receives the UPDATE and sends the route, unchanged, to its I-BGP peer, the North router. In this case, because the East router does not change the NEXT_HOP attribute for the NLRI 147.50.0.0/18, the next hop for this route sent will be 217.200.8.1, the egress interface for AS 8245. Therefore, the North and West routers will see the route to the 147.50.0.0/18 network with a NEXT_HOP of 217.200.8.1, and will consider this route unreachable. These routers will not advertise unreachable routes to E-BGP peers, and will not store the route in their main routing tables.

Figure 7-27 *NEXT_HOP with E-BGP Peers*

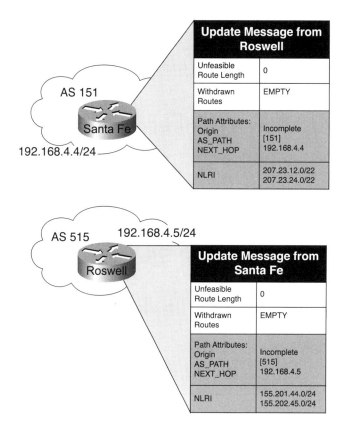

However, Figure 7-29 shows how this situation can be prevented using the **next-hop-self** command on the East router. After this command has been issued, the East router advertises the 147.50.0.0/18 route to the North router with a next hop of 204.168.52.1, and it advertises the same network to the West router with a next hop of 204.168.59.2. Because these are both reachable next hops, the North and West routers accept this route, advertise it to neighboring E-BGP routers, and store it in the main routing table.

Figure 7-28 *NEXT_HOP Attribute and I-BGP Peers*

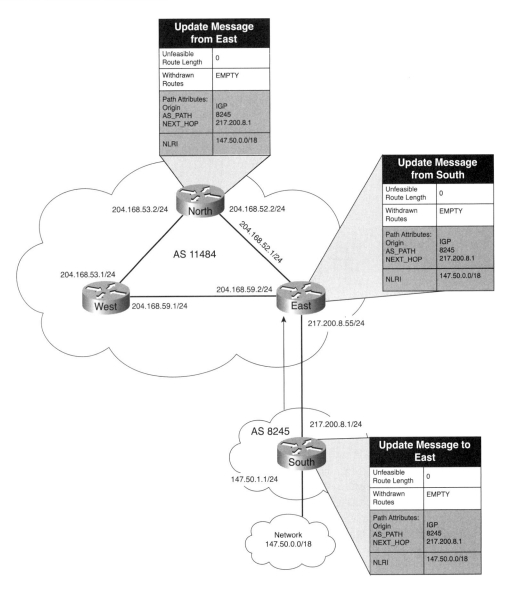

Figure 7-29 *NEXT_HOP Attribute and I-BGP Peers*

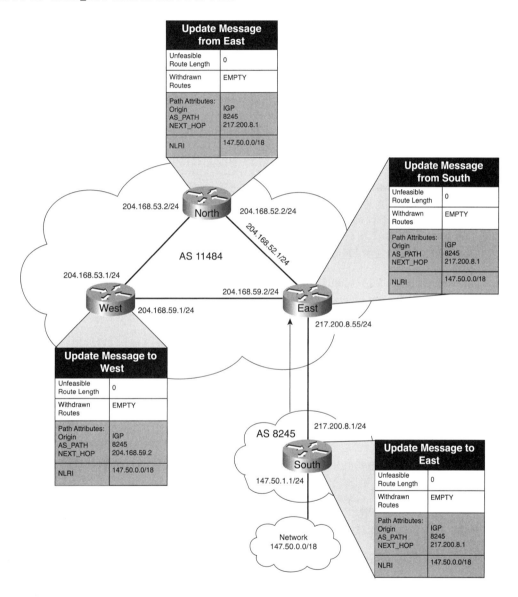

MED Attribute

The MULTI_EXIT_DISC (MED), or Multi Exit Discriminator, attribute is an optional nontransitive attribute used as a metric to specify the preferred entry path when there is more than one point of entry into a network. The MED attribute is basically a metric used to send other bordering autonomous systems information about the preferred network entry point. The MED value ranges from 0 to 4,294,967,295, with the lowest value being the preferred value, and is configured on a per-neighbor basis. The default MED value is 0. The MED attribute is not passed beyond the neighboring AS and is only compared when both external peers belong to the same neighboring AS; this metric applies only to the connection between externally configured peers. Before considering the use of the MED attribute, consult your service provider and inquire whether they accept the MED attribute, and how they prefer that it is used.

Figure 7-30 shows how the MED attribute is used between AS 3898 and AS 8021. In this example, AS 3898 has two exit points—one between the Edge 1 and Internet routers, network 211.146.2.248, which uses a DS3 connection; and another connection between the Internet and Edge 2 routers, network 211.146.2.252, which only uses a T1 connection. For the Internet router in AS 8021 to prefer the DS3 connection to the 123.45.67.0/24, 123.45.68.0/24, and 123.45.69.0/24 networks via the path advertised by the Edge 1 router, the Edge 2 router, which is connected to the Internet router via a T1 connection on the 211.146.2.252 network, advertises with a MED value of 50. The Edge 1 router advertises the same routes with the default MED value of 0. When the Internet router receives the routes from the Edge 1 and Edge 2 routers, it prefers the route from the Edge 1 router because it has a lower MED attribute.

Figure 7-30   *Using the MED Attribute to Select Paths*

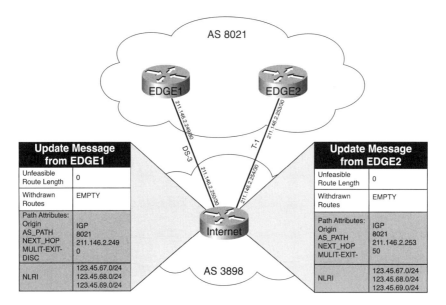

LOCAL_PREF Attribute

The LOCAL_PREF, *or* Local Preference, attribute is a well-known discretionary attribute used between I-BGP peers as a metric to specify a preferred path to a destination when there is more than one path to that network. The LOCAL_PREF attribute is used to specify a degree of preference to a network that has more than one path to an external destination network. The LOCAL_PREF value ranges from 0 to 4,294,967,295, and, like the MED attribute, is also configured on a per-neighbor basis. The default value of the LOCAL_PREF attribute is 100; this attribute is not passed to E-BGP peers.

Figure 7-31 illustrates how the LOCAL_PREF attribute is used to specify a more desirable path to the Internet through multiple providers. AS 3679 has two Internet bordering routers, Internet 1 and Internet 2. Each Internet border router is connected to a different Internet service provider, shown in the figure as Provider 1 and Provider 2.

Figure 7-31 *Using LOCAL_PREF to Select Paths*

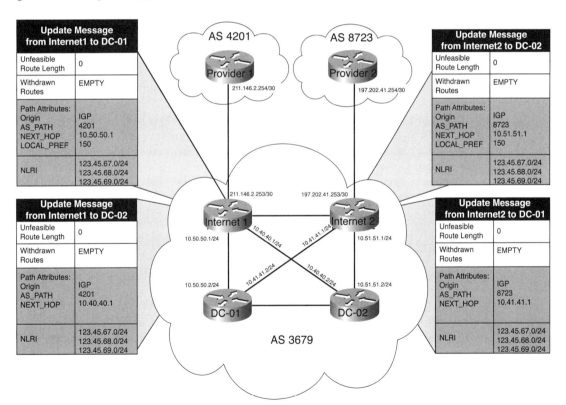

The Provider 1 and Provider 2 routers advertise the same three routes: 123.45.67.0/24, 123.45.68.0/24, and 123.45.69.0/24. The Internet border routers, Internet 1 and Internet 2, forward these routes to the directly connected BGP peer routers DC-01 and DC-02; however, Internet 1 is geographically closer to DC-01 and Internet 2 is closer to DC-02. Therefore, unless the connection from DC-01 to Internet 1 is down, DC-01 should prefer and use the routes originating from Internet 1, and the exact same applies for Internet 2, and DC-02. To achieve this effect, when Internet 1 sends routes to DC-01, it alters the LOCAL_PREF value from 0 to 150, and leaves the LOCAL_PREF value for the DC-02 router at the default value of 100. That way, unless the connection between Internet 1 and DC-01 is broken, DC-01 always prefers routes from the Internet 1 router; and if the connection does go down, routes from the Internet 2 router are used. This also applies to the DC-02 and Internet 2. The I-BGP peers always prefer the route with the largest local preference. Because the LOCAL_PREF values for the connection between Internet 1 and Internet 2 are not changed, those two routers always prefer to get the routes to the 123.45.67.0/24, 123.45.68.0/24, and 123.45.69.0/24 networks from their upstream providers (Provider 1 and Provider 2).

WEIGHT Attribute

The WEIGHT attribute is the only attribute covered in this book that applies only to Cisco routers. The WEIGHT attribute is another means to specify a preferred path to a destination network when more than one path exists. Larger weights are preferred to smaller weights, with 0 being the default value for a route received from a neighboring peer, and 32,768 being the default for locally generated routes. WEIGHT values range from 0 to 65,535. The WEIGHT attribute is not passed to *any routers*, E-BGP, or I-BGP; it is strictly a local BGP policy that applies to routes in the local BGP table.

NOTE   Because the WEIGHT attribute is the first item considered during the BGP path selection process, WEIGHT attribute modification can be a very useful tool that you can use when creating a local BGP routing policy.

NOTE   It is possible to use more than one route to a destination network and load balance over these routes. With the **maximum-paths** command, you can use up to six paths to a destination network.

Figure 7-32 shows how the WEIGHT attribute is modified to specify a preferred route to a network when more than one route exists in the BGP table. In this example, the Engineering router has two possible paths to reach the 10.7.8.0/24 network advertised by the Factory router.

In this case, the Engineering router should prefer the path through the Fast router over the path that passes through the Slow router. Because the decision to prefer the path over the Fast router more than the path using the Slow router is local to the Engineering Router, the WEIGHT attribute for the 10.7.8.0/24 route from the Fast router is changed to 1500. If the Fast router were to fail, traffic between the Engineering and Factory routers would still be passed using the path through the Slow router because its WEIGHT was left at the default value of 0.

Figure 7-32 *Locally Preferring Routes with WEIGHT*

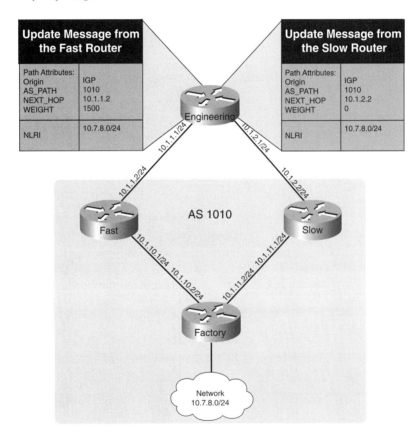

ATOMIC_AGGREGATE Attribute

The ATOMIC_AGGREGATE is a well-known discretionary attribute used to notify downstream neighbors that path information for a specific route has been lost. This information loss is caused when more specific paths are aggregated into a less-specific path. The ATOMIC_AGGREGATE attribute is just a flag set in the UPDATE packet that notifies the downstream routers that some path information has been lost during the aggregation. When the ATOMIC_AGGREGATE attribute is set, the downstream routers must not remove the attribute or send a more specific route to that network.

Figure 7-33 shows an example of the how the ATOMIC_AGGREGATE attribute is used to notify the Showroom router that the Warehouse router aggregated the NLRI to network 10.1.0.0/21. The ATOMIC_AGGREGATE flag is set to notify the Showroom router that it must not send more specific routes to the 10.1.0.0/21 network because path information was lost.

Figure 7-33 *ATOMIC_AGGREGATE Attribute*

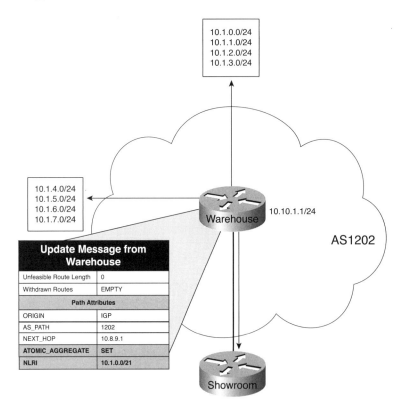

AGGREGATOR Attribute

The AGGREGATOR attribute is an optional transitive attribute that might be used if the ATOMIC_AGGREGATE attribute has been used on an NLRI. The AGGREGATOR attribute contains information about the speaker that aggregated the route. This attribute contains the BGP ID and AS number of the router that created the aggregate marking that route with the ATOMIC_AGGREGATE attribute. This information specifies the source of the less-specific aggregate route, which can be used to find where the more specific routes originated.

Figure 7-34 shows the AGGREGATOR in use for the route to the 10.1.0.0/21 network from Figure 7-33. In this example, the AGGREGATOR attribute was added to show that the router (BGP_ID 10.10.1.1 in AS 1202) aggregated the route.

Figure 7-34 *AGGREGATOR Attribute*

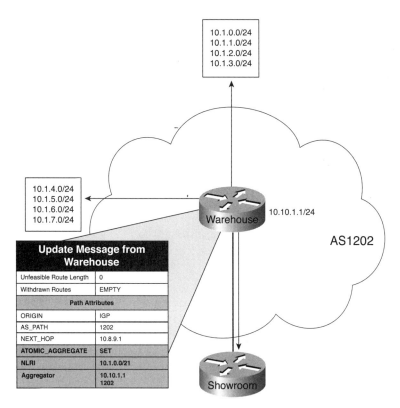

BGP COMMUNITY Attribute

BGP communities, defined in RFC 1997 (usages defined in RFCs 1998 and 2519), are an optional transitive attribute that define groups that follow the same policies. The policies assigned to communities affect the way routers belonging to the communities accept or deny incoming routes. They might also be used to specify a preference for particular routes. For a route to belong to a community, it must be locally configured to do so. All community-aware

BGP speakers belong to the *Internet* COMMUNITY by default. If a route with an unspecified COMMUNITY attribute is received, a new community might be added. If a route with a COMMUNITY attribute set is received, that COMMUNITY attribute might be modified. Because the COMMUNITY attribute is not automatically forwarded by BGP speakers, before sending the COMMUNITY attribute to an E-BGP peer, you should first coordinate the proposed community uses to the appropriate persons in that organization.

The BGP COMMUNITY attribute is a 32-bit, 4-octet value that contains the local AS number in the first 2 octets and the locally defined value in the last 2 octets. Communities might be defined in three ways: as a decimal, with a value ranging from 1 to 4,294,967,295; as a hexadecimal value in an *aa:nn* format with the first decimal number as the local AS number, and the last 2 octets as the local defined value; or third by name, using one of the well-known BGP COMMUNITY names.

Table 7-17 shows the various COMMUNITY values and their descriptions.

Table 7-17   *Well-Known BGP COMMUNITY Values*

COMMUNITY Value (Hex)	COMMUNITY Value (Decimal)	COMMUNITY Name	Description
0x0000000 to 0x0000FFFF	0 to 65535	Reserved	This range of COMMUNITY attributes has been reserved by IANA.
0xFFFF0000 to 0xFFFFFFFF	4294967041 to 4294967295	Reserved	This range of COMMUNITY attributes has been reserved by IANA.
0	0	Internet	The default community, which all BGP-Community aware routers belong to by default.
0xFFFFFF01	4294967041	NO_EXPORT	Routes with this COMMUNITY attribute must not be advertised outside of the local AS or confederation.
0xFFFFFF02	4294967042	NO_ADVERTISE	Routes with this COMMUNITY attribute must not be advertised to *any* peer.
0xFFFFFF03	4294967043	LOCAL_AS	Routes with this COMMUNITY attribute must not be advertised to any external confederation peer, referred to as NO_EXPORT-SUBCONFED in RFC 1997.

Figure 7-35 shows how the NO_EXPORT (0xFFFFFF01) community is used to keep internal network routes from being advertised to the public Internet. In this example, the Border router marks the 158.203.10.0/24, 158.203.20.0/24, and 158.203.30.0/24 routes as COMMUNITY NO_EXPORT and sends them to the ISP.com router. When the ISP.com router receives these routes, it might forward them to any router within its local AS, AS 2501, but no router within AS 2501 can forward that route beyond its local AS.

Figure 7-35 *Using the NO_EXPORT Community*

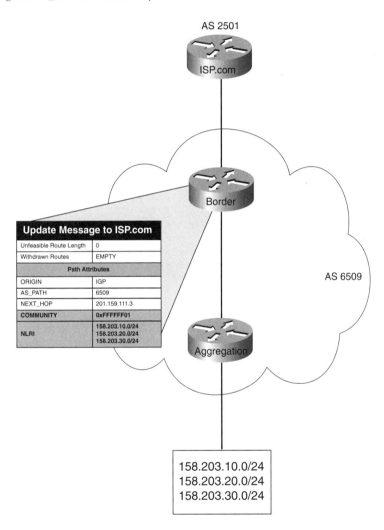

Two more BGP attributes are covered later in this chapter—the CLUSTER_LIST attribute, and the ORIGINATOR_ID attribute—both of which apply only to route reflectors. Each of these attributes is covered after an overview of BGP route reflector operation.

Route Reflectors

As mentioned earlier in this chapter, the BGP-4 protocol requires that all BGP peers belonging to the same AS form an I-BGP session with all other peers in that AS. The original BGP specifications assumed that an IGP protocol was running within each AS to synchronize all I-BGP sessions. Since the specification was written, however, more and more BGP users are no longer using IGP synchronization, and it has become very difficult for large networks running I-BGP to have I-BGP-speaking routers form a full-mesh topology. Figure 7-36 shows how many connections would be required between six routers if I-BGP were to run in a full mesh, without route reflectors or confederations.

Figure 7-36 *I-BGP Full Mesh Without Route Reflectors*

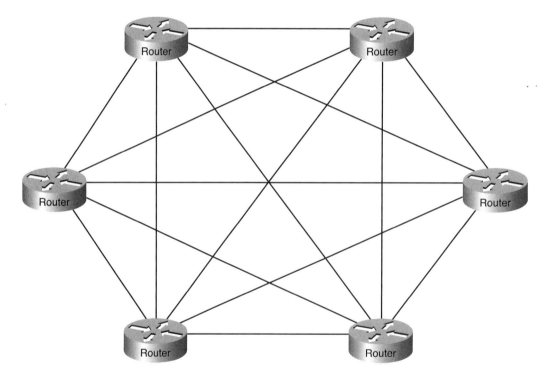

In this example, each of the six I-BGP speakers must form an I-BGP session with each peer in the local AS. As you can see, this configuration requires $n * (n - 1) / 2$, or 15 connections, which becomes unmanageable and unacceptable over large wide-area networks with expensive WAN connections. Each I-BGP session adds to the overall BGP memory and processor utilization load that each I-BGP router will have to support, and adds to the administrative headaches for the people who have to support the BGP routers. In an effort to solve this problem, route reflectors (specified in RFC 2796) and confederations (specified in 3065) were created. Confederations are covered later in this chapter.

Route reflectors are basically fully functional I-BGP speakers that form I-BGP sessions with other I-BGP speakers. However, router reflectors perform a second function: They forward routes from other I-BGP speakers to *route reflector clients.* Route reflector clients are BGP-speaking routers that only form I-BGP sessions with the route reflector, decreasing the number of I-BGP peering sessions and simplifying the BGP routing process. Figure 7-37 shows the same network previously shown in Figure 7-36. In the new figure, route reflectors are used to decrease the number of I-BGP sessions.

Figure 7-37 *Using Route Reflectors to Decrease the Number of I-BGP Sessions*

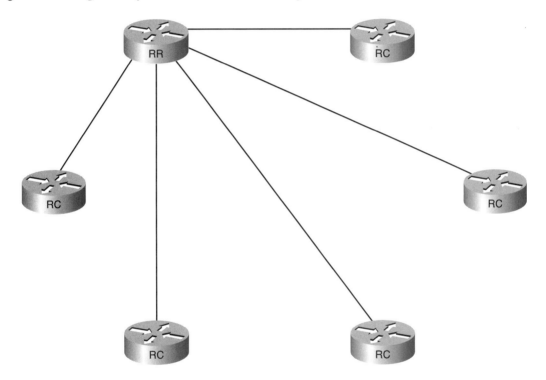

Notice in this figure that five of the six I-BGP peers, labeled RC, now form one I-BGP session with the route reflector, labeled RR.

In review, route reflectors advertise I-BGP routes to I-BGP neighbors, both the fully meshed neighbors who are not route reflector clients, and the route reflector clients, which they serve. Although route reflectors forward routes to route reflector clients, route reflector clients cannot forward routes to route reflector servers unless they are specifically configured to do so. The route reflector and the route reflector clients form *clusters*. More than one cluster can exist within an AS. Any I-BGP speakers that do not support route reflection must form I-BGP sessions with all other I-BGP routers, with the exception of route reflector clients, which behave as though they are fully meshed I-BGP peers with their route reflector. Route reflector clients require only I-BGP sessions with their route reflector, and the route reflector forms I-BGP connections with any routers that are not route reflector clients.

ORIGINATOR_ID Attribute

Route reflector clusters are identified by a 4-byte (32-bit) ORIGINATOR_ID attribute, which is the BGP ID for the route reflector. The ORIGINATOR_ID is a loop-prevention device that identifies a route reflector cluster by the IP address of the route reflector. If a route reflector finds its own ORIGINATOR_ID in an UPDATE message, it assumes that a routing loop has occurred and that message is ignored.

The ORIGINATOR_ID is an optional nontransitive attribute, described in RFC 2796 as the identifier for a route reflector cluster, which is used to prevent routing loops. If a route reflector receives a route without an existing ORIGINATOR_ID value, it adds its own BGP ID to the ORIGINATOR_ID. If the route reflector sees its own IP address in the ORIGINATOR_ID field, it ignores the update. Figure 7-38 shows how the ORIGINATOR_ID attribute is used with route reflectors within an AS.

CLUSTER_LIST Attribute

The CLUSTER_LIST attribute, also defined in RFC 2796, is an optional nontransitive attribute used to prevent loops when more than one route reflector cluster exists within an AS. The CLUSTER_LIST is a 4-byte value that contains a list of CLUSTER_ID values that describe the reflection path that a route passed through, similar to the AS_PATH attribute. Similar to the ORIGINATOR_ID, the CLUSTER_ID is the BGP ID of the router. When a route reflector receives an update, it checks the value of the CLUSTER_LIST attribute. If the CLUSTER_LIST field is empty, it adds its CLUSTER_ID to the field. If the field contains other entries, it prepends its local CLUSTER_ID to the list. If a route reflector receives an update with its own CLUSTER_ID in the CLUSTER_LIST, it assumes a routing loop exists and ignores the update. Figure 7-39 demonstrates how the CLUSTER_ID is prepended to the CLUSTER_LIST to prevent routing loops within an AS.

Figure 7-38 *ORIGINATOR_ID and Route Reflectors*

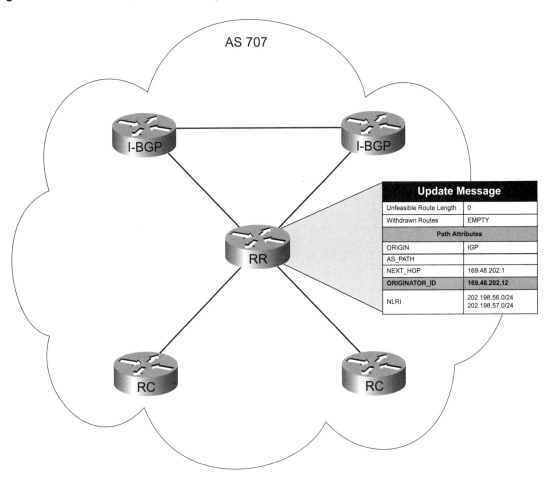

Figure 7-39 *CLUSTER_LIST Attribute*

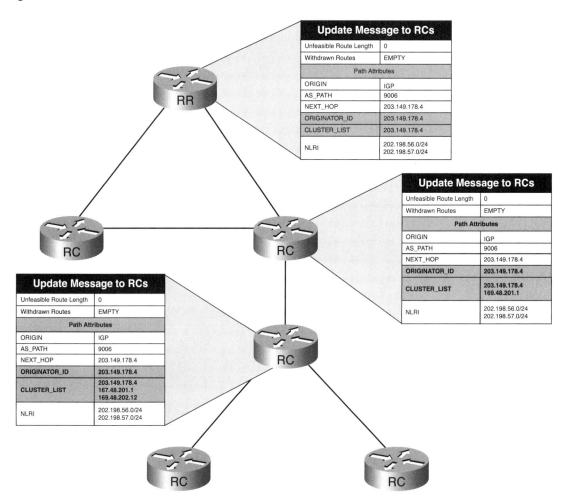

Confederations

Another way to solve the I-BGP full-mesh requirement is to use *confederations*. Defined in RFC 3065, BGP confederations are smaller sub-autonomous systems that can be created within a primary AS to decrease the size of BGP peer connections that are required between I-BGP peers. Figure 7-40 shows six routers before and after the creation of AS confederations.

Figure 7-40 *Before and After AS Confederations*

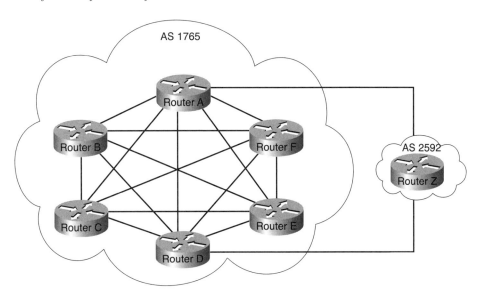

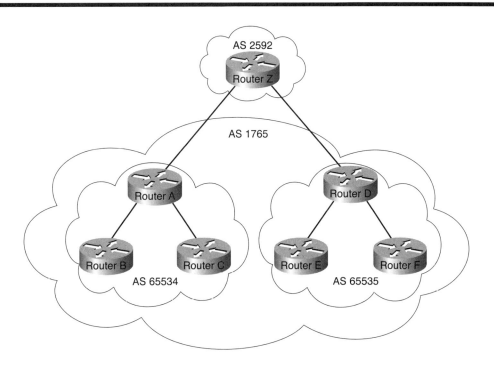

In the top diagram, all 6 peers in AS 1765 form a I-BGP full mesh, resulting in 6 * (6 – 1) / 2 = 15, $n * (n – 1) / 2$, I-BGP peering sessions between those 6 hosts, with Routers A and D forming E-BGP sessions with Router Z in AS 2592. The bottom diagram shows how two sub-autonomous systems, 65,534 and 65,535, are formed within AS 1765, decreasing the number of I-BGP peer sessions to three per sub-AS, with an E-BGP session between the sub-autonomous systems. Routers A and D still form an E-BGP session with Router Z in AS 2592, but Router Z is completely unaware of the existence of the AS confederations within AS 1756, the parent AS for the two sub-autonomous systems 65,534 and 65,535.

All BGP confederation peers follow the same rules that apply to I-BGP peers that do not belong to confederations. Each peer must have an I-BGP session with all other I-BGP peers in the sub-AS, and the NEXT_HOP, AS_PATH, MED, and LOCAL_PREF attributes remain unchanged as they are passed between peers belonging to the same sub-AS. Any AS containing confederations appears as one AS to all external BGP peers. Each sub-AS is assigned its own AS number, a private AS number that is invisible to peers outside the sub-AS. This private AS number is called a *member AS number*. The sub-autonomous systems belonging to an AS confederation are referred to as *member autonomous systems*. The parent AS containing the sub-AS confederations still maintains its own AS number. When confederations are in use, this number is referred to as a *confederation ID*. Because the peers within the sub-AS have a separate My AS value than other peers belonging to the parent AS, to facilitate communication with other routers within the parent AS, at least one peer that is a member of a confederation must form an E-BGP session with other peers belonging to any AS number other than that of the confederation. When a BGP update is sent from a peer belonging to a confederation to a peer outside the sub-AS, the sending peer uses its own sub-AS number. When the confederation peer sends an update to an E-BGP peer, it identifies itself using the AS confederation ID of the parent AS.

When confederations are in use, one of two new AS_PATH attributes apply. The AS_CONFED_SET and AS_CONFED_SEQUENCE AS_PATH path segment types are used to describe the path that a route followed as it passed through confederations. The AS_CONFED_SET segment type is an unordered list of sub-autonomous systems that a route has traversed, similar to the AS_SET segment type, and the AS_CONFED_SEQUENCE segment type contains an ordered list of member ASs that a route travels through. When updates are sent to external peers, the AS_CONFED_SET and AS_CONFED_SEQUENCE path segment types are replaced with the confederation ID belonging to the parent AS. Figure 7-41 illustrates how the AS_CONFED_SEQUENCE path segment type is used for an advertisement spanning multiple sub-autonomous systems before exiting the parent AS.

Figure 7-41 *AS_CONFED_SEQUENCE Path Segment Type*

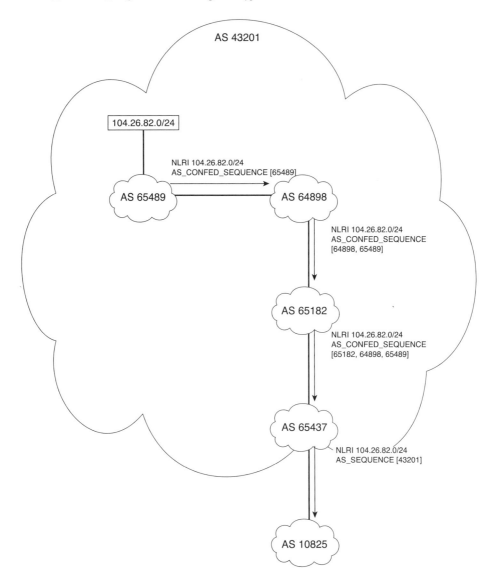

Figure 7-42 illustrates the various parts of a configuration and the roles that routers play, both inside and outside the confederation.

Figure 7-42 *How Confederations Work*

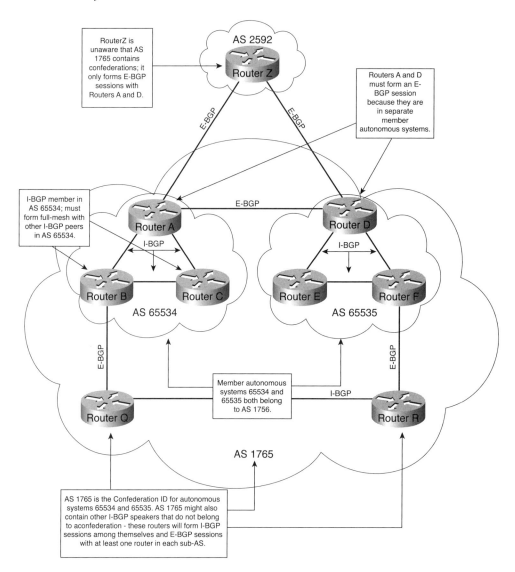

This figure identifies the basic characteristics of an AS containing confederations. Sub-AS 65,534 contains Routers A, B, and C. Each router in this sub-AS forms an I-BGP session with the other routers, forming a full mesh. Likewise sub-AS 65,535 contains Routers D, E, and F, which also form an I-BGP full mesh. Routers A and D form an E-BGP session across the two sub-autonomous systems, linking them together, and Routers B and F also form E-BGP with

Routers Q and R. All of these routers belong to AS 1765, the confederation ID for ASs 65,534 and 65,535.

Routers A and D are also the only routers in AS 1765 that interface with Router Z in AS 2592, the only peer relationship formed outside of AS 1765. Before routes that originated within AS 1765 can be passed to AS 2592, Routers A and D must modify the AS_PATH and replace the AS_CONFED_SEQUENCE value of either [65534] or [65535] with an AS_SEQUENCE value of [1765].

Peer Groups

When configuring one router with BGP multiple peer relationships, configurations can get quite complicated. Peer groups were created to simplify the configuration and troubleshooting process. Peer groups are created by making groups and assigning neighbors with the same policies to the groups. Peer group members inherit the policies assigned to the group. Chapter 9 covers peer group configuration and examples.

Route Selection Process

So, now that you know how BGP operates, how attributes influence routing decisions, and when to consider more complicated configurations, it is time to put this information together and use it to install routes in the main routing table. For a BGP speaker to move a route from its Adj_RIB_In to the Loc-RIB table, BGP performs a quite complicated route selection process. Unless the use of multiple paths has explicitly been configured, BGP speakers store only one route, the best route, in the main routing table. Only routes that the BGP process knows are reachable (from an IGP or directly connected) are considered for the BGP route selection process. The following BGP route selection process is described at the Cisco.com website at http://www.cisco.com/warp/public/459/25.shtml.

Step 1   Select the path with the *largest WEIGHT* (ranging from 0 to 65,535). Remember, WEIGHT is a Cisco proprietary attribute, is not forwarded to *any* peers, and only applies to the local router.

Step 2   If the WEIGHT attributes are equal, select the path with the *largest* LOCAL_PREF value (ranging from 0 to 4,294,967,295).

Step 3   If the WEIGHT and LOCAL_PREF values are equal, select the path that originated from the local router, either by local configuration or redistribution.

Step 4   If the WEIGHT, LOCAL_PREF, and local origination of the route are equal, select the route with the *shortest* AS_PATH.

Step 5   If all the previous attributes are equal, select the path with the *most desirable* ORIGIN. Remember, IGP is preferred, and EGP is considered before Incomplete.

Step 6 If the previous attributes are equal and there is more than one exit path to a network, prefer the path with the *lowest* MED value (ranging from 0 to 4,294,967,295).

Step 7 If the MED value is equal or not used, prefer E-BGP paths to I-BGP paths.

Step 8 If both paths are E-BGP (or both paths are not E-BGP), prefer the path with the lowest IGP metric.

If BGP multipath is enabled, and there are multiple external or confederation-external paths from the same neighboring AS or sub-AS, multiple paths are added to the Loc-RIB table at this point. The oldest path is considered the best path when forwarding updates to other routers.

Step 9 If the paths are external, select the *oldest* path (the path that was received first).

Step 10 If the paths were received at the same time, prefer the path that came from the peer with the *lowest* BGP-ID.

Step 11 If the route was received from a route reflector, select the path with the *lowest* CLUSTER_ID (BGP_ID of the route reflector) length.

Step 12 If the path was received from the same host, either peer or route reflector, select the path that came from the neighbor with the *lowest* peer IP address (the address of the directly [or nearest indirectly connected if not directly connected]) connected interface.

After the most desirable route has been selected, it is put into the main routing table and can be used to route packets.

Summary

BGP is an Exterior Gateway protocol that uses a path-vector algorithm to define the best path to a destination network. There are two types of BGP relationships, External BGP and Internal BGP—each type operates differently. Paths are not selected until BGP peers have transitioned through several states and established a peer relationship. OPEN messages are used during the peer session Establishment stage. After the neighboring routers have become peers, they exchange KEEPALIVE messages to verify connectivity and UPDATE messages to exchange routes. Upon a critical error, the peer experiencing the error condition sends a NOTIFICATION message to its peer, specifying the cause for the error and closing the BGP session. During the UPDATE process, BGP uses several attribute types to determine the best path to a destination network. After the best path has been selected, that path is stored in the main routing table and is ready for use.

Further Reading

Internet Routing Architectures, Second Edition, by Sam Halabi.

Routing TCP/IP, Volume II, by Jeff Doyle and Jennifer Dehaven Carroll.

Cisco BGP-4 Command and Configuration Handbook, by Dr. William R. Parkhurst.

BGP4 Inter-Domain Routing in the Internet, by John W. Stewart III.

RFC 1771, *A Border Gateway Protocol 4 (BGP-4)*, by Yakov Rekter and Tony Li.

RFC 1997, *BGP Communities Attribute*, by Ravi Chandra and Paul Triana.

RFC 1998, *An Application of the BGP COMMUNITY Attribute in Multi-Home Routing*, by Enke Chen and Tony Bates.

RFC 2395, *Protection of BGP Sessions via the TCP MD5 Signature Option*, by Andy Hefferman.

RFC 2519, *A Framework for Inter-Domain Route Aggregation*, by Enke Chen and John W. Stewart, III.

RFC 2892, *Capabilities Advertisement with BGP-4*, by Ravi Chandra and John G. Scudder.

RFC 2918, *Route Refresh Capability for BGP-4*, by Enke Chen.

RFC 2796, *BGP Route Reflection—An Alternative to Full Mesh IBGP*, by Tony Bates, Ravi Chandra, and Enke Chen.

CHAPTER 8

Introduction to BGP-4 Configuration

Configuring Border Gateway Protocol (BGP) in a production environment can be one of the most daunting tasks that network professionals encounter in their career. Depending on your BGP protocol and configuration knowledge, the BGP peering requirements, the network policy, and general network stability, designing and implementing a solid BGP network might be one of the largest design challenges that you face. BGP router configuration mode contains hundreds of possible commands, which makes it one of the most customizable routing protocols available today. BGP also uses several other features in Cisco IOS Software that complement the commands available in BGP router configuration mode, such as access lists, route maps, autonomous system path (AS path) access lists, IP prefix lists, community lists, and regular expressions. These features combined with the other BGP configuration commands create a large toolbox for use in BGP configuration. Over the next two chapters, this book covers many of these commands and shows you how to use them to create and implement solid BGP network models.

This chapter covers the basic BGP configuration prerequisites and briefly covers some of the BGP processes that run on a Cisco router. The chapter then takes you through a detailed step-by-step BGP neighbor configuration and network advertisement, using some hands-on practical examples. While configuring BGP in this chapter, you have the opportunity to analyze and verify the BGP configuration using BGP **show** and **debug** commands as troubleshooting tools. This chapter also introduces several BGP configuration tips and other tools that you can use to decrease troubleshooting time and to help you get more use from Cisco IOS Software. These tools are used to take a close look at BGP operation and can also be used to troubleshoot common BGP problems. The output of each command is listed in detail so that you can see exactly what the router is doing and read the command output like a pro.

This chapter provides the foundation for the final BGP chapter, Chapter 9, "Advanced BGP Configuration," which covers topics such as route reflectors, confederations, redistribution, route aggregation, and BGP tuning.

BGP Configuration Prerequisites

When modeling a BGP network, you need to consider many configuration prerequisites. You must consider the amount of memory and processor available on your routers and the software feature sets required to create the scenarios that properly model the network. As a best practice, before configuring BGP, always make sure that the routers running BGP are capable of doing so. Get a snapshot of the current operating environment, and check the available and used memory to verify that debugging BGP does not crash the router.

If the router does not have enough memory, and there is no way to increase the amount of memory on the router, you can do a few things to prevent configuration disasters. First, check your feature set using the **show version** command. If you are running an enterprise feature set and you will not be using all the other features, such as IPX, AppleTalk, or DEC protocols, try using a more scaled-down version of Cisco IOS Software such as the IP feature sets. Second, display the running processes and the running configuration, and find some protocols or features that can be disabled to make more memory available to BGP. Third, disable console logging (log to the buffer or syslog), and use the **scheduler allocate** command to prevent router reloads. Finally, save your configuration before debugging; that way, in the event that the router does reload, you still have your configuration.

Assessing the Router's Capacity for BGP

After BGP has been configured on a Cisco router, four processes are started: BGP Open, BGP Scanner, BGP Router, and BGP I/O. The *BGP Open* process is used to establish the TCP session between BGP speakers. The BGP Open process ends after a TCP session for the BGP peers has been established and is only visible at the beginning of BGP session establishment. The *BGP I/O* process performs all BGP packet processing and performs the queuing of BGP UPDATE and KEEPALIVE messages. The *BGP Scanner* process scans, or walks, the BGP table, a data structure called a *Radix Trie*, for next-hop reachability changes. By default, the scanner runs every 60 seconds and is shown while debugging BGP as *nettable_scan* and *nettable_walker*. Finally, the *BGP Router* process handles the establishment of peer sessions. The BGP Router process also handles the actual BGP decision process, determining which routes are stored in the main IP routing table; it also processes new routes and advertises routes to peers. Example 8-1 shows the four BGP processes as displayed using the **show processes cpu | include BGP** command.

Example 8-1   *Four BGP Processes*

```
Alki# show processes cpu | include BGP
CPU utilization for five seconds: 0%/0%; one minute: 0%; five minutes: 0%
 PID Runtime(ms)   Invoked    uSecs   5Sec   1Min   5Min TTY Process
  21          0          1        0  0.00%  0.00%  0.00%   0 BGP Open
  84         81       6085       13  0.00%  0.02%  0.00%   0 BGP Router
  85        693      13436       51  0.00%  0.00%  0.00%   0 BGP I/O
  86       2547        201    12671  0.00%  0.06%  0.06%   0 BGP Scanner
```

Notice in the prior example that there were four BGP processes running at the time that the **show processes cpu** snapshot was taken. The BGP Router, BGP I/O, and BGP Scanner processes always run after BGP has been configured. The BGP Open process only runs when BGP triggers the initial TCP session, and only runs until the TCP session is established, so you can tell that this command was issued at the beginning of a BGP session, right after BGP was configured. The **show processes history** command enables you to display a summarized graphical representation of the CPU utilization history. This command might prove useful when troubleshooting performance problems on a production router.

TIP   Output modifiers, like the one shown in Example 8-1, enable you to display more concise information from a command. In the preceding example, the | **include BGP** output modifier was used to limit the output of the **show processes cpu** command to include items containing the string "BGP." Output modifiers are case sensitive, and you might need to experiment with the output string to find the information that you want to display. When commands used with output modifiers are combined with command aliases, you have yet another tool that can help you customize your use of Cisco IOS Software. Use of aliases and output identifiers is covered in more detail later in this chapter.

The highlighted section of the command output was added into this example to show the command output description. It does not normally appear, unless specified, when output modifiers are used. Example 8-2, using the **show processes memory | include BGP** command, shows the BGP processes that are currently utilizing memory.

Example 8-2   *Output from the* **show processes memory | include bgp** *Command*

```
Alki# show processes memory | include  BGP
Total: 29184828, Used: 5148284, Free: 24036544
 PID TTY  Allocated      Freed    Holding    Getbufs    Retbufs Process
  21  0          0          0       6928          0          0 BGP Open
  84  0      52560        492      10324          0          0 BGP Router
  85  0          0          0       6868          0          0 BGP I/O
  86  0        116          0       9992          0          0 BGP Scanner
```

In the preceding example, you can see the amount of memory that the Alki router has allocated to the BGP processes that are currently running. Once again, the highlighted section of the command was added into the command output to show the descriptions for the items displayed for the command. If the entire contents of the **show processes memory** command had been included in the command, the output would have been quite a few pages, so the output modifier was used to constrain the output of the **show** command to display only BGP processes. The **show memory | include BGP** command enables you to display the current memory allocation for BGP processes, as shown in Example 8-3. The highlighted section of the command output was added to display the output description.

Example 8-3 *BGP Memory Utilization*

```
Alki# show memory | include  BGP
Address     Bytes     Prev      Next Ref    PrevF    NextF Alloc PC  what
823A2F8C 0000000044 823A2D10 823A2FE4 001  -------  ------- 813BC2E0  BGP Router
823C1C5C 0000005000 823C1830 823C3010 001  -------  ------- 805A124C  BGP rcache-
chunk
823C3010 0000005000 823C1C5C 823C43C4 001  -------  ------- 805A1280  BGP fcache-
chunk
823C4408 0000060496 823C43C4 823D3084 001  -------  ------- 805A12E8  BGP (0) attr
823D3084 0000000044 823C4408 823D30DC 001  -------  ------- 813BC2E0  BGP Router
8241C8D4 0000000032 8241C7F8 8241C920 001  -------  ------- 8045F35C  BGP Router
8241D100 0000000072 8241D08C 8241D174 001  -------  ------- 813B0548  BGP Router
8241D358 0000000072 8241D250 8241D3CC 001  -------  ------- 813B0548  BGP Scanner
8241D704 0000032768 8241D6C0 82425730 001  -------  ------- 805A12E8  BGP (1) attr
82425774 0000020000 82425730 8242A5C0 001  -------  ------- 805A12E8  BGP (2) attr
8242A604 0000032768 8242A5C0 82432630 001  -------  ------- 805A12E8  BGP (3) attr
82432630 0000003000 8242A604 82433214 001  -------  ------- 805A1330  BGP attrlist
-chunk
82433214 0000001500 82432630 8243381C 001  -------  ------- 805A1364  BGP worktype
-chunk
8243381C 0000005000 82433214 82434BD0 001  -------  ------- 805A1398  BGP gwcache
-c
hunk
82434BD0 0000002000 8243381C 824353CC 001  -------  ------- 805A13CC  BGP NLRI-
chunk
824353CC 0000000432 82434BD0 824355A8 001  -------  ------- 805A1400  BGP SNPA-
chunk
824355EC 0000065536 824355A8 82445618 001  -------  ------- 805A146C  BGP (0)
update
8244565C 0000065536 82445618 82455688 001  -------  ------- 805A146C  BGP (1)
update
824556CC 0000065536 82455688 824656F8 001  -------  ------- 805A146C  BGP (2)
update
8246573C 0000065536 824656F8 82475768 001  -------  ------- 805A146C  BGP (3)
update
824757AC 0000065536 82475768 824857D8 001  -------  ------- 805A146C  BGP (4)
update
8248581C 0000065536 824857D8 82495848 001  -------  ------- 805A146C  BGP (5)
update
8249588C 0000065536 82495848 824A58B8 001  -------  ------- 805A146C  BGP (6)
update
824A58FC 0000065536 824A58B8 824B5928 001  -------  ------- 805A146C  BGP (7)
update
824B5928 0000065536 824A58FC 824C5954 001  -------  ------- 805A14D4  BGP battr
chunk
824C5954 0000000264 824B5928 824C5A88 001  -------  ------- 805A1508  BGP vpnv4
soo
```

The output of the preceding command shows the memory addresses used by the BGP processes. In this example, the Alki router only had one peer relationship, and BGP only had four routes in the table. When routers have many peers, with many routes containing many attributes, the **show memory | include BGP** command displays pages of information. If a router in a network model is to have multiple peers, it is a good idea to have plenty of memory available to BGP. In a lab environment, BGP will run on just about any router that is running a feature set that includes BGP; however, BGP performance depends greatly on the selected router platform, the processor(s), the amount and type of memory, the speed of the backplane, the number of routes received by peering routers, and the router configuration itself. If you are modeling a BGP network for production use, carefully select the router platform you intend to use in production to support BGP process and memory utilization. If you are configuring a production router to run BGP with full Internet tables, it is a good rule to check the current BGP Internet table size. Make sure that you have at least twice the amount of memory as the full Internet table so that you will be able to run BGP uninterrupted until the tables double in size.

BGP Configuration Tips

When configuring and troubleshooting BGP, you will use a number of commands on a regular basis. You can use quite a few tricks to help you become more efficient with Cisco IOS Software. For instance, you can use the Control (Ctrl) key in combination with other characters on the keyboard as editing shortcuts. These shortcuts can save you time when you are in a hurry or are having a bad day and you just can't type. These commands are also helpful in the event that you are required to use a terminal-emulation program that does not support the use of up and down arrows or other commands that you would normally use. Table 8-1 shows some of the most popular commands.

Table 8-1   *Cisco IOS Software Shortcuts*

Command	Description
Ctrl+A	Goes to beginning of line
Ctrl+B	Moves back one character
Ctrl+E	Goes to end of line
Ctrl+F	Moves forward one word
Ctrl+P	Repeats previous line
Ctrl+R	Repaints line
Ctrl+U	Deletes entire line
Ctrl+W	Deletes last word

Another commonly overlooked command that can help you customize your use of Cisco IOS Software is the **alias** command. The **alias** command enables you to create command aliases, which are used to represent commonly used commands. You create aliases in global configuration mode using the following command:

```
alias mode alias-name alias-string
```

In Example 8-4, you can see several command aliases used as shortcuts for various commonly used commands.

Example 8-4 *Command Aliases*

```
Alki# show  alias
Exec mode aliases:
  h                    help
  lo                   logout
  p                    ping
  r                    resume
  s                    show
  u                    undebug
  un                   undebug
  w                    where
  cib                  cle ip bgp *
  sb                   show ip bgp sum
Router configuration mode aliases:
  net                  network
```

Notice that there are several default aliases—**h**, **lo**, **p**, **r**, **s**, **u**, **un**, and **w**—and that I added three other aliases, **cib**, which represents the command **clear ip bgp ***; **sb**, which represents the command **show ip bgp summary**; and **net**, which represents the router configuration mode command **network**. Aliases are never necessary, but they can be valuable tools for the ever-efficient network engineer.

Another tool that was briefly mentioned earlier in the chapter is the output modifier. Output modifiers have been around for a long time but are rarely ever used. Output modifiers change the way output from a **show** command is displayed and are available for just about every **show** command in existence. Table 8-2 shows some examples.

Table 8-2 *Output Modifiers*

Output Modifier	Description
begin *string*	Displays the command output from the point specified by the string
exclude *string*	Displays everything, excluding information specified by the string
include *string*	Displays only items matching the string

Example 8-5 shows how each of the output modifiers are used to show specific output from the **show ip bgp** command. The first line shows the unmodified output of the command. The second highlighted line shows how the **include** statement was used to specify only the best reachable routes marked with the ***>** characters. Notice in this example that the use of the * with the ***>** characters were preceded by a slash **/*>**. If the slash had not been used, the router would have shown an error condition, **% Failed to compile regular expression** because the * character itself is a regular expression, which matches a series of characters, much like ***.*** does in DOS. The second highlighted example shows how the **exclude** command was used to exclude the display of routes with 600 in their AS_PATH. The final highlighted area shows how the **begin** modifier was used to prevent the output description information from being shown in the command output.

Example 8-5   *Examples of Output Modifiers*

```
Alki# show ip bgp
BGP table version is 4, local router ID is 1.1.1.1
Status codes: s suppressed, d damped, h history, * valid, > best, i - internal
Origin codes: i - IGP, e - EGP, ? - incomplete
   Network          Next Hop          Metric LocPrf Weight Path
*> 10.1.1.0/24      192.168.32.2           0            0 600 i
*> 10.2.2.0/24      192.168.32.2           0            0 600 i
*> 192.168.32.0/30  0.0.0.0                0        32768 I
Alki# show ip bgp | include /*
BGP table version is 4, local router ID is 1.1.1.1
Status codes: s suppressed, d damped, h history, * valid, > best, i - internal
Origin codes: i - IGP, e - EGP, ? - incomplete
   Network          Next Hop          Metric LocPrf Weight Path
*> 10.1.1.0/24      192.168.32.2           0            0 600 i
*> 10.2.2.0/24      192.168.32.2           0            0 600 i
*> 192.168.32.0/30  0.0.0.0                0        32768 I
Alki# show ip bgp | exclude 600
BGP table version is 4, local router ID is 1.1.1.1
Status codes: s suppressed, d damped, h history, * valid, > best, i - internal
Origin codes: i - IGP, e - EGP, ? - incomplete
   Network          Next Hop          Metric LocPrf Weight Path
*> 192.168.32.0/30  0.0.0.0                0        32768 I
Alki# show ip bgp | begin Network
   Network          Next Hop          Metric LocPrf Weight Path
*> 10.1.1.0/24      192.168.32.2           0            0 600 i
*> 10.2.2.0/24      192.168.32.2           0            0 600 i
*> 192.168.32.0/30  0.0.0.0                0        32768 i
```

Now that you have some tips that make BGP easier to configure, it is time to put your knowledge of Cisco IOS Software and skill together and learn to configure BGP on a Cisco router.

Configuring and Troubleshooting BGP Neighbor Relationships

Five major tasks must be completed for each BGP session. In this section, each of these tasks is examined, and a practical example is used to show all the items included in each task. Figure 8-1 shows the network used for the examples in this section.

Figure 8-1   *BGP Neighbor Configuration*

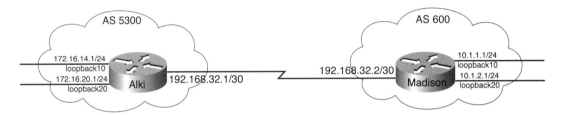

Prior to the configuration of a BGP neighboring session, the following tasks must be completed:

- If the remote BGP peer is not under your administrative control, you must find the IP address of the remote interface and the remote autonomous system number (ASN) for the remote peer, which in E-BGP is usually directly connected to your network's egress interface.

- The local and remote BGP peers must be able to reach each other using TCP port 179; therefore, the interface on the local router must be configured with an IP address, and the router must have a path to its remote peer.

- If the local router is not directly connected to its remote peer, another IGP or static route must be used to provide the routing information required to form a TCP session.

NOTE   Both sides of the BGP session must be fully configured before a BGP session can be established.

In this example, you configure an E-BGP session between the Alki router and the Madison router across a direct serial connection. The Alki router's serial 0/0 interface is configured to use the IP address 192.168.32.1/30, and the Madison router's serial 0 interface is 192.168.32.2/30. The Alki router will be advertising networks 172.16.14.0/24 and 172.16.20.0/24, so configure loopback 10 to use 172.16.14.1/24 and loopback 20 to use 172.16.20.1/24. The Madison router will advertise networks 10.1.1.0/24 and 10.1.2.0/24, so configure loopback 10 to use 10.1.1.1/24 and loopback 20 to use 10.1.2.1/24.

Step 1   Verify that the local BGP router can reach the remote router. The **ping** command enables you to verify connectivity to the remote router; if access lists or a firewall exist between the local and remote routers, however, you must verify that the packet filters will allow TCP traffic on port 179.

At this time, it is also a good idea to verify the IP addresses on both of the routers' serial interfaces using the **show ip interface brief** and **show interface serial** *interface-number* commands on both routers. Make sure that both interfaces are in the **interface is up, line protocol is up** state before continuing on to the next step.

Verify that the Alki and Madison routers can reach each other. Because there are no access lists between the two routers, you can safely assume that a ping test will verify the connection. Example 8-6 shows the serial interface configurations and the results of the ping tests.

Example 8-6   *Interface Configuration and Ping Tests*

```
Alki# show run | begin Serial0/0
interface Serial0/0
 ip address 192.168.32.1 255.255.255.252
Alki# ping 192.168.32.2
Type escape sequence to abort.
Sending 5, 100-byte ICMP Echos to 192.168.32.2, timeout is 2 seconds:
!!!!!
Madison# show run | begin Serial0
interface Serial0
 ip address 192.168.32.2 255.255.255.252
Madison# ping 192.168.32.1
Type escape sequence to abort.
Sending 5, 100-byte ICMP Echos to 192.168.32.1, timeout is 2 seconds:
!!!!!
```

After both interfaces are up and operating on Layer 3, it is time to configure BGP on each of the routers.

Step 2   To enable BGP in Cisco IOS Software, use the **router bgp** *as-number* command in global configuration mode. The *as-number* keyword identifies the local ASN. The values for the *as-number* variable range from 1 to 65,535, with 64,512 to 65,535 reserved for private autonomous system use.

```
    router bgp as-number
```

This command starts the following BGP processes (listed using the **show processes cpu** command) and allocates memory to those processes (listed using the **show processes memory** command) on the router:

— BGP Router

— BGP I/O

— BGP Scanner

Configure BGP on the Alki router; the Alki router is in AS 5300.

```
Alki(config)# router bgp 5300
Alki(config-router)#
```

You can use the **show processes cpu | include BGP** command to see that the BGP processes have started.

```
Alki(config-router)# do show processes cpu | include BGP
 80      4     111      36  0.00%  0.00%  0.00%   0 BGP Router
 84      0       1       0  0.00%  0.00%  0.00%   0 BGP I/O
 85     44       4   11000  0.00%  0.06%  0.01%   0 BGP Scanner
```

NOTE In the preceding example, the **do show processes cpu | include BGP** command was used to display the current BGP processes. If this same command were issued on a router with a failed TCP session between BGP peers, you would see instances of the BGP Open process, as shown here:

```
r2(config)# do show processes cpu | include BGP
  78       0     179       0  0.00%  0.00%  0.00%   0 BGP Open
  89       0     179       0  0.00%  0.00%  0.00%   0 BGP Open
  99       0     179       0  0.00%  0.00%  0.00%   0 BGP Open
 104  165252 3566960      46  0.00%  0.00%  0.00%   0 BGP Router
 105       0       1       0  0.00%  0.00%  0.00%   0 BGP I/O
 106    7108     890    7986  0.00%  0.03%  0.00%   0 BGP Scanner
 107       0     179       0  0.00%  0.00%  0.00%   0 BGP Open
```

If you were to issue the **show tcp brief all** command, you would notice that the router currently has no established TCP sessions but is listening for incoming TCP sessions. This is because no BGP peers have been configured on the Alki router, and the Madison router has not been configured yet.

```
Alki# show tcp brief all
TCB      Local Address        Foreign Address      (state)
8241BE64 *.*                  *.*                  LISTEN
```

Configure BGP on the Madison router; the Madison router is in AS 600.

```
Madison(config)# router bgp 600
```

After the **router bgp** *as-number* command has been issued, the router enters the BGP router configuration mode, where you can use the BGP commands shown in Example 8-7. These commands are covered in this chapter and in Chapter 9.

Example 8-7   *BGP Commands Available in Cisco IOS Software 12.2(7)T*

```
Madison(config-router)#?
Router configuration commands:
  address-family      Enter Address Family command mode
  aggregate-address   Configure BGP aggregate entries
  auto-summary        Enable automatic network number summarization
  bgp                 BGP specific commands
  default             Set a command to its defaults
  default-information Control distribution of default information
  default-metric      Set metric of redistributed routes
  distance            Define an administrative distance
  distribute-list     Filter networks in routing updates
  exit                Exit from routing protocol configuration mode
  help                Description of the interactive help system
  maximum-paths       Forward packets over multiple paths
  neighbor            Specify a neighbor router
  network             Specify a network to announce via BGP
  no                  Negate a command or set its defaults
  redistribute        Redistribute information from another routing protocol
  synchronization     Perform IGP synchronization
  table-map           Map external entry attributes into routing table
  timers              Adjust routing timers
  traffic-share       How to compute traffic share over alternate paths
```

Step 3   Specify information about the remote peer(s). The remote peer information is entered using the **neighbor** *ip-address* **remote-as** *remote-as-number* command as shown here:

> **neighbor** *ip-address* **remote-as** *remote-as-number*

This command specifies the IP address used to reach the remote BGP peer and the AS number to which the remote peer belongs.

Configure the Alki and Madison routers with their remote peer information using the **neighbor** command to specify the remote peer's IP address and remote AS number.

> Alki(config-router)# **neighbor 192.168.32.2 remote-as 600**
> Madison(config-router)# **neighbor 192.168.32.1 remote-as 5300**

Step 4   After configuring the local and remote peer autonomous systems, configure the networks that each of the BGP speakers will be advertising to its remote peer using the **network** command shown here:

> **network** network-address [mask *subnet-mask*] [route-map *route-map-name*]
> [backdoor]

The command enables you to specify the networks, and if the network is not classful, you can specify the subnet mask for the network. The *route-map* option allows for BGP attribute manipulation, and the **backdoor** keyword specifies the use of a BGP backdoor, both of which are covered later in this chapter.

Use the **network** command to configure the Alki router to advertise networks 172.16.14.0/24 and 172.16.20.0/24. Then use the same commands to configure the Madison router to advertise networks 10.1.1.0/24 and 10.1.2.0/24.

```
Alki(config-router)# network 172.16.14.0 mask 255.255.255.0
Alki(config-router)# network 172.16.20.0 mask 255.255.255.0

Madison(config-router)# network 10.1.1.0 mask 255.255.255.0
Madison(config-router)# network 10.1.2.0 mask 255.255.255.0
```

Step 5 After configuring the local and remote BGP peers, you can monitor the BGP status using one of several different BGP **show** and **debug** commands.

At this point, you should be able to verify several items on each of the routers. Using the **show tcp brief all** command, as shown in Example 8-8, you should see an established TCP session between the Alki and Madison routers on port 179, and you should also see the routers listening for TCP activity on port 179.

Example 8-8 *Using the **show tcp brief all** Command to Display TCP Connection State*

```
Alki# show tcp brief all
TCB        Local Address        Foreign Address      (state)
8248F4BC   192.168.32.1.11003   192.168.32.2.179     ESTAB
820E59F0   *.179                192.168.32.2.*       LISTEN
```

By issuing the **show ip bgp** command, shown in Example 8-9, you should see information about the BGP session and networks that are advertised by both peers.

Example 8-9 *Display BGP Routes Using the **show ip bgp** Command*

```
Alki# show ip bgp
BGP table version is 5, local router ID is 1.1.1.1
Status codes: s suppressed, d damped, h history, * valid, > best, i - internal
Origin codes: i - IGP, e - EGP, ? - incomplete
   Network          Next Hop          Metric LocPrf Weight Path
*> 10.1.1.0/24      192.168.32.2           0           0 600 i
*> 10.1.2.0/24      192.168.32.2           0           0 600 i
*> 172.16.14.0/24   0.0.0.0                0       32768 i
*> 172.16.20.0/24   0.0.0.0                0       32768 i
```

On the Alki router, notice that you can see networks 10.1.1.0/24 and 10.1.2.0/24 with a NEXT_HOP of 192.168.32.2 using the default MED, LOCAL_PREF, and WEIGHT attributes. You can also see that the route originated in AS 600 and has an ORIGIN attribute of **i** for IGP because it originated locally on the Madison router. To the left of each of the routes, you can see the asterisk (*) symbol, which means that the route has been verified as reachable by the BGP Scanner process, and the greater than (>) symbol means that the route is the best route to that network. When BGP has a valid best-path route to a network, it places that route in the main IP routing table and advertises it to any other external BGP peers.

You should also be able to issue the **show ip route** command to see the BGP routes in the main IP routing table and **ping** each of the loopback interfaces. Example 8-10 shows the output of the **show ip route** command from the Alki router, and Example 8-11 shows the **ping** tests from the Alki and Madison routers.

Example 8-10 *Displaying the Main IP Routing Table with the* **show ip route** *Command*

```
Alki# show ip route
Codes: C - connected, S - static, I - IGRP, R - RIP, M - mobile, B - BGP
       D - EIGRP, EX - EIGRP external, O - OSPF, IA - OSPF inter area
       N1 - OSPF NSSA external type 1, N2 - OSPF NSSA external type 2
       E1 - OSPF external type 1, E2 - OSPF external type 2, E - EGP
       i - IS-IS, L1 - IS-IS level-1, L2 - IS-IS level-2, ia - IS-IS inter area
       * - candidate default, U - per-user static route, o - ODR
       P - periodic downloaded static route
Gateway of last resort is not set
     172.16.0.0/24 is subnetted, 2 subnets
C       172.16.20.0 is directly connected, Loopback20
C       172.16.14.0 is directly connected, Loopback10
     10.0.0.0/24 is subnetted, 2 subnets
B       10.1.2.0 [20/0] via 192.168.32.2, 00:05:30
B       10.1.1.0 [20/0] via 192.168.32.2, 00:05:30
     192.168.32.0/30 is subnetted, 1 subnets
C       192.168.32.0 is directly connected, Serial0/0
```

Example 8-11 *Successful* **ping** *Tests on the Alki and Madison Routers*

```
Alki# ping 10.1.1.1
Type escape sequence to abort.
Sending 5, 100-byte ICMP Echos to 10.1.1.1, timeout is 2 seconds:
!!!!!
Success rate is 100 percent (5/5), round-trip min/avg/max = 32/35/36 ms
Alki# ping 10.1.2.1
Type escape sequence to abort.
Sending 5, 100-byte ICMP Echos to 10.1.2.1, timeout is 2 seconds:
!!!!!
Success rate is 100 percent (5/5), round-trip min/avg/max = 36/36/36 ms
```

To see the process that the routers used to set up the BGP session, advertise networks, and install them in the BGP table, use the **debug ip bgp** command. Because BGP only sends new or changed routes in UPDATE messages, you need to clear the BGP session using the **clear ip**

bgp command. Because there is only one BGP session on this router, you can use the *
character to tell BGP to clear all sessions, as shown in Example 8-12.

TIP   Be very careful with your use of the **clear ip bgp** * command on production routers; this
command closes all BGP sessions and will result in a network disruption if it is used on a
production network.

Example 8-12 *Debugging BGP*

```
Alki# debug ip bgp
BGP debugging is on
Alki# clear ip bgp *
01:10:18: BGP: 192.168.32.2 went from Established to Idle
Comment: BGP cleared session
01:10:18: %BGP-5-ADJCHANGE: neighbor 192.168.32.2 Down User reset
Comment: the ADJCHANGE message indicates the session with the 192.168.32.2
neighbor is down due to a user reset
01:10:18: BGP: 192.168.32.2 closing
Comment: The BGP session is being closed
01:10:38: BGP: 192.168.32.2 went from Idle to Active
01:10:38: BGP: 192.168.32.2 open active, delay 26900ms
Comment: The router sent a active host TCP open message
connection request and is awaiting a TCP session request from its passive
neighbor.
01:10:48: BGP: Applying map to find origin for 172.16.14.0/24
01:10:48: BGP: Applying map to find origin for 172.16.20.0/24
Comment: BGP is finding the ORIGIN for the 172.16.14.0/24 and 172.16.20.0/24
routes, which will be i for I-BGP
01:11:05: BGP: 192.168.32.2 open active, local address 192.168.32.1
01:11:05: BGP: 192.168.32.2 went from Active to OpenSent
Comment: The remote BGP session transitioned from Active to OpenSent meaning a
 TCP session has been established and OPEN message has been sent, the router is
 now waiting to receive an OPEN message from its peer.
01:11:05: BGP: 192.168.32.2 sending OPEN, version 4, my as: 5300
Comment: The router sent an OPEN message to its peer, 192.168.32.2, and the
message contained the BGP version: 4 and the MY_AS value 5300
01:11:05: BGP: 192.168.32.2 send message type 1, length (incl. header) 45
01:11:05: BGP: 192.168.32.2 rcv message type 1, length (excl. header) 26
Comment: The remote router sent an OPEN (type-1) message to this peer and it was
   successfully received
01:11:05: BGP: 192.168.32.2 rcv OPEN, version 4
01:11:05: BGP: 192.168.32.2 rcv OPEN w/ OPTION parameter len: 16
01:11:05: BGP: 192.168.32.2 rcvd OPEN w/ optional parameter type 2 (Capability)
len 6
01:11:05: BGP: 192.168.32.2 OPEN has CAPABILITY code: 1, length 4
01:11:05: BGP: 192.168.32.2 OPEN has MP_EXT CAP for afi/safi: 1/1
01:11:05: BGP: 192.168.32.2 rcvd OPEN w/ optional parameter type 2 (Capability)
len 2
```

Example 8-12 *Debugging BGP (Continued)*

```
01:11:05: BGP: 192.168.32.2 OPEN has CAPABILITY code: 128, length 0
01:11:05: BGP: 192.168.32.2 OPEN has ROUTE-REFRESH capability(old) for all
address-families
01:11:05: BGP: 192.168.32.2 rcvd OPEN w/ optional parameter type 2 (Capability)
len 2
01:11:05: BGP: 192.168.32.2 OPEN has CAPABILITY code: 2, length 0
01:11:05: BGP: 192.168.32.2 OPEN has ROUTE-REFRESH capability(new) for all
address-families
Comment: The remote peer's OPEN message contained the following data:
Comment: BGP version - 4
Comment: With Multiprotocol BGP and Route Refresh capabilities
01:11:05: BGP: 192.168.32.2 went from OpenSent to OpenConfirm
Comment: The session transitioned from OpenSent to OpenConfirm, the router is
 waiting on a KEEPALIVE message from its peer.
01:11:05: BGP: 192.168.32.2 send message type 4, length (incl. header) 19
01:11:05: BGP: 192.168.32.2 rcv message type 4, length (excl. header) 0
Comment: the router sent and received a KEEPALIVE (type-4) message and received a
 message from its peer.
01:11:05: BGP: 192.168.32.2 went from OpenConfirm to Established
Comment: The session transitioned from OpenConfirm to Established, now routes can
 be exchanged using UPDATE messages
01:11:05: %BGP-5-ADJCHANGE: neighbor 192.168.32.2 Up
Comment: The ADJCHANGED message indicating the BGP session with peer 192.168.32.2
 is up
```

The **debug ip bgp event** command shows detailed information about internal BGP events as they occur on the router, and the **debug ip bgp updates** command, shown in Example 8-13, displays detailed information on UPDATE messages as they are received.

Example 8-13 *Debugging BGP Updates*

```
Alki# debug ip bgp updates
BGP updates debugging is on
Alki# clear ip bgp *
01:33:30: %BGP-5-ADJCHANGE: neighbor 192.168.32.2 Down User reset
Comment: The session was reset upon user request
01:34:12: %BGP-5-ADJCHANGE: neighbor 192.168.32.2 Up
Comment: The BGP session with peer 192.168.32.2 is back up
01:34:12: BGP(0): 192.168.32.2 rcvd UPDATE w/ attr: nexthop 192.168.32.2, origin
 i, metric 0, path 600
Comment: The router received an update from peer 192.168.32.2 containing the
BGPattributes:
Comment: NEXT_HOP 192.168.32.2
Comment: ORIGIN: i
Comment: MED: 0
Comment: AS_PATH 600
01:34:12: BGP(0): 192.168.32.2 rcvd 10.1.1.0/24
01:34:12: BGP(0): 192.168.32.2 rcvd 10.1.2.0/24
```

continues

Example 8-13 *Debugging BGP Updates (Continued)*

```
Comment: The update contained NLRI paths 10.1.1.0/24 and 10.1.2.0/24
01:34:12: BGP(0): Revise route installing 10.1.1.0/24 -> 192.168.32.2 to main IP
 table
01:34:12: BGP(0): Revise route installing 10.1.2.0/24 -> 192.168.32.2 to main IP
 table
Comment: BGP found the routes to networks 10.1.1.0/24 and 10.1.2.0/24 valid best
paths and is installing them in the main IP routing table
01:34:12: BGP(0): nettable_walker 172.16.14.0/24 route sourced locally
01:34:12: BGP(0): nettable_walker 172.16.20.0/24 route sourced locally
Comment: The BGP Scanner (nettable_walker) found networks 172.16.14.0/24 and
172.16.20.0/24 sourced locally
01:34:12: BGP(0): 192.168.32.2 computing updates, afi 0, neighbor version 0,
table version 5, starting at 0.0.0.0
01:34:12: BGP(0): 192.168.32.2 send UPDATE (format) 172.16.14.0/24, next
192.168.32.1, metric 0, path
Comment: The router is sending an UPDATE message to 192.168.32.2 containing the
route 172.16.14.0/24 with the attributes of NEXT_HOP: 192.168.32.2, MED: 0
01:34:12: BGP(0): 192.168.32.2 send UPDATE (prepend, chgflags: 0x208)
172.16.20.0/24, next 192.168.32.1, metric 0, path
Comment: The router is sending an UPDATE message to 192.168.32.2 containing the
route 172.16.20.0/24 with the attributes of NEXT_HOP: 192.168.32.2, MED: 0
01:34:12: BGP(0): 192.168.32.2 1 updates enqueued (average=56, maximum=56)
01:34:12: BGP(0): 192.168.32.2 update run completed, afi 0, ran for 4ms, neighbor
 version 0, start version 5, throttled to 5
Comment: UPDATE messages were engueued for transport and then sent successfully
the BGP table version has been changed to 5
01:34:12: BGP: 192.168.32.2 initial update completed
Comment: The update is complete
```

If the BGP peers are not able to reach each other using TCP port 179, you can use a number of TCP troubleshooting commands to troubleshoot the connection. As a best practice (that will save you many a headache), however, it is better to verify the router configuration for inaccuracies before troubleshooting a problem that might end up being a typo.

- Verify that the local BGP ASN is entered correctly.

- Verify that the remote peer's BGP ASN and IP address are entered correctly.

- Verify that the interfaces connecting the two peers are up and operational.

- If the peers are not directly connected, verify that they have a valid route (to and from) to reach each other.

- Check routers along the path between the peers for access lists or route policies that might be dropping or rerouting BGP traffic.

- Check logs for interface instabilities. Are routes flapping along the route between the BGP peers? Are any of the interfaces heavily congested or dropping packets? Keep in mind that BGP uses rather small packets for OPEN and KEEPALIVE messages. These packets are delayed if other larger packets are monopolizing a congested interface.

- If something has changed in the path between the two BGP peers, verify that it is not affecting the BGP session—for example, a new switch configuration, new access lists, a firewall, new routing policies, and so on.

Don't spend time troubleshooting BGP when it is not the problem! Establish a general layered troubleshooting methodology; it will be the number one troubleshooting tool and your best friend when you encounter a problem.

Step 1 Layer 1

— Check your cabling; verify that all cables are connected and that the interface is in a line up and protocol up state. Don't spend time troubleshooting BGP when you have a Layer 1 problem.

— If you are using a serial link, make sure that you have set the correct clock rate. If you are using a channel service unit/data service unit (CSU/DSU), make sure it is properly configured and the line is up.

— If you are using an Ethernet interface, make sure that the speed and duplex are set correctly on the router and switch.

— Check the router and switch interfaces for errors; if there are errors, fix the error and then proceed with your troubleshooting.

If you are using a Token Ring interface, make sure the router is configured to use the right ring speed, and that it has a good connection to the multistation access unit (MSAU) or switch.

Step 2 Layer 2

— If you are using an Ethernet connection, make sure that the switch port has been assigned to the proper VLAN.

— Make sure that the VLAN is properly configured, and that there are no spanning-tree topology problems on the switch.

— On an ATM interface, verify that the maximum transmission unit (MTU) is properly configured on both sides of the connection.

— Verify that you are using the correct virtual path identifier/virtual channel identifier (VPI/VCI) pair, and that you have configured a valid ATM map for Layer 2 to Layer 3 connectivity.

On a Frame Relay connection, verify that your local and remote data-link connection identifiers (DLCIs) and Local Management Interface (LMI) type are correctly set to match the values generated on the switch.

— Verify that LMI is up and that the interface is not flapping.

— If you are making a PPP connection, make sure PPP is configured on both sides of the connection.

— Before proceeding to the next step, verify that your interface is not in a line up protocol down state.

Step 3 Layer 3

— Verify that you have configured the right IP address and subnet mask on the interface, check the other side of the connection, and verify that it is on the same subnet (if directly connected) or that it is what you think it is.

— Make sure there is a valid route to reach your destination in the IP routing table. Trace the connection through any routers along the path, and verify that they have a path to and from each of the routers that they must reach for packets to reach your source and destination networks.

— Check static routes for typos; make sure that any redistributed routes are actually being properly propagated.

— If multiple paths are in use, verify that there are no routing loops.

— If authentication is in use by any routing protocols, make sure that they are both using the correct passwords.

— On nonbroadcast multiaccess (NBMA) networks, such as ATM or Frame Relay, make sure that you have proper support for Layer 2 to Layer 3 mappings, and that protocols such as Open Shortest Path First (OSPF) are configured for the proper network type.

— Before proceeding to the next step, verify that you are able to reach the destination network from the source network and vice versa.

Step 4 Layer 4

— Check for any access lists or firewalls that might be dropping TCP packets.

— Verify that you have connectivity on TCP port 179. One BGP speaker, the passive TCP host, will receive a TCP request on port 179, and the other speaker, the active TCP host, will use a random TCP source port (beginning at 11,000) to initiate the TCP session.

— Check for retransmissions, out-of-order packets, or other TCP symptoms that might be pointing to network congestion or invalid configurations.

After verifying that all the prior conditions are not affecting the BGP session, use TCP **show** and **debug** commands to help narrow down the culprit. These commands, your BGP TCP connection troubleshooting tools, are listed in Table 8-3.

Table 8-3   *TCP Connection Troubleshooting Tools*

TCP Command	Command Description
show tcp	This command displays detailed information on each TCP session that the local router has formed with a remote peer. It can be used with BGP to show whether the local and remote BGP peers have formed an established TCP session, and show details about that session.
show tcp [brief][all] [I include 179]	This command displays a brief status of each of the TCP sessions that the local router has formed with a remote router. This is a basic summary command that you can use as another tool to verify the BGP TCP connection between peers.
debug ip tcp transactions	This command, which should be used with caution on a production router, displays information about TCP session changes. It enables you to troubleshoot a BGP TCP session, displaying information about TCP retransmissions or state changes.
debug ip tcp packet [in I out I address *IP-address* **I port** *port-number*]	This command displays detailed information about TCP packets. It can be used with the **in**, **out**, **address**, or **port** arguments to specify particular traffic, and must be used with extreme caution on a production router. With this command, you can monitor TCP packets sent and received by the local router. This information enables you to determine the cause of an unstable BGP TCP session and resolve route flapping or general connectivity issues.

If the **show tcp** command output for the peer IP address used for the BGP session is anything other than **ESTAB**, troubleshoot the TCP connection. The **show tcp** command, shown in Example 8-14, displays detailed information about the TCP session, and should, as a best practice, always be used as a TCP session troubleshooting command.

Example 8-14 **show tcp** *Command*

```
Alki# show tcp
Stand-alone TCP connection to host 192.168.32.2
Connection state is ESTAB, I/O status: 1, unread input bytes: 0
Local host: 192.168.32.1, Local port: 11009
Foreign host: 192.168.32.2, Foreign port: 179
Enqueued packets for retransmit: 0, input: 0  mis-ordered: 0 (0 bytes)
Event Timers (current time is 0x16681CC):
```

continues

Example 8-14 show tcp *Command (Continued)*

```
Timer          Starts    Wakeups              Next
Retrans        323       1                    0x0
TimeWait       0         0                    0x0
AckHold        320       164                  0x0
SendWnd        0         0                    0x0
KeepAlive      0         0                    0x0
GiveUp         0         0                    0x0
PmtuAger       0         0                    0x0
DeadWait       0         0                    0x0
iss: 3779523619  snduna: 3779529779  sndnxt: 3779529779    sndwnd:  16080
irs: 2902813429  rcvnxt: 2902819573  rcvwnd:        16099 delrcvwnd:    285
SRTT: 300 ms, RTTO: 303 ms, RTV: 3 ms, KRTT: 0 ms
minRTT: 20 ms, maxRTT: 300 ms, ACK hold: 200 ms
Flags: higher precedence, nagle
Datagrams (max data segment is 1460 bytes):
Rcvd: 556 (out of order: 0), with data: 320, total data bytes: 6143
Sent: 492 (retransmit: 1, fastretransmit: 0), with data: 321, total data bytes:
6159
```

Table 8-4 displays detailed information on the output of the **show tcp** command. You will probably never use all 20 lines of the command in day-to-day troubleshooting, but they might come in handy when you are troubleshooting TCP connection problems, such as too many retransmissions.

Table 8-4   show tcp *Command Output Explained*

Command Output	Output Description
`Stand-alone TCP connection to host 192.168.32.2`	Identifies TCP connection from the local router to host 192.168.32.2.
`Connection state is ESTAB`	Indicates an established TCP session.
	The **Connection state is** can be any of the following values:
	LISTEN—Indicates that the router is listening for a connection request
	SYNSENT—Indicates that the router is waiting for a connection request in return to a request that was sent (TCP-SYN message)
	SYNRCVD—Indicates that the router has sent and received a connection request and is now waiting for a connection acknowledgement (TCP-ACK message)
	ESTAB—Indicates an established TCP session TCP-SYN and ACK messages)

Table 8-4   **show tcp** *Command Output Explained (Continued)*

Command Output	Output Description
`Connection state is ESTAB` (*Continued*)	**FINWAIT1**— Indicates that the router is either waiting for a termination request or an acknowledgement to a previously sent termination request TCP-FIN ACK message)
	FINWAIT2— Indicates that the router is waiting for a termination request from a remote host (TCP-FIN message)
	CLOSEWAIT— Indicates that the router is waiting for a termination request from the user (TCP-FIN message)
	CLOSING—Indicates that the router is waiting for a termination request from a remote host (TCP-FIN message)
	LASTACK—Indicates that the router is waiting for a response to a termination request that was made to a remote host (TCP-FIN ACK message)
	TIMEWAIT—Indicates that the router is giving the remote host time to receive the connection termination request before closing the connection
	CLOSED—Indicates that there is no connection
	For a successful BGP session, the TCP session must always be in the ESTAB state.
`I/O status: 1`	Describes the status of the connection.
`unread input bytes: 0`	Indicates the number of bytes that have been read and are awaiting processing.
`Local host: 192.168.32.1, Local port: 11009`	Displays the local IP address and TCP port number.
	You can use this number to determine whether the local or remote router initiated the BGP session. If the TCP port is in the 11,000 range, the router initiated the session to a remote router at port 179.

continues

Table 8-4 show tcp *Command Output Explained (Continued)*

Command Output	Output Description
`Foreign host: 192.168.32.2, Foreign port: 179`	Displays the remote IP address and TCP port number for the connection.
	For BGP, you always look for values of 179 or a port in the 11,000 range.
`Enqueued packets for retransmit: 0, input: 0 mis-ordered: 0 (0 bytes)`	Displays the number of packets waiting to be retransmitted.
	Any value greater than 0 indicates packet retransmission and might point to TCP problems.

<pre>Event Timers (current time is 0x16681CC):
Timer   Starts   Wakeups   Next
Retrans   323   1   0x0
TimeWait   0   0   0x0
AckHold   320   164   0x0
SendWnd   0   0   0x0
KeepAlive   0   0   0x0
GiveUp   0   0   0x0
PmtuAger   0   0   0x0
DeadWait   0   0   0x0</pre>
	This section displays TCP timer information, in counter form for the current TCP session. (This information can be cleared with the **clear tcp statistics** command.)
	
	The *Event Timer* displays the amount of time that the system has been running in milliseconds.
	
	The *Timer* column describes the timers listed in the rows beneath.
	
	The *Starts* column describes the number of times that the counter has been started for this session.
	
	The *Wakeups* column describes the number of unacknowledged KEEPALIVES.
	
	The *Next* column shows the next time that the timer will go off.
	
	The *Retrans* timer displays the value of the timer used to time unacknowledged packets awaiting retransmission.
	
	The *TimeWait* timer shows the amount of time the system will wait to allow a remote system to receive a connection termination request.
	
	The *AckHold* timer is used to delay the transmission of acknowledgements to prevent network congestion.
	
	The *SendWnd* timer prevents TCP sessions from being lost due to missing acknowledgements.
	
	The *KeepAlive* timer is used to time the space between KEEPALIVE messages.

Table 8-4   **show tcp** *Command Output Explained (Continued)*

Command Output	Output Description
| ```
Event Timers (current time is 0x16681CC):
Timer          Starts    Wakeups       Next
Retrans          323          1        0x0
TimeWait           0          0        0x0
AckHold          320        164        0x0
SendWnd            0          0        0x0
KeepAlive          0          0        0x0
GiveUp             0          0        0x0
PmtuAger           0          0        0x0
DeadWait           0          0        0x0
``` | The *GiveUp* timer is the minimum time to wait before giving up on a pending resolution request. The *PmtuAger* timer is the timer that is used to keep track of the path MTU age-timer that can be changed using the **ip tcp path-mtu-discovery** [**age-timer** {*minutes* \| **indefinite**}] command. The *DeadWait* timer is the TCP DeadWait timer. |
`iss: 3779523619`	Displays the initial send sequence number, which is the initial sequence number sent during a new TCP session.
`snduna: 3779529779`	Displays the last unacknowledged sequence number that the router has sent.
`sndnxt: 3779529779`	Displays the next sequence number that will be sent.
`sndwnd:  16080`	Displays the remote host's TCP window size.
`irs: 2902813429`	Displays the initial receive sequence number.
`rcvnxt: 2902819573`	Displays the last sequence number that has been received and acknowledged.
`rcvwnd:     16099`	Displays the local router's TCP window size.
`delrcvwnd:    285`	Displays the delayed receive window which is the uncomputed value of the receive window.
`SRTT: 300 ms`	The smooth round-trip timer is a measurement of the average time that it takes a packet to be sent and acknowledged by the remote peer.
`RTTO: 303 ms`	The round-trip timeout in milliseconds.
`RTV: 3 ms`	The variance of the round-trip time in milliseconds.
`KRTT: 0 ms`	The new round-trip (K stands for Karn's algorithm) timeout. It measures the round-trip time, in milliseconds, for packets that have been retransmitted.
`minRTT: 20 ms`	The smallest round-trip timeout.
`maxRTT: 300 ms`	The largest round-trip timeout.

continues
```

Table 8-4 **show tcp** *Command Output Explained (Continued)*

Command Output	Output Description
`ACK hold: 200 ms`	The acknowledgment delay timeout used to delay acknowledgements to allow time to add data to the packet.
`Flags: higher precedence`	Specifies IP precedence values that might be present in the packets.
`nagle`	Specifies that the Nagle flag is set.
`Datagrams (max data segment is 1460 bytes):`	The largest data segment in bytes.
`Rcvd: 556 (out of order: 0, total data bytes: 6143`	The number of datagrams received. The number of datagrams that were received out of order. The total bytes of data received.
`Sent: 492 (retransmit: 1, fastretransmit: 0), with data: 321, total data bytes: 6159`	The number of datagrams sent. The number of datagrams that had to be retransmitted. The number of fast retransmissions. The number of datagrams that were sent that contained data. The total bytes of data received.

Two other frequently forgotten tools that enable you to troubleshoot a TCP connection are the **debug tcp transactions** and **debug tcp packet** commands. Output from the **debug tcp transactions** command is shown in Example 8-15.

Example 8-15 **debug ip tcp transactions** *Command*

```
Alki# debug ip tcp transactions
TCP special event debugging is on
Alki# clear ip bgp *
01:53:24: %BGP-5-ADJCHANGE: neighbor 192.168.32.2 Down User reset
Comment: BGP session reset at user request
01:53:24: TCP0: state was ESTAB -> FINWAIT1 [179 -> 192.168.32.2(11005)]
Comment: TCP session transitioned from ESTAB to FINWAIT1
01:53:24: TCP0: sending FIN
01:53:24: TCP0: state was FINWAIT1 -> FINWAIT2 [179 -> 192.168.32.2(11005)]
01:53:26: TCP0: FIN processed
01:53:26: TCP0: state was FINWAIT2 -> TIMEWAIT [179 -> 192.168.32.2(11005)]
Comment: TCP session was gracefully torn down and the router is waiting to close
the session between the two hosts on ports 179 and 110005
01:54:03: TCB8252932C created
01:54:03: TCP0: state was LISTEN -> SYNRCVD [179 -> 192.168.32.2(11006)]
Comment: BGP was listening for TCP connection request and received it on port
11006
```

Example 8-15 debug ip tcp transactions *Command (Continued)*

```
01:54:03: TCP0: Connection to 192.168.32.2:11006, received MSS 1460, MSS is 516
01:54:03: TCP: sending SYN, seq 1620953691, ack 2271616142
01:54:03: TCP0: Connection to 192.168.32.2:11006, advertising MSS 1460
01:54:03: TCP0: state was SYNRCVD -> ESTAB [179 -> 192.168.32.2(11006)]
Comment: The TCP session between the two routers on port 179 and 11006 was
successfully established
01:54:03: TCB820E59F0 callback, connection queue = 1
01:54:03: TCB820E59F0 accepting 8252932C from 192.168.32.2.11006
01:54:03: %BGP-5-ADJCHANGE: neighbor 192.168.32.2 Up
Comment: BGP session is ESTABLISHED
01:54:26: TCP0: state was TIMEWAIT -> CLOSED [179 -> 192.168.32.2(11005)]
01:54:26: TCB 0x82528E90 destroyed
Comment: The old TCP session between ports 179 and 11005 was closed the TCB
marker for the session was destroyed
```

After verifying that the TCP session between the routers is functioning properly, you can verify or troubleshoot the BGP session using the commands listed in Table 8-5.

Table 8-5   *BGP Neighbor Show and Debug Tools*

Command	Description
show ip bgp [*ip-address* | *prefix*]	Displays the BGP table, a summary, the table version, and the attributes associated with the paths listed in the table. The IP address or prefix can optionally be used to limit the information returned from the command.
show ip bgp neighbors [*ip-address*]	This command displays detailed information about each of the neighbors that the local router is configured to peer with, including the neighbor's BGP version, BGP router ID, finite-state machine (FSM) state, the number of messages received, and detailed TCP connection information. The IP address or prefix can optionally be used to limit the information returned from the command.
show ip bgp summary	This command displays a summarized version of the information about each of the BGP neighbors, including the neighbor's BGP router ID, table version, information about paths received from the neighbor, and the attributes assigned to those paths, the number of messages that have been sent and have been received, the FSM state, and the amount of time that the neighbor has been in the Established state.
debug ip bgp [*ip-address*]	The **debug ip bgp** command displays real-time information about all BGP peer relationships, showing FSM states, messages sent and received, capability negotiation, and routes received.

continues

Table 8-5 *BGP Neighbor Show and Debug Tools (Continued)*

Command	Description
debug ip bgp events	This command displays real-time information on BGP events, including BGP scanning, the local table for routes to be advertised, timers, and messages sent and received.
debug ip bgp [*ip-address*] **updates** [*access-list*] [**in** | **out**]	The **debug ip bgp updates** command displays real-time information about paths that have been received in UPDATE messages from peering BGP neighbors. This information includes paths received, installation of paths in the main IP routing table, and updates sent out to neighboring routers. The *IP-address* parameter enables you to specify updates from a specific neighbor. The **access-list** command enables you to limit the output from the command to certain updates. The **in** and **out** parameters enable you to specify incoming or outgoing updates.
debug ip bgp in [*ip-address*]	This command displays real-time information about incoming messages sent during a BGP session and paths that the local router has received from its neighbors.
debug ip bgp out [*ip-address*]	This command displays real-time information about outgoing messages sent during a BGP session and paths that the local router sends to its neighbors.
debug ip bgp keepalives	This command displays real-time information on KEEPALIVE messages sent and received by the local BGP speaker.
debug ip routing	This command enables you to help diagnose problems when BGP routes are not being added to the main IP routing table.

The **show ip bgp** Command

The **show ip bgp** command is a very handy tool that enables you to verify the local BGP configuration, check path attributes, and troubleshoot problems with BGP route advertisement. This command lists a brief summary of the status of each path; the next hop used to reach the path; and the MED, LOCAL_PREF, WEIGHT, AS_PATH, and ORIGIN attributes for the route. Example 8-16 shows an example of the **show ip bgp** command output, and Table 8-6 describes the output from that command.

Example 8-16 **show ip bgp** *Command Output Example*

```
Alki# show ip bgp
BGP table version is 5, local router ID is 172.16.20.1
Status codes: s suppressed, d damped, h history, * valid, > best, i - internal
Origin codes: i - IGP, e - EGP, ? - incomplete
   Network          Next Hop          Metric LocPrf Weight Path
```

Example 8-16 **show ip bgp** *Command Output Example (Continued)*

```
*> 10.1.1.0/24      192.168.32.2         0            0 600 i
*> 10.1.2.0/24      192.168.32.2         0            0 600 i
*> 172.16.14.0/24   0.0.0.0              0        32768 i
*> 172.16.20.0/24   0.0.0.0              0        32768 i
```

Table 8-6   **show ip bgp** *Command Output Explained*

Command Output	Output Description
`BGP table version is 5`	The current version of the BGP table. This number is increased each time the table changes.
`local router ID is 172.16.20.1`	The local BGP router ID. Unless explicitly configured, this number is generally the highest loopback IP address. The BGP router ID is explicitly set using the **bgp router-id** command.
	Notice that the BGP local router ID does not match the interface that the router is using for the BGP session. As a best practice, you should always configure your router to use a specific router ID to avoid any future issues that might occur if you add new BGP peers or want to load share over multiple BGP paths.
	When troubleshooting a BGP connection, if one of the BGP peers is not configured to use the proper IP address (the BGP router ID) for its remote peer, the BGP session will not come up. This might never become an issue when you are working with a router that only has one E-BGP peer with one directly connected interface; if the router has more than one E-BGP peer that is not directly connected, however, you might need to add a route and use the **ebgp-multihop** command to specify that the peers are not directly connected. The **ebgp-multihop** command is covered later in this chapter.

`Status codes:`
`s suppressed,`
`d damped,`
`h history,`
`* valid,`
`> best,`
`i - internal`
	The status codes display the status for each path in the BGP table.

	suppressed (s)—Routes that have been suppressed by the local BGP configuration and are not advertised to remote peers but are still contained in the local BGP tables.
	dampened (d)—Routes that are being dampened by a remote peer.
	history (h)—Shows that dampening is enabled for this route.
	valid (*)—Routes that have been verified as reachable; routes that are not marked with an asterisk sign are not used by BGP and will not be installed in the main routing table.
	best (>)—The best path to reach a destination. BGP stores all paths to each network destination; however, it only uses the best path for the main routing table and only advertises the best path to its neighbors.
	internal (i)—BGP learned the route by means of an IGP routing process.

continues

Table 8-6 show ip bgp *Command Output Explained (Continued)*

Command Output	Output Description

`Origin codes:`
`i - IGP`
`e - EGP`
`? - incomplete`
	The origin codes are the ORIGIN attribute for the route. The origin code can be found to the far-right side for each path in the output of this command.
	
	i - IGP—Learned through an I-BGP session. Most routes will have the **i** origin code because they were initially learned by means of local configuration.
	
	e - EGP—Learned through an EGP session. These routes are not often seen, unless the router is peering with an EGP peer.
	
	? - INCOMPLETE—The route was learned by an unknown origination. This origin is generally used if the route was learned by BGP through route redistribution with an IGP.

`Network`	The network that is being described by the command output in *IP address/ mask* form.
`Next Hop`	The NEXT_HOP attribute for the network. This is the next hop that BGP will use to reach the network. If this next hop is unreachable, the route will not be marked as valid. The NEXT_HOP attribute is also passed on by BGP to the main IP routing table and might cause reachability problems when used with I-BGP if it is not reachable by downstream routers.
`Metric`	The MED attribute, which is used when there are multiple exit points to a network. By default, this metric is set to 0 and must be explicitly configured.
`LocPrf`	The LOCAL_PREF attribute for the path, used when there are locally preferred paths to a network. The default LOCAL_PREF for I-BGP peers is 100.
`Weight`	The locally configured WEIGHT attribute for a path. The default weight for a locally originated route is 0, and the default weight for a route learned by means of a peer is 32,768. Remember, the WEIGHT attribute is Cisco proprietary and is not passed on to *any* BGP peer; it is only locally significant.
`Path`	The AS_PATH attribute for the path; this attribute lists the path of E-BGP autonomous systems that the route has passed through. The rightmost entries for the AS path is the originating AS. Locally originated routes—that is, paths that originated from the local AS—do not contain an autonomous system path entry until they leave the AS.

The **show ip bgp regexp** command can also be used with a regular expression to create AS path access lists, or just to find all routes originating from a particular autonomous system. AS access lists and regular expressions are covered in Chapter 9.

show ip bgp neighbors Command

The **show ip bgp neighbors** command is one of the commands that you will commonly use to troubleshoot and verify BGP peer sessions. This command displays a wealth of detailed information about each BGP peer session and the TCP parameters for each session. A number of lines in this command prove invaluable when troubleshooting BGP problems, and it should be one of your best tools to use for BGP. Example 8-17 shows the **show ip bgp neighbors** command output for the Alki router.

Example 8-17 **show ip bgp neighbors** *Command Output*

```
Alki# show ip bgp neighbors
BGP neighbor is 192.168.32.2,  remote AS 600, external link
  BGP version 4, remote router ID 192.168.32.2
  BGP state = Established, up for 01:15:35
  Last read 00:00:34, hold time is 180, keepalive interval is 60 seconds
  Neighbor capabilities:
    Route refresh: advertised and received(old & new)
    Address family IPv4 Unicast: advertised and received
  Received 168 messages, 0 notifications, 0 in queue
  Sent 174 messages, 0 notifications, 0 in queue
  Route refresh request: received 0, sent 0
  Default minimum time between advertisement runs is 30 seconds
 For address family: IPv4 Unicast
  BGP table version 5, neighbor version 5
  Index 1, Offset 0, Mask 0x2
  2 accepted prefixes consume 72 bytes
  Prefix advertised 12, suppressed 0, withdrawn 0
  Number of NLRIs in the update sent: max 2, min 0
  Connections established 6; dropped 5
  Last reset 01:16:14, due to User reset
Connection state is ESTAB, I/O status: 1, unread input bytes: 0
Local host: 192.168.32.1, Local port: 179
Foreign host: 192.168.32.2, Foreign port: 11006
Enqueued packets for retransmit: 0, input: 0  mis-ordered: 0 (0 bytes)
Event Timers (current time is 0xADA668):
Timer          Starts   Wakeups          Next
Retrans           81        0            0x0
TimeWait           0        0            0x0
AckHold           79       40            0x0
SendWnd            0        0            0x0
KeepAlive          0        0            0x0
GiveUp             0        0            0x0

PmtuAger           0        0            0x0
DeadWait           0        0            0x0
```

continues

Example 8-17 show ip bgp neighbors *Command Output (Continued)*

```
iss: 1620953691   snduna: 1620955275   sndnxt: 1620955275      sndwnd:  16270
irs: 2271616141   rcvnxt: 2271617706   rcvwnd:       16289  delrcvwnd:     95
SRTT: 300 ms, RTTO: 303 ms, RTV: 3 ms, KRTT: 0 ms
minRTT: 20 ms, maxRTT: 300 ms, ACK hold: 200 ms
Flags: passive open, nagle, gen tcbs

Datagrams (max data segment is 1460 bytes):
Rcvd: 126 (out of order: 0), with data: 79, total data bytes: 1564
Sent: 122 (retransmit: 0, fastretransmit: 0), with data: 80, total data bytes:
1583
```

This command enables you to troubleshoot a host of problems, fine-tune BGP performance, and verify configurations. For instance, the current BGP state and the time that the neighbor relationship has been established can be viewed by entering **show ip bgp neighbors | include BGP state**. The number of prefixes received and the amount of memory they consume can be referenced using **show ip bgp neighbors | include accepted**. The number of connections that have been established and dropped by the peers can be viewed using **show ip bgp neighbors | include Connections**. And you can quickly display the reason for the last connection reset by using **show ip bgp neighbors | include Last reset**. The output of the **show ip bgp neighbors** command is explained in detail in Table 8-7.

Table 8-7   **show ip bgp neighbors** *Command Output Explained*

Command Output	Output Description
`BGP neighbor is 192.168.32.2`	The IP address for the remote BGP peer.
`remote AS 600`	The remote BGP AS number.
`external link`	The BGP session type.
`BGP version 4`	The BGP version number (that was agreed on by both peers) for the session with the remote peer.
`remote router ID 192.168.32.2`	The remote peer's BGP router ID. Remember that this is not always the IP address of the directly connected interface.

Table 8-7   **show ip bgp neighbors** *Command Output Explained (Continued)*

Command Output	Output Description
`BGP state = Established`	The current BGP FSM state. Possible states are the following: Idle Connect Active OpenSent OpenConfirm Established You will probably only ever see the Idle, Active, and Established states.
`up for 01:15:35`	The amount of time that the current BGP session has been up (in an established state in a for: *hours*, *minutes*, and *seconds* format.
`Last read 00:00:34`	The last time a message from the remote peer was received and read.
`hold time is 180`	The current hold-timer value, which is the amount of time between messages from its peer. The default hold time is 180 seconds, which is 3 times the KeepAlive timer.
`keepalive interval is 60 seconds`	The KeepAlive timer interval for this session. The KeepAlive timer specifies the amount of time that a BGP peer waits before sending a KEEPALIVE message. If a KEEPALIVE is not received within 3 KEEPALIVE intervals, the hold timer expires, a NOTIFICATION message is sent, and the session terminates.

`Neighbor capabilities:`
`    Route refresh: advertised and received (old & new)`
`    Address family IPv4 Unicast: advertised and received`
	The negotiated capabilities for the session between the local and remote peers:
	
	For a list of BGP capabilities, refer to the "BGP Capabilities Advertisement" section in Chapter 7, "BGP-4 Theory."
	
	The route refresh capability allows for the request of dynamic inbound or outbound updates, without clearing the BGP session.

continues

Table 8-7 **show ip bgp neighbors** *Command Output Explained (Continued)*

Command Output	Output Description
```Neighbor capabilities: Route refresh: advertised and received (old & new) Address family IPv4 Unicast: advertised and received```	There are different IPv4 address families that might appear in this field, depending on the configuration. • IPv4 unicast • IPv4 multicast • VPNv4 unicast The address family for IPv4 unicast capability allows the propagation and reception of IPv4 unicast paths. The address family for IPv4 multicast capability allows the propagation and reception of IPv4 multicast paths a multiprotocol BGP function. The address family for IPv4 VPN capability allows the propagations and reception of IPv4 VPN unicast paths.
```Received 168 messages```	The total number of BGP messages received by this peer, including the following: • OPEN • UPDATE • KEEPALIVE • NOTIFICATION
```0 notifications```	The number of NOTIFICATION messages that have been received by this peer. NOTIFICATION messages are error conditions and should be examined, monitored, and noted upon arrival.
```0 in queue```	The number of messages waiting to be processed. A high number of messages in the queue could indicate congestion, lack of memory, CPU time, or a high number of BGP peers sending messages on a regular basis. The queue normally contains messages when a production router is currently exchanging updates with multiple peers. If this situation persists, it might be time to examine the router for BGP performance improvements.

Table 8-7   **show ip bgp neighbors** *Command Output Explained (Continued)*

Command Output	Output Description
`Sent 174 messages`	The total number of messages sent by the local router to the remote peer, including the following: • OPEN • UPDATE • NOTIFICATION • KEEPALIVE
`0 notifications`	The number of NOTIFICATION messages sent from the local router to the remote peer.
`0 in queue`	The number of messages in the queue waiting to be transmitted.
`Route refresh request: received 0, sent 0`	The number of ROUTE-REFRESH messages that have been sent to, or received from, the remote peer.
`Default minimum time between advertisement runs is 30 seconds.`	The default minimum time between UPDATE messages.
`For address family: IPv4 Unicast`	The address family for the BGP tables mentioned in the next field.
`BGP table version 5`	The current local BGP table version. This number increments each time a change occurs. Mismatched table numbers could indicate a problem between the BGP peers.
`neighbor version 5`	The current remote BGP table version.
`Index 1, Offset 0, Mask 0x2`	Internal BGP table information.
`2 accepted prefixes consume 72 bytes`	The number of prefixes accepted by the local peer and the amount of memory in bytes that those prefixes consume.
`Prefix advertised 12`	The number of prefixes advertised by the local peer.

continues

Table 8-7 show ip bgp neighbors *Command Output Explained (Continued)*

Command Output	Output Description
`suppressed 0`	The number of prefixes suppressed by the local peer.
`withdrawn 0`	The number of prefixes that have been withdrawn by the local peer. A high number of withdrawn routes could indicate route instability and can be corrected by fixing the instability or adding a static route with high administrative distance to a null interface.
`Number of NLRIs in the update sent: max 2, min 0`	The number of network layer reachability information (NLRI) or paths sent in UPDATE messages. **max**—Indicates the maximum number of NLRIs that were sent in a single UPDATE message. **min**—Indicates the minimum number of NLRIs that were sent in a single UPDATE messages.
`Connections established 6; dropped 5`	The number of sessions established between the local and remote peers since the last time the router booted. A high number of dropped sessions indicates a route-flapping condition and should be corrected to prevent route dampening.
`Last reset 01:16:14, due to User reset`	The time of the last BGP session reset (in hours: minutes: seconds format) and the reason for the reset.

Table 8-7   **show ip bgp neighbors** *Command Output Explained (Continued)*

Command Output	Output Description
| ```
Connection state is ESTAB, I/O status: 1, unread
  input bytes: 0
Local host: 192.168.32.1, Local port: 179
Foreign host: 192.168.32.2, Foreign port: 11006
Enqueued packets for retransmit: 0, input: 0
  mis-ordered: 0 (0 bytes)
Event Timers (current time is 0xADA668):
Timer        Starts   Wakeups           Next
Retrans          81        0            0x0
TimeWait          0        0            0x0
AckHold          79       40            0x0
SendWnd           0        0            0x0
KeepAlive         0        0            0x0
GiveUp            0        0            0x0
PmtuAger          0        0            0x0
DeadWait          0        0            0x0
iss: 1620953691  snduna: 1620955275  sndnxt: 1620955275
  sndwnd:  16270
irs: 2271616141  rcvnxt: 2271617706  rcvwnd:      16289
  delrcvwnd:      95
SRTT: 300 ms, RTTO: 303 ms, RTV: 3 ms, KRTT: 0 ms
minRTT: 20 ms, maxRTT: 300 ms, ACK hold: 200 ms
Flags: passive open, nagle, gen tcbs

Datagrams (max data segment is 1460 bytes):
Rcvd: 126 (out of order: 0), with data: 79,
  total data bytes: 1564
Sent: 122 (retransmit: 0, fastretransmit: 0),
  with data: 80, total data bytes: 1583
``` | The remaining part of the **show ip bgp neighbors** command output is the same as the **show tcp** command output. For details on these items, refer to Table 8-3. |

Essential parts of the **show ip bgp neighbors** command can be parsed using output modifiers (and command aliases, if configured) to view specific parts of the command output when troubleshooting. You can also use this command with the *ip-address* **advertised-networks** and *ip-address* **routes** keywords to view information on routes sent to or received from a specific neighbor, as shown in Example 8-18.

Example 8-18 *Displaying BGP Route Advertisements with the* **show ip bgp neighbors** *Command*

```
Madison# show ip bgp neighbors 192.168.32.1 advertised-routes
BGP table version is 3, local router ID is 10.1.1.10
Status codes: s suppressed, d damped, h history, * valid, > best, i - internal,
              r RIB-failure
Origin codes: i - IGP, e - EGP, ? - incomplete

   Network          Next Hop            Metric LocPrf Weight Path
*> 6.0.0.0          0.0.0.0                  0         32768 i
Madison# show ip bgp neighbors 192.168.32.1 routes
BGP table version is 3, local router ID is 10.1.1.10
```

continues
```

Example 8-18 *Displaying BGP Route Advertisements with the* **show ip bgp neighbors** *Command (Continued)*

```
Status codes: s suppressed, d damped, h history, * valid, > best, i - internal,
              r RIB-failure
Origin codes: i - IGP, e - EGP, ? - incomplete

   Network          Next Hop            Metric LocPrf Weight Path
*> 5.0.0.0          192.168.32.1             0             0 5300 i

Total number of prefixes 1
```

The first part of the preceding example shows how the **show ip bgp neighbors 192.168.32.1 advertised-routes** command is used to display routes advertised to peer 192.168.32.1. The second part of the example shows how the **show ip bgp neighbors 192.168.32.1 routes** command is used to display routes received from the 192.168.32.1 peer. These commands can prove very useful for troubleshooting BGP routing policies.

show ip bgp summary Command

The **show ip bgp summary** command displays a summarized version of the output displayed by the **show ip bgp neighbors** command, including information about each neighbor. This command enables you to obtain a brief snapshot of the state of each of the BGP peer sessions, to troubleshoot connection or performance issues, and to check the amount of memory that BGP is using to store path information. Example 8-19 shows an example of the output from the **show ip bgp summary** command, and Table 8-8 shows the descriptions for the output in detail.

Example 8-19 **show ip bgp summary** *Command Output*

```
Alki# show ip bgp summary
BGP router identifier 172.16.20.1, local AS number 5300
BGP table version is 5, main routing table version 5
4 network entries and 4 paths using 532 bytes of memory
2 BGP path attribute entries using 120 bytes of memory
1 BGP AS-PATH entries using 24 bytes of memory
0 BGP route-map cache entries using 0 bytes of memory
0 BGP filter-list cache entries using 0 bytes of memory
BGP activity 4/0 prefixes, 4/0 paths, scan interval 60 secs
Neighbor        V    AS MsgRcvd MsgSent   TblVer  InQ OutQ Up/Down  State/PfxRcd
192.168.32.2    4   600      20      21        5    0    0 00:16:47         2
```

Table 8-8   **show ip bgp summary** *Command Output Explained*

Command Output	Output Description
`BGP router identifier 172.16.20.1,`	The local BGP router ID.
`localAS number 5300`	The local AS number.
`BGP table version is 5,`	The local BGP table version.
`main routing table version 5`	The main IP routing table version.
`network entries and  paths using 532 bytes` `of memory`	The number of network entries, number of paths, and amount of memory consumed by those entries.
`2 BGP path attribute entries using 120` `bytes of memory`	The number of BGP path attribute entries and the amount of memory consumed by those entries.
`1 BGP AS-PATH entries using 24 bytes of` `memory`	The number of AS_PATH entries and the amount of memory used for those entries.
`0 BGP route-map cache entries using 0 bytes` `of memory`	The number of route map cache entries and the amount of memory that they consume.
`0 BGP filter-list cache entries using 0` `bytes of memory`	The number of filter list cache entries and the amount of memory used for those entries.
`BGP activity 4/0 prefixes`	The number of prefixes contained in the local BGP table.
`4/0 paths`	The number of paths contained in the local BGP table.
`scan interval 60 secs`	The interval at which the BGP Scanner scans the BGP tables for changes and reachability. The default BGP Scanner interval is 60 seconds, and can, with caution, be changed to a value between 5 and 60 seconds using the **bgp scan-time** command.
`Neighbor` `192.168.32.2`	The remote peer's IP address.
`V` `4`	The remote peer's BGP version.
`AS` `600`	The remote peer's AS number.

continues

Table 8-8 **show ip bgp summary** *Command Output Explained (Continued)*

Command Output	Output Description
MsgRcvd 20	The number of messages received from the remote peer (including OPEN, UPDATE, NOTIFICATION, and KEEPALIVE).
MsgSent 21	The number of messages sent to the remote peer (including OPEN, UPDATE, NOTIFICATION, and KEEPALIVE).
TblVer 5	The last version of the BGP table that was sent to the remote peer.
InQ 0	The number of incoming messages waiting to be processed.
OutQ 0	The number of outgoing messages waiting to be transmitted.
Up/Down 00:16:47	The amount of time that the BGP session between the two peers has either been up or down.
State/PfxRcd 2	The number of prefixes received from the remote peer once a BGP session has been established. The current BGP FSM state if the state is not established. • Idle • Connect • Active • OpenSent • OpenConfirm

Now that you have added the BGP **show** and **debug** commands to your BGP troubleshooting toolkit, in the next section, the use of BGP messages, another BGP troubleshooting tool, is introduced and explained.

Using BGP Messages as Symptoms

One of the best ways to troubleshoot a BGP problem is to use the BGP messages as diagnostic tools. Cisco IOS Software displays messages in a number of different ways, depending on configuration. As a normal best practice, you will probably disable console logging using the **no logging console** command, and use a virtual terminal line to perform all configuration and troubleshooting. Because the messages are not logged directly to the virtual terminal lines, unless you use the **terminal monitor** command each time you troubleshoot, you might not see the output from the BGP messages, unless you enable buffered logging using the **logging buffered** command to save the messages in memory.

Another Cisco IOS Software feature that is generally overlooked is the logging configuration. The default logging behavior is to log each event in the log according to the router's uptime. You might prefer this behavior, or you might want to have the router display messages in a date/time view. You can configure this using the **service timestamps debug datetime msec** and **service timestamps log datetime msec** commands. Using these commands, you can have the router display events with an accompanying date/time stamp rather than router uptime, which comes in quite handy when troubleshooting an event that occurred hours or days in the past.

After configuring the router's logging style, you can use the messages generated by the software processes to troubleshoot problems. Cisco IOS Software has five major message-logging conditions, varying in severity, as shown in Table 8-9.

Table 8-9 *Cisco IOS Software Event Conditions*

Event Condition Number	Event Condition	Condition Description
2	Critical	A critical condition requiring immediate action
3	Error	An error condition requiring immediate action
4	Warning	A warning condition showing an event that might cause issues
5	Notification	A notification message displaying a message about an important but normal event
6	Informational	Informational messages about an issue that exists but is not significant to router operation

BGP messages are displayed in the format shown in Figure 8-2.

Figure 8-2 *Cisco IOS Software Message Format*

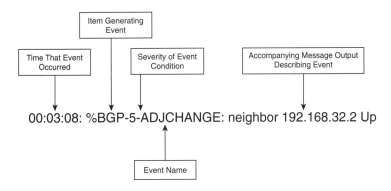

Based on the output displayed in the preceding figure, you can see that a BGP adjacency change event occurred with neighbor 192.168.32.2, and the BGP adjacency state changed to up. Example 8-20 shows how output from the **show logging** command enables you to diagnose and troubleshoot a BGP route-flapping problem in a matter of seconds.

Example 8-20 *Messages from the* **show logging** *Command*

```
00:00:51: %LINK-3-UPDOWN: Interface Serial0/0, changed state to down
00:00:52: %LINEPROTO-5-UPDOWN: Line protocol on Interface Serial0/0, changed
 state to down
00:02:23: %LINK-3-UPDOWN: Interface Serial0/0, changed state to up
00:02:24: %LINEPROTO-5-UPDOWN: Line protocol on Interface Serial0/0, changed
state to up
00:03:08: %BGP-5-ADJCHANGE: neighbor 192.168.32.2 Up
00:44:23: %LINK-3-UPDOWN: Interface Serial0/0, changed state to down
00:44:23: %BGP-5-ADJCHANGE: neighbor 192.168.32.2 Down Interface flap
00:44:24: %LINEPROTO-5-UPDOWN: Line protocol on Interface Serial0/0, changed
state to down
00:46:49: %LINK-3-UPDOWN: Interface Serial0/0, changed state to up
00:46:50: %LINEPROTO-5-UPDOWN: Line protocol on Interface Serial0/0, changed
state to up
00:47:22: %BGP-5-ADJCHANGE: neighbor 192.168.32.2 Up
```

In this example, you can see that interface Serial 0/0 repeatedly transitioned from an up to down state, causing the BGP peer relationship with neighbor 192.168.32.2 to flap as well. The BGP messages display inline with the LINK-3-UPDOWN messages, making the symptoms of the BGP route-flapping issue easier to diagnose. In this case, it is fairly easy to isolate the BGP route-flapping problem to an issue with connection on the Serial 0/0 interface. Table 8-10 displays a list of BGP messages and their descriptions.

Table 8-10 *BGP Messages*

BGP Message	Message Description
%BGP-2-INSUFMEM	This is a critical BGP message indicating that the router does not have sufficient memory to continue with the specified operation.
	This error frequently occurs on routers with insufficient memory to handle BGP operations. (You might see this error right before a reload when debugging BGP on a 2500 series lab router.) To remedy the situation, you might need to upgrade the router. If it cannot exceed the current memory configuration, upgrade the memory for the router, if possible, or use the **show memory** commands to find unnecessary processes and shut them down. If a lab router (not a production router—please) does not have the capacity to run BGP, you might need to save the configuration before debugging so that configurations are not lost during a reload.

Table 8-10 *BGP Messages (Continued)*

BGP Message	Message Description
%BGP-3-ADDROUTE	This error message indicates an error condition where the router cannot add a route.
%BGP-3-BADMASK	This error message indicates that the router was unable to install a route in the local routing table because of an error with the subnet mask for the prefix specified with the message accompanying the error.
%BGP-3-BADROUTEMAP	This error message indicates that one of the route maps (specified in the message accompanying the error) is not appropriate for its intended use.
%BGP-3-BGP_INCONSISTENT	This error indicates a BGP data structure inconsistency; this is an internal BGP error.
%BGP-3-DELPATH	This error indicates that an error occurred while trying to delete a path.
%BGP-3-DELROUTE	This error indicates that an error occurred while trying to delete a route from the router's internal BGP data structure, called a Radix Trie. This is an internal BGP error.
%BGP-3-INSUFCHUNKS	This error indicates an insufficient chunk definition; Cisco IOS Software allocates chunks to processes, similarly to memory allocation.
%BGP-3-MARTIAN_IP	This error message indicates that the local BGP speaker received a route with an invalid IP address or prefix on a remote router.
%BGP-3-MAXPATHS	This error message indicates that there are too many equal cost paths to a destination network. The output from this error includes the IP prefix and mask, what the error was about, and the current maximum number of allowed paths. You can fix this error by using the **maximum-paths** command under the BGP router configuration mode and specifying a higher number of paths (from 1 to 6).

continues

Table 8-10 *BGP Messages (Continued)*

BGP Message	Message Description
%BGP-3-MAXPFXEXCEEDED and %BGP-4-MAXPFX:	These messages indicate that the neighboring BGP speaker sent more prefixes than the local speaker is configured to receive. The IP address of the remote BGP speaker sending the updates, and the maximum prefix limitation number, in decimal, are displayed as output with these messages.
	The %BGP-3 message is an error message that specifies that the maximum number of prefixes has been reached, and the connection is being terminated. The %BGP-4 message is just a warning indicating that the number of prefixes was exceeded. The type of message received depends on the local BGP configuration.
	This is the command used to configure a maximum prefix limitation; its use is covered in Chapter 9.
%BGP-3-NEGCOUNTER	This is a BGP internal error that occurs when the number of prefixes received counter is a value less than 0.
%BGP-3-NOBITFIELD	This error message indicates that the router was unable to create an index entry for the peer displayed in the message output.
	This message occurs when the router does not have sufficient memory to open a BGP session with the remote peer; to correct this situation, either add more memory or close other unnecessary processes.
%BGP-3-NOTIFICATION	This error message indicates that the router received or sent a notification to the remote peer specified in the message output. The notification message type is also displayed in the message output, and the session with the remote peer is terminated.
%BGP-3-RADIXINIT	This error message indicates that the local router was unable to create the BGP Radix Trie because it was unable to allocate sufficient memory. To correct this condition, either add more memory or disable other unnecessary processes.
%BGP-5-ADJCHANGE	This notification message indicates that an adjacency change has occurred with the peer specified in the message output. The output from this message also specifies whether the BGP adjacency transitioned to either an up (Established) or down (Idle) state.
%BGP-5-VERSION_WRAP	This notification message indicates that the local BGP table exceeded the maximum allowed size and was wrapped.

Table 8-10   *BGP Messages (Continued)*

BGP Message	Message Description
%BGP-6-AS-PATH	This informational message indicates that the local router received an UPDATE message containing an invalid AS_PATH attribute. The message output includes the incorrect AS_PATH attribute and the sender's IP address.
%BGP-6-NEXTHOP	This informational message appears when the local speaker receives an update with an illegal NEXT_HOP attribute. When this event occurs, the route is ignored and BGP operation continues. The output of this message includes the IP address of the prefix received in the UPDATE message and the neighbor that sent the message.

The BGP Idle/Active Scenario

If you remember from the previous chapter, the BGP Finite-State Machine (FSM) transitions through several other states before reaching the Established state where BGP neighbors actually begin sending and receiving updates. As a brief review, Figure 8-3 shows how the BGP FSM transitions from the Idle to Established states.

Notice that if an error occurs between the Connect and OpenSent states, the FSM transitions to the Active state. If the FSM is still unable to transition from the Active state to the Connect or OpenSent state, it returns to the Idle state. Because the router actually stays only in Connect and OpenSent states for a brief amount of time while waiting to move on to the next state, one troubleshooting symptom to note is the constant transition between the Idle and Active states. If you take careful note when peers are alternating between the Active and Idle states, you will notice that the peer also transitions between the Connect state and if a TCP session is formed, the peer transitions between the OpenSent state as well. This problem generally occurs when there is an issue with the TCP session. If you used your layered troubleshooting methodology up to this point, and the peers are constantly transitioning from the Idle to Active states, you will verify Layers 1 through 3 are up and operating properly before troubleshooting BGP specifically.

Take the Alien network, shown in Figure 8-4, for example. In this example, the Mulder and Scully routers have been configured to peer with each other in AS 22801. Because both routers belong to AS 22801, they are I-BGP peers and do not have to be directly connected. Therefore, the Mulder router connects to router Krycek over network 148.201.100.0/24, which connects to the MrX router over the 148.202.100.0/24 network. Finally, the 148.202.100.0/24 network connects to the Scully router on the 148.203.100.0/24 network.

Figure 8-3 *BGP Finite-State Machine Review*

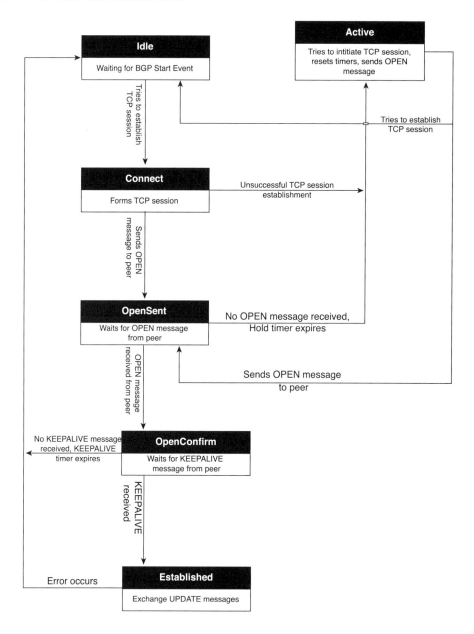

Figure 8-4   *The Alien Network*

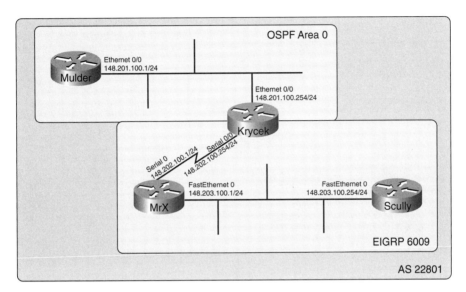

After configuring BGP, however, when the **show ip bgp summary** command is entered, you see that the routers are stuck in the Idle and Active states. Example 8-21 shows the configuration for the Mulder router. The Mulder router connects to the Krycek router over interface FastEthernet 0, and that interface is running in OSPF area 0.

Example 8-21 *Mulder Router Configuration*

```
hostname Mulder
<text omitted>
!
interface Ethernet0
 ip address 148.201.100.1 255.255.255.0
!
router ospf 1
 network 148.201.100.0 0.0.0.255 area 0
!
router bgp 22801
 bgp log-neighbor-changes
 network 10.1.1.0 mask 255.255.255.0
 network 10.2.2.0 mask 255.255.255.0
 neighbor 148.203.100.254 remote-as 22801
```

The Krycek router is connected to the Mulder router on its Ethernet 0/0 interface, which runs in OSPF area 0. The Krycek router also connects to the MrX router across a serial interface, which is running EIGRP process 6009. Example 8-22 shows the configuration for the Krycek router and the output of the **show ip route** command showing connectivity to and from the Mulder and Scully networks.

Example 8-22 *Krycek Router Configuration*

```
hostname Krycek

<text omitted>
!
interface Ethernet0/0
 ip address 148.201.100.254 255.255.255.0
!
interface Serial0/0
 ip address 148.202.100.254 255.255.255.0
!
router eigrp 6009
 passive-interface Ethernet0/0
 network 148.202.0.0
 auto-summary
!
router ospf 1
 passive-interface Serial0/0
 network 148.201.100.0 0.0.0.255 area 0
!
Krycek# show ip route
     148.201.0.0/24 is subnetted, 1 subnets
C       148.201.100.0 is directly connected, Ethernet0/0
     148.202.0.0/24 is subnetted, 1 subnets
C       148.202.100.0 is directly connected, Serial0/0
D    148.203.0.0/16 [90/2172416] via 148.202.100.1, 00:45:21, Serial0/0
```

Example 8-23 shows the configuration for the MrX router, which connects to the Krycek router on interface Serial 0 and the Scully router on interface FastEthernet 0.

Example 8-23 *MrX Router Configuration*

```
hostname MrX
<text omitted>
!
interface Serial0
 ip address 148.202.100.1 255.255.255.0
!
interface FastEthernet0
 ip address 148.203.100.1 255.255.255.0
!
router eigrp 6009
 network 148.202.0.0
 network 148.203.0.0
 auto-summary
```

Finally, Example 8-24 shows the configuration for the Scully router.

Example 8-24 *Scully Router Configuration*

```
hostname Scully
<text omitted>
!
interface FastEthernet0
 ip address 148.203.100.254 255.255.255.0
!
router eigrp 6009
 network 148.203.0.0
 auto-summary
!
router bgp 22801
 bgp log-neighbor-changes
 network 192.168.8.0
 network 192.168.9.0
 neighbor 148.201.100.1 remote-as 22801
```

Example 8-25 shows the output of the **show ip bgp summary** and **show ip bgp neighbors** commands, which give several hints as to the cause of the problem.

Example 8-25 *Troubleshooting Command Details*

```
Scully# show ip bgp summary
BGP router identifier 192.168.1.1, local AS number 22801
BGP table version is 1, main routing table version 1
Neighbor        V    AS MsgRcvd MsgSent   TblVer  InQ OutQ Up/Down  State/PfxRcd
148.201.100.1   4 22801       0       0        0    0    0 never    Active
Scully# show ip bgp neighbor
BGP neighbor is 148.201.100.1,  remote AS 22801, internal link
  BGP version 4, remote router ID 0.0.0.0
  BGP state = Active
  Last read 00:23:24, hold time is 180, keepalive interval is 60 seconds
  Received 0 messages, 0 notifications, 0 in queue
  Sent 0 messages, 0 notifications, 0 in queue
  Route refresh request: received 0, sent 0
  Default minimum time between advertisement runs is 5 seconds
 For address family: IPv4 Unicast
  BGP table version 1, neighbor version 0
  Index 1, Offset 0, Mask 0x2
  0 accepted prefixes consume 0 bytes
  Prefix advertised 0, suppressed 0, withdrawn 0
  Connections established 0; dropped 0
  Last reset never
  No active TCP connection
```

Notice that the **show ip bgp summary** command shows that the remote peer 148.201.200.1 is in an Active state and no messages have been sent or received on this connection. This would indicate that a BGP session has never been established between these peers. Next, notice that the **show ip bgp neighbor** command does not include the BGP router ID for the remote host, which means that the local host has never connected to the remote host to learn the router ID. Also notice that zero connections have been established or dropped, there have never been reset connections, and there are currently no active TCP connections. If you follow the troubleshooting methodology mentioned earlier in the chapter, you will probably use the following steps to investigate the cause of the missing TCP session.

Step 1   Verify Layer 1 connectivity.

— Use **show** commands to verify that the Ethernet interfaces are up on the Mulder and Scully routers.

— Verify that each router along the path between Mulder and Scully is up and operational.

Step 2   Verify Layer 2 connectivity.

— Check to make sure that there are no Layer 2 problems on any of the routers along the path between the Mulder and Scully routers.

Step 3   Verify Layer 3 connectivity.

— Verify Layer 3 connectivity between the Mulder and Scully routers.

— Ping from the Mulder router to the Scully router, and check the local routing table for a route to the remote peer's network.

```
Mulder# ping 148.203.100.254
Type escape sequence to abort.
Sending 5, 100-byte ICMP Echos to 148.203.100.254, timeout is 2 seconds:
.....
Success rate is 0 percent (0/5)
Mulder# show ip route 148.203.100.0
% Network not in table
```

Now it can be established that there is a Layer 3 routing problem between the Mulder and Scully networks. Because I-BGP requires an IGP to provide the underlying network connectivity between peers, it is impossible for the Mulder and Scully routers to form the TCP session required to become fully established BGP peers and exchange routes. By testing the IP connectivity between the two peers, you can immediately establish that the Mulder and Scully routers cannot reach each other, and you can move on to the Krycek router, examine its routing table, and try some ping tests.

```
Krycek# show ip route | begin Gateway
Gateway of last resort is not set
     148.201.0.0/24 is subnetted, 1 subnets
C       148.201.100.0 is directly connected, Ethernet0/0
     148.202.0.0/24 is subnetted, 1 subnets
C       148.202.100.0 is directly connected, Serial0/0
D    148.203.0.0/16 [90/2172416] via 148.202.100.1, 01:00:08, Serial0/0
```

```
Krycek# ping 148.201.100.1
Type escape sequence to abort.
Sending 5, 100-byte ICMP Echos to 148.201.100.1, timeout is 2 seconds:
!!!!!
Success rate is 100 percent (5/5), round-trip min/avg/max = 4/4/4 ms
Krycek# ping 148.203.100.1
Type escape sequence to abort.
Sending 5, 100-byte ICMP Echos to 148.203.100.1, timeout is 2 seconds:
!!!!!
Success rate is 100 percent (5/5), round-trip min/avg/max = 4/4/4 ms
```

Now that you have verified that the Krycek router can reach both the Mulder and Scully routers, you can then move on to the MrX router and verify IP connectivity again.

```
MrX# show ip route | begin Gateway
Gateway of last resort is not set
     148.202.0.0/16 is variably subnetted, 2 subnets, 2 masks
C       148.202.100.0/24 is directly connected, Serial0
D       148.202.0.0/16 is a summary, 01:17:13, Null0
     148.203.0.0/16 is variably subnetted, 2 subnets, 2 masks
C       148.203.100.0/24 is directly connected, FastEthernet0
D       148.203.0.0/16 is a summary, 01:17:13, Null0
MrX# show ip route 148.201.100.0
% Network not in table
```

By using the **show ip route | begin Gateway** command on the MrX router, you find that it does not have a route to the Mulder router; therefore, the Scully router will not have a route to the 148.201.100.0/24 network either. After revisiting the Krycek router and finding that the redistribution between OSPF and EIGRP had not been configured, and you take the action to fix that problem, the connection between the Mulder and Scully routers should be up.

```
Mulder# show ip route
     10.0.0.0/24 is subnetted, 2 subnets
C       10.2.2.0 is directly connected, Loopback20
C       10.1.1.0 is directly connected, Loopback10
     148.201.0.0/24 is subnetted, 1 subnets
C       148.201.100.0 is directly connected, Ethernet0
     148.202.0.0/24 is subnetted, 1 subnets
O E1    148.202.100.0 [110/30] via 148.201.100.254, 00:02:26, Ethernet0
O E1 148.203.0.0/16 [110/30] via 148.201.100.254, 00:02:26, Ethernet0
Scully# show ip route
     148.201.0.0/24 is subnetted, 1 subnets
D EX    148.201.100.0 [170/2223616] via 148.203.100.1, 00:00:53, FastEthernet0
D       148.202.0.0/16 [90/2172416] via 148.203.100.1, 01:19:24, FastEthernet0
     148.203.0.0/24 is subnetted, 1 subnets
C       148.203.100.0 is directly connected, FastEthernet0
Scully# ping 148.201.100.1
Type escape sequence to abort.
Sending 5, 100-byte ICMP Echos to 148.201.100.1, timeout is 2 seconds:
!!!!!
Success rate is 100 percent (5/5), round-trip min/avg/max = 36/37/40 ms
Scully# show ip bgp summary
BGP router identifier 192.168.1.1, local AS number 22801
BGP table version is 1, main routing table version 1
2 network entries and 2 paths using 266 bytes of memory
1 BGP path attribute entries using 60 bytes of memory
0 BGP route-map cache entries using 0 bytes of memory
0 BGP filter-list cache entries using 0 bytes of memory
BGP activity 2/0 prefixes, 4/2 paths, scan interval 15 secs
Neighbor        V    AS MsgRcvd MsgSent   TblVer  InQ OutQ Up/Down  State/PfxRcd
148.201.100.1   4 22801       8       6        1    0    0 00:00:11         2
```

BGP Neighbor Configuration

Before configuring BGP, it is important to understand some basic rules of configuration between I-BGP and E-BGP configuration. In the next section, both BGP types are covered, with examples that show how BGP can be configured to support different network topologies:

- Directly connected I-BGP configurations
- I-BGP connections configured across an IGP backbone
- E-BGP direct connections
- E-BGP multihop configurations
- E-BGP transit autonomous system configurations
- Configuring BGP peers to interact with IGPs

IBGP Peer Relationships

As mentioned in Chapter 9, I-BGP peer relationships rely on a full mesh of I-BGP speakers and the routing tables provided by IGP routing protocols to provide basic routing between each of the BGP peers. Because I-BGP peers do not need to be directly connected, there can be any number of IGP routers that do not participate in BGP routing between two I-BGP speakers, and as long as the two speakers have routes to each other, they can form a BGP peering relationship and exchange BGP routes.

BGP Synchronization

As a rule, I-BGP speakers must have their BGP routes synchronized with the routes from their IGP routing table before those routes will be considered usable. If an I-BGP peer is not synchronized with its IGP or does not have an IGP process running, that peer will not advertise networks or install BGP routes in the main IP routing table. There are two ways to correct a synchronization issue: First, when an IGP is running and you do not want to use it for synchronization, you use the **no synchronization** command. Second, if you are not running an IGP, use the **no synchronization** command to disable BGP/IGP synchronization.

Practical Example: I-BGP Synchronization Experiment

In this example, I-BGP is used to advertise remote BGP networks, symbolized by loopback IP addresses. This example demonstrates how IGP synchronization affects BGP routing and how I-BGPs operate in a fully meshed environment. Figure 8-5 shows the network used in this example.

Figure 8-5 *The SD-6 Network*

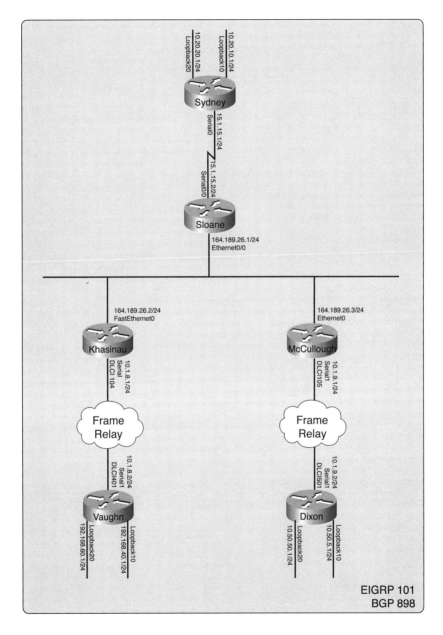

In this example, you use the IP addresses and DLCIs in Table 8-11.

Table 8-11 *Interface and IP Addresses for This Practical Example*

Router	Interface	Serial Encapsulation and/or DCLI	IP Address
Sydney	Serial0	56 kbps PPP with Compression	15.1.15.1/24
Sydney	Loopback10	None	10.20.10.1/24
Sydney	Loopback20	None	10.20.20.1/24
Sloane	Serial0/0	56 kbps PPP with Compression	15.1.15.2/24
Sloane	Ethernet0/0	None	164.189.26.1/24
Khasinau	FastEthernet0	None	164.189.26.2/24
Khasinau	Serial1	Frame Relay DLCI 104	10.1.8.1/24
McCullough	Ethernet0	None	164.189.26.3/24
McCullough	Serial0	Frame Relay DLCI 105	10.1.9.1/24
Vaughn	Serial1	Frame Relay DLCI 401	10.1.8.2/24
Vaughn	Loopback10	None	192.168.40.1/24
Vaughn	Loopback20	None	192.168.60.1/24
Dixon	Serial1	Frame Relay DLCI 501	10.1.9.2/24
Dixon	Loopback10	None	10.50.5.1/24
Dixon	Loopback20	None	10.50.50.1/24

Step 1 Configure the Frame Relay switch as shown in Table 8-12. For help configuring Frame Relay switching, refer to Chapter 1 in *CCIE Practical Studies, Volume I*.

Table 8-12 *Frame Relay Switch Configuration*

Interface	DLCI	Interface	DLCI
Serial4	104	Serial2	401
Serial2	401	Serial4	104
Serial1	105	Serial3	501
Serial3	501	Serial1	105

Example 8-26 shows the configuration for the Frame Relay switch and the Frame Relay routes present after configuring the switch.

Example 8-26 *Configuration for the Frame Relay Switch*

```
hostname Frame-Relay-Switch
!
frame-relay switching
!
interface Serial1
 no ip address
 encapsulation frame-relay IETF
 frame-relay lmi-type ansi
 frame-relay intf-type dce
 frame-relay route 105 interface Serial3 501
!
interface Serial2
 no ip address
 encapsulation frame-relay IETF
 frame-relay lmi-type ansi
 frame-relay intf-type dce
 frame-relay route 401 interface Serial4 104
!
interface Serial3
 no ip address
 encapsulation frame-relay IETF
 frame-relay lmi-type ansi
 frame-relay intf-type dce
 frame-relay route 501 interface Serial1 105
!
interface Serial4
 no ip address
 encapsulation frame-relay IETF
 frame-relay lmi-type ansi
 frame-relay intf-type dce
 frame-relay route 104 interface Serial2 401

Frame-Relay-Switch# show frame-relay route
Input Intf      Input Dlci      Output Intf     Output Dlci     Status
Serial1         105             Serial3         501             active
Serial2         401             Serial4         104             active
Serial3         501             Serial1         105             active
Serial4         104             Serial2         401             active
```

Step 2 Configure Frame Relay between Khasinau and Vaughn using IP addresses and DLCIs from Table 8-11. Also, configure the loopback IP addresses on the Vaughn router. At this time, you should be able to verify that the Vaughn and Khasinau routers can reach each other using the IP addresses on their serial interfaces. Example 8-27 shows the Frame Relay configurations for the Khasinau and Vaughn routers.

Example 8-27 *Khasinau and Vaughn Router Configurations*

```
hostname Khasinau
!
interface Serial0
 ip address 10.1.8.1 255.255.255.0
 encapsulation frame-relay IETF
 clockrate 1300000
 frame-relay map ip 10.1.8.2 104 broadcast
 frame-relay lmi-type ansi

hostname Vaughn
!
interface Loopback10
 ip address 192.168.40.1 255.255.255.0
!
interface Loopback20
 ip address 192.168.60.1 255.255.255.0
!
interface Serial1
 ip address 10.1.8.2 255.255.255.0
 encapsulation frame-relay IETF
 clockrate 1300000
 frame-relay map ip 10.1.8.1 401 broadcast
 frame-relay lmi-type ansi
```

Step 3   Configure Frame Relay between McCullough and Dixon using IP addresses
and DLCIs from Table 8-11. At this point, you should also configure the
loopback IP addresses on the Dixon router and verify that the McCullough
and Dixon routers can reach each other using the IP addresses on their serial
interfaces. Example 8-28 shows the Frame Relay configuration for the
McCullough and Dixon routers.

Example 8-28 *McCullough and Dixon Router Configurations*

```
hostname McCullough
!
interface Serial1
 ip address 10.1.9.1 255.255.255.0
 encapsulation frame-relay

 clockrate 1300000
 frame-relay map ip 10.1.9.2 105 broadcast
 frame-relay lmi-type ansi

hostname Dixon
!
interface Loopback10
 ip address 10.50.5.1 255.255.255.0
!
interface Loopback20
```

Example 8-28 *McCullough and Dixon Router Configurations (Continued)*

```
 ip address 10.50.50.1 255.255.255.0
 !
interface Serial1
 ip address 10.1.9.2 255.255.255.0
 encapsulation frame-relay IETF
 clockrate 1300000
 frame-relay map ip 10.1.9.1 501 broadcast
 frame-relay lmi-type ansi
```

Step 4   Configure an Ethernet network between the Sloane, Khasinau, and McCullough routers using IP addresses from Table 8-11. Then enable EIGRP on the Sloane, Khasinau, Vaughn, and McCullough routers and assign them to EIGRP AS 101. Do not configure EIGRP to include the loopback addresses on the Vaughn and Dixon routers. Verify that all routers can reach all interfaces on all other routers (except the loopback addresses) before proceeding to Step 5. Example 8-29 shows the configuration for the Ethernet and EIGRP configuration for the Sloane, Khasinau, Vaughn, McCullough, and Dixon routers, and their routing tables.

Example 8-29 *Ethernet and EIGRP Configurations for the Sloane, Khasinau, Vaughn, McCullough, and Dixon Routers*

```
hostname Sloane
!
interface Ethernet0/0
 ip address 164.189.26.1 255.255.255.0
!
router eigrp 101
 network 167.189.26.0 0.0.0.255
 no auto-summary
Sloane# show ip route
     10.0.0.0/24 is subnetted, 2 subnets
D       10.1.9.0 [90/2195456] via 164.189.26.3, 00:08:06, Ethernet0/0
D       10.1.8.0 [90/2195456] via 164.189.26.2, 00:01:50, Ethernet0/0
     164.189.0.0/24 is subnetted, 1 subnets
C       164.189.26.0 is directly connected, Ethernet0/0
```

```
hostname Khasinau
!
interface FastEthernet0
 ip address 164.189.26.2 255.255.255.0
!
router eigrp 101
 network 10.1.8.0 0.0.0.255
 network 164.189.26.0 0.0.0.255
 no auto-summary
```

continues

Example 8-29 *Ethernet and EIGRP Configurations for the Sloane, Khasinau, Vaughn, McCullough, and Dixon Routers (Continued)*

```
Khasinau# show ip route
     10.0.0.0/24 is subnetted, 2 subnets
D       10.1.9.0 [90/2172416] via 164.189.26.3, 00:02:21, FastEthernet0
C       10.1.8.0 is directly connected, Serial0
     164.189.0.0/24 is subnetted, 1 subnets
C       164.189.26.0 is directly connected, FastEthernet0
```

```
hostname Vaughn
!
router eigrp 101
 network 10.1.8.0 0.0.0.255
 no auto-summary
```

```
Vaughn# show ip route
C    192.168.60.0/24 is directly connected, Loopback20
C    192.168.40.0/24 is directly connected, Loopback10
     10.0.0.0/24 is subnetted, 2 subnets
D       10.1.9.0 [90/2684416] via 10.1.8.1, 00:04:03, Serial1
C       10.1.8.0 is directly connected, Serial1
     164.189.0.0/24 is subnetted, 1 subnets
D       164.189.26.0 [90/2172416] via 10.1.8.1, 00:04:03, Serial1
```

```
hostname McCullough
!
interface Ethernet0
 ip address 164.189.26.3 255.255.255.0
!
router eigrp 101
 network 10.1.9.0 0.0.0.255
 network 164.189.26.0 0.0.0.255
 no auto-summary
```

```
McCullough # show ip route
     10.0.0.0/24 is subnetted, 2 subnets
C       10.1.9.0 is directly connected, Serial1
D       10.1.8.0 [90/2195456] via 164.189.26.2, 00:06:50, Ethernet0
     164.189.0.0/24 is subnetted, 1 subnets
C       164.189.26.0 is directly connected, Ethernet0
```

```
hostname Dixon
!
router eigrp 101
 network 10.1.9.0 0.0.0.255
 no auto-summary
```

```
Dixon# show ip route
     10.0.0.0/24 is subnetted, 4 subnets
C       10.1.9.0 is directly connected, Serial1
D       10.1.8.0 [90/2707456] via 10.1.9.1, 00:07:41, Serial1
C       10.50.50.0 is directly connected, Loopback20
```

Example 8-29 *Ethernet and EIGRP Configurations for the Sloane, Khasinau, Vaughn, McCullough, and Dixon Routers (Continued)*

```
C       10.50.5.0 is directly connected, Loopback10
        164.189.0.0/24 is subnetted, 1 subnets
D       164.189.26.0 [90/2195456] via 10.1.9.1, 00:10:35, Serial1
```

Step 5   Configure the serial link between the Sydney and Sloane routers and the loopback interfaces on the Sydney router. Then enable EIGRP routing process 101 to allow the Sydney router to ping all interfaces except the loopback interfaces on the Vaughn and Dixon routers. Do not allow the Sydney router to advertise its loopback interfaces using EIGRP. Example 8-30 shows the configuration and routing table from the Sydney and Sloane routers.

Example 8-30 *Configuration and Routing Table for the Sydney Router*

```
hostname Sydney
!
interface Loopback10
 ip address 10.20.10.1 255.255.255.0
!
interface Loopback20
 ip address 10.20.20.1 255.255.255.0
!
interface Serial0
 ip address 15.1.15.1 255.255.255.0
!
router eigrp 101
 network 15.1.15.0 0.0.0.255
 no auto-summary
!
Sydney# show ip route
        10.0.0.0/24 is subnetted, 4 subnets
D       10.1.9.0 [90/2707456] via 15.1.15.2, 00:02:23, Serial0
D       10.1.8.0 [90/2707456] via 15.1.15.2, 00:02:23, Serial0
C       10.20.20.0 is directly connected, Loopback20
C       10.20.10.0 is directly connected, Loopback10
        164.189.0.0/24 is subnetted, 1 subnets
D       164.189.26.0 [90/2195456] via 15.1.15.2, 00:02:23, Serial0
        15.0.0.0/24 is subnetted, 1 subnets
C       15.1.15.0 is directly connected, Serial0

hostname Sloane
!
interface Ethernet0/0
 ip address 164.189.26.1 255.255.255.0
!
interface Serial0/0
 ip address 15.1.15.2 255.255.255.0
```

continues

Example 8-30 *Configuration and Routing Table for the Sydney Router (Continued)*

```
!
router eigrp 101
 network 15.1.15.0 0.0.0.255
 network 164.189.26.0 0.0.0.255
 no auto-summary

Sloane# show ip route | begin Gateway
Gateway of last resort is not set

     10.0.0.0/24 is subnetted, 2 subnets
D       10.1.9.0 [90/2195456] via 164.189.26.3, 00:07:09, Ethernet0/0
D       10.1.8.0 [90/2195456] via 164.189.26.2, 00:07:50, Ethernet0/0
     164.189.0.0/24 is subnetted, 1 subnets
C       164.189.26.0 is directly connected, Ethernet0/0
     15.0.0.0/24 is subnetted, 1 subnets
C       15.1.15.0 is directly connected, Serial0/0
```

Step 6   Configure BGP between the Sydney, Vaughn, and Dixon routers to advertise
          the loopback interfaces between BGP peers. Assign each of these routers
          to BGP AS 898. Do not allow the BGP peers to automatically summarize
          network addresses. Use the **show ip bgp** command to verify that the routes
          for each of the peering routers appear in the BGP routing tables. Example 8-31
          shows the BGP configuration for each of the routers and their BGP routing
          tables.

Example 8-31 *BGP Configurations and BGP Tables for the Sydney, Vaughn, and Dixon Routers*

```
Sydney# show run | begin bgp
router bgp 898
 bgp log-neighbor-changes
 network 10.20.10.0 mask 255.255.255.0
 network 10.20.20.0 mask 255.255.255.0
 neighbor 10.1.8.2 remote-as 898
 neighbor 10.1.9.2 remote-as 898
 no auto-summary

Sydney# show ip bgp
BGP table version is 3, local router ID is 10.20.20.1
Status codes: s suppressed, d damped, h history, * valid, > best, i - internal
Origin codes: i - IGP, e - EGP, ? - incomplete

   Network          Next Hop          Metric LocPrf Weight Path
*> 10.20.10.0/24    0.0.0.0                0         32768 i
*> 10.20.20.0/24    0.0.0.0                0         32768 I
*  i10.50.5.0/24    10.1.9.2               0    100      0 i
*  i10.50.50.0/24   10.1.9.2               0    100      0 i
*  i192.168.40.0    10.1.8.2               0    100      0 i
*  i192.168.60.0    10.1.8.2               0    100      0 i
```

Example 8-31 *BGP Configurations and BGP Tables for the Sydney, Vaughn, and Dixon Routers (Continued)*

```
Vaughn# show run | begin bgp
router bgp 898
 bgp log-neighbor-changes
 network 192.168.40.0
 network 192.168.60.0
 neighbor 10.1.9.2 remote-as 898
 neighbor 15.1.15.1 remote-as 898
 no auto-summary
Vaughn# show ip bgp
BGP table version is 3, local router ID is 196.168.60.1
Status codes: s suppressed, d damped, h history, * valid, > best, i - internal
Origin codes: i - IGP, e - EGP, ? - incomplete

   Network          Next Hop         Metric LocPrf Weight Path
* i10.20.10.0/24    15.1.15.1             0    100      0 i
* i10.20.20.0/24    15.1.15.1             0    100      0 i
* i10.50.5.0/24     10.1.9.2              0    100      0 i
* i10.50.50.0/24    10.1.9.2              0    100      0 i
*> 192.168.40.0     0.0.0.0               0           32768 i
*> 192.168.60.0     0.0.0.0               0           32768 i
```
```
Dixon# show run | begin bgp
router bgp 898
 bgp log-neighbor-changes
 network 10.50.5.0 mask 255.255.255.0
 network 10.50.50.0 mask 255.255.255.0
 neighbor 10.1.8.2 remote-as 898
 neighbor 15.1.15.1 remote-as 898
 no auto-summary
Dixon# show ip bgp
BGP table version is 3, local router ID is 10.50.50.1
Status codes: s suppressed, d damped, h history, * valid, > best, i - internal
Origin codes: i - IGP, e - EGP, ? - incomplete

   Network          Next Hop         Metric LocPrf Weight Path
* i10.20.10.0/24    15.1.15.1             0    100      0 i
* i10.20.20.0/24    15.1.15.1             0    100      0 i
*> 10.50.5.0/24     0.0.0.0               0           32768 i
*> 10.50.50.0/24    0.0.0.0               0           32768 I
* i192.168.40.0     10.1.8.2              0    100      0 i
* i192.168.60.0     10.1.8.2              0    100      0 i
```

If you configured each of the BGP peers in a full mesh, you would notice that each of the routers received the routes to the loopback interfaces on their peers. However, none of the routers store the routes to the loopback interfaces as the best (>) routes. This is because the loopback interface routes are not synchronized with routes in the main IP routing table. To determine whether a route synchronized is an issue, use the **show ip bgp** command and look for routes that show up as best (>). BGP only stores valid routes in the main routing table, and only the valid (*), best (>) routes are sent to peering BGP speakers.

Step 7   Now that you can see the effect that synchronization has on I-BGP peers, disable BGP synchronization, reset the BGP sessions between the peers, and check the BGP table again. Example 8-32 shows the effect of the **no synchronization** command on the Sydney router.

Example 8-32 *Disabling BGP Synchronization on the Sydney Router*

```
Sydney(config)# router bgp 898
Sydney(config-router)# no synchronization
Sydney# show ip bgp
BGP table version is 7, local router ID is 10.20.20.1
Status codes: s suppressed, d damped, h history, * valid, > best, i - internal
Origin codes: i - IGP, e - EGP, ? - incomplete

   Network          Next Hop          Metric LocPrf Weight Path
*> 10.20.10.0/24    0.0.0.0                0          32768 i
*> 10.20.20.0/24    0.0.0.0                0          32768 I
*>i10.50.5.0/24     10.1.9.2               0    100      0 i
*>i10.50.50.0/24    10.1.9.2               0    100      0 i
*>i192.168.40.0     10.1.8.2               0    100      0 i
*>i192.168.60.0     10.1.8.2               0    100      0 i
```

Step 8   To allow the BGP routers to ping their peers' loopback interfaces, you need to configure redistribution between BGP and EIGRP. To do so, you need to enter BGP configuration mode and enable BGP to IGP redistribution first, using the **bgp redistribute-internal** command, and then enable BGP redistribution on the EIGPR process as well. After EIGRP has reconverged, you will see the routes to the loopback networks in the main routing table on all routers, and you should be able to ping all addresses on all routers. The external EIGRP routes should also have replaced the BGP routes in the Sydney, Vaughn, and Dixon routers because external EIGRP has a lower administrative distance than BGP (external EIGRP 170, I-BGP 200). Example 8-33 shows the final configuration and routing table from the Sydney router.

Example 8-33 *Final Configuration and Routing Table for the Sydney Router*

```
hostname Sydney
!
interface Loopback10
 ip address 10.20.10.1 255.255.255.0
!
```

Example 8-33 *Final Configuration and Routing Table for the Sydney Router (Continued)*

```
interface Loopback20
 ip address 10.20.20.1 255.255.255.0
!
interface Serial0
 ip address 15.1.15.1 255.255.255.0
!
router eigrp 101
 redistribute bgp 898 metric 56 200 255 1 1500
 network 15.1.15.0 0.0.0.255
 no auto-summary
!
router bgp 898
 no synchronization
 bgp redistribute-internal
 bgp log-neighbor-changes
 network 10.20.10.0 mask 255.255.255.0
 network 10.20.20.0 mask 255.255.255.0
 neighbor 10.1.8.2 remote-as 898
 neighbor 10.1.9.2 remote-as 898
 no auto-summary

Sydney# show ip route | begin Gateway
Gateway of last resort is not set
D EX 192.168.60.0/24 [170/2758656] via 15.1.15.2, 00:00:25, Serial0
D EX 192.168.40.0/24 [170/2758656] via 15.1.15.2, 00:00:25, Serial0
     10.0.0.0/24 is subnetted, 6 subnets
D       10.1.9.0 [90/2707456] via 15.1.15.2, 00:37:45, Serial0
D       10.1.8.0 [90/2707456] via 15.1.15.2, 00:38:26, Serial0
D EX    10.50.50.0 [170/2758656] via 15.1.15.2, 00:08:21, Serial0
C       10.20.20.0 is directly connected, Loopback20
C       10.20.10.0 is directly connected, Loopback10
D EX    10.50.5.0 [170/2758656] via 15.1.15.2, 00:08:21, Serial0
     164.189.0.0/24 is subnetted, 1 subnets
D       164.189.26.0 [90/2195456] via 15.1.15.2, 00:39:36, Serial0
     15.0.0.0/24 is subnetted, 1 subnets
C       15.1.15.0 is directly connected, Serial0

Sydney# ping 10.50.5.1
Type escape sequence to abort.
Sending 5, 100-byte ICMP Echos to 10.50.5.1, timeout is 2 seconds:
!!!!!
Success rate is 100 percent (5/5), round-trip min/avg/max = 56/58/60 ms

Sydney# ping 192.168.40.1
Type escape sequence to abort.
Sending 5, 100-byte ICMP Echos to 192.168.40.1, timeout is 2 seconds:
!!!!!
Success rate is 100 percent (5/5), round-trip min/avg/max = 40/41/44 ms
```

Example 8-34 shows the complete configuration and routing table for the Sloane router. Example 8-35 shows the complete configuration and routing table for the Khasinau router. Example 8-36 shows the same type of information for the McCullough router.

Example 8-34 *Final Configuration and Routing Table for the Sloane Router*

```
hostname Sloane
!
interface Ethernet0/0
 ip address 164.189.26.1 255.255.255.0
!
interface Serial0/0
 ip address 15.1.15.2 255.255.255.0
!
router eigrp 101
 network 15.1.15.0 0.0.0.255
 network 164.189.26.0 0.0.0.255
 no auto-summary

Sloane# show ip route | include via|is
Gateway of last resort is not set
D EX 192.168.60.0/24 [170/2246656] via 164.189.26.3, 00:16:58, Ethernet0/0
D EX 192.168.40.0/24 [170/2246656] via 164.189.26.3, 00:16:58, Ethernet0/0
     10.0.0.0/24 is subnetted, 6 subnets
D       10.1.9.0 [90/2195456] via 164.189.26.3, 00:54:18, Ethernet0/0
D       10.1.8.0 [90/2195456] via 164.189.26.2, 00:54:59, Ethernet0/0
D EX    10.50.50.0 [170/2246656] via 164.189.26.3, 00:24:54, Ethernet0/0
D EX    10.20.20.0 [170/46277376] via 15.1.15.1, 00:26:04, Serial0/0
D EX    10.20.10.0 [170/46277376] via 15.1.15.1, 00:26:04, Serial0/0
D EX    10.50.5.0 [170/2246656] via 164.189.26.3, 00:24:54, Ethernet0/0
     164.189.0.0/24 is subnetted, 1 subnets
C       164.189.26.0 is directly connected, Ethernet0/0
     15.0.0.0/24 is subnetted, 1 subnets
C       15.1.15.0 is directly connected, Serial0/0
```

Example 8-35 *Final Configuration and Routing Table for the Khasinau Router*

```
hostname Khasinau
!
interface FastEthernet0
 ip address 164.189.26.2 255.255.255.0
!
interface Serial1
 ip address 10.1.8.1 255.255.255.0
 encapsulation frame-relay IETF
 clockrate 1300000
 frame-relay map ip 10.1.8.2 104 broadcast
 frame-relay lmi-type ansi
!
!
router eigrp 101
```

Example 8-35 *Final Configuration and Routing Table for the Khasinau Router (Continued)*

```
network 10.1.8.0 0.0.0.255

network 164.189.26.0 0.0.0.255
no auto-summary

Khasinau# show ip route | include via|is
Gateway of last resort is not set
D EX 192.168.60.0/24 [170/2223616] via 164.189.26.3, 00:21:11, FastEthernet0
D EX 192.168.40.0/24 [170/2223616] via 164.189.26.3, 00:21:11, FastEthernet0
     10.0.0.0/24 is subnetted, 6 subnets
D       10.1.9.0 [90/2172416] via 164.189.26.3, 00:58:31, FastEthernet0
C       10.1.8.0 is directly connected, Serial1
D EX    10.50.50.0 [170/2223616] via 164.189.26.3, 00:29:07, FastEthernet0
D EX    10.20.20.0 [170/46279936] via 164.189.26.1, 00:30:17, FastEthernet0
D EX    10.20.10.0 [170/46279936] via 164.189.26.1, 00:30:17, FastEthernet0
D EX    10.50.5.0 [170/2223616] via 164.189.26.3, 00:29:07, FastEthernet0
     164.189.0.0/24 is subnetted, 1 subnets
C       164.189.26.0 is directly connected, FastEthernet0
     15.0.0.0/24 is subnetted, 1 subnets
D       15.1.15.0 [90/2172416] via 164.189.26.1, 00:59:15, FastEthernet0
```

Example 8-36 *Final Configuration and Routing Table for the McCullough Router*

```
hostname McCullough
!
interface Ethernet0
 ip address 164.189.26.3 255.255.255.0
!
interface Serial1
 ip address 10.1.9.1 255.255.255.0
 encapsulation frame-relay IETF
 clockrate 1300000
 frame-relay map ip 10.1.9.2 105 broadcast
 frame-relay lmi-type ansi
!
router eigrp 101
 network 10.1.9.0 0.0.0.255
 network 164.189.26.0 0.0.0.255
 no auto-summary

McCullough# show ip route | include via|is
Gateway of last resort is not set
D EX 192.168.60.0/24 [170/2221056] via 10.1.9.2, 00:23:34, Serial1
D EX 192.168.40.0/24 [170/2221056] via 10.1.9.2, 00:23:34, Serial1
     10.0.0.0/24 is subnetted, 6 subnets
C       10.1.9.0 is directly connected, Serial1
D       10.1.8.0 [90/2172416] via 164.189.26.2, 01:00:59, Ethernet0
D EX    10.50.50.0 [170/2221056] via 10.1.9.2, 00:31:30, Serial1
D EX    10.20.20.0 [170/46279936] via 164.189.26.1, 00:32:40, Ethernet0
```

continues

Example 8-36 *Final Configuration and Routing Table for the McCullough Router (Continued)*

```
D EX    10.20.10.0 [170/46279936] via 164.189.26.1, 00:32:40, Ethernet0
D EX    10.50.5.0 [170/2221056] via 10.1.9.2, 00:31:30, Serial1
     164.189.0.0/24 is subnetted, 1 subnets
C       164.189.26.0 is directly connected, Ethernet0
     15.0.0.0/24 is subnetted, 1 subnets
D       15.1.15.0 [90/2172416] via 164.189.26.1, 01:00:59, Ethernet0
```

Example 8-37 displays the final configuration, BGP table, and routing table for the Vaughn
router, and Example 8-38 shows the same type of data for the Dixon router.

Example 8-37 *Final Configuration and Routing Tables for the Vaughn Router*

```
hostname Vaughn
!
interface Loopback10
 ip address 192.168.40.1 255.255.255.0
!
interface Loopback20
 ip address 192.168.60.1 255.255.255.0
!
interface Serial1
 ip address 10.1.8.2 255.255.255.0
 encapsulation frame-relay IETF
 clockrate 1300000
 frame-relay map ip 10.1.8.1 401 broadcast
 frame-relay lmi-type ansi
!
router eigrp 101
 redistribute bgp 898 metric 1544 200 255 1 1500
 network 10.1.8.0 0.0.0.25
 no auto-summary
!
router bgp 898
 no synchronization
 bgp redistribute-internal
 network 192.168.40.0
 network 192.168.60.0
 neighbor 10.1.9.2 remote-as 898
 neighbor 15.1.15.1 remote-as 898

Vaughn# show ip bgp | begin Network
   Network          Next Hop          Metric LocPrf Weight Path
*>i10.20.10.0/24    15.1.15.1              0    100      0 i
*>i10.20.20.0/24    15.1.15.1              0    100      0 i
*>i10.50.5.0/24     10.1.9.2               0    100      0 i
*>i10.50.50.0/24    10.1.9.2               0    100      0 i
*> 192.168.40.0     0.0.0.0                0         32768 i
*> 192.168.60.0     0.0.0.0                0         32768 i
```

Example 8-37 *Final Configuration and Routing Tables for the Vaughn Router (Continued)*

```
Vaughn# show ip route | include via|is
Gateway of last resort is not set
C    192.168.60.0/24 is directly connected, Loopback20
C    192.168.40.0/24 is directly connected, Loopback10
     10.0.0.0/24 is subnetted, 6 subnets
D      10.1.9.0 [90/2684416] via 10.1.8.1, 01:05:52, Serial1
C      10.1.8.0 is directly connected, Serial1
D EX   10.20.20.0 [170/46791936] via 10.1.8.1, 00:39:46, Serial1
D EX   10.50.50.0 [170/2735616] via 10.1.8.1, 00:38:36, Serial1
D EX   10.20.10.0 [170/46791936] via 10.1.8.1, 00:39:46, Serial1
D EX   10.50.5.0 [170/2735616] via 10.1.8.1, 00:38:36, Serial1
     164.189.0.0/24 is subnetted, 1 subnets
D      164.189.26.0 [90/2172416] via 10.1.8.1, 01:05:52, Serial1
     15.0.0.0/24 is subnetted, 1 subnets
D      15.1.15.0 [90/2684416] via 10.1.8.1, 01:05:53, Serial1
```

Example 8-38 *Final Configuration and Routing Tables for the Dixon Router*

```
hostname Dixon
!
interface Loopback10
 ip address 10.50.5.1 255.255.255.0
!
interface Loopback20
 ip address 10.50.50.1 255.255.255.0
!
interface Serial1
 ip address 10.1.9.2 255.255.255.0
 encapsulation frame-relay IETF
 frame-relay map ip 10.1.9.1 501 broadcast
 frame-relay lmi-type ansi
!
router eigrp 101
 redistribute bgp 898 metric 1544 200 255 1 1500
 network 10.1.9.0 0.0.0.255
 no auto-summary
!
router bgp 898
 no synchronization
 bgp redistribute-internal
 bgp log-neighbor-changes
 network 10.50.5.0 mask 255.255.255.0
 network 10.50.50.0 mask 255.255.255.0
 neighbor 10.1.8.2 remote-as 898
 neighbor 15.1.15.1 remote-as 898
```

continues

Example 8-38 *Final Configuration and Routing Tables for the Dixon Router (Continued)*

```
Dixon# show ip bgp | begin Network
  Network           Next Hop          Metric LocPrf Weight Path
*>i10.20.10.0/24    15.1.15.1              0    100      0 i
*>i10.20.20.0/24    15.1.15.1              0    100      0 i
*> 10.50.5.0/24     0.0.0.0               0          32768 i
*> 10.50.50.0/24    0.0.0.0               0          32768 i
*>i192.168.40.0     10.1.8.2               0    100      0 i
*>i192.168.60.0     10.1.8.2               0    100      0 i

Dixon# show ip route | include vialis
Gateway of last resort is not set
B       192.168.60.0/24 [200/0] via 10.1.8.2, 00:33:41
B       192.168.40.0/24 [200/0] via 10.1.8.2, 00:33:41
        10.0.0.0/24 is subnetted, 6 subnets
C          10.1.9.0 is directly connected, Serial1
D          10.1.8.0 [90/2684416] via 10.1.9.1, 01:08:24, Serial1
D EX       10.20.20.0 [170/46791936] via 10.1.9.1, 00:42:47, Serial1
C          10.50.50.0 is directly connected, Loopback20
D EX       10.20.10.0 [170/46791936] via 10.1.9.1, 00:42:47, Serial1
C          10.50.5.0 is directly connected, Loopback10
        164.189.0.0/24 is subnetted, 1 subnets
D          164.189.26.0 [90/2172416] via 10.1.9.1, 01:08:24, Serial1
        15.0.0.0/24 is subnetted, 1 subnets
D          15.1.15.0 [90/2684416] via 10.1.9.1, 01:08:24, Serial1
```

NOTE   Redistribution between BGP and IGPs, and vice versa, can have serious effects on routing performance. Use BGP/IGP redistribution with caution on production networks.

I-BGP **next-hop self** Command

One problem that frequently creeps up when multihoming BGP networks is unreachable BGP routes. This generally occurs when E-BGP to I-BGP relationships have just been configured and downstream I-BGP speakers cannot reach the next hop advertised by the router that peers directly with the routers sending E-BGP updates. Although the router peering with the upstream E-BGP peers can reach the addresses of its E-BGP peers, other routers that are downstream from this router do not have routes to the E-BGP peers, so those routers cannot reach the next hop advertised in the BGP updates. This action is by design, and this happens because I-BGP-speaking routers do not alter the NEXT_HOP attribute as they forward routes to other I-BGP peers. Figure 8-6 shows how routes sent from upstream routers, Chunk and Sloth, have NEXT_HOP attributes that are unchanged as they pass through the Mikey router onto Data and Brand.

Figure 8-6   *I-BGP NEXT_HOP Behavior*

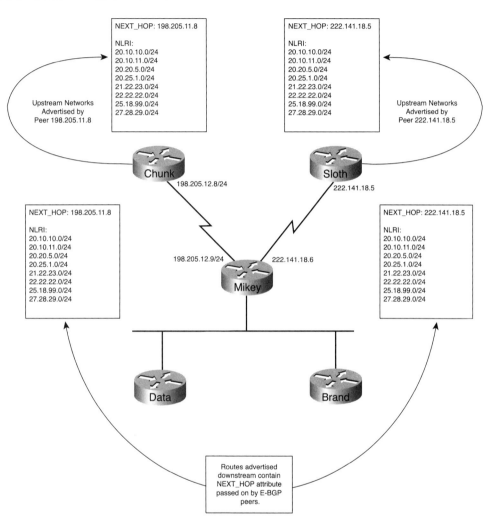

To change the NEXT_HOP attribute on an I-BGP peer to that of the local router, you just need to complete three steps.

Step 1   Enable BGP routing.

```
Mikey(config)# router bgp 10101
```

Step 2   Configure BGP neighbor relationships.

```
Mikey(config-router)# neighbor 198.205.12.8 remote-as 811      ← E-BGP peer
Mikey(config-router)# neighbor 222.141.18.5 remote-as 945      ← E-BGP peer
Mikey(config-router)# neighbor 192.168.1.2 remote-as 10101     ← I-BGP peer
Mikey(config-router)# neighbor 192.168.1.3 remote-as 10101     ← I-BGP peer
```

Step 3   Modify the NEXT_HOP attribute using the **neighbor** *ip-address* **next-hop-self** command.

```
Mikey(config-router)# neighbor 192.168.1.2 next-hop-self    ← Change attribute
Mikey(config-router)# neighbor 192.168.1.3 next-hop-self    ← Change attribute
```

Changes to the NEXT_HOP attribute can be seen when the **show ip bgp** command is issued. Example 8-39 shows how the NEXT_HOP attribute appears on the Data router before the **next-hop-self** command is used on the Mikey router, and Example 8-40 shows the same command on the same router after the **next-hop-self** command is added to the configuration on the Mikey router.

Example 8-39 *Before Changing the NEXT_HOP Attribute*

```
Data# show ip bgp | begin Network
   Network         Next Hop          Metric LocPrf Weight Path
*> 2.0.0.0         157.68.90.1            0    100     0 3456 i
*> 3.0.0.0         157.68.90.1            0    100     0 3456 i
```

Example 8-40 *After the* **next-hop-self** *Command*

```
Data# show ip bgp | begin Network
   Network         Next Hop          Metric LocPrf Weight Path
*>i2.0.0.0         192.168.1.1            0    100     0 3456 i
*>i3.0.0.0         192.168.1.1            0    100     0 3456 i
```

Practical Example: I-BGP Next-Hop Manipulation

This example shows the effects that the **next-hop-self** command has on I-BGP routing within an autonomous system. This example requires five Cisco routers with the interfaces shown in Table 8-13.

Table 8-13   *Router Interface Requirements*

Router	Ethernet, Fast Ethernet, or Token Ring Interfaces	Serial Interfaces
Skinner	0	1
Kritchgau	0	1
Langle	1	2
Byers	1	0
Frohike	1	0

Before configuring any routers, make sure the routers are cabled, as shown in Figure 8-7. This example requires two back-to-back serial cables and three Ethernet cables connected to a hub, switch, or MSAU. If you are using a switch, all interfaces should be placed in the same VLAN.

Figure 8-7   *The Conspiracy Network Diagram*

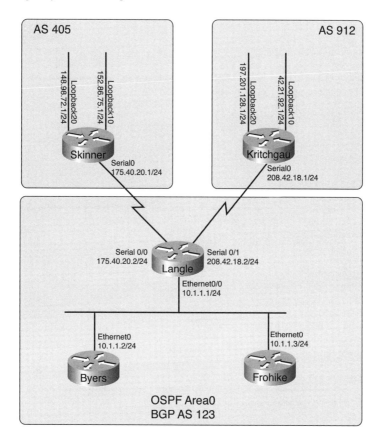

Step 1   Configure all IP addresses as specified in Figure 8-7. Verify that all interfaces are up before proceeding to Step 2. Configure OSPF on all I-BGP-speaking routers in AS 123, putting all interfaces on these routers in area 0. Do not configure OSPF on the Skinner or Kritchgau routers. Example 8-41 shows the IP addressing and OSPF configuration for the Skinner, Langle, Byers, and Frohike routers.

Example 8-41 *Configuration for Step 1 on Skinner, Langle, and Byers Routers*

```
Skinner# show run | begin Loopback
interface Loopback10
 ip address 152.86.75.1 255.255.255.0
!
interface Loopback20
 ip address 148.98.72.1 255.255.255.0
!
interface Serial0
 ip address 175.40.20.1 255.255.255.0
```

```
Kritchgau# show run | begin Loopback
interface Loopback10
 ip address 42.21.92.1 255.255.255.0
!
interface Loopback20
 ip address 197.201.128.1 255.255.255.0
!
interface Serial0
 ip address 208.42.18.1 255.255.255.0
```

```
Langle# show run | begin Ethernet
interface Ethernet0/0
 ip address 10.1.1.1 255.255.255.0
!
interface Serial0/0
 ip address 175.40.20.2 255.255.255.0
!
interface Serial0/1
 ip address 208.42.18.2 255.255.255.0
 clock rate 1300000
!
router ospf 1
 network 10.1.1.0 0.0.0.255 area 0
```

```
Byers# show run | begin Ethernet
interface Ethernet0
 ip address 10.1.1.2 255.255.255.0
!
router ospf 1
 network 10.1.1.0 0.0.0.255 area 0
```

```
Frohike# show run | begin Ethernet
interface Ethernet0
 ip address 10.1.1.3 255.255.255.0
!
router ospf 1
 network 10.1.1.0 0.0.0.255 area 0
```

Step 2   Configure the E-BGP sessions between the Skinner and Langle routers and the Kritchgau and Langle routers. Configure the Skinner and Kritchgau routers to advertise the networks belonging to their loopback interfaces via BGP. Have the Langle router advertise the 10.1.1.0/24 network to both of its E-BGP peers. Before moving on to Step 3, make sure that the Langle router can ping all IP addresses on the loopback interfaces of the Skinner and Kritchgau routers. Example 8-42 shows the BGP configurations for each of the BGP routers and the routing table from the Langle router.

Example 8-42 *BGP Configurations for the Skinner, Kritchgau, and Langle Routers*

```
Skinner# show run | begin bgp
router bgp 405
 bgp log-neighbor-changes
 network 148.98.72.0 mask 255.255.255.0
 network 152.86.75.0 mask 255.255.255.0
 neighbor 175.40.20.2 remote-as 123
 no auto-summary

Kritchgau# show run | begin bgp
router bgp 912
 bgp log-neighbor-changes
 network 42.21.92.0 mask 255.255.255.0
 network 197.201.128.0
 neighbor 208.42.18.2 remote-as 123
 no auto-summary

Langle# show run | begin bgp
router bgp 123
 bgp log-neighbor-changes
 network 10.1.1.0 mask 255.255.255.0
 neighbor 175.40.20.1 remote-as 405
 neighbor 208.42.18.1 remote-as 912
no auto-summary
Langle# show ip route | begin Gateway
Gateway of last resort is not set
     1.0.0.0/32 is subnetted, 1 subnets
C       1.1.1.1 is directly connected, Loopback0
B    197.201.128.0/24 [20/0] via 208.42.18.1, 00:01:54
     152.86.0.0/24 is subnetted, 1 subnets
B       152.86.75.0 [20/0] via 175.40.20.1, 00:05:21
     175.40.0.0/24 is subnetted, 1 subnets
C       175.40.20.0 is directly connected, Serial0/0
     42.0.0.0/24 is subnetted, 1 subnets
B       42.21.92.0 [20/0] via 208.42.18.1, 00:01:54
     10.0.0.0/24 is subnetted, 1 subnets
C       10.1.1.0 is directly connected, Ethernet0/0
     148.98.0.0/24 is subnetted, 1 subnets
B       148.98.72.0 [20/0] via 175.40.20.1, 00:05:22
C    208.42.18.0/24 is directly connected, Serial0/1
```

Step 3   Configure I-BGP connections between the Langle, Byers, and Frohike
routers. Before moving on to the next step, verify that Byers and Frohike
received the E-BGP routes from the Skinner and Kritchgau routers.
Example 8-43 shows the BGP configuration and BGP table for the Langle
router, Example 8-44 shows the same data for the Byers router, and
Example 8-45 shows the configuration and BGP data for the Frohike
router.

Example 8-43 *BGP Configuration and BGP Table for the Langle Router*

```
Langle# show run | begin bgp
router bgp 123
 bgp log-neighbor-changes
 network 10.1.1.0 mask 255.255.255.0
 neighbor 10.1.1.2 remote-as 123
 neighbor 10.1.1.3 remote-as 123
 neighbor 175.40.20.1 remote-as 405
 neighbor 208.42.18.1 remote-as 912

Langle# show ip bgp | begin Network
   Network          Next Hop          Metric LocPrf Weight Path
*> 10.1.1.0/24      0.0.0.0                0         32768 i
*> 42.21.92.0/24    208.42.18.1            0             0 912 i
*> 148.98.72.0/24   175.40.20.1            0             0 405 i
*> 152.86.75.0/24   175.40.20.1            0             0 405 i
*> 197.201.128.0    208.42.18.1            0             0 912 i
```

Example 8-44 *BGP Configuration and BGP Table for the Byers Router*

```
Byers# show run | begin bgp
router bgp 123
 bgp log-neighbor-changes
 neighbor 10.1.1.1 remote-as 123
 neighbor 10.1.1.3 remote-as 123
Byers# show ip bgp | begin Network
   Network          Next Hop          Metric LocPrf Weight Path
*>i10.1.1.0/24      10.1.1.1               0    100      0 i
* i42.21.92.0/24    208.42.18.1            0    100      0 912 i
* i148.98.72.0/24   175.40.20.1            0    100      0 405 i
* i152.86.75.0/24   175.40.20.1            0    100      0 405 i
* i197.201.128.0    208.42.18.1            0    100      0 912 i
```

Example 8-45 *BGP Configuration and BGP Table for the Frohike Router*

```
Frohike# show run | begin bgp
router bgp 123
 bgp log-neighbor-changes
 neighbor 10.1.1.1 remote-as 123
 neighbor 10.1.1.3 remote-as 123
```

Example 8-45 *BGP Configuration and BGP Table for the Frohike Router (Continued)*

```
Frohike# show ip bgp | begin Network
   Network          Next Hop          Metric LocPrf Weight Path
*>i10.1.1.0/24      10.1.1.1               0    100      0 i
*  i42.21.92.0/24   208.42.18.1            0    100      0 912 i
*  i148.98.72.0/24  175.40.20.1            0    100      0 405 i
*  i152.86.75.0/24  175.40.20.1            0    100      0 405 i
*  i197.201.128.0   208.42.18.1            0    100      0 912 i
```

Step 4   After configuring BGP between the Langle, Byers, and Frohike routers, you might have noticed that the Byers and Frohike routers received the routes from the upstream E-BGP peers of the Langle router but did not install them in the routing table. The reason why the routes were not installed in the table is because they are not reachable using the IP address of the next hop that was advertised by the Langle router. To correct this problem, use the **next-hop-self** command on each of the I-BGP sessions on the Langle router, and then reset the BGP sessions using the **clear ip bgp *** command. After the BGP sessions have come back up and the Langle router advertises its routes from the upstream router, it will modify the NEXT_HOP attribute on all routes sent to Byers and Frohike. Example 8-46 shows the configuration for the Langle router after the addition of the **next-hop-self** command, and Example 8-47 shows the resulting BGP and IP routing tables for the Byers and Frohike routers.

Example 8-46 *Langle Router's BGP Configuration*

```
Langle# show run | begin bgp
router bgp 123
 no synchronization
 bgp router-id 177.164.8.5
 bgp log-neighbor-changes
 network 10.1.1.0 mask 255.255.255.0
 neighbor 10.1.1.2 remote-as 123
 neighbor 10.1.1.2 next-hop-self
 neighbor 10.1.1.3 remote-as 123
 neighbor 10.1.1.3 next-hop-self
 neighbor 175.40.20.1 remote-as 405
 neighbor 208.42.18.1 remote-as 912
 no auto-summary
```

Example 8-47 *Resulting BGP and IP Routing Tables*

```
Byers# show ip bgp
BGP table version is 6, local router ID is 10.1.1.2
Status codes: s suppressed, d damped, h history, * valid, > best, i - internal
Origin codes: i - IGP, e - EGP, ? - incomplete
   Network          Next Hop          Metric LocPrf Weight Path
*>i10.1.1.0/24      10.1.1.1               0    100      0 I
*>i42.21.92.0/24    10.1.1.1               0    100      0 912 i
*>i148.98.72.0/24   10.1.1.1               0    100      0 405 i
*>i152.86.75.0/24   10.1.1.1               0    100      0 405 i
*>i197.201.128.0    10.1.1.1               0    100      0 912 i
Byers# show ip route | begin Gateway

Gateway of last resort is not set
B    197.201.128.0/24 [200/0] via 10.1.1.1, 00:01:09
     152.86.0.0/24 is subnetted, 1 subnets
B       152.86.75.0 [200/0] via 10.1.1.1, 00:01:09
     42.0.0.0/24 is subnetted, 1 subnets
B       42.21.92.0 [200/0] via 10.1.1.1, 00:01:09
     10.0.0.0/24 is subnetted, 1 subnets
C       10.1.1.0 is directly connected, Ethernet0
     148.98.0.0/24 is subnetted, 1 subnets
B       148.98.72.0 [200/0] via 10.1.1.1, 00:01:09
Byers# ping 197.201.128.1
Type escape sequence to abort.
Sending 5, 100-byte ICMP Echos to 197.201.128.1, timeout is 2 seconds:
!!!!!
Success rate is 100 percent (5/5), round-trip min/avg/max = 4/4/8 ms
Byers# ping 152.86.75.1
Type escape sequence to abort.
Sending 5, 100-byte ICMP Echos to 152.86.75.1, timeout is 2 seconds:
!!!!!
Success rate is 100 percent (5/5), round-trip min/avg/max = 36/36/40 ms

Frohike# show ip bgp | begin Network
   Network          Next Hop          Metric LocPrf Weight Path
*>i10.1.1.0/24      10.1.1.1               0    100      0 i
*>i42.21.92.0/24    10.1.1.1               0    100      0 912 i
*>i148.98.72.0/24   10.1.1.1               0    100      0 405 i
*>i152.86.75.0/24   10.1.1.1               0    100      0 405 i
*>i197.201.128.0    10.1.1.1               0    100      0 912 i
Frohike# show ip route | begin Gateway
Gateway of last resort is not set
B    197.201.128.0/24 [200/0] via 10.1.1.1, 00:02:24
     152.86.0.0/24 is subnetted, 1 subnets
B       152.86.75.0 [200/0] via 10.1.1.1, 00:02:24
     42.0.0.0/24 is subnetted, 1 subnets
B       42.21.92.0 [200/0] via 10.1.1.1, 00:02:24
     10.0.0.0/24 is subnetted, 1 subnets
C       10.1.1.0 is directly connected, Ethernet0
     148.98.0.0/24 is subnetted, 1 subnets
B       148.98.72.0 [200/0] via 10.1.1.1, 00:02:24
```

Example 8-47 *Resulting BGP and IP Routing Tables (Continued)*

```
Frohike# ping 42.21.92.1
Type escape sequence to abort.
Sending 5, 100-byte ICMP Echos to 42.21.92.1, timeout is 2 seconds:
!!!!!
Success rate is 100 percent (5/5), round-trip min/avg/max = 4/5/8 ms
Frohike# ping 152.86.75.1
Type escape sequence to abort.
Sending 5, 100-byte ICMP Echos to 152.86.75.1, timeout is 2 seconds:
!!!!!
Success rate is 100 percent (5/5), round-trip min/avg/max = 36/36/40 ms
```

Now that you can see the effects that the use of I-BGP full-mesh configurations, BGP synchronization, and **next-hop-self** commands have, it's time to move on to E-BGP peer configurations and look at some of the issues that you will encounter when working with E-BGP configurations.

E-BGP Peer Relationships

E-BGP peer relationships are, undoubtedly, the most common type of BGP peering relationship that most enterprise network professionals will encounter. Regardless of how many peers one BGP speaker has, only a few types of connections can occur between E-BGP peers.

- **Directly connected peers**—Peers that are directly connected; usually over a WAN connection between the customer and the service providers, or between transit peers.

- **Indirectly connected peers**—E-BGP peers that must cross one or more non-BGP-speaking routers to reach each other.

Configuring direct E-BGP connections is an extremely straightforward process involving only three steps.

Step 1   Enable BGP routing using the **router bgp** *as-number* command.

Step 2   Configure BGP peers using the **neighbor** *ip-address* **remote-as** *remote-as-number* command. E-BGP peer relationships are formed if the AS number entered during the configuration of the **neighbor** command is not the same as locally configured AS number.

Step 3   (Optional) Specify the networks that the local peer is to advertise using the **network** *network* [**mask** *subnet-mask*] command. Similar to the EIGRP **network** command, the BGP **network** command specifies networks that the local peer will advertise; if those networks do not fall exactly between the classful boundaries, the subnet masks define those networks.

Figure 8-8 shows an example of the direct E-BGP configuration between the Sideshow and Crusty routers.

Figure 8-8 *Directly Connected E-BGP Peers*

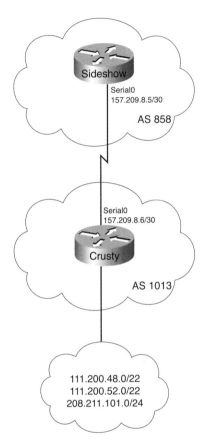

In this example, the Sideshow and Crusty routers form an E-BGP peer connection over a serial connection on the 157.209.8.4/30 network. The Sideshow router is in AS 858 and does not advertise BGP networks; the Crusty router belongs to AS 1013 and advertises networks 111.200.48.0/22, 111.200.52.0/22, and 208.211.101.0/24. Example 8-48 shows the Sideshow router configuration and the routes as seen by the Sideshow router, and Example 8-49 shows the configuration for the Crusty router.

Example 8-48 *Sideshow Router Configuration*

```
Sideshow# show run | begin bgp
router bgp 858
 bgp log-neighbor-changes
 neighbor 157.209.8.6 remote-as 1013
 no auto-summary
```

Example 8-48 *Sideshow Router Configuration (Continued)*

```
Sideshow# show ip bgp
BGP table version is 8, local router ID is 157.209.8.5
Status codes: s suppressed, d damped, h history, * valid, > best, i - internal
Origin codes: i - IGP, e - EGP, ? - incomplete
   Network          Next Hop          Metric LocPrf Weight Path
*> 111.200.48.0/22  157.209.8.6            0             0 1013 i
*> 111.200.52.0/22  157.209.8.6            0             0 1013 i
*> 208.211.101.0    157.209.8.6            0             0 1013 i
```

Example 8-49 *Crusty Router Configuration*

```
Crusty# show run | begin bgp
router bgp 1013
 bgp log-neighbor-changes
 network 111.200.48.0 mask 255.255.252.0
 network 111.200.52.0 mask 255.255.252.0
 network 208.211.101.0
 neighbor 157.209.8.5 remote-as 858
 no auto-summary
```

Exceeding BGP Limitations with E-BGP Multihop

Because the BGP-4 specification does not allow E-BGP speakers to form peer relationships unless they are directly connected, you must plan for indirect external BGP configurations. You need to know whether special design considerations are required for BGP to operate properly when the peers must pass through other routers to form peer relationships and exchange update messages.

The **neighbor** *ip-address* **ebgp-multihop** command specifies that the remote peer specified by the **neighbor** statement is not directly connected. This command is used to connect E-BGP speakers that must traverse one or more hops to form a successful E-BGP session. The **neighbor** *ip-address* **ebgp-multihop** command uses the following syntax:

```
neighbor ip-address ebgp-multihop [number-of-hops]
```

To specify the number of hops that must be crossed to reach a neighbor (ranging from 1 to 255), or, if you are unsure of the number of hops required, you can accept the default value of 255, although the default is not always recommended because it might allow for suboptimal routing across long paths.

You must complete five steps to create successful E-BGP peering relationships between peers.

Step 1   Verify that the local and remote routers have routes to reach each other before configuring BGP using the **show ip route** *neighbor-ip-address* command.

Step 2 Enable the local BGP process using the **router bgp** *as-number* command.

Step 3 Configure the remote peer's IP address and AS number using the **neighbor** *ip-address* **remote-as** *remote-as-number* command.

Step 4 Configure the networks that are to be advertised by the local peer using the **network** command.

Step 5 Enable E-BGP multihop using the **neighbor** *ip-address* **ebgp-multihop** *number-of-hops* command.

In the network shown in Figure 8-9, for example, notice that the Murtagh and Geilis routers are indirectly connected by means of the Willoughby router. The Murtagh router belongs to AS 1743, and the Geilis router belongs to AS 1968, so they must be able to form an E-BGP peer relationship by sending BGP messages through the Willoughby router, which does not participate in BGP.

Figure 8-9 *Running E-BGP Across Multiple Hops*

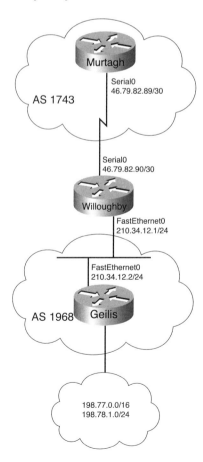

This shows how the **ebgp-multihop** keyword was used to enable BGP routing between the Murtagh and Geilis routers. Notice how the **neighbor 210.34.12.2 ebgp-multihop 2** command is used in Example 8-50 to specify that the Geilis router can be up to two hops away, and that a static route is used to tell the Murtagh router how to reach the 210.32.12.0/24 network, the route to the Geilis router.

Example 8-50 *Murtagh Router Configuration*

```
Murtagh# show run | begin bgp
router bgp 1743
 bgp log-neighbor-changes
 neighbor 210.34.12.2 remote-as 1968
 neighbor 210.34.12.2 ebgp-multihop 2
 !
ip classless
ip route 210.34.12.0 255.255.255.0 46.79.82.90
```

To verify that the E-BGP multihop configuration is working, use the **show ip bgp neighbor** command (or **show ip bgp neighbors | i external|state|hops** for an abbreviated summary of E-BGP neighbors), and look for an established connection. Example 8-51 shows the output of the **show ip bgp neighbors** and **show ip bgp neighbors | i external|state|hops** commands for the Murtagh router.

Example 8-51 **show ip bgp neighbors** *Command Output*

```
Murtagh# show ip bgp neighbors
BGP neighbor is 210.34.12.2,  remote AS 1968, external link

  BGP version 4, remote router ID 198.78.1.1
  BGP state = Established, up for 00:16:08
  Last read 00:00:08, hold time is 180, keepalive interval is 60 seconds
  Neighbor capabilities:
    Route refresh: advertised and received(old & new)
    Address family IPv4 Unicast: advertised and received
  Received 25 messages, 0 notifications, 0 in queue
  Sent 25 messages, 0 notifications, 0 in queue
  Route refresh request: received 0, sent 0
  Default minimum time between advertisement runs is 30 seconds
 For address family: IPv4 Unicast
  BGP table version 5, neighbor version 5
  Index 1, Offset 0, Mask 0x2
  2 accepted prefixes consume 72 bytes
  Prefix advertised 0, suppressed 0, withdrawn 0
  Number of NLRIs in the update sent: max 0, min 0
  Connections established 2; dropped 1
  Last reset 00:16:53, due to Peer closed the session
  External BGP neighbor might be up to 2 hops away.
 Connection state is ESTAB, I/O status: 1, unread input bytes: 0
 Local host: 46.79.82.89, Local port: 179
```

continues

Example 8-51 show ip bgp neighbors *Command Output (Continued)*

```
Foreign host: 210.34.12.2, Foreign port: 11020
Byers# show ip bgp neighbors | i external|state|hops
BGP neighbor 210.34.12.2,  remote AS 1968, external link
  BGP state = Established, up for 00:16:08
  External BGP neighbor might be up to 2 hops away.
```

If the **ebgp-multihop** keyword had not been used for each indirect E-BGP session, the **show ip bgp neighbors** command will show you several hints about the problem, as shown in Example 8-52.

Example 8-52 *Diagnosing Indirect E-BGP Peering Problems*

```
Murtagh# show ip bgp neighbors
BGP neighbor is 210.34.12.2,  remote AS 1968, external link
  BGP version 4, remote router ID 0.0.0.0
  BGP state = Idle
  Last read 00:00:09, hold time is 180, keepalive interval is 60 seconds
  Received 0 messages, 0 notifications, 0 in queue
  Sent 0 messages, 0 notifications, 0 in queue
  Route refresh request: received 0, sent 0
  Default minimum time between advertisement runs is 30 seconds
 For address family: IPv4 Unicast
  BGP table version 1, neighbor version 0
  Index 1, Offset 0, Mask 0x2
  0 accepted prefixes consume 0 bytes
  Prefix advertised 0, suppressed 0, withdrawn 0
  Number of NLRIs in the update sent: max 0, min 0
  Connections established 0; dropped 0
  Last reset never
  External BGP neighbor not directly connected.
  No active TCP connection
```

For instance, the first highlighted line shows that the local BGP speaker is unaware of the remote peer's BGP router ID, indicating that the local router has never seen the remote peer's BGP router ID. Also, notice that the BGP session is in the Idle state, which generally indicates that there was a problem establishing a TCP session between the peers. No BGP messages have been sent or received from the remote peer, as indicated by the zero sent and received BGP messages, and no connections have been established or dropped. The reason for the problem is clearly displayed in the line "External BGP neighbor not directly connected." In addition, the final line of the command output clearly shows that there is no active TCP connection between the peers. If you are having problems connecting E-BGP-speaking routers, you should always use the **show ip bgp neighbors** command for help diagnosing error conditions. Example 8-53 shows the configurations for the Willoughby and Geilis routers.

Example 8-53 *Willoughby and Geilis Router Configurations*

```
hostname Willoughby
!
interface Serial0
 ip address 46.79.82.90 255.255.255.252
!
interface FastEthernet0
 ip address 210.34.12.1 255.255.255.0
!
router ospf 1
 network 46.79.82.88 0.0.0.3 area 0
 network 210.34.12.0 0.0.0.255 area 0
```

```
hostname Geilis
!
interface Loopback10
 ip address 198.77.1.1 255.255.0.0
!
interface Loopback20
 ip address 198.78.1.1 255.255.255.0
!
interface FastEthernet0
 ip address 210.34.12.2 255.255.255.0
!
router ospf 1
 network 210.34.12.0 0.0.0.255 area 0
!
router bgp 1968
 bgp log-neighbor-changes
 network 198.77.0.0 mask 255.255.0.0
 network 198.78.1.0
 neighbor 46.79.82.89 remote-as 1743
 neighbor 46.79.82.89 ebgp-multihop 2
 no auto-summary
```

Now that you have a practical view about how BGP is configured and how to troubleshoot BGP connection problems, it is time to examine how BGP interacts with other routing protocols, how it stores routes in the table, and how it can be configured to advertise local networks.

BGP and IGP Interaction

One thing that you must always remember when using BGP as your AS routing protocol is that, unlike distance-vector and link-state protocols such as OSPF and EIGRP, BGP is a path-vector routing protocol. It does not route packets based on hops, costs, or other metrics like IGP protocols; it routes based on AS paths. Keeping this in mind will save hours of troubleshooting when you notice BGP behaving differently than IGP protocols.

Keep in mind these rules when using BGP with other IGP protocols:

- BGP will not put routes that it cannot verify reachability for in the main IP routing table.

- For routers to successfully use BGP routes, they must always have a route to the next-hop IP address in the main IP routing table.

- Unless otherwise configured, BGP stores only the best path to a destination network in the main IP routing table. However, you can use the BGP **maximum-paths** command, discussed in Chapter 9, to configure more than one path.

- BGP advertises only the best path to a destination network. You can control BGP path selection using BGP attributes, and you can control the best path selection process using certain Cisco IOS Software BGP configuration commands, which are discussed in Chapter 9.

- BGP follows its own best path decision process to find the most efficient path; this path is stored in the main routing table.

- BGP forms peer relationships only with explicitly configured peers, and only advertises networks that it was explicitly configured to advertise.

- BGP does not redistribute its routes into IGPs unless explicitly configured to do so.

- BGP is an extremely customizable protocol; it can be as dynamic or static as it is configured to be. You can advertise and control route policies in a number of different ways.

Using BGP as a Routing Protocol

You can use BGP to complement your existing IGP protocols in several ways. The easiest way to design a BGP network is first to analyze your IP addressing, verifying that you have created a network design that allows for route aggregation and route table conservation. Suppose, for instance, that you are responsible for designing a national enterprise network, and that you have been assigned a /22 block of public IP addresses to use across that network. In this case, you have to decide where to put your primary data-center locations, how to allocate IP addresses to take advantage of your routing protocols. During this process, you must create policies that specify which router to filter, how route aggregation and summarization will be accomplished, and how these routes will be advertised (to internal peers, to external partners, and the Internet).

Assume that your company has decided to build four major data centers that will peer with two service providers for Internet routing, and that you will use OSPF for your internal IGP routing protocol. Also assume that you were assigned the 109.248.4.0/22 block of IP addresses and AS number 444. You can break that IP allocation into four /24 networks and spread those across the nation, with one /24 per data center. Table 8-13 shows how you can break the /22 network into four /24 networks and spread them across the nation to sites in Los Angeles, Dallas, Chicago, and Boston.

Table 8-14   *IP Addressing for a Nationwide Enterprise Network*

Los Angeles	Dallas	Chicago	Boston
109.248.4.0/24	109.248.5.0/24	109.248.6.0/24	109.248.7.0/24

To provide hierarchical routing for your new network, you need to aggregate those addresses at each Internet border router and advertise the aggregate networks to each of the service providers at each data center. To provide carrier redundancy, each data center will require at least two E-BGP connections, and, to create a full I-BGP mesh, there will need to be an I-BGP connection between each of the Internet border routers inside of your autonomous system. To provide a successful design to your company, you have to make sure that the OSPF design sends its updates to the BGP routers, and that each of the Internet border routers has information about the routes it learned from the OSPF routing process. You need to do this so that, in the event that one of the border routers becomes unavailable, the other three routers can successfully advertise your network to the Internet. Figure 8-10 shows a high-level example of how the autonomous system border routers in this example can be arranged to handle routes for each state for which the data center provides routing.

Figure 8-10 *Autonomous System Border Router Arrangement for National Network with Four Data Centers*

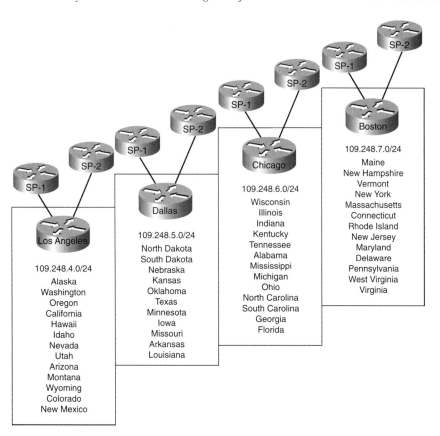

In this example, OSPF enables you to advertise and summarize the /27 or /28 networks that are used for smaller sites, using the OSPF ASBR routers to aggregate those smaller networks into /24 blocks that can be sent, through a firewall, to the Internet border routers, where they will be advertised to the Internet.

Now that you have an idea of how you can use BGP in a practical real-world example, let's look at how BGP uses the main IP routing table to store and advertise its routes, how IGPs learn BGP routes, and how to configure BGP to advertise different network types.

BGP and IP Routing Tables

In Chapter 7, you saw a brief overview of how BGP used its tables to store and advertise routes, and you learned the process that BGP uses to update the main IP routing table so that the routes can be used to forward traffic. Now you will see how you need to configure BGP to perform these functions, and what you can do to control the routing policies.

How BGP Stores Routes

Before BGP advertises a route to a peer, it always checks the validity of the route. Therefore, if the route originated locally, BGP checks to see whether the route exists in the main IP routing table, or whether the route was received from a peering router. It verifies that it can reach the next hop for that route. If either of these cases is not true, the router only stores the route in its BGP routing table, as you can see using the **show ip bgp** command, and the router does not advertise the route to any of its peers or store it in the main IP routing table.

NOTE   Always check your typing before troubleshooting BGP. Cisco IOS Software enables you to type any valid IP address as a network using the **network** command. If you accidentally mistype a network address (for instance **10.1.1.1 mask 255.255.255.0**, rather than **10.1.1.0 mask 255.255.255.0**), the router will accept the network configuration, and you might spend time trying to figure out why BGP is not advertising the 10.1.1.0/24 network, when you really configured it to advertise the 10.1.1.1/24 network.

Advertising Local Networks

There are quite a few ways to advertise networks to BGP peers; the command that you use to advertise the networks depends on a few variables. For example, you might want BGP to control exactly which networks BGP advertises to its remote peers. You might want to advertise any network that the router is directly connected to, or you might want to advertise static routes to networks, to "nail them down" so that when the path to that network changes, the route that BGP advertises to its upstream peers stays the same. Or, under certain circumstances, you might want to advertise an entire IGP routing process to the remote peers. BGP enables you to control how you advertise networks, by giving you different options on route origination. These options include the following:

- Using the **network** command
- Redistributing connected networks
- Redistributing static routes
- Redistributing IGP routes

This section shows you how to use the commands listed here to advertise networks to BGP peers. The network shown in Figure 8-11 is used for the following examples.

Figure 8-11 *Reservoir Network*

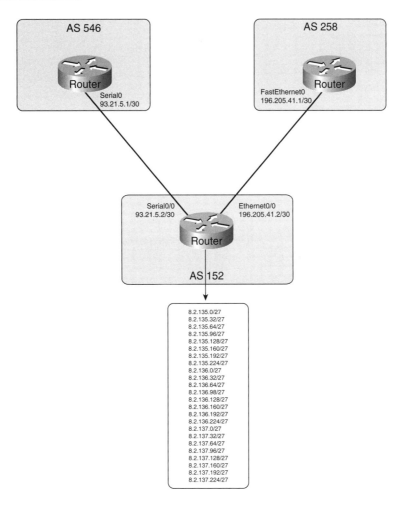

AS 546

AS 258

Router

Router

Serial0
93.21.5.1/30

FastEthernet0
196.205.41.1/30

Serial0/0
93.21.5.2/30

Ethernet0/0
196.205.41.2/30

Router

AS 152

8.2.135.0/27
8.2.135.32/27
8.2.135.64/27
8.2.135.96/27
8.2.135.128/27
8.2.135.160/27
8.2.135.192/27
8.2.135.224/27
8.2.136.0/27
8.2.136.32/27
8.2.136.64/27
8.2.136.98/27
8.2.136.128/27
8.2.136.160/27
8.2.136.192/27
8.2.136.224/27
8.2.137.0/27
8.2.137.32/27
8.2.137.64/27
8.2.137.96/27
8.2.137.128/27
8.2.137.160/27
8.2.137.192/27
8.2.137.224/27

Advertising Connected Networks

As previously mentioned, if you have a need to dynamically advertise directly connected networks, you might choose to redistribute connected networks into the local BGP process, which will limit the amount of static configuration. Take a look at the router in Example 8-54, for instance; more than 20 loopback interfaces need to be advertised using BGP.

Example 8-54 *Advertising Many Directly Connected Networks*

```
Black# show ip interface brief
Interface              IP-Address      OK? Method Status      Protocol
Ethernet0/0            196.205.41.2    YES manual up              up
Serial0/0              93.21.5.2       YES manual up              up
Loopback2              8.2.135.1       YES manual up              up
Loopback3              8.2.135.33      YES manual up              up
Loopback4              8.2.135.65      YES manual up              up
Loopback5              8.2.135.97      YES manual up              up
Loopback6              8.2.135.129     YES manual up              up
Loopback7              8.2.135.161     YES manual up              up
Loopback8              8.2.135.193     YES manual up              up
Loopback9              8.2.135.225     YES manual up              up
Loopback10             8.2.136.1       YES manual up              up
Loopback11             8.2.136.33      YES manual up              up
Loopback12             8.2.136.65      YES manual up              up
Loopback13             8.2.136.97      YES manual up              up
Loopback14             8.2.136.129     YES manual up              up
Loopback15             8.2.136.161     YES manual up              up
Loopback16             8.2.136.193     YES manual up              up
Loopback17             8.2.136.225     YES manual up              up
Loopback18             8.2.137.1       YES manual up              up
Loopback19             8.2.137.33      YES manual up              up
Loopback20             8.2.137.65      YES manual up              up
Loopback21             8.2.137.97      YES manual up              up
Loopback22             8.2.137.129     YES manual up              up
Loopback23             8.2.137.161     YES manual up              up
Loopback24             8.2.137.193     YES manual up              up
Loopback25             8.2.137.225     YES manual up              up
```

You could advertise all these networks using the BGP **network** command, which would require quite a bit of configuration and no dynamic route additions or subtractions, and allow for plenty of room for typos, as shown in Example 8-55.

Example 8-55 *Using the* **network** *Command to Advertise Networks*

```
Black# show run | begin bgp
router bgp 152
 bgp log-neighbor-changes
 network 8.2.135.0 mask 255.255.255.224
 network 8.2.135.32 mask 255.255.255.224
 network 8.2.135.64 mask 255.255.255.224
```

Example 8-55 *Using the* **network** *Command to Advertise Networks (Continued)*

```
 network 8.2.135.96 mask 255.255.255.224
 network 8.2.135.128 mask 255.255.255.224
 network 8.2.135.160 mask 255.255.255.224
 network 8.2.135.192 mask 255.255.255.224
 network 8.2.135.224 mask 255.255.255.224
 network 8.2.136.0 mask 255.255.255.224
 network 8.2.136.32 mask 255.255.255.224
 network 8.2.136.64 mask 255.255.255.224
 network 8.2.136.98 mask 255.255.255.224
 network 8.2.136.128 mask 255.255.255.224
 network 8.2.136.160 mask 255.255.255.224
 network 8.2.136.192 mask 255.255.255.224
 network 8.2.136.224 mask 255.255.255.224
 network 8.2.137.0 mask 255.255.255.224
 network 8.2.137.32 mask 255.255.255.224
 network 8.2.137.64 mask 255.255.255.224
 network 8.2.137.96 mask 255.255.255.224
 network 8.2.137.128 mask 255.255.255.224
 network 8.2.137.160 mask 255.255.255.224
 network 8.2.137.192 mask 255.255.255.224
 network 8.2.137.224 mask 255.255.255.224
 neighbor 93.21.5.1 remote-as 546
 neighbor 196.205.41.1 remote-as 258

Black# show ip bgp
BGP table version is 32, local router ID is 8.2.137.225
Status codes: s suppressed, d damped, h history, * valid, > best, i - internal
Origin codes: i - IGP, e - EGP, ? - incomplete
   Network          Next Hop          Metric LocPrf Weight Path
*> 8.2.135.0/27     0.0.0.0                0         32768 i
*> 8.2.135.32/27    0.0.0.0                0         32768 i
*> 8.2.135.64/27    0.0.0.0                0         32768 i
*> 8.2.135.96/27    0.0.0.0                0         32768 i
*> 8.2.135.128/27   0.0.0.0                0         32768 i
*> 8.2.135.160/27   0.0.0.0                0         32768 i
*> 8.2.135.192/27   0.0.0.0                0         32768 i
*> 8.2.135.224/27   0.0.0.0                0         32768 i
*> 8.2.136.0/27     0.0.0.0                0         32768 i
*> 8.2.136.32/27    0.0.0.0                0         32768 i
*> 8.2.136.64/27    0.0.0.0                0         32768 i
*> 8.2.136.128/27   0.0.0.0                0         32768 i
*> 8.2.136.160/27   0.0.0.0                0         32768 i
*> 8.2.136.192/27   0.0.0.0                0         32768 i
*> 8.2.136.224/27   0.0.0.0                0         32768 i
*> 8.2.137.0/27     0.0.0.0                0         32768 i
*> 8.2.137.32/27    0.0.0.0                0         32768 i
*> 8.2.137.64/27    0.0.0.0                0         32768 i
   Network          Next Hop          Metric LocPrf Weight Path
*> 8.2.137.96/27    0.0.0.0                0         32768 i
```

continues

Example 8-55 *Using the* **network** *Command to Advertise Networks (Continued)*

```
*> 8.2.137.128/27   0.0.0.0                0          32768 i
*> 8.2.137.160/27   0.0.0.0                0          32768 i
*> 8.2.137.192/27   0.0.0.0                0          32768 i
*> 8.2.137.224/27   0.0.0.0                0          32768 i
```

Alternatively, you could use the **redistribute connected** command to tell BGP to automatically redistribute all directly connected networks, as shown in Example 8-56.

Example 8-56 *Using the* **redistribute connected** *Command*

```
Black# show run | begin bgp
router bgp 152
 no synchronization
 bgp log-neighbor-changes
 redistribute connected
 neighbor 93.21.5.1 remote-as 546
 neighbor 196.205.41.1 remote-as 258

Black# show ip bgp
BGP table version is 5, local router ID is 8.2.137.225
Status codes: s suppressed, d damped, h history, * valid, > best, i - internal
Origin codes: i - IGP, e - EGP, ? - incomplete
   Network          Next Hop           Metric LocPrf Weight Path
*> 8.0.0.0          0.0.0.0                 0          32768 ?
*> 93.0.0.0         0.0.0.0                 0          32768 ?
*> 196.205.41.0     0.0.0.0                 0          32768 ?
```

Notice that when you use the **redistribute connected** command, as in the preceding example, BGP automatically summarizes networks at their classful boundaries. It is fairly unusual to have networks that can be summarized on their classful network boundaries; to overcome the default BGP behavior, you can use the **no auto-summary** command to tell BGP not to summarize networks, as shown in Example 8-57.

Example 8-57 *Using the BGP* **no auto-summary** *Command*

```
Black# show run | begin bgp
router bgp 152
 bgp log-neighbor-changes
 redistribute connected
 neighbor 93.21.5.1 remote-as 546
 neighbor 196.205.41.1 remote-as 258
 no auto-summary

Black# show ip bgp
BGP table version is 28, local router ID is 8.2.137.225
```

Example 8-57 *Using the BGP* **no auto-summary** *Command (Continued)*

```
Status codes: s suppressed, d damped, h history, * valid, > best, i - internal
Origin codes: i - IGP, e - EGP, ? - incomplete
   Network          Next Hop          Metric LocPrf Weight Path
*> 1.1.1.1/32       0.0.0.0                0          32768 ?
*> 8.2.135.0/27     0.0.0.0                0          32768 ?
*> 8.2.135.32/27    0.0.0.0                0          32768 ?
*> 8.2.135.64/27    0.0.0.0                0          32768 ?
*> 8.2.135.96/27    0.0.0.0                0          32768 ?
*> 8.2.135.128/27   0.0.0.0                0          32768 ?
*> 8.2.135.160/27   0.0.0.0                0          32768 ?
*> 8.2.135.192/27   0.0.0.0                0          32768 ?
*> 8.2.135.224/27   0.0.0.0                0          32768 ?
*> 8.2.136.0/27     0.0.0.0                0          32768 ?
*> 8.2.136.32/27    0.0.0.0                0          32768 ?
*> 8.2.136.64/27    0.0.0.0                0          32768 ?
*> 8.2.136.96/27    0.0.0.0                0          32768 ?
*> 8.2.136.128/27   0.0.0.0                0          32768 ?
*> 8.2.136.160/27   0.0.0.0                0          32768 ?
*> 8.2.136.192/27   0.0.0.0                0          32768 ?
*> 8.2.136.224/27   0.0.0.0                0          32768 ?
*> 8.2.137.0/27     0.0.0.0                0          32768 ?
   Network          Next Hop          Metric LocPrf Weight Path
*> 8.2.137.32/27    0.0.0.0                0          32768 ?
*> 8.2.137.64/27    0.0.0.0                0          32768 ?
*> 8.2.137.96/27    0.0.0.0                0          32768 ?
*> 8.2.137.128/27   0.0.0.0                0          32768 ?
*> 8.2.137.160/27   0.0.0.0                0          32768 ?
*> 8.2.137.192/27   0.0.0.0                0          32768 ?
*> 8.2.137.224/27   0.0.0.0                0          32768 ?
*> 93.21.5.0/30     0.0.0.0                0          32768 ?
*> 196.205.41.0/30  0.0.0.0                0          32768 ?
```

Advertising Static Routes

One way to make BGP announce very stable routes to the Internet is to "nail the routes down" using static routes to null0 with a high administrative distance. This causes the router to advertise the network specified by the static route to its neighbors. Because the static route to null0 has a high administrative distance (such as 253), any routes received from other routing protocols are preferred for use in the main IP routing table. Dynamic routes, learned from IGP neighbors, can change or even disappear. BGP will still advertise the "nailed-down" networks, without interruption, because of the static routes. Example 8-58 shows how you use the **redistribute static** command, static routes to null0, and the **no auto-summary** command to create stable Internet-facing routes.

Example 8-58 *Redistributing Static Routes*

```
Black# show run | begin bgp
router bgp 152
 no synchronization
 bgp log-neighbor-changes
 redistribute static
 neighbor 93.21.5.1 remote-as 546
 neighbor 196.205.41.1 remote-as 258
 no auto-summary
!
ip classless
ip route 8.2.135.0 255.255.255.224 Null0 254
ip route 8.2.135.32 255.255.255.224 Null0 254
ip route 8.2.135.64 255.255.255.224 Null0 254
ip route 8.2.135.96 255.255.255.224 Null0 254
ip route 8.2.135.128 255.255.255.224 Null0 254
ip route 8.2.135.160 255.255.255.224 Null0 254
ip route 8.2.135.192 255.255.255.224 Null0 254
ip route 8.2.135.224 255.255.255.224 Null0 254
ip route 8.2.136.0 255.255.255.224 Null0 254
ip route 8.2.136.32 255.255.255.224 Null0 254
ip route 8.2.136.64 255.255.255.224 Null0 254
ip route 8.2.136.96 255.255.255.224 Null0 254
ip route 8.2.136.128 255.255.255.224 Null0 254
ip route 8.2.136.160 255.255.255.224 Null0 254
ip route 8.2.136.192 255.255.255.224 Null0 254
ip route 8.2.136.224 255.255.255.224 Null0 254
ip route 8.2.137.0 255.255.255.224 Null0 254
ip route 8.2.137.32 255.255.255.224 Null0 254
ip route 8.2.137.64 255.255.255.224 Null0 254
ip route 8.2.137.96 255.255.255.224 Null0 254
ip route 8.2.137.128 255.255.255.224 Null0 254
ip route 8.2.137.160 255.255.255.224 Null0 254
ip route 8.2.137.192 255.255.255.224 Null0 254
ip route 8.2.137.224 255.255.255.224 Null0 254
```

```
Black# show ip bgp
BGP table version is 25, local router ID is 1.1.1.1
Status codes: s suppressed, d damped, h history, * valid, > best, i - internal
Origin codes: i - IGP, e - EGP, ? - incomplete
   Network          Next Hop            Metric LocPrf Weight Path
*> 8.2.135.0/27     0.0.0.0                  0         32768 ?
*> 8.2.135.32/27    0.0.0.0                  0         32768 ?
*> 8.2.135.64/27    0.0.0.0                  0         32768 ?
*> 8.2.135.96/27    0.0.0.0                  0         32768 ?
*> 8.2.135.128/27   0.0.0.0                  0         32768 ?
*> 8.2.135.160/27   0.0.0.0                  0         32768 ?
*> 8.2.135.192/27   0.0.0.0                  0         32768 ?
*> 8.2.135.224/27   0.0.0.0                  0         32768 ?
*> 8.2.136.0/27     0.0.0.0                  0         32768 ?
*> 8.2.136.32/27    0.0.0.0                  0         32768 ?
*> 8.2.136.64/27    0.0.0.0                  0         32768 ?
```

Example 8-58 *Redistributing Static Routes (Continued)*

```
*> 8.2.136.96/27     0.0.0.0             0        32768 ?
*> 8.2.136.128/27    0.0.0.0             0        32768 ?
*> 8.2.136.160/27    0.0.0.0             0        32768 ?
*> 8.2.136.192/27    0.0.0.0             0        32768 ?
*> 8.2.136.224/27    0.0.0.0             0        32768 ?
*> 8.2.137.0/27      0.0.0.0             0        32768 ?
*> 8.2.137.32/27     0.0.0.0             0        32768 ?
   Network           Next Hop      Metric LocPrf Weight Path
*> 8.2.137.64/27     0.0.0.0             0        32768 ?
*> 8.2.137.96/27     0.0.0.0             0        32768 ?
*> 8.2.137.128/27    0.0.0.0             0        32768 ?
*> 8.2.137.160/27    0.0.0.0             0        32768 ?
*> 8.2.137.192/27    0.0.0.0             0        32768 ?
*> 8.2.137.224/27    0.0.0.0             0        32768 ?
```

Notice that each of the routes is stored in the BGP table ready to be advertised to any remote peers; if an IGP route exists, the router forwards all traffic for the networks specified by the **redistribute static** command on to the correct destination, allowing IGP routes to change or disappear with no BGP service interruption. Just keep in mind that if you use a static route to null0, you still have to have a route to the destination network with a lower administrative distance; otherwise, the router actually forwards the routes to interface null0—the bit bucket.

Advertising Routes Learned via IGPs

The last, and least desirable, way to locally originate routes into BGP is to redistribute IGP routes into BGP dynamically. This is not a recommended practice because IGP routes tend to change rather often, and you (and anyone that you peer with) will not want BGP to constantly add, change, or remove IGP redistributed routes on a regular basis. However, you can configure BGP to have IGP routes redistributed directly into BGP by using the **redistribute** *protocol* command. Example 8-59 shows how routes advertised by an OSPF process are dynamically redistributed into BGP. This example shows the routes received by OSPF, the OSPF/BGP configuration, and the final BGP table.

Example 8-59 *Redistributing IGP Routes into BGP*

```
Black# show run | begin ospf
router ospf 1
 log-adjacency-changes
 network 8.2.138.0 0.0.0.3 area 0
Black# show ip route
      196.205.41.0/30 is subnetted, 1 subnets
C        196.205.41.0 is directly connected, Ethernet0/0
      8.0.0.0/8 is variably subnetted, 25 subnets, 2 masks
O        8.2.137.129/32 [110/65] via 8.2.138.2, 00:02:29, Serial0/1
O        8.2.136.129/32 [110/65] via 8.2.138.2, 00:02:29, Serial0/1
```

continues

Example 8-59 *Redistributing IGP Routes into BGP (Continued)*

```
O       8.2.135.129/32 [110/65] via 8.2.138.2, 00:02:29, Serial0/1
O       8.2.137.161/32 [110/65] via 8.2.138.2, 00:02:29, Serial0/1
O       8.2.136.161/32 [110/65] via 8.2.138.2, 00:02:30, Serial0/1
O       8.2.135.161/32 [110/65] via 8.2.138.2, 00:02:30, Serial0/1
O       8.2.137.193/32 [110/65] via 8.2.138.2, 00:02:30, Serial0/1
O       8.2.136.193/32 [110/65] via 8.2.138.2, 00:02:30, Serial0/1
O       8.2.135.193/32 [110/65] via 8.2.138.2, 00:02:31, Serial0/1
O       8.2.137.225/32 [110/65] via 8.2.138.2, 00:02:31, Serial0/1
O       8.2.136.225/32 [110/65] via 8.2.138.2, 00:02:31, Serial0/1
O       8.2.135.225/32 [110/65] via 8.2.138.2, 00:02:31, Serial0/1
C       8.2.138.0/30 is directly connected, Serial0/1
O       8.2.137.1/32 [110/65] via 8.2.138.2, 00:02:31, Serial0/1
O       8.2.136.1/32 [110/65] via 8.2.138.2, 00:02:31, Serial0/1
O       8.2.135.1/32 [110/65] via 8.2.138.2, 00:02:31, Serial0/1
O       8.2.137.33/32 [110/65] via 8.2.138.2, 00:02:31, Serial0/1
O       8.2.136.33/32 [110/65] via 8.2.138.2, 00:02:31, Serial0/1
O       8.2.135.33/32 [110/65] via 8.2.138.2, 00:02:31, Serial0/1
O       8.2.137.65/32 [110/65] via 8.2.138.2, 00:02:31, Serial0/1
O       8.2.136.65/32 [110/65] via 8.2.138.2, 00:02:31, Serial0/1
O       8.2.135.65/32 [110/65] via 8.2.138.2, 00:02:31, Serial0/1
O       8.2.137.97/32 [110/65] via 8.2.138.2, 00:02:31, Serial0/1
O       8.2.136.97/32 [110/65] via 8.2.138.2, 00:02:32, Serial0/1
O       8.2.135.97/32 [110/65] via 8.2.138.2, 00:02:32, Serial0/1
     93.0.0.0/30 is subnetted, 1 subnets
C       93.21.5.0 is directly connected, Serial0/0
Black# show run | begin bgp
router bgp 152
 no synchronization
 bgp log-neighbor-changes
 redistribute ospf 1 match internal external 1 external 2
 neighbor 93.21.5.1 remote-as 546
 neighbor 196.205.41.1 remote-as 258
 no auto-summary
Black# show ip bgp
BGP table version is 26, local router ID is 1.1.1.1
Status codes: s suppressed, d damped, h history, * valid, > best, i - internal
Origin codes: i - IGP, e - EGP, ? - incomplete
   Network          Next Hop          Metric LocPrf Weight Path
*> 8.2.135.1/32     8.2.138.2             65         32768 ?
*> 8.2.135.33/32    8.2.138.2             65         32768 ?
*> 8.2.135.65/32    8.2.138.2             65         32768 ?
*> 8.2.135.97/32    8.2.138.2             65         32768 ?
*> 8.2.135.129/32   8.2.138.2             65         32768 ?
*> 8.2.135.161/32   8.2.138.2             65         32768 ?
*> 8.2.135.193/32   8.2.138.2             65         32768 ?
*> 8.2.135.225/32   8.2.138.2             65         32768 ?
*> 8.2.136.1/32     8.2.138.2             65         32768 ?
*> 8.2.136.33/32    8.2.138.2             65         32768 ?
*> 8.2.136.65/32    8.2.138.2             65         32768 ?
*> 8.2.136.97/32    8.2.138.2             65         32768 ?
*> 8.2.136.129/32   8.2.138.2             65         32768 ?
*> 8.2.136.161/32   8.2.138.2             65         32768 ?
*> 8.2.136.193/32   8.2.138.2             65         32768 ?
```

Example 8-59 *Redistributing IGP Routes into BGP (Continued)*

```
*> 8.2.136.225/32   8.2.138.2            65        32768 ?
*> 8.2.137.1/32     8.2.138.2            65        32768 ?
*> 8.2.137.33/32    8.2.138.2            65        32768 ?
   Network          Next Hop        Metric LocPrf Weight Path
*> 8.2.137.65/32    8.2.138.2            65        32768 ?
*> 8.2.137.97/32    8.2.138.2            65        32768 ?
*> 8.2.137.129/32   8.2.138.2            65        32768 ?
*> 8.2.137.161/32   8.2.138.2            65        32768 ?
*> 8.2.137.193/32   8.2.138.2            65        32768 ?
*> 8.2.137.225/32   8.2.138.2            65        32768 ?
*> 8.2.138.0/30     0.0.0.0               0        32768 ?
```

Notice in the preceding example that redistribution between IGP and BGP is a fairly straightforward process, only requiring one or two commands (depending on your **auto-summary** requirements). However, the amount of routes redistributed into BGP could be rather large, and the routes will only be as stable as the networks that the IGPs are advertising. It is best to save this command for when absolutely necessary.

Lab 14: BGP Routing

As you have learned in this chapter, there are many ways to use BGP in a production network; the most common use is to use BGP to multihome a network to two or more service providers for Internet access. The following lab concentrates on the different BGP connection types and provides an application for BGP route testing using Voice over IP (VoIP).

Lab Exercise

In this lab, you configure BGP peering relationships between the "I-Scream for Coffee" 32-flavor network and use the BGP routing as a backbone for routing between the external networks hosted by the Mint and Chocolate routers in autonomous systems 203 and 507, and the internal networks hosted by the Vanilla, Strawberry, Latte, and Americano routers in AS 409. To test your skill in BGP routing, you have to send test calls between the phones on the Chocolate and Latte routers.

Lab Objectives

- Use E-BGP and I-BGP with associated commands to perform routing between autonomous systems.
- Allow BGP routes to pass through access lists.
- Configure BGP around IGP routers, without enabling BGP on all routers.
- Use the routes provided by BGP to make test calls over phones connected between routers in different autonomous systems.

Equipment Needed

- Seven Cisco routers (two with voice modules to allow for VoIP testing).
- Six routers will require only one or two serial interfaces, and three routers will require serial and Ethernet or Token Ring interfaces.
- One hub, switch, or MSAU, which is required to connect the three multiaccess routers.

Physical Layout and Prestaging

- Cable the routers as shown in Figure 8-12. The Mint, Chocolate, Vanilla, and Strawberry routers can be connected using back-to-back serial cables.

Figure 8-12   *The I-Scream for Coffee Network*

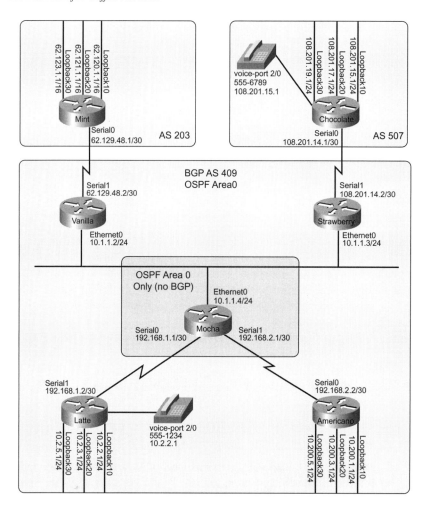

- The Vanilla, Strawberry, and Mocha routers require back-to-back serial and Ethernet (or Token Ring) connections.

- The Mocha, Latte, and Americano routers also require back-to-back serial connections.

- Configure all IP addresses on the loopback, serial, and Ethernet interfaces, as shown in Figure 8-12.

- Enable OSPF routing on all routers except for Mint and Chocolate; with the exception of the loopback interfaces, all interfaces on these routers should belong to OSPF area 0. Make sure OSPF advertisements are not sent out non-OSPF interfaces.

To successfully complete this lab, follow these steps:

Step 1   Configure E-BGP peering sessions between the Mint and Vanilla routers; assign the Mint router to AS 203 and the Vanilla router to AS 409. After configuring BGP on the Mint and Vanilla routers, configure BGP on the Chocolate and Strawberry routers. Put the Chocolate router in AS 507 and the Strawberry router in AS 409. Advertise all external loopback interfaces from AS 203 and AS 507, using BGP without using the **network** command. Do not allow BGP routers to perform auto summarization. Test the BGP router configurations using the **show ip bgp** and **show ip bgp summary** commands. To verify TCP reachability for the sessions, use the **show ip bgp neighbors** and **show tcp brief all** commands.

Step 2   Configure an I-BGP connection between the Strawberry and Vanilla routers, and verify that the Mint, Vanilla, Chocolate, and Strawberry routers can all reach each other's BGP routes.

Step 3   Configure I-BGP between the Vanilla, Latte, and Americano routers and the Strawberry, Latte, and Americano routers. Configure the Latte and Americano routers to advertise their loopback and serial IP addresses into BGP. Verify that all BGP routers can reach all other routers.

Step 4   Test the configuration using an application. To do this, make voice calls between the Chocolate and Latte routers. To configure VoIP on the Chocolate and Latte routers, create dial peers, add destination patterns and an IP address or physical port, and then dial from the phones. (For more information on VoIP configuration, refer to *CCIE Practical Studies,* Volume I.)

Lab Walkthrough

After cabling all the routers, verify connectivity using the **show cdp neighbors** and **show ip interface brief** commands; this will save a lot of time troubleshooting cabling and clock rate problems. After verifying Layer 2 connectivity, assign IP addresses to each of the routers using the information from Figure 8-12. After assigning all IP addresses, verify Layer 3 connectivity between directly connected networks using the **ping** command. Now that you have verified that all routers can reach each other, enable OSPF routing on all routers and put all of their interfaces in area 0. Each router should use the nonloopback interface with the highest IP address as the OSPF router ID. After enabling OSPF, verify that all routers have routes to all other OSPF routers using the **show ip route**, **show ip ospf neighbors**, and **show ip ospf interfaces** commands, and verify that they can ping each other before proceeding to Step 1.

Step 1   Configure E-BGP peering sessions between the Mint and Vanilla routers; assign the Mint router to AS 203 and the Vanilla router to AS 409. After configuring BGP on the Mint and Vanilla routers, configure BGP on the Chocolate and Strawberry routers. Put the Chocolate router in AS 507 and the Strawberry router in AS 409. Advertise all external loopback interfaces from AS 203 and AS 507, using BGP without using the **network** command. Do not allow BGP routers to perform auto summarization. Test the BGP router configurations using the **show ip bgp** and **show ip bgp summary** commands. To verify TCP reachability for the sessions, use the **show ip bgp neighbors** and **show tcp brief all** commands. Example 8-60 shows the configuration for the Mint and Vanilla routers, and Example 8-61 shows the configuration for the Chocolate and Strawberry routers.

Example 8-60 *BGP Configuration for the Mint and Vanilla Routers*

```
Mint# show run | begin bgp
router bgp 203
 no synchronization
 bgp log-neighbor-changes
 redistribute connected
 neighbor 62.129.48.2 remote-as 409
 no auto-summary

Vanilla# show run | begin bgp
router bgp 409
 no synchronization
 bgp log-neighbor-changes
 neighbor 62.129.48.1 remote-as 203
 no auto-summary
Vanilla# show ip bgp
BGP table version is 17, local router ID is 62.129.48.6
Status codes: s suppressed, d damped, h history, * valid, > best, i - internal,
Origin codes: i - IGP, e - EGP, ? - incomplete
```

Example 8-60 *BGP Configuration for the Mint and Vanilla Routers (Continued)*

```
     Network          Next Hop         Metric LocPrf Weight Path
*>  62.120.0.0/16    62.129.48.1           0               0 203 ?
*>  62.121.0.0/16    62.129.48.1           0               0 203 ?
*>  62.123.0.0/16    62.129.48.1           0               0 203 ?
*>  62.129.48.0/30   62.129.48.1           0               0 203 ?
```

Example 8-61 *BGP Configuration for the Chocolate and Strawberry Routers*

```
Chocolate# show run | begin bgp
router bgp 507
 no synchronization
 bgp log-neighbor-changes
 redistribute connected
 neighbor 108.201.14.2 remote-as 409
 no auto-summary

Strawberry# show run | begin bgp
router bgp 409
 no synchronization
 bgp log-neighbor-changes
 neighbor 108.201.14.1 remote-as 507
 no auto-summary
Strawberry# show ip bgp
BGP table version is 11, local router ID is 108.201.14.10
Status codes: s suppressed, d damped, h history, * valid, > best, i - internal,
Origin codes: i - IGP, e - EGP, ? - incomplete

     Network           Next Hop         Metric LocPrf Weight Path
*>  108.201.14.0/30   108.201.14.1          0               0 507 ?
*>  108.201.15.0/24   108.201.14.1          0               0 507 ?
*>  108.201.17.0/24   108.201.14.1          0               0 507 ?
*>  108.201.19.0/24   108.201.14.1          0               0 507 ?
```

Step 2 Configure an I-BGP connection between the Strawberry and Vanilla routers, and verify that the Mint, Vanilla, Chocolate, and Strawberry routers can all reach each other's BGP routes. Example 8-62 shows how I-BGP was configured on the Vanilla and Strawberry routers, and the routes that are exchanged between those routers.

Example 8-62 *I-BGP Configuration for the Strawberry and Vanilla Routers*

```
Strawberry(config)# router bgp 409
Strawberry(config-router)# neighbor 10.1.1.2 remote-as 409
Strawberry(config-router)# neighbor 10.1.1.2 next-hop-self
Strawberry# show ip bgp | begin Network
```

continues

Example 8-62 *I-BGP Configuration for the Strawberry and Vanilla Routers (Continued)*

```
   Network          Next Hop          Metric LocPrf Weight Path
*>i62.120.0.0/16    10.1.1.2              0    100     0 203 ?
*>i62.121.0.0/16    10.1.1.2              0    100     0 203 ?
*>i62.123.0.0/16    10.1.1.2              0    100     0 203 ?
*>i62.129.48.0/30   10.1.1.2              0    100     0 203 ?
*> 108.201.14.0/30  108.201.14.1         0            0 507 ?
*> 108.201.15.0/24  108.201.14.1         0            0 507 ?
*> 108.201.17.0/24  108.201.14.1         0            0 507 ?
*> 108.201.19.0/24  108.201.14.1         0            0 507 ?

Vanilla(config)#router bgp 409
Vanilla(config-router)#neighbor 10.1.1.3 remote-as 409
Vanilla(config-router)# neighbor 10.1.1.3 next-hop-self
Vanilla# show ip bgp | begin Network
   Network          Next Hop          Metric LocPrf Weight Path
*> 62.120.0.0/16    62.129.48.1          0            0 203 ?
*> 62.121.0.0/16    62.129.48.1          0            0 203 ?
*> 62.123.0.0/16    62.129.48.1          0            0 203 ?
*> 62.129.48.0/30   62.129.48.1          0            0 203 ?
*>i108.201.14.0/30  10.1.1.3             0    100     0 507 ?
*>i108.201.15.0/24  10.1.1.3             0    100     0 507 ?
*>i108.201.17.0/24  10.1.1.3             0    100     0 507 ?
*>i108.201.19.0/24  10.1.1.3             0    100     0 507 ?
```

The preceding example also demonstrated how the **neighbor** *ip-address*
next-hop-self command was used to alter the NEXT_HOP attribute for
routes passed between the I-BGP peers. Also, notice that after configuring
BGP routing between the Vanilla and Strawberry routers, even though the
routers have valid routes in their BGP tables, the Vanilla router cannot ping
the Chocolate router's networks, and the Strawberry router cannot ping the
Mint router's networks, as shown here:

```
Vanilla# ping 108.201.14.1
Type escape sequence to abort.
Sending 5, 100-byte ICMP Echos to 108.201.14.1, timeout is 2 seconds:
.....
Success rate is 0 percent (0/5)
Strawberry# ping 62.129.48.1

Type escape sequence to abort.
Sending 5, 100-byte ICMP Echos to 62.129.48.1, timeout is 2 seconds:
.....
Success rate is 0 percent (0/5)
Strawberry#
```

After verifying that the Mint router could ping the Vanilla router and that the
Strawberry router could ping the Chocolate router, the problem is identified
on the Chocolate (or Mint, whichever you look at first) router, namely that
the Chocolate router does not know how to reach anything on the 10.0.0.0/8

network (the Vanilla and Strawberry router's ping source IP address). To fix this problem, add a network statement to the Strawberry and Vanilla routers to advertise the 10.1.1.0/24 network to both the Mint and Chocolate routers and try again. Example 8-63 shows the Strawberry BGP network configuration addition and the subsequent changes that result in the Chocolate router's IP routing table. This example also shows that, after the Chocolate router receives the route to the 10.1.1.0/24 network, all four BGP routers can now ping all the BGP networks.

Example 8-63 *Adding a Route to the 10.1.1.0/24 Network*

```
Strawberry(config)#router bgp 409
Strawberry(config-router)# network 10.1.1.0 mask 255.255.255.0
Chocolate# show ip route | begin Gateway
Gateway of last resort is not set
     10.0.0.0/24 is subnetted, 1 subnets
B       10.1.1.0 [20/0] via 108.201.14.10, 00:00:32
     108.0.0.0/8 is variably subnetted, 5 subnets, 3 masks
S       108.201.14.10/32 [1/0] via 108.201.14.2
C       108.201.15.0/24 is directly connected, Loopback10
C       108.201.14.0/30 is directly connected, Serial0
C       108.201.17.0/24 is directly connected, Loopback20
C       108.201.19.0/24 is directly connected, Loopback30
Chocolate# ping 10.1.1.2
Type escape sequence to abort.
Sending 5, 100-byte ICMP Echos to 10.1.1.2, timeout is 2 seconds:
!!!!!
Success rate is 100 percent (5/5), round-trip min/avg/max = 40/42/44 ms
Vanilla# ping 108.201.14.1
Type escape sequence to abort.
Sending 5, 100-byte ICMP Echos to 108.201.14.1, timeout is 2 seconds:
!!!!!
Success rate is 100 percent (5/5), round-trip min/avg/max = 4/4/8 ms
```

Step 3   Configure I-BGP between the Vanilla, Latte, and Americano routers and the Strawberry, Latte, and Americano routers. Configure the Latte and Americano routers to advertise their loopback and serial IP addresses into BGP. Verify that all BGP routers can reach all other routers. Example 8-64 shows the configuration and BGP table for the Vanilla router.

Example 8-64 *Configuration and BGP Table for the Vanilla Router*

```
Vanilla# show run | begin bgp
router bgp 409
 no synchronization
 bgp log-neighbor-changes
 network 10.1.1.0 mask 255.255.255.0
```

continues

Example 8-64 *Configuration and BGP Table for the Vanilla Router (Continued)*

```
 neighbor 10.1.1.3 remote-as 409
 neighbor 10.1.1.3 next-hop-self
 neighbor 62.129.48.1 remote-as 203
 neighbor 192.168.1.2 remote-as 409
 neighbor 192.168.2.2 remote-as 409
 no auto-summary
Vanilla# show ip bgp
BGP table version is 435, local router ID is 62.129.48.6
Status codes: s suppressed, d damped, h history, * valid, > best, i - internal
Origin codes: i - IGP, e - EGP, ? - incomplete
   Network          Next Hop          Metric LocPrf Weight Path
* i10.1.1.0/24      10.1.1.3               0    100      0 i
*>                  0.0.0.0                0          32768 i
*>i10.2.2.0/24      192.168.1.2            0    100      0 ?
*>i10.2.3.0/24      192.168.1.2            0    100      0 ?
*>i10.2.5.0/24      192.168.1.2            0    100      0 ?
*>i10.200.1.0/24    192.168.2.2            0    100      0 ?
*>i10.200.3.0/24    192.168.2.2            0    100      0 ?
*>i10.200.5.0/24    192.168.2.2            0    100      0 ?
*> 62.120.0.0/16    62.129.48.1            0             0 203 ?
*> 62.121.0.0/16    62.129.48.1            0             0 203 ?
*> 62.123.0.0/16    62.129.48.1            0             0 203 ?
*> 62.129.48.0/30   62.129.48.1            0             0 203 ?
*>i108.201.14.0/30  10.1.1.3               0    100      0 507 ?
*>i108.201.15.0/24  10.1.1.3               0    100      0 507 ?
*>i108.201.17.0/24  10.1.1.3               0    100      0 507 ?
*>i108.201.19.0/24  10.1.1.3               0    100      0 507 ?
*>i192.168.1.0/30   192.168.1.2            0    100      0 ?
*>i192.168.2.0/30   192.168.2.2            0    100      0 ?
```

Now, take a look at the Latte router. Notice that the Latte router is not storing the external BGP routes as reachable; they have *, but no >, meaning they are valid, but not reachable, as shown in Example 8-65.

Example 8-65 *Latte Router's BGP Table*

```
Latte# show ip bgp
BGP table version is 6, local router ID is 10.2.5.1
Status codes: s suppressed, d damped, h history, * valid, > best, i - internal
Origin codes: i - IGP, e - EGP, ? - incomplete
   Network          Next Hop          Metric LocPrf Weight Path
*>i10.1.1.0/24      10.1.1.3               0    100      0 i
* i                 10.1.1.2               0    100      0 i
*> 10.2.2.0/24      0.0.0.0                0          32768 ?
*> 10.2.3.0/24      0.0.0.0                0          32768 ?
*> 10.2.5.0/24      0.0.0.0                0          32768 ?
* i62.120.0.0/16    62.129.48.1            0    100      0 203 ?
* i62.121.0.0/16    62.129.48.1            0    100      0 203 ?
* i62.123.0.0/16    62.129.48.1            0    100      0 203 ?
* i62.129.48.0/30   62.129.48.1            0    100      0 203 ?
```

Example 8-65 *Latte Router's BGP Table (Continued)*

```
  * i108.201.14.0/30    108.201.14.1           0    100      0 507 ?
  * i108.201.15.0/24    108.201.14.1           0    100      0 507 ?
  * i108.201.17.0/24    108.201.14.1           0    100      0 507 ?
  * i108.201.19.0/24    108.201.14.1           0    100      0 507 ?
  *> 192.168.1.0/30     0.0.0.0                0          32768 ?
     Network            Next Hop        Metric LocPrf Weight Path
  *>i192.168.2.0/30     192.168.2.2            0    100      0 i
```

The routes are not reachable because the upstream BGP neighbors are
advertising them with the original E-BGP next hop of 62.129.48.1 and
108.201.14.1 rather than local, reachable networks that the Latte and
Americano are aware of (by means of OSPF). The answer to this problem is
very simple and requires only a few steps—add the **next-hop-self** statement
to all the I-BGP-speaking routers; clear the BGP process; add two routes to
the Mocha router, telling it how to get to the 62.0.0.0/8 and 108.201.0.0/16
networks; and disable synchronization on all the I-BGP speaking routers so
that they will not wait for OSPF routes to those networks. After making those
configuration changes, check the routes again. Example 8-66 shows the steps
taken to correct the I-BGP routing problem and the solution.

Example 8-66 *Steps to Correct the I-BGP Routing Problem*

```
Vanilla# show run | begin bgp
router bgp 409
 no synchronization
 bgp log-neighbor-changes
 network 10.1.1.0 mask 255.255.255.0
 neighbor 10.1.1.3 remote-as 409
 neighbor 10.1.1.3 next-hop-self
 neighbor 62.129.48.1 remote-as 203
 neighbor 192.168.1.2 remote-as 409
 neighbor 192.168.1.2 next-hop-self
 neighbor 192.168.2.2 remote-as 409
 neighbor 192.168.2.2 next-hop-self

Strawberry# show run | begin bgp
router bgp 409
 no synchronization
 bgp log-neighbor-changes
 network 10.1.1.0 mask 255.255.255.0
 neighbor 10.1.1.2 remote-as 409
 neighbor 10.1.1.2 next-hop-self
 neighbor 108.201.14.1 remote-as 507
 neighbor 192.168.1.2 remote-as 409
 neighbor 192.168.1.2 next-hop-self
 neighbor 192.168.2.2 remote-as 409
 neighbor 192.168.2.2 next-hop-self
```

continues

Example 8-66 *Steps to Correct the I-BGP Routing Problem (Continued)*

```
 no auto-summary

Mocha# show run | begin ip route
ip route 62.0.0.0 255.0.0.0 10.1.1.2
ip route 108.201.0.0 255.255.0.0 10.1.1.3

Latte# show run | begin bgp
router bgp 409
 no synchronization
 bgp log-neighbor-changes
 network 10.2.2.0 mask 255.255.255.0
 network 10.2.3.0 mask 255.255.255.0
 network 10.2.5.0 mask 255.255.255.0
 network 192.168.1.0 mask 255.255.255.252
 neighbor 10.1.1.2 remote-as 409
 neighbor 10.1.1.2 next-hop-self
 neighbor 10.1.1.3 remote-as 409
 neighbor 10.1.1.3 next-hop-self
 neighbor 192.168.2.2 remote-as 409
 neighbor 192.168.2.2 next-hop-self
 no auto-summary

Americano# show run | begin bgp
router bgp 409
 no synchronization
 network 10.200.1.0 mask 255.255.255.0
 network 10.200.3.0 mask 255.255.255.0
 network 10.200.5.0 mask 255.255.255.0
 network 192.168.2.0 mask 255.255.255.252
 neighbor 10.1.1.2 remote-as 409
 neighbor 10.1.1.2 next-hop-self
 neighbor 10.1.1.3 remote-as 409
 neighbor 10.1.1.3 next-hop-self
 neighbor 192.168.1.2 remote-as 409
 neighbor 192.168.1.2 next-hop-self
 no auto-summary
```

Example 8-67 shows the Latte BGP table before the changes, and Example 8-68 shows the BGP table after the changes. In the first example, notice that the 62.120.0.0/16, 62.121.0.0/16, 62.122.0.0/16, 62.129.48.0/30, 108.201.14.0/30, 108.201.15.0/24, 108.201.17.0/24, and 108.201.19.0/24 networks are not reachable, and in the second example, after you add the **next-hop-self** statement and fix the bad next-hop routing problem, they are all reachable.

Example 8-67 *Latte BGP Table Before* **next-hop-self**

```
Latte# show ip bgp
BGP table version is 6, local router ID is 10.2.5.1
Status codes: s suppressed, d damped, h history, * valid, > best, i - internal
Origin codes: i - IGP, e - EGP, ? - incomplete
   Network          Next Hop         Metric LocPrf Weight Path
*>i10.1.1.0/24      10.1.1.3              0    100      0 i
*  i                10.1.1.2              0    100      0 i
*> 10.2.2.0/24      0.0.0.0              0          32768 ?
*> 10.2.3.0/24      0.0.0.0              0          32768 ?
*> 10.2.5.0/24      0.0.0.0              0          32768 ?
*  i62.120.0.0/16   62.129.48.1          0    100      0 203 ?
*  i62.121.0.0/16   62.129.48.1          0    100      0 203 ?
*  i62.123.0.0/16   62.129.48.1          0    100      0 203 ?
*  i62.129.48.0/30  62.129.48.1          0    100      0 203 ?
*  i108.201.14.0/30 108.201.14.1         0    100      0 507 ?
*  i108.201.15.0/24 108.201.14.1         0    100      0 507 ?
*  i108.201.17.0/24 108.201.14.1         0    100      0 507 ?
*  i108.201.19.0/24 108.201.14.1         0    100      0 507 ?
*> 192.168.1.0/30   0.0.0.0              0          32768 ?
   Network          Next Hop         Metric LocPrf Weight Path
*>i192.168.2.0/30   192.168.2.2          0    100      0 I
```

Example 8-68 *Latte BGP Table After* **next-hop-self**

```
Latte# show ip bgp
BGP table version is 15, local router ID is 10.2.5.1
Status codes: s suppressed, d damped, h history, * valid, > best, i - internal
Origin codes: i - IGP, e - EGP, ? - incomplete
   Network          Next Hop         Metric LocPrf Weight Path
*>i10.1.1.0/24      10.1.1.2              0    100      0 i
*  i                10.1.1.3              0    100      0 i
*> 10.2.2.0/24      0.0.0.0              0          32768 ?
*> 10.2.3.0/24      0.0.0.0              0          32768 ?
*> 10.2.5.0/24      0.0.0.0              0          32768 ?
*>i62.120.0.0/16    10.1.1.2             0    100      0 203 ?
*>i62.121.0.0/16    10.1.1.2             0    100      0 203 ?
*>i62.123.0.0/16    10.1.1.2             0    100      0 203 ?
*>i62.129.48.0/30   10.1.1.2             0    100      0 203 ?
*>i108.201.14.0/30  10.1.1.3             0    100      0 507 ?
*>i108.201.15.0/24  10.1.1.3             0    100      0 507 ?
*>i108.201.17.0/24  10.1.1.3             0    100      0 507 ?
*>i108.201.19.0/24  10.1.1.3             0    100      0 507 ?
*> 192.168.1.0/30   0.0.0.0              0          32768 ?
   Network          Next Hop         Metric LocPrf Weight Path
*>i192.168.2.0/30   192.168.2.2          0    100      0 I
```

```
Latte# ping 108.201.14.1
Type escape sequence to abort.
```

continues

Example 8-68 *Latte BGP Table After* **next-hop-self** *(Continued)*

```
Sending 5, 100-byte ICMP Echos to 108.201.14.1, timeout is 2 seconds:
!!!!!
Success rate is 100 percent (5/5), round-trip min/avg/max = 40/42/44 ms
```

> **Step 4**   Test the configuration using an application. To do this, make voice calls
> between the Chocolate and Latte routers. To configure VoIP on the Chocolate
> and Latte routers, create dial peers, add destination patterns and an IP address
> or physical port, and then dial from the phones. (For more information on
> VoIP configuration, refer to *CCIE Practical Studies, Volume I*.) Example 8-69
> shows the voice configuration for the Chocolate router, and Example 8-70
> shows the voice configuration for the Latte router.

Example 8-69 *Chocolate Router's Voice Configuration*

```
Chocolate# show run | begin dial
dial-peer voice 5551234 voip
 destination-pattern 5551234
 session target ipv4:10.2.2.1
 !
dial-peer voice 5556789 pots
 destination-pattern 5556789
 port 2/0
```

Example 8-70 *Latte Router's Voice Configuration*

```
Latte# show run | begin dial
dial-peer voice 5556789 voip
 destination-pattern 5556789
 session target ipv4:108.201.15.1
 !
dial-peer voice 5551234 pots
 destination-pattern 5551234
 port 2/0
```

Now that the introductory BGP configuration and troubleshooting commands have been
covered, it is time to look into the features that make BGP the most powerful protocol available
for IP routing. Chapter 9 covers advanced BGP features, such as the use of the BGP attribute,
route filtering and policy, route aggregation, manipulating the best path selection process, and
tuning BGP. Example 8-71 shows the final configurations for all routers in this lab.

Example 8-71 *Final Router Configurations for Lab 11*

```
hostname Mint
!
interface Loopback10
 ip address 62.120.1.1 255.255.0.0
!
interface Loopback20
 ip address 62.121.1.1 255.255.0.0
!
interface Loopback30
 ip address 62.123.1.1 255.255.0.0
!
interface Serial0
 ip address 62.129.48.1 255.255.255.252
clockrate 1300000
!
router bgp 203
 no synchronization
 bgp log-neighbor-changes
 redistribute connected
 neighbor 62.129.48.2 remote-as 409
 no auto-summary
```

```
hostname Vanilla
!
interface Ethernet0
 ip address 10.1.1.2 255.255.255.0
!
interface Serial1
ip address 62.129.48.2 255.255.255.252
!
router ospf 1
router-id 10.1.1.2
 log-adjacency-changes
 passive-interface Serial1
 network 10.1.1.0 0.0.0.255 area 0
 network 62.129.48.0 0.0.0.3 area 0
!
router bgp 409
 no synchronization
 bgp log-neighbor-changes
 network 10.1.1.0 mask 255.255.255.0
 neighbor 10.1.1.3 remote-as 409
 neighbor 10.1.1.3 next-hop-self
 neighbor 62.129.48.1 remote-as 203
 neighbor 192.168.1.2 remote-as 409
 neighbor 192.168.1.2 next-hop-self
 neighbor 192.168.2.2 remote-as 409
 neighbor 192.168.2.2 next-hop-self
 no auto-summary
```

continues

Example 8-71 *Final Router Configurations for Lab 11 (Continued)*

```
hostname Chocolate
!
voice-port 2/0
!
voice-port 2/1
!
dial-peer voice 5551234 voip
 destination-pattern 5551234
 session target ipv4:10.2.2.1
!
dial-peer voice 5556789 pots
 destination-pattern 5556789
 port 2/0
!
interface Loopback10
 ip address 108.201.15.1 255.255.255.0
!
interface Loopback20
 ip address 108.201.17.1 255.255.255.0
!
interface Loopback30
 ip address 108.201.19.1 255.255.255.0
!
interface Serial0
 ip address 108.201.14.1 255.255.255.252
!
router bgp 507
 no synchronization
 bgp log-neighbor-changes
 redistribute connected
 neighbor 108.201.14.2 remote-as 409
 no auto-summary
!
```

```
hostname Strawberry
!
interface Ethernet0
 ip address 10.1.1.3 255.255.255.0
!
interface Serial1
 ip address 108.201.14.2 255.255.255.252
 clockrate 1300000
!
router ospf 1
 router-id 10.1.1.3
 log-adjacency-changes
 passive-interface Serial1
 network 10.1.1.0 0.0.0.255 area 0
 network 108.201.14.0 0.0.0.3 area 0
```

Example 8-71 *Final Router Configurations for Lab 11 (Continued)*

```
!
router bgp 409
 no synchronization
 bgp log-neighbor-changes
 network 10.1.1.0 mask 255.255.255.0
 neighbor 10.1.1.2 remote-as 409
 neighbor 10.1.1.2 next-hop-self
 neighbor 108.201.14.1 remote-as 507
 neighbor 192.168.1.2 remote-as 409
 neighbor 192.168.1.2 next-hop-self
 neighbor 192.168.2.2 remote-as 409
 neighbor 192.168.2.2 next-hop-self
 no auto-summary
```

```
hostname Mocha
!
interface Ethernet0
 ip address 10.1.1.4 255.255.255.0
!
interface Serial0
 ip address 192.168.1.1 255.255.255.252
 clock rate 1300000
!
interface Serial1
 ip address 192.168.2.1 255.255.255.252
!
router ospf 1
 log-adjacency-changes
 network 10.1.1.0 0.0.0.255 area 0
 network 192.168.1.0 0.0.0.3 area 0
 network 192.168.2.0 0.0.0.3 area 0
!
ip classless
ip route 62.0.0.0 255.0.0.0 10.1.1.2
ip route 108.201.0.0 255.255.0.0 10.1.1.3
```

```
hostname Latte
!
voice-port 2/0
!
voice-port 2/1
!
dial-peer voice 5556789 voip
 destination-pattern 5556789
 session target ipv4:108.201.15.1
!
dial-peer voice 5551234 pots
 destination-pattern 5551234
 port 2/0
```

continues

Example 8-71 *Final Router Configurations for Lab 11 (Continued)*

```
!
interface Loopback10
 ip address 10.2.2.1 255.255.255.0
!
interface Loopback20
 ip address 10.2.3.1 255.255.255.0
!
interface Loopback30
 ip address 10.2.5.1 255.255.255.0
!
interface Serial0
 ip address 192.168.1.2 255.255.255.252
!
router ospf 1
 log-adjacency-changes
 network 10.2.2.0 0.0.0.255 area 0
 network 10.2.3.0 0.0.0.255 area 0
 network 10.2.5.0 0.0.0.255 area 0
 network 192.168.1.0 0.0.0.3 area 0
!
router bgp 409
 no synchronization
 bgp log-neighbor-changes
 redistribute connected
 network 10.200.1.0 mask 255.255.255.0
 network 10.200.3.0 mask 255.255.255.0
 network 10.200.5.0 mask 255.255.255.0
 network 192.168.1.0 mask 255.255.255.252
 neighbor 10.1.1.2 remote-as 409
 neighbor 10.1.1.2 next-hop-self
 neighbor 10.1.1.3 remote-as 409
 neighbor 10.1.1.3 next-hop-self
 neighbor 192.168.2.2 remote-as 409
 neighbor 192.168.2.2 next-hop-self
 no auto-summary
```

```
hostname Americano
!
interface Loopback10
 ip address 10.200.1.1 255.255.255.0
!
interface Loopback20
 ip address 10.200.3.1 255.255.255.0
!
interface Loopback30
 ip address 10.200.5.1 255.255.255.0
!
interface Serial0
 ip address 192.168.2.2 255.255.255.252
 clockrate 1300000
!
```

Example 8-71 *Final Router Configurations for Lab 11 (Continued)*

```
router ospf 1
 log-adjacency-changes
 network 10.200.1.0 0.0.0.255 area 0
 network 10.200.3.0 0.0.0.255 area 0
 network 10.200.5.0 0.0.0.255 area 0
 network 192.168.2.0 0.0.0.3 area 0
 !
router bgp 409
no synchronization
 network 10.200.1.0 mask 255.255.255.0
 network 10.200.3.0 mask 255.255.255.0
 network 10.200.5.0 mask 255.255.255.0
 network 192.168.2.0 mask 255.255.255.252
 neighbor 10.1.1.2 remote-as 409
 neighbor 10.1.1.2 next-hop-self
 neighbor 10.1.1.3 remote-as 409
 neighbor 10.1.1.3 next-hop-self
 neighbor 192.168.1.2 remote-as 409
 neighbor 192.168.1.2 next-hop-self
 no auto-summary
```

Further Reading

Cisco IOS Configuration Fundamentals, by Cisco Systems Inc., Riva Technologies

TCP/IP Principles, Protocols, and Architectures, by Douglas E. Comer

Internet Routing Architectures, Second Edition, by Sam Halabi with Danny McPherson

Routing TCP/IP, Volume II, by Jeff Doyle and Jennifer DeHaven Carroll

Cisco BGP-4 Command and Configuration Handbook, by William R. Parkhurst

CHAPTER 9

Advanced BGP Configuration

The preceding chapter discussed several BGP troubleshooting concepts, examined simple BGP designs, and showed how to advertise various types of BGP networks. Together, the last two chapters provided the foundation, or a review of BGP concepts, that allow for a more technical discussion of the advanced topics covered in this chapter. This chapter demonstrates ways to use BGP to support larger, more stable networks and explains how to implement advanced routing policies. This chapter covers the following topics:

- BGP router authentication
- How to simplify large network implementations with route reflectors and confederations
- The effective use of BGP peer groups
- Advanced BGP redistribution methods
- BGP route filtering, suppression, and conditional advertisements
- Route dampening
- Route aggregation and policies
- The use of BGP backdoors
- How to configure BGP to support different route table sizes and maintaining symmetric routes
- Tuning BGP performance

BGP Neighbor Authentication

One of the easiest ways to reduce security risks on a BGP network is to use BGP peer authentication. The Cisco implementation of BGP uses the TCP MD-5 signature as specified in RFC 2385. This algorithm takes a key, the password entered during configuration, and performs an MD-5 hash on the key, and sends the resulting hash to the remote peer. The password itself is never sent over the connection.

Only one configuration step is required to use BGP MD-5 password authentication; that step is enabling password authentication on a peer-by-peer basis using the **neighbor** *ip-address* **password** *password* command, shown here:

```
neighbor {ip-address | peer-group} password [0-7] password-string
```

This command also has an optional parameter, which enables you to use a previously encrypted password by specifying the password level of 7, as follows:

```
SlyDog(config-router)# neighbor 8.8.9.1 password 7 1511021F0725
```

Both sides of an authenticated BGP peer session must use the same password. If a router receives a BGP OPEN message with an invalid password, it sends a NOTIFICATION message with the OPEN message error stating that there has been an authentication failure. Example 9-1 shows how password authentication is used to protect a session between two E-BGP peers.

Example 9-1   *BGP MD-5 Password Authentication*

```
Mariner# show run | begin bgp
router bgp 5151
 bgp log-neighbor-changes
 neighbor 217.204.187.8 remote-as 1578
 neighbor 217.204.187.8 password cisco

OtherGuys# show run | begin bgp
router bgp 1578
 bgp log-neighbor-changes
 neighbor 217.204.187.7 remote-as 5151
 neighbor 217.204.187.7 password cisco
```

Although the use of MD-5 authentication does not completely guarantee the safety of a BGP session, it does reduce the risk of a BGP session attack.

Simplifying Large BGP Networks

One issue that eventually appears in almost any large BGP network is that of design complexity. When you have a large number of BGP-speaking routers that have a large number of BGP peers, either internally or externally, you eventually need to reassess the network design to determine ways to create a simpler, more scalable network. Proactive network professionals plan their network so that each of the routers has the capacity to hold a large BGP Routing Information Base (RIB) and plan for future network growth while considering the many factors that affect the network design and implementation, some of which are listed here:

- The number of routers participating in E-BGP peering sessions and the number of peers that must be configured

- The number, size, and frequency of the BGP updates sent between the peering routers

- Asymmetric routes caused by multiple paths

- The number of paths that must be sent between peers prior to network convergence, and the delay that the convergence time has upon network applications

- The possibility of route dampening due to route instability

- The full-mesh requirement for I-BGP peers
- Long, complicated router configurations, with the possibility for human error during router configuration

You can deal with each of these issues in several ways. This section examines how the use of route reflectors and confederations help solve the I-BGP full-mesh problem, and how peer groups and route aggregation can help control the size and complexity of large BGP implementations.

Route Reflectors

BGP *route reflectors*, defined in RFC 1966, provide a simple solution to the I-BGP full-mesh problem for large I-BGP implementations. As a quick review, there are two entities in a route reflector scenario: the server and the clients. Each route reflector server requires an I-BGP peer connection to each of its clients. However, the clients require only a connection to the route reflector server. The server sends updates to each of the client routers through the I-BGP connection, eliminating the need for a fully meshed topology. Figure 9-1 shows a before and after look at an I-BGP network in need of help.

Figure 9-1   *Before and After Route Reflectors*

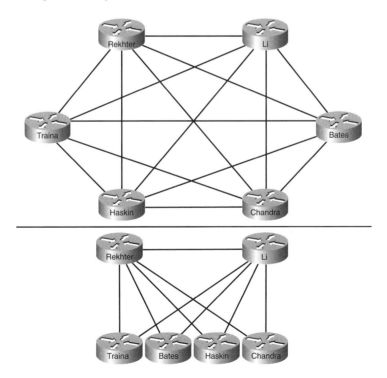

In the first part of the figure, each of the 6 routers has an I-BGP peer connection to each of its peers, creating 15 I-BGP connections. The second part of the figure shows how route reflectors simplify the I-BGP configuration for each of the six routers—with Routers Rekhter and Li acting as route reflector servers; and Routers Traina, Haskin, Bates, and Chandra acting as route reflector clients to the Rekhter and Li routers. When route reflector clients are homed to two or more route reflector servers, path redundancy is still maintained, and the configurations are greatly simplified.

You must complete two steps to create a route reflector server, sometimes referred to as a *route server*. This process is demonstrated here using the network in Figure 9-2.

Figure 9-2   *Route Reflection*

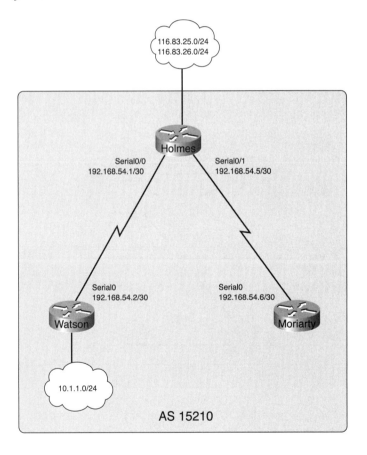

Step 1   Configure I-BGP peer connections for each of the BGP peers with which the route reflector server will peer. Example 9-2 shows the initial BGP configuration for the Holmes router.

Example 9-2 *Configuring the Holmes Router as a Route Reflector Server*

```
Holmes# show run | begin bgp
 router bgp 15210
 no synchronization
 neighbor 192.168.54.2 remote-as 15210
 neighbor 192.168.54.6 remote-as 15210
```

Step 2   On the route reflector server, configure each of the neighbors that are to act
as route reflector clients using the **neighbor** *ip-address* **route-reflector-
client** command. Example 9-3 shows the route reflector server configuration
from the Holmes router.

Example 9-3 *Holmes Router's Route Reflector Configuration*

```
 neighbor 192.168.54.2 route-reflector-client
 neighbor 192.168.54.6 route-reflector-client
```

No special configuration steps need to occur to make a router act as a route reflector client. All
you need to do is configure the client to peer with the route reflector server. Example 9-4 shows
the BGP configuration for the Watson and Moriarty route reflector clients.

Example 9-4 *BGP Configuration for the Route Reflector Clients*

```
Watson# show run | begin bgp
router bgp 15210
 no synchronization
 neighbor 192.168.54.1 remote-as 15210

Moriarty# show run | begin bgp
router bgp 15210
 no synchronization
 neighbor 192.168.54.5 remote-as 15210
```

The **show ip bgp neighbors | include BGP neighbor|Route-Reflector** command displays a
brief summary of the routers that the route reflector server is providing routes to, as shown in
Example 9-5.

Example 9-5 *Displaying Route Reflector Client Summary*

```
Holmes# show ip bgp neighbors | include BGP neighbor|Route-Reflector
BGP neighbor is 192.168.54.2,  remote AS 15210, internal link
  Route-Reflector Client
BGP neighbor is 192.168.54.6,  remote AS 15210, internal link
  Route-Reflector Client
```

To verify a route learned from a route reflector server, use the **show ip bgp** *ip-prefix* command, as shown in Example 9-6.

Example 9-6 *Displaying Route Reflector Server Information*

```
Moriarty# show ip bgp 10.1.1.0/24
BGP routing table entry for 10.1.1.0/24, version 8
Paths: (1 available, best #1, table Default-IP-Routing-Table)
Flag: 0x208
  Not advertised to any peer
  Local
    192.168.54.2 from 192.168.54.5 (10.1.1.1)
      Origin IGP, metric 0, localpref 100, valid, internal, best
      Originator: 10.1.1.1, Cluster list: 116.83.26.1
```

In the preceding example, the Moriarty router shows that the route to 10.1.1.0/24 contains two new BGP attributes: the ORIGINATOR attribute, which specifies the BGP router ID for the router that originated the route; and the CLUSTER_LIST attribute, which specifies the BGP cluster ID for the route. The BGP cluster ID is the BGP router ID of the route reflector server that originated the route. The *cluster list* is a loop-avoidance mechanism designed to prevent routers belonging to a route reflector cluster from accepting routes that originated within the local cluster from routers that belong to a different cluster. If a route reflector receives a route that contains its own cluster ID in the cluster list, it ignores that route.

NOTE   If a route has passed through more than one route reflector cluster, there is more than one cluster ID in the route's cluster list. Each route reflector that forwards a route on to its clients prepends its own local cluster ID to the cluster list. For more information on these BGP attributes, refer to the "Route Reflectors" section in Chapter 7, "BGP-4 Theory."

Confederations

Another way to manage the full-mesh requirement for I-BGP peers is to configure BGP confederations. As a quick review, *BGP confederations* break large I-BGP autonomous systems into smaller, more manageable sub-autonomous systems known as *member autonomous systems*. Comparing the example shown earlier in Figure 9-1 to the confederation solution shown in Figure 9-3, you can see how the same network could be reconfigured using BGP confederations.

Figure 9-3 *Before and After BGP Confederations*

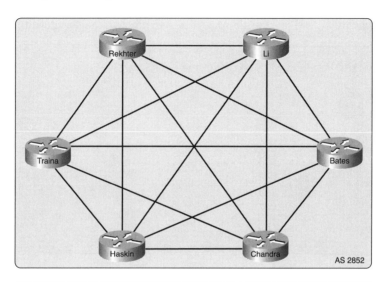

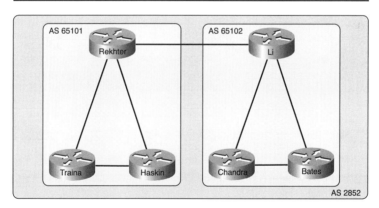

Notice in this example that confederations break Routers Rekhter, Traina, and Haskin into member autonomous systems 65,101 and routers Li, Chandra, and Bates into sub-AS 65,102. All routers in both AS 65,101 and AS 65,102 still belong to AS 2852, decreasing the number of I-BGP peer connections that have to be configured. Also, notice that each of the I-BGP routers within a sub-AS is still fully meshed with the other I-BGP peers in the same sub-AS. This brings attention to a key point about confederation use: Although confederations are a simpler solution to the I-BGP full-mesh problem, they still require full-mesh peer relationships within each sub-AS, so they still must be designed carefully to allow for growth.

You must complete five steps to configure confederations in a BGP AS. This process is described here using the network shown in Figure 9-4.

Figure 9-4 *The Good-Old-Boy Network*

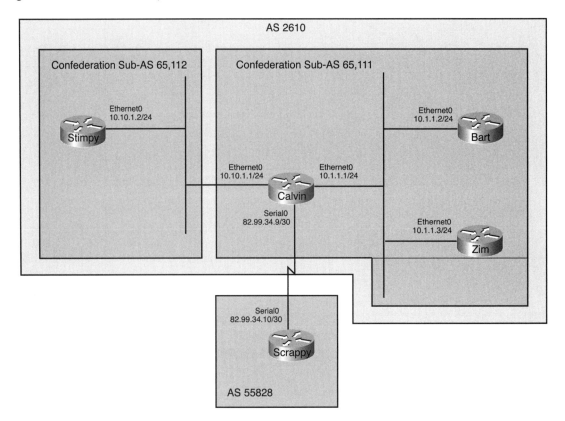

Step 1   Enable BGP routing using the member AS number as the BGP AS number, as shown here on the Calvin router:

```
Calvin(config)# router bgp 65111
```

In this example, the Calvin Router belongs to BGP sub-AS (member AS) 65,111, so the local BGP routing process is started using AS number 65,111.

Step 2 Configure the *confederation identifier*; this is the AS number that the parent
AS uses when peering with other external BGP neighbors.

```
Calvin(config-router)# bgp confederation identifier 2610
```

The BGP confederation ID defines the parent AS that the two sub-
autonomous systems, AS 65,111 and AS 65,112, both belong to.

Step 3 Configure fully meshed I-BGP sub-AS neighbor relationships using
the sub-AS number as the remote ASN for all internal I-BGP peers. In the
following example, the Calvin router peers with its I-BGP neighbors, the Bart
and Zim routers, in BGP sub-AS 65,111:

```
Calvin(config-router)# neighbor 10.1.1.2 remote-as 65111
Calvin(config-router)# neighbor 10.1.1.3 remote-as 65111
```

Step 4 Configure other BGP neighbors within the same parent AS, but not the same
confederation sub-AS as external neighbors, by specifying their sub-AS
number as the BGP remote AS number. Other confederation peers from
different sub-autonomous systems must also be identified as external
confederation peers using the **bgp confederation peers** *sub-AS number*
command, as shown here on the Calvin router:

```
Calvin(config-router)# neighbor 10.10.1.2 remote-as 65112
Calvin(config-router)# bgp confederation peers 65112
```

You can use the **bgp confederation peers** command to define multiple
confederation peer autonomous systems. When defining multiple
confederation peer autonomous systems, you can use this command in two
ways, and each method will have the same result:

— Enter the **bgp confederation peers** command followed by each of the
confederation peer AS numbers, separated by spaces.

— Enter one instance of the **bgp confederation peers** *member-AS number*
command for each confederation peer ID.

Step 5 Configure any E-BGP neighbors (peers that do not belong to the parent or
sub-autonomous systems) as you normally would configure any other E-BGP
peer. Each external peer will peer with each internal confederation peer using
the parent ASN. The external BGP neighbors are unaware of the I-BGP
confederation information from peers in other autonomous systems because
all confederation information is stripped from the AS_PATH before updates
are sent to neighboring external peers:

```
Calvin(config-router)# neighbor 82.99.34.10 remote-as 55828
```

The Calvin router forms an E-BGP peering session with the Scrappy router using its local confederation ID because the Calvin router belongs to parent AS 2610. In turn, the Scrappy router
must peer with the Calvin router using its parent AS number (the confederation ID) because that
is the only AS number of which it is aware.

NOTE	When configuring routers that belong to AS confederations, always pay close attention to the type of AS to which each peer belongs. When working with confederations, remember these three simple rules:

> - Member AS peers (peers belonging to the same sub-AS) only require a normal I-BGP neighbor definition using the **neighbor** *ip-address* **remote-as** *remote-AS-number* command.
>
> - External confederation peers (peers that belong to the same I-BGP parent AS, but different member AS numbers) require two steps: defining a peer with the **neighbor** *ip-address* **remote-as** *remote-ASN* command and the **bgp confederation peers** *remote-AS-number* command.
>
> - External BGP peers are configured using the standard E-BGP commands; however, the remote E-BGP peer will not be aware of any BGP confederation information. So, you must always make sure to use the **bgp confederation identifier** *parent-AS-number* command to define the parent AS.

To verify the configuration for each of the BGP confederation peers, use the **show ip bgp neighbors** command. This command shows each neighbor from a sub-AS as *under common administration*, as follows:

```
Calvin# show ip bgp neighbors 10.1.1.2
BGP neighbor is 10.1.1.2,  remote AS 65111, internal link
  BGP version 4, remote router ID 10.1.1.2
  Neighbor under common administration
  BGP state = Established, up for 00:00:45
  Last read 00:00:45, hold time is 180, keepalive interval is 60 seconds
  Neighbor capabilities:
    Route refresh: advertised and received(old & new)
    Address family IPv4 Unicast: advertised and received
  Received 3 messages, 0 notifications, 0 in queue
  Sent 4 messages, 0 notifications, 0 in queue
  Route refresh request: received 0, sent 0
  Default minimum time between advertisement runs is 5 seconds
```

Now that you have seen how BGP confederations can create sub-AS that simplify internal BGP configurations, examine a practical BGP confederation example.

Practical Example: BGP Confederations

In this example, using the network shown in Figure 9-5, BGP confederations split AS 7614 into two member autonomous systems, AS 65,500 and AS 65,501. This example explores a number of facets of BGP confederation configuration. It shows you how to perform the following:

- Configure peers within a member AS

- Configure special E-BGP-style peers that are within the same parent AS, but belong to a different member AS

- Configure confederation peers to interact with standard E-BGP peers

Figure 9-5   *Using Confederations to Simplify an AS*

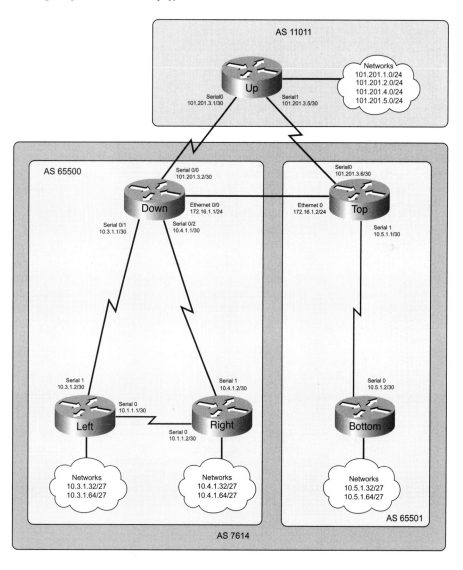

This example requires five Cisco routers with the interfaces shown in Table 9-1.

Table 9-1   *Router Interface Requirements*

Router Name	Ethernet, FastEthernet or Token Ring Interfaces	Serial Interfaces
Up	0	2
Down	1	3
Top	1	2
Right	0	2
Left	0	2
Bottom	0	1

Before configuring any routers, make sure that they are physically connected, as shown in Figure 9-5. This example, requires six back-to-back serial cables, and two Ethernet or Token Ring cables connected to a hub, switch, or multistation access unit (MSAU). If you are using a switch, all interfaces should be placed in the same VLAN:

Step 1   Configure all IP addresses as specified in the preceding figure. Place all members of AS 7614 in EIGRP process 1709. Do not send EIGRP updates out to the Up router. Verify that all interfaces are up and all routers in EIGRP 1709 can ping each other before proceeding to Step 2. Example 9-7 shows how the routing table from the Bottom router should look after completing this step.

Example 9-7   *Bottom Router's Routing Table*

```
Bottom# show ip route | include is|via
     101.0.0.0/30 is subnetted, 2 subnets
D       101.201.3.4 [90/2681856] via 10.5.1.1, 00:09:45, Serial0
D       101.201.3.0 [90/2707456] via 10.5.1.1, 00:09:45, Serial0
     172.16.0.0/24 is subnetted, 1 subnets
D      172.16.1.0 [90/2195456] via 10.5.1.1, 00:09:45, Serial0
     10.0.0.0/30 is subnetted, 4 subnets
D       10.3.1.0 [90/2707456] via 10.5.1.1, 00:09:45, Serial0
D       10.1.1.0 [90/3219456] via 10.5.1.1, 00:08:53, Serial0
C       10.5.1.0 is directly connected, Serial0
D       10.4.1.0 [90/2707456] via 10.5.1.1, 00:09:46, Serial0
```

Step 2   Configure BGP routing between the Down, Right, and Left routers. Put all routers in member AS 65,500 and parent AS 7614; BGP routes should not be summarized on classful boundaries. Example 9-8 shows the resulting BGP configuration for the Down router.

Example 9-8   *BGP Configuration for the Down Router*

```
Down# show run | begin bgp
router bgp 65500
 no synchronization
 bgp log-neighbor-changes
bgp confederation identifier 7614
 neighbor 10.3.1.2 remote-as 65500
 neighbor 10.3.1.2 route-reflector-client
 neighbor 10.3.1.2 next-hop-self
 neighbor 10.4.1.2 remote-as 65500
 neighbor 10.4.1.2 route-reflector-client
 neighbor 10.4.1.2 next-hop-self
 no auto-summary
```

The highlighted portions of the preceding example show that the member AS number is defined using the **router bgp 65500** command, and the parent AS is defined using the **bgp confederation identifier 7614** statement. If those statements had not been used, the router would have participated only in the private AS 65,500 and not been part of the parent AS. The **next-hop-self** command alters the BGP NEXT_HOP attribute for outgoing routes to the peer and changes it to the IP address for the local BGP speaker. The **route-reflector-client** command forwards routes learned by means of I-BGP peering sessions so that each of the I-BGP routers in member AS 65,500 has two routes to each network. Example 9-9 shows the BGP configurations for the Right and Left routers at the end of Step 2.

Example 9-9   *Left and Right Router Configurations*

```
Left# show run | begin bgp
router bgp 65500
 no synchronization
 bgp log-neighbor-changes
 bgp confederation identifier 7614
 network 10.3.1.32 mask 255.255.255.224
 network 10.3.1.64 mask 255.255.255.224
 neighbor 10.1.1.2 remote-as 65500
 neighbor 10.1.1.2 route-reflector-client
 neighbor 10.1.1.2 next-hop-self
 neighbor 10.3.1.1 remote-as 65500
 neighbor 10.3.1.1 route-reflector-client
 neighbor 10.3.1.1 next-hop-self
 no auto-summary

Right# show run | begin bgp
router bgp 65500
```

continues

Example 9-9   *Left and Right Router Configurations (Continued)*

```
 no synchronization
 bgp log-neighbor-changes
 bgp confederation identifier 7614
 network 10.4.1.32 mask 255.255.255.224
 network 10.4.1.64 mask 255.255.255.224
 neighbor 10.1.1.1 remote-as 65500
 neighbor 10.1.1.1 route-reflector-client
 neighbor 10.1.1.1 next-hop-self
 neighbor 10.4.1.1 remote-as 65500
 neighbor 10.4.1.1 route-reflector-client
 neighbor 10.4.1.1 next-hop-self
```

Step 3   Configure BGP routing on the Top and Bottom routers, place each router in member AS 65,501, and parent AS 7,614. Neither of these routers should auto-summarize any routes. Example 9-10 shows the resulting configuration for the Top and Bottom routers.

Example 9-10 *BGP Configuration for the Top and Bottom Routers*

```
Top# show run | begin bgp
router bgp 65501
 no synchronization
 bgp log-neighbor-changes
 bgp confederation identifier 7614
 neighbor 10.5.1.2 remote-as 65501
 neighbor 10.5.1.2 next-hop-self
 no auto-summary
```

```
Bottom# show run | begin bgp
router bgp 65501
 no synchronization
 bgp log-neighbor-changes
 bgp confederation identifier 7614
 network 10.5.1.32 mask 255.255.255.224
 network 10.5.1.65 mask 255.255.255.224
 neighbor 10.5.1.1 remote-as 65501
 no auto-summary
```

Step 4   Configure BGP routing between the Up, Down, and Top routers. Verify that the Up router receives the correct ASN from the Down and Top routers, and that the Right, Left, and Bottom routers can reach the routes advertised by the Up router. Example 9-11 shows the BGP configuration and BGP RIB for the Up router.

Example 9-11 *BGP Configuration and BGP RIB for the Up Router*

```
Up# show run | begin bgp
router bgp 11011
 no synchronization
 bgp log-neighbor-changes
 network 101.201.1.0 mask 255.255.255.0
 network 101.201.2.0 mask 255.255.255.0
 network 101.201.4.0 mask 255.255.255.0
 network 101.201.5.0 mask 255.255.255.0
 neighbor 101.201.3.2 remote-as 7614
 neighbor 101.201.3.6 remote-as 7614
 no auto-summary
Up# show ip bgp | begin Network
   Network          Next Hop         Metric LocPrf Weight Path
*  10.3.1.32/27     101.201.3.6                        0 7614 i
*>                  101.201.3.2                        0 7614 i
*  10.3.1.64/27     101.201.3.6                        0 7614 i
*>                  101.201.3.2                        0 7614 i
*  10.4.1.32/27     101.201.3.6                        0 7614 i
*>                  101.201.3.2                        0 7614 i
*  10.4.1.64/27     101.201.3.6                        0 7614 i
*>                  101.201.3.2                        0 7614 i
*  10.5.1.32/27     101.201.3.2                        0 7614 i
*>                  101.201.3.6                        0 7614 i
*  10.5.1.64/27     101.201.3.2                        0 7614 i
*>                  101.201.3.6                        0 7614 i
*> 101.201.1.0/24   0.0.0.0               0         32768 i
*> 101.201.2.0/24   0.0.0.0               0         32768 i
*> 101.201.4.0/24   0.0.0.0               0         32768 i
*> 101.201.5.0/24   0.0.0.0               0         32768 i
```

When configuring E-BGP peer relationships with confederation members, always remember to use the parent AS number for the remote AS. Example 9-12 shows the resulting configuration for the Down router.

Example 9-12 *BGP Configuration and BGP Routing Table for the Down Router*

```
Down# show run | begin bgp
router bgp 65500
 no synchronization
 bgp log-neighbor-changes
 bgp confederation identifier 7614
 bgp confederation peers 65501
 neighbor 10.3.1.2 remote-as 65500
 neighbor 10.3.1.2 route-reflector-client
 neighbor 10.3.1.2 next-hop-self
```

continues

Example 9-12 *BGP Configuration and BGP Routing Table for the Down Router (Continued)*

```
 neighbor 10.4.1.2 remote-as 65500
 neighbor 10.4.1.2 route-reflector-client
 neighbor 10.4.1.2 next-hop-self
 neighbor 101.201.3.1 remote-as 11011
 neighbor 172.16.1.2 remote-as 65501
 neighbor 172.16.1.2 next-hop-self
 no auto-summary
Down# show ip bgp | begin Network
   Network          Next Hop          Metric LocPrf Weight Path
 * i10.3.1.32/27    10.1.1.1               0    100     0 i
 *>i                10.3.1.2               0    100     0 i
 * i10.3.1.64/27    10.1.1.1               0    100     0 i
 *>i                10.3.1.2               0    100     0 i
 *>i10.4.1.32/27    10.4.1.2               0    100     0 i
 * i                10.1.1.2               0    100     0 i
 *>i10.4.1.64/27    10.4.1.2               0    100     0 i
 * i                10.1.1.2               0    100     0 i
 *> 10.5.1.32/27    172.16.1.2             0    100     0 (65501) i
 *> 10.5.1.64/27    172.16.1.2             0    100     0 (65501) i
 *  101.201.1.0/24  172.16.1.2             0    100     0 (65501) 11011 i
 *>                 101.201.3.1            0            0 11011 i
 *  101.201.2.0/24  172.16.1.2             0    100     0 (65501) 11011 i
 *>                 101.201.3.1            0            0 11011 i
 *  101.201.4.0/24  172.16.1.2             0    100     0 (65501) 11011 i
 *>                 101.201.3.1            0            0 11011 i
 *  101.201.5.0/24  172.16.1.2             0    100     0 (65501) 11011 i
 *>                 101.201.3.1            0            0 11011 i
```

In order for the Down router to form a special E-BGP type confederation peer relationship with the Top router, the bgp confederation peer 65501 statement is required. This statement tells the router that AS 65501 is also a peer member AS in the 7614 parent AS. Example 9-13 shows the BGP configuration and **show ip bgp RIB** information for the Top router.

Example 9-13 *BGP Configuration and the Resulting BGP RIB for the Top Router*

```
Top# show run | begin bgp
router bgp 65501
 no synchronization
 bgp log-neighbor-changes
 bgp confederation identifier 7614
 bgp confederation peers 65500
 neighbor 10.5.1.2 remote-as 65501
 neighbor 10.5.1.2 next-hop-self
 neighbor 101.201.3.5 remote-as 11011
 neighbor 172.16.1.1 remote-as 65500
 neighbor 172.16.1.1 next-hop-self
 no auto-summary
Top# show ip bgp | begin Network
   Network          Next Hop          Metric LocPrf Weight Path
```

Example 9-13 *BGP Configuration and the Resulting BGP RIB for the Top Router (Continued)*

```
*> 10.3.1.32/27     172.16.1.1          0    100    0 (65500) i
*> 10.3.1.64/27     172.16.1.1          0    100    0 (65500) i
*> 10.4.1.32/27     172.16.1.1          0    100    0 (65500) i
*> 10.4.1.64/27     172.16.1.1          0    100    0 (65500) i
*>i10.5.1.32/27     10.5.1.2            0    100    0 i
*>i10.5.1.64/27     10.5.1.2            0    100    0 i
*> 101.201.1.0/24   101.201.3.5         0           0 11011 i
*                   172.16.1.1          0    100    0 (65500) 11011 i
*> 101.201.2.0/24   101.201.3.5         0           0 11011 i
*                   172.16.1.1          0    100    0 (65500) 11011 i
*> 101.201.4.0/24   101.201.3.5         0           0 11011 i
*                   172.16.1.1          0    100    0 (65500) 11011 i
*> 101.201.5.0/24   101.201.3.5         0           0 11011 i
*                   172.16.1.1          0    100    0 (65500) 11011 i
```

At this point, you can ping all interfaces on all routers. If each I-BGP speaker has two routes to all the networks that originate in sub-AS 65,500, and you can successfully ping each interface on each router, you have completed this example. Example 9-14 shows the complete configurations for each of the routers from this experiment.

Example 9-14 *Complete Router Configurations*

```
Up# show run | begin int
interface Loopback100
 ip address 101.201.1.1 255.255.255.0
!
interface Loopback101
 ip address 101.201.2.1 255.255.255.0
!
interface Loopback102
 ip address 101.201.4.1 255.255.255.0
!
interface Loopback103
 ip address 101.201.5.1 255.255.255.0
!
interface Serial0
 ip address 101.201.3.1 255.255.255.252
!
interface Serial1
 ip address 101.201.3.5 255.255.255.252
!
router bgp 11011
 no synchronization
 bgp log-neighbor-changes
 network 101.201.1.0 mask 255.255.255.0
 network 101.201.2.0 mask 255.255.255.0
 network 101.201.4.0 mask 255.255.255.0
```

continues

Example 9-14 *Complete Router Configurations (Continued)*

```
 network 101.201.5.0 mask 255.255.255.0
 neighbor 101.201.3.2 remote-as 7614
 neighbor 101.201.3.6 remote-as 7614
 no auto-summary
```

```
Down# show run | begin int
interface Ethernet0/0
 ip address 172.16.1.1 255.255.255.0
 !
interface Serial0/0
 ip address 101.201.3.2 255.255.255.252
 !
interface Serial0/1
 ip address 10.3.1.1 255.255.255.252
 clock rate 1300000
 !
interface Serial0/2
 ip address 10.4.1.1 255.255.255.252
 clock rate 1300000
 !
router eigrp 1709
 passive-interface Serial0/0
 network 10.3.1.0 0.0.0.3
 network 10.4.1.0 0.0.0.3
 network 101.201.3.0 0.0.0.3
 network 172.16.1.0 0.0.0.255
 no auto-summary
 !
router bgp 65500
 no synchronization
 bgp log-neighbor-changes
 bgp confederation identifier 7614
 bgp confederation peers 65501
 neighbor 10.3.1.2 remote-as 65500
 neighbor 10.3.1.2 route-reflector-client
 neighbor 10.3.1.2 next-hop-self
 neighbor 10.4.1.2 remote-as 65500
 neighbor 10.4.1.2 route-reflector-client
 neighbor 10.4.1.2 next-hop-self
 neighbor 101.201.3.1 remote-as 11011
 neighbor 172.16.1.2 remote-as 65501
 neighbor 172.16.1.2 next-hop-self
 no auto-summary
```

```
Top# show run | begin int
interface Ethernet0
 ip address 172.16.1.2 255.255.255.0
 !
interface Serial0
 ip address 101.201.3.6 255.255.255.252
 clockrate 1300000
 !
```

Example 9-14 *Complete Router Configurations (Continued)*

```
interface Serial1
 ip address 10.5.1.1 255.255.255.252
!
router eigrp 1709
 passive-interface Serial0
 network 10.5.1.0 0.0.0.3
 network 101.201.3.4 0.0.0.3
 network 172.16.1.0 0.0.0.255
 no auto-summary
!
router bgp 65501
 no synchronization
 bgp log-neighbor-changes
 bgp confederation identifier 7614
 bgp confederation peers 65500
 neighbor 10.5.1.2 remote-as 65501
 neighbor 10.5.1.2 next-hop-self
 neighbor 101.201.3.5 remote-as 11011
 neighbor 172.16.1.1 remote-as 65500
 neighbor 172.16.1.1 next-hop-self
 no auto-summary
```

```
Left# show run | begin int
interface Loopback100
 ip address 10.3.1.33 255.255.255.224
!
interface Loopback200
 ip address 10.3.1.65 255.255.255.224
!
interface Serial0
 ip address 10.1.1.1 255.255.255.252
 clockrate 1300000
!
interface Serial1
 ip address 10.3.1.2 255.255.255.252
!
router eigrp 1709
 network 10.1.1.0 0.0.0.3
 network 10.3.1.0 0.0.0.3
 no auto-summary
!
router bgp 65500
 no synchronization
 bgp log-neighbor-changes
 bgp confederation identifier 7614
 network 10.3.1.32 mask 255.255.255.224
 network 10.3.1.64 mask 255.255.255.224
 neighbor 10.1.1.2 remote-as 65500
 neighbor 10.1.1.2 route-reflector-client
 neighbor 10.1.1.2 next-hop-self
```

continues

Example 9-14 *Complete Router Configurations (Continued)*

```
 neighbor 10.4.1.1 remote-as 65500
 neighbor 10.3.1.1 route-reflector-client
 neighbor 10.3.1.1 next-hop-self
 no auto-summary
```

```
Right# show run | begin int
interface Loopback100
 ip address 10.4.1.33 255.255.255.224
!
interface Loopback200
 ip address 10.4.1.65 255.255.255.224
!
interface Serial0
 ip address 10.1.1.2 255.255.255.252
!
interface Serial1
 ip address 10.4.1.2 255.255.255.252
!
router eigrp 1709
 network 10.1.1.0 0.0.0.3
 network 10.4.1.0 0.0.0.3
 no auto-summary
!
router bgp 65500
 no synchronization
 bgp log-neighbor-changes
 bgp confederation identifier 7614
 network 10.4.1.32 mask 255.255.255.224
 network 10.4.1.64 mask 255.255.255.224
 neighbor 10.1.1.1 remote-as 65500
 neighbor 10.1.1.1 route-reflector-client
 neighbor 10.1.1.1 next-hop-self
 neighbor 10.4.1.1 remote-as 65500
 neighbor 10.4.1.1 route-reflector-client
 neighbor 10.4.1.1 next-hop-self
 no auto-summary
```

```
Bottom# show run | begin int
interface Loopback100
 ip address 10.5.1.33 255.255.255.224
!
interface Loopback200
 ip address 10.5.1.65 255.255.255.224
!
interface Serial0
 ip address 10.5.1.2 255.255.255.252
```

Example 9-14 *Complete Router Configurations (Continued)*

```
 clockrate 1300000
!
router eigrp 1709
 network 10.5.1.0 0.0.0.3
 no auto-summary
!
router bgp 65501
 no synchronization
 bgp log-neighbor-changes
 bgp confederation identifier 7614
 network 10.5.1.32 mask 255.255.255.224
 network 10.5.1.65 mask 255.255.255.224
 neighbor 10.5.1.1 remote-as 65501
 no auto-summary
```

Private Autonomous Systems

Like private RFC 1918 IP addresses, a range of private AS numbers is reserved for networks that do not require a public AS number. Private ASNs (ranging from 64,512 to 65,535) are commonly used in two ways: They can be used between two private BGP networks, or as member AS numbers in BGP confederations. If you recall back to Chapter 7, you will remember that the default behavior for BGP confederations states that the member AS number must be removed from the AS path as the path is advertised to E-BGP neighbors. Although you manually do not have to remove the private AS number from confederation members before exiting an AS (the router will do this for you), you do need to remove private AS numbers from private BGP networks before advertising them to the public Internet.

You can remove private AS numbers from the AS path at an AS egress point before the path is advertised to an external peer. To remove private AS numbers from an AS path, use the **neighbor** *ip-address* **remove-private-as** command for each E-BGP peer that you configured. For example, looking at the network shown in Figure 9-6, notice that the Neon router sends the advertisement for networks 135.23.78.0/24 and 135.23.79.0/24 to the routers in AS 57,648 with an AS path of 64,785.

The upstream Nitrogen router receives the update for these networks that have the AS path value of [57648, 64785]. To remove the 64,785 AS from the path, you add the **remove-private-as** command to the E-BGP neighbor configuration on the Oxygen and Fluorine routers. You also need to clear the BGP session on these routers to apply the changes. Before you remove the private AS numbers, the BGP RIB on the Nitrogen router would look like the table shown in Example 9-15.

Figure 9-6 *Elements Network with Private Autonomous System Numbers*

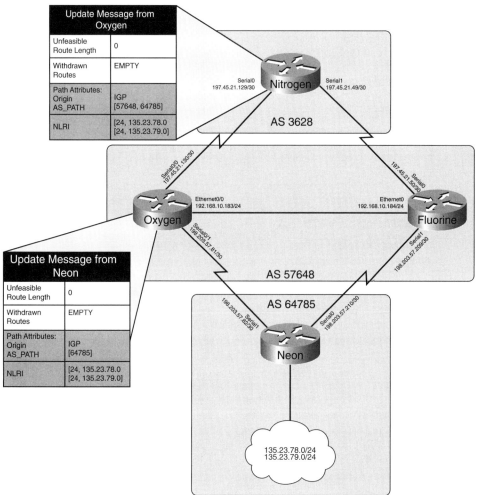

Example 9-15 *Nitrogen BGP RIB*

```
Nitrogen# show ip bgp | begin Network
   Network          Next Hop          Metric LocPrf Weight Path
*  135.23.78.0/24   197.45.21.130                     0 57648 64785 i
*>                  197.45.21.50                       0 57648 64785 i
*  135.23.79.0/24   197.45.21.130                     0 57648 64785 i
*>                  197.45.21.50                       0 57648 64785 i
```

Example 9-16 shows the BGP configuration for the Oxygen router after the **remove-private-as** command was used.

Example 9-16 *Using the* **remove-private-as** *Command on the Oxygen Router*

```
Oxygen# show run | begin bgp
router bgp 57648
 no synchronization
 bgp log-neighbor-changes
 neighbor 192.168.10.184 remote-as 57648
 neighbor 192.168.10.184 next-hop-self
 neighbor 197.45.21.129 remote-as 3628
 neighbor 197.45.21.129 remove-private-as
 neighbor 198.203.57.82 remote-as 64785
 no auto-summary
```

After adding the **remove-private-as** command and clearing the BGP session on the Oxygen router, the private AS number, 64,785, is removed from the AS path, as shown in Example 9-17.

Example 9-17 *BGP RIB from the Nitrogen Router*

```
Nitrogen# show ip bgp | begin Network
   Network          Next Hop          Metric LocPrf Weight Path
*> 135.23.78.0/24   197.45.21.130                     0 57648 i
*                   197.45.21.50                      0 57648 64785 I
*> 135.23.79.0/24   197.45.21.130                     0 57648 i
*                   197.45.21.50                      0 57648 64785 I
```

Now that the **remove-private-as** command has been issued, you can also see that the Nitrogen router now prefers the new route with the shorter AS path as well. To correct that problem, issue the **remove-private-as** command on the Fluorine router, clear the BGP session, and the Nitrogen router will once again prefer the path to networks 135.23.78.0/24 and 135.23.79.0/24 through the Fluorine router, as shown in Example 9-18.

Example 9-18 *Final Nitrogen BGP RIB*

```
Nitrogen# show ip bgp | begin Network
   Network          Next Hop          Metric LocPrf Weight Path
*  135.23.78.0/24   197.45.21.130                     0 57648 i
*>                  197.45.21.50                      0 57648 i
*  135.23.79.0/24   197.45.21.130                     0 57648 i
*>                  197.45.21.50                      0 57648 i
```

Simplifying Configurations with Peer Groups

Large, complex configurations tend to appear in more advanced BGP implementations. For each individual peer that you configure, you might require a **neighbor** statement, **next-hop-self** statements, route filtering, route aggregation, attribute modification, and so on, making the configurations complicated and difficult to read. The solution to this problem is to use BGP peer groups.

In Cisco IOS Software, BGP peer groups are used with BGP to simplify configuration tasks by incorporating repetitive statements into one or more peer groups. Each neighbor is assigned to a peer group, and the router determines that peer's configuration based on that of the peer group.

Three steps are required to create a peer group:

Step 1 Create the peer group using the **neighbor** *peer-group-name* **peer-group** command.

Step 2 Add groupwide configuration elements to the peer group as you would any other BGP neighbor, using the **neighbor** *peer-group-name* statement command for each item.

Step 3 Assign BGP peers with common group traits to the peer group using the **neighbor** *ip-address* **peer-group** command.

For example, the network shown in Figure 9-7 is a great candidate for peer group use.

Figure 9-7 *Shadow-Box Network*

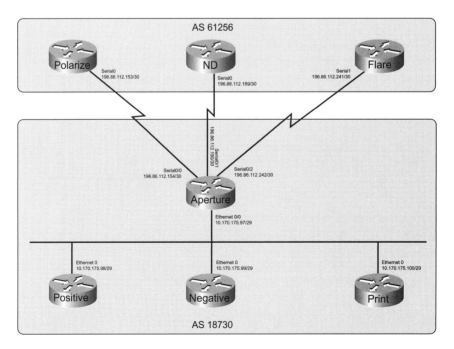

In this example, the Aperture router has three external BGP connections to routers in AS 61,256, and three internal BGP connections to its peers in AS 18,730. Each of these BGP peering sessions has the same basic configuration, as shown in Example 9-19.

Example 9-19 *BGP Configuration for the Aperture Router*

```
Aperture# show run | begin bgp
router bgp 18730
 no synchronization
 bgp log-neighbor-changes
 neighbor 10.170.175.98 remote-as 18730
 neighbor 10.170.175.98 password tough-password
 neighbor 10.170.175.98 route-reflector-client
 neighbor 10.170.175.98 next-hop-self
 neighbor 10.170.175.99 remote-as 18730
 neighbor 10.170.175.99 password tough-password
 neighbor 10.170.175.99 route-reflector-client
 neighbor 10.170.175.99 next-hop-self
 neighbor 10.170.175.100 remote-as 18730
 neighbor 10.170.175.100 password tough-password
 neighbor 10.170.175.100 route-reflector-client
 neighbor 10.170.175.100 next-hop-self
 neighbor 196.86.112.153 remote-as 61256
 neighbor 196.86.112.153 password secret
 neighbor 196.86.112.189 remote-as 61256
 neighbor 196.86.112.189 password secret
 neighbor 196.86.112.241 remote-as 61256
 neighbor 196.86.112.241 password secret
 no auto-summary
```

The preceding configuration shows that the Aperture router contains 18 statements for six BGP sessions. Each external session has a remote AS and password configuration, and each internal session has a **remote-as**, **password**, **next-hop-self** statement, and route reflector configuration. If any new statements are to be added to the configuration, they must be added on a peer-by-peer basis. The addition of any new peers also requires at least two more lines of configuration. The combination of peers and new configuration statements would create quite a long and tedious configuration. To solve this problem, two peer groups can be created, one for external peers in AS 61,256, and one for internal peers in AS 18,730. Each of the configuration statements for each peer group is added into the peer group configuration, and after the groups have been configured, each of the external and internal neighbors requires only one line of configuration, as shown in Example 9-20.

Example 9-20 *Aperture Router Configuration with Peer Groups*

```
Aperture# show run | begin bgp
router bgp 18730
 no synchronization
 bgp log-neighbor-changes
 neighbor External peer-group
 neighbor External remote-as 61256
 neighbor External password secret
 neighbor Internal peer-group
 neighbor Internal remote-as 18730
 neighbor Internal password tough-password
 neighbor Internal route-reflector-client
 neighbor Internal next-hop-self
 neighbor 10.170.175.98 peer-group Internal
 neighbor 10.170.175.99 peer-group Internal
 neighbor 10.170.175.100 peer-group Internal
 neighbor 196.86.112.153 peer-group External
 neighbor 196.86.112.189 peer-group External
 neighbor 196.86.112.241 peer-group External
 no auto-summary
```

Now that you have seen how to simplify large network implementations using route reflectors, confederations, and peer groups, it is time to learn how to simplify routing tables using BGP route aggregation techniques.

Route Aggregation

Another way to simplify large BGP implementations, is to decrease the size of the BGP RIBs by aggregating BGP routes. Route aggregation is a simple process that can help keep Internet routing tables down in size, lowering the number of routes that must be passed between neighboring BGP routers during updates. The following route aggregation schemes are covered in this section:

- General route aggregation;
- Route aggregation with filtering
- Route suppression
- Conditional route advertisement

By default, BGP advertises only aggregated routes if a more specific route exists in the main IP routing table. If you specify an aggregate for a collection of routes that the BGP scanner is not aware of, the aggregate is not advertised. By default, aggregated routes lose the attribute values that applied to the individual, more specific routes; however, you can change this behavior by using route maps that contain lists of routes and attributes to apply to those routes or the aggregate. Controlling BGP update traffic with route aggregation is a simple, easily configured process requiring only three steps:

Step 1   Specify networks that are to be aggregated using the **network** command.

Step 2   Use the **aggregate-address** command to specify the way the networks should be summarized. The syntax for the **aggregate-address** command in Cisco IOS Software Release 12.2(12)T is as follows:

```
aggregate-address ip-address aggregate-mask [advertise-map route-map-name ]
   [as-set] [attribute-map route-map-name] [route-map route-map-name]  [summary-
   only] [suppress-map route-map-name]
```

Step 3   (Optional) Specify any additional aggregation schemes that are to be used.

You can use a number of optional commands with BGP route aggregates by using the **aggregate-address** command. Table 9-2 shows these optional command values and their descriptions.

Table 9-2   *Optional* **aggregate-address** *Commands*

Command Name	Description
advertise-map	Specifies a route map containing a list of routes that an AS_SET attribute will apply to. This command can also be used to specify routes the routes that will be aggregated.
as-set	Creates an AS_SET attribute for the aggregated route. The AS_SET stores the aggregated subset of AS paths within a larger aggregated AS path for situations when the path contains different AS path values.
attribute-map	Allows for the custom specification of BGP attributes based on user-defined information.
route-map	Similar to the **attribute-map** command, this command allows for the manipulation of aggregate attributes.
summary-only	Limits the output of BGP advertisements to the aggregate address—filtering all the individual routes that create the aggregate.
suppress-map	Specifies more specific routes that are to be suppressed based on user-defined information contained in a route map.

When an aggregate route is created, both the new aggregate route and all other more specific routes are advertised to each BGP peer. If this is not the desired effect you had in mind, you can control this behavior by using the **summary-only** command. The new route, by default, contains the ATOMIC_AGGREGATE and AGGREGATOR attributes. The ATOMIC_AGGREGATE attribute specifies that the route has been aggregated, and path information for the specific routes that were aggregated has been lost. The AGGREGATOR attribute gives information about the router that originally aggregated the route.

It is possible to retain the AS path information for the paths being aggregated at the aggregation point using the **as-set** command, which creates an AS_SET path segment type within the AS_PATH field of the UPDATE message containing the information about the aggregated routes.

Example 9-21 shows how route aggregation summarizes the 156.202.148.x networks into one aggregated network, 156.202.148.0/24, between the Day and Night routers shown in Figure 9-8.

Figure 9-8   *Day and Night Network*

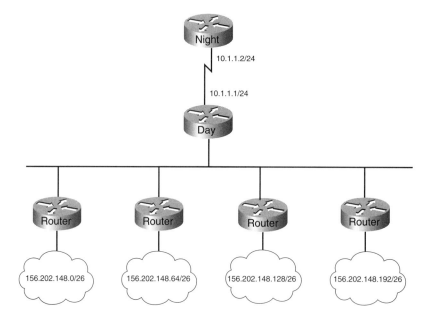

Example 9-21 *Aggregating Routes and Filtering Specific Routes*

```
Day# show run | begin bgp
router bgp 8
 bgp log-neighbor-changes
 network 10.1.1.0 mask 255.255.255.0
 network 156.202.148.0 mask 255.255.255.192
 network 156.202.148.64 mask 255.255.255.192
 network 156.202.148.128 mask 255.255.255.192
 network 156.202.148.192 mask 255.255.255.192
 aggregate-address 156.202.148.0 255.255.255.0 summary-only
 neighbor 10.1.1.2 remote-as 9
```

In this example, the **aggregate-address** command aggregates the four 156.202.148.0/26 networks into one 156.202.148.0/24 summary route. The **summary-only** statement tells the router to suppress the individual routes that created the summary, advertising only the 156.202.148.0/24 network to remote peers. To verify that the command is working properly, you can use the **show ip bgp** and **show ip bgp neighbors 10.1.1.2 advertised-routes** commands on the Day router, as shown in Example 9-22.

Example 9-22 show ip bgp *Command Output from the Day Router*

```
Day# show ip bgp | begin Network
   Network          Next Hop          Metric LocPrf Weight Path
s> 156.202.148.0/26 0.0.0.0                0          32768 i
*> 156.202.148.0/24 0.0.0.0                           32768 i
s> 156.202.148.64/26
                    0.0.0.0                0          32768 i
s> 156.202.148.128/26
                    0.0.0.0                0          32768 i
s> 156.202.148.192/26
                    0.0.0.0                0          32768 i
Day# show ip bgp neighbors 10.1.1.2 advertised-routes | begin Network
   Network          Next Hop          Metric LocPrf Weight Path
*> 10.1.1.0/24      0.0.0.0                0          32768 I
*> 156.202.148.0/24 0.0.0.0                           32768 i
```

Notice how the specific routes for the 156.202.148.0/24 aggregate network, highlighted in the preceding example, with the /26 mask are displayed with the **s>** characters, indicating a suppressed route; and the aggregate route, 156.202.148.0/24, is displayed with the ***>** characters, indicating that it is the best valid route to that network. Also, notice that when the **show ip bgp neighbors 10.1.1.2 advertised-routes** command is issued, you can see that the router is advertising only the 156.202.148.0/24 summary network. Example 9-23 shows the BGP-specific information for the 156.202.148.0/24 network.

Example 9-23 show ip bgp 156.202.148.0/24 *Command Output from the Day Router*

```
Day# show ip bgp 156.202.148.0/24
BGP routing table entry for 156.202.148.0/24, version 7
Paths: (1 available, best #1, table Default-IP-Routing-Table)
  Advertised to non peer-group peers:
  10.1.1.2
  Local, (aggregated by 8 10.1.1.1)
    0.0.0.0 from 0.0.0.0 (10.1.1.1)
      Origin IGP, localpref 100, weight 32768, valid, aggregated, local,
atomic-aggregate, best
```

Notice that the route for the 156.202.148.0/24 network contains the AGGREGATE and ATOMIC_AGGREGATE attributes, specifying that the Day router (10.1.1.1 in AS 8) aggregated the route, and that the path information for that route might have been lost during the aggregation. The **as-set** argument can also be used with the **aggregate-address** command to store the AS_SET path information for the route. In Figure 9-9, for example, the Day router is aggregating the 156.202.148.0/26 networks into a larger 156.202.148.0/24 aggregate network advertisement, which it then forwards to the Night router. In this example, the 156.202.148.0/26 networks each originate from a different AS. The **as-set** keyword can be used with the **aggregate-address** command to add the list of individual AS numbers, which were removed during the aggregation process, back to the AS_PATH attribute for the aggregate route. Example 9-24 shows the Night router's BGP RIB entry for the 156.202.148.0/24 network before the **as-set** keyword is used, and Example 9-25 shows the configuration change for the Day router, and the resulting BGP route change on the Night router.

Figure 9-9 *Detailed Day and Night Network*

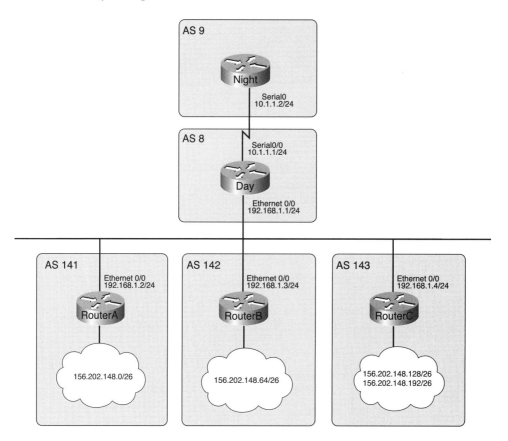

Example 9-24 *Night Router's BGP Entry for the 156.202.148.0/24 Network (Before)*

```
Night# show ip bgp 156.202.148.0/24
BGP routing table entry for 156.202.148.0/24, version 13
Paths: (1 available, best #1, table Default-IP-Routing-Table)
  Not advertised to any peer
  8, (aggregated by 8 10.1.1.1)
    10.1.1.1 from 10.1.1.1 (10.1.1.1)
      Origin IGP, localpref 100, valid, external, atomic-aggregate, best
```

Example 9-25 *Using the AS_SET Value to Preserve Individual AS_PATH Values*

```
Day# show run | begin bgp
router bgp 8
 no synchronization
 bgp log-neighbor-changes
 aggregate-address 156.202.148.0 255.255.255.0 summary-only
 neighbor 10.1.1.2 remote-as 9
 neighbor 192.168.1.2 remote-as 141
 neighbor 192.168.1.3 remote-as 142
 neighbor 192.168.1.4 remote-as 143

Night# show ip bgp 156.202.148.0/24
BGP routing table entry for 156.202.148.0/24, version 18
Paths: (1 available, best #1, table Default-IP-Routing-Table)
  Not advertised to any peer
  8 {141,142,143}, (aggregated by 8 10.1.1.1)
    10.1.1.1 from 10.1.1.1 (10.1.1.1)
      Origin IGP, localpref 100, valid, external, best
```

After the **as-set** statement has been added to the **aggregate-address** command, and the BGP session has been cleared, the Night router now shows a more detailed AS_PATH entry for the 156.202.148.0/24 route. That route now lists the 141, 142, and 143 ASNs in the AS_PATH attribute, and that list is referred to as an AS_SET.

You can use static routes to a null interface with a high administrative distance to prevent route flapping caused by network instabilities related to individual networks that have been aggregated. Remember, for BGP to advertise a route, it must first learn the route from its main IP routing table. If you use a static route with high administrative distance to a null interface, you allow the router to prefer routes learned by IGP protocols, while BGP can rely on the stability of the static route. In the event that the IGP protocol stops advertising the route, the router will begin sending all packets for that network to the null interface—the bit bucket; however, the BGP routes that the router advertises to upstream routers will not flap. Example 9-26 shows how you can use a static route to help aggregate the 189.28.145.0/24 network.

Example 9-26 *Using Static Routes to the Null Interfaces for Route Stability*

```
Doh# show run | begin bgp
router bgp 104
 no synchronization
 bgp router-id 10.1.1.1
 bgp log-neighbor-changes
 network 189.28.145.0 mask 255.255.255.128
 network 189.28.145.128 mask 255.255.255.128
 aggregate-address 189.28.145.0 255.255.255.0 summary-only
 neighbor 10.1.1.2 remote-as 9
 no auto-summary
 !
ip route 189.28.145.0 255.255.255.128 Null0 253 permanent
ip route 189.28.145.128 255.255.255.128 Null0 253 permanent

Doh# show ip bgp | begin Network
   Network          Next Hop          Metric LocPrf Weight Path
s> 189.28.145.0/25  0.0.0.0                0         32768 i
*> 189.28.145.0/24  0.0.0.0                          32768 i
s> 189.28.145.128/25
                    0.0.0.0                0         32768 i
```

Now that you have seen how BGP route aggregation is preformed, it is time to move on to more advanced BGP route aggregation and advertisement schemes, such as route suppression and conditional route advertisement.

Aggregation and Route Suppression

Another way to control routing advertisements for aggregated routes is to use route suppression to suppress the advertisement of certain networks; suppressed routes can also be unsuppressed on a neighbor-by-neighbor basis. You can use the optional **summary-only** command with the **aggregate-address** command to suppress all the more specific routes; and you can use *suppress maps* and *unsuppress maps* to specify exactly which routes should or should not be suppressed. By using route aggregation with route suppression, you can filter specific longer prefixes from the aggregated routing advertisements.

Four steps are required to use route aggregation with route suppression:

Step 1   Start BGP routing and configure neighbor relationships and networks that are to be advertised. If necessary, use the **no auto-summary** command to disable classful route summarization.

Step 2   Use an access or prefix list to specify the networks that are to be suppressed.

Step 3   Create the route map that will be used as a suppress map for the aggregated network. This route map should specify the access or prefix list that tells the router which prefixes to suppress.

Step 4 Configure route aggregation using the **aggregate-address** command with the
suppress-map statement to specify the aggregate and the suppressed routes.
The command structure used to specify route aggregation with suppression
is as follows:

```
aggregate-address ip-prefix mask [suppress-map route-map-name]
```

To verify that the longer prefixes belonging to the aggregated routes are correctly suppressed,
use the **show ip bgp** command or the **show ip bgp neighbors** *neighbor-address* **advertised-
routes** command. The **show ip bgp** command displays the suppressed routes with the **s>**
characters in the status field, and the **show ip bgp neighbors** *ip-address* **advertised-routes**
command displays only the routes that are actually advertised to the specified neighbor.

Consider, for instance, the network shown in Figure 9-10. The Rainier router is connected to
the Adams and Vernon routers and is sending two prefixes in each of its advertisements, the
aggregate for the 194.69.12.0/22 network and the more specific route to the 194.69.14.0/24
network.

Figure 9-10 *Route Suppression and the Volcano Network*

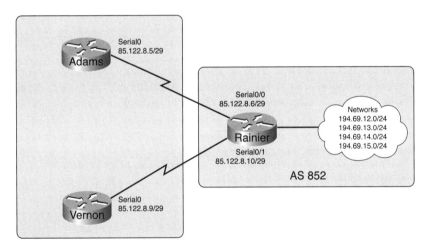

Example 9-27 shows how the **aggregate-address** command specifies the 194.69.12.0/22 prefix.
The hide-me suppress map specifies that any network contained in IP prefix list 10 will be
suppressed, whereas the Rainier router still advertises the more specific route to the 194.69.14.0/24
network. You can use the **suppress-map** command when you want to advertise a summary
route, and only particular specific routes.

Example 9-27 *Using a Suppress Map with the Summary Only Statement*

```
Rainier# show run | begin bgp
router bgp 852
 no synchronization
 bgp log-neighbor-changes
 network 194.69.12.0
 network 194.69.13.0
 network 194.69.14.0
 network 194.69.15.0
 aggregate-address 194.69.12.0 255.255.252.0 suppress-map hide-me
 neighbor 85.122.8.5 remote-as 7518
 neighbor 85.122.8.5 description Adams Peer
 neighbor 85.122.8.9 remote-as 7518
 neighbor 85.122.8.9 description Vernon Peer
 no auto-summary
!
ip prefix-list 10 seq 5 permit 194.69.12.0/24
ip prefix-list 10 seq 10 permit 194.69.13.0/24
ip prefix-list 10 seq 15 permit 194.69.15.0/24
!
route-map hide-me permit 10
 match ip address prefix-list 10
```

In Example 9-28, notice that the BGP RIB for the Rainier router contains three suppressed routes and two valid, best routes. These results are achieved using route aggregation with the **suppress-map** statement, as shown previously in Example 9-27.

Example 9-28 *BGP RIB from the Rainier Router*

```
Rainier# show ip bgp | begin Network
   Network          Next Hop          Metric LocPrf Weight Path
s> 194.69.12.0      0.0.0.0                0            32768 i
*> 194.69.12.0/22   0.0.0.0                             32768 i
s> 194.69.13.0      0.0.0.0                0            32768 i
*> 194.69.14.0      0.0.0.0                0            32768 i
s> 194.69.15.0      0.0.0.0                0            32768 i
```

To make a router suppress routes for certain peers and advertise them to others, use the **neighbor** *ip-address* **unsuppress-map** *route-map-name* command. Example 9-29 shows how that command advertises all the specific 194.69.x.0 routes to the Vernon router, while still using route suppression with the Adams router.

Example 9-29 *Using* **unsuppress-map** *to Unsuppress Previously Suppressed Routes*

```
Rainier# show run | begin bgp
router bgp 852
 no synchronization
 bgp log-neighbor-changes
```

Example 9-29 *Using* **unsuppress-map** *to Unsuppress Previously Suppressed Routes (Continued)*

```
  network 194.69.12.0
  network 194.69.13.0
  network 194.69.14.0
  network 194.69.15.0
  aggregate-address 194.69.12.0 255.255.252.0 suppress-map hide-me
  neighbor 85.122.8.5 remote-as 7518
  neighbor 85.122.8.5 description Adams Peer
  neighbor 85.122.8.9 remote-as 7518
  neighbor 85.122.8.9 description Vernon Peer
  neighbor 85.122.8.9 unsuppress-map hide-me
  no auto-summary
  !
 ip prefix-list 10 seq 5 permit 194.69.12.0/24
 ip prefix-list 10 seq 10 permit 194.69.13.0/24
 ip prefix-list 10 seq 15 permit 194.69.15.0/24
 !
 route-map hide-me permit 10
  match ip address prefix-list 10
```

In the preceding example, the **hide-me unsuppress map**, which is also used as the **hide-me suppress map**, states that the routes specified in IP prefix list 10 will not be suppressed for neighbor 85.122.8.9, the Vernon router. You can verify this by issuing the **show ip bgp** command on the Vernon router. Example 9-30 shows the resulting BGP tables from the Vernon and Adams routers.

Example 9-30 *Routes Advertised by the Rainier Router to the Vernon and Adams Routers*

```
Vernon# show ip bgp | begin Network
   Network          Next Hop         Metric LocPrf Weight Path
*> 194.69.12.0      85.122.8.10           0           0 852 i
*> 194.69.12.0/22   85.122.8.10                       0 852 i
*> 194.69.13.0      85.122.8.10           0           0 852 i
*> 194.69.14.0      85.122.8.10           0           0 852 i
*> 194.69.15.0      85.122.8.10           0           0 852 i

Adams# show ip bgp | begin Network
   Network          Next Hop         Metric LocPrf Weight Path
*> 194.69.12.0/22   85.122.8.6                        0 852 i
*> 194.69.14.0      85.122.8.6            0           0 852 i
```

Now that you have seen how you can use route suppression to suppress or unsuppress routes on a neighbor-by-neighbor basis, the next section examines how you can use conditional route advertisement to conditionally advertise routes to BGP neighbors.

Conditional Route Advertisement

Conditional route advertisements provide a method of user-defined route advertisement that allows for more control over the way routes are advertised. Conditional route advertisements enable you to specify a set of conditions to track the state of a route using a route map called a **non-exist-map**, and if that route does not exist, advertise another route specified by another route map called an **advertise-map**. Advertise maps can be used by themselves to provide conditional route advertisements, with the **aggregate-address** command to specify routes that should contain the AS_SET AS_PATH attribute during route aggregation, or as a condition to advertise an aggregated route.

The **non-exist-map** specifies the network that will be tracked in the BGP RIB. While the routes in **non-exist-map** exist, the routes specified by the **advertise-map** statement will not be advertised. If the route specified by the **non-exist-map** is withdrawn, however, the route specified by the **advertise-map** will be advertised until the **non-exist-map** routes reappear. Conditional route advertisement can be used with multihomed networks to prevent asymmetric routes or alone to provide additional routing functionality.

Four steps are required to configure conditional route advertisement:

Step 1   Configure BGP peering with the other routers that are to be involved in the route advertisements.

Step 2   Create a **non-exist-map** using a standard route map statement. This route map should specify an access or prefix list that identifies the network prefix that is to be tracked. Make sure to configure the access or prefix list specified in the route map.

Step 3   Create an **advertise-map** using a standard route map statement that specifies the access or prefix list describing the network prefixes that should be advertised when the networks specified by the **non-exist-map** are withdrawn from the BGP RIB. Also, create an access or prefix list that specifies the prefixes that should be advertised.

Step 4   Apply the route maps to the BGP neighbor using the **neighbor** *ip-address* **advertise-map** *route-map-name* **non-exist-map** *route-map-name* command.

In Figure 9-11, for example, the Speedy router is connected to the Tom and Jerry routers via an Ethernet connection. The Tom router is advertising the 129.40.18.0/24 network, and the Jerry router is advertising the 129.40.20.0/24 network. The Speedy router advertises both of these networks to the Tweety router in AS 714.

Figure 9-11 *Conditional Route Advertisement on the Cartoon Network*

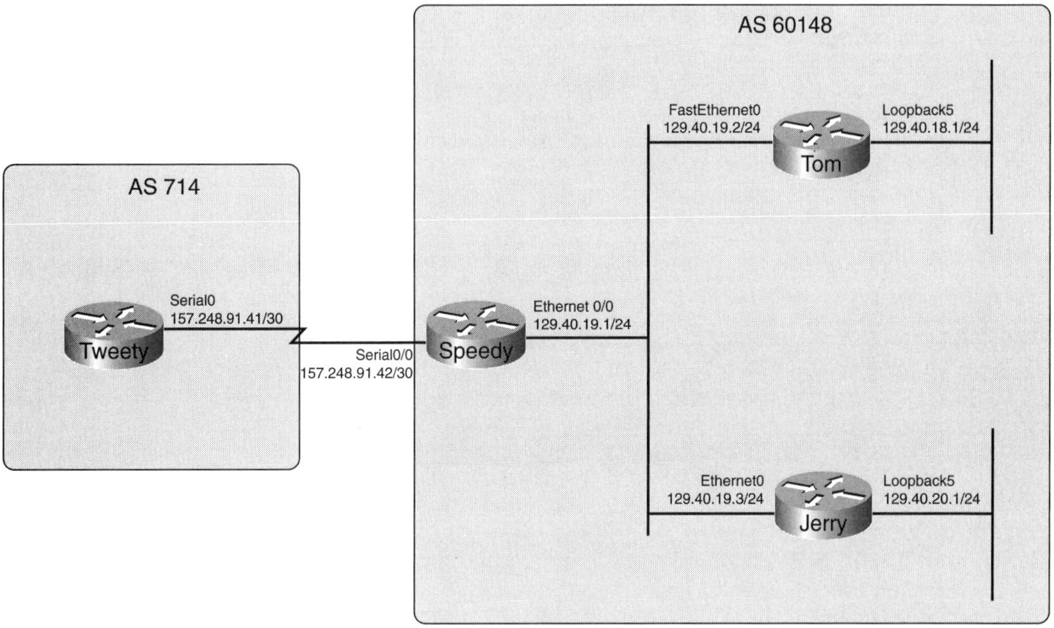

Example 9-31 shows the BGP RIB entries for the Tweety router. In this example, the Tweety router is receiving all routes (129.40.18.0/24, 129.40.19.0/24, and 129.40.20.0/24) from the Speedy router.

Example 9-31 *Tweety Router's BGP RIB*

```
Tweety# show ip bgp | begin Network
   Network          Next Hop          Metric LocPrf Weight Path
*> 129.40.18.0/24   157.248.91.42                      0 60148 i
*> 129.40.19.0/24   157.248.91.42          0           0 60148 i
*> 129.40.20.0/24   157.248.91.42                      0 60148 I
```

Example 9-32 shows how a conditional route advertisement manipulates the routes advertised by the Speedy router.

Example 9-32 *Conditional Advertisement on the Speedy Router*

```
Speedy# show ip bgp | begin bgp
router bgp 60148
 no synchronization
 network 129.40.19.0 mask 255.255.255.0
 neighbor 129.40.19.2 remote-as 60148
 neighbor 129.40.19.2 description Tom Router
 neighbor 129.40.19.3 remote-as 60148
 neighbor 129.40.19.2 description Jerry Router
 neighbor 157.248.91.41 remote-as 714
 neighbor 129.40.19.2 description Tweety Router
 neighbor 157.248.91.41 advertise-map advertise-me non-exist-map not-in-table
 no auto-summary
!
ip prefix-list 1000 seq 5 permit 129.40.18.0/24
!
ip prefix-list 1001 seq 5 permit 129.40.20.0/24
!
route-map not-in-table permit 10
 match ip address prefix-list 1001
!
route-map advertise-me permit 10
 match ip address prefix-list 1000
```

The not-in-table route map is used as the **non-exist-map** to specify the 129.40.20.0/24 network, and the advertise-me route map is used to specify the network that is to be conditionally advertised. As long as the 129.40.20.0/24 route exists in the Speedy router's routing table, the 129.40.18.0/24 route will not be advertised. If the 129.40.20.0/24 route is withdrawn, however, the 129.40.18.0/24 route is advertised in its place. Example 9-33 shows the Tweety router's routing table after the conditional route advertisement was added.

Example 9-33 *Tweety Routing Table After Conditional Routing*

```
Tweety# show ip bgp | begin Network
   Network          Next Hop         Metric LocPrf Weight Path
*> 129.40.19.0/24   157.248.91.42         0             0 60148 i
*> 129.40.20.0/24   157.248.91.42                       0 60148 i
```

As you can see in the preceding example, after the Speedy router was configured to conditionally advertise the 129.40.18.0/24 network it began to suppress the advertisement of the 149.40.18.0/24 network. If the Jerry router stops advertising the 129.40.20.0/24 network, however, the Speedy router withdraws the advertisement for the 129.40.20.0/24 network, and starts advertising the 129.40.18.0/24 network in its place. Example 9-34 shows the Speedy router conditionally routing the 129.40.18.0/24 network after the Loopback5 interface is disabled on the Jerry router.

Example 9-34 *Conditionally Advertising the 129.40.18.0/24 Network*

```
Jerry(config)# interface loopback 5
Jerry(config-if)# shutdown

Speedy# show ip bgp | begin Network
   Network          Next Hop          Metric LocPrf Weight Path
*>i129.40.18.0/24   129.40.19.2            0    100      0 i
*> 129.40.19.0/24   0.0.0.0                0         32768 i

Tweety# show ip bgp | begin Network
   Network          Next Hop          Metric LocPrf Weight Path
*> 129.40.18.0/24   157.248.91.42                    0 60148 i
*> 129.40.19.0/24   157.248.91.42          0          0 60148 i
```

You can monitor conditional route advertisement using the **show ip bgp neighbors** *ip-address* [| **begin Condition**] command, as shown in Example 9-35.

Example 9-35 *Using the* **show ip bgp neighbors** *Command to Monitor Conditional Route Advertisement*

```
Speedy# show ip bgp neighbors 157.248.91.41 | begin Condition
   Condition-map not-in-table, Advertise-map advertise-me, status: Withdraw
```

When the condition map, specified with the **non-exist-map**, is not available, the status of the conditional advertisement is *Advertise*, and the route specified by the Advertise map is advertised to the peer.

Now that you are armed with an understanding of BGP route suppression and aggregation, it is important to understand how you can use BGP route filtering to help define network policy. The next section introduces route filtering, and the following sections show how to use route filtering along with BGP attributes to filter routes and modify path selection.

Filtering BGP Routes

You can filter BGP routes in a number of ways; filtering incoming or outgoing routes from neighbors using distribute lists, route maps, prefix lists, filter lists, by BGP attribute, or by BGP COMMUNITY attributes. This section introduces basic BGP route filtering using route maps, distribution lists, and prefix lists.

Basic BGP route filtering is similar to the configuration of route filtering used with IGP protocols. A list of network prefixes is created, using access lists, or prefix lists, and that information is applied either to a specific neighbor or neighbors, a peer group, or as a blanket application to all BGP peers. The major difference between BGP and IGP route filtering is the number of options that BGP provides for filter selection criteria.

Using Distribute Lists to Filter Network Prefixes

The simplest way to filter BGP routes is to use a distribute list, either as a blanket statement for all peers or applied to specific peers using the **neighbor** statement. To apply a distribute list to all peers for all incoming or outgoing routes, follow these steps:

Step 1 Create an access or prefix list that specifies the traffic that is to be filtered.

Step 2 From BGP router configuration mode, create the distribution list that will be used to filter all incoming or outgoing UPDATE messages. Distribute lists use the following syntax:

```
distribute-list {access-list-number | access-list-name | gateway prefix-list-
    name | prefix prefix-list-name [gateway prefix-list-name]} {in [interface-name
    interface-number] | out [interface-name interface-number | bgp | connected | egp
    | eigrp | igrp | ospf | rip | static]}
```

NOTE The optional **gateway** statement in the **distribute-list gateway** *prefix-list-name* command enables you to filter all routes from a particular peer; the peer for route filtration is specified by a prefix list.

You can apply only one distribution list to incoming and outgoing (either or both) updates at any time. Distribution lists can also be applied to UPDATE messages from a particular interface using the optional *interface-name* and *number* statement at the end of a list. For instance, the Willis router is currently receiving routes to all the networks shown in Example 9-36.

Example 9-36 *Willis BGP RIB*

```
Willis# show ip bgp | begin Network
   Network          Next Hop          Metric LocPrf Weight Path
*> 23.75.18.0/24    62.128.47.6                        0 11151 5623 i
*> 23.75.19.0/24    62.128.47.6                        0 11151 5623 i
*> 23.75.20.0/24    62.128.47.6                        0 11151 5623 i
*> 23.75.21.0/24    62.128.47.6                        0 11151 5623 i
*> 23.75.22.0/24    62.128.47.6                        0 11151 5623 i
*> 23.75.23.0/24    62.128.47.6                        0 11151 5623 i
*> 23.75.24.0/24    62.128.47.6                        0 11151 5623 i
*> 23.75.25.0/24    62.128.47.6                        0 11151 5623 i
*> 23.75.26.0/24    62.128.47.6                        0 11151 5623 i
*> 189.168.56.0/23  62.128.47.198          0            0 645 i
*> 189.168.58.0/23  62.128.47.198          0            0 645 i
*> 189.168.60.0/23  62.128.47.198          0            0 645 i
*> 189.168.62.0/23  62.128.47.198          0            0 645 i
*> 189.168.64.0/23  62.128.47.198          0            0 645 i
*> 189.168.66.0/23  62.128.47.198          0            0 645 i
*> 189.168.68.0/23  62.128.47.198          0            0 645 i
*> 189.168.70.0/23  62.128.47.198          0            0 645 i
   Network          Next Hop          Metric LocPrf Weight Path
```

Example 9-36 *Willis BGP RIB (Continued)*

```
*> 189.168.72.0/23   62.128.47.198            0             0 645 i
*> 189.168.74.0/23   62.128.47.198            0             0 645 i
*> 189.168.76.0/23   62.128.47.198            0             0 645 i
*> 189.168.78.0/23   62.128.47.198            0             0 645 i
*> 189.168.80.0/23   62.128.47.198            0             0 645 i
*> 189.168.82.0/23   62.128.47.198            0             0 645 i
*> 189.168.84.0/23   62.128.47.198            0             0 645 i
*> 189.168.86.0/23   62.128.47.198            0             0 645 i
*> 189.168.88.0/23   62.128.47.198            0             0 645 i
```

To filter all routes, except for routes to the prefix 23.75.0.0/16, you create an access list specifying the 23.75.0.0/16 network prefix and use that access list with a distribute list to filter all incoming routes. Example 9-37 shows the Willis BGP configuration and the results of its application. In this case, the distribute list applies globally to all BGP neighbors.

Example 9-37 *Willis Router Configuration and Postconfiguration BGP RIB*

```
Willis# show run | begin bgp
router bgp 2001
 no synchronization
 bgp log-neighbor-changes
 neighbor 62.128.47.6 remote-as 11151
 neighbor 62.128.47.194 remote-as 645
 neighbor 62.128.47.198 remote-as 645
 distribute-list 1 in
 no auto-summary
!
access-list 1 permit 23.75.0.0 0.0.255.255
Willis# show ip bgp | begin Network
   Network          Next Hop           Metric LocPrf Weight Path
*> 23.75.18.0/24    62.128.47.6                          0 11151 5623 i
*> 23.75.19.0/24    62.128.47.6                          0 11151 5623 i
*> 23.75.20.0/24    62.128.47.6                          0 11151 5623 i
*> 23.75.21.0/24    62.128.47.6                          0 11151 5623 i
*> 23.75.22.0/24    62.128.47.6                          0 11151 5623 i
*> 23.75.23.0/24    62.128.47.6                          0 11151 5623 i
*> 23.75.24.0/24    62.128.47.6                          0 11151 5623 i
*> 23.75.25.0/24    62.128.47.6                          0 11151 5623 i
*> 23.75.26.0/24    62.128.47.6                          0 11151 5623 i
```

As previously mentioned, you can also use the **distribute-list** command with a **neighbor** statement to filter traffic to or from a specific neighbor or peer group. You can accomplish this type of BGP route filtering using the following command:

```
neighbor {ip-address | peer-group} distribute-list {access-list-number |
    access-list-name} {in | out}
```

For example, using the BGP configuration from the previous example, and a neighbor distribute list, you can filter all but two routes from peer 62.128.47.6. Example 9-38 shows the required commands and the resulting BGP routes.

Example 9-38 *Filtering Incoming Routes from a Specific Peer*

```
Willis# show run | begin bgp
router bgp 2001
 no synchronization
 bgp log-neighbor-changes
 neighbor 62.128.47.6 remote-as 11151
 neighbor 62.128.47.6 distribute-list 50 in
 neighbor 62.128.47.194 remote-as 645
 neighbor 62.128.47.198 remote-as 645
 no auto-summary
 !
access-list 50 permit 23.75.18.0 0.0.0.255
access-list 50 permit 23.75.19.0 0.0.0.255
Willis# show ip bgp neighbors 62.128.47.6 routes | begin Network
   Network          Next Hop            Metric LocPrf Weight Path
*> 23.75.18.0/24    62.128.47.6                          0 11151 5623 i
*> 23.75.19.0/24    62.128.47.6                          0 11151 5623 i
```

Using Prefix Lists to Filter BGP Routes

For a simpler, more readable route filtration configuration, you can also apply prefix lists directly to BGP peers using the **neighbor** {*ip-address* | *peer-group*} **prefix-list** *prefix-list-name* {**in** | **out**} command.

IP prefix lists offer a simpler, more intuitive alternative to the access list. IP prefix lists enable you to use a list name or number that specifies a sequence of **permit** or **deny** statements. By specifying the prefix list sequence number, you can edit each statement in an IP prefix list individually, without removing and reapplying the entire list. Prefix lists also remove the burden of wildcard mask calculation. If you want to specify a particular host IP—for example, 110.80.8.118/32—type the following:

```
ip prefix-list bad-host seq 100 deny 110.80.8.118/32
```

If you were to add several 62.128.0.0/23 networks to the local BGP configuration on the Willis router, and then issue the **show ip bgp neighbor 62.128.47.6 advertised-routes** command, for instance, you would see the routes advertised in Example 9-39.

Example 9-39 *Networks Currently Advertised to Peer 62.128.47.6*

```
Willis# show ip bgp neighbors 62.128.47.6 advertised-routes | begin Network
   Network          Next Hop            Metric LocPrf Weight Path
*> 62.128.60.0/23   0.0.0.0                  0           32768 i
*> 62.128.64.0/23   0.0.0.0                  0           32768 i
*> 62.128.68.0/23   0.0.0.0                  0           32768 i
*> 62.128.72.0/23   0.0.0.0                  0           32768 i
```

Example 9-39 *Networks Currently Advertised to Peer 62.128.47.6 (Continued)*

```
*> 62.128.76.0/23   0.0.0.0                      0        32768 i
*> 189.168.56.0/23  62.128.47.198                0            0 645 i
*> 189.168.58.0/23  62.128.47.198                0            0 645 i
*> 189.168.60.0/23  62.128.47.198                0            0 645 i
*> 189.168.62.0/23  62.128.47.198                0            0 645 i
*> 189.168.64.0/23  62.128.47.198                0            0 645 i
*> 189.168.66.0/23  62.128.47.198                0            0 645 i
*> 189.168.68.0/23  62.128.47.198                0            0 645 i
*> 189.168.70.0/23  62.128.47.198                0            0 645 i
*> 189.168.72.0/23  62.128.47.198                0            0 645 i
*> 189.168.74.0/23  62.128.47.198                0            0 645 i
*> 189.168.76.0/23  62.128.47.198                0            0 645 i
*> 189.168.78.0/23  62.128.47.198                0            0 645 i
*> 189.168.80.0/23  62.128.47.198                0            0 645 i
*> 189.168.82.0/23  62.128.47.198                0            0 645 i
*> 189.168.84.0/23  62.128.47.198                0            0 645 i
*> 189.168.86.0/23  62.128.47.198                0            0 645 i
*> 189.168.88.0/23  62.128.47.198                0            0 645 i
```

Now, suppose you want to allow only local 62.128.x.0 networks to be advertised to neighbor 62.128.47.6. To accomplish this task, add an IP prefix list and call that list from the **neighbor** command, as shown in Example 9-40.

Example 9-40 *Using a Prefix List to Filter BGP Routes*

```
Willis# show run | begin bgp
router bgp 2001
 no synchronization
 bgp log-neighbor-changes
 network 62.128.60.0 mask 255.255.254.0
 network 62.128.64.0 mask 255.255.254.0
 network 62.128.68.0 mask 255.255.254.0
 network 62.128.72.0 mask 255.255.254.0
 network 62.128.76.0 mask 255.255.254.0
 neighbor 62.128.47.6 remote-as 11151
 neighbor 62.128.47.6 prefix-list route-filter out
 neighbor 62.128.47.194 remote-as 645
 neighbor 62.128.47.198 remote-as 645
 no auto-summary
!
ip prefix-list route-filter seq 5 permit 62.128.0.0/16 le 23
Willis# show ip bgp neighbors 62.128.47.6 advertised-routes | begin Network
   Network          Next Hop          Metric LocPrf Weight Path
*> 62.128.60.0/23   0.0.0.0                    0        32768 i
*> 62.128.64.0/23   0.0.0.0                    0        32768 i
*> 62.128.68.0/23   0.0.0.0                    0        32768 i
*> 62.128.72.0/23   0.0.0.0                    0        32768 i
*> 62.128.76.0/23   0.0.0.0                    0        32768 i
```

This IP prefix list provides the same type of functionality as an access list with a 0.0.1.255 wild-card mask. The 62.128.0.0/16 le 23 prefix list allows any network that begins with 62.128.x.x with a 23-bit subnet mask. If you decide to change from access lists and try IP prefix lists, be careful to check your syntax before applying the prefix list to a neighbor. Remember, that just like access lists, prefix lists end with an implicit deny; so, if you use a **deny** statement at the beginning of a list, you must include a **permit** statement at some point in the list to allow other traffic. The use of the **ge** and **le** commands might be a bit tricky at first; remember that the mask used for the prefix must match the exact prefix for all filtered routes. The **ge/le** statements match a range of subnet masks, like an inverse wildcard mask. For more help configuring IP prefix lists, refer to Appendix D, "IP Prefix Lists."

Using Route Maps to Filter BGP Routes

Another more sophisticated approach to route filtering is to use a **neighbor** statement with an associated route map. There are a number of basic ways that route maps can be used to filter BGP routes: by attribute, network prefix, next-hop value, or route type. When filtering BGP routes, the **match** command specifies the item to match, and the route map itself is then applied to a neighbor or peer group. Table 9-3 lists the route map **match** command types supported by BGP.

Table 9-3   *BGP-Related Route Map* **match** *Commands*

Match Command	Description
as-path *as-path-access-list-number*	Matches the AS_PATH attribute specified by an *as-path-access-list number* (ranging from 1 to 199). AS_PATH access lists and other AS_PATH functionality is covered later in this chapter.
community *community-list-number* [**exact-match**]	Matches the community value specified by the community list. There are two types of community lists: standard (ranging from 1 to 99) and extended (ranging from 100 to 199). The **exact-match** command can be used to specify an exact match. Community lists and other BGP COMMUNITY attribute functionality is covered later in this chapter.
ip address {*access-list-number* | *access-list-name* | **prefix-list** *prefix-list-name*}	Matches the IP prefix specified by the access or prefix list.
ip next-hop {*access-list-number* | *access-list-name* | **prefix-list** *prefix-list-name*}	Matches the NEXT_HOP attribute of a route. The NEXT_HOP value is specified by the trailing access list or prefix list. The NEXT_HOP attribute, and its uses, is covered later in this chapter.

Table 9-3   *BGP-Related Route Map* **match** *Commands (Continued)*

Match Command	Description
ip route-source {*access-list-number* | *access-list-name* | **prefix-list** *prefix-list-name*}	Matches the source IP address of the peer that sent the route. The peer's IP address is specified by an access or prefix list. The **match ip route-source** command is supported only for outbound route maps.
metric *metric-value*	Matches a MULTI_EXIT_DISC (MED) value; metric matches are not supported for in- or outbound route filtering. The MED attribute, and its uses, is covered later in this chapter.
route-type {**internal** | **external** | **local**}	Matches a locally generated route (sourced from 0.0.0.0 using **show ip bgp**). The **match route-type** command is supported only for outbound route filtering. Make sure to test the results obtained using the **route-type local** command; this command matches any locally originated routes, including routes that entered a BGP process by redistribution.
tag *tag-value*	Matches a tag value. The use of BGP tags was covered earlier in Chapter 2, "Configuring Route Maps and Policy-Based Routing."

Only two steps are required to configure BGP basic route filtering with route maps:

Step 1   Create a route map using the **route-map** command, and from route map configuration mode, use **match** commands to specify the attributes that are to be matched. (Route map configuration is covered in detail in Chapter 2.)

Step 2   Apply the route map to a neighbor or peer group using the following command:

```
neighbor {ip-address | peer-group-name} route-map route-map-name {in | out}
```

The following example shows how you can use a simple route map to limit route advertisements to locally generated routes. Example 9-41 shows the routes that the Willis router is currently advertising to peer 62.128.47.6 before the application of route map filtering.

Example 9-41 *Routes Advertised by Willis to Peer 62.128.47.6 Before Applying the Route Map*

```
Willis# show ip bgp neighbors 62.128.47.6 advertised-routes | begin Network
   Network          Next Hop        Metric LocPrf Weight Path
*> 23.75.18.0/24    62.128.47.6                       0 11151 5623 i
*> 23.75.19.0/24    62.128.47.6                       0 11151 5623 i
*> 23.75.20.0/24    62.128.47.6                       0 11151 5623 i
*> 23.75.21.0/24    62.128.47.6                       0 11151 5623 i
*> 23.75.22.0/24    62.128.47.6                       0 11151 5623 i
*> 23.75.23.0/24    62.128.47.6                       0 11151 5623 i
*> 23.75.24.0/24    62.128.47.6                       0 11151 5623 i
*> 23.75.25.0/24    62.128.47.6                       0 11151 5623 i
*> 23.75.26.0/24    62.128.47.6                       0 11151 5623 i
*> 62.128.0.0/23    0.0.0.0             0          32768 i
*> 62.128.4.0/23    0.0.0.0             0          32768 i
*> 62.128.8.0/23    0.0.0.0             0          32768 i
*> 62.128.12.0/23   0.0.0.0             0          32768 i
*> 62.128.16.0/23   0.0.0.0             0          32768 i
*> 62.128.20.0/23   0.0.0.0             0          32768 i
*> 62.128.24.0/23   0.0.0.0             0          32768 i
*> 62.128.28.0/23   0.0.0.0             0          32768 i
*> 62.128.32.0/23   0.0.0.0             0          32768 i
*> 62.128.36.0/23   0.0.0.0             0          32768 i
*> 62.128.40.0/23   0.0.0.0             0          32768 i
*> 62.128.44.0/23   0.0.0.0             0          32768 i
*> 62.128.48.0/23   0.0.0.0             0          32768 i
   Network          Next Hop        Metric LocPrf Weight Path
*> 62.128.52.0/23   0.0.0.0             0          32768 i
*> 62.128.56.0/23   0.0.0.0             0          32768 i
*> 62.128.60.0/23   0.0.0.0             0          32768 i
*> 62.128.64.0/23   0.0.0.0             0          32768 i
*> 62.128.68.0/23   0.0.0.0             0          32768 i
*> 62.128.72.0/23   0.0.0.0             0          32768 i
*> 62.128.76.0/23   0.0.0.0             0          32768 i
*> 189.168.56.0/23  62.128.47.198      0              0 645 i
*> 189.168.58.0/23  62.128.47.198      0              0 645 i
*> 189.168.60.0/23  62.128.47.198      0              0 645 i
*> 189.168.62.0/23  62.128.47.198      0              0 645 i
*> 189.168.64.0/23  62.128.47.198      0              0 645 i
*> 189.168.66.0/23  62.128.47.198      0              0 645 i
*> 189.168.68.0/23  62.128.47.198      0              0 645 i
*> 189.168.70.0/23  62.128.47.198      0              0 645 i
*> 189.168.72.0/23  62.128.47.198      0              0 645 i
*> 189.168.74.0/23  62.128.47.198      0              0 645 i
*> 189.168.76.0/23  62.128.47.198      0              0 645 i
*> 189.168.78.0/23  62.128.47.198      0              0 645 i
*> 189.168.80.0/23  62.128.47.198      0              0 645 i
*> 189.168.82.0/23  62.128.47.198      0              0 645 i
*> 189.168.84.0/23  62.128.47.198      0              0 645 i
   Network          Next Hop        Metric LocPrf Weight Path
*> 189.168.86.0/23  62.128.47.198      0              0 645 i
*> 189.168.88.0/23  62.128.47.198      0              0 645 i
```

Example 9-42 shows how one simple little route map filters all routes from any source other than locally generated routes to the members of the all-peers peer group.

Example 9-42 *Using the* **route-type local** *Command to Filter Routes*

```
Willis# show run | begin bgp
router bgp 2001
 no synchronization
 bgp log-neighbor-changes
 network 62.128.60.0 mask 255.255.254.0
 network 62.128.64.0 mask 255.255.254.0
 network 62.128.68.0 mask 255.255.254.0
 network 62.128.72.0 mask 255.255.254.0
 network 62.128.76.0 mask 255.255.254.0
 neighbor all-peers peer-group
 neighbor all-peers route-map route-filter out
 neighbor 62.128.47.6 remote-as 11151
 neighbor 62.128.47.6 peer-group all-peers
 neighbor 62.128.47.194 remote-as 645
 neighbor 62.128.47.194 peer-group all-peers
 neighbor 62.128.47.198 remote-as 645
 neighbor 62.128.47.198 peer-group all-peers
 no auto-summary
!
route-map route-filter permit 10
 match route-type local
```

After this configuration is applied, the Willis router will advertise only the routes shown in Example 9-43 to any peer belonging to the all-peers peer group. This example uses the **show ip bgp neighbors** *peer-group* **advertised-routes** command to display the routes that are advertised to the all-peers peer group.

Example 9-43 **show ip bgp neighbors peer-group advertised-routes** *Command*

```
Willis# show ip bgp neighbors 62.128.47.6 advertised-routes | begin Network
   Network          Next Hop          Metric LocPrf Weight Path
*> 62.128.60.0/23   0.0.0.0                0         32768 i
*> 62.128.64.0/23   0.0.0.0                0         32768 i
*> 62.128.68.0/23   0.0.0.0                0         32768 i
*> 62.128.72.0/23   0.0.0.0                0         32768 i
*> 62.128.76.0/23   0.0.0.0                0         32768 i
```

You might have noticed that the route map **set** commands are not shown in Table 9-3; this is because the route map **set** commands provide more advanced BGP functionality—BGP attribute manipulation. Another even more powerful use for BGP route maps involves the manipulation of BGP attributes and BGP route dampening. Each of these subjects is covered later in this chapter. BGP attribute values are usually manipulated using the **set** command under route map configuration mode and applying the route map to a neighbor or peer group using the **neighbor** {*ip-address* | *peer-group*} **route-map** *route-map-name* {**in** | **out**} command. The following list shows a brief hint of the **set** commands that are covered in the next section:

- **as-path prepend** *as-path-number*
- **as-path tag** *as-path-string*
- **comm-list** *community-list-number* [**delete**]
- **community** [*community-value-decimal* | *aa:nn-format*]
- **community additive**
- **community internet**
- **community local-as**
- **community no-advertise**
- **community no-export**
- **community none**
- **dampening** *half-life-value reuse-penalty-value suppress-penalty-value*
- **ip default next-hop** *ip-address*
- **ip default next-hop verify-availability**
- **local-preference** *value*
- **metric** [**+** | **-**] *metric-value*
- **origin** {**egp** *as-number* | **igp** | **incomplete**}
- **tag** *tag-value*
- **weight** *weight-value*

Using BGP Attributes to Create Routing Policies

In the previous few chapters, this book covered BGP mechanics, neighbor configuration, MD-5 authentication, and route aggregation. This section shows how you can use BGP attributes to tie all the previous technologies together and use BGP as the robust routing protocol that it is. This section explores the configuration of various attribute types, and the many ways that they might be used with BGP, including how to do the following:

- Filter inbound or outbound routes
- Customize route redistribution
- Special route aggregation
- Manipulate the BGP route selection process
- Specify preferred network ingress or egress points

- Next-hop modification
- Modify how upstream or downstream peers will propagate specific routes

You can use attributes in a number of ways to modify BGP routing on a Cisco router—using route maps, attribute maps, prefix lists, AS path access lists, regular expressions, and more. This section introduces each attribute's most common configuration uses and presents ways that you can use attributes to make stronger, more resilient BGP networks. Attributes mentioned in this chapter are described in more technical detail in Chapter 7; therefore, each attribute is presented along with references to its accompanying explanation.

Modifying the ORIGIN Attribute to Affect Path Selection

The ORIGIN attribute, which describes the origin of a network prefix in BGP, is one of the key decision factors in the BGP path selection process. There are only three possible BGP ORIGIN types: IGP, EGP, and INCOMPLETE. BGP always prefers an IGP origin, then EGP, and finally, an INCOMPLETE origin. The ORIGIN for each route can be displayed using the **show ip bgp** command; the ORIGIN attribute is the last attribute shown on the right side of the **show ip bgp table** in Example 9-44.

Example 9-44 *Displaying a Route's ORIGIN Attribute*

```
Vernon# show ip bgp | begin Origin
Origin codes: i - IGP, e - EGP, ? - incomplete
   Network          Next Hop          Metric LocPrf Weight Path
*> 194.69.12.0      85.122.8.10            0              0 852 i
*> 194.69.12.0/22   85.122.8.10                           0 852 i
*> 194.69.13.0      85.122.8.10            0              0 852 i
*> 194.69.14.0      85.122.8.10            0              0 852 i
*> 194.69.15.0      85.122.8.10            0              0 852 i
```

You can also display the BGP attributes for each route using the **show ip bgp** *ip-prefix* command. The ORIGIN is shown in the lower-left corner in Figure 9-12.

Figure 9-12 *Using the* **show ip bgp** *Command to Display BGP Attributes*

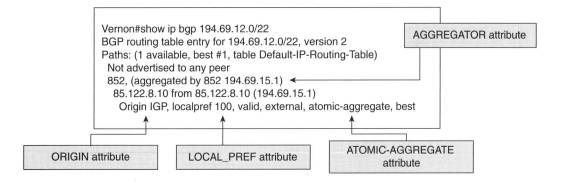

Unless a route has entered BGP by means of redistribution, the ORIGIN attribute for each route will normally be IGP. The ORIGIN attribute is near the top of the BGP route selection process (number five in the decision process), so in certain instances, it might be useful to modify the ORIGIN for a route under some conditions. Three steps are required to change the origin for a route:

Step 1   Configure BGP peers and specify the networks that are to be advertised.

Step 2   Create a route map that changes the BGP ORIGIN attribute to the desired value (IGP, EGP, or INCOMPLETE).

Step 3   (Multiple choices) To apply the route map to a network statement, use the **network** *ip-prefix* **mask** sub*net-mask* **route-map** *route-map-name* command.

To apply the route map to an aggregate network, use the **aggregate-address** *ip-prefix subnet-mask* **attribute-map** *route-map-name* [**summary-only**] command.

To apply the route-map to all advertisements to or from a certain neighbor or peer group, use the **neighbor** {*ip-address* | *peer-group-name*} **route-map** *route-map-name* {**in** | **out**} command.

TIP   When you make configuration changes, you might need to reset the BGP process to apply the changes. To clear a BGP process without resetting all sessions, use the **clear ip bgp * soft [in | out]** command.

To test the effect that changes to the ORIGIN attribute have on the BGP route selection process on the Willis router, shown in Figure 9-13, change all outbound BGP updates using the **neighbor** *ip-address* **route-map** *route-map-name* command. Example 9-45 shows the BGP entries for the 189.168.x.0 networks before the change.

Example 9-45 *Willis Router's BGP Table for the 189.168.x.0 Networks*

```
Willis# show ip bgp 189.168.0.0/16 longer-prefixes
BGP table version is 119, local router ID is 62.128.47.5
Status codes: s suppressed, d damped, h history, * valid, > best, i - internal,
Origin codes: i - IGP, e - EGP, ? - incomplete

   Network          Next Hop          Metric LocPrf Weight Path
*  189.168.56.0/23  62.128.47.198          0             0 645 i
*>                  62.128.47.194          0             0 645 i
```

Example 9-45 *Willis Router's BGP Table for the 189.168.x.0 Networks (Continued)*

```
*   189.168.58.0/23  62.128.47.198           0           0 645 i
*>                   62.128.47.194           0           0 645 i
*   189.168.60.0/23  62.128.47.198           0           0 645 i
*>                   62.128.47.194           0           0 645 i
*   189.168.62.0/23  62.128.47.198           0           0 645 i
*>                   62.128.47.194           0           0 645 i
*   189.168.64.0/23  62.128.47.198           0           0 645 i
*>                   62.128.47.194           0           0 645 i
*   189.168.66.0/23  62.128.47.198           0           0 645 i
*>                   62.128.47.194           0           0 645 i
*   189.168.68.0/23  62.128.47.198           0           0 645 i
*>                   62.128.47.194           0           0 645 i
*   189.168.70.0/23  62.128.47.198           0           0 645 i
*>                   62.128.47.194           0           0 645 i
*   189.168.72.0/23  62.128.47.198           0           0 645 i
    Network          Next Hop         Metric LocPrf Weight Path
*>                   62.128.47.194           0           0 645 i
*   189.168.74.0/23  62.128.47.198           0           0 645 i
*>                   62.128.47.194           0           0 645 i
*   189.168.76.0/23  62.128.47.198           0           0 645 i
*>                   62.128.47.194           0           0 645 i
*   189.168.78.0/23  62.128.47.198           0           0 645 i
*>                   62.128.47.194           0           0 645 i
*   189.168.80.0/23  62.128.47.198           0           0 645 i
*>                   62.128.47.194           0           0 645 i
*   189.168.82.0/23  62.128.47.198           0           0 645 i
*>                   62.128.47.194           0           0 645 i
*   189.168.84.0/23  62.128.47.198           0           0 645 i
*>                   62.128.47.194           0           0 645 i
*   189.168.86.0/23  62.128.47.198           0           0 645 i
*>                   62.128.47.194           0           0 645 i
*   189.168.88.0/23  62.128.47.198           0           0 645 i
*>                   62.128.47.194           0           0 645 i
```

NOTE   For simplicity sake, the BGP Attributes network shown in Figure 9-13 is used in all examples for this section.

Example 9-46 shows the configuration for the Kimberly router. In this case, the Kimberly router has been configured to send all locally originated routes to neighbor 62.128.47.97, the Willis router, with the ORIGIN attribute changed to INCOMPLETE. The Willis router is shown in Example 9-47.

Figure 9-13 *BGP Attributes Network*

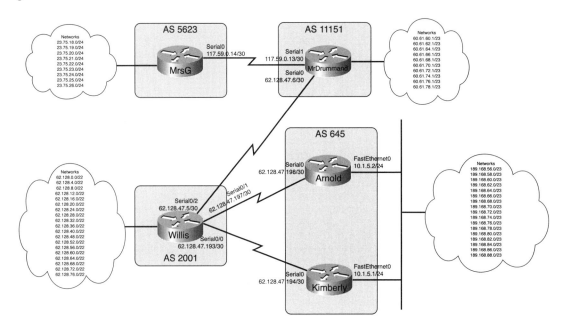

Example 9-46 *Kimberly Router's Beginning BGP Configuration*

```
Kimberly# show run | begin bgp
router bgp 645
 no synchronization
 bgp router-id 10.1.5.1
 bgp log-neighbor-changes
 network 189.168.56.0 mask 255.255.254.0
 network 189.168.58.0 mask 255.255.254.0
 network 189.168.60.0 mask 255.255.254.0
 network 189.168.62.0 mask 255.255.254.0
 network 189.168.64.0 mask 255.255.254.0
 network 189.168.66.0 mask 255.255.254.0
 network 189.168.68.0 mask 255.255.254.0
 network 189.168.70.0 mask 255.255.254.0
 network 189.168.72.0 mask 255.255.254.0
 network 189.168.74.0 mask 255.255.254.0
 network 189.168.76.0 mask 255.255.254.0
 network 189.168.78.0 mask 255.255.254.0
 network 189.168.80.0 mask 255.255.254.0
 network 189.168.82.0 mask 255.255.254.0
 network 189.168.84.0 mask 255.255.254.0
 network 189.168.86.0 mask 255.255.254.0
```

Example 9-46 *Kimberly Router's Beginning BGP Configuration (Continued)*

```
 network 189.168.88.0 mask 255.255.254.0
 neighbor 10.1.5.2 remote-as 645
 neighbor 10.1.5.2 route-reflector-client
 neighbor 10.1.5.2 next-hop-self
 neighbor 62.128.47.193 remote-as 2001
 neighbor 62.128.47.193 route-map change-origin out
 no auto-summary
!
route-map change-origin permit 10
 match route-type local
 set origin incomplete
```

Example 9-47 *Willis Router's BGP RIB After the ORIGIN Attribute Change*

```
Willis# show ip bgp | include 645
*> 189.168.56.0/23  62.128.47.198          0          0 645 i
*                   62.128.47.194          0          0 645 ?
*> 189.168.58.0/23  62.128.47.198          0          0 645 i
*                   62.128.47.194          0          0 645 ?
*> 189.168.60.0/23  62.128.47.198          0          0 645 i
*                   62.128.47.194          0          0 645 ?
*> 189.168.62.0/23  62.128.47.198          0          0 645 i
*                   62.128.47.194          0          0 645 ?
*> 189.168.64.0/23  62.128.47.198          0          0 645 i
*                   62.128.47.194          0          0 645 ?
*> 189.168.66.0/23  62.128.47.198          0          0 645 i
*                   62.128.47.194          0          0 645 ?
*> 189.168.68.0/23  62.128.47.198          0          0 645 i
*                   62.128.47.194          0          0 645 ?
*> 189.168.70.0/23  62.128.47.198          0          0 645 i
*                   62.128.47.194          0          0 645 ?
*> 189.168.72.0/23  62.128.47.198          0          0 645 i
*                   62.128.47.194          0          0 645 ?
*> 189.168.74.0/23  62.128.47.198          0          0 645 i
*                   62.128.47.194          0          0 645 ?
*> 189.168.76.0/23  62.128.47.198          0          0 645 i
*                   62.128.47.194          0          0 645 ?
*> 189.168.78.0/23  62.128.47.198          0          0 645 i
*                   62.128.47.194          0          0 645 ?
*> 189.168.80.0/23  62.128.47.198          0          0 645 i
*                   62.128.47.194          0          0 645 ?
*> 189.168.82.0/23  62.128.47.198          0          0 645 i
*                   62.128.47.194          0          0 645 ?
*> 189.168.84.0/23  62.128.47.198          0          0 645 i
*                   62.128.47.194          0          0 645 ?
*> 189.168.86.0/23  62.128.47.198          0          0 645 i
*                   62.128.47.194          0          0 645 ?
*> 189.168.88.0/23  62.128.47.198          0          0 645 i
*                   62.128.47.194          0          0 645 ?
```

Also, notice that the Willis router now prefers all routes from the Arnold router, 62.128.47.198. Example 9-48 shows the Willis router's IP routing table.

Example 9-48 *Willis Router's IP Routing Table*

```
Willis# show ip route | include 189
      189.168.0.0/23 is subnetted, 17 subnets
B        189.168.60.0 [20/0] via 62.128.47.198, 00:02:48
B        189.168.62.0 [20/0] via 62.128.47.198, 00:02:48
B        189.168.56.0 [20/0] via 62.128.47.198, 00:02:48
B        189.168.58.0 [20/0] via 62.128.47.198, 00:02:48
B        189.168.84.0 [20/0] via 62.128.47.198, 00:02:48
B        189.168.86.0 [20/0] via 62.128.47.198, 00:02:48
B        189.168.80.0 [20/0] via 62.128.47.198, 00:02:48
B        189.168.82.0 [20/0] via 62.128.47.198, 00:02:48
B        189.168.88.0 [20/0] via 62.128.47.198, 00:02:48
B        189.168.68.0 [20/0] via 62.128.47.198, 00:02:48
B        189.168.70.0 [20/0] via 62.128.47.198, 00:02:48
B        189.168.64.0 [20/0] via 62.128.47.198, 00:02:48
B        189.168.66.0 [20/0] via 62.128.47.198, 00:02:48
B        189.168.76.0 [20/0] via 62.128.47.198, 00:02:48
B        189.168.78.0 [20/0] via 62.128.47.198, 00:02:48
B        189.168.72.0 [20/0] via 62.128.47.198, 00:02:48
B        189.168.74.0 [20/0] via 62.128.47.198, 00:02:48
```

As you can see, the ORIGIN attribute can be used to manipulate the BGP route selection process. Now that you have seen an example of ORIGIN attribute modification, it is time to look at how you can use the AS_PATH attribute to affect path selection. Although the ORIGIN attribute can be modified to alter the best path decision, ORIGIN attribute modification is not the best choice for BGP path selection.

Using the AS_PATH Attribute to Affect Path Selection

Every time a routing update passes from one AS to another, the AS_PATH attribute is updated to store the path that the route has taken to reach its current location. As you might remember from Chapter 7, the AS_PATH field in the BGP UPDATE message contains the AS path, in a right-to-left format, beginning with the originating AS, as shown in Example 9-49.

Example 9-49 *Displaying the AS_PATH Attribute for a BGP Route*

```
MrsG# show ip bgp 189.168.88.0/23
BGP routing table entry for 189.168.88.0/23, version 699
Paths: (1 available, best #1, table Default-IP-Routing-Table)
  Not advertised to any peer
Please add shading to next line
  11151 2001 645
    117.59.0.13 from 117.59.0.13 (117.59.0.13)
      Origin IGP, localpref 100, valid, external, best
```

In the preceding example, you can see that the route to the 189.168.88.0/23 network originated in AS 645 at the Arnold router, then passed to AS 2001, the Willis router, and then to AS 11,151, the MrDrummand router, before reaching its current location, the MrsG router. The AS_PATH information is intended to be a BGP loop-prevention mechanism; if a router sees its own AS number in the path, the route is assumed to have looped and is ignored.

NOTE   The **neighbor** *ip-address* **allowas-in [number-of-occurrences]** command allows routers running Cisco IOS Software to accept up to 10 occurrences of the local AS number in the AS_PATH attribute of incoming BGP updates. Use this command with extreme caution, as it disables BGP's prime loop-prevention method.

The AS path information is also used to provide several other features, including BGP AS_PATH filtering, BGP RIB lookups using regular expressions, and the AS_PATH information that also affects the BGP decision process. Remember, the BGP route selection process selects a route based on the following items:

1 Largest WEIGHT attribute.

2 Largest LOCAL_PREF attribute.

3 Locally originated routes (Next hop 0.0.0.0 in the BGP RIB).

4 Shortest AS_PATH attribute.

5 Best route ORIGIN attribute: IGP, EGP, INCOMPLETE.

6 Lowest MED attribute.

7 E-BGP routes are preferred over I-BGP routes (and also have lower administrative distance).

8 The oldest route first. (Older routes are more stable.)

9 The path that originated from the router with the lowest BGP router ID.

10 If the router is a route reflector, the lowest CLUSTER_ID attribute length.

11 Routes received from the peer with the lowest IP address.

It is a common, though not recommended, practice to use the AS path as a decision factor in Internet route selection. As an experiment, go to an Internet looking-glass website and find routes containing AS paths with the same AS number repeated several times; this is referred to as *AS path prepending*. AS path prepending adds the local AS number to the current location (the leftmost AS path position) in the AS path as many times as the user specifies. It is not generally recommended because Internet routes travel through many autonomous systems, and as each route leaves each AS, the AS border routers also prepend their local AS number to the path, so there is no guaranty that the AS numbers that you originally prepended to the path will always have the desired effect. While exploring the Internet routing tables, you might even notice some routes that have up to 20 entries the in the AS_PATH. This is most likely because two or more entities prepended their AS number to the AS_PATH, and at the time you are viewing the route, it might have passed through several autonomous systems. There are several other more efficient route attribute manipulation techniques.

To manipulate the AS path on a Cisco router, use the **set as-path prepend** *as-number* command in a route map and specify the AS values that you want to add to the route. Only two steps are required to prepend an AS number to an AS path:

Step 1   Create a route map and access or prefix list specifying the networks that are to be AS prepended and identify the AS that is to be added to the path. To change the AS path for all locally originated routes, use the **match route-type local** command, which matches all routes originated by the local router. (This might not be a good idea on a large public network.)

Step 2   Apply the route map to the desired neighbors or peer groups.

NOTE   Although it is possible to prepend any AS value to the AS_PATH by adding a random AS number to increase the size of the AS path, this is not a good practice to follow in the field. Prepending your local AS will not hurt anything on your local network or your direct peers' networks, but the routes with the randomly prepended ASNs might actually flow through the AS that owns the AS number that you randomly selected, causing serious (and very embarrassing) problems. Most service providers have a policy on AS prepending. Always consult your service provider's policies before configuring BGP attributes. If you plan to use AS prepending in your network, be a good Internet neighbor and prepend only the number of AS numbers required for the situation.

Because Cisco's implementation of BGP compares the AS_PATH length (as the fourth best path decision factor), when one AS has more than one entrance point, you can use AS_PATH prepending to make one path longer than the other. This causes the upstream BGP peers to prefer the route with the smaller AS_PATH attribute. If the Kimberly router prepends its own AS number (AS 645) to all locally originated routes sent to the Willis router, for example, this causes the Willis router to prefer routes from the Arnold router. If the connection between the Willis and Arnold routers is lost, the Willis router removes the Arnold router's routes and uses the routes from the Kimberly router. When the connection between the Willis and Arnold routers is repaired, and BGP routes are exchanged, the Willis router will, once again, prefer routes from the Arnold router. Example 9-50 shows how autonomous system prepending is used in the Attributes network. In this example, autonomous system 645 has two exit points: the Arnold router, and the Kimberly router.

Remove the change-origin route map, used in the preceding example, before trying the next example.

Example 9-50 *Prepending ASNs to the AS_PATH*

```
Kimberly# show run | begin bgp
router bgp 645
 no synchronization
 bgp router-id 10.1.5.1
 bgp log-neighbor-changes
 network 189.168.56.0 mask 255.255.254.0
 network 189.168.58.0 mask 255.255.254.0
 network 189.168.60.0 mask 255.255.254.0
 network 189.168.62.0 mask 255.255.254.0
 network 189.168.64.0 mask 255.255.254.0
 network 189.168.66.0 mask 255.255.254.0
 network 189.168.68.0 mask 255.255.254.0
 network 189.168.70.0 mask 255.255.254.0
 network 189.168.72.0 mask 255.255.254.0
 network 189.168.74.0 mask 255.255.254.0
 network 189.168.76.0 mask 255.255.254.0
 network 189.168.78.0 mask 255.255.254.0
 network 189.168.80.0 mask 255.255.254.0
 network 189.168.82.0 mask 255.255.254.0
 network 189.168.84.0 mask 255.255.254.0
 network 189.168.86.0 mask 255.255.254.0
 network 189.168.88.0 mask 255.255.254.0
 neighbor 10.1.5.2 remote-as 645
 neighbor 62.128.47.193 remote-as 2001
 neighbor 62.128.47.193 route-map prepend out
 no auto-summary
 !
route-map prepend permit 10
 match route-type local
 set as-path prepend 645
```

After the Willis router receives the updates from the Kimberly router, it no longer prefers the routes sent by the Kimberly router, which had the lowest BGP router ID and IP address. This is because the AS_PATH length for the Kimberly router's routes is now longer than the AS_PATH length of the routes that originated from the Arnold router. Example 9-51 shows a sample BGP route from the Willis router.

Example 9-51 *BGP Route Information for a Prepended Route*

```
Willis# show ip bgp 189.168.56.0/23
BGP routing table entry for 189.168.56.0/23, version 276
Paths: (2 available, best #1, table Default-IP-Routing-Table)
Flag: 0x820
  Advertised to non peer-group peers:
  62.128.47.6 62.128.47.194
  645
    62.128.47.198 from 62.128.47.198 (10.1.5.2)
      Origin IGP, metric 0, localpref 100, valid, external, best
  645 645
    62.128.47.194 from 62.128.47.194 (10.1.5.1)
      Origin IGP, metric 0, localpref 100, valid, external
```

Filtering BGP Routes Using the AS_PATH Attribute

One of the easiest ways to filter large numbers of routes is to filter by AS number using an AS path access list. If you are not familiar with regular expressions, the first time you use AS path access lists you might find the AS_PATH filtering process to be rather confusing, causing unexpected results. Creating elegant AS path access lists requires you to become familiar with the use of regular expressions. But, relax, breathe deeply, and read on, because you are now going to learn regular expressions the easy way.

NOTE   Cisco IOS Software uses many of the same regular expressions that you might have seen in the UNIX/Linux world. If you are not familiar with regular expressions, you can find an appendix dealing directly with that subject in the *Cisco IOS Dial Solutions* book, or on the documentation website under "dial solutions."

How to Use Regular Expressions

One of the first things that scares people about regular expressions is the strange-looking structure that they use. If you are like most of the non-math majors out there, you might have found that expressions such as ^400$ look more like abbreviations for foreign currency than AS_PATH values; however, this regular expression simply means the following:

^ = "beginning with"

$ = "ends with"

or begins and ends with ASN 400

So, this statement simply means beginning and ending with the number 400; this regular expression matches only one instance of the AS number 400. Right about now you might be asking, why can't you just type "400" and be done with it? The reason is that the number 400 matches any string beginning, ending, or containing the number 400. There are a number of ways that the special characters used in regular expressions can be applied to represent different character strings. The best way to find the AS path sequence that you need is to use the **show ip bgp regexp** *regular-expression* command. When you use this command, you can test to find all the possible matches that the router finds for each regular expression before using the best expression in a route filter. Example 9-52 shows how the **show ip bgp regexp** command finds any instances of the AS path 645.

Example 9-52 **show ip bgp regexp** *Command*

```
Willis# show ip bgp regexp _645_
     Network          Next Hop          Metric LocPrf Weight Path
 *   10.1.1.0/24      62.128.47.198                        0 645 800 234 6768 i
 *>                   62.128.47.194          0             0 645 400 i
 *   10.2.2.0/24      62.128.47.198                        0 645 800 234 6768 i
 *>                   62.128.47.194          0             0 645 100 400 i
 *   10.3.3.0/24      62.128.47.198                        0 645 800 234 6768 i
 *>                   62.128.47.194          0             0 645 400 400 100 i
 *> 189.168.56.0/23   62.128.47.194          0             0 645 645 645 645 i
 *> 189.168.58.0/23   62.128.47.194          0             0 645 645 645 645 i
 *> 189.168.60.0/23   62.128.47.194          0             0 645 645 645 645 i
 *> 189.168.62.0/23   62.128.47.194          0             0 645 645 645 645 i
 *> 189.168.64.0/23   62.128.47.194          0             0 645 645 645 645 i
 *> 189.168.66.0/23   62.128.47.194          0             0 645 645 645 645 i
 *> 189.168.68.0/23   62.128.47.194          0             0 645 645 645 645 i
 *> 189.168.70.0/23   62.128.47.194          0             0 645 645 645 645 i
 *> 189.168.72.0/23   62.128.47.194          0             0 645 645 645 645 i
 *> 189.168.74.0/23   62.128.47.194          0             0 645 645 645 645 i
 *> 189.168.76.0/23   62.128.47.194          0             0 645 645 645 645 i
     Network          Next Hop          Metric LocPrf Weight Path
 *> 189.168.78.0/23   62.128.47.194          0             0 645 645 645 645 i
 *   189.168.80.0/23  62.128.47.198          0             0 645 800 234 6768 i
 *>                   62.128.47.194          0             0 645 645 645 645 i
 *   189.168.82.0/23  62.128.47.198          0             0 645 800 234 6768 i
 *>                   62.128.47.194          0             0 645 645 645 645 i
 *   189.168.84.0/23  62.128.47.198          0             0 645 800 234 6768 i
 *>                   62.128.47.194          0             0 645 645 645 645 i
 *   189.168.86.0/23  62.128.47.198          0             0 645 800 234 6768 i
 *>                   62.128.47.194          0             0 645 645 645 645 i
 *   189.168.88.0/23  62.128.47.198          0             0 645 800 234 6768 i
 *>                   62.128.47.194          0             0 645 645 645 645 i
```

TIP

If you experiment with the **show ip bgp regexp** command and find that a particular regular expression is not working, even though you absolutely know it should, check again! You might have accidentally hit the Spacebar at the end of the regular expression; doing so changes the meaning of the regular expression and prevents it from making the appropriate match. That is also why it is a good idea to give any regular expressions a test run before application in production environments.

Table 9-4 shows the special characters that you can use with regular expressions, the character definitions, and examples of their use.

Table 9-4   *Special Characters Used for Regular Expressions*

Character	Meaning	Examples
^ caret Used at beginning of expression.	Begins with *item*	^1 = begins with 1. This means that any other characters behind 1 also match this string. For example: 1 400 500 or 123 456 7891
$ dollar Used at end of expression.	Ends with *item*	400$ = ends with 400. This means that any other characters before the string 400 will also match this regular expression. For example: 645 400 or 645 100 400 400 However, the regular expression ^400$ means begins and ends with 400. ^$ matches an empty AS path.
* asterisk Used at the end of an expression.	0 or more of item.	40* = contains 0 or more instances of the string 4. This could match: 645 645 400 645 100 4 645 400 400 100 44 645 775 801 212 ^645* matches any string that begins with 645. For example: 645 100 400 645 645 645

Table 9-4   *Special Characters Used for Regular Expressions (Continued)*

Character	Meaning	Examples
. period Used anywhere in an expression.	Any character (including space).	.645 matches any instance of *character*-645, but only 645. For example: 1645 645 645 777 645 645 645 645. matches any string containing 645-character. For example: 645 645 645 100 645 400 189 201 13645 .* matches any as path, including a blank path.
+ plus Cannot be used at the beginning of an expression.	1 or more of *item* preceding + character.	645+ matches 1 or more instances of the 645 string. For example: 6451 65 400 100 400 100 645 645 645 645
- hyphen Used between brackets to specify a range.	Used between starting and ending points of a range.	Used in a range specified by brackets [x-x]. *See brackets [].
? question mark Used at the end of an expression. Requires the use of the CTRL-v characters before the ? character can be used as a character.	0 or 1 instances of *item*.	645? matches anything that contains any 645 string. For example: 645 645 645 645 645 645 400 123 400 400 645 ^645? begins with 645 and could end with anything.

continues

Table 9-4   *Special Characters Used for Regular Expressions (Continued)*

Character	Meaning	Examples
_ underscore	Matches special characters such as the following: **,** comma ( ) parenthesis { } braces beginning of string end or string blank space	Used when creating complex expressions with special characters. For example: _645_ matches any as path containing 645: 645 645 645 645 645 800 234 645
() parenthesis	Matches confederation identifiers in AS_PATH and can also be used create number patterns.	(65501)$ matches any as path ending with the string (65501). For example: 101 (65501)
[] brackets	Range of characters.	[0–9] matches any string of numbers, but does not match empty AS_PATHs. For example: 645 645 400 100 11151 2001 5623 11151 2001 [058]$ matches any as path containing a last character of 0, 5, or 8. For example: 645 645 645 800 234 6768 645 400 400 100 ^356_[0–9] matches any as path that begins with 356 and has more than one trailing ASN. For example: 356 789 012 356 012 356 356

TIP	Do not forget to use the **CTRL-V** key sequence when entering the ? character; otherwise, you will constantly be asking Cisco IOS Software for help.

After you are comfortable creating regular expressions, you can use those expressions to create AS path access lists.

AS Path Access Lists and Regular Expressions

Similar to regular numbered access lists used for IP traffic, AS path access lists are numbered access lists that match traffic based on an AS path value. This AS value is specified using a regular expression. Also, similar to IP access lists, each AS path access lists ends with an explicit **deny any**. AS path access lists are created using the following command:

```
ip as-path access-list list-number {permit | deny} regular-expression
```

Suppose, for instance, that the Willis router has a new requirement to block all network prefixes containing the AS_PATH value of 645. This can easily be accomplished using an AS_PATH access list that denies any instance of 645 in the AS_PATH, as shown in Example 9-53.

Example 9-53 *Using AS Path Access Lists to Filter BGP Routes Containing 645*

```
Willis# show run | include as-path
ip as-path access-list 1 deny _645_
ip as-path access-list 1 permit .*
```

In the preceding example, AS path access list 1 is used to deny any AS path containing the string 645, whereas all other traffic is permitted. The regular expression **_645_** describes any string containing the value 645, and the **.*** regular expression allows any other path values.

Like most parameters in BGP, there are two ways to apply an AS path access list: using a route map, or by applying a filter list. Both ways are examined in this section. Consider the route map configuration first.

Three steps are required to configure AS path prefix filtering using route maps:

Step 1   Create the AS path access list that will be used to specify the AS path regular expression.

Step 2   Create a route map to tell the router how to use the AS path access list.

Step 3   Apply the route map to a BGP neighbor or peer using the **neighbor** {*ip-address* | *peer-group*} **route-map** *route-map-name* {**in** | **out**} command.

If you are going to apply the access list using a route map, you must define a route map that tells the router how to use the AS path access list. As mentioned earlier in Table 9-3, the **match as-path** *as-path-access-list-number* command specifies the AS path that is to be matched. For example, **route-map filter-as**, shown in Example 9-54, is used to match AS path access list 1.

Example 9-54 *Using a Route Map with an AS Path Access List*

```
Willis# show run | begin route-map
route-map filter-as permit 10
 match as-path 1
```

After you create the route map, you can then apply it to a neighbor or peer group. Example 9-55 shows the completed AS path access list filtering configuration for the Willis router.

Example 9-55 *Applying a Route Map to a BGP Peer*

```
Willis# show run | begin bgp
router bgp 2001
 no synchronization
bgp router-id 62.128.47.5
 bgp log-neighbor-changes
 network 62.128.0.0 mask 255.255.252.0
 network 62.128.4.0 mask 255.255.252.0
 network 62.128.8.0 mask 255.255.252.0
 network 62.128.12.0 mask 255.255.252.0
 network 62.128.16.0 mask 255.255.252.0
 network 62.128.20.0 mask 255.255.252.0
 network 62.128.24.0 mask 255.255.252.0
 network 62.128.28.0 mask 255.255.252.0
 network 62.128.32.0 mask 255.255.252.0
 network 62.128.36.0 mask 255.255.252.0
 network 62.128.40.0 mask 255.255.252.0
 network 62.128.48.0 mask 255.255.252.0
 network 62.128.52.0 mask 255.255.252.0
 network 62.128.56.0 mask 255.255.252.0
 network 62.128.60.0 mask 255.255.252.0
 network 62.128.64.0 mask 255.255.252.0
 network 62.128.68.0 mask 255.255.252.0
 network 62.128.72.0 mask 255.255.252.0
 network 62.128.76.0 mask 255.255.252.0
 aggregate-address 62.128.44.0 255.255.255.252
 neighbor 62.128.47.6 remote-as 11151
 neighbor 62.128.47.6 route-map filter-as out
 neighbor 62.128.47.194 remote-as 645
 neighbor 62.128.47.198 remote-as 645
```

Example 9-55 *Applying a Route Map to a BGP Peer (Continued)*

```
  no auto-summary
 !
 ip as-path access-list 1 deny _645_
 ip as-path access-list 1 permit .*
 !
 route-map filter-as permit 10
  match as-path 1
```

In the preceding example, route map filter-as is used to deny any instance of ASN 645 for all outgoing updates to the MrDrummand router. The **permit .*** regular expression is used to allow all other AS numbers.

BGP filter lists provide a simpler, less granular approach to AS path access list filtering. Filter lists are used only to filter BGP routes by AS path.

Only two steps are required to configure BGP route filter routes based on the AS path:

Step 1   Create an AS path access list that specifies the AS path that is to be matched.

Step 2   Apply the route map to a BGP neighbor or peer using the following command:

> **neighbor** {*ip-address* | *peer-group*} **filter-list** *as-path-access-list-number*
> {**in** | **out**}

Example 9-56 shows how the **filter list** command accomplishes the same effect as the route map shown earlier in Example 9-55.

Example 9-56 *Using a Filter List to Filter BGP Traffic by AS Path*

```
Willis# show run | begin bgp
router bgp 2001
 no synchronization
 bgp router-id 62.128.47.5
 bgp log-neighbor-changes
 network 62.128.0.0 mask 255.255.252.0
 network 62.128.4.0 mask 255.255.252.0
 network 62.128.8.0 mask 255.255.252.0
 network 62.128.12.0 mask 255.255.252.0
 network 62.128.16.0 mask 255.255.252.0
 network 62.128.20.0 mask 255.255.252.0
 network 62.128.24.0 mask 255.255.252.0
 network 62.128.28.0 mask 255.255.252.0
 network 62.128.32.0 mask 255.255.252.0
```

continues

Example 9-56 *Using a Filter List to Filter BGP Traffic by AS Path (Continued)*

```
 network 62.128.36.0 mask 255.255.252.0
 network 62.128.40.0 mask 255.255.252.0
 network 62.128.48.0 mask 255.255.252.0
 network 62.128.52.0 mask 255.255.252.0
 network 62.128.56.0 mask 255.255.252.0
 network 62.128.60.0 mask 255.255.252.0
 network 62.128.64.0 mask 255.255.252.0
 network 62.128.68.0 mask 255.255.252.0
 network 62.128.72.0 mask 255.255.252.0
 network 62.128.76.0 mask 255.255.252.0
 aggregate-address 62.128.44.0 255.255.255.252
 neighbor 62.128.47.6 remote-as 11151
 neighbor 62.128.47.6 filter-list 1 out
 neighbor 62.128.47.194 remote-as 645
 neighbor 62.128.47.198 remote-as 645
 no auto-summary
!
ip as-path access-list 1 deny _645_
ip as-path access-list 1 permit .*
```

You can use AS path access lists to filter network prefixes in a number of ways:

- In multihomed environments, the **^$** regular expression can be used to prevent local autonomous systems from providing transit services between two upstream service providers, allowing only outgoing route advertisements that have an empty AS_PATH attribute.

- Provide only partial BGP RIB updates to downstream neighbors by using the **^AS$** regular expression.

- Use an AS path access list to allow only locally sourced updates to exit to an upstream neighbor, by using the **_AS_** regular expression.

- Filter certain AS paths from incoming or outgoing updates, by using a combination of complex regular expressions and AS path access lists.

Modifying the NEXT_HOP Attribute for Path Manipulation

You can manipulate routing by using BGP attributes in several ways. One of the simplest modifications you can make is to change the next hop for a route. As you learned in the preceding chapter, the NEXT_HOP attribute is changed each time a route crosses an AS border, but not when a route is advertised within an AS. In Figure 9-14, for example, there are four routers: Eany in AS 12,512; and Meany, Miney, and Moe in AS 61,382.

Figure 9-14 *How BGP Modifies the NEXT_HOP Attribute*

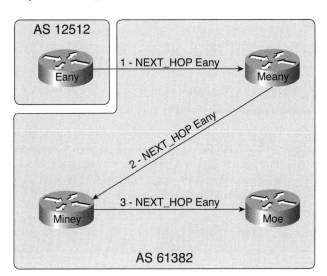

This figure shows a logical representation of how the NEXT_HOP attribute changes as a route passes through routers in different autonomous systems. First, the route passes between two autonomous systems as it is forwarded between the Eany and Meany routers. In this case, the NEXT_HOP attribute of the route is modified at the egress interface by the Eany router. The Eany router modifies the NEXT_HOP attribute and passes the route to the Meany router. By default, the Meany router does not alter the NEXT_HOP value before it passes the route to the Miney router because the route originated from an external AS. When the Miney router advertises the route to the Moe router, it does not change the NEXT_HOP attribute because, unless specified to do otherwise, I-BGP speakers do not modify the NEXT_HOP attribute.

NOTE   The NEXT_HOP attribute is covered in detail in the "The NEXT_HOP Attribute" section of Chapter 7.

It is usually necessary to change the NEXT_HOP attribute for routes forwarded between I-BGP speakers when an I-BGP speaker is forwarding a route learned by means of an update from an E-BGP peer. Unless the I-BGP neighbor has been configured with a gateway of last resort pointing to its upstream I-BGP peer, it will be unable to reach the E-BGP router's IP address. You can correct this situation in three ways:

- Originate a default route using the **neighbor** {*ip-address* | *peer-group*} **default-originate** command.

- Redistribute BGP routes in an IGP (if an IGP is in use).

- Use the **next-hop-self** command to alter the NEXT_HOP attribute for I-BGP routes.

NEXT_HOP attribute modification is accomplished using the **neighbor** {*ip-address* | *peer-group*} **next-hop-self** command. Sometimes, you might not want to modify the outgoing NEXT_HOP attribute for a route; in which case, you can use the **neighbor** {*ip-address* | *peer-group*} **next-hop-unchanged** command. So, you might ask, what do you do when you want to modify a NEXT_HOP attribute in other ways? Simple, the NEXT_HOP attribute can also be modified by using a route map.

NOTE   Be careful changing the NEXT_HOP attributes for a route. If that path fails, traffic might not reroute correctly.

Three steps are required to manually change the NEXT_HOP attribute for a route:

Step 1   Create an access or prefix list that specifies the networks that the attribute changes will apply to. If all routes to a particular neighbor or peer group are to be changed, you can skip this step.

Step 2   Create a route map that references the access or prefix list created in Step 1 and use the **set next-hop** {*ip-address* | *peer-address* | **verify-availability**} command.

NOTE   The **verify-availability** command can be used only for incoming routes.

Step 3   Apply the route map to a neighbor or peer group using the **neighbor** {*ip-address* | *peer-group*} **route-map** *route-map-name* {**in** | **out**} command.

If two more routers are added into AS 645, as shown in Figure 9-15, for instance, the Arnold and Kimberly routers need to be configured to peer with the new routers, provide reflected routes, and modify the outgoing NEXT_HOP attribute for all externally originated routes.

Figure 9-15 *Adding Two New Routers to the Mix*

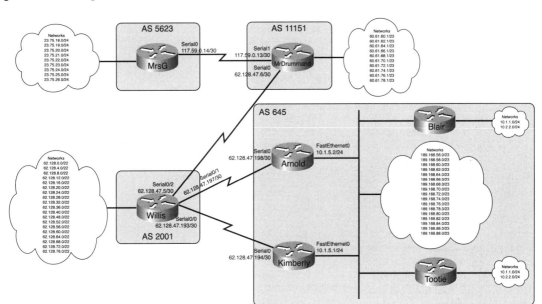

In this example, it would be easy to use the **next-hop-self** command to allow the Blair and Tootie routers to reach the external networks. For the sake of this example, however, a route map is used instead. Although the **next-hop-self** is simpler in most cases, sometimes you might need to modify the next hop and not want to use the NEXT_HOP value generated using the **next-hop-self** command. For example, you might want to point the next hop to an external firewall that is not advertised to I-BGP peers; in this case, you might want to use a route map to manually set the next hop. Example 9-57 shows how you can use a simple route map to change the NEXT_HOP attribute for all routes bound to a particular neighbor.

Example 9-57 *Using Route Maps to Modify the NEXT_HOP Attribute*

```
Arnold# show run | begin bgp
router bgp 645
 no synchronization
 bgp router-id 10.1.5.2
 bgp log-neighbor-changes
 network 189.168.56.0 mask 255.255.254.0
 network 189.168.58.0 mask 255.255.254.0
 network 189.168.60.0 mask 255.255.254.0
```

continues

Example 9-57 *Using Route Maps to Modify the NEXT_HOP Attribute (Continued)*

```
         network 189.168.62.0 mask 255.255.254.0
         network 189.168.64.0 mask 255.255.254.0
         network 189.168.66.0 mask 255.255.254.0
         network 189.168.68.0 mask 255.255.254.0
         network 189.168.70.0 mask 255.255.254.0
         network 189.168.72.0 mask 255.255.254.0
         network 189.168.74.0 mask 255.255.254.0
         network 189.168.76.0 mask 255.255.254.0
         network 189.168.78.0 mask 255.255.254.0
         network 189.168.80.0 mask 255.255.254.0
         network 189.168.82.0 mask 255.255.254.0
         network 189.168.84.0 mask 255.255.254.0
         network 189.168.86.0 mask 255.255.254.0
         network 189.168.88.0 mask 255.255.254.0
         neighbor 10.1.5.3 remote-as 645
         neighbor 10.1.5.1 route-reflector-client
         neighbor 10.1.5.1 next-hop-self
         neighbor 10.1.5.3 route-reflector-client
         neighbor 10.1.5.3 route-map next-hop out
         neighbor 10.1.5.4 remote-as 645
         neighbor 10.1.5.4 route-reflector-client
         neighbor 10.1.5.4 route-map next-hop out
         neighbor 62.128.47.197 remote-as 2001
 no auto-summary
 !
 route-map next-hop permit 10
  set ip next-hop 10.1.5.2
```

In the preceding example, the next-hop route map is used to change the NEXT_HOP attribute of the FastEthernet interface of the Arnold router. This same effect could have been achieved using the **next-hop-self** command.

Using the MED Attribute to Specify the Best Path

When you have a multihomed network, you can use the *Multi Exit Discriminator* (MED) attribute to specify the preferred entry point for an AS. The MED attribute is a BGP metric that makes E-BGP neighbors aware of the preferred entry point to a network. As a nontransitive BGP attribute, the MED is not advertised beyond the directly connected AS border, and is applied only on a peer-by-peer basis.

NOTE   The technical specifications for the MED attribute are covered in the "The MED Attribute" section of Chapter 7.

Only three steps are required to set the MED attribute for an AS. You might optionally apply a different MED value for each AS bordering router, or modify how the BGP decision process will use the MED attribute:

Step 1   (Optional) Create an access list that specifies to which traffic the MED value is to be applied.

Step 2   Create a route map specifying the MED value for the entry point. The default MED value is 0, and this can be changed to any value ranging from 1 to 4,294,967,295, with the lowest value being preferred. The metric is applied using the **set metric** [+ | - *metric-value*] command within a route map configuration mode. The optional + and - parameters change a preexisting metric.

Step 3   Apply the route map to a neighbor using the **neighbor** {*ip-address* | *peer-group*} **route-map** *route-map-name* {**in** | **out**} command.

Step 4   (Optional) Use the **bgp always-compare-med**, **bgp bestpath med confed**, **bgp bestpath med missing-as-worst**, or **bgp deterministic-med** commands to modify how BGP uses the MED attribute during the best path selection process. Table 9-5 shows how each of these commands apply and when they are used.

Table 9-5   *Best Path MED Modifications*

MED Command	Command Definition
bgp always-compare-med	Allows the BGP best path selection process to compare BGP MED attributes received from E-BGP peers that belong to different autonomous systems
bgp bestpath med confed	Allows BGP to compare MED attributes received from confederation peers
bgp bestpath med missing-as-worst	Specifies that BGP should consider a path to be the worst option if the MED attribute is not present
bgp deterministic-med	Allows BGP to compare MED values from different E-BGP peers in the same AS

NOTE   Although the MED attribute can be applied to incoming or outgoing paths, you should always use the MED to specify the preferred network entry point to E-BGP peers, and the LOCAL_PREFERENCE attribute to specify the preferred network exit point for I-BGP peers.

After you apply the new metric to a neighbor, you can verify its use by using the **show ip bgp** command on the remote peer. The MED attribute displays as the Metric value, as shown in Example 9-58.

Example 9-58 *Using the* **show ip bgp** *Command to Verify the MED Attribute*

```
Willis# show ip bgp regexp ^645$
    Network          Next Hop           Metric LocPrf Weight Path
*   10.1.1.0/24      62.128.47.194         100            0 645 i
*>                   62.128.47.198          50            0 645 i
*   10.2.2.0/24      62.128.47.194         100            0 645 i
*>                   62.128.47.198          50            0 645 i
*   189.168.56.0/23  62.128.47.194         100            0 645 i
*>                   62.128.47.198          50            0 645 i
*   189.168.58.0/23  62.128.47.194         100            0 645 i
*>                   62.128.47.198          50            0 645 i
*   189.168.60.0/23  62.128.47.194         100            0 645 i
*>                   62.128.47.198          50            0 645 i
*   189.168.62.0/23  62.128.47.194         100            0 645 i
*>                   62.128.47.198          50            0 645 i
*   189.168.64.0/23  62.128.47.194         100            0 645 i
*>                   62.128.47.198          50            0 645 i
*   189.168.66.0/23  62.128.47.194         100            0 645 i
*>                   62.128.47.198          50            0 645 i
*   189.168.68.0/23  62.128.47.194         100            0 645 i
```

To illustrate the use of the MED attribute, it can be applied to the Arnold and Kimberly routers in AS 645. Before a MED attribute was applied to the paths advertised by the two AS 645 border routers, the Willis router preferred the paths advertised by the Kimberly router because it had a lower IP address. By changing the MED attribute, an attribute that is ranked higher in the BGP decision process, on the Arnold router to a value lower than that of the Kimberly router, the preferred path to AS 645 will be changed. Example 9-59 shows how the MED attribute is changed on the Arnold and Kimberly routers.

Example 9-59 *Changing the MED Attribute for AS 645 on the Arnold and Kimberly Routers*

```
Arnold# show run | begin bgp
router bgp 645
 no synchronization
 bgp router-id 10.1.5.2
 bgp log-neighbor-changes
 network 189.168.56.0 mask 255.255.254.0
 network 189.168.58.0 mask 255.255.254.0
 network 189.168.60.0 mask 255.255.254.0
 network 189.168.62.0 mask 255.255.254.0
 network 189.168.64.0 mask 255.255.254.0
 network 189.168.66.0 mask 255.255.254.0
 network 189.168.68.0 mask 255.255.254.0
 network 189.168.70.0 mask 255.255.254.0
 network 189.168.72.0 mask 255.255.254.0
 network 189.168.74.0 mask 255.255.254.0
 network 189.168.76.0 mask 255.255.254.0
 network 189.168.78.0 mask 255.255.254.0
```

Example 9-59 *Changing the MED Attribute for AS 645 on the Arnold and Kimberly Routers (Continued)*

```
 network 189.168.80.0 mask 255.255.254.0
 network 189.168.82.0 mask 255.255.254.0
 network 189.168.84.0 mask 255.255.254.0
 network 189.168.86.0 mask 255.255.254.0
 network 189.168.88.0 mask 255.255.254.0
 neighbor 10.1.5.1 remote-as 645
 neighbor 10.1.5.1 route-reflector-client
 neighbor 10.1.5.1 next-hop-self
 neighbor 10.1.5.3 remote-as 645
 neighbor 10.1.5.3 route-reflector-client
 neighbor 10.1.5.3 next-hop-self
 neighbor 10.1.5.4 remote-as 645
 neighbor 10.1.5.4 route-reflector-client
 neighbor 10.1.5.4 next-hop-self
 neighbor 62.128.47.197 remote-as 2001
 neighbor 62.128.47.197 route-map MED out
 no auto-summary
 !
 route-map MED permit 10
 set metric 50
```

```
Kimberly# show run | begin bgp
router bgp 645
 no synchronization
 bgp router-id 10.1.5.1
 bgp log-neighbor-changes
 network 189.168.56.0 mask 255.255.254.0
 network 189.168.58.0 mask 255.255.254.0
 network 189.168.60.0 mask 255.255.254.0
 network 189.168.62.0 mask 255.255.254.0
 network 189.168.64.0 mask 255.255.254.0
 network 189.168.66.0 mask 255.255.254.0
 network 189.168.68.0 mask 255.255.254.0
 network 189.168.70.0 mask 255.255.254.0
 network 189.168.72.0 mask 255.255.254.0
 network 189.168.74.0 mask 255.255.254.0
 network 189.168.76.0 mask 255.255.254.0
 network 189.168.78.0 mask 255.255.254.0
 network 189.168.80.0 mask 255.255.254.0
 network 189.168.82.0 mask 255.255.254.0
 network 189.168.84.0 mask 255.255.254.0
 network 189.168.86.0 mask 255.255.254.0
 network 189.168.88.0 mask 255.255.254.0
 neighbor 10.1.5.2 remote-as 645
 neighbor 10.1.5.2 route-reflector-client
 neighbor 10.1.5.2 next-hop-self
 neighbor 10.1.5.3 remote-as 645
 neighbor 10.1.5.3 route-reflector-client
 neighbor 10.1.5.3 next-hop-self
```

continues

Example 9-59 *Changing the MED Attribute for AS 645 on the Arnold and Kimberly Routers (Continued)*

```
 neighbor 10.1.5.4 remote-as 645
 neighbor 10.1.5.4 route-reflector-client
 neighbor 10.1.5.4 next-hop-self
 neighbor 62.128.47.193 remote-as 2001
 neighbor 62.128.47.193 route-map MED out
 no auto-summary
 !
route-map MED permit 10
 set metric 100
```

Using the LOCAL_PREF Attribute to Specify Network Exit Points

The local preference (LOCAL_PREF) attribute is used with an AS to modify the desirability for routes with more than one possible path that can be used to exit the local AS. As its name implies, the LOCAL_PREF attribute is passed only between I-BGP peers; the LOCAL_PREF attribute is not forwarded to external peers.

NOTE   It is sometimes hard to remember the difference between the LOCAL_PREF and the MED attributes. One easy way to remember which attribute does which task is to look at the name — LOCAL_PREF applies only to local peers, and the Multi Exit Discriminator (MED) tells external peers the preferred entry point into your AS. The MED attribute is not compared for routes from I-BGP peers, and the LOCAL_PREF attribute is not compared for routes from E-BGP peers.

Like the MED, the LOCAL_PREF attribute is applied on a peer-by-peer basis using a route map. The default value of the LOCAL_PREF attribute is 100, and it can be changed to any value from 1 to 4,294,967,295; the largest LOCAL_PREF value is always preferred. Three steps are required to modify the LOCAL_PREF for a path:

Step 1   (Optional) Create an access or prefix list that specifies the networks to which the LOCAL_PREF will apply.

Step 2   Create a route map to assign the LOCAL_PREF using the **set local-preference** *value* command in route map configuration mode.

Step 3   Apply the route map to a neighbor or peer group using the **neighbor** {*ip-address* | *peer-group*} **route-map** *route-map-name* {**in** | **out**} command.

NOTE   Remember that the LOCAL_PREF attribute is not passed to external peers; so, if you want to modify LOCAL_PREF that will be used for external networks, you must apply the route map to incoming traffic.

To demonstrate the use of the LOCAL_PREF attribute, it is applied on the Arnold and Kimberly routers for all incoming routes from the Willis router, as they are passed to the Blair and Tootie routers. In this example, the Arnold router tells the Blair router to prefer its routes, and the Kimberly router tells the Tootie router to prefer its own routes. Both the Arnold and Kimberly routers still send routes to the other routers using the default LOCAL_PREF values. Example 9-60 shows the configuration on the Arnold and Kimberly routers.

Example 9-60 *Setting the LOCAL_PREF Configuration on the Arnold and Kimberly Routers*

```
Arnold# show run | begin bgp
router bgp 645
 no synchronization
 bgp router-id 10.1.5.2

<networks excluded>
 bgp log-neighbor-changes
 neighbor 10.1.5.1 remote-as 645
 neighbor 10.1.5.1 route-reflector-client
 neighbor 10.1.5.1 next-hop-self
 neighbor 10.1.5.3 remote-as 645
 neighbor 10.1.5.3 route-reflector-client
 neighbor 10.1.5.3 next-hop-self
 neighbor 10.1.5.3 route-map local-pref out
 neighbor 10.1.5.4 remote-as 645
 neighbor 10.1.5.4 route-reflector-client
 neighbor 10.1.5.4 next-hop-self
 neighbor 62.128.47.197 remote-as 2001
 no auto-summary
!
route-map local-pref permit 10
 set local-preference 500

Kimberly# show run | begin bgp
router bgp 645
 no synchronization
 bgp router-id 10.1.5.1
 bgp cluster-id 3181926401
 bgp log-neighbor-changes
 neighbor 10.1.5.2 remote-as 645
 neighbor 10.1.5.2 route-reflector-client
 neighbor 10.1.5.2 next-hop-self
```

continues

Example 9-60 *Setting the LOCAL_PREF Configuration on the Arnold and Kimberly Routers (Continued)*

```
 neighbor 10.1.5.3 remote-as 645
 neighbor 10.1.5.3 route-reflector-client
 neighbor 10.1.5.3 next-hop-self
 neighbor 10.1.5.4 remote-as 645
 neighbor 10.1.5.4 route-reflector-client
 neighbor 10.1.5.4 next-hop-self
 neighbor 10.1.5.4 route-map local-pref out
 neighbor 62.128.47.193 remote-as 2001
 no auto-summary
!
route-map local-pref permit 10
 set local-preference 500
```

In the preceding example, route map local-pref sets the LOCAL_PREF for all routes from Arnold router to the Blair router to 500, and likewise, for the Kimberly and Tootie routers. Example 9-61 shows excerpts of the BGP RIB from the Blair and Tootie routers.

Example 9-61 *BGP RIBs from the Blair and Tootie Routers After Changing the LOCAL_PREF Attribute*

```
Blair# show ip bgp regexp _11151_
BGP table version is 95, local router ID is 10.2.2.1
Status codes: s suppressed, d damped, h history, * valid, > best, i - internal,
              r RIB-failure
Origin codes: i - IGP, e - EGP, ? - incomplete
   Network          Next Hop            Metric LocPrf Weight Path
* i23.75.18.0/24    10.1.5.1                   100        0 2001 11151 5623 i
*>i                 10.1.5.2                   500        0 2001 11151 5623 i
* i23.75.19.0/24    10.1.5.1                   100        0 2001 11151 5623 i
*>i                 10.1.5.2                   500        0 2001 11151 5623 i
* i23.75.20.0/24    10.1.5.1                   100        0 2001 11151 5623 i
*>i                 10.1.5.2                   500        0 2001 11151 5623 i
* i23.75.21.0/24    10.1.5.1                   100        0 2001 11151 5623 i
*>i                 10.1.5.2                   500        0 2001 11151 5623 i
* i23.75.22.0/24    10.1.5.1                   100        0 2001 11151 5623 i
*>i                 10.1.5.2                   500        0 2001 11151 5623 i
* i23.75.23.0/24    10.1.5.1                   100        0 2001 11151 5623 i
*>i                 10.1.5.2                   500        0 2001 11151 5623 i
* i23.75.24.0/24    10.1.5.1                   100        0 2001 11151 5623 i
*>i                 10.1.5.2                   500        0 2001 11151 5623 i
* i23.75.25.0/24    10.1.5.1                   100        0 2001 11151 5623 i
*>i                 10.1.5.2                   500        0 2001 11151 5623 i
* i23.75.26.0/24    10.1.5.1                   100        0 2001 11151 5623 i
   Network          Next Hop            Metric LocPrf Weight Path
*>i                 10.1.5.2                   500        0 2001 11151 5623 I

Tootie# show ip bgp regexp _11151_
BGP table version is 307, local router ID is 10.2.2.2
```

Example 9-61 *BGP RIBs from the Blair and Tootie Routers After Changing the LOCAL_PREF Attribute (Continued)*

```
Status codes: s suppressed, d damped, h history, * valid, > best, i - internal
Origin codes: i - IGP, e - EGP, ? - incomplete
   Network          Next Hop          Metric LocPrf Weight Path
*>i23.75.18.0/24    10.1.5.1               500        0 2001 11151 5623 i
* i                 10.1.5.2               100        0 2001 11151 5623 i
*>i23.75.19.0/24    10.1.5.1               500        0 2001 11151 5623 i
* i                 10.1.5.2               100        0 2001 11151 5623 i
*>i23.75.20.0/24    10.1.5.1               500        0 2001 11151 5623 i
* i                 10.1.5.2               100        0 2001 11151 5623 i
*>i23.75.21.0/24    10.1.5.1               500        0 2001 11151 5623 i
* i                 10.1.5.2               100        0 2001 11151 5623 i
*>i23.75.22.0/24    10.1.5.1               500        0 2001 11151 5623 i
* i                 10.1.5.2               100        0 2001 11151 5623 i
*>i23.75.23.0/24    10.1.5.1               500        0 2001 11151 5623 i
* i                 10.1.5.2               100        0 2001 11151 5623 i
*>i23.75.24.0/24    10.1.5.1               500        0 2001 11151 5623 i
* i                 10.1.5.2               100        0 2001 11151 5623 i
*>i23.75.25.0/24    10.1.5.1               500        0 2001 11151 5623 i
* i                 10.1.5.2               100        0 2001 11151 5623 i
*>i23.75.26.0/24    10.1.5.1               500        0 2001 11151 5623 i
* i                 10.1.5.2               100        0 2001 11151 5623 i
```

Notice in both examples that the routers prefer the routes with the larger LOCAL_PREF attribute. The Blair router prefers routes from the Arnold router, and the Tootie router prefers routes from the Kimberly router.

Using the WEIGHT Attribute to Influence Path Selection

Unlike the MED and LOCAL_PREF attributes, the Cisco proprietary WEIGHT attribute, which specifies a locally preferred path, is only locally significant; this attribute is not forwarded to *any* peer. The WEIGHT attribute is a value ranging from 0 to 65,535. The default WEIGHT attribute for a locally originated route is 32,768, and the default weight for all other routes is 0.

Three steps are required to set the WEIGHT for a path:

Step 1   (Optional)Create an access or prefix list that specifies the paths that should be matched for WEIGHT manipulation.

Step 2   Create a route map to apply the access or prefix list and the WEIGHT attribute value using the **set weight** *value* command.

Step 3   Apply the route map to a neighbor or peer group using the **neighbor** {*ip-address* | *peer-group*} **route-map** *route-map-name* **in** command.

NOTE	Even though Cisco IOS Software enables you to apply a route map that modifies the WEIGHT attribute for outbound routes, this command will have no effect because the WEIGHT attribute is not passed to any peers.

Suppose, for example, that the Tootie router should always prefer routes from the Kimberly router (10.1.5.1), unless that router is not available. One easy way to accomplish this task is to set the WEIGHT attribute for all incoming routes from the Kimberly router to a high value. Example 9-62 shows how this might be accomplished using the WEIGHT attribute.

Example 9-62 *Using the WEIGHT Attribute to Set Route Preference*

```
Tootie# show run | begin bgp
router bgp 645
 no synchronization
 bgp log-neighbor-changes
 network 10.1.1.0 mask 255.255.255.0
 network 10.2.2.0 mask 255.255.255.0
 neighbor 10.1.5.1 remote-as 645
 neighbor 10.1.5.1 next-hop-self
 neighbor 10.1.5.1 route-map Heavy-Routes in
 neighbor 10.1.5.2 remote-as 645
 neighbor 10.1.5.2 next-hop-self
 neighbor 10.1.5.3 remote-as 645
 neighbor 10.1.5.3 next-hop-self
no auto-summary
!
route-map Heavy-Routes permit 10
 set weight 150
```

In the preceding example, route map Heavy-Routes sets the WEIGHT value to 150. This route map was then applied to incoming routes from the Arnold router, making those routes more desirable, and producing the results shown in Example 9-63.

NOTE	Before configuring this example, the local-pref route map was removed from the Kimberly and Arnold routers; however, the WEIGHT attribute would still have precedence over LOCAL_PREF (even though the LOCAL_PREF and WEIGHT attributes accomplished the same thing) because it is higher on the BGP path selection process.

Example 9-63 *Tootie BGP RIB After WEIGHT Attribute Modification*

```
Tootie# show ip bgp regexp _5623_
BGP table version is 111, local router ID is 10.1.5.4
Status codes: s suppressed, d damped, h history, * valid, > best, i - internal,
              r RIB-failure
Origin codes: i - IGP, e - EGP, ? - incomplete

   Network           Next Hop            Metric LocPrf Weight Path
*>i23.75.18.0/25     10.1.5.1                   100      150 2001 11151 5623 i
* i                  10.1.5.2                   100        0 2001 11151 5623 i
*>i23.75.19.0/24     10.1.5.1                   100      150 2001 11151 5623 i
* i                  10.1.5.2                   100        0 2001 11151 5623 i
*>i23.75.20.0/24     10.1.5.1                   100      150 2001 11151 5623 i
* i                  10.1.5.2                   100        0 2001 11151 5623 i
*>i23.75.21.0/24     10.1.5.1                   100      150 2001 11151 5623 i
* i                  10.1.5.2                   100        0 2001 11151 5623 i
*>i23.75.22.0/24     10.1.5.1                   100      150 2001 11151 5623 i
* i                  10.1.5.2                   100        0 2001 11151 5623 i
*>i23.75.23.0/24     10.1.5.1                   100      150 2001 11151 5623 i
* i                  10.1.5.2                   100        0 2001 11151 5623 i
*>i23.75.24.0/24     10.1.5.1                   100      150 2001 11151 5623 i
* i                  10.1.5.2                   100        0 2001 11151 5623 i
*>i23.75.25.0/24     10.1.5.1                   100      150 2001 11151 5623 i
* i                  10.1.5.2                   100        0 2001 11151 5623 I
*>i23.75.26.0/24     10.1.5.1                   100      150 2001 11151 5623 i
   Network           Next Hop            Metric LocPrf Weight Path
* i                  10.1.5.2                   100        0 2001 11151 5623 i
```

Because the WEIGHT attribute is the number one item on the BGP route selection process, modifying the WEIGHT attribute causes the Tootie router to prefer routes with high WEIGHT before routes with high LOCAL_PREF.

Many Uses of the COMMUNITY Attribute

The BGP COMMUNITY attribute is one of the most powerful BGP attributes available. Communities can filter or modify routes by community number, by community list, or by adding a well-known community value to a route. You can use communities for filtering routes by setting the COMMUNITY attribute for a route for later use or by matching a pre-assigned community value. Along with the standard-numbered community values, there are also named values that you can use to assign a more readable value to a path. Table 9-6 shows a review of the well-known BGP community values mentioned earlier in Chapter 7.

Table 9-6   *Well-Known BGP Community Values*

Community Value (Hex)	Community Value (Decimal)	Community Name	Description	Cisco IOS set community Command
0x0000000 to 0x0000FFFF	0 to 65535	Reserved	This range of COMMUNITY attributes have been reserved by IANA.	Decimal number between 0 to 65,535 or *aa:nn* format
0xFFFF0000 to 0xFFFFFFFF	4294967041 to 4294967295	Reserved	This range of COMMUNITY attributes have been reserved by IANA.	Decimal number between 65,536 to 4,294,967,295 or *aa:nn* format
0	0	Internet	The default community, to which all BGP community-aware routers belong by default.	**internet**
0xFFFFFF01	4294967041	NO_EXPORT	Routes with this COMMUNITY attribute must not be advertised outside of the local autonomous system or confederation.	**no-export**
0xFFFFFF02	4294967042	NO_ADVERTISE	Routes with this COMMUNITY attribute must not be advertised to *any* peer.	**no-advertise**
0xFFFFFF03	4294967043	LOCAL_AS	Routes with this COMMUNITY attribute must not be advertised to any external confederation peer, referred to as NO_EXPORT-SUB-CONFED in RFC 1997.	**local-as**

Five steps are required to set the BGP COMMUNITY attribute:

Step 1   (Optional) Create an access or prefix list to specify the paths that are to be modified. If the networks are not specified with a **match** statement, the route map will apply to all routes.

Step 2   Create a route map and specify a **set community** statement to change the COMMUNITY attribute using the **set community** {*decimal-number* | *aa:nn-format* | **additive** | **internet** | **local-as** | **no-advertise** | **no-export** | **none**} command.

Step 3   If you use the aa:nn community format, make sure to use the **ip bgp-community new-format** command. This command changes the way Cisco IOS Software displays the community value from the default hexadecimal view to the newer aa:nn view.

Step 4   Apply the route map to a neighbor or peer group using the **neighbor** {*ip-address* | *peer-group*} **route-map** *route-map-name* {**in** | **out**} command.

Step 5   Enable COMMUNITY attribute advertising by using the **neighbor** {*ip-address* | *peer-group*} **send-community** command.

As previously mentioned, communities are set using a route map containing a **set** statement; Table 9-7 shows the possible community values that can be set within a route map in Cisco IOS Software Release 12.2(12)T.

Table 9-7   *Route Map* **set** *COMMUNITY Commands*

Command	Description
Community number in *decimal-number* format	A number between 1 and 4,294,967,295
Community number in *aa:nn-format*	A BGP COMMUNITY attribute number in *aa:nn* format
additive	Adds a value to an existing community value
internet	Sets the community value to the well-known Internet value—the default for all BGP speakers
local-as	A well-known COMMUNITY attribute that specifies that the matching paths must not be advertised outside the local autonomous system
no-advertise	A well-known COMMUNITY attribute that specifies that the matching paths must not be advertised to *any* peer
no-export	A well-known COMMUNITY attribute that specifies that the matching paths must not be advertised to any external peers
none	Removes the COMMUNITY attribute

The next example shows how you can use the BGP NO_EXPORT community to prevent a BGP neighbor from propagating a specific route. In this example, the Arnold router is advertising the 10.1.1.0/24 and 10.2.2.0/24 networks with the BGP well-known community value of NO_EXPORT. Example 9-64 shows the BGP configuration for the Arnold router.

Example 9-64 *Using the BGP Well-Known NO_EXPORT COMMUNITY Attribute*

```
Arnold# show run | begin bgp
router bgp 645
 no synchronization
 bgp router-id 10.1.5.2
 bgp log-neighbor-changes
 neighbor 10.1.5.1 remote-as 645
 neighbor 10.1.5.1 route-reflector-client
 neighbor 10.1.5.1 next-hop-self
 neighbor 10.1.5.3 remote-as 645
 neighbor 10.1.5.3 route-reflector-client
 neighbor 10.1.5.3 next-hop-self
 neighbor 10.1.5.4 remote-as 645
 neighbor 10.1.5.4 route-reflector-client
 neighbor 10.1.5.4 next-hop-self
 neighbor 62.128.47.197 remote-as 2001
 neighbor 62.128.47.197 send-community
 neighbor 62.128.47.197 route-map community out
 no auto-summary
!
ip prefix-list local-list seq 5 permit 10.1.1.0/24
ip prefix-list local-list seq 10 permit 10.2.2.0/24
!
route-map community permit 10
 match ip address prefix-list local-list
 set community no-export
```

In the preceding example, the Arnold router is configured to advertise the 10.1.1.0/24 and 10.2.2.0/24 networks with the NO_EXPORT community by creating the "community" route map specifying the local-list prefix list, which referenced the 10.1.1.0/24 and 10.2.2.0/24 networks. The NO_EXPORT community was assigned to the networks using the **set community no-export** command, the route map was applied to the 62.128.47.197 neighbor, the Willis router, and BGP community advertisement was enabled using the **send-community** command. Example 9-65 shows the effects that this configuration had on the Willis and MrDrummand routers.

Example 9-65 *Willis Router's BGP RIB Entries After Community Filtering*

```
Willis# show ip bgp 10.1.1.0/24
BGP routing table entry for 10.1.1.0/24, version 191
Paths: (2 available, best #2, table Default-IP-Routing-Table, not advertised to
EBGP peer)
  Not advertised to any peer
  645
    62.128.47.194 from 62.128.47.194 (10.1.5.1)
      Origin IGP, metric 100, localpref 100, valid, external
  645
    62.128.47.198 from 62.128.47.198 (10.1.5.2)
      Origin IGP, localpref 100, valid, external, best
```

Example 9-65 *Willis Router's BGP RIB Entries After Community Filtering (Continued)*

```
             Community: no-export
Willis# show ip bgp 10.2.2.0/24
BGP routing table entry for 10.2.2.0/24, version 192
Paths: (2 available, best #2, table Default-IP-Routing-Table, not advertised to
EBGP peer)
  Not advertised to any peer
  645
    62.128.47.194 from 62.128.47.194 (10.1.5.1)
      Origin IGP, metric 100, localpref 100, valid, external
  645
    62.128.47.198 from 62.128.47.198 (10.1.5.2)
      Origin IGP, localpref 100, valid, external, best
      Community: no-export

MrDrummand# show ip bgp 10.1.1.0/24
% Network not in table
MrDrummand# show ip bgp 10.2.2.0/24
% Network not in table
```

Notice that the Willis router now shows the route as *not advertised to EBGP peer.* This is a direct result of the NO_EXPORT community application. Also, notice that the MrDrummand router did not receive any advertisement for the 10.1.1.0/24 or 10.2.2.0/24 networks after the change. The preceding example demonstrates how the BGP COMMUNITY attribute can be used to filter a route using well-known communities. The next section shows how you can use BGP community lists to specify routes that match multiple BGP community values.

Community Lists

BGP community lists provide a way to specify a list of BGP COMMUNITY attributes that are to be matched. There are four different types of BGP community lists; the list types, command syntax, and descriptions are shown in Table 9-8.

Table 9-8 *Community List Guide*

Community List Type	Syntax	Description
Standard numbered	**ip community-list** *number* {**permit** | **deny**} {*decimal-number* | *aa:nn-number* | **internet** | **local-as** | **no-advertise** | **no-export**}	A numbered access lists, ranging from 1 to 99, that lists BGP communities as either numbers or well-known names
Expanded numbered	**ip community-list** *number* {**permit** | **deny**} *regular-expression*	A numbered access lists, ranging from 100 to 199, that lists BGP communities using regular expressions

continues

Table 9-8   *Community List Guide (Continued)*

Community List Type	Syntax	Description
Standard named	**ip community-list standard** *list-name* {**permit** I **deny**} {*decimal-number* I *aa:nn-number* I **internet** I **local-as** I **no-advertise** I **no-export**}	A named access lists, ranging from 1 to 99, that lists BGP communities as either numbers or well-known names
Expanded named	**ip community-list expanded** *list-name* {**permit** I **deny**} *regular-expression*	A named access lists, ranging from 100 to 199, that lists BGP communities using regular expressions

The **show ip community-list** command enables you to display the local community list configuration, and the **show ip bgp community** *community* command lists any BGP paths from the RIB that match the specified community. The **show ip bgp community-list** {*list-name* I *list-number*} command displays BGP RIB entries that match the specified community lists. Example 9-66 shows examples of each of the community list types.

Example 9-66 *Community List Examples*

```
ip community-list 1 permit no-export
ip community-list 100 permit ^645
ip community-list standard my-community permit local_as
ip community-list expanded your-community permit 645$
```

The first community list matches any RIB table entry with the NO_EXPORT COMMUNITY attribute. The second community list, list 100, matches any RIB entry with a COMMUNITY attribute beginning with the string 645. The third community list, list my-community, matches any RIB entry with the LOCAL-AS COMMUNITY attribute. And the last community list matches any community ending with the string 645. The community lists are specified using a route map **match** statement. Table 9-9 shows the community **match** commands and their descriptions.

Table 9-9   *Well-Known BGP Community* **match** *Statements*

Command	Description
match community {*standard-list-number* I *expanded-list-number* I *list-name*}	Matches a predefined community list: Standard community lists range from 1 to 99. Expanded community lists range from 100 to 199.
match extcommunity {*standard-list-number* I *expanded-list-number* I *list-name*}	Matches extended multiprotocol BGP community lists: Standard lists range from 1 to 99. Expanded lists range from 100 to 199.

The next example shows how you can use the BGP COMMUNITY attribute to set and filter BGP communities. In Example 9-67, you can see that the Kimberly router is using the community route map to set two communities.

Example 9-67 *Setting Community Values with a Route Map on the Kimberly Router*

```
Kimberly# show run | begin bgp
router bgp 645
 no synchronization
 bgp router-id 10.1.5.1
 bgp log-neighbor-changes
 network 189.168.56.0 mask 255.255.254.0
 network 189.168.58.0 mask 255.255.254.0
 network 189.168.60.0 mask 255.255.254.0
 network 189.168.62.0 mask 255.255.254.0
 neighbor 10.1.5.2 remote-as 645
 neighbor 10.1.5.2 route-reflector-client
 neighbor 10.1.5.2 next-hop-self
 neighbor 10.1.5.3 remote-as 645
 neighbor 10.1.5.3 route-reflector-client
 neighbor 10.1.5.3 next-hop-self
 neighbor 10.1.5.4 remote-as 645
 neighbor 10.1.5.4 route-reflector-client
 neighbor 10.1.5.4 next-hop-self
 neighbor 62.128.47.193 remote-as 2001
 neighbor 62.128.47.193 send-community
 neighbor 62.128.47.193 route-map community out
 no auto-summary
!
ip bgp-community new-format
!
ip prefix-list 1 seq 5 permit 189.168.56.0/22
!
ip prefix-list 2 seq 5 permit 189.168.60.0/22
!
route-map community permit 10
 match ip address prefix-list 1
 set community 645:100
!
route-map community permit 20
 match ip address prefix-list 2
 set community 645:200
!
route-map community permit 30
```

In the preceding example, the Kimberly router used the community route map to set the BGP COMMUNITY attribute for the 189.168.56.0/22 network to 645:100 and the 189.168.60.0/22 network to 645:200. The community route map was then applied to the 62.128.47.193 neighbor, the Willis router, and the COMMUNITY attribute was sent using the **send-community** command. Example 9-68 shows how the Willis router uses the communities advertised by the Kimberly router to filter routes.

Example 9-68 *Filtering Routes on the Willis Router Using the COMMUNITY Attribute*

```
Willis# show run | begin bgp
router bgp 2001
 no synchronization
 bgp log-neighbor-changes
 neighbor 62.128.47.6 remote-as 11151
 neighbor 62.128.47.6 send-community
 neighbor 62.128.47.6 route-map use-community out
 neighbor 62.128.47.194 remote-as 645
 neighbor 62.128.47.198 remote-as 645
 no auto-summary
!
ip bgp-community new-format
ip community-list 1 permit 645:100
ip community-list 2 permit 645:200
!
route-map use-community permit 10
 match community 1
 set community no-advertise
!
route-map use-community permit 20
 match community 2
 set community no-export
!
route-map use-community permit 30
 set community internet
```

In the preceding example, the Willis router uses route map use-community sequence 10 to match routes containing the 645:100 community value and advertise them with the NO_ADVERTISE COMMUNITY attribute. Sequence 20 of this route map also sets any routes containing the 645:200 COMMUNITY attribute to the well-known NO-EXPORT community value; all other routes are set to the default Internet community value. The use-community route map is then applied to the MrDrummand router (62.128.47.6). This configuration can be verified using the **show ip bgp** *ip-prefix* command on the MrDrummand router as shown in Example 9-69.

Example 9-69 *Resulting BGP RIB Entries on the MrDrummand Router*

```
MrDrummand# show ip bgp 189.168.56.0/23
BGP routing table entry for 189.168.56.0/23, version 137
Paths: (1 available, best #1, table Default-IP-Routing-Table, not advertised to
any peer)
  Not advertised to any peer
  2001 645
    62.128.47.5 from 62.128.47.5 (62.128.76.1)
      Origin IGP, localpref 100, valid, external, best
```

Example 9-69 *Resulting BGP RIB Entries on the MrDrummand Router (Continued)*

```
          Community: no-advertise
MrDrummand# show ip bgp 189.168.58.0/23
BGP routing table entry for 189.168.58.0/23, version 138
Paths: (1 available, best #1, table Default-IP-Routing-Table, not advertised to
any peer)
  Not advertised to any peer
  2001 645
    62.128.47.5 from 62.128.47.5 (62.128.76.1)
      Origin IGP, localpref 100, valid, external, best
        Community: no-advertise
MrDrummand# show ip bgp 189.168.60.0/23
BGP routing table entry for 189.168.60.0/23, version 115
Paths: (1 available, best #1, table Default-IP-Routing-Table, not advertised to
EBGP peer)
  Not advertised to any peer
  2001 645
    62.128.47.5 from 62.128.47.5 (62.128.76.1)
      Origin IGP, localpref 100, valid, external, best
        Community: no-export
MrDrummand# show ip bgp 189.168.62.0/23
BGP routing table entry for 189.168.62.0/23, version 116
Paths: (1 available, best #1, table Default-IP-Routing-Table, not advertised to
EBGP peer)
  Not advertised to any peer
  2001 645
    62.128.47.5 from 62.128.47.5 (62.128.76.1)
      Origin IGP, localpref 100, valid, external, best
        Community: no-export
```

As you can see, the MrDrummand router received the routes from the Willis router with the attributes set. The MrDrummand router is not currently advertising the 189.168.56.0/22 route because it is marked **no-advertise**, and the route to the 189.168.60.0/22 network is not advertised because the MrDrummand router does not have any I-BGP neighbors to which it can forward the NO-EXPORT attribute.

The next example shows how communities enable you to change other BGP attributes. In this example, the Kimberly router is sending the Willis router routes containing the 645:600 BGP COMMUNITY attribute.

Example 9-70 *Kimberly Router Configuration*

```
Kimberly# show run | begin bgp
router bgp 645
 no synchronization
 bgp router-id 10.1.5.1
 bgp log-neighbor-changes
<networks omitted>
 neighbor 10.1.5.2 remote-as 645
```

continues

Example 9-70 *Kimberly Router Configuration (Continued)*

```
 neighbor 10.1.5.2 route-reflector-client
 neighbor 10.1.5.2 next-hop-self
 neighbor 10.1.5.3 remote-as 645
 neighbor 10.1.5.3 route-reflector-client
 neighbor 10.1.5.3 next-hop-self
 neighbor 10.1.5.4 remote-as 645
 neighbor 10.1.5.4 route-reflector-client
 neighbor 10.1.5.4 next-hop-self
 neighbor 62.128.47.193 remote-as 2001
 neighbor 62.128.47.193 send-community
 neighbor 62.128.47.193 route-map change-attr out
 no auto-summary
 !
ip bgp-community new-format
 !
route-map change-attr permit 10
 set community 645:600
```

As you can see, the Kimberly router uses route map change-attr to set the COMMUNITY attribute for all routing updates to 645:600. That route map is then applied to the Willis router (62.128.47.193). When the Willis router receives the routes, a local route map matches the 645:600 community value and sets the LOCAL_PREF value for the Kimberly routes, as shown in Example 9-71.

Example 9-71 *Using the COMMUNITY attribute to Change the LOCAL_PREF Attribute*

```
Willis# show run | begin bgp
router bgp 2001
 no synchronization
 bgp log-neighbor-changes
 neighbor 62.128.47.6 remote-as 11151
 neighbor 62.128.47.194 remote-as 645
 neighbor 62.128.47.194 route-map change-pref in
 neighbor 62.128.47.198 remote-as 645
 no auto-summary
 !
ip bgp-community new-format
ip community-list standard change-pref1 permit 645:600
 !
route-map change-pref permit 10
 match community standard change-pref1
 set local-preference 250
```

In the preceding example, the Willis router used the change-pref route map to set the LOCAL_PREF attribute for all incoming routes from the Kimberly router to 250. This makes the Willis router prefer to use the Kimberly router to reach all networks in AS 645. Example 9-72 shows the BGP RIB for AS 645 in the Willis router.

Example 9-72 *Local BGP RIB for the Willis Router*

```
Willis# show ip bgp regexp ^645$
     Network           Next Hop          Metric LocPrf Weight Path
 *> 10.1.1.0/24       62.128.47.194              250      0 645 i
 *                    62.128.47.198                       0 645 i
 *> 10.2.2.0/24       62.128.47.194              250      0 645 i
 *                    62.128.47.198                       0 645 i
 *  189.168.56.0/23   62.128.47.198         0             0 645 i
 *>                   62.128.47.194         0   250        0 645 i
 *  189.168.58.0/23   62.128.47.198         0             0 645 i
 *>                   62.128.47.194         0   250        0 645 i
 *  189.168.60.0/23   62.128.47.198         0             0 645 i
 *>                   62.128.47.194         0   250        0 645 i
 *  189.168.62.0/23   62.128.47.198         0             0 645 i
 *>                   62.128.47.194         0   250        0 645 i
 *  189.168.64.0/23   62.128.47.198         0             0 645 i
 *>                   62.128.47.194         0   250        0 645 i
 *  189.168.66.0/23   62.128.47.198         0             0 645 i
 *>                   62.128.47.194         0   250        0 645 i
 *  189.168.68.0/23   62.128.47.198         0             0 645 i
```

Using Multiple Paths

Multihoming a network to one or more providers is one of the most common tasks that you will encounter on an enterprise BGP network. You can configure multihomed networks in one of the following ways:

- One router multihomed to one service provider with multiple links
- One router multihomed to more than one service provider
- More than one router multihomed to one service provider
- More than one router multihomed to more than one service provider

Although there are a number of ways to configure a multihomed network, it is always best to follow the same rules each time. Careful planning is required to achieve maximum results in a multihomed network; you always want to verify that your upstream service provider supports your configuration, before attempting to multihome your network. Most service providers have BGP policies that they provide to any customer considering a multihomed network, some of which are listed here:

- The use of **ebgp-multihop** command (with or without load balancing)
- A list of supported BGP attributes
- Public IP address and AS number policies
- The use of service provider IP addresses and private ASNs
- Route filtering policies
- Route aggregation policies (Most service providers will not accept routes smaller than /24.)

- BGP version number
- Authentication method, policies, and passwords
- Route dampening policies

After determining your network requirements and acquiring the necessary addresses and circuits, you can begin to design your multihomed solution. Because loopback interfaces never go down, they are commonly used as multihoming anchoring devices. One of the most common multihoming practices is to use a loopback interface as the BGP update source. Another requirement for a multihomed network is AS path filtering—you do not want your upstream service providers to use your network as a transit AS. You must also filter any private address space and aggregate your internal networks prior to advertisement. Several basic tasks are required to multihome a network:

Step 1   Set up the E-BGP peer routing; your network will, most likely, be peering with a router that is not under you administrative control, so you must arrange a routing policy in advance.

Step 2   If the router will have more than one connection to another router, you should provide your loopback interface to the remote service provider and use the loopback interface's IP address as your update source. This is accomplished using the **neighbor** {*ip-address* | *peer-group*} **update-source** *interface-name interface-number* command. If you will be using the **update-source** command, it is best to configure the router to use that IP address as the BGP router ID using the **bgp router-id** *ip-address* command and specify the loopback IP.

Step 3   If you will be peering with a router that is not directly connected because you used a loopback interface, you must use the **neighbor** {*ip-address* | *peer-group*} **ebgp-multihop** *number-of-hops* command. Because you can specify the number of hops that are allowed when using this command, it should be used with some caution; your service provider could end up routing your traffic across long distances trying to reach an interface that is only two hops away. When using the **ebgp-multihop** command, always specify the maximum number of hops.

Step 4   If you will be load sharing using more than one interface, use the **maximum-paths** *number-of-paths* command. This command allows the BGP process to use multiple paths, rather than one best path for load-sharing purposes.

Step 5   If you will be using more than one router at the transit peering point, use the **next-hop-self** command between the I-BGP peers so that routes will be advertised with a reachable NEXT_HOP attribute.

Step 6   If you will be using more than one router to peer with more than one service provider, filter all external routes using an AS path filter list containing an empty AS path (^$). This prevents one service provider from using your AS as a transit to the other service providers network.

Step 7   Verify that your router is not propagating any private RFC 1918 addresses using an access list and distribute list, or route map, to specify the private networks.

Step 8   Perform route aggregation before advertising routes to your upstream provider. To conserve Internet route table space, always send the smallest prefix possible.

Step 9   Configure any BGP attributes that you will use for path selection and route policy. Set the LOCAL_PREF for I-BGP routing preferences, set the MED for E-BGP AS entrance preferences, and set any COMMUNITY attributes that you will use for route policy.

For instance, look at the network shown in Figure 9-16. In this example, the Internal_Border router has two connections to its upstream neighbor, the External router. For the Internal_Border router to successfully use both serial links it must be configured to do so using the previously outlined steps.

Figure 9-16   *Multihoming a Network to a Single Provider*

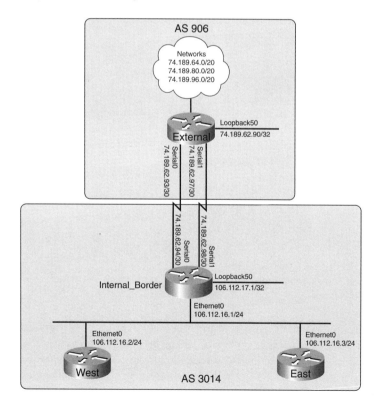

Example 9-73 shows the configuration used on the Internal_Border and External border routers. In this example, the Internal_Border uses loopback interface 50 to peer with the loopback interface on the External router.

Example 9-73 *Multihoming the External and Internal_Border Routers*

```
External# show run | begin bgp
router bgp 906
 no synchronization
 bgp router-id 74.189.62.90
 network 74.189.62.92 mask 255.255.255.252
 network 74.189.62.96 mask 255.255.255.252
 network 74.189.64.0 mask 255.255.240.0
 network 74.189.80.0 mask 255.255.240.0
 network 74.189.96.0 mask 255.255.240.0
 neighbor 106.112.17.1 remote-as 3014
 neighbor 106.112.17.1 ebgp-multihop 2
 neighbor 106.112.17.1 update-source Loopback50
 no auto-summary
!
ip route 106.112.17.1 255.255.255.255 74.189.62.94
ip route 106.112.17.1 255.255.255.255 74.189.62.98

Internal_Border # show run | begin bgp
router bgp 3014
 no synchronization
 bgp router-id 106.112.17.1
 bgp log-neighbor-changes
 network 106.112.16.0 mask 255.255.255.0
 aggregate-address 106.112.16.0 255.255.248.0 summary-only
 neighbor 74.189.62.90 remote-as 906
 neighbor 74.189.62.90 ebgp-multihop 2
 neighbor 74.189.62.90 update-source Loopback50
 neighbor 106.112.16.2 remote-as 3014
 neighbor 106.112.16.2 route-reflector-client
 neighbor 106.112.16.2 next-hop-self
 neighbor 106.112.16.3 remote-as 3014
 neighbor 106.112.16.3 route-reflector-client
 neighbor 106.112.16.3 next-hop-self
 no auto-summary
!
ip route 74.189.62.90 255.255.255.255 74.189.62.93
ip route 74.189.62.90 255.255.255.255 74.189.62.97
```

The preceding example shows how the External router uses the **ebgp-multihop 2** command to specify that the remote neighbor 74.189.62.90 might be up to two hops away. The **update-source loopback 50** command tells the router to send BGP messages with the IP address of the loopback50 interface. When this command is used, the update-source interface, which is usually a loopback interface, is also advertised as the next hop for all routes. Both the External and Internal_Border routers require routes telling them how to find the loopback interfaces for the BGP sessions.

Also, notice the configuration on the Internal_Border router. Like the External router, the Internal_Border router uses the **ebgp-multihop 2** and **update-source loopback 50** commands to specify that the router will use its loopback50 IP address to send BGP messages, and it also specifies that the remote peer's IP address might be up to two hops away. The Internal_Border router is also configured to advertise its Ethernet0 IP address as the next hop for all routing updates for the East and West I-BGP peers in AS 3014, and each of those routers is also a route reflector client. The Internal_Border router also aggregates all network advertisements before sending them off to the External router. Example 9-74 shows the resulting routing tables from the External router.

Example 9-74 *External Router's Routing Tables*

```
External# show ip bgp | begin Network
   Network          Next Hop          Metric LocPrf Weight Path
*> 74.189.62.92/30  0.0.0.0                0            32768 i
*> 74.189.62.96/30  0.0.0.0                0            32768 i
*> 74.189.64.0/20   0.0.0.0                0            32768 i
*> 74.189.80.0/20   0.0.0.0                0            32768 i
*> 74.189.96.0/20   0.0.0.0                0            32768 i
*> 106.112.16.0/21  106.112.17.1                        0 3014 i
External# show ip route | include vialis
     106.0.0.0/8 is variably subnetted, 2 subnets, 2 masks
B        106.112.16.0/21 [20/0] via 106.112.17.1, 00:00:43
S        106.112.17.1/32 [1/0] via 74.189.62.98
                         [1/0] via 74.189.62.94
     74.0.0.0/8 is variably subnetted, 6 subnets, 3 masks
C        74.189.62.90/32 is directly connected, Loopback50
C        74.189.62.92/30 is directly connected, Serial0
C        74.189.96.0/20 is directly connected, Loopback30
C        74.189.80.0/20 is directly connected, Loopback20
C        74.189.62.96/30 is directly connected, Serial1
C        74.189.64.0/20 is directly connected, Loopback10
```

In this example, you can see that the route to the 106.112.16.0/21 network can be reached using either the 74.189.62.94 or 74.189.62.98 next-hop IP addresses; therefore, if one interface fails, the other interface can quickly resume BGP routing with little to no interruption in service. Example 9-75 shows the **debug ip routing** command output during a simulated interface failure.

NOTE Use extreme caution when performing **debug** commands on production routers. Try to limit command output using access lists, disable console logging, and use a syslog server to capture log output. It is easy to crash a router by debugging on a production router.

Example 9-75 *Debug Output During an Interface Failure*

```
Internal_Border(config)# interface serail0
Internal_Border(config-if)# shutdown
01:59:37: is_up: 0 state: 6 sub state: 1 line: 0
01:59:37: RT: interface Serial0 removed from routing table
01:59:37: RT: del 74.189.62.92/30 via 0.0.0.0, connected metric [0/0]
01:59:37: RT: delete subnet route to 74.189.62.92/30
Comment: routes using Serial 0 interface are removed
01:59:37: RT: add 74.189.62.92/30 via 74.189.62.90, bgp metric [20/0]
01:59:38: RT: del 74.189.62.90/32 via 74.189.62.93, static metric [1/0]
Comment: route to External router loopback over Serial 0 is removed
01:59:39: %LINK-5-CHANGED: Interface Serial0, changed state to administratively
down
01:59:39: is_up: 0 state: 6 sub state: 1 line: 0
01:59:40: %LINEPROTO-5-UPDOWN: Line protocol on Interface Serial0, changed state
to down
01:59:40: is_up: 0 state: 6 sub state: 1 line: 0
01:59:41: RT: del 74.189.62.92/30 via 74.189.62.90, bgp metric [20/0]
01:59:41: RT: delete subnet route to 74.189.62.92/30
00:47:14: RT: del 74.189.64.0/20 via 74.189.62.90, bgp metric [20/0]
00:47:14: RT: delete subnet route to 74.189.64.0/20
00:47:14: RT: del 74.189.80.0/20 via 74.189.62.90, bgp metric [20/0]
00:47:14: RT: delete subnet route to 74.189.80.0/20
00:47:14: RT: del 74.189.96.0/20 via 74.189.62.90, bgp metric [20/0]
00:47:14: RT: delete subnet route to 74.189.96.0/20
00:47:38: RT: del 74.189.62.90/32 via 74.189.62.93, static metric [1/0]
00:47:38: RT: del 74.189.62.90/32 via 74.189.62.93, static metric [1/0]
00:48:14: RT: add 74.189.64.0/20 via 74.189.62.90, bgp metric [20/0]
00:48:14: RT: add 74.189.80.0/20 via 74.189.62.90, bgp metric [20/0]
00:48:14: RT: add 74.189.96.0/20 via 74.189.62.90, bgp metric [20/0]
```

Example 9-76 shows the IP routing table on the Internal_Border router during the interface outage. Notice that all the routes are still in the table and still pointing to the loopback interface; the only change is the route to the loopback interface.

Example 9-76 *IP Routing Table During Interface Outage*

```
Internal_Border# show ip route
     106.0.0.0/8 is variably subnetted, 3 subnets, 2 masks
B       106.112.16.0/21 [200/0] via 0.0.0.0, 00:13:18, Null0
C       106.112.16.0/24 is directly connected, Ethernet0
C       106.112.17.0/24 is directly connected, Loopback50
S     74.189.62.90/32 [1/0] via 74.189.62.97
B       74.189.96.0/20 [20/0] via 74.189.62.90, 00:45:00
B       74.189.80.0/20 [20/0] via 74.189.62.90, 00:45:00
C       74.189.62.96/30 is directly connected, Serial1
B       74.189.64.0/20 [20/0] via 74.189.62.90, 00:45:01
```

Practical Example: Multihoming a BGP Network

This example demonstrates all the tasks required to multihome a BGP network using two routers with multiple paths to two service providers. This example demonstrates the use of the multihoming commands, and shows how they are used in practice. Figure 9-17 shows the network that is used for this example.

Figure 9-17 *All-Weather Network*

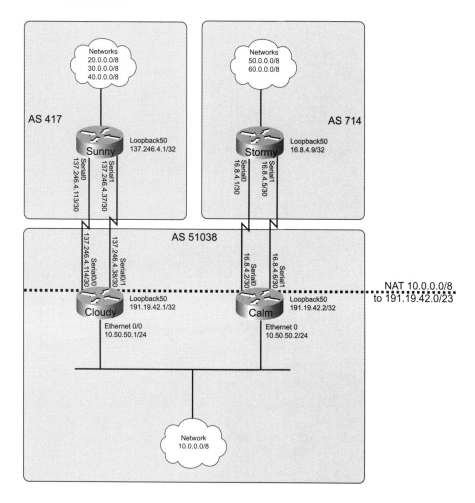

This example requires four Cisco routers, each with two serial interfaces; two of the routers also require an Ethernet interface. The routers in this example use the IP address and interface assignments shown in Table 9-10.

Table 9-10   *IP Address and Interface Assignments*

Router	Interface Name/Number	IP Address
Sunny	Loopback5	20.0.0.1/8
	Loopback10	30.0.0.1/8
	Loopback15	40.0.0.1/8
	Loopback50	137.246.4.1/32
	Serial0	137.246.4.113/30
	Serial1	137.246.4.37/30
Stormy	Loopback5	50.0.0.1/8
	Loopback10	60.0.0.1/8
	Loopback15	70.0.0.1/8
	Loopback50	16.8.4.9/32
	Serial0	16.8.4.1/30
	Serial1	16.8.4.5/30
Cloudy	Ethernet0/0	10.50.50.1/24
	Serial0/0	137.246.4.114/30
	Serial0/1	137.246.4.38/30
	Loopback50	191.19.42.1/32
Calm	Ethernet 0/0	10.50.50.2/24
	Loopback50	191.19.42.2/32
	Serial0	16.8.4.2/30
	Serial1	16.8.4.6/30

Step 1   Configure IP addresses and verify that each router can ping its directly connected next hop before proceeding to Step 2.

Step 2   Before configuring BGP, make sure that the Sunny and Cloudy routers can reach each other's Loopback50 IP addresses. Do not use an IGP protocol. The following example shows the routes configured on both of the routers. Example 9-77 shows the static routes configured on the Sunny and Cloudy routers.

Example 9-77 *Configuring Static Routes on the Sunny and Cloudy Routers*

```
Sunny# show run | begin ip route
ip route 191.19.42.1 255.255.255.255 137.246.4.114
ip route 191.19.42.1 255.255.255.255 137.246.4.38

Cloudy# show run | begin ip route
ip route 137.246.4.1 255.255.255.255 137.246.4.37
ip route 137.246.4.1 255.255.255.255 137.246.4.113
```

In this example, two very specific static routes are added to each router, allowing the routers to reach each other's loopback interface without specifying the entire network prefix.

Step 3   Configure BGP routing on the Sunny router. Assign this router to ASN 417, and use the Loopback50 IP address as the BGP router ID. Also disable auto-summarization. Advertise the three networks from the loopback interfaces using **network** statements. The Sunny router should peer with the Cloudy router by loopback interface only. Configure the Sunny router to peer with the Cloudy router's Loopback50 interface. Example 9-78 shows the BGP configuration for the Sunny router.

Example 9-78 *BGP Configuration for the Sunny Router*

```
Sunny# show run | begin bgp
router bgp 417
 synchronization
 bgp router-id 137.246.4.1
 bgp log-neighbor-changes
 network 20.0.0.0
 network 30.0.0.0
 network 40.0.0.0
 neighbor 191.19.42.1 remote-as 51038
 neighbor 191.19.42.1 ebgp-multihop 2
 neighbor 191.19.42.1 update-source Loopback50
 no auto-summary
!
ip route 191.19.42.1 255.255.255.255 137.246.4.114
ip route 191.19.42.1 255.255.255.255 137.246.4.38
```

In the preceding example, BGP was configured to allow two hops between E-BGP neighbors using the **ebgp-multihop** command, the loopback interface was specified using the update-source command, and the BGP router ID was changed using the **bgp router-id** command.

Step 4 Configure the Cloudy router to run in AS 51,038, and configure this router to peer with the Sunny router's loopback interface. Verify that both routers can successfully start and maintain a BGP session. Example 9-79 shows the BGP configuration for the Cloudy router; this example also displays the output from the **show ip bgp summary** command on the Cloudy and Sunny routers.

Example 9-79 *BGP Configuration for the Cloudy Router and* **show ip bgp summary** *Command Output from the Cloudy and Sunny Routers*

```
Cloudy# show run | begin bgp
router bgp 51038
 synchronization
 bgp router-id 191.19.42.1
 bgp log-neighbor-changes
 neighbor 137.246.4.1 remote-as 417
 neighbor 137.246.4.1 ebgp-multihop 2
 neighbor 137.246.4.1 update-source Loopback50
 no auto-summary
 !
 ip route 137.246.4.1 255.255.255.255 137.246.4.37
 ip route 137.246.4.1 255.255.255.255 137.246.4.113
Cloudy# show ip bgp summary
BGP router identifier 191.19.42.1, local AS number 51038
BGP table version is 4, main routing table version 4
3 network entries and 3 paths using 411 bytes of memory
1 BGP path attribute entries using 60 bytes of memory
1 BGP AS-PATH entries using 24 bytes of memory
0 BGP route-map cache entries using 0 bytes of memory
0 BGP filter-list cache entries using 0 bytes of memory
BGP activity 3/0 prefixes, 3/0 paths, scan interval 60 secs

Neighbor        V    AS MsgRcvd MsgSent   TblVer  InQ OutQ Up/Down   State/PfxRcd
137.246.4.1     4   417       7       6        4    0    0 00:02:13          3

Sunny# show ip bgp summary
BGP router identifier 137.246.4.1, local AS number 417
BGP table version is 4, main routing table version 4
3 network entries and 3 paths using 411 bytes of memory
1 BGP path attribute entries using 60 bytes of memory
0 BGP route-map cache entries using 0 bytes of memory
0 BGP filter-list cache entries using 0 bytes of memory
BGP activity 3/0 prefixes, 3/0 paths, scan interval 60 secs

Neighbor        V    AS MsgRcvd MsgSent   TblVer  InQ OutQ Up/Down   State/PfxRcd
191.19.42.1     4 51038       6       7        4    0    0 00:02:43          0
```

Like the Sunny router, the Cloudy router is configured using loopback interfaces, **ebgp-multihop**, and a predefined BGP router ID.

Step 5 Configure the Cloudy router to peer with the Calm router; do not use an IGP for I-BGP peer routing. Without using any route filtering, prevent the Cloudy router from advertising any RFC 1918 networks to the Sunny router. After configuration, the networks behind the Cloudy router should still be able to ping any upstream neighbor. Use half of the 192.19.42.0/23 network for this purpose, but configure BGP to advertise one route for the entire 23-bit block. Verify that the Cloudy router can reach the Sunny router's loopback interfaces using the 10.50.50.1 source address. Example 9-80 shows the configuration for the Cloudy router.

Example 9-80 *Cloudy Router Configuration for Step 5*

```
Cloudy# show run | begin interface Ethernet0/0
interface Ethernet0/0
 ip address 10.50.50.1 255.255.255.0
 ip nat inside
!
interface Serial0/0
 ip address 137.246.4.114 255.255.255.252
 ip nat outside
!
interface Serial0/1
 ip address 137.246.4.38 255.255.255.252
 ip nat outside
 clockrate 1300000
Cloudy# show run | begin bgp
router bgp 51038
 no synchronization
 bgp router-id 191.19.42.1
 bgp log-neighbor-changes
 network 191.19.42.0 mask 255.255.255.0
 neighbor 10.50.50.2 remote-as 51038
 neighbor 10.50.50.2 next-hop-self
 neighbor 137.246.4.1 remote-as 417
 neighbor 137.246.4.1 ebgp-multihop 2
 neighbor 137.246.4.1 update-source Loopback50
 no auto-summary
!
ip nat pool public 191.19.42.3 191.19.42.254 prefix-length 24
ip nat inside source list 8 pool public
ip route 137.246.4.1 255.255.255.255 137.246.4.37
ip route 137.246.4.1 255.255.255.255 137.246.4.113
ip route 191.19.42.0 255.255.255.0 Null0 253
!
access-list 8 permit 10.0.0.0 0.255.255.255
```

The **no synchronization** command allows BGP routing with the Calm router, without the presence of an IGP. Network Address Translation (NAT) allows the Cloudy router to hide the internal RFC 1918 network 10.50.50.0/24 from

the Sunny router. A NAT pool named public is created to NAT the rest of the
10.0.0.0/8 networks, which are not shown in the network diagram, to the public network 191.19.42.0/24. The first two IP addresses are skipped because
they are already in use. A static route to Null 0, with high administrative distance, ensures that a route to the 191.19.42.0/23 network exists in the main
IP routing table, so the network can be advertised via BGP to the Sunny
router. If you are having trouble with NAT, use the **debug ip nat** command
to debug NAT translations, and use the **show ip bgp neighbor** *ip-address*
advertised-routes command to verify that the Sunny router is receiving the
proper route to the 191.19.42.0/23 network. You can verify connectivity by
using an extended ping. The output of the **debug ip nat**, **show ip bgp neighbor 137.246.4.1 advertised-routes** and extended ping tests are shown in
Example 9-81.

Example 9-81 *Verifying Step 5*

```
Cloudy# show ip bgp neighbors 137.246.4.1 advertised-routes | begin Network
   Network          Next Hop            Metric LocPrf Weight Path
*> 191.19.42.0/23   0.0.0.0                            32768 i
Cloudy# debug ip nat
Cloudy# ping
Protocol [ip]:
Target IP address: 20.0.0.1
Repeat count [5]:
Datagram size [100]:
Timeout in seconds [2]:
Extended commands [n]: y
Source address or interface: 10.50.50.1
Type of service [0]:
Set DF bit in IP header? [no]:
Validate reply data? [no]:
Data pattern [0xABCD]:
Loose, Strict, Record, Timestamp, Verbose[none]:
Sweep range of sizes [n]:
Type escape sequence to abort.
Sending 5, 100-byte ICMP Echos to 20.0.0.1, timeout is 2 seconds:
!!!!!
Success rate is 100 percent (5/5), round-trip min/avg/max = 20/20/20 ms
Cloudy#
*Mar  5 06:16:51.307: NAT: s=10.50.50.1->191.19.42.3, d=20.0.0.1 [165]
*Mar  5 06:16:51.327: NAT*: s=20.0.0.1, d=191.19.42.3->10.50.50.1 [165]
*Mar  5 06:16:51.331: NAT: s=10.50.50.1->191.19.42.3, d=20.0.0.1 [166]
*Mar  5 06:16:51.347: NAT*: s=20.0.0.1, d=191.19.42.3->10.50.50.1 [166]
*Mar  5 06:16:51.351: NAT: s=10.50.50.1->191.19.42.3, d=20.0.0.1 [167]
*Mar  5 06:16:51.371: NAT*: s=20.0.0.1, d=191.19.42.3->10.50.50.1 [167]
*Mar  5 06:16:51.371: NAT: s=10.50.50.1->191.19.42.3, d=20.0.0.1 [168]
*Mar  5 06:16:51.391: NAT*: s=20.0.0.1, d=191.19.42.3->10.50.50.1 [168]
*Mar  5 06:16:51.395: NAT: s=10.50.50.1->191.19.42.3, d=20.0.0.1 [169]
*Mar  5 06:16:51.415: NAT*: s=20.0.0.1, d=191.19.42.3->10.50.50.1 [169]
```

Step 6   Configure static routing between the loopback50 addresses on the Stormy and Calm routers. Verify connectivity between the Loopback50 interfaces on these routers before continuing to Step 7. Example 9-82 shows the static routes configured on the Stormy and Calm routers.

Example 9-82 *Static Routes on the Stormy and Calm Routers*

```
stormy# show run | include ip route
ip route 191.19.42.2 255.255.255.255 16.8.4.2
ip route 191.19.42.2 255.255.255.255 16.8.4.6

Calm# show run | include ip route
ip route 16.8.4.9 255.255.255.255 16.8.4.1
ip route 16.8.4.9 255.255.255.255 16.8.4.5
```

Routing between the loopbacks of the Stormy and Calm routers is configured using specific static routes.

Step 7   Now configure BGP routing on the Stormy router. Assign this router to ASN 714 and use the Loopback50 IP address as the BGP router ID. Disable auto-summarization. Configure the Stormy router to peer with the Calm router using the Loopback50 interfaces only, and advertise the three networks from the loopback interfaces using **network** statements. Example 9-83 shows the BGP configuration for the Stormy router.

Example 9-83 *BGP Configuration for the Stormy Router*

```
stormy# show run | begin bgp
router bgp 714
 no synchronization
 bgp router-id 16.8.4.9
 bgp log-neighbor-changes
 network 50.0.0.0
 network 60.0.0.0
 network 70.0.0.0
 neighbor 191.19.42.2 remote-as 51038
 neighbor 191.19.42.2 ebgp-multihop 2
 neighbor 191.19.42.2 update-source Loopback50
 no auto-summary
!
ip route 191.19.42.2 255.255.255.255 16.8.4.2
ip route 191.19.42.2 255.255.255.255 16.8.4.6
```

Similar to the Sunny router, the Stormy router is configured using the **bgp router-id**, **ebgp-multihop**, and **update-source** commands.

Step 8 Configure BGP routing on the Calm router; configure this router to peer with the Stormy and Cloudy routers. Remember, the Cloudy router is not allowed to use an IGP for I-BGP routing. The Calm and Stormy routers should peer with each other's Loopback50 IP addresses. Configure the Calm router to advertise the 191.19.42.0/23 network to the Stormy router. Verify that the Cloudy router receives the full table from the Sunny and Stormy routers, and that all routers can ping all interfaces on all routers, which might require another NAT translation, before continuing to Step 9. Example 9-84 shows the BGP configuration for the Calm router.

Example 9-84 *BGP Configuration for the Calm Router*

```
Calm# show run | begin bgp
 router bgp 51038
 no synchronization
 bgp router-id 191.19.42.2
 bgp log-neighbor-changes
 network 191.19.43.0 mask 255.255.255.0
 aggregate-address 191.19.42.0 255.255.254.0 summary-only
 neighbor 10.50.50.1 remote-as 51038
 neighbor 10.50.50.1 next-hop-self
 neighbor 16.8.4.9 remote-as 714
 neighbor 16.8.4.9 ebgp-multihop 2
 neighbor 16.8.4.9 update-source Loopback50
 no auto-summary
!
ip nat pool public 191.19.43.3 191.19.43.254 prefix-length 24
ip nat inside source list 8 pool public
ip route 16.8.4.9 255.255.255.255 16.8.4.5
ip route 16.8.4.9 255.255.255.255 16.8.4.1
ip route 191.19.43.0 255.255.255.0 Null0 253
!
access-list 8 permit 10.0.0.0 0.255.255.255
```

The Calm router is configured using the same commands as the Cloudy router. Next, NAT is enabled using a NAT pool and an access list and then applied to the inside and outside interfaces; a static route to Null0 adds the route to the IGP routing table, so the public network can be advertised to the Stormy router. Then, the **next-hop-self** command is added to the Calm router to ensure that the Calm and Cloudy routers advertise a valid, reachable next hop, as shown in Example 9-85.

Example 9-85 *BGP RIB for the Calm Router*

```
Calm# show ip bgp | begin Network
   Network          Next Hop         Metric LocPrf Weight Path
*>i20.0.0.0         10.50.50.1            0    100      0 417 i
*>i30.0.0.0         10.50.50.1            0    100      0 417 i
*>i40.0.0.0         10.50.50.1            0    100      0 417 i
```

Example 9-85 *BGP RIB for the Calm Router (Continued)*

```
*> 50.0.0.0          16.8.4.9             0            0 714 i
*> 60.0.0.0          16.8.4.9             0            0 714 i
*> 70.0.0.0          16.8.4.9             0            0 714 i
*> 191.19.42.0/23    0.0.0.0                        32768 i
*  i                 10.50.50.1                100      0 i
s> 191.19.43.0/24    0.0.0.0              0         32768 i
```

Extended pings and the **show ip nat translations** command enable you to verify that all routing and NAT statements are properly configured, as shown in Example 9-86.

Example 9-86 *Verifying the BGP and NAT Configuration on the Calm Router*

```
Calm# ping
Protocol [ip]:
Target IP address: 20.0.0.1
Repeat count [5]:
Datagram size [100]:
Timeout in seconds [2]:
Extended commands [n]: y
Source address or interface: 10.50.50.2
Type of service [0]:
Set DF bit in IP header? [no]:
Validate reply data? [no]:
Data pattern [0xABCD]:
Loose, Strict, Record, Timestamp, Verbose[none]:
Sweep range of sizes [n]:
Type escape sequence to abort.
Sending 5, 100-byte ICMP Echos to 20.0.0.1, timeout is 2 seconds:
!!!!!
Success rate is 100 percent (5/5), round-trip min/avg/max = 24/30/40 ms
Calm#

Cloudy# ping
Protocol [ip]:
Target IP address: 50.0.0.1
Repeat count [5]:
Datagram size [100]:
Timeout in seconds [2]:
Extended commands [n]: y
Source address or interface: 10.50.50.1
Type of service [0]:
Set DF bit in IP header? [no]:
Validate reply data? [no]:
Data pattern [0xABCD]:
Loose, Strict, Record, Timestamp, Verbose[none]:
Sweep range of sizes [n]:
Type escape sequence to abort.
```

continues

Example 9-86 *Verifying the BGP and NAT Configuration on the Calm Router (Continued)*

```
Sending 5, 100-byte ICMP Echos to 50.0.0.1, timeout is 2 seconds:
!!!!!
Success rate is 100 percent (5/5), round-trip min/avg/max = 4/12/32 ms
Calm# show ip nat translations
Pro Inside global     Inside local      Outside local     Outside global
--- 191.19.42.3       10.50.50.1        ---               ---
```

Step 9 Configure a route filter that prevents the Sunny and Stormy routers from reaching each other's networks using any routers in AS 51,038 as a transit network. Example 9-87 shows the filter configuration for the Cloudy and Calm routers.

Example 9-87 *Filtering Transit Routes*

```
Cloudy# show run | begin bgp
router bgp 51038
 no synchronization
 bgp router-id 191.19.42.1
 bgp log-neighbor-changes
 network 191.19.42.0 mask 255.255.255.0
 aggregate-address 191.19.42.0 255.255.254.0 summary-only
 neighbor 10.50.50.2 remote-as 51038
 neighbor 10.50.50.2 next-hop-self
 neighbor 137.246.4.1 remote-as 417
 neighbor 137.246.4.1 ebgp-multihop 2
 neighbor 137.246.4.1 update-source Loopback50
 neighbor 137.246.4.1 filter-list 8 out
 no auto-summary
!
ip nat pool public 191.19.42.3 191.19.42.254 prefix-length 24
ip nat inside source list 8 pool public
ip classless
ip route 137.246.4.1 255.255.255.255 137.246.4.37
ip route 137.246.4.1 255.255.255.255 137.246.4.113
ip route 191.19.42.0 255.255.255.0 Null0 253
ip as-path access-list 8 permit ^$

Calm# show run | begin bgp
router bgp 51038
 no synchronization
 bgp router-id 191.19.42.2
 bgp cluster-id 1253916250
 bgp log-neighbor-changes
 network 191.19.43.0 mask 255.255.255.0
 aggregate-address 191.19.42.0 255.255.254.0 summary-only
 neighbor 10.50.50.1 remote-as 51038
 neighbor 10.50.50.1 next-hop-self
```

Example 9-87 *Filtering Transit Routes (Continued)*

```
 neighbor 16.8.4.9 remote-as 714
 neighbor 16.8.4.9 ebgp-multihop 2
 neighbor 16.8.4.9 update-source Loopback50
 neighbor 16.8.4.9 filter-list 8 out
 no auto-summary
 !
ip nat pool public 191.19.43.3 191.19.43.254 prefix-length 24
ip nat inside source list 8 pool public
ip route 16.8.4.9 255.255.255.255 16.8.4.1
ip route 16.8.4.9 255.255.255.255 16.8.4.5
ip route 191.19.43.0 255.255.255.0 Null0 253
ip as-path access-list 8 permit ^$
!
access-list 8 permit 10.0.0.0 0.255.255.255
```

An AS path access list number 8 is created to permit only locally generated routes containing an empty autonomous system path (indicated by the ^$ regular expression) to be advertised to the Cloudy and Calm routers' E-BGP peers. This prevents the Sunny and Stormy routers from receiving routes to each other's networks, saving AS 51,038 from becoming a transit AS as shown here. Example 9-88 shows the BGP tables on the Sunny and Stormy routers after the application of the AS path filters.

Example 9-88 *Viewing the Final BGP Tables on the Sunny and Stormy Routers*

```
Sunny# show ip bgp | begin Network
   Network          Next Hop          Metric LocPrf Weight Path
*> 20.0.0.0         0.0.0.0                0          32768 i
*> 30.0.0.0         0.0.0.0                0          32768 i
*> 40.0.0.0         0.0.0.0                0          32768 i
*> 191.19.42.0/23   191.19.42.1            0              0 51038 i

Stormy# show ip bgp | begin Network
   Network          Next Hop          Metric LocPrf Weight Path
*> 50.0.0.0         0.0.0.0                0          32768 i
*> 60.0.0.0         0.0.0.0                0          32768 i
*> 70.0.0.0         0.0.0.0                0          32768 i
*> 191.19.42.0/23   191.19.42.2                           0 51038 i
```

The preceding lab reviewed many of the topics covered in this chapter, including multihoming networks using loopbacks for stability, using AS path access lists to filter ASNs, and using routes to the null interface to advertise a network that is not in the IGP routing table. Example 9-89 shows the complete router configurations for this practical example.

Example 9-89 *Complete Router Configurations for this Experiment*

```
Sunny# show run | begin Loopback
interface Loopback5
 ip address 20.0.0.1 255.0.0.0
!
interface Loopback10
 ip address 30.0.0.1 255.0.0.0
!
interface Loopback15
 ip address 40.0.0.1 255.0.0.0
!
interface Loopback50
 ip address 137.246.4.1 255.255.255.255
!
interface Serial0
 ip address 137.246.4.113 255.255.255.252
!
interface Serial1
 ip address 137.246.4.37 255.255.255.252
!
router bgp 417
 synchronization
 bgp router-id 137.246.4.1
 bgp log-neighbor-changes
 network 20.0.0.0
 network 30.0.0.0
 network 40.0.0.0
 neighbor 191.19.42.1 remote-as 51038
 neighbor 191.19.42.1 ebgp-multihop 2
 neighbor 191.19.42.1 update-source Loopback50
 no auto-summary
!
ip route 191.19.42.1 255.255.255.255 137.246.4.114
ip route 191.19.42.1 255.255.255.255 137.246.4.38
```

```
Cloudy# show run | begin Loopback
interface Loopback50
 ip address 191.19.42.1 255.255.255.255
!
interface Ethernet0/0
 ip address 10.50.50.1 255.255.255.0
 ip nat inside
!
interface Serial0/0
 ip address 137.246.4.114 255.255.255.252
 ip nat outside
!
interface Serial0/1
 ip address 137.246.4.38 255.255.255.252
 ip nat outside
 clockrate 1300000
!
```

Example 9-89 *Complete Router Configurations for this Experiment (Continued)*

```
router bgp 51038
 no synchronization
 bgp router-id 191.19.42.1
 bgp log-neighbor-changes
 network 191.19.42.0 mask 255.255.255.0
 aggregate-address 191.19.42.0 255.255.254.0 summary-only
 neighbor 10.50.50.2 remote-as 51038
 neighbor 10.50.50.2 next-hop-self
 neighbor 137.246.4.1 remote-as 417
 neighbor 137.246.4.1 ebgp-multihop 2
 neighbor 137.246.4.1 update-source Loopback50
 neighbor 137.246.4.1 filter-list 8 out
 no auto-summary
!
ip nat pool public 191.19.42.3 191.19.42.254 prefix-length 24
ip nat inside source list 8 pool public
ip route 137.246.4.1 255.255.255.255 137.246.4.37
ip route 137.246.4.1 255.255.255.255 137.246.4.113
ip route 191.19.42.0 255.255.255.0 Null0 253
ip as-path access-list 8 permit ^$
!
access-list 8 permit 10.0.0.0 0.255.255.255
```

```
stormy# show run | begin Loopback
interface Loopback5
 ip address 50.0.0.1 255.0.0.0
!
interface Loopback10
 ip address 60.0.0.1 255.0.0.0
!
interface Loopback15
 ip address 70.0.0.1 255.0.0.0
!
interface Loopback50
 ip address 16.8.4.9 255.255.255.255
!
interface Serial0
 ip address 16.8.4.1 255.255.255.252
 clockrate 1300000
!
interface Serial1
 ip address 16.8.4.5 255.255.255.252
 clockrate 1300000
!
router bgp 714
 no synchronization
 bgp router-id 16.8.4.9
 bgp log-neighbor-changes
 network 50.0.0.0
 network 60.0.0.0
```

continues

Example 9-89 *Complete Router Configurations for this Experiment (Continued)*

```
 network 70.0.0.0
 neighbor 191.19.42.2 remote-as 51038
 neighbor 191.19.42.2 ebgp-multihop 2
 neighbor 191.19.42.2 update-source Loopback50
 no auto-summary
!
ip route 191.19.42.2 255.255.255.255 16.8.4.2
ip route 191.19.42.2 255.255.255.255 16.8.4.6
```

```
Calm# show run | begin Loopback
interface Loopback50
 ip address 191.19.42.2 255.255.255.255
!
interface Ethernet0
 ip address 10.50.50.2 255.255.255.0
 ip nat inside
!
interface Serial0
 ip address 16.8.4.2 255.255.255.252
 ip nat outside
!
interface Serial1
 ip address 16.8.4.6 255.255.255.252
 ip nat outside
!
router bgp 51038
 no synchronization
 bgp router-id 191.19.42.2
 bgp log-neighbor-changes
 network 191.19.43.0 mask 255.255.255.0
 aggregate-address 191.19.42.0 255.255.254.0 summary-only
 neighbor 10.50.50.1 remote-as 51038
 neighbor 10.50.50.1 next-hop-self
 neighbor 16.8.4.9 remote-as 714
 neighbor 16.8.4.9 ebgp-multihop 2
 neighbor 16.8.4.9 update-source Loopback50
 neighbor 16.8.4.9 filter-list 8 out
 no auto-summary
!
ip nat pool public 191.19.43.3 191.19.43.254 prefix-length 24
ip nat inside source list 8 pool public
ip route 16.8.4.9 255.255.255.255 16.8.4.5
ip route 16.8.4.9 255.255.255.255 16.8.4.1
ip route 191.19.43.0 255.255.255.0 Null0 253
ip as-path access-list 8 permit ^$
!
access-list 8 permit 10.0.0.0 0.255.255.255
```

Administrative Distance and Its Effects on BGP

When BGP and IGPs are used together for IP routing, as they generally will be in an enterprise network, you might sometimes want a router to prefer an IGP route to an E-BGP route. Under normal circumstances, this will not be possible because routers always prefer E-BGP routes because they have a lower administrative distance. The Cisco IOS Software uses the administrative distances shown in Table 9-11.

Table 9-11   *Default Administrative Distances*

Administrative Distance	Protocol
0	Directly connected networks
1	Static routes
20	E-BGP
90	Internal EIGRP
100	IGRP
110	OSPF
115	IS-IS
120	RIP
170	External EIGRP
200	I-BGP
255	Unknown

You can deal with these situations in a couple of ways. You could increase the administrative distance of an IGP protocol or increase the administrative distance for E-BGP routers using the **distance** *distance-value* command (or **distance bgp** *external-distance internal-distance local-distance* command for E-BGP routes); however, the effects of this command are rather broad and might produce unwanted results. Another more granular approach is to use the **bgp backdoor** command to alter routes on a network-by-network basis.

What Backdoors Are and How You Use Them

BGP backdoors are designed to change E-BGP administrative distance to allow IGP routes to have administrative preference in the IP routing table. The **BGP backdoor** command basically takes the specified E-BGP routes and changes the administrative distance from 20 to 200, the same distance as an I-BGP route, allowing IGP routes to take administrative precedence in the routing table. In Figure 9-18, for example, the Pike router has two paths to the 102.231.6.0/29 network—one by means of the Pine router and the other through the Union router.

Figure 9-18 *Administrative Distance and Routing on the Downtown Network*

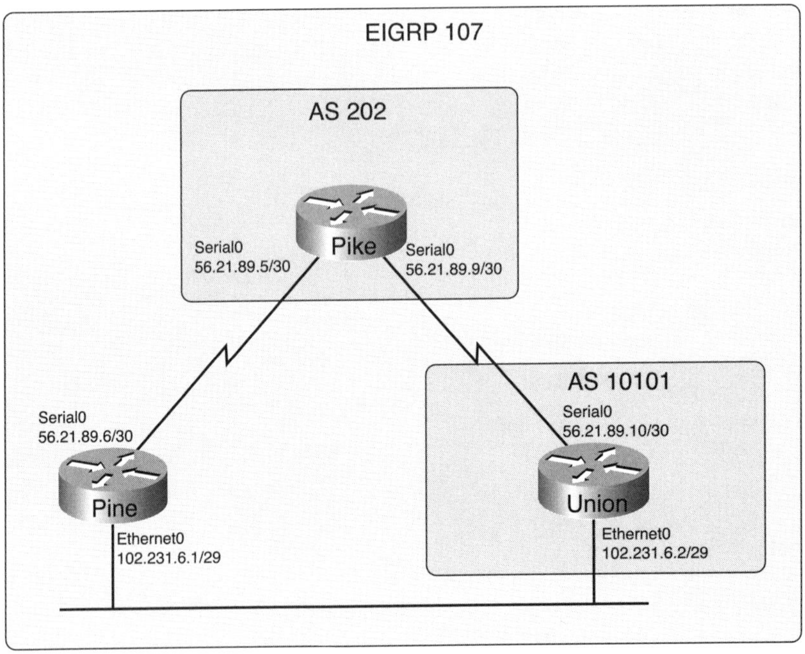

Because the Pike and Pine routers are not BGP neighbors, the Pike router stores only one route to the 102.231.6.0/29 network. The reason the Pike router ignores the EIGRP route is that that route has an administrative distance of 90, which is higher than the Union router's E-BGP administrative distance of 20, as shown in Example 9-90.

Example 9-90 *Pike Router's Routing Table Before the Backdoor*

```
Pike# show ip route | begin subnet
     102.0.0.0/29 is subnetted, 1 subnets
B       102.231.6.0 [20/0] via 56.21.89.10, 00:05:49
     56.0.0.0/30 is subnetted, 2 subnets
C       56.21.89.4 is directly connected, Serial0
C       56.21.89.8 is directly connected, Serial1
```

To allow the Pike router to use the two EIGRP routes to the 102.231.6.0/29 network, you can just configure a BGP backdoor for that network. BGP backdoors are configured using the **network** *network-prefix* **mask** *network-mask* **backdoor** command. You would be correct in thinking that the BGP **network** command cannot be used to generate a BGP advertisement for an indirectly connected network; however, in this case, the **network** command is used locally to change the administrative distance of a backdoor route. BGP does not advertise the route as a local route; the administrative distance for the route is simply altered, allowing the EIGRP routes to be administratively preferred by the main IP routing table. Example 9-91 shows how the BGP **backdoor** command is used to change the IP routing preference for the 102.231.6.0/29 network.

Example 9-91 *Changing the Administrative Distance with a BGP Backdoor*

```
Pike# show run | begin eigrp
router eigrp 107
 network 56.21.89.4 0.0.0.3
 network 56.21.89.8 0.0.0.3
 maximum-paths 2
 no auto-summary
 no eigrp log-neighbor-changes
!
router bgp 202
 no synchronization
 bgp log-neighbor-changes
 network 56.21.89.8 mask 255.255.255.252
 network 102.231.6.0 mask 255.255.255.248 backdoor
 neighbor 56.21.89.10 remote-as 10101
 no auto-summary
```

Example 9-92 shows the resulting changes to the IP routing table. After this configuration is applied, the administrative distance for the BGP route is changed, and the E-BGP route is removed from the main IP routing table. At this time, the two EIGRP routes are added because they now have a lower administrative distance. Also, notice that the **show ip bgp 102.231.6.0/29** command still shows the route as the best route and the BGP network is still not advertised to any peer.

Example 9-92 *Pike Router Configuration After the BGP Backdoor*

```
Pike# show ip route | begin subnet
     102.0.0.0/29 is subnetted, 1 subnets
D       102.231.6.0 [90/2195456] via 56.21.89.10, 00:01:14, Serial1
                    [90/2195456] via 56.21.89.6, 00:01:14, Serial0
     56.0.0.0/30 is subnetted, 2 subnets
C       56.21.89.4 is directly connected, Serial0
C       56.21.89.8 is directly connected, Serial1
Pike# show ip bgp 102.231.6.0/29
BGP routing table entry for 102.231.6.0/29, version 6
Paths: (1 available, best #1, table Default-IP-Routing-Table)
Flag: 0x800
  Not advertised to any peer
  10101
    56.21.89.10 from 56.21.89.10 (10.2.2.1)
      Origin IGP, metric 0, localpref 100, valid, external, best
```

Now that you understand the many ways that BGP can be configured for routing and policy enforcement, it's time to examine how BGP enables you to control Internet routing table stability, by means of route dampening, and some of the ways that BGP can be tuned to perform more efficiently.

BGP Route Dampening

BGP route dampening controls the effects of route flapping between E-BGP peers. Route dampening is generally used to help service providers prevent one customer's router or circuit problems from affecting the stability of the provider's network by withdrawing problem BGP routes. There are two ways to enable route dampening: The first is to globally enable route dampening for all BGP peers using the **bgp dampening** command; the second is to use a route map to specify certain routes that are to be dampened and the parameters that are to be applied to the dampened networks. The following syntax shows the **bgp dampening** command and its optional parameters.

```
bgp dampening [[route-map route-map-name] | [half-life] | reuse-limit start-
    suppress suppress-duration]]
```

Using the **bgp dampening** command, route dampening can be configured three ways:

- Global route dampening using default parameters
- Global route dampening using custom parameters
- Specific route dampening using custom parameters

Table 9-12 shows the optional **bgp dampening** command parameters and their descriptions.

Table 9-12 *BGP Route Dampening Parameters*

Dampening Command	Description
half-life	The amount of time to wait before decrementing the dampening penalty, ranging from 1 to 45 minutes. The default half-life is 15 minutes.
reuse-limit	The value between 1 and 20,000 that is compared to the penalty value to determine route reusability. If the penalty is greater than the suppress limit, the route will be suppressed; if not, it will be reused. The default suppress limit is 750.
start-suppress	This value between 1 and 20,000 specifies the penalty that will be used if a route is suppressed. The default route suppression penalty is 2000 for each route flap.
suppress-duration	This value specifies the maximum duration that a route will be suppressed. The range for the suppress duration is from 1 to 255 minutes. The default suppress duration is 4 times the half-life, or in other words 60 minutes.
route-map *route-map-name*	Specifies that a route map will be used to specify the route dampening parameters. Route maps are used to specify the routes that dampening policies should apply to. The same route dampening parameters apply when a route map is used.

After route dampening has been activated, a route flap penalty of 1000 points is assessed to the affected route. The router maintains a history for each route that has flapped, and that history stores the dampening information on a route-by-route basis. The *half-life* value is used to decrease the time suppression penalty by one-half after a route flaps. Therefore, if a route ceases to flap, it will not be dampened and the history will eventually be cleared. If the route flaps again, another penalty is imposed, and after the *suppress-limit* has been reached, the route is dampened. When a route has been dampened, it will not be advertised to other BGP peers until the *suppress-duration* has expired.

NOTE   The BGP route dampening penalty is initially set to 1000 points and cannot be changed; however, all other parameters are user configurable. You can accept the default values or create your own custom dampening policy based on the particular network requirements.

Look at the network shown in Figure 9-19. In this figure, the Service_Provider router in AS 18,901 is configured with a route dampening policy that dampens routes using the default dampening parameters with the exception of the half-life. In this case, the half-life is changed to 5 minutes, as shown in Example 9-93.

Figure 9-19 *Service Provider to Customer Network*

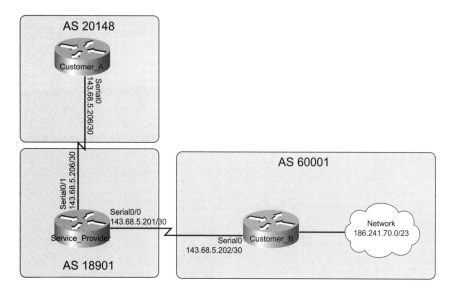

Example 9-93 *BGP Configuration for the Service_Provider Router*

```
Service_Provider# show run | begin bgp
router bgp 18901
 no synchronization
 bgp log-neighbor-changes
 bgp bestpath dampening 5
 bgp dampening 5
 network 143.68.5.200 mask 255.255.255.252
 network 143.68.5.204 mask 255.255.255.252
 neighbor 143.68.5.202 remote-as 60001
 neighbor 143.68.5.206 remote-as 20148
 no auto-summary
```

By default, the **bgp best path dampening** command is automatically entered after the **bgp dampening** command has been issued in later 12.2 releases of Cisco IOS Software. This command is also used to enable and disable route dampening. There are several ways to verify and track the BGP route dampening configuration, the most detailed of which is the **show ip bgp dampened parameters** command. Example 9-94 uses the **show ip bgp dampening parameters** command to show the BGP route dampening parameters for the Service_Provider router.

Example 9-94 **show ip bgp dampening parameters** *Command*

```
Service_Provider# show ip bgp dampening parameters
 dampening 5 750 2000 20
  Half-life time      : 5  mins      Decay Time       : 775 secs
  Max suppress penalty: 12000        Max suppress time: 20 mins
  Suppress penalty    : 2000         Reuse penalty    : 750
```

This command displays all the parameters for the local BGP route dampening policy, and in this case, it shows that the Service_Provider router has been configured with a 5-minute half-life. The alteration of the half-life parameter changed the maximum suppress time, so suppressed routes will not be as harshly penalized. Example 9-95 shows the default BGP route dampening parameters.

Example 9-95 *Default BGP Route Dampening Parameters*

```
Service_Provider# show ip bgp dampening parameters
 dampening 15 750 2000 60 (DEFAULT)
  Half-life time      : 15 mins      Decay Time       : 2320 secs
  Max suppress penalty: 12000        Max suppress time: 60 mins
  Suppress penalty    : 2000         Reuse penalty    : 750
```

The **show ip bgp dampening flap-statistics** command displays detailed information for all dampened routes; in this case, the Service_Provider router has dampened the route to the 186.241.70.0/23 network because it flapped four times. Example 9-96 uses the **show ip bgp**

dampening flap-statistics command to show that the route has been dampened for 3 minutes and 34 seconds and will be eligible for reuse in 10 minutes and 20 seconds.

Example 9-96 show ip bgp dampening flap-statistics *Command*

```
Service_Provider# show ip bgp dampening flap-statistics
BGP RIB version is 13, local router ID is 1.1.1.1
Status codes: s suppressed, d damped, h history, * valid, > best, i - internal,
Origin codes: i - IGP, e - EGP, ? - incomplete
   Network         From           Flaps Duration Reuse    Path
*d 186.241.70.0/23  143.68.5.202    4    00:03:34 00:10:20 60001
```

The **clear ip bgp dampening** command enables you to clear the dampened route and the flap statistics associated with the route.

Many steps can be taken to prevent BGP route dampening from occurring using the techniques covered earlier in this chapter; for instance, the Customer_B router could have been configured using some of the following BGP features:

- Multiple links and loopback interfaces to prevent network outages

- Aggregating routes into smaller, more stable prefixes so that one network failure will not affect all routes advertised to the upstream neighbor

- Creating static routes to Null0 to nail down unstable IGP routes

It will always be in your service provider's best interest to protect the stability of their network using BGP route dampening. Their policies might adversely affect a poorly configured network, so you should always try to configure your network with the most stable, redundant BGP configuration possible.

Tuning BGP Performance

Configuring and troubleshooting BGP sessions can be time intensive. Each time you change a BGP parameter, you must clear the session to propagate the changes. Clearing BGP sessions using the **clear ip bgp** *ip-address* * command is time-consuming and causes network outages. In the past, the **neighbor** {*ip-address* | *peer-group*} **soft-reconfiguration inbound** and **clear ip bgp** * *ip-address* **in** commands have helped the situation by allowing for the "soft" reconfiguration of incoming BGP routes. This meant that BGP peers were required to store the inbound BGP routing table in memory, increasing the load that the BGP configuration put on a router.

With the introduction of the route refresh capability, described in RFC 2918, and introduced to Cisco IOS Software in Release 12.2(6)T, dynamic incoming and outgoing soft resets are now both allowed. To find out whether a peer router supports the route refresh capability, use the **show ip bgp neighbors** *ip-address* | **begin capabilities** command, as shown in Example 9-97

Example 9-97 show ip bgp neighbors | begin capabilities *Command*

```
Service_Provider# show ip bgp neighbors 143.68.5.202 | begin capabilities
  Neighbor capabilities:
    Route refresh: advertised and received(old & new)
    Address family IPv4 Unicast: advertised and received
  Received 341 messages, 2 notifications, 0 in queue
  Sent 312 messages, 0 notifications, 0 in queue
  Default minimum time between advertisement runs is 30 seconds
 For address family: IPv4 Unicast
  BGP table version 251, neighbor version 251
  Index 1, Offset 0, Mask 0x2
  Route refresh request: received 7, sent 1
  1 accepted prefixes consume 40 bytes
  Prefix advertised 462, suppressed 0, withdrawn 2
```

Notice that the preceding example shows that the 143.68.5.202 neighbor supports the route refresh capability and has used it to refresh routes seven times. After you establish that the route refresh capability is supported, you can begin using the new **clear ip bgp * soft [in | out]**, as shown in Example 9-98.

Example 9-98 *Debugging IP BGP During a Route Refresh Request*

```
Service_Provider# clear ip bgp * soft
*Mar  1 09:18:01.817: BGP: service reset requests
*Mar  1 09:18:01.821: BGP: 143.68.5.202 sending REFRESH_REQ(5) for afi/safi: 1/1
*Mar  1 09:18:01.821: BGP: 143.68.5.202 send message type 5, length (incl.
header) 23
```

If the remote refresh capability is supported by both peers in a BGP session when a route refresh message is sent, the remote peer resends its outgoing BGP updates without clearing the BGP session. If the remote peer does not support the route refresh capability, the peer ignores the request, and you either need to use the **soft-reconfiguration** command for that neighbor or the standard **clear ip bgp** {* | *ip-add*ress | *peer-group*} command and reset the BGP session. The remote peer will still receive the route refresh capability but will be unable to use it; however, because the router will be unable to understand the requests, it will ignore any messages containing route refresh requests, and any subsequent route refresh capability advertisements, as shown in Example 9-99.

Example 9-99 *Debugging an Ignored Route Refresh*

```
Older_Router# debug ip bgp
BGP debugging is on
00:20:58: BGP: 10.1.1.1 unrecognized OPEN parameter (0x2/0x6)
00:20:58: BGP: 10.1.1.1 unrecognized OPEN parameter (0x2/0x2)
Older_Router# show ip bgp neighbors
BGP neighbor is 10.1.1.1,  remote AS 8, internal link
 Index 2, Offset 0, Mask 0x4
```

Example 9-99 *Debugging an Ignored Route Refresh (Continued)*

```
  Inbound soft reconfiguration allowed
  BGP version 4, remote router ID 10.1.1.1
  BGP state = Established, table version = 1, up for 00:00:53
  Last read 00:00:52, hold time is 180, keepalive interval is 60 seconds
  Minimum time between advertisement runs is 5 seconds
  Received 10 messages, 0 notifications, 0 in queue
  Sent 8 messages, 0 notifications, 0 in queue
  Prefix advertised 0, suppressed 0, withdrawn 0
  Connections established 2; dropped 1
  Last reset 00:01:00, due to Soft reconfig change
  0 accepted prefixes consume 0 bytes
  0 denied but saved prefixes consume 0 bytes
  0 history paths consume 0 bytes
```

Conserving Memory via BGP Configuration

BGP is a memory- and processor-intensive protocol. At some point in your career, you will most likely run into a situation where you must run BGP on a router that does not have enough resources to support the existing BGP system requirements. A couple of options can help you handle with this situation: Upgrade the memory, upgrade the router, filter incoming routes, or limit the number of prefixes that BGP will accept. Assuming that you cannot immediately upgrade the router itself, the memory, or processor, your best options will be route filtering or limiting incoming BGP prefixes. Example 9-100 shows the **show ip bgp summary** command output obtained by using an Internet looking glass on a real Internet router. (The IP addresses have been changed.)

Example 9-100 *Internet Routing Table Statistics*

```
  BGP router identifier 6.6.6.6, local AS number 123
  BGP table version is 8438778, main routing table version 8438778
  114591 network entries and 337412 paths using 23262159 bytes of memory
  82050 BGP path attribute entries using 4923540 bytes of memory
  15 BGP rrinfo entries using 360 bytes of memory
  40359 BGP AS-PATH entries using 1046148 bytes of memory
  162 BGP community entries using 7100 bytes of memory
  54353 BGP route-map cache entries using 869648 bytes of memory
  21745 BGP filter-list cache entries using 260940 bytes of memory
  Dampening enabled. 79 history paths, 20 dampened paths
  BGP activity 227228/2798971 prefixes, 8600655/8263243 paths, scan interval 15 secs
```

Using Partial BGP Routing Tables to Minimize Memory Use

One of the best ways to limit the BGP RIB size using route filters is to accept only partial BGP RIB updates. There are two ways to run BGP with partial tables: Ask your service provider to filter outbound routes to your network and only send you partial tables; or your can filter your own incoming routes. The easiest and safest way to configure partial BGP RIBs is to use an AS path access list with a filter list that will match AS paths beginning and ending with your service provider's AS.

For example, using the network shown earlier in Figure 9-19, the Customer_B router is running out of memory and can no longer handle the full Internet routing table that is being sent by the Service_Provider router. To fix this situation, you can use an AS path access list to limit the number of AS paths received from the upstream router's E-BGP neighbor, as shown in Example 9-101. And the upstream service provider can send you a default route so that your router can still have a route reach to other Internet networks.

Example 9-101 *Filtering for Partial BGP RIBs*

```
Customer_B# show run | begin bgp
router bgp 60001
 no synchronization
 bgp log-neighbor-changes
 network 186.241.70.0 mask 255.255.254.0
 neighbor 143.68.5.201 remote-as 18901
 neighbor 143.68.5.201 filter-list 101 in
 no auto-summary
!
ip as-path access-list 101 permit ^18901$
```

In this example, AS path access list 101 is used to filter any routes that do not begin and end with AS number 18,901, which limits the number of incoming routes to 63, as shown in Example 9-102.

Example 9-102 *Customer_2 Router's BGP RIB After Incoming Route Filters Are Implemented*

```
Customer_B# show ip bgp summary | begin Neighbor
Neighbor        V    AS MsgRcvd MsgSent   TblVer  InQ OutQ Up/Down   State/PfxRcd
143.68.5.201    4 18901     116     123      248    0    0 01:33:35        63
```

There are a few different ways to deal with the memory problem (listed in the order of least memory utilization):

- Accept only the default route from each service provider.

- Accept only the default and service provider–originated routes from each service provider.

- Accept only the default and service provider plus customer routes from each service provider.

The choice of implementation is up to you. Just remember that if you do not accept a full routing table, to reach any Internet network, you must accept a default route.

Configuring Incoming BGP Prefix Limitations

Another way to limit incoming BGP routes is to use the **maximum-prefix** command. When using the **maximum-prefix** command, you have two options after the number of prefixes has been reached: automatically disabling the BGP session, or sending a warning message. If you absolutely must not allow the router to exceed a certain number of routes, you can use the **maximum-prefixes** command to close BGP sessions from offending BGP peers using the **neighbor** {*ip-address* | *peer-group*} **maximum-prefix** *limitation-number* command, with a limitation number ranging from 1 to 4,294,967,295. Example 9-103 shows what happens when the **maximum-prefix** command is used on the Customer_B router.

Example 9-103 *Using the* **maximum-prefix** *Command to Close BGP Sessions*

```
Customer_B# show run | begin bgp
router bgp 60001
 no synchronization
 bgp log-neighbor-changes
 network 186.241.70.0 mask 255.255.254.0
 neighbor 143.68.5.201 remote-as 18901
 neighbor 143.68.5.201 maximum-prefix 50
 neighbor 143.68.5.201 filter-list 101 in
 no auto-summary
!
ip as-path access-list 101 permit ^18901$
Customer_B# show ip bgp summary | begin Neighbor
Neighbor         V    AS MsgRcvd MsgSent   TblVer  InQ OutQ Up/Down  State/PfxRcd
143.68.5.201     4 18901    138     147        0    0    0 00:02:20 Idle (PfxCt)
Customer_2# show logging | include %BGP
*Mar  1 02:48:01.731: %BGP-5-ADJCHANGE: neighbor 143.68.5.197 Down Neighbor
deleted
*Mar  1 02:48:53.927: %BGP-3-MAXPFXEXCEED: No. of prefix received from
143.68.5.201 (afi 0): 63 exceed limit 50
*Mar  1 03:08:05.507: %BGP-3-MAXPFXEXCEED: No. of prefix received from
143.68.5.201 (afi 0): 63 exceed limit 50
*Mar  1 03:33:04.307: %BGP-3-MAXPFXEXCEED: No. of prefix received from
143.68.5.201 (afi 0): 63 exceed limit 50
*Mar  1 03:33:04.307: %BGP-5-ADJCHANGE: neighbor 143.68.5.201 Down BGP
Notification sent
*Mar  1 03:33:04.307: %BGP-3-NOTIFICATION: sent to neighbor 143.68.5.201 3/1
(update malformed) 0 bytes
```

In the preceding example, if peer 143.68.5.201 sends more than 50 prefixes, the BGP session will be torn down, and a %BGP-3-MAXPFXEXCEED message will be logged. In this case, the BGP session will not be reinitialized until the session has manually been reset, and the maximum number of incoming routes has not been exceeded. After the situation has been corrected and the BGP connection has been restarted, the connection will come back up. Another less intrusive way to handle this situation is to use the **maximum-prefix** command with the optional

warning-only parameter; this command issues only a warning when the maximum number of prefixes has been exceeded. When this command is used in conjunction with syslog reporting, you can monitor the number of BGP prefixes and take action when syslog messages are received. Example 9-104 shows how the **maximum-prefix warning-only** command sends a warning trap to the syslog server at 186.241.70.89, when 80 percent of the 50 maximum prefix limitation has been reached.

Example 9-104 *Using a* **maximum-prefix** *Warning to Send Warning Traps*

```
router bgp 60001
 no synchronization
 bgp log-neighbor-changes
 network 186.241.70.0 mask 255.255.254.0
 neighbor 143.68.5.201 remote-as 18901
 neighbor 143.68.5.201 maximum-prefix 50 80 warning-only
 neighbor 143.68.5.201 filter-list 101 in
 maximum-paths 2
 no auto-summary
!
ip as-path access-list 101 permit ^18901$
!
logging 186.241.70.89
Customer_2# show logging | include %BGP
*Mar  1 04:04:40.462: %BGP-4-MAXPFX: No. of prefix received from 143.68.5.201
 (afi 0) reaches 41, max 50
*Mar  1 04:04:40.470: %BGP-3-MAXPFXEXCEED: No. of prefix received from
143.68.5.201 (afi 0): 51 exceed limit 50
```

Practice Scenarios

Lab 15: Multihoming a BGP Network

The previous few chapters covered BGP theory and basic and advanced BGP configuration, and briefly suggested ways that BGP can optimize Internet routing in a production environment. The following lab focuses on a multihomed BGP configuration, using a real-life BGP scenario to test advanced BGP configuration topics. HTTP web traffic tests the final network reachability.

Lab Exercise

In this lab scenario, you configure a simulated Internet web browsing experience using the 24-hour network backbone and two upstream service provider networks. The 24-hour network has two Internet border routers that peer with three upstream routers belonging to two upstream Internet service providers. This lab requires you to model an Internet connection, use common load-sharing techniques to utilize the most of the network resources, implement common security practices to mitigate simple security threats, and test the network connectivity using HTTP web browsing from an internal PC on the 24-hour network.

Lab Objectives

This lab demonstrates many of the topics covered in the preceding three chapters and shows how to use them in a redundant network design:

- BGP multihoming
- Load sharing between two autonomous systems
- Route aggregation
- BGP MD-5 authentication
- Using route reflectors for I-BGP
- I-BGP network exit preference
- Redistributing static routes
- Using peer groups to simplify configuration
- Filtering routes using AS path and community values
- Using DHCP and NAT with BGP to hide internal RFC 1918 network addresses

Equipment Needed

- One Cisco router with five serial interfaces to act as a Frame Relay switch.
- Six Cisco routers with at least one serial and one Ethernet interface.
- One Cisco router with two serial interfaces. (One of these routers requires one Ethernet interface.)
- One switch connecting the five multiaccess routers in separate VLANs.
- One PC with an Ethernet NIC capable of running TCP/IP with DHCP and a web browser.
- Portions of this lab are best suited for Cisco IOS Software versions up to or greater than 12.2(11)T.

Physical Layout and Prestaging

For this experiment, you use the network layout shown in Figure 9-20. The routers in AS 104 and AS 60 simulate Internet service provider networks Internet Service Provider-1 and Internet Service Provider-2. The Drazen and Palmer routers are the 24-hour network border routers, and all other routers are internal 24-hour network routers.

Figure 9-20 *The 24-Hour Network*

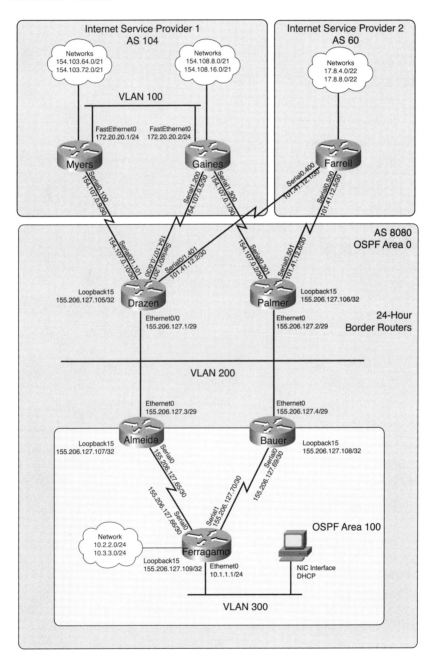

- Cable the routers as shown in Figure 9-20. The Myers, Gaines, Farrell, Drazen, and Palmer routers should be connected to the Frame Relay switch using the interface numbers shown in Table 9-13 and can be connected using back-to-back serial cables.

- Configure the Frame Relay switch using the interfaces and DLCI numbers shown in Table 9-13.

Table 9-13   *Frame Relay Switch Parameters*

Frame Switch Interface	Router Interface	Frame Switch Interface	Router DLCI	Router Interface	Router DLCI
Serial1	Myers Serial0.100	Serial0	100	Drazen Serial0/1.101	101
Serial2	Gaines Serial1.200	Serial0	200	Drazen0/1.201	201
Serial2	Gaines Serial1.300	Serial3	300	Palmer Serial0.301	301
Serial4	Farrell Serial0.400	Serial0	400	Drazen Serial0/1.401	401
Serial4	Farrell Serial0.500	Serial3	500	Palmer Serial0.501	501

Example 9-105 shows the **show frame relay route** command output from the Frame Relay switch.

Example 9-105 *Frame Relay Switch Configuration*

```
Frame-Relay-Switch # show frame-relay route
Input Intf     Input Dlci     Output Intf     Output Dlci     Status
Serial0        101            Serial1         100             active
Serial0        201            Serial2         200             active
Serial0        401            Serial4         400             active
Serial1        100            Serial0         101             active
Serial2        200            Serial0         201             active
Serial2        300            Serial3         301             active
Serial3        301            Serial2         300             active
Serial3        501            Serial4         500             active
Serial4        400            Serial0         401             active
Serial4        500            Serial3         501             active
```

- Connect the Ethernet interfaces on the Myers, Gaines, Drazen, Palmer, Almeida, and Bauer routers to the Ethernet switch, as previously shown in Figure 9-20.

- Attach the Almeida and Bauer routers to the Ferragamo router, as shown in Figure 9-20.
- Verify that each router interface on each router is in an up/up state.
- Do not configure DHCP on the Ferragamo router or PC yet.

Lab Exercises

Step 1 Configure all IP addresses, as shown in Table 9-14, and assign all Ethernet interfaces to the VLANs shown in the same table.

Table 9-14 *IP Addressing for This Network Model*

Router Name	Router Interface	IP Address	Ethernet VLAN
Myers	FastEthernet0	172.20.20.1/24	100
	Loopback100	154.103.64.1/21	
	Loopback200	154.103.72.1/21	
	Serial0.100	154.107.0.9/30	
Gaines	FastEthernet0	172.20.20.2/24	100
	Loopback100	154.108.8.1/21	
	Loopback200	154.108.16.0/21	
	Serial1.200	154.107.0.5/30	
	Serial1.300	154.107.0.1/30	
Farrell	Loopback100	17.8.4.1/22	50
	Loopback200	17.8.8.0/22	
	Serial0.400	101.41.12.1/30	
	Serial0.500	101.41.12.5/30	
Drazen	Ethernet0/0	155.206.127.1/29	200
	Loopback15	155.206.127.105/32	
	Serial0/1.101	154.107.0.10/30	
	Serial0/1.201	154.107.0.6/30	
	Serial0/1.401	101.41.12.2/30	
Palmer	Ethernet0	155.206.127.2/29	200
	Loopback15	155.206.127.106/32	
	Serial0.301	154.107.0.2/30	
	Serial0.501	101.41.12.6/30	

Table 9-14   *IP Addressing for This Network Model (Continued)*

Router Name	Router Interface	IP Address	Ethernet VLAN
Almeida	Ethernet0	155.206.127.3/29	200
	Loopback15	155.206.127.107/32	
	Serial0	155.206.127.65/30	
Bauer	Ethernet0	155.206.127.4/29	200
	Loopback15	155.206.127.108/32	
	Serial0	155.206.127.69/30	
Ferragamo	Ethernet0	10.1.1.1/24	300
	Loopback15	155.206.127.109/32	
	Loopback100	10.2.2.1/24	
	Loopback200	10.3.3.1/24	
	Serial0	155.206.127.66/30	
	Serial1	155.206.127.70/30	
PC	Ethernet NIC	DHCP	300

Step 2   Configure OSPF routing for the Drazen, Palmer, Almeida, Bauer, and Ferragamo routers. Put only the Ethernet interfaces of the Drazen, Palmer, Almeida, and Bauer routers in OSPF area 0:

— Assign the loopback interfaces on the Drazen and Palmer routers to area 0 as well. The Ferragamo router and the serial interfaces on the Almeida and Bauer routers should be in area 1.

— Use the Loopback15 interface IP address as the OSPF router ID for each OSPF router.

— Have the Almeida and Bauer routers send the default route to all downstream neighbors.

Step 3   Configure load balancing on the Ferragamo router so that the OSPF will use both of the upstream serial interfaces to forward packets to the 155.206.127.0/29 network. Use the appropriate commands to enable load balancing so that packets belonging to the same flow take the same route.

Step 4   Configure the Ferragamo router to be a DHCP server for the 10.1.1.0/24 network. The router should also assign the fiction.org domain name to its DHCP clients. After configuring the DHCP service on the router, configure the PC to request a DHCP lease from that router and verify the configuration by pinging the loopback interface on the Drazen router.

Step 5   After building the internal network, adding a host, and enabling routing, you can now focus on the BGP portion of the lab. Begin by configuring the external service providers in AS 104, the Myers and Gaines routers. Enable BGP routing on the Myers and Gaines routers. After you complete this task, each router should be able to see the /21 networks that are internally advertised between these routers.

Step 6   Next, configure E-BGP routing between the Service Provider-1 routers in AS 104 and the 24-hour border routers in AS 8080. Use peer groups to simplify the BGP configurations:

— Have the AS 8080 border routers use their Loopback15 IP addresses as their BGP router IDs, and multihome each router using the loopback address as the peering point. In this instance, one static route per neighbor per router is permitted on the AS 104 routers.

— Do not allow the Service Provider-1 routers to advertise the 172.20.20.0/24 network to any external peers. You cannot use a distribute list to perform this task.

— Do not allow the service provider routers to use the AS 8080 border routers as a transit network to reach each other's /21 networks.

— After this step is complete, the routers in AS 8080 should see all /21 networks behind the AS 104 routers.

Step 7   To complete the E-BGP Internet peering sessions, you need to configure a BGP session between the Farrell router in AS 60 and the 24-hour border routers. These BGP sessions should be configured using all the rules specified in Step 6:

— Use peer groups to allow for future peer additions.

— Have the AS 8080 border routers use their Loopback15 IP addresses as their BGP router IDs; one static route per neighbor is permitted on the Farrell router.

— Do not allow the service provider routers to use the AS 8080 border routers as a transit network to reach each other's networks.

— After this step is complete, the routers in AS 8080 should see all external networks advertised by the service provider routers.

Step 8   The BGP peer configuration would not be complete if there weren't an I-BGP connection between the 24-hour border routers and their peering partners, the Almeida and Bauer routers:

— Configure I-BGP peer relationships between these routers, using the Loopback15 interfaces as the peering points.

— Use peer groups to simplify the configuration on the border routers and do not fully mesh the routers in this network.

— Summarize all 155.206.127.0 networks at the AS 8080 border routers; do not advertise any routes smaller than /24.

— Verify that configuration by pinging the Internet networks from the Ferragamo router.

Step 9   To make the most efficient use of the connections between the border routers and the service provider's networks, configure the Service Provider-1 routers to prefer routes from the Drazen router, and configure the Service Provider-2 router to prefer routes from the Palmer router; neither the MED nor AS_PATH attributes can be used to accomplish this task. Locally generated routes should always have the highest preference:

— The Drazen router should prefer routes from the Myers router, with a secondary preference for the Farrell router; and the Palmer router should prefer routes from the Farrell, with the Gaines router as a secondary preference before the Myers router. Locally generated routes should always have the highest preference.

Step 10   As a security precaution, disable any CDP, HTTP web access, and any unnecessary features on the 24-hour border routers:

— Also create an antispoof access list that will prevent any RFC 1918 private IP addresses and internal addresses.

— Make sure that OSPF routes are not allowed out of the 24-hour network.

— Leave HTTP web service enabled on the Internet-facing routers; they will be used to simulate Internet web servers.

— Configure the HTTP services to use the IP address of the Loopback100 interface.

Step 11 To hide the RFC 1918 private networks from the Internet, configure the 24-hour border routers to NAT all internal networks to the public Internet-routable IP addresses shown in Table 9-15:

— Make sure all IP address blocks are aggregated to the fullest extent. All specific routes should be suppressed; only the aggregate should be advertised to external neighbors.

— To verify customer Internet connectivity, use a web browser to enter the HTTP web configuration site on each of the service provider networks.

Table 9-15   *Internal to External NAT Addresses*

Internal Network	External Network
10.1.1.0/24	155.206.124.0/24
10.2.2.0/24	155.206.125.0/24
10.3.3.0/24	155.206.126.0/24

Lab Walkthrough

Step 1 Configure all IP addresses as shown in Table 9-14 and assign all Ethernet interfaces to the VLANs shown in the same table.

Step 2 Configure OSPF routing for the Drazen, Palmer, Almeida, Bauer, and Ferragamo routers. Put only the Ethernet interfaces of the Drazen, Palmer, Almeida, and Bauer routers in OSPF area 0.

— Assign the loopback interfaces on the Drazen and Palmer routers to area 0 as well. The Ferragamo router and the serial interfaces on the Almeida and Bauer routers should be in area 1:

— Use the Loopback15 interface IP address as the OSPF router ID for each OSPF router.

— Have the Almeida and Bauer routers send the default route to all downstream neighbors.

This task builds the IGP routing solution for the internal 24-hour network. After OSPF has been configured, all the internal routers should be able to reach all interfaces on all other internal routers, except for the Internet-facing serial interfaces. This review begins with the Almeida and Bauer routers. One of the first, hidden tasks in this step required the configuration of a default route to the HSRP IP address for the Internet border routers. After the default route has been configured, OSPF can be enabled and interfaces should be assigned to the areas previously mentioned. The **default-information originate** command sends the default route to the other OSPF neighbors. Example 9-106 shows the OSPF configuration for the Almeida router.

Example 9-106 *Almeida Router's OSPF Configuration*

```
Almeida# show run | begin ospf
router ospf 1
 router-id 155.206.127.107
 log-adjacency-changes
 area 1 stub
 network 155.206.127.0 0.0.0.7 area 0
 network 155.206.127.64 0.0.0.3 area 1
 network 155.206.127.107 0.0.0.0 area 0
 default-information originate always metric-type 1
 !
ip route 0.0.0.0 0.0.0.0 155.206.127.5
```

After OSPF has been configured, all the internal routers should reach all OSPF-enabled interfaces. The default route should also have been advertised; this introduces a small problem, though. Unless you configure a distribution list to filter incoming routes on the Drazen or Palmer routers, they will receive the default route sent out in the LSAs originating from the Almeida and Bauer routers. After you configure and apply a distribution list denying the default route, 0.0.0.0/32, this problems should be corrected. You can test the OSPF configuration using the **show ip route** and **ping** commands on the Ferragamo, Drazen, and Palmer routers. Example 9-107 shows the routing table from the Drazen and Ferragamo routers.

Example 9-107 *Drazen and Ferragamo Routing Tables*

```
Drazen# show ip route | begin Gateway
Gateway of last resort is not set
     155.206.0.0/16 is variably subnetted, 7 subnets, 3 masks
C       155.206.127.0/29 is directly connected, Ethernet0/0
O       155.206.127.106/32 [110/11] via 155.206.127.2, 00:31:55, Ethernet0/0
O       155.206.127.107/32 [110/11] via 155.206.127.3, 00:31:55, Ethernet0/0
C       155.206.127.105/32 is directly connected, Loopback15
O       155.206.127.108/32 [110/11] via 155.206.127.4, 00:31:55, Ethernet0/0
O IA    155.206.127.64/30 [110/74] via 155.206.127.3, 00:31:55, Ethernet0/0
O IA    155.206.127.68/30 [110/74] via 155.206.127.4, 00:31:55, Ethernet0/0
     101.0.0.0/30 is subnetted, 1 subnets
C       101.41.12.0 is directly connected, Serial0/1.401
     154.107.0.0/30 is subnetted, 2 subnets
C       154.107.0.4 is directly connected, Serial0/1.201
C       154.107.0.8 is directly connected, Serial0/1.101
     10.0.0.0/8 is variably subnetted, 3 subnets, 2 masks
O IA    10.1.1.0/24 [110/84] via 155.206.127.3, 00:31:56, Ethernet0/0
                    [110/84] via 155.206.127.4, 00:31:56, Ethernet0/0
O IA    10.3.3.1/32 [110/75] via 155.206.127.3, 00:31:56, Ethernet0/0
```

continues

Example 9-107 *Drazen and Ferragamo Routing Tables (Continued)*

```
                         [110/75] via 155.206.127.4, 00:31:56, Ethernet0/0
O IA    10.2.2.1/32 [110/75] via 155.206.127.3, 00:31:56, Ethernet0/0
                         [110/75] via 155.206.127.4, 00:31:56, Ethernet0/0
─────────────────────────────────────────────────────────────────────────
Ferragamo# show ip route | begin Gateway
Gateway of last resort is 155.206.127.65 to network 0.0.0.0
     155.206.0.0/16 is variably subnetted, 7 subnets, 3 masks
O IA    155.206.127.0/29 [110/74] via 155.206.127.69, 00:35:02, Serial1
                          [110/74] via 155.206.127.65, 00:35:02, Serial0
O IA    155.206.127.106/32 [110/75] via 155.206.127.69, 00:32:22, Serial1
                           [110/75] via 155.206.127.65, 00:32:22, Serial0
O IA    155.206.127.107/32 [110/65] via 155.206.127.65, 00:35:02, Serial0
O IA    155.206.127.105/32 [110/75] via 155.206.127.65, 00:33:44, Serial0
                           [110/75] via 155.206.127.69, 00:33:44, Serial1
O IA    155.206.127.108/32 [110/65] via 155.206.127.69, 00:35:02, Serial1
C       155.206.127.64/30 is directly connected, Serial0
C       155.206.127.68/30 is directly connected, Serial1
     10.0.0.0/24 is subnetted, 3 subnets
C       10.3.3.0 is directly connected, Loopback200
C       10.2.2.0 is directly connected, Loopback100
C       10.1.1.0 is directly connected, Ethernet0
O*E1 0.0.0.0/0 [110/84] via 155.206.127.65, 00:35:03, Serial0
               [110/84] via 155.206.127.69, 00:35:03, Serial1
```

Step 3   Configure load balancing on the Ferragamo router so that the OSPF uses both of the upstream serial interfaces to forward packets to the 155.206.127.0/29 network. Use the appropriate commands to enable load balancing so that packets belonging to the same flow take the same route.

   This step actually does not require much configuration. By default, OSPF stores up to four equal-cost paths in the routing table. To enable per-destination load balancing over the two serial interfaces, you must enable CEF switching using the **ip cef** command. Once again, by default, the **ip cef** command enables CEF switching using the universal per-destination algorithm for load balancing. You can use the IP routing table and CEF table to verify the configuration. Example 9-108 shows the Ferragamo router's IP routing table and **show ip cef summary** command output.

Example 9-108 *Ferragamo Router's Routing Table and CEF Summary*

```
Ferragamo# show ip route | include vialis
Gateway of last resort is 155.206.127.69 to network 0.0.0.0
     155.206.0.0/16 is variably subnetted, 7 subnets, 3 masks
O IA    155.206.127.0/29 [110/74] via 155.206.127.65, 00:18:00, Serial0
                          [110/74] via 155.206.127.69, 00:18:00, Serial1
O IA    155.206.127.106/32 [110/75] via 155.206.127.65, 00:18:00, Serial0
                           [110/75] via 155.206.127.69, 00:18:00, Serial1
O IA    155.206.127.107/32 [110/65] via 155.206.127.65, 00:18:00, Serial0
```

Example 9-108 *Ferragamo Router's Routing Table and CEF Summary (Continued)*

```
O IA    155.206.127.105/32 [110/75] via 155.206.127.65, 00:18:00, Serial0
                           [110/75] via 155.206.127.69, 00:18:00, Serial1
O IA    155.206.127.108/32 [110/65] via 155.206.127.69, 00:18:00, Serial1
C       155.206.127.64/30 is directly connected, Serial0
C       155.206.127.68/30 is directly connected, Serial1
     10.0.0.0/24 is subnetted, 3 subnets
C       10.3.3.0 is directly connected, Loopback200
C       10.2.2.0 is directly connected, Loopback100
C       10.1.1.0 is directly connected, Ethernet0
O*E1 0.0.0.0/0 [110/84] via 155.206.127.69, 00:18:01, Serial1
               [110/84] via 155.206.127.65, 00:18:01, Serial0
Ferragamo# show ip cef summary
IP CEF with switching (Table Version 28), flags=0x0
  28 routes, 0 reresolve, 0 unresolved (0 old, 0 new)
  31 leaves, 18 nodes, 22734 bytes, 31 inserts, 0 invalidations
  4 load sharing elements, 1264 bytes, 4 references
  universal per-destination load sharing algorithm, id CD1F18C5
  2 CEF resets, 0 revisions of existing leaves
  refcounts:  4907 leaf, 4864 node
Adjacency Table has 3 adjacencies
```

Step 4 Configure the Ferragamo router to be a DHCP server for the 10.1.1.0/24
network. The router should also assign the fiction.org domain name to its
DHCP clients. After configuring the DHCP service on the router, configure
the PC to request a DHCP lease from that router, and verify the configuration
by pinging the loopback interface on the Drazen router.

DHCP configuration is a straightforward task, after creating a DHCP pool
and assigning DHCP parameters to the pool, the only remaining task is the
exclusion of the Ferragamo router's Ethernet IP address. After the DHCP
server configuration is finished, and the PC has been configured to request a
DHCP IP address, it should immediately be able to ping the Drazen router's
IP address. Example 9-109 shows the **ipconfig** command output and a
successful ping from a Windows PC.

Example 9-109 **ipconfig** *and* **ping** *Commands as Issued from the PC*

```
G:\>ipconfig
Windows 2000 IP Configuration
Ethernet adapter Local Area Connection:
        Connection-specific DNS Suffix  . : fiction.org
        IP Address. . . . . . . . . . . : 10.1.1.2
        Subnet Mask . . . . . . . . . . : 255.255.255.0
        Default Gateway . . . . . . . . : 10.1.1.1
G:\>ping 155.206.127.105
Pinging 155.206.127.105 with 32 bytes of data:
Reply from 155.206.127.105: bytes=32 time=20ms TTL=253
```

continues

Example 9-109 **ipconfig** *and* **ping** *Commands as Issued from the PC (Continued)*

```
Reply from 155.206.127.105: bytes=32 time<10ms TTL=253
Reply from 155.206.127.105: bytes=32 time<10ms TTL=253
Reply from 155.206.127.105: bytes=32 time<10ms TTL=253
Ping statistics for 155.206.127.105:
    Packets: Sent = 4, Received = 4, Lost = 0 (0% loss),
Approximate round trip times in milli-seconds:
    Minimum = 0ms, Maximum =  20ms, Average =  5ms
```

Step 5   After building the internal network, adding a host, and enabling routing, you can now focus on the BGP portion of the lab. Begin by configuring the external service providers in AS 104, the Myers and Gaines routers. Enable BGP routing on the Myers and Gaines routers. After you complete this task, each router should see the /21 networks that are internally advertised between these routers.

The I-BGP configuration between the Myers and Gaines routers is only dependent on one key factor: disabling IGP synchronization. After BGP is enabled, the networks and neighbors are configured, and synchronization is disabled, each router should reach its peers' /21 networks. Example 9-110 shows the IP routing table for the Myers router.

Example 9-110 *Myers Router's IP Routing Table*

```
Myers# show ip route | include is|via
Gateway of last resort is not set
     154.103.0.0/21 is subnetted, 2 subnets
C       154.103.72.0 is directly connected, Loopback200
C       154.103.64.0 is directly connected, Loopback100
     154.108.0.0/21 is subnetted, 2 subnets
B       154.108.16.0 [200/0] via 172.20.20.2, 00:07:57
B       154.108.8.0 [200/0] via 172.20.20.2, 00:07:57
     154.107.0.0/30 is subnetted, 1 subnets
C       154.107.0.8 is directly connected, Serial0.100
     172.20.0.0/24 is subnetted, 1 subnets
C       172.20.20.0 is directly connected, FastEthernet0
```

Step 6   Next, configure E-BGP routing between the Service Provider-1 routers in AS 104 and the 24-hour border routers in AS 8080. Use peer groups to simplify the BGP configurations:

— Have the AS 8080 border routers use their Loopback15 IP addresses as their BGP router IDs, and multihome each router using the loopback address as the peering point. In this instance, one static route per neighbor per router is permitted on the AS 104 routers.

— Do not allow the Service Provider-1 routers to advertise the 172.20.20.0/24 network to any external peers. You might not use a distribute list to perform this task.

— Do not allow the service provider routers to use the AS 8080 border routers as a transit network to reach each other's /21 networks.

— After this step is complete, the routers in AS 8080 should see all /21 networks behind the AS 104 routers.

This step contains several subtasks that must be completed accurately for the remainder of the lab to work properly. To facilitate BGP routing between the Internet Service Provider-1 and 24-hour border routers, you must use the **ebgp-multihop** command on the Internet Service Provider-1 routers and **update-source Loopback 15** command on the 24-hour routers. If you do not use these commands, the BGP session between the routers will never start, and you see the following message on the Internet Service Provider-1 routers:

```
Connections established 0; dropped 0
  Last reset never
  External BGP neighbor not directly connected.
  No active TCP connection
```

If you added a static route to each of the loopback IP addresses on the Internet Service Provider-1 routers, when the **multihop** and **update-source** commands are added to the appropriate routers, a BGP session should start. Example 9-111 shows the BGP configuration for the Gaines and Drazen routers.

Example 9-111 *Multihoming the Gaines and Drazen Routers*

```
Gaines# show run | begin bgp
router bgp 104
 no synchronization
 bgp log-neighbor-changes
 network 154.108.8.0 mask 255.255.248.0
 network 154.108.16.0 mask 255.255.248.0
 network 172.20.20.0 mask 255.255.255.0
 neighbor AS8080 peer-group
 neighbor AS8080 remote-as 8080
 neighbor AS8080 ebgp-multihop 2
 neighbor 155.206.127.105 peer-group AS8080
 neighbor 155.206.127.106 peer-group AS8080
 neighbor 172.20.20.1 remote-as 104
 no auto-summary
!
ip route 155.206.127.105 255.255.255.255 154.107.0.6
ip route 155.206.127.106 255.255.255.255 154.107.0.2
```

continues

Example 9-111 *Multihoming the Gaines and Drazen Routers (Continued)*

```
Drazen# show run | begin bgp
router bgp 8080
 no synchronization
 bgp log-neighbor-changes
network 154.107.0.8 mask 255.255.255.252
 network 154.206.127.0 mask 255.255.255.248
 neighbor AS104 peer-group
 neighbor AS104 remote-as 104
 neighbor AS104 update-source Loopback15
 neighbor 154.107.0.5 peer-group AS104
 neighbor 154.107.0.9 peer-group AS104
 no auto-summary
```

After the BGP session is established, and routes are exchanged, you need to find a way to prevent the service provider routers from advertising the 172.20.20.0/24 private network to external AS peers. Because you cannot use a route filter to accomplish this task, there is only one other way to hide that network: assigning the local AS COMMUNITY attribute to the service provider routers. This attribute allows the route to be advertised internally but prevents it from being sent to any external BGP neighbors. Example 9-112 shows the BGP configuration for the Myers router.

Example 9-112 *Using the Well-Known LOCAL_AS Community on the Myers Router*

```
Myers# show run | begin bgp
router bgp 104
 no synchronization
 bgp log-neighbor-changes
 network 154.103.64.0 mask 255.255.248.0
 network 154.103.72.0 mask 255.255.248.0
 network 172.20.20.0 mask 255.255.255.0 route-map hide-network
 neighbor AS8080 peer-group
 neighbor AS8080 remote-as 8080
 neighbor AS8080 ebgp-multihop 2
 neighbor 155.206.127.105 peer-group AS8080
 neighbor 172.20.20.2 remote-as 104
 no auto-summary
!
ip route 155.206.127.105 255.255.255.255 154.107.0.10
!
route-map hide-network permit 10
 set community local-as
```

As you can see, the Myers router uses the hide-network route map to set the local AS community for the 172.20.20.0/24 network, and because the local AS COMMUNITY attribute does not need to be advertised beyond the local AS, you do not need to use the **send-community** command.

The last part of Step 3 specified that you must not allow the service provider network to use AS 8080 as a transit network to reach internally generated routes. This task requires the addition of an AS path filter list on the 24-hour routers. A simple one-line AS path access list, which allows only the advertisement of internally generated routes using the **^$** regular expression to specify an empty AS path applied to all outgoing routes, achieves that effect. This is demonstrated by Example 9-113, which shows the BGP configuration for the Palmer router.

Example 9-113 *Applying a Filter List on the Palmer Router*

```
Palmer# show run | begin bgp
router bgp 8080
 no synchronization
bgp log-neighbor-changes
 network 155.206.127.0 mask 255.255.255.248
 neighbor AS104 peer-group
 neighbor AS104 remote-as 104
 neighbor AS104 update-source Loopback15
 neighbor AS104 filter-list 100 out
 neighbor 154.107.0.1 peer-group AS104
 no auto-summary
!
ip as-path access-list 100 permit ^$
```

Step 7   To complete the E-BGP Internet peering sessions, you need to configure a BGP session between the Farrell router in AS 60 and the 24-hour border routers. These BGP sessions should be configured using all the rules specified in Step 6:

— Use peer groups to allow for future peer additions.

— Have the AS 8080 border routers use their Loopback15 IP addresses as their BGP router IDs; one static route per neighbor is permitted on the Farrell router.

— Do not allow the service provider routers to use the AS 8080 border routers as a transit network to reach each other's networks.

— After this step is complete, the routers in AS 8080 should see all external networks advertised by the service provider routers.

If you configured these routers using the same steps that you used in the previous step, you should have two newly established BGP sessions between the Drazen, Palmer, and Farrell routers. The Myers and Gaines routers should reach the 155.206.127.0/29 network, and the networks for each of the serial interfaces on the AS 8080 border routers, but they should not have any routes to the 17.8.4.0/22 or 17.8.8.0/22 networks. Example 9-114 shows the BGP RIB for the Myers router.

Example 9-114 *Myers Router's BGP RIB After the Application of a Filter List*

```
Myers# show ip bgp | begin Network
   Network          Next Hop         Metric LocPrf Weight Path
* i101.41.12.0/30   155.206.127.105       0    100      0 8080 i
*>                  155.206.127.105       0             0 8080 i
*> 154.103.64.0/21  0.0.0.0               0         32768 i
*> 154.103.72.0/21  0.0.0.0               0         32768 i
* i154.107.0.4/30   155.206.127.105       0    100      0 8080 i
*>                  155.206.127.105       0             0 8080 i
* i154.107.0.8/30   155.206.127.105       0    100      0 8080 i
*>                  155.206.127.105       0             0 8080 i
*>i154.108.8.0/21   172.20.20.2           0    100      0 i
*>i154.108.16.0/21  172.20.20.2           0    100      0 i
* i155.206.127.0/29 155.206.127.106       0    100      0 8080 i
* i172.20.20.0/24   172.20.20.2           0    100      0 i
*>                  0.0.0.0               0         32768 I
```

The Drazen and Palmer routers should have routes to each of their external BGP neighbors' networks, with the exception of the 172.20.20.0/24 network in AS 104. Example 9-115 shows the BGP RIB for the Drazen router.

Example 9-115 *Drazen Router's BGP RIB After the Filter List Application*

```
Drazen# show ip bgp | begin Network
   Network          Next Hop         Metric LocPrf Weight Path
*> 17.8.4.0/22      101.41.12.1           0             0 60 i
*> 17.8.8.0/22      101.41.12.1           0             0 60 i
*> 101.41.12.0/30   0.0.0.0               0         32768 i
*  154.103.64.0/21  154.107.0.5                        0 104 i
*>                  154.107.0.9           0             0 104 i
*  154.103.72.0/21  154.107.0.5                        0 104 i
*>                  154.107.0.9           0             0 104 i
*> 154.107.0.4/30   0.0.0.0               0         32768 i
*> 154.107.0.8/30   0.0.0.0               0         32768 i
*  154.108.8.0/21   154.107.0.5           0             0 104 i
*>                  154.107.0.9                         0 104 i
*  154.108.16.0/21  154.107.0.5           0             0 104 i
*>                  154.107.0.9                         0 104 i
```

And finally, the Farrell router's BGP RIB should contain entries for all the networks advertised by the Drazen and Palmer routers, except the routes to networks in AS 104, as shown in Example 9-116.

Example 9-116 *Farrell Router's BGP RIB After the Filter List*

```
Farrell# show ip bgp | begin Network
   Network          Next Hop          Metric LocPrf Weight Path
*> 17.8.4.0/22      0.0.0.0               0          32768 i
*> 17.8.8.0/22      0.0.0.0               0          32768 i
*> 101.41.12.0/30   155.206.127.105       0              0 8080 i
*> 154.107.0.4/30   155.206.127.105       0              0 8080 i
*> 154.107.0.8/30   155.206.127.105       0              0 8080 i
*> 155.206.127.0/29 155.206.127.106       0              0 8080 I
```

Step 8   The BGP peer configuration would not be complete if there weren't an I-BGP connection between the 24-hour border routers and their peering partners, the Almeida and Bauer routers:

— Configure I-BGP peer relationships between these routers, using the Loopback15 interfaces as the peering points.

— Use peer groups to simplify the configuration on the border routers and do not fully mesh the routers in this network.

— Summarize all 155.206.127.0 networks at the AS 8080 border routers. Do not advertise any routes smaller than /24.

— Verify that configuration by pinging the Internet networks from the Ferragamo router.

This step requires several steps to accomplish successful network ping test verification. First, you must configure a peer group on the Drazen and Palmer routers. This peer group should contain all the characteristics that apply to the neighbors that will be added to the peer group (namely, the Almeida and Bauer routers). Each of the border routers need to serve as route reflectors for the downstream 24-hour routers and require the use of the **update-source** and **next-hop-self** to allow for full BGP routing capabilities. Example 9-117 shows the I-BGP configuration for the Drazen router.

Example 9-117 *I-BGP Configuration for the Drazen Router*

```
Drazen# show run | include AS8080
 neighbor AS8080 peer-group
 neighbor AS8080 remote-as 8080
 neighbor AS8080 update-source Loopback15
 neighbor AS8080 route-reflector-client
 neighbor AS8080 next-hop-self
 neighbor 155.206.127.106 peer-group AS8080
 neighbor 155.206.127.107 peer-group AS8080
 neighbor 155.206.127.108 peer-group AS8080
```

After the border routers have been configured, you can then move on and configure I-BGP for the Almeida and Bauer routers. The Bauer and Almeida routers configuration is straightforward and should require only two commands per peer: the **remote-as** and **update-source** commands. Example 9-118 shows the BGP configuration and BGP RIB for the Bauer router.

Example 9-118 *I-BGP Configuration and BGP RIB from the Bauer Router*

```
Bauer# show run | begin bgp
router bgp 8080
 no synchronization
 bgp log-neighbor-changes
 network 155.206.127.68 mask 255.255.255.0
 neighbor 155.206.127.105 remote-as 8080
 neighbor 155.206.127.105 update-source Loopback15
 neighbor 155.206.127.106 remote-as 8080
 neighbor 155.206.127.106 update-source Loopback15
 no auto-summary
Bauer# show ip bgp | begin Network
   Network          Next Hop         Metric LocPrf Weight Path
*>i17.8.4.0/22      155.206.127.105       0    100      0 60 i
* i                 155.206.127.106       0    100      0 60 i
*>i17.8.8.0/22      155.206.127.105       0    100      0 60 i
* i                 155.206.127.106       0    100      0 60 i
* i101.41.12.0/30   155.206.127.105       0    100      0 i
*>i                 155.206.127.105       0    100      0 i
*>i154.103.64.0/21  155.206.127.105       0    100      0 104 i
* i                 155.206.127.106            100      0 104 i
*>i154.103.72.0/21  155.206.127.105       0    100      0 104 i
* i                 155.206.127.106            100      0 104 i
*>i154.107.0.0/30   155.206.127.105            100      0 104 i
* i                 155.206.127.106       0    100      0 104 i
*>i154.107.0.4/30   155.206.127.105       0    100      0 i
* i                 155.206.127.105       0    100      0 i
* i154.107.0.8/30   155.206.127.105       0    100      0 i
*>i                 155.206.127.105       0    100      0 i
*>i154.108.8.0/21   155.206.127.105            100      0 104 i
* i                 155.206.127.106       0    100      0 104 i
*>i154.108.16.0/21  155.206.127.105            100      0 104 i
* i                 155.206.127.106       0    100      0 104 i
* i155.206.127.0/24 155.206.127.106            100      0 i
*>i                 155.206.127.106            100      0 i
```

The final task in the I-BGP configuration step requires the aggregation of the 155.206.127.0/24 network and should be performed on the border routers using the summary parameter to suppress the summarized routers. Notice that the Ferragamo router cannot reach any external service provider network until this step has been completed. This is because the upstream service providers do not have a route to the 155.206.127.64/30 and 155.206.127.68/30 networks. (You should never send /30 routes to service providers; they will generally not accept any routes smaller than /24.) After you have aggregated the networks, you see that the Ferragamo router can ping all the Internet service provider networks using its default route, using a configuration similar to that shown in Example 9-119.

Example 9-119 *Palmer Router's Route Aggregation Configuration*

```
Palmer# show run | begin bgp
router bgp 8080
 no synchronization
 bgp router-id 154.206.127.106
 bgp cluster-id 2614001514
 bgp log-neighbor-changes
 network 155.206.127.0 mask 255.255.255.248
 aggregate-address 155.206.127.0 255.255.255.0 summary-only
 neighbor AS104 peer-group
 neighbor AS104 remote-as 104
 neighbor AS104 update-source Loopback15
 neighbor AS104 filter-list 100 out
 neighbor AS60 peer-group
 neighbor AS60 remote-as 60
 neighbor AS60 update-source Loopback15
 neighbor AS60 filter-list 100 out
 neighbor AS8080 peer-group
 neighbor AS8080 remote-as 8080
 neighbor AS8080 update-source Loopback15
 neighbor AS8080 route-reflector-client
 neighbor AS8080 next-hop-self
 neighbor 101.41.12.5 peer-group AS60
 neighbor 154.107.0.1 peer-group AS104
 neighbor 155.206.127.105 peer-group AS8080
 neighbor 155.206.127.107 peer-group AS8080
 neighbor 155.206.127.108 peer-group AS8080
 no auto-summary
```

After the aggregate has been added to the border routers, the Internet service provider routers should all receive a route to the 155.206.127.0/24 network, and the Ferragamo router should ping the service provider networks from all 155.206.127.0 networks, as shown in Example 9-120.

Example 9-120 *Farrell Postaggregation BGP RIB and the Ferragamo Ping Test*

```
Farrell# show ip bgp | begin Network
   Network          Next Hop         Metric LocPrf Weight Path
*> 17.8.4.0/22      0.0.0.0               0        32768 i
*> 17.8.8.0/22      0.0.0.0               0        32768 i
*> 155.206.127.0/24 155.206.127.106               0 8080 i
*                   155.206.127.105               0 8080 i
```

Example 9-120 *Farrell Postaggregation BGP RIB and the Ferragamo Ping Test (Continued)*

continues

```
Ferragamo# ping
Protocol [ip]:
Target IP address: 154.103.64.1
Repeat count [5]:
Datagram size [100]:
Timeout in seconds [2]:
Extended commands [n]: y
Source address or interface: 155.206.127.66
Type of service [0]:
Set DF bit in IP header? [no]:
Validate reply data? [no]:
Data pattern [0xABCD]:
Loose, Strict, Record, Timestamp, Verbose[none]:
Sweep range of sizes [n]:
Type escape sequence to abort.
Sending 5, 100-byte ICMP Echos to 154.103.64.1, timeout is 2 seconds:
!!!!!
Success rate is 100 percent (5/5), round-trip min/avg/max = 8/9/16 ms
```

Step 9   To make the most efficient use of the connections between the border routers and the service provider networks, configure the Service Provider-1 router to prefer routes from the Drazen router, and configure the Service Provider-2 router to prefer routes from the Palmer router. Neither the MED nor AS_PATH attributes can accomplish this task. Locally generated routes should always have the highest preference:

—   The Drazen router should prefer routes from the Myers router, with a secondary preference for the Farrell router; the Palmer router should prefer routes from the Farrell, with the Gaines router as a secondary preference before the Myers router. Routes that were locally generated from a certain router should always have the highest preference.

There are several ways to set a preferred route in BGP; one of the easiest and most common ways to set a preferred route is to prepend AS path information to the less-desirable route, or to set the MED attribute for the more desirable route. When the external peer receives the routes with the new attributes, the BGP route selection algorithm prefer the routes with the shorter AS path, or the lowest MED attribute. Another, more customizable approach to this problem is to set and match a certain BGP COMMUNITY attribute and use a route map on the receiving side to set the WEIGHT attribute to a higher value, making the route more attractive. Example 9-121 shows how the Drazen router uses **route map external-pref** to set the BGP community value for locally generated routes specified by the **match route-type local** command to 104:8080, and the COMMUNITY attribute for all other outgoing routes is set to 104:111. The **ip bgp-community new-format** command allows for the use of the more readable aa:nn community format.

Example 9-121 *Changing the COMMUNITY Attribute on the Drazen Router*

```
Drazen# show run | include AS104|new-format
 neighbor AS104 peer-group
 neighbor AS104 remote-as 104
 neighbor AS104 update-source Loopback15
 neighbor AS104 send-community
 neighbor AS104 route-map external-pref out
 neighbor AS104 filter-list 100 out
 neighbor 154.107.0.5 peer-group AS104
 neighbor 154.107.0.9 peer-group AS104
ip bgp-community new-format
Drazen# show run | begin route-map external-pref permit 10
route-map external-pref permit 10
match route-type local
 set community 104:8080
!
route-map external-pref permit 20
 set community 104:111
```

After the external peers in AS 104 receive the routes with the new community attributes, they can, in turn, use the same type of route map to set the WEIGHT attribute. Example 9-122 shows how the Gaines router uses IP community lists 10, 11, and 80 to match the incoming community values and to set the weight based on these values.

Example 9-122 *Using the COMMUNITY Attribute to Change the Weight on the Gaines Router*

```
Gaines# show run | begin AS8080
 neighbor AS8080 peer-group
 neighbor AS8080 remote-as 8080
 neighbor AS8080 ebgp-multihop 2
 neighbor AS8080 route-map preference in
 neighbor 155.206.127.105 peer-group AS8080
 neighbor 155.206.127.106 peer-group AS8080
 neighbor 172.20.20.1 remote-as 104
 no auto-summary
!
ip bgp-community new-format
ip community-list 10 permit 104:8080
ip community-list 11 permit 104:111
ip community-list 80 permit internet
!
route-map preference permit 10
 match community 10
```

continues

Example 9-122 *Using the COMMUNITY Attribute to Change the Weight on the Gaines Router (Continued)*

```
 set weight 10000
 !
route-map preference permit 20
 match community 11
 set weight 2000
 !
route-map preference permit 30
 match community 80
```

In the preceding example, route map preference 10 matches the community string 104:8080, from community list 10, and increase the WEIGHT attribute of matching routes from the default of 0 to a new value of 10,000. Route map preference 20 matches the 104:111 COMMUNITY attribute using community list 11, and route map preference 30 matches the default Internet community and does not alter any attribute. If the route map preference 30 had not been present, the route map would have acted like an access list and denied all other routes. Example 9-123 shows the resulting BGP RIB from the Gaines router.

Example 9-123 *Gaines Router BGP RIB After the New Weight Adjustment*

```
Gaines# show ip bgp | begin Network
   Network          Next Hop        Metric LocPrf Weight Path
*>i154.103.64.0/21  172.20.20.1          0    100      0 i
*>i154.103.72.0/21  172.20.20.1          0    100      0 i
*>  154.108.8.0/21  0.0.0.0              0         32768 i
*>  154.108.16.0/21 0.0.0.0              0         32768 i
*   155.206.124.0/22 155.206.127.106                   0 8080 i
*  i                155.206.127.105           100      0 8080 i
*>                  155.206.127.105                2000 8080 i
*  i172.20.20.0/24  172.20.20.1          0    100      0 i
*>                  0.0.0.0              0         32768 i
```

The second part of the step required the configuration of internal preference on routes coming into the 24-hour network. At first glance, you might want to use the LOCAL_PREF attribute to change the preference for the routes; if you read the question closely, however, you notice that the LOCAL_PREF attribute does not work in this case because the LOCAL_PREF attribute is passed to all neighbors inside of AS 8080, which will not produce the required results. The other way to accomplish this task is to use **set** and **match** with the COMMUNITY attribute and use that attribute to change the WEIGHT for the route like you did in the first part of this step. This time, the task is a little trickier to accomplish because there are three orders of precedence. Example 9-124 shows how this was accomplished on the Drazen router.

Example 9-124 *Altering Route Precedence on the Drazen Router*

```
Drazen# show run | include AS104|AS60
 neighbor AS104 peer-group
 neighbor AS104 remote-as 104
 neighbor AS104 update-source Loopback15
 neighbor AS104 send-community
 neighbor AS104 route-map internal-pref in
 neighbor AS104 route-map external-pref out
 neighbor AS104 filter-list 100 out
 neighbor AS60 peer-group
 neighbor AS60 remote-as 60
 neighbor AS60 update-source Loopback15
 neighbor AS60 send-community
 neighbor AS60 route-map internal-pref in
 neighbor AS60 route-map external-pref2 out
 neighbor AS60 filter-list 100 out
 neighbor 101.41.12.1 peer-group AS60
 neighbor 154.107.0.5 peer-group AS104
 neighbor 154.107.0.9 peer-group AS104
Drazen# show run | include community-list
ip community-list 4 permit 104:104
ip community-list 10 permit internet
ip community-list 14 permit 104:222
ip community-list 44 permit 104:333
Drazen# show run | begin route-map internal-pref permit 10
route-map internal-pref permit 10
 match community 4
 set weight 10000
!
route-map internal-pref permit 20
 match community 14
 set weight 2000
!
route-map internal-pref permit 30
 match community 44
 set weight 1000
!
route-map internal-pref permit 40
 match community 10
```

In the preceding example, the internal-pref route map specifies the weight
that is to be assigned to routes with each COMMUNITY attribute. Route map
internal-pref 10 uses community list 4 to set the weight for all locally
originated routes (routes containing the 104:104 community attribute that
was set on the Myers and Gaines routers) to 10,000. The next iteration of this
route map matches traffic originating from the Myers router (this value was
set on the Myers router as 104:22), the next iteration specifies routes from the

Gaines router (this value was set on the Gaines routers as 104:333), and the last statement permits any other routes leaving their COMMUNITY attribute untouched. Example 9-125 shows the resulting BGP RIB.

Example 9-125 *Specifying Preference in the Drazen BGP RIB*

```
Drazen# show ip bgp | begin Network
   Network          Next Hop         Metric LocPrf Weight Path
* i17.8.4.0/22      155.206.127.106       0    100      0 60 i
*>                  101.41.12.1           0             0 60 i
* i17.8.8.0/22      155.206.127.106       0    100      0 60 i
*>                  101.41.12.1           0             0 60 i
* i154.103.64.0/21  155.206.127.106            100      0 104 i
*>                  154.107.0.9           0         10000 104 i
*                   154.107.0.5                    1000 104 i
* i154.103.72.0/21  155.206.127.106            100      0 104 i
*>                  154.107.0.9           0         10000 104 i
*                   154.107.0.5                    1000 104 i
* i154.108.8.0/21   155.206.127.106       0    100      0 104 i
*                   154.107.0.9                    2000 104 i
*>                  154.107.0.5           0         10000 104 i
* i154.108.16.0/21  155.206.127.106       0    100      0 104 i
*                   154.107.0.9                    2000 104 i
*>                  154.107.0.5           0         10000 104 i
s> 155.206.124.0/24 0.0.0.0               0         32768 i
* i155.206.124.0/22 155.206.127.106            100      0 i
*>                  0.0.0.0                        32768 i
s> 155.206.125.0/24 0.0.0.0               0         32768 i
s> 155.206.126.0/24 0.0.0.0               0         32768 i
r>i155.206.127.64/30
   Network          Next Hop         Metric LocPrf Weight Path
                    155.206.127.107       0    100      0 i
#
```

Step 10 As a security precaution, disable any CDP, HTTP web access, and any unnecessary features on the 24-hour border routers:

— Also create an antispoof access list that prevents any RFC 1918 private IP addresses and internal addresses.

— Make sure that OSPF routes are not allowed out of the 24-hour network.

— Leave HTTP web service enabled on the Internet-facing routers; they will be used to simulate Internet web servers.

— Configure the HTTP services to use the IP address of the Loopback100 interface.

Example 9-126 shows some of the commands that might have been issued, depending on the Cisco IOS Software version.

Example 9-126 *Disabling Services on a Cisco Router*

```
no service pad
no service dhcp
no ip identd
no service finger
no ip source-route
no ip bootp
no service tcp-small-servers
no service tcp-small-servers
!
interface Ethernet0/0
 no mop enabled
 no cdp enable
 ip access-group 101 in
!
router ospf 1
 passive-interface Serial0/1
 passive-interface Serial0/1.101
 passive-interface Serial0/1.201
 passive-interface Serial0/1.401
!
no ip http server
access-list 101 deny    ip 10.0.0.0 0.255.255.255 any
access-list 101 deny    ip 192.168.0.0 0.0.255.255 any
access-list 101 deny    ip 172.0.0.0 0.31.255.255 any
access-list 101 deny    ip 154.206.127.0 0.0.0.255 any
access-list 101 permit any any
!
no cdp run
```

Step 11 To hide the RFC 1918 private networks from the Internet, configure the 24-hour border routers to NAT all internal networks to the public Internet-routable IP addresses shown earlier in Table 9-15:

— Make sure all IP address blocks are aggregated to the fullest extent; all specific routes should be suppressed, and only the aggregate should be advertised to external neighbors.

— To verify customer Internet connectivity, use a web browser to enter the HTTP web configuration site on each of the service provider networks.

This step requires a few NAT and BGP configuration steps to work properly. First, you must configure NAT so that any internally routed networks are statically translated to an external IP address; if this step is not configured correctly, packets will not be forwarded and returned properly. To configure NAT for this situation, you need to configure a static network translation, as shown in Example 9-127.

Example 9-127 *NAT Configuration for the Drazen Router*

```
Drazen# show run | include nat inside source
ip nat inside source static network 10.1.1.0 155.206.124.0 /24
ip nat inside source static network 10.2.2.0 155.206.125.0 /24
ip nat inside source static network 10.3.3.0 155.206.126.0 /24
```

You can check for a successful NAT translation using the **show ip nat translations** command. When the PC issues a ping packet that is destined for any Internet IP address, you should see a successful translation on one of the border routers. Example 9-128 shows the NAT translations for the Drazen router.

Example 9-128 *Drazen Router's NAT Table*

```
Drazen# show ip nat translations
Pro Inside global     Inside local      Outside local      Outside global
--- 155.206.124.2     10.1.1.2          - - -              - - -
Subnet translation:
Inside global   Inside local   Outside local   Outside global /prefix
155.206.124.0   10.1.1.0       - - -           - - -          /24
155.206.125.0   10.2.2.0       - - -           - - -          /24
155.206.126.0   10.3.3.0       - - -           - - -          /24
```

For the upstream Internet service provider networks to reach the newly translated IP addresses, they must be advertised on the border routers by BGP. After you add the 155.206.124.0/24, 155.206.125.0/24, and 155.206.126.0/24 networks to the BGP process, these networks can be aggregated into one larger network—155.206.124.0/22. Example 9-129 shows the new BGP configuration changes on the Drazen router.

Example 9-129 *Drazen Router NAT/BGP Configuration Changes*

```
network 155.206.124.0 mask 255.255.255.0
network 155.206.125.0 mask 255.255.255.0
network 155.206.126.0 mask 255.255.255.0
aggregate-address 155.206.124.0 255.255.252.0 summary-only
```

After BGP has been properly configured, the last remaining step is to add local routes to the border routers so that they advertise the new BGP networks. This can be accomplished by adding three static routes to the Null0 interface, each with a high administrative distance. Example 9-130 shows the resulting BGP RIB on the Gaines router.

Example 9-130 *Final Gaines BGP RIB*

```
Gaines# show ip bgp | begin Network
   Network          Next Hop          Metric LocPrf Weight Path
*>i154.103.64.0/21  172.20.20.1            0    100      0 i
*>i154.103.72.0/21  172.20.20.1            0    100      0 i
*> 154.108.8.0/21   0.0.0.0                0          32768 i
*> 154.108.16.0/21  0.0.0.0                0          32768 i
*  i155.206.124.0/22 155.206.127.105           100      0 8080 i
*>                  155.206.127.105                 10000 8080 i
*                   155.206.127.106                  2000 8080 i
*  i172.20.20.0/24  172.20.20.1            0    100      0 i
*>                  0.0.0.0                0          32768 i
```

This step in this lab calls for a test on the PC located in the 10.1.1.0/24 network. To test the
routing and NAT configuration, use a web browser to open the default administrative website
on each of the Internet service provider networks. You have completed this lab after each
browser session is successfully opened. Figure 9-21 shows a successful web session from the
PC to the Farrell router.

Figure 9-21 *Successful Web Browsing Using NAT*

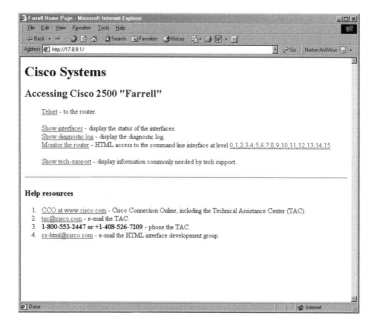

At this point, each of the routers should reach all other networks, except for the service providers, who are not allowed to use the 24-hour network for transit service. The border routers should perform BGP Internet path selection, route aggregation, simple security services, and NAT services for internal RFC 1918 networks. The Almeida and Bauer routers should load share and forward Internet traffic toward the border routers, and the Ferragamo router should provide DHCP service for the PC in the 10.1.1.0/24 network. Example 9-131 shows the complete configurations for each router in this lab.

Example 9-131 *Complete Router Configurations*

```
hostname Frame-Relay-Switch
!
frame-relay switching
!
interface Serial0
 no ip address
 encapsulation frame-relay
 frame-relay lmi-type ansi
 frame-relay intf-type dce
 frame-relay route 101 interface Serial1 100
 frame-relay route 201 interface Serial2 200
 frame-relay route 401 interface Serial4 400
!
interface Serial1
 no ip address
 encapsulation frame-relay IETF
 frame-relay lmi-type ansi
 frame-relay intf-type dce
 frame-relay route 100 interface Serial0 101
!
interface Serial2
 no ip address
 encapsulation frame-relay IETF
 frame-relay lmi-type ansi
 frame-relay intf-type dce
 frame-relay route 200 interface Serial0 201
 frame-relay route 300 interface Serial3 301
!
interface Serial3
 no ip address
 encapsulation frame-relay IETF
 frame-relay lmi-type ansi
 frame-relay intf-type dce
 frame-relay route 301 interface Serial2 300
 frame-relay route 501 interface Serial4 500
!
interface Serial4
 no ip address
 encapsulation frame-relay IETF
 frame-relay lmi-type ansi
 frame-relay intf-type dce
 frame-relay route 400 interface Serial0 401
 frame-relay route 500 interface Serial3 501
```

Example 9-131 *Complete Router Configurations (Continued)*

```
Myers# show run | begin hostname
hostname Myers
!
interface Loopback100
 ip address 154.103.64.1 255.255.248.0
!
interface Loopback200
 ip address 154.103.72.1 255.255.248.0
!
interface FastEthernet0
 ip address 172.20.20.1 255.255.255.0
!
interface Serial0
 no ip address
 encapsulation frame-relay
 clockrate 1300000
 frame-relay lmi-type ansi
!
interface Serial0.100 multipoint
 ip address 154.107.0.9 255.255.255.252
 frame-relay map ip 154.107.0.10 100 broadcast
!
router bgp 104
 no synchronization
 bgp log-neighbor-changes
 network 154.103.64.0 mask 255.255.248.0
 network 154.103.72.0 mask 255.255.248.0
 network 172.20.20.0 mask 255.255.255.0 route-map hide-network
 neighbor AS8080 peer-group
 neighbor AS8080 remote-as 8080
 neighbor AS8080 ebgp-multihop 2
 neighbor AS8080 send-community
 neighbor AS8080 route-map preference in
 neighbor AS8080 route-map external-pref out
 neighbor 155.206.127.105 peer-group AS8080
 neighbor 172.20.20.2 remote-as 104
 no auto-summary
!
ip route 155.206.127.105 255.255.255.255 154.107.0.10
ip http server
ip bgp-community new-format
ip community-list 11 permit 104:111
ip community-list 80 permit internet
!
route-map preference permit 10
 match community 11
 set weight 2000
!
```

continues

Example 9-131   *Complete Router Configurations (Continued)*

```
route-map preference permit 20
 match community 80
!
route-map external-pref permit 10
 match route-type local
 set community 104:104
!
route-map external-pref permit 20
 set community 104:222
!
route-map hide-network permit 10
 set community local-as
```

```
Gaines# show run | begin host
hostname Gaines
!
!
interface Loopback100
 ip address 154.108.8.1 255.255.248.0
!
interface Loopback200
 ip address 154.108.16.1 255.255.248.0
!
interface FastEthernet0
 ip address 172.20.20.2 255.255.255.0
!
interface Serial1
 no ip address
 encapsulation frame-relay
 clockrate 1300000
 frame-relay lmi-type ansi
!
interface Serial1.200 multipoint
 ip address 154.107.0.5 255.255.255.252
 frame-relay map ip 154.107.0.6 200 broadcast
!
interface Serial1.300 multipoint
 ip address 154.107.0.1 255.255.255.252
 frame-relay map ip 154.107.0.2 300 broadcast
!
router bgp 104
 no synchronization
 bgp log-neighbor-changes
network 154.108.8.0 mask 255.255.248.0
 network 154.108.16.0 mask 255.255.248.0
 network 172.20.20.0 mask 255.255.255.0 route-map hide-network
 neighbor AS8080 peer-group
 neighbor AS8080 remote-as 8080
 neighbor AS8080 ebgp-multihop 2
 neighbor AS8080 send-community
 neighbor AS8080 route-map preference in
 neighbor AS8080 route-map external-pref out
```

Example 9-131 *Complete Router Configurations (Continued)*

```
 neighbor 155.206.127.105 peer-group AS8080
 neighbor 155.206.127.106 peer-group AS8080
 neighbor 172.20.20.1 remote-as 104
 no auto-summary
!
ip route 155.206.127.105 255.255.255.255 154.107.0.6
ip route 155.206.127.106 255.255.255.255 154.107.0.2
ip http server
ip bgp-community new-format
ip community-list 10 permit 104:8080
ip community-list 11 permit 104:111
ip community-list 80 permit internet
!
route-map preference permit 10
 match community 10
 set weight 10000
!
route-map preference permit 20
 match community 11
 set weight 2000
!
route-map preference permit 30
 match community 80
!
route-map external-pref permit 10
 match route-type local
 set community 104:104
!
route-map external-pref permit 20
 set community 104:333
!
route-map hide-network permit 10
 set community local-as
```

```
Farrell# show run | begin host
hostname Farrell
!
interface Loopback100
 ip address 17.8.4.1 255.255.252.0
!
interface Loopback200
 ip address 17.8.8.1 255.255.252.0
!
interface Serial0
 no ip address
 encapsulation frame-relay
 clockrate 1300000
 frame-relay lmi-type ansi
!
```

continues

Example 9-131 *Complete Router Configurations (Continued)*

```
interface Serial0.400 multipoint
 ip address 101.41.12.1 255.255.255.252
 frame-relay map ip 101.41.12.2 400 broadcast
!
interface Serial0.500 multipoint
 ip address 101.41.12.5 255.255.255.252
 frame-relay map ip 101.41.12.6 500 broadcast
!
router bgp 60
 no synchronization
 bgp log-neighbor-changes
 network 17.8.4.0 mask 255.255.252.0
 network 17.8.8.0 mask 255.255.252.0
 neighbor AS8080 peer-group
 neighbor AS8080 remote-as 8080
 neighbor AS8080 ebgp-multihop 2
 neighbor AS8080 send-community
 neighbor AS8080 route-map preference in
 neighbor AS8080 route-map external-pref out
 neighbor 155.206.127.105 peer-group AS8080
 neighbor 155.206.127.106 peer-group AS8080
 no auto-summary
!
ip route 155.206.127.105 255.255.255.255 101.41.12.2
ip route 155.206.127.106 255.255.255.255 101.41.12.6
ip http server
ip bgp-community new-format
ip community-list 11 permit 60:111
ip community-list 60 permit internet
!
route-map preference permit 10
 match community 11
 set weight 2000
!
route-map preference permit 20
 match community 60
!
route-map external-pref permit 10
 match route-type local
 set community 60:60
!
route-map external-pref permit 20
 set community 60:222

Drazen# show run | begin host
hostname Drazen
!
no ip source-route
!
no ip bootp server
!
interface Loopback15
```

Example 9-131 *Complete Router Configurations (Continued)*

```
 ip address 155.206.127.105 255.255.255.255
!
interface Ethernet0/0
 ip address 155.206.127.1 255.255.255.248
  ip nat inside
!
interface Serial0/1
 no ip address
 encapsulation frame-relay
 clockrate 1300000
 frame-relay lmi-type ansi
!
interface Serial0/1.101 multipoint
 ip address 154.107.0.10 255.255.255.252
 ip access-group 101 in
 ip nat outside
 frame-relay map ip 154.107.0.9 101 broadcast
!
interface Serial0/1.201 multipoint
 ip address 154.107.0.6 255.255.255.252
 ip access-group 101 in
 ip nat outside
 frame-relay map ip 154.107.0.5 201 broadcast
!
interface Serial0/1.401 multipoint
 ip address 101.41.12.2 255.255.255.252
 ip access-group 101 in
 ip nat outside
 frame-relay map ip 101.41.12.1 401 broadcast
!
router ospf 1
 router-id 155.206.127.105
 log-adjacency-changes
 passive-interface Serial0/1
 passive-interface Serial0/1.101
 passive-interface Serial0/1.201
 passive-interface Serial0/1.401
 network 155.206.127.0 0.0.0.7 area 0
 network 155.206.127.105 0.0.0.0 area 0
 distribute-list 1 in
!
router bgp 8080
 no synchronization
 bgp log-neighbor-changes
 network 154.206.127.0 mask 255.255.255.248
 network 155.206.124.0 mask 255.255.255.0
 network 155.206.125.0 mask 255.255.255.0
 network 155.206.126.0 mask 255.255.255.0
 aggregate-address 155.206.124.0 255.255.252.0 summary-only
 neighbor AS104 peer-group
```

continues

Example 9-131 *Complete Router Configurations (Continued)*

```
 neighbor AS104 remote-as 104
 neighbor AS104 update-source Loopback15
 neighbor AS104 send-community
 neighbor AS104 route-map internal-pref in
 neighbor AS104 route-map external-pref out
 neighbor AS104 filter-list 100 out
 neighbor AS60 peer-group
 neighbor AS60 remote-as 60
 neighbor AS60 update-source Loopback15
 neighbor AS60 send-community
 neighbor AS60 route-map internal-pref in
 neighbor AS60 route-map external-pref2 out
 neighbor AS60 filter-list 100 out
 neighbor AS8080 peer-group
 neighbor AS8080 remote-as 8080
 neighbor AS8080 update-source Loopback15
 neighbor AS8080 route-reflector-client
 neighbor AS8080 next-hop-self
 neighbor 101.41.12.1 peer-group AS60
 neighbor 154.107.0.5 peer-group AS104
 neighbor 154.107.0.9 peer-group AS104
 neighbor 155.206.127.106 peer-group AS8080
 neighbor 155.206.127.107 peer-group AS8080
 neighbor 155.206.127.108 peer-group AS8080
 no auto-summary
!
ip nat inside source static network 10.1.1.0 155.206.124.0 /24
ip nat inside source static network 10.2.2.0 155.206.125.0 /24
ip nat inside source static network 10.3.3.0 155.206.126.0 /24
ip route 155.206.124.0 255.255.255.0 Null0 254
ip route 155.206.125.0 255.255.255.0 Null0 254
ip route 155.206.126.0 255.255.255.0 Null0 254
no ip http server
ip bgp-community new-format
ip community-list 4 permit 104:104
ip community-list 10 permit internet
ip community-list 14 permit 104:222
ip community-list 44 permit 104:333
ip as-path access-list 100 permit ^$
!
access-list 1 deny    0.0.0.0
access-list 1 permit any
access-list 101 deny   ip 10.0.0.0 0.255.255.255 any
access-list 101 deny   ip 192.168.0.0 0.0.255.255 any
access-list 101 deny   ip 172.0.0.0 0.31.255.255 any
access-list 101 deny   ip 154.206.127.0 0.0.0.255 any
access-list 101 permit ip any any
no cdp run
!
route-map external-pref2 permit 10
match route-type local
 set community 60:8080
```

Example 9-131 *Complete Router Configurations (Continued)*

```
!
route-map external-pref2 permit 20
 set community 60:111
!
route-map internal-pref permit 10
 match community 4
 set weight 10000
!
route-map internal-pref permit 20
 match community 14
 set weight 2000
!
route-map internal-pref permit 30
 match community 44
 set weight 1000
!
route-map internal-pref permit 40
 match community 10
!
route-map external-pref permit 10
match route-type local
 set community 104:8080
!
route-map external-pref permit 20
 set community 104:111
```

```
Palmer# show run | begin host
hostname Palmer
!
no ip source-route
!
interface Loopback15
 ip address 155.206.127.106 255.255.255.255
!
interface Ethernet0
 ip address 155.206.127.2 255.255.255.248
 ip nat inside
!
interface Serial0
 no ip address
 encapsulation frame-relay
 clockrate 1300000
 frame-relay lmi-type ansi
!
interface Serial0.301 multipoint
 ip address 154.107.0.2 255.255.255.252
 ip access-group 101 in
 ip nat outside
 frame-relay map ip 154.107.0.1 301 broadcast
!
```

continues

Example 9-131 *Complete Router Configurations (Continued)*

```
interface Serial0.501 multipoint
 ip address 101.41.12.6 255.255.255.252
 ip access-group 101 in
 ip nat outside
 frame-relay map ip 101.41.12.5 501 broadcast
!
router ospf 1
 router-id 155.206.127.106
 log-adjacency-changes
 passive-interface Serial0
 passive-interface Serial0.301
 passive-interface Serial0.501
 network 155.206.127.0 0.0.0.7 area 0
 network 155.206.127.106 0.0.0.0 area 0
 distribute-list 1 in
!
router bgp 8080
 no synchronization
 bgp router-id 154.206.127.106
 bgp log-neighbor-changes
network 155.206.124.0 mask 255.255.255.0
 network 155.206.125.0 mask 255.255.255.0
 network 155.206.126.0 mask 255.255.255.0
 network 155.206.127.0 mask 255.255.255.248
 aggregate-address 155.206.124.0 255.255.252.0 summary-only
 neighbor AS104 peer-group
 neighbor AS104 remote-as 104
 neighbor AS104 update-source Loopback15
 neighbor AS104 send-community
 neighbor AS104 route-map internal-pref in
 neighbor AS104 route-map external-pref out
 neighbor AS104 filter-list 100 out
 neighbor AS60 peer-group
 neighbor AS60 remote-as 60
 neighbor AS60 update-source Loopback15
 neighbor AS60 send-community
 neighbor AS60 route-map internal-pref in
 neighbor AS60 route-map external-pref2 out
 neighbor AS60 filter-list 100 out
 neighbor AS8080 peer-group
 neighbor AS8080 remote-as 8080
 neighbor AS8080 update-source Loopback15
 neighbor AS8080 route-reflector-client
 neighbor AS8080 next-hop-self
 neighbor 101.41.12.5 peer-group AS60
 neighbor 154.107.0.1 peer-group AS104
 neighbor 155.206.127.105 peer-group AS8080
 neighbor 155.206.127.107 peer-group AS8080
 neighbor 155.206.127.108 peer-group AS8080
 no auto-summary
!
ip nat inside source static network 10.1.1.0 155.206.124.0 /24
```

Example 9-131 *Complete Router Configurations (Continued)*

```
ip nat inside source static network 10.2.2.0 155.206.125.0 /24
ip nat inside source static network 10.3.3.0 155.206.126.0 /24
ip route 155.206.124.0 255.255.255.0 Null0 254
ip route 155.206.125.0 255.255.255.0 Null0 254
ip route 155.206.126.0 255.255.255.0 Null0 254
no ip http server
ip bgp-community new-format
ip community-list 10 permit internet
ip community-list 11 permit 60:60
ip community-list 11 permit 104:104
ip community-list 14 permit 104:333
ip community-list 60 permit 60:222
ip as-path access-list 100 permit ^$
!
access-list 1 deny    0.0.0.0
access-list 1 permit any
access-list 101 deny   ip 10.0.0.0 0.255.255.255 any
access-list 101 deny   ip 192.168.0.0 0.0.255.255 any
access-list 101 deny   ip 172.0.0.0 0.31.255.255 any
access-list 101 deny   ip 154.206.127.0 0.0.0.255 any
access-list 101 permit ip any any
no cdp run
!
route-map external-pref2 permit 10
match route-type local
 set community 60:8080
!
route-map external-pref2 permit 20
 set community 60:111
!
route-map internal-pref permit 10
 match community 11
 set weight 10000
!
route-map internal-pref permit 20
 match community 60
 set weight 2000
!
route-map internal-pref permit 30
 match community 14
 set weight 1000
!
route-map internal-pref permit 40
 match community 10
!
route-map external-pref permit 10
match route-type local
 set community 104:8080
!
route-map external-pref permit 20
```

continues

Example 9-131 *Complete Router Configurations (Continued)*

```
Almeida# show run | begin host
hostname Almeida
!
ip cef
!
interface Loopback15
 ip address 155.206.127.107 255.255.255.255
!
interface Ethernet0
 ip address 155.206.127.3 255.255.255.248
!
interface Serial0
 ip address 155.206.127.65 255.255.255.252
clockrate 1300000
!
router ospf 1
 router-id 155.206.127.107
 log-adjacency-changes network 155.206.127.0 0.0.0.7 area 0
 network 155.206.127.64 0.0.0.3 area 1
 network 155.206.127.107 0.0.0.0 area 0
 default-information originate always metric-type 1
!
router bgp 8080
 no synchronization
 bgp log-neighbor-changes
 network 155.206.127.64 mask 255.255.255.252
 neighbor 155.206.127.105 remote-as 8080
 neighbor 155.206.127.105 update-source Loopback15
 neighbor 155.206.127.106 remote-as 8080
 neighbor 155.206.127.106 update-source Loopback15
 no auto-summary
!
ip route 0.0.0.0 0.0.0.0 155.206.127.5

Bauer# show run | begin host
hostname Bauer
!
ip cef
!
interface Loopback15
 ip address 155.206.127.108 255.255.255.255
!
interface Ethernet0
 ip address 155.206.127.4 255.255.255.248
!
interface Serial0
 ip address 155.206.127.69 255.255.255.252
 clockrate 1300000
!
router ospf 1
 router-id 155.206.127.108
```

Example 9-131 *Complete Router Configurations (Continued)*

```
  log-adjacency-changes network 155.206.127.0 0.0.0.7 area 0
  network 155.206.127.68 0.0.0.3 area 1
  network 155.206.127.108 0.0.0.0 area 0
  default-information originate always metric-type 1
 !
 router bgp 8080
  no synchronization
  bgp log-neighbor-changes
  network 155.206.127.68 mask 255.255.255.0
  neighbor 155.206.127.105 remote-as 8080
  neighbor 155.206.127.105 update-source Loopback15
  neighbor 155.206.127.106 remote-as 8080
  neighbor 155.206.127.106 update-source Loopback15
  no auto-summary
 !
 ip route 0.0.0.0 0.0.0.0 155.206.127.5
```

```
Ferragamo# show run | begin host
hostname Ferragamo
!
ip dhcp excluded-address 10.1.1.1
!
ip dhcp pool workstations
   network 10.1.1.0 255.255.255.0
   default-router 10.1.1.1
   domain-name fiction.org
!
interface Loopback100
 ip address 10.2.2.1 255.255.255.0
!
interface Loopback200
 ip address 10.3.3.1 255.255.255.0
!
interface Ethernet0
 ip address 10.1.1.1 255.255.255.0
!
interface Serial0
 ip address 155.206.127.66 255.255.255.252
!
interface Serial1
 ip address 155.206.127.70 255.255.255.252
!
router ospf 1
 log-adjacency-changes network 10.1.1.0 0.0.0.255 area 1
 network 10.2.2.0 0.0.0.255 area 1
 network 10.3.3.0 0.0.0.255 area 1
 network 155.206.127.64 0.0.0.3 area 1
 network 155.206.127.68 0.0.0.3 area 1
```

Further Reading

RFC 2385, *Protection of BGP Sessions via the TCP MD5 Signature Option*, by A. Heffernan

Cisco IOS Dial Solutions, by Cisco Systems, Inc.

www.apnic.net—Asia Pacific Network Information Centre

www.arin.net—The American Registry for Internet Numbers

www.ripe.net—RIPE Network Coordination Centre

www.isoc.org—The Internet Society

www.nanog.org—The North American Network Operators' Group

CCIE Practice Labs

CCIE Preparation and Practice Labs

CCIE Preparation

> To achieve success, whatever the job we have, we must pay a price. Success is like anything worthwhile. It has a price. You have to pay the price to win and you have to pay the price to get to the point where success is possible. Most important, you must pay the price to stay there…sacrifice, perseverance, competitive drive, selflessness, and respect for authority is the price that each and every one of us must pay to achieve any goal that is worthwhile. Once you agree upon the price you and your family must pay for success, it enables you to ignore the minor hurts, the opponent's pressure, and the temporary failures.
>
> —Vince Lombardi

Entering into the ranks of the CCIEs means you are becoming a member of the most elite and skilled groups of networking engineers in the world. And the price for membership is steep. You will be required to commit yourself, and be tested to a level few people will ever know. The pressure during the months and days leading up to the test can be immense, and you will be required to perform near flawlessly under its weight.

Fortunately, you are not alone in this quest. As we head full speed into the information age, despite the dot.com bust, the need for highly skilled network engineers will always be there. As more and more engineers prepare for this test and others, more tools are becoming available. Study groups, such as routerie.com and groupstudy.com, are great places to get help from other people studying for the tests (from the only ones "who can feel your pain"). New books on routing protocols, switching, security, and many other topics are becoming available every year.

As you can see, becoming a CCIE will require a serious commitment on your part in terms of time, finances, and personal sacrifice.

The equipment needed to model CCIE labs can be very expensive. Companies such as Ascolta Training, Skyline Computer, Network Learning, and others offer labs, ISDN switches, and CCIE prep material at a reasonable rate. This can help limit the number of routers and switches you will need in your own lab. For details on setting up your CCIE lab, refer to *CCIE Practical Studies,* Volume I (*CCIE PSV1*), Chapter 1, "Modeling the Internetwork."

This text will serve as only one of many that you will have to read during your studies. The following books are a brief list of the ones that will be of great value during your studies:

Stevens: *TCP/IP Illustrated,* Volume I

Comer: *Internetworking with TCP/IP*

Pearlman: *Interconnections: Routers and Bridges*, Second Edition

Doyle: *Routing TCP/IP,* Volume I

Doyle/Carroll: *Routing TCP/IP,* Volume II

Solie: *CCIE Practical Studies,* Volume I

Solie/Lynch: *CCIE Practical Studies,* Volume II

Halabi: *Internetwork Routing Architectures*, Second Edition

Clark/Hamilton: *Cisco LAN Switching*

Caslow: *Bridges, Routers, and Switches*

Cisco Press: *CCIE Design and Case Studies*, Second Edition

Diker-Pildush: *Cisco ATM Solutions*

Cisco Press: *Troubleshooting IP Routing Protocols*

Cisco IOS Software 12.1 and 12.2 configuration guides (as many as you can bear to read)

The following list is by no means a complete list of CCIE study topics. However, it does offer a solid starting point for a list of topics with which the CCIE candidate should become *very familiar*:

- Frame Relay
    - Frame Relay switching
    - Frame Relay subinterfaces
    - Point-to-point links and multipoint links
    - Frame Relay map statements: bridge, LLC, DLSW, and other keywords
    - RFC 1490 encapsulation
    - Bridging over Frame
    - Voice over Frame
    - PPP over Frame
    - Frame Relay ARP and inverse ARP operation
    - Frame Relay traffic shaping
- HDLC
    - Compression types

- PPP
  - PPP authentication: PAP/CHAP
  - PPP callback
  - PPP multilink
  - DDR techniques
  - Virtual dialer profiles
  - Compression types
  - IPCP
- ISDN
  - Dialer maps/DDR
  - Know how to handle routing protocols over ISDN, such as RIP, EIGRP, OSPF, and so on
  - Snapshot routing
  - Dialer watch
  - OSPF demand circuits
- BGP
  - BGP theory, including BGP operation on a Cisco router
  - I-BGP versus E-BGP
  - BGP synchronization rule
  - Route reflectors
  - Hiding autonomous system numbers and creating private autonomous systems
  - Authentication
  - BGP backdoors
  - Route maps and route redistribution
  - Autonomous system path filters
  - BGP path selection process and path manipulation: MED, LOCAL_PREF, WEIGHT, and so on
  - BGP confederations
  - BGP communities
  - Advertising supernets, summarization
  - BGP interaction with IGPs
  - BGP attributes
  - Autonomous system path and community filtering, including regular expressions

- — Prefix suppression
- — Conditional route advertisements
- — Route dampening
- OSPF
  - — Redistribution to and from every routing protocol
  - — Summarization with summary address and area range statements
  - — OSPF over Frame
  - — OSPF demand circuits
  - — Route maps and route filters with OSPF
  - — OSPF costs and administrative distance
  - — Stub areas, NSS areas, backbone areas, and LSA propagation
  - — Authentication: Type I and Type II
  - — Authenticating area 0
  - — Designated router and BDR selection: **priority** command
  - — Default route propagation
- EIGRP
  - — EIGRP for IP
  - — Redistribution to and from every routing protocol
  - — Summarization
  - — Route maps and route filters with EIGRP
  - — MD5 authentication
  - — EIGRP over ISDN
  - — Split-horizons issues with multipoint networks
  - — Administrative distance of all routing protocols
  - — EIGRP stub networks
- RIP
  - — Redistribution to and from every routing protocol
  - — Snapshot routing/RIP over ISDN
  - — Split-horizons issues with multipoint networks
  - — RIPv1, issues from lack of VLSM support
  - — RIPv2
  - — RIP unicast updates

- IS-IS
  - Redistribution to and from every routing protocol
  - CLNS
  - IS-IS over Frame Relay
  - IS-IS type 1 and type 2 routes
- DLSw
  - TCP, FST, direct and Frame Relay peers
  - Backup peers
  - Promiscuous peers
  - Border peers and peer groups
  - Costed peers
  - Explorer control and LLC control with DLSw LSAP filters
- Bridging
  - Transparent bridging
  - Spanning-tree control
  - IEEE 802.1w and IEEE 802.1s
  - Bridging over Frame Relay
  - Source-route bridging
  - Remote source-route bridging
  - Translational bridging
  - Explorer control and flooding
  - LSAP filters
  - Integrated routing and bridging
  - Default gateways
- Controlling routing and traffic
  - Standard access lists
  - Extended access lists
  - Named access lists
  - Timed access lists
  - Dynamic and reflexive access lists
  - Route maps and policy routing
  - Propagating default routes

- Queuing
  - Generic and Frame Relay traffic shaping
  - RSVP, WRED basic configurations
  - Examining router configuration optimization
  - Route switching: process, fast, CEF, NetFlow, optimum, and distributed
  - Compression techniques—Predictor and Stacker
  - Quick ATM PVC theory and configuration review, including new IOS **atm** commands
  - ATM verses Frame Relay
  - ATM quality of service
  - Integrated services with RSVP
  - Differentiated services with IP ToS, Precedence, DSCP, and WRED
  - FIFO Queueing
  - Weighted Fair Queuing
  - Priority Queuing
  - Custom Queuing
  - Class-Based Weighted Fair Queuing
  - Low Latency Queuing
  - IP RTP Priority
  - Generic and Frame Relay traffic shaping and class-based shaping
  - Traffic policing
  - Committed access rate
- General IOS
  - Access server configuration
  - Jump register configuration
  - Password recovery for Catalyst and routers
  - EXEC control: timeouts, privilege levels, and so on
  - Security: encrypted tunnels, CONS, and vty access
  - Console and system logging
- IOS features
  - NAT: dynamic, static, and pooled and TCP overload
  - NTP: NTP authentication and stratum settings
  - DNS
  - HSRP: tracking and priority

- — IDRP
- — DHCP
- — Snapshot routing
- — Dialer watch
- — Mobile IP
- — ARP manipulation
- — SNMP: read/write keys, set and get traps
- — UDP flooding: **ip forward** command
- — GRE tunneling and authentication
- Catalyst
  - — Catalyst 3550 VLAN creation
  - — VTP domains
  - — Advanced spanning-tree control
  - — Spanning Tree: IEEE 802.1b, IEEE 802.1w and IEEE 802.1s
  - — Port security and IP access control
  - — VLAN maps
  - — ISL, 802.1Q trunking
  - — VLAN propagation and control over trunks
  - — Routing between VLANs
  - — Multicast routing
  - — SVIs and routed ports
  - — Layer 3 switching/routing
  - — STP load sharing with 802.1s
  - — Voice VLANs
  - — Layer 2 and Layer 3 EtherChannel
- Multicast routing
  - — Joining multicast groups
  - — Sparse and dense mode operation
  - — IGMP and CGMP
  - — Multicast issues on the Catalyst 3550

- ATM
  - Classical IP, routing over ATM
  - VPI, VCD, and VCI definition
  - ARP control
  - PVC mapping
- Voice
  - Voice over IP
  - Voice over Frame
  - Voice over ATM
  - FXO and FXS and E&M circuits
  - H.323
- VPN (mostly for the Security lab exam)
  - Encryption types
  - IPSec-protected GRE tunnels
  - IPSec transport and tunnel mode
  - Transform sets, crypto maps
  - "Key" authentication
  - CA authentication
- Removed Topics (The following topic have been removed for 2003.)
  - ATM LANE
  - AppleTalk
  - LAT
  - DECnet
  - Apollo
  - Banyan VINES
  - ISO CLNS
  - XNS
  - X.25
  - IGRP
  - IPX
  - Token Ring and Token Ring switching
  - Catalyst 5500 or CAT-OS configuration

The official equipment list for the CCIE Routing and Switching lab (November 2003) is as follows:

- 2600 series routers
- 3600 series routers
- Catalyst 3550 series switches
- 3700 series routers
- From July 7, 2003 to August 31, 2003, the CCIE program will be migrating to Cisco IOS Software 12.2. During the migration period, all exams will still be based on Cisco IOS Software 12.1 content and objectives. Note: Cisco IOS Software 12.2-specific features and commands will not be tested until September 1, 2003.

CCIE Practice Labs

The CCIE practice labs are designed to give you an accurate representation of what a CCIE lab exam actually looks like. Some labs are complete CCIE labs, which require hardware to support voice, ATM, and two Cisco 3550s; others have less stringent hardware requirements. The labs are also designed to be easily modifiable to your own hardware requirements. We realize that everyone does not have access to ATM, voice, and 3550s; therefore, every lab has different hardware requirements.

Before each lab, a complete equipment list is provided and prestaging information is included—such as the Frame Relay switch configuration, backbone router configuration, and so on. Use this information to model your own CCIE lab.

There was some debate during the creation of *CCIE PSV1* as to whether to include the answers for the practice labs. Many people, myself included, thought that by providing the answers, people would focus more on matching the answers themselves than on practicing the lab. However, we do realize the answers are sometimes very helpful to see. A Custom Queuing problem is a good example of this. For these and by reader request, we have decided to include answers on a CD-ROM. We also have included additional information and some networking utilities on the CD-ROM for you.

For further lab information and updates, check out the Cisco Press website, www.ciscopress.com.

Do not forget that practice is the most critical part of your studies. Spending hours to get just one of these problems to work on your first time through is very common. As a matter of fact, if we don't stump you somewhere, we did not do our job well. The labs have routing loops, route-feedback issues, split horizons, and all those nice things built in to them. We have come to call these "CCIE landmines." Without actually practicing the lab, you can miss many of these *fun* adventures. Try your best to resist the temptation to look at the answers if you are puzzled by one of the problems. Sometimes the best way to learn is by spending a lot of time looking for and understanding the solution. The goal is not to come up with a solution; that is implied. The ultimate goal is *practice*, *practice*, and *practice*.

With that in mind, we present to you five CCIE practice labs.

CCIE Practice Lab: Broken Arrow

Equipment List:

- 1 Frame Relay Switch: 4 serial ports
- ISDN simulator/switch with 2 BRI ports
- ATM switch with 2 ATM interfaces
- 3 lab routers: 1 Ethernet and 1 serial interface
- 1 lab router: 1 Ethernet, 1 ATM, 1 serial, 1 ISDN BRI interface
- 1 lab router: 1 Ethernet and 1 ISDN BRI interface
- 1 lab router: 2 Ethernet interfaces
- 1 lab router: 1 Ethernet and 1 ATM interface
- 2 Ethernet 3550 switches with the EMI software, 2 fiber ports or crossover cables for interconnection

Prestaging—Frame Switch and ATM Configuration

Configure the Frame Relay switch with the PVCs as depicted in Figure 10-1. Do not time yourself on this portion of the lab. The Frame Relay switch configuration is a global configuration and will be used for all labs but the third one. Not all the PVCs in the diagram are used during this lab. The PVCs indicated with a solid line are the ones used in this lab; the PVCs indicated with a dotted line are not used during this lab. Configure the ATM switch at this time, using the ATM configuration, and attach one interface to r3 and one to r7. Example 10-1 lists the configurations for the Frame and ATM switches.

Figure 10-1 *Frame Relay Switch Configuration*

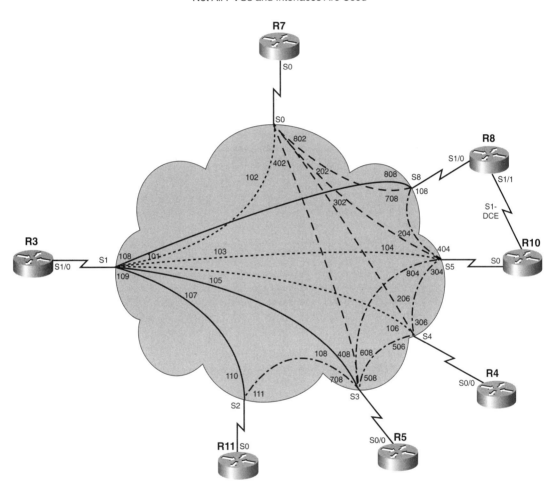

Frame Relay DLCI Map
Not All PVCs and Interfaces Are Used

Example 10-1 *Frame Relay and ATM Switch Configurations*

```
hostname frame_switch
!
frame-relay switching
!
interface Serial0
 no ip address
 encapsulation frame-relay
 no fair-queue
 clockrate 2000000
 frame-relay intf-type dce
 frame-relay route 102 interface Serial1 101
 frame-relay route 202 interface Serial5 204
 frame-relay route 302 interface Serial4 206
 frame-relay route 402 interface Serial3 408
 frame-relay route 802 interface Serial8 708
!
interface Serial1
 no ip address
 encapsulation frame-relay
 clockrate 2000000
 frame-relay intf-type dce
 frame-relay route 101 interface Serial0 102
 frame-relay route 103 interface Serial5 104
 frame-relay route 105 interface Serial4 106
 frame-relay route 107 interface Serial3 108
 frame-relay route 108 interface Serial8 808
 frame-relay route 109 interface Serial2 110
!
interface Serial2
 no ip address
 encapsulation frame-relay
 clockrate 64000
 frame-relay intf-type dce
 frame-relay route 110 interface Serial1 109
 frame-relay route 111 interface Serial3 708
!
interface Serial3
 no ip address
 encapsulation frame-relay
 clockrate 64000
 frame-relay intf-type dce
 frame-relay route 108 interface Serial1 107
 frame-relay route 408 interface Serial0 402
 frame-relay route 508 interface Serial4 506
 frame-relay route 608 interface Serial5 804
 frame-relay route 708 interface Serial2 111
!
interface Serial4
 no ip address
 encapsulation frame-relay
 clockrate 64000
```

Example 10-1 *Frame Relay and ATM Switch Configurations (Continued)*

```
 frame-relay intf-type dce
 frame-relay route 106 interface Serial1 105
 frame-relay route 206 interface Serial0 302
 frame-relay route 306 interface Serial5 304
 frame-relay route 506 interface Serial3 508
 !
interface Serial5
 no ip address
 encapsulation frame-relay
 clockrate 64000
 frame-relay intf-type dce
 frame-relay route 104 interface Serial1 103
 frame-relay route 204 interface Serial0 202
 frame-relay route 304 interface Serial4 306
 frame-relay route 404 interface Serial8 108
 frame-relay route 804 interface Serial3 608
 !
interface Serial8
 no ip address
 encapsulation frame-relay
 clockrate 64000
 frame-relay intf-type dce
 frame-relay route 108 interface Serial5 404
 frame-relay route 708 interface Serial0 802
 frame-relay route 808 interface Serial1 108
 !
no ip classless
 !
end
```

LIGHTSTREAM CONFIGURATION

```
hostname r12_ls1010
 !
atm address 47.0091.8100.0000.0061.705b.4001.0061.705b.4001.00
 !
interface ATM0/0/0
 no keepalive
 !
interface ATM0/0/1
 no keepalive
 atm pvc 1 88  interface  ATM0/0/0 1 77
 !
interface ATM0/0/2
 no keepalive
 !
interface ATM2/0/0
 no ip address
 no keepalive
 atm maxvp-number 0
```

continues

Example 10-1 *Frame Relay and ATM Switch Configurations (Continued)*

```
!
interface Ethernet2/0/0
 no ip address
!
no ip classless
!
line con 0
line aux 0
line vty 0 4
 login
!
end
```

The following portion of the lab is timed and should begin after the configuration and physical installation of all hardware.

Rules

- No static routes or floating static routes are allowed unless specifically stated.
- Follow the instructions exactly. Be careful to only propagate routes where and when instructed. Only use the PVCs as directed by the instructions.
- You can use the configuration guides and the CD-ROM for your only reference material.
- You have 8.5 hours to complete this portion of the lab. Do not talk to anyone during this phase.
- It is recommended that you read the entire lab before beginning.

Figure 10-2 *Network Diagram for Broken Arrow*

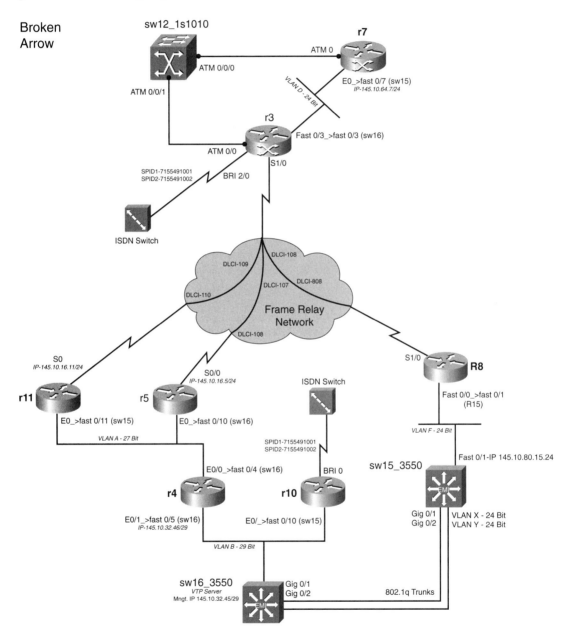

Section I: IP Setup

1   Use the IP subnet 145.10.1.19/27 on the E0 interface of r11.

2   Create virtual interfaces with the following subnets:

   — LB20-145.10.128.64/26 on r11

   — LB20-172.19.1.0/24 and LB21-172.18.1.0/24 on r10

   — LB20-206.191.1.0/24 on r5

   — VLAN X – 145.10.192.15/24 on sw15_3550

   — VLAN Y – 145.10.193.15/24 on sw15_3550

3   Use the network 145.10.0.0 for all other subnets and host addresses:

   — VLAN A: 27-bit subnet

   — VLAN B: 29-bit subnet

   — VLAN D: 24-bit subnet

   — VLAN F: 24-bit subnet

Section II: Catalyst Configuration

1   Configure an 802.1Q trunk between sw15_3550 and sw16_3550. Use the Gig 0/1 and Gig 0/2 interfaces for redundancy. Do not put IP addresses on the Gigabit interfaces. (You can use two 100BASE-T interfaces for this lab.)

2   Configure sw16_3550 to be a VTP server and sw15_3550 to be the client. Use PSV2 as the VTP domain name and ccie as the VTP password.

3   Configure the VLANs as depicted in Figure 10-2. Do not use VLAN 1.

4   Configure sw16_3550 as the root for all VLANs present and future, except for VLAN 800. sw15_3550 should be the root for VLAN 800 and serve as the secondary root for the remaining VLANs. If a new VLAN is created , it will follow these STP guidelines without additional configuration.

5   Configure Telnet access to all switches and do not use VLAN 1. The management addresses should be reachable from anywhere in the lab. sw15_3550 should be managed by VLAN F and VLAN B should be used for management on the sw16_3550 switch. Use cisco as the password.

6   Configure IEEE 802.1w RSTP between the two switches. Ensure that if a Gigabit Ethernet trunk drops, 99 percent of the traffic will still get through. That is, RSTP should converge the network in less than a second, not 50 seconds. Test by extended pings from r11 to r5 with a Gigabit Ethernet link failure. A 99-percent success rates indicates that RSTP is

working. RSTP should converge quickly on all interfaces, including ones with routers. (The two Gigabit interfaces can be substituted with two Fast Ethernet interfaces. It will not change the functionality of the lab.)

7 Ensure that all ports in use are taking advantage of 802.1w, including host/router ports.

Section III: OSPF, RIP, and Frame Relay

1 Configure the Frame Relay network between r3, r11, and r5 such that they share the same IP subnet 145.10.16.0/24.

2 Configure the Frame Relay network to be in OSPF area 0 between the routers r3, r11, and r5. Do not configure static OSPF neighbors.

3 Configure VLAN A to be in OSPF area 100. Routers r11, r5, and r4 all have an Ethernet interface in area 100. Configure VLAN D and the Frame Relay network to be in OSPF area 0.

4 Configure the Frame Relay network between r3 and r8. Configure this network and VLAN F to be in a RIP domain.

5 Use the IP address of 145.10.80.15 on interface FastEthernet 0/1 on sw15_3550. Configure this interface to exchange unicast RIP updates with r8.

6 Configure Layer 3 switching, if needed, such that all VLANs can ping each other for full IP reachability. Ensure that you can ping an address on VLAN X and VLAN Y from r11.

7 Ensure full IP reachability between the OSPF domain and the RIP domains.

8 Configure a tag equal to the host name of the router of autonomous system boundary routers (ASBRs) for the routes redistributed into OSPF. If r2 is an ASBR, for instance, when you redistribute any routing protocols into OSPF on r2, set a tag value of 2 for those routes.

9 Configure the routers r3 and r8 such that all RIP routes have an administrative distance of 95.

Section IV: EIGRP Integration

1 Configure EIGRP with AS 2003 between r10, r4, and sw16_3550.

2 Advertise the loopback networks of LB21-172.19.1.0/24 and LB20-172.18.1.0/24 on r10 via EIGRP. Prevent the RIP domains from ever seeing the 172.19.1.0/24 route. R7 should see both 172 routes.

3 Ensure full IP reachability between the EIGRP, OSPF, and RIP domains. Be sure that r10 can ping r7, VLAN X, and VLAN Y on sw15_3550.

Section V: Traffic Control and ISDN

1 Configure r4 such that Telnet traffic from VLAN B destined toward VLAN D will pass through r5. Pings from VLAN B destined toward VLAN D will go through r11. All other traffic should follow the directions in the route/forwarding table.

2 Configure the ISDN network between r10 and r3. Use the following guidelines:

— Configure r10 to only place the calls when IP connectivity is lost in any manner.

— Use PPP CHAP for authentication; use cisco as the password.

— The dialer should not remain up all the time due to routing protocols.

— Do not use static routes; routing should be dynamic.

— You can configure additional routing protocols to route across the ISDN link.

— R10 should pick up the second B channel with minimal load.

— The link should drop after 3 minutes of idle time.

Section VI: BGP

1 Configure BGP between r4 and r10.

— All I-BGP routes should be reachable in the BGP table; no NEXT_HOP attributes can be altered. You cannot use route reflectors or confederations.

— Place both routers in AS 144.

— Each router must use its VLAN B IP address for BGP identification.

— R4 should only advertise the 145.10.0.0/18 and 206.191.1.0/24 networks. One static route to an interface only (no IP addresses) can be used for this item.

— R10 should only advertise the 145.10.64.0/18 and 145.10.128.0/18 networks.

— Neither router should advertise private address space.

— Both routers should explicitly use the BGP soft-reset enhancement.

— Both routers should also have valid, reachable BGP routes to their neighbors' aggregate networks.

2 Configure BGP between r7 and the two routers in AS 144.

— Place r7 in AS 12501.

— Configure this router to use its Ethernet IP address as the BGP router ID.

— The AS 144 routers should also peer with the Ethernet IP address.

— Create two loopback interfaces: one in the 193.164.80.0/20 network and one in the 214.148.12.0/22 network.

— Advertise those networks to the E-BGP peers.

— Make r7 prefer routes to the 145.10.0.0/18, 145.10.64.0/18, and 206.191.1.0/24 networks from r4; you can not use the AS_PATH attribute for this task.

— Add r3 to AS 12501; use the directly connected interfaces for each neighbor as BGP peering points. Do not advertise new routes from this router.

3 Add r11 and r5 to AS 144; use the directly connected interfaces for each neighbor as BGP peering points. Do not advertise new routes from these routers. These routers should use their serial interfaces as their BGP router ID.

— Make r11 peer with r3, r4, and r5.

— Make r5 peer with r3, r11, and r4.

— R8 and the switches should not participate in BGP routing or learn BGP routes. All BGP routers should be able to ping any other BGP-advertised networks.

Section VII: QoS and ATM

1 Configure the ATM interfaces between r7 and r3.

— R7 should use VPI/VCI 1/77 and R3 should use 1/88.

— Both routers should have the capability to add other multipoint connections to this circuit at some point in the future.

— Both routers must have explicit PVC configurations; the ATM switch should not be relied upon for PVC configuration.

— Both routers should use the best ATM class of service for bursty data traffic, with an SCR of 1.544 and a PCR of 2.048 bps.

— Use BGP to advertise the /20 summary of the ATM network without using the **network** command. Do not advertise this network by means of IGP protocols. Remember not to advertise private networks.

— During periods of congestion, the Frame Relay-attached routers should drop packets based on IP precedence values; traffic from network 145.10.32.0/29 should have the highest noncontrol precedence value.

— Configure these routers to use the best congestion avoidance algorithm to prevent tail drop based on the IP precedence values.

Section VIII: DLSW+

1 Configure a DLSw TCP peer between VLAN B on r10 and VLAN D on r3. The peer should stay active and not disconnect while the ISDN link converges.

2 Configure another DLSw TCP peer from VLAN A on r5 to VLAN D on r3. This peer should only become active for NetBIOS traffic originating on VLAN A. The peer should drop 3 minutes after the last circuit disconnects.

3 You cannot configure **remote-peer** statements on r3.

CCIE Practice Lab: !!! Boom . . .

Equipment List:

- 1 Frame Relay switch: 4 serial ports
- ISDN simulator/switch with 2 BRI ports
- 2 lab routers: 1 Ethernet interface
- 1 lab router: 1 Fast Ethernet, 1 serial, 1 ATM, 1 ISDN BRI interface
- 1 lab router: 1 Ethernet, 1 ISDN BRI, 1 serial interface
- 1 lab router: 2 Ethernet interfaces
- 1 lab router: 1 Serial and 1 Ethernet interface
- 1 Ethernet 3550 switch with the EMI software, 2 fiber ports or crossover cables for interconnection
- 1 Ethernet 35xx Ethernet switch capable of Fast or Gigabit EtherChannel

Prestaging—Frame Relay Switch, Backbone Routers, and ATM Configuration

Configure the Frame Relay switch with the PVCs as depicted in Figure 10-3. Do not time yourself on this portion of the lab. Not all the PVCs in the diagram are used. The PVCs indicated by the solid lines are the ones you will use. Also configure the backbone routers r5 and r11 and the ATM switch. Example 10-2 lists the configurations for the Frame and ATM switches. Example 10-3 lists the configuration for the backbone routers r5 and r11.

Figure 10-3 *Frame Relay Switch Configuration*

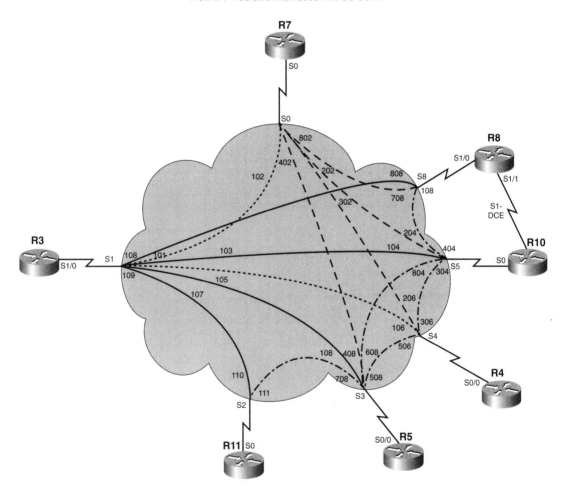

Master Frame Relay DLCI Map
Not All PVCs and Interfaces Will Be Used

Example 10-2 *Frame Relay and ATM Switch Configurations*

```
hostname frame_switch
!
frame-relay switching
```

continues

Example 10-2 *Frame Relay and ATM Switch Configurations (Continued)*

```
!
interface Ethernet0
 no ip address
 shutdown
!
interface Serial0
 no ip address
 encapsulation frame-relay
 no fair-queue
 clockrate 2000000
 frame-relay intf-type dce
 frame-relay route 102 interface Serial1 101
 frame-relay route 202 interface Serial5 204
 frame-relay route 302 interface Serial4 206
 frame-relay route 402 interface Serial3 408
 frame-relay route 802 interface Serial8 708
!
interface Serial1
 no ip address
 encapsulation frame-relay
 clockrate 2000000
 frame-relay intf-type dce
 frame-relay route 101 interface Serial0 102
 frame-relay route 103 interface Serial5 104
 frame-relay route 105 interface Serial4 106
 frame-relay route 107 interface Serial3 108
 frame-relay route 108 interface Serial8 808
 frame-relay route 109 interface Serial2 110
!
interface Serial2
 no ip address
 encapsulation frame-relay
 clockrate 64000
 frame-relay intf-type dce
 frame-relay route 110 interface Serial1 109
 frame-relay route 111 interface Serial3 708
!
interface Serial3
 no ip address
 encapsulation frame-relay
 clockrate 64000
 frame-relay intf-type dce
 frame-relay route 108 interface Serial1 107
 frame-relay route 408 interface Serial0 402
 frame-relay route 508 interface Serial4 506
 frame-relay route 608 interface Serial5 804
 frame-relay route 708 interface Serial2 111
!
interface Serial4
 no ip address
 encapsulation frame-relay
 clockrate 64000
```

Example 10-2 *Frame Relay and ATM Switch Configurations (Continued)*

```
 frame-relay intf-type dce
 frame-relay route 106 interface Serial1 105
 frame-relay route 206 interface Serial0 302
 frame-relay route 306 interface Serial5 304
 frame-relay route 506 interface Serial3 508
!
interface Serial5
 no ip address
 encapsulation frame-relay
 clockrate 64000
 frame-relay intf-type dce
 frame-relay route 104 interface Serial1 103
 frame-relay route 204 interface Serial0 202
 frame-relay route 304 interface Serial4 306
 frame-relay route 404 interface Serial8 110
 frame-relay route 804 interface Serial3 608
!
interface Serial6
 no ip address
!
interface Serial7
 no ip address
!
interface Serial8
 no ip address
 encapsulation frame-relay
 clockrate 64000
 frame-relay intf-type dce
 frame-relay route 108 interface Serial5 404
 frame-relay route 708 interface Serial0 802
 frame-relay route 808 interface Serial1 108
!
interface Serial9
 no ip address
 shutdown
!
interface BRI0
 no ip address
 shutdown
!
no ip classless
!
line con 0
line aux 0
line vty 0 4
 login
!
end

--------------------------- backbone routers ------------->
```

Example 10-3 *Backbone Router r5 and Backbone Router r11 Configurations*

```
hostname backbone_router_r5
!
clns routing
!
!
voice-port 1/0/0
!
voice-port 1/0/1
!
voice-port 1/1/0
!
voice-port 1/1/1
!
dlsw local-peer peer-id 141.200.5.5 promiscuous
dlsw icanreach netbios-name backbone_rtr5
dlsw bridge-group 1
!
interface Ethernet0/0
 ip address 141.200.5.5 255.255.255.0
 ip router isis
 bridge-group 1
!
interface Serial0/0
 no ip address
 encapsulation frame-relay
 no ip mroute-cache
!
interface Serial0/0.1 point-to-point
 ip address 140.200.1.1 255.255.255.0
 ip router isis
 no ip mroute-cache
 frame-relay interface-dlci 108
!
interface Serial0/1
 no ip address
 shutdown
 clns router isis
!
router isis
 redistribute connected metric 30 metric-type internal level-1
 distance 140
 net 00.0001.0050.736b.7800.00
!
ip classless
!
!
bridge 1 protocol ieee
!
end
-------------------------------------->
```

Example 10-3 *Backbone Router r5 and Backbone Router r11 Configurations (Continued)*

```
hostname backbone_router_r11
!
ip subnet-zero
!
isdn voice-call-failure 0
!
interface Loopback20
 ip address 192.200.16.11 255.255.255.0
 no ip directed-broadcast
!
interface Loopback21
 ip address 192.200.17.11 255.255.255.0
 no ip directed-broadcast
!
interface Loopback22
 ip address 192.200.18.11 255.255.255.0
 no ip directed-broadcast
!
interface Loopback23
 ip address 192.200.19.11 255.255.255.0
 no ip directed-broadcast
!
interface Loopback24
 ip address 192.200.20.11 255.255.255.0
 no ip directed-broadcast
!
interface Ethernet0
 description to fast 0/11 on sw15_3550
 ip address 129.200.17.11 255.255.255.0
 no ip directed-broadcast
!
<<<text omitted>>>
!
router rip
 network 129.200.0.0
 network 192.200.16.0
 network 192.200.17.0
 network 192.200.18.0
 network 192.200.19.0
 network 192.200.20.0
!
end
```

The following portion of the lab is timed and should begin after the configuration and physical installation of all hardware.

Rules

- No static routes or floating static routes are allowed unless specifically stated.
- Follow the instructions exactly. Be careful to only propagate routes where and when instructed. Only use the PVCs as directed by the instructions.

- You can use the configuration guides and the CD-ROM for your only reference material.
- You have 8.5 hours to complete this portion of the lab. Do not talk to anyone during this phase.
- It is recommended that you read the entire lab before beginning.

Figure 10-4   *Network Diagram for !!! Boom . . .*

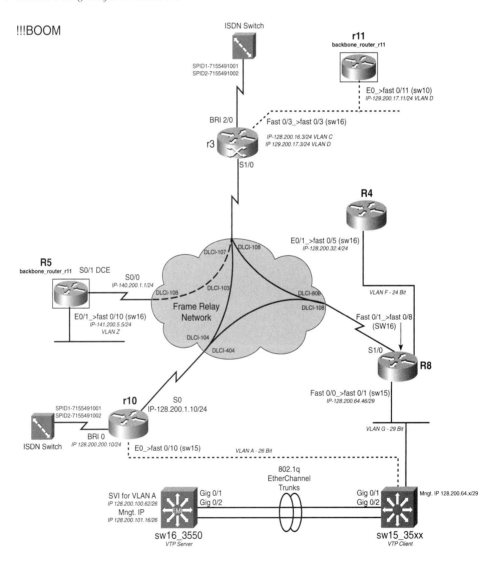

Section I: IP Setup

1 Use the IP addresses as depicted in Figure 10-4 and address the network accordingly. Note: Not all the IP addresses can be assigned at this time.

2 Use the IP addresses 128.200.16.3/24 and 129.200.17.3/24 on the Fast 3/0 interface of r3. Use VLAN C for subnet 128.200.16.0/24 and VLAN D for the 129.200.17.0/24 subnet.

3 Use the IP address of 128.200.32.4/24 on r4's E0/1. This interface is in VLAN F.

4 R8 has the Fast 0/1 interface in VLAN F and the Fast 0/0 interface in VLAN G. Use the IP address of 128.200.64.46/29 on the Fast 0/0 interface.

5 R10 will use the IP address of 128.200.1.10/24 on its s0 interface.

6 Use the network 128.200.0.0 for all other subnets and host addresses:

- VLAN A: 26-bit subnet
- VLANs C, D, F, X, Z: 24-bit subnet
- VLAN G: 6 usable host addresses

Section II: Catalyst Configuration

1 Configure an 802.1Q Gigabit EtherChannel trunk between sw15_35xx and sw16_3550 using the Gig 0/1 and Gig 0/2 interfaces. (You can substitute 100BASE-T interfaces for this lab.) Do not put IP addresses on the Gigabit interfaces. The EtherChannel trunk should be configured for PAgP.

2 Configure the VLANs as depicted in Figure 10-4.

3 Configure sw16_3550 to be a VTP server and sw15_35xx to be the client. Use ccie as the VTP domain name and password protect it.

4 Allow full configuration access to the switches by doing the following:

- Configure a management address of 128.200.101.16/24 on VLAN X on sw16_3550. Configure a management address in VLAN G on sw15_3550. Users should authenticate with the username ccie and use a password of psv2.

- Allow only two Telnet sessions per switch. If a third Telnet session is opened to the same switch, it will fail. The switches should be configurable and reachable from all routers in the lab.

Section III: OSPF, Layer 3 Switching, and Frame Relay

1 Configure a fully meshed Frame Relay network between r3, r10, and r8 such that they share the same IP subnet 128.200.1.0/24. You can only use subinterfaces on r3. You cannot change the IP OSPF network type on Frame Relay interfaces.

2   Configure the Frame Relay network to be in OSPF area 0 between r3, r10, and r8.

3   Configure VLAN A to be in OSPF area 200.

4   Do not run OSPF on the backbone to r11 VLAN D, r8 VLAN F, and r8 VLAN G.

5   Configure VLAN X on sw16_3550 to be in OSPF area 300. Configure VLAN A on the sw16_3550 to be in OPSF area 200.

6   When a link-state type 5 is created on a router, it should be tagged with the router number that created it. If r4 creates a link-state type 5, for example, it should have a tag of 4. Ensure that the OSPF domain will have full IP connectivity to the RIP, EIGRP, and IS-IS domains.

Section IV: RIP, EIGRP, IS-IS Integration

1   Configure VLAN D to be in a RIP domain, which connects to the backbone router r11. When you connect to the backbone router r11, you should receive the following RIP routes: 192.200.16.0/24, 192.200.17.0/24, 192.200.18.0/24, 192.200.19.0/24, and 192.200.20.0/24. Ensure that all OSPF routers can reach these routes.

2   Configure EIGRP on VLAN F and VLAN G only. Do not use the passive interface commands to accomplish this. Allow full reachability between the EIGRP, OSPF, and RIP domains.

3   Configure IS-IS between r3 and the backbone r5. Ensure that you see the IS-IS route 141.200.5.0/24 from the backbone r5.

4   Ensure that all routing domains can reach each other. Ensure that sw16_3550 can send 100 straight pings to all the OSPF and IS-IS Frame Relay interfaces, the IS-IS route 141.200.5.0/24, and 192.200.x.x routes from the RIP domain.

Section V: Route Filtering and Control

1   Prevent the backbone r11 from seeing any of the IS-IS routes, 140.200.1.0/24, and 141.200.5.0/24. Accomplish this with a two-line ACL.

2   Allow r4 to see only the even subnets from the RIP domain. Accomplish this with a two-line ACL.

Section VI: ISDN

1 Configure the ISDN network between r10 and r3. Use the following guidelines:

— Use the IP address of 128.200.200.10/24 on r10. This subnet should be in OSPF area 0.

— The dialer should not remain up all the time due to routing protocols. Configure r10 to only place the calls upon loss from the Frame Relay service.

— Use PPP CHAP for authentication; use cisco_isdn as the password.

— Do not use static routes; routing should be dynamic.

— R10 should pick up the second B channel when the link is used over 32 kbps of outbound traffic.

— The link should drop after 5 minutes of idle time.

Section VII: BGP

Unless otherwise specified, static routes are not allowed in this section. Do not advertise BRI interfaces into BGP. Unless otherwise specified, BGP routes cannot be redistributed into IGP routing protocols. All routers should prefer IGP routes to any BGP routes. All BGP routes should be aggregated to the smallest network prefix before being advertised to E-BGP neighbors. Have each BGP peer relationship use a static update source and BGP router ID. All routers should use the least possible configuration lines for their BGP configuration; BGP peers should be organized according to autonomous system number.

1 Configure BGP routing for r3, r8, and r10; put all of these routers in AS 5300. Have each of these routers peer with router 5 over the frame relay network. All AS 5300 routers should advertise all directly connected networks, and routes advertised to external peer should be summarized using the least number of network prefixes.

2 In addition to the previous configuration items, r3 should be configured to peer with r11, propagating all r11 routes to its I-BGP peers.

3 Configure BGP routing on r5; put this router in AS 12 and configure it to peer with the routers in AS 5300. Advertise the connected networks; then create loopbacks on the 4.0.0.0/8 and 5.5.0.0/16 networks and advertise these networks to all BGP neighbors.

4 The BGP router on r11 is in AS 500. Configure it to peer with r3. This router should use BGP authentication with all neighbors, using the password abc123. Create two loopbacks on r11, assigning them to networks 11.0.0.0/8 and 12.0.0.0/8, and advertise these networks to all BGP peers. Configure this router so that the routes sent to routers in AS 5300 will not propagate the route; no changes can be made on the AS 5300 routers to support this configuration.

5 Configure BGP routing on r4. Put this router in AS 101 and configure it to peer with router r8. Create two loopback interfaces on r4, assigning one to the 118.116.0.0/24 network and the other to the 117.116.115.0/24 network; advertise this network and all other connected networks to r8.

6 Configure r8 to hide r4's 117.116.115.0/24 network from r5 and, without making changes on r3 or r10, prevent the other AS 5300 routers from advertising that network to any peers.

7 Configure a single static route on sw16_3550 to the network 141.200.5.0/24 on backbone router r5. Do not use a default route.

Section VIII: QoS

1 Configure r8 with a policy that limits bandwidth consumption on its Frame Relay interface based on packet size. Use the packet size and bandwidth percentages shown in Table 10-1. Follow Cisco's interface bandwidth and queuing recommendations when allocating bandwidth restrictions.

Table 10-1 *r8 Policy Parameters*

Packet Size	Bandwidth Limitation
64 to 127	28%
128 to 255	10%
256 to 511	18%
512 to 767	9%
768 to 1024	6%
Other	Queue using WFQ

Section IX: DLSW+

1 Configure a DLSw TCP peer between VLAN A on r10 and 141.200.5.5 on r5, the backbone router. You should see backbone_rtr5 in the DLSW reachability cache when this is complete.

2 If you lose connectivity to the 141.200.5.5 peer, another peer should become active on r5 that peers to r4's VLAN F, where the backup server resides. You cannot use a **remote-peer** statement on r5.

3 When the peer is active from r10 to r4, r4 should advertise the NetBIOS host backup r4. This peer should remain active up to 3 minutes after connectivity to the primary peer is restored.

CCIE Practice Lab: The Intimidator

Equipment List:

- 1 Frame Relay switch: 4 serial ports
- 7 lab routers: 1 Ethernet and 2 serial interfaces
- 2 lab routers: 1 Fast Ethernet, 2 serial, and 1 voice (1750s)
- 1 Ethernet 35xx Ethernet switch capable of extended VLANs

Prestaging—Frame Relay Switch and Backbone Router Configuration

Configure the Frame Relay switch with the PVCs as depicted in Figure 10-5. Do not time yourself on this portion of the lab. Configure the backbone routers bb-1, bb-2, and bb-3. Example 10-4 lists the configurations for the Frame Relay switch and the backbone routers, bb-1, bb-2, and bb-3.

Example 10-4 *Frame Relay and Backbone Router Configurations*

```
hostname frame_switch
!
ip subnet-zero
!
no ip domain-lookup
!
frame-relay switching
!
interface Serial0
 no ip address
 encapsulation frame-relay IETF
 frame-relay lmi-type ansi
 frame-relay intf-type dce
 frame-relay route 304 interface Serial1 403
 frame-relay route 305 interface Serial2 503
 frame-relay route 306 interface Serial3 603
!
interface Serial1
 no ip address
 encapsulation frame-relay IETF
 clockrate 1300000
 frame-relay lmi-type ansi
 frame-relay intf-type dce
 frame-relay route 403 interface Serial0 304
!
interface Serial2
 no ip address
 encapsulation frame-relay IETF
 clockrate 1300000
 frame-relay lmi-type ansi
```

continues

Example 10-4 *Frame Relay and Backbone Router Configurations (Continued)*

```
 frame-relay intf-type dce
 frame-relay route 503 interface Serial0 305
 !
interface Serial3
 no ip address
 encapsulation frame-relay IETF
 logging event dlci-status-change
 frame-relay lmi-type ansi
 frame-relay intf-type dce
 frame-relay route 603 interface Serial0 306
 !
no cdp run
 !
end
--------------------- bb-1 config --------------------->
hostname bb-1
 !
logging buffered 4096 debugging
no logging console
ip subnet-zero
no ip source-route
 !
no ip domain lookup
 !
interface Loopback10
 ip address 177.164.12.1 255.255.252.0
 !
interface Loopback20
 ip address 177.164.16.1 255.255.252.0
 !
interface Loopback30
 ip address 2.0.0.1 255.0.0.0
 !
interface Loopback40
 ip address 8.0.0.1 255.0.0.0
 !
interface Loopback50
 ip address 16.0.0.1 255.0.0.0
 !
interface Ethernet0/0
 ip address 55.9.6.1 255.255.255.248
 half-duplex
 !
interface Serial0/0
 ip address 177.164.8.5 255.255.255.252
 clockrate 1300000
 !
interface Serial0/1
 ip address 177.164.8.9 255.255.255.252
```

Example 10-4 *Frame Relay and Backbone Router Configurations (Continued)*

```
!
interface Serial0/2
 no ip address
 shutdown
!
ip classless
no ip http server
!
end
-------------------- bb-2 config -------------------->
hostname bb-2
no logging console
!
ip subnet-zero
no ip domain lookup
!
interface Loopback10
 ip address 55.9.8.1 255.255.248.0
!
interface Loopback20
 ip address 55.9.16.1 255.255.248.0
!
interface Loopback30
 ip address 2.0.0.2 255.0.0.0
!
interface Loopback40
 ip address 8.0.0.2 255.0.0.0
!
interface Loopback50
 ip address 16.0.0.2 255.0.0.0
!
interface Ethernet0
 ip address 55.9.6.2 255.255.255.248
!
interface Serial0
 ip address 55.9.5.6 255.255.255.252
 clockrate 1300000
!
interface Serial1
 ip address 55.9.5.10 255.255.255.252
!
ip classless
ip http server
!
end
-------------------- bb-3 config -------------------->
hostname bb-3
!
logging buffered 4096 debugging
no logging console
```

continues

Example 10-4 *Frame Relay and Backbone Router Configurations (Continued)*

```
!
ip subnet-zero
!
no ip domain lookup
!
interface Loopback10
 ip address 168.101.12.1 255.255.252.0
!
interface Loopback20
 ip address 168.101.16.1 255.255.252.0
!
interface Loopback30
 ip address 2.0.0.3 255.0.0.0
!
interface Loopback40
 ip address 8.0.0.3 255.0.0.0
!
interface Loopback50
 ip address 16.0.0.3 255.0.0.0
!
interface FastEthernet0
 ip address 55.9.6.3 255.255.255.248
 speed auto
!
interface Serial0
 ip address 192.168.2.1 255.255.255.252
!
interface Serial1
 ip address 168.101.8.1 255.255.255.252
 clockrate 1300000
!
ip classless
no ip http server
!
call rsvp-sync
!
voice-port 2/0
!
voice-port 2/1
!
dial-peer cor custom
!
!
end
```

Figure 10-5 *Frame Relay Switch Configuration*

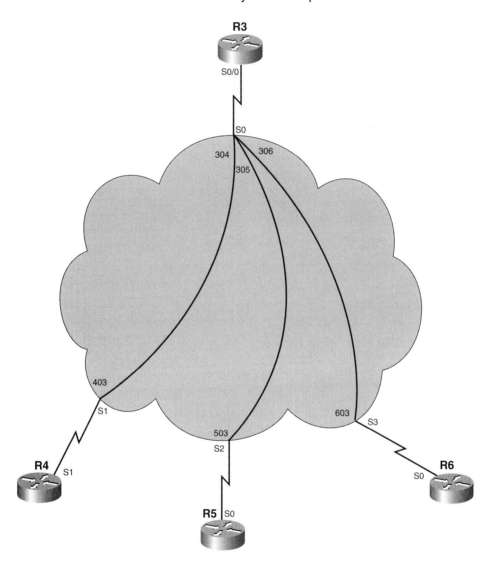

The following portion of the lab is timed and should begin after the configuration and physical installation of all hardware.

Rules

- No static routes or floating static routes are allowed unless specifically stated. This lab allows you to use a very limited amount of static routes. When you can use a static route, it is clearly noted.

- Follow the instructions exactly. Be careful to only propagate routes where and when instructed. Only use the PVCs as directed by the instructions.

- You can use the configuration guides and the CD-ROM for your only reference material.

- You have 8.5 hours to complete this portion of the lab. Do not talk to anyone during this phase.

- It is recommended that you read the entire lab before beginning.

Section I: IP Setup

1 Use the IP addresses as depicted in Figure 10-6 and address the network accordingly. Note: Not all the IP addresses can be assigned at this time.

   — Use the IP subnet of 10.12.13.0/24 for VLAN A, joining r1, r2, and r3.

   — Use the IP address of 10.12.64.5 on r5's E0 port. This interface is in VLAN C.

   — R4 will use the IP address of 192.168.2.2/30 on its s0 interface to the backbone router bb-3.

   — R6, r4, and r3 all share the same IP subnet on the WAN and should be configured as such. R6 serial 0 interface should have an IP address of 10.12.12.51/29, and r4 should have an IP address of 10.12.12.50/29 on its serial interface.

   — Use the network 10.12.0.0 for all other subnets and host addresses:

   VLANs A, B, C: 24-bit subnet

Section II: Catalyst Configuration

1 Configure *all* the VLANs as depicted in Figure 10-6. Do not use VLAN 1. The valid VLAN range you can use is 2000 to 3000.

2 Name the VTP domain name labx. Configure STP such that if new switches are added to the backbone subnet of 55.9.6.0/29, sw16_3550 will remain root.

3 Configure the switch with the IP address of 10.12.13.2/24. Configure the switch such that it can be reachable via IP. The switch should be reachable if r1, r2, or r3 goes down.

Figure 10-6 *Network Diagram for the Intimidator*

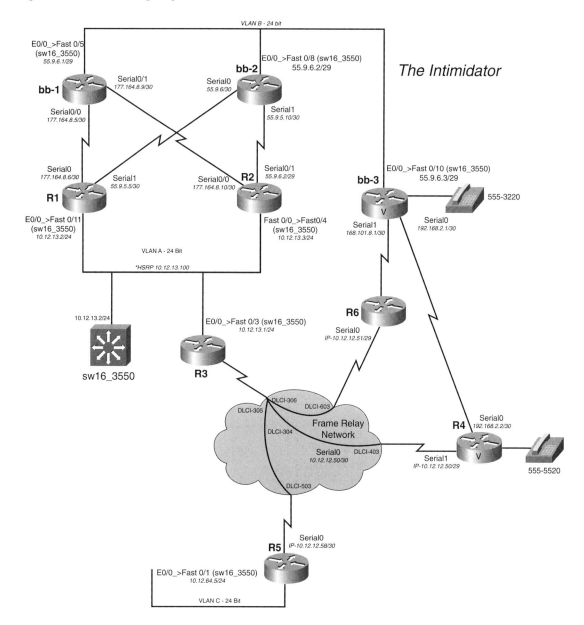

Section III: OSPF and Frame Relay

1 Configure a partial-mesh Frame Relay network between r3, r6, and r4 such that they share the same IP subnet. You can only use subinterfaces on r3.

2 Configure VLAN A to be in OSPF area 0.

3 Configure the Frame Relay network to be in OSPF area 100 between the routers r3, r6, and r4. You cannot use **neighbor** statements.

4 Configure area 100 such that all external link states will appear as link-state type 7s on r6 and r4.

Section IV: EIGRP Integration

1 Configure EIGRP on VLAN C and the Frame Relay network between r3 and r5.

2 Configure r5 to be an EIGRP stub router. Ensure that r5 will advertise VLAN C. Allow full reachability between the EIGRP and OSPF domains. Ensure that r5 can ping the serial interfaces of bb-3 and the LAN interfaces of r1 and r2.

Section V: HSRP

1 Configure HSRP for VLAN A, such that r1 will be primary. Use the IP address of 10.12.13.100 as the shared IP address.

2 If r1 loses its serial interface, r2 will be primary. If r1 and r2 lose both of their serial interfaces, r3 should become primary.

Section VI: BGP

1 Each router should use an explicitly configured BGP router ID. This ID should be the lowest IP address belonging to the locally generated public address space. For example, bb-1 would use 177.164.8.5 for its BGP router ID. All BGP speakers should use the largest available update packet size. Do not allow the backbone routers (bb-1, bb-2, or bb-3) to use the lab routers (r1, r2, and r6) as a transit.

2 Configure BGP for the backbone routers using the information shown in Table 10-2.

3 Wherever possible, network prefixes should be aggregated to the smallest mask size.

4 Routers bb-1 and bb-3 should use bb-2 as a transit network to reach each other.

Table 10-2   *Backbone BGP Configuration*

Router	Autonomous System Number	Remote Peer	Advertised Networks
bb-1	65	bb-2's Ethernet0 interface	177.164.8.0/22
			177.164.12.0/22
			177.164.16.0/22
		R2's serial0/0 interface	177.164.8.0/22
			177.164.12.0/22
			177.164.16.0/22
			2.0.0.0/8
			8.0.0.0/8
			16.0.0.0/8
		R1's serial0 interface	177.164.8.0/22
			177.164.12.0/22
			177.164.16.0/22
			2.0.0.0/8
			8.0.0.0/8
			16.0.0.0/8
bb-2	104	bb-1's Ethernet0/0 interface	55.9.0.0/21
			55.9.8.0/21
			55.9.16.0/21
		R1's serial1 interface	55.9.0.0/21
			55.9.8.0/21
			55.9.16.0/21
			2.0.0.0/8
			8.0.0.0/8
			16.0.0.0/8

continues

Table 10-2 *Backbone BGP Configuration (Continued)*

Router	Autonomous System Number	Remote Peer	Advertised Networks
		R2's serial0/1 interface	55.9.0.0/21
			55.9.8.0/21
			55.9.16.0/21
			2.0.0.0/8
			8.0.0.0/8
			16.0.0.0/8
bb-3	12	R6's serial1 interface	168.101.8.0/22
			168.101.12.0/22
			168.101.16.0/22
			2.0.0.0/8
			8.0.0.0/8
			16.0.0.0/8
		bb-2's Ethernet0 interface	168.101.8.0/22
			168.101.12.0/22
			168.101.16.0/22
		bb-1's Ethernet0/0 interface	168.101.8.0/22
			168.101.12.0/22
			168.101.16.0/22

5 Enable BGP routing on r1.

6 Put this router in AS 10142 and advertise the locally connected 196.200.32.0/20 network to all neighbors.

7 This router should peer with bb-1, bb-2, and r2; each peer should be set up to use the directly connected IP address for BGP peering.

8 Locally originated routes should be aggregated to the smallest prefix size.

9 This router should also advertise the other 196.200.x.0 networks from r2 and r6; however, these routes should be advertised so that their external peers prefer the routes from their originating peer router. The AS_PATH attribute cannot be used for this step. Two static routes can be added to this router for this step.

10 Enable BGP routing on r2.

11 Put this router in AS 10142 and advertise the locally connected 196.200.48.0/20 network to all neighbors.

12 This router should peer with bb-1, bb-2, and r1; each peer should be set up to use the directly connected IP address for BGP peering.

13 Locally originated routes should be aggregated to the smallest prefix size.

14 This router should also advertise the other 196.200.x.0 networks from r1 and r6; however, these routes should be advertised so that their external peers prefer the routes from their originating peer router. The AS_PATH attribute cannot be used for this step. Two static routes can be added to this router for this step.

15 Configure r1 so that it prefers routes to the 2.0.0.0/8 and 8.0.0.0/8 networks from bb-1 and the route to 16.0.0.0/8 network from bb-2. These settings should not be passed to any routers, and the AS_PATH attribute cannot be used for this step.

16 Enable BGP routing on r6.

17 Put this router in AS 10142 and advertise the locally connected 196.200.64.0/20 network to all neighbors.

18 This router should peer with bb-3, r1, and r2; each peer should be set up to use the directly connected IP address for BGP peering.

19 Locally originated routes should be aggregated to the smallest prefix size.

20 This router should also advertise the other 196.200.x.0 networks from r1 and r2; however, these routes should be advertised so that their external peers prefer the routes from their originating peer router. The AS_PATH attribute cannot be used for this step. Two static routes can be added to this router for this step.

21 Configure BGP routing between r1 and r6 and r2 and r6. Configure these routers to reach each other's locally originating BGP networks using Layer 2 VPN interfaces.

Section VII: Voice

1 Configure Voice over IP between these two routers using the 192.168.2.0/30 network as follows:

2 Attach a phone to port 2/0 on r4. This phone will be assigned the 555-5520 phone number.

3 Attach a phone to port 2/0 on bb-3. This phone will use the 555-3220 phone number.

4 Use the g723r63 codec for each voice connection.

5 Configure r5 so that when the phone is picked up, it automatically calls bb-3.

6 Configure bb-3 so that it dials r5 whenever either the 555-5520 or 811 numbers are dialed.

Section VIII: QoS

1 Configure each outbound backbone connection on routers r1, r2, and r6 so that they will drop traffic based on IP precedence values during periods of congestion.

2 Configure r3 with the following policy:

— All traffic on TCP port 80 should be limited to 20% of the Ethernet0/0 interface's bandwidth. Any HTTP traffic should proactively be dropped using WRED.

— All other traffic should be queued using Weighted Fair Queuing.

— Configure RSVP for all voice calls between the two Voice over IP callers; make sure that RSVP only allows enough bandwidth for the two callers and that the EF-PHB is used for all calls.

— Configure each Voice over IP session to request guaranteed rate QoS and use the EF-PHB for all incoming calls.

Section IX: DLSW+

1 Configure a DLSw+ peer between VLAN A on r3 and VLAN C on r5. Configure the peer such that it supports RFC 1490, with reliable delivery and local acknowledgment.

2 Configure the peer such that only SNA traffic will be allowed to cross the DLSw+ connection.

CCIE Practice Lab: Enchilada II

Equipment List:

- 1 Frame Relay switch: 5 serial ports
- ISDN simulator/switch with 2 BRI ports
- ATM switch with 2 ATM interfaces
- 2 lab routers: 1 Ethernet and 1 serial interface
- 1 lab router: 1 Fast Ethernet, 1 serial, 1 ATM, and 1 ISDN BRI
- 1 lab router: 1 Ethernet, 1 ISDN BRI, and 1 serial
- 1 lab router: 2 Ethernet and 1 serial
- 1 lab router: 1 ATM
- 1 lab router: 1 Ethernet
- 1 Ethernet 3550 switch with the EMI software, with 2 fiber ports or crossover cables for interconnection
- 1 Ethernet 35xx Ethernet switch

Prestaging—Frame Relay Switch, Backbone Routers, and ATM Configuration

Configure the Frame Relay switch with the PVCs as depicted in Figure 10-7. Do not time yourself on this portion of the lab. Not all the PVCs in the diagram are used. Also, configure the backbone routers r5 and r11 and the ATM switch. Example 10-5 lists the configurations for the Frame and ATM switches. Example 10-6 lists the configuration for the backbone routers r5 and r11.

Figure 10-7 *Frame Relay Switch Configuration*

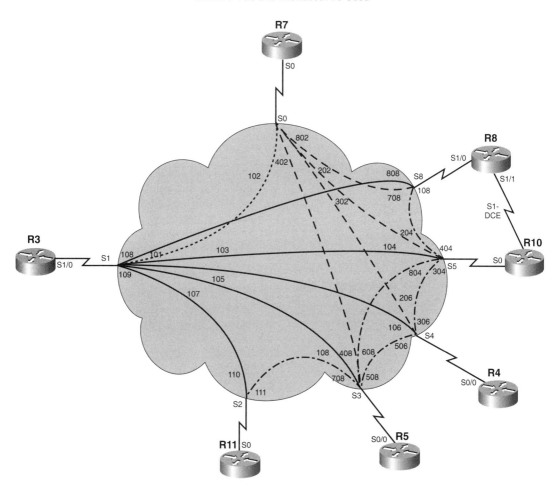

Master Frame Relay DLCI Map
Not All PVCs and Interfaces Are Used

Example 10-5 *Frame Relay and ATM Switch Configurations*

```
hostname frame_switch
!
frame-relay switching
!
interface Ethernet0
 no ip address
 shutdown
!
interface Serial0
 no ip address
 encapsulation frame-relay
 no fair-queue
 clockrate 2000000
 frame-relay intf-type dce
 frame-relay route 102 interface Serial1 101
 frame-relay route 202 interface Serial5 204
 frame-relay route 302 interface Serial4 206
 frame-relay route 402 interface Serial3 408
 frame-relay route 802 interface Serial8 708
!
interface Serial1
 no ip address
 encapsulation frame-relay
 clockrate 2000000
 frame-relay intf-type dce
 frame-relay route 101 interface Serial0 102
 frame-relay route 103 interface Serial5 104
 frame-relay route 105 interface Serial4 106
 frame-relay route 107 interface Serial3 108
 frame-relay route 108 interface Serial8 808
 frame-relay route 109 interface Serial2 110
!
interface Serial2
 no ip address
 encapsulation frame-relay
 clockrate 64000
 frame-relay intf-type dce
 frame-relay route 110 interface Serial1 109
 frame-relay route 111 interface Serial3 708
!
interface Serial3
 no ip address
 encapsulation frame-relay
 clockrate 64000
 frame-relay intf-type dce
 frame-relay route 108 interface Serial1 107
 frame-relay route 408 interface Serial0 402
 frame-relay route 508 interface Serial4 506
 frame-relay route 608 interface Serial5 804
 frame-relay route 708 interface Serial2 111
```

Example 10-5 *Frame Relay and ATM Switch Configurations (Continued)*

```
!
interface Serial4
 no ip address
 encapsulation frame-relay
 clockrate 64000
 frame-relay intf-type dce
 frame-relay route 106 interface Serial1 105
 frame-relay route 206 interface Serial0 302
 frame-relay route 306 interface Serial5 304
 frame-relay route 506 interface Serial3 508
!
interface Serial5
 no ip address
 encapsulation frame-relay
 clockrate 64000
 frame-relay intf-type dce
 frame-relay route 104 interface Serial1 103
 frame-relay route 204 interface Serial0 202
 frame-relay route 304 interface Serial4 306
 frame-relay route 404 interface Serial8 110
 frame-relay route 804 interface Serial3 608
!
interface Serial6
 no ip address
!
interface Serial7
 no ip address
!
interface Serial8
 no ip address
 encapsulation frame-relay
 clockrate 64000
 frame-relay intf-type dce
 frame-relay route 108 interface Serial5 404
 frame-relay route 708 interface Serial0 802
 frame-relay route 808 interface Serial1 108
!
interface Serial9
 no ip address
 shutdown
!
interface BRI0
 no ip address
 shutdown
!
no ip classless
!
end
----------------------------- ATM --------------------------->
```

continues

Example 10-5 *Frame Relay and ATM Switch Configurations (Continued)*

```
hostname ls1010
!
!
atm address 47.0091.8100.0000.0061.705b.4001.0061.705b.4001.00
!
interface ATM0/0/0
 no keepalive
 no atm auto-configuration
 no atm address-registration
 no atm ilmi-enable
 no atm ilmi-lecs-implied
!
interface ATM0/0/1
 no keepalive
 no atm auto-configuration
 no atm address-registration
 no atm ilmi-enable
 no atm ilmi-lecs-implied
 atm pvc 1 101  interface  ATM0/0/0 1 102
!
interface ATM0/0/2
 no keepalive
!
interface ATM0/0/3
 no keepalive
!
!
interface ATM1/1/3
 no keepalive
!
interface ATM2/0/0
 no ip address
 no keepalive
 atm maxvp-number 0
!
interface Ethernet2/0/0
 no ip address
!
no ip classless
logging buffered
!
line con 0
line aux 0
line vty 0 4
 login
!
end
--------------------------- backbone routers ------------->
```

Example 10-6 *Backbone Router r5 and Backbone Router r11 Configurations*

```
hostname backbone_router_r5
!
ip tcp path-mtu-discovery
!
voice-port 1/0/0
!
voice-port 1/0/1
!
voice-port 1/1/0
!
voice-port 1/1/1
!
interface Loopback0
 ip address 201.201.5.5 255.255.255.0
!
interface Loopback4
 ip address 4.4.4.4 255.0.0.0
!
interface Loopback6
 ip address 6.6.6.6 255.0.0.0
!
interface Loopback12
 ip address 12.1.1.1 255.0.0.0
!
interface Loopback55
 ip address 5.5.5.5 255.255.0.0
!
interface Ethernet0/0
 ip address 10.1.2.5 255.255.255.0
!
interface Serial0/0
 ip address 10.1.1.5 255.255.255.0
 encapsulation frame-relay
 ip ospf network point-to-point
 no ip mroute-cache
 frame-relay interface-dlci 108
!
interface Serial0/1
 no ip address
 shutdown
!
router ospf 2003
 network 10.1.0.0 0.0.255.255 area 500
 area 500 stub
!
router bgp 65001
 no synchronization
 bgp router-id 10.1.1.5
 bgp confederation identifier 10001
```

continues

Example 10-6 *Backbone Router r5 and Backbone Router r11 Configurations (Continued)*

```
 bgp confederation peers 65002
 network 4.0.0.0
 network 5.5.0.0 mask 255.255.0.0
 network 6.0.0.0
 network 12.0.0.0
 neighbor AS65001 peer-group
 neighbor AS65001 remote-as 65001
 neighbor AS65001 route-reflector-client
 neighbor AS65001 update-source Serial0/0
 neighbor AS65001 next-hop-self
 neighbor 10.1.1.3 peer-group AS65001
 no auto-summary
!
ip classless
!
logging buffered 4096 debugging
!
end

---------------------------------------->
hostname backbone_router_r11
!
ip subnet-zero
ip tcp path-mtu-discovery
!
isdn voice-call-failure 0
!
interface Loopback20
 ip address 192.200.16.11 255.255.255.0
 no ip directed-broadcast
!
interface Loopback21
 ip address 192.200.17.11 255.255.255.0
 no ip directed-broadcast
!
interface Loopback22
 ip address 192.200.18.11 255.255.255.0
 no ip directed-broadcast
!
interface Loopback23
 ip address 192.200.19.11 255.255.255.0
 no ip directed-broadcast
!
interface Loopback24
 ip address 192.200.20.11 255.255.255.0
 no ip directed-broadcast
!
interface Loopback88
 ip address 88.8.8.8 255.255.0.0
 no ip directed-broadcast
```

Example 10-6 *Backbone Router r5 and Backbone Router r11 Configurations (Continued)*

```
!
interface Ethernet0
 description to fast 0/11 on sw15_3550
 ip address 192.168.2.11 255.255.255.0
 no ip directed-broadcast
 ip ospf message-digest-key 2 md5 trustno1
!
interface Serial0
 no ip address
 no ip directed-broadcast
 no ip mroute-cache
 shutdown
!
interface Serial1
 no ip address
 no ip directed-broadcast
 shutdown
!
router ospf 2003
 area 0 authentication message-digest
 network 192.168.2.11 0.0.0.0 area 0
 network 192.200.0.0 0.0.255.255 area 200
!
router bgp 96
 bgp router-id 192.168.2.11
 bgp cluster-id 2177372427
 network 88.8.0.0 mask 255.255.0.0
 neighbor 192.168.2.1 remote-as 10001
 neighbor 192.168.2.1 password :)router
 neighbor 192.168.2.1 update-source Ethernet0
!
ip classless
no ip http server
!
end
```

The following portion of the lab is timed and should begin after the configuration and physical installation of all hardware.

Rules

- No static routes or floating static routes are allowed unless specifically stated.
- Follow the instructions exactly. Be careful to only propagate routes where and when instructed. Only use the PVCs as directed by the instructions.
- You can use the configuration guides and the CD-ROM for your only reference material.

- You have 8.5 hours to complete this portion of the lab. Do not talk to anyone during this phase.

- It is recommended that you read the entire lab before beginning.

- Make an accurate and precise network illustration.

Figure 10-8 *Network Diagram for Enchilada II*

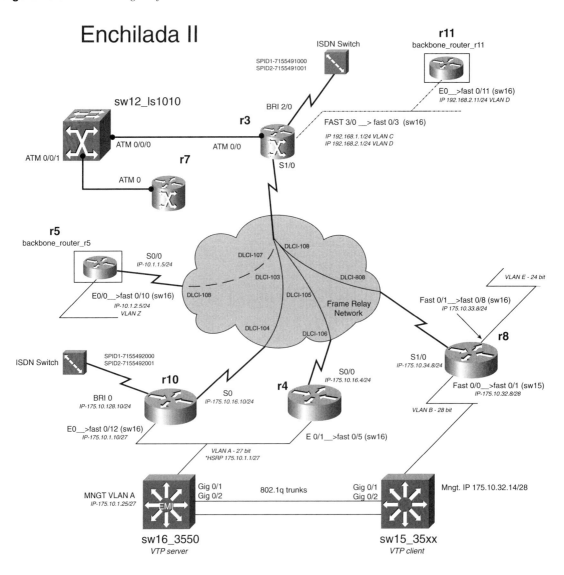

Section I: IP Setup

1 Use the IP addresses as depicted in Figure 10-8 and address the network accordingly. Note: Not all the IP addresses can be assigned at this time.

2 Use the IP subnets 192.168.1.0/24 and 192.168.2.0/24 on the Fast 3/0 interface of r3. Use VLAN C for subnet 192.168.1.0/24 and VLAN D for the 192.168.2.0/24 subnet.

3 Use the IP address of 175.10.1.10/27 on r10's E0 interface. This interface is in VLAN A, along with r4's e0/1 interface.

4 R8 has the Fast 0/1 interface in VLAN E and the Fast 0/0 interface in VLAN B. Use the IP address of 175.10.33.8/24 on the Fast 0/1 interface and 175.10.32.8/28 on the Fast 0/0 interface.

5 Use the network 175.10.0.0 for all other subnets and host addresses:

— VLAN: 27-bit subnet

— VLAN B: 28-bit subnet

— VLANs C, D, E, Z: 24-bit subnet

Section II: Catalyst Configuration

1 Configure an 802.1Q Gigabit trunk between sw15_35xx and sw16_3550 using the Gig 0/1 and Gig 0/2 interfaces. (You can substitute 100BASE-T interfaces for this lab.) Do not put IP addresses on the Gigabit interfaces.

2 Configure the VLANs as depicted in Figure 10-8. Do not use VLAN 1.

3 Configure sw16_3550 to be a VTP server and sw15_35xx to be the client. Use PSV2 as the VTP domain name and authenticate VTP with the password cisco.

4 Configure sw16_3550 to support 802.1w RSTP and 802.1s MSTP. Create three STP instances; use the following guidelines:

— Instance 0: VLAN 1, STP priority 8192

— Instance 1: VLANs 100–200, STP priority 4096

— Instance 2: VLANs 2–99, 201–4094, STP priority 16834

— Make sure 802.1w works with 802.1d on the sw15_35xx switch. That is, the VLAN priority for the VLANs noted above should be the same on sw15_35xx.

— Ensure that ports on the switch that are connected to hosts are configured for 802.1w.

5 Sw16_3550 should be reachable using the IP address 175.10.1.25/27, and sw15_35xx should be reachable via the IP address 175.10.32.14/28. You cannot configure a default or static route on sw16_3550.

Section III: EIGRP, Layer 3 Switching, and Frame Relay

1   Configure a partial-mesh Frame Relay network between r3, r10, and r4. You can only use subinterfaces on r3.

2   Configure EIGRP over the Frame Relay network between r3, r10, and r4. Use the autonomous system ID of 2003.

3   Configure EIGRP on VLAN A between r10, r4, and sw16_3550. Enable Layer 3 switching on sw16_3550 to accomplish this.

Section IV: RIP, OSPF Integration

1   Configure OSPF between r3 and the backbone router r11. Configure VLAN C to be in OSPF area 100 and VLAN D in OSPF area 0.

Authenticate OSPF area 0 with Type II authentication.

2   When you connect to the backbone router r11, you should receive the following OSPF routes: 192.200.16.0/24, 192.200.17.0/24, 192.200.18.0/24, 192.200.19.0/24, and 192.200.20.0/24. Ensure that all routers can reach these routes, including the RIP and EIGRP domains.

3   Configure OSPF between r3 and the backbone router r5 over the Frame Relay network. Configure the Frame Relay network to be in area 500. Area 500 should be configured as a stub area.

4   Configure RIPv2 between r3 and r8. VLAN E and VLAN B should run RIPv2, too.

Use MD5 authentication for RIP updates over the Frame Relay link.

Section V: Route Filtering and HSRP

1   R10 and r4 should have EIGRP external routes 192.200.16.0/24, 192.200.17.0/24, 192.200.18.0/24, 192.200.19.0/24, and 192.200.20.0/24. R10 should only propagate the odd 192.200.0.0 subnets to sw16_3550. R4 should only propagate the even 192.200.0.0 subnets to sw16_3550.

2   Configure HSRP between r10, r4, and sw16_3550. Use 175.10.1.1/27 for the HSRP address.

Authenticate HSRP updates between all devices. Use the password trustno1.

R10 should be the default primary router. If r10 loses it serial interface, r4 should become primary. If r4 loses its serial interface and the r10 serial interface is down, sw16_3550 should become the HSRP primary.

Section VI: ISDN

1 Configure the ISDN network between r10 and r3. Use the following guidelines:

— Use the IP address of 175.10.128.10/24 on r10. This subnet should be in the EIGRP domain.

— The dialer should not remain up all the time due to routing protocols. Configure r10 to only place the calls upon losing the 192.168.2.0/24 and 192.168.1.0/24 routes.

— Use CHAP for authentication; use cisco_isdn as the password

— Do not use static routes; routing should be dynamic.

— The link should drop after 5 minutes of idle time.

Section VII: ATM

1 Configure an ATM PVC from r3's atm0/0 port to r7's atm0 port; use subinterface for this purpose.

2 Use the ATM encapsulation method that is most suited to bursty data traffic.

3 Configure the ATM circuit to support bursty delay-tolerant VBR traffic; this circuit should be configured to use a sustained cell rate of 8 T1s and a peak cell rate that supports the full bandwidth of the interface.

4 Use the 62.1.8.0 network with a 30-bit subnet mask for this network.

Section VIII: BGP

1 All BGP routers should peer with each other using statically assigned BGP router IDs; BGP routing updates should use the largest possible packet sizes. Unless otherwise specified, you cannot use route reflectors to accomplish tasks in this lab. BGP will only be used to advertise loopback networks; do not configure BGP to advertise any 10 networks. When routers have more than one peer in the same autonomous system, use a peer group to simplify the configuration. At the end of this section, all BGP routes should be reachable on all BGP routers. Add and advertise the following networks shown in Table 10-3.

Table 10-3 *Lab 4 BGP Networks*

Advertising Router	Network
r3	62.1.8.0/24
	3.0.0.0/8
r4	32.1.1.0/24
	32.2.2.0/24
r5	4.0.0.0/8
	5.5.0.0/16
	6.0.0.0/8
	12.0.0.0/8
r7	52.1.1.0/24
	54.1.0.0/16
	62.1.8.0/30
r10	22.1.1.0/24
	24.24.24.24/24

2 Enable BGP routing on routers r3, r5, and r7. Configure all of these routers to peer with each other in AS 65001; these routers should also belong to parent AS 10001.

Configure r3 to peer with r11 in AS 96; these routers should use BGP authentication using the password ":)router".

R3 should also peer with r7 over the ATM network and r5 over the Frame Relay network; one route reflector statement is allowed on r3, r5, and r7 for this purpose.

R7 should be able to reach all networks r3 can reach; one default route is allowed on r7 for this purpose.

3 Configure BGP routing on routers r4 and r10; put these routers in AS 65002; these routers also belong to parent AS 10001.

R4 should also peer with r3 in AS 65001. All routers in AS 65002 should receive and be able to reach all BGP routes sent by r3 and vice versa.

Section IX: DLSW+

1 Configure a DLSw TCP peer between VLAN A on r4 and VLAN B or r8. Explorers and DLSw traffic from r4's VLAN A should only be allowed onto r8's VLAN B.

2 Configure a DLSw TCP peer between VLAN D on r3 and VLAN E of r8. Only explorers and DLSw traffic from VLAN D can reach r8's VLAN E.

3 DLSw traffic from these two peers should not interact with each other.

Section X: NAT

1 Configure NAT such that all users on VLAN B share a single IP address when accessing any internal lab equipment. If sw15_35xx issues a ping to r3, for instance, it should be translated.

Section XI: Multicast Routing

1 Configure multicast routing on r3, r10, and r7.

2 Use a rendezvous address of 175.10.16.3. R10 and r3 should both be able to ping the multicast address of 224.0.10.10 on the ATM interface of r7.

CCIE Practice Lab: Kobayashi Maru

Equipment List

- 1 Frame Relay switch: 4 serial ports
- ISDN simulator/switch with 2 BRI ports
- ATM switch with 2 ATM interfaces
- 1 lab router: 1 Ethernet and 1 serial interface
- 1 lab router: 1 Ethernet, 1 serial interface, and 1 FXS voice port
- 1 lab router: 1 Fast Ethernet, 1 serial, 1 ATM, and 1 ISDN BRI
- 1 lab router: 1 Ethernet, 1 ISDN BRI, and 2 serial
- 1 lab router: 2 Ethernet and 1 FXS voice port
- 1 lab router: 2 Ethernet and 1 serial
- 1 lab router: 1 ATM
- 1 Ethernet 3550 switch with the EMI software, 1 fiber port or crossover cable for interconnection
- 1 Ethernet 35xx Ethernet switch

Prestaging—Frame Relay Switch, Backbone Routers, and ATM Configuration

Configure the Frame Relay switch with the PVCs as depicted in Figure 10-9. Do not time yourself on this portion of the lab. Not all the PVCs in the diagram are used. Example 10-7 lists the configurations for the Frame Relay and ATM switches.

Figure 10-9 *Frame Relay Switch Configuration*

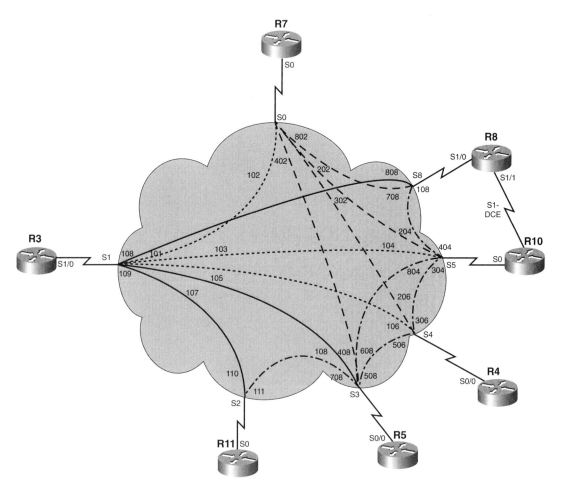

Master Frame Relay DLCI Map
Not All PVCs and Interfaces Are Used

Example 10-7 *Frame Relay and ATM Switch Configurations*

```
hostname frame_switch
!
frame-relay switching
!
interface Ethernet0
```

Example 10-7 *Frame Relay and ATM Switch Configurations (Continued)*

```
 no ip address
 shutdown
!
interface Serial0
 no ip address
 encapsulation frame-relay
 no fair-queue
 clockrate 2000000
 frame-relay intf-type dce
 frame-relay route 102 interface Serial1 101
 frame-relay route 202 interface Serial5 204
 frame-relay route 302 interface Serial4 206
 frame-relay route 402 interface Serial3 408
 frame-relay route 802 interface Serial8 708
!
interface Serial1
 no ip address
 encapsulation frame-relay
 clockrate 2000000
 frame-relay intf-type dce
 frame-relay route 101 interface Serial0 102
 frame-relay route 103 interface Serial5 104
 frame-relay route 105 interface Serial4 106
 frame-relay route 107 interface Serial3 108
 frame-relay route 108 interface Serial8 808
 frame-relay route 109 interface Serial2 110
!
interface Serial2
 no ip address
 encapsulation frame-relay
 clockrate 64000
 frame-relay intf-type dce
 frame-relay route 110 interface Serial1 109
 frame-relay route 111 interface Serial3 708
!
interface Serial3
 no ip address
 encapsulation frame-relay
 clockrate 64000
 frame-relay intf-type dce
 frame-relay route 108 interface Serial1 107
 frame-relay route 408 interface Serial0 402
 frame-relay route 508 interface Serial4 506
 frame-relay route 608 interface Serial5 804
 frame-relay route 708 interface Serial2 111
!
interface Serial4
 no ip address
 encapsulation frame-relay
```

continues

Example 10-7 *Frame Relay and ATM Switch Configurations (Continued)*

```
 clockrate 64000
 frame-relay intf-type dce
 frame-relay route 106 interface Serial1 105
 frame-relay route 206 interface Serial0 302
 frame-relay route 306 interface Serial5 304
 frame-relay route 506 interface Serial3 508
!
interface Serial5
 no ip address
 encapsulation frame-relay
 clockrate 64000
 frame-relay intf-type dce
 frame-relay route 104 interface Serial1 103
 frame-relay route 204 interface Serial0 202
 frame-relay route 304 interface Serial4 306
 frame-relay route 404 interface Serial8 110
 frame-relay route 804 interface Serial3 608
!
interface Serial6
 no ip address
!
interface Serial7
 no ip address
!
interface Serial8
 no ip address
 encapsulation frame-relay
 clockrate 64000
 frame-relay intf-type dce
 frame-relay route 108 interface Serial5 404
 frame-relay route 708 interface Serial0 802
 frame-relay route 808 interface Serial1 108
!
interface Serial9
 no ip address
 shutdown
!
interface BRI0
 no ip address
 shutdown
!
no ip classless
!
end
---------------------------- ATM Switch ----------------->
hostname ls1010
!
atm address 47.0091.8100.0000.0061.705b.4001.0061.705b.4001.00
```

Example 10-7 *Frame Relay and ATM Switch Configurations (Continued)*

```
!
interface ATM0/0/0
 no keepalive
 no atm auto-configuration
 no atm address-registration
 no atm ilmi-enable
 no atm ilmi-lecs-implied
!
interface ATM0/0/1
 no keepalive
 no atm auto-configuration
 no atm address-registration
 no atm ilmi-enable
 no atm ilmi-lecs-implied
 atm pvc 1 101  interface  ATM0/0/0 1 102
 atm pvc 3 103  interface  ATM0/0/0 7 107
!
interface ATM0/0/2
 no keepalive
end
```

The following portion of the lab is timed and should begin after the configuration and physical installation of all hardware.

Rules

- No static routes or floating static routes are allowed unless specifically stated.

- Follow the instructions exactly. Be careful to only propagate routes where and when instructed. Only use the PVCs as directed by the instructions.

- You can use the configuration guides and the CD-ROM for your only reference material.

- You have 8.5 hours to complete this portion of the lab. Do not talk to anyone during this phase.

- It is recommended that you read the entire lab before beginning.

Section I: IP Setup

1 Use the IP addresses as depicted in Figure 10-10 and address the network accordingly. Note: Not all the IP addresses can be assigned at this time.

2 Use the IP address 172.16.128.1 on the Fast 3/0 interface of r3. Subnet 172.16.128.0/24 will be VLAN C.

Figure 10-10 *Network Diagram for Kobayashi Maru*

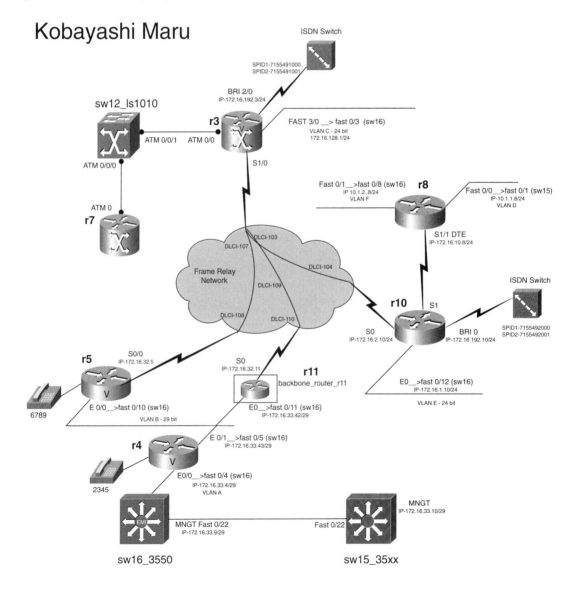

3 Use the IP address of 172.16.33.42/29 on r11's E0 interface. This interface is in VLAN B, along with r4's e0/1 interface and r5's e 0/0 interface.

4 R8 has the Fast 0/1 interface in VLAN F and the Fast 0/0 interface in VLAN D. Use the IP address of 10.1.2.8/24 on the Fast 0/1 interface and 10.1.1.8/24 on the Fast 0/0 interface.

5 R10 has its e0 interface in VLAN E; use the IP address of 172.16.1.10/24 for it.

6 R4's e 0/0 interface is in VLAN A and has the IP address of 172.16.33.4/29.

7 Use the network 172.16.0.0 for all other subnets and host addresses:

— VLAN A: 29-bit subnet

— VLAN B: 29-bit subnet

— VLANs C, D, E, F: 24-bit subnet

Section II: Catalyst Configuration

1 Configure the VLANs as depicted in Figure 10-8. Do not use VLAN 1:

— VLAN A = VLAN 2034

— VLAN B = VLAN 2033

— VLAN C = VLAN 1026

— VLAN D = VLAN 10 (on sw15_35xx)

— VLAN E = VLAN 1025

— VLAN F = VLAN 10

2 Connect the Catalyst switches together via back-to-back cable. Ensure that both switches are reachable from the lab using the following address: sw16_3550 = 172.16.33.9/29 and sw15_35xx = 172.16.33.10/29. Do not configure 802.1Q or ISL trunks. You cannot configure a default or static route on sw16_3550.

3 Configure sw16_3550 and the sw15_35xx to use ccie_psv2 as the VTP domain name. Choose the VTP mode that is most desirable to your network design.

4 Configure sw16_3550 to support 802.1w RSTP and 802.1s MSTP. Configure any host ports to support RSTP.

5 Configure MSTP such that all extended VLANs on sw16_3550 will be the root for spanning tree. Normal-range VLANs should use the default STP values.

6 Configure a MAC address of 0001.0001.aaaa on VLAN 2034 of sw16_3550.

Section III: OSPF, EIGRP, Layer 3 Switching, and Frame Relay

1   Configure a partial-mesh Frame Relay network between r3, r5, and r11. You can use subinterfaces wherever you desire.

2   Configure OSPF over the Frame Relay network between r3, r5, and r11. The Frame Relay network is in OSPF area 0. Configure VLAN C on r3 to be in area 51.

3   Configure VLAN B between r5, r11, and r4 to be in OSPF area 100.

4   Change the OSPF hello timer of r5's S0/0 interface to 60 seconds.

5   Configure EIGRP on VLAN A between r4 and sw16_3550. Use the autonomous system ID of 2003. Enable Layer 3 switching on sw16_3550 to accomplish this.

6   EIGRP-originated routes should appear as OSPF external type 1 routes with a tag of 4 on all OSPF routers.

7   Ensure full IP reachability from the EIGRP and OSPF domain. Sw15_35xx should be able to ping VLAN C and vice versa.

Section IV: IS-IS and RIP Integration

1   Configure IS-IS between r3 and r10 over the Frame Relay network. Advertise VLAN E via IS-IS.

2   Configure the serial link between r10 and r8. Configure the link such that it supports Lempel-Ziv (LZ)-based compression algorithms.

3   Configure RIP between r10 and r8. Do not advertise VLAN D and VLAN F via RIP. RIP should not use broadcast routing updates.

4   Integrate RIP and IS-IS fully into the existing OSPF/EIGRP domains. Ensure full reachability between all routing domains.

5   On r3, tag any redistributed routes with an original administrative distance of 0 with a tag of 3333. Tag redistributed routes with an original administrative distance of 115 with a tag of 3, and tag routes with an original administrative distance of 1 with a tag of 777.

Section V: NAT and DHCP

1   Configure NAT on r8 using the following guidelines:

   — Users on VLAN D, 10.1.1.0/24, will share 5 IP addresses (172.16.16.2 through 172.16.16.6).

   — R8 Fast 0/0 IP address, 10.1.1.8, will always be translated to 172.16.16.100.

   — Users on VLAN F will use PAT.

2 Ensure that users on VLAN D and VLAN F can ping sw16_3550 and sw15_35xx and are translated accordingly.

3 Configure the users on VLAN C on r3 to use DHCP. The server should advertise 172.16.128.1 as the default gateway. Reserve four host addresses on VLAN C in the DHCP pool for future use.

Section VI: Multicast Routing and NTP

1 Configure r8 as an NTP server and sw16_3550 to receive NTP updates. When sw16_3550 synchronizes with the server, it should have a stratum of 6.

2 Configure multicast routing on r3, r4, and r5. Use sparse mode and configure the multicast address of 224.0.10.3 on the Fast 3/0 interface of r3.

3 Configure r4 and r5 such that they can ping the multicast address of 224.0.10.3.

Section VII: ISDN

1 Configure the ISDN network between r10 and r3. Use the following guidelines:

— Use the IP address of 172.16.192.10/24 on r10.

— The dialer should not remain up all the time due to routing protocols.

— Configure r10 to only place the calls upon losing the 172.16.128.0/24 route/VLAN C. Both B channels should pick up immediately.

— Use PPP CHAP for authentication; use cisco_isdn as the password.

— You can use static routes.

— The link should drop after 5 minutes of idle time.

Section VIII: ATM

1 Configure an ATM PVC from r3's atm0/0 port to r7's atm0 port; use subinterfaces for this purpose.

2 Use the ATM encapsulation method that is most suited to bursty data traffic.

3 Configure the ATM circuit to support bursty delay-tolerant traffic with an unspecified bit rate; this circuit should be configured with a peak cell rate that supports the full bandwidth of the interface.

4 Use the 10.55.1.8 network with a 30-bit subnet mask for this network.

Section IX: BGP

1 All BGP routers should peer with each other using statically assigned BGP router IDs; BGP routing updates should use the largest possible packet sizes. BGP will only be used to advertise loopback networks; do not configure BGP to advertise any 10 networks. When routers have more than one peer in the same autonomous system, use a peer group to simplify the configuration. At the end of this section, all BGP routes should be reachable on all BGP routers. Add and advertise the networks shown in Table 10-4.

Table 10-4 *Lab 5 BGP Networks*

Advertising Router	Network
r3	198.201.5.0/24
	109.201.11.0/24
	10.55.1.8/30
r4	164.8.8.0/24
	164.10.10./24
r5	36.101.11.0/24
	37.101.12.0/24
r7	208.161.8.0/24
	208.164.8.0/24

2 Configure BGP on r3 and r7; put both of these routers in AS 97.

3 Configure r7 to peer with r3 over its ATM interface. R7 should be configured so that the 208.164.8.0/24 network will never be propagated beyond AS 97; one configuration line is allowed on r3 for this purpose.

4 R3 should peer with r5 and r11 in AS 148 over the Frame Relay network.

5 Configure BGP on routers r5 and r11.

6 R5 should peer with r3, r4, and r11.

7 R11 will peer with r3, r4, and r5.

8 Configure r11 so that routes from r4 will be less desirable to any other router that receives routes from this router.

9 Configure BGP on r4; put this router in AS 65 and configure it to peer with r5 and r11 over its Ethernet interface.

Section X: Voice

1 Configure Voice over IP between r5 and r4.

2 R4 should use the 2345 phone number on its 1/0/0 voice port. This lab requires that you use the 164.8.8.1 IP address for voice calls.

3 R5 should use the 6789 phone number on its 1/0/0 port, and you must use the 36.101.11.1 IP address for all voice calls.

4 Callers from r4 should also be able to reach r5 when the 411 phone number is dialed; only one command is allowed on r4 for this purpose.

Section XI: DLSW+

1 Configure a DLSw Fast Sequence Transport peer between r10 VLAN E and VLAN B or r5. Configure DLSw such that only NetBIOS traffic can traverse the peer.

Appendixes

Cisco IOS Software Limitations and Restrictions

Cisco IOS Software Limitations and Restrictions

These limitations apply to Cisco IOS Software Release 12.1(11)EA1:

- Storm control or traffic suppression (configured by using the **storm-control** {**broadcast** | **multicast** | **unicast**} **level** *level* [*.level*] interface configuration command) is supported only on physical interfaces; it is not supported on EtherChannel port channels even though you can enter these commands through the command-line interface (CLI).

- The Cisco RPS 300 Redundant Power System (RPS) supports the Catalyst 3550 multilayer switch and provides redundancy for up to six connected devices until one of these devices requires backup power. If a connected device has a power failure, the RPS immediately begins supplying power to that device and sends status information to other connected devices that it is no longer available as a backup power source. As described in the device documentation, when the RPS LED is amber, the RPS is connected but down. However, this might merely mean that the RPS is in standby mode. Press the Standby/Active button on the RPS to put it into active mode. You can view RPS status through the CLI by using the **show rps** privileged EXEC command. For more information, refer to the *RPS 300 Hardware Installation Guide*.

- You can connect the switch to a PC by using the switch console port, the supplied rollover cable, and the DB-9 adapter. You need to provide a RJ-45-to-DB-25 female DTE adapter if you want to connect the switch console port to a terminal. You can order a kit (part number ACS-DSBUASYN=) with this RJ-45-to-DB-25 female DTE adapter from Cisco.

- Modifying a multicast boundary access list does not prevent packets from being forwarded by any multicast routes that were in existence before the access list was modified if the packets arriving on the input interface do not violate the boundary. However, no new multicast routes that violate the updated version of the multicast boundary access list are learned, and any multicast routes that are in violation of the updated access list are not relearned if they age out.

   After updating a multicast boundary, the workaround is to use the **clear ip mroute** privileged EXEC command to delete any existing multicast routes that violate the updated boundary. (Error code: CSCdr79083)

- When an IP packet with a cyclic redundancy check (CRC) error is received, the per-packet per-DSCP counter (for DSCP 0) is incremented. Normal networks should not have packets with CRC errors. (Error code: CSCdr85898)

- The **mac-address** interface configuration command does not properly assign a MAC address to an interface. This command is not supported on Catalyst 3550 switches. (Error code: CSCds11328)

- If you configure the Dynamic Host Configuration Protocol (DHCP) server to allocate addresses from a pool to the switch, two devices on the network might have the same IP address. Pooled addresses are temporarily allocated to a device and are returned to the pool when not in use. If you save the configuration file after the switch receives such an address, the pooled address is saved, and the switch does not attempt to access the DHCP server after a reboot to receive a new IP address. As a result, two devices might have the same IP address.

  The workaround is to make sure that you configure the DHCP server with reserved leases that are bound to each switch by the switch hardware address. (Error code: CSCds55220)

- The **show ip mroute count** privileged EXEC command might display incorrect packet counts. In certain transient states (for example, when a multicast stream is forwarded only to the CPU during the route-learning process and the CPU is programming this route into the hardware), a multicast stream packet count might be counted twice. Do not trust the counter during this transient state. (Error code: CSCds61396)

- When changing the link speed of a Gigabit Ethernet port from 1000 Mbps to 100 Mbps, there is a slight chance that the port will stop transmitting packets. If this occurs, shut down the port and re-enable it by using the **shutdown** and **no shutdown** interface configuration commands. (Error code: CSCds84279)

- In IP multicast routing and fallback bridging, certain hardware features are used to replicate packets for the different VLANs of an outgoing trunk port. If the incoming speed is line rate, the outgoing interface cannot duplicate that speed (because of the replication of the packets). As a result, certain replicated packets are dropped. (Error code: CSCdt06418)

- When you use the **no interface port-channel global** configuration command to remove an EtherChannel group, the ports in the port group change to the administratively down state.

  When you remove an EtherChannel group, enter the **no shutdown** interface configuration command on the interfaces that belonged to the port group to bring them back on line. (Error code: CSCdt10825)

- In the output displayed after a **show interface** *interface-id* privileged EXEC command, the *Output Buffer Failures* field shows the number of packets lost before replication, whereas the Packets Output field shows the successful transmitted packets after replication. To determine actual discarded frames, multiply the output buffer failures by the number of VLANs on which the multicast data is replicated. (Error code: CSCdt26928)

- Internet Group Management Protocol (IGMP) packets classified by quality of service (QoS) to map the differentiated services code point (DSCP) value and the class of service (CoS) value in a QoS policy map might only modify the DSCP property and leave the CoS value at zero. (Error code: CSCdt27705)

- If you assign both tail-drop threshold percentages to 100 percent by using the **wrr-queue threshold** interface configuration command and display QoS information for this interface by using the **show mls qos interface statistics** privileged command, the drop-count statistics are always zero even if the thresholds were exceeded. To display the total number of discarded packets, use the **show controllers ethernet-controllers** *interface-id* privileged EXEC command. In the display, the number of discarded frames includes the frames that were dropped when the tail-drop thresholds were exceeded. (Error code: CSCdt29703)

- Open Shortest Path First (OSPF) path costs and Interior Gateway Routing Protocol (IGRP) metrics are incorrect for switch virtual interface (SVI) ports. You can manually configure the bandwidth of the SVI by using the **bandwidth** interface configuration command. Changing the bandwidth of the interface changes the routing metric for the routes when the SVI is used as an outgoing interface. (Error code: CSCdt29806)

- On the Catalyst 3550, coldStart and warmStart traps are not consistently sent. (Error code: CSCdt33779)

- Remote Monitoring (RMON) collection functions on physical interfaces, but it is not supported on EtherChannels and SVIs. (Error code: CSCdt36101)

- Multicast router information is displayed in the **show ip igmp snooping mrouter** privileged EXEC command when IGMP snooping is disabled. Multicast VLAN Registration (MVR) and IGMP snooping use the same commands to display multicast router information. In this case, MVR is enabled, and IGMP snooping is disabled. (Error code: CSCdt48002)

- When a VLAN interface has been disabled and restarted multiple times by using the **shutdown** and **no shutdown** interface configuration commands, the interface might not restart following a **no shutdown** command. To restart the interface, re-enter a **shutdown** and **no shutdown** command sequence. (Error code: CSCdt54435)

- When you configure the **ip pim spt-threshold infinity** interface configuration command, you want all sources for the specified group to use the shared tree and not use the source tree. However, the switch does not automatically start to use the shared tree. No connectivity problem occurs, but the switch continues to use the shortest-path tree for multicast group entries already installed in the multicast routing table. You can enter the **clear ip mroute *** privileged EXEC command to force the change to the shared tree. (Error code: CSCdt60412)

- If the number of multicast routes configured on the switch is greater than the switch can support, it might run out of available memory, which can cause it to reboot. This is a limitation in the platform-independent code.

  The workaround is to not configure the switch to operate with more than the maximum number of supported multicast routes. You can use the **show sdm prefer** and **show sdm prefer routing** privileged EXEC commands to view approximate maximum configuration guidelines for the current SDM template and the routing template. (Error code: CSCdt63354)

- Configuring too many multicast groups might result in an extremely low memory condition and cause the software control data structure to go out of sync, causing unpredictable forwarding behavior. The memory resources can only be recovered by issuing the **clear ip mroute** privileged EXEC command. To prevent this situation, do not configure more than the recommended multicast routes on the switch. (Error code: CSCdt63480)

- The **dec** keyword is not supported in the **bridge** *bridge-group* **protocol** global configuration command. If two Catalyst 3550 switches are connected to each other through an interface that is configured for IP routing and fallback bridging, and the bridge group is configured with the **bridge** *bridge-group* **protocol dec** command, both switches act as if they were the spanning-tree root. Therefore, spanning-tree loops might be undetected. (Error code: CSCdt63589)

- When you configure an EtherChannel between a Catalyst 3550 and a Catalyst 1900 switch, some Catalyst 3550 links in the EtherChannel might go down, but one link in the channel remains up, and connectivity is maintained.

  The workaround is to disable the Port Aggregation Protocol (PAgP) on both devices by using the **channel-group** *channel-group-number* mode on interface configuration command. PAgP negotiation between these two devices is not reliable. (Error code: CSCdt78727)

- When the switch is operating with equal-cost routes and it is required to learn more unicast routes than it can support, the CPU might run out of memory, and the switch might fail.

  The workaround is to remain within the documented recommended and supported limits. (Error code: CSCdt79172)

- The behavior of a software access control list (ACL) with QoS differs from a hardware ACL with QoS. On the Catalyst 3550 switch, when the QoS hardware rewrites the DSCP of a packet, the rewriting of this field happens before software running on the CPU examines the packet, and the CPU sees only the new value and not the original DSCP value.

When the security hardware ACL matches a packet on input, the match uses the original DSCP value. For output security ACLs, the security ACL hardware should match against the final, possibly changed, DSCP value as set by the QoS hardware. Under some circumstances, a match to a security ACL in hardware prevents the QoS hardware from rewriting the DSCP and causes the CPU to use the original DSCP.

If a security ACL is applied in software (because the ACL did not fit into hardware, and packets were sent to the CPU for examination), the match probably uses the new DSCP value as determined by the QoS hardware, regardless of whether the ACL is applied at the input or at the output. When packets are logged by the ACL, this problem can also affect whether or not a match is logged by the CPU, even if the ACL fits into hardware and the permit or deny filtering was completed in hardware.

To avoid these issues, whenever the switch rewrites the DSCP of any packet to a value different from the original DSCP, security ACLs should not test against DSCP values in any of their access control elements (ACEs), regardless of whether the ACL is being applied to an IP access group or to a VLAN map. This restriction does not apply to ACLs used in QoS class maps.

If the switch is not configured to rewrite the DSCP value of any packet, it is safe to match against DSCP in ACLs used for IP access groups or for VLAN maps because the DSCP does not change as the packet is processed by the switch.

The DSCP field of an IP packet encompasses the two fields that were originally designated Precedence and ToS (type of service). Statements relating to DSCP apply equally to either IP precedence or IP ToS. (Error code: CSCdt94355)

- Disabling autonegotiation on a gigabit interface converter (GBIC) interface by using the **speed nonegotiate** interface configuration command might cause the interface to show that the physical link is up, even when it is not connected. (Error code: CSCdv29722)

- If you configure a trunk port for Dynamic Trunking Protocol (DTP) nonegotiate mode and change the encapsulation type from Inter-Switch Link (ISL) to 802.1Q by using the **switchport trunk encapsulation** interface configuration command, the port becomes an access port and is no longer trunking. (Error code: CSCdv46715)

- On earlier versions of Catalyst 3550-24 switches, if a 10/100BASE-TX port on the switch is connected to a Catalyst 2820 or Catalyst 1900 switch through an ISL trunk at 100 Mbps, bidirectional communication cannot be established. The Catalyst 2820 or Catalyst 1900 switch identifies the Catalyst 3550-24 switch as a Cisco Discovery Protocol (CDP) neighbor, but the Catalyst 3550-24 switch does not recognize the Catalyst 2820 or Catalyst 1900 switch. On these switches, you should not use ISL trunks between the Catalyst 3550-24 and a Catalyst 2820 or Catalyst 1900 switch. Configure the link as an access link instead of a trunk link.

This problem has been fixed in hardware on Catalyst 3550-24 switches with motherboard assembly number 73-5700-08 or later. To determine the board level on your switch, enter the **show version** privileged EXEC. Motherboard information appears toward the end of the output display. (Error code: CSCdv68158)

- When IGMP filtering is enabled and you use the **ip igmp** profile global configuration command to create an IGMP filter, reserved multicast addresses cannot be filtered. Because IGMP filtering uses only Layer 3 addresses to filter IGMP reports and due to mapping between Layer 3 multicast addresses and Ethernet multicast addresses, reserved groups (224.0.0.x) are always allowed through the switch. In addition, aliased groups can leak through the switch. For example, if a user is allowed to receive reports from group 225.1.2.3, but not from group 230.1.2.3, aliasing will cause the user to receive reports from 230.1.2.3. Aliasing of reserved addresses means that all groups of the form y.0.0.x are allowed through. (Error code: CSCdv73626)

  If you use the **ip igmp max-groups** interface configuration command to set the maximum number of IGMP groups for an interface to 0, the port still receives group reports from reserved multicast groups (224.0.0.x) and their Layer 2 aliases (y.0.0.x). (Error code: CSCdv79832)

- The switch might reload when it is executing the **no snmp-server host** global configuration command. This is a rare condition that can happen if SNMP traps or informs are enabled and the SNMP agent attempts to send a trap to the host just as it is being removed from the configuration and if the IP address of the host (or the gateway to reach the host) has not been resolved by Address Resolution Protocol (ARP).

  The workaround is to ensure that the target host or the next-hop gateway to that host is in the ARP cache (for example, by issuing a **ping** command) before removing it from the SNMP configuration. Alternatively, disable all SNMP traps and informs before removing any hosts from the SNMP configuration. (Error code: CSCdw44266)

- When you access CISCO-STACK-MIB portTable, the mapping might be off by one from the mapping given by the switch. The objects in this table are indexed by two numbers: portModuleIndex and portIndex. The allowable values for portModuleIndex are 1 through 16. Because 0 is not an allowable value, the value 1 represents module 0.

  The workaround is to use the value 1 to represent module 0. (Error code: CSCdw71848)

- If a port on the Catalyst 3550 switch that is running the Multiple Spanning Tree Protocol (MSTP) is connected to another switch that belongs to a different Multiple Spanning Tree (MST) region, the Catalyst 3550 port is not recognized as a boundary port when you start the protocol migration process by using the **clear spanning-tree detected-protocols interface** *interface-id* privileged EXEC command. This problem occurs only on the root bridge, and when the root bridge is cleared, the boundary ports are not shown because the designated ports do not receive any bridge protocol data units (BPDUs) unless a topology change occurs. This is the intended behavior.

The workaround is to configure the Catalyst 3550 switch for Per VLAN Spanning Tree (PVST) by using the **spanning-tree mode pvst** global configuration command bridge, and then change it to MSTP by using the **spanning-tree mode mst** global configuration command. (Error code: CSCdx10808)

- If you apply an ACL to an interface that has a QoS policy map attached and the ACL is configured so that the packet should be forwarded by the CPU, or if the configured ACL cannot fit into the ternary content addressable memory (TCAM), all packets received from this interface are forwarded to the CPU. Because traffic forwarded to the CPU cannot be policed by the policer configured on the interface, this traffic is not accurately rate limited to the configured police rate.

  The workaround, when QoS rate limiting is configured on an interface, is to configure applied ACLs so that packets are not forwarded by the CPU or reduce the number of ACEs in the ACL so that it can fit into the TCAM. (Error code: CSCdx30485)

- Catalyst 3550 switches do not take into account the Preamble and Inter Frame Gap (IFG) when rate limiting traffic, which could result in a slightly inaccurate policing rate on a long burst of small-sized frames, where the ratio of the Preamble and IFG to frame size is more significant. This should not be an issue in an environment where the frames are a mix of different sizes.

- If the switch fails for any reason while you are exiting VLAN configuration mode (accessed by entering the **vlan database** privileged EXEC command), there is a slight chance that the VLAN database might get corrupted. After resetting from the switch, you might see these messages on the console:

  ```
  %SW_VLAN-4-VTP_INVALID_DATABASE_DATA: VLAN manager received bad data of type
  device
  type: value 0 from vtp database
  $SW_VLAN-3-VTP_PROTOCOL_ERROR: VTP protocol code internal error
  ```

  The workaround is to use the **delete flash:vlan.dat** privileged EXEC command to delete the corrupted VLAN database. Then reload the switch by using the reload privileged EXEC command. (Error code: CSCdx19540)

- When a Cisco RPS 300 Redundant Power System provides power to a switch, after the switch power supply is restored, the RPS 300 continues to provide power until the RPS mode button is pressed. At this point, some switches restart, depending on how quickly the switches' internal power supply resumes operation. (Error code: CSCdx81023)

- Inserting GigaStack gigabit interface converter (GBIC) modules in the switch causes an increase in the CPU usage. (Error code: CSCdx90515)

- Hot Standby Routing Protocol (HSRP) does not support configuration of overlapping addresses in different VPN routing and forwarding (VRF) tables. (Error code: CSCdy14520)

- When 1000 VLANs and more than 40 trunk ports are configured, and the spanning-tree mode changes from MSTP to PVST or vice versa, this message appears on the console:

  ```
  %ETHCNTR-3-RA_ALLOC_ERROR: RAM Access write pool I/O memory allocation failure
  ```

  There is no workaround. However, it is recommended that you reload the switch by using the **reload** privileged EXEC command. To avoid this problem, configure the system with fewer VLANs and fewer trunk ports, or use the **switchport trunk allowed vlan** interface configuration command to reduce the number of active VLANs on each trunk port. (Error code: CSCdx20106)

Cluster Limitations and Restrictions

These limitations apply to cluster configuration:

- When there is a transition from the **cluster active** command switch to the **standby** command switch, Catalyst 1900, Catalyst 2820, and Catalyst 2900 4-MB switches that are cluster members might lose their cluster configuration. You must manually add these switches back to the cluster. (Error codes: CSCds32517, CSCds44529, CSCds55711, CSCds55787, CSCdt70872)

- When a Catalyst 2900 XL or Catalyst 3500 XL **cluster** command switch is connected to a Catalyst 3550 switch, the command switch does not find any cluster candidates beyond the Catalyst 3550 switch if it is not a member of the cluster. You must add the Catalyst 3550 switch to the cluster. You can then see any cluster candidates connected to it. (Error code: CSCdt09918)

- When clustering is enabled, do not configure SNMP community strings of more than 59 bytes, or clustering SNMP might not work correctly. (Error code: CSCdt39616)

- If both the **active command-switch** and the **standby** command switch fail at the same time, the cluster is not automatically re-created. Even if there is a third passive command switch, it might not re-create all cluster members because it might not have all the latest cluster configuration information. You must manually re-create the cluster if both the **active** and **standby command** switches simultaneously fail. (Error code: CSCdt43501)

Cluster Management Suite Limitations and Restrictions

These limitations apply to Cluster Management Suite (CMS) configuration:

- Host names and Domain Name System (DNS) server names that contain commas on a cluster command switch, member switch, or candidate switch can cause CMS to behave unexpectedly. You can avoid this instability in the interface by not using commas in host names or DNS names. Also, do not enter commas when entering multiple DNS names in the IP Configuration tab of the IP Management window in CMS.

- ACEs that contain the **host** keyword precede all other ACEs in standard ACLs. You can reposition the ACEs in a standard ACL with one restriction: No ACE with the **any** keyword or a wildcard mask can precede an ACE with the **host** keyword.

- CMS performance degrades if the topology view is open for several hours on a Solaris machine. The cause might be a memory leak.

    The workaround is to close the browser, reopen it, and launch CMS again. (Error code: CSCds29230)

- If you are printing a topology view or front-panel view that contains many devices and are running Solaris 2.6 with JDK1.2.2, you might get an "Out of Memory" error message.

    The workaround is to close the browser, reopen it, and launch CMS again. Before you perform any other task, bring up the view that you want to print, and click Print in the CMS menu. (Error code: CSCds80920)

- If a PC running CMS has low memory and CMS is running continuously for 2 to 3 days, the PC runs out of memory.

    The workaround is to relaunch CMS. (Error code: CSCdv88724)

- When a VLAN or a range of VLANs is already configured and you specify VLAN filter for a SPAN session, the current configuration for that session is overwritten with the new entry. Although the CLI appends new entries after the existing ones, CMS re-creates the whole session, overwrites the current entry, and provides only a single VLAN filter per entry.

    The workaround is to use the CLI; it is the only method for specifying multiple VLANs for filtering in a Switched Port Analyzer (SPAN) session. (Error code: CSCdw93904)

Important Notes

Cisco IOS Software Notes

These notes apply to Cisco IOS Software configuration:

- If you configure a port ACL on a physical interface on a switch that has VLAN maps or input router ACLs configured, or if you configure a VLAN map or input router ACL on a switch that has port ACLs configured, a "CONFLICT" message is generated but the configuration is accepted. The port ACL action has priority on that port over actions in a router ACL or VLAN map applied to the VLAN to which the port belongs.

    The result is that packets received on that physical port will be permitted or denied based on the port ACL action without regard to any **permit** or **deny** statements in router ACL or VLAN map, whereas packets received on other physical ports in the VLAN will still be permitted or denied based on router ACLs or VLAN maps applied to the VLAN. If the port ACL is applied to a trunk port, it overrides any other input ACLs applied to all VLANs on the trunk port.

- The default system maximum transmission unit (MTU) for traffic on the Catalyst 3550 switch is 1500 bytes. The 802.1Q tunneling feature increases the frame size by 4 bytes. Therefore, when you configure 802.1Q tunneling, you must configure all switches in the 802.1Q network to be able to process maximum frames by increasing the switch system MTU size to at least 1504 bytes. You configure the system MTU size by using the **system mtu** global configuration command.

- Beginning with Cisco IOS Software Release 12.1(8)EA1, to configure traffic suppression (previously configured by using the **switchport broadcast**, **switchport multicast**, and **switchport unicast** interface configuration commands), you use the **storm-control {broadcast | multicast | unicast} level** *level* [*.level*] interface configuration commands. For more information about these commands, refer to the *Catalyst 3550 Multilayer Switch Command Reference*.

- When you are configuring a cascaded stack of Catalyst 3550 switches by using the GigaStack GBIC and want to include more than one VLAN in the stack, be sure to configure all the GigaStack GBIC interfaces as trunk ports by using the **switchport mode trunk** interface configuration command and to use the same encapsulation method by using the **switchport encapsulation {isl | dot1q}** interface configuration command. For more information about these commands, refer to the *Catalyst 3550 Multilayer Switch Command Reference*.

- If the 1000BASE-T GBIC (WS-G5482) is not securely inserted, the switch might fail to recognize it or might display an incorrect media type following a **show interface** privileged EXEC command entry. If this happens, remove and reinsert the GBIC.

- Beginning with Cisco IOS Software Release 12.1(11)EA1, the **mac address-table aging-time** command replaces the **mac-address-table aging-time** command (with the hyphen). The **mac-address-table aging-time** command (with the hyphen) will become obsolete in a future release.

- Beginning with Cisco IOS Software Release 12.1(11)EA1, the **vtp** privileged EXEC command keywords are available in the **vtp** global configuration command. The **vtp** privileged EXEC command will become obsolete in a future release.

Cluster Notes

This note applies to cluster configuration:

- The **cluster setup** privileged EXEC command and the **standby mac-address** interface configuration command have been removed from the CLI and the documentation because they did not function correctly.

CMS Notes

These notes apply to CMS configuration:

- If you use CMS on Windows 2000, it might not apply configuration changes if the enable password is changed from the CLI during your CMS session. You have to restart CMS and enter the new password when prompted. Platforms other than Windows 2000 prompt you for the new enable password when it is changed.

- CMS does not display QoS classes that are created through the CLI if these classes have multiple **match** statements. When using CMS, you cannot create classes that match more than one **match** statement. CMS does not display policies that have such classes.

- If you use Internet Explorer version 5.5 and select a URL with a nonstandard port at the end of the address (for example, www.add.com:84), you must enter **http://** as the URL prefix. Otherwise, you cannot launch CMS.

- Within an ACL, you can change the sequence of ACEs that have the **host** keyword. However, because such ACEs are independent of each other, the change has no effect on the way the ACL filters traffic.

- If you use the Netscape browser to view the CMS GUI and you resize the browser window while CMS is initializing, CMS does not resize to fit the window.

  Resize the browser window again when CMS is not busy.

- CMS does not start if the temporary directory on your computer runs out of memory. This problem can occur because of a bug in the 1.2.2 version of the Java plug-in. The plug-in creates temporary files in the directory whenever it runs CMS, and the directory eventually runs out of plug-in space.

  The workaround is to remove all the jar_cache*.tmp files from the temporary directory. The path to the directory is different for different operating systems:

  — Solaris: /var/tmp

  — Windows NT and Windows 2000: \TEMP

  — Windows 95 and 98: \Windows\Temp

Read-Only Mode in CMS

CMS provides two levels of access to the configuration options. If your privilege level is 15, you have read-write access to CMS. If your privilege level is from 1 to 14, you have read-only access to CMS. In the read-only mode, some data is not displayed, and an error message appears when these switches are running these software releases:

- Catalyst 2900 XL or Catalyst 3500 XL member switches running Release 12.0(5)WC2 or earlier

- Catalyst 2950 member switches running Release 12.0(5)WC2 or earlier
- Catalyst 3550 member switches running Release 12.1(6)EA1 or earlier

In the front-panel view or topology view, CMS does not display error messages. In the front-panel view, if the switch is running one of the software releases listed previously, the device LEDs do not appear. In topology view, if the member is a Long-Reach Ethernet (LRE) switch, the customer premises equipment (CPE) connected to the switch does not appear. The Bandwidth and Link graphs also do not appear in these views.

To view switch information, you need to upgrade the member switch software. For information about upgrading switch software, see the "Downloading Software" section.

Unsupported CLI Commands in Release 12.1(11)EA1

This section lists some of the CLI commands that are displayed when you enter the question mark (?) at the Catalyst 3550 switch prompt but are not supported in this release, either because they are not tested, or because of Catalyst 3550 hardware limitations. This is not a complete list. The unsupported commands are listed by software feature and command mode.

Access Control Lists: Unsupported Privileged EXEC Commands

```
access-enable [host] [timeout minutes]
access-template [access-list-number | name] [dynamic-name] [source] [destination]
[timeout minutes]
clear access-template [access-list-number | name] [dynamic-name] [source] [destination]
```

ARP: Unsupported Global Configuration Commands

```
arp ip-address hardware-address smds
arp ip-address hardware-address srp-a
arp ip-address hardware-address srp-b
```

ARP: Unsupported Interface Configuration Commands

```
arp probe
ip probe proxy
```

FallBack Bridging: Unsupported Privileged EXEC Commands

```
clear bridge [bridge-group] multicast [router-ports | groups | counts] [group-address]
[interface-unit] [counts]
clear vlan statistics
show bridge [bridge-group] circuit-group [circuit-group] [-mac-address]
  [dst-mac-address]
show bridge [bridge-group] multicast [router-ports | groups] [group-address]
show bridge vlan
show interfaces crb
show interfaces {ethernet | fastethernet} [interface | slot/port] irb
show subscriber-policy range
```

FallBack Bridging: Unsupported Global Configuration Commands

```
bridge bridge-group bitswap_13_addresses
bridge bridge-group bridge ip
bridge bridge-group circuit-group circuit-group pause milliseconds
bridge bridge-group circuit-group circuit-group source-based
bridge cmf
bridge crb
bridge bridge-group domain domain-name
bridge irb
bridge bridge-group mac-address-table limit number
bridge bridge-group multicast-source
bridge bridge-group route protocol
bridge bridge-group subscriber policy policy
subscriber-policy policy [[no | default] packet [permit | deny]]
```

FallBack Bridging: Unsupported Interface Configuration Commands

```
bridge-group bridge-group cbus-bridging
bridge-group bridge-group circuit-group circuit-number
bridge-group bridge-group input-address-list access-list-number
bridge-group bridge-group input-lat-service-deny group-list
bridge-group bridge-group input-lat-service-permit group-list
bridge-group bridge-group input-lsap-list access-list-number
bridge-group bridge-group input-pattern-list access-list-number
bridge-group bridge-group input-type-list access-list-number
bridge-group bridge-group lat-compression
bridge-group bridge-group output-address-list access-list-number
bridge-group bridge-group output-lat-service-deny group-list
bridge-group bridge-group output-lat-service-permit group-list
bridge-group bridge-group output-lsap-list access-list-number
bridge-group bridge-group output-pattern-list access-list-number
bridge-group bridge-group output-type-list access-list-number
bridge-group bridge-group sse
bridge-group bridge-group subscriber-loop-control
bridge-group bridge-group subscriber-trunk
bridge bridge-group lat-service-filtering
frame-relay map bridge dlci broadcast
interface bvi bridge-group
x25 map bridge x.121-address broadcast [options-keywords]
```

HSRP: Unsupported Global Configuration Commands

```
interface Async
interface BVI
interface Dialer
interface Group-Async
interface Lex
interface Multilink
interface Virtual-Template
interface Virtual-Tokenring
```

HSRP: Unsupported Interface Configuration Commands

```
mtu
standby mac-refresh seconds
standby use-bia
```

HSRP: Interface Configuration Commands

```
switchport broadcast level
switchport multicast level
switchport unicast level
```

NOTE   These commands were replaced in Cisco IOS Software Release 12.1(8)EA1 by the **storm-control {broadcast | multicast | unicast} level** *level* [*.level*] interface configuration command.

IP Multicast Routing: Unsupported Privileged EXEC Commands

```
debug ip packet
```

Displays packets received by the switch CPU. It does not display packets that are hardware switched.

```
debug ip mcache
```

Affects packets received by the switch CPU. It does not display packets that are hardware switched.

```
debug ip mpacket [detail] [access-list-number [group-name-or-address]
```

Affects only packets received by the switch CPU. Because most multicast packets are hardware switched, use this command only when you know that the route will forward the packet to the CPU.

```
debug ip pim atm
show frame-relay ip rtp header-compression [interface type number]
show ip mcache
```

Displays entries in the cache for those packets that are sent to the switch CPU. Because most multicast packets are switched in hardware without CPU involvement, you can use this command, but multicast packet information is not displayed.

```
show ip mpacket
```

Supported but is only useful for packets received at the switch CPU. If the route is hardware switched, the command has no effect because the CPU does not receive the packet and cannot display it.

```
show ip pim vc [group-address | name] [type number]
show ip rtp header-compression [type number] [detail]
```

Displays PIM and RTP header compression information.

IP Multicast Routing: Unsupported Global Configuration Commands

```
ip pim accept-rp {address | auto-rp} [group-access-list-number]
ip pim message-interval seconds
```

IP Multicast Routing: Unsupported Interface Configuration Commands

```
frame-relay ip rtp header-compression [active | passive]
frame-relay map ip ip-address dlci [broadcast] compress
frame-relay map ip ip-address dlci rtp header-compression [active | passive]
ip igmp helper-address ip-address
ip multicast helper-map {group-address | broadcast} {broadcast-address | multicast-
address} extended-access-list-number
ip multicast rate-limit {in | out} [video | whiteboard] [group-list access-list] [source-
list access-list] kbps
ip multicast use-functional
ip pim minimum-vc-rate pps
ip pim multipoint-signalling
ip pim nbma-mode
ip pim vc-count number
ip rtp compression-connections number
ip rtp header-compression [passive]
```

IP Unicast Routing: Unsupported Privileged EXEC or User EXEC Commands

```
clear ip accounting [checkpoint]
clear ip bgp {* | address | peer-group-name} soft [in | out]
clear ip bgp dampening
clear ip bgp address flap-statistics
clear ip bgp prefix-list
show cef [drop | not-cef-switched]
show ip accounting [checkpoint] [output-packets | access-violations]
show ip bgp dampened-paths
show ip bgp flap-statistics
show ip bgp inconsistent-as
show ip bgp regexp regular expression
show ip prefix-list regular expression
```

IP Unicast Routing: Unsupported Global Configuration Commands

```
ip accounting-list ip-address wildcard
ip as-path access-list
ip accounting-transits count
ip cef accounting [per-prefix] [non-recursive]
ip cef traffic-statistics [load-interval seconds] [update-rate seconds]]
ip flow-aggregation
ip flow-cache
ip flow-export
ip gratuitous-arps
ip local
ip prefix-list
ip reflexive-list
router bgp
router egp
router-isis
router iso-igrp
router mobile
router odr
router static
```

IP Unicast Routing: Unsupported Interface Configuration Commands

```
ip accounting
ip load-sharing [per-packet]
ip mtu bytes
ip route-cache
ip verify
ip unnumbered type number
```

All **ip security** commands.

Unsupported BGP Router Configuration Commands

NOTE   These Border Gateway Protocol (BGP) commands have not been tested for the Catalyst 3550 and are not supported for the switch in Cisco IOS Software Release 12.1(11)EA1. This is not a complete list.

```
address-family vpnv4
address-family ipv4 [multicast | unicast]
default-information originate
neighbor advertise-map
neighbor advertisement-interval
neighbor allowas-in
neighbor default-originate
neighbor description
neighbor distribute-list
neighbor prefix-list
neighbor route-reflector client
neighbor soft-reconfiguration
neighbor version
network backdoor
table-map
```

Unsupported VPN Configuration Commands

All

NOTE   The switch does support the multi-VPN routing/forwarding (multi-VRF) commands shown in the command reference for this release.

Unsupported Route Map Commands

```
match route-type { level-1 | level-2}
set as-path {tag | prepend as-path-string}
set automatic-tag
set dampening half-life reuse suppress max-suppress-time
```

```
set ip destination ip-address mask
set ip next-hop
set ip precedence value
set ip qos-group
set metric-type internal
set tag tag-value
```

MSDP: Unsupported Privileged EXEC Commands

```
show access-expression
show exception
show location
show pm LINE
show smf [interface-id]
show subscriber-policy [policy-number]
show template [template-name]
```

MSDP: Unsupported Global Configuration Commands

```
ip msdp default-peer ip-address | name [prefix-list list]
```

Because BGP/Multiprotocol BGP (MBGP) is not supported, use the **ip msdp peer** command instead of this command.

RADIUS: Unsupported Global Configuration Commands

```
aaa nas port extended
radius-server attribute nas-port
radius-server configure
radius-server extended-portnames
```

SNMP: Unsupported Global Configuration Commands

```
snmp-server enable informs
```

Spanning Tree: Unsupported Global Configuration Commands

```
spanning-tree etherchannel guard misconfig
```

VLANs: Unsupported User EXEC Commands

```
ifindex
private-vlan
```

APPENDIX B

RFCs

Table B-1 lists some of the more common RFCs found throughout this book. You can find all RFCs online at www.rfc-editor.org/cgi-bin/rfcsearch.pl. Just insert the RFC number in the search field.

Table B-1   *RFCs Referenced in This Book*

Document	Title	Update Notes
RFC 3392	*Capabilities Advertisement with BGP-4*	
RFC 3260	*New Terminology and Clarifications for Diffserv*	
RFC 3248	*A Delay Bound Alternative Revision of RFC 2598*	
RFC 3065	*Autonomous System Confederations for BGP*	
RFC 2918	*Route Refresh Capability for BGP-4*	
RFC 2892	*Capabilities Advertisement with BGP-4*	
RFC 2796	*BGP Route Reflection — An Alternative to Full Mesh IBGP*	
RFC 2750	*RSVP Extensions for Policy Control*	
RFC 2697	*A Single Rate Three Color Marker*	
RFC 2598	*An Expedited Forwarding PHB*	Updated by RFC 3246
RFC 2597	*Assured Forwarding PHB Group*	Updated by RFC 3260
RFC 2519	*A Framework for Inter-Domain Route Aggregation*	
RFC 2475	*An Architecture for Differentiated Services*	Updated by RFC 3260
RFC 2474	*Definition of the Differentiated Services Field (DS Field) in the IPv4 and IPv6 Headers*	Updated by RFC 3260

continues

Table B-1   *RFCs Referenced in This Book (Continued)*

Document	Title	Update Notes
RFC 3392	*Capabilities Advertisement with BGP-4*	
RFC 2385	*Protection of BGP Sessions via the TCP MD5 Signature Option*	
RFC 2362	*Protocol Independent Multicast-Sparse Mode*	
RFC 2309	*Recommendations on Queue Management and Congestion Avoidance in the Internet*	
RFC 2330	*Framework for IP Performance Metrics*	
RFC 2205	*Resource ReSerVation Protocol (RSVP) — Version 1 Functional Specification*	Updated by RFC 2750
RFC 1998	*An Application of the BGP Community Attribute in Multi-home Routing*	
RFC 1105	*Border Gateway Protocol (BGP)*	Obsoleted by RFC 1163
RFC 1075	*Distance Vector Multicast Routing Protocol*	

APPENDIX C

Bibliography

The following table provides information about the sources consulted during the creation of this book.

Resource	Title	Web Page	Chapter	Author
Bridging and IBM Networking Command Reference, Cisco IOS Software Release 12.0				Cisco
Cisco — Configuring IP Multicast Guides				Cisco
Cisco — Understanding Service Access Point Access Control Lists	"Understanding Service Access Point Access Control Lists"			Cisco
Cisco IOS Desktop Switching Software Configuration Guide	"Creating and Maintaining VLANs"		Chapter 5	Cisco
Router Products Configuration Guide	"Configuring DLSw+"		Chapter 30	Cisco
Software Configuration Guide – Release 5.4	"Configuring Fast EtherChannel and Gigabit EtherChannel"		Chapter 7	Cisco
Software Configuration Guide – Release 6.1			Chapter 9 Chapter 12	Cisco
Cisco IOS 12.1 and 12.2 Configuration Guides and Command Reference				Cisco
Software Configuration Guide, Release 5.2	"Configuring Spanning Tree"		Chapter 8	Cisco

continues

Resource	Title	Web Page	Chapter	Author
Statement of Direction	"10 Gigabit Ethernet Position Statement"			Cisco
Website	"Understanding and Configuring FastEtherChannel on Cisco Switching and Routing Devices"	www.cisco.com		Cisco
Website	"Understanding and Configuring Spanning-Tree Protocol (STP) on Catalyst Switches"	Cisco.com/warp/public/473/5.html		
Website	"Using the border Gateway Protocol for Interdomain Routing"	www.cisco.com		
Website	"Configuring a Gateway of Last Resort Using IP Commands"	Cisco.com/warp/public/105/default.html		
Data sheet	"Cisco 1000BASE-T GBIC"			Cisco
Router Products Configuration and Reference	"Configuring Transparent Bridging"		Chapter 1	
Website	"Connectors and Cables"	Cisco.com/univercd/cc/td/doc/product/lan/c2900x1/gbic/ig_gbic/mamopins.html		
Layer 3 Switching Software Feature and Configuration Guide	"Configuring Bridging"			

Resource	Title	Web Page	Chapter	Author
Website	"Configuring BGP"	Cisco.com/ univercd/cc/td/doc/ product/software/ ios113ed/113ed_cr/ np1_c/ 1cbgp.htm#xtocid2 382823		
Website	"Configuring ISO CLNS"	Cisco.com/ univercd/cc/td/doc/ product/software/ ios113ed/113ed_cr/ np3_c/3cclns.htm		
Website	"The American Registry for Internet Numbers"	www.arin.net		
Website	"The Internet Society"	www.isoc.org		
Website	"The North American Network Operators' Group"	www.nanog.org		
Website	"Asia Pacific Network Information Centre"	www.apnic.net		
Website	"RIPE Network Coordination Centre"	www.ripe.net		
	"BGP4 Inter-Domain Routing in the Internet"			John W. Stewart III
Website	"Catalyst 3550 limitation and Restrictions"	www.cisco.com		
CCIE Practical Studies, Volume I				Karl Solie
Cisco BGP-4 Command and Configuration Handbook				Dr. William R. Parkhurst

continues

Resource	Title	Web Page	Chapter	Author
Cisco Catalyst 3550 Software and Hardware Configuration Guides and Command Reference	"Configuring 802.1s and 802.1w STP"	www.cisco.com		Cisco website
Cisco Internetwork Troubleshooting				Laura Chappell Dan Farkas
Cisco IOS 12.0 Quality of Service				Cisco
Cisco IOS Configuration Fundamentals				
Cisco IOS Dial Solutions				Cisco
CCIE Professional Development: Cisco LAN Switching				Kennedy Clark Kevin Hamilton
Cisco Voice Over Frame Relay, ATM, and IP		www.cisco.com		Cisco
Converged Network Architectures				Oliver C. Ibe
Deploying Cisco Voice Over IP Solutions		www.cisco.com		Cisco
Developing IP Multicast Networks, Volume I				Beau Williamson
Integrating Voice and Data Networks				Scott Keagy
Interconnections: Bridges, Routers, Switches, and Internetworking Protocols				Radia Perlman
Internet Performance Survival Guide				Geoff Huston
Internet Routing Architectures, Second Edition				Sam Halabi Danny McPherson

Resource	Title	Web Page	Chapter	Author
Internet Routing Architectures, Second Edition				Sam Halabi
Internetworking SNA with Cisco Solutions				George Sackett Nancy Sackett
Internetworking Troubleshooting Handbook, Second Edition				
Internetworking Troubleshooting Handbook, Third Edition				Faraz Shamim Zaheer Aziz Johnson Liu Abe Martey
Internetworking with TCP/IP, Volume I				Douglas Comer
IP Quality of Service				Srinivas Vegesna
IP Telephony				Bill Douskalis
Managing Cisco Network Security				Michael Wenstrom
Network Consultants Handbook				Matthew J. Castelli
Network Routing Architectures				Sam Halabi
Performance and Fault Management				Paul L. Della Maggiora Christopher E. Elliott Robert L. Payone, Jr. Kent J. Phelps James M. Thompson
Putting VoIP to Work: Softswitch Network Design and Testing				Bill Douskalis

continues

Resource	Title	Web Page	Chapter	Author
Routing TCP/IP, Volume 1				Jeff Doyle
Routing TCP/IP, Volume II				Jeff Doyle Jennifer DeHaven Carroll
TCP/IP Principle, Protocols, and Architectures				Douglas E. Comer
The Protocols TCP/IP Illustrated, Volume I				W. Richard Stevens

IP Prefix Lists

Prefix lists became available in Cisco IOS Software Release 12.0(3)T. You can use prefix lists as a simpler alternative to standard IP access lists for routing advertisement filtering with routing protocols. Although prefix lists are most commonly put to use in Border Gateway Protocol (BGP) configurations, this appendix demonstrates other ways that you can use prefix lists to support other routing protocols such as Enhanced Interior Gateway Routing Protocol (EIGRP). Prefix lists introduce a more streamlined way to create filters for network prefix advertisements by following these rules:

- Like access lists, prefix lists are processed sequentially from top to bottom. When a match is made, processing stops and the rest of the entries are not read.

- Entries can be added to the prefix lists at any time.

- An empty prefix lists permits all prefixes by default.

- Prefix lists do not use wildcard masks like access lists; they use a subnet length mask (for instance, /24).

- Unlike access lists, lines in prefix lists can be edited by the use of the sequence number.

- Prefix lists contain an implicit **deny any** at the end of each list.

- Sequence numbers are automatically generated; however, automatic sequence generation can be stopped.

Prefix lists are configured from global configuration mode using the following command:

```
ip prefix-list list-name | list-number [sequence sequence-value] deny | permit
network-address/length [ge ge-value] [le le-value]
```

Table D-1 shows the meaning for the prefix list syntax.

Table D-1   *IP Prefix List Syntax*

Command/Argument	Description
*list-name	list-number*	Specifies the name or number of the prefix list.
seq *sequence-value*	(Optional) Sequence number. If the sequence number is not entered manually, an automatic sequence number is generated. These numbers are generated sequentially starting with 5 and incrementing by 5.
**deny	permit**	Specifies whether prefixes are permitted or denied upon a match.
network-address	Network address to be matched, entered in dotted-decimal format.
/length	Length of the subnet mask in bits.
ge *ge-value*	(Optional) Specifies the minimum range of prefixes to be matched.
le *le-value*	(Optional) Specifies the maximum range of prefixes to be matched.

As previously mentioned, you can use prefix lists with distribute lists in router configuration mode to filter routing advertisements. Configuration of IP prefix lists is straightforward; changes in prefix lists are simple to configure as well. Figure D-1 provides a step-by-step introduction to prefix list configuration using the network.

Figure D-1   *Artista Network*

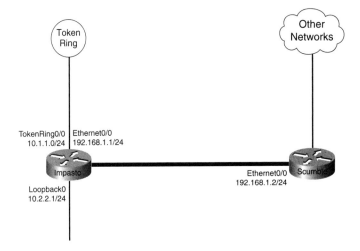

The following example shows how prefix lists can be used to filter incoming routing updates with the EIGRP routing protocol:

Step 1   Define your prefix lists; in this example, prefix list Internal is used to specify eight 192.168.0.0/24 network prefixes:

```
ip prefix-list Internal seq 5 deny 192.168.0.0/24
ip prefix-list Internal seq 10 deny 192.168.1.0/24
ip prefix-list Internal seq 15 deny 192.168.2.0/24
ip prefix-list Internal seq 20 deny 192.168.3.0/24
ip prefix-list Internal seq 25 deny 192.168.4.0/24
ip prefix-list Internal seq 30 deny 192.168.5.0/24
ip prefix-list Internal seq 35 deny 192.168.6.0/24
ip prefix-list Internal seq 40 deny 192.168.7.0/24
```

Step 2   Create a distribution list that specifies your previously configured prefix list:

```
router eigrp 100
distribute-list prefix Internal in
```

To verify that the prefix list worked, from another router issue a **show ip route** command. Example D-1 shows what the routing table looked like before the distribution list was configured.

Example D-1   *Routing Table Prior to Distribution List*

```
Impasto# show ip route eigrp
D     192.168.10.0/24 [90/409600] via 192.168.1.2, 00:00:03, Ethernet0/0
D     192.168.11.0/24 [90/409600] via 192.168.1.2, 00:00:03, Ethernet0/0
D     192.168.4.0/24 [90/409600] via 192.168.1.2, 00:00:47, Ethernet0/0
D     192.168.5.0/24 [90/409600] via 192.168.1.2, 00:00:47, Ethernet0/0
D     192.168.6.0/24 [90/409600] via 192.168.1.2, 00:00:47, Ethernet0/0
D     192.168.7.0/24 [90/409600] via 192.168.1.2, 00:00:47, Ethernet0/0
D     192.168.2.0/24 [90/409600] via 192.168.1.2, 00:00:47, Ethernet0/0
D     192.168.3.0/24 [90/409600] via 192.168.1.2, 00:00:47, Ethernet0/0
```

Example D-2 shows the same routing table after applying the distribution list and clearing the routing from the Impasto router.

Example D-2   *Routing Table After Distribution List Application*

```
Impasto# clear ip route *
Impasto# show ip route eigrp
D     192.168.10.0/24 [90/409600] via 192.168.1.2, 00:00:41, Ethernet0/0
D     192.168.11.0/24 [90/409600] via 192.168.1.2, 00:00:41, Ethernet0/0
```

Notice that the routes mentioned by the prefix list have been removed from the routing tables. Example D-3 shows the full configuration for the Impasto router used in this example.

Example D-3 *Using IP Prefix Lists*

```
interface Loopback0
 ip address 10.2.2.1 255.255.255.0
 !
interface Ethernet0/0
 ip address 192.168.1.1 255.255.255.0
 !
interface TokenRing0/0
 ip address 10.1.1.1 255.255.255.0
 !
router eigrp 100
 network 10.0.0.0
 network 192.168.1.0
 distribute-list prefix Internal in
 no auto-summary
 !
ip prefix-list Internal seq 5 deny 192.168.0.0/24
ip prefix-list Internal seq 10 deny 192.168.1.0/24
ip prefix-list Internal seq 15 deny 192.168.2.0/24
ip prefix-list Internal seq 20 deny 192.168.3.0/24
ip prefix-list Internal seq 25 deny 192.168.4.0/24
ip prefix-list Internal seq 30 deny 192.168.5.0/24
ip prefix-list Internal seq 35 deny 192.168.6.0/24
ip prefix-list Internal seq 40 deny 192.168.7.0/24
ip prefix-list Internal seq 45 permit 0.0.0.0/0 le 32
```

Example D-4 demonstrates how you can use the **ge** and **le** arguments to filter routes based on minimum and maximum prefix matches. For this example, you need the same two routers with the same configurations. On the Impasto, create four loopback interfaces with the addresses 11.1.1.1/24, 11.2.1.1/16, 11.30.1.1/13, and 11.200.1.1/10. The Impasto and Scumble routers will run EIGRP in autonomous system number 100; the Impasto router will advertise networks 10.0.0.0, 192.168.1.0, and 11.0.0.0; and summarization should be disabled on both routers.

Example D-4 *Preparing the Impasto Router*

```
interface Loopback0
 ip address 10.2.2.1 255.255.255.0
 no ip directed-broadcast
 !
interface Loopback10
 ip address 11.1.1.1 255.255.255.0
 !
interface Loopback11
 ip address 11.2.1.1 255.255.0.0
 !
interface Loopback12
 ip address 11.30.1.1 255.248.0.0
```

Example D-4 *Preparing the Impasto Router (Continued)*

```
 !
 interface Loopback13
  ip address 11.200.1.1 255.192.0.0
 !
 interface Ethernet0/0
  ip address 192.168.1.2 255.255.255.0
 !
 router eigrp 100
  network 10.0.0.0
  network 11.0.0.0
  network 192.168.1.0 0.0.0.255
  no auto
```

Example D-5 shows the addition of the new 11.0.0.0 networks, displaying the routing table on the Scumble router.

Example D-5 *R2's Routing Table*

```
Scumble# show ip route | include is|via
Gateway of last resort is not set
C    192.168.10.0/24 is directly connected, Loopback10
C    192.168.11.0/24 is directly connected, Loopback20
C    192.168.4.0/24 is directly connected, Loopback2
C    192.168.5.0/24 is directly connected, Loopback3
     10.0.0.0/24 is subnetted, 2 subnets
D       10.2.2.0 [90/156160] via 192.168.1.1, 00:02:02, FastEthernet0
D       10.1.1.0 [90/178688] via 192.168.1.1, 00:02:02, FastEthernet0
C    192.168.6.0/24 is directly connected, Loopback4
     11.0.0.0/8 is variably subnetted, 4 subnets, 4 masks
D       11.2.0.0/16 [90/156160] via 192.168.1.1, 00:02:02, FastEthernet0
D       11.1.1.0/24 [90/156160] via 192.168.1.1, 00:02:02, FastEthernet0
D       11.24.0.0/13 [90/156160] via 192.168.1.1, 00:02:02, FastEthernet0
D       11.192.0.0/10 [90/156160] via 192.168.1.1, 00:02:02, FastEthernet0
C    192.168.7.0/24 is directly connected, Loopback5
C    192.168.1.0/24 is directly connected, FastEthernet0
C    192.168.2.0/24 is directly connected, Loopback0
C    192.168.3.0/24 is directly connected, Loopback1
```

After creating the loopbacks and verifying EIGRP operation, create an IP prefix list that allows only the Impasto router to advertise the 11.1.0.0 networks with prefixes ranging from /16 to /32. Apply this prefix list to filter EIGRP routes leaving the Impasto router as shown in Example D-6.

Example D-6 *Applying the IP Prefix List*

```
ip prefix-list Trial-2 seq 5 permit 11.1.0.0/16 le 32
!
router eigrp 100
 distribute-list prefix Trial-2 out
```

After you apply the prefix list on the Impasto router, the Scumble router's routing table will contain only the route to the 11.1.1.0/24 network. The other 11.0.0.0 networks with masks that range from 16 to 32 bits have been removed, and network 10.2.2.0/24 has also been removed, as shown in Example D-7.

Example D-7 *Scumble Router's Routing Table After IP Prefix List*

```
Scumble# show ip route | include is|via
Gateway of last resort is not set
C    192.168.10.0/24 is directly connected, Loopback10
C    192.168.11.0/24 is directly connected, Loopback20
C    192.168.4.0/24 is directly connected, Loopback2
C    192.168.5.0/24 is directly connected, Loopback3
C    192.168.6.0/24 is directly connected, Loopback4
     11.0.0.0/24 is subnetted, 1 subnets
D       11.1.1.0 [90/156160] via 192.168.1.1, 00:02:30, FastEthernet0
C    192.168.7.0/24 is directly connected, Loopback5
C    192.168.1.0/24 is directly connected, FastEthernet0
C    192.168.2.0/24 is directly connected, Loopback0
C    192.168.3.0/24 is directly connected, Loopback1
```

Now, remove the 11.1.1.1/24 interface and add loopback interfaces 11.1.1.0/29, 11.1.1.32/29, and 11.1.1.64/29 to the configuration on the Impasto router; check the routing table on the Scumble router again. It should look like Example D-8.

Example D-8 *Experimenting with an IP Prefix List*

```
Impasto(config)# interface loopback 11
Impasto(config-if)# ip address 11.1.1.1 255.255.255.248
Impasto(config-if)# interface loopback 14
Impasto(config-if)# ip address 11.1.1.33 255.255.255.248
Impasto(config-if)# interface loopback 15
Impasto(config-if)# ip address 11.1.1.65 255.255.255.248

Impasto# show ip route | include is|via
Gateway of last resort is not set
D    192.168.10.0/24 [90/409600] via 192.168.1.2, 00:06:53, Ethernet0/0
D    192.168.11.0/24 [90/409600] via 192.168.1.2, 00:06:53, Ethernet0/0
     10.0.0.0/24 is subnetted, 2 subnets
C       10.2.2.0 is directly connected, Loopback0
C       10.1.1.0 is directly connected, TokenRing0/0
     11.0.0.0/8 is variably subnetted, 6 subnets, 4 masks
C       11.2.0.0/16 is directly connected, Loopback11
C       11.1.1.0/29 is directly connected, Loopback10
C       11.24.0.0/13 is directly connected, Loopback12
C       11.1.1.32/29 is directly connected, Loopback14
C       11.1.1.64/29 is directly connected, Loopback15
C       11.192.0.0/10 is directly connected, Loopback13
C    192.168.1.0/24 is directly connected, Ethernet0/0
```

For the next part of this experiment, remove the outgoing Trial-2 prefix from EIGRP 100 and change the prefix list to any 11.1.0.0/16 network prefixes greater than 25 bits in length. (This will include the loopback interfaces that were just created in the preceding step but permit everything else.) After you have edited the prefix list, reapply it, as shown in Example D-9.

Example D-9 *Experimentation Continued*

```
router eigrp 100
 no distribute-list prefix- Trial-2 out

ip prefix-list Trial-2 seq 5 deny 11.1.0.0/16 ge 25
ip prefix-list Trial-2 seq 10 permit 0.0.0.0/0 le 32


router eigrp 100
 distribute-list prefix- Trial-2 out
```

After you have applied the changes, the Scumble router's routing table should show the reappearance of the 10.0.0.0 networks and the 11.0.0.0 networks with masks greater than 16. The loopbacks created in the preceding step should have been removed, as shown in Example D-10.

Example D-10 *Scumble Router's Routing Table After Changing Prefix List Trial-2*

```
Scumble# clear ip route *
Scumble# show ip route | include is¦via
Gateway of last resort is not set
C    192.168.10.0/24 is directly connected, Loopback10
C    192.168.11.0/24 is directly connected, Loopback20
C    192.168.4.0/24 is directly connected, Loopback2
C    192.168.5.0/24 is directly connected, Loopback3
     10.0.0.0/24 is subnetted, 2 subnets
D       10.2.2.0 [90/156160] via 192.168.1.1, 00:00:16, FastEthernet0
D       10.1.1.0 [90/178688] via 192.168.1.1, 00:00:16, FastEthernet0
C    192.168.6.0/24 is directly connected, Loopback4
     11.0.0.0/8 is variably subnetted, 3 subnets, 3 masks
D       11.2.0.0/16 [90/156160] via 192.168.1.1, 00:00:16, FastEthernet0
D       11.24.0.0/13 [90/156160] via 192.168.1.1, 00:00:16, FastEthernet0
D       11.192.0.0/10 [90/156160] via 192.168.1.1, 00:00:16, FastEthernet0
C    192.168.7.0/24 is directly connected, Loopback5
C    192.168.1.0/24 is directly connected, FastEthernet0
C    192.168.2.0/24 is directly connected, Loopback0
C    192.168.3.0/24 is directly connected, Loopback1
```

Example D-11 shows the completed configuration for the Impasto router.

Example D-11 *Complete Configuration for the Impasto Router*

```
interface Loopback0
 ip address 10.2.2.1 255.255.255.0
 !
interface Loopback10
 ip address 11.1.1.1 255.255.255.248
 !
interface Loopback11
 ip address 11.2.1.1 255.255.0.0
 !
interface Loopback12
 ip address 11.30.1.1 255.248.0.0
 !
interface Loopback13
 ip address 11.200.1.1 255.192.0.0
 !
interface Loopback14
 ip address 11.1.1.33 255.255.255.248
 !
interface Loopback15
 ip address 11.1.1.65 255.255.255.248
 !
interface Ethernet0/0
 ip address 192.168.1.1 255.255.255.0
 !
interface TokenRing0/0
 ip address 10.1.1.1 255.255.255.0
 !
router eigrp 100
 network 10.0.0.0
 network 11.0.0.0
 network 192.168.1.0
 neighbor 192.168.1.2
 distribute-list prefix Trial-2 out
 distribute-list prefix Internal in
 no auto-summary
 !
ip prefix-list Internal seq 5 deny 192.168.0.0/24
ip prefix-list Internal seq 10 deny 192.168.1.0/24
ip prefix-list Internal seq 15 deny 192.168.2.0/24
ip prefix-list Internal seq 20 deny 192.168.3.0/24
ip prefix-list Internal seq 25 deny 192.168.4.0/24
ip prefix-list Internal seq 30 deny 192.168.5.0/24
ip prefix-list Internal seq 35 deny 192.168.6.0/24
ip prefix-list Internal seq 40 deny 192.168.7.0/24
ip prefix-list Internal seq 45 permit 0.0.0.0/0 le 32
 !
ip prefix-list Trial-2 seq 5 deny 11.1.0.0/16 ge 25
ip prefix-list Trial-2 seq 10 permit 0.0.0.0/0 le 32
```

With a little practice, you might use the simpler prefix lists in place of access lists for all routing protocols, not just for BGP.

INDEX

Symbols & Numerics

R

T

U

V

W-Z

learn

NOW
I HAVE THE POWER TO MAKE
YOU MORE PRODUCTIVE ON THE JOB.
I CAN PREPARE YOU TO MEET
NEW CHALLENGES.

I AM A CISCO CAREER CERTIFICATION.
ADD ME TO YOUR TOOLBOX WITH
AUTHORIZED TRAINING FROM
CISCO LEARNING PARTNERS...
PAY EASILY WITH CISCO
LEARNING CREDITS.

It is the power to acquire new skillsets, and expand your capabilities. Only Cisco Learning Partners can put you ahead of the curve. Visit **www.cisco.com/go/learningpartners.**

CISCO SYSTEMS

THIS IS THE POWER OF THE NETWORK. now.

Cisco Press

Learning is serious business.

Invest wisely.

Cisco Security Certification

CCSP™ Cisco Secure PIX® Firewall Advanced Exam Certification Guide (CCSP Self-Study)
Christian Degu, Greg Bastien
1-58720-067-8 • **Available Now**

The CSPFA exam is one of the five component exams to the CCSP certification. *CCSP Cisco Secure PIX Firewall Advanced Exam Certification Guide* provides CSPFA exam candidates with a comprehensive preparation tool for testing success. With pre- and post-chapter tests, a CD-ROM-based testing engine with more than 200 questions, and comprehensive training on all exam topics, this title brings the proven exam preparation tools from the popular Cisco Press Exam Certification Guide series to the CSPFA candidate. It also serves as a learning guide for networkers interested in learning more about working with the PIX Firewall line of products.

CCIE® Practical Studies: Security (CCIE Self-Study)
Andrew Mason, Dmitry Bokotey
1-58705-110-9 • **Available June 2003**

The Cisco Certified Internetworking Expert (CCIE) Certification from Cisco Systems is the most prestigious certification in the networking industry. In 2001, Cisco introduced the CCIE in Security. This exam, a combination of a written qualification exam with a one-day intensive lab exam is a highly sought after affirmation of a networkers security skills. A key to success in the intensive lab exam is hands-on understanding of how the security principles and concepts are executed in a real network. *CCIE Practical Studies: Security* provides a series of lab scenarios that help a CCIE candidate or advanced-level networker gain that expertise. The labs show how, with or without a lab of actual equipment, different concepts are applied. Chapters include background and technology overviews, directions on how to set up a practice lab, case study-based scenarios that show the step-by-step implementation of these concepts, and comprehensive labs that mimic those in the one-day lab exam. *CCIE Practical Studies: Security* serves as an invaluable guide in gaining networking security experience and in CCIE testing success.

CCIE Security Exam Certification Guide (CCIE Self-Study)
Henry Benjamin
1-58720-065-1 • **Available Now**

CCIE Security Exam Certification Guide is a valuable self-study aid in preparing for the Security Qualification Exam. The book covers security and application protocols, security technologies, general and Cisco-specific security applications, as well as related general networking and operating system issues.

CCIE Professional Development

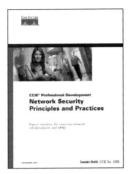

Network Security Principles and Practices
(CCIE Professional Development)

Saadat Malik

1-58705-025-0 • **Available Now**

Network Security Principles and Practices is a comprehensive guide to network security threats and the policies and tools developed specifically to combat those threats. Starting with a general discussion of network security concepts and design philosophy, the book shows readers how they can build secure network architectures from the ground up. Taking a practical, applied approach to building security into networks, the book focuses on showing readers how to implement and verify security features and products in a variety of environments. Security aspects of routing protocols are discussed and various options for choosing and using them analyzed. The book goes into a detailed discussion of the security threats posed by increasingly prevalent LAN to LAN Virtual Private Networks and remote access VPN installations and how to minimize large vulnerabilities caused by these non-traditional network portals. Firewalls, including the PIX and IOS® firewalls, and underlying protocols are presented in depth. Intrusion detection is fully examined. The book shows the reader how to control dial-in access by setting up access servers with AAA, PPP, TACACS+, and Radius. Finally, protections at the service provider are discussed by showing the reader how to provision security at the service provider level.

ciscopress.com

Cisco BGP-4 Command and Configuration Handbook (CCIE Professional Development)

William R. Parkhurst

1-58705-017-X • **Available Now**

Cisco BGP-4 Command and Configuration Handbook is an exhaustive practical reference to the commands contained within BGP-4. For each command/subcommand, author Bill Parkhurst explains the intended use or function and how to properly configure it. Then, he presents scenarios to demonstrate every facet of the command and its use, along with appropriate show and debug commands. Through the discussion of functionality and the scenario-based configuration examples, Cisco BGP-4 Command and Configuration Handbook helps you gain a thorough understanding of the practical side of BGP-4.

Routing TCP/IP, Volume II (CCIE Professional Development)

Jeff Doyle, Jennifer DeHaven Carroll

1-57870-089-2 • **Available Now**

This book presents a detailed examination of exterior routing protocols (EGP and BGP) and advanced IP routing issues, such as multicast routing, quality of service routing, IPv6, and router management. Students learn IP design and management techniques for implementing routing protocols efficiently. Network planning, design, implementation, operation, and optimization are stressed in each chapter.

Cisco CCNP BSCI Certification

CCNP® BSCI Exam Certification Guide (CCNP Self-Study), Second Edition

Clare Gough

1-58720-078-3 • **Available Now**

CCNP BSCI Exam Certification Guide, Second Edition, is a comprehensive exam self-study tool for the CCNP/CCDP/CCIP BSCI exam, which evaluates a networkers ability to build scalable, routed Cisco internetworks. This book, updated with more than 100 pages of IS-IS protocol coverage, addresses all the major topics on the most recent BSCI #640-901 exam. This guide enables readers to master the concepts and technologies upon which they will be tested, including extending IP addresses, routing principles, scalable routing protocols, managing traffic and access, and optimizing scalable internetworks. CCNP candidates will seek out *CCNP BSCI Exam Certification Guide* as timely and expert late-stage exam preparation tool and useful post-exam reference.

CCNP Self-Study: Building Scalable Cisco Internetworks (BSCI)

Catherine Paquet, Diane Teare

1-58705-084-6 • **Available Now**

CCNP Self-Study: Building Scalable Cisco Internetworks (BSCI) is a Cisco authorized, self-paced learning tool for CCNP, CCDP, and CCIP preparation. The book teaches readers how to design, configure, maintain, and scale routed networks that are growing in size and complexity. The book focuses on using Cisco routers connected in LANs and WANs typically found at medium-to-large network sites. Upon completing this book, readers will be able to select and implement the appropriate Cisco IOS® Software services required to build a scalable, routed network.

Cisco CCNP Certification

CCNP Preparation Library (CCNP Self-Study), Third Edition
Various Authors
1-58705-131-1 • **Available Now**

CCNP Preparation Library, Third Edition, is a Cisco authorized library of self-paced learning tools for the four component exams of the CCNP certification. These books teach readers the skills in professional level routing, switching, remote access and support as recommended for their respective exams, including for the new Building Scalable Cisco Internetworks (BSCI) exam.

Based on the four component exams of the CCNP certification, this four-book library contains *CCNP Self-Study: Building Scalable Cisco Internetworks* (BSCI), *Building Cisco Multilayer Switched Networks*, *Building Cisco Remote Access Networks*, and *Cisco Internetwork Troubleshooting*. These books serve as valuable study guides and supplements to the instuctor-led courses for certification candidates. They are also valuable to any intermediate level networker who wants to master the implementation of Cisco networking devices in medium to large networks.

Cisco CCNP Certification Library (CCNP Self-Study), Second Edition
Various Authors
1-58720-080-5 • **Available Now**

Cisco Certified Network Professional (CCNP) is the intermediate-level Cisco certification for network support. This is the next step for networking professionals who wish to validate their skills beyond the Cisco Certified Network Associate (CCNA®) level or who want to have a path to the expert level certification of CCIE. CCNP tests a candidates skill in installing, configuring, operating, and troubleshooting complex routed LANs, routed WANs, switched LANs, and dial access services. Where CCNA requires candidates to pass a single exam, CCNP requires candidates to pass four written exams, including 640-901 BSCI, 640-604 Switching, 640-605 Remote Access, and 640-606 Support.

The official exam self-study guides for each of these exams are now available in this value priced bundle. These books, *CCNP BSCI Exam Certification Guide*, *CCNP Switching Exam Certification Guide*, *CCNP Remote Access Exam Certification Guide*, and *CCNP Support Exam Certification Guide*, present the certification candidate with comprehensive review and practice of all the key topics that appear on each of the CCNP exams.

Learning is serious buisiness. **Invest wisely.**

Cisco CCNP Certification

Internetworking Technologies Handbook, Third Edition
Cisco Systems, Inc.
1-58705-001-3 • **Available Now**

Internetworking Technologies Handbook, Third Edition, is an essential reference for every network professional. *Internetworking Technologies Handbook* has been one of Cisco Press' best-selling and most popular books since the first edition was published in 1997. Network engineers, administrators, technicians, and support personnel use this book to understand and implement many different internetworking and Cisco technologies. Beyond the on-the-job use, *Internetworking Technologies Handbook* is also a core training component for CCNA and CCDA® certifications. It is a comprehensive reference that enables networking professionals to understand and implement contemporary internetworking technologies. You will master terms, concepts, technologies, and devices used in today's networking industry, and will learn how to incorporate internetworking technologies into a LAN/WAN environment.

This Third Edition features new chapters on cable technologies, wireless technologies, and voice/data integration. After reading this book, networking professionals will possess a greater understanding of local and wide-area networking and the hardware, protocols, and services involved. *Internetworking Technologies Handbook* offers system optimization techniques that will strengthen results, increase productivity, and improve efficiency--helping you make more intelligent, cost-effective decisions for your network environment.

ciscopress.com

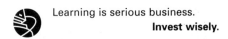

CISCO SYSTEMS/PACKET MAGAZINE
ATTN: C. Glover
170 West Tasman, Mailstop SJ8-2
San Jose, CA 95134-1706

Place
Stamp
Here

☐ **YES!** I'm requesting a **free** subscription to *Packet*™ magazine.

☐ No. I'm not interested at this time.

☐ Mr.
☐ Ms.

First Name (Please Print) _____ Last Name _____

Title/Position (Required) _____

Company (Required) _____

Address _____

City _____ State/Province _____

Zip/Postal Code _____ Country _____

Telephone (Include country and area codes) _____ Fax _____

E-mail _____

Signature (Required) _____ Date _____

☐ I would like to receive additional information on Cisco's services and products by e-mail.

1. Do you or your company:
- A ☐ Use Cisco products
- B ☐ Resell Cisco products
- C ☐ Both
- D ☐ Neither

2. Your organization's relationship to Cisco Systems:
- A ☐ Customer/End User
- B ☐ Prospective Customer
- C ☐ Cisco Reseller
- D ☐ Cisco Distributor
- E ☐ Integrator
- F ☐ Non-Authorized Reseller
- G ☐ Cisco Training Partner
- I ☐ Cisco OEM
- J ☐ Consultant
- K ☐ Other. (specify): _____

3. How many people does your entire company employ?
- A ☐ More than 10,000
- B ☐ 5,000 to 9,999
- C ☐ 1,000 to 4,999
- D ☐ 500 to 999
- E ☐ 250 to 499
- F ☐ 100 to 249
- G ☐ Fewer than 100

4. Is your company a Service Provider?
- A ☐ Yes
- B ☐ No

5. Your involvement in network equipment purchases:
- A ☐ Recommend
- B ☐ Approve
- C ☐ Neither

6. Your personal involvement in networking:
- A ☐ Entire enterprise at all sites
- B ☐ Departments or network segments at more than one site
- C ☐ Single department or network segment
- F ☐ Public network
- D ☐ No involvement
- E ☐ Other (specify): _____

7. Your Industry:
- A ☐ Aerospace
- B ☐ Agriculture/Mining/Construction
- C ☐ Banking/Finance
- D ☐ Chemical/Pharmaceutical
- E ☐ Consultant
- F ☐ Computer/Systems/Electronics
- G ☐ Education (K–12)
- U ☐ Education (College/Univ.)
- H ☐ Government—Federal
- I ☐ Government—State
- J ☐ Government—Local
- K ☐ Health Care
- L ☐ Telecommunications
- M ☐ Utilities/Transportation
- N ☐ Other (specify): _____

CPRESS

PACKET

Packet magazine serves as the premier publication linking customers to Cisco Systems, Inc. Delivering complete coverage of cutting-edge networking trends and innovations, *Packet* is a magazine for technical, hands-on users. It delivers industry-specific information for enterprise, service provider, and small and midsized business market segments. A toolchest for planners and decision makers, *Packet* contains a vast array of practical information, boasting sample configurations, real-life customer examples, and tips on getting the most from your Cisco Systems' investments. Simply put, *Packet* magazine is straight talk straight from the worldwide leader in networking for the Internet, Cisco Systems, Inc.

We hope you'll take advantage of this useful resource. I look forward to hearing from you.

Cecelia Glover
Packet Circulation Manager
packet@external.cisco.com
www.cisco.com/go/packet

PACKET™